The Insider's Guide to the Colleges

2001

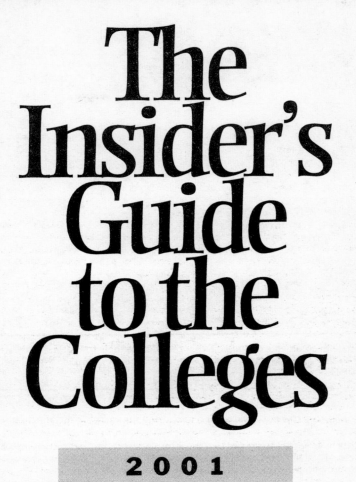

The Insider's Guide to the Colleges

2001

Compiled and Edited
by the Staff of the
Yale Daily News

St. Martin's Griffin
New York

Visit *The Insider's Guide to the Colleges* Web site at http://www.yale.edu/ydn.

The editors have sought to ensure that the information in this book is accurate at press time. Because policies, costs, and statistics do change from time to time, readers should verify important information with the colleges.

Contents

The Insider's Guide to the Colleges

2001

Preface

Congratulations! Although your head may be spinning and the college admissions process may seem daunting, you have begun your search on the right foot by picking up a copy of this book. Our staff has worked very hard on this new edition of *The Insider's Guide to the Colleges* to provide you with the tools necessary to give you an advantage in this hectic process.

We have one central objective, and that is to give you the *real* picture of what it's like to be a college student and not bore you with glossy brochure talk. After all, we have been through the process ourselves, and we owe it to you to tell you the truth. We tell you what we would love to have known when we were in your shoes. Through writing the book, we have discovered that there is more to college life than what is offered by any single institution. College is the godlike professor who stays after class to help you with a difficult concept in economics, and the dorm room friends whose late-night study breaks keep you from going insane. It is the dining hall where the lines are long and the food is bad, and the roommate who skips class and lets you cry on her shoulder after you get a D on your first English paper. College is gallons of coffee, alcohol, laughter, and stress.

All of this is well and good, but you are probably still thinking that it does not help you much. After all, you have to get there first. You can apply to no more than a handful of colleges from among thousands. Maybe you have a hazy idea of what you are looking for, but how do you even begin to narrow your choices?

That is where *The Insider's Guide* fits in. In this 27th edition, we provide a snapshot of life at 311 (7 additions in this edition!) colleges and universities in the United States and Canada. *The Insider's Guide* has changed a lot in twenty-seven years. In 1973, *The Insider's Guide* was little more than a handful of sarcastic, condescending articles by "Yale Men" about the "lesser Ivy League schools." Today, we strive for accurate and witty reports that capture the spirit and essence of a college. Most importantly, we give you the inside scoop on these places, directly from the students who attend these institutions.

We research each school in *The Insider's Guide* by interviewing friends (and friends of friends) at each of the 311 colleges covered. This allows us not only to keep in touch with high school buddies, but also gives *The Insider's Guide* a unique perspective from students whose opinions we trust. It also means that we are only as accurate as our sources. Though we have worked hard to ensure that each article is factually correct and current, you should still do additional research. As a good rule of thumb, never rely solely on any one source to decide something as important as choosing the right college. It is critical that you make every effort to learn as much about the school (or schools) of your choice before making a commitment.

In addition to the reports on each college, *The Insider's Guide* includes a number of special features to help you in your search. "The College Finder" gives you a rundown on some schools according to selected attributes. "Getting In" takes you step-by-step through all the intricacies of the admission process. In "The College Spectrum," we discuss some of the most important factors to consider when differentiating among schools, as well as give you a look at some of the current trends in college life. "Introduction for International Students" provides some tips on applying to American schools if you live outside the United States. "Disabled Student Services" introduces students with learning or physical disabilities to some of the issues they should be aware of when applying to college. Finally, we have included "Terms You Should Know," a humorous look at some of the often confusing jargon used in the world of college life.

We are confident that this edition of *The Insider's Guide* is even more lively and informative than its predecessors. We wish you all the best in finding the best match

for your interests and talents and hope
that you will think of us when you finally
buy your first college sweatshirt. —*Seung
C. Lee and Alexandra M. Rethore*

Editors-in-Chief
Seung C. Lee
Alexandra M. Rethore

Executive Editors
Brian Abaluck
Melissa K. Chan
William Chen
Jeffrey Kaplow
Marti Page
Alison Pulaski

Associate Editors
Jane H. Hong
Ellen L. Moskowitz
Shu-Ping Shen
Engin Yenidunya

Statistics Editor
Julita Ramirez

Senior Editor
Lisa E. Smith

Senior Writers
Robert G. Berschinski
Stephanie Manson
Johnny Swagerty
Jennifer B. Wang

Staff Writers
Amanda A. Ambroza
Kyla M. Dahlin
Alyssa Blair Greenwald
Nicole Jabaily
Conor Knighton
Sean McBride
Jessica Morgan
Edward Mundy
Yakut Seyhanli

Contributing Writers
Chiraag Bains
Jessica Bondell
Jason Friedrichs
Lauren Gold
Florence Han
Ludwig Johnson
Robert Lee
Melissa J. Merritt
Ann Sun
Kenneth Tseng
Robert Wong

Acknowledgments

Special thanks to Carrie McGinnis, our editor at St. Martin's Press, who has been instrumental in getting this book out on time and in excellent shape. We would also like to thank all the interviewees who were kind enough to let us get a personal peek into their lives and their colleges: Without you, this book would not have been possible.

Jamie Aaronson
Kristin Abbate
Kevin Adams
Jon Adler
Mathieu Ahlstrom
Ammar Ahmed
Gus Alberelli
Sylvia Alonso
Jozef Amado
Jessica Anderson
Jeff Atkins
Camille Atkinson
Lynne Bachand
Philip Bailey
Can Bakir
Stefanie Bala
Sarah Barkley
S.E. Barr
Ryan P. Barrows
Suzy Bass
Elizabeth Bates
Tatiana Becker
Kristine Behm
Kayce Bell
Chip Bennett
Robin Benson
Miles Berger
Denise Bilbao
Raffi Bilek
Pavel S. Blagov
Mary Bolt
Sonia M. Borrell
Alex Bragg
Virginia R. Brandt
Christin Brown
Jarrett Byrnes
Alberto Caban Jr.
Maria Caltabiano
Ashley Campbell
Greg Canfield
Abraham Caplan

Ursula Carliss
Leslie Carr
Matt Carter
Kristen Cartus
Maja Catipovic
Andrew Cencini
Taia Cesana
Janney Chang
Elaine Chao
Pei-Sze Cheng
Kate Childers
John Choi
Eugene Chung
Andrew Clark
Sarah Clarke
Enijin Cole
Vince Conte
Gracile Cook
Rob Curtis
Julie Cyphers
Mark Davis
Martha Davis
Dedric Day
Shirah Dedman
Michael DeLorenzo
Jaime Devereaux
Michael R. Dietrich
Gizem Dorter
Cameron Douglass
Joseph J. Doyle
Kelli Doyle
Anthony "Drazzy Draz" Draucikas
Sara Edelman
Joseph Esposito
Valerie Esser
Sarah Evans
Eileen Everett
Mark Farber
Dana Feinstein
Amanda Ferguson-Cradler
Rachel Fink
Noah Fisch
Erica Fisher
Kathleen M. Fregeau
Alison Mara Friedman
Marcus Friesen
Kelly Frisby
David Fuller
Lucy Garcia
Katharine Gatz
Selim Gokay

Acknowledgments

Melanie Goode
Ian Gopez
Paulina Grossman
Yola Habif
Laura J. Harris
Ethney Harrison
Karen Henderson
Kaysie Hermes
Thomas Hernandez
Kim Higbie
Anna L. Hillbrand
Joe Hoffman
Mary Holt
Anna Hong
Sibel Horada
Colleen Hsia
Carolyn Hunter
Hee-Jung Hwang
Ross Irwin
Lisa Jabaily
Nalo Jackson
Jane Jih
Carol Johnson
Kaleisha Johnson
Peter Johnson
Sarah Johnson
Victor Johnson
Lindsay Johnston
Meredith Jones
Olivia Jones
Tiffany Jones
Michael Joven
Deborah Kaufman
Bob Keary
Jocelyn Kenyon
Rashel Kesilman
Julie Kidd
Henry Kim
Tess Kim
David Knouf
Darrel Ko
Wendy Kobayashi
Galya Kohen
Ari Krepostman
Lynn Kuo
Sam Kusnetz
Kristin Kwasniewski
Elaine Lai
Wayne Lai
Stephanie Lambert
Kimberly Lau
Jung Min Lee
Dani Leiman
Steven Leong
Josh Levine
Nicole Levy

Tammy Li
Chris Liao
Angela Little
Jaemi Loeb
John Lofranco
Sue Lovoy
Cuitlahuac Lujan
Amber Luong
Staci Lyvers
John Mangin
Seth Manrow
Jeffrey Mansell
Eric Martens
Marissa Martinez
Michael Mayer
Lidia Meana
Maria Medlen
Keesha Melendez
Jay Le Melledo
Scott Merrill
Simon Messing
Teresa Metcalf-Johnson
Trisha Milazzo
Nicholas Miller
Vanessa Milsom
Jessica Minyard
Michelle Mitchell
Anne Moriarty
Isil Muderrisoglu
Tim Munn
Scotty Naigles
Kyle Najarian
Catherine Neuschler
Brianna Neville
Sarah Nuss-Waren
David Oehl
Meghan O'Mara
Stephen Osserman
Tanla Ozuzun
Andrea Partemore
Mukti Patel
Prapiksha Patel
Matt Pelowski
Ronald Petty
Natalie Pheasant
Andrew Philpott
Alissa Poisson
Jordan Posamentier
Harsha Ramachandra
Anne Reedstrom
Yonju Rhee
Jonathan Ritter
Sabin Rividi
Erin Rodgers
Trevor Rutledge-Leverenz
Ozer Sancak

Nalia Sanchez
Miguel Santos-Neves
Ipek Sarac
Shadron Sellman
Serra Semi
Steve Sendecki
Heather Shapiro
Shane Shariffskul
Jae Sung Shim
Yoko Shimizu
Laura Sideman
Matt Siedsma
Amanda Smith
Amy Smith
Andrea Smith
Andy Smith
Brad Smith
Courtney E. Smith
Jennifer Smith
Jaime Snape
Jay Snyder
Micah Spooner-Wyman
Jill Sprague
Stacy Steinhoff
Edward Stern
Volkan Stodolsky
Doug Strain

Keren Surowitz
Sarah Taylor
Irina Telyukova
William Terrin
Adam Thomas
Teneshia Thurman
Linda Tieu
Derrick Tung
Jodi Turrell
Joe Ursic
Toni Ann Vicari
Veena Villivalam
Sean Voscamp
David de Voursney
Marissa Wagner
Rita Wang
Rachel Wasser
Johanna Weinstock
Robert Whipple
Emily Woods
Forrest Woolery
Bean Worley
Jason Wirth
Ian Yohai
Juliette Yu
Selin Zalma

How to Use This Book

How We Select the Colleges

One of the most difficult problems we wrestle with is which schools should be included in *The Insider's Guide*. Out of the more than 2,000 four-year degree-granting institutions in the nation, we cover 311. The most important factor in our decision is the academic quality of the schools we select. Approximately 200 of the schools in the book qualified based on the excellence and breadth of their offerings alone. With that criterion established, making the other selections became more difficult. One key factor we carefully consider is the size of the colleges and universities in question. We make a particular effort to include a broad selection of larger universities, most of which are state-affiliated. Further, we have included at least one such school from each of the fifty states. Although the overall quality of larger universities is often comparable to schools we chose not to include, these larger universities frequently have better facilities and offer more varied opportunities than do smaller institutions. Many have one or two outstanding programs that make them noteworthy. Finally, because large universities enroll thousands of students every year, more readers are likely to consider them on a list of prospective colleges.

We have also made every effort to include a broad cross section of smaller colleges. The smaller the school, the more we tended to view the quality of the student body—which we measured by admissions selectivity, average high-school class rank, SAT profiles, etc.—as the key criterion. Choosing among small liberal arts colleges is especially difficult because there are so many that are "selective" or "competitive" in admissions. However, like most admissions offices, we consider geographical distribution a virtue, so when faced with difficult choices, we favored colleges in less heavily represented regions of the country.

The Insider's Guide also includes a selection of two types of specialized schools—technical institutes and schools strong in the creative and performing arts. *The Insider's Guide*'s modest sampler of some of the better institutions across the nation is designed primarily to whet your appetites and to encourage you to continue your own independent research.

In sum, this book includes colleges we believe to be among the best and most noteworthy in North America. This does not imply in any way that you cannot get a good education at colleges that are not included in this year's *The Insider's Guide*. Nor, of course, does it mean that you are guaranteed a happy and prosperous four years if you attend any one of them. Rather, we believe that every school in *The Insider's Guide* offers students the raw materials for constructing an excellent education.

It's All Up to You

After your initial browse through *The Insider's Guide*, we suggest that you read the front section carefully and then go back and take a more careful look at the articles on the colleges that caught your eye. The opening features of the book are designed to help you zero in on what is unique and important about the schools you might be considering. The things we discuss in general terms in the introductory parts should give you a new perspective on the colleges as well as suggest options you had not considered before.

As you read through the *Guide*, you will notice that we have avoided the temptation to pigeonhole the colleges with some kind of catchall rating system, or worse, numerically rank these schools. Our reason is that the "best" college for one individual may come near the bottom of the list for another. Each person has his or her own particular set of wants and needs, so it would be pointless for us to try to objectively rank the schools.

Even so, people inevitably ask, "Can't you rate the colleges just on the basis of academic quality?" We think not. There are too many variables—from the many factors that contribute to the quality of a department and school as a whole to the articulateness and accessibility of the professor who happens to be your academic advisor. Furthermore, it is useless to try to compare a college of 2,000 with a university of 10,000 (or a university of 10,000 with one of 40,000) on any other basis than individual preference.

Despite all the reasons not to, report-edly reliable sources such as national magazines often insist on publishing numerical rankings of colleges. It is our hope that you can ignore such rankings when you find them elsewhere, or at the very least, take them with a healthy grain of salt.

We are dedicated to the notion that the quality of a college is largely in the eye of the beholder. What we want to do is help you to train your eye so that you can pick the college that is best for you. *The Insider's Guide* describes, explains, and interprets, but the choice is always yours.

Getting In

The task of applying to college can seem as intimidating as the thickness of this book. In the spring of your sophomore year in high school your Aunt Betsy, whom you have not seen in three years, pinches your cheek and asks you where you are going to college. *How the heck should I know?* you think to yourself. That fall, your mother tells you that the boy down the street with the 4.0 grade point average is taking the SAT prep course for the fifth time to see if he can get a perfect score and win thousands in scholarship money. You reply that you are late for school. We know you keep ducking the subject, but the hints keep coming with increasing regularity. You start dreading dinner time, which has suddenly become a time for "serious" conversations about schools with your parents. You find yourself choking on your broccoli. Pretty soon a few of your friends are visiting the guidance office periodically to talk to counselors or leaf through college catalogs. Finally, you decide to make an appointment yourself.

When you first talk to your counselor, preferably as soon as possible in your junior year, you may have only just begun to feel comfortable in high school, let alone prepared to think about college. The entire prospect still seems far away, but picking and getting into a good school takes a lot of work and organization. The earlier you begin the search, the better. A visit to your counselor is a good way to start. Most are very helpful, but a few should make you wary—such as those who do not want to disappoint anyone, and those who want to keep their track records unblemished. The first group will assure you that you do not have a thing to worry about getting into the college of your choice. Although these counselors may be paying you a hard-earned compliment, it still pays to read everything you can about the schools that interest you and to follow application procedures carefully. The second group will tell you not to apply to any school whose admissions they consider "too competitive," and will try to limit your alternatives. Listen to reason, but trust your instincts. Getting a sense of how helpful your counselor will be is important. The good ones can be enormously valuable as advisors and confidants throughout the admissions process.

The next step is to read articles that interest you, ask questions, and begin to think about what factors about a school make a difference for you. What do you want in a college? A strong science department? A friendly atmosphere? A great social life? While your academic needs should be your primary concern at the outset, be wary of concentrating on only one or two academic departments and making them the sole basis of your judgments. In college, most people change their mind two or three times before finally settling on a major. If you do change your major midway through your sophomore year, you do not want it to affect the overall quality of your coursework or force you to transfer because your college does not offer a good program in your new area of interest.

We realize that you cannot possibly think of all the angles. No one can say for sure what your interests will be three or four years from now, or what things will ultimately prove most important to you at the college you attend. By taking a hard look at yourself now, and proceeding carefully as you begin looking at the colleges, you can be reasonably sure that you are investigating the right colleges for the right reasons.

In the early winter of your junior year, you will receive your PSAT scores (discussed later, in "The Tests"). Unless you request otherwise, you will also be deluged with mail from colleges throughout the nation. The College Search Service of the College Board provides these colleges with the names and addresses of students who scored in various percentiles, and the schools crank out thousands of form letters to those whose scores show promise.

At first, making sense of your flood of mail may seem impossible. Glossy brochures tend to portray a diverse group of students frolicking happily and thinking deep thoughts on every page. "They're all the same," recalled one college freshman, happy to be finished with the process. Each brochure speaks of "rich diversity" and "academic rigor" and dozens of other high-minded ideals that are often nothing more than hollow catchphrases. Likewise, any campus can look beautiful through the lens of an admissions-office photographer. Just remember that the building that looks so picturesque in the fading twilight could be part of the law school, miles from where the undergraduates study and live.

You should also consider that the schools who select you for their mailings might not be the ones you would choose. Schools can recruit you for any number of reasons: You could be from a part of the country that the school feels is underrepresented in its student body, or your test scores could be higher than their average, and they would like you to bring them up! Chances are you will have to take the initiative to get the mailing information on some of the schools that truly interest you.

Brochures and viewbooks can be useful if they are read critically. What themes does the college stress most? What is not mentioned? What does the SAT or ACT profile look like? Look for hard facts to back up the flowery prose. If nothing else, viewbooks reveal something about how the college perceives itself, as well as what it aspires to be. It is not much to go on, but then again you also do not have time to do a thorough analysis of all 2,000 four-year colleges in the nation.

There is one source of information that is often overlooked just because it is close at hand, namely your parents. They, and other adults who know you well, probably have some good ideas about which schools you ought to consider. Take their advice seriously and investigate the alternatives they suggest. Adults frequently have a better perspective on you as an individual than would most people in your age group. Do not, however, let anyone dictate which colleges you "must" consider. It is important to come to an understanding with your parents early on that the college choice is ultimately yours alone. You are the one who has to live with that choice for four years, not them. If money is a potential problem, reach an agreement on that as well. How much can your family afford to pay? Some colleges might offer substantial financial aid. How much will you be expected to contribute? It is much better to deal with these questions in the opening months of the process than to wait until later when emotions are running high.

There are two important things to bear in mind as you consult the opinions of others. First, every piece of advice you will get will be a reflection of a particular person's own life experiences and is likely to be highly subjective. Second, opinions are frequently based on stereotypes that are often false, outdated, or misleading. Still, these are the shortcuts most applicants use to begin narrowing their choices, an unfortunate but necessary phase. The more people you talk to, the better perspective you gain on the colleges you are considering. The primary purpose of this book is to give you an inside look at the colleges. If you like what you have heard about a particular school, follow up with some careful research and find out if it lives up to its name.

As the field narrows, you should begin to dig deeper. See what the guides have to say about schools that interest you. Do you know anyone in college? Do you know anyone who knows anyone in college? Talk to them. You do not have to interview everyone you know, but you may find that real students are your best resource. Do not be afraid to ask "real" questions (for example, Is State U really the party school it is made out to be?). Get the "facts" from your college guides, and opinions and insights from the people who really know the school—the students. College nights and visits from admissions officers can also be useful because you get to see and talk to a representative of the college in the flesh. As with the viewbooks, read between the lines. College reps are there to sell the school and will be reluctant to confess any serious problems with it. It is up to you to be critical in evaluating what they say.

At this point, all the things we have been mentioning are just bits and pieces, but if you start adding them up, you will begin to get an idea of what the college experience is like on each campus. We realize that college may still seem miles away.

Being editor of the school paper or winning the league championship often seems a thousand times more important than reading through stacks of college literature that all looks much the same anyway. You will be tempted to put off thinking about college until later. Resist the temptation. Getting off on the right foot is important, and it will take some serious effort. We hesitate to say "earlier the better," for the fear of striking panic in the hearts of every parent, but the summer after sophomore year is not too bad a time to slowly start looking around.

The Visit

The summer vacation between junior and senior years is the best time to get serious about college visits. Your list of potential colleges should be narrowed to about 15 schools by this point.

The purpose of a college visit is not to get the basic information you already have. You can find out all about the academic particulars from the glossy promotional literature that each school is sure to send you. The goal, instead, is to figure out how each campus feels and how much you like it. You will want to see how the students act toward each other to know if you would be comfortable there. Said one student about visiting an Ivy League school, "I just wanted to see if they looked normal, or if they all wore preppy sweaters and drove BMWs. I wanted to be able to picture myself there."

The best time to visit schools is during the academic year. It is the best time to see prospective colleges in action; this is how they will look if you decide to attend. You want to see daily life. It is best to avoid the exam periods and breaks when students usually are not around. Also, you will want to schedule interviews with admissions officers as far in advance as possible. However, we warn you, from speaking with friends who work for Yale's admissions office, the on-campus interview is much more grueling and critical. Unless the school's admissions office hints that it is preferable to do an on-campus interview, opt for the alumnus in-

terview instead. Largely, the idea that on-campus interviews are more important than alumni interviews is a myth.

Before you go, take some time for a little preparation. You will need to develop a system for evaluating the strengths and weaknesses of each college you see. Make up a short list of characteristics to have in mind when you visit: What is the atmosphere of the campus—is it fun and games or conducive to studying? How crowded are the freshman dorms? Try to think of a uniform way to record your findings, especially if you are visiting several colleges on one trip. By focusing on carefully selected criteria, it will be much easier to compare schools later in the process. Take a look at "The College Spectrum" section of this book for some ideas.

Staying on campus overnight with undergraduates is a good idea. Contact them through friends or ask the admissions office to help you find a host (most will be glad to do so). The prospect of staying with students might sound intimidating, but most hosts are genuinely interested in helping you. After a night or two, you will hopefully be sorry to leave. The real differences among most colleges are in daily life, so pay careful attention. "I found that it didn't matter much if I stayed over or not, as long as I got to talk to students," one recent applicant said. "But if you do stay over, Friday night is the best time." That's when you get to see what the students' social life is really like. And if you are staying with socially withdrawn hosts, just strike out on your own if you are feeling brave; just don't do anything you'll regret later.

"The best advice I got," another prospective student said, "was to talk to students. It's tough . . . I'm kind of shy. But it's worth it to ask." Indeed, the best source of information is the living, breathing student body. You will be surprised by how willing most students are to divulge the dark secrets of their daily lives. After all, most campuses have a healthy dose of school spirit. Who would miss a chance to promote their favorite place?

You can also learn a lot from the nonverbal clues students emit. Size up the typical student. Are his eyes glazed? Is her vocabulary limited to the word "intense" and "dude?" Is he tripping over his own feet, weighed down by a calculator, two slide rules, and physics and chemistry textbooks? These are caricatures, of course, but if you can identify some common thread running through most of the students on campus, you should be well on your way to an intelligent evaluation of the college.

Keep in mind that college life does not consist entirely of classes. Sample the food, which is, after all, a necessity of life. Check out the dorms. Take the campus tour. Though you are sure to be inundated with obscure facts about the college that do not interest you, it can be useful to see the buildings themselves and the campus as a whole. Look closely at the facilities. If you have questions, do not hesitate to ask. The tour guide is usually a student, so do not let the opportunity pass if there is something you really want to know.

Most important, though, is to get a sense of the campus atmosphere. How does it feel to walk across the main quad? Does the mood seem intellectual or laid-back? Do T-shirts read "Earth Day Every Day" or "Coed Naked Beer Games"? Look for postings of events; some campuses are alive and vibrant, others will seem pretty dead. Focus on these characteristics while you are on campus; you can read about the distribution requirements at home.

Should you bring your parents along when you visit? Maybe. If you feel comfortable going alone, leave them home. Although they mean no harm, parents can sometimes get in the way. If Mom or Dad takes a wrong turn and starts driving the car around on the main quad (it has happened before), your embarrassment may cloud your impression of a school you might otherwise have loved.

If your parents do go along, make sure you take some time to roam around on your own. Take the tours together, but send Mom and Dad to a hotel while you sleep in the dorm. In all fairness, having your parents along can be a good thing as long as they know when to step back and let you go your own way. They know you as well as anyone, and they might see things you miss. The drive home is often an excellent time to discuss with them the pros and cons of the school that you just visited.

The Interview

Just about every college applicant dreads the interview. It can be the most nerve-wracking part of the college application process. But relax—despite the horror stories you might have heard, the interview will rarely make or break your application. If you are a strong candidate, don't be too cocky (many have fallen this way); if your application makes you look like a hermit, be lively and personable. Usually the interview can only help you, and at some schools it is nothing more than an information session. "I was constantly surprised at how many questions they let me ask," one applicant reported.

It is best to look at the interview as your chance to highlight the best parts of your application and possibly to explain the weakest parts without being whiny or making excuses. Are your SAT scores on the low side? Did your extracurricular section seem a little thin? An interview gives you the opportunity to call attention to your successes in classes despite your scores, or explain that of the three clubs you listed, you founded two and were president of the third.

There are a few keys to a successful interview. The first is to stand out from the crowd. Keep in mind that the interviewer probably sees half a dozen or more people every day, month after month. If you can make your interviewer laugh, interest him or her in something unusual you have done, or somehow spice up the same old questions and answers, you have had a great interview. Don't just say that you were the president of something; you *must* be able to back up your titles with interesting and genuine stories. Second, do not try to be something you are not. Tell the truth. By doing so, you will be more relaxed and confident. Even if you feel that the "real you" isn't that interesting or amazing, think hard about your years of high school; you'll surprise yourself with the stories that will surface in your mind.

A few days before the actual interview, think about some of the questions you might be asked. Some admissions officers begin every interview by asking, "Why do you want to go to this school, and why should we let you?" You should not have memorized speeches for every answer, but try not to get caught off guard. Make sure you really know why you want to attend this college. Even if you are not sure, think of a plausible reason and be prepared to give it. Students often make the mistake of giving a canned answer, which is okay given most answers are similar, but admissions officers look to admit students who want to take advantage of all that is available at their school. Your answer must include the three essential elements of a good reply: your interests, whether academic or extracurricular; what you believe the school will provide; and how and why you are excited about the opportunity to take advantage of them. Other common questions include those about your most important activities, what you did with your summers, and what vision you may have for your future.

A note of caution: If your interview takes place after you have submitted your application, the interviewer might ask you questions about some of the things you included. One student wrote on his application that he read *Newsweek* religiously. During his interview, the admissions officer asked the student about a story in a recent issue of the magazine. The student had no idea what the interviewer was talking about. He was not accepted. Back up your claims or don't talk the talk.

It is always an excellent idea to indicate that you have a special interest in something, but make sure the interest is genuine—you may wind up with an hour-long conversation on the topic. Do not start talking about how you love learning about philosophy if you have only dabbled in it once. Do not try to use big words simply to sound impressive during what should be just a friendly chat. An open, thoughtful manner can do as much as anything else to impress your interviewer.

Having a successful interview usually amounts to being spontaneous in a contrived situation. If you are nervous, that is okay. Said one applicant, "I felt sick and I didn't eat for a day before the interview." The most common misconception is that admissions officers are looking for totally confident individuals who know every-

thing and have their entire future planned out. Almost the opposite is true. An admissions officer at a selective private college said, "We do not expect imitation adults to walk through the door. We expect to see people in their last year or two of high school with the customary apprehensions, habits, and characteristics of that time of life." Admissions officers know that students get nervous. They understand.

If everything in your life is not perfect, do not be afraid to say so when appropriate. For example, if the conversation comes around to your high school, there is no need to cover up if problems do exist. It is okay to say you did not think your chemistry lab was well equipped. An honest, realistic critique of your school or just about anything else will make a better impression than false praise ever could. Even more, someone with initiative who overcomes adversity is often more appealing to an interviewer than a person who goes to the "right" high school and coasts along.

If something you say does not come out quite right, try to react as you would with a friend. If the interviewer asks about your career plans, it is all right to say you are undecided. As a high school student, no one expects you to have all the answers— that is why you are going to college. Above all, remember that the admissions officer is a person, interested in getting to know you as an individual. As one interviewer explained, "I'm not there to judge the applicants as scholars. I'm just there to get a sense of them as people."

Do not get so worried about saying all the right things that you forget to listen carefully to the interviewer. The purpose of the interview is not to grill you, but to match you and the school in the best interest of both. Sometimes the interviewer will tell you, either during the interview or in a follow-up letter, that you have little chance of getting in. If she says so or implies it, know that such remarks are not made lightly. On the other hand, if she is sincerely encouraging, listen to that, too. If an interviewer suggests other schools for you to look into, remember that she is a professional and take note. Besides, many interviewers appreciate a student's ability to listen as well as to talk.

Your interviewer might ask you whether you have a first choice, particularly if her college is often seen as a backup. If the school is really not your first choice, fudge a little. Mention several colleges, including the one you are visiting, and say you have not made up your mind yet. Your first choice is your business, not hers. If the school really is your first choice, though, feel free to say so, and to give a good reason why. A genuine interest can be a real plug on your behalf.

Also know that you can direct the conversation. Do not worry about occasional lapses as some interviewers wait to see how you will react to a potentially awkward situation. Calmly ask a question, or mention something that really interests you. It is your job to present the parts of you and your background that you want noted.

Selective colleges need reasons to accept you. Being qualified on paper is not always enough. Think of the interviewer's position: "Why should we accept you instead of thousands of other qualified applicants?" The answer to that question should be evident in every response you give. Use the interview to play up and accentuate your most memorable qualities. Show flashes of the playful sense of humor that your English teacher cites in his or her recommendation; impress the interviewer with the astute eye for politics about which your math teacher raves.

Too many applicants are afraid to talk confidently about their accomplishments. If the interviewer is impressed by something, do not insist that it was not much, or he might believe you. If he is not impressed by something you think is important, tactfully let him know that he should be. But do not, under any circumstances, be "too cool" for the college. One well-qualified applicant to a leading college was turned down when the interviewer wrote, "It obviously isn't going to be the end of his world if he doesn't get in. And it won't be the end of our world, either." If there is any quality you want to convey, it is a sincere interest in the school. Always come to the interview armed with a good question or two and not one whose answer is easily found in the college's viewbook. Do not ask if they have an economics department, for example—ask the average class size in introductory economics courses.

You will probably wonder what to wear. This is no life or death decision, but remember that your appearance is one of the first things the interviewer will notice about you. Wear something you will be comfortable in—a jacket and a tie or a nice dress are fine. Do not, however, be too casual. Faded jeans and a T-shirt will give the impression that you are taking the interview too lightly.

One crucial point: Keep your parents a thousand feet and preferably a thousand miles away from the interview session. When parents sit in, interviews tend to be short, boring, and useless. If the interviewer feels you cannot handle an hour without your parents, she might be concerned about your ability to survive the pressures of college life. Take the risk of hurting your parents' feelings and ask them to wait outside.

Once the interview is over, it is perfectly all right for your parents to ask any questions they may have if the interviewer walks with you back to the waiting room. Even if this makes you uncomfortable, do not let it show. Admissions officers can learn as much about you by the way you treat your parents as they do in the interview. The interviewer is not judging your parents. As long as you conduct yourself calmly and maturely, you have got nothing to worry about.

All of this advice applies for interviews given by alumni as well as those conducted by admissions staff. Alumni interviewers usually carry slightly less weight with the admissions office, but they are valuable contacts with the schools and should not be taken lightly.

What if you do not have an interview at all? Perhaps you live too far away, and you cannot get to the school itself. Or, perhaps you feel that your lack of poise is so serious that it would work against you in any interview you had. Talk it over with your guidance counselor. In general, geographic isolation is a valid excuse for not having an interview, and most colleges will not hold it against you. Yet, if the college is fairly close and makes it clear that applicants should have an on-campus interview if at all possible, make the effort to go. Otherwise, the college will assume that for some reason you were afraid to interview, or worse, that you simply did not care enough to have one. If the prospect is genuinely terrifying, schedule your first interview for a safety school, or ask your guidance counselor to grant you a practice interview. You might discover that the process is not as horrible as you originally thought.

The Tests

Standardized tests are known (not necessarily correctly) as the great equalizers. Whether you are an Olympic hopeful, a musical prodigy, or a third-generation legacy, you cannot avoid taking them. Whether you attend prep, private, public, or parochial school, your scores are meant to indicate the quantity and quality of education you have had in the past as well as your potential to excel in the future. Certainly, tests do not tell the whole story; grades, recommendations, extracurricular activities, application essays, and personal interviews round out the picture. Scores are often the only uniform admissions criteria available, and regardless of your opinion of them, they are necessary.

The Scholastic Assessment Test (SAT), by far the best known of admissions tests, is required by virtually all of the nation's highly selective colleges. The SAT is designed to measure verbal and mathematical abilities—as opposed to achievement—so theoretically you cannot study for it. After being administered in the same format for decades, the test changed slightly in March 1994. In the verbal section, antonym questions were replaced by a section on vocabulary in context, and more questions on reading comprehension and comparisons were added. For the first time, students were allowed to use a calculator for the math sections, which each included ten new "student-produced response" (fill-in-the-blank) questions along with 50 multiple-choice questions.

According to the Educational Testing Service (ETS), which administers the test, the format changes were minor, and they did not affect the way colleges used the test in their admissions decisions. Of course, it is difficult to speculate whether some colleges may lean more or less heavily on the new test in making their decisions. However, because ETS made the changes to improve the test's accuracy in determining students' scholastic ability, colleges are likely to find it a better indicator than before.

Beginning April 1, 1995, ETS also began reporting SAT scores on a "recentered" scale. The SAT was originally calibrated so that the average scores for the math and verbal sections would be 500 each, giving an average SAT score of 1000. These scores had slowly slipped over several decades to an average of 900—some say as a result of a declining American educational system, although others argue that the perceived "decrease" is not surprising considering that today's 1.8 million SAT-takers are much more representative of American education as a whole than the 10,000 primarily affluent prep-school students who took the SAT when it was implemented in 1941. The recentering returns the average SAT score to 1000 and thus gives the average test-taker a 100-point boost over the old system, which sounds encouraging only until you realize that almost everybody else gets a similar boost, and that as a result, your percentile "rank" will not change. Ultimately, the recentering, like the changes in the actual test, redistribute scores more evenly along the 200–800 score scale and therefore makes it easier for a school to differentiate between applicants. A few prestigious colleges and universities with many high-scoring applicants have complained that the recentering blurs the distinctions between top students' scores (yes, it is easier to get a 1600 now), although ETS and the College Board would argue that this is precisely why they changed the scoring; admissions committees should not be using minute differences in test scores to split hairs between applicants.

When you take the test, be sure to take advantage of two services offered by ETS upon registration. The first concerns the disclosure of your scores to recruiters. If you mark "yes" in the appropriate box, any colleges engaged in recruiting can find out the range in which your scores fall, and may send information about their programs directly to you. You might consider some of these pamphlets junk mail, but some of them might help you form the list of colleges to which you intend to apply. The SATs are also the qualifying round for the Presidential Scholar Award, a highly selective competition not as well known as the Merit Scholarship program (see "The Money").

The second service will mail your test scores to specified colleges. ETS will mail your scores directly to the admissions office of up to six colleges at no extra cost. If you have a "bad day," you have three days to cancel the mailing. If you take the test again, however, the form that reports the results of your second try will also contain the results of your previous attempt, so the colleges to which you apply will know about your bad day sooner or later.

Previously, the American College Test (ACT) was required mostly by colleges in the southern and western regions of the country, but now more colleges are accepting it as a substitute for the SAT I and SAT II tests. The ACT test consists of reading, math, science reasoning, and English grammar sections, each of which takes an hour. The ACT differs from the SAT in that it explicitly attempts to measure past achievement rather than aptitude. Many students feel that the ACT is easier, since wrong answers are not penalized.

Many of the more selective colleges also require up to three SAT II exams, formerly called Achievement Tests (also administered by ETS). Available subjects include English, a variety of foreign languages, math, history, and several of the sciences. Colleges may weigh these scores as heavily as the SAT I, so these tests should not be taken lightly. SAT II scores were also changed to reflect the re-centering. By now, you may have already taken the Preliminary Scholastic Assessment Test (PSAT). The PSAT is good practice for the SAT and high scores can qualify you for merit scholarships, although the scores themselves will mean very little after you have taken the SAT.

Advanced Placement (AP) exams are another animal altogether, since their purpose is not to get you into college, but instead to earn you credits once you get there. Administered in May, each test covers a specific subject area. Different schools require different scores for granting college credit. Some will offer credit but still require you to take classes in a subject that you aced on the AP exam. Since the tests require in-depth knowledge of specific subjects, do not put them off. If you plan on taking the American history AP test, take it right after you finish your American History course, be it sophomore or senior year. The fresher the material is in your mind, the better your score will be. In addition, the AP test scores can only help your college applications if you take them before your senior year and score high.

The most reliable way to keep up-to-date on test dates, sites, and registration deadlines is through your high school guidance office. After the PSAT, which most schools administer to sophomores or juniors every fall, you will be on your own about when and where you take the tests. Find out which ones are required by the colleges you are interested in way ahead of time; deadlines have a way of sneaking up on you. It is a good idea to begin taking the tests by the spring of your junior year. If you take the SAT in March or May of your junior year and do not do as well as you think you should, you will have a couple of other opportunities to improve your scores. The required SAT IIs should also be taken by June of the junior year so that if you decide to apply to an early-action or early-decision program, you will have completed the required testing.

Avoid postponing required testing until November, December, or January of your senior year. One new college student who put off the SAT until the last minute recalled his freshman faculty advisor saying to him, "I just don't understand it . . . you went to one of the best high schools in Chicago and did very well. How could your SAT scores have been so low?" He told her how lucky he felt just getting into college; he had contracted a nasty flu and thrown up before, during, and after the test! On the other hand, do not repeat the tests over and over. The ETS reports that students can gain an average of 25 points on both the verbal and math sections of the SAT if they take the test a second time. Two or three shots at the SATs are sufficient, and there is no need to sit for every SAT II imaginable.

If you have got the time and money, you might also consider taking a prep course given by a professional test-preparation service. Ideally, the object of the SAT is to measure raw ability, so studying should be forbidden. National test-prep companies like Kaplan and the Princeton Review, as well as dozens of local companies, remind us that our world is not an ideal one. There is a continuing debate among educators about whether these courses actually raise scores—but they certainly cannot hurt. The ETS maintains that there is "no surefire way to practice for standardized tests designed to predict aptitude." The testing agency adds that some students improve their scores after coaching, whereas others do better by preparing themselves. Coaching programs generally cost hundreds of dollars and seem to be most useful to students who are poor test-takers or who feel that they have a great deal of room for improvement. If you do take a prep class, take it seriously. You may have six or seven other high school classes to worry about and those might seem more important, but you cannot hope to get your money's worth if you do not attend all of the sessions and complete any homework. In general, the longer the program, the more likely it is to boost your scores.

If you choose not to take a practice course, at least read the instructions on the ETS practice exams carefully and thoroughly. You should not have to waste time during the exam rereading instructions. If you do choose to study by taking practice exams, treat them seriously. Simulating the test-taking environment (real questions, no interruptions, strict time limits) is a good exercise in familiarizing yourself with the situation so you will not freak out when it is for real. The official ETS book of practice tests, *10 SATs*, and commercially marketed practice books (the ones produced by the companies that also teach prep courses are the best) contain sample SATs.

In our opinion, one of the most effective ways to prepare for the SAT is to take as many practice tests as possible under simulated testing conditions. Actual SATs are much better than the practice tests in

SAT preparation books. True to its title, *10 SATs* has official SATs from two previous years. It is published annually and is available in most bookstores or can be ordered directly from ETS. Set aside three hours every Saturday for the ten Saturdays before the test; try to make it the same three hours when you will be taking the real exam. Instruct family, friends, and your dog to leave you alone for those hours. Such a regimen will give you a keener sense of the overall structure of the test and help you to work faster during the actual exam, and might help you relax a bit. Chances are that your actual score will hover somewhere close to your practice test scores.

A good student who is confident about test taking will probably do just as well studying on his or her own. One student endured a practice course only to score 100 points below what he received on a practice test he took before entering the course. He then prepared on his own with *10 SATs*, took the SAT a second time, and not only gained the 100 points but bettered his original practice score by 50 points. One thing to keep in mind: Although test preparation may or may not boost your SAT scores, it can make a huge difference on the SAT IIs, which measure your knowledge of a subject the way conventional tests do.

The night before the exam, get plenty of sleep. Do not cram the night before. Relax. "My teacher encouraged us to go out and have a good time the night before," recalled one first-year college student. "So I went to the movies as a distraction. I think it worked!" On the day of the test eat a full breakfast, dress comfortably, and do not forget to bring two pieces of ID, a couple of number-two pencils, and a pencil sharpener. Make sure you are up early and know where you will be taking the test as well as how to get there. The test center may be overcrowded, there may be no airconditioning or heat, and a hundred construction workers may be drilling outside the nearest window—be prepared for anything!

The key to success on the SAT is to keep calm. During the exam, keep track of how many problems there are, and allot time accordingly. Read and attempt to answer every question since you do not get more credit for the hard ones than the easy ones. The SAT is one of the few standardized tests that penalizes the taker for wrong answers. The best overall rule is to eliminate one or more of the possible answers and try to select from the remaining choices. If you really have no idea about a question, it is best to leave it blank. Just remember to also leave a blank on your answer sheet!

A word of warning: Do not even think about cheating. It is not worth it, and your chances of getting caught and blackballed from college are high. To weed out cheaters, the ETS uses the mysterious K-index, a statistical tool that measures the chance of two students selecting the same answers. If your K-index is suspect, a form letter goes out to the colleges you are interested in, delaying your score until you retake the exam or prove your innocence. Know that looking at another person's test is not the only activity that the ETS considers cheating. Going back to finish work on a previous section is also against the rules. Do not tempt fate—a low score is better than no score at all.

At the beginning of this section, we stressed that standardized tests are important. How important? It varies. Generally speaking, the more selective the school, the less your scores will matter. At many state schools, admission depends almost entirely on test scores and grades. If you score above the cutoffs, you are in. At very competitive colleges, tests are just one of many factors. According to the dean of admissions at Harvard University, "If scores are in the high 500 to low 700 range, they probably have a fairly small impact on our decisions." Each of the schools in this book lists a mean SAT score. Remember that half of the students accepted to that college scored below the mean. Unless you score far below or far above the mean of your desired college, in most cases the SAT will not make or break your chances of getting in. If your scores are not quite up to snuff, but you have attended an inner-city school or a school in an area of the country where educational standards are below the norm, your apparent deficit might, in fact, indicate real strength—as long as you have passed certain minimum levels. Remember that a combined 700-point minimum is necessary to participate in NCAA athletic programs.

Many students mistakenly believe that the SAT is the only test that "really matters" in competitive college admissions. In fact, SAT II scores taken as a whole are usually of equal importance. Although most claim that SAT IIs are not taken into account for admissions, many colleges actually view these scores as a more accurate predictor of future performance than the SAT. In almost every case, your high school record is more important than your SAT scores. A strong performance in high school can sometimes compensate for weak scores, but standardized tests alone rarely make up for a poor showing in the classroom. If scores are exceptionally high or low, however, they do tend to take on more importance in the eyes of the admissions officer. The fact, for better or worse, is that currently test scores are an important factor in college admissions; try your best to make it an advantage point for you and don't panic if you don't get 1600.

The Application

By the time the leaves start to change in the fall of your senior year, you should decide on four to eight schools to apply to. If you are fairly certain about your first-choice school, you may apply to as few as two or three others, but if you are looking at highly selective schools, seven or eight is a more realistic number.

Ideally, the colleges you choose should range from highly selective to less so. A common tendency among applicants is to aim too low or too high. Do not let high median SAT scores and low acceptance rates at your two favorite schools intimidate you and keep you from applying. Even if the odds are against you, you will be happier attending your third choice knowing you at least tried for the other two. However, do not go to the opposite extreme of overconfidence and forget to choose a "safety school"—one where your chances of getting in are excellent and where you'll also be comfortable and happy. "At my school, we use the 2-2-2 plan," explained one senior. "Two 'safeties,' two 'middles,' and two 'reaches.'"

Once you have decided where you want to apply, start thinking about when. Make a list of when each application is due, and think about completing them in that order. You can put the schools most important to you closer to the front so you will not rush through them, or save them for last when you have had the most practice. If you truly want to go to a school, get the application in on time, preferably early. If a school needs to weed an applicant pool of thousands down to a few hundred, nothing is easier than immediately eliminating a late application.

Once you start considering due dates, you will want to decide whether to apply under any of the various "early" programs. These typically include early decision, early action, and rolling admissions. Early decision and early action are similar. Both require you to submit your application in the fall, usually mid-October to early November, and both will notify you by mid- to late December. The key difference is that early decision is binding, whereas early action is not. An early-decision candidate signs a contract stating that if he or she is accepted, he or she will enroll. Be sure to read carefully any early-decision agreement you sign. All applications to other schools usually must be withdrawn, and the student will most likely pay some sort of retainer fee immediately. Failure to comply with the agreement can lead to rather disagreeable consequences, typically blackballing from other schools. Needless to say, a student can apply to only one school as an early decision.

Early decision should only be used if you have a clear first choice in mind since it allows no room for flexibility. It does have advantages, however. Applying for early decision expresses a clear interest in the school and may give you an advantage over regular applicants. In addition, if you get accepted, you will be spared many of the hassles of the application process (and you can be wearing your college sweatshirt as early as Christmas vacation of senior year). If you feel your credentials will greatly improve during the first semester of your senior year, though, you might not want early deci-

sion. Rejections are final, regardless of when they arrive, and robbing yourself of an opportunity to put your best application forward for the sake of an earlier reply is not wise.

Early action is offered primarily by a few Ivy League schools, although other schools are beginning to offer similar programs. Because early action is not binding, it offers convenience without commitment, but for this reason it may not give as much of an advantage to the applicant. Typically only the top applicants are accepted, with borderline cases deferred for consideration with the main applicant pool.

Rolling admissions is another process offered by some schools, usually those that are larger and less selective. The process is a simple one. You send in the completed application, the staff considers it, and sends you a reply within a few weeks. Rolling admissions means you are judged on your own merits as opposed to being judged against the rest of a pool, but the relative difficulty of gaining acceptance increases as the spaces fill up, so apply as early as possible. Rolling admissions lets many students ensure acceptance to a "safety" school early in the process.

Once you know when to apply, you must begin the process of filling out the application, and there are some general rules to follow. Read the entire application carefully, cover to cover, before you begin. Always fill out or type the applications yourself. Never allow more than one person's handwriting to appear on anything you send to the admissions office. If you must write by hand, again, do so yourself and do it neatly. Keep ink color consistent throughout the entire application as well. If you use a word processor or computer for your essay, select a basic font, preferably the one that looks most like a typewriter, and use the best printer you can find.

You will find that each application has a certain "style." Some are very stiff and formal; others make an attempt to be casual. You can let the style of the application help you determine how to fill it in. Some schools insist that the application must be handwritten, for example, and others strongly encourage you to type. Some colleges do not make it easy to follow their own suggestions. "My Emory University application encouraged me to write, but there were no lines on the page!" complained one new freshman. Do the best you can.

Applications are usually divided into several sections. Treat every section as important, and use every page to your advantage. If a section gives you some degree of freedom to answer, do not repeat information you have listed elsewhere. The following explanations of the sections include some things you should remember when filling out your application.

- *Personal Information.* This usually is the first section, and is fairly straightforward. Certain questions of race or ethnic background may be optional, but it is not a bad idea to answer them, as they cannot hurt you and may help you. Again, do not try to be something you are not. Having a third cousin twice removed who has a Cherokee grandfather does not make you a Native American in the eyes of the admissions office. This part of the application may also ask for specifics about your parents—their careers, college degrees, and places of birth. You might want to write all this out on an index card to keep with your applications, so you only have to ask once.

- *Standardized Tests.* This section, also straightforward, tells you which tests are required, and gives you a place to list your scores and dates of past exams. You will most likely have to send an official copy of all your exam results to the school, through the Educational Testing Service. Make sure you request the copy of this report early enough for it to arrive before the deadline.

- *Extracurricular Activities.* Here is your first chance to be more than a statistic. Along with your essay, your activities define your personality in the eyes of the admissions office. Take the time to list them as the college requests. "Some schools want them chronologically, some want them in order of importance," said one recent applicant. If

it does not say, use the order of importance, and check this order against the rest of your application. If you intend to write your essay about your experiences as a hospital volunteer and you list it as your fifth most important activity, the committee will have doubts, either about the sincerity of your essay or the accuracy of your list. Make sure your information does not contradict itself.

As for which activities to list, remember that quality consistently takes precedence over quantity. Two or three activities to which you have committed yourself and that reflect your character in some manner will far outweigh membership in 20 clubs that you dropped after your first year. The general rule is that there are very few "superstars" of extracurriculars such as nationally ranked athletes or concert musicians in any applicant pool, and that activity lists are designed more to give some depth to your application than to tip the scales of an admissions committee in either direction.

- *Transcript.* Grades are a vital part of any application. There is little we can do at this point to help you improve them, but you can work on their presentation. Your percentile class rank counts for a lot, and those with the strongest applications will be in about the top ten percent. With any luck, you have taken the majority of your classes in the "meat and potatoes" disciplines: math, English, science, and so on. Colleges are not likely to be impressed with sociology, psychology, and other frill courses some high schools offer unless you have also mastered the basics. Senioritis makes offbeat electives tempting, but watch out. If the school of your choice sees that you have selected "Leadership Skills" instead of AP English, they will be somewhat less than impressed.

One more thing to remember: It is vitally important that any honors classes you have taken are marked as such on your transcript. (See your counselor to make sure.) If you are not taking honors classes, try to schedule some for your senior year. It can be damaging not to have taken the most rigorous courses offered at your school. Include any transcripts from summer programs at other schools or universities as well. Taking a college-level course shows initiative and is always a plus with the admissions office.

• *Recommendations.* Many colleges require one or more letters of recommendation. In cases where they are optional, the recommendation of a guidance counselor or teacher may not guarantee your acceptance, but it certainly will not hurt. Look for teachers who know you personally, perhaps as coaches or advisors. You should obviously choose teachers in subjects that are your strong points. Writing skills are highly valued by any college, so English teachers are a good choice, especially if your verbal test scores are strong. You should once again aim for a balance of subjects and viewpoints in selecting your teachers. Make sure they receive all of the necessary information in plenty of time to meet the deadline, and make sure to follow up. "I casually asked my bio teacher about my recommendation on the day before the deadline, and he hadn't even written it yet!" Most teachers are quite careful and considerate, but it never hurts to remind them when the deadline is near.

Most recommendation forms have a line at the bottom asking the student to waive his or her rights to see the completed recommendation. Unless you are extremely uncomfortable about allowing your recommendations to be submitted without your approval, sign the waiver. It shows that you have faith in those who have worked with you. Besides, many teachers will let you see what they have written anyway. "My teachers showed me the results voluntarily. I think they put a lot of time and effort into them, and they want us to know," said one applicant. A few schools demand confidentiality, including The College of William and Mary, which asks that the teacher seal the letter in an envelope and then sign over the flap.

• *The Essay.* Last but not least, you must write The Essay. Too many students needlessly stress out over the essay. If you think about it, the essay is, along with the interview, the only part of the application process that lets you determine the form and/or presentation. Even better, you get to go back and correct the parts of your essay that do not come out right the first time. There are some guidelines to follow, though.

Be concise. If the essay gives you a length limit, adhere to it. Pick a topic that not only will interest an admissions officer, but also truly interests you. Trying to write about something that you do not really care about just because you think it will make a good topic will only result in an essay no one else will care about either. Be yourself. If that means writing about a topic someone else might deem trivial, let an interesting, expressive essay be your answer to their criticism.

Begin thinking about your essay almost immediately, and do not be afraid to simply sit down and let some words pour out. Revision is the key to truly good writing, and under no circumstances should you send in a first draft. Procrastination, as tempting as it might be, can result in an inferior product. If you begin early enough, your writing will be relaxed and natural, and can be revised and tinkered with until it reaches the desired level of perfection. Writing your college essay the night before you mail it is a pressure-cooker situation that can only lead to disappointment. If you can, ask a teacher or counselor to work with you, not only to give grammatical and stylistic advice, but also to check for typos. Under no circumstances should you write on an application form until your essay is perfect.

Many schools ask what seem to be similar questions, but unless they are exactly alike, do not use the same essay more than once. Sometimes rewriting the introduction and conclusion can do the trick, but get a second opinion. Trying to make an essay written for one application "fit" a specific question from another college can be a fairly obvious ploy, and one that will only make you look bad. "I ended up writing about ten essays," explained one college freshman. "I wanted to be sure they were specific enough."

Essentially, your goal in writing an essay is to clearly and concisely discuss yourself by discussing something different. Your writing style should say as much about you as your words. To say people find you funny is one thing, but to make a reader laugh is quite another. You do not need an admissions officer to tell you which is more effective. Speak in your own voice and do so consistently throughout. Being humorous or unorthodox can make you memorable, but only if you are good at it and it is consistent with the tone of the rest of the application.

- *Miscellaneous.* If you feel that something about you speaks strongly in your favor, and it cannot be included in the application proper, think about sending it anyway. Many schools accept portfolios from aspiring artists and tapes from musicians. This does not, however, include such gimmicks as videotapes of your friends extolling your virtues, or sending your application inside a cake. Essentially, if your "creative writing sample" still needs to be written, do not bother. It probably is not worth the extra effort and certainly isn't the purpose of sending additional materials. Think "past accomplishments" when you are trying to decide if something should be sent.

Above all, be certain that your application is neat, honest, and all your own. Never put down anything fake, half-true, or almost true. Admissions officers have sensitive bullshit detectors, and if something in your work sets off their alarms, you've kissed your chances at that college goodbye.

Once all the stamps are licked and envelopes sealed, try to relax. This may be easier said than done, but if you are like most students, the months before your deadlines will have been frazzled ones. Go out, have fun, and enjoy the rest of your senior year. April is just around the corner. . . .

The Wait

We realize, of course, that no matter what we say, you will worry. From the day the final application goes in, students across the nation torture themselves with the ever-present "What if?" What if my first-term grade report got lost in the mail? What if my physics teacher forgot to send in my recommendation? What if ETS reports my SAT scores to the wrong schools? For some applicants, this period of suspense will be short-lived. Those who apply on a rolling admissions plan will have to wait only the few weeks it takes their application to be processed, while early-action and early-decision applicants should have their suspense ended (or prolonged) around December.

For those of you remaining, the pressure can be intense. "The whole school was waiting," recalled one college student. "We had all applied to the same schools, and we were all wondering who was going to get in!" The following information may help you understand what really happens while you are waiting.

Some colleges have relatively uncomplicated ways of evaluating applications. Many state universities use simple cutoffs for grades and SATs, accepting everyone who is qualified. At more selective colleges, however, the process is much more complex. After all the applications are in, every piece of information about each applicant, from the application to jotted notes from an interview, is assembled in a folder. Much of the applicant pool is academically qualified to attend; therefore, non-academic factors play a more important role. Each admissions office has its own criteria for organizing and reading the folders. Many do them by secondary school, others by state or region; sometimes all the "legacy" applicants (sons and daughters of alumni) are evaluated together. Each college starts with a rough idea of the optimal mix of "types" to enroll. Instead of being judged against absolute standards, applicants are evaluated relative to others who apply. Your fate will probably be determined by how well you rate within your subgroup.

Ethnic-minority status can be an important advantage in college admissions. Talented African-American students are much in demand. Being of Latino or Native-American descent also can be an asset. Recent years have seen a tremendous rise in the number of qualified Asian Americans applying to prestigious colleges. Consequently, their acceptance rates have seen a steady decline at these schools—so much so that questions have been raised as to whether limits have been imposed on the number of Asian Americans admitted each year.

Aside from ethnicity, chance diversity factors (as opposed to special talents or skills developed through a student's own initiative) are of limited importance. Relatives who attended the college or university may be an important asset at some schools and mean little at others. The same goes for geographic distribution. In general, the less successful a college is in attracting students from your school or region, the better your chances for admission. If you live very close to a selective college, you will sometimes get a break because the school wants to keep good relations with the community by admitting more local students. All these factors are far less important than the other parts of your application, but they can give you an advantage among applicants with similar qualifications, and sometimes that makes all the difference.

At most schools each folder is read and evaluated by one to three admissions officers. Many colleges have numerical ratings that are assigned to every application. Some rate the academic and non-academic sides of the folder; other systems are more complex. After a folder has been read, usually one of the staff will present it to the admissions committee as a whole for final action. Faculty members frequently are involved in the deliberations, either to contribute professional opinions on artwork, music, and so on or as full-fledged members of the committee. Coaches and alumni groups can also have their say about particular students they would like to see admitted.

Inevitably, the folders of marginal applicants get closer scrutiny than those of clear "admits" or "denies." Particularly close calls are saved until the end for final action by the committee. Sometimes, the director or dean of admissions retains a number of "wild card" acceptances for applicants denied admission by the full committee.

Although the process is subjective, it is by no means haphazard. Many admissions officers are recent graduates who vividly remember what it is like to be an applicant, and others on the committee bring many years of admissions experience to the evaluation process. In addition, each college has built-in safeguards to ensure that admissions officers with headaches or hemorrhoids do not bias the process.

Finally, after the admissions machine has ground to a halt, decision letters arrive in mailboxes across the nation. "My dad had about 1,000 copies of that acceptance letter made. And then he framed it!" reported one triumphant acceptee. "It's true what they say about a thick or thin envelope!" said one recent graduate, "but not for early action—the acceptances arrive in a thin envelope for those."

Making the waiting list, once a booby prize or a sop to the child of a potentially disgruntled alumnus, has come to have value in this age of overlapping acceptances. If schools underestimate the number of accepted candidates who will reject them, there will be holes in the incoming freshman class, which will be filled from the waiting list. Even so, the waiting list is usually a long shot. Final notification may not come until well into the summer, so for safety's sake it is best to accept an offer of admission from another school, even if it means sending in a nonrefundable room deposit.

If you happen to be denied admission to a college you especially wanted to attend, never call the admissions office to vent your anger or ask why. If you are not satisfied, have your counselor make a discreet inquiry sometime later. As one admissions officer told us, "If somebody is contemplating transferring a year later, a bitter encounter with the admissions office can seal that person's doom forever."

When it comes to the final decision, go with your instincts. In the end, the best choice is probably the place where you will feel most comfortable.

The Money

Getting into the college of your choice is not the end of your worries, as four very expensive years lie ahead. Presently, the annual costs at the most expensive colleges are past the $25,000 mark, with some already costing more than $115,000 for a four-year education. Few families can afford this expensive price tag, especially if there is more than one member of the family going to college, but there are millions of dollars out there in the form of scholarship money each year. You should not hesitate to apply to a college because of its cost of attendance, so you should always look into the possibility of financial aid.

The most important step of the financial-aid process is to get organized (as with any step in the college application process). The money is not going to come to you, so you have to look for it. A good place to start is with your high-school guidance office. Often guidance counselors receive information about various types of scholarships (more on that later) and will usually post them somewhere in the school. Take note of these announcements and fill out the applications and you're on your way. The applications can be time consuming, but if you are well organized, there should be no problem. The following Web sites also provide information and services for students seeking financial aid: *www.finaid.org* and *www. fastweb.com*. The more persistent you are in your search, the better your chances are of finding all the funds you need.

By far the best sources of aid are the colleges themselves. Most colleges earmark large sums of money for financial aid and also distribute much of the money available from federal and state governments. Depending on the school, some may award only on the basis of need while others award on the basis of need and/or merit or achievement. The policies at various schools differ widely.

Carefully read the bulletins provided by the colleges you are considering. If you have any questions, write to the admissions or financial-aid office right away. Find out what their admissions policy is regarding financial-aid applicants. Some of the nation's wealthier schools have "need-blind admissions," which means that your application for admission is considered with no regard to your ability to pay. However, at some schools, financial need may affect the admissions decisions, especially in borderline cases where preference may be given to those with the ability to pay. Even if you do not think you can afford it, apply to the school and for financial aid. Then, just wait and see. Sometimes it is cheaper to attend a more expensive college because they sometimes provide superior aid packages. Of course this is not always the case, but it does prove that you should never decide against a school because of money until you have a financial-aid offer (or rejection) in your hand.

As a financial-aid applicant, you will soon notice all the paperwork involved. Most colleges require you to file a standardized needs-analysis form to determine an expected family contribution (EFC). Depending on the school, the form will either be the College Board's Financial Aid Form (FAF), the Free Application for Federal Student Aid (FAFSA), or occasionally the ACT Program's Family Financial Statement (FFS). The school will also have its own financial form for you to fill out, which you have to send along with the family's income tax forms for verification. The school will determine a reasonable family contribution for one year. (The student is also usually expected to contribute around $1,000 from summer earnings.) To come up with an estimate, a formula established by Congress is used. The formula takes into account family income, expenses, assets, liabilities, savings accounts, and other data. The cost of attendance minus this expected family contribution yields an approximate financial need. The school then designs a financial-aid package that may consist of a low-interest, federally guaranteed loan, a work-study job, and a combination of different types of grants. This would lead one to believe that all packages would be similar, yet this is not at all true. Even though all schools receive the recommended family contribution, they do not all use the same formula. The family contribution will thus vary slightly, but there will not be a big difference. The differences in aid packages comes mainly from the way the school issues money. Some schools may require you to get more loans, or they might give you more money.

Some schools will always make better offers than others. Wealthier schools guarantee to meet the full "demonstrated" need of every applicant they accept. At other colleges, however, the financial-aid package may leave an "unmet" need that you will have to cover on your own. In unfortunate cases like these, students can bear the extra financial burden or choose a college that gives them a better offer.

There are a few things you can do to improve your chances of receiving an adequate financial-aid package from a school. First of all, be efficient in getting all the forms in as early as possible. Some schools have a limited supply of funds available for financial aid, and the earlier they look at your application, the better your chance of receiving a larger share. Getting your forms in early shows a good-faith effort on your part, and schools are more likely to be cooperative with you if they feel you are being cooperative with them. Another thing you can do is write a letter to the financial-aid office explaining any special family circumstances that are not reflected on the financial-aid forms. If you do not let the school know about such situations, there is no way they can take them into account.

If a school offers you a financial-aid package that you consider inadequate despite your best efforts to let them know about your family situation, all is still not lost. After you have been accepted at the school, make a polite call to the school's financial-aid office. If you noted any special circumstances either on the financial-aid form or in a separate letter, ask if they took them into account when determining the award. Sometimes letters or comments get overlooked in the haste to get the aid awards out on time. If they say they took the circumstances into account, or if you did not mention any, tell them that you would really like to attend the school but do not think you can without more aid. If another school has offered you more aid, mention that, especially if the school is a competitor of the one

you're talking to. Calling may not help, but they are not going to withdraw your acceptance once you are in.

If you are eligible for money on the basis of need, then the school may list some federal government assistance. The first of the types of federal government assistance are grants. Grants do not have to be paid back, unlike loans, but they are also harder to obtain. The federal government offers two grants: the Federal Pell Grant and the Federal Supplemental Education Opportunity Grants. You have to demonstrate "exceptional" financial need for either, but the latter is harder to obtain since the government does not guarantee as much. A Pell Grant is as high as $2,340, and the FSEOG is as high as $4,000 annually.

The federal government also offers lower-interest loans. If you demonstrate "exceptional" financial need, you may be eligible for a Perkins Loan, which can be loaned at 5 percent interest up to a maximum of $3,000. There are two types of Stafford Loans, one subsidized and the other unsubsidized. The subsidized Stafford Loan is only for people who demonstrate financial need, and it has a cap of 8.25 percent interest. The government pays for the interest while you are in school and during the grace period after you graduate. The unsubsidized loan is for those who do not demonstrate financial need, and they have to pay interest the whole time. There is also a new loan called the Federal Direct Student Loan, which is just like the Stafford except that the lender is the federal government and not a bank.

There is also a federal government-sponsored loan for parents called the PLUS loan. It is particularly valuable for those who qualify for little or no financial aid. Each year, parents are allowed to borrow the full amount of tuition less any financial aid the student receives. The loan requires good credit, repayment while the child is still in school, and interest rates that are not far from market rates. Still, it can help to ease the burden on middle-class families.

You will also probably be required to take a job through the federal work-study program. Many applicants worry that working part-time will detract from study or, equally important, playtime. Yet, if you work on campus, you certainly will not be the only one: Most colleges report that about half of their students hold term-time jobs. It is possible to take a full load of courses, participate in extracurricular activities, and work 10 or 15 hours per week, all while maintaining a good grade point average. Although freshmen tend to get the least exciting jobs on campus, in later years you may well find yourself working on interesting research, in a lab, or in a library job.

Many private colleges also provide scholarships based on academic, athletic, or artistic ability. As competition among colleges for the best students intensifies, more and more colleges are offering lucrative merit awards to well-qualified students. There are many excellent schools, including many state universities, that offer merit scholarships in ever-increasing numbers. The best source of information is your high-school counselor and state Department of Education.

Be sure not to overlook the millions of dollars of aid available from private sources. Organizations ranging from General Motors to the Knights of Columbus offer money for college, often as prizes to assist students from your community. Sometimes large companies offer scholarships to children of their employees, so have your parents find out if their employers have such programs. There are also several scholarships out there related to specific majors, religions, or even ethnic heritage. Or if you scored very high on the PSAT, you could be in the running for a National Merit Scholarship. There is often a catch to merit-based awards, however: If you qualify for awards from private sources, your school will often deduct some or all of the amount from any need-based aid you receive.

The only other significant federal aid available that is not based on need is ROTC (Reserve Officers Training Corps) scholarships. Thousands of dollars are available annually for students willing to put in several years in a branch of the armed forces. Sometimes they will even repay a portion of the federal government loans. More and more, federal aid is being reserved exclusively for the very needy. Many families with incomes over $35,000

who qualify for PLUS loans must now pass a needs test to get Stafford Loans. Yet, if you play your cards right, your family should not have to undergo severe financial hardship to put you through school.

Advice for Transfers

If you are already in college and are thinking about transferring to another school, the preceding comments are mostly old hat. Theoretically, you know what to do now, but there are a number of new considerations that all potential transfers should keep in mind. The most important is the actual decision to transfer. If you are unhappy, it is easy to blame your school first. However, the cause of your troubles might not be your school in particular, but college itself, so do not assume that you will automatically be happy at another university. One dejected Ivy League student formed a transfer club during his freshman year and recruited friends to join him. Now, he is a happy senior at his original school, thankful that he and his friends ultimately decided not to transfer. Another student left Stanford in search of what she thought were "greener pastures," but found New England "cold, gray, and without pastures at all." According to one transfer student, "It's a big risk. You have to really want to leave where you were or really want to go where you will be."

Most schools accept transfer students who have up to two years of credit at another university. It is safer, however, to transfer after your first year, because your old university will be more likely to take you back if you change your mind. One student advised that it is better to take a leave of absence from your original school than to withdraw completely. This way, if you do not like the new school, you will have an "escape hatch" and little trouble returning. If you received financial aid from your former institution, make sure the schools you are applying to can offer an adequate aid package.

Another new consideration is the application itself. Be aware that colleges tend to consider a transfer student in a different light from a high school senior. Few students tend to leave top private universities, so the acceptance rate for transfers tends to be much lower than that for first-time applicants. The situation can be different for state schools. One student at UC Berkeley reported that many of her classmates spent two years at Bay Area community colleges, then transferred to Berkeley to complete their degrees and benefit from the prestigious name. Each school looks for different students, but grades, recommendations, and the essay that explains why you want to transfer are usually the three most important parts of the application. Standardized tests and extracurricular activities are not as important. College grades will carry far more weight than your high-school grades. Although you rarely will be able to transfer out of a college at which you are getting low grades, admissions committees understand that many a high-school or freshman-year dilettante suddenly gets serious. It may not be too late. If your grade point average just shot up from 2.0 to 3.7, a tougher school than your current one may well accept you. As much as you might want to leave your school, do not ease up on classes.

Recommendations from college professors will be important. An English professor at Louisiana State University who is writing your recommendation, for example, might personally know an English professor at Tulane. In such a case your recommendation will naturally go much further than one from an unknown high-school teacher.

Because colleges will expect you to prove that you have developed and matured in your first year or two of college and to show why you absolutely cannot stay at your old school, your essay (and interview, if you can arrange one) is critical. Be definite about why you want to transfer and what you expect to find. Academic reasons are best; personal ones (such as a heartfelt need to live in a more rural setting after suddenly developing acrophobia in your skyscraper dormitory) are only as persuasive as you can make them. Never mention a long-distance love unless the two of you are married. It helps if the department in which you want to major is under-subscribed at the new school.

If you do transfer, consider your housing options carefully. College housing is often best because experienced students will be all around to answer your questions. Whether or not your dormmates are friendly is "the luck of the draw, but you can expect them to at least be responsive and civil," said one transfer student. Another successful transfer felt that sharing a room with a fellow transfer student in a regular dorm was ideal because "when you have two people in the same situation, you help each other, and when you have regular students close by, it's easy to make new friends." Once acclimated, transfers tend to be extremely adept at getting involved in campus life at their new schools. One Stanford admissions dean noted that "it's not unusual for transfers to take a lot of leadership positions."

The College Spectrum

At first glance, the sheer number of colleges included in this book might seem a bit overwhelming—clearly you would never consider applying to 300 schools. Since colleges and their student bodies vary in so many ways, it can be difficult to identify schools at which you would feel comfortable. One way to get some perspective on different colleges is to identify where they stand in terms of various criteria—to figure out where they fall on a continuum we call the College Spectrum. Another is to be aware of the general social, political, and academic trends that schools are experiencing at the turn of the century.

We are not attempting to judge which types of schools are best, but instead to present a variety of perspectives and observations that can help students with the decision-making process. Our hope is that you consider all of these factors and sharpen your sense of the differences among schools, so that you can find the one that is best for you.

Size

The total enrollments of the schools in this book range from about 250 at Vermont's Marlboro College to nearly 50,000 at the University of Texas at Austin. Considering the size of the campus you want to attend is helpful in the initial narrowing-down process; the feel of a school can be very dependent on how small or large its student body is.

Academically, two important areas of comparison between large and small schools are class size and the accessibility of senior faculty. In this case, smaller colleges decidedly have the advantage simply because a smaller population usually translates into smaller classes. Students at small schools have greater opportunities for one-on-one student-faculty inter-action. At large schools, students are more likely to complain of impersonal instruction and "being treated as a Social Security number."

To make up for this apparent disadvantage, many larger schools offer special programs intended to create the sense of community among professors and students that small colleges enjoy. Different universities have different approaches. Some offer honors programs for a limited number of students; others divide the whole undergraduate student body into separate living units. Some schools house all the students who are in special programs together, occasionally with faculty living in the same residence halls. Generally, students in such programs all take the same or similar courses, most of which are divided into small, discussion-oriented groups. Bear in mind that many honors and special programs are highly selective; do your best to make a realistic assessment of your chances to be included.

Another important factor to remember is that no matter how large a school is, not all of the classes it offers will be huge and overcrowded, and some of the huge classes will break into smaller discussion groups. Thus, although courses are generally larger, you can find small ones of interest. If you are considering a large university, take a close look at the quality of its special programs. Very often, there is a gap between the description of the program in the pages of a glossy admissions brochure and the reality.

Also, pay attention to who teaches the classes. At most liberal arts colleges, only professors do. Many large universities pad their student-faculty ratios by including graduate students, or they advertise discussion classes that turn out to be taught by people who are still working toward a Ph.D. By reading guides such as this one and by talking to students, you can find out roughly how many graduate students teach and whether or not senior professors teach undergraduates; this also gives you a good idea of how much the administration cares about the typical undergraduate student. Many times, courses taught by graduate students allow for a rapport between teachers and students that does not happen with some of the stodgier old professors. However, if graduate students appear to dominate the teaching, even if only for the freshman year, you should definitely consider this as you make your decision.

For highly specialized fields that require extensive facilities, the resources at small schools are generally limited. If you want to major in mineral engineering, for instance, neither the facilities nor the course offerings at most small colleges will suffice. For facilities not associated with technical research, such as the gym or the library, size and showiness are not nearly as important as accessibility. You will not care how many racketball courts the gym has as long as one is available when you want to play. Instead of asking how many volumes there are in the library, find out whether everyone has full access to all its resources. The same goes for labs: A large school may have state-of-the-art equipment, but it will not do you much good if only graduate students and professors get to work with it. While the facilities at smaller schools may be less impressive than those at big universities, they are often more accessible to undergraduates.

You should also carefully examine the scope and breadth of the curriculum offered. A course catalog may be packed with myriad offerings, but remember that in four years you will only be able to take a fraction of those, and that a larger student population means more competition to get into the classes you want to take. Some small colleges supplement and expand their own course selection by offering cross-registration with nearby large schools or a consortium of local colleges. Thus, if you are looking for a small college, but are concerned about the depth of the course offerings, you might want to consider one that has a close relationship with neighboring schools.

Social life, too, is affected by the size of a school. Consider carefully what kind of social life you plan to have and which type of school would be more conducive to your particular interests. The people you

associate with will likely be determined by your extracurricular interests—a sports team, the school newspaper, or student government. This is especially true for universities that do not provide more than one year of campus housing. The key is finding your own comfortable niche within any school. While there are usually more niches in large colleges, finding yours may require some initiative. The larger the school, the more subgroups there are likely to be within the student body. Fraternities and sororities are also more abundant and popular on bigger campuses. (Be careful, however, of large or small schools that tend to put too much pressure on being part of Greek life or on any other kind of affiliation.) An advantage to being a member of a very large community is that the supply of new faces never runs out. If you get tired of one circle of friends, you can always find another. But when you are on your own in the midst of all those people it is also possible to feel very lonely.

Typically, small colleges offer a stronger sense of community than larger ones. You probably will have an easier time fitting in and getting involved with activities. Such intimacy also has its drawbacks. On particularly small campuses, students can develop the feeling that "everybody knows everybody else's business," as one student put it. Another all too common problem at smaller schools are cliques. The social liabilities at a small college often do not become apparent until after you have been enrolled for a year or two. By the middle of your sophomore year you might feel as if you have met everyone. ("I was on a first-name basis with my entire class within a month," said one student at a small college in Ohio. "Sometimes I just want to meet new people.") Social stagnation can set in, and it might be difficult to break stereotypes or images that others have of you. To remedy this, many smaller schools offer popular junior-term exchanges or junior-year abroad programs that allow students to experience a change of environment. If you are considering a small school, particularly an isolated one, find out if it offers such programs.

One common misconception about smaller schools is that they are inevitably more homogeneous and have less school pride or spirit. On the contrary, many of them, especially the more selective ones, have just as many different types of people as do most large universities, only in smaller numbers. Although larger schools, especially those with a big emphasis on athletics, may have tremendous school spirit, smaller ones foster their own brand of pride, usually stemming from rich tradition and a strong sense of community.

Location

Students often have misconceptions about the differences between urban and rural schools because they know only their hometown atmospheres. Many college applicants are oblivious to the opportunities (and challenges) of going out of their own state, or even out of their own region, for college.

Going away to college can be an intimidating experience. However, it can also be invigorating and rewarding. If you are from a rural area and are considering the big move to the city, expect a lot of adjustment (to noise, traffic, people, crime, the hectic pace), but try not to make or accept any assumptions about "the horrors of city life."

The most important reason for rural and small-town people to consider attending a college in or near a city is that it is a good way to find out how the other half lives. Four more years of living in the country may sound appealing, but sooner or later you will probably want to try living in a big city. Although the transition to both college life and city life will make things more difficult at first, you may actually enjoy yourself sooner than you think. Do not let your wish to live in a particular city, however, outweigh other factors when you are looking at schools.

On the same note, applicants from cities tend to believe that they will "need" the cultural resources of a city during their college years. If you fall into that category, do not underestimate the ability of the college and its surrounding community to keep you busy. After academic work, extracurricular activities, dorm parties, visiting speakers, football games, and the multitude of other school-sponsored events, few students have time to go to the theater or the opera every other night.

The most important thing to remember about rural campuses in general is that they tend to be more self-contained, both physically and socially, than most urban campuses. Many people head off to rural colleges expecting four carefree years studying by the shores of Walden Pond. In fact, these schools are sometimes academic pressure cookers. At a rural school, it is harder to get away, especially on the spur of the moment, when the academic grind gets oppressive. Then again, for some students a naturally beautiful and isolated environment may be the most conducive for a productive and successful academic life.

The biggest drawback of a rural school is the ease with which it is possible to fall out of touch with the "real world." In academic circles, it is called the "ivory tower" effect. It dulls the social consciousness and warps perceptions of how the world works. College, after all, is supposed to prepare you for adult life, which often includes facing the realities of poverty and crime.

Another point to consider is how far from home you want to be. Are you comfortable leaving the Golden Gate Bridge for the Brooklyn Bridge, or does being three hours away from your family make your knees start to quake? Distance is a very personal decision.

Your life will change in college, whether you travel far away or not. As tempting as it seems, it is generally not a good idea to sacrifice your choice of schools just to remain near high-school friends. Staying close to home does not keep your old relationships from changing, although it might make you feel secure to know that you can go home for the weekend if that is what you need or want. Make sure you are honest with yourself about your reasons for choosing a school either far away or nearby. Further, consider how the location will affect your life: Take the weather, the people, homesickness, phone bills, travel expenses, and your personal appetite for adventure into account.

Public or Private?

Choosing between a public or private school is a lot like buying a car. Some people think it is best to buy an inexpensive, fuel-efficient model that simply gets you where you want to go. Others head straight for a luxury-car dealership for a model that is more prestigious, has a better trade-in value a few years down the road, and may have several perks.

As with cars, the most obvious difference between public and private schools is their cost. As tuition at private institutions has skyrocketed in recent years, public universities have become an increasingly attractive option. Although less prestigious and usually less selective for in-state students than their private counterparts, many public universities offer solid departments in a wide range of fields, as well as top-notch honors programs for the most ambitious. Facilities at many state universities frequently equal and sometimes surpass those at the best private ones. While some of the wealthier private schools can offer extensive financial-aid packages, the fact remains that there is a large and ever-widening gap in the relative costs of attending public and private schools.

Academic offerings at both types of schools often do not differ to any great extent. Outside the classroom, however, differences become apparent. Highly selective private colleges have an intellectual atmosphere rarely matched at state universities. At any good college, public or private, much of the valuable learning takes place through interaction with students of backgrounds different from your own. Rarely do state universities approach the type of geographic diversity found at private ones, since by law they must reserve most of their places for state residents.

While some applicants consider attending a state university second-best compared to an elite private school, others make a public institution their first choice. Why might someone pass up the opportunity to attend a big-name school in favor of a state university? Some people find the atmosphere at many of the prestigious private colleges just a bit too self-centered. At a good state university, you might not find the geographic and cultural diversity of a private college, but you might just find a different type of diversity among the students. Some people may prefer the natural diversity of a public school to the carefully selected diversity of an elite private college.

It is important not to let your assumptions or prejudices about either type of school sway your decision. Not all private school students "prepped together" at the same boarding school and have names like Kip or Muffy, and not all state schools are centered on Greek life and football.

Coed or Single-Sex?

Since coeducation became the norm at American universities in the 1960s, the number of single-sex schools in the nation has dropped steadily. There are only four men's colleges remaining in this book: Deep Springs College, Hampden-Sydney College, Morehouse College, and Wabash College. The numerical decline does not at all reflect a decline in the quality of these schools or a desire among their students to admit women. Students at all-male schools state with some consistency that the absence of the opposite sex allows unsurpassed dedication to academics and a friendlier, more fraternal atmosphere. Weekends are far from single-sex: road-tripping to nearby women's colleges and frat parties with women are still the pillars of social life. Not surprisingly, the few colleges that remain all-male tend to be traditional, conservative places.

Women's colleges are more abundant than men's colleges. Many women feel that women's colleges have more to offer them than coeducational institutions. While opponents of single-sex education might say that "sheltering" women does not prepare them for the "real world," advocates insist that four years at a women's college provides an invaluable opportunity to develop one's identity as a woman in a culture that historically has been defined in very masculine terms. In defending her institution, one professor remarked, "Yes, it's segregation, but so is taking a young plant and keeping it in its own pot with enriched soil, until it grows strong enough to withstand the rigors of the garden." At most women's colleges, women's experience is a clear and constant focus. While all-male schools tend to be conservative, all-female schools tend to espouse liberal views on topics such as abortion, AIDS, sexuality, and environmental protection. Sometimes sparks fly among those with different points of view, but the atmosphere tends to be thought-provoking, especially for those who have not confronted such issues before.

The female environment generally offers more support and leadership opportunities, and many graduates of women's colleges consider their institutions as important forces driving their success. One graduate of a women's college said she now feels "more confident when in a room full of males or in competition with males." Women's colleges are also an escape from sexual discrimination; because there are no men, there is no possibility of higher grades going to those who have not necessarily done better work. For many, these are considerations that make keeping women's colleges alive a valuable cause: In 1990, students at Mills College fought successfully to keep their school from going coed. Several women's colleges are part of coed consortia, such as Mount Holyoke and Smith, whose students can take classes at nearby coed Amherst and Hampshire Colleges and the University of Massachusetts. Others are paired with all-male or coed colleges, as Barnard is with Columbia.

The majority of college-bound seniors will be enrolling in a coeducational school, and for most of these students, entering such a college environment requires little, if any adjustment. At some larger universities you may have to get used to coed dormitories and/or bathrooms. These setups are not nearly as uncomfortable (or as advantageous) as you might think. Most university dormitories are coed by floor, although some are coed by hallway. At some universities it is even possible for men to live next door to women. On the other side of the spectrum, single-sex dormitories still exist.

Make sure to check the housing information to see if the offerings match your preferences.

Advising

Not everybody is expected to ace college classes from day one, and even fewer people enter college knowing what they want to study for the next four years. Most colleges offer some sort of help for those who are struggling with a class or deciding which classes to take.

There is no way to predict whether you will need tutoring at your future college, but it can be reassuring to know beforehand that your school of choice has a safety net of academic help waiting for you if you stumble. Because many schools require knowledge of a foreign language and a smattering of math and the sciences for graduation, it is likely that these schools will provide tutoring for those who need it, free of charge. If a designated tutor is not available, it is the duty of the professors and teaching assistants (TAs), who are better prepared to answer questions about the homework than a generic dorm monitor, to fill in the void. Professors and their TAs, who are usually grad students in the department offering the class, must hold office hours. (Whether the professors or TAs are easy to understand once you speak with them is a different matter.) Study groups with classmates are a useful last resort, but it is usually up to you to organize them. Many colleges provide their students with a writing tutor, which can be a tremendous resource for those willing to admit that their papers, though well-reasoned, could be better written.

Academic advising is often not as accessible as academic tutoring. Although some colleges pair their students with a faculty advisor starting freshman year, faculty advisors often are not a useful source of information on classes outside of their specific department. If you are concerned about the administration leaving you in the cold when it comes time to enroll in your classes, talk with freshmen to see how helpful their advisors are. Most of the students *The Insider's Guide* questioned about academic advising agreed that upperclassmen who had just passed through the stress of choosing a major were the best people to consult. Upperclassmen are also a prime resource for advice on choosing classes outside of your major, because they most often share your viewpoint as a student and have tried a wide variety of classes during their college years.

A Minority Perspective on the College Spectrum

As a minority student or a person of color, there might well be some additional factors to consider in your decision. You may, for example, be searching for a school with a high population of minority students or for a school that is predominantly African-American. A school with a high minority population may prove to be more supportive and even more comfortable. Regardless of size, though, a strong minority community can be helpful during the next four years and can even help reduce the racism and ignorance on some campuses.

Another factor to consider is the general attitude of both the administration and the student body. Unfortunately, racism still exists at many colleges, but do not assume a defensive attitude while visiting schools. Instead, be aware of possible situations and attitudes that may make you feel excluded and uncomfortable. What might have seemed like a diverse college in the brochures may not seem so open-minded after all. Take note of how integrated the minority community is, and what the school does to recognize and support other cultures. Some schools may foster a pressure to conform; if the school has a large population of a certain race, there may be a distinct sense of separatism. For some this may provide a stronger sense of belonging, while for others it will only increase the stress of college life.

To determine the true attitude of the administration, look at how it attempts to support the minority communities. Some schools assign ethnic counselors to help

minority students adjust to college life. Some students appreciate this; others resent it. One student reported that her school was doing so much to accommodate her minority status she felt separated, rather than integrated. Many students, however, get used to the idea of special resources and ultimately find them supportive.

Another thing to look at is the extracurricular life. What kinds of organizations are there for specific minority groups, or minority students in general? The school may have cultural centers and politically oriented associations that focus on the traditional arts and dances of their culture. With any luck, the school's primary form of minority student recognition will not be an ethnic theme dinner once a semester.

For African-American students, an important decision may be whether to attend a predominantly black college over another school. Despite the improving financial situations of most private black colleges, you are likely to find better facilities and larger academic departments at predominantly white schools. Unfortunately, the continuing decline of federal funding is likely to exacerbate this situation, since black colleges rely heavily on such resources. Nevertheless, many students choose to attend a predominantly black college for many of the same reasons other students choose to attend a single-sex school. Some black students find them a more congenial and accepting community that is more conducive to personal growth. Likewise, students have a better chance to attain key leadership positions at a college where they do not have minority status. At a predominantly black school, the African-American experience is one of the central issues on campus. What does it mean to be a black person in America at the turn of the century? Of what importance is African-American heritage? At predominantly black schools, these questions are addressed in a manner and with a fervor unrivaled by other institutions.

In this book, we include reports on five of the best-known predominantly black schools in the United States: Howard University in Washington, D.C.; Spelman and Morehouse Colleges in Georgia; Florida

A&M University; and Tuskegee University in Alabama. For a more complete listing, we suggest you consult *The Black Student's Guide to Colleges* by Barry Beckham and published by Beckham House.

Ultimately, you have to decide where you will feel most comfortable. Whatever your choice, it is important to remember that your ethnicity is an integral part of yourself and is not something you should have to compromise in choosing a school.

Sexual Minorities

So far, we have spoken primarily of ethnic minorities. Gay men, lesbians, and bisexuals are also minorities, but unlike ethnic minorities, no college we know of has a recruitment program to attract them. The task of finding a school that will allow you to make your collegiate years the best they can be is largely up to you. One of the most important things to consider when choosing a school is whether you will be comfortable with the people around you, and whether other people (students, professors, administrators, even "townies") will be comfortable with you. Look for a place where your sexuality is respected and where there are others of the same sexuality with whom you can share your experiences. "One of the reasons why I chose [a liberal women's college] was because I knew it would have a very welcoming and accepting environment," said one student. "I think you'll find more lesbians here than at a traditional, conservative, coeducational school because it has a very safe atmosphere. It is not only easier to come out of the closet to your friends, but also to yourself," said one student.

So how can a gay or lesbian applicant assess the atmosphere at a particular college? The best way is to visit the campus, but there are also a number of other ways to evaluate schools. By looking through the official literature that a school mails to its prospective students, you can evaluate the attitudes of the administration. Check to see if there is a gay and lesbian student center. If there is not one, and this is most often the case, look for gay groups on the official list of clubs and organizations. If there are none, this could mean one of

three things: the administration refuses to officially recognize the gay and lesbian population; the homosexual population is "underground," or reluctant to attract publicity, perhaps due to potentially negative reactions on campus; or an openly homosexual population does not exist on campus. It is also helpful to browse the course catalog. Homosexual topics in history, modern culture, and the arts are subjects of legitimate academic inquiry; the absence of such course offerings might reflect the administration's ambivalence toward alternative sexual orientations.

Consider closely the vital statistics of a school. Urban schools tend to be more open-minded than small rural schools (see "Location"). Students at schools with a politically liberal climate tend to be more accepting of differences in lifestyles and backgrounds than do those at conservative schools. Schools with a large Greek scene tend to be more conservative as well (see "Greek Life and Other Social Options"). Greek systems can be oppressive toward homosexuality; many fraternity traditions reject alternative lifestyles. According to one gay student, on campuses where there are lots of fraternities, "it's cool to be macho, and they don't think homosexuality is macho at all."

These are all good indicators, but a campus visit is the best way to find out how other students view the gay community. Look for posters announcing lectures concerning homosexuality, rallies for homosexual causes, or simply meetings of gay, bisexual, or lesbian groups. Read the campus newspapers to see if they cover any prominent gay/lesbian issues. If so, what slant does the writer take on the issue? Are there publications dedicated solely to gay issues? Observe how people dress, and how the rest of the students react to alternative dress styles. If a number of people express themselves in an eccentric manner and onlookers treat them no differently than regularly dressed students, those are good indications that the school accepts individuality and self-expression.

Although the aim of this book is to help you choose a college, not to help you adjust once you get there, here are some suggestions to help homosexuals avoid potentially uncomfortable situations. If there are gay and lesbian student groups, seek them out. "Seeing that there are other people just like you will give you confidence in your sexuality, and for somebody who hasn't met many homosexuals before, they are a gigantic leap socially," one undergraduate suggested. Obviously, some people are more comfortable about their sexuality than others. If you are not yet comfortable, "remember that homosexuality is nothing to be ashamed of," one student said, "and that being homosexual does not have to dominate your life." Realize that coming out to roommates does not need to be as earthshattering as the beginning of World War III. Bring it up in the proper context (for example, if a roommate is trying to set you up for a blind date) and do not be afraid to discuss the issue further as your roommates might be more uncomfortable than you.

Politics

How politically active a campus is may affect how comfortable you are there. A generation ago, political activism was as common as bell bottoms and tie-dye. Today, however, many students treat it as an extracurricular activity. "There is a hard core of committed activists on the left and right who believe that the struggle is everything, but most people don't seem to have a whole lot of time for that," said one student at Princeton University. In fact, one student remarked that a majority of her fellow students stay away from politics for social reasons: Many people at her college look down on those with strong convictions because they assume them to be closeminded.

Some schools, most often small liberal arts colleges, are highly politicized. "At my school, you don't just put your name on name tags, you put your cause, your oppressor, your god, and your sexual orientation," one student remarked. At less politically active schools, apathetic students might be in the majority. This does not mean, however, that those who espouse strong opinions and wish to discuss them have been silenced. Before you select a school, check to see if it has a political forum that sponsors speakers and discussions. Most schools have politically oriented journals, both conservative and liberal, that provide outlets for issueoriented thinking. Many schools also have party-affiliated organizations like the College Democrats and the College Republicans. Such partisan organizations tend to be most active in the year of a presidential election. Instead of joining political organizations, many students channel their activism into volunteer programs to confront such problems as urban blight or environmental destruction head-on.

If you have gotten the impression that campus activism has been institutionalized and domesticated in recent years, you are not too far off base. The average campus in the last decade was not the hotbed of radical reform that it may have been in the past. Nevertheless, certain incidents and issues garner communitywide attention. On Columbus Day at one school, for example, indignant students covered the sidewalks with brightly colored chalk-marked polemics against racism and genocide. The gay- and lesbian-rights activists at a different school sponsored a kiss-in where same-sex couples clustered around the campus's central promenade and necked.

Gay rights, AIDS awareness, and race-related issues are commonly on the collegiate slate of activist causes. Today, political correctness (PC), manifested by a tolerance for others' ideas and political orientations and an attempt to be inoffensive to any and all groups in speech as well as in print, is something of a secondary issue. Although PC was a hot topic on campus in the early 1990s, the debates on the spelling of the word "woman" and whether your floormate is disabled or "differently abled" seem to have faded. According to one student, "Political correctness is only an issue among the watchdog groups of the right and left."

The PC contingent has won some battles. Many schools now require students to take courses that focus on non-Western cultures, or courses aimed at raising sensitivity to minority issues and concerns. One student reported that the administration at his college goes so far as to hassle non-PC groups; although a gay rights coalition was not reprimanded for announcing events with explicitly sexual posters, a reactionary group on the same campus faced executive investigation for the minor infringement of staying in a classroom too late at night.

As a general rule, the more liberal the campus, the more concerned students are about political issues. If you enjoy informal political debates or thrive on dinner conversations about the Middle East or Proposition 187, you might want to consider a more liberal school, even if you are a Bush Republican.

By visiting a college you can learn just how important politics are to the student body. Read posters and student newspapers to gauge whether the political climate on campus is right for you. The best schools might be those that can absorb all viewpoints, so that no matter what you think, there will be others who will embrace your thoughts, challenge them, or respect your decision not to vocalize them.

Preprofessionalism vs. Liberal Arts

Preprofessionalism is a term you will see again and again throughout this book. All college curriculums are not created equal. Depending on what track or what major you choose, you will be receiving either a preprofessional or a liberal arts education.

Majors that do not lead directly to a specific career fall into the liberal arts category. Even if a student plans to be an accountant, for example, he or she might get a liberal arts degree in philosophy or math, and then go on to study accounting at the appropriate professional school. The goal of a liberal arts education is to teach students how to think creatively and analytically, thus preparing them to pursue any career.

The get-ahead attitude of the 1980s generated strong interest in both preprofessional and liberal arts programs, and these interests have continued into the 1990s. There are pros and cons to each track. Some argue that a liberal arts program is the key to a solid education, while others believe that a liberal arts degree can be a waste of four years and thousands of dollars for students who already have their career plans mapped out. Many preprofessional programs require that a student take general education courses in liberal arts departments. In fact, almost all colleges insist that you take some courses outside your chosen field.

If you do not yet know your interests well enough to decide up front which option is for you, it may help you to know that the largest colleges and universities have both liberal arts and preprofessional students. The University of Michigan, for example, has a strong undergraduate school of business; many students in Michigan's liberal arts school also plan to go into business eventually but are pursuing a B.A. in a more general field first.

If you know exactly what you want from a school in terms of career preparation, then you probably will feel right at home at a preprofessional institution. However, be aware that getting a liberal arts education and getting a good job are not mutually exclusive. Furthermore, many students report that preprofessional schools tend to have a more competitive atmosphere that is unpleasant to those students who enjoy the intellectual exchange more common in purely liberal arts environments.

The 1980s also saw renewed interest in the various ROTC (Reserve Officers Training Corps) programs. These scholarships from the four branches of the armed forces help pay for tuition, books, and room and board during college. When you graduate, you are committed to four, five, or possibly eight years of reserve or active duty, depending on the program. As the supply of financial aid declines and the cost of a college education increases, many more students are viewing ROTC scholarships as a viable alternative.

Be very thorough when investigating ROTC programs. The system works differently at different schools. You will also want to explore the way that ROTC is received at your school. Some colleges tend to be very anti-military, and you may find yourself part of a controversial program on or off campus. Also keep in mind that your participation in the program does mean that you could be called to service, as a few graduates realized in a hurry during the Gulf War. Yet, the benefits of an ROTC program can be substantial for a student who joins after careful research and consideration.

Greek Life and Other Social Options

Social life at a given college is largely determined by the type of student body it attracts and by its location. At Arizona State, the fraternity scene is particularly dominant. At Loyola University, downtown Chicago clubs rule the party scene. At Harvard, intimate parties in the residences are typical Friday night fare. Your own social taste can be an important factor in choosing the type of school you want to attend.

Many students believe that fraternities and sororities are an American college staple—and the rise of the national drinking age to 21 during the 1980s has assured the Greeks an important role in campus social activity. The reason is, as one student put it, that at most schools "frats don't card." Membership in Greek organizations has increased dramatically in the past several years. Many once-defunct chapters have been revived and many new ones established.

Frats of the last decade generally had a cleaner image than their ancestral counterparts. At most schools, the notorious hazing rituals once associated with pledge initiation have been de-emphasized or abolished altogether. In addition, many Greek organizations have strengthened ties with charitable organizations and have become increasingly active in community service. On some campuses, the fraternities and sororities are the most active social-service organizations. Many new and revived Greek organizations, especially the sororities, are focusing on volunteerism. You may find that being in a sorority means more than socializing; it might also involve working on Saturdays in a soup kitchen with a group of socially conscious women.

Yet despite their best efforts, the Greeks still come under fire. Some of the old problems remain. In recent years, several pledges have been killed or seriously injured in connection with Greek-sponsored events. Hazing accidents and alcohol-related mishaps have carried the *Animal House* image into the present, and at schools where frats are one of the few places students can party, the image is likely to stick.

Whether Greek life appeals to you or not, make sure you understand how important the Greeks are at the school you choose. Going against the grain could make your social life different from most. Then again, that might be fine with you. You will also find that at many schools, it is perfectly normal to rush and also perfectly normal not to rush. While the Greeks are a presence on most campuses, at only a few do students report genuine social pressure to be part of the group.

While some other force besides Greek life may rule the scene at a given school, the odds are that alcohol has something to do with it. The sixties are long gone, and at most schools the use of hard drugs is no longer common. Among college students, alcohol is the current drug of choice.

Alcohol policies differ greatly from school to school. At some, there is a tacit understanding that students may drink in their rooms as long as they are not conspicuous about it. Other colleges are cracking down on underage drinking, eager to put an end to "party school" reputations. Many students escape the restrictions by moving off campus, which at some colleges leads to a fragmented social scene. Alcohol on campus continues to be an issue of debate among college administrations, and it is possible that the struggle will move to the federal level; in coming years, colleges might have to prove they actively oppose illegal drinking before they can receive federal money.

Visiting a school is the best way to be sure you will be comfortable with the social scene. Some would argue that the largest schools have a great number of cliques. However, it is also true that the largest schools have the most diverse social groups, due to the sheer numbers of personalities on campus.

Most college applicants worry about meeting people they will like, then find when they get to college that making friends was easier than they expected. Your interests will largely determine whom you meet. Therefore, you should be sure you find a school that has groups to represent your interests. Do you like journalism? Make sure that your school has an active newspaper. Pay attention to the social options you see. Fraternities, sororities, athletic groups, cultural groups, musical groups, and other activities can all be a part of your social experiences at college. Find what you think may be the right combination, and you will meet the right people.

Security

Security as an issue on college campuses is not simply a response to a few well-publicized campus murders. Although the tragedies at other colleges are by no means insignificant, crime in general is increasing on campuses across the country. In response to this trend, recent federal legislation has made it mandatory for all colleges receiving federal aid (which is almost every one) to publish crime statistics in several categories. At your request, the appropriate office (usually the public relations or admissions offices) at any college or university should release to you the crime count for the last calendar year.

Many colleges have also taken measures to beef up security. If you visit a campus and notice very stringent security measures (at the University of Pennsylvania, for example, you have to show your ID just to get into the quadrangle), remember that this means two things: there is a need for security measures, and the administration is responding to this need.

There are a number of features that any safety-conscious campus should have. Doors to individual dorm rooms and to the building entrances should be equipped with locks. All walkways should have bright lights, not only so that you can see, but so friends and classmates would be able to see you from a distance in case of danger. Another important security measure is a safety phone system with one-touch access to an emergency line. Each safety phone should have a distinct light to make it easily recognizable at night.

Ideally, there should be enough units so that you are never more than a half block from a phone. For getting around campus late at night, colleges should provide bus service or student safety escorts, free of charge. At least one of these services should be available 24 hours a day and should travel to every possible destination on campus. Every school should employ some type of security guard, whether unarmed monitors in or near the dorms or full-time police officers responsive solely to students and the affairs of the college.

Security problems are not limited to urban campuses. Some rural schools have crime rates as high as the urban ones. The sad truth is that many crimes are committed by other students, not outsiders. Why is campus crime such an issue now? College students are ideal targets—they keep expensive stereo and computer equipment in badly guarded areas, and they often walk alone across dark, seemingly safe campuses.

Therefore, it is important to understand that you cannot judge the safety of a campus simply by eyeing it from the safe confines of the viewbook's glossy photographs. Yet, by using a little common sense and preventive measures, the security problems of a given school should not prevent you from attending that school. By making yourself aware of potential problems and following the school's security guidelines, you can improve your chances of enjoying a safe four years. Security may be a fundamental problem with college life, but you can certainly do something about it.

Computers

Like it or not, computers are taking over. You cannot turn on the TV anymore without hearing a news report about "cyber" something-or-other or the "information superhighway"—of course, that is if you are old-fashioned enough to get your news from a boring old television set instead of downloading it off the Internet. Whether you are a literature major, art major, or major procrastinator, you are going to be using a computer of some sort, either your own or the university's. With that in mind, here is a list of things to look for when evaluating a college's computing facilities.

- *Twenty-four-hour computer rooms.* At some point you are going to have to type a paper at 3 A.M. and your machine will be broken. Make sure there is a at least one room on campus that is available 24 hours a day. Ideally, the computers are recent models; a room with five Mac Pluses does not cut it these days.

- *Internet access from your dorm room.* Most colleges provide e-mail accounts and access to the huge international network called the Internet. The lame way to do this is to give you modem access, which usually means a slower connection and busy phone lines every time you check your e-mail. The cool way is to wire all the dorm buildings so that you have direct access, often through Ethernet, without using a phone line at all.

- *Public printing.* If the school offers free laser printing, you are in luck. If you have to pay for it, you are also lucky, but not nearly as much.

- *Support staff.* Are there students (or paid staff) available to rescue your term paper when it mysteriously vanishes from your floppy disk the day before it is due? Are there enough of them to deal with the entire campus? One computing assistant for every 75 people is a pretty good ratio.

- *Macs and PCs.* Unless the college requires you to use a specific type of machine, make sure it provides adequate support for both types. If the college requires you to buy a Mac (or a PC), that is actually a pretty good thing, because it means that the cost of purchasing a computer is factored into financial aid.

- *The administration's position on computing.* Does the college want to stay cutting-edge, or does it want to squeeze the last breath of life out of every obsolete machine it owns? Is the computer situation big on the administration's list of priorities? Does the administration favor free speech or censorship over

the network? Does the president of the college have an e-mail account?

- *Access to professors.* Look for professors who are accessible over the network. Many of them will answer questions via e-mail. More and more professors now allow students to turn in assignments over the network, which can save you a trek across campus on a cold winter day.

Few colleges will score high in every category, but as long as the school you are looking at is adequate in all areas, it will suitable for your needs.

A Final Note About Quality of Life

A final but crucial criterion for your decision is the overall quality of life you can expect to have at college. A school might have the best archaeology program in the nation, but if you are not happy at the school, there is no point in going.

While it is true that academics are the most important reason to go to college, they are not the only reason. Do not lose sight of the fact that we are talking about four or more years of your life. You should set your priorities not just in terms of academics, but also in terms of social life, extracurricular activities, housing, and even the weather. Do not go to the University of Miami if you cannot stand the sun! Will your freshman room be smaller than your closet at home? Will you have to share it with three other people? Is the food identifiable? Are you comfortable with the people you see walking down the street? Does the administration listen to the students? Is there a movie theater nearby? All of these factors make a difference in the way you will feel about a school. The best way to analyze them is to visit the school and to get your hands on a student newspaper. Do you like what you see?

You may also want to check that what you like about a school will still be there when you enroll. In recessionary times, more and more schools, both public and private, face a shortage of funds and are finding themselves forced to make budget cuts. This can take many forms: reducing the number of tenured professors, cutting entire departments or programs within departments, delaying campus renovations and additions, cutting sports teams and extracurricular activities, or a combination of the above. If you were your school's star varsity soccer player and want to continue playing soccer in college, check that the team is not rumored to be the next victim of the budget ax. If you are set on majoring in linguistics, find out how big that department is; frequently the smaller and less popular departments are the first to go. Talk to students and faculty to see how potential cuts could affect your interests. As recent newspaper and magazine headlines will tell you, even the best-known and supposedly best-endowed schools are tightening their purse strings.

We hope we have been able to give you a stronger idea about some of the decisions you will be making as you continue this process. Just remember that only you can make the final decision. —*Diana Sherman*

Introduction for International Students

International students, including Americans living abroad as well as citizens of foreign countries, might face special problems in submitting applications that conform to the standards and conventions American colleges expect from their applicants. Some of these deserve special consideration. They include the "strange" American insistence on external tests such as the SAT or the ACT, getting recommendations from teachers rarely confronted with American recommendation forms, the problem of writing the kind of essay that will best combine your cultural background with the style expected by American admissions officers, and assembling a list of extracurricular activities even if your school does all it can to de-emphasize them.

Unlike schools in many other countries, virtually all American colleges insist that applicants take standardized tests such as the Scholastic Assessment Test and the SAT IIs. These tests may be hard to come by, depending on the country, but the more selective schools tend not to accept otherwise qualified applicants without standardized test scores. In most countries, American consulates or high schools offer the SAT and ACT tests, as do many international schools. In Europe, several of the American cultural centers offer additional testing sites in metropolitan areas. The best way of finding out where the nearest testing center is located is to write to the Educational Testing Service (Rosedale Road, Princeton, New Jersey 08541) well in advance. A low score on the SATs can be compensated by many other factors in an application.

A word to the wise about the TOEFL (Test of English as a Foreign Language). Many colleges say that if English is your first language or language of instruction you do not have to take this test. If your verbal SAT scores are exceptionally high and you are confident about your language skills, you should not bother to take it. However, if you are in doubt about whether your SAT verbal scores are high enough, or you think you can do exceptionally well on the TOEFL, take it. Even if you are an American citizen or have grown up speaking English all your life, a near perfect TOEFL score can never hurt. Since many colleges substitute it for the verbal part of the SAT, a low verbal SAT score can be compensated to an extent by a high TOEFL result. Those who speak English only as a second language, of course, ought to take the TOEFL, since it is considerably easier than memorizing the rarely used vocabulary required in the verbal SAT.

At many schools, international students are eligible for acceleration credits. These credits, assigned by the individual colleges, permit students who hold foreign secondary-school degrees considered superior to the American high school degree to accelerate and graduate in less than four years' time—sometimes even one or two full years earlier, depending on the college. At most colleges, international students must apply for acceleration credits during their first year, so you must take action yourself if you want the opportunity to graduate early. Some of the more selective schools can be picky about awarding these credits; applicants should make sure to ask what their prospective college's guidelines are. Similarly, a college's language requirement for undergraduates can usually be met with a foreign high school diploma, but some schools require students to take placement exams when they enroll. Taking the College Board Advanced Placement (AP) exams before college is an effective way to avoid the hassle. A good score on any of these exams can translate directly into college credit.

Foreign students should be aware of two basic facts about the AP exams. First, they tend to be difficult to arrange. Although many people outside the United States take the SAT or the ACT, international students usually have to look harder for AP testing and must often arrange it themselves. If there is an American high school in your country, approach the guidance counselors directly and ask to be allowed to take the APs with their students. (In this, as in most other instances involving college applications, good relations with an American civilian or military high school are useful, especially since guidance counselors frequently are accessible and are excellent sources for all kinds of information about the application process.) Second, if you are in the early years of secondary school and know that you may want to apply to colleges in the United States, it makes sense to take AP exams as you complete certain courses of study. Doing well on a biology AP exam is next to impossible if you have not studied that subject for several years, even though your general level of knowledge may be superior to that acquired by students in the American high school system. Taking the tests not only helps to prove to college admissions officers that you have real proficiency in a subject, it can also entitle you to immediate "advanced placement" in college courses—a serious advantage for many international students. Unlike the SATs, for which all the scores you have received are reported when you request an official transcript to be sent to a college admissions office, individual AP scores are not reported directly to the colleges. So, if you do poorly on one of the tests, you can simply forget about it or retake the test without making a bad impression on the admissions board.

The most important issue, however, is the application itself. In getting teachers to write recommendations for you, be sure to approach those who not only know you, but are also apt to write enthusiastically about you. Many teachers, especially those in English-oriented school systems, tend to be more reluctant to award superlatives than their American counterparts. An otherwise perfectly qualified candidate's application could be marred by an amusingly cynical teacher's wry comment, "An excellent student, but I hardly know him outside the classroom. Appears to have a somewhat sound character." Obviously, recommendations should not go overboard, but if the recommendation form includes boxes for the teacher to check, his or her opinions of your academic and personal achievement ought to be in the highest category. In the essay sections, again, personality counts: The more personal insight the teacher can provide the better, and a rounded description can be more convincing than a one-sided laudation.

The lack of a "guidance counselor" at your school in no way means that your headmaster has to fill out the counselor recommendation form. Instead, have a teacher whom you know well, perhaps outside the classroom, fill it out. Especially in large schools, getting an administrative official who has never seen or heard from you to comment on aspects of your personal character is a formal statement without much meaning, and can have disastrous effects on your application.

A few words on translations: Even though many colleges will accept teacher recommendations in foreign languages and have them translated at their facilities, it is often a good idea to have them translated in your own country. A translation obviously makes the recommendation easier for the admissions officers to read. Also, since schools rarely require official translations, they offer the possibility of working with your teachers to do your own translations, especially if your own proficiency in English exceeds theirs. Generally, the more the recommendation is a communal effort, the better it will be.

The same applies to the parts of the application you have to fill out yourself. Most of the important general hints have been discussed in the preceding sections of this book, but international students unprepared for American college application essays can often be baffled by the empty page that says, in effect, "Write whatever you want, but remember that anything you say can be held against you." Some schools prepare special application forms for international students that require only a curriculum vitae (similar to a resume) and a book discussion instead of the "creative" essays the American applicants must complete. Do not feel you need to comply with this format; if you feel comfortable writing about yourself creatively, do not hesitate to submit the regular "American" application form. Do remember that many of the other international applicants to colleges will be as qualified as you are, so your essay and the personal impression you make are crucial, especially at the more selective colleges. It is important not only to write about concrete achievements, but also to be creative and to present an idea of what kind of person you are, even if this seems insubstantial compared to the more stringent essays required for university administration in other countries. Your cultural or family background can often be of more interest to admissions officers than the fact that you won a national academic award.

Many foreign schools do not place a great deal of emphasis on extracurricular activities, but as can be judged from the space they are allotted in the application forms you receive, they are of utmost importance to American schools. Contrary to many other university systems, American colleges frequently prefer a "well-rounded" applicant to someone who has received the highest marks in all his classes but has done little else. This means that you have to look actively for extracurriculars to include in your resume in order to make you competitive with other applicants. Activities you choose are obviously dependent on your own interests, but it is important to find your slot, even if this means founding your own newspaper or working for charitable organizations. Even though extracurriculars may be frowned upon in your educational system, they count in the U.S. An insincere pursuit of various activities is pointless, but demonstrated commitment to one or two activities that reflect aspects of your character are vital to a strong application. College admissions officers, of course, are aware of the differences among individual countries and have different expectations of American high school students than of international applicants. All this means, however, is that extracurricular involvement in a school system that de-emphasizes such activities shows all the more personality and strength of character.

It is important to note that many American colleges group all students applying from abroad into one category, with a limited number of admissions officers evaluating the applications. Frequently, all applicants from abroad—full American citizens, students with one American parent, and foreign nationals—are grouped according to the country they applied from. Some schools, especially the more selective ones, are rumored to have quotas on the number of international students they admit, in order to achieve a particular geographical and cultural mix. This can mean two things: If you are one of several dozen applicants from a Western European country, the competition for the few spaces available may be extremely stiff. On the other hand, if you are from a country that has few other applicants, you might stand a better chance of being admitted.

A consequence of this selection process poses a difficult question to American citizens who apply from abroad. You should consider whether or not you want to submit yourself to the "international student quota"—which may prefer "real" international students to Americans who went to high school in foreign countries—and take the chance of being one of only two or three students admitted from that country. In some countries, the actual percentage of acceptance to some of the more selective schools is lower than the American average acceptance rate. Depending on the individual case, it may be advisable to apply as a regular American student with an international background rather than compete with native residents for a limited number of acceptance slots.

Financial aid to international students can range from limited to nonexistent. Many colleges will send international applicants brochures that include all kinds of information on financial aid for Americans; only upon direct inquiry do they respond that they simply do not give financial aid to international students. This situation, unfair as it seems, is not likely to change in the near future. Some of the very large and wealthy colleges can afford to be virtually need-blind in their international admissions, but make sure you know the policy at every college you intend to apply to. There is no point in going through the entire application process only to find out that once admitted, you won't receive the aid you need to attend the school.

Federal regulations for visas vary from country to country. Generally, once you are accepted to an American university, you can obtain a student visa without much difficulty. However, do not expect to be able to work in the United States outside the university. Financial-aid recipients can usually work within their colleges, but finding an outside job is next to impossible unless you have a green card (a government document proving that you're a permanent U.S. resident) or outright American citizenship.

Despite these complications, do not despair. As an applicant from a foreign country, you have a distinct advantage over many American applicants. Getting into an American college might appear difficult, but at most of them, your cultural and educational background make you an attractive addition to their student roster. —*Amy Kappelman*

Disabled Student Services

This section is included in *The Insider's Guide* to give students with physical and learning disabilities an idea of additional considerations they might have in applying to or choosing a college.

Learning disabilities are defined as a collection of biological conditions that impede a person's ability to process and disseminate information. They are more common than any other disability. It has been estimated that as many as 5 percent of American schoolchildren are so affected. Leonardo da Vinci, Sir Winston Churchill, and President Woodrow Wilson were all learning-disabled. Physical disabilities are most often categorized as impairments of speech, vision, hearing, or mobility, but often include "hidden" disabilities like heart conditions or diabetes.

Students with disabilities are a rapidly growing element of the expanding collegiate student base. Many attend special schools that cater specifically to the disabled, but others are taking advantage of recent federal and state legislation demanding that non-specialty schools become accessible to the disabled. The accompanying rise in the disabled student body has prompted many institutions to accommodate students voluntarily (instead of after a legal battle), making many of the schools in this book within reach of the disabled student. Kay Runyan-Brown, the former coordinator of learning-disabled services for the Disabled Students' Program at the University of California/Berkeley, strongly encourages applicants to visit prospective campuses during the application process. "Visiting can allow for personal interviews, which deal with services available, the pace of campus life, and the expectations the LD Office has of prospective candidates," she said.

Advances in technology have given rise to many helpful services for disabled students. Many word-processing programs and pocket computers are equipped with spelling and grammar checkers. Students with reading disabilities should make sure voice synthesizers are available at their school of choice, while those with dexterity impairments should be on the lookout for computers with the voice recognition feature. Those for whom a traditional collegiate program of lectures, reading assignments, and timed essay tests is a problem should ask about visual learning equipment. Multimedia encyclopedias on CD-ROM, which provide photos, movie clips, animation, and sound effects, are excellent learning tools that exploit the potential of visual learning. Because such technology is often brand new or even experimental, try to consider schools that are on the cutting edge of the information age.

Runyan-Brown suggests that students with learning disabilities identify themselves early on in the admissions process. Self-identification remains a personal choice, yet it is often crucial in order for your application to be placed in the proper context with the rest of the applicant pool or for you to be placed on a housing preference list.

Runyan-Brown also recommends that parents help guide LD candidates in finding out which colleges have strong support services, and then help the students examine their own needs to see what kinds of services they could not do without. "A lot of learning-disabled students do not go about the application process in an organized fashion; they simply don't know how to do it. And I think that is where the parents come in, in helping them organize themselves," she said. In the application process, a good way to encourage proper understanding of special needs is to have someone who knows you and your efforts to overcome disability write a letter of support that can be included in your college applications. A school principal or guidance counselor is a good choice. Have the letter describe your specific situation and encourage the admissions and student-affairs committees to take it into account.

Be on the lookout for universities that have a Disabled Students Office with counselors who can steer you clear of tough obstacles and unnecessary frustrations. Federal law requires that schools provide assistance for LD students, such as alternative testing. Unfortunately, professors may not assume responsibility for making suitable arrangements. A good counselor can notify professors with learning-disabled students and help the professor make accommodations.

Not all colleges operate a disabled-student services office. Many schools provide accommodations informally, as needed, through the Dean of Student Affairs. In these cases, Runyan-Brown recommends that the LD student learn the federal statutes applying to disabled-students' rights (Public Law PL 94-142 and Section 504 of the Rehabilitation Act of 1973 [Public Law PL 93-112]). "When you are at a school that doesn't have a formal program, being able to verbalize and understand your learning disability so that you can help someone else understand it is the way to be your own best advocate," she said. You might prefer a school without a formal program. According to Bill Scales, Director of Disabled Student Services at the University of Maryland, an "overly comfortable environment is an unrealistic preparation for real life."

Physically disabled students also have special needs. In July 1992, the Americans with Disabilities Act went into effect, ensuring that campuses be legally responsible for providing reasonable accommodation and access for disabled students. Subpart C of Section 504 of PL 93-112, on the books since 1973, mandates that campus facilities be made readily accessible for disabled students' use. A prevailing interpretation of this legislation, however, is that a school need not create a totally barrier-free environment, just one that does not significantly hinder the participation

of students with disabilities. The case of Chris Powell, a University of Maryland undergraduate with limited motor control due to cerebral palsy, as reported by the *Washington Post*, reveals that hindrances still exist. The university is 95 percent accessible, but for Chris, getting up the ramp to his classroom building was always a struggle, the electric handicap doorway did not always function, he was not always able to push the small buttons for the elevators, the chairs in the classrooms were not designed for disabled students, and he had to rely on others' class notes because taped lecture notes were not available.

Bill Blanchard, at UC/Berkeley's Disabled Students Program, stresses the importance of the campus visit for physically disabled applicants. In addition to the regular campus tour, they should acquire a map and case the entire layout. Blanchard advises paying particular attention to the accessibility of key structures, such as libraries and the department building of the student's intended major. It is illegal for a college to be inaccessible, but some are more accessible than others. It is also important to contact the campus disabled-student services office and to meet and chat with enrolled students who have similar disabilities.

Lastly, it is important to remember that students with either physical or learning disabilities should be free to approach the college selection process in the same way as other students. He or she should understand throughout the admissions process that college opportunities do exist and that acceptance to (and rewarding attendance at) competitive schools is a realistic possibility for the motivated disabled student. —*Marc Schwarz*

Terms You Should Know

Advanced Placement (AP)—College credit earned by students while still in high school. Many high schools offer specially designed AP courses that prepare students for the College Board's AP Exams. Administered in May, they can qualify students who score well for advanced standing when they enroll in college.

American College Test (ACT)—Test administered to high school juniors and seniors by the American College Testing Program. Traditionally it has been used as an admissions criterion primarily by Midwestern schools. Some Southern and Western schools use it as well.

American College Testing Program (ACTP)—The organization that produces the American College Test (ACT) and the Family Financial Statement (FFS). Many Midwestern universities use the ACT and the FFS in admissions instead of the SAT and the Financial-Aid Form (FAF). (See also "Family Financial Statement" and "Financial-Aid Form.")

arts and sciences (also called liberal arts)—A broad term that encompasses most traditional courses of study, including the humanities, social sciences, natural sciences, mathematics, and foreign languages. A liberal arts college is also a college of arts and sciences. (See also "humanities" and "social sciences.")

bagging—You're in bed. It's 9:30 A.M. You've got a class at 9:30. You are about to "bag" this class.

beer goggles—People start to look interesting when you've had too much to drink. If you hook up as a result of this phenomenon, you've been looking through "beer goggles."

candidate's reply date—The May 1 deadline, observed by most selective colleges, by which the applicant must respond to an offer of admission, usually with a nonrefundable deposit of several

hundred dollars. Colleges that require students to respond by May 1 in almost all cases notify them of their acceptance on or before April 15.

College Board—The organization that sponsors the SAT, the SAT IIs, the Advanced Placement tests, and the Financial-Aid Form (FAF). College Board admissions tests are developed and administered by the Educational Testing Service (ETS). (See also "Advanced Placement" and "Financial-Aid Form.")

Common Application—A form produced by a consortium of about 100 colleges (mainly selective liberal arts schools) that may be filled out and sent to member colleges in lieu of each school's individual application.

comprehensive exams (comps)—Tests, administered by some colleges (usually during the senior year), designed to measure knowledge gained over a student's entire college career. Schools that give comps usually require students to pass the test in their major field in order to graduate.

computing assistant (CA)—A university employee, often an undergraduate, who helps students with all varieties of computing problems, from how to use a word processor to how to download games from the network.

consortium—A group of colleges affiliated in some way. The extent of the association can vary widely. Some consortiums—usually among colleges in close proximity—offer a range of joint programs that may include cross-registration, interlibrary loans, residential exchanges, and coordinated social, cultural, and athletic events.

co-op job—A paid internship, arranged for a student by his or her college, that provides on-the-job training, usually in an occupation closely related to the student's major.

core curriculum—A group of courses all students in a college must take in order to graduate. Core curricula are becoming widespread.

couch duty—There are two people in your bedroom that you share with your roommate, and you are not one of them. Guess where you get to sleep? Also known as "sexile."

cramming—The process by which students attempt to learn a semester's worth of course material in a short period, often 24 to 48 hours. Cola, coffee, and/or caffeine pills are the staples of most all-night cramming sessions.

crew (rowing)—A sport, more familiar to those who live on or near either coast than to those from the South and Midwest, in which teams of two, four, or eight oarsmen or oarswomen race in long, narrow boats, usually on inland waterways. Crew is very "Ivy," very popular at many schools, and usually requires no high school experience.

deferral—A college's postponement of the decision to accept or reject an early-action applicant. The applicant's file is entered in with those of regular-action candidates and is reviewed once again, this time for a final decision.

distribution requirements—Requirements stipulating that students take courses in a variety of broad subject areas in order to graduate. The number and definition of subject areas and the number of courses required in each varies from school to school. Typical categories include the humanities, social sciences, fine arts, natural sciences, foreign languages, and mathematics. Unlike a core curriculum, distribution requirements do not usually mandate specific courses that students must take. (See also "humanities," "social sciences," and "core curriculum.")

dry—as in "dry campus." A school that does not allow alcohol for any students in its dorms or other campus facilities.

early action—A program that gives students early notification of a college's admissions decision. Like early decision, a student can apply early action only to one school, but unlike early decision, it does not require a prior commitment to enroll if accepted. Early action—far less common than early decision—is primarily associated with the Ivy League school that offers it: Brown. Deadlines for early-action applications are usually in late fall, with notification in December, January, or February. An applicant accepted under early action usually has until May 1, the candidate's reply date, to respond to the offer of admission. (See also "early decision" and "candidate's reply date.")

early decision—A program under which a student receives early notification of a college's admissions decision if the student agrees in advance to enroll if accepted. Students may apply early decision to only one college; it should be a clear first choice. Application deadlines for early decision are usually in November, with decision letters mailed by mid-December.

Ethernet—A direct, high-speed means of access to the World Wide Web and the Internet, as well as a way to keep in touch with friends via e-mail. Most campuses are either "wired" with Ethernet, or will be in the near future.

family contribution—The amount of money that a family can "reasonably" be expected to pay toward a student's education, as determined by one of the two standardized needs-analysis forms. (See also "Financial-Aid Form" and "Family Financial Statement.")

Family Financial Statement (FFS)—The financial-needs analysis form submitted to the American College Testing Program (ACTP), which, like the FAF, determines the expected family contribution. Colleges that use the American College Test (ACT) for admissions purposes usually require a copy of the FFS report from students applying for financial aid. (See also "American College Testing

Program," "family contribution," and "Financial-Aid Form.")

fee waiver—Permission, often granted upon request, for needy students to apply for college admission without having to pay the application fee.

Financial-Aid Form (FAF)—The financial-needs analysis form submitted to the College Board by students applying for financial aid. Like the Family Financial Statement (FFS), it yields the expected family contribution. Colleges that require the Scholastic Assessment Test (SAT) for admission typically use the FAF as the basis for financial-aid awards. (See also "Family Financial Statement," "family contribution," and "College Board.")

financial-aid package—The combination of loans, grants, and a work-study job that a school puts together for a student receiving financial aid.

five-year plan—The practice of stretching a four-year degree program over a five-year period.

four-one-four—An academic calendar consisting of two regular four-month semesters with a short "winter" or "January" term in between. Variations include four-four-one and three-three-two. In most cases, these numbers refer to the number of courses a student is expected to complete in each segment of the year, although at some schools they refer to the number of months in each segment.

freshman 15—A reference to the number of pounds students often gain during the freshman year. Usually caused by a combination of too little exercise, unlimited helpings in the dining hall, too many late-night runs for pizza, and overconsumption of alcoholic beverages.

government aid—Money that federal or state governments make available to students, most of which is administered through the colleges on the basis of need. Government aid can come in the form of grants, loans, and work-study jobs. Stafford Loans (formerly Guaranteed Student Loans) and PLUS parent loans of up to $2,625 and $4,000 per year, respectively, are made available through commercial lending institutions. For further information on government aid programs, contact the state and federal departments of education.

grade inflation—A situation in which average work is consistently awarded a higher letter grade than it would normally earn. At most schools, the grade for average work is about a B-/C+. But in classes or entire colleges with grade inflation, it can be as high as a B or even B+.

Greek system—The fraternities and sororities on a particular campus. They are called "Greek" because most take their names from combinations of letters in the Greek alphabet.

gut—A course widely known to be very easy, often with enrollments well into the hundreds. Guts are traditionally favorites among second-semester seniors.

hook up—To enjoy a person's nonplatonic company, often used in reference to a one-night deal. A very vague term that can range from an innocent kiss to sex, depending on usage.

humanities—Subjects in which the primary focus is on human culture. Examples include philosophy, language, and literature. (See also "social sciences.")

independent study—A course, usually in a student's major field, in which he or she studies independently and meets one-on-one with a professor on a topic of the student's choosing. Some colleges require an independent study essay or research paper for graduation.

interdisciplinary major—A major that combines two complementary subjects from different fields, such as biology and psychology. Students completing these majors take courses in each area as well as courses that explicitly join the two.

International Baccalaureate (IB)—A high school program found across the world which, like AP courses, can earn a student advanced standing upon college enrollment.

intramurals—Athletic leagues informally organized within a college. Students are free from the burden of tryouts and play with and against fellow classmates.

language requirement—A rule at many colleges that requires students to study a foreign language before graduation. Two years on the college level are usually required, although credit from Advanced Placement or SAT IIs often allows students to bypass the requirement.

legacy—An applicant whose mother or father is a graduate of a particular school. Students with legacy status are often given preferential treatment in admissions.

merit scholarship—A financial grant for some part of college costs, usually awarded for academic achievement or special skill in an extracurricular activity and not based on need. Private corporations and many colleges offer merit scholarships.

need-based aid—Money awarded solely on the basis of need, usually administered through the colleges. Some schools agree to pay the difference between their total fees and the expected family contribution; others pay only part of it, leaving some "unmet" need. Most financial-aid packages consist of some combination of three components: grants, loans, and work-study jobs. Some of the money comes from the college's own resources, although part is financed by federal and state governments. (See also "government aid.")

need-blind admissions—A policy in which the applicant's ability to pay does not affect the college's consideration of his or her application. Some schools with need-blind admissions also guarantee to meet the full demonstrated financial need of all accepted applicants as determined by one of the two standardized needs-analysis forms; others do not. (See

also "family contribution," "Financial-Aid Form," and "Family Financial Statement.")

office hours—A period during which a professor agrees to be available in his or her office for the purpose of talking with students about their coursework. Professors are not always required by their colleges to have office hours, but most do anyway.

open admissions—A policy under which any applicant with a high school diploma is accepted. State universities that have this policy usually limit open admission to state residents.

parietals—Regulations that govern the times when students of one sex may visit dorms or floors housing the opposite sex. Usually found only at the most conservative schools nowadays.

pass/fail or CR/F or CR/D/F—An option offered by some schools in some classes. A student may enroll in a class and simply receive credit or failure (or a D in "CR/D/F") for it on his or her transcript instead of a specific grade: God's gift to college students everywhere.

PLUS parent loans—A component of the Stafford Loan, for parents. (See also "government aid.")

problem set—An annoying weekly assignment you're inevitably faced with in any given science or quantitative class. This thankless task will keep you up till 2 A.M. Sunday nights but can count for anywhere from 1/50th of your grade to 1/2. Previously known as homework.

quad—An abbreviation for "quadrangle"; many dorm complexes are built in squares (quadrangles) with a courtyard in the middle. Quad can also refer to a suite of dormitory rooms in which four students live together.

quarter system—An academic calendar under which the school year is divided into four quarters, three of which constitute a full academic year. Less common than the semester system, it is most often used by large universities with extensive programs in agricultural and technical fields.

resident advisor/assistant (RA)—A student, usually an upperclassman, who lives in a dorm and helps to maintain regulations and enforce school policy, as well as offer advice and support to dorm residents. RAs receive compensation from the school for their services, usually in the form of free room and board.

rolling admissions—A policy under which a college considers applications almost immediately after receiving them. Decision letters are mailed within a month after the application is filed. Colleges with rolling admissions continue to accept applications only until the class is filled, so it is best to apply early.

Scholastic Assessment Test (SAT)—Test administered to high school juniors and seniors by the College Board of the Educational Testing Service, with math, verbal, and written language sections. Used as an admissions criterion at most colleges nationwide.

senior project—Many majors at many colleges require seniors to complete a special project during their senior year. Depending upon your major and institution, this could involve a thesis (anywhere from 15 to 100 pages), a research project, some sort of internship, or all of the above. Some colleges offer seniors a choice between taking comps or doing a project.

social sciences—Subjects that deal systematically with the institutions of human society, most notably economics and political science. The behavioral sciences, which include psychology, sociology, and anthropology, are often included in this group as well.

study break—An institutionalized form of procrastination involving food and talk. Often informally arranged—"I'm sick of calculus, let's take a study break at— (insert name of local hangout)"—but can be sponsored by RAs, cultural groups, or even school administrators. Some nights, study breaks can take more of your time than the actual studying.

teaching assistant (TA)—A graduate student who assists a professor in the presentation of a course. Usually the professor gives two to four lectures a week for all the students in the class; the TAs hold smaller weekly discussion sections.

three-two program (3-2)—A program in which students can study three years at one school, followed by two at another, more specialized school. Upon completion, many of these programs award both the bachelor's and the master's degrees.

town-gown relations—The contact between a college (students, employees, buildings) and its host town (citizens, businesses, local government) and the set of issues around which this contact revolves. Such issues include taxes, traffic, local employment practices, and government services like road maintenance, sewage, and trash collection. Because a town and its university can be dependent on each other, good town-gown relations are important to both sides.

townie—A resident of a college town or city who is not enrolled in the college, but who might sit beside you at the local pub. Usually involves a "them vs. us" mentality.

trimesters—An academic calendar that divides the school year into three terms of approximately equal length. Schools on the trimester system generally have one term before the winter break and two after.

tutorial major (also called self-designed or special major)—A program offered by many schools in which a student can plan his or her own major, combining the offerings of two or more traditional majors, usually in consultation with a faculty member. An example is Medieval studies, in which the student might study the history, literature, philosophy, and art of the period, taking courses from a number of departments.

waiting list—A list of students who are not initially accepted to a certain school, but who may be admitted later, depending on the number of accepted students who enroll. Most colleges ultimately accept only a small fraction of the students on the waiting list, who are notified during the summer.

work-study—Campus jobs, for financial-aid recipients, that are subsidized by the federal government. Work-study jobs are a component of most need-based financial-aid packages. Students typically work 10 to 20 hours a week to help finance their education.

The College Finder

With so many colleges from which to choose, how can you zero in on one that is right for you? The lists that follow are designed to help you match your interests with a selected group of colleges. Our hope is that The Finder will introduce you to a number of colleges you might not otherwise have considered.

Regions

New England: Connecticut, Maine, Massachusetts, New Hampshire, Rhode Island, Vermont. Also includes Eastern Canada.

Mid-Atlantic: Delaware, District of Columbia, Maryland, New Jersey, New York, Pennsylvania, West Virginia.

Midwest: Illinois, Indiana, Iowa, Kansas, Kentucky, Michigan, Minnesota, Missouri, Nebraska, North Dakota, Ohio, South Dakota, Wisconsin.

Southeast: Alabama, Arkansas, Florida, Georgia, Louisiana, Mississippi, North Carolina, South Carolina, Tennessee, Virginia.

West: Alaska, Arizona, California, Colorado, Hawaii, Idaho, Montana, New Mexico, Nevada, Oklahoma, Oregon, Texas, Utah, Washington, Wyoming. Also includes Western Canada.

Schools with 1,500 Undergraduates or Fewer

New England
Bennington College
Hampshire College
Marlboro College
Simmons College
United States Coast Guard Academy
Wheaton College

Mid-Atlantic
Bard College
Bryn Mawr College

Cooper Union for the Advancement of Science and Art
Drew University
Eastman School of Music
Goucher College
Haverford College
Juilliard School, The
Manhattanville College
Sarah Lawrence College
St. John's College
Stevens Institute of Technology
Swarthmore College
Trinity College
Wells College

Midwest
Albion College
Alma College
Antioch College
Beloit College
Centre College
Cornell College
Earlham College
Grinnell College
Kalamazoo College
Knox College
Lake Forest College
Lawrence University
Wabash College

Southeast
Agnes Scott College
Birmingham-Southern College
Hampden-Sydney College
Hendrix College
Hollins College
Millsaps College
New College of the University of South Florida
North Carolina School of the Arts
Randolph-Macon Woman's College
Rhodes College
Sweet Briar College
University of the South (Sewanee)
Wofford College

West
California Institute of Technology
California Institute of the Arts
Claremont McKenna College
Deep Springs College
Harvey Mudd College

Mills College
Occidental College
Pitzer College
Pomona College
Reed College
Scripps College
St. John's College (NM)
University of Dallas
University of Redlands
Whitman College

Schools with 1,501 to 3,000 Undergraduates

New England
Amherst College
Babson College
Bates College
Bowdoin College
Clark University
Colby College
Connecticut College
Holy Cross, College of the
Middlebury College
Mount Holyoke College
Rhode Island School of Design
Smith College
Trinity College
Wellesley College
Wesleyan University
Williams College
Worcester Polytechnic Institute

Mid-Atlantic
Adelphi University
Alfred University
Allegheny College
Barnard College
Catholic University of America
Clarkson University
Colgate University
Dickinson College
Franklin & Marshall College
Gettysburg College
Hamilton College
Hobart and William Smith College
Lafayette College
Muhlenberg College
Parsons School of Design
Skidmore College
St. Bonaventure University
St. Lawrence University
Susquehanna University

Union College
Vassar College
Yeshiva University

Midwest
Carleton College
Denison University
DePauw University
Gustavus Adolphus College
Kenyon College
Macalester College
Oberlin College
Ohio Wesleyan University
Rose-Hulman Institute of Technology
St. Olaf College
Valparaiso University
Wittenburg University
Wooster, The College of

Southeast
Davidson College
Florida Institute of Technology
Furman University
Morehouse College
Spelman College
Stetson University
Tuskegee University
Washington and Lee University

West
Colorado College
Colorado School of Mines
Lewis and Clark College
Oral Roberts University
Pepperdine University
Puget Sound University
Rice University
Trinity University
University of Denver
University of Tulsa
Willamette University

Schools with Over 20,000 Students

New England
Boston University
Carleton University
McGill University
Northeastern University
University of Massachusetts/Amherst
University of Toronto
University of Western Ontario

Mid-Atlantic
New York University
Pennsylvania State University
Rutgers, The State University of New
    Jersey
SUNY/Buffalo
Temple University
University of Maryland/College Park
University of Pennsylvania
University of Pittsburgh
West Virginia University

Midwest
Indiana University
Iowa State University
Kansas State University
Kent State University
Michigan State University
Ohio State University
Purdue University
Southern Illinois University/Carbondale
University of Cincinnati
University of Illinois/Urbana-Champaign
University of Iowa
University of Kansas
University of Kentucky
University of Michigan
University of Minnesota
University of Missouri/Columbia
University of Nebraska/Lincoln
University of Wisconsin

Southeast
Auburn University
Florida State University
George Mason University
Louisiana State University & A&M
    College
North Carolina State University
University of Florida
University of Georgia
University of North Carolina/Chapel Hill
University of South Carolina
University of Tennessee/Knoxville
University of Virginia
Virginia Polytechnic Institute and State
    University

West
Arizona State University
Brigham Young University
California State University/San Diego
Colorado State University
Texas A&M University/College Station
Texas Tech University
University of Arizona

University of British Columbia
University of California/Berkeley
University of California/Davis
University of California/Los Angeles
University of Colorado/Boulder
University of Houston
University of New Mexico
University of Oklahoma
University of Southern California
University of Texas/Austin
University of Utah
University of Washington
Washington State University

Some Schools Over 200 Years Old

Bowdoin College
Brown University
College of William and Mary
Columbia College of Columbia University
Dartmouth College
Dickinson College
Franklin & Marshall College
Georgetown University
Hampden-Sydney College
Harvard and Radcliffe College
Princeton University
Rutgers, The State University of New
    Jersey
St. John's College
Union College
University of Delaware
University of Georgia
University of North Carolina/Chapel Hill
University of Pennsylvania
University of Pittsburgh
University of Tennessee/Knoxville
University of Vermont
Washington and Lee University
Williams College
Yale University

Some Schools Less Than 50 Years Old

California Institute of the Arts
Eugene Lang College of the New School
    for Social Research
Evergreen State College

Florida Institute of Technology
George Mason University
Hampshire College
Harvey Mudd College
New College of the University of South Florida
North Carolina School of the Arts
Oral Roberts University
Pitzer College
SUNY/Stony Brook
United States Air Force Academy
University of California/Irvine
University of California/Riverside
University of California/Santa Cruz
University of Dallas
University of Waterloo

Single-Sex Schools

Women
Agnes Scott College
Barnard College
Hollins College
Mills College
Mount Holyoke College
Randolph-Macon Woman's College
Scripps College
Simmons College
Smith College
Spelman College
Sweet Briar College
Trinity College (D.C.)
Wellesley College
Wells College

Men
Deep Springs College
Hampden-Sydney College
Morehouse College
Wabash College

Predominantly Male Schools (More Than Two-Thirds Male)

California Institute of Technology
Carnegie Mellon University
Clarkson University
Colorado School of Mines
Georgia Institute of Technology

Harvey Mudd College
Rensselaer Polytechnic Institute
Rose-Hulman Institute of Technology
Stevens Institute of Technology
United States Air Force Academy
United States Coast Guard Academy
United States Military Academy
United States Naval Academy
Worcester Polytechnic Institute

Predominantly Female Schools (More Than Two-Thirds Female)

Adelphi University
Bennington College
Bryn Mawr College
CUNY/Hunter College
Eugene Lang College of the New School for Social Research
Goucher College
Manhattanville College
Parsons School of Design
Sarah Lawrence College
Wheaton College

Some Schools with High Minority Enrollment (More Than 30%)

New England
Harvard and Radcliffe College
Massachusetts Institute of Technology
Wellesley College
Wesleyan University
Yale University

Mid-Atlantic
Barnard College
Columbia College of Columbia University
Cooper Union for the Advancement of Science and Art
CUNY/City College of New York
CUNY/Hunter College
CUNY/Queens College
Drexel University
Howard University
Johns Hopkins University
Juilliard School, The
New York University

Rutgers, The State University of New Jersey
Stevens Institute of Technology
SUNY/Stony Brook
Swarthmore College
Temple University
Trinity College (D.C.)
University of Pennsylvania

Midwest
De Paul University/Southeast
Florida A&M University
Morehouse College
Old Dominion University
Spelman College
Tuskegee University
University of Miami

West
California Institute of Technology
California Polytechnic State University/San Luis Obispo
California State University/Fresno
California State University/San Diego
Claremont McKenna College
New Mexico State University
Occidental College
Oral Roberts University
Pitzer College
Pomona College
Scripps College
Stanford University
University of Alaska/Fairbanks
University of California/Berkeley
University of California/Davis
University of California/Irvine
University of California/Los Angeles
University of California/Riverside
University of California/San Diego
University of California/Santa Barbara
University of California/Santa Cruz
University of Hawaii/Manoa
University of Houston
University of New Mexico
University of Southern California

Schools Accepting 30% or Less of Their Applicant Pool

Amherst College
Brown University
California Institute of Technology

Claremont McKenna College
Columbia College of Columbia University
Cooper Union for the Advancement of Science and Art
Dartmouth College
Deep Springs College
Georgetown University
Harvard and Radcliffe College
Juilliard School, The
Massachusetts Institute of Technology
North Carolina School of the Arts
Northwestern University
Princeton University
Rice University
Stanford University
Swarthmore College
United States Air Force Academy
United States Coast Guard Academy
United States Military Academy
United States Naval Academy
Williams College
Yale University

Schools Accepting 31% to 50% of Their Applicant Pool

Babson College
Barnard College
Bates College
Boston College
Bowdoin College
California Institute of the Arts
Carnegie Mellon University
Colby College
Colgate University
Connecticut College
Cornell University
Davidson College
Duke University
Eastman School of Music
Emory University
George Washington University
Hamilton College
Harvey Mudd College
Haverford College
Holy Cross, College of the
Howard University
Johns Hopkins University
Middlebury College
New York University
Pomona College

Queen's University
Rhode Island School of Design
Sarah Lawrence College
SUNY/Binghamton (Binghamton University)
Trinity College
Tufts University
University of British Columbia
University of California/Berkeley
University of California/Los Angeles
University of Notre Dame
University of North Carolina/Chapel Hill
University of Pennsylvania
University of Richmond
University of Southern California
University of Virginia
University of Waterloo
University of Western Ontario
Vassar College
Wake Forest University
Washington and Lee University
Washington University
Wellesley College
Wesleyan University
William and Mary, College of

Rose-Hulman Institute of Technology
Rutgers, The State University of New Jersey
Smith College
Spelman College
SUNY/Stony Brook
Syracuse University
Union College
University of California/San Diego
University of Chicago
University of Miami
University of Rochester
Vanderbilt University
Whitman College

Schools Accepting 51% to 60% of Their Applicant Pool

Bard College
Boston University
Brandeis University
Bryn Mawr College
Bucknell University
California Polytechnic State University/San Luis Obispo
Carleton College
Colorado College
Franklin & Marshall College
Georgia Institute of Technology
James Madison University
Lafayette College
Lehigh University
Macalester College
McGill University
Morehouse College
New Jersey, The College of
Parsons School of Design
Pennsylvania State University
Pepperdine University
Pitzer College

Private Schools

New England
Amherst College
Babson College
Bates College
Bennington College
Boston College
Boston University
Bowdoin College
Brandeis University
Brown University
Clark University
Colby College
Connecticut College
Dartmouth College
Fairfield University
Hampshire College
Harvard and Radcliffe College
Holy Cross, College of the
Marlboro College
Massachusetts Institute of Technology
McGill University
Middlebury College
Mount Holyoke College
Northeastern University
Rhode Island School of Design
Simmons College
Smith College
Trinity College
Tufts University
Wellesley College
Wesleyan University
Wheaton College
Williams College
Worcester Polytechnic Institute
Yale University

Mid-Atlantic
Adelphi University
Alfred University
Allegheny College
American University
Bard College
Barnard College
Bryn Mawr College
Bucknell University
Carnegie Mellon University
Catholic University of America
Clarkson University
Colgate University
Columbia College of Columbia
    University
Cooper Union for the Advancement of
    Science and Art
Cornell University
Dickinson College
Drew University
Drexel University
Eastman School of Music
Eugene Lang College of the New School
    for Social Research
Fordham University
Franklin & Marshall College
George Washington University
Georgetown University
Gettysburg College
Goucher College
Hamilton College
Haverford College
Hobart and William Smith College
Hofstra University
Howard University
Johns Hopkins University
Juilliard School, The
Lafayette College
Lehigh University
Manhattanville College
Muhlenberg College
New York University
Parsons School of Design
Princeton University
Rensselaer Polytechnic Institute
Rochester Institute of Technology
Sarah Lawrence College
Skidmore College
St. Bonaventure University
St. John's College
St. Lawrence University
Stevens Institute of Technology
Susquehanna University
Swarthmore College
Syracuse University

Trinity College
University of Pennsylvania
University of Rochester
Union College
Vassar College
Villanova University
Wells College
Yeshiva University

Midwest
Albion College
Alma College
Antioch College
Beloit College
Carleton College
Case Western Reserve University
Centre College
Cornell College
Creighton University
Denison University
DePaul University
DePauw University
Earlham College
Grinnell College
Gustavus Adolphus College
Kalamazoo College
Kenyon College
Knox College
Lake Forest College
Lawrence University
Loyola University of Chicago
Macalester College
Marquette University
Northwestern University
Oberlin College
Ohio Wesleyan University
Rose-Hulman Institute of
    Technology
St. John's University/College of St.
    Benedict
St. Olaf College
University of Chicago
University of Notre Dame
Valparaiso University
Wabash College
Washington University
Wittenburg University
Wooster, The College of

Southeast
Agnes Scott College
Birmingham-Southern College
Davidson College
Duke University
Emory University

Florida Institute of Technology
Furman University
Hampden-Sydney College
Hendrix College
Hollins College
Millsaps College
Morehouse College
Randolph-Macon Woman's College
Rhodes College
Spelman College
Stetson University
Sweet Briar College
Tulane University
Tuskegee University
University of Richmond
University of the South (Sewanee)
University of Miami
Vanderbilt University
Wake Forest University
Washington and Lee University
Wofford College

West
Baylor University
Brigham Young University
California Institute of Technology
California Institute of the Arts
Claremont McKenna College
Colorado College
Colorado School of Mines
Deep Springs College
Harvey Mudd College
Lewis and Clark College
Mills College
Occidental College
Oral Roberts University
Pepperdine University
Pitzer College
Pomona College
Puget Sound University
Reed College
Rice University
Scripps College
Southern Methodist University
St. John's College (NM)
Stanford University
Texas Christian University
Trinity University
University of Dallas
University of Denver
University of Redlands
University of Southern California
University of Tulsa
Whitman College
Willamette University

Some Schools with Religious Affiliation

Agnes Scott College
Albion College
Allegheny College
Alma College
American University
Baylor University
Birmingham-Southern College
Brigham Young University
Catholic University of America
Centre College
Creighton University
Davidson College
DePauw University
Duke University
Earlham College
Emory University
Fairfield University
Georgetown University
Gustavus Adolphus College
Hampden-Sydney College
Holy Cross, College of the
Kenyon College
Lafayette College
Lake Forest College
Loyola University of Chicago
Macalester College
Marquette University
Millsaps College
Muhlenberg College
Notre Dame
Ohio Wesleyan University
Pepperdine University
Randolph-Macon Woman's College
Rhodes College
Southern Methodist University
St. Bonaventure University
St. John's University/College of St. Benedict
St. Olaf College
Susquehanna University
Texas Christian University
Trinity College (D.C.)
Trinity University
University of Dallas
University of Denver
University of Notre Dame
University of the South (Sewanee)
University of Tulsa
Valparaiso University
Villanova University

Willamette University
Wittenburg University
Wofford College
Wooster, The College of

New England
Amherst College
Babson College
Bates College
Bennington College
Bowdoin College
Brandeis University
Clark University
Colby College
Connecticut College
Fairfield University
Hampshire College
Holy Cross, College of the
Marlboro College
Middlebury College
Mount Holyoke College
Simmons College
Smith College
Trinity College
Wellesley College
Wesleyan University
Wheaton College
Williams College

Mid-Atlantic
Allegheny College
Bard College
Barnard College
Bryn Mawr College
Clarkson University
Colgate University
Dickinson College
Drew University
Franklin and Marshall College
Gettysburg College
Goucher College
Hamilton College
Haverford College
Hobart and William Smith Colleges
Manhattanville College
Muhlenberg College
Sarah Lawrence College
Skidmore College
St. John's College (MD)

St. Lawrence University
Swarthmore College
Trinity College (D.C.)
Union College
Vassar College
Wells College

Midwest
Albion College
Alma College
Antioch College
Beloit College
Carleton College
Centre College
Cornell College
Denison University
DePauw University
Earlham College
Grinnell College
Gustavus Adolphus College
Kalamazoo College
Kenyon College
Knox College
Lake Forest College
Lawrence University
Macalester College
Oberlin College
Ohio Wesleyan University
St. Olaf College
Wabash College
Wittenburg University
Wooster, The College of

South
Agnes Scott College
Birmingham-Southern College
Davidson College
Furman University
Hampden-Sydney College
Hendrix College
Hollins College
Millsaps College
Morehouse College
New College of the University of South
    Florida
Oral Roberts University
Randolph-Macon Woman's College
Rhodes College
Rice University
University of Dallas
University of Richmond
University of the South (Sewanee)
University of Tulsa
Spelman College
Stetson University
Sweet Briar College

Trinity University
Washington and Lee University
Wofford College

West
Claremont McKenna College
Colorado College
Deep Springs College
Lewis and Clark College
Mills College
Occidental College
Pitzer College
Pomona College
Puget Sound University
Reed College
Scripps College
St. John's College (NM)
University of Redlands
Whitman College
Willamette University

Rose-Hulman Institute of Technology
Stetson University
Stevens Institute of Technology
Susquehanna University
Texas Christian University
Trinity University
Union College
University of Mississippi
University of Pennsylvania
University of Richmond
University of the South (Sewanee)
Valparaiso University
Vanderbilt University
Villanova University
Wabash College
Wake Forest University
Washington and Lee University
Whitman College
Willamette University
William and Mary, College of
Wofford College
Worcester Polytechnic Institute

Large Fraternity/Sorority Systems (More Than 30%)

Albion College
Allegheny College
Birmingham-Southern College
Bucknell University
Centre College
Colgate University
Cornell College
Creighton University
Dartmouth College
Denison University
DePauw University
Dickinson College
Duke University
Emory University
Franklin & Marshall College
Furman University
Gettysburg College
Johns Hopkins University
Lafayette College
Lehigh University
Massachusetts Institute of Technology
Miami University
Millsaps College
Muhlenberg College
Northwestern University
Ohio Wesleyan University
Puget Sound University
Rensselaer Polytechnic Institute
Rhodes College

Schools with No Fraternities or Sororities

Agnes Scott College
Amherst College
Antioch College
Bard College
Barnard College
Bates College
Bennington College
Boston College
Brandeis University
Brigham Young University
Bryn Mawr College
California Institute of the Arts
California Institute of Technology
Carleton College
Carleton University
Claremont McKenna College
Clark University
Colby College
Connecticut College
CUNY/City College of New York
CUNY/Hunter College
CUNY/Queens College
Deep Springs College
Drew University
Earlham College
Eugene Lang College of the New School
    for Social Research

Evergreen State College
Fairfield University
Fordham University
Georgetown University
Goucher College
Grinnell College
Hampshire College
Harvard University
Harvey Mudd College
Haverford College
Hendrix College
Hollins College
Holy Cross, College of the
Juilliard School, The
Kalamazoo College
Lewis and Clark College
Macalester College
Manhattanville College
Marlboro College
McGill University
McMaster University
Middlebury College
Mills College
Mount Holyoke College
New College of the University of South
    Florida
North Carolina School of the Arts
Oberlin College
Oral Roberts University
Parsons School of Design
Pitzer College
Princeton University
Queen's University
Randolph-Macon Woman's College
Reed College
Rhode Island School of Design
Rice University
Sarah Lawrence College
Scripps College
Simmons College
Skidmore College
Smith College
St. Bonaventure University
St. John's College (MD and NM)
St. John's University/College of St.
    Benedict
St. Olaf College
Sweet Briar College
Trinity College (D.C.)
United States Air Force Academy
United States Coast Guard Academy
United States Military Academy
United States Naval Academy
University of California/Santa Cruz
University of Dallas
University of Notre Dame

University of Toronto
University of Washington
University of Waterloo
University of Western Ontario
Vassar College
Wellesley College
Wells College
Wheaton College
Williams College
Yeshiva University

Some Schools with Very High Graduation Rates

Amherst College
Bates College
Brown University
Bryn Mawr College
Bucknell College
California Institute of Technology
Carleton College
Claremont McKenna College
Colby College
Colgate University
Columbia College of Columbia University
Connecticut College
Cornell University
Dartmouth College
Davidson College
Dickinson College
Duke University
Emory University
Florida A&M University
Georgetown University
Hamilton College
Harvard and Radcliffe College
Haverford College
Holy Cross, College of the
Johns Hopkins University
Kenyon College
Middlebury College
Mount Holyoke College
Northwestern University
Rhode Island School of Design
University of Notre Dame
University of Richmond
University of the South (Sewanee)
Swarthmore College
Trinity College (CT)
Union College
United States Air Force Academy
Villanova University
Washington and Lee University

William and Mary, The College of
Yale University

Tuition, Room and Board

Note: Schools with asterisks (*) have tuition figures listed for the 2000–2001 academic year. When a school is followed by (I), that figure refers to in-state tuition only; out-of-state tuition is higher.

Under $6,000

NEW ENGLAND
United States Coast Guard Academy*

MID-ATLANTIC
CUNY/City College of New York (I)
CUNY/Hunter College (I)
CUNY/Queens College
United States Military Academy
United States Naval Academy

MIDWEST
Kansas State University (I)
University of Nebraska/Lincoln (I)
University of North Dakota (I)
University of South Dakota (I)
University of Wisconsin (I)

SOUTHEAST
Florida A&M University (I)
North Carolina School of the Arts (I)
North Carolina State University (I)
University of Mississippi (I)

WEST
Brigham Young University
Deep Springs College*
New Mexico State University (I)
United States Air Force Academy
University of Idaho (I)
University of Texas/Austin (I)

$6,000 to $11,999

NEW ENGLAND
Carleton University (I)
McGill University

McMaster University (I)
Queen's University (I)
University of Connecticut (I)
University of Maine/Orono (I)
University of Massachusetts/
  Amherst (I)*
University of New Hampshire (I)
University of Rhode Island (I)
University of Toronto (I)
University of Waterloo (I)
University of Western Ontario (I)

MID-ATLANTIC
CUNY/City College of New York
CUNY/Hunter College
New Jersey, The College of (I)
Pennsylvania State University (I)
Rutgers, The State University of New Jersey (I)
SUNY/Albany
SUNY/Binghamton (I)
SUNY/Buffalo (I)
SUNY/Stony Brook (I)
Temple University (I)
University of Delaware (I)
University of Maryland/College Park (I)
University of Pittsburgh (I)
West Virginia University (I)*

MIDWEST
Bowling Green State University (I)
Illinois State University (I)*
Indiana University (I)
Iowa State University
Kansas State University (I)
Kent State University (I)
Miami University (I)
Michigan State University (I)
Ohio State University (I)
Ohio University (I)
Purdue University (I)
Southern Illinois University/
  Carbondale (I)
University of Cincinnati (I)
University of Illinois/Urbana-Champaign (I)
University of Iowa (I)*
University of Kansas
University of Kentucky
University of Michigan (I)
University of Minnesota (I)
University of Missouri/Columbia (I)
University of Nebraska/Lincoln
University of North Dakota
University of South Dakota
University of Wisconsin

SOUTHEAST

Auburn University
Clemson University
Florida A&M University
Florida State University (I)
George Mason University (I)
Georgia Institute of Technology (I)
James Madison University (I)
Louisiana State University & A&M
  College
Mississippi State University
New College of the University of South
  Florida
North Carolina State University
Old Dominion University (I)
University of Alabama
University of Arkansas
University of Florida (I)
University of Georgia
University of Mississippi
University of North Carolina/Chapel Hill
University of South Carolina
University of Tennessee/Knoxville
University of Virginia (I)
Virginia Polytechnic Institute and State
  University (I)
William and Mary, College of (I)

WEST

Arizona State University
California Polytechnic State University/
  San Luis Obispo
California State University/Chico
California State University/Fresno
California State University/San Diego
Colorado School of Mines (I)
Colorado State University (I)
Evergreen State College
New Mexico State University
Oklahoma State University
Oregon State University
Texas A&M University/College Station (I)
Texas Tech University
University of Alaska/Fairbanks
University of Arizona
University of British Columbia (I)
University of California/Berkeley (I)*
University of California/Davis (I)
University of California/Irvine (I)
University of California/Los Angeles (I)
University of California/Riverside (I)
University of California/San Diego (I)
University of California/Santa Barbara (I)
University of California/Santa Cruz (I)
University of Colorado/Boulder (I)
University of Hawaii/Manoa (I)

University of Houston
University of Idaho
University of Montana
University of Nevada/Reno
University of New Mexico
University of Oklahoma
University of Oregon (I)
University of Texas/Austin
University of Utah
University of Washington (I)
University of Wyoming
Washington State University (I)

$12,000 to $17,999

NEW ENGLAND

Carleton University
Queen's University
University of Maine/Orono
University of Massachusetts/Amherst*
University of Rhode Island
University of Toronto
University of Vermont (I)
University of Waterloo
University of Western Ontario

MID-ATLANTIC

Cooper Union for the Advancement of
  Science and Art
Howard University
New Jersey, The College of
Pennsylvania State University
Rutgers, The State University of New
  Jersey
SUNY/Binghamton
SUNY/Buffalo
SUNY/Stony Brook
Temple University
University of Delaware
University of Maryland/College Park
West Virginia University*
Yeshiva University

MIDWEST

Bowling Green State University
Creighton University
DePaul University
Illinois State University*
Indiana University
Kansas State University
Kent State University
Miami University
Michigan State University
Ohio State University

Ohio University
Purdue University
Southern Illinois University/Carbondale
University of Cincinnati
University of Illinois/Urbana-Champaign
University of Iowa*
University of Minnesota
Universitysity of Missouri/Columbia

SOUTHEAST

Florida State University
George Mason University
Georgia Institute of Technology
Hendrix College
James Madison University
Morehouse College
North Carolina School of the Arts
Old Dominion University
Spelman College
Tuskegee University
University of Florida
Virginia Polytechnic Institute and State
    University
Wake Forest University

WEST

Baylor University*
Colorado State University
Oral Roberts University
Rice University
Texas A&M University/College Station
Texas Christian University
University of British Columbia
University of California/Davis
University of California/Irvine
University of California/Santa Barbara
University of Colorado/Boulder
University of Dallas
University of Hawaii/Manoa
University of Oregon
University of Tulsa
University of Washington
Washington State University

$18,000 to $23,999

NEW ENGLAND

McMaster University
University of Connecticut
University of New Hampshire

MID-ATLANTIC

Adelphi University
Catholic University of America

Drew University
Drexel University
Fordham University
Hofstra University
Juilliard School, The
Muhlenberg College
Rochester Institute of Technology
St. Bonaventure University
Trinity College (D.C.)
University of Pittsburgh
Wells College

MIDWEST

Alma College
Case Western Reserve University*
Centre College*
DePauw University
Earlham College
Grinnell College
Gustavus Adolphus College*
Knox College
Loyola University of Chicago
Marquette University*
Rose-Hulman Institute of Technology*
St. John's University/College of St.
    Benedict
St. Olaf College
University of Michigan
Valparaiso University
Wabash College
Wittenburg University

SOUTHEAST

Agnes Scott College*
Birmingham-Southern College
Florida Institute of Technology
Furman University*
Hampden-Sydney College
Hollins College*
Millsaps College
Randolph-Macon Woman's College
Rhodes College
Stetson University
Sweet Briar College
University of Richmond*
University of the South (Sewanee)
University of Virginia
Washington and Lee University
William and Mary, College of
Wofford College

WEST

California Institute of Technology
California Institute of the Arts
Colorado School of Mines
Mills College

Puget Sound University
Southern Methodist University
Trinity University
University of California/Berkeley*
University of California/Los Angeles*
University of California/Riverside
University of California/San Diego
University of California/Santa Cruz
University of Denver
University of Redlands

Over $24,000

NEW ENGLAND
Amherst College
Babson College*
Bates College
Bennington College*
Boston College
Boston University*

Bowdoin College
Brandeis University
Brown University
Clark University
Colby College
Connecticut College
Dartmouth College
Fairfield University
Hampshire College
Harvard and Radcliffe College*
Holy Cross, College of the*
Marlboro College
Massachusetts Institute of Technology
Middlebury College
Mount Holyoke College*
Northeastern University
Rhode Island School of Design
Simmons College*
Smith College
Trinity College
Tufts University
University of Vermont

A Word About Statistics

Every college description in this book is preceded by a statistical profile. The figures are the most recent available. The data are supplied by the colleges themselves. When no figures were available, the symbol "NA" (not available) has been used. For the most up-to-date information, you should contact the colleges directly.

Please note that in general, except where doing so would be misleading, all percentages have been rounded off to the nearest whole-number percent. As an example, statistically speaking, there is no significant difference between an acceptance rate of 30 percent and 30.4 percent; in fact, even a difference of 3 to 5 percent would hardly be noticeable in everyday life situations.

As a rule, the statistics provided by a school are for the most recent year for which that school has information: in most cases, either the 1997–1998 or 1996–1997 academic year.

Below the name of each school is listed the **World Wide Web (WWW) site** and admissions office e-mail address for that school.

The **address** and **undergraduate admissions** phone numbers are the ones that a school's admissions office prefers applicants to use when corresponding.

Location describes the setting of a college: rural, suburban, small city, or urban. Of course, this can only give a general idea of a campus's surroundings.

Private/public refers to private schools versus "state" schools. **Founded** is the year that the school first accepted students. **Religious affiliation** indicates whether a school is affiliated with a particular religious establishment, either directly or indirectly.

Undergraduate enrollment is the number of full-time undergraduate students for the most recent year available at press time.

Total enrollment gives the total number of students, including not only full-time undergraduates, but also part-time students, graduate, and professional students, and in some cases, evening and extension students.

Subtracting the number of undergraduates from the total enrollment will give an estimate of the number of graduate students; the ratio of undergraduates to graduate students will give you a rough indication of the relative emphasis a given university places on each.

Percent male/female (M/F) gives the percentage of undergraduates of each sex.

Percent minority is the percentage of enrolled students who indicated on their applications that they consider themselves members of a minority group. This figure is followed by percentages of students in three broad minority groups— African American, Asian American, and Hispanic—to give a measure of the ethnic diversity of the school. International students are not included in this figure.

Percent in-state/out-of-state is the percentage of enrolled undergraduates who are residents of the state in which the school is located. (For Canadian schools, the percentage given is the percentage of students from within Canada.) This figure gives a rough idea of the regional diversity of the school. Obviously, the in-state numbers will usually be much higher for public schools than for private schools, though in almost all cases, states provide incentives for private schools to take in-state students.

The figures for membership in **fraternities/sororities** are based on the approximate percentage of male students joining fraternities and female students joining sororities, as reported by the administration. Fraternity and sorority enrollment over 30 percent usually indicates a strong Greek system. Note that fraternity and sorority figures do not include non-Greek exclusive clubs or secret societies. Also, "NA" means that a school did not report a figure, while "0%" indicates that a school does not have fraternities or sororities.

Number of applicants is the number of completed first-year undergraduate applications received by the university.

Percent accepted is the number of applicants accepted for the most recent entering freshman class (in the case, usually the class of 2003) divided by the total number of applicants.

This is an imperfect measure of a college's selectivity, and does not necessarily reflect academic quality, since many factors can influence acceptance rates. Some schools with reputations for being easy after admission tend to attract larger numbers of applicants; public schools offer lower in-state tuition, often an attractive incentive for in-state applicants. Even winning sports teams can increase application numbers. And there are many other factors that can influence the quality and size of the applicant pool, from school to school and even year to year.

Despite these caveats, "percent accepted" can be a revealing statistic: Colleges that accept a relatively small percentage of their applicants are usually in the best position to maintain their academic quality. When the acceptance rate is less than one-third, you can be assured the school is one of the best around.

Percent accepted who enroll is the number of students who enroll divided by the number accepted. This figure, commonly called the "yield" by admissions offices, is another way to assess how well a school attracts qualified applicants. Since many applicants are accepted at multiple schools, the yield is a good indicator of which schools are first-choice schools, and which are "safety" schools: The latter usually have yields below 40 percent.

The main use of yields is to compare schools that have similar applicant pools; state universities tend to have high yields because some applicants are in-state students who don't apply anywhere else.

Number of transfers tells the number of students who were accepted for transfer to that institution each year. Keep in mind that "NA" here does not mean that there were no transfers, only that the schools did not report a number. A few schools, though, do not accept transfers.

This number gives an indication of the college's receptivity to transfer applicants. Colleges with many transfers are often fair to good academic institutions with one important feature (e.g., location, a particular program) that sets them apart

from other institution. Schools in or near Washington, D.C., are a good example because of their proximity to the seat of national government. Most schools with high transfer rates have as many students going as coming. Those who decide that whatever is there is not for them are continually replaced by fresh faces from other colleges. The transfer figure should not be considered an index of a school's popularity, since many limit transfers to a small number, and a few cases forbid them entirely. *The Insider's Guide* prints the number accepted rather than the number matriculated, because the former number better represents the opportunity to transfer than the latter. For example, if a school accepts 90 transfers, but only 4 matriculate, the "90" figure more accurately reflects the potential for a successful transfer acceptance.

Size of entering class is the number of first-years and transfers on campus at the beginning of the year.

The application deadline is the final deadline for completed applications (except for second-term grade reports and late admissions tests) for freshman students.

Many schools offer early-decision or early-action plans that allow students to submit applications for evaluation before the normal deadline. Early-decision usually requires a commitment to enroll if accepted (except in unusual circumstances), while early-action plans usually give you until April to decide. The main advantage of these plans is that you can have a definite answer by December or January. If you are interested in any of these plans, contact the schools for more information—the earlier the better.

A large number of schools have "rolling" admissions, where applications are reviewed in the order received. In most cases, however, these schools have priority deadlines after which applications are at a disadvantage.

A note to transfer students: As a general rule, transfer applications have a later deadline (often one to two months) than freshman applications. Nevertheless, the earlier you submit your application, the better.

Many colleges do not report **mean SAT scores** (SAT I), as they do not wish to discourage potential applicants by doing so; instead they either report a range of SAT scores, or none at all. If no figure is listed for the mean SAT, then the school is probably one of many that no longer report mean SAT scores. Keep in mind, though, a mean score implies there are approximately as many students with higher SAT scores as students with lower SAT scores. Some schools, notably in the South and Midwest, prefer the ACT (American College Test); for these schools, a single number (on a scale of 1 to 36) is reported. Where a school has reported both, only the SAT I score is provided; in most cases, though, schools will accept either test.

Middle 50% SAT range is the figure the College Board prefers schools to use in discussing actual SAT scores. The range represents where half of a particular school's new freshman students' scores fell. So, a mathematics range of 550 to 650 would mean that half of the incoming freshmen had SAT mathematics scores somewhere between 550 and 650. The middle 50 percent range are the numbers between the twenty-fifth and seventy-fifth percentile boundaries; someone whose SAT score falls on the seventy-fifth percentile scored higher than 75 percent of the people who took that particular test. The same applies for someone whose SAT score falls on the twenty-fifth percentile; the median is a score at the fiftieth percentile. So, if your SAT score falls within the middle 50 percent range, you are on par, SAT-wise, with previously successful applicants. But remember that this does not mean you have a 50-50 chance of getting in; instead, view this figure as an indication of your own competitiveness against the overall applicant pool that the school receives.

Most popular majors lists the three most popular majors among students in the most recent graduating class (usually class of 1999). Remember, though, that popularity is not necessarily a measure of quality; also, the exact number of students majoring in any given field can vary widely from year to year, though certain schools are particularly well-known for specific programs (e.g., criminology, biomedical engineering, government, journalism).

The **retention rate** is the percentage of first-year students who remain enrolled at a given institution for their second (sophomore) year.

The **graduation rate** represents the percentage of students who successfully graduate within a specific amount of time: for example, "80% within 5 years." Most schools report a five-year graduation rate, as many now expect students to take five years to complete a degree program, while others report four- or six-year graduation rates.

Library figures list the physical number of volumes in the possession of the library. This includes book, audio and video recordings, but not micro-reproductions or volumes available through cooperative programs with other libraries.

Tuition and fees and **room and board** figures are given for the most recent year available. (The College Finder lists those schools that have provided tuition figures for the 2000–2001 academic year.) In cases where costs differ for in-state and out-of-state students, both figures are given. Also, many public schools charge tuition that vary with the course load taken.

Remember that these figures are meant as an estimate of the cost of a year at a given institution, and do not include such costs as travel, books, and personal expenses. Their main usefulness is as a relative measure of how expensive one college is to another.

On-campus housing, first-year gives the percentage of students living in school-controlled housing for their first year. This figure is given primarily for the benefit of students applying to state universities, many of which have reputations for literally leaving new students out in the cold. Be prepared to seek off-campus arrangements early if a school's housing percentage is less than 90 percent, or if no figure is listed.

Also, schools that reported first-year students are guaranteed on-campus housing are listed with a (G) after the percentage. Schools that stated they require first-years to live on-campus are designated by an (R). Most schools, though, make exemptions for older students, married students, and/or students living nearby.

For **financial aid, first-year** figures, schools were asked to report the percentage of the entering class receiving need-based financial assistance from the institution out of those applying for aid (in some cases, though, schools responded with the total percentage of students on financial aid). This does not include students receiving only merit-based scholarships, federal loans not given out by the institution, and students who did not apply for aid. These figures are most relevant for comparing similar institutions. Questions about specific financial aid programs should be addressed to the schools.

A Note About Some Statistics We Do Not Include

We do not list student-faculty ratios in our statistics because we believe that such ratios form an inappropriate basis for judging student-faculty interaction. Large universities often pad their ratios by counting graduate students who teach undergraduate courses as faculty. Other schools distort their figures by including part-time professors, or full-time research and emeritus faculty who do not teach at all.

Many public universities maintain quotas for resident students who transfer from community colleges. These minimums usually are set by state laws enacted to encourage and provide motivated community-college students the opportunity to apply to major public universities within their respective home state. Often such transferees comprise a substantial proportion of a state university's incoming transfer students. If such minimums are on public record, this figure might be included in future editions of *The Insider's Guide* in order to serve this large body of students transferring from community college.

Previous editions of this guide included a percentage of international students. *The Insider's Guide* is aimed primarily at an American readership. Since the international student percentage was never greater than 9 percent in previous editions, the figure was dropped in favor of one that would better serve the needs of a predominantly American audience (percentage of students from in-state/out-of-state). International students should not feel slighted by this.

Alabama

Auburn University

Address: 202 Mary Martin Hall, Auburn AL 36849	**Percent African-American:** 6.0%	**Middle 50% SAT range:** 520–620 V, 510–630 M
Phone: 334-844-4080	**Percent Hispanic:** 1.0%	
E-mail address: admissions@mail.auburn.edu	**Percent Asian:** 1.0%	**Middle 50% ACT range:** NA
Web site URL: www.auburn.edu	**Percent in-state / out-of-state:** 69% / 31%	**Mean ACT:** 23
Location: suburban	**Percent Pub HS:** 83%	**3 Most popular majors:** business, engineering, education
Founded: 1856	**Fraternities:** 16%	
Private or Public: public	**Sororities:** 28%	**Retention:** 81%
Religious affiliation: none	**Number of Applicants:** 9,638	**Graduation rate:** 29%
Undergraduate enrollment: 18,538	**Percent Accepted:** 92%	**Library:** 2.5 million volumes
Total enrollment: 21,525	**Percent Accepted who enroll:** 41%	**Tuition and Fees:** $2,760 in; $8,280 out
Percent Male / Female: 52% / 48%	**Entering:** 3,166	**Room and Board:** $4,930
Percent Minority: 8.0%	**Transfers:** 0	**On-campus housing:** 16%
	Application Deadline: 1 Sept	**Financial aid, first-year:** 11%
	Mean SAT: 562 V, 580 M	

"Why do they have two mascots?" As you turn off the interstate on the way to Auburn University you'll drive over large tiger-paw prints showing you the way to the campus. Upon your arrival you'll meet Aubie the Tiger, who was the 1997 NCAA mascot national champion. But at football games, you'll sing the War Eagle fight song and witness The Eagle in his cage outside Jordan-Hare Stadium. What does it all mean? At Auburn University, a school that prides itself on both its football and its friendliness, one emblem just isn't enough.

Two Heads Are Better Than One

Auburn University is divided into 12 different colleges. Students graduate with a major from one of these colleges, which include Agriculture; Architecture, Design, and Construction; Business; Education; Engineering; Forestry; Nursing; Human Sciences; Liberal Arts; Pharmacy; Science and Mathematics; and Veterinary Medicine. Once students declare their major at the end of their sophomore year, they are not ultimately bound to it and a change of major even between different colleges is easily accomplished. With some noted exceptions, Auburn students are pleased overall with their academic experiences. Grading is seen as fair, and homework is not too much of a burden, although as one student put it, "Your time here is all what you make of it. You can walk out without ever picking up a book, but you can also study your head off." While there are certainly exceptions, education is largely known as a "slack" major, while engineering and veterinary medicine are both considered "tough" and "prestigious." In addition to its tough subject matter, the math and science departments at Auburn also draw student criticism due to some of the faculty members. One student stated, "My teacher seemed to fall asleep during his own lecture, so I went in for a little personal help during office hours, and he fell asleep there too!" Other complaints stem from the fact that getting a professor or TA who speaks fluent English is often a rarity, although another student noted that the university is currently addressing this problem.

To Dorm or Not to Dorm

Freshmen aren't required to live on campus, so many choose among other options available to them. For those who do decide to reside in university housing, there are two main areas of the campus to live in: the Quad and the Hill. Dorms in both of these areas are divided by sex but have regular visiting hours for students of the opposite sex. Dorms are also segregated according to student interests. For example, there is Sewell, the dorm for athletes, and Broun and Harper, which house many honors-program students. Another point of interest surrounding dorm life is that the majority of the dorms are strictly female. For unknown reasons, many more Auburn women decide to spend their freshman year in the dorms than their male counterparts.

For the majority of students who live off campus, housing options are plentiful. Many students decide to rent apartments or houses. Residential complexes often have reputations associated with them, like the College Park Apartments, which is known as "party central." Other options include the Commons, an interesting blend of apartment and dorm that is not run by the university but still supplies younger students with an RA system in order to help them with any problems they may have adjusting to college life.

Students rate the food at Auburn's two main dining halls, War Eagle Court and Terrell, "just average," but they consider their overall food choices plentiful. There are several fast-food chains around campus for students on the go, as well as other university-run options like the Dow Deli, where students can make their own pizza and sandwiches. There is no common meal plan at Auburn, but students can and often do make use of their "Tiger Club" card to send the bill for any food purchases home to Mom and Dad. For more upscale dining, the town of Auburn hosts a large array of popular restaurants like Applebee's and Ruby Tuesday's, along with local favorites like Gutherie's, where students joke that one can choose from "chicken fingers, chicken fingers, or chicken fingers."

Y'all Come Back Now, Ya Hear?

Socially, Auburn considers itself one of the preeminent universities nationwide. Students pride themselves on their southern hospitality and amiability, although the university is somewhat homogeneous. "There is definitely a student stereotype here," said one upperclassman, "and those who don't fit in might feel a little out of it."

> **"There is definitely a student stereotype here," said one upperclassman, "and those who don't fit in might feel a little out of it."**

On weekends, Auburn students know how to have fun. "Friday night party, Saturday night party, and Sunday recuperate" is how one student described her weekend schedule. Most of these parties occur either in private apartments or at the many fraternities and sororities around campus. The Greek scene of Auburn is somewhat different from that at other large Southern universities. While the Greek presence is large, the frats and sororities don't have their own houses and students reside in the dorms. Thus, the first three floors of most dorms are populated with members of one particular fraternity or sorority.

This doesn't keep the Greeks from having a good time, however. Their large band parties and dressy formals keep members entertained and active. The band parties are attractive to Greek and non-Greek alike, and while police are required to be present at these get-togethers, students claim limitations on underage drinking are virtually never enforced. The cops do, however, enforce one popular safety rule known as "Sober Drivers" at major parties. Volunteers give their services to get partiers home safely at the end of the night, and are required to be on call at all times. Students say that non-Greeks don't feel particularly pinched by a lack of activity at Auburn.

Sports also play a large role in campus activities for all levels of commitment. Auburn football is followed with incredible zeal, especially when such noted rivals as the University of Georgia, Florida, and of course, Alabama, come knocking. While no other varsity sport garners the attention given to football, Auburn plays host to a large group of well-supported intercollegiate teams. For those who take their sports a little less seriously, there are also many intramural and pickup games occurring on the campus at all times, as well as a bevy of local lakes and parks to which students frequently retreat.

Many students also engage themselves with a large array of social and community service organizations present around the campus. Popular groups include the University Program Council, commonly known as the UPC, which strives to bring famous entertainers and musicians to campus, and Campus Crusade for Christ, which regularly boasts over 800 members. Service groups also include Habitat for Humanity, which builds housing for the underprivileged in the area, Impact and Uplift, two groups that work with local families and children, and the Circle K, which works in conjunction with the local Kiwanas Club in community efforts.

A Walk in the Park

When asked to describe the campus, virtually every Auburn student replies "beautiful," "pretty," and "green." The campus is large enough that students don't feel cramped, yet not so big that getting from place to place is a problem. Grass and trees abound, and comparable redbrick buildings complete the campus.

When asked which of these buildings is the most noteworthy, most students reply with authority, "the Haley Center." This behemoth of college life contains the university bookstore, cafeteria, and most of the large lecture halls on the campus. It is shaped into four quadrants that point (as rumor has it) toward four parts of Auburn life in decreasing importance, from Jordan-Hare Football Stadium to Draughton Library to Foy Student Union and finally to a four-way intersection. Perhaps the importance of the intersection rests in Auburn's large automobile population. Cars have caused a slight dilemma on the campus due to a limited number of parking spaces. Most Auburn students do bring a vehicle to school, because as one student puts it, "a car is not a necessity for getting to classes, but socially it's a big plus." In fact, Auburn students seem to regard their entire collegiate experience as a big plus, and with two mascots, how could you go wrong? —*Robbie Berschinski*

FYI
The three best things about attending Auburn are "the beautiful campus, the school spirit, and the academic diversity."
The three worst things about attending Auburn are "the size, the foreign-speaking TAs, and living in Alabama."
The three things that every student should do before graduating from Auburn are "go to a 'Beat 'Bama' pep rally, relax during Splash into Spring week, and run in the 2.7 mile Cake Race across campus."
One thing I'd like to have known before coming here is "how humid it is."

Birmingham-Southern College

Address: 900 Arkadelphia Road, Birmingham, AL 35254
Phone: 205-226-4686
E-mail address: admissions@bsc.edu
Web site URL: www.bsc.edu
Location: urban
Founded: 1856
Private or Public: private
Religious affiliation: Methodist
Undergraduate enrollment: 1,447
Total enrollment: 1,531
Percent Male/Female: 41%/59%
Percent Minority: 18.0%

Percent African-American: 13.0%
Percent Hispanic: 0%
Percent Asian: 4.0%
Percent in-state/out-of-state: 89%/11%
Percent Pub HS: NA
Fraternities: 65%
Sororities: 65%
Number of Applicants: 757
Percent Accepted: 96%
Percent Accepted who enroll: 43%
Entering: 358
Transfers: 0
Application Deadline: rolling

Mean SAT: 598 V, 588 M
Middle 50% SAT range: 540–670 V, 520–660 M
Middle 50% ACT range: NA
Mean ACT: 26
3 Most popular majors: business administration, biology, English
Retention: 84%
Graduation rate: 48%
Library: 250,000 volumes
Tuition and Fees: $14,450 in; $14,450 out
Room and Board: $5,365
On-campus housing: 82%
Financial aid, first-year: 47%

Passing through the scenic town of Birmingham, Alabama, one would not expect to come across a thriving academic institution. But this is precisely what one does find, in the form of Birmingham-Southern College—a community that combines tough academics with a good dose of Southern charm.

Classroom Interaction

Faculty-student interaction is a foremost consideration at BSC. Introductory classes seldom exceed 35 students, and most upper-level classes enroll 15 people or less. Professors teach just about everything, but some qualified upperclassmen act as professors' assistants for either credit or pay. Students universally praise the student-faculty relationships as one of BSC's greatest assets. "Teachers push you to do your best," remarked one undergraduate. Their relationships tend to be "very good, positive, and close" when students make the effort. Others lauded professors for being "very accessible" and for trying to foster a "collaborative effort to absorb the material."

The curriculum is reportedly rigorous and students tend to study a lot because "standards are high." "It's a tough school," added another student. Birmingham-Southern has a core curriculum of general education requirements that all undergraduates must fulfill; students say they meet them as a matter of course. "It's not hard to find a class that you like that also fulfills your general education requirement."

Business and natural sciences are two of the most popular majors. The English department also gets high marks, and BSC has a "good reputation in the Southeast for theater." "Most classes demand a good deal of time," said one student, and the natural sciences are particularly notable for their difficulty level. Organic chemistry and genetics are especially notorious courses, but that degree of rigor is what attracts some students in the first place.

4-1-4

Birmingham-Southern works on a 4-1-4 calendar in which students take four classes in the fall term, one in January (called the "Interim"), and another four in the spring. The Interim allows students to explore unconventional areas, do independent research, engage in internships, or study abroad in countries like Spain, Rome, Russia, or Italy. Special seminar courses are also offered during this term. Seniors' interim work must be related to their major. The Leadership Studies Program and Service Learning Program are two other program options at BSC. Qualified BSC applicants may be eligible for the collegiate honors program, which provides an "intense work load, but pretty good discussion." Honors classes are all taught in seminar format. Fewer than 50 students are chosen for this program each year.

Undergrad Life

The vast majority of BSC undergraduates are white, middle and upper-middle class students from Alabama and other southeastern states. The minority population is low, and few students are openly gay. The political environment is "very conservative." Tradition is paramount at BSC. Sports do not play a large role in campus life—BSC does not even have a football team. Rather, the Panthers' areas of expertise tend to be soccer, basketball, and baseball. Soccer has a particularly strong following and usually brings out many fans. Intramurals are popular with some, but games are not widely attended. The academic facilities are reportedly "good for the most part." The newly renovated Norton Campus Center contains a food court, movie theater, computers for games, seating, and conference areas. The library, the Charles Andrew Rush Learning Center, is only "adequate," according to one student, but has a "wonderful computer network." Students do their hardcore studying either there or in their dorm rooms.

Greek Dominance

Many students write for *Hilltop News*, the weekly campus paper, work with the Student Government Association, and volunteer in the community. Student Outreach Day, a community-service event, always draws a good turnout.

"Greeks dominate the campus," according to Greeks and independents alike. Most students go Greek, and many claim they find Greek life one of the most rewarding aspects of their college experience. Frat members say they have found a sense of belonging within the college. Others feel the Greeks are exclusive, however, and warn that "unless you plan to go Greek, prepare to be frustrated." Pressure to rush can be "a big deal," but Greek par-

ties are officially open to everyone. Alcohol is common, and people drink "a lot." The administration's stance toward alcohol is relaxed, but drugs are not tolerated. The Cellar, a coffeehouse, is a popular student hangout. Thursdays are open-mike night, and bands frequently perform on campus. Live music is definitely a staple of the social life at BSC. Entertainment Fest and Southern Comfort are annual concert festivals that students love. Past performers have included Blues Traveler, Drivin' and Cryin', and the Connells.

> **"Unless you plan to go Greek, prepare to be frustrated."**

All students are required to live on campus or with a close relative until they are 21 years old. All dorms are single-sex with different visitation policies for those of the opposite sex. Option 4, the most liberal, allows 24-hour visitation, but no cohabitation. Hansen and Bruno reportedly are the best all-male and all-female dorms, respectively. Some of the older buildings are not well maintained, according to residents. On-campus student apartments rented by the college are a popular option because some consider the neighboring communities unsafe. Security measures are taken seriously, and campus police are always available, according to students.

Eclectic Architecture

The campus itself is hilly and the architecture is "eclectic." Building styles range from neoclassical to modern. The campus is self-contained, and everything is within "a five-minute walk."

All students who live on campus are required to purchase a comprehensive meal plan, but opinions differ dramatically on the quality of the vittles. One commented that the cafeteria workers were "wonderful and under-appreciated." Pizza Hut and Chick-Fil-A are popular alternatives to dining hall grub. For more exotic fare, Money's and the Purple Onion offer Mediterranean cuisine around the clock. Small classes and a faculty truly devoted to education are the hallmarks of

Birmingham-Southern College. Tradition and a Southern demeanor combine to produce an environment with great cama- raderie and opportunity in this small college situated in an old Southern city. —*Melissa Droller and Staff*

FYI

The three best things about attending Birmingham-Southern are "that it's a small campus where everyone, including professors, knows your name, small class sizes make it possible for you to learn and interact with everyone, and everyone here is very friendly."

The three worst things about attending Birmingham-Southern are "it's a small campus so everyone knows *everything* about you—even when you don't want them to, there's not too much diversity in the student body, and the surrounding neighborhood isn't so nice."

The three things every student should do before graduating from Birmingham-Southern are "go to Southern Comfort and Entertainment Fest, stand outside on Guys Bid Day, the day when guys run down the hill to whichever fraternities they received a bid from and want to join, and get involved in some type of service activity so you get to know the area."

One thing I'd like to have known before coming here is "people at this school party a whole lot, but they study just as much."

T u s k e g e e   U n i v e r s i t y

Address: Old Administration Building, Suite 101, Tuskegee, AL 36088	**Percent African-American:** 98.0%	**Mean SAT:** 400 V, 500 M
Phone: 334-727-8500	**Percent Hispanic:** 1.0%	**Middle 50% SAT range:** NA
E-mail address: admis@acd.tusk.edu	**Percent Asian:** 1.0%	**Middle 50% ACT range:** NA
Web site URL: www.tusk.edu	**Percent in-state / out-of-state:** 32% / 68%	**Mean ACT:** 20
Location: rural	**Percent Pub HS:** 80%	**3 Most popular majors:** electrical engineering, biology, business administration
Founded: 1881	**Fraternities:** 6%	
Private or Public: private	**Sororities:** 5%	**Retention:** 77%
Religious affiliation: none	**Number of Applicants:** 3,073	**Graduation rate:** 50%
Undergraduate enrollment: 2,708	**Percent Accepted:** 90%	**Library:** 310,000 volumes
Total enrollment: 3,023	**Percent Accepted who enroll:** 33%	**Tuition and Fees:** $9,500 in; $9,500 out
Percent Male / Female: 40% / 60%	**Entering:** 906	**Room and Board:** $4,900
Percent Minority: 93.0%	**Transfers:** 0	**On-campus housing:** 0%
	Application Deadline: 15 July	**Financial aid, first-year:** 88%

Founded in 1881 by Booker T. Washington, Tuskegee University (formerly Tuskegee Institute) has drawn generations of African-American men and women searching for a strong higher education and for cultural enrichment. Tuskegee's close-knit student community lives and studies in the shadow of one of America's most important African-American universities.

Changing Tradition

Tuskegee was founded upon the concept that African-Americans ought to train in specific, technical fields in order to gain a competitive stance in the job market. This approach has changed over the years, however, and today the school provides its undergraduates with a liberal arts education. Even with the change in curriculum, all freshmen are required to take an orientation course, which consists of history of the university—including the mandatory reading of Booker T. Washington's *Up from Slavery*—and advice for adapting to college life. Other requirements include two semesters each of English and math.

Most Tuskegee students are engineering or science majors. Pre-vet, pre-med, and nursing programs receive high student praise. Many introductory classes enroll between 40 and 50 students, but the average class size ranges from 20 to 30 students. The small class sizes and the fact that very few courses use TAs allow for interaction between students and faculty. Overall, students give Tuskegee's academics a high rating, calling the school "demanding." However, some students lament what they called "recent budget cuts" that have increased the faculty-student ratio and cut into instruction quality. *The Guide* could not independently confirm this allegation.

Tuskegee's history is clearly visible around its campus. Some of the brick buildings were built by students when the school was founded. Many of these buildings' interiors have been recently renovated. Although administrators claim that these renovations have produced air-conditioning, increased Ethernet access, and an overall increase in comfort, students complain that the renovations were "incomplete because of funding problems." Despite such recent work, however, students argue that the library still "needs work." It is small and limited in resources, and as a result students doing research projects often have to travel to nearby Auburn University to find information. In an effort to improve their library system, Tuskegee joined an interlibrary loan system and began a renovation project, to be completed shortly.

In Loco Parentis, or Just Loco

Dorms are the other main source of student complaints. Students must remain on campus for their freshman and sophomore years. One student called the dorms "ancient." A typical room is sparsely furnished. "You had better bring things that make you feel at home," said one undergrad, because "there's no real cozy feeling." Also, because the school's traditional atmosphere lends itself to conservative social rules, all dorms are single-sex, and members of the opposite sex are never permitted to visit each other's rooms. To help enforce these rules, male and female dorms are separated by a 10-minute walk. In addition, the university staff keeps a close eye on dorms; students are not allowed to be on the "wrong" side of campus after 11 P.M. and, if caught, may face punishment.

> "The town of Tuskegee offers nothing except seclusion from the modern world, but you learn a lot trapped in the wilderness."

As a result of the strict rules and old facilities, many upperclassmen choose to move off campus. One student said of the coed policies, "I love my campus, but I had to leave it because of the rules." In an attempt to persuade more students to stay, however, the administration has announced plans for the construction of new on-campus apartments, but little has been said about the relaxation of rules.

Students tend to meet in the student union, which contains a movie theater, a grill, a game room, and offices for student organizations. The new cafeteria is another popular meeting place. Students report that the food quality is "ten times better" than it was several years ago. Tuskegee's many clubs and organizations also help to bring students together. Some of the biggest clubs are the state clubs, which unite students hailing from the same states to plan activities relating to their home turf. African-American groups such as the National Society of Black Engineers are also popular. Students are active in community service, and many students volunteer at the local hospital. Football and basketball games generate great excitement at Tuskegee. Students are sure to use their tickets for games against Morehouse College and Alabama State University. Homecoming is one of the biggest social events of the year. Aside from football, however, varsity sports tend not to be so popular.

Student Solidarity

Social life at Tuskegee changes with the season. In the fall, football brings the student body together. In the spring, Greek Weeks and Springfest attract large crowds. While the Greek system is a strong presence on campus, students report that they do not feel an urge to rush.

There is little animosity between the fraternities, but they reportedly have a "friendly rivalry." Officially, alcohol is prohibited on campus and students who are caught with it face fines or other penalties. As a result, on-campus drinking is not a big activity; those wishing to drink can just search for off-campus parties.

Many students consider the town of Tuskegee "slow," but students agree that it contains the basics for college life. And, as one student put it, "Tuskegee has a lot of potential to grow," adding, "but you come for the school—not the town." Tuskegee students say their campus is safe and claim that it is "getting better." Additional lights have been installed around campus in the past few years, and security patrols keep increasing. Security

is "much, much better about patrolling both night and day," said one student. It has "really increased from years past," she added.

Tuskegee has a history of enriching young minds both culturally and academically. To this day, students take pride in the beliefs upon which their school was founded. The administration is more conservative and tradition-bound than the student body, but students are willing to accept this conservatism in return for the Tuskegee experience. As one student said, "There are a lot of good people here and you can meet a lot of great minds—not to mention we're friends for life. People might complain about things here, but in the end, you don't want to leave."
—Melissa Chan and Staff

FYI

The three best things about attending Tuskegee are "the teachers are very helpful, the people are friendly, and the parties are *excellent*."

The three worst things about attending Tuskegee are "the administration seems to have no respect or regard for the students, the registration process takes 3 days, and the dorms are really run-down."

The three things every student should do before graduating from Tuskegee are "try the food at the Chicken Coop, go to Homecoming, and visit the George Washington Carver Museum on campus."

One thing I'd like to have known before coming here is "that you need a car to survive here—the nearest mall is like 20 minutes away. The town of Tuskegee offers nothing except seclusion from the modern world, but you learn a lot trapped in the wilderness."

University of Alabama

Address: Box 870132, Tuscaloosa, AL 35487-0132
Phone: 1-800-933-BAMA
E-mail address: admissions@ua.edu
Web site URL: www.ua.edu
Location: suburban
Founded: 1831
Private or Public: public
Religious affiliation: none
Undergraduate enrollment: 14,645
Total enrollment: 18,744
Percent Male/Female: 48%/52%
Percent Minority: 16.5%

Percent African-American: 14.1%
Percent Hispanic: 0.6%
Percent Asian: 0.8%
Percent in-state/out-of-state: 73%/27%
Percent Pub HS: NA
Fraternities: 16%
Sororities: 21%
Number of Applicants: 9,569
Percent Accepted: 88%
Percent Accepted who enroll: 42%
Entering: 2,720
Transfers: 1,231
Application Deadline: rolling
Mean SAT: 523 V, 532 M

Middle 50% SAT range: 450–590 V, 460–600 M
Middle 50% ACT range: 20–26
Mean ACT: 22
3 Most popular majors: business administration, communication, education
Retention: 80%
Graduation rate: 55%
Library: 2,187,000 volumes
Tuition and Fees: $2,872 in; $7,722 out
Room and Board: $4,154
On-campus housing: 70%
Financial aid, first-year: NA

University of Alabama students have an enormous amount of pride in their school. It's not just the beautiful architecture ("This place must have more Greek columns than Athens!") that gets raves from undergrads. Rather, in the words of one senior, "The spirit I saw here is what attracted me in the first place. I've lived in college towns and have never seen anything like this place on a game day." In all likelihood, if you attend the University of Alabama, a significant portion of your free time is going to be spent supporting tremendously successful athletic teams. In addition, Alabama students manage to fit academics and many extracurricular activities into their busy lives on the warm, southern campus.

The Necessities

Ferguson Center, the student union, houses the supply store, post office, dining hall, small movie theater, and food court with fast-food chain restaurants such as Burger King, Blimpie, Manchu Wok, and Chick-Fil-A. Taco Casa, students claim, "puts Taco Bell to shame!" On the meal plan, students buy 5, 10, or 15 meals a week plus $200 of credit per semester to use at the Ferguson Center and restaurants near campus. Students agree the food is acceptable for cafeteria cuisine. "It's nothing to write home about," one student said, and another added he "wouldn't call it home cooking." What does get raves, however, is the City Café's homemade biscuits with molasses on top.

For students who don't reside in Greek houses, dorm life is typical of campus living, getting "pretty loud" at times. "The dorms are not an ideal living situation, but you don't spend much time in them anyway." Freshmen are not required to live on campus, but for those who want to, suites with bathrooms and kitchens are available, as are coed and single-sex dorms. Friedman Hall is popular for its newer stoves and refrigerators. A junior advised that the smaller dorms tend to have bigger rooms.

Academics at Alabama

While many students study in their rooms, many study in Gorgas Library, which is the main library. Other options include the Science and Engineering Library, the Business Library (where many go to socialize while studying), Mclure Library, and the Arts and Sciences Library. The options of what to study are diverse as well. In addition to the College of Arts and Sciences, Alabama houses a business school and colleges of engineering, nursing, and communications. Other schools include the College of Education, the College of Human Environmental Sciences, and the College of Social Work. At the College of Arts and Sciences (which contains undergraduate liberal arts majors as well as many pre-professional programs) distributional requirements ensure that graduates of UA are well-rounded. These requirements include writing-intensive courses, computer or foreign-language literacy, humanities, literature, fine arts, history, social and behavioral sciences, natural sciences, and mathematics. 'Bama undergrads may take advantage of the prestigious honor program for incoming freshmen with high test scores and grades. This program allows for more student-faculty interaction, since participants work and research with professors. Also prestigious is the Computer-Based Honors Program. Along with the program's prestige comes a lot of hard work: One student recalled an assignment in which he was given a week to learn JAVA an write a complex program for presentation. The Women's Honors Program also allows students to capitalize on the intellectual resources of the University.

One of the biggest concerns for UA students is the lack of recognition given to its solid academics. Despite the school's vibrant and respected business and law schools, its noted communications program, and the successful accounting department, for the most part, UA's academics go unrecognized. Some students lament the lack of recognition; others consider UA "our little secret."

Crimson and White

As the team with the most national championships of any other college football team, the Crimson Tide garners the passion and spirit of many loyal Alabama fans. It would not be an overstatement to say that football is life for much of the student body. Much of the excitement centers around an intense rivalry with

Auburn University. Not to be outdone, the women's gymnastics team, the men's baseball team, and the girls' softball team are also impressive. Intramural sports are also popular: Students devote time to flag football, Ultimate Frisbee, soccer, and basketball. One popular place where students can be found playing casual sports is the Quad. One student remarked, "With its oaks and gentle breeze, this ten-acre park in the middle of campus makes the school's character."

The Machine

Besides athletics, Greek life is one of the main binding factors among University of Alabama students. *Esquire* magazine once ran an article on the country's most powerful fraternity located at Alabama, titled "The Machine." The article reported that this UA organization, a secret fraternity of fraternities, allegedly controlled student government.

> **"The homecoming pep rally is an unforgettable event involving "fireworks, the Million Dollar Band, old alumni, a four-story bonfire, and 20,000 of your closest friends."**

According to students, the majority of voters in SGA elections still are Greek, and although Alabama students held a constitutional convention on the electoral system, a staff member of the *Crimson White*, the campus daily newspaper, said he believes the changes were purely cosmetic. "In a race in which a Greek was running, a Greek won," he said of a recent SGA election. Despite the strong presence and influence of fraternities and sororities, students say there is no great pressure to rush and that it is possible to have a social life, if not political power, outside the Greek system. Students note that other popular activities are the Campus Crusade for Christ, the *Crimson White* newspaper, the national championship-winning debate team, the honorary organizations, and the community services groups. Active theatre, dance, and music programs also contribute to the diversity of cultural entertainment that UA has to offer.

The University of Alabama is known as a party school by outsiders and students don't go out of their way to discourage this view. Homecoming in late October is the biggest social event of the year. The homecoming pep rally is an unforgettable event involving "fireworks, the Million Dollar Band, old alumni, a four-story bonfire, and 20,000 of your closest friends." During homecoming, students can see the bond between the school and the community as "frat boys rally next to families."

In the spring, a big-name band performs on campus. Past performers have included Jimmy Buffett, Tom Petty, and James Taylor. On the weekends, students frequent the Strip, a street lined with restaurants, bars, and clubs. Many students have cars to get around in Tuscaloosa, which many call a typical college town. About five minutes away is the community of Northport, while Birmingham is less than an hour's drive. Something that every student should do, one senior claims, is to "drive somewhere insane on the weekend before exams and drive straight back that night." Popular roadtripping destinations have included Atlanta and the beach. On weekends without big basketball or football games, many students head home or to nearby Auburn.

The UA Student

"Most people think of UA as a typical white, southern, Greek school with a lot of alcohol. Few people actually fit the stereotype. There are students from many backgrounds here, though most are from Alabama and, reflecting the region, the majority are white." Students say they believe that all races and religions are welcome at UA, though they acknowledge that their school is relatively conservative. Efforts by the Student Government Association are aimed at improving diversity awareness and relations, to ensure a comfortable environment for all students on UA's campus. —*Marti Page*

FYI

The three best things about attending UA are "the Quad, football season, and flexibility of classes."

The three worst things about attending UA are "the lack of recognition for academics, the distance between classes, and the division between the Greek and independent students."

The three things that every student should do before graduating from UA are "eat breakfast at City Café at 5 in the morning after an all-nighter, attend the homecoming pep rally, and road trip to random locations."

One thing I'd like to have known before coming here is "that the University of Alabama is truly what you make of it."

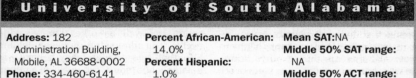

University of South Alabama

Address: 182 Administration Building, Mobile, AL 36688-0002

Phone: 334-460-6141

E-mail address: admiss@jagural.usouthal.edu

Web site URL: www.usouthal.edu

Location: urban

Founded: 1963

Private or Public: public

Religious affiliation: none

Undergraduate enrollment: 9,360

Total enrollment: NA

Percent Male/Female: 43%/57%

Percent Minority: 19.0%

Percent African-American: 14.0%

Percent Hispanic: 1.0%

Percent Asian: 3.0%

Percent in-state/out-of-state: 75%/25%

Percent Pub HS: 92%

Fraternities: 10%

Sororities: 8%

Number of Applicants: 2,661

Percent Accepted: 94%

Percent Accepted who enroll: 48%

Entering: 1,201

Transfers: 0

Application Deadline: 10 Sept

Mean SAT: NA

Middle 50% SAT range: NA

Middle 50% ACT range: NA

Mean ACT: 23

3 Most popular majors: nursing, health and physical education, adult degree program

Retention: 63%

Graduation rate: 25% (within 5 years)

Library: NA

Tuition and Fees: $2,475 in; $4,950 out

Room and Board: $2,883

On-campus housing: 21%

Financial aid, first-year: 84%

The University of South Alabama, "South" or "USA" to students, offers a bit of everything. It provides both a traditional Greek scene for the typical college-age student, and unique dorm accommodations for older students. The campus itself reflects a mixture of environments—the main campus sprawls across several grassy acres in the western outskirts of Mobile, but many classes, particularly in the health-related fields, are located in the much more urban downtown area. Although relatively young, South is growing into a more traditional university as it ages.

Academic Options

South offers a variety of academic options to students, including traditional degrees, an honors program, and several degrees geared toward older students returning to school. The university is divided into nine colleges: Arts and Sciences, Computer and Information, Business, Education, Medicine, Nursing, Engineering, Allied Health, and Continuing Education. The core requirements differ from college to college; however, all students must take two classes with a writing emphasis, although they do not have to be English classes. Workloads vary according to majors as well. Health-related majors, such as nursing and physical therapy, are considered strong departments, and students must have GPAs in the 3.8 range to be considered for admission to the BS/MS programs in these majors in their junior year. The Continuing Education program offers many night classes for students who work during the day and many students pursue this option. "Going to school here certainly is convenient for those of us who work all day," notes one night student.

Students generally praise their professors as "very helpful, not intimidating at all." Most classes are small enough to allow professor-student interaction, with average class size between 20 and 40 students. Professors teach nearly all the classes, which are primarily in lecture format. Students complain that due to poor English-speaking skills, math professors are close to impossible to understand, but reading the textbook usually gave adequate instruction. Professors are happy to meet with students during office hours. "Go visit your professors," one student advised. "It's the best advice that I got freshman year—professors are helpful and inspiring as well as being nice people." The Honors Program offers opportunities for extended involvement with faculty. It pairs students with a faculty mentor with whom they do research and community service projects.

Registration for new students is conducted on campus during orientation. Everyone else registers over the phone, and priority is dictated by GPA. There are caps to classes, but students say they can often get around these by talking to professors and administrators. South recently changed its academic calendar from the quarter to the semester system. One student wonders if professors have completely adapted to the longer terms, commenting that the number of tests in some classes have not changed despite the lengthier time period.

Commuter Campus?

In years past, South has been primarily a commuter school, with many of its students living in Mobile or surrounding areas and driving to class every day. This is still the case, for the most part, and, as a result, commuters' interactions in campus social life are limited. Clubs meet in the afternoon, for instance, which is an inconvenient time for students who work full-time. Many attribute the lack of school spirit to the fact that so many students live off campus and don't participate in campus events. "You have to jump into campus life here; nothing is going to pull you in like the school spirit that other schools have," says a frustrated student.

There are signs that this longstanding trend is beginning to fade, however. More efforts are being made to involve commuters—a newsletter, for example, tells commuter students about campus events. The recent completion of on-campus housing for Greek organizations is in part aimed at increasing student residence on campus. Another sign of growth is the Mitchell Center, the new home to the basketball team and site of concerts (Indigo Girls and Better Than Ezra played recently) as well as other campus-wide events. The administration began fielding a football team, which many believe will bolster school spirit, especially in a region so focused on football. Alumni are very active in this effort as well and view a football team as necessary to put South on par with other state universities that have strong football programs, namely Alabama and Auburn.

Few live on campus all four years, but for those who do, dorm life is a great opportunity to meet other students. Epsilon dorms are newer, and their interior hallways are more conducive to getting to know others in the dorm. Other dorms include Beta and Gamma, which have apartmentlike setups, and Delta, which resembles a hotel. All freshmen who live on campus must have the university meal plan. But limited cafeteria hours on weekends reportedly create problems for meal plan holders. Resident assistants in each dorm occasionally sponsor activities to build community spirit. "Living in dorms is a terrific way to meet people—most of the people I hang out with now I met freshman year in dorms," raves one junior. South recently implemented the Essence Program, designed to ease the transition to college life and encourage greater student involvement. It has several components, including living on campus, eating together with other students in the program, and an emphasis on mentoring and advising.

BYOB

The Greek system is responsible for most of the campus's social scene. Membership isn't huge, but Greeks have a strong presence on campus since most of the students who join sororities or fraternities are also active in other activities at South. Non-Greeks are welcome at all social functions except date parties. The campus is officially dry, so frat parties do not usually supply alcohol (they can obtain licenses for special occasions). Party-goers are encouraged to bring their own drinks. Written warnings are given for alcohol violations and for storing alcohol in dorm rooms. Nevertheless, students emphasize that South is a dry campus "in name only."

> South students are "not extreme— you don't see a bunch of people with spikes or piercings running around here."

A myriad of other activities cater to a range of interests. Outdoor movies, clubs relating to a particular major or interest (like backpacking or rock climbing), and student government are some popular extracurricular activities. Religious alternatives are numerous, and include student fellowships, Bible studies, and mission trips. Students can also found a club if they so desire. Organizations often develop theme weeks to focus attention on a particular issue, like rape awareness, and speakers regularly visit campus in conjunction with these events. Sports are another option for students—the basketball team has made recent appearances in the NCAA Tournament and the baseball team regularly plays in the postseason. Intramurals cater to less serious athletes, and the on-campus gym is more than adequate for students looking for a good workout.

While the university's administration has made several changes to enrich the life of the school, characteristics of the student body remain the same. Nearly all students are from Alabama or surrounding states. Many are older students returning for a degree as they change careers, or they are parents going back to school—as many as half the students are over twenty-one. Regardless of their age, students seem pretty uniform. One undergrad described her fellow classmates as "not extreme—you don't see a bunch of people with spikes or piercings running around here."

With the advent of new programs and buildings (the Mitchell Center and a new Fine Arts building are recent additions), South is going through growing pains as well. Poor investing, by the committee that controls the school's endowment, has led to the loss of a substantial amount of money. The administration is facing questions as it tries to institute a football team and over the student protest against the school's dry campus status. Nevertheless, the concerted effort to improve the quality of students' experiences have resulted in many changes that are fostering a great sense of community in this deep South school. —*Alexa Frankenberg*

FYI
The three best things about attending South are "helpful, knowledgeable professors, strong programs in health-related fields, and a wide variety of activities."
The three worst things about attending South are "no school spirit, parking, and no football team."
The three things that every student should do before graduating from South are "play ooze-ball (volleyball in a knee-deep mud pit), go to an event in the Mitchell Center, and take advantage of the fine arts offerings."
One thing I'd like to have known before coming here is "that it's much different from other colleges in that it lacks school spirit."

Alaska

Address: P.O. Box 757480, Fairbanks, AK 99775-7480
Phone: 907-474-7500
E-mail address: fyapply@uaf.edu
Web site URL: www.uaf.edu
Location: suburban
Founded: 1917
Private or Public: public
Religious affiliation: none
Undergraduate enrollment: 6,225
Total enrollment: 9,012
Percent Male/Female: 42%/58%
Percent Minority: 26.0%

Percent African-American: 4.0%
Percent Hispanic: 2.0%
Percent Asian: 3.0%
Percent in-state/out-of-state: 87%/13%
Percent Pub HS: NA
Fraternities: 1%
Sororities: 1%
Number of Applicants: 2,812
Percent Accepted: 82%
Percent Accepted who enroll: 33%
Entering: 667
Transfers: 0
Application Deadline: 1 Aug

Mean SAT: 462 V, 495 M
Middle 50% SAT range: NA
Middle 50% ACT range: NA
Mean ACT: NA
3 Most popular majors: education, biological sciences, business administration
Retention: 64%
Graduation rate: 26%
Library: 1.8 million volumes
Tuition and Fees: $2,190 in; $6,810 out
Room and Board: $4,150
On-campus housing: NA
Financial aid, first-year: 62%

At the University of Alaska at Fairbanks, Alaska's first state university, moose promenade through the streets and boiling water dumped outside freezes before reaching the ground. One student reported that even nose hairs become tiny icicles in the sub-zero Alaskan air. Yet, students who are hardy enough to brave the not-so-hospitable climate receive a unique and rewarding educational experience.

Unusual Academic Opportunities

All University of Alaska at Fairbanks (UAF) undergraduates must take a preliminary course in library skills as well as fulfill distributional requirements in communications, humanities, social sciences, mathematics, and the natural sciences. The university also offers an honors program that requires the completion of 27 credits as well as a senior thesis. Classes within this program range from "Aesthetic Appreciation" to "Differential Equations." UAF offers classes in environmental engineering, military science, and wildlife management. Additionally, there are two schools that provide students with excellent internship and research opportunities: the School of Fisheries and Ocean Sciences, and the School of Mineral Engineering. For example, one special program enables students to spend a semester in the Arctic, offering an "amazing field-study experience."

Students are quick to point out that UAF is also the home of Denali, a supercomputer with one of the largest memories in the world. Although mostly graduate students and other researchers use it, Denali is accessible to undergrads as well. As one student notes, "Denali is just another example of the kind of unique, hands-on educational opportunities we are so lucky to have at our fingertips."

Another academic highlight is the renowned University of Alaska Museum, which attracts visitors every year, making the university a top tourist attraction in the state. Over a million objects, from fine arts to biological specimens, are housed in the museum's imposing, modern architectural framework.

Other prominent facilities enhance the UAF campus, too. Students at UAF hibernate in the all-hours room of the central Elmer E. Rasmuson Library for serious studying. The main social retreat is Wood Center, a two-level student center that includes a bowling alley, arcade, pub, and food court. Students report that because the university ran short on funding while the Wood Center was under construction, its two staircases actually lead nowhere. UAF is currently engaged in the middle of a 4-year, $20 million dorm renovation plan, so the "staircases will have to wait for now!"

A Mixed Bag

Most UAF students live on campus for their first and second years. The eight dorms are divided into Upper and Lower Campus. Seven of the dorms are coed, while one is all-female. Students report that Lower Campus residence halls, especially McIntosh (the all-female dorm), are smaller and have a stronger community atmosphere. Alcohol-free housing is also available in Nerland Hall and suite-style living is available in the newly renovated Wickersham Hall.

Recently, dorm renovations for both the inside and the outside of existing buildings on the Lower Campus have spruced up campus. In addition to renovations, the university also undertook the construction of a new multimillion-dollar residence hall specifically for Native Alaskan students. The dorm provides 25 to 30 students with an environment that will ease the transition from village to university life.

In addition to the eight dorms at UAF, there is the Student Apartment Complex, which offers students a chance to experience the feeling of living off campus without "actually having to deal with the nitty-gritty details of living off." Roughly half the student body lives off campus in Fairbanks, mostly in small cabins or special sections of local hotels reserved for students. Thus, undergraduate living at UAF is "a mixed bag and you can pretty much find a living arrangement that suits your needs."

The town of Fairbanks is a few minutes' drive or, alternatively, a short, $1.50 bus trip away from central campus. Fairbanks boasts a movie theater, several malls, restaurants, bars, and grocery stores. Though many students have cars, they report that "parking on campus is a hassle, although a shuttle bus does run from parking lots to the main campus."

UAF security "keeps an eye on those who live off- and on-campus." Security includes campus police patrols, nightly escort services, exterior lighting for pathways, and emergency phones strategically placed around campus. Guests also must leave a picture ID at the check-in desk upon entering any residence hall.

Eats and Social Treats

Students who live on campus must be on a meal plan, which one student thought "would explain the reason why half of the university lives off campus!" The food at the university's dining hall, called Commons, inspires descriptions that range from "bland" to "disgusting and fattening." Nevertheless, Commons is one of the more popular places for students to hang out and socialize. As one student joked, "Even if you don't know what to talk about, you can always chat about your eats—always a good topic of conversation." For alternative fare, students head over to the Wood Center, which offers hungry undergraduates pizza, hamburgers, and coffee. The Wood Center also becomes a place for entertainment as well. In the past, the Bust-a-Gut comedy series at the Wood Center Pub has featured big-name stand-up comedians, such as Chuck Milligan, Greg Fitsimmons, and Scott Falconbride. As one senior said, "These events are a big treat for us."

The majority of entertainment and social activity for UAF students, however, relies heavily on the weather. Popular outdoor activities include cross-country and downhill skiing and sledding. Students say that since the winters are so dark and cold, drinking is often prevalent "to warm us up." One student felt that the administration follows an "out of sight, out of mind" policy toward drinking on campus.

In the fall, UAF students celebrate the coming of winter with Starvation Gulch, a carnival that includes a bonfire contest and "celebrity auction" for such treats as dinner with the university president. In April, UAF students commemorate the arrival of spring with events like Spring Meltdown, Spring Breakup, and All Case Day (an event where students try to "drink a case of beer before midnight"). Students also participate in mud volleyball games and, from several stories up, a watermelon toss and egg drop. No matter the season, UAF students enjoy school-sponsored dances and ice-skating in their own indoor rink.

The harsh winter weather limits UAF's intercollegiate outdoor sports program, but students and the surrounding community enthusiastically support the university's Nanooks Division I hockey team (whose name comes from the Eskimo word for polar bear). The cross-country ski team also performs well, and the rifle team, despite little fan support, ranks among the best in the NCAA. Other varsity sports include basketball and volleyball. Intramural sports (IMs) are popular on campus, especially volleyball, basketball, hockey, and broomball (hockey without the skates). At the Student Recreation Center, students take advantage of a climbing wall, indoor track, weight room, swimming pool, and ice arena either to hone their skills for IMs or simply to keep in shape.

A Little Spice in Life

While many UAF students are from Alaska (the school's Rural Student Services helps students from small villages adjust to college), a good number of international students enroll, mostly from Canada and Russia. Native Americans make up the largest and most closely-knit minority group.

Undergrads range from the "preppy" to "granola" outdoorsy types who live in cabins year-round. UAF also has a large nontraditional (older) student population. Although one student described the general political attitude as "apathetic and independent," many undergrads are politically active in matters that directly affect them, such as defending their departments from budget cuts. Many also aspire to return to their native villages after graduation to help their respective communities.

> **"Living and learning here is a remarkable experience."**

Extracurricular activities at UAF include a weekly newspaper titled the *Sun Star*, the Associated Students of UAF (student government), and the student-run radio station. Students are active in everything from College Republicans to specialized groups such as the Student Ceramics Art Guild. As one student said, "You have the freedom to do pretty much whatever you want." Greek life is also a new social option at UAF, though so far, there is only one sorority and one fraternity (the only one in Alaska). Both focus on community service and neither has attracted a large membership.

Students cite the quality of residential life, low tuition price, and academic offerings as UAF's strong points, but some warn that undergrads unaccustomed to Alaska's long, dark winters can easily become depressed. Alaska is not for everyone. For those hardy people who do decide on UAF, "living and learning here is a remarkable experience."—*Melissa Chan*

FYI
The three best things about attending UAF are "the hands-on educational opportunities, the abundance of outdoor fun, and the friendly student-body."
The three worst things about attending UAF are "the lack of parking, the terrible dining food, and the freezing *cold!*"
The three things that every student should do before graduating are "visit the University of Alaska Museum (It really has lots of cool stuff), take a winter nightcap to warm up, and partake in 'Arrival of Spring' celebrations."
One thing I'd like to have known before coming here is "that it gets so cold here your nose hairs freeze!"

Arizona

Arizona State University

Address: P.O. Box 870112, Tempe, AZ 85287-0112
Phone: 602-965-7788
E-mail address: ugradadm@asuvm.inre.asu.edu
Web site URL: www.asu.edu
Location: suburban
Founded: 1885
Private or Public: public
Religious affiliation: none
Undergraduate enrollment: 47,000
Total enrollment: 33,268
Percent Male/Female: 48%/52%
Percent Minority: 21.0%

Percent African-American: 3.0%
Percent Hispanic: 11.0%
Percent Asian: 5.0%
Percent in-state/out-of-state: 77%/23%
Percent Pub HS: NA
Fraternities: 7%
Sororities: 4%
Number of Applicants: 11,434
Percent Accepted: 77%
Percent Accepted who enroll: 40%
Entering: 5,191
Transfers: 0
Application Deadline: 15 Jan

Mean SAT: 543 V, 557 M
Middle 50% SAT range: 480–600 V, 490–610 M
Middle 50% ACT range: NA
Mean ACT: 23
3 Most popular majors: psychology, education, business
Retention: 73%
Graduation rate: 48%
Library: 3 million volumes
Tuition and Fees: $2,058 in; $8,710 out
Room and Board: $4,500
On-campus housing: 17%
Financial aid, first-year: 56%

In a climate where you can wear shorts 10 months out of the year, it is no wonder that most students at Arizona State care more about their tan lines than their grade-point average. Situated in Tempe, in the heart of what the locals call the Valley of the Sun, Arizona State is often a victim of its location. The sun provides the students with what is, in one undergrad's opinion, "a nine-month vacation." And as much as the university has tried, with numerous new programs over the past few years, ASU has not yet shed its reputation as one of the nation's top party schools.

Serious Sun Devils

The Sun Devils of Arizona State are a curious lot. Amid all of the distractions and beautiful weather, there are those who are serious about their studies. Arizona State's best programs are primarily preprofessional, and students rate the business, engineering, architecture, and broadcasting colleges as the university's best.

The music school is also highly regarded. The main student complaint is the overall size of Arizona State, which has more than 32,000 undergrads and 47,000 students overall. "Seemingly simple things like registration for classes in my major can sometimes become a real hassle because of a required signature of a professor who has, on short notice, decided to take a vacation," one student said. To help ease this problem, Arizona State has implemented a phone registration process that has enabled students to check their grades, class schedules, and even their financial charges.

Introductory classes tend to be huge: Classes such as Introduction to Sociology and Human Sexuality often enroll as many as 500 students. Undergrads report, however, that as they progress in their major, the class size radically decreases. Another student complaint centers on the English skills of some TAs. According to one undergrad, "Chemistry is hard enough as it is. It almost becomes impossible when the lab assistant can't speak English."

Students can sidestep some of these problems in ASU's nationally regarded Honors College. Housed in McClintock Hall at the center of the university, the program accepts top high school applicants as well as undergraduates who have performed well. The program includes such benefits as priority at registration and extended library checkout, as well as the opportunity to enroll in honors seminars taught by the university's best professors.

Living Off

With rare exceptions, only freshmen live in the campus dorms. The rest of the students can choose to live in nearby apartments, condominiums, or Greek houses. On campus, students have the choice of single-sex, coed, or theme dorms. Off-campus, students say having a car is a virtual necessity. Public transportation is poor in Tempe, and long distances between many of the city's attractions cause even the most ambitious student to acquire a car. Arizona State does, however, provide ample parking on campus for a relatively small fee. Many students also purchase a bike to travel around the vast campus.

Between classes, students have a wide variety of activities to pass the time. Many choose just to lounge around the many lawns and quads, while others opt to study in the university library or hit the Memorial Union, the student center. Students generally rate the library system as "good" and "easy-to-use." Hayden, the main university library, is centrally located and provides students with ample study space and high-tech research equipment. Inside the enormous Memorial Union are various restaurants, a movie theater, a video arcade, lounges, and the popular basement bowling alley.

The Best Bodies on Campus

ASU's intercollegiate athletic program is perennially regarded as one of the best in the nation. The baseball and golf teams are among the nation's best annually. Every Saturday night, almost religiously, thousands of students head over to Sun Devil Stadium to watch the football team

compete before they go, just as ritualistically, to the fraternity parties. The varsity athletes, however, are not the only ones working up a sweat. The enormous and well-equipped Student Recreation Complex is home to thousands of students who hope to add muscle to their already tanned and toned bodies. As one student said, "The lack of competition in the classroom is more than made up for by the extreme competitiveness for the best bodies on campus."

Many students also take advantage of Phoenix's professional sports scene. Football, basketball, baseball, and hockey games all take place during the academic year. The Arizona Cardinals play on campus in Sun Devil Stadium. For just a 20-minute drive west of campus, students can enjoy Arizona Diamondbacks games in the Bank One Ballpark and Phoenix Suns games in the Bank One Ballpark and American West Arena, respectively, in downtown Phoenix.

Party Central

At the same time, no one can completely forget the world-class social life at ASU that attracts so much media attention and annual rankings by college and national publications alike. The social life is heavily divided between those who are 21 (or, students say, those who have a fake ID) and those who are not. For the under-21 crowd, students say that dorm, apartment, and fraternity parties are the primary sites to socialize. Greek life at ASU is influential, with 36 chapters and over 3,000 pledges. Many students report feeling some pressure to rush, as "there is really no better way to meet other people."

> **"You really have to be dedicated to be a good student here."**

For the over-21 crowd, Tempe offers students a large choice of bars, dance clubs, and pool halls that attract almost every eligible student. In fact, Mill Avenue, the city's most famous street for bars and entertainment, has become so crowded by partying university students that police have enacted measures to stop the frequent cruising by voyeuristic drifrom U of A without going to a b-ball game at McKale." Home basketball games feature "the Ooh-Aah Man," an unofficial mascot who strips down to his spandex pants to lead spectators in chants of "ooh-aah" in hopes of inspiring the team to victory. Football is also a great tradition at U of A, and each season climaxes with "the Game" against archrival Arizona State. Whatever the sport, wherever the event, U of A students are sure to be there in large numbers and in full support of their teams.

Sun, Sun, and More Sun

Undergrads like to say that "the sun always shines on the U of A," and this applies as much to the social scene as to any other part of campus life. Thursday-night fraternity and sorority parties mark the beginning of the weekend. The Greek system is alive and well at U of A, and joining it is reportedly the best way to meet people on campus, although students say there is never pressure to join or even to go to a frat party. One sophomore reported that "the U of A scene is a juxtaposition of Greeks, cool, artsy 1950s-ish beatniks, and fun, sun-loving, bright-eyed students."

The city of Tucson also has many hot spots for students (especially those over 21), including popular dance clubs and bars such as the Velvet Tea Garden, Bisonwithces, Gotham, the Rialto, and Club Congress. For weekend getaways, Mexico is only one hour away. The less adventurous crowd is content with theme parties (and the alcohol that often accompanies them) on campus.

Extracurricular activities at U of A reflect the diversity of the student population: ethnic organizations, political forums, literary publications, and environmental groups are especially popular. But what if there isn't a club to meet a student's interests? "Just start your own—it's that easy!" one undergrad said.

Many students call the U of A campus breathtaking. Students enjoy warm weather all year-round, and wake up each morning to mountains and palm trees outside their windows. U of A also houses a beautiful cactus garden that attracts many visitors.

> "With such great weather, it can be difficult to concentrate on the university's varied academic offerings—a dilemma U of A students face daily."

Buildings on campus all have the same redbrick, Spanish architectural style. The campus is fairly self-contained, but at the same time, is well integrated into the city of Tucson, and many students get involved with the surrounding community through volunteer programs and environmental projects. The university reportedly has a good relationship with the Tucson community, and students claim that Tucson has all the benefits of a medium-sized city without the big-city problems.

Although a large percentage of U of A students are from Arizona, one senior said that there "really is no typical student here." One thing most students do seem to have in common is a strong sense of school spirit.

At the University of Arizona, students choose the combination of academics, sports, and socializing that suits them best. The relaxed environment and warm weather only add to the pleasure of university life. As one student said, "I don't think I could ever leave here—it would be like ending my dream vacation." —*Joel Karansky and Staff*

FYI
The three best things about attending U of A are "the excellent school spirit, the fabulous social scene (there is always something going on), and the sun, the sun, the sun!"
The three worst things about attending U of A are "the dorms (some are overcrowded and yucky), intro classes (they are too big and are often taught by TAs), and a weak advising/counseling system."
The three things that every student should do before graduating are "live off campus for at least a year, go to a Wildcats' basketball game, and take a weekend trip to Mexico."
One thing I'd like to have known before coming here is "bring the car, forget the warm-weather clothes."

Arkansas

Hendrix College

Address: 1600 Washington Avenue, Conway, AR 72032
Phone: 501-450-1362
E-mail address: adm@hendrix.edu
Web site URL: www.hendrix.edu
Location: suburban
Founded: 1876
Private or Public: private
Religious affiliation: United Methodist
Undergraduate enrollment: 1,143
Total enrollment: 1,147
Percent Male / Female: 16% / 84%

Percent Minority: 12.0%
Percent African-American: 5.0%
Percent Hispanic: 2.0%
Percent Asian: 4.0%
Percent in-state / out-of-state: 65% / 35%
Percent Pub HS: NA
Fraternities: 0%
Sororities: 0%
Number of Applicants: 962
Percent Accepted: 88%
Percent Accepted who enroll: 34%
Entering: 331
Transfers: 32
Application Deadline: (15 Jan priority) & rolling

Mean SAT: 632 V, 603 M
Middle 50% SAT range: 590–690 V, 560–670 M
Middle 50% ACT range: 25–31
Mean ACT: 28
3 Most popular majors: psychology, history, biology
Retention: 86%
Graduation rate: 62%
Library: 197,995 volumes
Tuition and Fees: $12,340 in; $12,340 out
Room and Board: $4,625
On-campus housing: 99%
Financial aid, first-year: 60%

Imagine canoeing down a turbulent river with nine friendly strangers. As you and your companions try to remain on course, a bond forms. Or, imagine participating in a charity house-painting project in which you and your fellow workers feel the satisfaction of lending a helping hand. These activities are a sampling of the many programs designed to welcome first-year students to Hendrix. In a week-long freshman orientation, students can choose one of 15 different trips that range from camping, rock climbing, and spelunking to visiting Memphis. These excursions allow students to get acquainted with both faculty and upperclassmen. One freshman explained, "I immediately felt like I belonged to the school after the program."

"The Best College in the State"

Students at Hendrix, a small liberal arts college in the small town of Conway, Arkansas, quickly identify their school as the "best college in the state," an assertion supported by its strong academic programs. Hendrix has a core curriculum that includes a foreign-language requirement, three courses in the sciences, and courses in English composition and literature. Along with these requirements, first-year students must enroll in Western Intellectual Traditions (WIT), a course that lasts two-thirds of the academic year and covers all elements of Western thought and history with lectures by professors from various departments, including history and physics. Students consider WIT a tough but definitely worthwhile experience. One student said, "At the beginning, I thought WIT would be quite a hassle, and it was a lot of work, but I definitely feel that it was an interesting and vital experience that gave me a wider perspective on my studies."

Hendrix runs on a trimester system with three terms, averaging 10 weeks each. Students take three classes every trimester with each class meeting daily. Hendrix students feel that the science departments are the strongest, especially for pre-med students majoring in biology and chemistry. One student said, "Hendrix is very strong in the sciences; it has an exceptional record of getting students into prestigious medical schools." Some students feel that the school places too much emphasis on the sciences at the expense of the fine arts and theater departments.

One of the best things about Hendrix is its student-faculty relations. The largest lecture classes are usually no larger than 50 students, and most upper-level classes enroll no more than 10 to 15. All faculty members at Hendrix teach undergrads—there are no research fellows. As a result of small class sizes, student-faculty interaction is universally described as "amazing," and professors are reported to be very accessible.

In previous editions of *The Guide*, we reported that "registration is not a hassle at Hendrix." However, when we shared the good news with current students, they laughed at us. The new consensus? "It is a huge hassle, complicated by rude and inefficient office workers, long lines, and general poor organization. It's universally dreaded."

Academics are reportedly rigorous, with studying taking up a large portion of students' time during the week. According to one student, "The amount of reading expected for many of the courses is unreal."

Natural Surroundings

One student described the self-contained Hendrix campus as "aesthetically pleasing, with red brick as its recurring theme." A particularly beautiful section of campus is said to be its "pecan shell" courtyard, lined with trees, large rocks, and benches, with a fountain and goldfish pond, which students say make it "a relaxing study spot." Students give the suburb of Conway low marks; one student said it is "not exactly the quintessential college town" and another reported that it "offers very little for college kids," although the suburban nature of the surrounding community poses few security problems on campus.

To find activity, most students make the 25-minute trek to Little Rock on weekends, where the night life is a little more exciting.

The facilities at Hendrix are considered "very well maintained," and several new buildings are in the works. Students consistently praise Hendrix's newly constructed Bailey Library, which is much larger than the old, underground library. The administration is planning new science facilities. However, the construction of the Jack Frost Campus Center, once slated for completion in late 1997, has been postponed for lack of funding. Students have placed lawn chairs and tables outside of the construction site, where they sit on sunny days. The new "center" is at the "campus crossroads, so you can usually see everybody if you sit there long enough. . . . Few campuses are this groovy."

Most Hendrix students live on campus. There are three male dorms, three female dorms, and one coed dorm. Most students live in doubles, although there are some singles. All campus residents are required to buy a full meal plan, a policy some students despise for its expense and inflexibility. There is one cafeteria, and students are ambivalent about the food. One student said, "The food is decent, as cafeteria food goes, but the menu is very monotonous and repetitive."

Extracurricular Activities

One of the most popular extracurricular activities is the radio station, KHDX, which was recently rated one of the top college radio stations in the nation. Students are also active in the Student Senate and in the production of a biweekly newspaper, the *Profile*, and the *Aonian*, a literary magazine.

Varsity sports do not have a huge presence at Hendrix. With its recent change from NAIA to NCAA Division II status, the college no longer offers athletic scholarships. There is no football team, but the basketball, soccer, and swimming teams are all well supported and fairly successful. Students are active in intramurals. The Mabee Center athletic facility contains modern exercise amenities, such as aerobics rooms, a weight area, and exercise machines.

Dorm-based Social Scene

Hendrix has no Greek system, and since the town of Conway provides little in the way of entertainment, social life centers on the dorms. Many students describe their dorm as "a close-knit community." Each dorm holds dances and parties throughout the year. The Student Social Committee also organizes special events and often brings guest entertainers to campus. Some annual events sponsored by the social committee and the dorms include the Miss Hendrix Pageant, where men dress up as women, and Kampus Kitty Week, a carnival that raises money for charity. Some of the biggest social events of the year are the on-campus "Warehouse Dances" sponsored by the Student Social Committee. Some students say the alcohol policy is not heavily enforced on campus, and for many, alcohol plays a central role in the social life on weekends. On the issue of sex, the small community of Hendrix has no secrets: "If someone has sex here, at least 50 people will know about it within a week."

Students at Hendrix are primarily from Arkansas, although the school is drawing more and more students from other states in the South as its reputation grows. Even so, students say that "the vast majority of Hendrix students are upper-middle-class...white kids." Some argue, "Hendrix's diversity isn't ethnic; rather, it's in the varied interests and idiosyncrasies of its students." However varied students' interests might be, Hendrix's social scene is known as "cliquish," and non-conformist students we talked to were quite bitter. *The Guide* once remarked in the past that "you will always fit in at campus." That may be true. But, it is equally true that you are more likely to fit in if you are an upper-class-white moderate conservative. Hendrix's bohemian reputation might be a product of affluence and convenience.

> **"Hendrix's diversity isn't ethnic; rather, it's in the varied interests and idiosyncrasies of its students."**

Hendrix, then, is a small college with all the advantages and disadvantages of its breed. It has a strong regional academic presence, and its science programs are strong for a liberal arts college. Its students are tightly knit, and many enjoy their Hendrix experience. Students who do not fit in to the Hendrix mesh are less sanguine. —*Melissa Chan and Staff*

FYI

The three best things about attending Hendrix are "that everyone is so different here, the campus is truly beautiful, and our core curriculum."

The three worst things about attending Hendrix are "its homogeneity, there are no Greeks, and people can be cliquish."

The three things that every student should do before graduating from Hendrix are "to get a place to stay off campus, buy some food – the dining hall sucks, put down the marijuana and start planning your future."

One thing I'd like to have known before coming here is "what Alabama Slammers are."

University of Arkansas

Address: 2801 South University Avenue, Little Rock, AR 72204
Phone: 501-569-3127
E-mail address: admissions@ualr.edu
Web site URL: www.ualr.edu
Location: urban
Founded: 1871
Private or Public: public
Religious affiliation: none
Undergraduate enrollment: 11,679
Total enrollment: 8,559
Percent Male/Female: 53%/47%
Percent Minority: 27.0%

Percent African-American: 21.0%
Percent Hispanic: 1.0%
Percent Asian: 4.0%
Percent in-state/out-of-state: 98%/2%
Percent Pub HS: NA
Fraternities: 14%
Sororities: 19%
Number of Applicants: 4,499
Percent Accepted: 90%
Percent Accepted who enroll: 55%
Entering: 2,229
Transfers: 0
Application Deadline: 1 Aug

Mean SAT: NA
Middle 50% SAT range: NA
Middle 50% ACT range: 19.8-26.0
Mean ACT: 19
3 Most popular majors: psychology, biology, liberal arts
Retention: 59%
Graduation rate: 15% (in 5 years)
Library: 1.5 million volumes
Tuition and Fees: $1,131 in; $2,916 out
Room and Board: $2,435
On-campus housing: 100%
Financial aid, first-year: 70%

Meandering through the Fayettville campus of the University of Arkansas is the nostalgic Senior Walk. The name of every senior is carefully etched into the sidewalks so that current students can gaze at the years of tradition, pride, and spirit that have made this university an exciting place for students to spend their college years.

Hitting the Books

Undergrads at the University of Arkansas can enroll in one of several colleges: the College of Education and Health Professions; the College of Engineering; Dale Bumpers College of Agricultural, Food and Life Sciences; J. William Fulbright College of Arts and Sciences; Sam M. Walton College of Business Administration; and the School of Architecture. Each college has its own graduation requirements and honor programs. Many students complain that engineering and accounting are substantially more challenging than other majors, but even these majors do not demand terribly exhausting workloads. One sophomore noted that "accounting is not necessarily hard for me because I really enjoy it." Another mentioned that her engineering classes were "challenging, but

manageable because of really helpful professors and TAs."

The accessible faculty is one of the most appreciated benefits of taking classes at the University of Arkansas. Professors hold regular office hours and even go to meals with students. Some students, however, regret that not all classes are taught by professors. Teaching assistants supervise labs, and they occasionally teach introductory freshman classes. Intro and core courses can top 400 students, and even some of the upper-level courses can be large.

When asked what he would like to have known before coming to the University of Arkansas, one student answered that he would have benefited from understanding that "you need to cut loose your freshman year and try new things while still doing your homework and going to most of your classes." Many students find that being responsible and doing the reading, labs, research, or problem set requires a trip to the recently expanded Mullins Library. While this four-story structure may appear "ominous-looking," its broad collection of books and convenient access to online catalogs make it a great place to conduct research. Those who prefer less somber surroundings sometimes opt to study in their rooms, study lounges, or outside. Students who have to finish labs can study in the recently constructed chemistry and biochemistry research center or the newly remodeled physics research building.

Razorback Pride

Students at the University of Arkansas clamor to watch the school's highly spirited Razorback games. Because Arkansas has no professional teams, the community also rushes to purchase tickets to basketball and football games. The football team has enjoyed much success, and the basketball team has flourished under the talented coaching of Nolan Richardson. The university's track team stands as a perennial powerhouse. School pride swells at any of the Razorback sporting events. One sophomore described how "going to your first football and basketball game as a freshman gives you chills." Athletic fanaticism reaches its heights as "thousands of people stand up in red and white and 'call the hogs.'" Yet another student declared that "every student should experience a basketball game! The new Bud Walton Arena can get so loud and fun." The rivalries between Tennesse, Ole Miss, Alabama, and LSU are pretty intense. New to this list of rivals is Texas, thanks to Arkansas's victory in the 2000 Cotton Bowl. Arkansas hopes to extend its impressive legacy of "over thirty national championships in the last fifteen years!"

> **"You need to cut loose your freshman year and try new things while still doing your homework and going to most of your classes."**

The fervor for spectator sports extends to the school's intramurals. Because they allow students to meet more friends and because the program is so well organized, many get involved and "get rather competitive." Greeks, hallmates, groups of friends, clubs, and study groups can form their own teams as well. Students prepare for intramurals by working out at the university's gym, the HPER (House of Physical Education and Recreation). The "Hyper" building provides tracks, pools, racquetball courts, weight rooms, dance floors, basketball courts, and multipurpose rooms. Most students appreciate the convenience of this rec space and use it fairly often.

Students are less appreciative of the campus housing. One student claimed "the dorms aren't anything special." Other students disagree, reporting that Gregson and Gibson are "pretty nice because they have been remodeled and are in the middle of campus." Student opinion is unanimous, however, when it comes to Pomfret and Humphreys. "They're the worst," explained one junior. Many find that the alternative off-campus housing is convenient and inexpensive. One popular off-campus residence is the College Park Apartments, just 20 minutes from campus. Students who don't have cars can get to campus by taking the university-supplied shuttle bus. Many students take advantage of this service because parking is such a hassle. "You have to park such a long way from everything and people get parking tickets all the time."

Fayetteville Fun

Fayetteville "makes for a great college town," according to one student. Its size—"you have the feel of a city, but you also feel like you are in a small town"—allows for safety but also provides for a lot of fun. Students frequent Dickson Street often because it runs through the heart of campus. Here, undergrads can find an array of good restaurants and popular bars like George's and River City, where students can play pool.

Students can also pick from a lot of weekend activities on campus. Some choose to relax by watching a movie on one of the large-screen cable TVs, while others flock to the Arkansas Union. This huge campus hangout offers a movie theater with new releases on Friday night, and it also has a large ballroom where past gubernatorial debates have been held. In addition to these entertainment spaces, students can find a post office and a travel agency in the Arkansas Union. Non-alcoholic events include the Red-Eye party, an annual event that features bands, dancing, and other entertainment.

Students who want to go out on weekends can usually find a party at one of the fraternities or sororities. Despite the fact that only a limited number of students actually pledge, Greek life is prevalent on campus because the houses are in the middle of campus. There's no pressure to rush, but some claim that "being Greek lets you meet a lot more people your freshman year." Non-Greek students don't have any problem going to the frat parties. Although the administration "is *trying* to get strict on the alcohol policy," kegs and alcohol somehow find their way into Greek housing. Students say that "you won't get in trouble unless you are just a stupid drunk or flaunting it."

Keeping Busy

In addition to the intramurals and academics, students can participate in various on-campus organizations and activities. In fact, one senior recommended that "getting involved on campus is the best way to love your time here." Students can immerse themselves in KUAF radio or UATV, the campus television station. Students who are interested in campus publications can contribute to the *Arkansas Traveler*, the campus newspaper that is released three times each week, *The Harbinger* magazine, or the yearbook.

Students enjoy the University of Arkansas because "everyone is so friendly," and because there is so much school spirit. Alumni constantly return for big games or to see their names in the Senior Walk. But all Razorbacks make sure not to step on the year 1900, because according to legend, students who step on that year will take longer to graduate. But hey, for some that might just be motivation to tread on 1900. —*Staff*

FYI
The three best things about attending the University of Arkansas are "the city, the friendly students, and the athletics."
The three worst things about attending the University of Arkansas are "the wind, the parking, and the food."
The three things every student should do before graduating are "get involved, go to a football game, go to the Bud Walton Arena."
One thing I wish I'd known before coming here is "that I'd have to do so much walking around the hilly campus."

California

California Institute of Technology

Address: 1200 East California Boulevard, Pasadena, CA 91125
Phone: 626-395-6341
E-mail address: ugadmissions@caltech.edu
Web site URL: www.admissions.caltech.edu
Location: suburban
Founded: 1891
Private or Public: private
Religious affiliation: none
Undergraduate enrollment: 901
Total enrollment: 1,973
Percent Male/Female: 72%/28%

Percent Minority: 34.0%
Percent African-American: 2.0%
Percent Hispanic: 5.0%
Percent Asian: 27.0%
Percent in-state/out-of-state: 34%/66%
Percent Pub HS: 79%
Fraternities: 0%
Sororities: 0%
Number of Applicants: 2,944
Percent Accepted: 18%
Percent Accepted who enroll: 47%
Entering: 218
Transfers: NA
Application Deadline: 1 Jan

Mean SAT: 715 V, 768 M
Middle 50% SAT range: 680–770 V, 740–800 M
Middle 50% ACT range: NA
Mean ACT: NA
3 Most popular majors: engineering/applied science, biology, electrical engineering
Retention: 91.0%
Graduation rate: 86.0%
Library: 530,000 volumes
Tuition and Fees: $19,476
Room and Board: $6,000
On-campus housing: 100%
Financial aid, first-year: 58%

During prefrosh orientation at the California Institute of Technology, prospective students receive T-shirts depicting a beaver—Caltech's mascot—about to take a drink from a fire hose. This reference to the slogan, "Getting an education at Caltech is like drinking from a fire hose," is a warning to freshmen of what to expect from four years at one of the most prestigious science and engineering institutions in the world. As if just getting in wasn't hard enough, getting through four years at Caltech means surviving what students regard as the toughest educational program in the country. While the pressure gives rise to a strong sense of community, and students help each other as best they can, there is a huge amount of work to be done, and "most people are very stressed a lot of the time."

Eager Beavers Wanted

Caltech students ("Techers") are required to take a total of 486 credit units over four years. With the academic year divided into three terms, this equates to an average of 40.5 units (hours per week students are expected to spend on work in or out of class) per term. But students point out that at this rate, it would be impossible to finish Caltech's required courses; a typical load consists of 45 to 48 units, and some students take 50 or more. Students add that the number of units is fewer than the number of hours they really work. Most courses are worth 9 units, but students report that "some problem sets can take 18 hours."

Professors, not TAs, teach all courses at Caltech. However, brilliant researchers don't always make good teachers. Many of the professors are "excellent researchers," remarked one student, "but this does not mean in any way whatsoever that they can teach." "I like all of them as people," said another, "but it's difficult to find profs that teach well. Some of the profs who care the most about students are also the worst teachers." For help with coursework, students usually turn to TAs, who received higher ratings from students; "There are some TAs who should be doing the lecturing," said one student. Both professors and TAs, though, are readily accessible for help, "if you know where to find them."

The largest classes at Caltech are the freshman core courses, which contain the entire freshman class of 200 to 250. Most other classes are smaller, but sophomores can still have "two classes with about 100 people." Students in lecture courses are divided into recitation sections run by TAs. Because changing sections is usually easy, students report, "The good TAs might have three or four times more students" than others.

In terms of workload, Techers are hit hard from the beginning: All students spend freshman year and most of sophomore year taking Caltech's core program, which includes five terms of math and physics, two of chemistry, one of biology, and two lab courses, and covers topics like calculus, quantum mechanics, and special relativity. Though Caltech is overwhelmingly science-oriented, students are also required to take a total of 12 courses in the humanities and social sciences. While there are non-science departments, "they don't get much respect" said one student. "People should not come to Caltech if they're not 100 percent sure that the sciences are all that they care about."

Information Overload

Whether studying science or the humanities, undergrads find almost nothing at Caltech easy. "We do everything vigorously," said one student. "There's not a whole lot of hand-waving." As a result, students say, Techers must learn much more than students at any other school. "One student transferred to Harvard after sophomore year. She didn't have to take any more physics to finish their physics major."

Of course, long hours of work are required to master the immense amount of information students are responsible for. "Everyone's working," said one student. "There are 24 hours in the day, minus 6 hours sleeping, 1 hour commuting, 1 hour playing around, and 2 hours eating, so I guess I spend 14 hours working and going to class." Freshmen are graded pass/fail in their core classes for the first two terms, which is "a much needed thing" as new students try to adjust. But things still are not easy—"Being up until 4 is quite usual here, even for freshmen," said one student. "I'm not gonna sleep more than 7 hours a night. It can easily dip down to 3 or 4 hours."

To help each other out, students commonly work in groups. "We're encouraged to collaborate on homework. There's no way you'd survive if you didn't," said one student. It is agreed that "complaining about the work fosters a big sense of community."

However, the high level of pressure does not result in academic dishonesty. Students are governed by the Caltech Honor System, which is founded on the rule that "no member of the Caltech community shall take unfair advantage of any other member of the community." Because of the Honor System, students are given access to labs, libraries, and most any other building on campus at all hours. When a take-home final is given, with instructions forbidding the use of textbooks, notes, or certain calculator functions, "you're expected to do it, and people do. Because of that, the honor system works. There's a huge amount of responsibility and trust given to students."

The House System

In order to create a sense of community among students, Caltech is organized into seven undergraduate houses, which bear some resemblance to fraternities. At the beginning of freshman year, students spend a week touring the houses, eating and spending the night at each one. At the end of the week, students make their preferences known, and the houses go about deciding which students they will accept; once assigned to a house, students get to select their roommates. A great deal of freedom is given to the students with regard to house life: Students supervise the election of a house president and other officials. Also, students can do whatever they like to their rooms—"paint them, build things in them, whatever. We're the ones who have to live with it."

The house often becomes like "an extended family," so much so that many students are isolated from activities outside their house—"that's a bad thing about it, but that says it works," said one student. The house community also serves as a support network, "helping you stay afloat, because there's a ton of work." Students select their own residential advisers (RAs), who can be anyone from a grad student to the soccer coach, and some upperclassmen are given duties as counselors. Houses organize their own social events, which can be anything from a party to a miniature golfing trip.

The vast majority of students live in Caltech housing, but as there isn't enough room for everyone in the houses, some students stay in nearby Caltech-affiliated apartments, or in other places on campus, which are considered "off-campus" because they are disconnected from the houses. Sophomores are often kicked "off-campus," because only freshmen are guaranteed spots in houses, and seniors and juniors get priority among upperclassmen. Even though the house is less the center of social life for "off-campus" students, "people will still come by after class; not living in the house, but still very much a part of it." The three North houses consist mainly of doubles, while the four South houses have doubles, singles, and triples.

Students on Caltech's meal plan receive 10 meals a week: 5 lunches and 5 dinners. The kitchen, however, is open during breakfast hours, and students can get snacks or take food to eat later. Dinner is served in the houses by student waiters who eat before everyone else and bring food to the tables. Opinions of the food vary from "the food is not very good here; however, we just try to deal with it" to "I don't find it that bad, but there are some dishes it's better not to eat."

Saturday Night Nuclear Holocaust

Social life at Caltech centers in large part on the houses, but "there are lots of activities that go on that aren't house-related." There is, understandably, less partying and drinking than at most schools: "There is drinking here, but not a huge amount. It's impossible to get wasted all the time and not flame out." There are usually parties at one of the houses every weekend, but "they're very different from the parties at other schools." Caltech students commonly throw parties with themes like "Nuclear Holocaust" (complete with burning buildings and glowing green lights) and do such things as flood courtyards in order to set up a floating bar on a boat in the center of the yard.

With the amount of work students have to do, time must be made to unwind. "There's always something to do; it's just a question of being able to do it." But students recognize the need to take breaks from studying, so parties are always "big events." For those who wish to go off campus, there are movies theaters and video stores nearby, and the city of Pasadena is "within a reasonable driving distance. Stuff you want to do is pretty close, but you still have to have a friend with a car." The nearest mountain range is only three miles away, should students feel like going hiking. Lake Arrowhead and Big Bear Mountain (which is popular with skiers) are also accessible by car.

The campus itself is described as "a great place to do everything except go to school. People come here to take wedding pictures." Though students may not always have time to stop and enjoy it, the campus features lots of grass and trees, as well as certain science inside-jokes, such as lamps in the figure-eight shape of an atomic p-orbital. There is a noted contrast between the buildings of the original campus, which were constructed in the first half of the 20th century, and some of the newer buildings. One such building is the 10-story Millikan Library (named after the scientist who measured the charge of the electron), which is described as "the ugliest building around." Students find the campus "very safe," while the area off campus not as safe. "There have been a few instances of people having problems with attempted muggings." Students who need a ride to or from somewhere off campus can make use of a campus escort system.

Athletics: A Different Approach

Extracurricular activities are both abundant and popular as a means of relieving stress: "Anyone can participate in anything here," said one student. This statement applies particularly to varsity sports, which are the choice of many students. "We have people on the varsity soccer team who have never played soccer." There are not enough women at Caltech to start a woman's soccer team, but this is of no import, as "we've had girls on the boys' soccer team." Students admit that "we're pretty bad—our basketball team hasn't won a conference game in 12 years." But in Caltech athletics, winning is less a concern than making sure everyone gets to play "who comes to practices and makes the effort."

Intra-house athletics, which are popular as well, share this philosophy. "It's very rare that they'll exclude you because you're not very good," said one student. Added another, "When you come to games, it's not just because you support the school, it's because you know the entire team." Despite the popularity of its sports programs, Caltech does not recruit high school athletes, lest academic standards be lowered. It is universally understood that "academics come first," so coaches will accommodate students who miss practice in order to finish work.

Other popular activities include a weekly newspaper, the *California Tech*, student-run plays, and other productions, and "a surprising number" of a cappella singing groups, given the small undergraduate population. Among the wide variety of activities, "you can find pretty much anything."

There is also Caltech's reputation for student pranks, which over the years have become tradition. While "vicious" pranks might involve nothing more than toilet-papering some trees, some of the more elegant and complicated pranks (assembling a car in someone's room, for example) are planned weeks or months in advance. On Senior Ditch Day, underclassmen, in order to get into absent seniors' rooms and "redecorate," must break through "stacks," which can consist of complex puzzles, or something as simple as a wall of bricks. Successful underclassmen are rewarded with food ("bribes") the seniors leave behind to prevent the rearrangement of their rooms.

> There are usually parties at one of the houses every weekend, but "they're very different from the parties at other schools."

Such eccentricity is one way for students to alleviate some of the pressures that are a part of life at what they call "the hardest school in the nation." Caltech students recognize that the massive workload is something that comes with the territory: "You have to be willing to work, because it's easy to fail." But to those willing to accept the challenge of Caltech and play the part of the beaver with the fire hose, the potential benefits are worth it. As one student said, "I read in some article on Caltech that 'you work your butt off, but you come out an academic badass.' I think I'd agree that that sums it up pretty well." —*Chiansan Ma*

FYI
The three best things about attending Caltech are "the smart students, awesome pranks, and your marketability and skills after four rigorous years."
The three worst things about attending Caltech are "the really hard courseload, not enough attractive women/men, and small student body."
The three things that every student should do before graduating from Caltech are "take part in Senior Ditch Day, learn to surf, and join a varsity team."
One thing I'd like to have known before coming here is "when they said hard work, they meant *really* hard work."

California Institute of the Arts

Address: 24700 McBean Parkway, Valencia, CA 91355
Phone: 805-292-2787
E-mail address: admiss@calarts.edu
Web site URL: www.calarts.edu
Location: suburban
Founded: 1961
Private or Public: private
Religious affiliation: none
Undergraduate enrollment: 777
Total enrollment: 1,125
Percent Male/Female: 55%/45%
Percent Minority: 10.0%

Percent African-American: 6.0%
Percent Hispanic: 1.0%
Percent Asian: 1.0%
Percent in-state/out-of-state: 52%/48%
Percent Pub HS: NA
Fraternities: 0%
Sororities: 0%
Number of Applicants: 1,250
Percent Accepted: 43%
Percent Accepted who enroll: 24%
Entering: 453
Transfers: NA
Application Deadline: 1 Feb

Mean SAT: NA
Middle 50% SAT range: NA
Middle 50% ACT range: NA
Mean ACT: NA
3 Most popular majors: animation, graphic design, film/video
Retention: 92.0%
Graduation rate: 38.0%
Library: 80,000 volumes
Tuition and Fees: $19,020 in; $19,020 out
Room and Board: $5,500
On-campus housing: NA
Financial aid, first-year: 75%

There's rarely a dull moment at the California Institute of the Arts. On its small campus in Valencia, California, students are constantly creating new ways to portray life, whether it be through devising a new interpretation of Hamlet, preparing for an exhibit opening, making a song completely out of Chewbacca sounds, or celebrating at the "My Bloody Valentine" party. Although the students are from an array of different backgrounds, they are tied together by their love of and total immersion in the arts. The result is a true cornucopia of passionate artists and an extremely focused yet admittedly eccentric student body.

Arts Aplenty

There is never a lack of daily activities at CalArts. Between academic responsibilities and alluring extracurricular activities, some students are at school for as much as 14 hours each day—and loving every minute of it. One sophomore's biggest complaint was that "classes are too short." CalArts is divided up into five different schools: music, art, dance, film/video, and theater. Within each school, there is a rough progression of classes that everyone must take, though

this schedule is more defined in the music, theater, and dance schools. While academic requirements are different in each school, a senior found that "school politics make it hard to get into classes that aren't required. You really have to work at getting in the good classes, and it doesn't always pan out." However, students are required to take some classes outside of their school, and introductory courses in other schools are relatively easy to get into.

The assignments at CalArts are not traditional essay papers. One art student recounted, "I had to make art out of garbage and then sell it to someone. Then, I had to use the money to buy candy and bring it to class!" Students are also encouraged to join forces in their extracurricular activities; for many productions, theater students will make movies with the help of film students while music students write the score and art students create the sets.

Students are required to take 48 credits in the Critical Studies department in order to gain a strong liberal arts foundation. Some students feel restricted by these "annoying" requirements, but many find the Critical Studies department a wonderful opportunity to explore unusual fields.

One theater student was taking Narcissism, Holography, and a Theater Management class to fulfill his requirement, and found Critical Studies to be "a little tedious, but you can find some gems in there." For the most part, students consider Critical Studies little more than an interesting obstacle in their pursuit of the arts.

Cutting-Edge Arts

CalArts professors receive rave reviews from all students. "The student-teacher ratio is seven to one, and they can really focus on me. That's why I'm here," remarked one student. The professors are not just instructors, but usually also active participants in their field. "The training here is absolutely phenomenal. My theater professor just took time off from Broadway to teach at CalArts, and she's going back to be in a production with Uma Thurman. We're being trained by the professionals for the professionals," reported a junior. Professors are very accessible and friendly, and the school also manages to attract an impressive crop of guest speakers. Noted alum Ed Harris frequently makes appearances, while jazz virtuosos Charlie Hayden and Tim Allen have each held workshops recently. "There is always someone cutting edge here."

Although the CalArts campus is minuscule by most standards, students can lay claim to some of the best art resources on the West Coast. There are studios and practice spaces galore, not to mention the acclaimed Walt Disney Modular Theater, constructed entirely out of 3'x3'x3' blocks. Hydraulic pistons make it possible to raise and lower segments of the wall, floor, and ceiling, paving the way for some bizarre sets. It is rumored that scenes from *The Empire Strikes Back* were filmed there, and one junior recalled a terrific modernized version of *Edward II* reorganized under the auspices of "the Mod." The animation department has just received expanded studios, and CalArts also boasts one of the biggest photo enlargers in the country. However, some students claim that getting access to facilities, even in your own school, can be trying.

Everyday Life With Not Your Everyday People

Students can live off campus all four years, but those who remain on campus don't complain about much. "The rooms are huge, and I have my own sink in the bathroom." However, not all experiences are positive. One student complained, "Ants really ruined my freshman year." The halls are also well-decorated by the students. "There is some really fantastic artwork; they make all these illusions. One hallway looks like it goes on forever. It's amazing!" Resident advisors preside over the dorms, but like most CalArts students, they are fairly laid-back. "They might come in to tell us to stop smoking weed if they can smell it, but usually they're pretty cool." Half the students are blessed with a view directly over the courtyard and site of the CalArts heated swimming pool, which has inspired some unusual behavior. "I never expected so much skinny-dipping when I decided to come here!" exclaimed a junior.

Many cook at home or eat out, but CalArts does have a pretty good cafeteria. "Even though it's got a pretty wide range of choices, after a while it gets monotonous. But overall, it's pretty decent." Meals can be cooked to order and the food is considered fresh by most, although some students have gripes with the "rip-off" meal plan. If the meal plan gets old, there is always the student-run Mom's Cafe or the Tatum Coffee Lounge on campus. For those up for a journey, the Claimjumper in Valencia was lauded, but students also have the entire city of Los Angeles to peruse for an incredible array of dining options.

Tiny Town, Tall Talent

Valencia itself is considered one of the main drawbacks to CalArts. Although it boasts plenty of movie theaters, bowling alleys, and restaurants, students complain that "Valencia is really a cookie-cutter, soccer mom kind of place. You can always pick out the students." There is a Six Flags Magic Mountain in town, but to many "there's only so many times you can twist around the looping loops or swish down a hundred feet without getting bored." Fortunately, Valencia is only 20 minutes from

L.A. and a half hour from the country, so students have a smorgasbord of options. Many have cars, and for those not swamped with rehearsals, jaunts into L.A. transpire several times a week. Students swing at the Derby, go clubbing around Hollywood, or just go out for a bite to eat.

Those who opt to stay on campus are not living in a ghost town. The Rendezvous is a popular drinking hole, and there are always performances or art openings sponsored by the school. "Most Saturday nights there are raving parties on campus too; I usually don't go anywhere," remarked a junior. CalArts is renowned for its wild Mardi Gras party and especially the annual Halloween party, which necessitates the LAPD for security. "The costumes are awesome. Last year there was some guy dressed up as Jesus, and he actually nailed a cross through the thin skin in his hands!" Creativity even pervades the graduation ceremonies. There are no cap and gowns; instead, each year, commencement is based on a theme. Last year the theme was the circus, so "the dean dressed up as a magician, people wore outfits, they served peanuts and hot dogs, and there was hay everywhere. It was wild!"

Yet very little at CalArts is as wild as the students who go there. "People here are very eccentric and different. They are all really into their work and have green hair and a lot of piercings," remarked a junior. Another student admitted, "There are a lot of freaks. But they're nice freaks." CalArts students find ways to express themselves in all aspects of life, from their work to their appearance.

This sense of individuality is heightened by CalArts' lack of organized sports teams. "Someone made up a T-shirt last year that said 'CalArts Varsity Football,' but that's as close as we get to having a sports team." While arts are the main focus, many students miss sports—there isn't even a school gym! "There's no school spirit. I kind of wish we all had something to rally around like a football team." Fortunately, for the casual athlete, Nerf football and ultimate Frisbee games have been know to pop up in students' spare time.

> **"Someone made up a T-shirt last year that said 'CalArts Varsity Football,' but that's as close as we get to having a sports team."**

If you like doodling in the margins during boring classes, the California Institute of the Arts is probably not for you. These students are extremely dedicated to their artwork and goals, and the overflowing creativity pervades everything from their personal appearance to their environment and even to their parties. But don't be scared off if you're not a pro just yet. For the truly motivated, CalArts provides an unparalleled opportunity to develop and refine your understanding of art as well as your ability to create it. —*Matt Stewart and Staff*

FYI
The three best things about attending CalArts are "the super-talented students, renowned faculty, and the California weather."
The three worst things about attending CalArts are "the strenuous workload, no school spirit, and it's easy to feel burned out once in a while."
The three things that every student should do before graduating from CalArts are "take a good dose of non-art classes, attend many student shows and presentations, and hit the L.A. club district."
One thing I'd like to have known before coming here is "how your interests can change dramatically."

California State University System

The California State University system has continually grown since the enactment of the Donahoe Higher Education Act of 1960, which brought together a collection of individual colleges to form the California State University. The expansive system now contains 22 colleges, including the first public university in California, San Jose State University, and the most recently established campus, CSU Monterey Bay. A 23rd campus is planned to open in Ventura County within the next few years and will be founded as CSU Channel Islands.

From the metropolitan Los Angeles campus to rural CSU Sonoma to the coastal San Diego State, the individual campuses that make up the system are distinctive and vary greatly. San Diego State University, known for its party atmosphere and close proximity to fine beaches, is the largest campus, with about 31,000 full-time students. Maritime Academy and CSU Monterey Bay are the smallest, with total enrollments of 450 and 1,960, respectively.

CSU or UC?

Although often overshadowed by the better-known University of California system, the CSU system offers many features that the UC system does not. With campuses located throughout the state, the CSU system allows many Californians the option of commuting to a college close to home. For students concerned with the high costs of financing higher education, the tuition of the California State Universities are half that of UC schools, while still providing larger and better resources than two-year junior colleges. Even for an out-of-state student seeking California weather, the CSU system is still an attractive deal.

Differences and Similarities

All CSU schools offer financial aid and over 60% of the students are currently receiving aid. The larger campuses offer Division I varsity sports, while the smaller schools are in Division II. All campuses have organized club and intramural sports. Each campus differs greatly and prospective students should research the academic focus, size, location, and student makeup of each campus before deciding. To help high school students decide which of the twenty-three campuses is right for them, Cal State has implemented a specialized website named CSUMentor System (www.csumentor. edu). This site is very helpful and anyone interested in CSU should check it out.

Education, Not Just Research

The most popular undergraduate majors in the system are business and management, social science, and interdisciplinary studies. At the graduate level, education, business, and management majors top the list. The CSU system gives out more degrees in business, computer science, and engineering than all other California schools combined, reflecting the career-oriented focus of the programs.

Unlike the research-oriented UC system, CSU schools concentrate most of their resources on undergraduate teaching.

Unlike the research-oriented UC system, CSU schools concentrate most of their resources on undergraduate teaching. Although the professors are less prestigious, it is for this reason that they can spend less of their efforts maintaining their reputation and more time focused on teaching. As tuition skyrockets at private colleges, the CSU system's offer of a good education at a reasonable price looks better and better. —*Seung Lee and Staff*

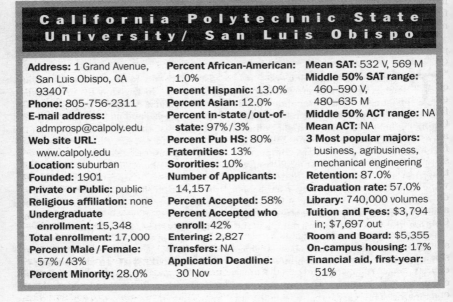

California Polytechnic State University/ San Luis Obispo

Address: 1 Grand Avenue, San Luis Obispo, CA 93407

Phone: 805-756-2311

E-mail address: admprosp@calpoly.edu

Web site URL: www.calpoly.edu

Location: suburban

Founded: 1901

Private or Public: public

Religious affiliation: none

Undergraduate enrollment: 15,348

Total enrollment: 17,000

Percent Male / Female: 57% / 43%

Percent Minority: 28.0%

Percent African-American: 1.0%

Percent Hispanic: 13.0%

Percent Asian: 12.0%

Percent in-state / out-of-state: 97% / 3%

Percent Pub HS: 80%

Fraternities: 13%

Sororities: 10%

Number of Applicants: 14,157

Percent Accepted: 58%

Percent Accepted who enroll: 42%

Entering: 2,827

Transfers: NA

Application Deadline: 30 Nov

Mean SAT: 532 V, 569 M

Middle 50% SAT range: 460–590 V, 480–635 M

Middle 50% ACT range: NA

Mean ACT: NA

3 Most popular majors: business, agribusiness, mechanical engineering

Retention: 87.0%

Graduation rate: 57.0%

Library: 740,000 volumes

Tuition and Fees: $3,794 in; $7,697 out

Room and Board: $5,355

On-campus housing: 17%

Financial aid, first-year: 51%

Well-respected as one of the top tech schools in the nation, Cal Poly places heavy emphasis on academics, offering students small classes and many required labs in a "learn-by-doing" atmosphere. But, despite the rigorous academic standards, students still describe Cal Poly as a "laid-back surfer-dude" type of school. Situated in a small coastal town only 15 minutes from the beach, Cal Poly offers a unique college experience through its mix of academic challenge and laid-back atmosphere.

Hands-On Learning

Cal Poly's "learn-by-doing" philosophy distinguishes it from most other schools. Beginning freshman year, students are required to take numerous labs, which one student described as "challenging and pretty tough, but you really do learn a lot from them." The general-ed (GE) requirements demonstrate this modern approach to learning: 15 credits each are required in science and technology distributions (labs included), as well as in Social, Political, and Economic Institutions and Life Understanding (psychology). Combined with more traditional requirements of communication and the arts and humanities, the GEs are described as "fair," and contribute to the progressive learning philosophy of Cal Poly.

Another aspect of the "learn-by-doing" philosophy is the commitment to small classes. Even freshman year and at the introductory level, "large" classes usually only hold 40 to 50 students, and the 24 person upper-level classes and labs are the norm. A sixth-year super-senior reported that he'd only been in a class with 100 students twice. These small class sizes facilitate active discussions with professors, who are largely well-liked and easily accessible. Students comment that professors believe "they're really here to lecture and teach, not just to do research." This undoubtedly contributes to the learning environment. Of course, small classes have their disadvantages, too: Reportedly getting into desired classes is very difficult, even for required ones. This causes students to complain that "athletes have priority in the registration process" and "the faculty is under-staffed." However, there are ways around this problem, which mostly entail "crashing classes," or sitting in on a desired but full course during the first week and requesting the professor to sign a form, giving a student permission to enroll.

Despite its California, laid-back atmosphere and close proximity to the beach, Cal Poly is no party school. Classes are "tough, usually not a joke," and the short quarter system creates an almost rushed environment. One student commented, "I feel like I have a test every other week." Certain areas, like the Business School, are considered "fluffy," but most students feel challenged by the rigorous academic schedule. Undergraduates recommend taking light course loads in order to do well in classes, which, combined with the difficulty of getting into desired courses, adds to the almost six-year average stay at Cal Poly before graduation.

Not surprisingly for a tech school, most students are engineering, technology, or science-related majors. And although the courses are challenging, students did not complain much about academics in general. Students have come to work hard in a progressive learning environment. This has led to Cal Poly's excellent reputation, especially in California's industry sector. Cal Poly graduates are highly sought after, both in California and out-of-state.

Life in SLO

The town of San Luis Obispo, or "SLO" in campus slang, is a small, comfortable town on the California coastline, halfway between Los Angeles and San Francisco. Cal Poly plays an important role in the economy of the city, and one student commented, "If the school weren't here, SLO wouldn't be here." Like their counterparts at other colleges in small cities, students at Cal Poly complained that there isn't much to do in the town. Although students frequent a select number of town bars, they most often look toward the campus to entertain themselves. "Life in SLO is pretty slow."

Although the campus itself is technically dry, parties abound in the off-campus housing that surrounds campus. Most students will go to house parties on the weekends and the occasional fraternity fiesta. The Greek system is small and not strong at Cal Poly, leading students to comment that the frats "are only in the

background, and not noticeable." On top of that, some say that frat parties are only "okay."

Partly because of the intense academic atmosphere and strict enforcement of the dry campus, the party scene is not raging; instead students describe it as "pretty kick-back." Drugs are reportedly commonplace in the community of SLO, but among the students, mostly upperclassmen experiment with "soft drugs."

The administration and student body all take advantage of Cal Poly's great weather. Every Thursday afternoon the school hosts "U-U Hour" (University Union Hour), where no classes are scheduled and different bands play outside in the university's main quad. Students attend this popular event and use the time to "sit with friends, chill out, and enjoy ourselves." On the weekends, students get away from campus and head to the outdoors. Pismo Beach, renowned for surfing, is only 15 minutes away, and students often go there to swim, sun, and surf. Students can also bike or hike in the range of grassy, rolling hills that lie just to the east of SLO.

Surfer Dudes and Brainiacs

Even with its rigorous academics, California's laid-back atmosphere and "surfer-dude" feeling prevail at Cal Poly, partly because of the short distance to the beach. Students describe the school as a "flip-flop kind of place" where shorts and T-shirts are the norm. The character of the student body also reflects the surfer mindset. One female student said, "Freshman year in one of my labs there was this surfer guy in the class. He had a big blond afro, wore baggy shorts and tank tops, and seemed like a brain-dead kind of guy. I ended up being his lab partner, and I found out he was actually a computer engineering major. Now, I think he's one of the smartest guys I know." Because of its proximity to tubular surfing spots, many students will surf in the morning, go to class in the afternoon, and study at night. Another part of the California character, that of the "trendy, made-up sorority girl," also exists in full force at Cal Poly. However, Cal Poly's rigorous entrance standards ensure that all who come to the school are not merely "all tan and no brain."

In general, the student body at Cal Poly is dominated by white, upper-middle-class Californians. Shiny, new convertibles fill parking lots and undergraduates can be "very image-conscious, sometimes snobby," but most students agree that this facet of Cal Poly life is easily ignored. The school reportedly doesn't boast too much diversity, but this seems to be changing as more minority students—especially women and Asian-Americans— enroll.

Unfortunately, school spirit can be lacking at times. There seems to be a rift between athletes and engineers, and professors may have negative biases toward athletes in general. However, "when a team starts to win its games, the sport suddenly becomes really popular." The men's basketball team competes at the Division I-A level, and its home games are well attended by undergraduates. Many students participate in intramurals, so much that "it seems like there is always an IM game on the fields around campus."

Because of the academic atmosphere, extracurriculars are centered around academics as well. Most students participate in academic clubs, such as the Micro-Biology Society and the Society of Women Engineers. Between challenging classes, academic clubs, and enjoying California opportunities, Cal Poly students keep plenty busy.

> **"Despite the rigorous academic standards, students still describe Cal Poly as a laid-back 'surfer dude' type of school."**

At few other schools can students obtain a hands-on technical education in small classes and labs, join academic clubs, take advantage of California's weather, beaches, and landscape, and all the while live in a "chill," laid-back atmosphere. With the myriad of unique attributes that attracts students to Cal Poly, it is no wonder students choose to stay so many years. —*Johnny Swagerty*

FYI
The three best things about attending Cal Poly are "small, intense, hands-on academic environment, the laid-back atmosphere, and the close proximity to the beach."
The three worst things about attending Cal Poly are "difficulty of getting into courses, the boring town of SLO, and the average six-year stay."
The three things that every student should do before graduating from Cal Poly are "enjoying U-U hour, learning to surf at Pismo Beach, and purchasing a great pair of flip-flops."
One thing I'd like to have known before coming here is "that the stereotype of surfer-dude and sorority chick does prevail here, but the irony is that they are all smart!"

California State University/Chico

Address: Admissions Office, 400 West First Street, Chico, CA 95929-0722
Phone: 800-54-CHICO
E-mail address: info@csuchico.edu
Web site URL: www.csumentor.edu
Location: small city
Founded: 1891
Private or Public: public
Religious affiliation: none
Undergraduate enrollment: 11,007
Total enrollment: 13,919
Percent Male/Female: 49%/51%

Percent Minority: 18.0%
Percent African-American: 3.0%
Percent Hispanic: 10.0%
Percent Asian: 5.0%
Percent in-state/out-of-state: 98%/2%
Percent Pub HS: 84%
Fraternities: 8%
Sororities: 9%
Number of Applicants: 5,343
Percent Accepted: 83%
Percent Accepted who enroll: 35%
Entering: 1,561
Transfers: NA
Application Deadline: 30 Nov

Mean SAT: 486 V, 487 M
Middle 50% SAT range: 430–530 V, 430–540 M
Middle 50% ACT range: NA
Mean ACT: NA
3 Most popular majors: liberal studies, business administration, psychology
Retention: 79.0%
Graduation rate: 50.0%
Library: 1,700,000 volumes
Tuition and Fees: $2,080 in; $9,460 out
Room and Board: $5,031
On-campus housing: 85%
Financial aid, first year: 17%

California State University/Chico is set among the foothills of the Sierra Nevada Mountains. The campus is replete with matching brick buildings, "tons of trees and flowers," and the Big Chico Creek running through its center. Strolling around Chico, one often finds students and locals wandering through the twice-weekly farmers' market that fills the streets of the small town; its homey feel welcomes students warmly.

A Varied Environment

Though some students feel isolated, others rave about the beauty of their surroundings. "Ten minutes from here there is snow, and five minutes the other direction is fishing, hiking, and the best mountain biking in the country." Students are quick to take advantage of their beautiful location. The salmon fishing is reported to be fantastic, and Chico also boasts Feather Falls, the sixth-largest waterfall in the country. A university-sponsored program, "Adventure Outings," takes groups of students on outdoor expeditions. They also offer day-long classes on subjects such as wilderness survival. The group has sponsored whitewater rafting,

long hiking trips, and even ventured outside of the country. Students looking for a less formal hike or mountain-biking trip walk downtown to Bidwell Park, a huge area with watering holes, places to relax, and a massive trail system.

Hitting the Books

Students don't flock to Chico for the environment alone; many believe that the small class size and the accessible professors are the school's best assets. The undergraduate program consists of six academic colleges as well as a School of Nursing and a College of Business. While core requirements are strenuous, students have few complaints. The average class size is 35 students. Students study diligently during the week, but admit that their books gather dust when the weekend hits.

TRAC, a telephone registration process, makes selecting classes easy, allowing students to plan their schedules up to two years ahead of time. Students report having very little trouble getting into the classes they want. An honors program is available to incoming freshmen with a high school GPA of 3.5 or higher. This program offers more one-on-one attention from professors, smaller classes with an average of 12 students, and an off-campus Honors House. Even if not enrolled in the honors program, students get to know their professors very well. "You see your professors out and about with the students." TAs are very rare, but when present, they get rave reviews as being very in touch with students' needs. Students claim that the friendly atmosphere and the size of the school leads to more networking with professors and other students, and therefore better jobs after graduation.

Dorm Living

Freshmen live in the dorms, which are co-ed by hall, and consist of small double rooms with "jail beds." The Resident Assistants program in the dorms is quite strict, as the campus is "supposed to be . . . uhh, is, a dry campus." Any student caught with alcohol on campus must endure harsh penalties including community service and attendance at alcohol-related classes. Shafta is a dorm specifically for transfer students, while Whitney Hall is the largest dorm and the only one containing a dining hall. Sophomores traditionally move into Creekside Apartments and the upperclassmen to other off-campus complexes. The dorms tend to be noisy, and have recently become overcrowded. During the 1998–1999 school year, over 400 students were denied dorm housing.

Students linger over meals in the dining hall to chat about the weekend, but upperclassmen tend to avoid eating there altogether. Rather, they choose to use their meal cards at the student union, the BMU, sometimes referred to as "the Moo." Here students gather at the Rainbow Cafe, a snack area where they can pay or use their meal cards. Students also frequent other area restaurants.

Wildcat Spirit

Cheering for the school colors—maroon and white—is also a popular activity. The football team was cut completely two years ago in order to fund golf and swimming teams, though few students seem upset by the loss. The gym itself is unpopular, with students choosing instead to join independent local gyms. The basketball and baseball teams are particularly popular, as they have recently advanced far into their respective divisional playoffs.

The Greeks

The Greek system at Chico is a prominent part of campus life. Approximately 20 percent of students join either a sorority or fraternity. The Greeks also sponsor intramural games for less serious athletes, and this often attracts students to the Greek system. Though a division exists between those within the system and those outside of it, students claim that the division is neither extreme nor hostile. The Greek organizations on campus host parties, which are well attended. Students do not date traditionally, but rather travel in large groups. The largest Greek-sponsored activity is Greek Week, a week filled with activities, including relay races to benefit various charities.

Halloween is the biggest social event of the year; people park all along the streets and get out their folding chairs to watch the costume parade—a town tradition. During this party, which lasts the whole week, the population of Chico nearly doubles. Parties abound, and students wander the streets attending haunted houses and admiring each others' costumes.

> "The students are laid-back party animals."

Local bands often frequent the Chico campus, and distinguished visitors are also common. The Cherry Poppin' Daddies and Red Hot Chili Peppers are bands who have recently played in front of the Rose Garden, a large grassy area backed by a large garden of roses. Prominent speakers such as the president of the Honda Corporation have also made appearances. A Free Speech area allows campus groups to voice their opinions and gain support for their causes.

Chico is home to the Sierra Nevada Brewery, and many students are proud to drink their locally brewed ales. Going to bars is a favorite weekend activity, with the Bear, a restaurant and bar, and the Crazy Horse, which has a mechanical bull, rating among the top hot spots off-campus. The beverage of choice remains beer, though martinis are a close second. Texas Tea, a stronger version of a Long Island Iced Tea, is thought to have developed in Chico. Students also say that marijuana is prevalent on campus.

Students laud the friendliness of Chico, and say that it is not unusual to smile and wave as they stroll across campus. The student body in general is quite liberal. In fact, the town of Chico holds the largest per capita lesbian population in California. Largely consisting of preppy, middle-class students, diversity at Chico is small, but improving. Described as "laid-back party animals," students are very happy with their experiences at Chico. "It is the typical college experience that you see in the movies," explained one student. Renowned for their partying, Chico students describe themselves as social: "We're like an island, secluded, but we still know how to have a good time." —*Cynthia Matthews*

FYI

The three best things about attending Chico are "the beautiful campus, the opportunities for fantastic outdoors activities, and the small classes headed by visible, caring professors."

The three worst things about attending Chico are "strict drinking rules, overcrowded dorms, and the lack of diversity."

The three things that every student should do before graduating from Chico are "see Feather Falls, participate in Adventure Outing, and share a glass of Sierra Nevada's best with a friend."

One thing I'd like to have known before coming here is "how big the Greek life is here."

California State University/Fresno

Address: 5150 North Maple Avenue, Fresno, CA 93740-0057
Phone: 559-278-2261
E-mail address: donna_mills@csufresno.edu
Web site URL: www.csufresno.edu
Location: urban
Founded: 1961
Private or Public: public
Religious affiliation: none
Undergraduate enrollment: 14,518
Total enrollment: 18,113
Percent Male/Female: 45%/55%
Percent Minority: 48.0%

Percent African-American: 6.0%
Percent Hispanic: 29.0%
Percent Asian: 12.0%
Percent in-state/out-of-state: 99%/1%
Percent Pub HS: 99%
Fraternities: 5%
Sororities: 5%
Number of Applicants: 5,114
Percent Accepted: 74%
Percent Accepted who enroll: 79%
Entering: 5,386
Transfers: NA
Application Deadline: 30 July
Mean SAT: 453 V, 473 M

Middle 50% SAT range: 390–510 V, 410–530 M
Middle 50% ACT range: NA
Mean ACT: NA
3 Most popular majors: business administration, liberal studies, agricultural sciences
Retention: 80.0%
Graduation rate: 37.0%
Library: 900,000 volumes
Tuition and Fees: $1,754 in; $9,134 out
Room and Board: $5,659
On-campus housing: 7%
Financial aid, first-year: 67%

Looking for an urban agriculture school, or interested in education, engineering, or health sciences? In the center of California, between San Francisco and Los Angeles, lies California State University, Fresno (a.k.a. Fresno State University). In the past decade, the city has developed into the metropolitian home of many software and Internet companies, and the university has matured by its own right into a diverse and well-respected state school.

Diversity is one of Fresno's strongest points. As one student put it, "There is awesome racial and ethnic diversity at this school, which I have not seen in many places. It truly makes it fantastic." In the heart of the San Joaquin Valley, Fresno has the resources and enthusiasm that make for an incredible agricultural department. And, it doesn't stop there. Fresno students all have particular interests and ideas, preventing the school from becoming an exclusively agriculture school. According to students, Fresno has highly respected education, engineering, health sciences, and criminology departments. "It can be hard to get into the more popular majors, but it's totally worth it," one student commented.

The Brain Part

Freshman and sophomore years at Fresno are mostly spent fulfilling General Education requirements, commonly known as the "breadth." These classes strive to "expose students to a variety of disciplines within a structured framework." Beginning in the 1999–2000 school year, a new format has been adopted, expanding the program and dividing it into four basic categories. Now students are required to take their 21-class GE requirements from each of the 4 groups: Foundation, Breadth, Integration, and Multicultural/International Studies.

Along with this change in format, Fresno State has adopted an ambitious program to improve the school, both academically and socially. The staff and faculty's "Vision for the 21st Century" includes the development of an honors program, an intensification of research projects, and an increase in the overall diversity of the campus. The president of the university and his staff are "extremely committed to this school and its improvement," said one student.

The "breadth" allows students to explore many different areas before selecting a major, and is rarely an obstacle when it comes to taking classes in which one is interested. A second-year student confessed, "There are usually a few classes in the divisions that are required by your major anyway." Some of the required courses

include a speech course and an English class. Many frosh are daunted by the prospect of giving speeches, but that, according to one third-year, is the point. "Every student should take a good speech class their freshman year; it helps bring out some of those shy ones."

Getting into the classes you want is rarely a problem. Even students in popular majors, such as animal science, still find that they are almost never barred from a class and that most of the introductory courses remained relatively small. However, in some instances, when the phone registration system fails to cap the numbers registered, popular courses could end up with nearly 300 people. On average, introductory science courses enroll between 80 and 100 students, but most English and speech courses for freshman are capped at 30. While few students have had problems with TAs teaching courses, others, like one junior, have "had a few problems with teachers not being able to speak English too well."

There aren't any notorious "slacker majors," or awful classes that everyone avoids. As one student pointed out, "Everyone has their own hopes and aspirations, which of course gives way for diversity"—one of Fresno's greatest qualities.

To escape the distractions of dorm or apartment life, many students choose to study in the Henry Madden Library, which is large and modern enough to accommodate a number of different study areas. Moreover, the digital card catalog is accessible from any computer on campus.

The Life Part

Student life at Fresno centers on the University Student Union (USU). This building contains many student resources, including a food court, bank, post office, Tower Records, information center, lounge, balcony (for enjoying the beautiful California weather), administrative offices, graphic design center, and meeting rooms for student organizations. In the recreation center one can find billiards, bowling, chess, cards, pinball, video games, and even dominos. "One could never leave the college and still have an awesome four years," noted one student. However, most students do choose to leave campus occasionally. While Fresno is not a "commuter school," a fair number of students do live at home, and most choose to live off campus after freshman year. Generally people have cars, and live in one of the "tons of apartments located very close to campus and at reasonable costs" that are within a 5 to 10 minute drive away.

Dorms are without question a "great way for frosh to meet people," and most of them are organized "like mini-apartments." The bathrooms are single sex and "the facilities are actually very nice." However, the dorms come with Resident Advisors (RAs) and certain "strictly enforced" regulations. Only eight people are allowed in a room at a time, and quiet hours are enforced from 11 P.M. to 7 A.M. on weekdays, and from 1 A.M. to 7 A.M. on weekends. In addition, there are no kegs allowed on campus.

When not in their rooms, students participate in a variety of activities, from varsity athletics, to part-time jobs, to community service. On weekends, one sophomore found that "Fresno does not have that much to offer if you are under 21." However, there are movie theaters, restaurants, and clubs located near campus. People do date regularly, and it is not uncommon to see couples walking around the school. Great date spots are Romano's Macaroni Grill, the Bulldog Café, and later in the evening, Williker's or Baja's. Fresno is equidistant from San Francisco and Los Angeles. Both are a four-hour drive away, a longish, but not impossible, weekend excursion. Closer by are Shaver Lake and Yosemite, two "beautiful escapes from urban life."

The Outside World

Fresno State's 327-acre main campus and its 1,083-acre University Farm are located at the northeast edge of Fresno, California, at the foot of the Sierra Nevada mountain range. The San Joaquin Valley, one of the richest agricultural areas in the world, surrounds the city. Fresno is the sixth largest metropolitan area in California and has all the amenities of a major urban area.

The campus itself is spread out enough to seem full of lawn and trees, yet not so large that one can't walk to classes. In the middle of campus sits "a large fountain with a row of roses up the center of campus . . . with trees and a grassy area." Directly across are the Student Union and the bookstore.

> "If I had to go back and pick a school again, I would pick Fresno . . . the campus is beautiful and the diversity among students and faculty is incredible."

While crime is a problem off campus, special designated paths on school property are very well lit at night, and there are emergency phones scattered throughout campus. About on-campus crime, one student warned, "just like anywhere else, be wary; it's a cool place to meet people, but always keep your eyes open." A third-year added, "I feel safe on campus for the most part, but having a late class is not always a good thing." While for many students living in such an urban environment is quite a shock, the sizable number of students from surrounding areas creates an excellent town-gown relationship. Fresno State has grown up with the city, for the benefit of both, and that connection is not easily forgotten. Every year the Associated Student Body puts on Vintage Days, a celebration where people from all over the Central Valley come together for wine tastings, antique auto shows, sales, and other entertainment. Non-students also follow the University's dynamic sports teams religiously, and the Red Wave (Fresno fans, wearing their color, "cardinal") have managed to break multiple records in numbers of spectators attending competitions.

The Cheering Part

Varsity sports, ranging from football to the equestrian team, are a huge part of Fresno State life. Recently, 11,000 seats were added to Bulldog Stadium to accommodate the increasing number of fans. The Red Wave financially supports the entire Fresno athletic program. Their athletic boosters club, the Bulldog Foundation, has had the number-one fund drive since 1986. While football reigns as the most popular sport on campus, the men's basketball team is "a close second," thanks in part to new coach Jerry Tarkanian, who's been making a splash and leading the team to numerous victories. Enthusiasm for athletics infects everyone at Fresno. As one student put it, "The sports here at Fresno are awesome. I really don't know too much about their programs, but the facilities and the games are always good."

And those facilities are about to get even better. Scheduled to open in the fall of 2001 is the Save Mart Center, a new arena for Bulldog basketball, volleyball, and wrestling. Sponsored primarily by Save Mart and Pepsi, this facility will not only hold sporting events, but concerts and cultural gatherings as well. It will also include classrooms, banquet facilities, shops, and a gym. The enthusiasm of the student body and the surrounding population for sports is what allows this all to happen.

Fresno State is a school with "an endless amount of opportunities, and a highly involved staff." It enjoys an urban setting minutes away from a rural area, meaning students have the best of both worlds. The school is diverse both in students and in faculty, allowing learning to span far beyond the classroom. —*Kyla Dahlin*

FYI
The three best things about attending Fresno State are "the people, the low cost of living, and the campus."
The three worst things about Fresno State are "the crime, the weather, and all the agriculture majors."
The three things everyone should do before graduating from Fresno State are "go to Shaver Lake, go to Vintage Days, and participate in as many activities as possible."
One thing I'd like to have known before coming here is "that you *must* be a sports fan . . . or at least pretend to be one."

The Claremont Colleges

The Claremont Colleges are a cluster of five small liberal arts colleges and two graduate schools, nestled in a suburban valley about 35 miles east of Los Angeles. The member colleges are Claremont McKenna, Harvey Mudd, Pitzer, Pomona, and Scripps, as well as Claremont Graduate University and Keck Graduate Institute, both of which are separate from the undergraduate colleges. Each college is independent, with its own faculty, campus, and academic focus. However, the schools' closeness gives their respective students the best of both worlds: the feel of a small college with the resources of a large university.

Academic Integration
Cross-registration of classes between the colleges is easy and commonplace. The five campuses make up about 12 blocks total, so commuting is not a problem. Since each college has a particular academic focus and expertise, students can take advantage of specialized instruction in almost every subject. Claremont McKenna offers 26 majors, with strengths in economics, government, and international relations. Harvey Mudd specializes in science and engineering, with the option of a five-year master's program. Pitzer offers liberal arts majors with an emphasis on social and behavioral sciences. Pomona offers a variety of majors in the arts, humanities, and social and natural sciences with a para-professional bent. Scripps is a liberal arts college for women. All the libraries are integrated, as is the campus bookstore.

Campus-wide Activities
The Claremont Colleges are also linked through athletic, social, and extracurricular activities. Pitzer and Pomona together comprise a NCAA Division III team, while Claremont McKenna, Harvey Mudd, and

Scripps make up another. However, most athletic competition is usually among one another. Parties thrown in one college draw people from the other colleges. And there are several all-college parties thrown throughout the year. Many student organizations are comprised of undergrads from all the colleges, including the *Claremont Collage*, the student daily newspaper; the Claremont Colleges Model U.N.; and the Claremont Shades, an a cappella group. The Claremont Center is the hub for social groups, organizations, and administrations on each campus and orchestrates the activities of all five schools.

As integrated as the five colleges are, they still retain distinct characteristics, and prospective students should look to find the right fit. As one student summed it up, "It's really a matter of your academic interests as well as your personality. There is something for everyone at each of the colleges, but one college will definitely be the best fit." —*Seung Lee*

Claremont McKenna College

Address: 890 Columbia Avenue, Claremont, CA 91711
Phone: 909-621-8088
E-mail address: admission@mckenna.edu
Web site URL: www.mckenna.edu
Location: suburban
Founded: 1946
Private or Public: private
Religious affiliation: none
Undergraduate enrollment: 1,025
Total enrollment: 1,025
Percent Male/Female: 55%/45%
Percent Minority: 35.0%

Percent African-American: 5.0%
Percent Hispanic: 13.0%
Percent Asian: 18.0%
Percent in-state/out-of-state: 53%/47%
Percent Pub HS: 72%
Fraternities: 0%
Sororities: 0%
Number of Applicants: 3,043
Percent Accepted: 28%
Percent Accepted who enroll: 32%
Entering: 252
Transfers: 29
Application Deadline: 15 Jan
Mean SAT: 690 V, 690 M

Middle 50% SAT range: 620–720 V, 640–730 M
Middle 50% ACT range: 27–32
Mean ACT: 29
3 Most popular majors: economics, government, psychology
Retention: 94.0%
Graduation rate: 87.0%
Library: 2,011,000 volumes
Tuition and Fees: $20,780 in; $20,780 out
Room and Board: $7,060
On-campus housing: 100%
Financial aid, first-year: 71%

Although the school enrolls fewer than a thousand undergrads, students at Claremont McKenna College do not feel isolated, claustrophobic, or bored. Instead, they are immersed in the social opportunities of the five-college system and the challenges of its rigorous academic standards. The "work hard/party hard" ethic is the rule here, but mixed with the laid-back atmosphere and newness of southern California, Claremont McKenna creates a unique environment of its own.

Five Colleges = Five-Star Social Life

A distinguishing feature of Claremont McKenna is its membership in the five-college Claremont Colleges System, which also includes Pomona, Pitzer, Harvey Mudd, and Scripps. Students may cross-register in classes, facilities are open to all undergrads, and no social barriers prevent students from interacting with those from the other colleges. Most students agree that CMC is the kind of place where everyone knows everyone, including the professors, but the other schools provide additional social options. One junior commented, "It's small, but you can make it as big as you want it to be."

Within the five-college system, students pull resources together in order to party hard. Almost every weekend there is a five-college party, hosted in various conference rooms, dining halls, and other facilities in the schools. Professional DJ's are hired or student bands play, and attendance can reach over 200; not surprisingly, undergrads report that these parties are usually pretty fun. College councils organize the especially popular theme nights, such as Monte Carlo, a formal event with jazz music and faux gambling, and the Screw Your Roommate, a semiformal dance where roommates set each other up on blind dates. The vibrant five-college scene keeps most social activity on campus, and students rarely venture into the town of Claremont on the weekends.

Claremont is regarded as a retirement community and its lack of entertainment options draw disgruntled comments from students. Students at CMC report that it is not a huge party school but "you can go out around three nights a week, if you get your work done."

The CMC administration seeks a happy medium between tolerance of campus parties and the enforcement of strict rules. In recent years, the number of kegs allowed per weekend in school-sponsored functions has been reduced to six, but students attest that "you won't be thrown out of school if you're caught with beers in your backpack." Kids who don't drink reportedly do not feel out of the social circle; the college provides a variety of other activities, many students don't binge drink, and there is a popular substance-free dorm if students so choose. Drug use at CMC usually doesn't extend beyond alcohol, as only a few students report smoking pot. There is also no Greek system within the five colleges.

Besides parties, a variety of events are organized on campus by individual dorms, the CMC College Council, or the Five College Council, with activities ranging from small get-togethers to movies to semi-formal dances. Both the Dave Matthews Band and Third Eye Blind played at the college in 1999, much to the understandable delight of students. Also, the college sponsors a weekly series of dinner lectures known as Athenaeum, which has brought speakers such as James Earl Jones and the California schools superintendent to speak.

Small Classes, Big Selection

As one would expect from a school with an enrollment of a thousand, class sizes are small at CMC. A typical class consists of about 25 students, and a 75-person class is considered big. Thanks to the five-college system, students can choose from a wide variety of classes from all five schools and use common facilities, such as the newly built Joint Science Center.

Students voice overwhelmingly high opinions for the academics at CMC. They never find it difficult to get into desired courses or the required general education (GE) classes. The GE classes are described as challenging and fair. Professors welcome interaction with students both in and out of class. One student attested, "We eat lunch and dinner with our professors all the time. They even come to our parties." Also, it is common for undergraduates to be an integral part of professors' research projects. One senior reported, "Here professors will actually ask students to work on their projects, and they expect them to do real research."

CMC boasts a high academic standard, so classes are not a breeze. Reportedly it is very difficult to get an A or A- in a course, and students definitely believe that they have a lot of work. These aspects of CMC life may not be as popular as the student/professor interaction, but it guarantees the respected academic reputation of the school.

Equal but Separate

Although the five-college system is extremely integrated, the student body at Claremont McKenna never loses its unity or identity. There are many opportunities for CMC students to meet and hang out with the other 3000 undergrads at the neighboring schools, but social circles rarely extend beyond CMC. One student claimed, "People interact but identify with their own school." Another student added, "I know people in the other schools, but most of my friends are from Claremont. But it's a good thing—the system is unifying rather than restrictive."

Diversity has increased at CMC in recent years, but students still say that it has room to increase further. The majority of the kids are from white, upper-middle-class backgrounds in California, but one student reported that people here aren't "snobby or spoiled." However, the student body is changing: More and more states and foreign countries are represented, enrollment of women and minorities is rising, and the political balance is shifting toward moderate after years of conservative domination.

Besides studying hard, most CMC students fill their time with a wide variety of campus clubs and organizations, and like many other aspects of CMC, these clubs often involve all five colleges. Because of the popularity of the economics and business-related majors, academic organizations such as the Accounting and Student Investment Clubs are quite popular. A few atypical clubs exist at Claremont, such as the James Madison Society and the Winston Churchill Society, which convene to smoke cigars and drink fine wine, respectively.

Intra-Claremont Rivalry

By far the most popular undergraduate organization is sports. Students estimate that between 40 and 60 percent of students participate in at least one varsity sport in their four-year career, and almost everyone plays intramurals. The campus is filled with fields and grassy areas, and combined with California's sunny weather, CMC creates a great atmosphere for athletic competition. A student commented, "There is always a pick-up game of soccer or ultimate Frisbee going on, or maybe just a couple people throwing a baseball." On the varsity level, the Clare-

mont College System's five colleges are divided into two teams, one team consisting of Claremont McKenna, Harvey Mudd, and Scripps Colleges and the other made up by Pitzer and Pomona. Basketball draws the largest student crowds, and the big game between the two Claremont teams can get wild: People dress up and supporters of each team try to steal the opponent's mascot.

CMC boasts many other traditions enjoyed by undergrads. Apart from the usually chaotic basketball festivities, on students' birthdays it is customary to "pond" them, or throw them numerous times into one of several campus fountains.

> **"It's small, but you can make it as big as you want it to be."**

Dorm life is something else that distinguishes CMC from colleges across the nation. Almost 100 percent of students live on-campus all four years, choosing between the dorms or, as upperclassmen, on-campus apartments. Dorms are not segregated by year; students meet a variety of people from all class levels, interests, and ages with whom they share floors and buildings. Also, the RA system is very friendly. One student commented, "My RAs were not alcohol police, but focused on becoming friends with residents and being involved in dorm life."

Claremont McKenna does not fit the typical idea of a liberal arts college. By combining the benefits of a small school, such as interaction with professors, small classes, and a lively on-campus social life, with the resources, facilities, and class selection of a mid-size university, CMC provides students with the best of both worlds. —*Johnny Swagerty*

FYI

The three best things about attending CMC are "the five-college system, small classes, and great student-professor relations."

The three worst things about attending CMC are "the town of Claremont, the need for diversity, and L.A. smog."

The three things that every student should do before graduating from CMC are "go to a five-college party, attend an Athenaeum lecture, and participate in intermurals."

One thing I'd like to have known before coming here is "how much I would love the CMC experience—the tough academics, the students, and a sense of community that includes your professors."

H a r v e y   M u d d   C o l l e g e

Address: 301 East 12th Street, Claremont, CA 91711-5990
Phone: 909-621-8011
E-mail address: admission@hmc.edu
Web site URL: www.hmc.edu
Location: suburban
Founded: 1955
Private or Public: private
Religious affiliation: none
Undergraduate enrollment: 693
Total enrollment: 699
Percent Male/Female: 74%/26%
Percent Minority: 30.5%

Percent African-American: 1.0%
Percent Hispanic: 25.0%
Percent Asian: 4.0%
Percent in-state/out-of-state: 39%/61%
Percent Pub HS: NA
Fraternities: 0%
Sororities: 0%
Number of Applicants: 1,642
Percent Accepted: 33%
Percent Accepted who enroll: 32%
Entering: 170
Transfers: 9
Application Deadline: 15 Jan

Mean SAT: 700 V, 760 M
Middle 50% SAT range: 660–770 V, 730–800 M
Middle 50% ACT range: NA
Mean ACT: NA
3 Most popular majors: engineering, computer science, physics
Retention: 96.0%
Graduation rate: 79.0%
Library: 2,000,000 volumes
Tuition and Fees: $22,083 in; $22,083 out
Room and Board: $8,017
On-campus housing: 100%
Financial aid, first-year: 72%

If you like math and science—that is, if you *really* like math and science—then Harvey Mudd College might be right up your alley. Located in suburban Claremont, California, Harvey Mudd offers students a rigorous and self-motivated education with top-quality academics and outstanding professors in a slightly unusual environment. Mudd students pride themselves on their strong work ethic, as well as the seemingly endless hours spent completing physics problem sets and math projects. They're also quick to point out the lighter side of life at Mudd—they live in a "crazy, weird, eccentric place," and they know how to break free from stress. "We may study a lot, but we're not nearly as uptight as Caltech," one junior pointed out. Mudd, like any other college, has its share of parties, student activities, and unique traditions.

Science Anyone?

Mudders are the first to point out the intensity of their curriculum. According to one junior, "The whole school is basically an honors program." Most of Mudd students' first two years are filled with core requirements, which amount to a total of 12 science and math courses, and additional humanities courses. Gut courses are unheard of, unless you consider Introductory Bio a walk in the park. Students estimate spending four to six hours a night on homework, and they insist this does not include time spent procrastinating.

Harvey Mudd College offers students only six majors: physics, chemistry, biology, math, computer science, and engineering. However, the opportunities to diversify one's education are growing. Students are offered the option of a double major, or more recently, the option to "off-campus major." The off-campus-major program allows students to complete requirements for a major at one of the other Claremont colleges while still graduating with a degree from Harvey Mudd. With the academically diverse mix of the Claremont system, students can major in subjects ranging from music to Chinese, while still benefiting from their own math/science-rich environment. However, the off-campus major is a relatively new policy, and has not yet become popular among the science-hungry Mudders.

Most students praise the individual classes and professors at Mudd, noting that most classes have only 25 enrolled students. Some introductory lecture courses enroll up to 175 students, but these classes also have smaller tutorials led by professors. One student noted, "It's not particularly difficult to get into the classes you want to take—you might not get a time slot or a professor you want, but you aren't really restricted in your choice of actual courses." All courses at Mudd are taught by professors, and students appreciate the individual attention they receive. "The professors are easily accessible, and most are very good. They're excited to talk to students one on one, and being a small school, they usually recognize you and remember your name outside of class," noted one student.

Mudders raved about the "Clinic Program." It is very popular among engineering majors, but students in other majors can also participate. A large company, such as Kodak, develops a year-long program in cooperation with Harvey Mudd, and students work together on a particular problem or project for the company. They design a system and give the company a working prototype at the end of the year, one that actually gets used by the company. Students were quite pleased with the clinic program, and boasted of the superiority of Mudd's program to other schools' similar programs.

Campus and Community

"[The founders] decided that they really like cinder block when they built Mudd," explained one junior. The modern cinder-block style is predominant on the small campus, which is about the size of a city block. Many buildings are accentuated with "warts," small square protrusions from the sides of buildings, which serve no functional purpose other than helping to differentiate Mudd from most other schools. Mudd is within walking distance from the other Claremont Colleges, thus helping to provide a change of scenery for most students. Another much appreciated aspect of the college's location is the relative closeness to Los Angeles, which allows students with cars to escape from the high-stress academic atmosphere and let loose in the city.

Only freshmen are required to live on campus, but most other Mudders choose to do so anyway. Students generally have positive responses toward their living quarters. There are seven dorms on campus, which consist of doubles and singles, some of which are grouped as suites into quads, sextets, or octets. South dorm, for example, is nearly all singles, while Linde has suites of six, and Atwood has suites of eight. Each dorm has its own distinct personality, or "dormunity," as Mudd students like to call it. "West dorm is really loud; the jugglers and martial artists live in East—they also have an old fire pit they use for a hot tub on weekends; North dormers stay to themselves more," noted one student who happened to live in the unicycler dorm. All dorms are co-ed; one female student lived in a suite with three males, and was quick to point out the logical nature of her living situation. As only a Mudder would phrase it, "There's a pi:1 ratio of guys to girls here, so it makes sense." One can only guess where the extra 0.14159 . . . came from. Students report that the dorm rooms are moderately sized and well furnished, with Ethernet connections in all the rooms. Mudd dorms each have a few proctors (similar to RAs), but "they're not very strict—it's a pretty relaxed atmosphere in the dorms."

All Mudd students living on campus must have a meal plan, which most students consider pretty flexible. Harvey Mudd has one main dining hall, but hungry Mudders can look to any of the five dining halls of the Claremont colleges for their meals. In addition, there are restaurants in the area to provide a bit of variety to one's diet. However, don't look too hard for a McDonald's—the town of Claremont does not allow chain restaurants or stores within the city limits. The Mudd Hole, a student hangout, also provides snacks to students looking to relax among the pool tables and video games.

Mudd shares its library and athletic facilities with the other four Claremont colleges. A new recreation center just opened on campus, and is growing in popularity among Mudders. "It takes a while to rip us away from our computers," noted one student.

Attractions and Distractions

Yes, despite what some may believe, there is life outside of academia at Harvey Mudd, and students take advantage of their convenient location and unique student body to get the most out of their free time. As one student points out, "Most Mudders have average IQs higher than the rest of the world, so it's a very interesting atmosphere."

Watching television is a big part of any college campus social life, and Mudd students have their own favorites such as *The X-Files* and *The Simpsons*. Many students also often pile into cars and hit the L.A. club scene. "It's so cool to be able to leave campus and go dancing in Hollywood," noted one junior. Like most other colleges, Mudd is also no stranger to the alcohol/party scene. "Dorms throw parties every couple of weekends because there are no frats, but on any given weekend, there are always some random, small things going on," noted one student. "There's not much pressure to drink for those who choose not to, but if you do, there's pressure to drink more. The social life doesn't revolve around liquor, but it's always available."

Dating is a tricky issue at Mudd, because of the lopsided ratio of guys to girls. A male student pointed out, "We spend a lot of time at Scripps [a women's college within the Claremont system]." Mudd is not completely lacking in romantic relationships, though, and students point out that a lot of people are involved in relationships, or at least random hookups.

Students can also participate in a slew of student activities, such as the Gonzo Unicycling Club, the Shades singing group, swing dancing, intramurals, club, and varsity sports (varsity teams are formed together with Scripps and Claremont Colleges). Inter-collegiate sports competition consists of competing against the combined teams from Pitzer and Pomona Colleges. While athletic activities are available to students, they are not a big priority for most people. Said one student, "Most Mudders don't care too much about attending sporting events; our school spirit comes from being nerdy together."

Other types of stress relief for Mudders include getting drunk and running around all five of the Claremont colleges campuses and jumping in every body of water in sight. Even the annual food fight in North dorm, and the Mudders' common hatred of their academic rival, Caltech, brings the students closer together. One large-scale prank involved stealing a giant cannon from Caltech, who had previously stolen it from the National Guard. Added one Mudder, "Large trucks and heavy manpower were used."

Harvey Mudd students consider themselves to be extremely close-knit and community-oriented. "The way it's designed, if you weren't a part of the community and wanted to exclude yourself, you wouldn't survive. It's a team effort because we all work so hard and are usually in high-speed mode," said one sophomore.

> **"There is a pi:1 ratio of guys to girls here."**

Harvey Mudd College is no scene out of *Animal House*. Its intense academic programs require a great deal of effort from students, and in turn, the school offers students one of the most respected science and math curricula in the country. Students are always quick to mention their concentrated workload. However, Mudd is more than just math and science classes, and most people truly enjoy the stimulating and often silly environment in which they find themselves. Members of the diverse student body always seem to be able to find ways to amuse themselves and have fun when they are not working, whenever those precious times come. Students get a kick out of their own craziness, but it's justified by the intensity of their academic programs. As one Mudder explained, "We really do work that hard."
—*Melissa Andersen*

FYI
The three best things about attending Mudd are "the intensity, the ability to intensely concentrate on one subject, and the personal attention from the professors."
The three worst things about attending Mudd are "the intensity, the lack of females, and the cinder-block campus!"

The three things that every student should do before graduating from Mudd are "academically diversify by taking a non-science course at a Claremont college, participate in the Clinic Program, and revel in the eccentric student body."

One thing I'd like to have known before coming here is "what a crazy, intense, and amusing environment Mudd really is."

Pitzer College

Address: 1050 North Mills Avenue, Claremont, CA 91711-6101
Phone: 909-621-8129
E-mail address: admission@pitzer.edu
Web site URL: www.pitzer.edu
Location: suburban
Founded: 1963
Private or Public: private
Religious affiliation: none
Undergraduate enrollment: 880
Total enrollment: 880
Percent Male / Female: 40% / 60%
Percent Minority: 35.0%

Percent African-American: 6.0%
Percent Hispanic: 15.0%
Percent Asian: 11.0%
Percent in-state / out-of-state: 59% / 41%
Percent Pub HS: 50%
Fraternities: 0%
Sororities: 0%
Number of Applicants: 1,831
Percent Accepted: 64%
Percent Accepted who enroll: 18%
Entering: 180
Transfers: NA
Application Deadline: 1 Feb

Mean SAT: 601 V, 584 M
Middle 50% SAT range: NA
Middle 50% ACT range: NA
Mean ACT: NA
3 Most popular majors: psychology, sociology, art
Retention: NA
Graduation rate: 58.0%
Library: 2,000,000 volumes
Tuition and Fees: $23,226 in; $23,226 out
Room and Board: $6,214
On-campus housing: 75%
Financial aid, first-year: 50%

Considered the most carefree school of the Claremont Colleges, this small college has made a unique name for itself. As one of five schools that make up the Claremont system, Pitzer's academic flexibility, numerous extracurricular activities, and great location combine to make it "an extremely fun and diverse environment to be in." True, Pitzer's activities provide "a lot of distractions to take you off track," but students promise that "there's a very supportive community here that will help you along the way."

No Shortage of Academic Options

Because it has a relatively small student body of less than a thousand undergraduates, the faculty to student ratio at Pitzer is low, which allows students to have a good deal of interaction with their professors. "It's awesome—you get so much help," says one student. "Even if a class is hard, it's so easy to do well because professors are always ready and willing to help you." Class sizes in general range anywhere from 7 to 20 students, and even introductory courses are small. Says one student, "I don't think I had a class that enrolled more than 40 students." Close contact with professors is enhanced by a college-sponsored program in which students invite faculty members to their dining halls to discuss courses or just to get to know each other better. The contact with professors is so close that some instructors occasionally have classes right in their own homes.

There are few complaints about the limited number of required courses. According to one student, "The requirements are really easy to fulfill and they don't hinder your ability to take the classes you really want to take."

Among the most popular and strongest

of Pitzer's departments, according to students, are sociology and psychology. Because of the popularity of some departments, classes fill up quickly, and students can get shut out. Students aren't limited to Pitzer's courses, however, for everyone has the option of taking others at any of the Claremont colleges. These joint courses provide the wealth of academic options that makes Pitzer "everything you can ask for in a college, academically."

Location, Location, Location

Pitzer is about 40 minutes outside Los Angeles. Its location attracts a very diverse student body: People of different ethnicity, opinions, fashions, interests and backgrounds, hailing from California to Illinois to the Middle East, all flock to Pitzer. Students do report, however, that there is a "liberal leaning" among those who attend.

Pitzer students appreciate the safety and cleanliness of the city of Claremont. Although it has "lots of pretty houses and trees," students complain that "it's not a college town." Still, they enjoy the restaurants and shops in the area that provide them with the opportunity to relax and get away from campus for a while. Students have the freedom to roam about Claremont, in part, because the area is basically "free from crime." The overall consensus is that the city is a "peaceful place to be."

Where Should I Live?

Like many other private schools, Pitzer requires all freshmen to live on campus. Sophomores and juniors can live off campus, but they must apply for permission to do so. Most students, however, opt for on-campus housing, which consists of three dorms: Holden, Mead, and Sanbourn Halls. All freshmen and almost all sophomores live in Holden, nicknamed the "suburbs," and Sanbourn, also called the "ghetto." Upperclassmen live in Mead, which is referred to as the "projects." Despite the name, however, Mead is characterized by large apartment-style suites and huge rooms and is also known as the "Party Hall." Within these dorms, there are numerous theme halls, in which students can choose to live. Students who want a noise-free environment live in

"Hush Hall" in Holden, which is known for its quiet and serene atmosphere. "Involvement Tower" in Mead Hall is designed for students who want a support network of other students for their academic, as well as their non-academic, concerns. And "Wellness Quarter" in Sanbourn is occupied by students who neither smoke nor drink.

There is one dining hall on campus, McConnell, which serves the entire Pitzer student body, and many students complain about the quality of food it serves. "Sometimes the food is good; sometimes it's not," explained one undergrad. "Students frequently dash off to Collins [at Pomona] to satisfy their hunger," says another student. All students who live on campus are required to purchase a meal plan, but they have the freedom to eat at any of the other dining halls in the Claremont Colleges. In addition, they can use their meal plan at the Gold Mine and the Groove House, two on-campus eateries, up to twice each week. Other options include going to one of many off-campus restaurants and cafés.

What's on Campus?

Newly built facilities include the Gold Mine, the Groove House, and the Gold Center, where students can get their minds off school work. The Gold Mine is a student-run eatery where students can grab a quick bite to eat or substitute their regular dining hall meals. The Groove House is a coffeehouse frequented by students who want to relax, talk to friends, or just simply catch up on some reading. The student union building, the Gold Center, allows students to "kick back and unwind after a long, hard day of studying." It contains an arcade room, a swimming pool, a TV room complete with pool and ping-pong tables, and a weight room. It also includes meeting rooms that are used by various campus organizations.

Varsity sport teams are shared by the colleges, something unique to the Claremont system. Pitzer and Pomona team up to form the Sage Hens, and Harvey Mudd, Scripps, and Claremont McKenna come together to form an opponent team. There is a strong rivalry between these two teams, and although students concede that athletics are not a big deal, sporting events between these two teams are sure to draw crowds.

Since Pitzer doesn't have its own library, many students go to Honnold at Pomona, which is the most popular of all the campus libraries. Those looking for the mathematics and hard sciences books usually go to Sprague library at Harvey Mudd. Dennison, the Scripps library, specializes in books on the fine arts and humanities. Students enjoy this variety; according to one, "It gives me the opportunity to go to any library I'm in the mood for."

What To Do?

Pitzer offers many extracurricular activities that keep students active and involved. Students can write for the daily newspaper, *The College*, which covers current events for all five colleges, or they can host a radio program on the student-run radio station, also managed by all five colleges. Community service is one of the more popular ways in which students get involved. Other activities range from student government, which is considered to be very influential, to intramural sports. These activities equip Pitzer with "every opportunity to get involved with something." You can tutor at high schools, volunteer at community centers, or participate in campus activities. Basically, "all you have to do is just figure out what you want to do and then do it."

On the weekends, many students hit the party scene. Most activities are held in Mead Hall. Events sponsored by a student organization that spans all five colleges take place in McKenna Auditorium. Students' choices of parties are diverse, ranging from dance parties that play hip-hop, dance, or house music, to wild concerts with live bands, to parties that serve "lots and lots" of alcohol. Drugs and alcohol are part of the party scene and it's not too hard to find them if that's what you're looking for. According to one student, students drink freely because "Pitzer is not really strict about cracking down on them." Instead, claims one, the administration "[tells] you that whatever you do is your business."

Besides the typical weekend parties, Pitzer throws a couple of well-known parties every year. OSCAR, a student activity group, organizes a party called "The Super Tri Fly," featuring hip-hop and house music. The once-a-semester party called "Screw Your Homey" involves setting people up on a blind date. However, the social event considered by students to be the best of the year is the weekend-long party called "Kahoutek." Celebrating the coming of the spring, it attracts some big-name bands and arts and crafts from all over southern California.

> "The requirements are really easy to fulfill and they don't hinder your ability to take the classes you really want to take."

Beyond the confines of the Claremont campus, students needing an escape can flock to the many attractions of Los Angeles and the surrounding area. Nearby, students can shop and hang out at the Montclair Mall or catch a movie at the local cinema, Edward's. For students with cars, Los Angeles is a popular destination. The beaches, Hollywood, sports events, and Disneyland are just some of the many places students go on the weekends.

Pitzer is a diverse and vibrant community that thrives on the opportunities offered by the larger Claremont Colleges community. Students enjoy thes opportunities, claiming that "you have a great time at Pitzer; overall, it's a really great and exciting place to be." —*Edward Mundy*

FYI

The three best things about attending Pitzer are "accessibility to professors, great opportunities to study abroad, and its diversity."

The three worst things about attending Pitzer are "prevalent drug use, you have to go to the Pomona library to get some quiet study time, and you get absolutely no privacy."

The three things that every student should do before graduating from Pitzer are "travel abroad (it's so easy to do), get really drunk the day before finals, and pull at least one all-nighter each semester."

One thing I'd like to have known before coming here is "that there was so much drug use here."

Pomona College

Address: 333 North College Way, Claremont, CA 91711-6312
Phone: 909-621-8134
E-mail address: admissions@pomona.edu
Web site URL: www.pomona.edu
Location: suburban
Founded: 1887
Private or Public: private
Religious affiliation: none
Undergraduate enrollment: 1,549
Total enrollment: 1,549
Percent Male/Female: 53%/47%
Percent Minority: 40.0%

Percent African-American: 4.5%
Percent Hispanic: 10.0%
Percent Asian: 18.5%
Percent in-state/out-of-state: 39%/61%
Percent Pub HS: 70%
Fraternities: 9%
Sororities: 0%
Number of Applicants: 3,612
Percent Accepted: 32%
Percent Accepted who enroll: 35%
Entering: 390
Transfers: 16
Application Deadline: 1 Jan

Mean SAT: 720 V, 710 M
Middle 50% SAT range: 670–760 V, 670–750 M
Middle 50% ACT range: 29–33
Mean ACT: 32
3 Most popular majors: biology, psychology, history
Retention: 99.0%
Graduation rate: 94.0%
Library: 2,000,000 volumes
Tuition and Fees: $24,170
Room and Board: $8,170
On-campus housing: 100%
Financial aid, first-year: 51%

Even in the great multitudes of California's outstanding educational institutions, Pomona College stands tall among the masses. Pomona is a relatively small school, but the quality of its academic program has propelled it to high standing. In recent years, *U.S. News & World Report* has ranked Pomona among the top national liberal arts colleges in the nation. In addition to its intimate feel, Pomona enjoys the resources of a larger university through its affiliation with the Claremont McKenna system. To its credit, Pomona has risen to the top ranks through an unusual blend of traditional and innovative methods.

Unique Academics

Besides attracting some of the nation's best students, Pomona's liberal arts approach ensures that every student is provided with a broad education. Besides the usual courses that reportedly produce sleep-deprived students, Pomona has its own unique selection of courses. All first-year students have to take an ID1 course, which is a writing/thinking-intensive class. Although it may sound like a typical class, Mind, Culture, and Sport allows students to chat, think, and play sports on the same day the paper is due. Furthermore,

Pomona requires its freshmen to take a P.E. class for the first semester. The courses range from aikido to Brazilian jujitsu techniques—talk about a liberal education! However, Pomona still keeps its share of the classics. Even at a school with such academic diversity, the most popular majors include psychology, economics, English, political science, and chemistry.

Although Pomona has an abundance of social opportunities, any prospective student should understand one important aspect about Pomona's social scene. One student describes it as "a socially awkward place where there doesn't seem to be a set group of friends that you hang around with." Many students claim that the school is so small that "even if there were cliques on campus, you would know at least two or three people in that group." Pomona's small size makes social life quite different. For the most part, Pomona is one of those "you know everybody" schools. As one student put it, "The whole school is almost one big group of friends."

Drinking is a common part of most colleges and Pomona is no exception. Pomona's social scene generally centers on parties, so alcohol often finds its way into the mix. Says one student, "The rules for alcohol at Pomona are very, very liberal." Another quips, "The rules are almost amusing because nobody cares if you are of age or not." Take heart, though, if you are not into drinking. "There are many non-drinkers on campus, so it's not a big thing if you don't drink."

Living at Pomona

Even if you're not into the activities on campus, there is so much to do in and around the community. Pomona College is close to Ontario Mills Mall and about an hour away from Los Angeles. Of course, many students claim that a car is a must. Echoes of "I really need a car" can be heard all over campus. But students say the great likelihood is that you will have a friend who drives, so if you are vehicularly challenged, you won't be left stranded and bored.

Some think that size is all that matters. In the case of Pomona College, small size definitely does matter. Pomona has among the lowest student-to-faculty ratio (8 to 1) of any college and 74 percent of classes have fewer than 20 students. "Most classes are taught by professors and there is a very free and open climate when it comes to class discussions." Students report great individual attention from the professors.

If all that isn't enough for you, one of the greatest advantages of going to Pomona College is its affiliation with the other Claremont colleges. Based on the Oxford University system, the Claremont Colleges are a group of five colleges that include Pomona, Claremont McKenna, Pitzer, Scripps, and Harvey Mudd. As a Pomona student, you have the opportunity to enroll in each college's courses. If you opt to take courses from the college that specializes in a particular field, you are essentially getting the best of five worlds.

Social Pecking Order

Pomona's social life is lively and enriching. Pomona's mascot is the Sage Hen. If you're one of those people who are just into hanging around, then Pomona has a huge student center called the Coup. "The Coup is a great place to meet fellow Sage Hens, eat, study, and of course sleep," says a current student. However, if you require more than hanging around, Pomona can deliver. You can try a whole host of activities that range from the Filipino Club to the Hawaii Club. Sports definitely abound. Pomona is a Division III school and you can try your hand at varsity sports or intramurals—whatever strikes your fancy.

Students say the food at Pomona inspires many different eating habits. One student claims that "no one even touches the beef and everyone is slowly becoming a vegetarian." Apparently, the food at Pomona not only inspires vegetarian conversions, but a general migration to Claremont McKenna College. If you're dying for some decent food, "you will have to hike over to Claremont McKenna for the best grub."

Most freshmen live on South Campus, which is a group of dorms made up of long, big hallways. Rooms vary in size from small to large. Pomona's dorms are generally described "as happy living quarters, filled with camaraderie and bonding. They are definitely livable places."

> **"For the most part, Pomona is one of those 'You know everybody' schools."**

Pomona is an extremely open and tolerant community. There are lots of interracial couples and ample opportunities for relationships abound. One student noted that, "although there are not very many homosexual people at Pomona, many people here respect other's beliefs and behaviors." It is apparently very common to see posters on people's doors that sport such phrases as "I respect 'Queer' [name of homosexual support group] rights." Overall, many see Pomona as a community that is very accepting of diversity.

So what makes Pomona rise above the rest? Pomona is like the David of colleges surrounded by many Goliaths. It may be small, but there are so many advantages and beneficial aspects of a Pomona

education that it definitely warrants consideration from anyone looking for a small-college environment with all the advantages of a university education.
—*Aaron Johanson*

FYI

The three best things about attending Pomona are "the students are amazing, the professors really care, and the weather is spectacular."

The three worst things about attending Pomona are "a poor relationship with the surrounding community, the lack of school spirit, and the lack of diversity."

The three things that every student should do before graduating Pomona are "go to a professor's house for dinner, go skiing and to the beach all in one day, and be part of a live television audience in Hollywood."

One thing I'd like to have known before coming here is "no need for winter clothing!"

Scripps College

Address: 1030 Columbia Avenue, Claremont, CA 91711
Phone: 800-770-1333
E-mail address: admission@scrippscollege.edu
Web site URL: www.scrippscollege.edu
Location: suburban
Founded: 1926
Private or Public: private
Religious affiliation: none
Undergraduate enrollment: 768
Total enrollment: 768
Percent Male/Female: 0%/100%
Percent Minority: 32.0%

Percent African-American: 3.0%
Percent Hispanic: 6.0%
Percent Asian: 15.0%
Percent in-state/out-of-state: 42%/58%
Percent Pub HS: 53%
Fraternities: 0%
Sororities: NA
Number of Applicants: 1,063
Percent Accepted: 70%
Percent Accepted who enroll: 28%
Entering: 213
Transfers: 11
Application Deadline: 1 Feb
Mean SAT: 640 V, 620 M

Middle 50% SAT range: 580–660 V, 540–640 M
Middle 50% ACT range: NA
Mean ACT: 27
3 Most popular majors: psychology, politics & international relations, biology
Retention: 88.0%
Graduation rate: 69.0%
Library: 2,000,000 volumes
Tuition and Fees: $21,130 in; $21,130 out
Room and Board: $7,870
On-campus housing: 100%
Financial aid, first-year: 51%

If life among independent, motivated women strolling between Spanish Mediterranean architecture, sprawling lawns, and rose gardens sounds appealing, check out Scripps College! This small, all-female institution boasts the intimacy and community of a single-sex school, and the resources and entertainment of the surrounding four colleges and nearby Los Angeles.

Students are quick to point out that they are not members of a stereotypical women's college. "It's not about feminism and activism, but about equality and com-munity spirit." The advantages of a single-sex environment range from the supportive environment and relaxed atmosphere, to the attention given to women's educational issues. Most students did not choose Scripps because of its all-female status, but rather fell in love with the school itself.

All in the Family

Scripps is part of a consortium with Claremont McKenna, Pomona, Pitzer, and Harvey Mudd. Students cross-register frequently, and claim that doing so is easy, and often rewarding. "Going to one of the other schools is just like walking to another part of campus." Claremont McKenna, Pitzer, and Scripps have a Joint Science Center, where resources, and often classes, are shared between the schools. This state-of-the-art facility (completed in 1992) allows Scripps to benefit from resources that it would not be able to afford alone.

Students rate academics highly, praising their professors as well as their small classes. The campus is evenly divided between humanities and science majors. With an average of 10 to 15 students in a Scripps class, and up to 150 in a joint science lecture, personal attention is one of Scripps's greatest attributes. There are no teaching assistants, and the professors are helpful and always willing to talk.

A core curriculum is required of all Scripps students. Students must also fulfill general requirements, which include three semesters of a foreign language, one of laboratory science, two of social sciences, and one inter-cultural class. Students note that these requirements are not difficult to meet.

Scripps registers students by randomly choosing a letter, and proceeding alphabetically from that point, circling back around to cover the letters passed initially. This provides a fair way to register students, though some students are occasionally denied their first-choice classes.

The Scripps campus is located in the rather upscale town of Claremont, dubbed "the village" by students, and student interaction with the townspeople is very congenial. The campus is built in a loose square, with lawns and walled gardens filling the middle. A set of steps forming a semi-circle in the middle of campus is laughingly called "the Miss America Steps." Add Spanish Mediterranean architecture and rose gardens to these lawns, and it is easy to understand why the Scripps campus is a National Historic Landmark. Students feel extremely safe on the Scripps campus. It is a quiet and closed community in which students "never feel endangered." The dorms have an escort policy stating that a Scripps student must always accompany visitors to the dorms.

Home Sweet Home

Dorms at Scripps vary widely but all have resident assistants. Scripps has a few newer dorms, which are largely suite-style, with air-conditioning, and several older dorms, which students often prefer. "The older dorms have more character, with larger rooms, vaulted ceilings, and just more charm," one student explained. Designed to foster a close community, the older dorms each have a living room with a piano and a fireplace, as well as a "browsing room" in which students may make use of uninterrupted quiet, reference books, and couches. One particularly unique dormitory, Toll Hall, has a star-shaped fountain in its courtyard with balconies running around it. Students call residing in this part "living on star court."

Students live in double rooms their first year, and singles thereafter. In the past two years, campus housing was tight, but a new dorm is currently under construction, which should alleviate the space crunch. Further campus additions include a new Commons, built to replace the three smaller dining halls located in Toll Hall, Browning Hall, and Kimberly Hall. This single dining hall will make dining more accessible to students from the other colleges without jeopardizing dorm security. This centralized building will also house administrative offices, student organizations, and mailboxes.

A new food service was introduced recently, and students were not happy with the results. Students unhappy with the menu can use their meal plans at grills and pizza places off-campus, as well as at the Motley Coffee House, which shows movies every Friday night and hosts bands every Sunday night.

Athletics, Activities, and Dateless Dances?

Sports are played in conjunction with the other four colleges, with Pitzer and Pomona forming one league, and Claremont McKenna, Scripps, and Harvey Mudd forming another. There is intense rivalry between the two leagues. Within the Scripps league students can participate in intramural sports. Though many Scripps students are involved in sports, the

Scripps campus houses few athletic facilities. One of these facilities is a small gym, with plans for a new, expanded gym facility under way.

Other extracurricular activities abound, from student government to NOW, the National Organization for Women, or the literary magazine. One sorority recently opened a local chapter on campus, though it received a lot of student resistance. This chapter associates largely with the three fraternities at Pomona, and is not a large part of campus life.

Weekend activities often involve cultural events such as concerts, guest speakers, or art openings. Some of Scripps' most memorable speakers include the Supreme Court Justice Sandra Day O'Connor, author Jane Smiley, and former president of NATO Parliament, Karsten Voigt. Students also travel to the other colleges for Five College parties. Until this year, a Five College Organization worked to organize a large party at one campus each weekend. This organization has broken up for administrative reasons, and is currently being reconstructed. The Dean of Students organizes several Saturday afternoon trips into Los Angeles. Students might also spend several weekends a semester visiting L.A. or going to Disneyland.

Scripps students attend several formal occasions a year, one where Scripps women get dressed up and go to a dance on their campus without dates. A more conventional Spring Formal is also held on the Scripps campus.

> **"Going to one of the other schools is just like walking to another part of campus."**

Other Scripps traditions include freshman signing their names in a book of Scripps students, and seniors having a special champagne brunch, after which some streak across the campus. The Dean of Students serves students cookies and tea during the traditional Scripps Tea.

Students at Scripps form a tight community based on mutual support. "Scripps is a small college with personal attention, yet you don't know every person that you see every day." For many, Scripps presents the best of both worlds, one where diverse students can bond and "not be on guard all the time," experience small class sizes, and yet reap the benefits of an active college town. —*Cynthia Matthews*

FYI

The three best things about attending Scripps are "that professors are truly interested in helping their students; the dynamics of a women's college: mutual respect and support, an openness to new ideas, and a lack of cut-throat competitiveness; and the combination of a small college with a high teacher/student ratio and the five-college consortium."

The three worst things about attending Scripps are "the smog, the location, and the housing crunch (which will soon be alleviated with the new dorm)."

The three things that every student should do before graduating Scripps are "go to one of Professor Hao Huang's concerts, take a professor to the Motely for coffee and talk about anything but class work, and find an excuse to spend time in the Rare Books room in Denison Library."

One thing I'd like to have known before coming here is "it all goes by too quickly!"

Deep Springs College

Address: Application Committee, Box 45001, Dyer, CA 89010
Phone: 760-872-8088
E-mail address: apcom@deepspring.edu
Web site URL: http://www.deepsprings.edu
Location: rural
Founded: 1917
Private or Public: private
Religious affiliation: none
Undergraduate enrollment: 26
Total enrollment: 26
Percent Male/Female: 100%/0%

Percent Minority: 0%
Percent African-American: NA
Percent Hispanic: NA
Percent Asian: NA
Percent in-state/out-of-state: 99%/1%
Percent Pub HS: NA
Fraternities: 0%
Sororities: 0%
Number of Applicants: 120
Percent Accepted: 11%
Percent Accepted who enroll: 100%
Entering: 13
Transfers: NA

Application Deadline: 15 Nov
Mean SAT: NA
Middle 50% SAT range: 700–800 V, 700–800 M
Middle 50% ACT range: NA
Mean ACT: NA
3 Most popular majors: NA
Retention: 96.0%
Graduation rate: 92.0%
Library: 26,000 volumes
Tuition and Fees: NA
Room and Board: NA
On-campus housing: 100%
Financial aid, first-year: 100%

Have you ever wished that you could run your school, just for a day? Do you want to fire that English teacher, or introduce a new class into your curriculum? Do you want to learn how to milk a cow or discuss the intersection of community and law until three in the morning? If so, Deep Springs College might be the place for you.

Deep Springs is a unique all-male institution of 26 students. In addition to being a liberal arts college, it is a working cattle ranch and alfalfa farm. The campus of Deep Springs is the only installation in a long, high-desert valley in eastern California, with the campus at one end of the valley and a saltwater lake at the other. In between the two lies an oasis of alfalfa fields and cottonwood trees that are home to various forms of wildlife. This small area becomes every Deep Springer's home for two years—leaving the valley during the seven-week terms is forbidden except when special permission is granted. There are two or three breaks of variable length (from one to three weeks) dispersed throughout the year.

Student-Run College

One of the most interesting of the many unique aspects of Deep Springs is its self-governing student body. The students are responsible for almost the entire administration of the school. Students divide themselves into four committees: curriculum, applications, communications, and review. The curriculum committee hires and fires the faculty and determines what classes to offer; the applications committee is in charge of reading the 200-plus applications received each year and choosing between 10 and 13 new students for admission; the communications committee produces the school's newsletters, brochure, and other publications; and the review committee, the most "traditional" of the committees, reviews all the students during and after their first year, making sure it wants to invite everyone back. Students praise these committees, as they "provide a unique environment of responsibility and involvement" in their college experience. The committees meet three or four nights per week, in addition to the all-school meeting every Friday night, which begins at eight and sometimes lasts until three in the morning. Deep Springers certainly earn their reputation as an "uncommonly thoughtful" group.

Down on the Farm

Besides being administrators, students must also be farmers while at school. Deep Springs is an almost entirely self-sufficient farm, meaning that work must be done every day of the week. Students "labor" on the farm about 20 to 30 hours per week, rotating duties ranging from harvesting and planting to milking the cow, which someone has to do every morning at six (yes, even on Saturday).

In addition, students must stay on top of a large class load. Since students choose the curriculum, all of the classes are popular—that is, all nine of them. The classes are focused on the humanities, with two required courses in composition and public speaking. With fewer than 30 students, all classes are seminars, and any college student can tell you that that means no slacking. Of course, as one second–year student put it, "Deep Springs does not attract slackers." The faculty consists of only six members, who all "leave their lights on" for the students.

Students can get a two-year associate degree upon graduating from Deep Springs, but the degree is not the focus at all. Most students end up transferring to the nation's top colleges to earn their bachelor's degree. In recent years, the students who chose to transfer went to Yale, Harvard, Swarthmore, and the University of Chicago.

> **"The faculty consists of only six members, who all 'leave their lights on' for the students."**

With so many responsibilities, do students have any time at all? "Hell no!" said a second-year student. However, as anywhere, students do always seem to make time to enjoy themselves. Popular activities at Deep Springs include running, biking, and hiking in the beautiful, untouched area of southern California. While there are no organized athletics, there is a very "humble" gym, and people will often take part in pickup games of soccer, basketball, or frisbee.

There are three strict rules at Deep Springs. First, students may not leave the valley for any reason while school is in session except for family emergency. No smoking is allowed anywhere near the campus: Fire on a farm with the nearest help 45 minutes away is not a good scenario. Third, drugs and alcohol are forbidden. However, during breaks Deep Springs is not dry. These breaks occur every seven weeks, and while some students must remain on campus at all times to keep up the farm, those whose turn it is to leave often go on trips together. Clearly Deep Springers spend a lot of time with each other. One student made the comment that his fellow Deep Springers "are like brothers—I love them, but sometimes I want to kill them."

The students who arrive at Deep Springs are those who did "incredibly well" in high school, and who usually have a strong background in community service. Students have come from all different backgrounds, although one student notes that it is usually kids from privileged backgrounds, or whoever "had the opportunity to work his butt off in high school." The composition of the school can change dramatically from year to year, and the strengths that each new student brings are truly felt. However, a student reported that the school is always looking to diversify.

No Coed Dances

When asked to describe Deep Spring's social life, one student summed it up with the word "ironic," saying that the students were "very aware that it is single-sex." But this same student was quick to dispel the stereotypes of Deep Springs' "really lame social scene or tendency toward "gay erotica." Deep Springs is, a second-year student mused, "somewhere between grunting and head-banging and touchy feely." While such a small school lacks the thrills of huge parties packed with people, blind dates, and pounding dances, it offers a different kind of experience based on the closeness of a single group of friends. No matter how close the men of Deep Springs become, phone bills are still "astronomical," and visitors are certainly welcomed, provided they will help out with the chores.

It is safe to say that the students at Deep Springs are truly happy to be there; if they weren't, there would be little incentive to stay. They generally praise the school's policy of isolation, pointing out that freedom from distraction gives them more time to think about their studies. One student said that in looking at other colleges he noticed that many fell short.

At Deep Springs, students give their lives a lot of consideration. It is this breeding of thoughtfulness that makes Deep Springs what one student called a "very successful experiment in education." —*Lucy McClellan*

FYI

The three best things about attending Deep Springs are "dilettantism (e.g., 'You're always doing something that you don't know how to do. It's encouraged'), the close relationship you have with everyone in the valley, and the sense of purpose."

The three worst things about attending Deep Springs are "the atmosphere of brutal honesty, the inability to escape the intensity, and the sheer masculinity of the place."

The three things that every student should do before graduating Deep Springs are "slide naked down the Eureka valley sand dunes in the light of the full moon (Deep Springs' most hallowed tradition), participate in the spring branding of a calf, and doing something legendary."

One thing I'd like to have known before coming here is "how hard it is to leave Deep Springs."

Mills College

Address: 5000 MacArthur Boulevard, Oakland, CA 94613
Phone: 510-430-2135
E-mail address: admission@mills.edu
Web site URL: www.mills.edu
Location: urban
Founded: 1946
Private or Public: private
Religious affiliation: none
Undergraduate enrollment: 746
Total enrollment: 1,169
Percent Male/Female: 0%/100%
Percent Minority: 28.0%

Percent African-American: 9.0%
Percent Hispanic: 7.0%
Percent Asian: 11.0%
Percent in-state/out-of-state: 79%/21%
Percent Pub HS: NA
Fraternities: 0%
Sororities: 0%
Number of Applicants: 474
Percent Accepted: 77%
Percent Accepted who enroll: 34%
Entering: 124
Transfers: NA
Application Deadline: 15 Feb

Mean SAT: NA
Middle 50% SAT range: 540–660 V, 520–610 M
Middle 50% ACT range: NA
Mean ACT: NA
3 Most popular majors: english, psychology, communication
Retention: NA
Graduation rate: 69.0%
Library: 220,000 volumes
Tuition and Fees: $18,262 in; $18,262 out
Room and Board: $7,296
On-campus housing: 100%
Financial aid, first-year: 80%

Mills College is a small, private, all-women's liberal arts college located in Oakland. Aside from the obvious difference in that all students are female, Mills offers something unique that students would not be able to get just anywhere: focus on the individual female student. The diverse student body includes a sizable group of "resumers" who are over the age of 23 and either returning to school or seeking a degree later in life. According to one senior, "Students come here for many different reasons, but what they find is a supportive and friendly atmosphere backed by a great education from top-notch professors."

Political Activism Is Alive and Kicking

When Propositions 187 and 209 affecting immigration and affirmative action, respectively, were heatedly debated back in 1997, students protested with as much fervor as students did in the '60s. In recent years, students have boycotted classes to protest the school's lack of faculty diversity and an ethnic studies department. Students report that the administration is doing much better at addressing student concerns. Currently, resumers are protesting that their special child-care needs and older-age concerns are not being met and are working to bring about change. Students involved in Amnesty International often hold protests and events to focus on political prisoners. Current hot issues include the Free Tibet movement and gay/lesbian rights.

Women's issues are also of great concern to students. The National Organization of Women (NOW) has a strong presence as do other organizations for the advancement of women's rights. Even those who are not politically active view the activism with high regard. Says one Mills woman, "Students here are very passionate about their beliefs and are very involved in bringing about change."

Activists Have Classes, Too

However, life isn't all protest and no work for students. All Mills women must take two classes from each of the four major academic divisions: humanities, fine arts, social sciences, and natural sciences. The curriculum guidelines also require two semesters of English and one course on multiculturalism. One student voiced a common complaint: "The multiculturalism requirement is a good idea, but only requiring one course hardly seems diverse." Students favor the English and music majors, but some criticize the math and computer science departments for their dwindling faculty, though the administration has made an effort to reverse this trend. Although the computer science department has recently hired a new professor, the math department is still less than fantastic. Some students report that the absence of male students limits production options in the theater department. However, the science and art departments tend to have integrated upper-level classes with the coed grad students, and one woman noted, "It's a nice change of pace."

Students herald small class size and individual attention as the most positive aspect of Mills College. Introductory

science courses rarely enroll more tha 70 students, and the majority of classe have no more than 25. Some classes hav capped enrollments, especially those i the art department, which give priority t art majors. "Classes in the art departmer are sometimes hard to get into, but othe than that it's pretty easy to get the classe you want." Students report that "profe sors are willing to negotiate paper dea lines and very understanding if student have problems, or unique situations." I addition to the offerings at Mills, student are allowed to cross-register one class pe semester at UC Berkeley or other nearb colleges if Mills doesn't offer a class i their topic of interest.

An Oasis in an Urban Desert

Students describe the Mills campus as a oasis in the middle of an urban enviror ment. Eucalyptus trees and a small strea add beauty to the picturesque Spanish style buildings that dot the campus. Mil Hall, the main administration building, u derwent extensive renovations after 1989 earthquake caused severe structur. damage. The main campus library, Olin L brary, holds over 210,000 texts, a rar book room, and cushy study rooms, b many still travel to nearby UC Berkeley do "serious research."

All residence halls include a kitchen, l brary, laundry, and computer room. Th favored dorms include Orchard Meadov with its homey atmosphere, and Eth Moore, despite its rather secluded hillsid location. While about half of the student choose to live off campus, those who liv on campus live in dorms with spaciou singles and shared common rooms.

While the dining halls provide salad ar pasta bars in addition to the hot entree students still complain about the foo though they admit that it is "better than a most other places." One student als lauded "the taco stand on the corner Fruitvale and High, which makes the be tacos I've ever had."

Social Options

While students feel defensive about the neighborhood of East Oakland, they d scribe Mills as being a pretty se contained campus with only one entrance onto the campus. "The school is located next to a major freeway on-ramp . . . so when students leave campus, they go far away." Others believe that the line of restaurants and coffee shops along the border of the campus provides a great atmosphere. "There are some really nice movie theaters in close range, including one that has couches for seats and serves food to you while you watch the movie." For the club scene, students take the Mills van shuttle service to the city of Berkeley. Students sometimes complain that the last shuttle pickup is at 10:30, leaving tardy students stranded. Nearby San Francisco also provides great entertainment opportunities.

Students, typically outfitted in jeans, tank tops, and Birkenstocks or running shoes, often stop at the Tea Shop, an on-campus beverage and food shop, to socialize or take a break from studies. The Black-and-White Dance and the Boat Dance are two annual campus activities. For the Boat Dance students and their dates dance the night away on a chartered boat that cruises around the San Francisco Bay. One student explained, "It's almost like a prom."

Students either participate actively in extracurricular organizations or ignore them altogether. A small, dedicated group of women publishes the *Mills Weekly*, the college newspaper. *The Walrus*, a literary magazine, comes out every semester.

The on-campus social scene is described as "reserved." Students report that many off-campus students tend to be resumers and they often do not participate as much in the day-to-day campus activity and social scene. For obvious reasons, the typical college frat parties are absent from the social scene and most students really like not having ragers around. One junior offered this advice: "The social life at Mills is really what you make of it. A lot of people tend to travel to San Francisco and partake in the great cultural life there. Others like to hang around and relax. But everyone finds their niche."

Mills College is a Division III school and therefore does not offer athletic scholarships. Few students consider athletics a big deal on campus, though they still support their teams. The crew team competes against top California teams, and a win over UC Berkeley is always a sweet victory. Varsity athletes and weekend athletes all use the Haas Pavilion, whose facilities include basketball and volleyball courts, as well as aerobic and weight-lifting rooms.

> "Students here are very passionate about their beliefs and are very involved in bringing about change."

While Mills women readily point out their perceived isolation, they are also quick to praise Mills strengths. Students of all ages can expect to find a supportive network of women who are as passionate about learning as they are. Mills students care about their school, know its history, and love it. Many children of alumnae, called "bent twigs," are currently enrolled, attesting to the ties that students have to their school. The women are strong, active, and as one busy student explained, all "have a million things going on; maybe too many things!" —*Seung Lee*

FYI

The three best things about attending Mills are the "focus on the individual female student, the political and social activism, and the shared passion for learning."

The three worst things about attending Mills are "the East Oakland neighborhood, the reserved social scene, and the weak computer science department and overly popular art department."

The three things that every student should do before graduating Mills are "attending the Boat Dance, enjoying the cultural/social opportunities in Berkeley and San Francisco, and taking the time to get to know women of all ages."

One thing I'd like to have known before coming here is "my fears about a all-women's college were wrong: Mills' women live in a supportive, wonderful environment."

Occidental College

Address: 1600 Campus Road, Office of Admissions, Los Angeles, CA 90041
Phone: 323-259-2700
E-mail address: admission@oxy.edu
Web site URL: www.oxy.edu
Location: suburban
Founded: 1917
Private or Public: private
Religious affiliation: none
Undergraduate enrollment: 1,482
Total enrollment: 1,516
Percent Male/Female: 43%/57%
Percent Minority: 48.0%

Percent African-American: 5.0%
Percent Hispanic: 17.0%
Percent Asian: 22.0%
Percent in-state/out-of-state: 55%/45%
Percent Pub HS: NA
Fraternities: 25%
Sororities: 25%
Number of Applicants: 1,866
Percent Accepted: 77%
Percent Accepted who enroll: 27%
Entering: 353
Transfers: NA
Application Deadline: 15 Jan

Mean SAT: 600 V, 600 M
Middle 50% SAT range: 530–650 V, 540–640 M
Middle 50% ACT range: NA
Mean ACT: NA
3 Most popular majors: English, psychology, economics
Retention: 89.0%
Graduation rate: 77.0%
Library: 470,000 volumes
Tuition and Fees: $22,709 in; $22,709 out
Room and Board: $6,551
On-campus housing: 100%
Financial aid, first-year: 60%

Just outside the bustling city limits of Los Angeles is the small campus of Occidental College, with its quiet lawns and balanced architecture. If you were to wander around the campus, you would probably find it uncannily familiar; Occidental was the site of the mythical "California University" that the kids of *Beverly Hills 90210* attended. But while camera crews used to crowd onto the campus weekly, now the *90210* gang has moved on, and most Oxy students agree that this is a good thing. The homogeneity of the popular show could not be farther from the true makeup of the Occidental student body, which hails from a wide variety of cultural, economic, and geographic backgrounds.

Oxy Academics

Oxy has a large number of core requirements that students describe as "a lot of work," but well worth it. One student said the courses "prepared me to be a better student as a whole," and that they laid a good base for later classes. Requirements include courses in history, science, math, foreign language, fine arts, and writing, as well as a special Cultural Studies course required for freshmen. For this requirement, first-years choose from four classes, which are different every semester. These are considered some of the best classes at Occidental, because they focus on current issues and are taught by passionate professors. The sciences are reportedly strong; one student went so far as to say "most students do something with chemistry or biology." Other popular majors include psychology, history, English, and sociology.

Occidental undergrads say that student-teacher relationships are very strong. Professors are often young, with new teaching styles and fresh ideas, and they are "very accessible and more than willing to assist in the individual education of the students." Classes generally have one professor, as well as one or two TAs, but most large classes enroll no more than 40 or 50 students, and smaller ones usually enroll around 12 to 18. Students usually get into the classes they want during registration, even though sizes are so limited; "No one will be denied a class that he/she wants, it just takes some running around and signing forms," one student said. Registration is done at the end of the previous semester, and seniors have priority, but in the fall, freshmen register during orientation, and a certain number of spots in classes are reserved for them.

Studying at Occidental is intense, but balanced. Students say that the time just before exams can be very stressful, but most of the time they feel fairly relaxed. Students are also "good about studying together and sharing information," one student said, and the atmosphere is one of cooperation, not competition. The library, considered adequate both for research and for studying, has group study rooms as well as quiet rooms. If students can't find the books or periodicals they need at Occidental, they can order the books from other local college libraries of Pomona and UCLA.

Living on the Oxy Campus

Most Occidental students live on-campus in the dorms (freshmen are required to do so), and those who live off-campus generally live within a few blocks of the college, creating a tight-knit community. Students cite Norris Hall as one of the best dorms, with mostly quads composed of two double bedrooms, a bathroom, and a large common room. There are also a few singles in Norris, and other halls contain either all singles or a mix of doubles and singles. Students say the rooms are "not luxurious, but they are large," and students are generally pleased with their options.

Some students report that there are only two sizes of rooms, "huge and tiny." But even the smaller rooms generally have enough space, and some have additional perks, like balconies. Off-campus housing may be cheaper, but students find that off-campus housing is often "ugly and out of the way." All dorms are coed, although some have single-sex wings, and bathrooms are all single-sex.

Many students who live off-campus choose fraternity or sorority houses. Occidental has three national fraternities and three local sororities, which organize a lot of events open to the entire campus. "A lot of Oxy life is centered around campus activities," one student said. The Associated Students of Occidental College (ASOC) plans campus social activities such as movie screenings every Friday, and parties such as the annual Sex at the Beach Party, which includes dancing and drinking in a mock-beach environment.

Students also hang out at the on-campus Tiger Cooler or the Ozone, a campus coffee shop.

On and Off Campus Fun

Whether into sports, community service, writing for a publication, or theater groups, "most students try and find the time to participate in extracurriculars." Some popular activities include the A-team (the admissions team); Tour Guides; *La Encina* (the yearbook); and the Tango/Swing Dance Club. Students also cheer on the O, X, and Y, three guys who go to all of the football and basketball teams and cheer like crazy.

Occidental also offers a variety of sports. Oxy competes in Division III, so sports are not a huge part of campus life, but students say that this means "the students who participate do it because they love the game." Large numbers of students turn out and cheer for both home and away games, particularly against their chief rival, Pomona College. Students say that the athletic facilities are "up to date and easily accessible," and completely open to non-athletes as well. For those who want to compete on a less intense level, Occidental organizes intramural football, basketball, volleyball, and softball. Teams are generally organized from within fraternities, dorms, or clubs, but anyone who wants to organize a team can do so.

> **"A lot of Oxy life is centered around campus activities."**

Even with so much to do on campus, many students are drawn off campus to Los Angeles or other nearby areas for entertainment. The college runs a free shuttle service to Pasadena's Old Town, but students say that having a car is a big advantage. With a car, students have access to countless restaurants, clubs, stores, and other entertainment in Los Angeles, or recreation areas like beaches and parks outside the city. Closer to campus, students can walk to coffee shops and restaurants in the surrounding suburban area when they need a break from traditional Oxy food.

Occidental students are very proud of their school's commitment to diversity. Ranked number one in the country for diversity, with roughly half of the student body comprised of minorities, Oxy students find that they have avoided some of the problems that other colleges face. At some other schools, students of different backgrounds may tend to divide off into cliques, but Oxy students find their classmates not only extremely tolerant, but also integrated. The strong, tight community and well-integrated diversity are what makes Occidental College stand out from busy Los Angeles and trendy Pasadena; students say they are glad that they can visit the city, but still live in their community. —*Melissa Andersen and Staff*

FYI

The three best things about attending Occidental are "strong teacher-student relationships, the atmosphere of cooperation, not competition, and the diversity of the student body."

The three worst things about attending Occidental are "the *90210* image (which is so far from the truth), the small library, and the poor off-campus living options."

The three things that every student should do before graduating Occidental are "get to know the incredible people, play intermurals, and enjoy the opportunities that L.A. offers, without having to deal with the negatives of living in the city."

One thing I'd like to have known before coming here is "that a school in such an urban area could be so tight-knit—a car is necessary if you need a break."

Pepperdine University

Address: 24255 Pacific Coast Highway, Malibu, CA 90263
Phone: 310-456-4392
E-mail address: admission-seaver@pepperdine.edu
Web site URL: www.pepperdine.edu
Location: suburban
Founded: 1955
Private or Public: private
Religious affiliation: Church of Christ
Undergraduate enrollment: 3,256
Total enrollment: 7,802
Percent Male/Female: 41%/59%
Percent Minority: 24.0%

Percent African-American: 6.0%
Percent Hispanic: 9.0%
Percent Asian: 7.0%
Percent in-state/out-of-state: 58%/42%
Percent Pub HS: NA
Fraternities: 20%
Sororities: 25%
Number of Applicants: 4,793
Percent Accepted: 46%
Percent Accepted who enroll: 29%
Entering: 626
Transfers: NA
Application Deadline: 1 Mar
Mean SAT: 590 V, 600 M

Middle 50% SAT range: 550–640 V, 550–650 M
Middle 50% ACT range: NA
Mean ACT: NA
3 Most popular majors: business administration, telecommunications, sports medicine
Retention: 85.0%
Graduation rate: 70.0%
Library: 480,000 volumes
Tuition and Fees: $21,240 in; $21,240 out
Room and Board: $6,840
On-campus housing: 65%
Financial aid, first-year: NA

Overlooking the Pacific Ocean from the hills of Malibu stands the coastal castle that is Pepperdine University. Students rave, "This place is absolutely gorgeous." But there is more here than sunny beaches and stunning views. Pepperdine is a Christian, conservative, private institution that offers an intimate academic experience shared among classmates from all over the world.

Caring Professors and Small Classes

Many students claim that the regular small class size (usually under 20 students) was a major factor in choosing

Pepperdine. Especially compared to the larger public universities in California, students here can brag about having "great relationships with professors." Profs are reportedly very understanding of students' needs. "They'll work really hard for you. They always give the extra effort." Between holding regular office hours and even inviting students over for dinner, the typical Pepperdine professor is accessible, friendly, and truly cares about the students.

Students are also very satisfied with the classroom instruction, a feeling shared by majors in all departments. Before choosing a major, students fulfill their general education requirements (GEs) which include courses in English, math, religion, Western Heritage, and physical education. Of the majors to choose from, business tends to be the most popular. Many students also major in communications.

Diversity . . . Students from All Over California?

The student body is a fairly diverse bunch. Although more than half of the student body comes from California, there are also many international students who "fit in just fine," according to one student. Most seem satisfied with the diversity on campus. "There is no stereotypical Pepperdine student and you can always wear what you want," reported one junior, although another student commented, "There are definitely those who always dress up." An undergraduate organization called Campus Life holds two major events each year to celebrate the cultural diversity at Pepperdine. For example, Rainbow Fest is a week-long festival full of multi-ethnic food tables and international dance presentations.

Sexy but Dateless Students

If you think the campus is pretty, just wait until you see the students. Complete with dark tans appropriate for sunny California, Pepperdine undergraduates are "a really good-looking bunch" and very health-conscious. However, there is one minor problem with these sunbathing studs and hot chicks: They don't date. "Nobody ever dates at Pepperdine; you just get engaged." There seems to be a general consensus on the two main ro-

mantic options—you're either in a serious relationship, or you're in no relationship at all. One student called this "the sore spot of Pepperdine." A female student agreed, lamenting, "the guys here are wimps." Yet many students say that the lack of dating is more than made up for by the intimate, long-lasting friendships that emerge on campus. "Some date, many don't, but everyone has great friends."

Social life is generally geared toward off-campus activities. Pepperdine is in such an exciting part of California it would be hard not to venture off campus during the weekends. Los Angeles, Santa Monica, and Hollywood are just a jump, skip, and a hop from Pepperdine. As one student happily reported, the surrounding cities offer "everything you'd ever want to do." Many students, especially freshmen, opt to go home for the weekends as well, since often home is not too far away, then return on Sunday for a hard day of studying.

This is not to say that on-campus life is dead. Greek life most definitely plays a role in Pepperdine's social scene; it engages over half of the student body and is growing more popular every year. Fraternities and sororities on campus have become part of their respective national charters since 1995, whereas before they were limited to being merely local organizations due to administrative restrictions. Students say one of the nice things about the societies is that it's not too difficult to get in if you're interested. One of the priorities of Campus Life is to make sure that all girls who want to get into a sorority can do so. Because Pepperdine is a dry campus (a policy that is strictly enforced), almost all drinking takes place away from campus.

To Convo or Not to Convo— Got No Choice

Pepperdine University is affiliated with The Church of Christ, a relationship not taken lightly by the student body and the administration. A strong religious atmosphere is an integral part of the Pepperdine experience. For the most part, students love this religious element tied in with their years of higher education. Although many students attend church regularly and are actively involved with the Campus Ministry (an undergraduate organization that focuses on community service projects), not everyone is devout. One student who doesn't consider herself to be very religious commented that the "presence is not overbearing." There are no requirements to attend church or the Bible studies on campus, but all undergraduates must attend the weekly convocation. "Convo" is a meeting held every Wednesday morning during which a variety of issues are discussed. Often guest speakers are featured, ranging from popular celebrities to local ministers, and not all discussions focus around a religious theme. Topics range from "community service to school spirit to 'how to be a better lover,'" said one senior. For the most part, students feel that convo is an important and interesting part of campus life at Pepperdine. "It truly builds a community feeling." The diverse meetings are cited as building an "awareness on important issues" that students often encounter during the rest of the week. However, some say that the mandatory aspect of convo makes it feel "more like an obligation." One student reported that at times, "some feel uncomfortable" attending the convocation if they are "not that serious about religion."

Community Clusters

Incoming freshmen can look forward to a dormitory experience "geared toward a community feeling." Freshman dorms are single-sex buildings, which typically hold 40 students. Each building has five suites with eight people in each suite. The suites have two bathrooms, a community living area, and four doubles. Although they are not air-conditioned, the mild and "not too humid" weather allows students to live comfortably. Most important, the small buildings really foster a sense of community. However, as with all deals, some restrictions apply: Members of the opposite sex are only permitted in the rooms from 11 A.M. to 11 P.M., although they can stay in the dorm room lobby until 2 A.M. Also, you must leave your door open if someone of the opposite sex is in your room. Each dormitory has a Resident Advisor and a

Student Advisor whom students can approach with questions and problems.

Juniors and seniors sometimes petition to live in on-campus apartments. The apartments, while still single-sex, have later time restrictions (you don't have to kick your partner out of your room until 1 A.M.).

Given the small student population, there is only one large dining hall, located at the Tyler Campus Center. Students select from a wide variety of different food stations, such as the Grill. For the most part, the food at Pepperdine is described as really good. And why not, it's catered by Marriott Services. Although students complain that the cafeteria cuisine can sometimes get boring, they take comfort in the fact that there's "always pizza."

Competitive Sports and Fun Activities

Pepperdine is also widely known for its excellence in varsity sports, with many teams often competing for Division I national championships. In recent years, Pepperdine has gained recognition with the men's water polo team 1997 national title, a consistently successful men's volleyball team, which has placed as high as second in the nation, and a talented men's basketball team. But don't be afraid if you're not an incredible athlete. Club and intramural teams play on more relaxed turf, and it is easy to get involved.

> **"Nobody ever dates at Pepperdine, you just get engaged."**

This "easy to get involved" mentality extends over most extracurricular activities at Pepperdine. Students generally feel they can find clubs that satisfy their interests and they are very easy to join. For singers, there is a Church of Christ a cappella group, which tours often. Pepperdine also has its own student-run radio and television stations.

A diverse student body, whose members share a common respect for Christian beliefs, characterizes Pepperdine University. These students enjoy the small, intimate, well-taught classes at Pepperdine. The campus on the coast of sunny California is beautiful. The weather is beautiful. Even the people are beautiful.

One word of advice, though—if you decide that Pepperdine is the place for you, don't be afraid to ask somebody out on a date. —*Carl Shephard*

FYI
The three best things about attending Pepperdine are "its location, its small class size and the abundance of attention given to students, and its standing as a reputable university."
The three worst things about attending Pepperdine are "the lack of school spirit, a poor Greek system, and too much emphasis on religion."
The three things that every student should do before graduating Pepperdine are "get an professional internship through the school, take a day off to enjoy the incredible weather and scenery, and make sure you acquire a car."
One thing I'd like to have known before coming here is "how much emphasis would be put on religion. There is quite a diverse crowd at Pepperdine, and many students feel that they are being forced to participate in the religious aspects of the school."

St. Mary's College of California

Address: P.O. Box 4800, Moraga, CA 94575-4800
Phone: 935-631-4224
E-mail address: smcadmit@stmarys-ca.edu
Web site URL: www.stmarys-ca.edu
Location: suburban
Founded: 1963
Private or Public: private
Religious affiliation: Roman Catholic
Undergraduate enrollment: 3,234
Total enrollment: NA
Percent Male/Female: 39%/61%

Percent Minority: 30.0%
Percent African-American: 7.0%
Percent Hispanic: 13.0%
Percent Asian: 9.0%
Percent in-state/out-of-state: 88%/12%
Percent Pub HS: NA
Fraternities: NA
Sororities: NA
Number of Applicants: 2,999
Percent Accepted: 83%
Percent Accepted who enroll: 23%
Entering: 573
Transfers: NA

Application Deadline: 1 Feb
Mean SAT: NA
Middle 50% SAT range: 600–690 V, 560–670 M
Middle 50% ACT range: NA
Mean ACT: NA
3 Most popular majors: business, communications, English
Retention: NA
Graduation rate: NA
Library: NA
Tuition and Fees: $17,458 in; $17,458 out
Room and Board: $7,370
On-campus housing: 100%
Financial aid, first-year: NA

Looking for a small Christian liberal arts college near a major urban center? Nestled among the hills east of Oakland and Berkeley, across the bay from San Francisco, lie the city of Moraga and St. Mary's College. With its white walls and red tile roofs, this school is as picturesque as any California mission, but filled with students living the modern college life. St. Mary's is one of 914 Christian Brother schools throughout the world, and one of 7 in the United States. The philosophies of the Brothers, followers of

Saint John Baptist De La Salle, patron saint of teachers in the Roman Catholic Church, are rooted in traditions of community support and service through education.

Life Is a Journey of Learning

Since it was founded, St. Mary's has dedicated itself to the education of the whole person. As one professor put it, "The capacity to think critically and live life as a journey of learning are not, after all, skills to be listed on a résumé. They are, rather, traits of the heart and the soul as much as of the mind." Students at St. Mary's enroll in one of four schools, the School of Liberal Arts, the School of Science, the School of Economics and Business Administration, or the Intercollegiate Nursing Program. All of these schools (except the INP) have different majors, and within each major there are concentrations to choose from. It is also possible to combine majors or double major. The most popular majors are psychology and business administration, though students can major in anything from computer science to physical education and recreation.

In order to graduate from St. Mary's, each student must participate in four seminar courses and two religion classes. Students feel that "the seminar program is a very important part of our education." It allows them to discuss topics more intimately and examine ideas further than a normal class would allow. The seminars generally involve the reading of classic literature, and topics range from "Greek Thought" to "19th and 20th Century Thought." The religion courses "have also provided insight into unfamiliar faiths and a foundation for my own beliefs," according to one student. Another pointed out, "religion classes are not all based in Catholicism," which provides for more objective perspectives in this area.

The school is experiencing a surge in popularity, but students complain that "due to increasing size, it is becoming more difficult to get the classes we want." Classes are also not as small as most incoming students had expected. But, according to one upperclassman, "[Classes] are still on the small side. My smallest class this semester has 11 students, my largest has 30." So while class sizes increase, "they are still small compared to most universities." There are no TAs at St. Mary's. All classes are taught by professors and "all teachers speak fluent English."

"Students strive to do well, but it is not a competitive atmosphere to the extent that they do not help one another." As one student pointed out, "The courses are not graded on a curve. If you deserve an A you get an A. This makes it less competitive and encourages students to work together."

The High Potential program is one that makes St. Mary's stand out from the crowd. This program is "for students who could not normally get into college on their grades." After an additional application process, students who, due to extenuating circumstances, did not do as well as they could have in high school, may be admitted. As one student put it, "It is a program that allows those that normally would not get the opportunity to go to college to go." This program, an interesting alternative to affirmative action, helps increase the school's diversity and helps deserving students.

Fun and Games

While St. Mary's is not a commuter school, weekends often involve dashing home for some home-cooked food and free laundry for the many students who grew up in the area. As one student put it, freshmen either "drink in the dorms or go home" on the weekends. Most people on campus own cars, and "if you don't, you'll know someone who does," so quick trips to Berkeley or San Francisco for a night of clubbing or bar hopping is always an option. Also, there are "buses that run from campus to BART [Bay Area Rapid Transit] regularly."

Student life, while fun, is not centered on the college. There is no Greek system, and one mildly disgruntled student pointed out that "student apathy is really bad here. There is no collective spirit or passion about anything on campus." But just because "everyone does their own thing" doesn't make it all bad. Students participate in many extracurriculars, like the Student Alumni Association and the service group run through Circle K (a national community service organization). Many students have jobs either on campus or in nearby cities, and play intramural or club sports.

Students say that there are plenty of attractive people—however, dating is fairly uncommon. According to one student, "there is a lot of sex, for some." Cliques exist, but it is easy to meet people through any sort of activity or class. Students complained that "people think we're all rich," and that there are virtually no interracial or homosexual couples on campus. While almost the entire student body is either

Catholic or Protestant, few of the activities are religious in nature and "we are not required to attend church services."

Every year there are several dress-up events, two boat dances on San Francisco Bay, a junior formal, a senior ball, and a casino night. Also, "two of the most popular events of the year are the Luau and Jamaica-me Crazy" theme dances for the entire school.

Freshman Dorms Build Character

Freshmen and sophomores are guaranteed housing, though it's not always the best. As one upperclassman put it, dorms "are small and crowded, sometimes housing three people to a room." Floors are divided by gender, and there are community bathrooms. Freshman dorms purportedly "build character."

All on-campus housing is overseen by RAs and Brother Counselors who live in the dorms. Though many in these positions are laid-back, the "level of discipline varies from person to person." The primary rules of the dorms are "no cohabitation past 2 A.M., no alcohol, and quiet times that vary." The dorms are clean and pest-free, but students warn, "don't live in Assumption Hall." Students who live off campus find rent to be high and proximity to the school not always guaranteed. However, this choice is often "a nice alternative to dorm life."

Dining hall food is, for the most part, good. The vegetarian options are "getting better," and flex dollars on the meal plans allow students a bit more variety. In addition to the cafeteria, there are "a Taco Bell, a grill, and a café" on campus.

Sporting

Both the men's and women's sports teams at St. Mary's are highly respected and receive a lot of attention from the student body. The most popular team to watch is men's basketball, and last year the women's basketball team won the West Coast Conference. Club sports and intramurals are also played by many at St. Mary's, and Gaels pride is a must.

> "Students strive to do well, but it is not a competitive atmosphere."

St. Mary's is a small liberal arts college with all the benefits of a major metropolitan area. It has cross-registration programs with the University of California at Berkeley, Cal State University, Hayward, Mills College, and Holy Names College. It is also connected to the Hearst Art Gallery. The Saint Albert Hall Library is extensive for such a small college, and through the Interborrowing Library Service, any book in the bay area is at your fingertips.

St. Mary's College is a typical college in many respects. However, it may serve prospective students well to consider how they feel about the administration's Catholic influence (minor though it may be) in the school's academic and social life. Most students report being very happy at St. Mary's and profess they'd to choose it again if given the opportunity. Given the mild Bay Area weather and vibrant on-campus life, who can blame them? —*Kyla Dahlin*

FYI

The three best things about attending St. Mary's are "having professors who know your name and getting to know them on a personal basis, walking through campus and knowing most of the people you see, and the collegiate seminars."

The three worst things about attending St. Mary's are "cafeteria food, getting housing, and the fact that rumors spread so quickly."

The three things that every student should do before graduating from St. Mary's are "to paint 'SMC' on the hill, attend the Luau and Jamaica-me Crazy dances, and go to 'the Grove.'"

One thing I'd like to have known before coming here is that "class sizes aren't as small as they are advertised."

Stanford University

Address: 520 Lasuen Hall, Old Union 232, Stanford, CA 94305-3005
Phone: 650-723-2091
E-mail address: undergrad.admission@stanford.edu
Web site URL: www.stanford.edu
Location: suburban
Founded: 1867
Private or Public: private
Religious affiliation: none
Undergraduate enrollment: 6,594
Total enrollment: 14,219
Percent Male/Female: 51%/49%
Percent Minority: 44.0%

Percent African-American: 8.0%
Percent Hispanic: 11.0%
Percent Asian: 24.0%
Percent in-state/out-of-state: 44%/56%
Percent Pub HS: 65%
Fraternities: 17%
Sororities: 12%
Number of Applicants: 17,919
Percent Accepted: 15%
Percent Accepted who enroll: 65%
Entering: 1,750
Transfers: 20
Application Deadline: 15 Dec
Mean SAT: NA

Middle 50% SAT range: 670–770 V, 690–780 M
Middle 50% ACT range: 28–33
Mean ACT: NA
3 Most popular majors: biology, economics, English
Retention: 99.0%
Graduation rate: 90.0%
Library: 7,000,000 volumes
Tuition and Fees: $24,441
Room and Board: $8,030
On-campus housing: 100%
Financial aid, first-year: 39%

Stanford students can be found wearing T-shirts that read, "Harvard: the Stanford of the East." As the T-shirt attests, Stanford has long been recognized as one of the top universities in the nation, competing with Ivy League schools such as Harvard, Yale, and Princeton for top students. However, Stanford boasts California weather, a slew of nationally ranked sports teams, and a relatively low-stress environment—things no East Coast school could dream of mentioning in its glossy brochures. Students feel that because Stanford does not stand out in merely one area, it stands out even more as a whole.

Cornucopia of Academic Offerings

The Stanford academic year is divided into three 10- to 11-week quarters, followed by a summer session. A total of 180 credits are required for graduation. Most courses are worth 4 to 5 units, and students generally take 14 to 18 units (4 classes) per quarter. Stanford also has general education requirements (GERs), which students must complete. A freshman core program—either Cultures, Ideas, and Values (CIV), or Introduction

to the Humanities (I-Hum)—is required, along with courses in each of the following groups: Science, Technology, and Math; Humanities and Social Sciences; and World Culture, American Culture, and Gender Studies. In addition to the GERs, students must meet writing and foreign language requirements. Course requirements generally are not a significant problem. As according to one student, "Often many of them fit into your major or interests."

Stanford students have a reputation for being laid-back and easygoing compared to their peers at other prestigious institutions. Although students report having on average 5 to 6 hours of work every day, "whether or not it gets done depends on the weather." Perhaps because of this reputation, a student reported, "It's a big thing here to not stress about work. . . . Everyone does their work; they just do it without complaining." "Generally there isn't any homework you have to turn in, so everybody does their estimate of what they can get away with. I think we're a little bit more relaxed," says another student, though there are always people who are "really intense." While the daily workload is generally not a problem, students claim that getting As is by no means easy, especially in science classes. "I guess the stereotypical thing to say about Stanford is that even if you don't know what's going on, you can get a B," said one student, "but to get an A you really need to work hard." As a result, there is competition—"You're always fighting against a pretty tough curve"—but students are quick to add that competition takes place "anonymously" rather than on a personal level and that "it's not a competitive place." Even though getting good grades may be difficult, "No one compares GPA or rankings." Students note a heavy contrast between humanities ("fuzzy") and science ("techie") classes, in "everything from structure to time to units to grades." It is widely agreed that science and engineering courses are more time-consuming and tend to cover more material faster; another significant difference between the two groups is that science classes require more written homework, rather than just reading. "You spend more time on a 5-unit techie class than a 5-unit fuzzie class. . . . It's harder to not turn in a problem set than it is to not do your reading, so you have to keep up a lot more," said one student. As at most major universities, students can expect some crowded introductory classes. Introductory economics courses, "far and away the biggest classes on campus," usually enroll over 700 students. Fortunately, class size "gets smaller pretty quickly" in higher-level courses, which generally enroll 60 to 70 students. Seminars and the highest-level courses usually have 20 students or fewer.

Stanford's most popular majors include economics, computer science, and biology, so lectures in these subjects tend to be largest. Both professors and teaching assistants (TAs) are described by students as "very, very qualified." Opinions of the faculty are almost overwhelmingly favorable, ranging from "pretty good" to "fabulous." But some students report that the quality of teaching is "not nearly as good in the sciences as they are in the humanities." All lecturing is done by professors, and lectures are broken up into discussion sections (usually made up of about 15 students) led by TAs, who are, according to one student, "often as good as the professors."

Student-faculty relations are also reputedly good, especially for a major research university like Stanford. Professors tend to be pretty friendly and open, and "they're always there for office hours." Some students note that reaching science and engineering professors tends to require more effort, since humanities classes are often smaller. But all professors are accessible through office hours or by appointment. Dorms also periodically hold "faculty nights," when students get to invite faculty members to dinner.

Feeling Lucky for the Housing Draw?

Entering Stanford freshmen are asked to give a preference between co-ed and single-sex dorms, and between freshman, four-class housing, and the new freshman/sophomore housing. Now with the freshman/sophomore housing, freshman can bond with their classmates but get advice from upperclassmen at the same time.

> **"We have a lot of very committed athletes—and they're smart, too."**

In order to help get freshmen started on the right foot, each dorm has its own Residential Adviser (RA), who is typically "active with freshmen, and very depended upon." Residential Fellows (RFs), faculty members affiliated with the dorms ("the parents of the dorm"), are meant to "add a family feel." Some students and faculty also serve as Academic Advisors (AAs), and certain dorms have live-in tutors. "The feeling of being taken care of really helped me freshman year," said one student. Some dorms have more active staffs than others.

Students report that rooms are "decent size" but claim that housing at Stanford is better than what they hear from friends about other schools. However, the university's lottery system for placing students in housing is the subject of complaints from many seniors, who would obviously favor a room draw based on seniority rather than a mere lottery. Groups of up to 8 students each draw a number and are given priority in choosing rooms based on the results of the draw.

Dorms usually house several hundred students. Row houses, apartment-like complexes housing 50 students, are also available but very hard to get. One student complained, "It's almost impossible to get a single in a dorm, and lots of students live in one-room doubles." Whether students get the housing they want depends largely upon luck, and the students often find themselves feeling "screwed."

Dining In

Several different meal systems are available at Stanford. Students' choices depend on where they live: Some dorms offer a set number of meals per week, others give students a certain number of meal "points" to be used by the end of the quarter. Some dorms allow students to choose between meal plans. Food in the dining halls is described as "generally not too bad, but some places are better than others." Students can eat at dining halls outside of their own dorms, but because the halls often use different meal plans and all have different management, "it's not always easy to eat wherever you want."

Beautiful Campus and Surroundings

Stanford's sprawling campus features many walkways and wide-open spaces among predominantly red-roofed buildings, which were supposedly built so that the university would be visible from the air. Trees and grass can also be found everywhere. The campus is so big that most students get around on bikes. With beautiful surroundings and near-constant California sunshine, the environment is described as "amazing." According to one enthusiastic student, "[The atmosphere] is one of the reasons I came here in the first place. I can't think of anything I'd change."

Students report that there are "always quite a few things going on" on campus. Most activities are planned by student organizations, but the administration also arranges events. "We always have guest lecturers and people visiting, but a smaller group of people pay attention to those things." Common hangouts for students include the Coffee House ("CoHo") and

Tressider Student Union, a student center featuring various eateries. Also popular are Sunday night movie showings, which are always preceded by a massive, auditorium-wide paper fight. "People bring their phone books. I feel bad for whoever has to clean up afterward," said one student. Every weekend, one can find lots of campus parties. Parties organized by fraternities can be found most weekends, and dorm-organized parties are also frequent. Alcohol is "definitely there, but I wouldn't say there's more than there is anywhere else," said one student. Any drinking that goes on is usually "not too crazy." The nearby town of Palo Alto draws mixed reviews from students. The area is described as "cute," but it is agreed that Palo Alto is "not quite a college town," and that as a result, a sense of isolation is common among students. For many, there is just not enough to do. Students report taking trips to Safeway (grocery store) or the Palo Alto Shopping Center, but otherwise "there aren't many hangouts," said one student. Despite Palo Alto's limitations, one student offered, "It's a nice town to look at. There are about a million really nice restaurants, but that's about it." In general, getting around off campus requires a car, or the services of a friend with a car (reportedly, not many students drive). Visits to San Francisco (a 45-minute drive) and other nearby cities are possibilities for a weekend trip, but "when things start to get hot and heavy academically, there's not a lot of that."

Finding a Niche

Students at Stanford agree that "people here do a lot." A wide variety of activities and student groups can be found on campus; "the campus is active enough so that if there's some niche that needs to be filled, someone will come along and fill it." Likewise, Stanford is large enough for anyone to find his or her own niche. The more popular activities include the marching band and a cappella singing groups. Many students also tutor at elementary schools in disadvantaged areas. Though fraternities organize many parties, students report that the Greek system "isn't very big here." Frats tend to be more popular than sororities, but neither have a large influence on social life. Stanford sports, on the other hand, command the attention of not only students but also that of sports fans all over the country. Stanford's varsity sports teams, among the best in the nation, get a lot of support from the student body. This winter alone, many a Stanford student could be found rooting for the home team as Stanford played Wisconsin in the annual Rose Bowl, and the school's winning basketball team is a perennial heavyweight in the NCAA Tournament. "We have a lot of very committed athletes—and they're smart, too," said one student, who also estimated that half of the *Stanford Daily* is taken up by the sports section. Intramural sports are also very popular, but the emphasis in IM sports is more on having fun than on winning. Even with the more popular sports, students say that Stanford is "still a very academic place." Because Stanford is so good in every area, students have trouble deciding which aspect of Stanford is their favorite. "It's hard to say — it really is all things to all people." However, students are proud that "people definitely seem more laid-back here" than at other top universities. Although the school is without a doubt one of the best academic institutions anywhere, it is ultimately this sense of balance that makes Stanford "a good place to live, as well as a great place to learn." —*Chiansan Ma*

FYI

The three best things about attending Stanford are "the weather, the beautiful campus, and the Rose Bowl."

The three worst things about attending Stanford are "the hard course loads, the housing lottery draw, and Palo Alto is boring."

The three things every student should do before graduating from Stanford are "attend the Rose Bowl and cheer for Stanford, play frisbee golf, and listen to a band in the CoHo."

One thing I'd like to have known before coming here is "how much Palo Alto is not a college town."

University of California System

The schools comprising the University of California System are renowned as some of the top research and academic institutions in the world. Since the founding of the first school in Berkeley in 1868, the UC schools have produced over 20 Nobel Prize winners. Currently, the system spans the entire state with universities in Berkeley, Davis, Irvine, Los Angeles, Riverside, San Diego, Santa Barbara, and Santa Cruz, and one medical school in San Francisco. Each of the eight undergraduate institutions receives a large number of applications from all over the nation and competition to enroll is high.

Distinctive Campuses

The foremost determining factor for many applicants is the location and climate of the schools. UCLA and Berkeley are in urban settings and offer the exciting bustle and sophistication of cities. San Diego, Irvine, Santa Barbara, and Santa Cruz are near beaches, settings that tend to lull their respective students to take a day off to surf or sunbathe. Davis and Riverside are in more secluded rural areas, surrounded by the tranquil outdoors. Perhaps because their urban atmospheres appeal to more people, LA and Berkeley tend to have the most applicants and most competitive admissions process. Academically, all eight schools are top-notch and were recently recognized by *U.S. News & World Report* as some of the best schools in both the national public universities category as well as the national universities category.

Fall of Affirmative Action

With the recent fall of affirmative action in California, a casualty of Proposition 209, the demographic shift in the student body of the UC schools was dramatic. At UCLA and Berkeley, the Asian-American population has skyrocketed to the mid-40 percent range, while African-American and Hispanic acceptance rates have suffered. In addition to the lower acceptance rates, many African-Americans and Hispanics who were accepted have declined admission in favor of more "minority-friendly" campuses with higher African-American and Hispanic enrollment. Many students have noticed that with this change has come greater self-enforced segregation among the student body. The future ramifications of this decision are still hard to foresee, but as of now, California has become the testing ground for a non-affirmative action educational policy.

Why Attend a UC School?

Despite the recent admissions changes and financial hardships, the hard fact is that the UC System provides a great education at a comparably cheap price. The tuition for an in-state resident is six times less than tuition at an Ivy League college, and out-of-state students still pay half what they would at a similar private college. With the warm and temperate California weather, it is no wonder that students from all over the U.S. and the world choose one of the UC System universities to spend four blissful years.
—*Seung Lee*

University of California / Berkeley

Address: Office of Undergraduate Admission and Relations, 110 Sproul Hall #5800, Berkeley, CA 94720-5800
Phone: 510-642-3175
E-mail address: ouras@uclink.berkeley.edu
Web site URL: www.berkeley.edu
Location: urban
Founded: 1926
Private or Public: public
Religious affiliation: none
Undergraduate enrollment: 22,261
Total enrollment: 30,290
Percent Male/Female: 50%/50%

Percent Minority: 60.0%
Percent African-American: 5.0%
Percent Hispanic: 12.0%
Percent Asian: 41.0%
Percent in-state/out-of-state: 89%/11%
Percent Pub HS: 84%
Fraternities: 10%
Sororities: 10%
Number of Applicants: 30,042
Percent Accepted: 28%
Percent Accepted who enroll: 44%
Entering: 3,570
Transfers: NA
Application Deadline: 30 Nov
Mean SAT: 655 V, 685 M

Middle 50% SAT range: 580–610 V, 620–730 M
Middle 50% ACT range: NA
Mean ACT: NA
3 Most popular majors: molecular/cell biology, English, psychology
Retention: 93.0%
Graduation rate: 77% (within 5 years)
Library: 8,500,000 volumes
Tuition and Fees: $4,184 in; $13,568 out
Room and Board: $8,122
On-campus housing: NA
Financial aid, first-year: 73%

Considered by many to be the best school in the University of California system, and ranked this year by *U.S. News & World Report* as the best public university in the country, UC Berkeley is an outstanding institution of higher learning. It has one of the highest percentages of Nobel laureates per capita in the world, over 20 Medals of Science, and 16 discovered elements to prove it too! Students are extremely proud of their school (affectionately called "Cal"), professors, and their first-rate education. Despite recent budgetary cuts, libraries and research facilities remain top-notch.

Large-Scale Academics

Berkeley is a huge school with over 20,000 students divided among several academic colleges. 17,000 of these students are in the College of Letters and Science. According to one student, "this makes it easier to get lost than at most schools, and you need to take the initiative in most situations and go after what you want." Students self-register for classes via the Telebears telephone process, and some complain that classes fill up before their assigned call-in time (freshmen and seniors usually get assigned earlier times than other students). Also, students who do not plan ahead may find it difficult to fulfill the extensive requirements necessary to graduate in four years. Students generally agree, however, that if you're aggressive and pushy, you can get what you want.

Introductory lectures can enroll upward of 1,000 students (excluding languages, which limit class size to 15) and are often co-taught by TAs, whom most students describe as "very competent and qualified—it's great to have a casual supplement to the professor," although there's "a small lake" of small upper-level seminars. The most popular majors are English, molecular and cell biology, and psychology. Other praised departments include political science, engineering, and history. Students describe academics at Berkeley as "hard, just plain hard—getting straight A's throughout high school doesn't mean a thing here. You can't get by with just kissing up to your professors, doing your busywork, and talking a lot in class." Science classes are reportedly among the hardest, and "it seems like half the people coming in pre-med give up by junior year."

Take Off That Red Shirt

Sports are very popular at Cal, and the school's mascot, the Golden Bear, "is the most loved creature on campus." Students report that the biggest game of the year by far is the Berkeley-Stanford football game. Months before this "contest for the Axe," students start chanting "take off that red shirt" (their archrival's school color), and "the festivities go on before, during, and long after the game, no matter

who wins." Those who don't "take off their red shirts" at the game can expect to get picked up and tossed around the stands "in a display that's wilder than any mosh pit." Men's crew and basketball are also popular and well attended, as are many women's sports such as volleyball and soccer. There's no shortage of athletic facilities, and almost everyone gets involved in intramural or club sports.

Extracurricular activities abound at Cal, from publications such as the *Daily Cal* and the humorous *Heuristic Squelch* to numerous political organizations, religious groups, public service organizations, and performance groups. One student observed, "It's almost impossible to find someone here who's not involved in something."

Many agree, however, that no single extracurricular stands out above the rest, and "everything has a place at Cal." Berkeley is well-known for its diversity, and ethnic studies is a popular major. The school is politically liberal with "a touch of '60s radicalism," although "absolutely every group, denomination, or sub-culture is represented."

The social life at Cal revolves around Greek organizations. Although some say this fosters social segregation, it allows students to form a small, intimate group of friends within such a large school. Although Berkeley is officially a drug-free campus, "drinking is one of the most popular social activities, and smoking pot is a close second." Apart from frat and sorority parties, "almost everyone takes advantage of the bars, clubs, restaurants, cafes, and bookstores in the city of Berkeley." If that's not enough, San Francisco is a 20-minute car ride away, and the northern California coast is very accessible through public transportation.

Dorms and Dining

Housing at Berkeley is guaranteed for all freshmen who turn in their forms and deposits on time. However, because the entering freshman class has increased in size last year, the school "had to convert some of the lounges into rooms and cram more people into the regular rooms." High-rise units One, Two, and Three consist mostly of double rooms on coed floors. This housing, located on the central campus, is considered the most social. Clark Kerr, Bowles, Foothill, and Stern are "newer, quieter, more comfortable, farther from everything, and more expensive" according to residents; Bowles and Stern are also single-sex, composed of all men and all women, respectively. These four dorms have mostly suites of 7 to 20 people. Students complain that going to and from classes is an "uphill-both-ways struggle." After freshman year, students can choose alternatives to dorm life, and live instead in fraternity and sorority houses, off-campus apartments (although inexpensive ones close to campus are rare), international, language, and cultural houses, or student-run co-ops.

Over the last couple of years, Berkeley has taken several measures to improve campus safety. The administration has increased outdoor lighting, as well as the number and visibility of security guards, installed emergency phones, and now provides a nighttime student escort service. If that doesn't make you feel safe enough, there is also a UC SWAT team and bomb squad.

Students who live on campus are required to buy a meal plan, and each dorm has its own cafeteria. Students can choose a plan of 10, 14, or 19 meals per week, but "most people here go with 14.

This gives you a good combo of cafeteria and restaurant variation," one student reported. When cafeteria food gets "repetitive, stale, and boring" despite the variety and the cereal, salad, and pasta bar options, students go to several eateries/student lounges around campus to satisfy their hunger. Many of these are located on "Gourmet Ghetto," which is open almost around the clock.

> "Everything here is fast-paced, hectic, fun, strenuous, sexy, or disordered."

Berkeley is "a serene, peaceful, and tree-covered campus where everything from the neo-classical/modern architecture to Strawberry Creek to the clock tower is conducive to learning." Another student had a different perspective: "Everything here is fast-paced, hectic, fun, strenuous, sexy, or disordered." At such a large and diverse institution, it takes initiative and action to create the ideal college experience, and expectations vary drastically from one student to the next. One student summed up UC Berkeley by saying, "I love it here, and I couldn't see myself anywhere else."
—*Chiansan Ma and Staff*

FYI

The three best things about attending UC Berkeley are "location (close to SF, transportation, nature), the big, beautiful campus, and food (name an ethnicity and you'll find it)."

The three worst things about attending UC Berkeley are "the price of the dorms, some classes are huge, and the administration."

The three things that every student should do before graduating from UC Berkeley are "live in a coop, take a class about something controversial, and go up to the top of the Campinille for the noon Carrillon concert (bring earplugs)."

One thing I would like to have known before coming here is "one has to have an active role in his/her education. Go to a professor's office hours to get help when you need it! Don't be shy."

University of California / Davis

Address: Admissions Office, University of California/Davis, Davis, CA 95616-8678
Phone: 530-752-2971
E-mail address: thinkucd@ucdavis.edu
Web site URL: www.ucdavis.edu
Location: suburban
Founded: 1863
Private or Public: public
Religious affiliation: none
Undergraduate enrollment: 19,403
Total enrollment: 23,092
Percent Male/Female: 45%/55%

Percent Minority: 41.0%
Percent African-American: 3.0%
Percent Hispanic: 1.0%
Percent Asian: 35%
Percent in-state/out-of-state: 97%/3%
Percent Pub HS: 85%
Fraternities: 10%
Sororities: 10%
Number of Applicants: 20,744
Percent Accepted: 66%
Percent Accepted who enroll: 26%
Entering: 3,287
Transfers: NA
Application Deadline: 20 Oct

Mean SAT: 556 V, 593 M
Middle 50% SAT range: 500–620 V, 520–650 M
Middle 50% ACT range: NA
Mean ACT: NA
3 Most popular majors: biological sciences, psychology, engineering
Retention: NA
Graduation rate: 77.0%
Library: NA
Tuition and Fees: $4,311 in; $13,596 out
Room and Board: $5,946
On-campus housing: 65%
Financial aid, first-year: NA

The University of California at Davis is not known for its great snowboarding conditions, and for good reason. "This place is flat," remarked a senior. "There are maybe two hills in the whole campus, and we're talking gentle slopes." Combined with the beautiful weather that characterizes northern California, would-be pro boarders may want to look elsewhere for a training ground. On the upside, the even landscape and balmy weather make UC Davis a haven for bikers. Up to 18,000 bike riders a day can be found on the campus's elaborate system of bike paths and circles, causing a student to remark that "we've got to have the most bikes per capita of any school. You don't need a car here, but I've got to have my bike."

Although it was founded as the agricultural counterpart to UC Berkeley, Davis's academics are no longer centered on agricultural programs. Its biology and organic chemistry departments are acclaimed, and the College of Engineering is also nationally ranked. The humanities and social science departments are gaining ground with the natural sciences, and are considered on par with other schools in the UC system.

Plenty of People

UC Davis's undergraduate college consists of four academic divisions: the College of Agricultural and Environmental Sciences (24 percent of undergrads), College of Engineering (14 percent), College of Letters and Sciences (43 percent), and Division of Biological Sciences (19 percent). With 5,200 acres, Davis is the largest of the nine UC campuses in area, and more than fills up the space with its 19,403 undergrads. Not surprisingly, classes are generally large, with some introductory classes—most notably math and chemistry—attracting crowds of up to 400 students.

While some classes are lauded, one student thought that her professors "are not as enthusiastic as they should be." Most students feel that the large class size is a big drawback. Another minus is that students usually only have access to their teaching assistants instead of the professors themselves. Most professors seemed interested in a chance to meet more students, but the large classes really require the students to be motivated and seek professors out. TAs lead weekly discussion sections in which students can more freely voice their opinion and supplement the material covered in lecture. Students find these sections useful, and a junior commented that despite the class size, "they really encourage you to do well here."

Students must accumulate 180 units in order to graduate, but "you can pass the requirements without realizing it. Just sign up for all the classes you like." Registering, which is done over the phone, can prove frustrating for most, and can bar lazy students from required classes. Scheduling preferences are given to upperclassmen and varsity athletes, although most students felt that you could usually get into a class you want with effort. Lucky students who get into Professor Donneley's chemistry class can learn about the oxidization of zinc in the presence of peroxide from the inventor of Sex Wax himself.

UC Davis runs on the 10-week quarter system, which makes for intense instruction over a relatively short time. This system draws some complaints in terms of vacation schedules because students find themselves "out of sync with friends from back home." Most students believe that grading is fair, but one commented that "you have to be really pro-active to get the most out of class."

Living in the Lap of Luxury

Although most students move off campus their second year, the recently renovated residences received rave reviews. Many suites have their own bathrooms and a living room, with each dorm generally holding about 200 students. Residential advisors do live with the freshmen, but are reportedly easygoing. According to one junior, "RAs are a joke really, as long as you figure out how to deal with them." Tercero is generally regarded as the worst dorm due to its proximity to the dairy and the odoriferous emanations of the bovine inhabitants, while Quarto is known as the party dorm. Upperclassmen usually live in apartments or houses nearby, which are "cheap, but hard to find."

For those with cars and energy, weekends are a cue to head to nearby Sacramento for clubbing and good food. Students who choose to stay on campus usually find some parties. While frats do exist at UC Davis, they hardly dominate the party scene. "I went to frat parties when I was a freshman and wanted to meet people, but now I just go to house parties," remarked a sophomore. "Actually, I wish people would party a little more here; it feels like it's the same group of people partying all the time." UC Davis also tries to entertain the students on an alcohol-free level. One such event consists of a get-together with a giant bonfire. Another campus-wide event is the Pajamarama, an annual late-night affair when the students go down to the train station to welcome returning alumni.

Several renowned speakers have visited Davis recently; Maya Angelou came in 1997, and Wavy Gravy, the MC for Woodstock, spoke in 1998. A freshman felt that UC Davis "has every single possible thing that you can think of," but a junior wished that "there could be more to do, but that's Davis." Some students also wish that there was a little more diversity at school. As a junior remarked, "This place isn't exactly a melting pot."

Satisfying the Munchies

University dining hall food is rarely renowned, but a junior admits that while "I wouldn't say it's excellent, I survive." A freshman commented that "if you think about it, you won't eat," while a sophomore said, "It started off good, but then I got really sick of it." The dining halls serve hot entrees, stock salad bars, and cater to both vegetarian and vegan needs. After freshman year, students are not required to purchase the meal plan, and usually eat out or cook for themselves. There is a plethora of restaurants in Davis, and one sophomore swore that "Davis must have the most Chinese restaurants in the world! Well, maybe other than China." Nearby Woodstock's pizza and trips to restaurants in Sacramento are highly recommended.

Intense Sports

The fabulous weather and open town setting offers students plenty of ways to burn off those Mu Shu Pork–induced pounds. "Sports are huge here," commented one freshman. "There are a ton of pickup sports," said a junior. "People are always outside playing soccer or something." However, those who opt to exercise on their own in the gym may be disappointed because, according to one junior, "the gym sucks." Luckily, renovations are currently under way. Although UC Davis doesn't offer athletic scholarships, the varsity sports program has done extremely well in NCAA Division II. The men's basketball team has recently been making yearly trips to the national championship, which they have also won, and the football and volleyball teams are competitive as well. A big draw for students is the annual Causeway Classic football game against regional rival Sacramento State University. The sports teams are supported by the largest student cheer organization in the country: the Aggiepack. Renowned for bringing school spirit to an incredible high, "they catapult food and shirts and stuff into the crowd. They really get the crowd going; it's awesome."

Small-Town Magic

Students make up about half the population of Davis, which gives the area a distinctive small-town flavor. As a result, Davis students have the same advantages and disadvantages that come with all small towns. Davis provides a peaceful and friendly environment, but it lacks things to do. There are farms around the campus, with plenty of field space and livestock. There is reportedly very little crime and one student admits, "I never lock my door. I don't need to." Bike theft is common, though. One senior felt restricted by Davis, and said, "I wish there was more activity. It's always the same." Regardless, most students agreed that there is usually more than enough to keep them busy on campus.

> "Lucky students who get into Professor Donneley's chemistry class can learn about the oxidization of zinc in the presence of peroxide from the inventor of Sex Wax himself."

All in all, UC Davis offers a comprehensive liberal education in a tightly knit small-town environment. If you don't mind leaving the snowboard at home and smelling a cow here and there, you can be rest assured that four years in Davis will leave you in great shape, both physically and intellectually. —*Matt Stewart*

FYI
The three best things about attending UC Davis are "the close-knit student community, the casual, popular sports scene, and the fabulous weather."
The three worst things about attending UC Davis are "the quarter system, overcrowded classes, and the annoying registration system."
The three things that every student should do before graduating UC Davis are "going to the Causeway Classic football game, making time to explore nearby Sacramento, and spending a night taste-testing at Davis' plethora of Chinese restaurants."
One thing I'd like to have known before coming here is "that a bike is necessary for survival, and so is a tolerance for the perfume of cows."

University of California / Irvine

Address: Office of Admissions, 204 Administration Building, Irvine, CA 92697-1075
Phone: 949-824-6703
E-mail address: oars@uci.edu
Web site URL: www.uci.edu
Location: suburban
Founded: 1885
Private or Public: public
Religious affiliation: none
Undergraduate enrollment: 14,400
Total enrollment: 16,129
Percent Male/Female: 47%/53%
Percent Minority: 72.0%

Percent African-American: 2.0%
Percent Hispanic: 11.0%
Percent Asian: 57.0%
Percent in-state/out-of-state: 99%/1%
Percent Pub HS: 88%
Fraternities: 1%
Sororities: 2%
Number of Applicants: 19,490
Percent Accepted: 63%
Percent Accepted who enroll: 25%
Entering: 2,781
Transfers: NA
Application Deadline: rolling

Mean SAT: NA
Middle 50% SAT range: NA
Middle 50% ACT range: NA
Mean ACT: NA
3 Most popular majors: biological sciences, economics, psychology
Retention: NA
Graduation rate: 36.0%
Library: 1,500,000 volumes
Tuition and Fees: $4,049 in; $9,384 out
Room and Board: $5,233
On-campus housing: 50%
Financial aid, first-year: 61%

A tiger strikes fear into its opponents and a lion roars to victory, but an anteater . . . eats its opponents like ants? While students at UC Irvine have ambivalent feelings about their anteater mascot, they are positively pleased with their choice of university. Located in the city of Irvine and just minutes from the beach, UCI boasts a diverse student body, a modern, beautiful campus, and nationally recognized academic departments.

Broad Academic Offerings

UCI has a lot of classes to offer its students. While academics are considered intense, students are happy with the diverse course offerings at UC Irvine. In addition to the large number of students majoring in biology, UCI offers majors in seven schools: Engineering, Social Ecology, Art, Humanities, Physical Sciences, Biological Sciences, and Social Sciences. UC Irvine is on the ten-week quarter system, and the first thing students mention when you ask them about their courses is the heavy workload. General education requirements (or "breadth requirements" as students call them) are extensive and varied, and include competence in a foreign language, three natural science courses, and

three writing courses. While some complained about the hassle of the requirements, they were quick to mention "cool and interesting" classes such as Greek literature and the history of jazz.

Students need 180 credits to graduate, and most undergrads take three to four classes a quarter. Some mentioned difficulties enrolling in classes at times, and anticipated taking five years to graduate. UCI is a huge public university with an undergraduate enrollment of over 12,000 students, and class size can often reach "intimidating proportions." Introductory courses often enroll about 400 students, though discussion sections with only about 15 to 20 students provide a more interactive atmosphere.

Extensive Facilities and UCI Spirit

UCI boasts a huge student center, with a great food court, an auditorium, and a music store. It is described as a center for student activity, and club meetings and casual gatherings often take place there. The Bren Center is a sports complex that houses popular basketball games and concerts throughout the year. Various bands have played at UCI, including Sarah

Maclachlan and Lisa Loeb. Students majoring in performing arts show off their talent at the Barcley Center.

Various religious organizations, community service programs, and clubs also give students something to do besides studying. Yet, though there are many extracurricular activities, UCI does not have a football team, which one student feels might bring out more school spirit. Football fans usually root for other schools, such as UCLA or USC. While Thursdays are "spirit days" on which students wear UCI paraphernalia, not many students adhere to this "tradition."

Picturesque Campus Close to the Beach

UCI is a modern campus in a suburban area close to Newport Beach and Costa Mesa, two very popular hangouts. It is a relatively new university, which accounts for its popular modernity. One student described it as "picturesque and pleasing to the eye." Tree-lined drives and green grass abound, and California's pleasant year-round climate enhances UCI's allure. Students reported feeling safe and happy with the quality of life.

Freshmen are guaranteed housing, and in their subsequent years usually seek off-campus housing in apartments and homes in town, which are plentiful. Two housing complexes called Mesa Court and Middle Earth are freshman residences, each accommodating about 1,200 students. There are two main dining halls, which students feel are not bad at all, although one student cautioned, "Keep away from the pasta sauces." A fairly large portion of the student body commutes, and as a result "parking can be a hassle at times."

Party on the Weekdays, Go Home on the Weekends

Students describe Irvine as boring, but say that the surrounding cities more than compensate. Partying starts as early as Wednesday night, as students head to clubs or the Irvine Spectrum, a huge complex with a movie theater, restaurants, and shops. There are plenty of places to shop and many head over to South Coast Plaza, one of the largest shopping malls in the United States, only a few minutes away. Since home for many students is really close, many head home for the weekend.

For those living in the dorms, the semi-annual formal is an opportunity to get dressed up and dance the night away. There are many parties in off-campus apartments, and students find that they can be great places to meet people. One undergrad felt that "being at such a huge school can be so alienating, but if you make an effort, it's not hard to get to know people." Alcohol is easy to get, but there isn't much pressure to drink. "You do your own thing. It's all good even if you don't drink," said a sophomore.

One student mentioned that besides L.A. or Newport Beach, the Greek scene is a good alternative. While the percentage of students involved in the Greek system is relatively small, fraternity and sorority mixers are cited as the places to go for parties. Thursday and Friday nights are party nights, and fraternities and sororities provide the alcohol. But there is very little pressure to participate in the Greek system, and ethnic fraternities and sororities are also options.

> **"At times life at UCI can seem like a fashion show."**

According to one student, "At times life at UCI can seem like a fashion show." Some students get really dressed up for class, and designer names are popular. Flashy cars are known in the parking lots, and many of them are "fixed up and lowered to the ground with great sound systems." However, many students don't feel a pressure to conform to this "fashion show," because they can easily blend into the large student body. A student explained, "Cars aren't necessary, since so many friends have one and you can always bum a ride off them."

Unlike some of the students' cars, UCI is not all show. Its excellent academics earn UCI recognition as one of the top public universities in the nation. Though UCI has a few disgruntled football fans, its vast resources and opportunities make it an easy choice for many students.
—*Sathya Oum*

FYI

The three best things about UCI are "the charming campus with good facilities, the proximity to L.A. and Newport Beach, and the great social scene during the week."

The three worst things about UCI are "Irvine, the intimidating class sizes, and the heavy workload due to the quarter system."

The three things that every student should do before graduating UCI are "move off campus—*fast*, ditch a day of classes and head to the beach, and go to a great concert at the Bren Center."

One thing I'd like to have known before coming here is "I would need a model's wardrobe and a car to match."

University of California / Los Angeles

Address: 405 Hilgard Avenue, Los Angeles, CA 90095

Phone: 310-825-3101

E-mail address: ugadm@saonnet.ucla.edu

Web site URL: www.saonet.ucla.edu/uars.htm

Location: urban

Founded: 1919

Private or Public: public

Religious affiliation: none

Undergraduate enrollment: 24,668

Total enrollment: 36,351

Percent Male/Female: 45%/55%

Percent Minority: 60.2%

Percent African-American: 4.9%

Percent Hispanic: 15.0%

Percent Asian: 38.0%

Percent in-state/out-of-state: 94%/6%

Percent Pub HS: 79%

Fraternities: 11%

Sororities: 9%

Number of Applicants: 35,681

Percent Accepted: 29%

Percent Accepted who enroll: 40%

Entering: 4,131

Transfers: 2249

Application Deadline: 30 Nov

Mean SAT: 620 V, 655 M

Middle 50% SAT range: 610–660 V, 650–700 M

Middle 50% ACT range: NA

Mean ACT: 26

3 Most popular majors: psychology, economics, political science

Retention: 97.0%

Graduation rate: 79.0%

Library: 7,401,780 volumes

Tuition and Fees: $3,698 in; $13,872 out

Room and Board: $7,692

On-campus housing: 85%

Financial aid, first-year: NA

Surrounded by the Santa Monica mountains and exclusive neighborhoods of Beverly Hills and Bel Air, it's easy to see why UCLA is one of the most popular UC schools. But don't let the ideal location fool you. UCLA is one of the most academically elite universities in America, its location being only one of its many enviable qualities.

Solid Academics

Although a relatively young university, UCLA has established a strong academic reputation firmly rooted in a commitment to undergraduates. "Even though some of my classes were quite large, the professors always advertised office hours where I routinely went to ask questions and really got to know the professor," one student said. Professors teach all of the lecture classes at UCLA, with TAs leading many of the discussion sessions. "The TAs were an invaluable source of information for me. Without their help, I quite honestly don't know how I would have survived!" another student said.

Many introductory math and science classes enroll up to 300 students. However, upper-level courses are much smaller. Students in introductory humanities courses report classes of as few as 20 students. Like many other schools in California, UCLA is on a modified-quarter system with three 10-week periods. This system accelerates the pace of learning: During a typical year, students take three sets of courses instead of the usual two. Students complain that one disadvantage of the quarter system is having to take midterms every few weeks. However, most students find the system manageable, even if they are not overly enthusiastic about it.

UCLA has a general education (GE) requirement that includes classes in a variety of departments. The College of Arts and Sciences requires undergrads to choose from an extensive list of classes in the humanities, social sciences, life sciences, physical sciences, and foreign languages, while the School of Engineering requires only seven humanities courses. Some GE requirements can be met with advanced placement credits earned in high school.

Choosing a major at UCLA can be a relatively complex procedure. Students must apply to a major upon completion of their prerequisites, and admission to many programs such as business economics or engineering is highly competitive. Undergraduates report that biology, engineering, economics, business economics, and chemistry are among the most popular majors and best departments. One student complained, "Everyone is a bio major," and many among them hope to enter the esteemed UCLA medical school.

Students rate the library system at UCLA very highly. Powell Library is the main campus library, and serves as mainly as a study center. Undergraduates report that they also study outside in the sun, in dorm study rooms, and in campus restaurants. Research is primarily done in the University Research Library and various graduate school libraries around campus.

Off Campus or On?

UCLA has many different housing options. Four high-rise dorms offer a social atmosphere to their primarily underclassmen tenants. Upperclassmen tend to choose to live in apartment-like, university-owned buildings. Students report that these accommodations, such as Sunset Village, provide more luxury in a "hotel-like" atmosphere that includes picnic and volleyball areas. Students report that while these apartments are quite social and friendly, they are nothing compared to the "roar and mania" of the freshman high-rises. Many students also choose to live off-campus, though students often travel to the neighboring towns of Santa Monica, Culver City, and Westwood to find affordable apartments. Many students do have cars despite the university-wide shortage of parking spaces.

Students rate the food at UCLA with great enthusiasm. Ackerman Union, the main student building, serves regular cafeteria-style meals, and is also home to Taco Bell and many similar restaurants that are part of the meal plan. Students can choose between plans of 11, 15, or 19 meals a week.

Far and Away

The campus is divided into North Campus, where the majority of humanities classes are held, and South Campus, where the math and science courses take place. Though UCLA tries hard to keep its buildings on campus, its huge size often defeats this goal. Students say that aside from the occasional rickety classroom, the university is doing a good job maintaining and upgrading the campus facilities.

Security is a main priority of the university, and the campus is "unquestionably safe even in the wee hours of the morning." Blue-light emergency phones and security escorts are easily available.

Students report great ethnic diversity at UCLA, although some claim that the diversity is misleading. Students from similar ethnic backgrounds tend to self-segregate, creating an uneasy tension between groups. Students are quick to point out, somewhat defensively, that this is true everywhere, and that race issues at UCLA are probably better than at most universities.

Divided Social Life

The social life at UCLA is often divided between those who live on campus and those who live off. Fraternity parties are the main attraction on campus, with frequent dorm and campus-wide parties drawing students as well. Students with cars often leave campus for the weekend to go home or visit friends; they also take advantage of nearby Los Angeles. Located just minutes away from the clubs of Sunset Boulevard and the beaches of Santa Monica, students rarely have trouble finding weekend entertainment.

Recently, *Sports Illustrated* rated UCLA the number one "jock school" in the nation. This distinction is well deserved. The enormous John Wooden Recreation Center provides all students the opportunity to sweat off those hours spent in the library. Intramural sports are also incredibly popular, and team spirit is high. In recent years, the varsity basketball, gymnastics, volleyball, and tennis teams have had huge national success. The football team is also highly supported and the rivalry between UCLA and the University of Southern California peaks each year when the football teams battle it out on the gridiron, often with both conference title and bowl game hopes at stake.

> **Students complain that one disadvantage to a quarter system is having to take midterms every few weeks.**

UCLA has much to offer its students. Along with its vast resources as a major university and its relatively low costs, UCLA provides an exceptional education with a spirited student body. With its enviable weather and superior education, students say it is no wonder that UCLA has few competitors. —*Sathya Oum and Staff*

FYI

The three best things about attending UCLA are "sunny weather, Los Angeles, and the diversity of the student body."

The three worst things about attending UCLA are "Los Angeles, huge lecture classes, bureaucracy."

The three things every student should do before graduating from UCLA are "go to a Bruins game, hang out on the beach, and party at Mardi Gras."

One thing I'd like to have known before coming here is "how dificult sciences classes would be."

University of California / Riverside

Address: 1120 Hinderaker Hall, Riverside, CA 92521
Phone: 909-787-4531
E-mail address: discover@pop.ucr.edu
Web site URL: www.ucr.edu
Location: suburban
Founded: 1905
Private or Public: public
Religious affiliation: none
Undergraduate enrollment: 9,130
Total enrollment: 9,898
Percent Male/Female: 47%/53%
Percent Minority: 69.0%
Percent African-American: 5.0%

Percent Hispanic: 21.0%
Percent Asian: 41.0%
Percent in-state/out-of-state: 98%/2%
Percent Pub HS: 86%
Fraternities: 12%
Sororities: 13%
Number of Applicants: 12,030
Percent Accepted: 80%
Percent Accepted who enroll: 24%
Entering: 2,145
Transfers: NA
Application Deadline: 30 Nov
Mean SAT: 512 V, 554 M

Middle 50% SAT range: 450–570 V, 490–620 M
Middle 50% ACT range: NA
Mean ACT: NA
3 Most popular majors: biology, psychology, business administration
Retention: 86.0%
Graduation rate: 43.0%
Library: 1,800,000 volumes
Tuition and Fees: $8,120 in; $13,510 out
Room and Board: $6,579
On-campus housing: 60%
Financial aid, first-year: NA

UC Riverside has an unfortunate reputation as a safety school for the more popular UCLA and Berkeley. However, its newness and smaller size offers its own charms to its students. The quiet town of Riverside affords the students a tranquil academic atmosphere, and as the school is a major research center, Riverside's undergraduate population is given great opportunities to participate in research activities.

"Boonie-hill"

Students characterize the town of Riverside, located east of downtown L.A., as "Boonie-hill." Even with grass and mountains in the background, the town inherits the smoggy air characteristic of L.A., but not the bustling urbanity. As one student reported, "It wouldn't be considered desolate, but it's definitely a lot quieter than parts of L.A. just 30 minutes away."

To date, UCR remains one of the smallest UCs; a five- to ten-minute minute walk is all it takes to walk from one edge of campus to the other. The architectural design of the campus is distinguished by its lack of uniformity. According to several students, there seems to be no underlying theme that connects the modern buildings. UCR is continually upgrading its campus, renovating its current buildings as well as constructing new ones. One of the three dorm buildings was recently refurbished, and others are continually being renovated. The improvements to the dorms have been met with great enthusiasm among the students. As one student said, "There's new carpeting, and the AC and heating can now be adjusted within each room. There's more than enough space—as long as your roommate isn't too messy." The majority of the dorms are doubles, but some residents have singles or triples. There are no suite arrangements. While the majority of freshmen live in the dorms, on-campus housing is not required, even for freshmen. Some students choose to live in apartments on- or off-campus, or in one of the many fraternity houses.

Studying Made Possible

With reportedly few attractions in the immediate area, "Riverside is a school where you can study because, well, there's not much else to do." One heralded aspect of UCR is the Biomed Program, a joint association with UCLA Medical School. Twenty-five spots are made available in UCLA Med each year for graduates of the program. Competition for these spots is fierce, and students often gripe about the curve being set by "those overachievers in the Biomed program." The most popular majors at UCR are business, engineering, and the natural sciences. As one senior noted, "I haven't met that many people in the humanities, but I am sure there are some out there." UCR expanded its science programs by building a new Science Library, which was completed in fall 1998.

With many classes being held in large lecture halls, a common complaint is the size of classes, particularly in the large introductory courses required for specific majors. Capping enrollment frustrates those who cannot get in, and prevents the professor from "giving us some individual attention." These classes, even when broken into discussion sections, often have 15 to 40 people. One student stated, "I wish that they would open up more sections of major impact classes. Course selection is done on the phone by appointment, and it sucks to be late."

It Can Get Pretty Gross

Food receives mixed reviews from students. Some indicate that food on-campus is "actually not that bad," while others state that "the slop we're served in the dorm dining halls is awful." Another student noted that "food here can get pretty gross." Not only does UCR offer dining hall facilities, but it also makes food stands available around campus that offer hamburgers, beef bowls, and other fast-food items. Those who choose to eat off campus find that the main road through Riverside also offers eateries including Baker's, Church's Chicken, and the Spaghetti Factory.

Night Life

While frats are popular, the Greek scene does not dominate campus activities. Rather, many students indicate that student organizations thrive alongside them. "There are a good deal of frats around, but there are also a lot of clubs where we hang out on weekends." Though frat parties are often exclusive, there are many dances open to the entire student body. There is also a UCR movie night once a week that is popular with students. Beyond that, however, students complain that they are left to find their own entertainment. Downtown Riverside is 5 to 10 minutes away, but few undergrads have cars, and those who do often "don't want to risk losing their parking spaces. So we're left to find another way to get off campus." With a social scene that sometimes lags on campus, some students argue, "Come on. It's L.A. There's always something to do; you just have to look around and deal."

> With a social scene that sometimes lags on campus, some students argue, "Come on. It's L.A. There's always something to do; you just have to look around and deal."

Sagging Spirit

Sports do not muster much school sprit at UCR, a Division II school. On the whole, students are reportedly "apathetic and saggy" about their teams. As one student stated, "Really, are we known for any sports at all? No, we're just known for the Biomed Program." While students do not appear to rally behind their teams, involvement in sports certainly exists. Intramural sports are particularly popular as friends sign up to form teams and play "for the sheer fun of it—you can't study all the time because it wears you down after a while."

Though the university is somewhat isolated from the heart of Los Angeles, many students praise UCR for enabling them to work in a much more "tranquil environment." Students often forget that UCR wasn't their first choice because of all that UCR has to offer. Its proximity to L.A. and its quiet setting allows students to concentrate on studying during the weekday and have fun during the weekends. If a good education is more important to you than bragging rights, UCR isn't a bad choice at all. —*Seung Lee and Staff*

FYI
The three best things about attending UCR are "the great faculty, its great location, and a very flexible program."
The three worst things about attending UCR are "the isolated campus, lack of sports, and self-segregated student body."
The three things that every student should do before graduating from UCR are "make use of the resources at UCLA, go celebrity sighting, and go to nearby national parks."
One thing I'd like to have known before coming here is "how homogeneous the student body is because most come from California."

University of California/ San Diego

Address: 9500 Gilman Drive, La Jolla, CA 92093-0337
Phone: 619-534-4831
E-mail address: admissionsinfo@ucsd.edu
Web site URL: www.admissions.ucsd.edu
Location: urban
Founded: 1965
Private or Public: public
Religious affiliation: none
Undergraduate enrollment: 15,837
Total enrollment: 18,324
Percent Male/Female: 51%/49%
Percent Minority: 40.0%

Percent African-American: 2.0%
Percent Hispanic: 1.0%
Percent Asian: 35.0%
Percent in-state/out-of-state: 98%/2%
Percent Pub HS: NA
Fraternities: 10%
Sororities: 10%
Number of Applicants: 28,089
Percent Accepted: 48%
Percent Accepted who enroll: 25%
Entering: 4,092
Transfers: NA
Application Deadline: 30 Nov

Mean SAT: 601 V, 640 M
Middle 50% SAT range: NA
Middle 50% ACT range: NA
Mean ACT: NA
3 Most popular majors: biocehmistry, biology, psychology
Retention: NA
Graduation rate: 74.0%
Library: 2,300,000 volumes
Tuition and Fees: $4,027 in; $13,545 out
Room and Board: $6,864
On-campus housing: 86%
Financial aid, first-year: 50%

A ten-minute drive from San Diego will take you to the sunny town of La Jolla, home to the University of California at San Diego. The first thing you might notice is the pleasant southern California climate; as a student you might be tempted by the beach and the surf conditions to skip classes for the afternoon. UCSD is known for attracting some of the best students in California, but it's the great seaside weather and quirky architecture on campus that truly make UCSD a standout. But as you explore the tree-lined paths of the UCSD campus, you might be asking yourself the following question: "What the heck is something called a 'Singing Tree' doing at a university?"

Variety of Studies

The UCSD school year is divided into fall, winter, and spring quarters, with a summer session serving as a fourth quarter. Students apply to one of five residential colleges within the university: Muir, Warren, Marshall, Revelle, and Roosevelt. Each college has a different academic slant, and requires students to take different required courses along with the general requirements of the university. Muir College places emphasis on the humanities and is popular among students who have not decided on a major. Warren stresses a comprehensive education, requiring two secondary programs of study outside the major. Marshall College emphasizes public involvement and an appreciation of diversity. Revelle is devoted to math and the sciences, and Roosevelt College focuses on international relations.

Classes are large for required courses, especially lower-level math and science classes, but there are "never more people than they can fit into a lecture hall." However, this does not say much, since the largest lecture halls hold up to 400 students. Discussion sections with TAs vary in size but usually never have more than 30 students. Like most universities, upper-level classes generally have smaller enrollment.

Overall, professors receive mixed reviews. Foreign professors, often encountered in math and science departments, are sometimes hard to understand ("I had a professor who kept saying one word. The whole time I couldn't figure out what it was. I think it was 'radical,'" said one student). Ratings for courses and professors can be found in CAPE (Course and Professor Evaluation), a student publication also containing comments on professors, which range from constructive to insulting to downright vulgar. "It should be taken with a grain of salt," said one student.

TAs can be a big help, as students commonly find student-professor relations "impersonal." Professors have open office hours but they "aren't always conducive to your schedule." TAs, on the other hand, are more accessible; they identify better with students since they are often undergraduates themselves. Sometimes a TA can be even younger than the students in the class. "One guy in our apartment is a TA for my bio class," one student commented. But another student complained that TAs "can to be arrogant, and really not care about students."

Registration is quick and can be done via phone or using the StudentLink Internet system (which is more efficient, though sometimes busy). Students with more credits get registration priority—for example, freshmen with AP credits register earlier. However, it's usually not hard for students to "crash" classes they haven't registered for—"I actually haven't heard of anyone not getting a class yet," said one student. Some professors, instead of letting you in, "will just tell you to go talk to the department."

Students typically take three or four classes per quarter. The amount of work "depends on your personality. Some people can slack off and do well—others hear the professor say one plus one equals two and they write it down and underline it in pink." Science majors reputedly have the heaviest workloads. Pre-med bio-engineering "is the road to death," while the economics major is called "a joke" by some. "Communications is regarded as 'the fake major,'" added another student. Also notable is the large number of pre-meds (science majors are popular, biology in particular), who are considered workaholics by many peers. "Pre-meds are of two kinds: with or without a soul," quipped one non-pre-med. There is competition between students, but not much—cooperative study groups are

common, and students' interest in eac others' grades rarely extends past curios ity—"We want to know where we stand but we're not all ready to kill each other

UCSD's "first rate" academic resource center around the towering Geisel Librar (named after Ted Geisel, a.k.a. Dr. Seus longtime La Jolla resident). The univer sity's main library, located at the center o campus, houses the Humanities, Eng neering, and Art and Architecture l braries. Through a shared electroni catalog, students can access holdings a any of the University of California can puses. However, students complain tha the library has "very limited hours, whic sucks. Some days (Fridays and Satu days) it closes at 6 P.M." The UCSD con puting resources receive praise. Thoug most students own their own computer they find the computers in residential co leges and academic departments very use ful and convenient.

Crazy Campus

UCSD's sprawling campus is characte ized by lots of trees and open spaces. Th campus is enlivened by creatively de signed buildings such as the previousl mentioned Geisel Library, a steppe tower with levels of varying width: th building is widest at the sixth story, wit smaller floors above and below. The St art Collection of Sculpture, a series o unique artworks, adds an air of eccentri ity to different places across campus. Th collection includes the Sun God (a hug sun-bird statue); a snake-shaped pat leading up a hill to the library; "Talking "Singing," and "Silent" trees (the sile one, appropriately, is next to the library and a huge red shoe. And where else ca students read the seven virtues and vice in big neon letters on the way to nigl classes? "LUST, FORTITUDE, ENVY flash the walls of Powell Laboratory i bright red and green. Opinions of the co lection range from "cool" to "lame."

Life on Campus

Students generally make friends withi their own colleges, fraternities, and club As UCSD is predominantly an academi institution, studying and homework com first for many. As a result, some student complain that their classmates are "anti-social" and "only into studying."

The vast majority of the UCSD student body comes from California. There are virtually equal numbers of men and women; Asian and Hispanic students account for most of the large minority population (minorities account for about half of the student body).

On-campus housing is guaranteed for two years; freshmen usually stay in a residential college dorm, sophomores in campus apartments. The size and style of freshman dorm rooms depends on the residential college; most freshmen are placed in two-person suites ("doubles"). For the remaining two years, students generally move into one of the condominiums and apartments nearby (some within walking distance of campus).

Dorm life can be "distracting"; "if you're working and leave the door open, people just walk in." Though students say food (which is "okay for dorm food") could be better, they can eat at any campus dining hall. Some dining halls serve better food, so students benefit by exploring their options.

Much time is spent hanging out in friends' dorm rooms or apartments. Due to strict policies concerning drinking on campus, alcohol must be slipped past Residential Advisors (RAs). Nevertheless, drinking is "definitely common," though because of regulations, "you need to go off-campus for the good parties."

For juniors and seniors, living off-campus usually requires a car (or bike, for those who live close to campus), or public transit for those who wish to avoid high parking costs and the annoyance of finding space in crowded lots. Sidewalks off-campus are packed with parked cars every morning. "Parking is bad, but people drive anyway," said one off-campus student.

The town of La Jolla is pleasant and safe, although "people always complain that it's too small." Restaurants such as California Pizza Kitchen, T.G.I. Friday's, and Islands (a beach-themed burger joint), as well as movie theaters and shopping malls, can be found at nearby shopping centers. Students with cars can head to San Diego, which boasts the world-famous San Diego Zoo and Sea World,

along with professional sports teams, performing arts centers, and a bustling downtown area. Crossing the border into Tijuana (where the legal drinking age is conveniently 18) is also popular. Although most students live on campus, "it's still very much a commuter school." Many students go home to San Diego or Los Angeles on weekends, leaving the campus "kind of dead."

What Football Team?

There's "always something going on somewhere" but the UCSD campus is large, and people aren't always aware of what's happening. One sees "notices all over" announcing events organized by colleges, clubs, or the university itself. A variety of clubs and organizations, devoted to everything from surfing and skiing to independent films and chess, can be found, but according to some, "they're not very popular—if more people did them maybe we'd have a more fun campus." Larger organizations, such as the Asian student associations, have lots of members, but "aren't really active except for a few events each year." Residential college organizations are more popular. Smaller groups, such as the Anime (Japanese animation movies) club, often have more devoted membership. Offbeat groups include the Society for Creative Anachronism, who, among other things, "make medieval armor and can be seen carrying swords and maces around." The Greek system is "definitely present" on campus—about 10 percent of students are members of fraternities or sororities—but it is described as "tame," partly due to the absence of official Greek housing.

> With the lack of school spirit, "there isn't anything that unifies us."

There's little enthusiasm for sports—"we're Division III, and we play no-name schools." The administration "isn't really big on sports, and neither are we. Maybe we'd root for the football team, if we had one." Intramural ("IM") sports are the choice of "quite a few people." The Recreation and Intramural Athletic Complex

(RIMAC) is a popular place to work out or take classes in "everything from kendo to swing dance." "People would rather play than watch," added another. Some think that with the lack of school spirit, "there isn't anything that unifies us."

Hanging Out

A popular hangout is the Price Center, which has a food court, game room, video arcade, the campus bookstore, and movie theatre. Going to the beach is another popular activity; from campus, it's a short walk to La Jolla Shores, a popular place not only for students but also for residents of La Jolla and San Diego, who crowd the beach on weekends. Surfing is common, but it is also possible to sit and study on the beach. For those who not only like to hang out but like to let it *all* hang out, Blacks Beach (the local nude beach) is only a short distance away.

In addition to a rising academic reputation (ranked sixth among public universities by *U.S. News & World Report* in 1998), what makes UCSD a great choice for many students is the location. "Being by the beach is awesome, and [San Diego] has a lot to offer." The climate is a big plus; even when hard at work in the library, students note that it's almost always sunny outside—"It's good to feel the ocean breeze on campus every day." Just ask the singing tree. —*Chiansan Ma and Staff*

FYI

The three best things about attending UCSD are the "intelligent, engaging faculty, beautiful location, and low cost of tuition."

The three worst things about attending UCSD are the "isolated campus, rampant nerdiness of students, and the lack of popular spectator sports."

The three things that every student should do before graduating from UCSD are "go to class more often, get to know your professors well, and take advantage of the beautiful location."

One thing I'd like to have known before coming here is "that parking can be a real pain."

University of California / Santa Barbara

Address: 1210 Cheadle Hall, Santa Barbara, CA 93106
Phone: 805-893-2881
E-mail address: appinfo@sa.ucsb.edu
Web site URL: www.admit.ucsb.edu
Location: suburban
Founded: 1919
Private or Public: public
Religious affiliation: none
Undergraduate enrollment: 17,699
Total enrollment: 20,056
Percent Male/Female: 46%/54%
Percent Minority: 35.0%

Percent African-American: 3.0%
Percent Hispanic: 15.0%
Percent Asian: 16.0%
Percent in-state/out-of-state: 94%/6%
Percent Pub HS: 82%
Fraternities: 10%
Sororities: 10%
Number of Applicants: 26,964
Percent Accepted: 53%
Percent Accepted who enroll: 26%
Entering: 3,781
Transfers: 1,314
Application Deadline: 30 Nov

Mean SAT: 578 V, 601 M
Middle 50% SAT range: NA
Middle 50% ACT range: NA
Mean ACT: 24
3 Most popular majors: business economics, sociology, communications
Retention: 89.0%
Graduation rate: 61.0%
Library: 2,571,000 volumes
Tuition and Fees: $3,844 in; $14,018 out
Room and Board: $7,156
On-campus housing: 46%
Financial aid, first-year: 58%

Picture yourself strolling down the beach on a sunny afternoon. The waves lap at your feet and the soft sand squishes between your toes. What a nice break from the stress of college life! But wait, this *is* college! At least for those who attend the University of California campus at Santa Barbara (UCSB). Though technically located in Galeta, ten miles outside of Santa Barbara, UCSB is bordered on three sides by the Pacific Ocean. Most students are California natives, and admit it is easy to be distracted from academia when the surf is calling.

A Top 5 School

Perennially regarded as one of the greatest party schools in the nation, UCSB does not disappoint. With a ban on kegs in all university housing, only about 2,500 undergrads choose to live on the campus itself. But with Galeta and Isla Vista right next door, there are about "20,000 college students living together," particularly in Isla Vista, one resident explained. Affectionately called I.V., Isla Vista is the center of UCSB party life. In addition to shops, cafes, and parks, "beer is available seven days a week" in I.V., either at apartment parties or at the "raging [frat house] parties."

Social activity peaks every October as students from UCSB and other local colleges celebrate Halloween. On other weekends, however, there is still a plethora of stuff to do, including dance recitals, movies, intramural sports, and the outdoor activities. "With Mother Nature looking so beautiful," many hike, mountain bike, or surf when they're not cheering for the popular UCSB Gauchos' varsity basketball and volleyball teams.

Seriously, We've Got Academia

Seeking to shed its timeworn image as a party school, however, UCSB has followed the lead of other UC schools and begun placing more emphasis on academics for the past decade. There was a recent increase in minimum admission requirements, and students remarked that "UCSB is not as big a party school as I thought it'd be. Sure, there's still parties up the gazoo, but you actually have to put in some effort to maintain good academic standing." Commonly regarded as some of the school's better departments, biology, environmental studies, engineering, economics, and psychology attract a good number of the undergraduate population. Marine biology is also popular, as is the perennial favorite Shakespeare course by Professor Frank McConnell.

Distinguished speakers have also graced the campus, many through the efforts of the Interdisciplinary Humanities Center. Recently, the fourteenth Dalai Lama of Tibet visited and spoke to UCSB students.

Classes tend to be large, like those at most state schools, particularly at the introductory level. Some lectures enroll as many as 800 students, though most are closer to 150. Additional instruction is usually provided in these large lecture courses through TA-lead discussion sessions. As one heads toward upper-level courses, however, classes are as small as 30. There is "not much one-on-one with professors, but if you find them in their offices, they're usually really easy to talk to," one student reported. "The [professors] are pretty chill. There isn't too much of a rift between students and professors, and you can usually see a couple of them getting a beer at the same bars we're at," added one undergrad.

UCSB also offers undergrads opportunities to explore various career fields while still in college. The UCSB Washington Center Program, for instance, assists students who want to pursue internships, research, or creative activities in the nation's capital. In addition, the Education Abroad Program provides students with overseas programs at nearly 100 colleges and universities in 32 countries throughout the world.

There *Is* a Campus to Be On

For the few living on campus, rooms tend to be small despite continual renovations. "They're always fixing or building something, but the dorms just don't seem to get any bigger." Several dorms have themes, including the Scholars Hall, the Multicultural Experience Hall, and the Performing and Creative Arts Hall. Inhabited mostly by freshmen, campus dorms are often geared toward helping freshmen adjust to college life. Likewise, one dorm is reserved for transfer students. Most upperclassmen, however, prefer to live in off-campus apartments in I.V. or Galeta. "Sure, it might actually be a little more expensive to live in a nice off-campus apartment, but most feel it's well worth it," said one such upperclassman. "Living off-campus is more like real life," explained one undergrad. "You take care of your own mess, but you get to do whatever you want."

Stores for all sorts of daily supplies are nearby, making life in an apartment a "very manageable chore." Cars aren't totally essential around campus, but "they really make travel a lot more manageable, especially when lugging home the groceries. But practically everyone has a car, so you can always bum a ride."

> **"Beer is available seven days a week."**

Some students living off-campus have also found life away from the college scene. A number have been elected to positions on the local and county boards, working to represent both the college and community interests. On campus, meanwhile, the student newspaper, *Daily Nexus*, is popular and well regarded. In each of the last four years, it has been rated either first or second in the statewide Newspaper Publishers Association's college newspaper competition.

Ongoing renovations around campus have resulted in "shutting down all the roads at times, but I think it's worth it," one student asserts. The fruits of this labor have been seen in a new recreation building and aquatic center, fondly known as the "Rec-Cen," which boasts two swimming pools and spacious workout rooms. Athletic types can also take advantage of the old Robertson Gym and Event Center. Also on campus is the Davidson Library, home of over 2 million volumes. There is a new humanities and social science building, as well as a student service center.

Well-Rounded

A member of one of the academically better state school systems and home to undergrads from all walks of life, UCSB, students argue, is a "total thing to do," a "complete package." It provides academic challenge, a friendly atmosphere, and a fabulous setting. With warm weather year-round, the oceanside location, and nearby mountains ideal for biking and hiking, it is often difficult to think of more ideal surroundings. Pull out the shades, get some sunscreen, add a desire for knowledge without the intensity found at more cutthroat schools, and you're all set.
—*William Chen*

FYI

The three best things about attending UCSB are "the beach, the weather, and the women/men."

The three worst things about attending UCSB are "the beach, the weather, and the women/men. With all these distractions, I'm amazed we actually get work done."

The three things that every student should do before graduating from UCSB are "live in Galeta, surf in the Pacific, and party on a random mid-week school night."

One thing I'd like to have known before coming here is "that this is actually a school—people learn."

University of California / Santa Cruz

Address: Office of Admissions, Cook House, 1156 High Street, Santa Cruz, CA 95064
Phone: 831-459-4008
E-mail address: admissions@cats.ucsc.edu
Web site URL: www.ucsc.edu
Location: suburban
Founded: 1954
Private or Public: public
Religious affiliation: none
Undergraduate enrollment: 9,159
Total enrollment: 10,215
Percent Male/Female: 41%/59%

Percent Minority: 31.0%
Percent African-American: 2.0%
Percent Hispanic: 14.0%
Percent Asian: 13.0%
Percent in-state/out-of-state: 91%/9%
Percent Pub HS: NA
Fraternities: NA
Sororities: NA
Number of Applicants: 13,866
Percent Accepted: 79%
Percent Accepted who enroll: 21%
Entering: 1,997
Transfers: NA
Application Deadline: 30 Nov

Mean SAT: 510 V, 510 M
Middle 50% SAT range: NA
Middle 50% ACT range: NA
Mean ACT: NA
3 Most popular majors: biology, psychology, literature
Retention: NA
Graduation rate: 37.0%
Library: 1,200,000 volumes
Tuition and Fees: $4,359 in; $13,933 out
Room and Board: $6,900
On-campus housing: 50%
Financial aid, first-year: 50%

What exactly can one guess about a university whose mascot is the banana slug? As the slug suggests, UC Santa Cruz is arguably the most liberal and laid-back of the University of California schools, and it is sometimes still associated with the hippie movement of the '60s. However, despite their relatively casual attitude, students find that the low-stress environment, along with a pleasant city and a beautiful campus that is literally built into the surrounding redwood forest, provides a great atmosphere for learning.

Grades Optional

The academic year at Santa Cruz is divided into four quarters, and because usually only three are attended in any given year, most students leave during the summer. A typical course load is 15 units, consisting of three courses, each worth 5 credits. Everyone must have 180 credits, or roughly 36 classes, to graduate.

Students speak very highly of the faculty, who are generally described as "really excellent." Registration for classes is done by phone or over the Internet and is "pretty cut-and-dry." Internet registration is considered "really easy" and "useful." Students who have completed more credits get registration priority. The most popular majors at UC Santa Cruz include psychology and biology—nearby Monterey Bay and its abundantly valuable marine life provides resources for students of marine biology. As at many universities, intro-level classes are the biggest and hardest to get into, especially classes in popular majors such as biology and photography.

The most distinctive aspect of the UCSC academic system is the grading policy; you can pass without . . . well . . . grades. Students are allowed to take as many courses pass/fail as they wish. Instead of a letter grade, students who choose the pass/fail option receive a written narrative evaluation from their professor or teaching assistant, assessing their performance in the course. This way, the emphasis is less on the grading curve and more on learning the material. However, in very large classes, the sheer number of students can mean that "you'll get an evaluation that's two lines long, which kinda kills the intent," but such cases are the exception rather than the rule, and students agree that "it's a really good system." Students also have the option of receiving a letter grade along with their evaluation. The majority of students in the more competitive majors (think pre-med) tend to opt for the grade to verify their efforts.

Not surprisingly, the pass/fail option means that for most classes, the level of competition is close to nil. "There's no need to do better than everyone else," said one student. "There's not a lot of pressure from your peers," agreed another. "It's you versus the course load." But students are quick to point out that "you've still gotta pass the class—if you pass by the skin of your teeth, you're still going to get the rundown of how you did in the evaluation." It is also observed that "you could get away with doing very little, and a lot of people do, but they don't do well. Don't come here if you're not self-motivated. There are too many opportunities to slack off." Although there are slackers on campus, other students are more focused on academics: "Once you get into what you like, you'll have a lot of work."

Meat Dish

Students are assigned to one of eight residential colleges, each with requirements that students take a special core course. Particular colleges also have reputations for drawing certain types of students. Crown College is said to attract more science majors, while Porter College is supposedly favored by performing arts majors. Students can also choose to live in substance-free, same-sex, or ethnic-theme dorms.

Freshmen generally live in a residential college dorm and usually move into an on-campus apartment ("a big room with a kitchen") for sophomore year, though staying in the dorms is also possible since "there's no trouble finding friends," especially within one's college. The majority of students move off campus after sophomore year in one of several nearby houses.

Life in the dorms is "social and loud at times," but parties are "easy to get away from since there's always somewhere quiet to go." Drugs and alcohol are pre-

sent, although "not obvious." "You don't have to look that hard," claimed another student. "You will find people smashed on Saturday morning." The administration has reportedly been "trying to buckle down [on drug use and drinking], but it's always there."

Dorm food is described as "not bad" and "bearable" overall. Yet students warn of hearing past comments such as "they try to make real meal-type foods and fail miserably," and "I once saw something that was labeled simply 'Meat Dish.'" Fortunately, students can choose to eat at any dining hall, and since the food quality varies from college to college, students who explore all of their options will have a better chance of avoiding the dining services' apparent fixation with things containing pasta and/or tofu.

School Upon a Hill

To those looking for outside entertainment, Santa Cruz offers "lots of options," including various restaurants, stores, and movie theaters. The university sits on a hill overlooking downtown Santa Cruz, which is only a short ride away on "the Magical #1 Bus," and is free for students making frequent trips between the campus and the city. The city is a very popular student hangout and easily accessible via car, bike, the bus, or even on foot. With the amount of leisure time students have, going off campus is "a big thing . . . almost a necessity," said one student. Many students also get around on bikes; some have cars, but "it's not necessary to have a car. You can get around without one." Students report that parking is "terrible."

Excursions to the city often involve going bowling or watching an independent film, but "sometimes it just involves going to Taco Bell." The downtown area is considered safe at night by some students, perhaps due to a recent increase in the police presence, but "it's not advisable to go out alone." Hiking, camping, and going to the beach are also popular, especially on weekends. For students with cars, San Jose is only 30 miles away, and a drive to San Francisco takes an hour and a half.

Higher praise is given to the campus itself, which was founded in 1965 and built with the surrounding redwood forest (home to the banana slug) in mind. While constructing the university, "they attempted to harm as little of the forest as possible," and as a result, many buildings are nestled among the trees. "Nature lovers out there, have we got a place for you!" Students use such words such as "beautiful" and "amazing" to describe their campus, and many comment on the frequent encounters with wildlife on campus, especially deer. Signs warning passersby to watch out for mountain lions are also a common sight. "The deer come on campus and eat the flowers," said one student, and "the mountain lions come on campus and eat the deer." UCSC's location also offers views of the surrounding forest and of the ocean; the two can sometimes be seen through the same window. The "cool environment" on campus and in the city is cited as the greatest thing about UC Santa Cruz by many students: "I could totally live here. Maybe when I'm really rich, I'll have a house here."

No Vibrant Campus Scene

Extracurricular activities are not a big part of life on campus, and there is "very little in the way of sports," at least at the varsity level. The swimming, water polo, and ultimate frisbee teams do get attention, but one student reports, "I've never seen anything posted for any sporting events." However, participating in intramural and club sports is very easy: "If you can get five people together and field a team, then you can play."

There are fraternities and sororities, but they are not overly influential. One student said, "There are some frosh who are surprised to know that we even have fraternities." The student body is described as "a lot of everything and everyone can find their niche." With such a loose, open environment on campus, "everyone's friendly," and "you can always find someone playing a guitar." As for activities during their spare time, students often take classes like self-defense and belly dancing, and "there's a lot of the environmental thing up here; CALPIRG (California Public Interest Research Group, a consumer/environmental watchdog agency) gets a lot of support." Overall, though, "students are more inclined toward their studies."

> "I could totally live here. Maybe when I'm really rich, I'll have a house here."

But students also note that recent university projects, including a new science library and the establishment of a school of engineering, reflect a shift toward the hard sciences and away from the liberal arts. The university, which is in the process of hiring new faculty in order to expand its engineering departments, "might get a little bigger" as a result of this shift. The growth of Santa Cruz itself may parallel that of the university, according to one student: "It's an expanding city desperately trying to stay small." Another student expressed worries that the development of the university may result in "more red tape," and that "UCSC might become more of a normal university, which is scary. There needs to be more places like this." —*Chiansan Ma*

FYI
The three best things about attending UCSC are "the narrative evaluations and the awesome pass/fail system, gorgeous campus nestled in a redwood forest, and free public transportation system that takes you almost anywhere."
The three worst things about attending UCSC are "that it's becoming more like every other UC college and they're slowly dismantling the narrative evaluation system, people pretend to be progressive but really aren't, and the way the UC system takes every opportunity to take money from you."
The three things that every student should do before graduating from UCSC are "walk the length of the campus (via trails, not roads!), celebrate Halloween or New Year's Eve on Pacific Ave., and make use of the UC transfer system and take classes in other UC schools."
One thing I'd like to have known before coming here is "how bad the financial aid system is."

University of Redlands

Address: P.O. Box 3080, Redlands, CA 92373-0999
Phone: 909-335-4074
E-mail address: admissions@uor.edu
Web site URL: www.redlands.edu
Location: suburban
Founded: 1959
Private or Public: private
Religious affiliation: none
Undergraduate enrollment: 1,480
Total enrollment: 1,508
Percent Male/Female: 45%/55%
Percent Minority: 24.0%

Percent African-American: 3.0%
Percent Hispanic: 11.0%
Percent Asian: 8.0%
Percent in-state/out-of-state: 69%/31%
Percent Pub HS: 87%
Fraternities: NA
Sororities: NA
Number of Applicants: 1,848
Percent Accepted: 84%
Percent Accepted who enroll: 28%
Entering: 309
Transfers: NA
Application Deadline: 1 July

Mean SAT: 560 V, 552 M
Middle 50% SAT range: NA
Middle 50% ACT range: NA
Mean ACT: NA
3 Most popular majors: social sciences, business administration and management, liberal arts and sciences
Retention: NA
Graduation rate: 56.0%
Library: 230,000 volumes
Tuition and Fees: $19,716 in; $19,716 out
Room and Board: $7,468
On-campus housing: NA
Financial aid, first-year: 75%

Redlands is a university that feels like a small liberal arts college. It is a place where professors give out their home phone numbers, where the largest class has about 40 students, and where everyone immediately finds out whom you are dating. Clearly its small size, coupled with its location in a small, sleepy southern California town, has benefits and drawbacks. The academics and general atmosphere are intimate but the social life can sometimes be a bit stifling.

A West Coast Orientation

Most Redlands students hail from California, and the rest are primarily from elsewhere in the West. There are "more students from abroad than from the East Coast." Although Redlands has become more diverse in recent years, one student reported that "a lot of people here talk about the lack of diversity." One student commented, "If you aren't from southern California, be prepared to either become like the others, or struggle to fit in with the rich, trendy majority." Students claim that homogeneity is especially apparent in the fraternities. Gay students face a small dating pool and a slightly unfriendly atmosphere. However, Redlands does have a Gay, Lesbian, Bisexual, Straight Union (GLBSU), which runs "Coming Out Week"

and displays a "closet" booth in the middle of campus where students can learn about homosexuality.

When Redlands was founded in the early 20th century by American baptists, the campus had two walkways on the main quad so males and females could walk separately to chapel. The administration allowed dancing for the first time in the late 1960s.

Times have changed: Frat brothers, as well as the soccer and baseball teams, now occasionally run naked from the chapel to the administration building. Unlike in decades past, traditional dating is uncommon. One student explained, "We used to be known as 'Wedlands.' My parents and all their friends met here and got married. But now the dating scene here sucks." "There are a lot of random hookups at all the parties," one student claimed. Another echoed that sentiment: "It's a small school. Be prepared for everyone to know whom you're dating the next day."

Palm Trees and Greek Columns

Redlands has distinctive Greek architecture, in a setting that is "like a desert motif, with a sprinkling of palm trees." Another student said that Redlands "has that college-campus feel. I can walk anywhere in ten minutes." With the construction of a new Hedco Biology and Chemistry Building under way, and the recently added Thompson Aquatic Center, the campus is undergoing a facelift. The student center provides career and tutoring services, homes for clubs, a cafeteria, a lounge, and other amenities. In general, students like the Redlands campus, though one longed for a multicultural student center.

Dorm rooms are "way above average," one resident said. Many rooms are doubles that share a bathroom with another double. The freshman dorm is "very active in terms of parties and socializing," one student said. Fairmont was recently remodeled and "feels like a hotel." In contrast, "East Hall resembles a jail, has small rooms, and is dirty." The Johnston dorms, where most residents are enrolled in the Johnston Center, are also "notorious for being nasty," but they are the center for frequent parties. Only students older than 23, married, or living with immediate family may choose to live off campus. Honor House, whose residents must meet GPA and community service requirements, is a five-minute walk from campus, and "many upperclassmen choose it to be away from the dorm-life scene." Other students choose to live in the university-owned Grove Apartments.

One student described Redlands food as "wretched" and "too expensive." Another student thought "lots of people complain but in reality it is a lot better than at other schools." This is fortunate, because the meal plan is mandatory, even for off-campus students. Like most college dining, the food "just gets old." "Weekend meals consist entirely of leftovers." Students bored with campus dining will find few alternatives in the town of Redlands beyond popular Mexican and pizza places and "a few really good coffeehouses." San Bernardino, 15 minutes away on the freeway, has "a huge array of restaurants," especially chains like Friday's and the Olive Garden.

One student described Redlands' location as about an hour and 10 minutes from the ocean, an hour and a half from Los Angeles, and 45 minutes from Palm Springs. The town of Redlands is described as "fairly white-collar and suburban." "It doesn't have a lot. Most people, if they don't have a car, have a best friend with a car." Ontario Mills, a mall that is "just huge," has 60 movie theaters and is about half an hour away. If one wishes to shop in Redlands proper, "there's always Wal-Mart," one student said.

Frat-Dominated Social Scene

The social scene at Redlands is varied, but many students complain that the fraternities dominate it, though only about 25 percent of the students are involved in the Greek system. One student categorized the student body as "the Greeks and the non-Greeks, which includes activists, nonconformists, devout Christians, jocks, and a huge pool of others." Non-Greek students complain that once friends plunge into the Greek system, they no longer associate with their old friends. "I didn't expect the Greek system to be so visible," students claimed. Freshmen can pledge a fraternity or sorority after their first semester. Students report that "there are tons of rumors about horrible pledging rituals, but nobody knows if they're true."

Frat parties often include alcohol, though non-drinkers also attend. The university offers many non-drinking alternatives. Friday at Five, a weekly music event, caters to people who do not drink. Crossroads, another Friday night activity, is completely alcohol-free, and, in the words of one student, "can be a comedian, a party, a hypnotist, or a game of broomball hockey." Redlands also has a chapter of Bacchus, which is a nationally recognized program that ensures that non-alcoholic alternatives are always available. Drugs, primarily marijuana, "are easy to obtain," one student reported, although hard drugs are almost nonexistent on campus.

Student-run social events at Redlands offer alternatives to parties. The social-affairs committee sponsors two or three major concerts a year. "The music department is really good, so there are lots of classical-music events," one student said. The Convocation Lecture Series brings to campus about eight speakers a year. Recent speakers included former surgeon general Jocelyn Elders and Arun Gandhi

(Mahatma Gandhi's grandson). Most events are "moderately well attended," one student said, but "most people don't realize how much there is to do here."

There are more than 60 clubs and organizations at Redlands, and "just about everybody belongs to one or two clubs." The *Bulldog Weekly* is well respected, as is the debate team and the student government (ASUR). Among the offbeat options is the Footbag Club, which plays hackey sack. Because Redlands has a small student body, one student said that as a freshman, "I got involved with lots of organizations and leadership positions. I had major opportunities." Redlands requires 80 hours of community service to graduate. Many students also have work-study jobs, but at Redlands they "are really cool," and can include on- and off-campus internships.

Although there are some successful sports teams at Redlands, "there is not tons of school spirit." The football team won its conference in 1996 and 1997, but "people go to football games out of a lack of anything else to do." The women's water polo team is outstanding, having recently won four consecutive national titles. In addition, many students play club or intramural sports.

Academic Life and Blessings of Smallness

Redlands' classes rarely exceed 25 students. One student said, "I like the size—a small school gives rise to faculty-student interaction. There are only three or four rooms that can hold more than 30 people." The largest classes, which are usually in the sciences, may have 35 to 40 students. Graduate students almost never take a part in leading undergraduate classes, as the graduate school, with satellites around southern California, is primarily an evening program. "Most students don't know the graduate school exists," one undergrad said. Even with such small classes, registration is no problem. According to one student, "I've never had a problem getting into a class. Even if a class is full, the professor will usually let you in." According to one senior, Redlands professors are willing "to give you experiences that you would never have at another place. They really try to make you

passionate about that subject." Professors are also very friendly, and students report that "they bring us food, hold parties at their houses, and play jokes on us."

Creative classes abound during the January term, when each student takes one class for three hours a day, four days a week. This format allows for intensive student-faculty interaction. Departments offer specialized classes year-round, though many unconventional classes are unique to the January term. For example, during a class on water in southern California, students made five field trips to dams and other nearby locations. Other students traveled to Tahiti to study the biology of the oceans. Professors even offer fun classes such as The History of Wine, complete with tasting, for students over 21.

> **"It's a small school. Be prepared for everyone to know whom you're dating the next day."**

Redlands' academic requirements expose students to many disciplines. The Liberal Arts Foundation requires all students, regardless of major, to take at least one class in each of almost a dozen categories. These categories include Human Behavior, Mathematics and Science, and Dominance and Difference. In the latter, students discuss dominant cultures and those whom they have oppressed. Foundation classes, which are generally survey classes on a broad topic, are "excellent when students don't view them as a burden." The most difficult classes at Redlands are in the sciences, especially organic chemistry, though students say no majors are particularly easy. Most students major outside of the sciences, and the humanities departments are all reportedly strong. Many departments are small enough to make it possible for majors to know the entire faculty. Redlands may have "fewer high-tech machines and labs, but we have more faculty-student interaction and we are an expanding university," one student said. The university is building four new math and science buildings "to be competitive in terms of technology with other southern California schools." There are also a number of special academic programs. Students in the Johnston Center for Integrated Studies can design their own majors—one Johnston student is majoring in wine making. Students in the Proudian Program make a presentation at the end of sophomore year, travel abroad during junior year, and then write about their experience in their senior year.

In Redlands' popular study-abroad program, "students can go anywhere in the world they want to. They are not constrained by which programs are considered worthy."

Redlands' small size allows for small classes, great student-faculty interaction, and amazing undergraduate opportunities in research and job experience. It can also lead to a somewhat stifling social scene and few off-campus social opportunities unless one has access to a car and a penchant for long drives. Yet overall, students love the campus, the dorms, and the on-campus activities. Redlands is a place where students "can study what they are passionate about." —*Cynthia Matthews and Staff*

FYI
The three best things about attending Redlands are "the small liberal arts college feel, fantastic, involved professors, and the January term."
The three worst things about attending Redlands are "too much gossiping, the mandatory meal plan (with terrible food), and the domination of the Greek system."
The three things that every student should do before graduating Redlands are "treat yourself to exciting January terms, go abroad for a semester, and take advantage of the high profile intellectuals and professors Redlands attracts."
One thing I'd like to have known before coming here is "how much of a struggle it is to fit in with rich, trendy California kids if you are an outsider."

University of Southern California

Address: University Park, Los Angeles, CA 90089-0912
Phone: 213-740-1111
E-mail address: NA
Web site URL: www.usc.edu
Location: urban
Founded: 1880
Private or Public: private
Religious affiliation: none
Undergraduate enrollment: 15,430
Total enrollment: 28,342
Percent Male/Female: 51%/49%
Percent Minority: 45.0%
Percent African-American: 6.0%

Percent Hispanic: 23.0%
Percent Asian: 14.0%
Percent in-state/out-of-state: NA
Percent Pub HS: NA
Fraternities: 20%
Sororities: 20%
Number of Applicants: 21,140
Percent Accepted: 46%
Percent Accepted who enroll: 29%
Entering: 4,166
Transfers: NA
Application Deadline: 21 Jan
Mean SAT: NA

Middle 50% SAT range: 540–650 V, 570–680 M
Middle 50% ACT range: NA
Mean ACT: NA
3 Most popular majors: business, engineering, social sciences
Retention: 92.0%
Graduation rate: 69.0%
Library: 3,300,000 volumes
Tuition and Fees: $20,480 in; $20,480 out
Room and Board: $6,748
On-campus housing: 65%
Financial aid, first-year: 61%

In the heart of South-Central Los Angeles awaits your chance to become a Trojan. Just exactly what does that mean? "It means you bleed garland and gold, and you despise UCLA." Besides having enormous pride in the University of Southern California, being a Trojan also means living in a "what-you-make-it" academic atmosphere with a diverse group of students who insist on having a great time in the process. Most students at USC are incredibly happy with their college choice, and they have great reasons that justify their pride in being Trojans.

Opportunistic Academics

The word that often describes academics at USC is "opportunity." "You have the opportunity to challenge yourself but you don't have to." For students with a passion for working hard toward their intellectual pursuits, there are plenty of incredible programs and plenty of work to do. But if you want, "you can also get by being a slacker." The two most popular majors are business and film, each with world-renowned reputations.

Applicants to USC must declare a particular major that they hope to pursue, but it is not binding. When you apply to USC, you automatically apply for a number of special academic programs and scholarships. Thirty to forty incoming freshmen will be offered admission to the BAMD program, a "sweet program for pre-meds." Students in the BAMD program are guaranteed admission to the medical school as long as you earn a minimum required score on the MCAT. Another program, Thematic Options, features an honors curriculum with intensive reading and writing courses. Students taking Thematic Options are housed together in their own dorm. There is also a Business Scholars Program offering freshman the chance to take advanced classes in the Business School.

Scholarships are given out according to the major that you declare on your application. The Business School is highly competitive, while the Public Policy and Management School and International Relations School are two of the least competitive. Students agree, "The way to get money is to apply to the less popular schools."

Whether or not you are in a special academic program, students generally rave about their classes and their professors, who are very accessible despite the large student body. "I usually have great relationships with my professors," said one enthusiastic student. The regular liberal arts curriculum at USC consists of 12 subject areas in which students must fulfill general education requirements. Proficiency in at least one foreign language is also required before graduation.

Excellent Social Scene

Students immerse themselves in the array of social activities that USC offers. A laid-back attitude prevails on campus, as students walk around in "flip-flops, T-shirts, and shorts" year-round, enjoying the beautiful sunny California weather. The location of the campus leaves almost nothing to be desired. Beverly Hills is 10 minutes away, and Westwood and Santa Monica are each 20 minutes away. "You can go surfing in the morning, and skiing in the afternoon." While students admit that owning a car is nice, it is not necessary, as you can always find a ride. "Even if you don't have a car, there are plenty of people who do."

While the opportunity to explore nearby cities is enticing, one does not have to move off campus to partake in a great social scene. "Greek life is very strong on campus." Twenty-eighth Street holds all the fraternity and sorority houses, and students are content with the numerous parties available to them each weekend. While many enjoy the Greek parties, there is no pressure to rush. USC also hosts a variety of bands throughout the year that perform on campus. As one student summed it up, "The social life at USC is, in one word, 'amazing.'"

If you're looking for love, USC might also be the place for you. "Relationships are great here." Contrary to many schools where students complain that the only two choices seem to be random hookups or marriage, the full spectrum of relationships is prevalent at USC. Dating is very popular. Perhaps acting as a catalyst to this wonderful dating setting, "USC is full of really beautiful people."

Living in Paradise

The beautiful people who attend USC can choose to live either in dorms or local apartments. Most incoming freshman choose the dorms, of which Flour Tower is the best option, according to students. The suites in Flour have four doubles, two bathrooms, a large living room, and a kitchen area. College University is regarded as "the most social dorm." Pardee and Marks Tower, which was recently renovated, are also popular dorm buildings. Each dorm has a Residential Advisor (in addition to Student Advisors by major), whom students say are easy to get along with, "cool, and really flexible." Dorms also offer a good, easy way to get involved with student government. "It's not too difficult to be an officer of a residential dorm, and then you can become really involved in the student government body." The dorm buildings themselves, like the campus as a whole, are "absolutely beautiful." The campus is flat and compact, making all buildings very accessible. Gates separate the USC campus from the outside world. "It's like a paradise and the architecture really brings out the life of the campus."

If you prefer an off-campus apartment, "you should check out Cardinal Gardens, a beautiful, recently renovated complex." While incoming freshmen sometimes have safety concerns regarding the neighborhoods surrounding USC, students soon come to feel that the "area is pretty safe." Emergency call boxes throughout the campus and police officers that constantly patrol the local area create a safe atmosphere for students.

Evil Kitchen

Students are offered a variety of food options at USC. All freshmen are on meal plans, which have less flexibility if you live in the dorms. The two main dining halls are EVK and Cafe 84. EVK, called "Evil Kitchen" by students, is generally regarded as "pretty nasty—stay away from there." But students seem satisfied with Cafe 84, which offers a variety of cuisine at different stations, such as Mexican, Chinese, and Italian food, in addition to cheeseburgers and french fries. Most meal plans offer "food points" for local establishments. Trojan Grounds, or "TG," is a "really cool" coffee shop that serves Starbucks coffee. There are also a variety of fast-food restaurants within a walk from campus, such as McDonald's, Taco Bell, and Subway, and most are open 24 hours a day. If you have a car, Jerry's Famous Deli in Beverly Hills is a really neat place to grab a bite to eat, "especially," says one student "around 3 A.M. You always see famous people; last week I ran into Scary Spice there!" Students who like

to cook their own food are advised to do their grocery shopping at Ralph's instead of the 32 Market, "which is too crowded and the food selection is not as good."

Extracurricular Activities

"It is very easy to get involved in extracurricular activities at USC." Student government and intramural sports are very popular. The band is also easy to join and students take pride in it. There are also funds—the Philanthropy Fund and the Leadership Fund—for which you can apply to get money for programs of public service or leadership that you wish to pursue.

Yet, watching and playing varsity sports by far dominates the realm of extracurricular activities at USC. "Football games are huge," and the school spirit is quite impressive. "There's an amazing amount of school pride. Once a Trojan, always a Trojan!" USC–UCLA is one of the hottest rivalries in the collegiate world. "Every football game, no matter who we're playing, we bash UCLA. The energy level is incredible." When asked about their football team's record, one student replied, "We've beaten UCLA more than they've beaten us. That's all that matters."

Basketball games are also well attended, as are most varsity sports. USC certainly places a strong emphasis on athletic activities. One student complained, "The system seems to cater to athletes." But one thing is certain: "The pride people take in flashing the Trojan colors is unparalleled."

Students at USC are both academically and culturally diverse. "There is a good cross-section of students and a diversity of intelligence." While most ethnic groups are well represented on campus, each group tends to hang out together. "There is not much mixing, and people form their own cliques," often along racial or ethnic lines. Students seem unanimously to praise the diversity of the student body while complaining about the self-imposed segregation.

All students graduating from USC will share at least one common bond: a tremendous alumni support network often called the "Trojan family." "There are lots of connections to be made here, especially in the business worlds."

USC offers a very healthy blend of intellectual and social life, complete with a diverse student body who take pride in their school, both during their college years and beyond. One student summed up USC as a place where "serious students can challenge themselves within their academic passion, and less-serious students can enjoy college while developing as scholars." All students seem to agree that living and learning at the beautiful campus of USC in sunny California makes one happy and proud to be a lifelong member of the Trojan family. —*Carl Shephard*

FYI

The three best things about attending USC are "its location in L.A., the connections you can make, and the Greek system."

The three worst things about attending USC are "the neighborhood, the declining party life, and the new students who seem to be more concerned with their grades than their social life because of the university's stricter admission requirements."

The three things that every student should do before graduating USC are "get an internship in the entertainment industry, be an extra in a movie, and network, network, network!"

One thing I'd like to have known before coming here is "that you should bring a car."

Colorado

Colorado College

Address: 14 East Cache La Poudre Street, Colorado Springs, CO 80903
Phone: 800-542-7214
E-mail address: Admission@Colorado College.edu
Web site URL: www.coloradocollege.edu/ admission
Location: small city
Founded: 1874
Private or Public: private
Religious affiliation: none
Undergraduate enrollment: 1,900
Total enrollment: 1,950
Percent Male/Female: 45%/55%

Percent Minority: 11.0%
Percent African-American: 3.0%
Percent Hispanic: 4.5%
Percent Asian: 3.5%
Percent in-state/out-of-state: 25%/75%
Percent Pub HS: 60%
Fraternities: 2%
Sororities: 4%
Number of Applicants: 3,650
Percent Accepted: 35%
Percent Accepted who enroll: 27%
Entering: 547
Transfers: 36
Application Deadline: 15 Jan

Mean SAT: 637 V, 644 M
Middle 50% SAT range: 600–680 V, 600–670 M
Middle 50% ACT range: 25-30
Mean ACT: 38
3 Most popular majors: biology, English, economics
Retention: 90%
Graduation rate: 93%
Library: 434,215 volumes
Tuition and Fees: $21,822 in; NA out
Room and Board: $5,568
On-campus housing: 100%
Financial aid, first-year: 57%

At Colorado College, it's easy to understand why the snowcapped mountains of Colorado, visible from any window, might tempt students from their studies and up to the slopes for extended ski trips. Fortunately for CC students, their school's unorthodox academic schedule, the block plan, leaves plenty of four-and-a-half-day breaks during the school year that are perfect for skiing, community service, and any other adventure CC students can think up.

Focusing and Concentrating

Students agree that the block plan, for better and for worse, is a unique aspect of their college and the main reason they chose to come to CC. The academic calendar is divided into eight three-and-a-half-week blocks, with four-and-a-half-day breaks in between each block. During a block, students immerse themselves in a single subject. "I get to concentrate on one thing; I learn more about what I'm taking, and I don't have to worry about a test in another class," one student said of the plan. The schedule, which students say is good for those with a "one-track mind," spares the residents of this small school the stress of juggling four or five different classes. Professors know they have their students' undivided attention, and it's not uncommon for them to take classes on overnight field trips or out for midnight viewing of the stars. Classes like geology and astronomy especially benefit from this freedom.

Although the block system can be intense and stressful, students said they don't feel an overwhelming sense of competition at CC. "It's what you put into it," said one student. Another agreed, "You can get away with slacking." With all classes held for two or three hour sessions in the morning, some students say they feel spoiled by having so much free time on their hands.

According to students, though, the plan

is not without its drawbacks, and can be quite rigorous. Classes are "intense" and if you miss more than one class or fall behind, especially in a language class, it can be very difficult to catch up before the next exam, since the learning for each class goes on during such a short, concentrated period of time. One student also commented that, due to the small class size, you can't just expect to skip unnoticed, and professors know if a student is not there. Academic life at CC is definitely not for everyone.

"Buying" Classes

The block plan isn't the only thing that's different about Colorado College—registration at CC is as unorthodox as the academic calendar. Students receive 80 "points" at the end of each spring for the next year. To register, they assign these points to courses they want to take, putting more points on preferred classes. Those who assign the most points to a particular class get priority.

Introductory classes and film courses are in high demand and sometimes hard to get. Human Sexual Behavior is reportedly among the most popular courses. Students who manage to "buy" their way into their class of choice reap the benefits of smaller class sizes. For the most part, classes taught by one professor have no more than 25 students, and classes taught by two professors have no more than 32. TAs, called "paraprofessionals," help with labs and tutoring, but don't teach classes.

Requirements at CC are described by students as "loose." During their four-year career in Colorado Springs, students must take two blocks each of lab and natural sciences, and by the end of sophomore year, four blocks of "Alternative Perspectives," two in Western culture classes and two in non-Western. The required courses are not seen as a heavy burden. "They're great, because otherwise I wouldn't have taken [these classes]," one student insisted. Although undergrads report that there are no gut courses at Colorado College, they admit that some classes are easier than others. Some less-challenging courses cited by students were Jazz and Exercise Physiology. An end may be near to even these less stressful block choices.

"They are making them harder," lamented one student. Geology, biology, economics, psychology, and English are all popular majors, and many students choose to double major.

Natural Beauty and Artificial Modernity

Located at the foot of Pike's Peak and the majestic Rocky Mountains, CC attracts many students for the scenery and the entertainment it provides. Skiing and other outdoor pursuits are definitely high priorities in the lives of most CC students. Despite the natural beauty and the fact that campus is within walking distance of the city's downtown, students are "not too impressed with Colorado Springs." The dominant style of buildings at the school has been described as "modern ugly," but the campus is framed by breathtaking mountains, so students say they love the setting and spend a lot of time within the confines of CC's campus.

Because of the block plan schedule, students have concentrated amounts of work to do in the afternoons, and Tutt Library is the place of choice for doing it. Dorms have study lounges as well, but in nice weather, many students opt to bask in the warm Colorado sun in Armstrong Quad, reading and dodging Frisbees. Some students complain that the library is not adequate for in-depth research, and often travel to the library at nearby University of Colorado in Colorado Springs for a better stock of books.

All dorms at CC have been renovated recently, or will be in the near future. There are three large dorms: Loomis, which houses most freshmen, is "definitely the loudest"; Mathias is a "very sterile" dorm with the reputation of being "full of jocks"; and Slocum is the "quiet dorm" with "substance-free wings." The dorms are coed, with mostly doubles and singles, but bathrooms are single-sex. Other on-campus housing options include five language houses, three fraternity houses (there are also three non-residential sororities), and a couple of theme houses. Themes change every year; last year CC was the proud home to an "eclectic arts" house and a "multicultural" house. First years and sophomores must live on campus, but some juniors and several seniors live in nearby off-campus housing.

Veggies for Granolas

Deciding how to eat can be as difficult for students at CC as choosing what class to take next block, though the options are fairly straightforward and flexible once you get used to them. First-year students may choose between five different meal plans, which offer combinations of meals in one of CC's dining halls, and a "flex-point" system that can be used at Benjamin's snack bar, housed in the Worner Student Center, and a campus convenience store. Rastall, the main cafeteria, serves standard college fare, described by some as "better than average." It serves a variety of entrées at each meal, in addition to a salad bar, grilled items, and pasta almost every day. Students advise avoiding the pasta, and added that the daily entrée is usually a student's best bet for an edible meal. The smaller Bemis, with less variety and shorter hours, is preferred by some because "the food's healthier and it has a really nice environment." Both dining halls serve vegetarian food.

When dorm food becomes too much for students to take, CC dining hall patrons head out for Mexican fare at La Casita or pizza and beer at Old Chicago's. One "really cool place" near campus is Poor Richard's, a coffee shop/bookstore/movie theater/pizza joint.

Like many Coloradans, students at CC take physical fitness seriously. Varsity and intramural sports are probably the most popular extracurricular activities at CC. The Division 1 Tigers men's hockey team draws the largest crowds on campus, especially when the school is playing its big rival, the University of Denver. The school's football and women's soccer teams also have large followings.

For the less serious sports enthusiast, CC's active intramural sports program provides an antidote to the freshman 15. Especially popular are hockey, flag football, broomball (played with a ball in tennis shoes on an ice rink), and ultimate Frisbee. Outdoor activities, like mountain climbing, camping, hiking, biking and (especially) skiing in the nearby mountains meet the needs of the more solitary CC student. Some students warn that frequent ski trips can burn a hole in your budget, however, and popular outdoor recreation spots are usually accessible only by car.

The less sports-minded can join student government, write for the college's weekly newspaper, the *Catalyst*, play in student bands, or perform with Room 46, CC's prominent a cappella group.

In addition to being outdoor fanatics, students at CC are generally Birkenstock-clad liberals. Some students describe their classmates as "crunchy granola" and "suffocatingly liberal," and grumble that their peers conform to nonconformity. Ethnic diversity is not CC's strong point either. For the most part, campus politics (which some students complained lack enthusiasm) stand in stark contrast to those of politically conservative Colorado Springs, the birthplace of Colorado's anti-gay amendment a few years ago. One student described CC as an "oasis in conservative Colorado Springs." Still, according to one student, "If you read between the lines, there's more diversity; people aren't just how they look."

> **"With the block plan, I get to concentrate on one thing; I learn more about what I'm taking, and I don't have to worry about a test in another class."**

Students report that alcohol and pot are the drugs of choice at CC, and because of the unorthodox class schedule at CC, which leaves some students with lots of extra time on their hands (so they claim), there are usually parties every night of the week. Frat parties, often themed, are common on campus. The most popular are the Harley-Davidson party, beach parties, and DU Sucks, an anti-University of Denver party. Still, with only four fraternities and an equal number of nonresidential sororities, there is no pressure to rush. As one student described it, the frat presence on campus is "low-key."

Room parties in the dorms are not unheard of, but "you have to be kind of discreet." Many students have turned to off-campus locations for their more drunken nighttime escapades. Still, most drinking takes place on or around campus, as Colorado Springs has a limited bar scene.

There are people on campus who do not drink, and students say even at a school the size of CC, it's possible to find a niche of people with similar social preferences. Movies, plays, and concerts—both on campus and in the city—provide alternatives to alcohol-centered social events. A few nondrinkers on campus have become militant recently, and are trying to lobby the administration to make the campus dry, or at least drier than it is. The social life is also greatly affected by the fact that there is a mass exodus off campus every four weeks on block breaks, somewhat breaking the continuity of socialization.

Many Colorado College students choose the school for its outdoorsy atmosphere and unconventional academics. A prevailing attitude is "do what you want, not what people tell you to do," and Colorado students do just that. —*Brian Abaluck and Staff*

FYI

The three best things about attending Colorado College are "the block plan when you are taking a class you love; the beautiful setting and all of the opportunities for activities that it affords; and block breaks every four weeks."

The three worst things about attending Colorado College are "the block plan when you are taking a class you hate; the ugly buildings; and the limited bar scene in Colorado Springs."

The three things every student should do before graduating are "play broomball; go on a cool road trip on block break; and take Human Sexual Behavior."

One thing I'd like to have known before coming here is "how liberal everyone is."

Colorado School of Mines

Address: 1811 Elm Street, Golden, CO 80501
Phone: 303-273-3220
E-mail address: admit@mines.edu
Web site URL: www.mines.edu
Location: small city
Founded: 1874
Private or Public: public
Religious affiliation: none
Undergraduate enrollment: 2,431
Total enrollment: 3,193
Percent Male/Female: 76%/24%
Percent Minority: 15.0%

Percent African-American: 2.0%
Percent Hispanic: 7.0%
Percent Asian: 6.0%
Percent in-state/out-of-state: 72%/28%
Percent Pub HS: 90%
Fraternities: 16%
Sororities: 16%
Number of Applicants: 1,950
Percent Accepted: 77%
Percent Accepted who enroll: 32%
Entering: 549
Transfers: 80
Application Deadline: 1 May

Mean SAT: 590 V, 650 M
Middle 50% SAT range: 590 V, 650 M
Middle 50% ACT range: 28
Mean ACT: 28
3 Most popular majors: chem. engr., mechanical engr., electrical engr.
Retention: 84%
Graduation rate: 64%
Library: 320,000 volumes
Tuition and Fees: $15,211 in; $15,311 out
Room and Board: $4,920
On-campus housing: 86%
Financial aid, first-year: 80%

Located at the base of the Rocky Mountains, the Colorado School of Mines campus as well as the Coors Brewery are the main hot spots of Golden, Colorado, a town of 15,000 people (of which about 3,000 attend the college). The university offers 14 bachelor of science degrees, 10 of which include the word "engineering," along with degrees in chemistry, economics, mathematics, and computer sciences. The bevy of engineering majors at Mines, says one student, makes for a very "homogeneous student body and a rather dull college experience."

Highly Academic Minded

Almost everyone would agree that students consider academics a top priority at the Colorado School of Mines. All students are required to take a number of courses including those in calculus, chemistry, economics, physics, physical education, and a course called Nature and Human Values (described as "a lousy excuse for a liberal arts class"). Freshmen are also required to take EPICS (Engineering Practices Introductory Course Sequence), in which groups are given a real-life project to solve each semester. Projects range from re-mediating mine tailing waste to making solar cookers. Basically, freshmen are "all in the same classes for the first year and a half." The larger classes, physics and chemistry, range from 100 to 200 students while most others enroll about 40 to 50. The larger classes are broken up into weekly recitations so students know that "you can get help if you need it." However, one senior described some of the required courses as "of no interest and kind of a waste of time, even though they give us a broad (academic) basis." These classes are tough and most students believe that the requirements are imposed "to weed out" those who cannot stay afloat, which accounts for the high class dropout rate. Indeed, students say that the first few months are "very overwhelming at first," though many tend to "get used to the pace and rigor as the semester rolls along." Nevertheless, one Mines student described the workload as "challenging, engaging, and gratifying." Students here are devoted to their studies and proud of the work that they do.

The school's heavy emphasis on engineering sets Mines apart from other schools. One student said that he came because "I always loved science and math classes, and hated English and history classes in high school. Here, I'm not required to take any of those classes." However, the Guy T. McBride Honors Program offers students a liberal arts dimension to their education. In this program, students are required to read one book a week and write an essay on it. Most students love that the Mines is generally focused on the areas that they enjoy the most, yet some students were bothered by the small number of liberal arts opportunities. This heavy emphasis on the sciences and engineering creates an environment often described as "intense," though not overly competitive.

Your Place or Mine?

The social life at Mines can be summed up by the fact that most students complain that it is "pretty lousy." The school enforces its no-tolerance policy for drugs. Although drinking goes on, especially at frat parties, security is required at all parties that serve alcohol. Guards work doors, check IDs, and give out wristbands in an effort to curb underage drinking.

Students report that Mines is not much of a party school. On weekends, many Mines students migrate toward UC Boulder or Colorado State University to find both the "girls and the parties." One student said that the party scene is "the worst in the country. I am from Anchorage, Alaska, and my high school parties were better than this." However, Golden does offer a few bars for the upper-age crowd as well as a movie theater, though many students indicated that neither option is a major source of distraction from the academic rigors of the school week. Other students turn to their computers, video games, or homework on the weekends.

Colorado also provides many modes of escape for students. Outdoor activities such as rock climbing, hiking, and camping are popular among students here. Students are frequently found skiing on the weekends, as Golden is not more than half an hour away from many top ski locales including Vail, Copper Mountain, and Winter Park. One student commented that the opportunities to interact with nature and the outdoors offered at Mines "are unlike anything else that any other school could offer."

The dating scene, however, suffers from the fact that 77 percent of the student body is male. One male student commented that "the girls who have a social life turn into sluts and the girls that were decent-looking in high school become goddesses." For women, the debilitated dating scene is also complicated because "all the guys are geeky losers." The best advice for those seeking love and romance is that "while most people here are very nice, most students would be best looking off- campus for love."

Mind and (Student) Body

Adjectives students use to describe their classmates are "un-athletic," "quiet," "smart," and "conservative." One student characterized the variety of students here as "about as diverse as the Ku Klux Klan." Nonetheless, most students are not greatly bothered by the lack of minorities. As for homosexuals, one student said that "this is not the campus to be openly gay on because it's way conservative."

Many students do raise complaints about other personal characteristics of the student population. One said that "many students don't interact much with the outside world. They just kinda sit in front of the computer all day—there are a number of people here who wake up at 6 A.M. to play on their computers." Multiplayer games such as Quake and Starcraft are very popular as most floors are known to have big games every day. Another student commented that "most people are nerds; they don't have any social life and live in the dorms all four years. They don't do anything but homework." One student concluded that the large portion of introverts "goes along with the type of people that major in engineering. They are not very social for the most part so the school is pretty much dead, and those people who want to party end up doing a lot of stuff off-campus."

The Colorado School of Mines is not the best place to be for those who are likely to be found picketing outside of state buildings or lobbying for better U.S.–Arab relations. As far as an activist scene, one student commented that "nobody seems to care because they are either just not interested or too busy doing a problem set." When asked about student involvement in campus life, one student responded with a "resounding no." The Greek system accounts for most of the philanthropic activity while most students get involved with the engineering department either through working with their professors or joining academic organizations.

This Life of Mine

Freshmen comprise a great majority of students in Mines's five residence halls. The four halls that offer "traditional" housing are comprised mostly of doubles and singles. Though housing is "comfortable," these are the older buildings that tend to be "old and dirty." Bathrooms are shared, closet space is limited, and most do not have carpeting. Apart from the traditional dorms are the more luxurious and more expensive Weaver Towers. Students in the Towers live in suites of six to eight people in "newer and nicer" facilities, particularly noted for their air-conditioning. Students receive postcards on which to rank their housing preferences, and dorm assignments are on a strictly first come, first served basis. However, most students move to nearby off-campus apartments after their first year because of a strict resident advising system and expensive on-campus meal plans. Although the food was described as "satisfying" and "good for a university," there were some complaints about meal variety and options.

> "I always loved science and math classes and hated English and history classes in high school, and here I'm not required to take any of those classes."

The Mines campus is very small, but "beautifully green." The main campus covers about one square mile and students report that they can walk from one end to another in just a few minutes. There are large common areas, such as Kassador Commons, where students can play Frisbee or set up tents for campus events. One student praised the wildlife around campus, remembering one day when he saw 30 wild deer passing in front of his dorm. This intimate size of the Mines community receives mixed reviews from the student body. One student stated, "I feel like I know the whole campus, and can talk to most of the students or faculty, but it is limiting because sometimes there is nothing I want to do here." Another student noted that the campus lacks a collegiate atmosphere when he stated "I drive through campuses of other universities and can almost always see students walking around or studying on the grass. Here, you hardly ever see that."

Golden is a generally safe town located only about 20 minutes from downtown Denver. Students have no problem commuting for the occasional sporting event or concert. The Coors Brewery is also nearby and offers students a couple of free beers at the end of every tour. Many students comment that they can smell the malt from the brewery from the dorm rooms. Golden also offers many popular off-campus opportunities to grab some food with friends, including McDonald's, Wendy's, Pizza Hut, and Subway. Other popular off-campus hangouts include the Ace Bar and the Buffalo Rose Saloon.

Taking to the (Mine) Field

Mines offers 16 varsity sports, the most by any state school in Colorado. About 20 percent of the student body is involved at the varsity level. Also, more than 35 percent of students actively participate in the intramural sports program at Mines. Soccer, ultimate Frisbee, flag football, and basketball are the most popular. School spirit, though, is generally considered "dead as a ghost." One student said that "sometimes the cheerleaders will yell; that's the closest thing to team sprit I can think of."

The Colorado School of Mines is a great place for those who can find their niche in a very rigorous and academically focused program. One insightful senior noted that the college is "so geared toward engineering that you want to go here and be an engineer or go to a different school—most people realize they don't want to be engineers and transfer." The Mines is a great place to be for those who enjoy a small campus life and a strong emphasis on the applied sciences.
—*Kurtland Ma and Staff*

FYI

The three best things about attending Mines are "gratification of hard work, focus on math and science, and great location (close to Denver, close to nature)."

The three worst things about attending Mines are "homogeneous student body, weeding out process (high student drop out rate), and the poor social life."

The three things that every student should do before graduating Mines are "taking a nonscience class, participating in outdoors activities for an escape, and looking for love and a life with the outside world off campus!"

One thing I'd like to have known before coming here is "how terrible the love life is for both men and women."

Colorado State University

Address: Spruce Hall, Fort
  Collins, CO 80523
Phone: 970-491-6909
E-mail address:
  admissions@colostate.edu
Web site URL:
  www.colostate.edu
Location: suburban
Founded: 1870
Private or Public: public
Religious affiliation: none
**Undergraduate
  enrollment:** 18,640
Total enrollment: 22,344
Percent Male / Female:
  48% / 52%
Percent Minority: 14.0%

Percent African-American:
  2.0%
Percent Hispanic: 6.0%
Percent Asian: 3.0%
**Percent in-state / out-of-
  state:** 79% / 21%
Percent Pub HS: NA
Fraternities: 14%
Sororities: 14%
Number of Applicants:
  10,367
Percent Accepted: 76%
**Percent Accepted who
  enroll:** 39%
Entering: 4,609
Transfers: 0
Application Deadline: 1 Jul

Mean SAT: 551 V, 561 M
Middle 50% SAT range:
  490–590 V, 500–610 M
Middle 50% ACT range: NA
Mean ACT: 24
3 Most popular majors:
  general business, liberal
  arts, biological science
Retention: 81%
Graduation rate: 26%
Library: 1.8 million volumes
Tuition and Fees: $2,933
  in; $10,155 out
Room and Board: $4,878
On-campus housing: 95%
Financial aid, first-year:
  38%

It's been called by *Your Future* one of the four "Best Places to Be Young." *Money Magazine* ranked it among the twenty safest cities in the U.S. *Reader's Digest* noted that it was the third best city in the country to live based on the absence of crime, low rate of drug and alcohol abuse, clean environment, and affordable cost of living. Where can you find such a city? Where the Great Plains meet the Rocky Mountains is the vibrant city of Fort Collins, and nestled in the heart of Fort Collins are 642 green acres, home of Colorado State University.

Students come from Colorado and beyond to enjoy the beauty of Fort Collins, experience the "exceptional academics" that come without exceptional costs, and join in the multitude of activities that CSU has to offer. Few are disappointed. Students report that they love CSU and its "exciting and relaxed" environment.

Hidden Resources

Students claim that the solid academics at CSU are consistently underrated. The university boasts eight academic colleges with concentrations in agricultural science; applied human science; business; engineering; literary arts; forestry and natural resources; veterinary medicine; and biomedical sciences. Students who

haven't decided on a major can postpone enrollment in a specific college and register with the more generic "open option." Although liberal arts are offered at the school, its strengths lie in the natural sciences. The well-respected veterinary school is ranked among the top in the nation; the business school is "top notch"; the forestry and natural resource management school is well respected; and the engineering program is earning increased attention, due in part to extensive facility renovations, an easily accessible internship program in Fort Collins, and great research opportunities.

With this respect, however, comes a "kind of challenging" workload. CSU requires its students to take classes from each of five general categories, including Communications and Reasoning; Natural Sciences; Arts and Humanities; Behavioral and Social Sciences; and Physical Education and Wellness. Although most students claim these requirements are relatively simple to fulfill, some students complain that they ensure that "there will always be that one semester when you cannot avoid an 8:00 A.M. class." Students also get frustrated with class sizes in some of the introductory courses, some of which enroll 200–300 students. Whether the class has 10 or 300 students, however, students claim that "professors genuinely care for their students on an individual level and make themselves accessible."

The workload varies by class. Many perceive studio art to be easy, but time consuming, and some students report that psychology is relatively easy. Science courses, particularly engineering, tend to be more challenging. One student joked that "if you're a genius, even the sciences will be easy, and if you're not, you'll have to work fairly hard."

So where do people do this hard work? Some students study in their rooms, but usually that's a luxury of people who have singles. Popular places to study include the Sunken Lounge at Lory Student Center, the newly renovated Morgan Library, or outside on the grass. Despite the work load that CSU students can expect, most guarantee that "there's always time to have fun!"

Fort Fun

The new Lory Student Center provides not only the Sunken Lounge for study, but also a popular place to take a break from the books. After the old facility was flooded, the school decided to renovate its main gathering place. After the student center underwent a complete renovation, the *New York Times* ranked Lory as one of the country's ten best student centers. With video arcades, pool tables, a ballroom, a theater, a computer store, a bookstore, restaurants, bowling alleys, comfortable places to sit and sleep, TVs, and more, Lory earned the high ranking that came as no shock to CSU students.

Other recent renovations on campus have included the engineering building, the environmental sciences building, and the student recreation center/gym. Students report that the engineering building is "very attractive," but the real enthusiasm is for the environmental sciences building, with its copper fountain cascading from three stories. Students consider the new gym to be a "great facility," but sorry professors, you're not allowed.

Students are required to live on campus for their freshman year. Those who live on campus prefer Corbett, the party dorm, and Braiden, the most centrally located dorm. Rooms tend to be small, but stu-

dents enjoy the "great big windows" from which you can enjoy Colorado's 300 days of sunshine. After freshman year, many students move off campus. Fort Collins offers many apartment complexes, like Rams Village, to its students.

Many opt to live off campus because the on-campus alcohol policy strictly states that no alcohol can be consumed in the dorms. Fraternities and sororities aren't a huge presence, though they do constitute about 10 percent of the student body. Students have a wide selection of bars and clubs in Fort Collins to choose from. Popular clubs include Ramskellar (on campus, actually), Linden's and Felipe's (in Old Town Fort Collins), Suite 152, the Matrix, the Martini Bar, and Washington's. Students who want to get a bite to eat off campus enjoy Coopersmith's, a brewery with reportedly good food, El Burrito and Rio Grande, Bisetti's, Canino's, the Charcoal Broiler, CB & Potts, Young's Vietnamese Cuisine, and the Red Dragon. Students also frequent several coffee places, including Starry Night, Starbucks, Déjà vu Coffeehouse, and the Coffee Connection.

300 Days of Sunshine

Colorado boasts nice weather, but Fort Collins has the added benefit of avoiding "those huge storms that Denver gets." Students capitalize on this weather by hanging outside, hiking, biking, roller blading, running, skiing (slopes are only 2 hours away), snowshoeing, and rock climbing. River rafting is popular, as are water sports on nearby Horsetooth Reservoir. With the exception of surfing, Fort Collins offers almost everything for the outdoor enthusiast.

This enthusiasm for outdoor activity extends to sports: CSU students enjoy participating in and/or watching the many sports that CSU has to offer. The women's basketball team has had a strong performance, making a bid for the NCAA tournament. The football team has also had strong showings, taking the title for the Mountain West Athletic Conference. Both the community and students come out to support the teams.

Intramurals are a popular activity on campus. Team lists, sometimes arranged by dorm floor or apartment complex, fill up quickly. Students are especially eager to play softball, basketball, innertube waterpolo, soccer, flag football, volleyball, tennis, racquetball, and in-line hockey (a new offering). Part of the popularity of intramurals stems from the fact that students recognize them as a fun way to get to know people and to get some exercise.

Student enthusiasm isn't limited to sports and outdoor activity; students have a wide selection of extracurricular activities from which to choose. Those interested in writing can work for the *Rocky Mountain Collegian,* and those interested in television can participate in Campus Television, which one student claimed "has won more Emmy's than the cast of *Seinfeld.*" His claim might be slightly exaggerated, but students agree that the television and the radio station, KCSU, are great. The arts are also popular at

CSU. The dance school hosts recitals, there are open auditions for plays and musicals, and there are frequent poetry and fiction readings. Community service is another activity that draws a number of students. CSU students can volunteer to tutor in the Fort Collins community, give time to the Northern Colorado AIDS Project, run and bike in marathons to help raise funding for various causes, and conduct food drives for the homeless and needy.

"There's always time to have fun!"

Students at CSU benefit not only from a strong academic program, but also from gorgeous surroundings and countless opportunities to get involved in social and community life. —*Marti Page*

FYI
The three best things about attending CSU are "being in Colorado; the opportunities on and off campus to learn, volunteer, and have fun; and the caring and devoted faculty."
The three worst things about attending CSU are "parking, limited library hours, and large student body."
The three things that every student should do before graduating from CSU are "go to a lady Rams basketball game, hike to the Aggies sign above Fort Collins, and go into Old Town on Friday night."
One thing I'd like to have known before coming here is "how spread out the campus is."

United States Air Force Academy

Address: HQ USAFA / RRS, 2304 Cadet Drive, Suite 200, USAF Academy, CO 80840-5025
Phone: 719-333-2520
E-mail address: rrmail.rr@usafa.af.mil
Web site URL: www.usafa.af.mil
Location: suburban
Founded: 1954
Private or Public: public
Religious affiliation: none
Undergraduate enrollment: 4,107
Total enrollment: 4,107
Percent Male / Female: 84% / 16%
Percent Minority: 17.0%

Percent African-American: 5.0%
Percent Hispanic: 7.0%
Percent Asian: 4.0%
Percent in-state / out-of-state: 5% / 95%
Percent Pub HS: NA
Fraternities: 0%
Sororities: 0%
Number of Applicants: 10,035
Percent Accepted: 12%
Percent Accepted who enroll: 100%
Entering: 1,204
Transfers: 0
Application Deadline: 31 Jan
Mean SAT: 626 V, 649 M

Middle 50% SAT range: 580–670 V, 610–690 M
Middle 50% ACT range: NA
Mean ACT: NA
3 Most popular majors: management / engineering management, biology, political science
Retention: 92%
Graduation rate: 80%
Library: 700,000 volumes
Tuition and Fees: 0%
Room and Board: $0
On-campus housing: 100%
Financial aid, first-year: 0%

Freshmen at the United States Air Force Academy undergo a rigorous academic and military regimen that occupies almost every waking minute, and cadets do not spend much time asleep. Arriving in late June, freshmen spend six weeks at "Basic," a boot camp that prepares them for academy life. They then begin the Academy's most difficult year. Those who choose to remain at the Academy report that their hard work definitely pays off. Looking back on his experience, one senior said, "Freshman year is really tough. It's not fun here, but it's rewarding. Now that I'm a senior, I love it."

A Cadet's Life

Cadets, nicknamed "zoomies," praise the Academy for providing leadership opportunities that will help them in later life, regardless of whether they continue to pursue a military career. The entire student body, called the Cadet Wing, is divided into 40 squadrons of approximately 100 cadets each. Cadets in the same squadron live together, eat together, and train together. Seniors, called "first classmen," hold major leadership positions in the squadron. One first classman is squadron commander each semester; his or her duties include assigning rooms, marching the squadron to breakfast and lunch, and knowing the schedule of every cadet in the squadron. Other cadets in the squadron make up the commander's staff.

Each squadron lives in either Vanderberg or Sijan halls, two large dorms with mostly two-person rooms. Many freshmen have triples, but almost all upperclassmen have doubles. Cadets with rooms in the same hallways share communal bathrooms, which are all single-sex. Female cadets live on the same floors as males, but because of the high male-to-female ratio, women often live far away from one another. "In the dorm, there's me and my roommate. The closest room with girls is quite a bit away," one cadet said. She added that women receive the same treatment as men and enjoy the same leadership opportunities.

The freshmen's day starts early in the morning, usually between 5:30 A.M. and 6 A.M., when they wake up and attend to their squadron duties. Squadron duties include delivering newspapers to upperclassmen's rooms and cleaning the squadron's offices and common areas. At 6:40, cadets line up for morning formation and march to Mitchell Hall ("Mitch's") for breakfast. Freshmen eat all their meals at attention, making as little noise as possible. The entire cadet wing takes its meals during the same 20-minute period, so cadets eat quickly. The food receives mixed reviews, though the cadets' main complaint was the lack of choices. Classes start at 7:30 and last until 11:30, when cadets line up again for another formation. They march into Mitch's for lunch and hurry to afternoon classes, which run from 12:30 to 3:30.

After class, a variety of activities occupy the cadets' time. Athletes head to practice, and some students attend club meetings. Popular extracurricular activities include the jump team, whose members parachute out of airplanes; KAFA, a campus radio station; the Drum and Bugle Corps; the *Warrior Update*, a student newspaper; and community service opportunities. Students report that service projects such as tutoring and working at soup kitchens "give you a chance to get off base, especially for us freshmen." Students without time commitments to varsity teams or certain clubs must play one intramural sport each semester; intramurals meet every other day.

Dinner is the Academy's only optional meal, so students can stay in if they need to study or rest. The cadets' evenings are unstructured. Freshmen, however, must be in their rooms studying after 8 P.M. Most cadets report going to sleep around midnight so that they can be ready for the next morning's early wake-up.

Academics

Academy cadets face the same academic challenges as students at any competitive college or university. Cadets often take twenty-one credit hours (or seven classes) in a semester, and some majors, such as aeronautical engineering, require even more course work. One student was surprised by "the other cadets' dedication to academics here." He added, "There's no letdown at all. You're taking so many classes." Students divide majors into technical and non-science "fuzzy" majors, where the non-science majors are considered slightly easier. Many aspiring pilots flock to the political science and management majors, which prompt some non-pilots to chant, "Wanna fly? Poli-sci." Cadets agree that even the somewhat less rigorous majors demand a great deal of work since "none of the majors are easy."

Many students have reported that they have "no problem getting into classes we want," but they also said the core curriculum often dictates most of their course selections. After satisfying the requirements for the core and her major, one senior said, "I haven't really had that much opportunity to choose my courses." Each year, the Academy assigns each freshman to an academic advisor and also to a sophomore who looks out for the cadets and ensures that they follow regulations. Students who studied a subject at an advanced level in high school or at another college before entering the Academy (transfer students enter as freshmen), may be able to place out of some core classes. Otherwise, students should count on taking classes in chemistry, calculus, one year of a foreign language, computer science, writing, and mechanics among other fields during their first year. In the last year or two, more elective choices become available, such as music appreciation, American philosophy, medical ethics, and "499 courses," which are independent research programs guided by the professors in various departments.

Weekend Leave

Weekends often provide a much needed break from academy life. Each cadet is assigned a host family in the Colorado Springs area, often a retired military serviceman, which provides a home for the cadets on weekends. After freshman year, cadets can leave campus on almost any weekend, and many students go to Denver, Fort Collins, or Boulder, the homes of Colorado State University and the University of Colorado, respectively. Cadets say that you can spot an academy student on leave in Colorado Springs by his demeanor. Cadets are generally "very conservative," "polite," and "very much in line."

For those who do not leave the base, the Academy plans social activities for freshmen in Hap Arnold Hall ("Arnie's"), which serves as a campus social center. Seniors are allowed to leave the base on weekdays after completing their military duties, so they often leave around 5 P.M. and return by 11 P.M. One thing that might prevent students from leaving base on a weekend is the "triple threat," which includes Saturday morning inspections ("Sami's"), a home football game (which all cadets must attend), and a parade put on by cadets for spectators. Weekends also allow students some free time to enjoy their surroundings. "It's just beautiful up here," one cadet said. "We're right in the mountains."

> "Many people complain, but with the challenges come definite rewards. I fly upside down every other day, and I haven't paid a dime."

Most cadets seem truly grateful for the opportunity to attend a top-notch school at absolutely no cost. One cadet said, "Many people complain, but with the challenges come definite rewards. I fly upside down every other day, and I haven't paid a dime." In return for a free education, cadets pledge to serve for at least five years in the Air Force after graduation; pilots accept an extra service requirement (so they cannot immediately use their expensive government-funded training to get jobs at commercial airlines). The Air Force pays for some graduates from the Academy to attend medical school, law school, and other postgraduate schools; however, years spent in professional school do not count toward a graduate's service requirement.

Cadets warn prospective students not to come to the Academy without learning a lot about it. As one cadet advised, "If you are a recruited athlete [who sometimes know less about academy life], make sure you find out more about this place because it can be really brutal if you don't know what you are getting into." Cadets consistently stress the importance of time management at the Academy and of having a real understanding of the place's military rigor. Overall, however, cadets consider the intense effort that the Academy demands more than worthwhile. Many genuinely respect the Air Force and what it stands for, and they look forward to putting their education and training to work both in and out of the military — *Ben Trachtenberg and Staff*

FYI
The three best things about attending the USAFA are "the free top-notch education, the campus is beautiful, and the camaraderie with fellow students."
The three worst things about attending the USAFA are "the entire freshman year, a lack of vacation time, and the bureaucracy."
The three things that every student should do before graduating from the USAFA are "the Jump (parachuting) program, take advantage of the skiing, and break the rules at least once."
One thing I'd like to have known before coming here is "how to study and write because you won't make it otherwise."

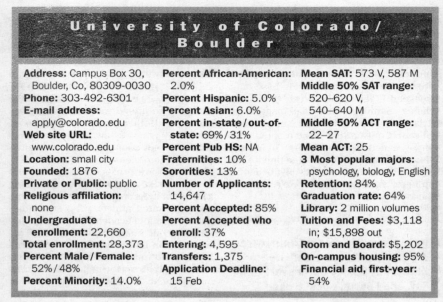

University of Colorado / Boulder

Address: Campus Box 30, Boulder, Co, 80309-0030
Phone: 303-492-6301
E-mail address: apply@colorado.edu
Web site URL: www.colorado.edu
Location: small city
Founded: 1876
Private or Public: public
Religious affiliation: none
Undergraduate enrollment: 22,660
Total enrollment: 28,373
Percent Male / Female: 52% / 48%
Percent Minority: 14.0%

Percent African-American: 2.0%
Percent Hispanic: 5.0%
Percent Asian: 6.0%
Percent in-state / out-of-state: 69% / 31%
Percent Pub HS: NA
Fraternities: 10%
Sororities: 13%
Number of Applicants: 14,647
Percent Accepted: 85%
Percent Accepted who enroll: 37%
Entering: 4,595
Transfers: 1,375
Application Deadline: 15 Feb

Mean SAT: 573 V, 587 M
Middle 50% SAT range: 520–620 V, 540–640 M
Middle 50% ACT range: 22–27
Mean ACT: 25
3 Most popular majors: psychology, biology, English
Retention: 84%
Graduation rate: 64%
Library: 2 million volumes
Tuition and Fees: $3,118 in; $15,898 out
Room and Board: $5,202
On-campus housing: 95%
Financial aid, first-year: 54%

In a valley at the foot of the Rocky Mountains, where the great plains abruptly meet the front range, sits the University of Colorado at Boulder. Known locally as CU, the beautiful campus is located just 25 minutes from Denver and 45 minutes from Eldora, the closest ski resort. Students can take advantage of the great outdoors, which is virtually in their backyards, without giving up city life. Boulder is a small city that is growing at a tremendous rate, but is still small enough to lack urban problems like high crime rates. The campus has a relaxed feeling about it, and some students say anyone who is easygoing would love CU's environment because "here, students do their own thing."

Academics— What You Make Them

At CU, academics are as easy or as tough as you make them. Students say that you can earn a degree from CU having worked hard or having hardly worked at all. Graduation requirements include a distribution core that requires students to be reasonably proficient in a foreign language, writing, critical thinking, and have basic mathematical skills. Among the best departments, according to undergrads, are engineering, the natural sciences, sociology, and business. Anthropology is an especially popular department. Professors are reportedly very approachable, and one student said he especially liked how most professors interact with students and love what they are doing. However, one student warned that some calculus professors are "brainy Nobel prize winners that really don't know how to teach," and who sometimes like to fail students. Another student said some profs are "egomaniacs." Overall, though, CU students are satisfied with their professors. Difficult classes include calculus, those in the natural sciences, and engineering classes, especially physical chemistry. Slackers reportedly major in open-option arts and sciences—otherwise known as the "arts and parties."

Freshmen tend to get stuck with leftover classes in the fall term because they register at orientation over the summer, and all other students register the previous April. Class size averages 200 to 500 for introductory and popular courses, but after freshman year the classes get progressively smaller, with an average class size of about 50. By senior year, classes usually range from 10 to 30 students. Large classes break into smaller sections taught by teaching assistants (TAs). Students report that TAs are usually good, despite the occasional problems with those TAs whose English is not strong. CU also has an honors program with smaller classes, averaging 9 to 10 students per class discussion in classes with 40 students or fewer. CU students also get their share of outside education when famous guest speakers come to campus. In recent years, guest speakers have included the CEO of the company that produces Tootsie Rolls (who came to a business class to lecture in addition to giving out product samples), Secretary of the Interior Bruce Babbitt, and Olympic diver Greg Louganis.

Much More Than Academics

At CU, life is much more than just academics. CU students have diverse interests, and can likewise choose from a large number of social options. Greeks are a definite presence in Boulder social life, but they don't offer the only option for fun on the weekends. The most popular Panhellenic groups are Alpha Chi Omega, Kappa Kappa Gamma, Kappa Alpha Theta, and Delta Gamma. The most active fraternities are Alpha Tau Omega, FIJI, Pi Kappa Phi, Pi Kappa Alpha, and Sigma Alpha Epsilon. Sororities are usually harder to rush than fraternities, since they are more formal and have more rules and regulations than frats. Frat parties are said to be "a blast," but they are officially dry. Many Greek bashes are inter-house, date, or theme parties. The Sink is a favorite watering hole for fraternity boys. However, if you are not into the frat scene, one student warns that it is hard to mix in with the crowd. Fraternities occasionally rent out dance clubs, which are especially well-attended affairs. But, it is a definite "scene." One student felt that, "Greek life is lots of skinny girls in trendy dresses and piles of wasted frat boys."

If you're not into the Greek scene, Nick's Sports restaurant is a popular hangout. On the weekend, students frequent the bars of Boulder, such as the Foundry, the Wallace, and the Walnut Brewery, which all offer "good music, good drinks, and lots of fun." There are also large school parties around campus.

Every year people attend the party "Xmas" dressed as Santas and elves (this party can draw a crowd in excess of 2,000 people). Many people go out on dates and one student said that "Fridays are pretty laid-back; they are the date night." However, students report that there are just as many random hookups. Although there are a lot of gay and lesbian couples, students say they are not as visible on campus as at some other schools. CU has a reputation as a party school, and many students agree with the stereotype to a degree, saying that "there are more people that party [than don't]" but that not everyone parties in the same way.

Chemical Fun

CU has had some alcohol-related problems in recent years, which students say have changed the relationship between police and undergrads from one of mutual tolerance to one of mutual disrespect. Recently, the police have been cracking down harder and harder on underage alcohol consumption, and students agree that being underage is much more of a problem if you want to drink than it used to be. Some students gripe that Boulder police are "horrible" because they never "let students be without giving them a hard time." Therefore, students basically "despise" them and there are several major "incidents" between students and police each year. The administration is as unpopular as the police among students for its regulations against kegs on campus ("but people get them anyway"), and the beer ban at sports events. Even with the crackdown, students say alcohol is still widely consumed both on and off campus, and there are more students that drink than that don't. However, being a nondrinker reportedly will not hinder your social life. Those who don't drink say they are not pressured to do so.

Drugs do not present as much of a problem on the CU campus as alcohol. Although CU is known to many as a "druggie school," a large number of students don't do drugs. Students agree that there are at least as many people who don't use drugs on a regular basis as those that do. The most common drug is marijuana, which almost everyone encounters at some point whether he or she is involved with drugs or not. According to one student, "Drugs are there for those that want them."

Kicking Back

Dorm life at CU is not for everyone. Freshmen are required to live on campus, but after freshman year more and more people move off campus. By senior year, a large percentage of students are living off campus. Dorms are said to be good, but some residents dislike the "childish rules that are not well-enforced"—like no alcohol. Dorms vote on quiet hours, and RAs are usually easy on the students they supervise. The best dorms are said to be Kittridge, because of its scenic location, as well as Baker, Reed, and Crosman. Libby Hall, Cheyenne/Arapaho, and Hallet are popular for social students because they party so much in them that the dorms have received national recognition for it. However, some residents complain that these dorms are too loud, too crowded, have bad facilities/small rooms, are ugly, or all of the above.

CU students are a very diverse group, and resist categorization. However, some say there is a "common CU student" if not a typical one: wealthy Caucasian. Some undergrads would like just a bit more diversity among the student body. Stereotypes of CU students include "hippies" and "granolas," as many come from suburban or urban environments and are trying to "get back to nature." Students at CU are very easygoing and friendly, and although there are cliques, you can choose to hang out with just about anyone. At CU, "you always feel welcome," one student said. Many people are the "outdoorsy" type, and love to camp, hike, bike, and join environmental clubs. Engineers, pre-meds, and math and science majors are all identified separately from other majors, largely because these majors require less partying and more work. The administration discourages cars because of the traffic problems and limited parking space in Boulder, though many students ride bikes. Despite this, one student said cars are popular because so many people like to travel to the mountains or to Denver.

Rocky Mountain High

Students agree that both the environment and location of CU make it one of the most beautiful campuses in the nation. The buildings are uniform in architectural style, and are quite attractive on the outside, but sometimes "junky on the inside." In recent years, additions to the Music School, the engineering building, and the Integrated Teaching and Learning Labs have provided for new, attractive sights on campus. The engineering addition is the only regular classroom building on campus that students need an ID to get into. The CU gym is very large and modern. Norlin Library offers students a quiet environment and all the resources they need for research. Folsom Stadium, where the varsity football team plays, has a gorgeous view of the front range of the Rockies. Since the CU campus is in a suburban area, students mostly feel safe there. However, in Boulder there "are a lot of weirdos running around that aren't dangerous, just really weird," and students recommend using caution.

The Buffs

Sports at CU are a major attraction. The football team has been in the top 25 in the nation for the past 10 years, and the basketball team "is on the way up" with a new coach. The CU Buffaloes, known locally as "the Buffs," have excellent sports teams and a popular mascot, Ralphie the buffalo. Popular sports include varsity football and basketball (mostly spectator sports, unless you are good enough to get on the teams), and skiing and snowboarding. Students pursue every other sport imaginable, including rock climbing on the Flatirons (huge stone slabs that jut out of the faces of mountains) and in nearby Eldorado Canyon. Intramurals are also popular. Saturday football is a tradition with many students, and the games against Nebraska and Oklahoma, CU's Big Eight archrivals, always fill the stadium. Of course, students have local professional teams to support as well, including the Broncos, the Avalanche, the Nuggets, and the Colorado Rockies.

The Stuff on the Table

One aspect of CU that students do not praise is the food. The dinning halls at CU serve food that draws such comments as "interesting," "barely tolerable," and "gets old fast after freshman year." Perhaps because of the food, students rarely hang out in the dining halls but instead "eat and leave." The campus meal plans give students the option to use their "dining dollars" at vending machines. The city of Boulder has many excellent restaurants, especially on the Pearl Street Mall (an outdoor mall popular with students). Students also go to Pearl Street for its "good" bars. Students often go to restaurants right off campus on the Hill. Pizza delivery and takeout is also a favorite option among undergrads.

The beautiful outdoors, the gorgeous campus, and the easygoing atmosphere all make CU a unique university. People in Boulder and on campus are generally accepting, tolerant, and liberal. The laid-back mood is so pervasive that students warn it can completely win you over. Students say they love their campus and their school and "would choose CU again in a minute." —*Alison Pulaski and Staff*

FYI

The three best things about attending CU are "outdoor activities, casual atmosphere, and geographic location."

The three worst things about attending CU are "parking sucks, ethnic diversity is limited and the groups are sometimes hostile towards each other, and police are lame...they are either over-reactive or under-reactive, and they are prejudiced towards college students."

The three things that every student should do before graduating CU are "hike to the Flatirons, do the Pearl Street Mall pub crawl, and see a concert at Fox Theater."

One thing I'd like to have known before coming here is "that you should have a good academic plan because advisors are clueless."

University of Denver

Address: 2199 S. University Blvd, Denver CO 80208
Phone: 303-871-2036
E-mail address: admission@du.edu
Web site URL: www.du.edu
Location: suburban
Founded: 1864
Private or Public: private
Religious affiliation: none
Undergraduate enrollment: 3,809
Total enrollment: 9,188
Percent Male / Female: 42% / 58%
Percent Minority: 16.0%
Percent African-American: 4.0%

Percent Hispanic: 6.0%
Percent Asian: 5.0%
Percent in-state / out-of-state: NA
Percent Pub HS: NA
Fraternities: 29%
Sororities: 22%
Number of Applicants: 3,303
Percent Accepted: 83%
Percent Accepted who enroll: 30%
Entering: 834
Transfers: NA
Application Deadline: 1 Feb
Mean SAT: 557 V, 560 M

Middle 50% SAT range: 490–610 V, 500–610 M
Middle 50% ACT range: NA
Mean ACT: 24
3 Most popular majors: biology, communication, psychology
Retention: 84%
Graduation rate: 54%
Library: 1,155,981 volumes
Tuition and Fees: $18,936 in; $18,936 out
Room and Board: $6,165
On-campus housing: 41%
Financial aid, first-year: 52%

At an elevation of 5,280 feet with 300 days of sunshine every year, the University of Denver is a paradise for the student who loves the outdoors. With the snowcapped Rocky Mountains nearby, access to the ski slopes is a hop, skip, and a jump away, while the city itself teems with enough life to satisfy any student. Of course, the academic reputation of the University of Denver is fairly strong as well. Thus, students who decide to obtain a degree from DU will reap the benefits of a study hard, play hard environment.

What TAs?

By far the distinguishing factor of DU academics is the predominantly small class size. Class enrollment ranges from as few as 6 students to approximately 60 students. The relationships between professors and students flourish in this more personalized setting, and the faculty for the most part "are approachable, knowledgeable, and grade fairly." The "one-on-one relationship we have with professors," says one student, "opens great opportunities for research." There are also very few TAs teaching except in science laboratories.

DU does have a core curriculum. All entering freshmen must take first-year English; one course in oral communications, math, computer science; and demonstrate proficiency in a foreign language. The DU Campus Connection ensures that freshmen adjust to the rigors of college life by assigning each one a faculty member who serves both as an academic advisor and a mentor for the entire first year. Special programs include the unique and highly selective Pioneer Leadership Program, which allows students to receive a minor in Leadership Studies that may be applied to any major. Students must apply to the Pioneer Leadership Program and be able to demonstrate leadership and devotion to community service. The Honors Program offers a variety of opportunities: seminars with lectures by guest scholars, a student-run Honors Association, special checkout privileges at Penrose Library, and special "honors floors" in each of the residence halls. Students in the Honors Program must take special honors courses while maintaining a GPA of 3.4 or higher.

The most difficult classes on campus are the courses on genetics and organic chemistry. As one student noted, "Since we are on a quarter system, if you miss a week of class, you can lose up to 10 percent of your grade in the course!" But, as another student said, "If you keep up and study hard, classes are not too strenuous." In addition, the university also hopes to "maximize the educational benefits that are associated with having a computer" by requiring all first-year students to purchase a laptop, beginning in fall of 1999.

One extremely popular DU offering is the Interterm classes. Because DU operates on a quarter system, the period of time between quarters, known as the Interterm, provides priceless opportunities for DU students. Each Interterm (in fall, winter, and spring), DU offers one-to-two-week classes that take students out of the classroom. Some popular classes include a painting class in Santa Fe, New Mexico; a business class that includes a trip to Wall Street in New York City; and a photojournalism class in Brazil.

The New and the Old

DU has a mix of old, almost Gothic-style buildings juxtaposed with brand-new structures. Evans Chapel near the student center has beautiful stained-glass windows, while not too far away, Penrose Library maintains a sleek, rectilinear style. The new science building, F. W. Olin Hall, is topped with a gleaming copper dome. DU will continue to make major capital improvements on buildings in coming years. A new business building, tennis pavilion, and the Wellness Center are slated for construction.

The architecture is not the only aesthetically pleasing characteristic of DU. There's a breathtaking view of the mountains, and also lots of "unique specimens of flowers and trees" scattered throughout campus. Besides the main University Park Campus, DU also has a "satellite" campus an inconvenient 10 miles away known as the Park Hill Campus. Students at Park Hill often complain about feeling disconnected from the rest of campus and the big hassle of having classes on both campuses.

DU also requires that students living outside a 90-mile radius of the school live on campus for the first two years. There are only two residence halls on campus: Centennial Halls and Johnson-McFarlane. Centennial Halls is comprised of twin high-rises 10 stories tall. Special features include a convenience store located in the residence hall as well as air-conditioned suites with furnished kitchens. Centennial Halls is where the Living-Learning Centers and Special Interest Floors are located. Living-Learning Centers are designed to bring American and international students together to "explore far-ranging global concerns." Each quarter, students take a one-credit course focusing on critical global issues. Special Interest Floors are available in the form of business floors, math and science floors, substance-free floors, and single-gender floors. Centennial Halls is also the home for students involved in the Honors Program. Johnson-McFarlane, commonly known as J-Mac, is a three-story building containing facilities similar to those at Centennial Halls. Students involved in the Pioneer Leadership Program live here, and J-Mac is considered the "tamer" of the two residence halls because Centennial Halls is "a-LOT wilder than J-Mac." Dorm food in these residence halls is regarded as "regular, nasty college food." As one senior stated, "Prepare to lose weight when you get here due to the terrible food."

Drink and Ski

"The city of Denver considers us at times a rich kid's school where all we do is drink and ski," commented one student. Admittedly, many students agree that there is some truth to the stereotype. Numerous students come from wealthy families, and a common joke among all undergrads is that they "drive Range Rovers that their Republican fathers bought for them." The preppy type of student definitely seems to be the majority on campus, but the "friendly, intelligent, mature, and generous" attitude of all DU students makes being a minority on campus comfortable.

Students say that alcohol is prevalent throughout campus. There are a few Greek houses going dry, though most are establishing a "bring your own beer" policy. At parties, students report plenty of random hookups, but a lot of serious dating also exists on campus as well. The Greek system at DU reportedly drives the social scene on campus. Little hostility exists between Greeks and non-Greeks, but one sophomore who decided not to rush said, "The Greek system runs the school. When I went through rush, people told me that if I wanted to be something on campus, I had to join a house." The frats and sororities open their parties to all students and hold big theme parties ranging from the "Beachcombers" (featuring sand and beach attire) to the very formal "Casino Royale" (where students gamble with fake money). There are parties and events not associated with the Greeks running throughout the year, which include fall homecoming, Winter Carnival, and May Daze in the spring. The DU Programming Board also sponsors weekly movies and guest speakers.

So Many Things to Do

"It is extremely easy to become involved at this school. All activities are open to everyone," exclaims one junior. The most popular organizations include students who work on the campus newspaper staff, the *Clarion*, the Alpine Club, and the DU Programming Board. Ethnic and cultural organizations and professional honors associations are also popular. Other, more specialized, organizations include the Forensics Club, the Kayak Club, and the Rescue Team. DU offers enough variety to satisfy almost any student. Many students participate in DU's club sports program, which allows students to join any team they like. No one is cut from a team, and "everyone has the chance to play in competition." Sports groups range from cycling to ultimate Frisbee to skiing (of course!). The most popular spectator sport is hockey. The Pioneers garner strong student support with DU "bleacher creatures," who often sit together in a designated section of the stadium to cheer loudly and stamp their feet incessantly during games.

> **"It is extremely easy to become involved in this school."**

Student enthusiasm and support for the Division I hockey team is a reflection of the general love the students have for their school. "People are very laid-back and casual here," says one student. DU undergrads at once enjoy the benefits of a city and the seclusion of suburban surroundings. Students agree that DU provides a solid undergraduate education while still allowing for an active social life and, more importantly, frequent ski trips to the Rockies. —*Melissa Chan and Staff*

FYI

The three best things about attending DU are "the proximity to the Rockies, the small class size and one-on-one relationships with professors, and Interterm classes."

The three worst things about attending DU are "the pressure of a quarter system, the terrible food, and the plethora of rich, preppy kids who have gone Greek."

The three things that every student should do before graduating DU are "take advantage of the Rockies, join the bleacher creatures at a hockey game, and enjoy the incredible social scene."

One thing I'd like to have known before coming here is "how much life at DU is a balance of work, partying, and skiing."

Connecticut

"Looking for a typical, small, New England liberal arts school? Well, in that case, Connecticut College is a great place to come," reported one sophomore. His description of his school as "typical," however, does not capture its honor code, close-knit community, great location, and solid academic programs that are hallmarks of the college.

The Best Programs

The best and most popular departments at Conn include government, psychology, economics, history, English, art, and dance. Although the humanities reign supreme in terms of popularity, this by no means indicates that the science departments are weak. Thanks to great facilities like the Connecticut College Arboretum and the new Olin Science Center, sciences are stronger than ever at Conn. Perhaps the main reason for the low levels of participation in the sciences is that many students dread the formidable pre-med track that requires introductory chemistry, re-

garded as the most difficult course at Conn.

In the true spirit of the liberal arts, students at Conn are required to take one course from each of seven different areas, including Physical and Biological Sciences, Mathematics and Logic, Social Science, Critical Studies in Literature and Arts, Creative Arts, Philosophy and Religious Studies, and Historical Studies. Students view the requirements as positive, not as some burden. "It's good because you go through the whole potpourri," said one student. This potpourri also contributes to the great flexibility offered to Conn students. One particularly impressed student noted that, "It's easy to design your own major, double major or minor, area of concentration, certificate program, or any other course of study you may desire, along with the dozens of already established programs." One complaint that students did voice was the requirement that students go to tutorials with their pre-major advisors during the first and second semesters. Students are also asked to attend at least six General Education events designed around an annual theme.

The international program is extremely popular at Conn. Students applaud the administration's belief in the importance of studying abroad. The college has recently become involved in CISLA , an intensive program that offers funding for students who want to pursue their self-designed projects. One of the students commented that CISLA "is a way to explore your dreams and learn about another culture."

Class sizes at Conn are usually small, but do include large lectures. Typically, upper-level seminars enroll only a few students, and the introductory courses are large. The classes are reportedly "challenging, but not overwhelming." Perhaps this relatively relaxed atmosphere can be attributed to the professors, who are "very approachable and personable." All classes at Conn are taught by professors, although TAs are there for tutoring. Office-hours meetings or e-mail are the most popular means for getting help from instructors.

Social Life—Unity on Campus

While the students do spend much time studying in Shain Library or their rooms, Conn students find room in their schedules to hang out with friends. "Students here get along and work well with others, probably because we're all stuck here together." Although New London "leaves much to be desired," the president is launching a campaign to integrate the school with the city development. Still, campus life is "active, busy, and fun." The Student Activities Council (SAC) provides events every Thursday, Friday, and Saturday night. Some of these activities include movies shown by the film society, performances by the a cappella singing groups or drama groups, and concerts. Although drinking does play a role in campus social activities, students agree that "you don't need to be drunk to have fun on this campus." Many students are attracted to Conn simply because there is no Greek life on campus. Not having a Greek system "doesn't impede the social life at all . . . it actually contributes to a certain unity on campus."

Extracurriculars

Students can enjoy a variety of activities at Connecticut College. Those interested in journalism can write for the *College Voice* or the *College Journal*. Those who have musical talent can join one of Conn's multiple singing groups or orchestra. Those particularly interested in broadcasting can participate in the operation of the school radio station, WCNI. Involvement in student government is also popular.

Sports also are a big part of student life at Conn. This Division III school receives much community support at games, especially in soccer and hockey. New on campus is the women's ice hockey team. Those students who do not wish to participate in a varsity sport can take advantage of the newly renovated Athletic Center. Conn also has a popular intramural sports program. Making intramurals especially entertaining is the friendly competition fostered by Dorm Olympics. This series of games also increases dorm loyalties.

Location and Rooming

Students comment favorably on the school's location. The campus is very safe according to one student who said, "I have never felt unsafe walking alone late at night because the campus is well lit and there are phones scattered throughout for emergency use." Although New London does not receive rave reviews as a college town in terms of fun, students enjoy the 721-acre campus that overlooks the Thames and the Long Island Sound. The on-campus Connecticut College Arboretum provides students a great place to study and conduct research, but is also an ideal place to visit for an outdoor experience.

The rooming situation at Conn is reportedly very good. Most freshmen live in doubles or triples, but all upperclassmen get singles. Dorms are coed and run by a house fellow. One alternate housing situation is the Unity House, a dorm staffed by a full-time director who works "to bring all sorts of people together, from race to ethnicity to culture to lifestyle." Other housing options include the Earth House for environmentally concerned students, Quiet Housing, Substance-Free Housing, and Thematic Housing. Three of the four previously "ugly" Plex dorms have undergone renovations, so that they are modernized, air conditioned, and have brand new furniture. Also, all the dorms now have cable television.

The dining halls are said to be "great" due to the reconstruction of Harris Dining Hall. Renovations have helped eliminate long lines and broaden dining options for students. Dining halls serve vegetarian as well as standard fare. Students can choose among several dining halls on campus, Harris being the largest. But each dining hall has its own special attributes. For example, Freeman is known as the "stir-fry dorm" and Harkness is the "deli dorm." Those looking for something different can go to the newly renovated Crozier-Williams Student Center (the "Cro"), where they can get pizza, mail a letter, or have a beer at the "Cro" bar.

Students and Their Honor Code

One student admitted that "Conn leaves something to be desired in terms of diversity." Students described the typical Conn student this way: "Rich, white, athletic, shops at Abercrombie and Fitch and North Face, drives a SAAB, and lives in a suburb of Boston."

One defining trait of Connecticut College is its honor code. Upon matriculation, every student must sign an agreement that he or she will abide by the honor code. In the academic vein, students agree that they will not cheat or plagiarize, rules that enable students to enjoy "completely self scheduled, unproctored exams." Students regard this as a "great perk because students can study as long as they need to, and take exams when they're ready." Socially, students agree to respect others and their lifestyles and space, and those who infringe on the honor code rules deal with the Judiciary Board, a board of students who "take their jobs seriously."

> "It's easy to design your own major, double major or minor, area of concentration, certificate program, or any other course of study you may desire."

Connecticut College is a place where students can learn in an academically supportive atmosphere with small classes and accessible professors. Conn students also learn the value of responsibility and integrity through the honor code. Conn students are proud of their school and see it as a constantly improving institution where they can make great friends. As one student said, "Conn is a fun and interesting place to go to school. I am excited about what my future here will bring." —*Marti Page and Staff*

FYI
The three best things about attending Connecticut College are "the small size allows for wide access to professors and their work, a cappella groups, and the flexibility in major design.
The three worst things about attending Connecticut College are that "students tend to be apathetic towards the outside world, the honor code is taken too lightly, and that politics get in the way of administration."
The three things every student should do before graduating are to "do an internship, go to Harkness beach, and sing in an a cappella group."
One thing I'd like to have known before coming here is that "students here don't always take their time as seriously as I'd expected."

Fairfield University

Address: 1073 N. Benson Road, Fairfield, CT 06430-5195
Phone: 203-254-4100
E-mail address: admis@fair1.fairfield.edu
Web site URL: www.fairfield.edu
Location: suburban
Founded: 1942
Private or Public: private
Religious affiliation: Catholic, Jesuit
Undergraduate enrollment: 3,151
Total enrollment: 5,127
Percent Male/Female: 47%/53%

Percent Minority: 11.0%
Percent African-American: 3.0%
Percent Hispanic: 4.0%
Percent Asian: 3.0%
Percent in-state/out-of-state: 26%/74%
Percent Pub HS: 50%
Fraternities: 0%
Sororities: 0%
Number of Applicants: 6,457
Percent Accepted: 61%
Percent Accepted who enroll: 22%
Entering: 837
Transfers: 31
Application Deadline: 1 Feb

Mean SAT: 575 V, 584 M
Middle 50% SAT range: 530–620 V, 540–620 M
Middle 50% ACT range: NA
Mean ACT: 25
3 Most popular majors: English, biology, psychology
Retention: 89%
Graduation rate: 81%
Library: 206,849 volumes
Tuition and Fees: $20,435 in; NA out
Room and Board: $7,380
On-campus housing: 100%
Financial aid, first-year: 65%

The roar of cheering fans and the chants of the Fairfield University Pep and Dance team resound beyond the boundaries of Alumni Field on campus. Red and white banners litter the bleachers, and the "Fairfield Fight Song" rings in the charged night air. Why this cause for celebration? These boisterous fans are geared up for the football season. After the Fairfield football team's 1996 debut, it has continued to "boost school spirit and add another dimension to social life at Fairfield." Although the football tradition at Fairfield has begun only recently, high energy levels are a long-standing tradition at this small Jesuit university.

Rolling Hills and Small Ponds

Set in southwestern Connecticut, the Fairfield University campus has rolling hills, small ponds, tall trees, and wide expanses of green lawn. Some students find the campus buildings "very modern and ugly," but all agree that the facilities are well-maintained and in good condition. One of the most prominent buildings at Fairfield is the Egan Chapel of St. Ignatius Loyola, located in the center of campus. One student reported that with its modern dome, "our chapel's appearance is like chocolate—you either love it or think it's awful!"

In keeping with the Jesuit philosophy of education, academics at Fairfield strive to create well-rounded students. Undergrads tend to feel "challenged, but not completely overwhelmed." One student said she was drawn to Fairfield because "while the education is strong, the program of study isn't so intense that I can't cultivate other interests beyond schoolwork."

The University is divided into four schools: the School of Arts and Sciences, the Business School, the School of Nursing, and the Graduate School. Students are kept busy with a long list of distribution requirements. Undergrads must take three semesters of English and two semesters each of math, science, language, history, social science, and fine arts. True to its Jesuit roots, students are also required to take two semesters each of religious studies, two semesters of philosophy, and one additional semester of either religious studies, philosophy, or applied ethics. One student praised the extensive core curriculum for "laying a terrific base to explore new areas while teaching us how to write really well." But, core courses also draw criticism; one student complained that they kept him "tied up in tedious classes." The registration process also draws complaints for "ridiculous lines and no guarantees about getting the classes you want."

Fairfield has a large honors program that invites students to apply upon admission to the college and also admits students after their freshman year on the basis of their first-year GPAs. Honor students are exempt from some of the classes in the core curriculum and follow an interdisciplinary program, which emphasizes writing.

Within the School of Arts and Science, the biology department is especially popular. "Biology at Fairfield is amazing—particularly for pre-med preparation," one student said. Many undergrads credit "wonderful professors" for making the English department strong. The religious studies program, while small in size, is also considered outstanding. Students are less enthusiastic about the foreign language departments. Some criticize the limited course selection and the "professors who can't even make sense of the English language, let alone a foreign one!" The accounting department is popular among undergrads at the Business School, while the School of Nursing draws talented students from around the country.

Incredible Personal Attention

For many students, small class size has proven to be one of the biggest advantages of Fairfield academics. As one student said, "You really get some incredible personal attention here." Introductory lecture classes rarely enroll more than 40 people, and seminars often have fewer than 12. Undergrads say small class sizes allow them to develop strong interactions with their professors and to have some "great discussions during class."

The housing system at Fairfield is conducive to promoting strong relationships among students. Housing is guaranteed for all four years, and most students report being generally pleased with their accommodations. Many underclassmen live in one of the dorms at the center of campus called the Quad, where the residents say the rooms are fairly large. Though there is not a dorm exclusively dedicated to first-years, a large majority of freshmen live in Dolan, a dorm comprised entirely of single rooms. The "sense of freshmen unity" fostered in Dolan is a highlight for

many residents, although some are unhappy with living in what they consider to be a "party dorm." Upperclassmen participate in a lottery for rooms in either the condominium-like townhouses or the popular beach houses at Latern Point, which are located a short distance from campus. Some juniors and seniors claim that the lottery system is a "huge hassle that causes a lot of resentment without providing an alternative to beach house living."

> **"Although the football tradition at Fairfield University has only recently begun, high energy levels are a long-standing tradition at this small Jesuit university."**

Campus residents are on either a 19 or a 14-meal-per-week plan, while off-campus students can elect for 7, 10, or 12 meals per week. While many students generally rate the food as "standard, but edible," freshmen living outside the Quad complain about the twenty-five minute trek up to the cafeteria. "Stagbucks" (the stag is Fairfield's mascot) can also be purchased in order to buy snacks during the day at the student-run deli. The town of Fairfield also boasts some popular restaurants like Spazzi's and Sidetracks.

Beach Parties

Latern Point is an integral part of social life at Fairfield, as many students head for keg parties on the beach during the weekend. Undergrads report that socializing at Fairfield usually involves alcohol. Although the Fairfield administration's alcohol policy strictly forbids students under the legal age to possess or consume alcohol on campus, drinking is the weekend activity of choice for many students. "I feel really bad about the kids on my floor that don't drink, because there isn't much to do beyond beach parties here on any given weekend," one senior resident advisor said.

In recent years the Fairfield University Student Association (FUSA) has tried to bring students back to campus for social activities, with some terrific results. In addition to the two major semi-formals

(Harvest and Dogwood-Midnight Madness during basketball season) and the huge Clam Jam weekend in the spring, FUSA also promotes student support of athletic events, concerts, and dances. A second event in the spring, the Spam Jam, is one of the biggest events of the year with concerts and parties spanning two days. One student emphasized that "Fairfield is not a 'suitcase' school, as we generally stay on campus during the weekends, attend FUSA events, and show our support for our school."

Many Fairfield students get involved with IRHG, Inter-Residence Hall Government. Others are active in religious and community service programs with the Campus Ministry. Music at Fairfield is well supported by students who participate in the glee club, marching band, and orchestra. Intramural sports also draw a crowd for flag football, soccer, and crew. Colorful signs posted around campus advertise a wide selection of group meetings and events.

Burgeoning School Spirit

Fairfield's women's soccer team is often nationally ranked, and the men's basketball team draws incredible support from the student body. With the addition of the football team in recent years, school spirit is running high. According to one student athlete, "It is great to be so well supported by the fans here—it makes you feel good to know that they are behind you."

Fairfield students characterize their classmates as largely Catholic, middle-class, and from New England. Some students have expressed concern about Fairfield's reputation as the "antithesis of diversity." Although many students believe that the administration has been working diligently to increase diversity some feel their school "still has a long way to go."

The Multicultural Task Force and other organizations have been working toward increasing tolerance and broadening the students' understanding of other cultures by inviting guest lecturers to campus and sponsoring ethnic and cultural awareness days. The administration's institution of a diversity requirement as part of the core curriculum has also drawn praise from many students. The requirement ensures that all undergraduates take at least one course about another culture, ethnic, or religious group during their four years. On the whole, Fairfield students consider themselves relatively enthusiastic about academics, eager to learn from one another, and bursting with school spirit. If the energy radiating from Alumni Field is any indication, this school has pride in both its Stags and its community.
—*Alexandra M. Rethore and Staff*

FYI
The three best things about attending Fairfield University are "Latern Point, Stagbucks, and biology."
The three worst things about attending Fairfield University are "the lack of diversity, foreign languages, and core requirements."
The three things every student should do before graduating from Fairfield University are "to live at Latern Point, to eat with Stagbucks, and to attend Spam Jam."
One thing I'd like to have known before coming here is "what a Stag is."

Trinity College

Address: 300 Summit Street, Hartford, CT 06016
Phone: 860-297-2180
E-mail address: admissions.office@trincoll.edu
Web site URL: www.trincoll.edu
Location: urban
Founded: 1823
Private or Public: private
Religious affiliation: none
Undergraduate enrollment: 1,905
Total enrollment: 2,371
Percent Male/Female: 51%/49%
Percent Minority: 20.0%

Percent African-American: 6.0%
Percent Hispanic: 5.0%
Percent Asian: 5.0%
Percent in-state/out-of-state: 18.0%/82.0%
Percent Pub HS: 45%
Fraternities: 19%
Sororities: 19%
Number of Applicants: 4,644
Percent Accepted: 40%
Percent Accepted who enroll: 31%
Entering: 567
Transfers: 23
Application Deadline: 15 Jan
Mean SAT: 630 V, 630 M

Middle 50% SAT range: 590–680 V, 590–680 M
Middle 50% ACT range: 26–29
Mean ACT: 27.3
3 Most popular majors: economics, English, political science
Retention: 92.0%
Graduation rate: 85.0%
Library: 1,000,000 volumes
Tuition and Fees: $24,490 in; $24,490 out
Room and Board: $6,890
On-campus housing: 100%
Financial aid, first-year: 47%

Although it is a small school with only 1,900 students, Trinity is an academically rigorous liberal arts college located in Connecticut's capital city, Hartford. The main part of the campus, Long Walk, is graced with rows of Gothic buildings jarringly offset by the ultramodern Life Sciences Center, nicknamed "Castle Grayskull" by students. The campus, as a whole, is lovely. As one enthusiastic freshman stated, "This place is paradise in so many ways, it really is."

Hitting the Books at Trinity

Trinity's small size promotes an intimate academic environment; students find professors friendly and accessible. One upperclassman philosophy major said, "Professors in the philosophy department are thrilled whenever students come up to them outside of class to talk about their work." Many students, however, often do not take advantage of professors' accessibility. "If you're not too shy to open your mouth, you'll get all the attention you can stand," commented a junior English major. TAs at Trinity are undergraduates who have taken a course and done well in it, and are used at Trinity only as lab assistants and leaders of review and extra help

sections, although they do grade homework assignments in many science courses. Class sizes are generally small (15–20), though there are some large introductory courses, such as freshman biology and freshman English, which may contain close to 100 students.

Trinity's academic requirements are fairly easy to fulfill. "There are few distribution requirements because the school really wants people to focus on their majors," said one student. To fulfill the distribution requirements, students must take one course in each of five general areas: Humanities, Numerical and Symbolic Logic, Arts, Social Sciences, and Life Sciences. Each freshman is also expected to take a non-traditional first-year seminar on an interdisciplinary topic like Images of Light or Representations of Gender. There is no foreign-language requirement. Many students complained about the mandatory math proficiency test, which is administered the first Sunday of school. "It's the first weekend of college," complained a sophomore, "everyone is hungover." To make matters worse, Trinity does not allow those with high SAT I or SAT II math scores to waive the exam. Students who do poorly are placed into

Math 101, a course generally regarded as a waste of time. Trinity's strongest departments were cited as English and the sciences, in which there are lots of research opportunities, even for freshman science majors. Facilities are notably "excellent," though music and theater arts are relatively small departments "without many course offerings," one junior said.

For particularly motivated students, Trinity offers an intensive two-year program in Western philosophy, history, and literature called Guided Studies. Guided Studies consists of three reading- and writing-intensive courses each semester for two years and is open to first-year students by invitation only. The program is rewarding, but also very limiting and restrictive to non-Classics or English majors, according to a freshman in the program. "I want to be a theater arts major, and being in Guided Studies makes it pretty hard for me to fulfill all my requirements," she said.

There are no easy-A courses at Trinity. Although one student recommended the History of Flight as an easy way to fulfill the Life Sciences requirement, another warned, "Even courses that sound like guts are not blow-off courses." Music Appreciation and Philosophy of Sports were two prominent examples of unexpectedly difficult courses.

Grading at Trinity was described as fair, neither too severe nor too lenient. Since As are not easy to come by, many students report that Bs are considered average. Very few people graduate with honors. "In my major [English], the profs really peer to see if you're straining before they'll give you a decent mark," said one junior. Political science was cited as one of the easier majors.

Socializing, Camp Trin-Trin Style

"It's like summer camp here," explained a sophomore. "Most people know how to have a good time." They do indeed—Trinity students work hard and party hard. Greeks are very active on the campus, but, since frat parties are generally open to all students, few people feel the need to become members. Frats do arrange and host popular campus theme parties, like "Gender Bender," "Tropical," and the ex-

tremely popular "Disco Inferno." "I never thought you could have so much fun in polyester," raved one junior. Another student said "Tropical" was the single worst thing about life at Trinity, a night "of too many drunk people with no control." Lately, student organizations have been hosting more parties.

As on many college campuses, drinking and smoking are widespread at Trinity; in fact, several upperclassmen suggested that a beer keg would be the most appropriate mascot for the school. However, students who do not drink are by no means social outcasts. "I know a lot of people who don't drink. They still go out on weekends, even to bars, and still have a good time," one sophomore commented. One student expressed pleasant surprise about the attitudes of his peers. "I am straight-edge, and it's not that hard to not drink here," he explained. "People are actually understanding and sometimes even impressed by your strength." Nevertheless, "students who don't drink are in the minority," a sophomore added. Pot is smoked by a large percentage of the campus population, at least according to the estimates of several upperclassmen. "I'm a freshman Residential Advisor," one sophomore explained, "and I'm trained to be alert for the smell of pot in any of the dorm rooms. But it's pretty easy for students to get away with it." Cigarettes are not prohibited on campus or even in dorms. In fact, students may smoke anywhere except in common rooms, lounges, and a few other areas that are designated smoke-free. One of the campus dorms offers two floors of smoke-free housing, which is available upon request.

The administration has made a concerted effort to crack down on underage drinking and drug use on campus, and students still find carding strict at the Tap, an on-campus bar. Among other measures, the administration in the fall of 1997 introduced a new class of enforcement officers called Junior Fellows. In 1993, kegs were banned in residence halls, although frats and other groups can make arrangements to use party halls, where kegs are allowed. Junior Fellows have the right to academically expel anyone they catch drinking illegally, but one student noted that Junior Fellows handle "a variety of issues" and most of their attention is focused on the freshman dorms

Although there is a school-sponsored shuttle system providing transportation into Hartford, students rarely go into the city. The school administration encourages weekend parties and other social events that keep students on campus at night. Trinity is located in Frog Hollow, a run-down area of Hartford that one junior characterized as a "ghetto." Broad Street, which borders the campus on one side, is not a good place to go walking at night. The campus itself, though, is fairly safe, at least in the opinion of many students. "There was one person accosted on the campus with a gun last year and made to hand over all his money, but that was just one incident," said a sophomore. "It's a very well lit, protected campus and I feel safe here."

Social life consists of party-hopping or hanging out with small groups of friends. Very little dating goes on at Trinity, according to students. "There is not much of a thing called love at Trinity," said one upperclassman, yet "there are a lot of random hook ups." The Trinity student body is more sexually active than most, according to one frustrated junior who said, "Being a person involved in a long-term relationship, I can, as a partial observer, say the sexual activity at Trinity is among the highest in the known universe." Sexual assault and sexual harassment are very prominent campus issues, although there have not been many reported instances of them in the past few years. "It's definitely a concern, because so much of the hooking-up that goes on here is alcohol-induced," said a sophomore Resident Advisor.

A Sell Point

Although the area may be somewhat dangerous, Trinity can still boast about its location in Hartford, which is the home of the Bushnell Theater and the Wadsworth Atheneum, the nation's oldest public art gallery. "The city is a selling point for the school," one sophomore said. "Some other liberal arts colleges are isolated from the real world." Another student added, "Hartford's not like New York or Boston, but it is a city and it does offer certain things." Music fans can always find an abundance of concerts in the city. Also, Hartford is a great source of internships for Trinity students. Until the late 1980s, Hartford was known as "the insurance company capital of the world." Although the city's economy has declined slightly in recent years, there are still many large business firms in Hartford willing to employ Trinity students. The administration is very encouraging and supportive of students who pursue internships, study-abroad opportunities, or other special programs. Trinity has a Rome campus of its own, but also allows people to participate in programs offered by foreign universities for credit. "Nearly everyone here goes abroad," said one sophomore. According to one junior who is currently studying in London, "All I had to do was fill out a simple form. Really, it couldn't have been much easier."

The campus, like a summer camp, is alive with spirit. "We are aggressive athletes, students, partygoers, and for the most part, we are ambitious beyond that," said a junior. Unlike summer camp cabins, however, Trinity dorms are comfortably furnished (although some gripe that the college-issued desks are far too small). Also, as is not the case at most summer camps, many students even like the food, which is provided by Marriott Catering. There are three on-campus dining halls: the standard cafeteria; the Cave, a grill and social center; and the Bistro, a dinner and lunch restaurant that serves smaller portions of better-quality food. All three are covered by the campus meal plan. There are not many restaurants nearby, and students rarely eat off campus.

Trinity's Extracurriculars

The Trinity student body is very athletic. The vast majority of people participate in varsity or intramural sports, with football and rugby being two popular choices. Even students who do not play a sport work out frequently. Outside of sports, the most popular extracurricular activities include a cappella singing groups and the student newspaper, the *Tripod*. Student government at Trinity is more active than on most campuses. "It has a strong voice in decisions made by the faculty," said a sophomore. Not surprisingly, the campus is not a hotbed of social activism, although "we do try to be very politically correct," one junior said.

Students rarely interact with the Hartford community, although the administration strongly encourages community service and is currently involved in massive neighborhood revitalization plans. There is a community service dorm at Trinity devoted to social activism, and there are several small, but devoted groups, such as Habitat for Humanity and tutoring groups. Fewer than 400 out of the 1,900 students at Trinity participate in community outreach programs. Trinity life is centered on campus activity. Ninety-two percent of Trinity students spend their four years on campus.

Currently, 16 percent of the student body consists of minorities. Starting with the class of 2001, the administration is making more of a commitment to increase the socio-economic diversity of the student body. "I'm impressed. There's a tremendous difference in diversity between the senior class and the incoming freshman class," said a sophomore. One junior noticed a surprising number of Slavic and Eastern European international students. "I don't know how they heard of Trinity," he commented in amazement.

The student body is predominantly preppy and consists mostly of students from wealthy, white families who have attended boarding schools. "J. Crew and North Face outfit our entire campus," one junior said. A frustrated student said the campus consists entirely of "rich, white conservative Republicans." One junior railed against Trinity social life, saying "Meeting new friends is completely dependent on your age and economic status, the sports you play, the music you listen to, and, rarely, your actual worth as a human being." Other students, however, had no problems meeting new people and found the campus comfortable socially.

Very few people are openly homosexual, although Trinity is by no means a homophobic school. Encouraging Respect of Sexualities (EROS) is one of the most socially active groups on campus. However, one student did say that "there are more homosexual and interracial couples on campus than you'd expect given our preppy reputation."

> **"It's like summer camp here. Most people know how to have a good time."**

By and large, though, Camp Trin-Trin is still a place where people buy their clothes from J. Crew, travel to Europe in the summer, and watch *Party of Five*, *Dawson's Creek*, and reruns of *Melrose Place*. One undergrad noted, however, that "the current freshman class is comprised of individuals who come from different backgrounds and styles," and they stand to break that Camp Trin-Trin image of Trinity. Overall, it is a place trying to redefine itself, a unique school that offers its students both an excellent liberal arts education and, in the apt words of a Trinity sophomore, "a good time." —*Erik Johnson and Staff*

FYI
The three best things about attending Trinity are "the small size, the parties, and the Freshman Seminar program."
The three worst things about attending Trinity are "the location, the math proficiency exam, and the homogeneity."
The three things that every student should do before graduating from Trinity are "to dress all out for the Disco Inferno, to go to the Wadsworth Atheneum, and to play an intramural sport."
One thing I'd like to have known before coming here is "that I'd have to revamp my wardrobe to be completely J. Crew and Abercrombie, or risk social exile."

United States Coast Guard Academy

Address: 31 Mohegan Avenue, New London, CT 06320-8103
Phone: 800-883-8724
E-mail address: admissions@cga.uscg.mil
Web site URL: www.cga.edu
Location: suburban
Founded: 1876
Private or Public: public
Religious affiliation: none
Undergraduate enrollment: 795
Total enrollment: 795
Percent Male/Female: 71%/29%
Percent Minority: 17.0%

Percent African-American: 5.0%
Percent Hispanic: 5.0%
Percent Asian: 6.0%
Percent in-state/out-of-state: 7%/93%
Percent Pub HS: NA
Fraternities: 0%
Sororities: 0%
Number of Applicants: 5,757
Percent Accepted: 7%
Percent Accepted who enroll: 64%
Entering: 257
Transfers: 0
Application Deadline: 15 Feb

Mean SAT: 614 V, 643 M
Middle 50% SAT range: 560–650 V, 610–680 M
Middle 50% ACT range: NA
Mean ACT: 26
3 Most popular majors: government, civil engineering, marine science
Retention: 89.0%
Graduation rate: 75.0%
Library: 180,000 volumes
Tuition and Fees: 0%
Room and Board: $0
On-campus housing: 100%
Financial aid, first-year: 0%

The United States Coast Guard Academy is not your average college. Life at the academy emphasizes military life, not social life. Although it's not for everyone, it offers the attractive combination of strong academics and an eventual career as a United States Coast Guard officer.

The academy offers eight major courses of study, including civil engineering, electrical engineering, mechanical engineering, naval architecture and marine engineering, marine and environmental sciences, operations research, and government and management (the only two non-engineering majors). Government is said to be the easiest major, but "that's just because it's tough to fail someone when they're writing papers interpreting things," one cadet said. However, cadets say all of the majors are challenging, mainly because cadets must balance military obligations, academics, and sports.

Coast Guard Courses

All cadets must take a set of core courses. The freshman curriculum includes Calculus I and II, Chemistry I and II, Organizational Behavior and Leadership, Nautical Science, Introduction to Engineering and Design, English Composition and Speech, among others. Essentially, cadets spend their freshman and sophomore years fulfilling the necessary requirements. Cadets must maintain a 2.0 cumulative GPA to remain at the academy, but it's also possible to make up failed core courses. Classes are small and range from 25 to 40 students. All are taught by professors. Courses also can be taken at Connecticut College, across the street from the academy. Most internships and training take place during the summers at Coast Guard stations or aboard ships.

The academy is a functioning Coast Guard base and is small compared to most college campuses. Built mainly in the 1930s, the buildings are brick and the landscape is meticulously kept. The hilly grounds fit "just beautifully against the background of the Thames River," according to one cadet. Regardless of rank, all cadets must live on academy grounds, in Chase Hall, the barracks/dorm. Rooms and roommates are reassigned every semester. Most cadets live in doubles; the few available singles go to lucky upperclassmen. Keeping the modestly furnished rooms spotless is a never-ending task, and aside from monthly formal inspection, cadets can receive demerits from wandering upperclassmen who spot a messy room. The emphasis on cleanliness and organization is reportedly designed to help future Coast Guard officers adapt to the close quarters that are the norm on a ship.

Before beginning your academic career at the academy, you must first survive the grueling six weeks of summer training known as "Swab Summer," which is organized and run by the junior class. During this time, the "swabs," or pre-freshmen, perform rifle drills, march, run obstacle courses, and learn military courtesy and customs. One cadet described the process as an "intense indoctrination into the military," an experience that is challenging mentally, physically, and emotionally. After the successful completion of Swab Summer, the pre-freshmen become fourth-class cadets and begin the rigorous academic schedule.

A typical day at the USCGA begins with morning formations at 6:20 A.M. Breakfast is at 6:40, and by 7:40 the cadets await personal inspection, when the shine on their shoes and the creases in their uniforms are checked carefully. The academic day continues from 8 A.M. to 3:40 P.M. and is followed by two hours of mandatory athletic activity. Dinner is served from 5 to 7 P.M. and is followed by a mandatory study period from 8 to 10 P.M., during which students either study in their own rooms, the library, or classroom buildings. At 10 P.M., when "Taps" is played, all cadets must be back in their rooms.

> "Cadets must balance military obligations, academics, and sports."

All cadets eat in the wardroom (the cafeteria) and are required to attend breakfast and lunch. These meals are eaten "family-style" in tables of ten with a mixture of all classes, freshmen through seniors. Dinner attendance is optional, except for freshmen: upper-class cadets can eat in the wardroom or take out using plastic containers. On the whole, cadets offer no complaints about the cuisine, although fourth-class cadets say meals are difficult because they must eat "braced up," without looking at their food. All meals are paid for by the academy, but cadets can eat off campus or order food from local fast-food restaurants. Plenty of fast-food joints and restaurants are located close by, and according to one cadet, "Campus Pizza is the big cadet hangout."

Academy Activities

The academy offers a variety of clubs, and most cadets participate in at least one or two. These include several campus bands, singing groups, a debate team, student government, and a political affairs association. Cadets interested in journalism publish a monthly magazine, the *Howling Gale*, and a yearbook, *Tide Rips*. However, the focus remains on academics, military life, and sports. The Coast Guard Bears compete in NCAA Division III. The Merchant Marine Academy is the big rival, and the two football teams compete every year for the Secretary's Cup. "Since everyone here is pretty athletic, we usually have good records," one student said. Cadets have a strong school spirit, and leading the way is the academy's mascot, the bear, which is affectionately referred to as "Obje" (the name is derived from "objectionable," the label the Humane Society gave to the academy's former practice of keeping a live bear mascot in a pen). Every cadet at the academy must participate in intercollegiate or intramural sports each year.

Life of Discipline

The social sphere is where the academy differs the greatest from most other colleges. Although cadets must remain on campus for most of the week, "liberty," or free time, allows them to venture off-campus occasionally for a break from the military regime. Underclassmen (juniors and below) cannot have cars and cannot leave campus until Friday night. Seniors get one night off a week, but can earn more. On the weekend, cadets only have time off until midnight on Fridays, 1 A.M. on Saturdays, and 8 P.M. on Sundays. Cadets say drugs and alcohol do not exist on campus. "We do have plenty of mixers and formal dances, though," reported one cadet. The towns of New London and Groton provide adequate distractions for cadets, and New York City, Boston, and Newport are also close enough (each less than two hours away) for road trips.

Upon graduation from the academy, the new officers of the Coast Guard patrol the seas while participating in such activities as drug enforcement, rescues, and protection of the American people in peacetime.

Cadets are required to serve five years after graduation, and many stay on past their period of mandatory service. Cadets strongly suggest that prospective students visit the academy before making a commitment, because it's not for everyone. They point out that although the life they live at the U.S. Coast Guard Academy is a disciplined one, rewards and opportunities are many. —*Melissa Droller and Staff*

FYI

The three best things about attending the Academy are "the academics here are very strong, the sports is great, and you gain a strong sense of discipline and achievement at the Academy."

The three worst things about attending the Academy are "6:30 A.M. roll call, the mandatory meetings we have, and trying to keep your uniform clean during meals."

The three things that every student should do before graduating from the Academy are "to join an extracurricular club (on top of everything else we already have), to head out to New York City or Boston one weekend, and hang out at Campus Pizza for hours."

One thing I'd like to have known before coming here is "there is no alcohol, only water."

University of Connecticut

Address: 2131 Hillside Rd, U-88, Storrs, CT 06269-3088
Phone: 860-486-3137
E-mail address: beahusky@uconn.edu
Web site URL: www.uconn.edu
Location: rural
Founded: 1881
Private or Public: public
Religious affiliation: none
Undergraduate enrollment: 12,325
Total enrollment: 15,936
Percent Male/Female: 48%/53%
Percent Minority: 15.2%

Percent African-American: 5.0%
Percent Hispanic: 5.7%
Percent Asian: 4.0%
Percent in-state/out-of-state: NA
Percent Pub HS: NA
Fraternities: 9%
Sororities: 4%
Number of Applicants: 11,781
Percent Accepted: 70%
Percent Accepted who enroll: 36%
Entering: 2,956
Transfers: 443
Application Deadline: 1 Mar
Mean SAT: 562 V, 573 M

Middle 50% SAT range: 500–610 V, 510–620 M
Middle 50% ACT range: NA
Mean ACT: NA
3 Most popular majors: psychology, English, human dev & family relations
Retention: 86.0%
Graduation rate: 68.0%
Library: 2,475,851 volumes
Tuition and Fees: $5,404 in; $13,922 out
Room and Board: $5,694
On-campus housing: 96%
Financial aid, first-year: 74%

The roars of the crowd chanting "GO HUSKIES!" echo throughout Gampel Pavilion as one of the nation's finest basketball teams takes the court. Overwhelming school spirit can be heard across the campus as students, alumni, and spectators rally for their team. However, UConn offers much more than a fine athletic program. The administration has made strides in recent years to shift UConn's focus to offering a solid liberal arts education to all of its students at an affordable price. Many changes are at work to change the perception of UConn as a regional school to that of a nationally recognized university.

Innovative Learning

The undergraduate education at the University of Connecticut offers a comprehensive focus on the liberal arts by requiring core curriculum credits that students are free to fulfill in the classes that best suit their interests. Credits are required in many disciplines including computers, science, philosophy, and art. In restrospect, one alumna found that UConn requires "more of a variety than many other state schools." Most students meet requirements by sophomore year. UConn is among the more technologically advanced schools in that most classrooms are equipped with Internet access and many classes are run primarily through the Internet. Through this new educational technology, students are able to do things like observe on-screen research occurring in a separate facility on campus.

Students apply to schools of specialized study by their junior year, and the majority of their remaining classes are taken within the focus of that school. Among the nine specialized schools, the most popular ones include the schools of pharmacy, engineering, and physical therapy. Widely known for its economics department, the business school is the most recognized school on campus. A challenging honors program is also available for those who seek more difficult work and smaller classes. Although there are a fair number of large introductory lectures, the average class size ranges from 18 to 25 students. Professors are described as easily accessible, but as one student commented, "In such a big school it's the responsibility of the student to seek the professor, but once you show the initiative they are usually willing to help."

Well-known as a party school, students find that it is hard to find good places to study. The Homer Babdige Library holds more then 2 million volumes, but is more of a place for social gatherings. Dorm rooms are rarely any better as a quiet refuge of scholarship. "It is really difficult to find an equal balance of fun and studying because there is always so much activity on such a large campus," said one student. With regard to getting work done,

another student joked, "We procrastinate like it's our job!"

The university also offers an extremely diverse student body that one student praises as "allowing a separate education" on people and their differences. One student said, "Because there are so many people, everyone eventually finds his or her niche."

The Party Niche

The majority of UConn students have no trouble finding their niche in the party scene. Fraternities, sororities, and Rugby House are all notorious for their huge parties, usually held outdoors on large fields. However, as one student observed, "Frats are not really a way to socialize. In order to have fun, most people bring a party with them and because [the frat parties] are so far away and crowded, it's usually not even worth it." Other parties take place in people's dorm rooms or in off-campus houses such as the Blue, White, Yellow, Brick, Stone, and Fire Houses. Popular hangouts on campus are Ted's (a restaurant), Civic Pub (a pool hall/bar), and Huskies (a bar/dance club). Although alcohol is the central focus of the party scene, as one non-drinker commented, "No one ever forces you to do anything."

UConn's social activity includes more than just parties. The campus is a popular stop on the tours of many famous entertainers such as Jewel, Reel Big Fish, Harry Belafonte, and David Spade of *Saturday Night Live* fame. The Student Union sponsors weekly dances and movie nights while the Student Union Board of Governors (SUBG) plans such large events as homecoming weekend, a winter party, and a star-studded spring weekend.

Located in rural Storrs, UConn is fortunately a virtually self-sufficient campus: most students' needs can be met by on-campus stores and facilities. However, many students miss the conveniences of living in the city and prospering from its entities. One student said, "I wish that we were closer to a mall or something just for convenience purposes."

Students say that dorms are barely in satisfactory condition due to the lack of money invested in their upkeep and renovation. However, better dorms include

Buckley, Shippe (which is all-female), and the recently built dorms on South Campus. Most freshmen choose to live in a dorm on North Campus known as "the jungle" because of the "wild parties." But one student noted that "all dorms throw parties, and 'the jungle' doesn't really stand out as a party dorm." Dormitories are both single-sex and coed, consisting of high-rises as well as smaller buildings. The majority of the rooms are doubles, with some singles and triples. Upper- and lower-classmen are mixed in the dorms, allowing for integration and bonding among the classes. Students who favor this set-up comment, "Living with [upperclassmen] is an advantage because they help with the adjustment period and are able to offer valued advice on picking classes and dealing with roommates." However, many freshmen were disappointed to find themselves with upperclassmen roommates because "it can be limiting if you aren't around anyone your own age." Floor regulations are relatively lax. As long as alcoholic beverages are not carried in their original containers, RAs usually don't bother students; however, underage students caught with alcohol can expect to find a much harder time with the campus police.

The food disappoints most on campus, and one student even accused the dining halls of serving food that is "at best, inedible." Although the food may be horrible, students enjoy the luxury of having an on-campus creamery that offers savory fresh-made ice cream and milk. However, students have to pay the price for this perk by enduring the "pleasant aroma" of the grazing cows.

Extracurricular activities and service-oriented clubs are in abundance at the University of Connecticut. Opportunities range from the *Daily Campus* newspaper to political unions to bands and singing groups. Many people join the Student Union Board of Governors to act as a voice in student government while others choose to pledge fraternities and sororities in order to be part of a smaller, closer community. The Public Interest Research Group (PIRG) is a protest group focused on improving government environmental issues. Other outlets of service allow students to volunteer with children, the el-

derly, and the state government in nearby Hartford, Connecticut's capital.

Basketball Fever

The men's and women's basketball teams are at the center of both UConn's sports program and the spirit of the students. Ranking among the top teams in the nation, UConn has not failed to be a major contender for both the NCAA Division I Big East Conference and national championships. In 1999, the men's team took home its first national championship. Men's and women's soccer have also become increasingly popular, as has football, each acquiring quite a number of dedicated fans in recent years. As observed by one student, "They go unrecognized, but there is a huge following." In its effort to upgrade the football team to Division I-A status, UConn and the state of Connecticut have finalized budget approvals to construct a state-of-the-art football facility. While many students anxiously await the vast improvement to the sports complex, many are disappointed that money will not be spent to renovate the run-down dorms that students are forced to live in on-campus.

"We procrastinate like it's our job!"

Intramurals are a source of entertainment and exercise for many students as well. Coed football and badminton promise exciting competitions and rivalries every year. Intramurals are a great way to be involved in sports for many students. One student declared, "I don't have a varsity sport, but intramurals let me enjoy playing anyway."

The educational and athletic offerings are growing through numerous construction and curriculum projects on campus. With a top-notch basketball program and a football team on the verge of going Division I-A, UConn's athletics receive national attention. UConn is also widely known for its intense social scene and *Animal House*-like parties. In addition, a very affordable tuition and strong academics make UConn an excellent choice for any student. —*Christine Bonanno and Staff*

FYI

The three best things about attending UConn are "the great people, basketball games, and the bars."

The three worst things about attending UConn are "walking to classes because they're so far away, the food, and the heavy workload."

The three things that every student should do before graduating from UConn are "go to Horsebarn Hill and watch the sun rise, order a calzone from D.P. Dough, and go to a basketball game."

One thing I'd like to have known before coming here is "to bring a fake I.D."

W e s l e y a n   U n i v e r s i t y

Address: 70 Wyllys Avenue, Middletown, CT 06459-0265

Phone: 860-685-3000

E-mail address: admissions@wesleyan.edu

Web site URL: www.wesleyan.edu

Location: suburban

Founded: 1831

Private or Public: private

Religious affiliation: none

Undergraduate enrollment: 2,750

Total enrollment: 2,900

Percent Male/Female: 49%/51%

Percent Minority: 23.0%

Percent African-American: 9.0%

Percent Hispanic: 6.0%

Percent Asian: 8.0%

Percent in-state/out-of-state: 9.0%/91%

Percent Pub HS: 58%

Fraternities: 10%

Sororities: 2%

Number of Applicants: 5,727

Percent Accepted: 32%

Percent Accepted who enroll: 39%

Entering: 715

Transfers: 70

Application Deadline: 1 Jan

Mean SAT: 666 V, 658 M

Middle 50% SAT range: NA V, NA M

Middle 50% ACT range: NA

Mean ACT: 28

3 Most popular majors: English, government, economics

Retention: 96.0%

Graduation rate: 78.0%

Library: 1.2 million volumes

Tuition and Fees: $24,330 in; $24,330 out

Room and Board: $6,510

On-campus housing: 100%

Financial aid, first-year: 50%

I f you are human, you'll find your place at Wesleyan. Renowned for its diverse student body, Wesleyan University is a comfortable place for nearly any student who has a real interest in learning, both inside and outside the classroom.

A Passion for Learning

Academics at Wesleyan take top priority. "There are no slackers here," said one student, "everyone comes here to work." Wesleyan students must fulfill six general educational requirements for graduation: they must take two classes in natural sciences, two in behavioral and social sciences, and two in arts and humanities. Because the requirements demand only that students take classes in particular academic areas, students are given considerable latitude in their choice of courses: "The requirements are really gen-

eral. Everyone here says that you fill them by accident." Each requirement group has its share of guts, however. "Rocks for Jocks" and "Drugs and Disease" are said to be notably easy classes that fulfill the natural science requirement.

For the most motivated students, Wesleyan also offers two interdisciplinary programs to which students apply during their sophomore year. The College of Letters combines work in English, writing and languages while the College of Social Studies (nicknamed the "College of Suicidal Sophomores") focuses on history, philosophy, political science, and sociology. "They're difficult to get into, and really hard once you're there, but they give you an amazing education," said a student of the colleges. For students whose interests are in both the humanities and the sciences, the Science and Society program enables participants to double major in one natural and one social science simultaneously, or to concentrate solely on science and medicine and their implications on society.

Classes at Wesleyan are taught exclusively by professors, but TAs lead section discussions for some of the larger classes. According to students, however, it is easy to stick to smaller classes, even to fulfill the requirements. Because Wesleyan students are passionate about learning, and because the professors are truly interested in their students' education, class discussions are intense and valuable. "Everyone here is really passionate about whatever they're discussing in class. Class discussions don't stop when we leave the classroom." The workload varies considerably by department and individual classes. Many humanities classes have "a ridiculous amount of reading and, if they're writing-intensive, an obscene amount of writing." The humanities at Wesleyan are a particular strength, with the English and history departments leading the way. Psychology and economics are also very popular departments.

According to some students, registration at Wesleyan can be "a royal pain," since it's entirely computer-based. But, according to one student, "you just have to show enough interest to the professor to get into the class. If you can't get in when you first try, just keep going and the prof will definitely let you in." The First-Year Initiative Program affords freshmen the opportunity to take small seminar classes in several departments, enabling them to get to know professors early on.

On-Campus Fun

While Wesleyan students take their academics seriously, they are fanatical about their social lives. Weekends offer almost every type of student the opportunity to get out, meet people, and have a good time. "There are a ridiculous amount of things to do on the weekends here. There are concerts, movies, shows, parties, dances, everything." And since the surrounding area of Middletown has little to offer students and is not considered by many to be the safest of places, most students stick around on weekends, making campus life busy and exciting. If students

do want to hang out off-campus, then a car is necessary for travel to New Haven. Students also go to Boston and New York City occasionally for cultural events clubbing.

The partying and drinking scenes are based on the fraternity and residential houses. Each weekend, several fraternities and residential houses throw parties that are open to all students. Fraternities, despite their active role in the party scene, are actually a small presence on campus. "We use them for the parties," said one student. Students at Wesleyan do admit to drinking and smoking pot. According to students, being underage is not a problem at all. "When you walk into a party, they mark your hand to show that you're over or under the drinking age. But once you get into the party, no one checks your hands and no one cares." Officially, students under 21 are not allowed to consume alcohol, and all advertised parties on campus must register with the administration and follow guidelines such as a required food-to-alcohol ratio if they plan to serve alcoholic beverages. Students claim that the administration is pretty lax about alcohol, though: the general rule seems to be "if they don't see it, they don't care," and behind closed doors, students say they can do almost whatever they want.

Even amid all this drinking, though, non-drinkers can find refuge. "You don't have to drink to have a good time. If you do, you do; if you don't, you don't. No one cares either way." Throughout the year, however, bigger events such as the Fall Ball, Spring Fling, Halloween Dance, and the '80s theme dance draw big crowds.

Parties at Wesleyan are also the center of the hook-up scene. Most students meet at parties and then get caught up in an "extended random hookup," as one student put it. Actual relationships at Wesleyan tend to be on one extreme or another. "You either have marriages or random hookups here," exclaimed one student. "There is no dating scene here, but there are lots of attractive people. There's just a lot of sex. It's sort of gross." All kinds of couples find acceptance at Wesleyan, as well. There are many homosexual and interracial couples and, according to students, they are accepted on campus.

"We're very PC here, PC is based on Wesleyan," said one student. "Everything is cool here."

The idea of PC may very well have had its roots at Wesleyan, since the campus is very diverse and open to virtually any sort of personality or activity. "Students here are from everywhere, of every ethnicity, very open-minded and very friendly," reported one student. Wesleyan students run the entire spectrum in nearly every facet of life: Some students are athletic and some never go to the gym; some are very wealthy and many are on financial aid; and the music tastes range from Sublime and Led Zeppelin to Ani DiFranco and alumna Dar Williams. Many students have tattoos, and even more have body piercing. Wesleyan students, however, are surprisingly "normal," one student said. "I was a little surprised when I got here because, from the school's reputation, I expected everyone to be a little bit weird, that everyone would be really strange and into really eclectic things," she said. "But everyone is more 'normal.' Kids are really laid-back, no one cares what you look like. It's a really comfortable, accepting, awesome environment."

Living and Eating

Campus living at Wesleyan is comfortable and varied. According to students, the administration is very good at matching students up freshman year with the residential needs they indicated on their housing forms: students can rank the dorm options in order of preference, and can also indicate if they want to live on "well-being" floors, which specifically forbid any use of drugs and alcohol. Freshmen live throughout the campus, but mostly in Clark ("the loud jock dorm") and Butterfield ("pretty isolated, but damn nice"). "The rooms freshman year are pretty big and they're really, really nice," said one student. Five or six RAs live in each dorm building and are "pretty cool about pretty much everything." One RA is on call every Friday and Saturday evening to take care of student needs. Floors and bathrooms are coed, but students can vote for the latter not to be.

After freshman year, students enter a lottery for housing, either with the group of people they want to live with, or alone if they want a single. In this lottery, drawn in order of seniority, each student or group gets to list its preferences of which dorm complex they wish to live in. Upperclassmen also have the option of living in residential houses, some of which cater to particular interests. For example, students can live in the Malcolm X House, La Casa, the Gay and Lesbian House, or one of a few literary societies. "The houses are awesome and throw the best parties," said one student.

Like the rest of the campus, dorm buildings are generally attractive, with the architecture ranging from colonial to Gothic. The main science building, though "really modern and ugly," provides a good, quiet place to study. When the weather is nice, students tend to study outdoors on one of the large greens—which are always bustling with people playing Frisbee, students on the way to class, and, often, classes themselves taking place outdoors. "When you look in a catalog and see people sitting there on the steps of a library or on the grass, you think it's just in the catalog," said one student. "But here, that's the way it really is. There are lots of trees, lots of green grass, people always outside, chilling out." The campus also has a large gym which many students use to work out.

Food at Wesleyan is one of the few areas that draw constant complaint. "Thank God Domino's delivers," said one student. As a freshman, students have the option of choosing a meal plan consisting of either 19 meals per week or 13 meals per week and flex points. The meals can only be eaten in a few places, the most popular of which is "Mocon," the McConaugh cafeteria, which always offers a salad bar, a deli bar, and a buffet of hot foods. At Mocon, students can count on finding a pasta dish, two soups, and grilled cheese sandwiches and hamburgers. The cafeteria is also extremely accommodating to vegetarians. Flex points can be used at various on-campus eateries and mini-grocery stores. As upperclassmen, students have more meal plan opportunities, including a point-based plan.

Beyond the Classroom

Outside class, Wesleyan students put their passion and energy to work. Wesleyan boasts more than 180 undergraduate organizations, many of which perform community service in Middletown. A cappella groups, theater troupes, and the student newspaper, *Argus*, are among the most popular student activities. "Activities here are awesome because they give you something to do and people to know without forcing you to identify yourself as one type of person," one student said. Students with a flair for writing can join the staff of *Hermes*, an alternative literary magazine, while those who were always the class clown when they were younger gravitate toward Gag Reflex, a comedy group whose extremely popular shows nearly always sell out. One student also reported that "tutoring at local high school and elementary schools is also really popular." In short, nearly anyone could find his or her niche in the extracurricular world of Wesleyan.

Athletics at Wesleyan take a low-key position. Students say that it is as if "there are two different worlds, there are the athletes and the non-athletes." For the athletes and devoted fans, Wesleyan sports are extremely important, and several teams are very successful. Reportedly, football, crew, and Ultimate Frisbee are particularly hard-core, competitive teams. Those interested in participating in athletics on a less competitive level can choose from a large and active array of noncompetitive club and intramural sports.

> "We're very PC—PC is based on Wesleyan. Everything is very cool here."

While Wesleyan students take themselves seriously in their academic lives, they have the same excitement for their lives outside of the classroom. Nicknamed "Diversity University," Wesleyan boasts a student body and a campus where everything is accepted and everything is encouraged, and everyone is welcome. —*Alan Schoenfeld and Staff*

FYI

The three best things about attending Wesleyan are "the politics, the nudity, and the chemicals."

The three worst things about attending Wesleyan are "the administration, the weather, and the food can be terrible."

The three things that every student should do before graduating from Wesleyan are "to attend a naked party at Art House, attend a football game, and go to a protest."

One thing I'd like to have known before coming here is "I wish I had a map of the tunnels."

Yale University

Address: P.O. Box 208234, New Haven, CT 06520-8234
Phone: 203-432-9300
E-mail address: undergraduate.admissions@yale.edu
Web site URL: www.yale.edu
Location: urban
Founded: 1701
Private or Public: private
Religious affiliation: none
Undergraduate enrollment: 5,440
Total enrollment: 11,059
Percent Male / Female: 50% / 50%
Percent Minority: 32.0%

Percent African-American: 8.0%
Percent Hispanic: 6.0%
Percent Asian: 17.0%
Percent in-state / out-of-state: 9.0% / 91%
Percent Pub HS: 54%
Fraternities: NA
Sororities: NA
Number of Applicants: 11,947
Percent Accepted: 18%
Percent Accepted who enroll: 62%
Entering: 1,333
Transfers: 30
Application Deadline: 31 Dec
Mean SAT: 720 V, 730 M

Middle 50% SAT range: 670–770 V, 670–760 M
Middle 50% ACT range: NA
Mean ACT: NA
3 Most popular majors: biology, history, economics
Retention: 98.0%
Graduation rate: 85.0%
Library: 10.8 million volumes
Tuition and Fees: $24,500 in; $24,500 out
Room and Board: $7,440
On-campus housing: 100%
Financial aid, first-year: 66%

In late November, Yale University paraphernalia glitters prominently in the stands; the school mascot, a bulldog named Handsome Dan, parades proudly along the edge of the field; and fight songs echo resolutely across the Yale Bowl. Generations of Yalies gather together to cheer their football team to victory against their Cambridge archrival in one of the most anticipated events of the year, "The Game." Indeed, the festivities in the stands and at the tailgates outside the Bowl are a strong display of the solidarity, spirit, and dynamism that pervade the campus of one of the nation's premier institutions, long after The Game weekend is over.

Located in the Elm City neighborhood of New Haven, Connecticut, the Yale campus offers undergraduates a glimpse of city living without sacrificing the intimacy of a suburban campus. As one junior stated, "living here lets me enjoy a city heartbeat in a friendlier, more relaxed environment." Modeled after England's Oxford and Cambridge, large Gothic buildings loom beside both Georgian and modern architectural styles. Many students are quick to call Yale "your quintessentially charming, traditional, New England campus—it's very impressive."

But this prominent liberal arts university provides more than just a beautiful campus for the enthusiastic undergraduates who matriculate each year.

A Rigorous Academic Pace

The incoming freshman class learns very quickly about the pace and rigor of academic life at Yale. Yale requires 36 course credits for graduation, compared to the standard 32 at other Ivy League schools. In fact, most Yalies exceed the 36 course requirements, finding themselves overwhelmed by the sheer volume of classes available in the "Blue Book" (the Yale College Programs of Study). As one junior stated, "poring over the Blue Book and making decisions about my courses gets harder each term. I just need a few more semesters to take all the classes I like!"

At the beginning of each semester, Yale students enjoy a two-week "shopping period," which enables them to attend as many different classes as they please without making an official commitment. While some students use shopping period as an extension of their vacation, many consider it a "great way to try to see as much of what Yale academics have to offer to make sure you don't get stuck taking something you will regret later."

Yale students are required to fulfill a series of distributional requirements during their first two years at the university. In addition to two years of study in a foreign language, students must take two courses in each of the following rough distribution groups: language and literature, history, social science, and natural science. Students can waive the language requirement by demonstrating proficiency on a Yale-administered test or on the AP exam. The Yale proficiency exams are reportedly very difficult, though; "I took six years of Spanish before coming to Yale, and I left the proficiency test wondering whether I had learned Portuguese by mistake," a sophomore said.

Aside from these basic requirements, Yale students are encouraged to experiment and take classes in as many different departments as they wish before officially choosing their major at the beginning of junior year. Popular majors include history, English, molecular biophysics and biochemistry (MB&B), political science, economics, and psychology. Some of Yale's comparatively weaker majors are ecology & evolutionary biology, which is a new major, and women's studies, which have fewer course offerings. In February, 2000, President Richard Levin announced a $500 million fund that will afford construction of a new general sciences and engineering complex and also fund for more faculty. This move is meant to show Yale's support for the sciences and attempt to mark Yale's sciences every bit as good as MIT's or Caltech's.

Each semester, the university also offers several Residential College Seminars, small classes taught by visiting professors or individuals in the community. Recent choices have ranged from Chinese Landscape Gardens to the Physics of Sailing to Bioethics to Writing for TV.

Freshmen often decide to apply to either the Perspectives on Science program, a lecture and discussion course designed for freshmen who are strong in math and science, or the Directed Studies program, a writing-intensive, yearlong interdisciplinary program open to roughly 10 percent of the class. The latter program, often labeled "Directed Suicide," requires a particularly high reading load and weekly papers that keep many "DS-ers"

chained to their desks on Thursday nights.

Yale has its share of "guts" to abate the intensity of the students' workload, and many learn to balance their workload with such courses. As one senior noted, "If there is one thing I have learned, it's that you have to strike a happy medium with your courses. Unless you want to pitch a tent in the library all term, then you need at least one class you can let slide." Electrical Engineering 101, the History of Jazz, and Astronomy 110 are favorites. Also, one student noted, "You're never gonna do all the reading for all of the classes. I've had professors tell me that we're supposed to be picking and choosing—it's a life skill." The Credit/D/Fail option is also a popular way to lighten the pressure of rigorous academics and encourage experimentation in new areas without the fear of a "crummy grade."

According to many Yalies, one of the highlights of Yale academics is the chance to learn from some of the most important scholars in academia. Students often look to such "star" professors as history's John Gaddis ("Mr. Cold War), religious studies' Wayne Meeks ("a guru of early Christianity"), history of art's Vicent Scully ("his fervor for art is infectious"), history's Jonathan Spence ("think brilliant Chinese history scholar who looks like Sean Connery"), and the English department's Harold Bloom ("the man has written literary criticism of every great piece of literature you can think of"). Undergrads particularly comment on the strong degree of student-faculty interaction, citing regular office hours as "one of the best ways to get to know profs more personally." One senior remarked, "I love the fact that I can feel comfortable chatting with my seminar professor over a cup of coffee at Willoughby's."

Yalies do not always have time to spend talking philosophy over espresso, as many find themselves working amid the intricate woodwork, arches, and cathedral ceilings of Sterling Memorial Library, the recently renovated "researcher's dream." The Yale library collection is the second largest in the nation, and its 10 million volumes are housed in almost 40 libraries spread across campus. For those undergraduates who prefer to study closer to home, the residential colleges each have their own individual libraries, which are open 24 hours a day.

Thanks to a recent donation, Yale has commenced construction of a $500 million Science Park. This project will provide new facilities and update many of the existing labs. The Science Park initiative will invite more faculty and researchers to utilize the technologically advanced facilities.

College Living

Just about every aspect of life at Yale is influenced by the residential college system. As freshmen, students are randomly assigned to one of the 12 residential colleges, where they live after they complete their first year on Old Campus. Each college preserves its own architectural style and traditions, and each residential college is overseen by the college master and dean who both live and work within the college. While the deans oversee student academics, masters often work closely with the college councils and student activities committees to improve student life.

Residential colleges are equipped with their own dining halls, music rooms, snack bars, computing facilities, laundry rooms, TV rooms, exercise facilities, and student kitchens. Some colleges have special features such as Davenport's darkroom, Silliman's movie theater ("Silliflicks"), Branford's printing press, Jonathan Edward's racquetball court, Berkeley's woodshop, and Calhoun's sauna. Rooms vary markedly across all the colleges, though generally, students live in medium or large suites which include both single and double bedrooms off of a common room with Gothic windows and poor overhead lighting.

Last year marked the beginning of a twelve year, $1 billion project to renovate one residential college every year. While Branford is being renovated during the 1999–2000 school year, Branfordians live in a newly constructed dorm, informally called "Swing Space," complete with small kitchenettes, overhead lighting, and private bathrooms. When the Branfordians move back into their college next year, the structural integrity of their college will remain the same, but they will enjoy the renovated interior with reconfigured rooms, generous lighting, and air conditioned common areas. Students in Berkeley, the first college to be renovated, rave about the improvements. One sophomore was so enthusiastic about the changes that she exclaimed, "I don't want to graduate; I'll just enjoy my spacious room-with-a-view for the rest of my life."

Students are universally enthusiastic about the residential college system. "I think it provides a support system for students," said one senior. "There's a sense of belonging for no other reason than your being randomly placed in this college," said another. Each college, and often each class within a college, has a certain reputation among the student body, and friendly intercollegiate rivalry is manifested at intramurals sports (IMs) and varsity football games (where members of each college invariably sit together, wave their college flags, and shout insults at the other colleges).

Yalies associate strongly with their colleges, and the social interaction is often centered around the residential college system. Annual parties such as the Silliman Safety Dance (an immensely popular all-'80s revival), the Pierson Inferno (a Halloween costume ball), Exotic Erotic (Timothy Dwight's "the less you wear, the less you pay"), and the Morse and Stiles Casino Night (a formal '20s event) are all sponsored by the residential colleges. The Holiday Balls are also a favorite student event as each college hires either a band or a disc jockey and students dress for "ball-hopping" to all 12 colleges in a single night.

A Time to Let Loose

The social scene at Yale also revolves in large part around non–college sponsored events. As one junior stated, "One of the biggest misconceptions about Yale is that we are all dork losers who hate a good time and are too busy saving the world or padding our resumes. It's just not true. There is a definitely hard core party network of people who love to let loose." Events such as Alpha Epsilon Pi's Jello Night, Swing Dance parties, Naples nights, and Co-op Dances (sponsored by the Lesbian, Gay, Bisexual and Transgendered Cooperative at Yale) draw a large crowd of Yalies on weekends. Students also show their support for student drama productions, dance performances, a cappella concerts and musical performances. Particularly popular productions include the Yale Symphony Orchestra's Halloween Extravaganza, the Anti-Gravity Society's Fire Show, Rhythmic Blue's contemporary dance show, and the Viola Question's improvisational comedy performances. The Yale Repertory Theater offers students discount prices to attend their most recent productions, which have included *Measure for Measure* and *A Streetcar Named Desire* for the 1998–99 season. The Yale University Art Gallery, British Art Center, and Peabody Museum all offer weekend symposiums on current exhibitions. Additionally, York Square Cinema primarily shows "artsy" films with only a smattering of first-run movies. However, for many students, it is a "favorite date spot for those of us who actually do the dating thing."

Several Yalies point to a prominent casual hookup scene as the only alternative to a "meager" dating environment. "You either have zip in the relationship department, or something really long and intense. There isn't much in between," one student remarked. Many Yalies are so committed to their academics and extracurricular activities that they often give dating a lower priority; "essentially dating gets lost in the shuffle."

On weekends, students are not likely to lose the chance to take advantage of the "incredible" variety of bars and restaurants in New Haven. As one junior noted, "one of the best things about living here is being able to break out of the dining hall doldrums and enjoy either Thai, Mexican, Japanese, Chinese, Italian, French, Cajun, American, or Middle Eastern fare." Some of the most popular dinner destinations in New Haven include Scoozi's, Thai Taste, Rainbow Gardens, Consiglio's, and Union League. To appease late-night cravings without breaking the bank, students frequent Krauzer's, Au Bon Pain, Xando's, Copper Kitchen, Durfee's, and Yorkside Pizza. Students often frequent nightspots such as Viva's, Kavanaugh's, Gecko's, Richter's, BAR, and Toad's Place, a nightclub that is particularly packed on Saturday nights with Yale students taking advantage of free admission with a valid Yale ID.

Serious Commitments

Partying isn't the only thing students take seriously. Extracurricular commitments have a high priority for many students who want to "take a breather from work and give something back to Yale." Organizations abound on campus and freshmen often find themselves inundated by the possibilities, particularly during the Freshman Bazaar in late August. Student interests are so varied that a mind-boggling number of extracurricular groups exist to accommodate them. Publications include the *Yale Daily News*, the nation's oldest college daily, and *Rumpus*, a humor paper/tabloid notorious for its selection of Yale's 50 Most Beautiful People each fall. According to one student, roughly 18 a cappella singing groups exist at Yale, of which the Whiffenpoofs and the SOBs (Society of Orpheus and Bacchus) are the oldest both at Yale and across the nation. For the dancing inclined, Yale Dancers, A Different Drum, and TAPS offer a variety of options. Debate and politics organizations, including the Yale College Student Union, the Yale Debate Association, and the Yale College Mock Trial Association also make their voices heard. Finally, community service organizations like TIES (Tutoring in Elementary Schools), Project SAT, and YHHAP (the Yale Hunger and Homelessness Action Project).

> "I love the fact that I can feel comfortable chatting with my seminar professor over a cup of coffee at Willoughby's."

Sports also have a significant presence on campus. There are approximately 30 varsity teams, including traditional favorites of spectators such as football and ice hockey, but also extremely successful fencing, crew, and squash teams for both men and women. Some varsity teams, such as lacrosse, tennis, soccer, and volleyball, were so popular that JV teams were recently established. There are also a wide variety of other club sports teams, including serious rugby and ultimate Frisbee teams for both men and women, and more informal badminton and croquet teams. In addition, there is a popular intramural sports program, in which students on residential college teams compete in fall, winter, and spring seasons for the prestigious "Tyng Cup."

A Yale Type?

Is there such a thing as a typical Yalie? According to one senior, "Its no big secret that Yale strives for diversity in its student body." Yalies come from all over the world, but the highest concentrations are from the Northeast. The college is considered diverse—politically, ethnically, economically, and religiously. Support networks exist for all students. Freshmen counselors are assigned to all incoming freshmen. Undergrads are also able to contact trained counselors at 2-TALK for sexual harassment and ECHO for eating disorder issues. Minority students have a particularly strong set of resources available, including ethnic counselors for the freshmen, deans for each campus racial group, and cultural centers such as the Asian American Cultural Center, Casa Cultural Julia de Burgos, and the Af-Am House.

The Yale community is an incredibly eclectic mix of students, activities, and extracurricular passions. With its tradition of academic excellence and its social and cultural diversity, Yale is undoubtedly an unparalleled place to spend those "bright college years," as the alma mater goes. Yalies are "a driven, enthusiastic, ambitious bunch." And, if the energy generated during Game weekend is any indication, these Bulldogs are bursting with pride. —*Alexandra M. Rethore and Staff*

FYI

The three best things about going to Yale are "the gorgeous campus, the awesome faculty, the constant activity and excitement on campus."

The three worst things about going to Yale are "incompetence of the Registrar's office, high tuition, and the cold winter."

The three things every student should do before graduating from Yale are "toast at Mory's, go to The Game, go to a Master's Tea."

One thing I wish I'd known before coming to Yale is "that the school doesn't celebrate any national holidays, so you never get three-day weekends."

Delaware

University of Delaware

Address: 116 Hullihen Hall, Newark, DE 19716
Phone: 302-831-8123
E-mail address: admissions@udel.edu
Web site URL: www.udel.edu
Location: suburban
Founded: 1743
Private or Public: public
Religious affiliation: none
Undergraduate enrollment: 15,443
Total enrollment: 18,230
Percent Male / Female: 42%/58%
Percent Minority: 12.0%

Percent African-American: 6.0%
Percent Hispanic: 2.0%
Percent Asian: 3.0%
Percent in-state / out-of-state: 42%/58%
Percent Pub HS: 75%
Fraternities: 15%
Sororities: 15%
Number of Applicants: 15,482
Percent Accepted: 67%
Percent Accepted who enroll: 35%
Entering: 3,212
Transfers: 0
Application Deadline: 15 Feb

Mean SAT: 560 V, 575 M
Middle 50% SAT range: 510–610 V, 520–630 M
Middle 50% ACT range: NA
Mean ACT: NA
3 Most popular majors: business management, education, engineering
Retention: 87%
Graduation rate: 54%
Library: 2.3 million volumes
Tuition and Fees: $9,668 in; $17,668 out
Room and Board: $0
On-campus housing: 0%
Financial aid, first-year: 44%

The University of Delaware is a large state college nestled in the rolling hills of picturesque Newark, Delaware. It is a place where intellectuals and frat boys co-exist in eternal bliss. As one Delaware freshman states, "we talk about everything from Heidegger to Heineken."

Rollin' with the Scholars— Academics

The University of Delaware offers the full range of the usual college majors. Particularly intense majors, according to some students, are engineering, visual communication, chemistry, and physics. Chemical engineering is of special interest to many students since the DuPont Company endowed the university with several million dollars to create a program that rivals the best technical schools in the United States. On the other end of the spectrum, for those not interested in "masochism," the psychology major is apparently a popular option for the "slacker student population."

In order to attract top-notch students the university has also implemented numerous programs. In particular, the Honors Program provides students with challenging classes with lower enrollment. Honors students praise the close contact between students and professors as "the most important aspect of joining this group. The Jefferson Scholars program offers would-be doctors guidance and aide in applying to medical school in an attempt to give them a competitive edge. For minority students interested in engineering there is the RISE (Resources to Insure Successful Engineers) program, which offers them tutelage and career counseling. In addition to these programs, Delaware also offers the Dean's Scholar Program whereby students can devise their own major.

When it comes to academic distributions, Delaware students are "fairly lucky." They are required only to fulfill basic core courses that include such courses as E110—otherwise known as Freshman

English. Full-time students are required to take 12 credits per semester but most studious Blue Hens opt for 15.

Many would-be college students are greatly concerned about having TAs as teachers. At Delaware, many large lecture courses are actually taught by the professors, but have TAs leading sections. Prefrosh, take heart: there are some excellent professors at the University of Delaware including big names such as Robert Straight and Katherine Varnes, whom one student calls "absolutely incredible!"

Although there are some large introductory courses, many students enjoy schedules where most of their classes do not have more than 30 or 35 students. Despite the perks of small classes and "incredible professors," one student complains that she has a mere 3.5 hours of sleep a night and has absolutely a "TON" of work.

To help students diminish the intensity of the workload the university offers a "winter term" which many eager students take advantage of during which students remain in school to take classes during their long winter break. The university, however, does not require anyone to partake in this term.

Students love to relax at some of the university's most popular study locations. Morris Library is called "indispensable" by one student and the Chemistry, Physics, or Honors Centers are notoriously quiet locales ideal for the angstridden student. Overall, "The University of Delaware has a strong academic program and what you get out of it depends on how you treat the courses."

For those looking to kick back, there are also some great off-campus hangouts that include the famous Klondike Kate's and the ever hip Iron Hill Brewery. According to several sources the Hartsoe House, located in Nonantum Hills, is *the* location for popular parties and cool music. Local musical talent includes Phil Lamplugh and his band The Grieder's. All three locations offer food and accept UD flex dollars, whereby students "pay" for off-campus food with specially distributed UD cards. Many students complain about the meal plan and the varying quality of the food, as one student does by calling Delaware's meal plan an absolute

"rip-off." Unfortunately, many students list dining hall food as one of the "worst aspects of university life—so thank goodness for UD."

Gettin' Jiggy Wit It—The Social Scene

Social life at UD centers heavily on the drinking scene. According to some upperclassmen, the freshmen can always be "spotted in huge groups desperately trying to locate parties they hear about through the grapevine." The upperclassmen, on the other hand, are the ones who throw these much-sought-after parties. On a more serious note, drugs exists on campus, but they are not widespread and mainly consist of marijuana usage.

There is a definite Greek scene on campus and as much as 15 percent of UD students belong to either a frat or a sorority. For those interested in rushing, the process of joining one is not "very difficult—these places are inclusive and want you if you want them." According to students, the most popular frats and sororities are Sigma Chi and Alpha Zeta Delta. Though Greek life is a presence on campus, it is not an integral part of the social scene at UD. Students wary of the drinking scene always have the option of attending a large number of on-campus non-alcoholic activities. There are frequent movies screened, as well as "Art Under the Stars."

Dating is rare at UD, though there is "no lack of random hookups." Sex is apparently commonplace on campus and "attractive individuals," according to several seniors, "abound." For students lucky enough to find a date, Klondike Kate's followed by a movie is always a popular option for a night on the town.

Many students report that it is very easy to meet new people on campus and most people form friendships with individuals from classes and activities. When asked about stereotypes of UD students, some boldly characterized their fellow classmates as "upper-middle-class white kids, beer guzzlers." Many students stated that "there is a definite categorization of the student body along the lines of athletes, Greeks, and nerds." In fact, a common complaint from students centers on the lack of diversity at the school. Many students come from Delaware and the surrounding mid-Atlantic states, so geographical diversity is not commonplace. As for racial diversity, there is very little interracial mixing on campus, though race relations are still described as "good and supportive."

A Burst of Extracurricular Enthusiasm

Extracurricular life at Delaware is booming. When asked about the workload at Delaware, one student replied that he was "swamped" with mainly extracurricular activities. Like any major state school Delaware has the ROTC, theater groups, and some singing groups. There is a very active Black Student Union, as well. The inter-varsity Christian Fellowship and the Greek groups are active in community service in and around Newark. Many students at Delaware enjoy actual paying jobs on and off the campus. Popular places of employment are clothing stores, restaurants, and a wide variety of on-campus jobs.

> "We talk about everything from Heidegger to Heineken."

Of all extracurricular activities, the largest and most popular one at Delaware is athletics. Delaware has a superb men's basketball team that has reached the NCAA Tournament and helps drum up school support for the Fighting Blue Hens. The football team is also a popular source of school spirit. The opening game versus archrival West Chester University is considered a highlight of the season.

Close Quarters at UD

Housing problems, with the recent increase in the number of students, is one of the greatest problems on campus today. Last year, some students were forced to live in common rooms until suitable accommodations could be found. Freshmen describe the dorms as comfortable but certainly not "palaces." One dorm to particularly avoid is the Dickinson dormitory. The RAs at Delaware are notoriously strict and hand out offenses for underage drinking and other frowned upon dormitory activities. One RA claimed that Delaware RAs are as "strict as they have to be" in order to enforce the alcohol policy on campus despite the fact that many students maintain that alcohol still flows freely at Delaware. Most upperclassmen move off campus and housing is apparently readily available to students in the Newark area. Some others choose, however, to live in the house of their respective fraternity or sorority. Theme houses, such as the French house, also exist on campus.

Ultimately, most students are content with their decision to attend the University of Delaware. With wonderful professors and interesting visiting speakers (from Chris Rock to Maya Angelou), the experiences students enjoy while at the UD are "eye opening and mind-expanding." Delaware students consider themselves healthy, somewhat sober, and very, very wise. —*Sean McBride*

FYI
The three best things about attending the University of Delaware are "the Ethernet connection, the traffic stops for students, and every time you do work friends try to get you to go to a party."
The three worst things about attending the University of Delaware are "the parking, the meal plan, and the inadequate showers."
The three things every student should do before graduating from the University of Delaware are "to learn how to take an ice block shot, walk around campus at night and appreciate the architecture and lighting, and to visit Nonantum Mills."
One thing I wish I'd known before coming here is "how many students there are from Jersey."

District of Columbia

American University

Address: 4400 Massachussetts Ave. NW, Washington, DC 20016-8001
Phone: 202-885-6000
E-mail address: afa@american.edu
Web site URL: www.american.edu
Location: urban
Founded: 1893
Private or Public: priv
Religious affiliation: United Methodist
Undergraduate enrollment: 5,533
Total enrollment: 10,894
Percent Male/Female: 40%/60%

Percent Minority: 18.0%
Percent African-American: 8.0%
Percent Hispanic: 6.0%
Percent Asian: 4.0%
Percent in-state/out-of-state: NA
Percent Pub HS: NA
Fraternities: NA
Sororities: NA
Number of Applicants: 7,554
Percent Accepted: 74%
Percent Accepted who enroll: 22%
Entering: 1,219
Transfers: NA
Application Deadline: 1 Feb

Mean SAT: 604 V, 582 M
Middle 50% SAT range: 550–650 V, 530–630 M
Middle 50% ACT range: 23–29
Mean ACT: 26
3 Most popular majors: international studies, political science, international business
Retention: 85%
Graduation rate: 65%
Library: 870,000 volumes
Tuition and Fees: $21,399 in; $21,399 out
Room and Board: $8,200
On-campus housing: 60%
Financial aid, first-year: 47%

American University's vibrant heartbeat is the nation's capital. For students at AU, the political epicenter of the world is part of their daily lives, but they still can live and study in a relaxed suburban setting. American University's choice location in northwest Washington, D.C., in combination with its first-rate academics, attracts students from all over the country and the world.

Tuesday Night Parties

Academics are foremost on everyone's mind at American. Although some manage to get by with less than Herculean effort, the typical student's top priority is academics. To graduate, students must fulfill the General Education guidelines, which require introductory and intermediate courses in each of five distribution groups. Students are definitely satisfied with the academic aspect of American. Many rate the classes "difficult, but not unbearable," with a moderate amount of competition. Instead of large lectures, classes at American usually enroll about 30 to 40 students. Classes are also broken down into small discussion sections. Students generally do not have a problem with enrollment, and few experience getting "locked out" of a class. Classes are arranged on a Monday–Thursday or Tuesday–Friday schedule, with Wednesdays reserved for labs or seminars. Compared to the traditional Monday–Wednesday and Tuesday–Thursday format some other schools use, this alternate configuration allows for an extra day of freedom dents come from Delaware and the surrounding mid-Atlantic states, so geographical diversity is not commonplace. As for racial diversity, there is very little interracial mixing on campus, though race relations are still described as "good and supportive."

A Burst of Extracurricular Enthusiasm

Extracurricular life at Delaware is booming. When asked about the workload at Delaware, one student replied that he was "swamped" with mainly extracurricular activities. Like any major state school Delaware has the ROTC, theater groups, and some singing groups. There is a very active Black Student Union, as well. The inter-varsity Christian Fellowship and the Greek groups are active in community service in and around Newark. Many students at Delaware enjoy actual paying jobs on and off the campus. Popular places of employment are clothing stores, restaurants, and a wide variety of on-campus jobs.

> **"We talk about everything from Heidegger to Heineken."**

Of all extracurricular activities, the largest and most popular one at Delaware is athletics. Delaware has a superb men's basketball team that has reached the NCAA Tournament and helps drum up school support for the Fighting Blue Hens. The football team is also a popular source of school spirit. The opening game versus archrival West Chester University is considered a highlight of the season.

Close Quarters at UD

Housing problems, with the recent increase in the number of students, is one of the greatest problems on campus today. Last year, some students were forced to live in common rooms until suitable accommodations could be found. Freshmen describe the dorms as comfortable but certainly not "palaces." One dorm to particularly avoid is the Dickinson dormitory. The RAs at Delaware are notoriously strict and hand out offenses for underage drinking and other frowned upon dormitory activities. One RA claimed that Delaware RAs are as "strict as they have to be" in order to enforce the alcohol policy on campus despite the fact that many students maintain that alcohol still flows freely at Delaware. Most upperclassmen move off campus and housing is apparently readily available to students in the Newark area. Some others choose, however, to live in the house of their respective fraternity or sorority. Theme houses, such as the French house, also exist on campus.

Ultimately, most students are content with their decision to attend the University of Delaware. With wonderful professors and interesting visiting speakers (from Chris Rock to Maya Angelou), the experiences students enjoy while at the UD are "eye opening and mind-expanding." Delaware students consider themselves healthy, somewhat sober, and very, very wise. —*Sean McBride*

FYI

The three best things about attending the University of Delaware are "the Ethernet connection, the traffic stops for students, and every time you do work friends try to get you to go to a party."

The three worst things about attending the University of Delaware are "the parking, the meal plan, and the inadequate showers."

The three things every student should do before graduating from the University of Delaware are "to learn how to take an ice block shot, walk around campus at night and appreciate the architecture and lighting, and to visit Nonantum Mills."

One thing I wish I'd known before coming here is "how many students there are from Jersey."

District of Columbia

American University's vibrant heartbeat is the nation's capital. For students at AU, the political epicenter of the world is part of their daily lives, but they still can live and study in a relaxed suburban setting. American University's choice location in northwest Washington, D.C., in combination with its first-rate academics, attracts students from all over the country and the world.

Tuesday Night Parties

Academics are foremost on everyone's mind at American. Although some manage to get by with less than Herculean effort, the typical student's top priority is academics. To graduate, students must fulfill the General Education guidelines, which require introductory and intermediate courses in each of five distribution groups. Students are definitely satisfied with the academic aspect of American. Many rate the classes "difficult, but not unbearable," with a moderate amount of competition. Instead of large lectures, classes at American usually enroll about 30 to 40 students. Classes are also broken down into small discussion sections. Students generally do not have a problem with enrollment, and few experience getting "locked out" of a class. Classes are arranged on a Monday–Thursday or Tuesday–Friday schedule, with Wednesdays reserved for labs or seminars. Compared to the traditional Monday–Wednesday and Tuesday–Thursday format some other schools use, this alternate configuration allows for an extra day of freedom in completing assignments. Due to American's unique scheduling system, Tuesdays have become a big party night on campus, along with the standard Friday and Saturday nights.

An honors curriculum is available for those seeking extra challenge. It requires participants to take several honors courses each semester for a total of 30 credits. The World Capitals program allows students to spend a semester or year in one of 11 international locations participating in seminars and internships. The Washington Semester Program enables students to take part in seminars with four to six speakers per week, including policy makers, practitioners, and business professionals, and also provides internship opportunities.

Several notable professors teach some of the most popular classes, including Charles Larson, an expert in African literature; the leader of Disney's Virginia division and public relations professor Lenny Steinhorn; and the former host of National Public Radio's "All Things Considered," a professor of communications, Sandy Unger. The most popular majors are those concerned with politics, such as communications, international service, and business. A literature or chemistry major may sometimes feel out of place, although everyone can "find his own niche," one student said.

Next Door Neighbors: Bill and Hillary

American's campus is small and enclosed, with an abundance of greenery as well as a bank, hair salon, travel agency, and other conveniences. However, the majority of student activities take place off-campus. D.C. is a bundle of resources for undergrads, from abundant internships to college-oriented stores like Urban Outfitters to great ethnic restaurants located in Georgetown. Students also enjoy hanging out at coffee shops in the nearby artsy Dupont Circle. The Metro (subway) is clean, inexpensive, and easy to navigate around town. A shuttle provided by the university also runs students from campus into the city free of charge.

Although the political scene is the main attraction and the dominating force of life at American, there is an extracurricular activity for just about everyone. The clubs are generously funded, and any motivated student seeking an activity that isn't offered can start his or her own club. American has its own television and radio stations and numerous political organizations. The Kennedy Political Union arranges for many prominent speakers, such as recent guests Oliver Stone and Marion Barry. Many students recall an "unbelievable" recent visit from President Clinton, who shook hands with hundreds of American undergrads.

Preppy and Loud Students

The student body is diverse, with a substantial representation of minorities. It's hard to go anywhere on campus without hearing another language being spoken, evidence for the claim that there are many international students at American. Students have a reputation for being slightly aloof and either "extremely nice or rather snotty," but undergrads say they have found plenty of friendly people. The majority of students are upper-middle-class and preppy, decked out in clothing from J. Crew or Abercrombie and Fitch.

Everything from Phish to classic rock such as the Grateful Dead can be heard blaring from the dorm windows at American, except during nightly quiet hours, which are strictly enforced throughout the semester. At midnight of the first night of finals week, all the students have a collective angst fest and scream out their windows for 10 minutes in a schoolwide stress reliever called "Primal Scream." Round-the-clock quiet hours are also a finals week tradition at American.

Greek life is present at American, but it is not all-consuming. The fraternities, which are all located off-campus, provide parties, but most agree that the best nightlife is in the bars and clubs of D.C. There are places for those both over and under 21. The Adams Morgan neighborhood is a popular bar/club scene for students who are 21 and over. Some other hot spots for partying are Odds, Tracks, Platinum, and Club Zei. Despite American's dry-campus policy, some students say drinking is as easy as "putting beer in a book bag." Alcohol and drug use is prevalent, although no more so than at any other college, according to the under-grads. The occasional formal dances, homecoming and Winter Ball, are held at unusual locations such as Union Station, a renovated train depot in D.C., or on cruise ships.

Plush Rooms, Gourmet Dining

American's dorms earn high praise from students. Freshmen are assigned to dorms, but upperclassmen can either choose their rooms through a lottery system or move off-campus. Dorm rooms are spacious, with air-conditioning, carpeting, and adequate storage space. The dorms are in two areas of campus, the "quiet Northside" and the "party oriented Southside." Some of the suites, which contain a kitchen, bathroom, and common rooms, are especially plush, offering what one resident called the "convenience of on-campus living with the semi-hominess of off-campus housing."

Students at American also rave about the food, which is catered by Marriott. One student called the food at American "better than [the food at] any other college I've visited." For vegans and vegetarians, there is a well-stocked salad bar and a vegetarian bar with veggie burgers and vegetarian chili.

At American, varsity sports are not the unifying force they are at some schools. There is no football team, which some students say hurts school spirit, but American has Division I soccer and basketball teams. Club and intramural sports supplement the varsity sports. Floors of residence halls, fraternities, or clubs can all create their own intramural teams in order to face-off for some friendly, or not-so-friendly, competition. Students praise the Bender arena, where athletic events as well as concerts are held, but some complain about the poor workout facilities.

> **American University provides the best of both worlds.**

American University puts its students at the forefront of the U.S. government in a uniquely multicultural environment. In the words of one junior, "American University provides the best of both worlds. We live in the politically charged urban setting of Washington, D.C., but we're located on a beautiful suburban campus." It's the ideal place for those who have a love for politics or just want to be part of an active and exciting university. —*Naomi Schoenbaum and staff*

FYI:
The three best things about attending American are "Washington, D.C., the World Capitals program, and the unique class schedule."
The three worst things about attending American are "the fact that there's no football team, the lack of school spirit, and the hyper-strict quiet hours."
The three things that every student should do before graduating from American are "de-stressing by hollering in the Primal Scream, listen to prominent speakers, and go abroad.
One thing I'd like to have known before coming to American is "that school spirit is so low."

The Catholic University of America

Address: Office of Undergraduate Admissions, 620 Michigan Avenue, Washington, DC 20064-0001
Phone: 800-673-2772
E-mail address: cua-admissions@cua.edu
Web site URL: www.cua.edu
Location: urban
Founded: 1887
Private or Public: private
Religious affiliation: Roman Catholic
Undergraduate enrollment: 2,412
Total enrollment: 5,616
Percent Male / Female: 45% / 55%

Percent Minority: 19.0%
Percent African-American: 9.0%
Percent Hispanic: 5.0%
Percent Asian: 5.0%
Percent in-state / out-of-state: 8% / 92%
Percent Pub HS: 39%
Fraternities: 1%
Sororities: 1%
Number of Applicants: 2,055
Percent Accepted: 69%
Percent Accepted who enroll: 39%
Entering: 618
Transfers: 0
Application Deadline: 15 Feb
Mean SAT: NA V, NA M

Middle 50% SAT range: 530–640 V, 520–630 M
Middle 50% ACT range: 22–27
Mean ACT: NA
3 Most popular majors: architecture, engineering, politics
Retention: 82%
Graduation rate: 70%
Library: 1.5 million volumes
Tuition and Fees: $18,200 in; $18,200 out
Room and Board: $7,765
On-campus housing: 100%
Financial aid, first-year: 79%

For some reason the idea of a "religious" school always seems to strike fear into the hearts of prospective students. Fear not, my friends! Despite its ominous name, CUA is not Vatican City. In fact, it might be more aptly characterized as the prototypical American institution of higher learning.

Although Roman Catholics are the majority at CUA, all faiths are not only tolerated but also openly studied. The administration encourages students to study and explore the numerous faiths of the world. According to one student, "There isn't the least bit of pressure to convert to anything!" Although Intro to Religion is a thorn in the sides of most freshmen, non-Catholic first-years report feeling very little discomfort in class.

God Loves Smart People

CUA does have numerous core requirements for many of its majors. Some students enjoy the regimentation while others find it particularly annoying. According to one student, "sometimes the core courses don't make sense in light of your major." Despite having an exceptional architecture program, students who intend to major in this field must fulfill requirements in such oddly incongruous courses as Religion and Philosophy. Many students regard the large introductory classes in math and English as rudimentary to the point of ridiculousness.

The core requirements, for most majors, include courses in English, the humanities, philosophy, social science, foreign language, science, and math. One of the more popular majors, and considered by some to be a slacker major, is political science. CUA is, after all, centered in Washington, D.C., the heart of what we fondly call the "political process." As a consequence, many of the incoming freshmen at Catholic are interested in political science, political philosophy, and history. There are myriad internships available for these future practitioners of democracy. Special programs in Europe are available particularly for the scholar of history, as well. English literature is also well-regarded as most of the professors have degrees from such esteemed institutions as Harvard and Yale. Professors are readily available to help out the student-in-need. As one student creatively put it, "My English professor is the best thing since Shakespeare and mangoes!"

In terms of the facilities on campus, students give them mixed reviews. The main library, Mullin, is good, in part because of the quiet rooms for studying. However, the card catalog is somewhat confusing and on occasion the book the student so desperately needs cannot be found. Membership in the D.C. College Consortium, consisting of CUA, Howard, George Washington, and American, helps many students find much-needed research material. The Library of Congress, the largest library in the United States, is also a few Metro stops away.

And on the Fifth Day He Created Dorms . . .

Are you tired of the same old cookie-cutter dorm room with your handheld fan being the only source of relief from the stifling humidity of the Mid-Atlantic? Do you like *Dawson's Creek* as much as the next college freshman? Go no further! CUA has two of the greatest luxuries afforded to the college freshman—air-conditioning and cable. And for you "playas" out there, CUA offers coed floors and wings, with the only all-female dorm being Conaty. The prize of these palatial housing options is Centennial Village. CUA has an odd policy regarding dorm visitation. All visitors must be signed in by 8 P.M. and must leave the dorm by 2 A.M. As a result, many students complain of a "booty gap" that exists at Catholic. Centennial Village is popular for several reasons, foremost of which are its guards who, according to one senior, are "easily bypassed." Those who cannot find housing in Centennial usually move off campus, a once popular option that has fallen by the wayside in recent years. Two apartment complexes near campus, Heights and the Cloisters, provide many upperclassmen with adequate housing. But why, you ask, has this option declined in popularity? According to one student, there is a growing racial tension in the neighborhood in and around Catholic. "The neighborhood seems to be getting worse, not better." Fewer and fewer upperclassmen opt to

live off campus because of the safety issue that now exists. The administration encourages students to avoid walking alone anywhere in the area. "The campus itself is incredibly safe with the guards and all . . . but just watch out when you step outside the gates. Use common sense and you'll be fine." The university provides escorts to concerned students.

But, living on campus is not all bad. The campus itself is "gorgeous" and overflowing with green things (a.k.a. trees and shrubs). Students have nicknamed the campus "The Mall II" after a more famous mall in Washington, D.C. On sunny days, students can be seen reading and doing other collegiate activities on the Mall. Students have also been able to enjoy a relatively new athletic center. Also nearby is the third largest Catholic Church—The National Shrine—in the world.

> "You just step outside and you're in the nation's capital. It's kind of awe-inspiring."

Finding food on campus is a different story. Catholic is notorious for "shitty" meals. A popular option among students is to eat in D.C., which has "some really fine restaurants." However, there are some decent meals on campus, where Taco Bell is a popular destination. The neighborhood around Catholic is also replete with fast-food joints and surly counter people.

God Hates Keggers

Don't go to CUA expecting to find kegs all over the place—the administration forbids underage drinking on campus. For hedonists there are a plethora of off-campus bars and pubs that'll liquor you up to your heart's content. But be forewarned that late night drinking in D.C. also means a late night walk through the less than hospitable streets of D.C. Thankfully for CUA students, emergency blue phones are in abundance on campus. They allow students to contact the police in the event of an emergency.

Although there is no Greek System, fun does exist on campus. The Program Board dominates campus social activities by bringing in cool bands and popular guests. They also sponsor such infamous dances as the "Screw Your Roommate Dance," which involves roommates setting each other up on blind dates. Other popular on-campus events are the Mistletoe Formal, and Movies on the Mall nights.

Although Catholic is a Division III school, sports are still popular on campus. The football team and basketball teams are perennial favorites. Although most teams at Catholic are Division III, the rugby team is at the Division I level and routinely performs well. Games against crosstown Jesuit rival Georgetown are heavily attended.

CUA, on the whole, is a place where students can allow their own individual talents to flourish. The social life in a major city, especially one chock full of college students, cannot be beat. "You just step outside and you're in the nation's capital. It's kind of awe-inspiring." Although the school has its Catholic traditions, which many students praise, DMX can also be routinely heard in the hallways. And as DMX would say, "Stop, Drop . . . and come to The Catholic University of America." —*Sean McBride*

FYI

The three best things about attending Catholic University are "the love, the independent minded student body, and the cool bands that visit."

The three worst things about attending Catholic University are "the neighborhood, Intro to Religion, and the food!"

The three things that every student should do before graduating from Catholic University are "go clubbing in D.C., visit the Shrine, and kick Georgetown's ass."

One thing I'd like to have known before coming here is "the condition of the surrounding area."

George Washington University

Address: Admissions Office, 2121 I Street NW, Washington, DC 20052
Phone: 202-994-6040
E-mail address: gwadm@dwis2.circ.gwu.edu
Web site URL: www.gwu.edu
Location: urban
Founded: 1821
Private or Public: private
Religious affiliation: Roman Catholic
Undergraduate enrollment: 8,154
Total enrollment: 19,356
Percent Male/Female: 46%/54%
Percent Minority: 22.0%

Percent African-American: 7.0%
Percent Hispanic: 4.0%
Percent Asian: 9.0%
Percent in-state/out-of-state: 7%/93%
Percent Pub HS: 70%
Fraternities: 15%
Sororities: 12%
Number of Applicants: 13,086
Percent Accepted: 49%
Percent Accepted who enroll: 28%
Entering: 1,787
Transfers: 0
Application Deadline: 1 Feb
Mean SAT: NA V, NA M

Middle 50% SAT range: 560–660 V, 560–660 M
Middle 50% ACT range: 24–29
Mean ACT: NA
3 Most popular majors: international affairs, psychology, biology
Retention: 89%
Graduation rate: 68%
Library: 1.9 million volumes
Tuition and Fees: $22,340 in; $22,340 out
Room and Board: $8,210
On-campus housing: 94%
Financial aid, first-year: 34%

Interested in politics? George Washington University may be the perfect school for you. Located in the nation's capital, George Washington University unavoidably fosters a highly political atmosphere, giving students the opportunity to work and intern in the United States government. GW's open campus allows students the ability not only to visit, but also to live among the cultural centers of Washington, D.C. Not far from the university is the White House, the National Mall, the Capitol Building, and numerous historical monuments, as well as museums and art galleries.

Future Politicians

In this environment, it is no wonder that students find GW's best departments to be political science and international affairs. These concentrations aren't the only solid ones, however. In recent years, GW's business school and the engineering department have become increasingly popular. Some students do not find that the science and math departments are as strong. Aspiring poets who want to try out the sciences can take introductory classes such as "baby chem" with little academic stress or challenge. Class sizes tend to vary at George Washington. Lecture courses and introductory courses can have as many as 150 students while some classes have fewer than ten. TAs do exist in GW's world of academia, but professors are extremely accessible and helpful. TAs are responsible for grading papers, conducting labs and sections. Students mainly seek their help before professors'.

GW also offers an honors program for students looking to focus more rigorously on academics. Approximately 100 freshmen are accepted into the Columbia Scholars Honors Program annually. Perks of the program include smaller class sizes and lectures by well-known visiting professors. Although some students find the workload heavy, they reportedly enjoy the program.

Social and Cultural Haven

In the center of one of the best college towns, GW students definitely defy the slogan "all work and no play." Although undergrads say the drinking scene is big, it is not the only form of entertainment. The bonuses of being in D.C. include the city's clubs, cafés, and bars. Georgetown is great for restaurants and casual bars, while Adams Morgan is another popular neighborhood of D.C. that is often patronized by the 21-and-over crowd. The city

also caters to students' intellectual side: the Smithsonian Museum, Kennedy Center for the Performing Arts, Corcoran Gallery, the National Geographic Museum, and historical sites such as the Lincoln Memorial give students great opportunities for cultural enrichment. Yet, there is a cost to all this cultural and social exploration. Students find that although there is always something to do, it often costs a lot of money to do it. From taking taxi rides to paying covers at bars, shopping in quaint boutiques to paying museum admissions, D.C. has the high fees to go with its high reputation.

Still, students say that there are also many non-monetary social options. These include frat parties as well as many free museums. Greek life is present on campus, with 17 fraternities and 12 sororities whose parties offer an alternative to weekly clubbing. In fact, some students prefer frat parties to the city scene. George Washington's urban campus is intermixed with city buildings—there is no central campus "quad" or senior dorm, yet despite this, one student boasts, "We do own a plot of grass, though." There are no football fields, but then again, there is no football team. The most popular varsity sports include basketball, crew, tennis, and soccer. Non-varsity athletes have the option to dabble in intramural sports.

Luxurious Alcatraz

Crime is a big concern at George Washington, as in any urban environment. University and city police work together to enforce security, but students say the best advice is to be sensible: travel with others and use the escort service. To ensure safety, dorms are monitored by security guards. Students must scan their ID cards to open the doors and then scan them again for the guard to gain entry. The cards are needed for access not only into dorms, but also the libraries and the gym. Students report that the dorm buildings seem more like apartments—some house over a thousand students. Many dorms are, in fact, converted apartment buildings or hotels. Students rave about the fact that many have private bathrooms, kitchens and even walk-in closets.

GW dorms vary widely in atmosphere and structure, however. Everglades is the quiet dorm, whereas Thurston, home to over a thousand freshmen, is very social. Moving off-campus is common after freshman year, since many apartments are just as close to academic buildings as the university dorms. About half of GW's students live off-campus, despite high rents in the area.

Good Studyin', Good Eatin'

With such a social atmosphere, from the housing to the city itself, it can be hard to find a quiet place to study. Popular spots include the main undergraduate library on campus, Gelman Library; the many computer clusters scattered throughout the campus; and the law or medical libraries. The city itself holds a wealth of information, of which students are encouraged to take advantage. For social studying, the main hangout is the Marvin Center, which offers plenty of snacking options.

As for meal plans, GW students brag about their system. Although the dining hall food itself is only average, undergrads have a point system that allows them to transfer points to places like Domino's, local sandwich shops, the Marvin Center, and even grocery stores. Although the meal plan is popular with those who are on it, many students prefer to cook for themselves.

Washington, D.C., offers ambitious students a plethora of internship opportunities as well as chances for permanent jobs. The obvious job and internship opportunities in politics are accompanied by a wide range of possibilities in the information technology sector. "D.C. is one of the biggest IT cities in the country," one student remarked, adding that many students intern with such companies as AOL, GTE, and Oracle.

One sorority's pledge is said in 14 different languages.

GW students express their appreciation not only for the diverse city atmosphere, but also for the diverse student body. Students come from all over the country and the world to George Washington because of its location in D.C. As one sorority president commented on the diversity, "Our pledge is said in 14 different languages, each language representing the native tongue of one of our sisters." George Washington University offers independent and disciplined students the chance to study and have fun in an incredibly vibrant and exciting city. —*Melissa Milazzo and Staff*

FYI:
The three best things about attending GW are "the prime D.C. location, the internship opportunities, and the spacious rooms."
The three worst things about attending GW are "the lack of a campus feel, the lack of safety, and cost of living in Washington, D.C."
The three things that every student should do before graduating from GW are "go to the Kennedy Center for the Performing Arts, go to Marvin Graw, and sing *Hail to the Buff,* the fight song."
One thing I'd like to have known before coming here is "that there's no football team."

Georgetown University

Address: Undergraduate Admissions, Georgetown University, Washington, DC 20057-1002
Phone: 202-687-3600
E-mail address: guadmiss@gunet.georgetown.edu
Web site URL: www.georgetown.edu
Location: urban
Founded: 1789
Private or Public: private
Religious affiliation: Roman Catholic
Undergraduate enrollment: 6,272
Total enrollment: 12,629
Percent Male/Female: 46%/54%

Percent Minority: 21.0%
Percent African-American: 6.0%
Percent Hispanic: 6.0%
Percent Asian: 8.0%
Percent in-state/out-of-state: 2%/98%
Percent Pub HS: 42%
Fraternities: 0%
Sororities: 0%
Number of Applicants: 13,417
Percent Accepted: 22%
Percent Accepted who enroll: 49%
Entering: 1,487
Transfers: 0
Application Deadline: 10 Jan
Mean SAT: NA V, NA M

Middle 50% SAT range: 630–730 V, 630–720 M
Middle 50% ACT range: 27–31
Mean ACT: NA
3 Most popular majors: international affairs, government, English
Retention: 98%
Graduation rate: 83%
Library: 2 million volumes
Tuition and Fees: $23,088 in; $23,088 out
Room and Board: $8,693
On-campus housing: 100%
Financial aid, first-year: 53%

Interested in politics, government, or international relations? Students at Georgetown University have the nation's capital as their classroom. Located in one of the most affluent areas of Washington, D.C., Georgetown undergrads have at their disposal the resources of one of the country's finest universities and the opportunity to experience life in a hub of national and international activity.

A World of Learning
In addition to the law, medical, and graduate schools, Georgetown offers undergraduates four different schools to which one applies specifically: the School of Business, School of Nursing, College of Arts and Sciences, and School of Foreign Service (SFS) which many cite as Georgetown's strongest program. Each of the colleges has slightly different academic guidelines. The College of Arts and Sciences requires two courses each in philosophy, English, theology, and natural sciences or math. Students must take one course each semester toward their major, which they declare during their sophomore year. Many students praise the history program and the humanities in general, but some find Georgetown's science department relatively weak. Well-known easy courses include Fun with Numbers and some sociology classes.

Business school undergrads take two classes of history or government, philosophy, theology, and English, as well as a semester each of psychology and sociology. SFS (School of Foreign Service) has perhaps the strictest set of core requirements, especially for freshman year, when students must take political theory, economics, theology, English, history, and a foreign language (proficiency is required for graduation). While the relatively small nursing school is considered one of the easier programs, SFS (also known by students as Safe from Science) is among the most rigorous courses of study available.

One of the biggest complaints among freshmen is Georgetown's large class size, especially in SFS. All classes are taught by professors, but many lectures break down into weekly small-group recitations led by TAs. Many students say their professors are what they like best about Georgetown. "They know what they're talking about and they really try to make it interesting," said one undergrad. "All my professors are characters with great personalities." Famous Georgetown profs include Ben Bradlee, Madeleine Albright, and Dean Galluchi.

That students are required to study theology is one of the more obvious results of Georgetown's Jesuit origins. Other manifestations of its Catholic roots include nuns on the faculty, crucifixes in the classrooms, representations of saints adorning the walls, and the administrative decision against condom distribution. "Sometimes you can really tell Georgetown is a Catholic school and other times it's not very pervasive," explained one student.

Georgetown draws students from a variety of geographic areas, including many international locations. Many students say, however, "the diversity is not as great" as they had expected. Self-segregation is a problem many undergrads identify. "Being a minority here tends to translate into a minority status." Students say there doesn't seem to be much of a gay community on campus, "at least not one that is clearly visible. There are definitely religious undertones which guide certain standards of behavior."

Students identify the stereotypical Georgetown students as Jane/Joe Hoya (after the school mascot—the Georgetown Hoyas), who is best described as "white cap, plaid shirt, khakis...clean-cut preppy East Coast kid." Many expressed their initial surprise at how dressed up students tend to get for classes and especially for evenings out. "The student image here is blond hair, blue eyes—a perfect Ken and Barbie . . . Sometimes people put too much pain into their fashion," said one student.

A More Social Side

"During the week, tension levels are so high that everyone goes crazy on the weekends, and it's one non-stop party," said one student. Clubbing seems to be a popular nighttime activity for weekend partying, which starts on Thursday night. Friday night tends to be slightly more low key, as many students decide to stay on-campus and hang out or party quietly in dorms.

All the freshmen dorms are dry dorms, and students who are caught with alcohol in the dorms are assigned community service and are fined $25 for the first offense, with increased punishments for subsequent offenses. As a result, many students go off-campus to party. Popular destinations include bars like the Tombs, Chadwicks, or Champs, or keg parties at off-campus upperclassmen apartments.

Drug use on campus is not very visible, according to several students. "If you use drugs, you're considered an outcast," said one student. "Pot is totally taboo." And although much of the social scene seems to be related to alcohol consumption, students claim non-drinkers do not feel left out and are under no pressure to drink. There are no official fraternities or sororities on campus. "There's a lot of other stuff to do—plays and movies every weekend—and there's all of D.C. for you to hang out in." Recent speakers include the U.S. national security advisor, the former king of Rwanda, and Jerry Springer.

Classic Hoyas

Tradition abounds at Georgetown. A favorite of the students is the Healy Howl, which began after parts of *The Exorcist* were filmed on campus. On Halloween everyone gathers on the quad, watches the movie, and howls at the nearby graveyard. Another superstition that new students at Georgetown learn early on is that if they want to graduate in four years, they should never step on the giant seal in the doorway of Healy Hall.

The campus itself is a mixture of seventeenth-century brick buildings with heavy Gothic influences and some modern buildings, all clustered together. "When you walk on campus, it looks so majestic," said one student. "And there's a lot of grass—it's very aesthetically pleasing." One complaint is that everything on campus is uphill—the entrance to one building will be on the first floor, but when you walk into the building next door, you're already on the fourth floor. "I'll be in such good shape by the time I graduate," joked one student.

Outside Academics

Freshmen live in one of four dorms on campus: Harbin and New South are older dorms built in typical dormitory style while Village C East and Village C West are newer dorms with smaller rooms and private bathrooms, considered by those who live there to be a "huge plus." Dorm halls are coed with common areas and kitchens on every floor, and students enjoy air-conditioning in their rooms. Undergrads from all five schools are mixed in the dorms, which "eliminates any feeling of segregation between colleges."

Georgetown has an RA (resident advisor) system that assigns an upperclassman to each freshman hall. Some RAs "hang out with us all the time and organize activities as a floor," while others are "really strict" in their role as police officers. RAs take turns patrolling the halls each night to keep the noise level down and watch for alcohol. Security is not an issue for Georgetown students, who feel quite safe with the security clerk on duty checking IDs until 3 A.M., when an electronic system goes into effect. "On our hall, we always keep our doors open—I feel perfectly secure," said one student.

Hallmates form the nucleus of a freshman's social circle, at least during the first several months. Huge groups are often seen heading off together for dinner in one of Georgetown's two dining halls. Students choose from a wide variety of meal plans (including "munch money," which can be used for some local takeout, groceries on campus, and snacks at Fast Break), although most do not consider the variety of dining hall food to be satisfactory. Standard fare includes such items as pasta, pizza, rice and vegetables, and a salad bar. Many students also enjoy weekend dinners out—Middle Eastern, Egyptian, Vietnamese, and Indian food can all be found nearby, in addition to more traditional cuisine.

The Washington, D.C., area offers many opportunities for participation in community service—D.C. Reads (elementary school tutoring), Increase the Peace (workshop seminars with troubled teens), and jail/inmate programs are just a few ways Georgetown students find their way out into the greater community. Many students also take advantage of D.C.'s political life and find internships with congressmen, at international firms, or at the Smithsonian Institute. Some feel frustrated that they do not take more advantage of their surroundings, especially since the Kennedy Center for Performing Arts and a multitude of museums, fairs, historical monuments, and off-campus lectures are all accessible by the Metro subway system.

Popular activities on campus include the International Relations Club and various special-interest groups for students from different areas of the country. Although many people come to Georgetown with backgrounds in student government, "it's kind of looked down upon here…student government has no power."

Lots of Georgetown students get involved in sports, whether on the varsity, intramural, or spectator level. The men's soccer team is one of the more popular teams to watch—fans bang pots and pans together to show their support at soccer games. Undergrads don't consider football to be a very big draw, but school spirit is definitely high during basketball season, as students flock to cheer on one of the top-ranked teams in the country.

> **"If you use drugs, you're considered an outcast," said one student. "Pot is totally taboo."**

The life of a Georgetown student is not easy. Like other colleges, the challenge of balancing rigorous academics, engaging activities, and an active social life can be quite trying at times. "Although the campus itself is serene and calm," said one student, "you never see people who aren't rushing somewhere with an agenda." Students say that after four years at Georgetown, they have gained more than just an academic education. Said one undergrad, "There's a great mix of studying and learning a lot with real-life experiences."
—*Marti Page and Staff*

FYI
The three best things about attending Georgetown are "the small, pretty campus; the tight-knit student body; and the location in Washington, D.C."
The three worst things about attending Georgetown are "the lack of racial diversity, the religious presence of nuns teaching classes, and class size."

The three things that every student should do before graduating from Georgetown are "walk through the cherry blossoms, eat a chicken madness at Weismiller's, and howl on Halloween."

One thing I'd like to have known before coming here is "that SFS was going to be so much work."

Howard University

Address: 2400 Sixth Street NW, Washington, DC 20059
Phone: 202-806-2700
E-mail address: admission@howard.edu
Web site URL: www.howard.edu
Location: urban
Founded: 1867
Private or Public: private
Religious affiliation: none
Undergraduate enrollment: 4,285
Total enrollment: 11,839
Percent Male/Female: 39%/61%
Percent Minority: 99.0%

Percent African-American: 88.0%
Percent Hispanic: 1.0%
Percent Asian: 1.0%
Percent in-state/out-of-state: 91%/9%
Percent Pub HS: 80%
Fraternities: 2%
Sororities: 3%
Number of Applicants: 3,322
Percent Accepted: 45%
Percent Accepted who enroll: 60%
Entering: 909
Transfers: 0
Application Deadline: 1 Apr

Mean SAT: 526 V, 493 M
Middle 50% SAT range: 430–640 V, 410–680 M
Middle 50% ACT range: NA
Mean ACT: NA
3 Most popular majors: biology, psychology, radio/TV/film
Retention: 0%
Graduation rate: NA
Library: 1.8 million volumes
Tuition and Fees: $8,750 in; $8,750 out
Room and Board: $5,250
On-campus housing: 100%
Financial aid, first-year: 60%

One of the nation's premier historically black universities, Howard has produced more African-Americans with advanced degrees than any other institution in the world. It is no surprise that Howard counts such distinguished people as Nobel Prize–winning author Toni Morrison and world-renowned singer Roberta Flack among its alumni.

Best Is Best

According to students, Howard's strongest areas are communications, business, and engineering. Undergrads attribute much of Howard's academic success to warm student-professor relationships. It is not unusual, students say, for professors to make themselves very available to their students, even giving out their home phone numbers. "The professors here have a particularly important philosophy in their teaching," one student said. "They truly want you to be the best you can be for yourself and for your community." Another student commented, "They want

you to succeed and then give back to the community. They feel that we have the power to strengthen the African-American community." Undergrads report that the work is very challenging, but they are rewarded by the knowledge they gain. They feel that, at Howard, excellence is not a goal—it is a requirement.

Those who desire further challenge can participate in the school's honors program, which students may qualify for after freshman year and which involves a heavier course load than the average five classes per semester. All students are required to take courses in physical education, African-American history, English, speech, and math. Students highly recommend the courses in African-American history and communications as among Howard's best. Others recommend the class on sexuality as an "easy A."

Undergrads at Howard say they mostly study in the Founder's Library, the undergraduate library, or in their rooms. The undergraduate library is popular among those who like to study in groups, while Founder's is the favorite for intense independent study.

Something for Everyone

With over 150 student organizations, students say it is extremely easy for everyone to get involved with campus life, meet friends, and have fun. Student government, intramural and varsity sports, and community service are among Howard's most popular activities. Undergrads have taken the university's highly renowned media groups far beyond campus boundaries. The student newspaper, *The Hilltop*, is internationally circulated. Students also produce an Emmy-nominated program called *Spotlight*, which is aired on one of the nation's few black-owned and operated television stations. WHUR, the campus radio station, has a large following in the Washington, D.C., metropolitan area.

A unique feature of Greek life at Howard and other black colleges is "stepping," an inter-fraternity and -sorority competition that mixes choreographed dance routines with stomping and taunting chants to a beat.

Students describe Howard's social scene as "adequate" in terms of excitement. Many students congregate outdoors on "the Yard," located at the heart of the campus; the Blackburn student center is also popular. Students say on-campus parties occur fairly frequently, but many also appreciate D.C.'s intense and varied club scene, including 18-and-over "college nights" at the Ritz, Mirage, and other hip spots. Howard's social scene tends to revolve around football games. Although many students say they are dedicated fans, others say they go to the games just to hear the marching band, nicknamed the Thundermachine, whose powerful drum section can make even the least rhythmic person get up and dance. School spirit is always high at games, but students say that it turns into a frenzy during homecoming, when the Howard Bisons battle

their bitter rival, Morehouse. Homecoming also features such activities as the Miss Howard Beauty Contest and a fashion show.

Most freshmen and sophomores live on campus; the majority of freshmen live in single-sex dorms. Cook Hall, which mainly houses sophomores, is considered Howard's best dorm for its walk-in closets, air conditioning, and student lounge equipped with a large-screen TV and weight room. Most upperclassmen that elect to live off-campus prefer the 10-story Howard Plaza Towers for its prime location.

Growing Diversity

Undergrads say Howard's population is becoming more diverse, with an increasing number of non-blacks matriculating each year. Many of these students cite Howard's strong academic reputation and D.C.-area campus as their reasons for attending the school: "I came here for the challenge," reported one, "and I stay here for the friends I've made."

Although part of Howard's agenda is to foster unity among its students, the campus environment welcomes a variety of ideas. According to one student, "It's very intellectually stimulating to be around people with such different opinions about everything from politics to sports." Some students feel that there are "a lot of snotty, rich" people on campus and that "going to class is like going to a fashion show." One student reported his first memorable experience upon arriving at Howard for the first time. "I was lucky—in the first couple of days a girl took me aside and told me exactly what clothes I needed to buy to fit in." Others, however, argue that such stereotyping is unfair. "You'll find all kinds of people here, all with different styles, and everyone is accepted."

A Greek History

There is a strong Greek presence on campus; in fact, many of the national black fraternities were founded at Howard. Students report that the Greeks at Howard are interested in more than just throwing wild parties: they also emphasize racial unity and community service as focusing on ways of uplifting all African-Americans. A unique feature of Greek life at Howard and other black colleges is "stepping," an inter-fraternity and -sorority competition that mixes choreographed dance routines with stomping and taunting chants to a beat. Yet, one student expressed some misgivings about the strong Greek presence on campus, saying some people have the impression that "if you are not Greek there must be something seriously wrong with you."

Most students declare that the best thing about Howard is the opportunity a Howard degree provides. One student declared, "When current community leaders want to reach out to the community leaders of tomorrow, to give them guidance and inspiration, they come to Howard because they know Howard teaches us more than math or engineering. It teaches us to lead." —*Dylan Howard*

FYI

The three best things about attending Howard are "the cultural solidarity, living in D.C., and the alumni network."

The three worst things about attending Howard are "social life is just okay, the utter lack of diversity, and PE requirements."

The three things that every student should do before graduating from Howard are "go clubbing, learn to 'step,' and go to a bunch of football games."

One thing I'd like to have known before coming here is "how strong our spirit is."

Trinity College

Address: 125 Michigan Avenue, NE, Washington, DC 20017
Phone: 202-884-9400
E-mail address: admissions@trinitydc.edu
Web site URL: www.trinitydc.edu
Location: urban
Founded: 1897
Private or Public: private
Religious affiliation: Roman Catholic
Undergraduate enrollment: 1,096
Total enrollment: 1,489
Percent Male/Female: 0%/100%
Percent Minority: 85.0%

Percent African-American: 55.0%
Percent Hispanic: 7.0%
Percent Asian: 3.0%
Percent in-state/out-of-state: 35%/65%
Percent Pub HS: 60%
Fraternities: 0%
Sororities: 0%
Number of Applicants: 293
Percent Accepted: 68%
Percent Accepted who enroll: 59%
Entering: 140
Transfers: 0
Application Deadline: rolling
Mean SAT: 490 V, 460 M

Middle 50% SAT range: 400–590 V, 400–590 M
Middle 50% ACT range: NA
Mean ACT: 21
3 Most popular majors: business administration, political science, English
Retention: 76%
Graduation rate: 56%
Library: 170,000 volumes
Tuition and Fees: $13,470 in; $13,470 out
Room and Board: $6,310
On-campus housing: NA
Financial aid, first-year: 85%

In the heart of the nation's capital is a place where women's issues always receive a fair hearing—Trinity College. This small college has been educating women in the liberal arts, while maintaining its Catholic roots, for a century. According to students, Trinity is a melting pot of political activity, tradition, new ideas, and learning.

New Ideas in Academics

Upon acceptance, undergraduate students enter the School of Arts and Sciences. Political science is said to be the most popular major and a strong department, likely influenced by the school's proximity to Washington, D.C. In order to graduate from Trinity, students must complete the Foundation for Leadership curriculum, which includes courses from six areas. Communication Skills enables students to develop critical reasoning and to speak or write a second language. Cultural Diversity explores the traditions and civilizations of different groups worldwide, and Knowledge and Beliefs involves the study of religious and intellectual perspectives. Traditions and Legacies looks at Western civilization, Scientific and Mathematical Inquiries requires study in those two areas, and Individual and Society investigates how individual and group behaviors affect societal institutions.

Within these areas, classes are designated as either Group One or Group Two, and students must take some of each group. For Group One, they must take a set number of hours. Then, students choose at least three out of the six areas available and take a Group Two course out of each of these. Most undergrads find these core requirements a bit on the extensive side, although they can usually complete them by the end of their sophomore year. One recent grad said, "You definitely have to keep it in mind, but it's really not a headache to fulfill." Recently, students have been given more choice within the core requirements. Instead of a list of specific courses, students now have more course options in the required areas of study, which makes the requirements less of a hassle.

> "The neighborhood isn't very good. When you walk onto campus, it's like stepping into a different world."

Small classes are the norm at Trinity. Classes range in size from 4 or 5 students to 20 at the most, and the majority have between 10 and 15 students. Students value the approachability of their professors. "The professors are involved in and become a part of your life," one sophomore stated. Unproctored tests are also routine for Trinity women, who are serious about upholding their honor code.

The code also includes restrictions on underage drinking and men in the dorms after hours, but rumor has it that reports of these social violations are less common. Trinity also offers a highly popular Weekend College Program for working women through which adult students may take classes on the weekends to earn their undergraduate degrees.

Social Life and Migration Patterns

The social scene at Trinity always involves both its own campus and the lively areas surrounding it. Transportation on the Metro, D.C.'s subway system, provides easy access to the movies, shopping (at Union Station, Pentagon City, and Dupont Circle), dance clubs, and bars. Other college hangouts in the neighborhood also enhance the social scene; undergrads frequently migrate to nearby Georgetown, Howard, and Catholic Universities for mixers or just to hang out in a coed environment. While the surrounding area has its attractions, the campus has its fair share of hangouts as well. Most popular is the Pub, which offers fast food, video games, billiards, occasional dances, and karaoke nights.

Certain campus social events and traditions are an integral part of the Trinity experience. Twice a year, each class convenes on one of the four floors of the Main dorm to sing canons. The college sponsors a Christmas party called the Holly Hop, and a Beaux-Arts weekend during the spring semester. Towards the end of the year, rising juniors don their graduation caps and gowns for the first time at a special mass. Class dinners and class color days take place as well, but according to one student, these are "nothing special."

Politicking and Other Activities

Because Trinity is in Washington, D.C., political involvement is naturally the most popular extracurricular activity for the Trinity undergrad. A good number of students work on Capitol Hill and are active on campus in various leadership roles. The student government plays an important role at Trinity and has a strong rapport with the administration. Interning is a common activity for students, sometimes to receive course credit and in other cases for enjoyment and experience. Some students travel to other states in order to work on political campaigns. In general, students interested in politics find that at Trinity their extracurricular activities and academic endeavors complement, if not overlap, each other.

It's Like Stepping into a Different World

Although very many Trinity students find politics near or at the top of their priority list, other activities also find their place. The monthly paper, the *Trinity Times*, and the literary magazine, the *Record*, attract aspiring writers. The school has a strong a cappella group, the Bells, and the Pan American Symphony Orchestra is in residence at Trinity and some students play for the orchestra. Some students also take piano or voice lessons for credit. Trinity has six varsity sports teams—lacrosse, soccer, tennis, field hockey, crew, and track and field—all of which are quite popular. Because of the small student body, the teams will accept anyone who wants to play. Trinity became a member of NCAA Division III in September 1995, and as a result both the number of participants and spectators have surged.

Living Standards

Overall, Trinity students are satisfied with the quality of the housing on campus. Although single rooms are not available to first-year students, the doubles are reportedly roomy. Some undergrads prefer Main for its convenient location, and Cuvilly Hall remains a favorite because of its spaciousness and easy staggering distance from the Pub. Seniors and some fortunate juniors live in Alumni Hall, which is popular for its two-bedroom suites with private bathrooms, underground tunnel leading to Main, and proximity to the cafeteria. Students are required to purchase a 19-meal plan the first semester of their first year, but after that they may choose either 19, 14, or 10 meals a week. Some students are also pushing for a pay-as-you-eat plan, citing the inflexibility and inefficiency of the set meal plans. Approximately 25 percent of all students, including commuters, live off-campus.

Relations between the school and the largely residential area that surrounds it are reportedly good, although the area surrounding the campus is not flourishing quite as well as the university. According to one senior, "The neighborhood isn't very good. When you walk onto campus, it's like stepping into a different world." Security, however, is not a problem. Campus buses leave for the Metro stations every twenty minutes, and escort services are always available. Trinity and its neighbors are working together on plans for a new campus center. The center has not begun yet, but plans are definite, and the college is set to break the ground at any time.

Trinity students say that over the years they have earned a reputation for being "white, Catholic, feminist snobs," but many report that this stereotype is outdated and incorrect. Trinity's Catholic population is down to approximately 50 percent, minority enrollment is increasing, and need-based student financial aid is prevalent. According to one first-year student, "There are some snobs—but the stereotype is really misleading."

At Trinity, women find a small, friendly environment, enlivened by the excitement of being in a major city. In the political center of the nation's capital, Trinity students thrive and learn, receiving hands-on experience to complement their work in the classroom. —*Lisa E. Smith and Staff*

FYI

The three best things about attending Trinity are "you're in the nation's capital, it is a small all women's community which has given a lot of students confidence in their academic life, and the people are always willing to help you here."

The three worst things about attending Trinity are "financial aid is weak, the dorm life is TERRIBLE—there is no air conditioning in the first-year dorms, and the school does not offer enough selection in terms of majors."

The three things that every student should do before graduating from Trinity are "to get a great internship, use this opportunity to network, and do something spectacular—there are a lot of opportunities here."

One thing I'd like to have known before coming here is "that Trinity is a hub of activity."

Florida

Florida A & M University

Address: Suite G-9 Foote-Hilyer Administration Center, Tallahassee, FL 32307
Phone: 850-599-3796
E-mail address: bcox@nsl.famu.edu
Web site URL: www.famu.edu
Location: urban
Founded: 1887
Private or Public: public
Religious affiliation: none
Undergraduate enrollment: 10,492
Total enrollment: 11,091
Percent Male / Female: 43%/57%
Percent Minority: 97.0%

Percent African-American: 95.0%
Percent Hispanic: 1.0%
Percent Asian: 1.0%
Percent in-state / out-of-state: 79.0%/21%
Percent Pub HS: 85%
Fraternities: 20%
Sororities: 20%
Number of Applicants: 4,883
Percent Accepted: 67%
Percent Accepted who enroll: 34%
Entering: 1,674
Transfers: 727
Application Deadline: 13 May
Mean SAT: NA V, NA M

Middle 50% SAT range: NA V, NA M
Middle 50% ACT range: NA
Mean ACT: 20
3 Most popular majors: business administration, health professions, liberal arts
Retention: 64.0%
Graduation rate: 27.0%
Library: 490,000 volumes
Tuition and Fees: $2,132 in; $8,788 out
Room and Board: $3,690
On-campus housing: 70%
Financial aid, first-year: 75%

While most of the country braves the winter cold, Florida A&M students, with sunblock and books in hand, settle back on well-manicured, flower-filled lawns. Located in quiet and scenic Tallahassee, Florida A&M University (also known as FAMU) provides solid educational opportunities in a variety of disciplines.

Preprofessionals

Academics at FAMU are centered on specific pre-professionals programs. Students report that the business, architecture, engineering, and pharmacy departments are among the strongest. While one senior particularly praised the administration for "teaching us practical information with tons of realistic applications instead of abstract ideas and principles that we will forget an hour after the final," another freshman complained that "my academic program is way too narrowly defined and there is little room for personal exploration." All classes at FAMU, including some recitation sections, are taught by professors. Graduate TAs only help with labs and occasionally substitute for faculty. While each department has its own specific requirements for graduation, all students must complete at least one course each in history, English, math, humanities, and a physical or biological science. The academic program on the whole is considered both "very manageable" and "reasonable, with enough work to make you feel like you are learning without being ridiculously overwhelmed."

Most of the facilities at FAMU are reportedly satisfactory. Although Coleman Library "needs a bigger collection," according to one student, it is a great space to "spread out your stuff, get focused, and accomplish a lot." Empty classrooms are also popular places to get to work when classes are done for the day. Several students said that the sports facilities are "small and mediocre at best" due to a lack of modern gym equipment. Yet, students are also quick to compliment the administration for investing in building improvements and point to the recent additions of a new music building and general classroom building.

An Off-Campus Student Body

Most undergraduates at FAMU live off campus in either rented houses or apartments. The situation draws mixed reviews. While an off-campus student body can be "great because you are really living on your own without dealing with the bullshit regulations that often accompany on-campus housing arrangements at other schools," others are not as convinced. One undergrad said "off-campus living is limiting socially because you are confined to your own group of friends and lose the close proximity that on-campus dorms offer." Residents consider campus housing "fine—nothing great, nothing awful." All students who live on-campus must be on a meal plan. The food ranges from "nasty" to "fair." Several students reported that the quality and variety of the meal plan has improved under a new policy that allows them to take their meals in delis and pizza places as well as in the school cafeterias. Off-campus, students enjoy eating at Jake's, "a greasy BBQ dive," and Shingle's, "a decent seafood restaurant."

FAMU's campus is relatively self-contained and somewhat separated from the town of Tallahassee. Students say town-gown relations are "great." Undergrads enjoy shopping, hanging out at several local clubs, or just wandering around the city's two malls. As one junior reported, "Everything you need is right here." Tallahassee is also only an hour and 15 minutes away from the beach. Fraternity parties are another social venue for those who have exhausted the Tallahassee club scene. Students agree that FAMU's top on-campus hangout is the "Set," a common area near the Student Union Building, which has a post office, TV room, bookstore, and market. As one sophomore said, "It is great to have the Set so that off-campus people like myself can still stay connected with the rest of the student body." One senior added, "It is

awesome to be able to come to campus for something more than just going to class."

Getting Involved

Many undergrads are quick to praise the active student government at FAMU for helping to get students involved in campus life. One person noted that student government leaders "have a really tough task trying to keep an off-campus student body involved with the school, but they do a terrific job." The student government is responsible for planning many social events throughout the year including their biggest event of the year, "Be-out day," which occurs in the spring and features food, games, and contests on the athletic field. It also organizes the extensive homecoming festivities, activities that "we all look forward to each year," one student said.

> Students rally behind the school mascot, the Rattler, and FAMU students show their school spirit during game weeks when the "whole school is covered" with orange and green, FAMU's colors.

Most undergraduates join extracurricular activities connected to their future professions, such as the pre-medical society. Some students also participate in FAMU's theater group, which stages four performances every semester. The gospel choir, several bands, and the *Faumuan*, FAMU's weekly paper, are also popular among students. Community service activities are largely sponsored by fraternities and sororities. Varsity sports also draw student support, and intramural competition is reportedly "fierce and fun." Students rally behind the school mascot, the Rattler, and FAMU students show their school spirit during game weeks when the "whole school is covered" with orange and green, FAMU's colors.

Diversity at FAMU?

The students at FAMU are predominantly in-state African-Americans. Some students have questioned the lack of diversity at FAMU. As one senior reported, "I love this community, but I also think there is much to be desired in terms of creating a more diverse student body—I look outside and everyone is so much like me." While not ethnically diverse, FAMU students say that they have very different interests and backgrounds. The small number of openly lesbian and gay students, however, are not organized, and according to one sophomore, not very welcome on campus. "Students are not very open-minded when it comes to that,"

said one student. FAMU undergrads also consider themselves more environmentally than politically aware.

FAMU offers an opportunity to take advantage of a strong pre-professional academic program in a warm, relaxed environment. In the words of one senior, "I am going out into the real world with not only solid academic training, but a host of life experiences that I won't soon forget."—*Jeff Kaplow and Staff*

FYI

The three best things about attending FAMU are "do theater, do sports, do something."

The three worst things about attending FAMU are "the largely in-state student body, orange and green school colors, and an off-campus culture."

The three things that every student should do before graduating from FAMU are "chill at the Set, volunteer in Tallahassee, and attend homecoming."

One thing I'd like to have known before coming here is "how much energy these people have."

Florida Institute of Technology

Address: 150 West University Blvd, Melbourne, FL 32901-6975
Phone: 407-674-8030
E-mail address: admissions@fit.edu
Web site URL: www.fit.edu
Location: NA
Founded: NA
Private or Public: pub
Religious affiliation: none
Undergraduate enrollment: 1,843
Total enrollment: NA
Percent Male / Female: 69% / 31%
Percent Minority: 12.0%

Percent African-American: 4.0%
Percent Hispanic: 6.0%
Percent Asian: 2.0%
Percent in-state / out-of-state: 55% / 45%
Percent Pub HS: NA
Fraternities: 18%
Sororities: 13%
Number of Applicants: 2,449
Percent Accepted: 76%
Percent Accepted who enroll: 24%
Entering: 395
Transfers: 47
Application Deadline: rolling

Mean SAT: 550 V, 580 M
Middle 50% SAT range: 500–610 V, 530–630 M
Middle 50% ACT range: 22–27
Mean ACT: 25
3 Most popular majors: marine bio, aviation management, mech eng
Retention: 76.0%
Graduation rate: 55.0%
Library: 368,517 volumes
Tuition and Fees: $17,300 in; NA out
Room and Board: $5,270
On-campus housing: 96%
Financial aid, first-year: 86%

After a day of classes at the Florida Institute of Technology, some students head for nearby beaches along Florida's Space Coast while others study under the tall palm trees on campus. The motivated preprofessional student who chooses FIT is rewarded not only

with its picturesque, tropical setting but also with its intense, challenging curriculum.

Sun and Studies

Despite the temptations of the sun and beach, students at FIT take academics seriously. The core curriculum includes heavy doses of science and math (something most FIT students are happy about), along with courses in English composition and rhetoric. Many FIT students have a strong sense of what they want to do later in life and focus on their major early in their college career at one of the five undergraduate schools: the College of Engineering, the College of Science and Liberal Arts, the School of Aeronautics, the School of Business, or the School of Psychology.

Each major requires an intensive curriculum in addition to the core requirements, so freshmen and sophomores have little flexibility in their schedules. According to one student, FIT "gives you a schematic for your major—there aren't too many electives." One sophomore described the first-year program as "rather difficult. They test you to see whether or not you can handle it." The rigorous course load, however, does not translate into cutthroat competition: students report that they "don't go after each other." On the contrary, study groups are popular, and some professors encourage team problem solving. Easy courses are hard to come by in the science departments, but many students use their elective opportunities to take stress-free courses such as scuba diving or sailing.

The College of Engineering is especially popular at FIT. The School of Aeronautics and the departments of oceanography and marine science are also well respected. According to one oceanography major, FIT is one of the few places where students receive "in-the-field" training from almost the first day of class. FIT maintains an extensive co-op program with many of the major companies on the Space Coast, which enables undergrads to alternate semesters in the classroom with semesters on the job. Students can become involved as early as sophomore year, and one participant said of his job experience, "You're not a gopher. You are asked to do the work and get it done. It is a real job." Students work (earning course credits and money) at places such as NASA, Rockwell International, Martin Marietta, McDonnell Douglas, Harris, and Lockheed.

Living Arrangements

Dorm life at FIT is quiet, but as one RA confirmed, "there are parties." The six campus dorms surround a large quad. Evans and Brownly are considered upper-class dorms, although some upperclassmen live on halls with freshmen in the other four dorms, two of which are single-sex. Most rooms are designed for three people, although freshmen generally live in doubles. Residents consider the rooms "quite large." Brownly Hall is especially popular: although the rooms are smaller on average, each has its own bathroom. All rooms at FIT are air-conditioned, and many also have ceiling fans. While freshmen must live on-campus, many upperclassmen move to the university-owned Southgate Apartments or to other off-campus housing. Southgate units typically have two or three bedrooms, a large living room, and a kitchen.

Students say they feel safe hanging out on campus. University security officers, most of whom are ex–law enforcement or ex-military officers, are on duty 24 hours a day. Call boxes are located around campus, and an escort service walks students from place to place at night.

Students call the food in FIT's Evans cafeteria "decent—it could be better, it could be worse." Freshmen are required to be on the meal plan. Students looking for tastier food head for the popular campus hangout called the Rat (short for Rathskeller), whose specialties include burgers, grilled chicken, and sub sandwiches. Pool tables, a large-screen TV, and small bar make the Rat a favorite place for eating, talking, and hanging out. The campus social scene is dominated by the school's seven fraternities and two sororities, which host the majority of the parties and other social activities at FIT. According to one student, "The most fun you have in Melbourne is at the fraternities and sororities. You're not going to die if you're not involved in one, but they're pretty big." Drinking is a popular pastime despite the administration's efforts to curb it, but students say that those who don't want to drink are under no pressure to do so.

The surrounding city of Melbourne, home to a large retirement community, has little to offer students (who have nick-named it "Melboring"). Many students drive or find rides to the bars, malls, and other entertainment venues outside the Melbourne area. Orlando is an hour away, and the beach is a mere ten minutes from campus. Hangouts just off campus include a pizza place called the Mighty Mushroom (locally known as "the 'Shroom"), the local bowling alley, and a miniature golf course. There is also a 7-Eleven store for late-night snack runs.

FIT's lopsided male-female ratio affects campus social life. Many male students lament that it is difficult to meet women, and one female student reported that the situation sometimes causes "a little tension" between the sexes. Another student pointed out that as more women enroll at FIT, the ratio and the tension are slowly improving.

The FIT student body hails from all parts of the globe, with especially large contingents from the Northeast, Florida, and the Caribbean. A burgeoning international community on campus has led to the formation of a number of ethnic clubs, including the Caribbean Students Association. FIT supports many extracurricular organizations, ranging from student government to the school newspaper, the *Crimson*, and from a biology fraternity to a theater group called the College Players.

The FIT Panthers compete in the NCAA Division II Sunshine State Athletic Conference. Popular varsity teams include women's volleyball, men's and women's basketball, crew, cross-country, softball, and baseball. The administration's efforts to start a football program have been unsuccessful so far; homecoming revolves around basketball instead. Many students are active in intramural flag football, inner-tube water polo, and cycling. For the size of the school, students consider the athletic facilities "pretty good."

> ## "Who else takes their calculators to the beach?"

In general, FIT students take a lot of pride in and are happy with their school. ("Who else takes their calculators to the beach?" one tanned undergrad questioned). As one student emphasized, "If you work hard, you will receive a good education here." And the weather and waves aren't bad, either. —*Ellen Lee Moskowitz and Staff*

FYI

The three best things about attending Florida Institute of Technology are "how Florida Tech gives scholarships to nearly everyone who applies, the proximity to the ocean where I can surf between classes or in the mornings, and the weather during the 'winter.'"

The three worst things about attending Florida Institute of Technology are "the campus apathy, the buildings are old and need improvements, and there's no flavor here because a lot of people here are engineer majors = boring."

The three things that every student should do before graduating from Florida Institute of Technology are "learn how to dive, go watch the shuttle lift off, and attend Daytona 500 at least once."

One thing I'd like to have known before coming here is "that the humidity is intense in the summer and fall."

Florida State University

Address: 2249 University Center, Tallahasse, FL 32306
Phone: 850-644-6200
E-mail address: admissions.admin.fsu.edu
Web site URL: www.fsu.edu
Location: suburban
Founded: 1851
Private or Public: public
Religious affiliation: none
Undergraduate enrollment: 24,699
Total enrollment: 30,519
Percent Male / Female: 45% / 55%
Percent Minority: 22.0%

Percent African-American: 12.0%
Percent Hispanic: 7.0%
Percent Asian: 3.0%
Percent in-state / out-of-state: 86.0% / 14%
Percent Pub HS: 89%
Fraternities: 10%
Sororities: 10%
Number of Applicants: 18,292
Percent Accepted: 75%
Percent Accepted who enroll: 38%
Entering: 5,213
Transfers: 3,458
Application Deadline: rolling

Mean SAT: 576 V, 571 M
Middle 50% SAT range: 520–620 V, 520–620 M
Middle 50% ACT range: NA
Mean ACT: 24
3 Most popular majors: biology, criminology, psychology
Retention: 85.0%
Graduation rate: 38.0%
Library: 2.2 million volumes
Tuition and Fees: $1,696 in; $8,685 out
Room and Board: $4,951
On-campus housing: 51%
Financial aid, first-year: 33%

Smokey and the Bandit, Striptease, and *Boogie Nights* are just some of the films starring Florida State's favorite alumnus, Burt Reynolds. In fact, this movie-star graduate is so popular, there is even a dorm named after him. Furthermore, many FSU students will concede that Reynolds dorm is probably the best dorm on campus. No matter where FSU students are living, however, be it Reynolds dorm or somewhere off-campus, they always find the time to party and to study in the warmth of Florida's sun.

Not Just Fun and Games

Although Florida State is consistently considered one of the biggest party schools in the nation, FSU students are quick to discount that stereotype. "People think we're just partyers, and that we're not as smart," said one sophomore. The academic requirements at FSU, however, are extensive. While most undergraduates enroll in the School of Arts & Sciences, there are several schools specializing in other programs, among which the School of Music, College of Engineering, and College of Business are some of the strongest. Depending on the student's major, there are different guidelines to fol-

low, but all students must earn course credits in English, mathematics, history, social sciences, humanities, and natural science. Other requirements include what one student called "x-and-y requirements," meaning cross-cultural studies, and the Gordon Rule, which states that each student must take a class that entails at least 3,000 words of writing. Regarding these requirements, one student said that "it's good to have a well-rounded education, but sometimes it gets to be too much. I already have so many classes dealing with my major." Another sophomore summed up the requirements simply by saying, "A lot of them are BS. Plus, I got a lot of credit from high school work, so I don't have to take the required stuff."

As for the classes themselves, FSU students unanimously cited psychology as an easy major, as well as communications. One student said that the communications major was "something you do when you don't know what else to do." Aside from psychology, reportedly easy classes include religion, sociology, most introductory classes, and Theater 300, which was considered by one student as "an easy A." Classes at FSU tend to be large. "Most classes number between 100 and 200 students including the liberal arts classes that fulfill a multicultural requirement. However, my biology class for non-majors has 1,600 kids!" said another student. Nevertheless, there are still plenty of small classes, particularly foreign language and music classes, which usually have 20 students or less. For students looking for a more academically challenging course load, the honors program is an option. One sophomore reported that the "honors geology class is a lot harder, it's no longer 'rocks for jocks.'" Honors students also reap the benefits of special housing. Aside from the honors classes, students say the hardest classes at FSU are found in the "real hard-core science classes, like physics and chemistry."

As for getting into classes, one student simply called it "a nightmare." "Registration's a mess because you have to make sure everything is right. You can never get through the phone registration line—it's just horrible." Another major grievance for FSU students regarding academics is "the fact that we have to take summer school for nine credit hours," which means about three summer courses. One sophomore reported that due to AP work, "I already have hours from high school, and if you take too many hours, they charge extra." Despite these disappointments, however, FSU students in general find the academic experience worthwhile. One music major said, "Overall, it's all right. You learn what you need to learn."

Social Options Galore

When Florida State Seminoles aren't studying, they can surely be found having fun on campus or in the surrounding city of Tallahassee. Be it simply hanging around in the dorms on the weekends, or going to clubs in the city, the social options at FSU seem endless. In Moore Auditorium, there are movie nights every few days, sponsored by the Student Government Association. These movies are popular because "the movies are good and you can go for free." If a movie doesn't seem like the right option, many students take advantage of Oglesby Union, the building where Moore Auditorium is located, but also where students can go bowling, eat, or even express themselves artistically in an art studio. Other students like to take advantage of the con-

certs put on by the music school, lectures, and the recitals found all over campus. On the weekends, students frequent the dance clubs of Tallahassee, as well as the popular coffeehouse, Epitome. Although Tallahassee "isn't Orlando, it has enough—essential stores, two malls." Plus, anyone who enjoys nature can visit nearby Jefferson Lake or take advantage of bike trails found in the area.

For those who are looking for campus parties, there are always those thrown by the Greeks. According to one freshman, "the Greek system is pretty big, but you don't have to be part of that scene to be 'in.'" One sophomore said, "our school doesn't seem to revolve around Greek life." Although alcohol may be available at these parties, it is probably not a wise idea to engage in excessive drinking on the FSU campus. "It's a dry campus, so you're not allowed to have anything on campus. But . . . if they don't see it, they can't do anything about it. However, they are beginning to crack down on underage drinking and if you're underage you'll get arrested," complained one student speaking about the administration.

Everyone's Friendly

Maybe it is due to the great weather, but FSU may be one of the friendliest campuses in the nation. As one student said, "People here are so friendly, you really have to be anti-human not to meet people." However, although the Seminoles are friendly people, there is a tendency to associate by academic department. "You won't see a lot of business majors mixing with the dance and theater types," said one freshman. Nevertheless, the student body is diverse. As one student put it, "We've got pretty much anything and everything—it's all sorts of different people."

Students report that although it is possible to get around campus without a car, most people, aside from freshman, do bring cars with them. Parking is, however, "really, really, really bad. It's just awful. There's never any student parking, and when you find a spot, people always hit your doors, because the spaces are so narrow." Parking is particularly rough on students living off-campus, who require a car to get to class. According to one such student, "I've driven around for an hour trying to find a parking space and subsequently missed class." In addition, the parking situation has not been alleviated by the building of a new campus police station on the site of one parking lot.

Campus Life

For FSU students, dormitories range from those that are "like a hotel: clean, nice, new furniture" to those with "cockroaches everywhere, with stains on the ceiling, and nasty smells emanating throughout the building." The dorm a student receives is dependent both on a first-come, first-serve basis and on class seniority. Thus, seniors who send in their forms early are most likely to get into Reynolds, Bryan, Gilchrist, or Broward, all of which were renovated within the last year or two. Students submitting their forms later may find themselves banished to Sally and Kellum on the other side of campus. "Those aren't just the dirty, nasty ones, but also the ones where people party nonstop," said one sophomore. Unfortunately for freshmen, they are more likely to be put in these dorms rather than the coveted hotel-like rooms. With the exception of all-female Dorman and Jennie Murphree Halls, FSU dorms are coed by floor. Even though seniors may choose the newer dorms, it is not unusual to find members of all classes living in the same area. There are RAs in each dorm, with at least one on each floor. For the most part they are considered friendly and helpful. Most upperclassmen prefer finding off-campus housing. Prices in the area range anywhere from $180 a month up to $500, but in general, there is usually reasonably priced housing available.

When asked about dining hall food, a surprisingly high number of FSU students simply say that they don't eat in the dining hall at all. One sophomore said, "I've probably eaten in the dining hall only once or twice since I got here." For the most part, almost all students either buy their own food or take advantage of the food court in the student union. This food court includes what one student terms as "the Chicking Hut," which stands for the popular fast-food restaurants—Chick-Fil-A, Burger King, and Pizza Hut. Also on-campus is the Gourmet Bean, where stu-

dents buy coffee and breakfast food. Off-campus, some students like to go to Pocket Emporium, where "there's Middle Eastern food. Really cheap and really good." Students choose not to stick with the FSU meal plan because they largely feel that it is a "rip-off" and slightly unorganized. "You have to use your FSU card and sometimes the system is down so you can't get food." One student who was on the meal plan was unhappy because she ended up using only half of the meals that she had to buy under the plan and then lost all the money she had spent on the meals she didn't use.

The Chop

Students desiring extracurricular activities have some options at Florida State. Clubs range from the Japanese Animation Club, where students get together to watch Japanese cartoons, to community service organizations. Other clubs on campus include the Flying High Circus, a live circus presented by students, and the martial arts clubs, where students can take anything from aikido to tae kwon do. Students at FSU are also health-conscious and can often be found in Leach Center, the new three-story gym. "Everyone goes there ALL the time!"

> "The food court includes what one student terms 'the Chicking Hut,' which stands for the popular fast-food restaurants Chick-Fil-A, Burger King, and Pizza Hut."

While extracurricular activities may not be as popular, sports is surely one of FSU's defining traits. "There is a lot of concentration given to sports and attention to the football team, but that's only because they are really good!" said one student. Football games are always packed and the students are always ready to do "the chop," the university's traditional way of showing team spirit with a downward movement of the arm to represent chopping with a tomahawk. As one student put it, it's "a mindless waving of the arm." A freshman said, "the games are so much fun. People paint their faces and wear T-shirts. It's a big deal." Although football is without question the dominant sport on campus, many students say that the men's crew team garners a good deal of respect. For those wishing to play sports, but not at a varsity level, there are intramurals as well as an indoor track, pool, and racquetball courts. The gym also offers some free classes to students, including kickboxing.

Southern Charm

The Florida State campus is described as "very large" and "very hilly." For those not so inclined to walking on this sort of terrain, there is a campus-wide bus system. One student described the university as "Southern and deceptively old-looking. Even the new buildings are built of red brick so that they all fit in." Students can often be found lounging on Landis Green, right in the middle of campus, near Strozier Library. Aside from the very recently added Leach Center and massive additions to the football stadium, FSU plans on building a large performing arts center in the near future.

Florida State Seminoles party heartily as well as put in their study time. One student said, "Every school has programs that are good, and FSU really does have some great ones." The incredible school spirit and the Southern hospitality of Florida State are certainly tempting, but one student did warn, "you have to like going to a big school. I like going to a big school and I love it here!" —*Shu-Ping Shen and Staff*

FYI
The three best things about attending Florida State University are "the excellent sports programs (all home events are free to students), school spirit is high and very contagious, and the party school atmosphere."

The three worst things about attending Florida State University are "32,000 other students attend this school—many times you feel like a number, parking is bad and getting increasingly worse, and the small surrounding city."

The three things every student should do before graduating from Florida State University are "to swim in the Wescott Fountain, paint themselves garnet & gold for the football games and do the Seminole 'chop,' and go out to the clubs."

One thing I wish I knew before coming here is "live on campus as a freshman, even the bad dorms are a good time."

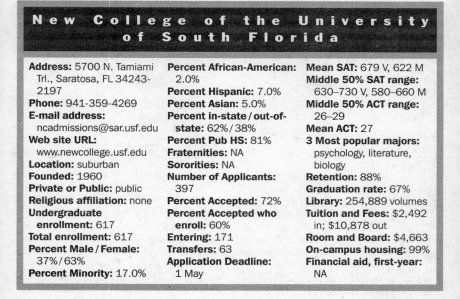

New College of the University of South Florida

Address: 5700 N. Tamiami Trl., Saratosa, FL 34243-2197

Phone: 941-359-4269

E-mail address: ncadmissions@sar.usf.edu

Web site URL: www.newcollege.usf.edu

Location: suburban

Founded: 1960

Private or Public: public

Religious affiliation: none

Undergraduate enrollment: 617

Total enrollment: 617

Percent Male / Female: 37% / 63%

Percent Minority: 17.0%

Percent African-American: 2.0%

Percent Hispanic: 7.0%

Percent Asian: 5.0%

Percent in-state / out-of-state: 62% / 38%

Percent Pub HS: 81%

Fraternities: NA

Sororities: NA

Number of Applicants: 397

Percent Accepted: 72%

Percent Accepted who enroll: 60%

Entering: 171

Transfers: 63

Application Deadline: 1 May

Mean SAT: 679 V, 622 M

Middle 50% SAT range: 630–730 V, 580–660 M

Middle 50% ACT range: 26–29

Mean ACT: 27

3 Most popular majors: psychology, literature, biology

Retention: 88%

Graduation rate: 67%

Library: 254,889 volumes

Tuition and Fees: $2,492 in; $10,878 out

Room and Board: $4,663

On-campus housing: 99%

Financial aid, first-year: NA

W ith a name like "New College" there's no mistaking the small Sarasota, Florida school for a traditional undergraduate institution. With only six hundred students and no grades or core curriculum, New College attendees report that their four years of striving for success takes place "in an experimental milieu."

Independent Intellectuals

New College students make much of the fact that self-motivation is key for success at their school. There is no core curriculum. Rather, students design their course plan with the help of a faculty advisor. Students can easily design their own majors, though many choose from the variety of already-established ones. Traditional liberal arts majors like anthropology, English literature, and biology are common. Students caution, though, that the "literature theory classes will completely exhaust your brain and overload your reading time." In addition, "Psychology is very popular . . . but the department walks you through the thesis, which is the most difficult aspect of New College." Some even get degrees in "general studies,"

which is "sort of a catchall." As for those who plan to continue their education, faculty members can suggest programs of study appropriate for future graduate students.

Another hallmark of the New College education is the lack of grades. Said one sophomore, "There can't really be competition—there's nothing to compete about." Nevertheless, one student did note that "it can be a hard adjustment from high school. You have to train yourself to study for the right reasons." Students don't point to any particularly strong area of faculty expertise, but note, rather, that they are all "high-caliber." Like the college as a whole, classes are almost universally small. As a result, professor-student interaction is lauded at New College. "You'll definitely have professors who know you well—some'll probably cook your whole class dinner." There are TAs, but they only assist professors and students and do not teach classes.

Students say that at least partly as a result of the atmosphere of "intellectualism," most students spend more time on academics than any other aspect of college. The Jane B. Cook Bancroft Library, the main library, is praised for having "the best librarian I've ever met." Because New College is a state school, it is part of an interlibrary book exchange program with other Florida colleges. Upperclassmen are also pleased that they get their own study carrels. Other places to study, which tend to be more social than Bancroft, are the student center and individual dorm rooms.

Time Flies When You're Saving the World

While studying occupies the biggest chunk of a New Collegian's life, many students are involved in extracurricular activities. The *Catalyst* is the weekly paper written by students. Other popular activities include student government (through the New College Student Alliance) and Amnesty International. Politically, "the overwhelming majority is liberal." A senior cautioned, though, that "more than being of one view or another we are openminded." Nevertheless, students noted that the campus isn't as good at activism as it is at "theorizing about activism." New College does not have a varsity sports program, but its athletic facilities include a gym, racquetball, tennis, and basketball courts, a soccer field, and a pool.

> "You'll definitely have professors who know you well—some'll probably cook your whole class dinner."

On the weekends, New College students party like their peers at other institutions—sort of. There are no fraternities or sororities, and students say that the social scene is "fairly laid-back." The majority of socializing takes place on campus. "Walls" are parties randomly thrown together whenever the urge hits. Crossdressing is reportedly popular at these parties. A more organized dance is the Palm Court Party (PCP), where a laidback atmosphere of tie-dyeing, listening to music, and dancing pervades. Students say that both drinking and drugs are prevalent at the school, though the latter is mostly confined to marijuana. "Cops look the other way most of the time," said one student. Outside of campus, Sarasota does not offer much for nighttime activity, though its tourist-friendly beaches are appreciated by New College students. Said one student, "Sarasota is a small, artsy town with not a lot to do, but it's beautiful and has more cultural opportunities than any other city in Florida. Which I guess makes me a bit sad for the rest of Florida . . ." Tampa is less than an hour way and students in need of a break from the quiet suburban life occasionally make the trip.

Sleeping and Snacking in Sarasota

Most freshmen and sophomores live on campus while upperclassmen generally move off campus. All B and Viking rooms are singles, while Pei residents share doubles. Viking is actually a converted motel, which some students say has "charm." The newer Dort and Goldstein dorms are said to be much better than their counterparts. Dort features large suites with single bedrooms, complete with appliances. In all the dorms, though, residents often keep their doors open, which contributes to a more suitelike atmosphere. Security concerns are minimal among students; locking doors is the only precaution most students take. There are two RAs for each dorm. Students enjoy the "very Florida" campus, calling the architecture "'70s Spanish" style. The school is located on a bay, which, "during good weather, is awesome." In general, students appreciate going to school in sunny Florida. "I don't know why my friends put up with snow up north!" said one.

Campus residents eat in one central cafeteria and are required to be on the meal plan. The food is prepared by the Marriott food service, and students can use their meal cards at the local convenience stores as well. Many undergrads complain about the quality of the food. As one student explained, "There's a reason we were ranked as the worst college food in the South." Students also enjoy eating at the Granary, a health-food restaurant, and at Taco Bell.

Lack of Cultural Diversity

While students have diverse interests, they generally come from similar backgrounds: white, upper-middle-class, and suburban. Said one student, "I wouldn't say New College is particularly diverse, unless you consider a school nearly 85 percent full of white, suburban, overly intelligent kids diverse. Of course, everyone welcomes diversity, but it's part of the 'program' here." The homosexual community is said to be "well-accepted." In general, said one student, "due to self-selection, we're a pretty alternative, easygoing bunch. Students are proud to be a part of their "thoughtful—in both senses of the word" community and don't mind missing the "traditional" college experience. "I belong here. I can't imagine most of us truly belonging anywhere else."
—*Ellen Moskowitz*

FYI

The three best things about attending New College are "freedom of education, meeting lots of strange and exciting people, and the intimate atmosphere of a small school."

The three worst things about attending New College are "freedom to accomplish nothing, living with lots of strange people, and the atmosphere of a small school where everyone knows everything about everyone else."

The three things that every student should do before graduating from New College are "dance naked in Palm Court, listen to one of John More's storytimes, and win a game of one-on-one with John Newman."

One thing I'd like to have known before coming here is "there's a small social sphere."

Rollins College

Address: 1000 Holt Ave, Winter Park, FL 32789
Phone: 407-646-2161
E-mail address: admission@rollins.edu
Web site URL: www.rollins.edu
Location: suburban
Founded: 1885
Private or Public: private
Religious affiliation: none
Undergraduate enrollment: 1,520
Total enrollment: 3,483
Percent Male/Female: 40%/60%
Percent Minority: 16.0%

Percent African-American: 2.0%
Percent Hispanic: 8.0%
Percent Asian: 3.0%
Percent in-state/out-of-state: 40%/60%
Percent Pub HS: 55%
Fraternities: 27%
Sororities: 27%
Number of Applicants: 1,854
Percent Accepted: 73%
Percent Accepted who enroll: 33%
Entering: 448
Transfers: 68
Application Deadline: 15 Feb
Mean SAT: 570 V, 580 M

Middle 50% SAT range: 520–620 V, 520–620 M
Middle 50% ACT range: 23–27
Mean ACT: NA
3 Most popular majors: psychology, economics/international business, English
Retention: 83%
Graduation rate: 68%
Library: 277,671 volumes
Tuition and Fees: $21,870 in; $21,870 out
Room and Board: $6,700
On-campus housing: 95%
Financial aid, first-year: 55%

"Don't forget to bring your suntan oil," joked a Rollins College student when describing the reputation Rollins has among its neighboring schools. With its Spanish Mediterranean architecture and majestic trees hung with Spanish moss, this college in the sunny climes of Winter Park, Florida, garners a certain amount of envy from other southern universities. Add to this the fact that *U.S. News & World Report* ranked Rollins number two behind the University of Richmond and above rival Stetson (number four) in its year 2000

"Top Southern Colleges and Universities" rankings, and you have a group of satisfied, if slightly smug, students.

Tom and Tammy Tar

Take Tom and Tammy Tar (the school mascots), for instance. "Tom's basically this big, brawny sailor guy, and Tammy's his, ahem, mate," one student explained. These tan, lean mascots inspire generations of Tars to sports excellence in the traditionally sports of golf, tennis, and crew. Rollins has several nationally ranked teams, including men's golf and men's and women's tennis. The Tom Tar men's and women's basketball team also do well in their tough Division II conference. One male student recently set a NCAA record for 93 consecutive games with three-point baskets. "Hey, we got it great. Nice weather, great sports... uh, oh yeah, I guess we study a little bit, too," one student said.

Working Hard

Rollins students study more than a little bit. "My reasons for coming here were academics first, and that other stuff second," said one studious freshman. Another student emphasized that "active participation in classes is essential for good grades." Rollins' three-story Olin Library comfortably seats the hard-core studiers on the basement floor, while the first floor is home to the more social studier. Rollins has several programs catering to such students: the Winter Term (or J term, short for January term), the Honors Degree Program, and the Rollins Advantage Program (RAP) are the primary vehicles for particularly motivated students. The J term, which was once mandatory for students, now consists of a totally optional term after the winter holidays in which classes meet three times per week for three hours, and finish with an exam before the start of the spring semester. Although the J term is no longer required, most students still take the opportunity to partake in the more hands-on classes that the shorter term provides. Students who do not stick around for the J term often go abroad or take internships in nearby Orlando, which, as one of the fastest-growing cities in the nation, is home to myriad large corporations, as well as Universal Studios and Disney World.

Hmmm . . . What To Study?

The business-oriented environment of Orlando makes the Rollins environment conducive to the study of economics, one of the most popular majors of the 28 that Rollins offers. Rollins's psychology, political science, English, and theater departments were also cited as popular, while some students report that the language departments are weaker. All students must satisfy course requirements before graduating, and while the requirements "help some people make up their minds about their possible major, I think they're a crock," said one undergraduate.

> "Hey, we got it great. Nice weather, great sports... uh, oh yeah, I guess we study a little bit, too."

Greeks play a large role in the Rollins social scene, with approximately 40 percent of students choosing to pledge. Some students say the Greek scene "really opens up a lot of social opportunities," while others feel that it makes the already close-knit community of Rollins "damn near suffocating." "I think that they're good for the campus as a whole, but some people just rush and then lose themselves in the organization, never really becoming an individual," one perceptive student said. But, according to one undergrad, "There is nothing on campus, so we either have to do the bar scene or hit an off-campus party." Since there are few school-wide dances (the annual President's Dance is an informal theme dance), Greek formals take prominence.

Dating and Relationships

On the topic of dating and coed relations, one student summed, "I'd say there's a lot of sex, I mean, hooking up here. Perhaps it's because we're so small that you hear about it all the time, but then again, maybe there's something in the water, because you hear about it all the time." Same-sex relationships are also treated with respect, and gay students can join R-FLAG, Rollins for Lesbians and Gays. International students make up only about 5 percent of the Rollins student population, but they do organize activities and contribute to campus life. Minority students are represented by LASA (Latin American Student Association), BSU (the Black Student Union), and the Muslim Student Association, among others. Since Rollins is small, these groups tend to coordinate campus events together. With a country club-like campus and over 70 student organizations to choose from, very few students opt to live off campus. Those who do "are the type that commute and just come to get their degrees. They're very rare," one junior said. The only incentive that students cited to move off campus is the quality of the dining hall food. "If you ask me, it pretty much bites," a disgruntled senior remarked, but several underclassmen said they were satisfied: "Even though the menu is ultra-predictable, they still do some novel stuff, like a teriyaki bar." Another student said, "You pay the same price everyone else does, then you're charged for each item of food you buy at the on-campus convenience store or at the dining hall. Problem is, everybody is always running out of money toward the end of the semester, so you've gotta call Mom and Dad and ask for more money." The Rollins administration takes a hard stance on alcohol, but ignores what some students see as a pressing campus drug problem. According to one undergraduate, "There's a lot of money here. A lot of kids should be in AA." A recent change allows for "catered kegs" at fraternity parties, which means an outside company is hired to provide beer to students with proper ID. According to several undergrads, a "surprising number" of students smoke pot, and "some of the rich, snobby types are involved in cocaine and heroin—it's really pretty sad." Despite these issues, Rollins students in general enjoy a laid-back life of sun, fun, and Orlando at a bargain that cannot be beat this side of the Mason-Dixon Line. Students interested in such a "work hard, play hard" atmosphere should consider applying to Rollins. —*Ellen Lee Moskowitz and Staff*

FYI

The three best things about attending Rollins are "the sun, the beautiful country club of a campus, and Florida."

The three worst things about attending Rollins are "the dining hall food, there are too many rich preppies, and a close-knit school can be stifling."

The three things every student should do before graduating are "to play golf, to play tennis, and to get a tan."

One thing I'd like to have known before coming here is "how big the Greek system is."

Stetson University

Address: 421 N. Woodland Blvd, Unit 8378, DeLand, FL 32720-3771
Phone: 904-822-7100
E-mail address: admissions@stetson.edu
Web site URL: www.stetson.edu
Location: small city
Founded: 1883
Private or Public: private
Religious affiliation: none
Undergraduate enrollment: 2,062
Total enrollment: 2,380
Percent Male/Female: 42%/58%
Percent Minority: 10.2%

Percent African-American: 3.5%
Percent Hispanic: 4.8%
Percent Asian: 1.5%
Percent in-state/out-of-state: 74%/26%
Percent Pub HS: 78%
Fraternities: 33%
Sororities: 26%
Number of Applicants: 1,913
Percent Accepted: 80%
Percent Accepted who enroll: 37%
Entering: 563
Transfers: 120
Application Deadline: 15 Mar

Mean SAT: 561 V, 557 M
Middle 50% SAT range: 510–620 V, 500–610 M
Middle 50% ACT range: NA
Mean ACT: NA
3 Most popular majors: general business, biology, psychology
Retention: 81.0%
Graduation rate: 60.0%
Library: 344,452 volumes
Tuition and Fees: $14,475 in; $14,475 out
Room and Board: $6,070
On-campus housing: 90%
Financial aid, first-year: 98%

Expect to be recognized by name at Stetson University by student and faculty alike. Named after the famous hat maker, this small university prides itself on the feeling of community that develops as students study, work, and party together on the warm central Florida campus.

Hatter Learning

Most students say they chose Stetson primarily for its academic programs. The University is composed of four colleges, three of which, the College of Arts and Sciences, School of Business, and School of Music, contain undergraduate majors. All students are required to fulfill general education requirements that serve to ensure a liberal arts background. These include computer literacy, foreign language, humanities, math, science, and religion. As one student said, the wide-ranging requirements "don't let you slack in any one area, even if you're not that interested in it. You come out of Stetson well-rounded." Top students selected into the honors program have the opportunity to replace some general education classes with smaller, higher-level ones. In addition, honors students have the option of creating their own majors. Freshman year, students may choose to balance out tough

core requirements with a "University Experience" class, usually chosen from the college in which one plans to major. UE classes (some of which involve field trips and learning time-management skills) are designed to introduce students to Stetson and participants remark that the laid-back courses are "a great way to meet the people you'll be studying with for four years." The school also offers study-abroad programs in seven countries.

Programs at the Business and Music schools are considered by students to be the strongest on campus. In addition, students note that smaller majors such as Computer Information Systems (which boasts a 100 percent job placement rate), Russian Studies, and Sports and Exercise Science are taught by expert faculty. Students universally agree that the student-faculty interaction fostered by the school's small environment is one of Stetson's best qualities. "Professors actually inquire about your life when you run into them at the Commons [the school's dining hall]!" remarked one freshman. UE classes are the only ones in which TAs assist professors.

It is not uncommon to see higher-level classes of two or three students held on benches under Stetson's palm and oak trees, but even introductory lectures rarely have more than 35 students. Though priority for registration is given to students with more credits, complaints about not getting into classes are rare.

Living and Eating

Rooms in freshman housing are typically a bit smaller than those in dorms reserved for upperclassmen but are also considered "friendlier." Lofts are popular spacesavers. All freshmen are housed in doubles with communal bathrooms, but as upperclassmen, students have the opportunity to be housed in suites. Of the eight dorms, two are all-female, one is all-male, and five are coed (separated by hall or wing). Smith is a predominantly freshman dorm with a reputation for being boisterous, while Nemec, a little less centrally located, maintains special housing for honors students who choose to live there. Emily and Stetson Halls are two of the more popular upperclassmen residential halls. During the school week and when finals time arrives, dorms have quiet-hours policies. All floors have RAs to help students deal with concerns ranging from roommate trouble to custodial problems. Upperclassmen may choose to live off campus, but most prefer to remain in the more affordable on-campus residences.

The Commons serves food that "ranges dramatically in quality," but Stetson students say that lingering with friends in the recently renovated dining hall makes mealtimes enjoyable. Meal-plan options include 5 to 17 meals a week that consist of a choice of entrée, side dishes, and a drink. The Commons recently began offering stir-fry and fresh pasta dishes a few times a week and an omelet station on Sundays. Vegetarians are guaranteed a well-stocked salad bar, but some note that partaking of the vegetarian entrées can be a questionable venture. Students may transfer unused meals into points that can be used at the Kiosk, an on-campus coffee shop, or the Hat Rack, which serves "slow fast-food" that's perfect "if you're in the mood for grease."

Life after Classes

A "quaint town," nearby DeLand provides students with the requisite grocery store and Denny's and offers Main Street for an afternoon stroll. Most students agree, though, that the Blind Pig Pub and Halftimes, two local bars, are DeLand's most popular offerings. Those looking for true night life head to Daytona or Orlando, making a car useful, though not necessary. Thursday is Stetson's big party night, which some students attribute to its being "a suitcase school." A large percentage of Hatters head home for the weekends, though recently the numbers have been dropping as the school is attracting more students from the Northeast.

> "Students universally agree that the student-faculty interaction fostered by the school's small environment is one of Stetson's best qualities."

Greek life is very influential at Stetson. Approximately 30 percent of the campus is affiliated, but students note that Greeks are the strongest voice in student government and essentially control intramurals. Those not affiliated are welcome at the majority of Greek parties, though some parties are restricted to Greeks until a certain hour. Stetson's notable parties, including Around the World (which serves a drink from a different nationality in every room) are held by the fraternities and sororities. A senior remarked that feeling left out if students are non-Greek depends on "what kind of person you are and how involved you are on and off campus." The campus recently became wet and students of legal age can serve limited amounts of alcohol in their rooms. Public Safety, Stetson's security, reportedly does not enforce drinking policy as stringently as DeLand's police force is reputed to. Drugs are minimal on campus and, in general, students do not find pressure to partake of drugs or alcohol.

The Stetson Student

Most students are involved in at least a few extracurricular activities at Stetson; some of the more popular ones include branches of national community service organizations, the weekly *Stetson Reporter*, the Baptist Student Union, and the

Council for Student Activities. The school does not have a football team, but strong men's baseball, basketball, and soccer teams help promote Hatter pride. Students say intramurals primarily involve members of fraternities and sororities. The new Hollis Wellness Center has made working out popular, "at least temporarily."

Most Hatters recognize (but do not necessarily praise) the homogeneity of the Stetson student body, typically describing each other as preppy and middle-to-upper class. Homosexuality is accepted at Stetson, though some students express doubt as to how fully. Students note that the student body includes a relatively small percentage of minorities.

In addition to a strong academic program, students say Stetson definitely fits the image of a small school—intimate and welcoming. Though an embarrassing incident at a fraternity party may potentially haunt you forever at Stetson, students find the advantages of a small school well worth the drawbacks. —*Ellen Lee Moskowitz and Staff*

FYI

The three best things about attending Stetson are "the small classes, getting to know your peers, and the quaint atmosphere of DeLand."

The three worst things about attending Stetson are "that there's no big football team, the food sucks, and the damn tuition costs!"

The three things that every student should do before graduating from Stetson are "to patronize the local bars, to participate in the Greek Life, and to get to know your profs."

One thing I'd like to have known before coming here is "how expensive it was—'Try to earn scholarships in high school!'"

University of Florida

Address: 201 Criser Hall, Box 114000, Gainesville, FL 32611-4000
Phone: 352-392-1365
E-mail address: freshman@ufl.edu, transfer@ufl.edu
Web site URL: www.ufl.edu
Location: NA
Founded: 1853
Private or Public: public
Religious affiliation: none
Undergraduate enrollment: 31,633
Total enrollment: 43,382
Percent Male/Female: 43%/57%
Percent Minority: 24.9%

Percent African-American: 7.3%
Percent Hispanic: 10.5%
Percent Asian: 6.4%
Percent in-state/out-of-state: NA
Percent Pub HS: NA
Fraternities: 15%
Sororities: 15%
Number of Applicants: 13,967
Percent Accepted: 60%
Percent Accepted who enroll: 44%
Entering: 3,717
Transfers: 45%
Application Deadline: 29 Jan
Mean SAT: NA V, NA M

Middle 50% SAT range: 570–670 V, 600–690 M
Middle 50% ACT range: 26–29
Mean ACT: NA
3 Most popular majors: business management, education, engineering
Retention: 91.0%
Graduation rate: 67.0%
Library: 3,401,279 volumes
Tuition and Fees: $2,210 in; $11,580 out
Room and Board: NA
On-campus housing: NA
Financial aid, first-year: 27%

While UF students are proud that their school has finally been noted as one of the top 50 universities in the country according to *U.S. News & World Report*, they'd toss that accolade aside for a repeat #1 ranking where outside opinion really matters: football. The school has a winning tradition in the sport, and the annual game against Florida State makes for the biggest weekend of the year, as well as one of the biggest pep rallies in the country. Gator-

Growl, as the pep rally is known, typifies both American college life and the UF experience—quality football, parties, and fun.

Pride's for More than Saturday

Students are proud of their fun-loving reputation but emphasize that their education is both high-quality and strenuous. As admission standards of recent years have risen markedly, the school's prestige has increased accordingly. The general education core curriculum requires students to complete classes in math, English, the biological sciences, the humanities, and social and behavioral sciences. Nearly all Gators note the reputation of UF's teachers and programs as having been a decisive factor in their college choice. In particular, architecture, journalism, and engineering are quality programs. Business-related majors are popular as well. Choice of major is a decision that should be made early at UF. Said one student, "If you are going to change your major, change it early. If not, expect to stay an extra year." An honors program is available, acceptance to which is based on SAT score and high school GPA. In addition, study abroad programs are gaining popularity. Gripes about the academic experience at UF include the lecture classes of as many as 700 students and the preponderance of graduate students in teaching positions. One junior noted, however, that the "personal attention" from TAs is a valuable asset.

Prowling Grounds

The main library, used for both studying and research, is Smathers Library, which houses 2.5 million volumes in two main centers and nine branches. Students report that they often study in other quiet places, such as computer labs or the Plaza of Americas park, due to the limited hours of the libraries. Social studying is based in the dorm lobbies. Other facilities available for student use on campus include the Florida Museum of Natural History, the Center for the Performing Arts, Harn Museum of Art, and the University Art Gallery. Further contributing to the breadth of Gators' opportunities are the world's largest citrus research center, a world-renowned institute for the study of the brain, a public television and radio station, and one of the largest health centers in the Southeast, the Shands Hospital. Students enjoy the Florida sunshine on a gorgeous campus characterized by a variety of brick and Gothic-style buildings. One section of campus is on the National Register of Historic Places.

Quarters and Cuisine

Dorm living does not get as much praise as the dorms themselves. While one upperclassmen said, "It's good to experience it," she acknowledged that, "people are always happy to move off campus after the first year." Living on campus is optional, and most take advantage of the option freshman year in order to get acquainted with their classmates. Only upperclassmen have the opportunity of getting into an ARF (apartment residence facility) and even these are rare. The rest of the dorms are generally small but comfortable doubles. There are RAs on every floor, and floor residents vote on visiting hours for members of the opposite sex. The only particularly undesirable dorms are Murphree and Buckman, which have no airconditioning.

Students say that their dining options have improved recently and that they appreciate not being forced into a meal plan. Many take advantage of the offer, though, and food ranges from cafeteria-style, to fast food at the Hub, to vegetarian at the Gator Dining Corner.

Living the Florida Life

The campus is mainly self-contained and Gators can easily keep themselves occupied on its grounds. Besides the opportunities to be a spectator at premier college sporting events, UF students can participate in popular intramural sports including football, soccer, and tennis. Extracurricular activities abound; students can't point to the most popular ones because "there's seemingly as many groups as there are students." The *Alligator*, a student-run daily newspaper and Florida Blue Key, a campus activity involvement organization, are two of the most well-known. Popular community service activities include Habitat for Humanity and volunteering for the Shands Hospital.

Greek life is influential at UF. The fraternities and sororities dominate social life but non-Greeks don't feel left out. "We can still go to the parties and there's plenty other ways to meet people. You probably have to make more of an effort, though, and that's why there's some pressure to rush." All year long, Gators expect opportunities for socializing and drinking. Drugs are "without question available, but completely avoidable."

Students report that Gainesville caters to the university and that movies, malls, and restaurants are easily accessible with a car. Local clubs such as Torches and Maui's are popular too. Tampa, Tallahassee, Jacksonville, and Orlando are all located within a two-hour drive, and students often make weekend trips to other colleges. Fans of the outdoors can take advantage of great year-round weather in Gainesville—and at the hour-away beaches located on the Gulf of Mexico or the Atlantic Ocean.

A Gator?

A junior laughed in response to the question, "Is there a student stereotype?" "With 42,000+ students we've got 'em all," he said. Florida students come from all over the country and from remarkably diverse cultural backgrounds. Cultural organizations like the Black Student Union are popular. The lesbian and gay communities are large and in general students point to a "live and let live" feeling on campus. "We all bleed orange and blue down here! FSU fans are the only thing we're not open-minded about."

> **"We all bleed orange and blue down here! FSU fans are the only thing we're not open-minded about."**

Students are curious about the changes that will occur at UF due to the loss of long-time president Vince Lombardi in November of 1999, noting that, "he is probably the best president UF has ever had." Nevertheless, the spirit UF students exhibit for more than football reflects confidence in their school. Said one junior, "If you are looking for a good academic school and you want to experience all that college has to offer then UF is your place." At first overwhelmed by the great size and many opportunities of the the University of Florida, students ultimately find niches at UF and unite to scream "If you're not a GATOR, you're GATORBAIT!" —*Ellen Moskowitz*

FYI

The three best things about attending University of Florida are "football, either the weather or the highly-ranked programs, and football."

The three worst things about attending University of Florida are "huge classes, parking (or lack thereof), and the sometimes sweltering heat."

The three things that every student should do before graduating from University of Florida are "watch the bats leave the bat house at dusk, attend a UF football game, and hang out on Payne's Prairie and watch the stars on a clear night."

One thing I'd like to have known before coming here is "that every freshman should come to summer classes before they come in the fall—it's a great time to meet new people."

University of Miami

Address: P.O. Box 248025, Coral Gables, FL 33124-4616
Phone: 305-284-4323
E-mail address: admissions@miami.edu
Web site URL: www.miami.edu
Location: suburban
Founded: 1925
Private or Public: private
Religious affiliation: none
Undergraduate enrollment: 8,235
Total enrollment: 13,715
Percent Male/Female: 45%/55%
Percent Minority: 50.0%
Percent African-American: 12.0%

Percent Hispanic: 32.0%
Percent Asian: 6.0%
Percent in-state/out-of-state: 54%/46%
Percent Pub HS: NA
Fraternities: 12%
Sororities: 12%
Number of Applicants: 12,264
Percent Accepted: 55%
Percent Accepted who enroll: 28%
Entering: 1,858
Transfers: 643
Application Deadline: 1 Mar
Mean SAT: NA V, NA M

Middle 50% SAT range: 520–630 V, 530–640 M
Middle 50% ACT range: 22–27
Mean ACT: NA
3 Most popular majors: biology, psychology, nursing
Retention: 82.9%
Graduation rate: 61.0%
Library: NA
Tuition and Fees: $22,526 in; $22,526 out
Room and Board: $7,934
On-campus housing: 72%
Financial aid, first-year: 71%

As the danger of a hurricane sets in, the ibis is the last bird to leave its home, and it quickly returns as soon as the storm blows over. As mascot for the University of Miami, the ibis could not be more appropriate. It stands brave in the face of storms just as Miami students stand strong in the face of academic challenges. The ibis is proud of its home in Miami, and like many UM students, hates to leave its beloved shores.

A-B-C Not So Easy as 1-2-3

The University of Miami is divided into several schools: arts and sciences, architecture, business administration, engineering, communication, education, international studies, law, medicine, music, marine and atmospheric science, continuing studies, graduate, and nursing. All freshmen enroll in the College of Arts and Sciences and do not enter a specific school until they declare a major, which is usually done second semester of sophomore year. Although each school has different requirements, all students must complete a core curriculum. These core classes are in the natural sciences, social sciences, and English. Students typically "don't mind the core at all because major requirements often overlap with required courses." Furthermore, UM's core forces students to take courses they might not otherwise choose. For example, one popular course in psychology calls for student participation in the graduate school's experiments. One student noted that he "was skeptical at first, but everyone found it to be fun and interesting."

Class size varies from subject to subject. Math and English classes have a maximum of 20 students, while science lecture courses tend to enroll about 200 students. The popularity of these courses is not surprising because the university's respected medical school offers a few undergraduate courses in the natural sciences. However, one student observed that while his biology lecture had 200 students at the beginning of the semester, it had dropped to half that size by finals. Many students agree that introductory biology and chemistry are "serious weeding-out courses," which explains why many students also consider the pre-med track to be the most difficult. In contrast, business and education majors are viewed as less rigorous.

Students find that they enjoy the majority of their classes because of the professors. One undergrad reported that professors, who teach both large and small classes, "beg for questions, and they adjust their schedules to make time outside of class for more questions or discussion." Students agree that professors are "approachable and there to help you." In particular, one student noted that "even in large lecture classes, professors recognize their students outside of the classroom." TAs offer review sessions before an exam and office hours for individual questions, but according to undergrads, the graduate students are there as a supplementary resource, not for primary instruction.

Freshmen are assigned to a faculty advisor to help them choose appropriate courses. When students declare their major, they are assigned to another advisor in the respective department. Overall, students agree that their "advisors are great and really supportive. They're there to help with all kinds of academic problems."

The University of Miami also offers special academic programs. The honors program requires a minimum 3.3 GPA and at least one honors class per semester. These classes are usually smaller and more intense than regular classes. There is also an honors program in medicine open only to Florida residents; students who qualify can earn undergraduate and graduate degrees in six years. While this is an extremely sought-after opportunity, only about 25 undergrads are admitted into the rigorous program each year. Although science is in the spotlight at UM, one student reported that "the university caters to just as many liberal-arts majors as it does to natural science majors."

The Neon Lights Are Bright on South Beach

When academic life becomes a little overwhelming, UM students find plenty of ways to relax, both on- and off-campus. On campus, the university frequently shows free movies, from sneak previews in the university's theater to old favorites shown on a big outdoor screen. The university also hosts theme "Patio Parties" where local bands play and extracurricular clubs set up booths to advertise their activities. Students enjoy these festivities because "there is always lots of food to eat and lots of people to meet." In addition, the Greek system thrives at the University of Miami. While some events are by invitation only, like fraternity and sorority mixers, most of the time fraternities plaster flyers all over campus, inviting everyone to their parties. While Greeks do play a large role in Miami's social scene, the University Center (the UC), where many students socialize and relax during the week, is a popular hangout. Right next door to the UC is the Rathskeller, affectionately known as the Rat, a campus bar that hosts comedians and bands. The Rat even offers a happy hour, but alcohol is served only to those over 21. As far as dating is concerned, some have "found their significant others, but most people tend to go out with lots of people," one student said.

The UM campus is recognizably diverse. Its proximity to a big city attracts students from all kinds of backgrounds. Although one student expected most of his classmates to be from Florida, he quickly learned that Miami lures many international students as well as students from the Northeast. Praised by undergraduates, Miami's diversity makes it "easy to meet people because all kinds of people are everywhere you look."

On weekends, many students explore the energetic life of Florida's southern coast, Coconut Grove or "the Grove," and South Beach. After a quick commute on the Metrorail, an aboveground subway system, students find the sand right at their feet. Many students "beach it" until the sun falls and "the nightclubs and bands begin to roar with music." Bayside, an oceanfront plaza with shops and boutiques, also lights up with weekend entertainment. One student noted that "both on- and off-campus, music is heard everywhere!" At on-campus parties, students report that alcohol has a strong presence, but neither kegs nor funnels are allowed. Beer is common, but students agree that whether you drink like a fish or don't drink a drop, "you can always have a good time."

Although there is always something to do at the University of Miami, many students refute the claim that Miami is a party school. One student admitted that he "thought Miami was much more of a party school until I became a student." Another recognized that "there is a balance between study hard and party hard, so that parties are rarely out of control, but people also know how to relax and enjoy themselves."

Miami, You've Got Style

Students generally approve of UM's coed dorms. Among them are Eaton, Stanford, Walsh, Pentland, McDonalds, and Hecht, also called "the Towers." These modern dorms surround Lake Osceola and are conveniently located near Miami's academic buildings. Since students are permitted to request a particular dorm, different dorms take on different personalities. For example, Eaton, which is generally regarded as the best dorm, houses mainly athletes, and Pentland tends to attract the international crowd. There also is a "singing dorm" for the musically inclined. First-years usually live in units of two doubles that share a bathroom. Upperclassmen commonly have singles or live in campus apartments with kitchenettes. Although all dorms are coed, floors are single-sex. Freshmen, who are required to live on-campus unless commuting from home, live in the same dorms as the upperclassmen. Freshmen are assigned a Residential Advisor, usually a senior or graduate student who can help with living problems or offer advice. Students generally find the RAs "pretty cool about everything." Overall, students agree that the dorms are modern and clean, although they "tend to be a little loud, at least without earplugs." This might explain why some students search for off-campus housing after their first year. Although the apartment search can be tiresome, it is not impossible, and some students opt to rent small houses in the area.

Dining at the University of Miami receives mixed reviews. There are two main cafeterias: Hecht-Stanford and Pierson-Mahoney. There is also a popular food court, called the Hurricane, which houses various fast-food eateries and a coffee stand. Students who live on-campus are required to purchase a meal plan of 8 to 21 meals per week. Some students say they might go to the dining hall to "talk with friends for hours rather than for the food." One student even claimed that "breakfast is the only edible meal," but another felt as if options were improving. Vegetarians find that the "salad bar is great, and it's pretty cheap, which makes it that much better." Off-campus, options include a Bennigan's, TGI Friday's, the Cheesecake Factory, and the Grove.

The campus of the University of Miami is comprised of mostly modern and brick buildings surrounded by the wealthy suburb of Coral Gables. The buildings are "mostly laid out in a circle so everything is pretty close and accessible," one student said. Having a car on campus is not necessary, but undergrads agree that "a car would definitely be nice when you want to venture to the beach." The Metrorail also provides transportation off campus, and many students use it frequently.

Other university facilities include a recently built Wellness Center, which students call a "bright, new facility with a great pool, beautiful gym, huge tennis courts, and even saunas." It also houses an indoor track, basketball courts, racquetball courts, and workout rooms. In addition to athletics, this huge center provides dance, aerobic, and nutrition classes. The university's historic football field, the Orange Bowl, is located nearby.

When students want to exercise their minds, Miami has several places to study. The most popular spot is Richter Library, which some say can be too popular because the volume of people can turn study hours into social hours. On the other hand, one student stressed that "if you want serious seclusion, find a cubicle in Richter and no one will bother you." Richter is open 24 hours a day and has copy machines and computer labs. Other quiet places include the medical, music, and law school libraries.

According to students, the campus lacks very little. It even is equipped with its own movie theater and game rooms. Many undergrads are impressed by the cleanliness of the campus. "Everything is spotless," observed one student. "There's no graffiti or trash." Even the dining halls are commended on their "spotlessness."

Get Up, Stand Up

The University of Miami prides itself on its history of strong athletic, extracurricular, and social spirit. Football, which is probably the most popular spectator sport, tempts Miami students to don their orange and green to show their support and spirit. UM's biggest football game is against its main rival, the Florida State Seminoles. Football season also heralds Miami's homecoming. Traditional homecoming activities begin two weeks prior to the football game. Dances, parties, and parades enliven the campus with school spirit. Other popular spectator sports include basketball, baseball, and soccer. In the past, the diving team has won national championships. Tickets to athletic events are free to all students. For the not-so-athletic student who still wants to get involved, Miami has an extensive intramural program. The most popular intramurals are flag football, soccer, and softball. Many people participate in intramurals because "anybody can join the teams; often the people who play aren't even aware of the rules."

Through organizations such as Link, Hurricane Help the Hometown, and Circle K, some UM students work with inner-city children and the elderly, build homes for the homeless, and assist the disabled. In addition to volunteer opportunities and other extracurriculars, the university also provides a wide range of work-study jobs. Students agree that having a job "isn't hard to balance because the university offers flexible hours. They really under-stand how hectic a student's life can become."

Traditional festivities also contribute to Miami's strong spirit. To honor one of their most famous graduates, the late reggae artist Bob Marley, the university annually hosts Marley Fest, a free reggae concert at South Beach. Architecture students carry out another annual tradition at Miami. Before homecoming, they build a boat, light it on fire, and set it out on Lake Osceola. Crowds of cheering students surround the lake to see whether the boat will sink or stay afloat. It is said that if the boat remains on top of the water the Miami Hurricanes will defeat their homecoming football rival.

> **"On weekends, many students explore the energetic life of Florida's southern coast, Coconut Grove, and South Beach."**

Undergrads laud the University of Miami for its abundant school spirit and respectable academic programs. Students find that encouragement from their professors, faculty, and their peers helps them become better people and prepare them for life after college. As one student claimed, "if you don't like the cold, but want to challenge yourself among palm trees and the beach, UM definitely fits the bill." —*Melissa Droller and Staff*

FYI

The three best things about attending the University of Miami are "the diversity, the Greek system, and it's a small school with 8,000 students—most people think it's a big school."

The three worst things about attending the University of Miami are "the parking is horrible, everything on campus is expensive, and the weather is so great that sometimes you just want to sit outside in the grass and forget about class."

The three things every student should do before graduating from the University of Miami are "go to the clubs on South Beach, go on a cruise to the Bahamas, and get involved in the volunteer activities Butler Volunteer Services offers."

One thing I wish I knew before coming here is "there is never any parking. If possible, try not to bring your car. It's impossible to find parking. They sell more spaces than there are!"

Georgia

Address: 141 College Avenue, Atlanta / Decatur, GA 30030
Phone: 404-471-6402
E-mail address: admissions@agnesscott.edu
Web site URL: www.agnesscott.edu
Location: urban
Founded: 1889
Private or Public: private
Religious affiliation: Presbyterian Church (USA)
Undergraduate enrollment: 879
Total enrollment: 887
Percent Male / Female: 0% / 100%

Percent Minority: 28.0%
Percent African-American: 18.0%
Percent Hispanic: 3.0%
Percent Asian: 4.0%
Percent in-state / out-of-state: 50% / 50%
Percent Pub HS: 80%
Fraternities: 0%
Sororities: 0%
Number of Applicants: 688
Percent Accepted: 77%
Percent Accepted who enroll: 45%
Entering: 241
Transfers: 25
Application Deadline: 1 Mar

Mean SAT: NA V, NA M
Middle 50% SAT range: 580–680 V, 530–640 M
Middle 50% ACT range: 24-29
Mean ACT: NA
3 Most popular majors: biology, English, psychology
Retention: 82%
Graduation rate: 66%
Library: 208,283 volumes
Tuition and Fees: $16,745 in; NA out
Room and Board: $6,900
On-campus housing: 98%
Financial aid, first-year: 72%

What is your favorite scary movie? *Scream 2*, perhaps? The beautiful college campus featured in the blockbuster movie is none other than all-female Agnes Scott College in Decatur, Georgia. Of course, Agnes Scott comes free of the gore and scary masks. The women who attend Agnes Scott swear that the luxurious buildings shown in the film are definitely for real and assert that the campus is one of the most appealing aspects of their school.

Beautiful Setting

Agnes Scott is a very small campus located six miles outside of Atlanta. According to one sophomore, "it only takes about 15 minutes to walk the entire campus." When asked what she most loved about her school, another student said, "I love the fact that it's a really nice-looking campus." The campus is built around the Quadrangle, simply called the "Quad," which one student described as "a nice,

green area in the middle of the campus." From the Quadrangle, one can soak in the splendor of Gothic architecture, which is a characteristic of many of the dorms and buildings on campus. According to the students, Agnes Scott possesses many other scenic locations where students can go to relax. Some cited the most peaceful place on campus as the amphitheater, an outdoor area that now largely goes unused. "A lot of people don't go down there, so it's a good place to go when you need to be alone." Another sophomore mentioned the "Secret Garden." To get there, "you have to walk through the first floor of the library, then walk down some steps, when you come to this really cute walled-in courtyard. It's a fun place to be." The "Secret Garden," however, is currently not accessible to students due to a massive renovation project that Agnes Scott is now undergoing. Hoping to increase enrollment to 1,000 students, renovations are being made to a number of buildings, including the library and the student center. These renovations should be complete in a few years. Nonetheless, the beauty and seclusion of the campus are still present and the students make sure to take advantage of it. Being on a small campus in a small city, however, does come with a number of drawbacks. Most students have cars, including freshmen, because certain student necessities are not readily available on campus. One student stated, "I wish we had a grocery store on-campus. To get to the nearest grocery store or the drug store, you have to have a car." Another student complained that "Agnes Scott really needs more coffeehouse sorts of establishments. I get tired of having to walk to a coffeehouse all the time." Despite any complaints the campus might garner from students, most students say they do feel safe. One student contended that "the public safety officers are pretty on top of everything, so I'm not terribly worried."

It is also on campus that Agnes Scott students celebrate Black Cat, which one student summed up as "our equivalent of homecoming." During the week-long celebration, the four classes—frosh to seniors—engage in "Color Wars." Each class is assigned a color, which it uses to determine a mascot. Students play jokes on each other during the week and upperclassmen try to guess what the frosh have chosen as their mascot. The celebration includes singing of "sister songs" and a bonfire. The juniors put on the Junior Production, a two-hour extravaganza consisting of skits poking fun at first-years, professors, the administration, and Agnes Scott in general. The week culminates in a big formal on Saturday night, where one of the classes is announced as the winner, based on various competitions, such as the one for best hall and door decorations.

Classes: Small but Challenging

Students of Agnes Scott say they study hard. As one student put it, the classes are "not-too-hard, but it's hard to get an A." The college sets specific and distribution standards for its students. The specific standards consist of two courses in En-

glish composition, intermediate competency in a foreign language, and two semester hours of physical education. The distribution standards require students to take courses in literature, history, philosophy, fine arts, and social sciences. In addition, one math course must be taken, as well as a natural science course including laboratory work. Regarding these requirements, one student said, "they're pretty lenient, really. Whatever you major in, you're going to go ahead and fulfill the standards somehow." Though the requirements are generally well accepted, one student did say that "parts of the requirements are sort of stupid."

Almost all students said that getting into classes was rarely a problem. Registration, as one student put it, "is very laid back. You fill out a registration card, go to the registration place at the assigned time, and they put it in the computer." Most students who do not get into their desired courses are freshman because they register a few days after the upperclasswomen and, as a result, some of the bigger, introductory classes may already be filled. One student praised academics at Agnes Scott as giving "lots of opportunities. You get to take a lot of classes. Very few classes fill up, and even then, they open up a new section." Students insist that class size is small. "I've never had a class with more than 30 people, and as a freshman, I was in a class composed of only four people including myself," said one student. The small size, however, is also a cause of grievance among many of the students. One sophomore said that due to the small enrollment, professors "care too much about attendance. They always know who's absent." Another student cited the small size of the college as contributing to the fact that "sometimes, they don't have as many classes as you might want." If course selection is indeed a problem, however, Agnes Scott students are given the option of taking classes at any other Atlanta university. "It's great because you can take the course and the school pays for your cab fare," exclaimed one student.

Students unanimously declared the sciences as the harder classes, although English is also rumored to have some fairly difficult courses. Biology and English appear to be the strongest departments, as well as the most popular majors. The English department has drawn a number of prominent female writers to come and speak, including Alice Walker, Jamaica Kincaid, and Margaret Atwood. Professors are reportedly "very accessible. They have office hours and the faculty hall doors are always open." Only professors teach courses, with the exception of instructors who teach foreign languages or lab components to the science classes, although in the latter case, there is always a professor involved as well. Students have generally been very pleased with their professors and appreciate the interdisciplinary approaches sometimes used in class. Another aspect of academic life that Agnes Scott students are particularly happy with is the International Education Office, which provides high quality study abroad programs to upperclasswomen.

The Draw of Atlanta

Although Agnes Scott students do study hard and some freshman say they stay on campus all the time, most of the students enjoy leaving the Agnes Scott campus to do some partying. "We're really close to downtown Atlanta, so we just go to parties there, usually frat parties at Georgia Tech," said one student. For those interested in dancing, there are reportedly lots of clubs for the over-21 crowd. Students without cars can take the MARTA, the local public transport system, and arrive in the city within 15 minutes. One freshman did say that, "There are some clubs where you only need to be 18, but some of the over-21 clubs have a college night anyway." While Atlanta may be popular, there are also things to do on the Agnes Scott campus. "They show movies on the Quad and sometimes we even have big-name comedians come, such as Bobcat Goldthwaite and Tommy Davidson," stated one student. Official parties are also thrown on campus, but one student said that "it's hard to get guys to come here from their own campuses." Free beer is always served at these parties, but "it's really silly because only about 10 people on the campus are old enough to drink and the administration is very strict about underage drinking." Other popular weekend options include eating out at restaurants or coffeehouses in Decatur.

Bad Food, Great Rooms

Many Agnes Scott students enjoy eating off-campus because the dining hall food does not receive terribly good reviews. One student did concede, however, "it's not bad for dining hall food. You can always find something edible." All Agnes Scott students are required to purchase a meal plan, which, in addition to a certain number of meals a week, includes a declining balance used when the dining hall is not open. Agnes Scott students have the option of going to Ebans dining hall or the snack bar, once termed Scotland Yard. One student griped about the dining hall hours, saying that, "the hours are pretty narrow and the system is sometimes slow." Vegetarian students are accommodated in the dining hall. "They have veggie burgers, yogurt, the salad bar, and there's always at least one vegetarian entrée." Due to the short hours, however, one student said, "I have to depend on the snack bar quite a bit." Students who go to the snack bar can choose from fast-food-style food, namely hamburgers. One upperclasswoman said, "Actually, I usually eat out unless I'm broke. There are good restaurants in the area, particularly in downtown Atlanta."

While the food is not stellar, Agnes Scott students certainly rave about the dorms. One student described the dorms as "huge." First-years live in two dorms, Winship and Walters. Most dorms have air-conditioning, and many frosh get singles. Due to the renovations, however, many students are now required to have roommates, which "isn't as luxurious, but it's still nice," said one student. All rooms have cable access and a phone line on each side, so it is possible for those students living in singles to use both a telephone and a modem at the same time, if necessary. After first year, room assignments are decided by lottery, with preference given to upperclasswomen. Agnes Scott students are required to live on campus, unless they are over 21 or are married. The college, however, recently purchased a nearby apartment building, which is also considered on-campus housing. In certain dorms, students have the option of living in language halls, where TAs of a particular language can be found and where foreign-language tables are held.

In Their Spare Time

Students like to joke that there are two stereotypical views of the Agnes Scott student: either she is a "preppy, Southern, well-off girl" or else she is a lesbian. They are quick to point out, though, that at Agnes Scott, neither of these stereotypes constitutes the majority. When they aren't watching TV or going to work out at Woodruff, the gym, the women at Agnes Scott also engage in extracurricular activities. According to one student, however, "there doesn't seem to be much of a presence from what I've seen. Community service isn't all that popular." Nevertheless, there are clubs for those interested in joining. There are a number of ethnic clubs for students of color and service clubs such as Circle K and the Campus Civitan, which focuses on helping the disabled. There are also organizations for ecology buffs, as well as outdoor activities, such as hiking and rafting.

Aside from extracurricular activities, some students do participate in sports. As one student declared, "We have them, but they're not very visible. Only the people who play them are into them." There isn't a particularly high level of school spirit, but students do attend some of the games nonetheless. The most visible teams at Agnes Scott are the softball team and the rugby team. Students not interested in intercollegiate sports can participate in activities at Woodruff gym. One sports club, the Century Club, makes a goal of running 100 miles by the end of the semester.

> **"We sometimes get flak for being a women's college, but they don't prepare us to be housewives. They're trying to empower us."**

Set in the heart of Georgia, Agnes Scott College provides a rigorous academic environment and the pleasures of both the suburbs and the big city. Agnes Scott students love their school and, for the most part, have never regretted their decision to go there. One sophomore said, "I definitely think this is a good school and that it's preparing me for my future." Regarding the fact that Agnes Scott is a women's school, another student commented, "We sometimes get flak for being a women's college, but they don't prepare us to be housewives. They're trying to empower us." —*Shu-Ping Shen and Staff*

FYI

The three best things about attending Agnes Scott are "there are no TAs—all classes are taught by professors; it's near Atlanta, a great city with many opportunities for internships and things for college kids to do; and classes are small, so there are lots of chances for class discussion."

The three worst things about attending Agnes Scott are "there is a great deal of bigotry and racism; not much variety in terms of things to do; and it is all girls, and some people here preach that virtually all men are evil and should not be trusted."

The three things every student should do before graduating from Agnes Scott are "study abroad—the school pays for it; get engaged—there's this great tradition that when you get engaged, you get thrown into this stinky pond behind the alumnae house; and mud wrestle on field day during Black Cat week."

One thing I'd like to have known before coming here is "that virtually every girl goes home for the weekend. The campus is very dead after about 7 P.M., and on the weekends there is no one around."

Emory University

Address: 200 B. Jones Center, Atlanta, GA 30322	**Percent African-American:** 10.0%	**Middle 50% SAT range:** 620–700 V, 645–715 M
Phone: 800-727-6036	**Percent Hispanic:** 3.0%	
E-mail address: admiss@emory.edu	**Percent Asian:** 15.0%	**Middle 50% ACT range:** 27–31
Web site URL: www.emory.edu	**Percent in-state/out-of-state:** 19%/81%	**Mean ACT:** NA
Location: urban	**Percent Pub HS:** 70%	**3 Most popular majors:** biology, political science, business
Founded: 1836	**Fraternities:** 33%	
Private or Public: private	**Sororities:** 33%	
Religious affiliation: United Methodist	**Number of Applicants:** 9,800	**Retention:** 92%
Undergraduate enrollment: 5,700	**Percent Accepted:** 41%	**Graduation rate:** 90%
	Percent Accepted who enroll: 30%	**Library:** 2,700,000 volumes
Total enrollment: 11,000	**Entering:** 1,200	**Tuition and Fees:** $23,130 in; $23,130 out
Percent Male/Female: 48%/52%	**Transfers:** 125	**Room and Board:** $7,750
	Application Deadline: 15 Jan	**On-campus housing:** 100%
Percent Minority: 28.0%	**Mean SAT:** NA V, NA M	**Financial aid, first-year:** 57%

Emory veers from tradition with its unconventional mascot—a skeleton named Dooley. Though he may not seem as tough as his bulldog and tiger rivals, during one week of the school year Dooley's human impersonator has the greatest kind of power—the ability to end a class by running in and water-gunning the professor. Though students do not claim that Emory is perfect, they agree that it, like Dooley, it is still alive and kicking.

Learning and Loving It

Students rave about Emory's academics. "Professors epitomize the idea of being there for the sake of the students," said one sophomore. Wole Soyinka, a Nobel laureate in literature, teaches at Emory, as does former U.S. president and political science professor, Jimmy Carter. Foreign-language professors are also cited as extremely good. While an estimated one-third of the freshman class enters with pre-med hopes (and a substantial percentage of the others are aiming for pre-law), tough introductory classes and the appeal of other programs lower these numbers by graduation.

Biology, psychology, and political science are the most popular majors, though business and English are also said to be quite strong as well. The physics and math departments are not so well regarded as the "material is tough to understand, and the professors even tougher." Students call Emory competitive, but "not cutthroat" and report that it has "a motivating atmosphere." One sophomore said that upon arrival, Emory students could be classified into two groups: "People who are ticked off that they didn't get into Harvard or Yale and those who recognize that Emory is a very good school." Students speculate that some of the competitive atmosphere may be a result of the former of the two mentalities, but claim that the sense of competition among classmates dissipates after they settle in.

In order to graduate, Emory students must fulfill distribution requirements that include courses in the natural sciences, history, aesthetics and values, a yearly writing requirement, and four one-credit physical education courses. While the physical education requirement includes a mandatory health class that some called "useless, unless you really want to know the physical manifestations of sexually transmitted diseases," students enjoy classes in social dancing and tennis as a break from the rigors of academic subjects.

Those looking for academic opportunities off-campus discover that Emory also offers popular study-abroad programs in countries including Mexico, Kenya, France, India, Israel, Italy, Japan, and Russia through its Center for International Programs Abroad (CIPA).

Content with Their Campus

Students describe Emory as "gorgeous. It is hilly and beautifully landscaped, complete with ravines and wonderful architecture." Emory is well-endowed, notably by Coca-Cola, and has funds that are specified for construction only. "I've been here for a year and a half and have seen one stretch of sidewalk torn up and replaced many times over. This place is well kept." Emory instituted a "Master Plan" four years ago that is still in place to alter the look of the campus. $250 million is committed to 9 new buildings, including a performing arts center, science centers, new recreational spaces; and continuing the plan of becoming more of a pedestrian campus are projects to remove cars and create more green space and walkways. Emory students can also boast about beautiful southern weather to their Ivy friends.

Awesome Atlanta

"Atlanta is an awesome city," said one student, an opinion which seems to be the consensus at Emory. Students are enamored with the variety of options that living in a big city provides. Emory itself is located in a peaceful, upscale neighborhood of ante-bellum houses, where the movie *Driving Miss Daisy* was filmed. Public transportation is described as mediocre, and as a result students say "a car is key." Freshmen, though, aren't permitted to have them. For students who do make it into the city, Braves games, the High Museum, the Fox Theater, and a shopping complex known as Underground Atlanta are popular destinations, as are the Lenox and Phipps malls, which run shuttles from campus on the weekends. Little Five Points is a "funky" area filled with coffee shops and retro stores, and the Buckhead neighborhood is a popular destination for students interested in clubbing at the Chili Pepper and the Cotton Club.

On-Campus Fun

"The only parties thrown on campus are all pretty much fraternity functions, so you really won't leave Emory without seeing Frat Row." The Greek system plays a big part in life at Emory. While "non-Greeks don't feel left out for the most part," some students express discontent that social options seem very limited from the perspective of a freshman deciding whether to rush. "The Greek system is too big, and it's too easy to feel excluded, but those who don't rush will find their niche with time." Although parties are not too wild for the most part, one student reported, "Two of the most raucous parties in the history of humanity have been thrown here, but are in danger of extinction at the hands of Emory administration: Bid Day, which celebrates the frats taking in their new pledges, and Dooley's Ball, on Halloween." Alcohol is prevalent and drug use is "somewhat surprisingly common, but primarily limited to marijuana," students report.

> **"Emory is a southern school with a 'northern, accepting mentality.'"**

Emory students are a very involved group. Popular organizations include the *Wheel* (a bi-weekly newspaper), Emory Hillel, Black Student Alliance, and the Student Government Association. Volunteer Emory is enormously popular, and is noted as "one of the strongest components of Emory's extracurricular scene." Emory has a strong Division III athletic program, but lacks (in the case of football) or has relatively weak (in the case of basketball) popular spectator sports.

Standard Fare

Students describe the food as "standard cafeteria fare—decent." Freshmen and on-campus upperclassmen are required to have a meal plan, with the latter permitted to choose a debit-card-like á la carte system. The "DUC" (Dobbs University Center) houses the main dining hall, in addition to the mailroom and bookstore. Cox Hall contains a number of fast-food restaurants including Burger King and Chick-Fil-A. Students also report that many eat in off-campus establishments.

Woodruff Center (named for the former Coca-Cola chairman) is the main gym and contains an indoor track, swimming pools, weight rooms, a dance studio, and a rock-climbing wall. Emory's largest library is the Woodruff library, and is open for studying twenty-four hours a day.

Freshmen are required to live on campus, primarily in doubles, and are, for the most part, housed in dorms that do not contain upperclassmen. All freshmen floors have an RA and two SAs (sophomore advisors). The Complex, which contains Thomas, Hopkins, and Smith Halls, is said to be spacious and convenient. Turman Hall is extremely far from central campus and Dobbs Hall, a newer dorm, has very small rooms. In addition, upperclassmen have the option of living in on-campus apartments.

A Community?

One RA noted that dorms provide the closest sense of community at Emory. Students bemoan the general lack of spirit and pride in their school. The university is statistically very diverse (with large populations of Asian, African-American, and Jewish students), but "certainly divided along many demographic lines." Students applaud Emory's tough stance against discrimination, but note that while homosexuality is accepted, "you don't really see it out in the open." Emory is a Southern school with a "Northern, accepting mentality." There are plenty of conservative students, but on the whole, the university is "the most liberal place in the region. We've had unfortunate incidents of intolerance here, but thankfully the great majority of students are not narrow-minded." Students are happy to be at Emory, saying that "Emory offers a great education at the expense of a smaller community. Prepare not only to work hard in the classroom, but also to seek out all of the opportunities to have a good time." —*Ellen Lee Moskowitz and Staff*

FYI

The three best things about attending Emory are "Emory strives to be innovative; internships are available at the Carter Center, at CNN, and at the Centers for Disease Control; and Emory genuinely values each student."

The three worst things about attending Emory are "how freshmen are not allowed to have cars on campus; the area surrounding Emory is far from a college town; and to get downtown, one must wait thirty minutes or more for a bus, followed by a thirty minute bus ride to a subway station."

The three things that every student should do before graduating from Emory are "to participate in the study abroad program, to apply for the scholars program, and to do an internship at the Carter Center."

One thing that I'd like to have known before coming here is "nothing—Emory sent tons of information about the university before I even applied, so I was not in the dark about the social or academic community at Emory."

Georgia Institute of Technology

Address: 225 North Avenue, Atlanta, GA 30332-0320
Phone: 404-894-4154
E-mail address: admission@success.gatech.edu
Web site URL: www.gatech.edu
Location: urban
Founded: 1885
Private or Public: public
Religious affiliation: none
Undergraduate enrollment: 10,255
Total enrollment: 14,072
Percent Male/Female: 71%/28%
Percent Minority: 30.0%

Percent African-American: 9.0%
Percent Hispanic: 3.0%
Percent Asian: 15.0%
Percent in-state/out-of-state: 66.0%/NA
Percent Pub HS: 75%
Fraternities: 25%
Sororities: 25%
Number of Applicants: 7,583
Percent Accepted: 69%
Percent Accepted who enroll: 44%
Entering: 2,307
Transfers: 455
Application Deadline: 15 Jan
Mean SAT: 630 V, 674 M

Middle 50% SAT range: 590–690 V, 630–730 M
Middle 50% ACT range: NA
Mean ACT: NA
3 Most popular majors: industrial engineering, electrical engineering, and mechanical engineering
Retention: 88.0%
Graduation rate: 70.0%
Library: 3,500,000 volumes
Tuition and Fees: $3,108 in; $10,350 out
Room and Board: $5,700
On-campus housing: 95%
Financial aid, first-year: 43%

Only at Georgia Tech can you find electrical engineers who, in accordance with tradition, yearly deactivate university alarm systems to steal a lighted T from atop Tech Tower. In fact, the mechanical engineers are known to help the electrical engineers in lowering the giant T to the ground. Although this tradition is a fairly expensive one, supposedly the university accounts for the T's replacement in their annual budget. However, only one offense is allowed per student, because after that the university reportedly draws the line between Yellow Jacket pride and crime.

Hit the Books, Buzz

Despite one student's claim that "Georgia Tech has a rigorous workload," students seem happy to work hard because of the great opportunities that await them after graduation. Georgia Tech's co-op program offers undergraduates semesters off to work in paid internship positions for course credit. Students must sign up by sophomore year to participate in this program. "Usually students stick to working for the same company throughout their time at GT and then end up working for them after graduation," one student said. However, while students are on campus, most are inundated with courses in math, computers, and engineering. One student pointed out, "We are definitely an engineering school, full of insane students who want to major in electrical or chemical engineering"—considered Tech's most difficult majors. Another competitive department is architecture, also known as "archi-torture."

Although GT is notorious for its difficult engineering courses, one student cautions, "If you think you'll have it easy in humanities and English courses because we're a tech school, think again because they're definitely just as hard." Unfortunately, students can't dodge these classes, either. All GT students must fulfill a core curriculum requirement, including courses in English, math, science, and the humanities. Most students try to get the core out of the way their first year. However, "the requirements are not a big deal," one undergrad said. Students agree that "the core helps you figure out what you want to specialize in before declaring your major," which is often done by the end of the first year.

After selecting a department, students are assigned an advisor, but it is "not difficult to change advisors, or your entire major for that matter." Many students enter Tech as a chemical engineering major and then change quickly after discovering that the workload is too strenuous for them. While the workload can be overwhelming, one undergrad said that "it is tolerable and doable, but if you don't work hard, you'll be gone after one term. It really is all about time management and how you want to use your free time." Some easier departments at GT reportedly include management and international relations. "Among engineering students, majors in international relations and management are known as a joke," said one student.

Students praise Georgia Tech's system for course registration—everything is done over the Internet. Although priority is given to athletes and upperclassmen, students do not have many problems getting into their first-choice classes. All classes are taught by professors, and graduate students offer smaller recitation sections for more individual attention. As students take higher-level classes, class size "slims down and more professors teach smaller classes," one student said. Another noted that "all professors are approachable and cool about answering all kinds of questions outside of the classroom." In all departments, grading is considered fair but tough. Although there is no official regulation on grade distribution, one student estimated that "about one-fifth of a class will get an A." Generally, students are pleased with GT's academics and the university's concentration on technology.

Georgia Tech requires all students to own a computer, and a lot of class work is computer-oriented. One impressed student said she "never thought she could have a class discussion without ever leaving her dorm room."

Buzz'n Around

In comparison to larger state schools, Georgia Tech does not have a huge social scene, but as one undergrad reported, "For an engineering school, there's lots of social activity and lots of parties." Although students say that Greek life does not dominate the school's social scene, many undergrads rush a fraternity or sorority. GT students stress that "you should at least rush because you meet a lot of great people," and another student added, "It's better to have rushed rather than not." On the GT campus, which is divided between East and West Campuses, fraternities are on East Campus and host most parties, which are open to all students.

However, the school does have fairly strict rules on alcohol, and one student concluded that "it's more of a BYOB [Bring Your Own Beer] kind of scene." The bigger parties of the year include a springtime, week-long Yacht Party and homecoming parties. The fraternities also participate in the traditional Rabbling Wreck Parade, in which each fraternity builds a car out of scrap metal and parades its creation around campus. Outside fraternities, parties in the International House and in off-campus housing are known to be sources of fun.

Many students also go into Atlanta on the weekends. Since bars are generally strict about IDs, clubs and bars predominantly attract upperclassmen. However, some nearby clubs host 18-and-over nights, which are popular among freshmen. Clubs that draw the Tech crowd include Northside Tavern, El Amigos, and Masquerade. While many students tend to go out in groups, casual dating also exists at Georgia Tech. As one student pointed out, "Girls definitely have the advantage in dating because there are three times as many men as there are women." As far as gay life, one student said, "It isn't really noticeable, but the campus supports an active gay and lesbian organization." According to another student, "Because we're in the South, there is still some unspoken homophobia."

In contrast to the party-hard fraternities and sororities, Georgia Tech also has Greek organizations that focus on community service and business. Students encourage involvement in "some of Tech's thousands of extracurricular organizations," like student government; MOVE, a community service club; and SWARM, a spirit group. Most undergrads "are involved in something outside of academics." Student organizations have been known to bring some big names to campus, including comedians Adam Sandler and Paula Poundstone.

Sporting events also offer students reasons to socialize. Basketball and football are Tech's largest spectator sports, but school pride extends to all athletic events, and most games attract a large cheering section. Tech baseball has a strong winning tradition, and the golf team has done well in past years. Evidence of widespread spirit covers the campus through Yellow Jacket clothing and spirit posters, and when it rains, the campus is dotted with Yellow Jacket umbrellas. One undergrad said that without a doubt, everyone is proud of "Buzz, our Yellow Jacket mascot."

Housing and Facilities

Most Georgia Tech students start their college careers living with other members of their class in a program called Freshman Experience. Although the program is not mandatory, one student guessed that "about 95 percent of freshmen participate." This program allows freshmen to live together in dorms with upperclassmen peer leaders, known as PLs. For the most part, students agree that "PLs are there to be your friend and help you adjust to college life." PLs also organize movie trips and socials that "help lonely freshmen find an instant group of friends." Students say the program "helps to form class unity among freshmen" and that "it's a great way to get to know your class." Of the freshmen dorms, Fitten and Montag are popular choices, as is Freemen which is known for its "quieter atmosphere." In short, one student summed up Freshman Experience as "just a lot of fun."

Those who choose not to participate in Freshman Experience can either commute from home or live in upperclass dorms. The dorms are divided between East and West Campus; most Freshman Experience dorms are on East Campus. Each dorm has a study lounge and air-conditioning; most also have workout rooms and TV rooms. Some dorms are single-sex and require members of the opposite sex to be escorted into the buildings. While recognizing the inconvenience, one student said, "This policy is for our own protection, and everyone generally accepts that." Another option, popular among upperclassmen, is to live in campus apartments, which were built for the Summer Olympic Games in 1996. Residents describe these accommodations as "new, plush apartments that are in high demand."

Georgia Tech dining options include typical cafeteria services, a campus food court, and local restaurants. Each campus, East and West, has its own dining hall, Britain and Woodruff respectively. GT does not require a meal plan except for participants in Freshman Experience. Although the food is "typical institutional food," the dining halls are "clean and offer a great place to socialize with friends," one student said. Another noted that the "vegetarian options are the best." In one undergrad's opinion, "West Campus has three times better food!" However, if institutional food is not your style, the Georgia Tech Student Center offers a food court that includes a Burger King, Pizza Hut, McDonald's, Chick-Fil-A, and more. Conveniently, these establishments accept GT "buzz cards" that bill students' accounts directly.

The Student Center also houses the university post office and student lounges. Since the center is open 24 hours a day, many students find the dining tables and lounges "provide a great place to study." Undergrads also study in empty classrooms, the library, or dorm lounges. However, many find that "computers are crucial for all class work, so studying in front of your desktop in your room is usually the norm."

> **"Everyone is proud of 'Buzz, our Yellow Jacket mascot.'"**

Taking a break from studying, students flock to their intramural fields and Athletic Complex, which one student described simply as "huge!" It is fully equipped with an Olympic-size pool (which was used in the 1996 Summer Games), a weight room, aerobics rooms, racquetball courts, a jogging track, and tennis courts. Located right outside West Campus dorms, the intramural fields and Athletic Complex are convenient for West

Campus residents. Not even limited daylight keeps GT students from exercise, because the intramural fields "have new lights, and are open 24 hours a day."

Undergrads say it takes about 25 to 30 minutes to walk completely around campus. Therefore, having a car "is absolutely a good thing," but on the flip side, one student warned, "Parking is atrocious, and the permits are too expensive." To limit the parking problem, freshmen cannot have cars during their first term. Students also recommend bikes to get from one side of the campus to another. Generally, the campus is "pretty modern" with "lots of interesting buildings," one student observed, "because all buildings are designed by architecture students or professors."

Although Georgia Tech is in the city and "you can see the skyscrapers of Atlanta" from campus, one student explained that "there are still lots of trees and open spaces. There are benches everywhere and lots of places to go to find fresh air." Although students have their complaints about Georgia Tech's workload, most seem willing to put the time into their courses to reap the rewards of an engineering diploma. Georgia Tech offers some of the best instruction available and nearby Atlanta some of the best opportunities. Through it all, one student said, "We live among friendly and outgoing people where there's potential to meet new people every day. I guess it's what Georgians like to call 'southern hospitality.'" —*Jeff Kaplow and Staff*

FYI

The three best things about attending Georgia Tech are "the city of Atlanta, MARTA—the city's great rail system, and the campus is beautiful."

The three worst things about attending Georgia Tech are "TBS—Tech Bitch Syndrome—because the guy to girl ratio is 3 to 1, girls here often treat guys as if they're disposable; the food; and the school is often underrated."

The three things every student should do before graduating from Georgia Tech are "to watch the sunrise from the top of the EE building, watch a play at the Fox Theater, and rush a frat to see what it's all about."

One thing I'd like to have known before coming here is "how bad first-year housing is."

Morehouse College

Address: 830 Westview Drive, SW Atlanta, GA 30314

Phone: 404-215-2632

E-mail address: apatillo@morehouse.edu

Web site URL: www.morehouse.edu

Location: urban

Founded: 1867

Private or Public: private

Religious affiliation: none

Undergraduate enrollment: 3,148

Total enrollment: 3,148

Percent Male/Female: 100%/0%

Percent Minority: 98.0%

Percent African-American: 98.0%

Percent Hispanic: 0.0%

Percent Asian: 0.0%

Percent in-state/out-of-state: 24.0%

Percent Pub HS: 82%

Fraternities: 2%

Sororities: 0%

Number of Applicants: 2,813

Percent Accepted: 64%

Percent Accepted who enroll: 46%

Entering: 828

Transfers: 85

Application Deadline: 15 Feb

Mean SAT: 526 V, 530 M

Middle 50% SAT range: 440–680 V, 470–680 M

Middle 50% ACT range: NA

Mean ACT: 23

3 Most popular majors: engineering, business administration, and biology

Retention: 82%

Graduation rate: 31.0%

Library: 550,000 volumes

Tuition and Fees: $9,624 in; $9,624 out

Room and Board: $6,214

On-campus housing: 45%

Financial aid, first-year: 85%

Undergrads may learn engineering or biology in their time at Morehouse, but most important, students say, they learn the true meaning and value of the word brotherhood. For many of Morehouse's illustrious alumni, such as Dr. Martin Luther King, Jr., brotherhood has been much more than just a buzzword. Morehouse, known affectionately by its graduates as the "House," changed their lives and, in turn, allowed them to change the world.

Men Only!

The only historically African-American all-male college in the United States, Morehouse prides itself on its traditions of brotherhood, which date back to the college's beginnings in 1867. Incoming students are taught the meaning of brotherhood early in their time at Morehouse with the tradition of Spirit Night. In this traditional ceremony, underclassmen link their arms and form a circle that upperclassmen try to break. Through this struggle, Morehouse men say they learn to hold on to their brotherhood above all else. As one freshman said, "Spirit Night made me realize how much I could trust my new friends. I'd only known them for a little while, but we all held on, supporting one another like we'd been together forever."

The tradition of brotherhood is supported by Morehouse's strong academic reputation, reflected today in the extensive General Studies requirements, which comprise 68 of the 124 credits needed to graduate. Each student must complete one-year courses in composition, literature, history of civilizations (which has a special focus on ancient African civilizations), social science, and physical education. Also required is one semester each of art, music, speech, religion, philosophy, physical science, and biological science, as well as two years of a foreign language. The completion of this rigorous academic program lends truth to the school's unofficial motto: "You can always tell a Morehouse man, but you can never tell him much." Academics are further supplemented with cultural instruction. Students are required to attend the Crown Forum, a weekly address by prominent African-American leaders that many students see as a vital part of the House's so-cial mission. "The speakers at the Crown Forum are one of the most important parts of a Morehouse education. Knowledge is just knowledge without the ability to make a difference in the real world. The speakers teach us that," one student said.

One major benefit of Morehouse's urban Atlanta location is its membership in the Atlanta University Center (AUC), a consortium of five schools including Clark Atlanta, Morris Brown, the Interdenominational Theological Center, and Morehouse's sister school, all-female Spelman. Morehouse students can cross-register at any of the other four AUC schools, provided that the chair of the department at each school grants permission and that the course is not offered at Morehouse if it is within the student's major.

Pre-professionals Rule

The most popular majors at Morehouse, biology, business, and engineering, hint at the student body's strong preference toward pre-professional subjects. For students who desire further challenge and achievement, the college offers "3-2" programs in engineering and architecture. After three years at Morehouse, students can earn an advanced degree (in two years) at such schools as Georgia Tech or the University of Michigan. Morehouse also has an honors program, beginning in the freshman year, that offers dedicated students more advanced classes and a special diploma. Students report that a definite "easy A" is Intro to Visual Art, whose toughest requirement reportedly involves "just visiting a few museums in the area."

Morehouse is also notable for its professors. Spike Lee, one alumnus, returns to lecture fairly often. Students describe their relationships with professors as "extremely close." Many students say that it is common for undergrads and teachers to have lunch together, or go to museums or parks outside of class. One student claimed that he got invited to dinner at professors' homes on a regular basis.

Although some students said that the academics at Morehouse can be very competitive, many declared that the tradition of brotherhood on campus extends into the classroom. "At Morehouse all of your fellow students want you to do well. If you are having trouble, all you have to do is ask the person sitting next to you. People are always tutoring one another," said one student.

Where'd Everybody Go?

One statistic that attests to Morehouse's challenging academic regimen is its low student retention rate. One student declared "it's definitely a tough school to be successful in—people drop out of here like flies," while another added that his junior class of 600 began as a freshman class of 900. Other academic problems related by undergrads include difficulty with getting into required classes. Occasionally, seniors are forced to postpone their graduation because they were shut out of one or two classes, students said. Students cited financial-aid problems as a common reason for leaving Morehouse.

Undergrads report that they spend much of their time studying at one of several libraries in the close vicinity of Morehouse. Woodruff Library, the central library for the five-member institutions of the Atlanta University Center, gets mixed reviews. While some students reported that it is especially good for "social" studying, others declared that the number and variety of students who share the library make resources hard to come by. Students who desire more quiet studying travel to the libraries at either Georgia State University or Emory. Hard-core studying takes place in the Frederick Douglass Commons, a student center at Morehouse where students have access to study rooms and materials. "What you learn here, they don't teach anywhere else."

> "These programs enable us to teach our code of brotherhood to younger students in Atlanta who are particularly in need of love and respect," one student said.

Undergrads live in seven dorms on campus. Graves Hall, the oldest building on campus, is reportedly the best, as it has air-conditioning. Hubert is said to be the least appealing, with no air-conditioning and small rooms. Students can unwind at Kilgore, a dorm that houses pool and Ping-Pong tables, big screen TVs, and a snack shop that stays open until midnight. Dorms have friendly rivalries and are unofficially identified by Greek letters and hand signals. Dorm restrictions include no alcohol and specific visiting hours for women. Some residents call restricted visitation "an initiation for freshmen," but admit that the rules are obeyed without much active enforcement. Undergrads seeking relaxed rules of conduct say the best bet is to move off-campus. Most students say they prefer private apartments on Fair Street to those in the West End, where there is college-owned housing removed from the main dorm area. However, residents say that facilities in this area are "run-down."

Students who live on campus are required to be on a full meal plan that they describe as "below average," but "improving." Those desperate for improved fare eat out at places like Spegal's, a popular pub and restaurant, or fast-food restaurants at West End, a mall close to campus.

Athletics play an important role at Morehouse. The most popular teams, football and basketball, draw dedicated fan support, particularly when Morehouse plays its perennial rivals Howard and Tuskegee. Students say the tennis team is also extremely popular and successful. Archer Hall, the gym, underwent several renovations for the 1996 Summer Olympics.

Reaching Out

Students say they are particularly proud of the extracurricular activities at Morehouse, citing a strong devotion to community service programs, particularly several mentoring programs in which students act as big brothers or academic tutors to inner-city youth. "These programs enable us to teach our code of brotherhood to younger students in Atlanta who are particularly in need of love and respect," one student said. Students are also quick to point out that the popular Glee Club performed at President Clinton's first inauguration. Other organizations, such as the Pre-Law Society, the Health Care Society, and the Business Association, reflect the high aspirations of Morehouse students.

Although some students report that they were skeptical about attending an all-male college at first, many say that Morehouse provides them with the best of both worlds. They feel the all-male environment on campus allows them to cultivate a strong feeling of brotherhood. In fact, undergrads say, the high female-to-male ratio of the AUC provides students with more than adequate opportunities to meet and party with women.

Students say that the Morehouse social scene is "perfect for the challenging academic atmosphere." The campus is reportedly calm during the week, to allow for plenty of studying. Over the weekend, however, students can choose from innumerable parties, AUC unity rallies, picnics, concerts, or excursions to a local nightclub called Club Garage. Many students say that homecoming is one of the prime social events of the year and is traditionally a time for graduates and their families to return to the House to reminisce. The largest social event of the year,

Freaknic, is one that is alternately loved or despised by the student body. While many students report the annual event, which consumes most of Atlanta, is the best party in the entire country, others complain that the large number of visiting students, reportedly 20,000 in recent years, absolutely prevents the students from being able to drive anywhere in downtown Atlanta.

Students consistently say that the one aspect that makes Morehouse unique is its deeply ingrained sense of tradition and brotherhood. As one student said, "What you learn here, they don't teach anywhere else. And I don't mean pre-law. I mean the overwhelming sense that you are truly a part of something great and that you can accomplish anything you want, simply because you are a Morehouse man. Even today, when students say they are only attending their college for a diploma and a few connections, being a Morehouse man still means something."—*Dylan Howard and Staff*

FYI

The three best things about attending Morehouse are "Spirit Night, solidarity, and being a Morehouse man."

The three worst things about attending Morehouse are "no women in classes, calm social scene during the week, and tough academics."

The three things that every student must do before graduating are "go to Freaknic, tutor inner-city youth, and go to Spegal's."

One thing I'd like to have known before coming here is "how many people drop out after the first year."

Spelman College

Address: 350 Spelman Lane, South West Atlanta, GA 30314
Phone: 800-982-2411
E-mail address: admiss@spelman.edu
Web site URL: www.spelman.edu
Location: urban
Founded: 1881
Private or Public: private
Religious affiliation: none
Undergraduate enrollment: 1,899
Total enrollment: 1,899
Percent Male / Female: 0% / 100%
Percent Minority: 99.0%

Percent African-American: 96.0%
Percent Hispanic: 1.0%
Percent Asian: 3.0%
Percent in-state / out-of-state: 22%/78%
Percent Pub HS: NA
Fraternities: 0%
Sororities: 5%
Number of Applicants: 3,102
Percent Accepted: 53%
Percent Accepted who enroll: 35%
Entering: 500
Transfers: 0
Application Deadline: 1 Feb

Mean SAT: 549 V, 524 M
Middle 50% SAT range: 500–590 V, 480–580 M
Middle 50% ACT range: NA
Mean ACT: 22
3 Most popular majors: psychology, biology, English
Retention: 86.0%
Graduation rate: 77.0%
Library: 350,000 volumes
Tuition and Fees: $9,250 in; $9,250 out
Room and Board: $6,560
On-campus housing: 62%
Financial aid, first-year: 80%

Spelman College strives to give each of its students more than just a diploma after four years of hard work; it also wants its graduates to walk away with a strong sense of cultural identity. As the first institute of higher learning specifically designed for African-American women, the college is in a unique position to do just that.

Challenging, Yet Worthwhile

Students describe Spelman academic life as "extremely rigorous." Every student is required to fulfill a core curriculum that consists of classes in the natural sciences, social sciences, fine arts, and humanities. In addition to these broad divisions, students are required to take several specific classes in black history such as African-American Women's Studies and the African Diaspora in the World. Although many students say the requirements are both necessary for a proper education and fulfilling in their own regard, most say the classes just add extra stress to students already worried about finishing the requirements for their major in four years. As one student put it, "I don't have as much time as I'd like to take classes in my major—I don't need this added stress."

Popular majors at Spelman include English, biology, chemistry, and psychology. Many students are preprofessional, preparing themselves for medical and law school. Undergrads stress that the most important aspect of Spelman academics is the faculty. One student said, "The professors here are incredibly nice and accessible. I haven't had a single class yet when I didn't feel completely comfortable with just walking up and talking to my teacher." Many students echoed this sentiment, declaring that the level of student-faculty interaction is unusually strong: "Teachers want to know you by your first name; they ask you to come by and talk all the time. It's important to them that they know you on a personal level," another student added. Many students said that this warmth is extremely valuable at Spelman, where "it makes the challenging classes seem possible and the extra work worthwhile."

To meet the academic challenge, students use the many study rooms located in each dorm. Spelman's Woodruff Library is shared by all of the other schools in the Atlanta University Center (AUC), including Morehouse, Clark Atlanta, and Morris Brown. Although the library is a long walk from the center of campus, students say it is particularly useful for research and serious studying, one of the perks of a university-like community.

No Alcohol

Woodruff does, however, provide common ground for Spelman students and those at their unofficial "brother" college, all-male Morehouse. Students say that much of their social life is centered off-campus, at parties hosted by local clubs or on the Morehouse campus. Undergrads say the strict rules of conduct, the campus ban on alcohol, and limited visiting hours for males may seriously limit the potential for an on-campus social scene.

Campus residents describe their dorms as "adequate," although this judgment varies greatly depending on which dorm a student lives in. The Living and Learning Center II earns high marks for cleanliness and convenience. The Laura Spelman house is ancient in comparison, described by one student as "old, rickety, hot, and unstable." McVicar, located above the infirmary, is also unpopular. Many upperclassmen opt to live off-campus in "nice residential neighborhoods" within 15 minutes of campus.

Another fact of campus life at Spelman is the required meal plan. Students say the cafeteria food is "pretty bad," although some feel that "in the not-so-grand scheme of college food, Spelman's is about average." As a result, many students opt to pay for food at the two campus eateries located in the Manley Student Center: the Grill (a burger joint), and Subway, the sandwich franchise. The most popular off-campus restaurant, Mick's, serves typical American fare.

Weekly Prayers

Many students attribute the strict code of conduct to Spelman's Christian philosophy. Students are required to attend weekly meetings that include a guest speaker and an opening prayer. Student opinions on the religious tradition vary widely. Some students say that religion is an extremely important part of their life and education. Others feel that it infringes upon their personal beliefs, and warn that the depth of religious sentiment can surprise new students. As one student said,

"The religious nature of the school isn't made clear during the admissions process; it's a feeling you get once you're here."

Spelman students say that the historical philosophy of the school administration is not indicative of current student sentiment at all. Many describe the political climate of the student body as liberal and engaging. Informal debates and discussions "rage daily." One student said that one important distinction between Spelman and other colleges is that at Spelman, students act on their political convictions. "If a Spelman student feels that there is some problem that needs to be solved, social or political, you better watch out because something is going to be done about it."

> **"Spelman is the perfect place for young, determined women to find themselves and to learn how they can really make a difference in the world."**

Spelman students say that sororities are very important to campus life. Although they lack actual houses, each sorority fosters a communal spirit as sisters plan social events and spend time together. Many students also join the wide variety of academic clubs available. Aside from sororities, students say the most popular extracurricular activities include journalism, student government, and community service in the neighboring low-income areas.

What's a Sport?

According to students, one aspect typical of college life that is lacking at Spelman is sports. Although the basketball team is noted for its devoted following, sports are not at the forefront of students' thoughts. One senior reported that she had just recently discovered Spelman even had a mascot. This does not mean that Spelman students are not athletically inclined, however. Many students say they regularly use the campus gym to keep in shape. For those less energetic, the required physical education classes can be happily spent in the campus bowling alley.

Spelman primarily attracts African-American women from the South, California, New York, and Washington, D.C., and is widely considered the most selective black women's college in the country. Some students believe this reputation leads to Spelman students being perceived as snobbish, which "may be true of some people here, but not generally."

Students assert that their time at Spelman has provided them with an experience unequaled at other colleges. One student said, "Spelman is the perfect place for young, determined women to find themselves and to learn how they can really make a difference in the world." —*Melissa Droller and Staff*

FYI

The three best things about attending Spelman are "the supportive environment fostered by students and professors, the rigorous academics, and the opportunity to get an education at an all-women's school but still have access to a co-ed social life through exchange with Morehouse."

The three worst things about attending Spelman are "the importance placed on sororities, the overemphasis on religion, and the food."

The three things every student should do before graduating from Spelman are "have dinner at Mick's, participate in a community service group, and engage in a discussion with someone who challenges your personal beliefs."

One thing I'd like to have known before coming here is "how important religion is to the institution."

University of Georgia

Address: 212 Terrell Hall, Athens, GA 30602-1633
Phone: 706-542-2112
E-mail address: contact us on web site
Web site URL: www.admissions.uga.edu
Location: small city
Founded: 1785
Private or Public: public
Religious affiliation: none
Undergraduate enrollment: 22,800
Total enrollment: 31,000
Percent Male/Female: 45%/55%
Percent Minority: 13.2%

Percent African-American: 7.0%
Percent Hispanic: 3.0%
Percent Asian: 3.0%
Percent in-state/out-of-state: 85%/15%
Percent Pub HS: 15%
Fraternities: 17%
Sororities: 20%
Number of Applicants: 13,400
Percent Accepted: 63%
Percent Accepted who enroll: 50%
Entering: 4,272
Transfers: 1,834
Application Deadline: 1 Feb

Mean SAT: 598 V, 597 M
Middle 50% SAT range: 550–650 V, 550–640 M
Middle 50% ACT range: 24–29
Mean ACT: 27
3 Most popular majors: business, education, biological sciences
Retention: 87%
Graduation rate: 65%
Library: 3.4 million
Tuition and Fees: $3,034 in; $10,276 out
Room and Board: $4,902
On-campus housing: 85%
Financial aid, first-year: NA

At the University of Georgia every student becomes very familiar with one new word that definitely wasn't on the SAT's. "Dawgs," short for "Bulldogs," is used to denote both the sports teams and the students at UGA.

UGA plays host to a total enrollment of approximately 30,000 students, and the size of the school, located in the "classic city" of Athens, allows for an immense range of activities, sports, clubs, and social groups. These benefits, coupled with the university's comprehensive list of degrees and programs, have made UGA one of the South's premier state universities.

Keeping the Hope Alive

At UGA, academics are spelled HOPE. This is because a large percentage of student tuition is paid by Georgia's HOPE grant—a fund created through state-lottery proceeds that allows any student who maintains a B average free tuition and $100 toward books each semester at any public state institution. The relatively cheap cost of attending UGA has made it popular among Georgia's top students, which is reflected in the school's admissions numbers. Students must now have noticeably higher GPA and average SAT scores than their predecessors in order to be eligible to walk around the famous Georgia "arch." (Though do not go through! It's campus lore that those who prematurely pass under the arch are doomed never to graduate.)

Once inside the hallowed halls, students have a large selection of classes from which to choose, ranging from pre-law and Greek lyrical poetry to calculus and chemistry. While opinions differ among students on whether the university caters more to the humanities- or science-focused student, both are thought to be very well-represented on campus. For those who take a long time to commit to any one path, the university allows students to wait until the end of their sophomore year to declare a major, prompting one student to notice that, for a good portion of their stay at UGA, "slackers major in undecided." Those students who wish to flex their mental might may choose to participate in the university's honors program. While time-consuming, (honors students must take at least nine honors classes throughout their career in order to graduate from the program), the honors program was cited in *U.S. News & World Report* as one of the nation's best. Other perks for honors students include smaller class size and more personal contact with their professors.

In general, students at UGA are happy with their professors—when they have them. Many classes are taught by teaching assistants and most class sizes are admittedly large, although they are usually cut down to weekly discussion sections of only 20 or so. TAs are reputedly good and grading fair, although some students reported occasional problems with the English-speaking abilities of their teachers.

Did Someone Say "Party?"

The social scene at UGA can be considered as much of an institution as the school itself. Dawgs love their football team, and throughout the fall much of campus life revolves around the weekly games. Tailgates and post-game parties are a rite of passage in Athens, and season tickets sell out months before the first kickoff.

Parties can be found at UGA seven days a week. The Greek system is very popular among students and annually holds the country's second-largest rush period. The approximately 40 fraternities and sororities at UGA are reputed to party hard, but non-Greeks are invited to many of the events and do not find themselves without social alternatives. One student sums up the atmosphere by stating that "Greeks have a great time, but if you're not in [a frat] then you hardly know they exist." Greek or not, the one thing that unites nearly all parties at UGA is the large quantity of alcohol, leading one student to exclaim, "a Dawg's favorite food is usually beer." As alternatives to the party scene, students can often be found just hanging out in each other's rooms or frequenting the nearby mall and movie theater.

And the Winner Is . . .

There's no doubt about it, the sport on the Georgia campus is football. With each home football game, Athens turns itself from a moderately busy college town into a sea of Dawg-crazed fans as students past and present swamp Sanford Stadium to see the boys in red.

While football is certainly the king of the sports scene at UGA, it is not the only game played. UGA fields powerhouses in a wide variety of intercollegiate athletics, including women's gymnastics. For those who take their sports a little less seriously, UGA offers a wide variety of club and intramural teams to fit any level of participation. Students who just want to keep in shape can use the university's state-of-the-art Ramsey Student Physical Activity Center. The Ramsey Center, as it's known, is a sprawling gym that contains among other things an indoor track, two pools complete with diving equipment, a rock-climbing wall, basketball and volleyball courts, and a large weight room.

Owing to the immensity of the student body at UGA, the options for extracurricular activities and social organizations are broad. Students with a journalistic bent can work for one of the many publications including the *Pandora Yearbook* or the student newspaper, the *Red and Black*. There are also several active religious groups on campus, including the Baptist Student Union and Campus Crusade for Christ. Habitat for Humanity was started in Georgia under President Jimmy Carter, and is very popular among the students on campus. Participants help build houses for economically challenged families in the community. A broad spectrum of organizations, as well as the fraternities and sororities at UGA, actively engage in community service activities as well.

A Dawg's Life

It is not mandatory for students to live in dorms at UGA for any period, although some do take advantage of this option. Two of the more popular dorms are Russell, which is known for its party atmosphere, and Oglethorpe. Many other students choose to live in Myers, but this un–air-conditioned dorm tends to elicit complaints until late fall rolls around. Female students who wish to live in a single-sex dorm can choose to live in Brumby, known on campus as "the virgin vault." Rules on dorm visitation vary from dorm to dorm and even floor to floor. The severity of the restriction ranges from no admittance at any time to 24-hour-a-day visitation—but students are allowed to place themselves according to their preferences. UGA has a comprehensive Resident Assistant program and at least one RA lives on every floor in each dorm. Students remark that RAs do not act as police, and are not overly strict.

While most students seem to be relatively happy with their dorm experiences, few remain in the university-provided housing for more than a year. Apartments abound on and around the campus, and the majority of upperclassmen choose to move off-campus after their freshman year. Students who live off-campus find that having a car is a must, and even the majority of those living on the campus have a car. One student summed up the situation at Georgia by saying "the traffic problem is getting rather large, but I can't imagine what I'd do here without a car."

One aspect of college life consistently given high marks is the food. Students on the meal plan can eat their meals at any of the three dining halls: Bolton, Oglethorpe (commonly known as "O-House"), and Snelling. As with the choice to live in dorms, the meal plan at UGA is totally optional, although most freshmen tend to take advantage of the university-supplied food. Some students who do not live in the dorms also purchase full or limited meal plans for weekday stops in the cafeterias. Food off-campus is rated as very good as well, although it can sometimes get expensive for one to eat all meals out. Many students avoid this situation by buying groceries and cooking for themselves in the apartments.

> "With each home football game, students past and present swamp Sanford Stadium to see the boys in red."

A large state university in a picturesque college town, UGA has something to offer each and every one of its students. Whether a challenging courseload or a never-ending series of parties, there is rarely a lack of things to keep someone busy at UGA. One simply has to find his or her own home among the "Dawgs."
—*Robbie Berschinski and Staff*

FYI
The three best things about attending UGA are "the city of Athens, the wonderful people, and the football."

The three worst things about attending UGA are "being so close to home since UGA is a state school, parking is horrible, and the administrative red-tape."

The three things that every student should do before graduating from UGA are "take time to enjoy the campus, go to the UGA-University of Florida football game, and do some kind of community service."

One thing I'd like to have known before coming here is "just how big the school really is."

Hawaii

University of Hawaii / Manoa

Address: 2600 Campus Road, Room 1 Honolulu, HI 96822
Phone: 808-956-8975
E-mail address: ar-info@hawaii.edu
Web site URL: www.uhm.hawaii.edu
Location: urban
Founded: 1907
Private or Public: public
Religious affiliation: none
Undergraduate enrollment: 11,785
Total enrollment: 17,344
Percent Male/Female: 46%/54%
Percent Minority: 84.0%

Percent African-American: 1.0%
Percent Hispanic: 1.0%
Percent Asian: 82.0%
Percent in-state/out-of-state: 95%/5%
Percent Pub HS: 69%
Fraternities: 3%
Sororities: 3%
Number of Applicants: 4,251
Percent Accepted: 67%
Percent Accepted who enroll: 52%
Entering: 1,481
Transfers: 1,883
Application Deadline: rolling

Mean SAT: 520 V, 565 M
Middle 50% SAT range: 470–570 V, 510–620 M
Middle 50% ACT range: NA
Mean ACT: NA
3 Most popular majors: biology, information and computer science, psychology
Retention: 82.0%
Graduation rate: 56.0%
Library: 3 million volumes
Tuition and Fees: $3,024 in; $9,504 out
Room and Board: $5,297
On-campus housing: 21%
Financial aid, first-year: 28%

Despite the exotic location, being a student at the University of Hawaii is not all about sitting on the beach, getting a tan, and surfing. The mission of the University of Hawaii is to provide quality education and training, to create knowledge, and to contribute to the cultural heritage of the community. At this major research institution, students not only enjoy their surroundings but also seek knowledge.

Academics

"There are too many core requirements here," one student said about the academic requirements at the University of Hawaii. Each student must take two years of a foreign language, in addition to numerous other arts and sciences courses. Many students take more than four years to graduate, due to the large number of core courses and the difficulty they have getting into classes. Registration at the university is a rigorous procedure, unless you're in the honors program, whose students receive priority. Despite the high demand for most classes, the student-to-teacher ratio is pretty low—most classes average 20 to 30 students. Introductory classes are reportedly much larger than the upper-level courses within a major. Attitudes about professors run the gamut. When asked about the quality of the teaching, many students replied "average." On the bright side, TAs are rare in upper-level courses, and one student described the grading as "generally easy." The University of Hawaii has been increasing its enrollment in recent years, and this has put more of a strain on resources. Undergrads report that geography, geology, science, and business courses are among the toughest at the University of Hawaii. One student said the university offers more to chemistry majors than other science majors because the chemistry department has more professors who are better teachers.

What's on for Tonight?

The social options at the University of Hawaii are ample. Many freshmen spend their weekends going to parties. Drinking and smoking are part of the social scene, but non-smokers and non-drinkers do not report feeling uncomfortable. Students say that not many of their classmates use illegal drugs. One undergrad described the typical freshman weekend as "Drink, party, smoke." There are few dress-up formal occasions on the weekends, and few students go on formal dates, but random hookups are a regular occurrence. "Yes, it's easy to meet new people," one student said. Students are reportedly open-minded about their social groups and can easily move in and out of different cliques on campus. Cliques do persist, however, even though fraternities and sororities are not major forces in the campus social scene.

One undergrad described the student stereotype at the University of Hawaii as "female, short, and Asian." In general, students are laid-back and most often wear T-shirts, shorts, and sandals to class. Some students find the campus population "homogeneous—Asian."

Where We Live

Freshmen who live on campus live in co-ed dorms with students in all class years. This situation provides for a great introduction to college life, as students avoid the craziness of all-freshman dorms. Campus housing has become limited as more and more students enroll in the university. Hawaii residents receive first priority, and those who don't get campus housing usually commute from home if possible, since a lot of students live nearby. The campus apartments, which offer more privacy and space than the regular dorms, are considered the best on-campus housing, but still, many students choose to live off-campus to avoid the hassle of competing for the vacancies.

The campus is "nice, lots of trees," as one student said. Another student described the buildings as "cramped and overcrowded." "One architecture professor characterized the buildings as the worst part of the campus," a student reported. The campus is near major bus routes, and students rave about the convenience of this transportation system, although there is some debate over the safety of the campus. Some students say they feel safe, others say they feel insecure at night on the campus. One student said, "In general, you shouldn't walk anywhere alone at night, no matter how safe the city, but [at UH] I would." Some students complain that the campus lacks a 24-hour eating establishment.

The dining hall food is "overpriced," according to many students. One said that the food is "pretty good for the first week, after that it's not so good." Another said the dining halls are "clean, big, and not bad." Although the campus social scene is open to movement between groups, the dining halls are characterized as more cliquey; students often eat with their friends from high school or even grade school. Extracurriculars do not dominate the lives of most university students, yet intramurals are popular. According to one student, "It's a commuter school," and most students work part-time.

> **"The University of Hawaii is not all about sitting on the beach, getting a tan, and surfing."**

Team spirit at the University of Hawaii abounds, though, and the school actively recruits athletes for its teams. Major sports teams participate in the Western Athletic Conference, and basketball and volleyball are two of the most popular sports. The football team has also made recent strides toward improvement. One student called the athletic facilities, particularly the new special events arena, "great, since the school spends the most funds on the sports program," but some students complain that the campus lacks a good track.

The three four-year campuses, seven community colleges, and five education centers that make up the University of Hawaii emphasize different levels of instruction, research, and service, but all focus on a Hawaiian and Pacific orientation

and an international leadership role. Students agree that the University of Hawaii is a great place to spend four or more years, as long as you learn early on how to balance the beach with your studies.
—*Rebecca Pace and Staff*

FYI

The three best things about attending the University of Hawaii are "the weather, meeting people from different ethnic backgrounds, and the live music every Friday night at Manoa Gardens (the bar on campus)."

The three worst things about attending the University of Hawaii are "the limited space to study in the library, the unkempt school grounds, and the continuing rise in tuition."

The three things every student should do before graduating from the University of Hawaii are "to check out the Oriental garden by Kennedy Theatre, attend a volleyball game, and relax at Manoa Gardens."

One thing I wish I knew before coming here is "tuition increased 11 times in 10 years here."

Idaho

University of Idaho

Address: P.O. Box 443133, Moscow, ID 83844-3133
Phone: 208-885-6326
E-mail address: nss@uidaho.edu
Web site URL: www.uidaho.edu/
Location: small town
Founded: 1889
Private or Public: pub
Religious affiliation: none
Undergraduate enrollment: 8,591
Total enrollment: 11,305
Percent Male / Female: 54% / 46%
Percent Minority: 6.5%
Percent African-American: 1.0%

Percent Hispanic: 2.0%
Percent Asian: 2.0%
Percent in-state / out-of-state: 73% / 27%
Percent Pub HS: 98%
Fraternities: 28%
Sororities: 21%
Number of Applicants: 4,827
Percent Accepted: 82%
Percent Accepted who enroll: 43%
Entering: 1,453
Transfers: 846
Application Deadline: rolling
Mean SAT: 550 V, 554 M

Middle 50% SAT range: 490–610 V, 490–620 M
Middle 50% ACT range: 21–26
Mean ACT: 23.6
3 Most popular majors: engineering, education, business
Retention: 80.0%
Graduation rate: 51.0%
Library: 1,566,081 volumes
Tuition and Fees: $2,348 in; $8,348 out
Room and Board: $3,952
On-campus housing: NA
Financial aid, first-year: 60%

One junior captured the essence of his years at the University of Idaho as "cheap, fun, and a great education." Tucked between the potato fields and rolling hills of Moscow, Idaho, the University of Idaho is wrapped up in its own world—a world immersed in frat parties, intramurals, and academics.

Engineering Future Engineers

Engineering is widely recognized as the toughest major on campus. Even so, undergrads flock to the department. The University of Idaho engineering programs are regarded as some of the best in the country. The university attracts candidates early on through an engineering camp for juniors in high school. Future engineering majors earn credit at the university during the intense two-week program. All undergrads, regardless of major, are required to fulfill basic core requirements. These include math, science, social science, and communications. The easiest classes are found in the PE department (one can get credit for playing football or bowling) and in general studies, but most students feel that "for the most part there are not too many easy classes."

Students were split in their feelings on class size and TAs. Some undergrads thought their TAs were generally very good while others thought they "suck royally." Feelings about class sizes ran along similar lines. Opinions on class size varied from "perfect" to "fine as long as the room is big enough" to "too big." Many introductory classes fall into the "too big" category, but are broken down into sections and labs taught by TAs.

Undergrads also have the option of enrolling in classes offered by Washington State University, located eight miles away in Pullman, Washington. Students are able to take classes at WSU that the U of I does not offer, though course selections are very limited.

It's All Greek to Me

With 18 fraternities and 8 sororities for the approximately 8,000-member campus, Greek life dominates every aspect of non-academic life at the U of I. About 28 percent of men and 21 percent of women go Greek. There is an unspoken but pronounced division between Greeks and independents. As one undergraduate put it, "There are two separate worlds. You're proud to be where you are."

Freshmen are free to choose their living arrangements. Their options include living in a fraternity or sorority house, living in a residence hall, or living off-campus. Just as each Greek house has its own personality, each dorm has its own character. Residents may choose their dorm, but dorms have unofficial designations such as "athletic" housing. Despite the variety of options, the administration has had to deal with a housing crunch in recent years, and dorms and Greek houses were renovated to provide extra space. There are also apartments available on campus. Many students opt for off-campus housing but find that a good location at a decent price is difficult to come by if they don't look early.

Greeks also dominate social and extracurricular life. There are fraternity and sorority parties nearly every weekend. There is no cover charge for the parties, but they are open only to those on the guest list (usually the membership list of other Greek houses). There have been no publicized problems with Greek life recently, though one fraternity chapter lost its charter a few years ago. However, underage drinking is "the epitome of the U of I. There are constant minor-in-possession citations." Greek life revolves around dances, cruises, socials, and philanthropic events. Strong friendships are a part of the package. A sorority member claims, "The friends that I have made through the Greek system will be my friends for life."

Those not involved in Greek life take quite a different view, "[The Greek system] has TOTAL control of this place. We have the second-largest Greek system in the Northwest here (next to U. of Washington). It sucks because the Greeks here think they are God's gift to life and everything else." However, social life outside of the Greek scene is abundant. Many undergrads take advantage of the nearby mountains and rivers to camp and hike. Others head for neighboring Pullman, Washington, or for Spokane, Washington, which is about an hour's drive away.

Where's the Kremlin?

Moscow, Idaho, itself has very limited opportunities. Described as a "typical college town," this tiny town of about 18,000 boasts fast food restaurants, movie theaters, a small mall, and an abundance of bars. Students complained that there is nothing social to do off campus. Many students own cars and escape from Moscow over the weekends. The U of I campus is fairly compact. It takes about 15 minutes to get from one end to the other. With both a small campus and a small town, students said they generally feel safe on campus and in town, although like anywhere there are "certain places [where] you don't walk after dark."

> **"I have only been on one date and I went to the rodeo!"**

Dating at the U of I is very low-key. A typical date involves attending a Greek event or going to the movies. Those who are not in serious relationships generally just try to meet people at parties. With such limited options, dating often gets creative. "I have only been on one date and I went to the rodeo! Whoa, pardner, easy!"

"Vandal"izing Fun

School spirit runs high among the University of Idaho Vandals, and sporting events are heavily attended. U of I athletes, both men and women, compete in NCAA Division I as members of the Big West Athletic Conference. The men and women Vandals represent the university in 14 varsity sports, including the recently added women's soccer program. The rivalry with the Boise State University Broncos is especially intense. Outstanding recreational facilities, available to the campus and the community, include an excellent 18-hole golf course, swimming pool, indoor and outdoor tracks, indoor and outdoor tennis courts, and racquetball courts.

Extracurricular activities are unfortunately quite limited at the U of I. The engineering department offers several organizations and teams, but these usually appeal only to students in the major. Outside of academic organizations, there is a large Christian group on campus that has some presence. The campus also hosts various concerts, including the widely known Lionel Hampton Jazz Festival held every spring. The most popular activity, by far, is intramural sports, although they are often "Greek dominated."

Despite its isolated location and the deep division between Greek and non-Greek undergrads, students love the U of I. Whether they are looking for an awesome social life or a decent education at a decent price, U of I meets its students' needs, and creates many fond memories for them along the way. Students feel that they are getting the "college experience." As one enthusiastic Vandal put it, "I thought that high school was the best time of my life, until I got to college. This is where my best memories are!" —*Jennifer Rogien and Staff*

FYI

The three best things about attending the University of Idaho are "the incredible Greek life, the Vandals are crazy fans, and the alcohol flows over the weekends."

The three worst things about attending the University of Idaho are "that there aren't a lot of extracurriculars, dating doesn't happen often, and this place is out of the ways."

The three things that every student should do before graduating from the University of Idaho are "make a road trip to one of the cities, attending a game against the Broncos, and participate in intramurals."

One thing I wish I knew before coming here is "how much Greek life dominates everything!"

Illinois

DePaul University

Address: 1 East Jackson Boulevard, Chicago, IL 60604-2287
Phone: 800-433-7285
E-mail address: admitdpu @wppost.depaul.edu
Web site URL: www.depaul.edu
Location: urban
Founded: 1898
Private or Public: private
Religious affiliation: none
Undergraduate enrollment: 11,186
Total enrollment: 16,747
Percent Male / Female: 40%/60%
Percent Minority: 32.0%

Percent African-American: 12.0%
Percent Hispanic: 12.0%
Percent Asian: 8.0%
Percent in-state / out-of-state: 81.0%/19%
Percent Pub HS: 64%
Fraternities: 2%
Sororities: 2%
Number of Applicants: 5,107
Percent Accepted: 72%
Percent Accepted who enroll: 32%
Entering: 1,209
Transfers: 1,787
Application Deadline: rolling
Mean SAT: 520–630 V, 500–620 M

Middle 50% SAT range: NA V, NA M
Middle 50% ACT range: NA
Mean ACT: 24
3 Most popular majors: accounting, finance, and communications
Retention: 83.0%
Graduation rate: 52% (within 5 years)
Library: 960,000 volumes
Tuition and Fees: $14,670 in; $14,670 out
Room and Board: $6,198
On-campus housing: 17%
Financial aid, first-year: 68%

Chosen by *Time* magazine and the *Princeton Review* as having the happiest student body of any college in the country in 1999, DePaul University manages to maintain a small-school, student-oriented atmosphere. It probably helps that classes are small and almost all taught by professors, and that the main campus is in one of the best parts of Chicago, Lincoln Park. One political science major referred to the neighborhood's inhabitants as "rich, young yuppies."

Safety is rarely an issue, whether in Lincoln Park or on the downtown campus, which is located near the Art Institute of Chicago. No wonder the students of DePaul are so pleased: they can go to the nation's third-largest city for fun, get a great education, and still find time for top-notch extracurricular activities and sports.

Educational Priorities

"The school is very passionate about making education the first priority," said a pleased senior. While DePaul offers more than 100 academic programs and more than 1,000 different courses, every single class is taught by a professor as opposed to a teaching assistant, like at other large schools. More than 88 percent of the faculty have Ph.D.s, and average class sizes max out at 25 students and can be as small as 5 students. Notable professors include Wayne Steger, who teaches political science; Deena Weinstein, the authority on rock concerts and audiences (one student said that "she knows everybody in the music industry"); and Lorilee Sadler of computer science, telecommunications and information systems. Professors and students maintain a comfortable atmosphere both in and out of class—the professors give out their home phone numbers on syllabi and are flexible with grading. As one freshman described, "You can call them up and be like, 'Hey, what happened with this grade?' A lot of times, they'll change it and be reasonable." Students are encouraged to participate in class, and one senior raved that the professors "encouraged individuality and helped guide me."

DePaul is known for being a humanities and business-oriented school, but one student pointed out that the "computer science program is gaining national attention" and that "the School of Computer Science is one of the largest in the country." Slackers can be found in any major, but, in particular, the exotic cat management major seems to attract a large share of the loafers for some reason.

DePaul is on a quarter system, and students must take at least three courses a quarter and maintain a 2.1 GPA. Those in the liberal arts program must take a core curriculum. First-year students have a special curriculum that they must follow, but they have "a lot of room for other classes," according to one freshman. Honors programs can be found in each college, and classes are even smaller in those; one honors student raved, "You end up taking the majority of your classes with the same group of people, and you get to know each other, which is nice when a school is large." However, a sophomore mentioned that while "my honors and political science classes are the most challenging, the rest seem like a joke at times." On the other hand, a freshman said that he felt like he had a ton of work, although he did say that it was manageable.

The professors are available to help those who need it. One invited students over to his house to help them with projects that he had assigned. Other positive aspects of classes at DePaul include, said a senior, "their locations. You can be in the Chicago Loop downtown in the center of business, then take a ten-minute train ride into Lincoln Park and be at a standard college campus that's surrounded with history and all kinds of things to do."

An Extracurricular Experience

Extracurricular activities are also a big part of student life. There are about 120 different student organizations: ethnic clubs, political groups, honor societies, a radio station, and many more. Students are often identified by the activity they are involved in. As one student put it, "Every-

one knows who works on the *DePaulia* [the student paper], partly because our lives revolve around it. It's like that for anyone, if they are really into one thing, they will be associated with it." Many students are involved with community service, and student government is also well respected. Perhaps gaining the most attention are the sports teams, which compete in NCAA Division I. In particular, the men and women's basketball teams, which recruit heavily, are popular and bring in a lot of fans.

While DePaul is a commuter school, students did not mention that as having an adverse effect on their social lives. The most obvious reason for this is that the "city is our campus. Even if you don't drink, there's still a lot of stuff to do." Similarly, another student said that "DePaul utilizes Chicago to the extreme; it's awesome." Students can go to concerts, bars, clubs, and plays, although one upperclassman remarked that freshmen just "find the nearest party and travel there in large packs." Students agreed that it was easy to meet people, that "people are very friendly." Good parties include swing dances, Halloween parties, '70s parties, and toga parties hosted by the fraternities. There is a lot of drinking, and one sorority member pointed out that "the Greek life is really starting to grow."

Punks v. *Dawson*

Because, as one senior put it, "DePaul is a very liberal school," students mentioned that there is a large gay population. "We live near one of the largest gay communities in the country, North Halstead," explained a freshman. Many students tend to be trendy, and a common stereotype is "a bunch of rich, Chicago, suburban kids." This stereotype might stem from the fact that, as one disgruntled junior pointed out, DePaul, as a rule, does not give scholarships to international students. Student dress tends to differ between the campuses. The Lincoln Park campus is really laid-back, while students at the downtown campus tend to be more dressed up. The student population is "pretty diverse," with a large number of Hispanic and African-American students, although there are not many Asian students. One thrilled female student also mentioned that "I think there are some fine-looking men here!" Music-wise, the punk scene is reputedly quite big, despite the somewhat antithetical popularity of *Dawson's Creek*.

> **One thrilled female student also mentioned that "I think there are some fine-looking men here!"**

Also big, although in a different sense, are the dorm (called "residence hall") rooms, for the few who opt to stay in them (students complain about the high prices of housing). All student rooms have private bathrooms, air-conditioning, and cable with movie channels; upperclassmen get to stay in "town houses and beautiful apartments with a killer view of the skyline." Freshmen must stay on-campus, but even their dorms are complete with "tall ceilings," an attribute not found at too many other universities. Centennial Hall is the best, while Corcoran is oldest but it will soon be torn down. Cafeteria food is good, but "gets boring," (DePaul has just one cafeteria) so students often go off-campus to eat. Popular restaurants include Potbelly's, My Pie, Demon Dogs, and "Taco Burrito Place is where every DePaul student goes after hitting the bars." Campus buildings are indistinguishable from the rest of the city, and anywhere on the undergraduate campuses students can be awed by the sight of the magnificent Chicago skyscrapers.

Winner? Chicago

So there are great academics, extracurricular activities, and parties. But what epitomizes DePaul University? Students seem to love, above all, their school's deep bond with the city of Chicago. As one senior reflected, "I got to do things here that I could never do at a huge university, and I'm in the center of a huge city." Just like Chicago, the DePaul community is connected through close-knit classes and a dedication to community service. Even the sororities and fraternities are friendly with each other, said one member. What creates this great atmosphere? As one freshman put it, "The city. It's all about the city." —*Jennifer Wang and Staff*

FYI

The three best things about attending DePaul are "the great diversity among the students, the very knowledgeable and approachable faculty, and the exciting and diverse atmosphere of Chicago."

The three worst things about attending DePaul are "the quarter system, the expectation that every student is rich, and the special treatment of the basketball team over the other varsity sports teams."

The three things that every student should do before graduating from DePaul are "go to the Midnight Madness pep assembly in the fall, take a class on a campus other than Lincoln Park, and see different areas of Chicago other the immediate Lincoln Park area."

One thing I'd like to have known before coming here is "that I wish that I could have been reminded to always keep an open mind!"

Illinois State University

Address: Campus Box 2200, Normal, IL 61790-3490

Phone: 309-438-2181

E-mail address: ugradadm@ilstu.edu

Web site URL: www.ilstu.edu

Location: small city

Founded: 1857

Private or Public: pub

Religious affiliation: none

Undergraduate enrollment: 17,705

Total enrollment: 20,470

Percent Male/Female: 42%/58%

Percent Minority: 11.3%

Percent African-American: 7.0%

Percent Hispanic: 2.0%

Percent Asian: 2.0%

Percent in-state/out-of-state: NA

Percent Pub HS: 90%

Fraternities: 10%

Sororities: 9%

Number of Applicants: 11,049

Percent Accepted: 75%

Percent Accepted who enroll: 37%

Entering: 3,080

Transfers: 1,824

Application Deadline: rolling

Mean SAT: NA V, NA M

Middle 50% SAT range: NA V, NA M

Middle 50% ACT range: 20–25

Mean ACT: 22.5

3 Most popular majors: elementary education, business administration, applied computer science

Retention: 78.0%

Graduation rate: 53.0%

Library: 1,398,742 volumes

Tuition and Fees: $4,210 in; $10,465 out

Room and Board: $4,248

On-campus housing: NA

Financial aid, first-year: 40%

L ocated in the small town of Normal, Illinois State University provides students with both the resources of a large university and the comforts of a small community. With its central quad containing all the academic buildings, and the residence halls surrounding the quad, the campus is very central and accessible to students. One student described the campus as "small enough that the environment is very comfortable and relaxed."

Intimate Academic Setting

The small feeling created by the comfort of the campus contrasts with the vast number of academic opportunities. The theater, political science, education, and accounting departments are all reportedly strong and competitive. Although one student described the academics as "not really hard, not really easy," another political science major described the classes as "challenging and interesting." Professors teach most classes, with some introductory classes taught by graduate assistants. Students rate the student-faculty interaction as "very good," and one student said that "compared to some universities we have a good, solid rela-tionship between students and faculty." Students also report that interaction is encouraged through many available resources to students, and the professors are very accessible during office hours. They are always "willing to do what they can for students."

According to one student, registering for classes is "not a problem." Students can easily register by phone or computer. Getting shut out of classes is not the problem at ISU that it is at other large universities. If a class is a requirement of a major, the administration puts a block on a certain number of openings. In this way, students who need the class for their major can apply to the specific department for a position in the class. Undergrads must also fulfill general requirements within the University Studies areas. These groups include humanities, natural sciences, social sciences, arts, mathematics, communications, contemporary life studies, and non-Western cultures and traditions. While some students pronounce the requirements a "waste of time," many find them enriching. Freshmen are assigned a general advisor when they arrive, and after declaring a major receive an advisor in their specific department. Students find this system helpful.

Freshmen also have the opportunity to participate in a recently implemented program called Connections, which brings small groups of students with common interests together in "learning communities." These groups take three classes together during the year, study together, and often form close social groups. One participant praised the program as a "great transition tool from high school to college."

Where We Work?

One undergrad explained that "students who are here for the education study a lot." The recently built Milner Library is a six-floor building with up-to-date resources. It is reportedly a good environment for serious studying. The second floor has equipment and resources that are available 24 hours, which students find helpful. Many students also study in the Prairie Room in the Bone Student Center. It is reportedly a popular place to study at any hour with "couches, TVs, and a really cozy atmosphere."

Dorm Life

Undergrads also study in their dorms. Freshmen and sophomores are required to live on campus in one of the 14 residence halls. The dorms on East campus, Hewett, and Manchester, are considered to be social. West campus, with the Tri Towers (Wilkins, Haynie, and Wright), is also a popular place to live. Waterson, where the floors are divided by a staircase, is sometimes considered "antisocial." While one student complained that "the rooms are pretty small," the university is currently in the process of a campus enhancement project to renovate all dorms. Adding computer access to the dorm rooms was recently approved as well. After their first two years, many students choose to either live in Greek housing or in apartments in Normal.

Eats

Students who do live in the dorms are required to be on a meal plan. The university runs on a debit-card system, where students use their IDs at any of the five dining halls on campus. There are two food courts, two all-you-can-eat cafeterias, and one coffeehouse/deli. One undergrad commented that "the food is average" while another student felt that it was "pretty gross." Most students do like the variety, however, and as part of the enhancement plan the dining halls are increasing their options and responding to student input. Now all the cafeterias always offer a vegetarian bar, a pizza bar, a sub bar, and many other choices.

There are also several places to eat off-campus. As one student explained, "Normal grew when ISU grew, so there are a lot more places now to eat and socialize off-campus." Popular options include Avanti's, an Italian restaurant close to campus, Micheleo's Pizza, and La Bamba, which serves "burritos as big as your head." The Pub, a bar and grill, is a popular place for older students to hang out.

Social Life

The town of Normal provides other social opportunities for students as well. Many students frequent the local bars, which admit 18-year-olds on certain nights. Popular bars include Rocky's, Spanky's, and the Pub. ISU has a very strong, established Greek system, with around 20 percent of students participating. For those who seek it out, it can be a major part of their lives, but one student reported that "it is not the major influence on campus." Frat parties are extremely popular on the weekends, but for those students not involved in Greek life, there are private parties and house parties. One student adds, though, "it is fine if you are not a partier. The town is pretty big and you can go to the movies or out to eat." There are also two malls in Normal, and the campus bus system provides students with transportation to off-campus locations, which makes it "okay not to have a car."

For extracurricular interests on campus, ISU has over 180 student organizations, ranging from political groups to dancing troupes to Habitat for Humanity. With so many interests represented, one student felt that "you have to make an effort to get very involved in a few things, because, with 20,000 students, it's easy to get lost here." ISU has a school newspaper, the *Daily Vidette*, which attracts a high amount of student involvement. The Student Government Association is also very strong. This year's student body president's main goal is to target different campus organizations to get more students involved in campus life.

An Athletic Lot

Many students are involved in athletics. As a Division I school, ISU has a very strong athletic reputation. Last year, the men's basketball team had a great year, earning a spot in the NCAA tournament. While the football team has not been great lately, the team is currently rebuilding under a new coach. The softball, baseball, and volleyball teams are reportedly strong as well. School spirit is "pretty good," reflected in the large number of students wearing various ISU apparel around campus.

People from Normal strongly support the university, attending athletic events and offering discounts in the local stores and restaurants. Along with varsity sports, intramurals are extremely popular and competitive, attracting Greeks, dorm residents, and any other students who want to participate.

Student Body

Along with a diversity in interests, the student population as a whole is diverse as well. Many different ideas and ethnicities

are well represented. However, one student, disappointed by the lack of interaction between ethnic groups, described the population as "not exactly unified," and the social atmosphere as "self-segregated." Support services for minority students include a multicultural center and the Minority Student Development Service, and many active groups on campus such as the Black Student Union. ISU also has one of the oldest LGB (lesbian, gay, and bisexual) groups in the country.

> Freshmen also have the opportunity to participate in a recently implemented program called Connections, which brings small groups of students with common interests together in "learning communities."

Students at Illinois State University praise the small-school feeling they get from this large university, and the incredible opportunities they encounter. As one student concluded, "Whatever you're looking for, you can find it at ISU. You just have to be willing to go out and look for it."—*Melissa Kantor and Staff*

FYI

The three best things about attending ISU are "small-school feel, decent school spirit, and a student government that really represents."

The three worst things about attending ISU are "self-segregation, invitation-only parties, and there are too many ways to get involved."

The three things that every student should do before graduating from ISU are "head to La Bamba, root for men's basketball, and wear ISU shirts."

One thing I'd like to have known before coming here is "how such a big place can feel like home."

Knox College

Address: 2 East South Street, Box K-148, Galesburg, IL 61401
Phone: 309-341-7100
E-mail address: admission@knox.edu
Web site URL: www.knox.edu
Location: small city
Founded: 1837
Private or Public: private
Religious affiliation: none
Undergraduate enrollment: 1,220
Total enrollment: 1,220
Percent Male/Female: 45%/55%
Percent Minority: 11.0%

Percent African-American: 3.0%
Percent Hispanic: 3.0%
Percent Asian: 5.0%
Percent in-state/out-of-state: 50%/50%
Percent Pub HS: 75%
Fraternities: 33%
Sororities: 12%
Number of Applicants: 1,357
Percent Accepted: 75%
Percent Accepted who enroll: 30%
Entering: 300
Transfers: 44
Application Deadline: 1 Feb

Mean SAT: NA V, NA M
Middle 50% SAT range: 550–680 V, 550–650 M
Middle 50% ACT range: 24–29
Mean ACT: NA
3 Most popular majors: biology, political science, economics
Retention: 88%
Graduation rate: 74%
Library: 169,661 volumes
Tuition and Fees: $21,174 in; NA out
Room and Board: $5,436
On-campus housing: 95%
Financial aid, first-year: 90%

Imagine arriving for your first day of college and before the day is done meeting every single student at the school. Welcome to Knox College. Every year begins with a tradition called Pump Handle, a two hour event where students line up and shake everyone's hand. This is just the first glimpse of the friendliness of a school "where everybody wants to know your name."

Reaching Your Potential

Academics at Knox push students to reach their academic potential. As one junior put it, "I don't know anyone who isn't working really hard." All Knox students must take two credits in each of the humanities, social studies, and math and science. Beyond this, first-years are required to enroll in a preceptorial, a discussion class about a variety of controversial topics. Preceps are taught by professors from all departments and are meant to foster personal growth. As a follow-up, seniors are given a choice between several advanced preceptorials. Although it has a strong liberal arts philosophy, Knox is particularly well known for its excellent science and math departments, though students said the computer science department leaves much to be desired. The

faculty has a lot to do with the excitement Knox students feel about learning. They are highly accessible and it is not uncommon to be invited to a prof's house for dinner. As one student explained, "They have a 'Yes you can!' philosophy. They make you want to learn."

"A different perspective is really important to the way we learn at Knox," stated one undergrad. As evidence of this philosophy, two of the unofficial rites of passage of a Knox student are study abroad and staying at Knox over the summer. In fact, there are even some majors that require time abroad. There is also a big emphasis on multiculturalism, with approximately 15 percent of students coming from outside the United States. A strong overseas recruiting program has drawn a large contingent of Indian students as well as students from East Asian nations. A very generous financial-aid program also promotes diversity on campus.

Social Life

One junior explained the social scene at Knox: "We live in a pretty small town, so it's not really going on." Another agreed, "You have to come up with your own fun." The biggest mainstay is the fraternity scene, which is always a popular option for first-year students. Being underage generally isn't a problem, and there is also a prevalent non-drinking scene. There are few formal events, but that doesn't mean that there is no dating. However, students complained that there is little casual dating and instead, most dating is serious.

The housing at Knox earns much praise, and one sophomore even said that it was the housing that drew him to Knox. The rooms are generally large and well maintained, but there is not much diversity in the type of rooms available within dorms. However, there can be a distinct differences between dorms. This is especially evident in dorms like Seymour, where first-year men are housed, which offers markedly inferior accommodations compared to the hotel-like Post dorm, where the first-year women are housed. There are also theme houses, which are an option after the first year, offering excellent living accommodations. The RA system has drawn praise as being "a little more intimate" than the typical college RA system. RAs tend to act a lot more like an older sibling and less like enforcers.

The food is generally described as run-of-the-mill college food, being neither spectacular nor inedible. One student described the food as "mundane," and a common student complaint is that they do not receive good value with their meal plan. There is an attempt to offer larger variety with facilities like the Oak Room, a special dining area where students can eat sit-down dinners.

Extracurriculars

According to one student, "The attitude surrounding extracurriculars at Knox is 'Join!'" People are very involved in many organizations and they are an important part of the Knox education. Music and drama are among the most popular activities, and multicultural groups also have a large presence on campus due to the high level of diversity at Knox. The student newspaper, the *Knox Student*, has also received many awards.

Sports at Knox tend to take a backseat to other interests. Recently, Knox's team name has changed from the Siwashers to the Prairie Fire because the former was considered a derogatory term for an alco-

holic Native American. Although many students see Knox sports as a joke, the teams do work very hard. The cross-country team and the men's golf team have achieved recent success.

Knox students still find plenty of time to participate in intramurals, which in many ways have a larger presence on campus than varsity sports. There is fierce competition in men's volleyball and ultimate Frisbee in particular, and basketball and soccer are popular as well. To support the non-varsity athlete, sports facilities are constantly improving. The latest change has been the addition of a new pool. Athletic facilities also include an excellent field house with basketball, volleyball, tennis courts, and an eight-mile track.

Traditions

One of the harbingers of summer is a special festival called "Flunk Day." No one knows when this day is going to be held. When it is announced, it is the responsibility of several drunk seniors to run around campus at 5 A.M., banging on pots and pans and letting the entire campus know that Flunk Day has arrived. Classes are canceled for the day and the campus turns into a big carnival with an amusement park appearing on campus overnight. Students and professors alike spend the day outside, sunning themselves, relaxing with friends, and taking the time to sit back and enjoy life.

"A different perspective is really important to the way we learn at Knox."

According to one student, "A different perspective is really important to the way we learn at Knox." Knox is truly a place that comforts students with its homey atmosphere, yet will challenge them to expand their minds in ways that might not always seem comfortable. The Knox education extends far beyond academics to prepare students to be successful in the real world. —*William Chen and Staff*

FYI

The three best things about attending Knox College are "the small student population, the closeness of people, and the philosophy behind teaching."

The three worst things about attending Knox College are "the small student population—there's fewer people to date; there's not much to do in Galesburg; and small schools come with smaller resources."

The three things that every student should do before graduating from Knox College are "study abroad, stay at Knox over the summer, and be immersed in the traditions."

One thing I'd like to have known before coming here is "that despite the desolate area, there's a great wealth of things to do, you just have to figure out what you want to do."

Lake Forest College

Address: 555 North Sheridan Road, Lake Forest, IL 60045
Phone: 800-828-4751
E-mail address: admissions@lfc.edu
Web site URL: www.lfc.edu
Location: suburban
Founded: 1857
Private or Public: private
Religious affiliation: none
Undergraduate enrollment: 1,193
Total enrollment: 1,193
Percent Male/Female: 43%/57%
Percent Minority: 14.0%

Percent African-American: 6.0%
Percent Hispanic: 4.0%
Percent Asian: 4.0%
Percent in-state/out-of-state: 95%/5%
Percent Pub HS: 67%
Fraternities: 20%
Sororities: 21%
Number of Applicants: 1,149
Percent Accepted: 79%
Percent Accepted who enroll: 33%
Entering: 299
Transfers: 68
Application Deadline: 1 Mar

Mean SAT: 570 V, 560 M
Middle 50% SAT range: 520–620 V, 500–610 M
Middle 50% ACT range: NA
Mean ACT: 25
3 Most popular majors: business/economics, English, psychology
Retention: 79.0%
Graduation rate: 61.0%
Library: 280,000 volumes
Tuition and Fees: $20,240 in; $20,240 out
Room and Board: $4,820
On-campus housing: 83%
Financial aid, first-year: 75%

Set in the wealthy suburb of Lake Forest, a five-minute walk from the beach of Lake Michigan, a fifty-minute drive from Chicago, and filled with close, extremely social, and hardworking professors and students, Lake Forest College sounds a bit too good to be true. Sure, it has the makings of a great vacation getaway, but a real, four-year college? Get out of here. There must be a catch.

It's a Ton of Fun

One junior, when asked when the weekend started at Lake Forest College, was confused by the question. "The weekend doesn't quit," he said. Then he added, "But people have got their priorities, and not a lot of people say their priority is to party." However, one student double majoring in computer science and business said that parties are great: "They're so much fun.

You go there, and it's 1,300 of your closest friends. If you bring a freshman to a party, it's like a dream for them. If an upperclassman brings a frosh, he'll introduce you to everyone, and everyone wants to know where you live, what do you do. It's so cool."

Lake Forest administration allows legal-age students to consume alcohol, as long as they're in their rooms behind closed doors. "They give us a little leeway; if we [mess] up there's consequences," explained one student. After being caught outside with alcohol three times, students are "kicked off housing."

When asked what differentiated Lake Forest from other schools, one student gushed, "The socialness. I can't even express it in words. It's unbelievable. When you go to class you say hi to everybody, if you go to a party, you know everybody.

If you don't know somebody, it's like a long-lost brother. You're like, 'Where have you been? Why don't I know you?' Everyone hangs out; everyone knows everyone. It's literally like an oversized family at our school." And when students are not at the parties, which usually take place on Fridays, they can easily hop on a train (the station is about a mile away; students drive and park their cars there) downtown for $1.75, or get a $5 unlimited weekend pass. As one English major put it, "We like to mix some culture in our social/party schedule." And of course, the city of Chicago speaks for itself.

Students who want to stay on campus and sober (some undergrads estimate that between 30 to 40 percent do not drink) have plenty of options, too. Lots of movies, sporting events, community service, and dry social activities run by the Student Council can be found, although one sophomore mentioned that the turnout at the events is pretty small, since "it's a small school, and people are too busy getting trashed." But even so, it seems hard to knock a social scene where, as one athlete put it, "Everyone is welcome everywhere."

The Academics Are Good

If the weekends "don't quit," then the classes could not be too challenging, right? No. Students all agreed that classes are difficult, entail a lot of work, and ultimately, are very rewarding. A junior said that after finishing a test one time, his professor gave him a high five, saying, "You studied so hard for this." Professors invite students to their houses for dinner, attend sporting events, and "want you to succeed and come back to visit and say 'Thanks for kicking my [butt] all through college—look where I am now,'" said a student. Students are close to their professors, who tend to be relatively young. Freshmen introductory courses are sometimes a source of complaint because they average 30 to 40 students, but upper-class courses max out at 25 and average between 6 and 10 students per class. Another junior said that "the professors are very competent and willing to let students exercise intellectual freedom and reward them accordingly."

In fact, some illustrious profs can be found at Lake Forest: the inventor of holography is in the physics department. There is also a world-renowned art historian, a nationally recognized postmodern theorist, and the leading authority on the philosophy of erotics. The "all-around, most competent, rewarding prof?" asks one student. "Bob Greenfield in the English department. Ph.D. Columbia, amazing." Students also mentioned Dawn Meyer in the music department, Jason Cody in chemistry, and Ben Goluboff in English. Professor Matheson in business/economics starts off every class with a joke to "loosen everybody up." Professor Guglielmi in the psychology department is "awesome, gets so pumped up in class. He'll throw chalk and erasers at you." There are no TAs, class participation is encouraged and necessary, and as one chemistry major quipped, "I'm taking organic chemistry, which is taught by two professors. Both meet with me on a regular basis. The Dean of the College helps me out. My advisor calls me in my room, to see if I need something. Professors really care. If there's anything that stands out about this school, it's that they really care, won't let you fail. They really encourage interaction and challenge you. Students rise to the occasion and really get a decent education."

The Sports Teams Are Good, Too!

The Lake Forest handball team is the best in the nation, literally, since there is only one division and Lake Forest is on top of it. Other sports are also top-notch. The men's swimming team has won three Midwest Conference titles in a row, even with only 12 swimmers in 1999–2000 and every team out to defeat them. The women's swim team was upset in 1998–99, taking second in the conference, but has a tradition of first-place finishes. Men's tennis has also won titles the last couple of years. The men's soccer team is reputedly good, but the most popular varsity teams are men's hockey and women's basketball.

Juniors referred to a poll of students taken every year that revealed "astronomical statistics. Sixty-five percent of the freshmen class has played varsity athletics. Forty percent were captains of their teams. Thirty percent had a varsity letter in three or more sports." As one student put it, "Our school goes out and gets people that are leaders, that can express their feelings, who are able to perform well in the academic world. A 36 ACT is not what they're looking for. They want students that are well-rounded."

Student organizations mentioned included the campus radio station, Student Council, an environmental organization that is helping out with the reforestation of Lake Forest, and GLASS, the gay, lesbian, and straight society, one of whose events was to watch the Grammys together and cheer on Madonna. The student in charge of the radio station, when asked what type of music the undergrads listened to, answered, "The music is just as diverse as the people who go here. People listen to anything from swing to alternative to jazz to metal to rap to R&B."

"Our school thrives on diversity," emphasized a junior. She went on to explain how students were from all over the place, both from all over the States and other countries. There are also "all sorts of minority groups, an intercultural relations center, and all sorts of scholarships." However, students tend to be quite wealthy. A junior, when asked what students typically wore to class, said, "Polo, Prada, and Banana Republic." Somewhat antithetically, he went on to say, "There is certainly a spectrum of other people [not predominantly wealthy] here." There are also quite a few homosexual and interracial couples. And what brings the diversity of students together? As one student put it, "Everyone drinks. All races, they all get drunk and plastered together."

The Dorms Finally Get Renovated

"The dorms are kind of in a sad condition right now," said a junior. "They started a big plan last summer [1999] to renovate. It will be much nicer next year." Deerpath, the freshman dorm that was built in the 1950s and has not been renovated since then, is getting a "major facelift. They're adding at least twelve new rooms, a fitness center, and a cafeteria. They're going all out on it this summer and touching up the other ones." Even without the renovations, students all agreed that the dorms

are "livable," a good thing, since not many can live off-campus because of the costly surrounding neighborhood. Lake Forest is home to multimillion-dollar houses, and "one of the most expensive places to live in the entire nation." (The town is not exactly a college town, although students did mention the popularity of the Lantern, which has Wednesday-night drink specials and Rainbows for Thursdays.)

> "The music is just as diverse as the people who go here. People listen to anything from swing to alternative to jazz to metal to rap to R&B."

The campus itself is "very, very beautiful. It's slightly hilly, but crisscrossed with ravines and an oak forest. It's just a mile or so from the lakefront." Buildings are red brick, and one building, Holt Chapel, is the center of an unusual tradition. Every year, "these super-religious people come out and all sit around it. They meditate and try to levitate the chapel. Just the concept of trying to levitate the 120-year-old building . . . it's pretty solid." There are three campuses: North, Middle, and South. Middle is where the classroom buildings are, and "it is a lug" from South Campus, where most of the students live (and where the parties are). Five dorms are on South Campus, and "all the jocks live down there because the sports center is down there. It's usually the crazy area," explained a Middle Campus resident. Along with the class buildings, there are two dorms on Middle Campus, including the Blackstone, which students need to apply to, to live in, since it is the "academic dorm." North Campus includes Cleveland Young, a residence hall for international students and those who have lived abroad. It was "just renovated. It's really, really nice," gushed one student.

Even the food is good, because Lake Forest switched to Aramark food service a few years ago, which does "a good job," say students. There's full salad and pasta bars daily, and "compared to other colleges, it's really good," said a junior. There are a couple of exceptions, however. "Some of the meats are bad, but it's tough to get good-quality meat," said one junior, while another mentioned, "They don't have enough seating, but it's getting fixed."

Ferris Bueller, Macaulay Culkin, Harrison Ford Are Right

So, it seems the catches are small and getting fixed, and the great parts of Lake Forest College are going to last. Reputedly, Lake Forest has produced the most CEOs of any small college. And even Hollywood likes Lake Forest. Movies like *Ferris Bueller's Day Off*, *Home Alone*, and *The Fugitive* have all been shot here. Students cannot stop gushing, and as one said, "all sorts of races and ages come together, it's a super-friendly campus." It seems there is not much to lose and a whole lot of fun, learning, and friends to gain when it comes to Lake Forest College. —*Jennifer Wang and Staff*

FYI:
The three best things about Lake Forest are "the beautiful campus, the friendly student body, and the caring *and* renowned faculty."
The three worst things about Lake Forest are "the freezing winters, a weak football team, and the eggs and hamburgers in the dining hall."
The three things that every Lake Forest student should do before graduating are "go to the Lantern and Rainbows, go to a Winter Ball, and spend the day touring Chicago."
One thing I wish I'd known before coming to Lake Forest is "how to juggle a moderate course load with all the activities on campus."

Loyola University

Address: 820 North Michigan Avenue, Chicago, IL 60611
Phone: 800-262-2373
E-mail address: admissions@luc.edu
Web site URL: www.luc.edu
Location: urban
Founded: 1870
Private or Public: private
Religious affiliation: Roman Catholic
Undergraduate enrollment: 7,669
Total enrollment: 13,604
Percent Male / Female: 36% / 64%
Percent Minority: 34.0%

Percent African-American: 8.0%
Percent Hispanic: 9.0%
Percent Asian: 14.0%
Percent in-state / out-of-state: 98.0%
Percent Pub HS: 60%
Fraternities: 7%
Sororities: 5%
Number of Applicants: 3,972
Percent Accepted: 82%
Percent Accepted who enroll: 27%
Entering: 1,188
Transfers: 871
Application Deadline: rolling

Mean SAT: 572 V, 570 M
Middle 50% SAT range: 520–630 V, 510–620 M
Middle 50% ACT range: NA
Mean ACT: 24
3 Most popular majors: psychology, business, biology
Retention: 83.0%
Graduation rate: 65.0%
Library: 1.7 million volumes
Tuition and Fees: $16,074 in; $16,074 out
Room and Board: $7,000
On-campus housing: 31%
Financial aid, first-year: 75%

In a city known for the Bulls, stuffed pizza, and the Sears Tower, Loyola University continually strives to make its mark with strong academics and a diverse student body.

Academic Flexibility

While seeking to be different, Loyola instills the traditional set of core requirements, hoping to ensure that students graduate with a well-rounded education. Among the requirements are three courses each in natural sciences and literature, two in history or social science, one in communicative and expressive arts, and one in the mathematical sciences. Unique to Loyola, however, are the requirements (three semesters each) in theology and philosophy. This is in keeping with the university's Jesuit affiliation. Despite the number of courses required in this core, few students are dissatisfied. They find that there is still enough academic flexibility: "It really provides you with alternatives," said one student. Class sizes are in general fairly small. While there are classes that exceed 150 students, like the popular Dr. Linda Heath psychology course, most classes enroll approximately 30, and some upper-level classes have as few as 4. Professors match the intimacy of their classes with personal accessibility. Reported one student, "most professors even give out their home numbers."

While there is a core requirement, students have reported that Loyola's strength lies in its division into five different campuses. Among the strongest is that which includes the nursing department. While business, communications, and biology are among the most popular, it is the 16-month intensive nursing program that draws the largest crowds and some of the fiercest competition; "there's a large pre-med/nursing crowd on campus," reported one sophomore, "and some of the requirements for that track are really hard." A selective program, nursing is open to application during undergrads' third year.

But Loyola is not just about nursing. There are a "lot of liberal arts people, as well." Since the recent merger with Mundelein College, Loyola's music department now offers instrumental as well as choral courses. To accommodate an expanded campus, there are shuttle buses that allow students to commute between the Lake Shore main campus which houses most of the undergraduate facilities, classes, and dorms and the four satellite campuses.

Living in Chicago

Freshman dorm life is the norm, and Loyola does not encourage moving off-campus until junior year, but many upperclassmen nonetheless eventually move out to nearby, furnished, campus apartments. All campus dorms are monitored by RAs, and are coed by floor. Opposite-sex visitors are not allowed on dorm floors after midnight during week-

days and 2 A.M. on weekends. "It is a Catholic school, you have to understand," explained one undergrad. In short, strict security dominates dorm life. But students do report the policy in campus apartments to be "a bit more open." While there is a sign-in at the door, ID cards need not be deposited for entry. And for those seeking even more freedom from regulations, Chicago provides all of life's essentials, from housing to eateries. Which is not to say that the food on campus is bad—most declared the food at Loyola's two cafeterias to be "tolerable." But nonetheless, "it is school food, and you just get sick of it after a while," one sophomore professed.

While most students do in fact remain on campus, with local transportation so convenient a large portion of Loyola's student body is made up of commuters. As such, these students have a markedly different experience in Loyola's social scene than do those who live on campus. While Loyola does offer many activities, ranging from Christian groups to ethnic clubs to the Lake Shore Student Government Association, there is a general consensus that these social offerings are somewhat lackluster. Proclaimed one student, "some organizations do stuff; a lot of people do their own thing." Added another, "Greeks are not big at all; we don't have enough people throwing parties." But the few frat houses present still garner enough support to sponsor the annual "Night on Ice" skating party held downtown.

While alcohol regulations are strictly enforced at dorm parties, students find alcohol readily available at off-campus parties or at city bars. Despite the apparently quiet campus, one commuter strongly recommended living on campus. "You really don't get to meet a lot of people if you always have to leave after class." The sports center at Loyola provides facilities for various levels of athletic involvement, from intramural to club sports. School spirit for team sports is not strong, however. Without a football team, Loyola students find themselves "supporting Chicago sports teams" more than they do their own.

But not all events are uninspired; Loyola students are reportedly among the most politically active in Chicago. Debates often rage over gay rights and abortion legislation, and some are vocal in their discontent with administrative policy—most noticeably against the student health center's policy of not distributing birth control.

Social Life? It's in Chicago

If Loyola's social scene sounds fairly tame, the plethora of resources in Chicago make up for it. Many students prefer Chicago nightlife, just a short bus ride or a train ride away. Along with excellent museums and other cultural attractions, the city has an abundance of dance clubs, comedy clubs, shops, and bars. Local coffeehouses like Coffee Chicago and Pannini Pannini are popular hangouts. Many also are fans of the vibrant local jazz and blues scene. Chicago even provides employment opportunities for students. Local companies recruit on campus, and

undergrads generally find the career-placement center adept in counseling and assisting with job searches.

> **Opposite-sex visitors are not allowed on dorm floors after midnight during weekdays and 2 A.M. on weekends.**

Impressively diverse for its size, Loyola offers, as one student said, "college life without a college town." With Chicago as an integral part of social and academic life, undergrads say they enjoy "more of the real world." If you're looking for a combination of strong pre-professional programs, solid liberal arts courses, and an exciting urban setting, Loyola offers this and more. —*William Chen and Staff*

FYI

The three best things about attending Loyola are "the location, the faculty, and the lake."

The three worst things about attending Loyola are "studying, the lack of a football team, and the weather."

The three things that every student should do before graduating from Loyola are "ride the Ferris wheel at Navy Pier, enjoy local ethnic restaurants, and sit on the rocks up by the lake."

One thing I'd like to have known before coming here is "not to take 8:30 classes."

Northwestern University

Address: 1801 Hinman Ave., Evanston, IL 60208-1260
Phone: 847-491-7271
E-mail address: ug-admission@northwestern.edu
Web site URL: www.ugadm.nwu.edu
Location: suburban
Founded: 1851
Private or Public: private
Religious affiliation: none
Undergraduate enrollment: 7,842
Total enrollment: 15,406
Percent Male/Female: 47%/53%
Percent Minority: 27.0%

Percent African-American: 6.0%
Percent Hispanic: 4.0%
Percent Asian: 17.0%
Percent in-state/out-of-state: 25%/75%
Percent Pub HS: 66%
Fraternities: 32%
Sororities: 36%
Number of Applicants: 15,460
Percent Accepted: 32%
Percent Accepted who enroll: 39%
Entering: 1,952
Transfers: 70
Application Deadline: 1 Jan
Mean SAT: NA V, NA M

Middle 50% SAT range: 630–720 V, 650–740 M
Middle 50% ACT range: 28–32
Mean ACT: NA
3 Most popular majors: economics, political science, engineering
Retention: 96%
Graduation rate: 91%
Library: 3,958,508 volumes
Tuition and Fees: $24,648 in; $24,648 out
Room and Board: $7,320
On-campus housing: 98%
Financial aid, first-year: 47%

At the heart of Northwestern University sity lies a solitary rock laden with uncountable layers of paint. Students will camp out overnight to stake their claim on this unofficial campus bulletin board in order to let their voices be heard. It displays everything from fraternity pride to campus events, such as AIDS Awareness Week and Gay/Lesbian Pride Week. The rock brings together and provokes dispute within a student body of boundless diversity, interest, talents and opinions. The rock is a monument to how so many diverse ideas can come together and create a community with strength and spirit.

Work Hard . . .

Northwestern is definitely the place to go for serious academics. The school year runs on a quarter system, and courses are taught in a 10-week period. This fast pace leaves little room for slacking. As one sophomore said, "You can study your butt off, but it doesn't guarantee a good grade. It is very easy to feel mediocre in the midst of such intelligent classmates." The faculty is excellent, but many students feel that they spend too much time on research.

Students must enroll in one of the six undergraduate schools: the College of Arts and Sciences (CAS), the School of Music, the Medill School of Journalism, the School of Speech, the School of Education and Social Policy, or the McCormick School of Engineering and Applied Sciences. Several of these schools have received high acclaim, especially Medill School of Journalism and the School of Music. Northwestern has several departments that are highly acclaimed, including theater, economics and biomedical engineering.

All of the University's colleges offer several highly selective honors programs. The best known is the Honors Program in Medical Education (HPME) that guarantees entrance into Northwestern's medical school after three years. There are also several honors programs in engineering, the Integrated Science Program (ISP), the Mathematical Experience for Northwestern Undergraduates (MENU) and Mathematical Methods in the Social Sciences (MMSS), all of which provide an opportunity for accelerated study in the field of choice.

Distributional requirements vary from college to college, but, for the most part, they are quite similar. In the College of Arts and Sciences, which has the largest enrollment, students are required to take two quarter classes from each of the six distributional groups: formal studies (math); natural sciences; social and behavioral sciences (sociology, economics, political science); historical studies; values (civilizations, philosophy, religion); and literature and fine arts. Freshmen also take two seminars with an emphasis on writing and literature.

Play Hard

Located right on the shore of Lake Michigan, Northwestern offers a picturesque college setting. The college is divided into the Chicago and Evanston campuses. Over a mile long, the Evanston campus is further divided into North and South campuses. South Campus is generally more quiet and houses most of the freshmen, while the fraternities and sororities are housed on North Campus, making it the place to party. With 40 percent of the students belonging to fraternities or sororities, the social scene focuses around Greek parties. However, recent administration crackdowns on underage drinking have pushed a significant amount of parties off-campus. Despite the freshman freeze on Greek parties that is in effect for the first quarter, first-years still find it easy to get into them. Northwestern's proximity to Chicago also spices up the social scene, and students find that their weekends often entail the half-hour trip to the Windy City.

The social scene also includes many formal events. There are formal parties practically every weekend. At a recent Winter Ball, 4,000 students attended. As one freshman commented, "There is always an opportunity to get dressed up." But, not all special events require getting dressed up. Every May, the university sponsors Armadillo Day (Dillo Day) in celebration of the coming of summer. The celebration lasts the entire weekend, as students move out onto the lakefill, which is the peninsula that the university built to extend out into Lake Michigan. It gives overworked students an opportunity to forget about all their worries and listen to different bands in an atmosphere reminiscent of the 1960s. As an upperclassmen

said, "It is a time where everyone sheds any reservations they might have."

There is a common view on campus that people are so caught up in studying that they do not have time to date. As a sophomore said, "There is not enough dating, not enough parties, and too much studying." In spite of Northwestern's intense academics, students who can find the time discover there is no lack of dating possibilities. As a freshman put it, "People are too busy doing their own thing."

> **"We are intelligent, but we definitely know how to have a good time."**

Extracurricular opportunities abound at Northwestern. As one student lamented, "There's just too much stuff to choose from!" Artistic groups, especially theater and a cappella troupes, are prominent. The Associated Student Government is also popular, though the students admit that "this is a very apathetic campus." Despite the apathy, Northwestern sponsors Dance Marathon, the second largest college philanthropic event in the nation. The entire campus is drawn into participating in this 30-hour fund-raising dance.

The student union, Norris University Center, is a great place for students to chill and houses several franchises, including Pizza Hut and Higher Grounds, which is open 24 hours a day during reading week and is a popular destination for people who want to study and be social.

Let the Games Begin!

Sports have long been an important part of Northwestern. Being a Big Ten school, they find themselves with stiff competition, but they have been able to hold their own as they proved by their back-to-back football championships in 1996 and 1997. Their strong spirit is embodied in the clock tower that is purple when the football team wins and white when they lose. Unfortunately, in the 1998 season there was a lot more white than purple. Beside football, the men's basketball team enjoys particular success, and women's sports in general are very popular, often ranking higher than the men's sports. Intramurals are a popular alternative that draw a great number of participants. The Sports Pavilion and Aquatic Center (SPAC) provides state-of-the-art facilities for athletes and non-athletes alike to work out. In fair weather, in-line skaters, joggers, and bicyclists are drawn to the path that runs along the lakefront offering a beautiful change in scenery.

It does not matter if Northwestern stu-

dents are studying or being social, they do it in style. Although there are many complaints that the school is too focused on academics, a balance between work and play does exist as long as you are prepared to look for it. As an upperclassman said, "We are intelligent, but we definitely know how to have a good time." —*Seung C. Lee and Staff*

FYI

The three best things about attending Northwestern are "the people, being a Big Ten school, and Chicago."

The three worst things about attending Northwestern are "the cold, the serious affect of Greek life, and the tough academic curriculum."

The three things that every student should do before graduating from Northwestern are "hang out in Chicago, play intramurals, and take a gut class to alleviate some of the pressure."

One thing I'd like to have known before coming here is "how snowy Chicago gets."

Southern Illinois University / Carbondale

Address: Mail Code 4710, Carbondale, IL 62901-4710
Phone: 618-536-4405
E-mail address: admrec@siu.edu
Web site URL: www.siu.edu
Location: suburban
Founded: 1869
Private or Public: public
Religious affiliation: none
Undergraduate enrollment: 17,817
Total enrollment: 21,908
Percent Male/Female: 56%/44%
Percent Minority: 18.0%

Percent African-American: 14.0%
Percent Hispanic: 2.0%
Percent Asian: 2.0%
Percent in-state/out-of-state: NA
Percent Pub HS: NA
Fraternities: 4%
Sororities: 2%
Number of Applicants: 10,323
Percent Accepted: 73%
Percent Accepted who enroll: 33%
Entering: 2,494
Transfers: 4,108
Application Deadline: rolling
Mean SAT: NA V, NA M

Middle 50% SAT range: NA V, NA M
Middle 50% ACT range: 17–24
Mean ACT: 22
3 Most popular majors: workforce education, health care management, psychology
Retention: 66.0%
Graduation rate: 37.0%
Library: 2.3 million volumes
Tuition and Fees: $3,716 in; $9,116 out
Room and Board: $3,745
On-campus housing: 24%
Financial aid, first-year: 57%

While Southern Illinois University has always been famous for its party-school image, the administration is making a conscious effort to direct attention back to academics. Numerous attempts at curbing undergraduate drinking and promoting alcohol-free fun have not earned a warm reception from students feeling the effects of the crackdown, however. Even though they

are not thrilled with the new changes, many are still impressed with SIU's building up of academic programs.

Southern Education

SIU undergraduates are convinced that their school is the best in southern Illinois; they cite their communications, psychology, and political science majors as proof of that assertion. Students are especially proud of their unique aviation program, one of the few existing programs of its kind in the country, which attracts top students interested in flying. Other undergrads participate in the equally distinctive hotel and restaurant management program. During their freshman and sophomore years, all undergrads are required to take courses within the core curriculum that range from English to the environment to music. While most introductory courses are large and many classes are taught by TAs, students are generally happy with the level of instruction. They rave about the professors, especially retired U.S. senator Paul Simon, who teaches a political science and a journalism course. Students claim that SIU is not strictly composed of humanities majors or science majors. In fact, many revel in the fact that their fellow students are involved in diverse fields. One student said that his three best friends were interested in forensic chemistry, art, and engineering.

The Social Scene

If you go to SIU and do not drink, you may feel left out. Practically all social functions revolve around drinking. Many underclassmen say they have no problem finding alcohol to fill their weekend, which usually begins around Wednesday and does not end until late Sunday. Upperclassmen spend most of their free time consuming alcohol at local Carbondale clubs and bars. Fraternities and sororities sponsor popular parties, although only about 15 percent of the student body goes Greek. One student chalks this up to the fact that "frats really don't recruit aggressively enough." Other undergrads feel that the number of students rushing will slowly decline in the next few years due to the unpopular Select 2000 program. Under this nationwide pilot study, SIU frats and sororities must all be dry by the turn of the millennium. Students say that some Greeks aren't really sure how to hold parties without alcohol.

By necessity, the alternatives to drinking are becoming more and more popular. The Student Programming Council, one of the most well-respected organizations on campus, coordinates film screenings and concerts. Acts as diverse as Garth Brooks and 311 have recently played SIU. Undergrads report that random hookups also are a favorite pastime and that there is not much steady dating. Students claim to be liberal on the whole, but homosexual and interracial couples reportedly are still not fully accepted in the mainstream. Undergrads also perceive that a large number of their classmates smoke pot. As one upperclassman said, regarding the alternatives to alcohol consumption, "Options are there, but people think they have to drink to have fun."

Cornfields and College

SIU students rave about the beauty of their campus. Instead of being located in the stereotypical midwestern flatlands and cornfields, SIU is situated among rolling hills, and a lake stands in the middle of campus. Minutes away, there are hundreds of acres of forest preserve. While town-gown relations are admittedly tense because many Carbondale residents dislike the seasonal influx of boisterous, reveling students, the town provides all of the amenities, including restaurants of practically every ethnicity.

> **Practically all social functions revolve around drinking.**

That is not to say that the dining hall food is bad, though. The typically dining-hall-jaded college student is rare at SIU; those who eat at the dining halls are content. Many upperclassmen both eat and live off-campus. Freshmen and sophomores are required to live on campus, and tend to be happy with their dorm rooms; most have doubles with air-conditioning, cable, and private bathrooms.

Extracurriculars

While fraternities and sororities are by far the most popular activities on campus, there are many different clubs to join. *The Daily Egyptian*, the campus newspaper, has won many awards and has one of the largest circulations in the country for a college newspaper. Minority groups, such as the Black Affairs Council and the Asian

Student Council, also attract many members. In addition, community service is an extremely popular activity on campus. The Saluki Volunteer Corps, named after the SIU mascot, an Egyptian hunting dog, actively raises money for needy groups and organizes volunteers. Many students also have jobs, both on- and off-campus. One student estimated that as much as 90 percent of the part-time workforce in Carbondale is composed of SIU students.

Saluki Athletics

Students describe the SIU recreational center as "awe-inspiring." It has six indoor basketball courts, twelve racquetball courts, and an Olympic-size pool. Some claim that this single building is responsible for most undergrads' above-average bodies. Popular intramurals are also a factor in keeping the student body in shape.

Many sports classes for athletes and non-athletes alike are offered each semester, and students describe these sports as fun and well-attended.

As for varsity sports, the actively recruited basketball team has a huge following throughout SIU. For three years in a row, the men's team has made it to the NCAA tournament. Football, on the other hand, has been decidedly less successful and consistently fails to gain much support. That could all change under the leadership of the new football coach, however.

There is a lot of change happening at SIU. Chancellor Joanne Argersinger came on board last fall and has been wildly successful by all accounts. These new appointments and the Select 2000 rule are the administration's attempts to focus on creating a new SIU geared toward academics and not drinking. —*William Chen and Staff*

FYI:
The three best things about attending SIU are "its gorgeous campus, an internationally diverse student body, and WIDB radio."
The three worst things about attending SIU are "the administration's alcohol policy, a lack of school spirit, and the drinking-centered social life."
The three things every student should do before graduating from SIU are "go abroad, watch a varsity basketball game, and see a play at the Shryock Auditorium."
One thing I wish I'd known before coming to SIU is "how central drinking is to weekend activities."

University of Chicago

Address: 1116 East 59th Street HM 186, Chicago, IL 60637
Phone: 773-702-8650
E-mail address: college-admissions@uchicago.edu
Web site URL: www.uchicago.edu
Location: urban
Founded: 1891
Private or Public: private
Religious affiliation: none
Undergraduate enrollment: 3,561
Total enrollment: 12,117
Percent Male/Female: 54%/46%
Percent Minority: 36.0%

Percent African-American: 4.0%
Percent Hispanic: 5.0%
Percent Asian: 27.0%
Percent in-state/out-of-state: 27%/73%
Percent Pub HS: 67%
Fraternities: 14%
Sororities: 5%
Number of Applicants: 5,472
Percent Accepted: 58%
Percent Accepted who enroll: 31%
Entering: 980
Transfers: 120
Application Deadline: 1 Jan

Mean SAT: NA V, NA M
Middle 50% SAT range: 640–740 V, 640–730 M
Middle 50% ACT range: NA
Mean ACT: NA
3 Most popular majors: economics, biology, psychology
Retention: 96.0%
Graduation rate: 83.0%
Library: 6 million volumes
Tuition and Fees: $21,485 in; $21,485 out
Room and Board: $7,275
On-campus housing: 95%
Financial aid, first-year: 69%

What differentiates Chicago from any other school is the fact that we are probably the only school that decided to tear down its football stadium to build a library," remarked one fourth-year student at the University of Chicago, summing up the atmosphere of the highly reputed school. However, the rigorous academics at U of C is exactly why students say they chose to attend the institution. With the highest total of Nobel Prize winners (70, including former students, faculty, and researchers; five are currently teaching) of any university in the nation, a Core program that ensures its students a well-rounded education, motivated peers, and many classes of less than 20 students, the university offers an incredible education for those who are not afraid to work hard and work often. As one sophomore happily reported, "I have never met a more masochistic group . . . [my school] has met and oftentimes exceeded my expectations."

Well-Rounded Masochists

"U of C is a mix of biology and economics and humanities and math and everything. There is a lot of work, but it's challenging, and in a strange and twisted way, fun," commented one pre-med computer science double major. Indeed, the University of Chicago offers strong programs for both humanities and math/science students and requires students to take 14 Common Core requirements. This consists of civilization, science, math, humanities, arts, foreign language, and social science courses in addition to 21 courses in a student's chosen concentration (U of C lingo for a major). Students enjoy the "good variety and depth" of the Core program, according to a sophomore, but are skeptical of the new 14-quarters requirement. The original 21-quarter requirement encourages better course distribution. As one economics and environmental studies major gushed, "I love it. Everyone is so much more well-rounded, and I feel like Core is a way I can take classes that I otherwise wouldn't take."

As for that masochism, students love the academics at Chicago, despite the astonishing workload and tough grading (a popular legend passed down from class to class is that no student has managed a 4.0

GPA in the past 60 years). As one political science and biology double major commented about the university's academics, "Great . . . too much work . . . but great." Students are given the opportunity to be "taught by brilliant and interesting people" said one sophomore, while a junior described the "many, many cool profs" as "really great people who teach well and are very approachable." The professors are not devoid of humor, however. One freshman spoke about her humanities professor, "One day he lectured us on the danger of running in the courtyard. He had tripped on a flagstone and landed on his face earlier that day. The next day, he came in with a broken arm. He wouldn't tell us how he really broke it, but he did say it was from playing basketball."

Most classes (humanities, social sciences, and foreign language) create the type of intimate setting where students can poke fun at their professors (and have good discussions), with class sizes between 10 and 25 students. Lectures are between 50 and 75 students, and, in some there is even student participation. Classes max out at around 150 students in the Core science classes, but even then "students can rest assured that they will receive enough attention should the need it," said a pre-med biology major. Students did not have any problems with too many teaching assistants, and those whom they had were "helpful but not overbearing," as one second-year student put it. However, a senior warned that "some of the TAs for science classes don't have the best English skills either."

Partying? I'd Rather Ponder Art

One sophomore who praised U of C's academics was less positive when asked how he felt about the social scene at his school. He said "It could be better . . . way too many people study all the time." When asked to describe the weekend lives of freshmen, one sophomore scathingly replied, "Drink and complain that there isn't anything to do. Idiots." In contrast, explained one senior, "Upperclassmen get out more. Students are really attracted to going to the city and absorbing all that has to offer culturally and entertainment wise, and the university does an excellent job of making that possible for students with bus services." One student said that the school administration is "pretty lax on alcohol. They want to up their social image so they kind of let things go." The Greek scene is still very small at the university; more than one student jeered, when asked which frats and sororities were the coolest: "They all think they're cool."

When weekends come around, students head in different directions. Some go to the few parties that are available. Others hang out at the local bars. Many students attend events put on by student organizations that have free food, dancing, and live music. Watching movies is also popular. "The campus movie theater is by far the best of any other school that I have seen. The movies are state-of-the-art, just like any public theater downtown," described a senior. Some students hit the north side of the city to go gallery- and museum-hopping. And of course there are those students who do not head anywhere, who, as one explained, "take the weekends to study at the library. And there are lazy people who sleep the whole weekend time away." Athletic events do not play a part in most students' weekends, although the men's basketball, wrestling, and the women's soccer team are reputedly quite good despite low fan attendance. As one junior put it, "I don't think any organization could garner that much respect from a significant portion of the student body, due to the students' whininess, cynicism, and apathy."

In spite of these apparently prevalent characteristics, a lot of students are involved in community service through one of the many (one student estimated 30) community service organizations, working, for example, tutoring area children. One "cynical" student attributed this popularity to the many "pre-meds trying to look good on applications." Most students are also involved in at least one of the 200-plus recognized student organizations.

Luxury Among Squalor

The campus is situated in the Hyde Park neighborhood, which is on the southeast side of the city. The area around campus "can be scary at times. The periphery can be dangerous if you are not careful, and the neighborhoods tend to be much worse, run-down, and less safe," warned one student. While both the large U of C police force (the second-largest privately owned police force in the nation, behind Columbia) as well as the Chicago police patrol the area, a third-year student said that "many bad things happen—people have been raped even in broad daylight in places where I have to walk in the neighborhood—I feel trapped." Fortunately, the students have a pleasant campus to be trapped on: the campus architecture is Gothic, with notably beautiful chapels and excellent libraries. This beautiful campus will become increasingly pleasant once the school's massive construction projects are completed. The school has announced it will build another residence hall, a parking structure, the Gerald Ratner Athletics Center, the Kovler Gym, the University Press building, and the Interdivisional Research Building. In addition to these structural changes, the University of Chicago is aiming to improve its neighborhood relations by launching the Midway Plan in which an urban horticultural center, a children's garden, a playground, playing fields, and added lighting will be introduced. The most notable addition in this plan is the Midway Skating Rink (with an observation deck, warming room, and café), where students and the community can ice-skate in the winter and rollerblade in the summer.

The dorms at the University of Chicago are superb, with the exception of Pierce Tower, which has the smallest rooms (one student referred to his frosh room as a "hamster cage") and communal bathrooms. Pierce Tower, like Woodward and Burton Judson, has its own dining hall, is large, and is closely situated to the other buildings on campus. Stony Island and Shoreland (which is a converted luxury hotel) are apartment dorms with kitchens and individual bathrooms but are farther from campus, as are Broadview and Blackstone, which offer many singles with bathrooms that are individual or shared by two to four people. Each dorm has its own personality, and a senior said, "I think students come to enjoy any dorm that they choose to live in." Nonetheless, most students move off-campus after their second year.

> **"I have never met a more masochistic group."**

Situated in one of the best cities in the world (stuffed pizza, Michael Jordan, Bessie the Cow, Kerry Wood, the Sears Tower, the Blues Fest . . . who could ask for more?), home to some of the most distinguished academics in the world, filled with some of the most motivated students in the world, the University of Chicago is simply one of the best educational institutions in the world. "Many people think that Chicago is incredibly stressful, incredibly difficult to succeed in, and very competitive," said a senior. "To a certain extent, that's all true. But, honestly, if you are willing to put forth the time and effort, you'll do just fine. There's more than enough time to get your work done and still have a life outside of school." And, hopefully, that life will include, before the four years are out, a Taste of Chicago.
—*Jennifer Wang and staff*

FYI:

The three best things about attending U of C are "the solid academics, the great dorms, and the faculty."

The three worst things about attending U of C are "the masochistic workload, the lack of safety in the Hyde Park neighborhood, and the fact that everyone studies all the time."

The three things that every student should do before graduating from U of C are "spend an entire day museum hopping, ruin your GPA with a big fat B, see a play at the Court Theatre."

One thing I'd like to have known before coming here is that "many weekends revolve around studying."

University of Illinois / Chicago

Address: 601 S. Morgan M/C 102, Chicago, IL 60607
Phone: 312-996-4350
E-mail address: uicadmit@uic.edu
Web site URL: www.uic.edu
Location: urban
Founded: 1965
Private or Public: public
Religious affiliation: none
Undergraduate enrollment: 16,374
Total enrollment: NA
Percent Male/Female: 45%/55%
Percent Minority: 5.0%

Percent African-American: NA
Percent Hispanic: NA
Percent Asian: NA
Percent in-state/out-of-state: 98%/2%
Percent Pub HS: 81%
Fraternities: NA
Sororities: NA
Number of Applicants: 10,524
Percent Accepted: 63%
Percent Accepted who enroll: 44%
Entering: 2,947
Transfers: NA
Application Deadline: NA

Mean SAT: NA V, NA M
Middle 50% SAT range: NA V, NA M
Middle 50% ACT range: NA
Mean ACT: NA
3 Most popular majors: business, health professions, engineering
Retention: NA
Graduation rate: NA
Library: NA
Tuition and Fees: $4,644 in; $10,920 out
Room and Board: $6,760
On-campus housing: NA
Financial aid, first-year: NA

"UIC is a very worldly school. It gets you ready for the real world," explained a third-year transfer student, summing up the difference between the University of Illinois at Chicago and her previous private college. UIC is not your typical life-in-a-fishbowl college, as concrete-clad UIC is right in the city with the looming Sears Tower and world-renowned theaters, restaurants, and stadiums at the students' disposal. Many save money by commuting and have jobs to put themselves through UIC, which is known for its affordability. Students warn that the school is 92 percent commuter, leading to little participation in extracurricular activities and a less than happening social scene, as the campus is dead after 4 P.M. Said a sophomore—"*No one* is around at all!" However, that's not to say UIC ignores its population. Students can find plenty of faculty support if they have the desire to conduct independent research or to start a club. An enthusiastic first-year said, "UIC is constantly looking to raise its profile in the educational system of Illinois."

Academics

Opinions differ as to whether UIC is more humanities- or math- and science-oriented, but one student said that the school is probably stronger in science because of the impressive research facilities and the medical school—UIC has the largest medical center campus in the nation. One second-year mentioned that the music program is "underfunded and small, but excellent." The school is strengthened by the presence of its students in the math- and science-oriented Guaranteed Professional Program Admissions (GPPA—affectionately pronounced "guppa"), in which select incoming freshmen (Illinois residents only) are automatically admitted into specific graduate programs at UIC. Especially well-known is the medical program, where students are guaranteed a medical school spot for three to five years without having to take the MCAT. Many GPPA students thus opt to finish their undergraduate career in three years. GPPA students still need to do pre-med requirements as specified by the medical school, including chemistry, biology, physics, and social science courses. These GPPA students up the curve in classes—cautioned one student, "stay away from the GPPA kids and the curve's a beautiful thing. With GPPA kids, the curve's definitely a lot higher."

While admission into the GPPA programs is quite competitive, regular admissions, according to a second-year student, are "too easy. Anyone can get into this school as long as you passed high school."

"However," added the same student, "our standards are going up, and within the next few years, academically, our standards will be as high as our brother school U of I at Champagne." Regular students need to maintain a 3.0 on a 5.0 scale to continue at UIC, while GPPA students must maintain a 4.5. Grading is pretty easy, although, one economics major said, "Sometimes there are teachers who, even though the whole class failed the test, choose not to curve the scores."

Classes range from "intimate," at around 20 students to "huge," with as many as 340 students in the large lecture courses. While one second-year student said that not many students participate in class—"it's a pretty apathetic campus," another pointed out that "students for the most part are very focused. The ones who don't pay attention don't show up."

Unfortunately, the lack of interest in many classes may stem from the plethora of TAs. "Discussion can be stupid and worthless, especially if you can't understand what the TA is saying," complained one student. Chemistry TAs have an especially bad rep, although biology TAs are "pretty good." Even some professors do not fare so well in their students' eyes. "Lecture is sometimes useless because you can always get notes off the Web or rely on others." Further, "labs are absolutely stupid in the general courses." Some professors who have good reputations on campus include Stanley Fish, a well-known writer and the Dean of Liberal Arts and Sciences; Professor Young, who somehow gets "rave reviews every year" despite teaching organic chemistry; Professor Ackles in psychology; and Professor Fetzer in chemistry.

Students agreed that the slacker major is psychology. One psych student was pleased that the major required just 27 credits (roughly 9 classes) out of the 120 credit hours needed to graduate. Other popular majors are criminal justice and biology, with biology being especially important to premed GPPA students since "it's only a few more classes more than the requirements for the program." "There are a lot of requirements for the Liberal Arts and Science College, but it's easy to understand if you talk to upperclassmen about them," said one freshman. The toughest class at UIC, students say, is physical chemistry—"everything else pales in comparison unless you're taking grad classes," said one victim. Other tough classes include an embryology class and calculus-based physics.

UIC takes care of its honors students, giving them priority in class choices, but this does not mean that it forgets the rest of its population. "The University has various counseling services that are available to aid with career placement, tutoring, advising, scheduling, and various other things that overwhelm the student body," described a third-year student. "There are even counseling services for those with math anxiety!"

Social Life—Well, Sort Of
Unfortunately, "unless you're part of the small Greek system, UIC isn't that much of a social school," reported one sorority member. Cool frats and sororities are Sigma Alpha Mu, the third largest national fraternity, and Alpha Sigma Tau. Anyone can rush, but pledging is selective. There is no hazing at UIC, and Greek mixers or exchanges are closed to nonmembers. Cool theme parties include Toga, Graffiti, Cowboys and Indians, Tropical, and Cops and Robbers. The administration does not allow minors to drink, and "athletes can not be associated with alcohol *period*," said one Greek.

Being underage poses problems at Chicago clubs and bars, as some card hard. "But there are always places that don't card. Most importantly, meet someone that's 21 and you'll be fine," assured one student. However, beware: while those of drinking age are allowed to drink in the dorms, "if they catch you drinking below age, you get one warning before getting kicked out," stated a freshman. Freshmen who do not go home tend "to go to the city, find one of maybe five parties, watch movies, or go clubbing." Upperclassmen do roughly the same, with the addition of visiting Hawkeyes, the closest campus bar. Students visit clubs at Rush and Division, as well. Especially popular are The Drink and The Crowbar, where Dennis Rodman has been known to hang out and party.

Because of the lack of resident students, there are very few campus-organized activities aside from those in the beginning of the year for freshmen to meet each other and members of the administration. However, it is easy to meet people in classes. "Most people are pretty friendly," said a second-year student. "You could stand in the middle of Inner Circle (a fast-food place) and meet someone new everyday," described a first-year student. Many students frequent the student center to hang out, exercise, and eat.

Student Body
At UIC, "there are racial cliques that just can't be beat. Indians and blacks and Asians all stick—it's just the way it is," one student said. But one freshman, after describing the cliques, said that ultimately, "it doesn't really matter because there are so many people that go to school here. You're bound to find a friend somewhere." As for significant others, upperclassmen tend to have long-term relationships while freshmen and sophomores "play the field and do more stupid stuff." Interestingly enough, despite the cliques which students say tend to form and remain cemented (especially among religious groups and athletes), one freshman declared that there are quite a few interracial couples. "This school isn't called University of Indians and Chinese for nothing. It's very, very diverse," said one second-year student. Many students mentioned the multitude of Indian, Korean, and Chinese students. As for dress, "there are really a lot of people that look like they're about to go clubbing at any moment, but you have your relaxed outfits and pajamas and grungier styles like anywhere else. I think for the most part people dress pretty well," observed a biology major. In general, the student population is "pretty middle-class," according to one student.

The Neighborhood
Most students said they feel safe on and around campus, as the campus police have a strong presence. However, one second-year student mentioned that she hears sirens pass by her room almost nightly. As in most places, it is generally unwise to walk around alone at night. "It's not a good-looking campus either," in-

sisted one student. "But within the next ten years or so, the school is planning to tear down the projects separating the east and west campuses. The older architecture at UIC, explained one student, "is built mostly with concrete and other rather blah-looking materials, and the windows are puny. The newer buildings are pretty nice, and lately the school has been working on beautifying the campus so it's getting better—more grass and flowers, less concrete." UIC buildings are riot-proof since they were built during the civil rights movement. For example, University Hall, the tallest building on campus, was built with the bottom narrower than the top so that people couldn't climb it in the event of a riot. Also, UIC is adding a south campus in the next five years, having bought up all the land in the surrounding neighborhoods.

Most students live off campus, either at home or in nearby apartments, although the school guarantees housing. Warned one student, "it's kind of a pain to live on the west side of campus and have classes on the east side." However, the west side "has more community" than the east. Students said that they were very happy with their freshman year dorms. One second-year student said that her floor "happened to bond very well together and we're all pretty tight." Specific dorms mentioned were PSR, which is an older dorm that is being torn down in two years, and SSR, a dorm for people over 21. In SSR, two to four people share a kitchen and a common room and have their own bedrooms. Exterminators come every month to the dorms, "whether you need them to or not," and while there is an RA system, RAs are reportedly not strict.

Food and Sports Perks

There are plenty of great restaurants off campus. Giordano's, the famed Chicago pizzeria, is a five-minute walk from school, and Greektown, which is open 24/7, is just another five minutes down from Giordano's. Little Italy and Chinatown are within walking distance as well. There is "pretty good food" on campus, said a first-year, ticking off Wendy's, Sbarro's, Subway, Taco Bell, and KFC. "The cafeteria food isn't too bad either. It's actually pretty good on the west side because all the doctors eat there for lunch."

The school's most popular sports team is by far the men's basketball team, as UIC does not have a football team. "Our homecoming is in February with a basketball game. Weird, huh?" said one student. Facilities for non-athletes are reportedly nice and well populated by bench-pressing giants. The athletes have a new $10-million-dollar Flames Athletic Center that regular students are not allowed to use. And while most students do not participate in extracurriculars, one student said that "the best thing about attending UIC is having one consistently nationally known dance team. We are ranked fifth in the nation."

> **"UIC has a lot to offer an ambitious student."**

UIC, with its location right in the hub of Chicago, has a lot to offer to the city-loving student: the advantages of its affordability and location counterbalance its being a mostly commuting student body. With its unique GPPA programs and top-notch research facilities, as one first-year student summed it up: "I believe UIC has a lot to offer to an ambitious student . . . you just have to look for opportunities." —*Jennifer Wang*

FYI
The three best things about attending UIC are "Chicago and all its splendiferous glory, 3:00 Pizza Puff runs at the still very much awake Greektown, and you never run out of people to meet—this place is crawling with people."
The three worst things about attending UIC are "dangers of city living, the lack of a college campus atmosphere, and the fact that almost everyone's a commuter — it makes it difficult to meet people, especially if you live on campus."

The three things that every student should do before graduating from UIC are "to explore the city, to get involved in a club or activity, and to share a 50-piece Chicken McNugget meal at the Rock 'n' Roll McDonald's with someone."

One thing that I'd like to have known before coming here is "that AP credit counts for massive amounts and if you want to register early, you need that credit. Take your APs, baby."

University of Illinois / Urbana-Champaign

Address: University of Illinois at Urbana-Champaign, 901 W. Illinois Street, Urbana, IL 61801
Phone: 217-333-0302
E-mail address: admission@oar.uiuc.edu
Web site URL: www.uiuc.edu
Location: small city
Founded: 1867
Private or Public: public
Religious affiliation: none
Undergraduate enrollment: 26,865
Total enrollment: 36,019
Percent Male/Female: 53%/47%

Percent Minority: 25.0%
Percent African-American: 7.0%
Percent Hispanic: 5.0%
Percent Asian: 13.0%
Percent in-state/out-of-state: 91.0%
Percent Pub HS: NA
Fraternities: 19%
Sororities: 22%
Number of Applicants: 18,140
Percent Accepted: 68%
Percent Accepted who enroll: 32%
Entering: 5,805
Transfers: 1,366
Application Deadline: 1 Jan

Mean SAT: 602 V, 638 M
Middle 50% SAT range: 540–650 V, 580–700 M
Middle 50% ACT range: NA
Mean ACT: NA
3 Most popular majors: biology, psychology, and electrical engineering
Retention: 92.0%
Graduation rate: 78.0%
Library: 9 million volumes
Tuition and Fees: $4,338 in; $10,954 out
Room and Board: $5,078
On-campus housing: 33%
Financial aid, first-year: 83%

The University of Illinois at Urbana-Champaign is a huge research university on the cutting edge of many academic fields. Its sprawling campus is also home to a diverse student body and an equally diverse set of undergraduate opportunities. In a school the size of U of I, there is no shortage of choices in any area of college life.

Academic Illinois

Academically, Illinois has many strong departments. Its engineering and business schools consistently rank in the top five in the nation. But while the university unquestionably draws some of the brightest minds in the state, some students are skeptical about its lofty claims. "They want it perceived as this prestigious academic institution," explained one undergrad. "They say that these are the top students in the state, but it's really more like anyone in the top 50 percent of their high school class." Another student agreed: "The reputation of this school is highly exaggerated."

Still, its reputation does help to bring an influx of new engineering majors to the university each fall, and the public perception of Illinois as a math and science school also affects the student body. "Illinois is definitely more friendly toward math and science than it is to the traditional humanities," explained one student. No matter the major, Illinois's graduation requirements are generally considered strict. It is not uncommon for students to take five years to complete all of their credit hours, and the university admits as much. "When we came to orientation, they basically told us that, yes, this is a four-year program, but probably many of us would graduate in five years," said one architecture major.

In contrast to the difficult requirements of the Schools of Engineering and Liberal

Arts and Sciences is the College of Agriculture, considered by many to be a back door into the university. "High school counselors tell you, if you're just on the edge of getting into Illinois, to apply to the agriculture school and transfer later," said one student.

The professors at Illinois are, on the whole, excellent, and students are generally happy about the level of teaching, even from TAs. Class size is not really a problem, since huge lectures usually break up into much smaller discussion and quiz sections, led by TAs. There are occasional complaints, however, especially in the sciences. "The entire math department can't speak English," moaned one undergrad. "It took me a week and a half to break the language barrier and start understanding some of what the TAs said."

A Greek Influence

Illinois is certainly not all work and no play. Students deal with the stress of their workload by throwing themselves wholeheartedly into the social scene. With around 60 fraternities, Illinois reportedly has the highest participation in Greek life in the nation. Consequently, the social life for most revolves around fraternities and sororities—so much so that some fraternities hold a pre-rush for incoming high school seniors before they've even arrived at the university. As one student put it, "Being the largest Greek campus in the nation, if you're not Greek, you're in trouble." Weekends find most Greek members at bars until late in the evening, when after-hours parties at frat houses begin.

The prevalence of bars on campus has a major influence on campus social life. "Social life at Illinois?" asked one student. "Two words: 'bars' and 'frats.'" Fake IDs are common, but most establishments allow entrance to 19-year-olds, and, once inside, some students report that alcohol is relatively easy to obtain. Campus police take a harder stand on underage drinking. "Bars around here are routinely busted," explained one undergrad. "The cops send [underage] students undercover to order drinks, then fine the bar and issue tickets if the student is served." Even so, drinking forms a large part of the campus social

life, and some students say non-drinkers sometimes feel excluded. Revelers seeking non-alcoholic entertainment can go to movies and concerts on campus. Many also frequent coffee shops or hang out in dorm rooms and the quad. Other common attractions near campus include movie theaters and a mall in Champaign. "There isn't much that isn't here," said one undergrad.

A "Free Flow Policy"

Students said that food in the campus dining halls is generally mediocre. Undergrads living in university housing must purchase a meal plan with either 20 or 14 meals per week. Illinois' "free flow" policy lets undergrads use their meal plan in any residential dining hall or any of 13 specialty restaurants run by the dining service. These themed eateries serve everything from traditional Italian fare to African-inspired entrees.

Dorm rooms, especially for freshmen, can be universally characterized with one word: tiny. "There are no lofts allowed or anything," said one student. "It's like living in a closet." Some administration regulations also draw student ire. In women's dorms, gentlemen callers must be accompanied at all times by a resident of the dorm, a rule that is strictly enforced. Residential advisors (RAs) live on the same floor as students and provide help and assistance when needed. But, the RAs also are there to enforce the rules of the university. As one student put it, "The RA is not your friend." The group of six dorms, widely known as the "six-pack," are considered to be party dorms, especially for freshmen. Many freshmen accept the inconvenient location, far from the center of campus and strategically located close to most frat houses, in exchange for the promise of an active social life. Whether close to the main quad or far away, the majority of students live on-campus, either in dorms or university-owned certified housing units.

The Illinois campus itself, located right on the border between Urbana and Champaign, is a throwback to its farm-town heritage. Morrow Plots, the oldest experimental agricultural field in the U.S., is a major campus landmark. "We're right in the middle of cornfields," said one student. "The campus seems very isolated." Most consider the campus a strong point of the university. "The campus, while large, is very centralized," explained one student. "There's main quad, where most of the classes are, and then the engineering and business quads. It doesn't seem as big as it actually is." The campus also has large open fields and tree-lined paths. "It's beautiful, just beautiful," said one student.

The student body is overwhelmingly from in-state. "People here are either from small farming towns or the suburbs of Chicago," explained one student. The small-town influence can be felt on campus. "Barn dances are huge, just huge," said one student. "And you know what that means—country music!" Most think of the student body as being relatively diverse, with large minority representation. "There is a lot of diversity," explained one student. "But, there's a lot of racial cliquing."

Active Illini

This diverse student body translates into a great variety of interests. Extracurricular activities are very popular on campus. "Clubs are especially big within academic departments," said one student. "For example, the engineers are usually in an engineering club, the computer scientists in a computer-related club, and on and on." At such a large school, however, it takes student initiative to discover what activities and events are occurring on campus. "Unless you go looking for things, you'll miss something," said one student.

In order to introduce new students to the incredible array of extracurricular opportunities at Illinois, the university holds Quad Day, in which hundreds of groups open booths on main quad, attempting to draw potential members from the student body. "We walked through on Quad Day for four hours, and didn't make it to every group," exclaimed one undergrad. One activity that draws immense participation is Illinois' intramural sports program. "Practically everyone does intramurals," said one student. "It seems like there's a thousand different teams to keep track of."

As a member of the Big Ten Confer-

ence, the Fighting Illini face some of the toughest athletic competition in the nation. Because of this, the school's varsity sports generate a tremendous amount of campus excitement. Recent athletic successes include a second place Big Ten finish by the women's basketball team, and a nationally ranked volleyball team.

As would be expected at a school where sports play such a large role, tradition and folklore abound. Assembly Hall, the Fighting Illini's basketball stadium, is often rumored to have been an architecture student's final project. As the story goes, the student received a failing grade, as the building included no inside supports, and the professor believed it would collapse. The student was vindicated, they say, after the applause of cheering fans failed to shake the building to the ground.

Students deal with the stress of their workload by throwing themselves wholeheartedly into the social scene.

Many students attend football games, but some perceive a lack of spirit on campus. "People go to the games, but it's like they're just going through the motions. They don't seem to even care about the teams," said one student. A recent controversy has involved the use of Chief Illini Wek as a mascot. While some value the tradition associated with the venerable mascot, many consider this use of an Indian Chief to be demeaning to Native Americans, forcing the administration to deny that Chief Illini Wek is an official mascot. Rather, he has become a "symbol" only loosely associated with the school.

From the large Greek scene to the famed failed architecture project, Illinois's all-encompassing diversity has an extraordinary effect on students' lives. "There's just so much going on," said one student. "It's such a huge school, with so much happening, and so many opportunities."
—*William Chen and Staff*

FYI:
The three best things about attending U of I are "the social atmosphere, the centralized campus, and the research facilities."
The three worst things about attending U of I are "the closet-sized dorm rooms, the fact that most people are from Illinois, and poor TAs."
The three things that every student should do before graduating from U of I are "play an intramural sport, go to Quad Day and sign up for a million activities, go see a basketball game."
One thing I wish I'd known before coming to U of I is "the size of the dorm 'rooms.'"

Wheaton College

Address: 501 College Ave, Wheaton, IL 60187
Phone: 630-752-5005
E-mail address: admissions@wheaton.edu
Web site URL: www.wheaton.edu
Location: suburban
Founded: 1860
Private or Public: private
Religious affiliation: Evangelical
Undergraduate enrollment: 2,340
Total enrollment: NA
Percent Male/Female: 48%/52%
Percent Minority: 9.0%

Percent African-American: 2.0%
Percent Hispanic: 3.0%
Percent Asian: 4.0%
Percent in-state/out-of-state: 21%/79%
Percent Pub HS: NA
Fraternities: NA
Sororities: NA
Number of Applicants: 1,910
Percent Accepted: 56%
Percent Accepted who enroll: 54%
Entering: 578
Transfers: NA
Application Deadline: 15 Jan

Mean SAT: NA V, NA M
Middle 50% SAT range: 600–700 V, 600–700 M
Middle 50% ACT range: NA
Mean ACT: NA
3 Most popular majors: English, music, Biblical studies
Retention: NA
Graduation rate: NA
Library: NA
Tuition and Fees: $14,930 in; $14,930 out
Room and Board: $5,080
On-campus housing: 100%
Financial aid, first-year: NA

When the Blanchard Hall bells ring, Wheaton students cannot help but smile. It is a school tradition that when a Wheaton couple becomes engaged, the two must climb the bell tower and ring the bell twenty-one times, in three sets of seven. Then they are to leave behind some sort of memorabilia or token in memory of their trip there. One of the school's most famous alumni, Christian evangelist Billy Graham, is reported to have visited the site himself more than 50 years ago with his then-fiancée Ruth. Every week, three or four couples follow his same path up the bell tower stairs.

Founded in 1860, Wheaton College is known today as one of America's premier Christian colleges. As one student joked, "People call us the Harvard of Christian colleges." And indeed it is true that many Wheaton students reject offers from top secular universities to attend Wheaton. For them, it is often a matter of where they think they will grow the most, and for many, the decision to come to Wheaton stems from a desire to learn in a Christian-friendly environment absent at secular institutions. Christian faith is a requisite for entrance to Wheaton, which asks its applicants to submit a personal testimony as well as a recommendation from a church pastor. At Wheaton, biblical Christian values underlie every aspect of life as the school strives to realize its motto, "Christo Et Regno Ejus" ("For Christ and His Kingdom").

In the Christian Classroom

When asked to name her favorite place on campus, one student jokingly replied, "My bed because I don't get to see it very often." Students at Wheaton work hard. All majors must fulfill a general education requirement, which includes two social science courses, Philosophy 101, two science courses, and two Bible classes concentrating on the Old and New Testaments. "We're definitely a liberal arts school," said one student. "I don't think most people realize that before coming here."

As a Christian college, Wheaton offers a number of specifically Christianity-related majors in addition to more traditional ones. Among those distinctive to Wheaton are biblical studies, Christian education, and various ministry-related music majors. Students say communications and Christian education are the easiest fields of study, while Chemistry and the sciences can be "absolutely killer." In the words of one science student, though, "Wheaton is really good if you're gonna major in Bible, but not so great if you're doing science. It is a liberal arts school, after all." Music students were said to work especially hard. "You never even see music majors because they're always in the conservatory practicing," one student noted.

Like students, all professors at Wheaton are Christian. Many will open their lectures by reciting a short prayer or bible verse. Students agree that having Christian professors can be both good and bad. As one student said, "It's good because we have the opportunity to learn in an academic atmosphere that is not hostile to the Christian faith." But because professors and students share a core of Christian beliefs, the classroom can sometimes "lack challenge and diversity of opinion." According to one student, "The environment here is conducive to close-mindedness because everyone thinks the same way. One person will say something and everyone else will just nod in agreement. Where's the challenge in that?" Another student added, "Sometimes it's like you're cheating yourself out of figuring out things for yourself by having it spoon-fed to you."

The Wheaton Pledge

Every semester, Wheaton students sign an official statement of responsibility, promising to uphold certain Christian values. In taking this Wheaton pledge, they agree to refrain from smoking, drinking alcohol, social dancing, and premarital sex. Most students do adhere to these guidelines, but there are exceptions. One student remarked, "I kinda had the impression that everyone here is a perfect Christian and never breaks any of the rules. But I've realized that's not true. It's kinda disappointing. Then again, Christians are human too—we all make mistakes."

In addition, students must attend a morning chapel service three times a week—Monday, Wednesday, and Friday. They are allowed up to 9 skips a semester; those students who miss more than 9 may be placed on "chapel probation." Students on probation cannot participate in school activities and lose seniority in housing privileges. "It's not too big a deal, though," said one student.

"Bro-Sis" Housing

Almost all Wheaton students live in dorms or university-owned apartments. First-year students are required to live in dorms. Fischer was named the most social freshman dorm, while Saint and Elliot were cited as the worst places to live because of their distance from main campus. Frosh do have a curfew—midnight on weeknights and 2 A.M. on weekends—but according to one upperclassman, "it's not enforced too strictly. Coming in late is okay as long as you don't do it too much."

Males are generally not allowed in female dorm rooms and vice versa except during special hours called "open floors," which take place twice a week for about three hours. One stipulation is that dorm room doors must be kept open throughout visits, so that floor RAs (Residential Advisors) can oversee everything that goes on.

Dorms operate on a "Bro-Sis" system, in which each male floor has a corresponding "sister floor." "Brother" and "sister" floors will regularly get together, for weekly dinners at Saga, the campus dining hall, and "raids," partylike get-togethers that happen a couple of times a semester. Wheaton has one dining hall to accommodate its 2,300 undergrads. Officially known as Centennial Cafeteria, students informally refer to it as "Saga" after the food service Wheaton employed during the '80s. Food is cited as "pretty good—

much better than what you'll find at some other schools." After hours, students can find munchies at the school eatery, called "The Stupe." Most students will only go there during certain times, though. "It's okay at night, but during the day, it's like a junior-high hangout, so we all kinda avoid it then," said one sophomore.

On Campus

Primarily residential, the town of Wheaton has been nationally recognized as one of America's safest cities. "I feel really comfortable walking around even at night," said one student. But most students will agree, local life can get really boring. The handful of coffee shops and restaurants near campus "all close at like 8!" lamented one student.

Wheaton is a dry, Greek-free campus. But even in the absence of traditional frat party life, students find lots to do. A couple of times a month, Wheaton will host popular Christian bands, with students attending in hordes. Classical music is also a big draw. The school conducts an Artist Concert Series of 6 or 7 concerts every year. Recent guests have included Dawn Upshaw and the Vienna Boys' Choir. Another popular event is a weekly Praise Night hosted by the campus World Christian Fellowship group every Sunday night. For a few hours, students will gather and sing Christian praise and worship songs. The school talent show and February formal are two other well-attended Wheaton events.

Wheaton does not permit its students to engage in social dancing. Square dancing performed to traditional American hoedown music is the only kind of dancing allowed, and it is only permissible at school-sponsored events. Square dances happen a few times a semester and remain popular despite the dance's "hickish" reputation. Most students will go as singles, but it is not uncommon for people to go with dates.

Going for an M.R.S. Degree

According to one student, dating at Wheaton tends to get "very complicated." "Everyone's pretty much looking for marriage, so dating here involves a lot of pressure," noted one sophomore. Another male student explained dating at Wheaton,

"The way it works, if you're seen walking around campus with a girl, people will jump to conclusions and automatically assume you're engaged. Needless to say, casual dating is lacking."

On the female side, a common joke circulating among Wheaton women is that "you've come to get your M.R.S. degree." One female student went so far as to call Wheaton a "meat market." Every week the school newspaper runs a section called "Up the Tower," listing newly engaged couples; a minimum of two or three pairs of names appear each week with numbers soaring near the end of each semester.

Off Campus

Many students own cars, a luxury which makes finding fun off campus considerably easier. A big nearby movieplex is a popular weekend destination. After shows, students often get coffee and talk at the local Borders or Barnes & Noble bookstores. The Front Street Cocina was cited as a fun place to satisfy cravings for salsa and other Mexican treats. Despite their popularity, however, cars are not a necessity. Said one student, "You can get by without a car, but it's nice to have one," and with on-campus parking becoming scarcer many students are choosing to leave their cars at home.

Twenty-five miles from Wheaton campus is Chicago. Many Wheaton students take trains there to enjoy the bustle of metropolitan life. Train fare is inexpensive—$5 for a weekend pass—and the trip takes less than an hour, making for a mass student exodus to the city on weekends.

Extracurriculars

Most Wheaton students are involved in at least one extracurricular campus activity. In particular, Christian campus ministry groups abound at Wheaton, ranging from local community service to international evangelism groups. Some well-known student organizations include the College Union, the school's social planners, who are in charge of bringing groups and speakers to campus, and Student Government, comprising Wheaton's student body representatives.

Many Wheaton students are musical, so participation in campus singing and music performance groups is naturally very high. One student joked, "I'm convinced that 99 percent of the people on this campus play the guitar. Moving in, almost everyone is carrying one."

Wheaton tends to lack ethnic diversity, but for the less than 10 percent minority student population, the Office of Minority Affairs organizes a number of ethnic organizations, such as Koinonia, the Asian-American group, and Unidad Cristiana, the Hispanic and Latino-American group.

Sports at both the intercollegiate and intramural levels are very popular among Wheaton students, with soccer being especially big. Last year, the Wheaton Crusaders set an NCAA record with their undefeated season. Wheaton students attend school games en masse, and the crowds tend to become "very enthusiastic," said one frequent attendee.

Always Changing

In 1980, world Christian evangelist Billy Graham led a crusade at Wheaton College, celebrating the completion of the Billy Graham Center, dedicated to advancing world evangelism. Almost two decades later, the Center houses its own museum, which uses art to chronicle world evangelism. As the Center adapts to changing world needs and conditions, it serves as a paradigm of advancement and useful adaptation.

> **"I'm convinced that 99 percent of the people on this campus play the guitar."**

Wheaton, too, is a dynamic being. But the school never loses its foundation rooted in faith. Amidst a changing world, the school strives to remain a Christ-

ian bastion of higher learning. But, as the new millennium begins, recognizing the school's need to adapt and grow, the Wheaton administration has announced a school-wide "New Century Challenge," which includes plans to foster greater ethnic diversity as well as more practical plans for building construction and renovation. An improved Sports and Recreation Center is now projected for completion by fall 2000. And having successfully finished a library renovation last summer, the administration has plans for a new student center underway.

In a further effort to keep up with the times, Wheaton has plans to change its mascot within the next few years. Historically, the school mascot has been the Crusaders, a modern take on the medieval Christian soldiers who fought for their faith. But, some people feel the current "Crusaders" image inaccurately depicts Christians and may unnecessarily offend. So, in the name of cultural sensitivity, Wheaton's current president, Dr. Duane Litfin, has expressed support for a change. The new mascot is unknown as of yet.

A Personal Decision

Amidst a changing world, Wheaton can be a great place for some to grow in their Christian faith. But, as one student warned, Wheaton life can quickly become a "super-saturation of the Christian experience." As always, the final decision is a personal one. But Christian students considering Wheaton are encouraged to really look at the school. As it has been for hundreds of Christian greats, it may be the stretch in the straight and narrow that leads them places they never dreamed they would go. —*Jane H. Hong*

FYI

The three best things about attending Wheaton are "the integration of faith and learning, good professor-student interaction, being in a Christian community that supports and encourages."

The three worst things about attending Wheaton are "the lack of ethnic diversity, its being kinda isolated from the rest of the world, and it's easy to over-commit yourself to too many things here."

The three things every student should do before graduating from Wheaton are "to go up the bell tower of Blanchard Hall—or in other words, get engaged; visit Chicago; live in an apartment."

One thing I wish I had known before coming here is "how easy it is here to cut yourself off from the real world."

Indiana

DePauw University

Address: 101 E.Seminary St., Greencastle, IN 46135
Phone: 765-658-4006
E-mail address: admission@depauw.edu
Web site URL: www.depauw.edu
Location: rural
Founded: 1837
Private or Public: private
Religious affiliation: United Methodist
Undergraduate enrollment: 2,216
Total enrollment: 2,216
Percent Male/Female: 44%/56%
Percent Minority: 11.0%

Percent African-American: 6.0%
Percent Hispanic: 3.0%
Percent Asian: 2.0%
Percent in-state/out-of-state: 51%/49%
Percent Pub HS: 89%
Fraternities: 75%
Sororities: 71%
Number of Applicants: 2,737
Percent Accepted: 74%
Percent Accepted who enroll: 30%
Entering: 581
Transfers: 15
Application Deadline: 1 Feb
Mean SAT: NA V, NA M

Middle 50% SAT range: 550–650 V, 560–650 M
Middle 50% ACT range: 24–28
Mean ACT: NA
3 Most popular majors: communication, English, economics
Retention: 84.0%
Graduation rate: 79.0%
Library: 254,806 volumes
Tuition and Fees: $19,420 in; NA out
Room and Board: $6,080
On-campus housing: 99%
Financial aid, first-year: 99%

In the small Indiana town of Greencastle, Marvin's is the home of good, greasy eats like the garlic cheeseburger (GCB). Venture inside and you will discover more than a thousand pictures covering the walls, of people holding "Marvin's Delivers" signs at locations across the globe, from Antarctica to the bottom of the ocean. Famous for delivering its GCBs at almost any hour of the day or night, Marvin's is just one of many traditions at DePauw University, a private liberal arts college located in Greencastle.

DePauw was founded in 1837 to provide students of all religious denominations with a sound liberal arts education. According to students, the current academic environment reflects those original intentions. A total of 31 course credits is required for a B.A. degree, along with distribution requirements in six categories: natural science and mathematics; social and behavioral sciences; literature and the arts; historical and philosophical understanding; foreign language; and self-expression, which includes classes in physical education, communications, and musical performance. DePauw students must also demonstrate proficiency in writing, quantitative reasoning (mathematical problem solving), and oral communication skills by taking classes in each of these three areas. In addition, students are required to attend a winter term held in January, an opportunity many DePauw students use to pursue internships and real-world experience in their field of study. Although the requirements are numerous, there are few complaints. Students describe the curriculum as "very challenging." One undergrad said, "Initially, most students here have to adjust to the difference in workload between college and high school."

DePauw has several honors programs for exceptionally talented and ambitious students. These include Management Fellows (a pre-business program), Media Fellows (focused on mass media—print and broadcast), and Science Research Fellows (focused on independent laboratory research). Students report that the humanities and social science departments at DePauw are exceptionally strong, while some find the sciences weaker. Many say the real strength of a DePauw education is the intimate learning environment provided by small classes and professors; DePauw has neither TAs nor large introductory courses. According to one student, the largest class has only about 90 students, and most have enrollments of less than 30. "I love the small classes and the fact that teachers actually know your name!" said one student.

A Huge Petrified Turtle?

The small size of DePauw's campus also contributes to the intimacy of the school. The walk from one end of campus to the other "takes about 10 minutes," said one student. Undergrads universally praise the beauty of the DePauw campus, noted for its attractive brick buildings, especially the centrally located East College, one of the oldest buildings at DePauw. Also, on the East Campus lawn is the Boulder, donated to the university in 1892 by a farmer who reportedly thought it was a huge petrified turtle. Every year, a group of adventuresome students streak around the Boulder to celebrate the first snowfall.

Going Greek

The intimacy of the school, the small student body, and the lack of entertainment options in Greencastle result in a social scene dominated by the Greek system. According to one student, "Social life exists only because of the Greek system." The high percentage of Greeks has a significant impact on the independent (non-Greek) students at DePauw. Those outside of the Greek system are more likely to be dissatisfied with the school, and some feel left out of the social scene. "At DePauw it is very hard not to go Greek. It is harder to make friends, especially if you're a quiet person," reported one student. Another student said that if you are not planning on going Greek at

DePauw, "there's a good chance you wouldn't stay here." For the majority who do make the plunge into Greek life, the rush process is a painless, noncompetitive, and relatively enjoyable experience. "Rush was one of the most unique experiences I've had. If you go to DePauw, you should rush just to check it out," said one freshman. Several students who had not planned on going Greek before coming to DePauw commented on how rush changed their stereotypes of fraternities and sororities.

However, members agree that one stereotype is true: fraternities and sororities provide a multitude of opportunities to drink and party, including theme parties and formals throughout the year. Delta Chi, for example, hosts a Hawaii Five-O party every year, complete with sand and 40-ounce drinks. Though kegs are officially banned on campus, some students say it is fairly easy to find alcohol, if you so desire, at Greek parties and local bars. Several restaurants also serve as popular hangouts, especially Marvin's, Hathaway's (slightly upscale), Jackson's (for breakfast), and the Phoenix Orient Chinese Restaurant.

These restaurants are a much-appreciated reprise from the standard fare served in the dining halls. The food was uniformly described as average to mediocre, primarily for the limited choices and "recycled menus." Vegan and vegetarian options are available, but that's where the variety ends. First-semester freshmen are required to purchase a full 21-meal plan—a requirement that annoys many. Beginning sophomore year, Greeks can take their meals in their respective houses, which many feel is a much more economical and tasty alternative to dining hall food.

Beginning sophomore year, the majority of Greek students move into their fraternity or sorority houses. All first-year students are required to live in on-campus dorms. The average freshman room "isn't anything special" but is fairly large; students share common bathrooms with hallmates. All dorms are coed; most have mixed floors, but a few floors remain single-sex. Many freshmen consider their RAs more as friends than authority figures. For those who do not go Greek, the university guarantees single rooms in Huber and other upperclass dorms.

Who Goes to DePauw?

The general consensus is that people at DePauw do not fit a certain stereotype. The school may be 80 percent Greek, but students described the Greek scene as different from those of larger state universities. "It's not as exclusive and elitist," said one student. The general fashion style is an eclectic mix that ranges from preppy to alternative. Most of the students are upper-middle-class, white in-staters, with a good mix of political conservatives and liberals (leaning more to the conservative side). The school has a visible gay and lesbian group that is generally accepted. Many undergrads believe that black, Latino, and Native American students are underrepresented at the university and thus have been the focus of recruitment efforts. A large number of scholarships are available for traditionally underrepresented minorities.

The majority of DePauw students get involved with some sort of extracurricular activity. Intramurals and exercise are popular pastimes, although several students complain that the gym and athletic facilities could be better. DePauw is a Division III school and offers no athletic scholarships, so sports teams are "good but not great." Basketball and football games are the best-attended events.

> **"Social life exists only because of the Greek system."**

The intense rivalry between DePauw and its long-standing local archrival Wabash comes to the forefront in the last football game of the season—the Monon Bell Game ("the Game"), when each school battles to proudly display the old railroad bell at its respective campus until the next Bell Game comes around. The nationally televised Monon Bell Game unifies all of DePauw, past and present, Greek and non-Greek, students and alumni, by demonstrating their spirit and pride. On game day, DePauw spirit peaks at a school deeply entrenched in both the academic liberal arts tradition and the Greek social system. —*Madhu Pocha and Staff*

FYI

The three best things about attending DePauw are "the low faculty-to-student ratio, the Greek system, and the friendly people."

The three worst things about attending DePauw are "the location, the weather sucks, and there's not a lot of entertainment options."

The three things every student should do before graduating from DePauw are "to attend a Monon Bell Game, do a roadtrip, and go abroad."

One thing I wish I knew before coming here is "what Greencastle has to offer."

Earlham College

Address: 801 National Road West, Richmond, IN 47374	**Percent African-American:** 8.0%	**Middle 50% SAT range:** 520–660 V, 500–630 M
Phone: 765-983-1600	**Percent Hispanic:** 2.0%	**Middle 50% ACT range:** 21–27
E-mail address: admission@earlham.edu	**Percent Asian:** 2.5%	**Mean ACT:** 35
Web site URL: www.earlham.edu	**Percent in-state / out-of-state:** 27% / 73%	**3 Most popular majors:** biology, psychology, English
Location: small city	**Percent Pub HS:** 75%	
Founded: 1847	**Fraternities:** 0%	**Retention:** 87%
Private or Public: private	**Sororities:** 0%	**Graduation rate:** 70%
Religious affiliation: Society of Friends, Quaker	**Number of Applicants:** 1,038	**Library:** 477,161 volumes
Undergraduate enrollment: 1,123	**Percent Accepted:** 84%	**Tuition and Fees:** $20,256 in; NA out
Total enrollment: 1,191	**Percent Accepted who enroll:** 34%	**Room and Board:** $4,810
Percent Male / Female: 43% / 57%	**Entering:** 322	**On-campus housing:** 96%
Percent Minority: 13.0%	**Transfers:** 26	**Financial aid, first-year:** 80%
	Application Deadline: 15 Feb	
	Mean SAT: 594 V, 565 M	

Many things have changed at this small Quaker college. Jeans and T-shirts have replaced the traditional Quaker plain dress. Liberal thinking has seeped through the conservatism. A student body that more closely resembles a cross section of America's young adults has replaced the once all-Quaker student population. Yet, after more than a century of modernization, Earlham College still holds on to many of the ideals upon which it was founded. In the flat plains of the Midwest, these traditions help make Earlham stand out.

Small Classes, Big Ideas

A classroom with seven people is a fairly common sight at Earlham—and it's not because students don't like going to class. The school's small size makes for small, intimate classes, like "Literature of the Industrial Age" and "Humanism and Personology." "Earlham provides opportunities to students that aren't available to my friends that go to larger universities. If there is something you wish to pursue in your studies, Earlham provides an informal, supportive, and comfortable setting in which to do it." As with most colleges, Earlham does have its share of large introductory lecture classes, but even these classes are reported to have only seventy or eighty people.

Professors teach every class at Earlham. As a result of small class sizes and Quaker tradition, students are on a first name basis with their teachers. Even the president of the school is greeted with a "Hey Doug!" But informal doesn't mean pushover. In fact, getting to know the professors helps students get to know the subject matter. One student gushed, "The professors are *wonderful*—they are accessible, challenging but caring about their students, and very passionate about the subject matter." One student explained the dedication of the professors: "If you move to Richmond, Indiana to teach for the pay that they provide at Earlham, you have to be pretty invested in your work." Professors play a part outside of the classroom, too. In addition to the usual invitations to dinner, or parties on the front lawn, professors are known to participate in student activities. "The oldest member of the English department, his daughter (also a professor), and two other professors performed Bananarama's 'Venus' at our annual air guitar show."

Academics at Earlham can be challenging, but you have to make the effort. Even the general education requirements, which can be a hassle to fulfill, are enriching experiences. Claimed one student, "The Freshman Humanities program, which is required, could have made Tolstoy a better writer." Students are also given opportunities to get into seminar-level classes as first-year students, although first-years ("we don't say freshmen") often aren't prepared for the level of difficulty in these seminar courses. Academic advisors are always willing to help students decide whether or not a class is right for them. Some classes that students recommend taking include German Film, "Topics in the History of Ideas: Thucydides and Plato," and "Theory and Practice of Nonviolence."

The Heart of It All

The center of the campus is a grassy circle known as "the Heart." "You can see just about every major building from the middle of the Heart." On a nice, spring afternoon, students are found playing Frisbee, barbecuing, or just relaxing on the Heart. The rest of the campus is a blend of '60s architecture, newly constructed buildings, and back-campus—an undeveloped area of campus great for quiet walks and peaceful thoughts. As a whole, the campus is beautiful and cozy; no streets run through it. Students are excited about the new field house, recently completed and housing new weight machines and an indoor pool. A new social sciences building and a fine arts building are under development.

The two opposite ends of the campus each have their own libraries: Lilly Library and the Science Library. Both libraries have computer labs where students can print out their reports and are considered good places to study. Lilly Library—the larger of the two libraries—has Japanese mats to sit on. Another important piece of the campus is the Runyan Center, which houses several classrooms, a small coffee shop, the bookstore, and a theater, and is attached to the dining hall. Most students find themselves at Runyan at least twice a day, if not more.

Living

The types of housing at Earlham vary, and most people are able to find an accommodation that works for them. The variety of housing options runs the gamut from Hoerner (the quiet dorm) to Barrett ("the loud dirty drugs dorm") to Warren and Wilson (the each-room-has-individual-adjustable-thermostats-and-air-conditioning dorm). All of the dorms have a kitchen on each floor and students often make their own meals for special occasions or just to get out of eating dining hall food. All of the dorms have RAs who help out for all four years that a student is on campus, and most of the RAs are reportedly "wonderful." Students also have the option of living in campus-owned housing, some of which is based on themes. Each theme house plans a theme week for the other students sometime during the year. For example, the residents of Peace House are responsible for planning Peace and Justice Week every year in the fall.

Students think that the food in the dining halls has been steadily improving, especially with the most recent addition of pizza. A vegetarian contingent has also gotten the college to add more "edible" vegetarian options, in addition to the usual meaty fare. One vegan student recommended the vegan potpie: "It's delicious."

Trials and Tribulations of a Small Town

The small town of Richmond, Indiana, doesn't provide the entertainment that Earlham's college kids crave. Outside of bowling, Wal-Mart, movies, Little Sheba's, and El Rodeo, students find that Richmond doesn't have much to keep them occupied. Instead, weekend jaunts up to Oxford, Ohio (home of Miami University), Indianapolis, and Dayton are common. Students do find that Richmond offers a lot in the way of volunteer activities, though, and most take advantage of these opportunities to help out their community. A select group is offered the Bonner Scholarship, which helps students pay for school in exchange for ten hours of volunteer work a week. Students say volunteering is a bonus in that it also gives them a chance to meet the people of Richmond. Small though the town is, students advise that prospective first-years "bring a car (or make friends with someone who has one) because it's hard to get around Richmond without one."

Living It Up

Earlham's extracurriculars are as numerous as students' interests. From Earlham Environmental Action Coalition to the radio station, from the Film Society to the Rainbow Tribe (Earlham has a history of supporting gay and bisexual students), most students find something that suits their interests. Within this bastion of liberalism ("a stifling political oneness"), one brave force battles to bring bipartisanship back to the campus: the Earlham Progressive Alliance—group activities include infiltrating the school newspaper staff.

Spectator sports are not popular at Earlham. Although not many people go to the football games or other athletic events, participation in team sports is common. The less athletically inclined can form an intramural team—IM soccer team names include "Southern Comfort" and "the Green Nuggets"—play a club sport, or just join a pick-up game of football on the Heart. Playing a varsity sport requires more of a commitment—about three hours per day—but success doesn't come without hard work. The men's soccer team is one of the most successful teams in its division and other Earlham teams have seen considerable success, as well.

> Outside of bowling, Wal-Mart, movies, Little Sheba's, and El Rodeo, students find that Richmond doesn't have much to keep them occupied.

Many Earlham students count going abroad as one of their best experiences in college. Earlham offers programs to such exotic locales as Japan, Kenya, Jerusalem, and others. And if a student wants to go someplace that isn't part of Earlham's off-campus program, the school gives them the opportunity to go abroad through other universities; their financial aid goes with them, too.

Runnin' the Hash

Earlham is a dry campus so no alcohol is sold on campus, but that doesn't mean that nobody drinks. "The Hash" has been an Earlham tradition for about 10 years: students follow a set trail of flour for 3 miles through the woods to find a body of water and a keg of beer at the end. Then a wild party ensues. "[The beer] is usually Schaeffer, the nectar of the gods. As you drink, standing in the water, the rest of the crowd sings bawdy Hash songs. There are a variety of rules and veteran Hashers have Hash names. The best part is that it's all underground—sort of. It's really hard to hide a flour trail."

The social atmosphere is very laid back, so those who don't feel like drinking find that "you can easily not drink and still have fun. There isn't pressure to drink. It's not the basis of a social life." The film society usually shows a movie every weekend and the Student Activities Board brings in comedians every now and then. The college often sponsors concerts (like Louis Belson, the jazz performer). Annual events include the Sunsplash—a reggae concert, the International Festival, and a lip-synching competition. Some people say that the best parties, though, are the small ones with their friends. "The best party I've been to was back-campus in the woods around a campfire. We had some musical instruments and played and sang into the night." For late-night cravings, Sunshine is open 24/7 and Papa John's delivers until 1:30 A.M. And for those who can't live without a hot cup of joe, Java Jazz is a little college-run coffee shop about a block off campus.

Quaker Friends

Earlham is not as racially diverse as most here would like. One athlete pointed out, "I'm concerned that the relatively few African Americans on campus are recruited by the sports teams. I think more should be recruited by the academic departments." Racial diversity aside, students are often very different and come from different parts of the country. However, students find themselves moving among the different groups on campus— the "gamers, jocks, activists, punks, hashers" although "there is a lot of permeability within these groups." Most people on campus are very friendly and will say "hi" to you if they see you. Chalk it up to Quaker tradition or Midwestern hospitality, Earlham is a great place to meet new

people. A third-year gives this piece of advice: "GET INVOLVED. LEAVE YOUR DORM ROOM. You will meet great people, get job skills, and have an excuse for never handing in work on time—works with some profs but not others."
—*Kenneth Tseng*

FYI

The three best things about attending Earlham are "accessible professors, the sense of community, and being able to take peace studies classes."

The three worst things about attending Earlham are "the food (I could just say that three times), the red tape associated with housing, and Richmond."

The three things that every student should do before graduating from Earlham are "take a walk on back-campus, do some volunteer work, go abroad for a year, and (four), gotta run the Hash."

One thing I'd like to have known before coming here is "when they say that the Midwest is flat, they ain't kidding."

Indiana University / Bloomington

Address: 300 North Jordan Avenue, Bloomington, IN 47405-7700	**Percent African-American:** 4.0%	**Mean SAT:** 466 V, 530 M
	Percent Hispanic: 2.0%	**Middle 50% SAT range:** 500–620 V, 510–630 M
Phone: 812-855-0661	**Percent Asian:** 3.0%	**Middle 50% ACT range:** NA
E-mail address: iuadmit@Indiana.edu	**Percent in-state / out-of-state:** 73% / 27%	**Mean ACT:** 24
Web site URL: www.indiana.edu / iub	**Percent Pub HS:** NA	**3 Most popular majors:** biology, psychology, journalism
Location: urban	**Fraternities:** 4%	
Founded: 1820	**Sororities:** 4%	**Retention:** 87.0%
Private or Public: public	**Number of Applicants:** 17,583	**Graduation rate:** 70.0%
Religious affiliation: none	**Percent Accepted:** 82%	**Library:** 5.7 million volumes
Undergraduate enrollment: 25,451	**Percent Accepted who enroll:** 35%	**Tuition and Fees:** $4,244 in; $12,900 out
Total enrollment: 34,937	**Entering:** 6,986	**Room and Board:** $5,492
Percent Male / Female: 47% / 53%	**Transfers:** 1,227	**On-campus housing:** 49%
Percent Minority: 9.0%	**Application Deadline:** 15 Feb	**Financial aid, first-year:** 38%

Ask 10 different students at Indiana University at Bloomington for the definition of a Hoosier, and expect to get 10 different answers. Located in the small city of Bloomington, IU can boast about its excellent academic reputation in addition to its nationally recognized basketball team. In fact, the only thing you may not learn at IU is the definition of a "Hoosier."

Tough Stuff

Academics at IU are reported to be tough, but not overwhelming. As one student noted, "It's only as bad as you make it." Music, journalism, and business are extremely popular majors at IU, and the business school is known to be especially demanding. While most students say that slackers are "weeded out" pretty quickly during the first year, others say the School of Public and Environmental Affairs has gained a reputation as "the school for business dropouts." Also, one student said that "the English department has a real attitude. It's impossible to get an A." The biggest academic complaints are about the strict language requirements (four semesters).

For those willing to work hard, the university offers several honors programs for both underclassmen and upperclassmen. On the other hand, when looking for those easy classes, students give warning about elective courses offered for credit through the HPER (Health, Physical Education, and Recreation) Departments like archery and tae kwon do. "The teachers all know that you're probably taking them for an easy A, so they make it tough on you."

Overall, students are happy with the classes and professors at IU, but some complain about large intro classes freshman year. Freshmen are last to register, and one student said that you can "sign up early and get a 30-person class, later and get a 300." However, even the smallest classes usually break up into smaller sections taught by TAs. In a sea of over 25,000 undergrads, students say that sometimes they feel like "just a number." "However," as one student countered, "something about big universities that people don't take into consideration is that once you're accepted into your chosen school . . . it feels like a family."

The Resources at IU

One of the advantages of a large university are the resources it can offer. Indiana is home to the nation's largest student center, a building that includes restaurants, eateries, a bookstore, a movie theater, a bowling alley, pool tables, and a four-star hotel. Also, the Recreational Sports Building, which students love to brag about, was recently finished.

Though Hoosiers complain about the food in the dining halls, there are plenty of other places to eat around campus, and most dorms now include fast-food chains like McDonald's and Sbarro's Pizza.

Most freshmen and sophomores live in the dorms, since a large number of upperclassmen decide to live in fraternity and sorority houses or apartments off-campus. As one student described it, "people flock off-campus after freshman year." Students who do live in the dorms say they are not too bad. Most housing is coed by floor with several RAs. Students claim each dorm has a definite personality and some say that "you can usually tell what someone is like by which dorm they live in."

For example, Ashton is known for its academics, Eigenmann for its international student population, and Collins Living-Learning Center is the place for "free spirits" on campus.

Though a majority of students are from in-state, undergrads agree that there is no stereotypical Hoosier. Some people come in with a set group of friends from high school, but it is "very easy to meet people here." Many students mention the very liberal attitudes of students and their open-mindedness. Bloomington has a large gay and lesbian population, and the IU campus is "well known for its gay rights activism."

Greek Glory

A typical Hoosier is known as a big party fiend, and it is no coincidence that the fraternity and sorority presence on the IU campus is huge. One student reported that sometimes tension exists between Greeks and independents. While some said non-drinkers do not feel out of place (campus is "technically" dry), other students disagree, saying that "a large portion of the social life does revolve around alcohol." Drugs, mostly marijuana, are on campus, but they are "only around if you are into it." A typical weekend for underclassmen includes frat parties every night. Many of these parties are exclusive and tickets are checked at the door. However, many upperclassmen, even those who are frat members, tend to prefer the local bar scene. Other than bars, students talk about the lack of off-campus activities, saying "everything closes early here." Frequent road trips to Chicago, St. Louis, Indianapolis, or a weekend at home are also common.

One of the most anticipated events at IU is the annual "Little 500" bike race (the subject of the film *Breaking Away*, which was filmed in Bloomington). Students from all different organizations on campus participate, the days beforehand are filled with parties, and it is said to be "one of the wildest weeks ever."

100 Percent Basketball

"Basketball, basketball, basketball. That's what IU is!" Bobby Knight's team is legendary around the country, and IU school spirit reaches its peak during March Mad ess, the month of NCAA playoffs, known ere as "Hoosier Hysteria." Students can asily get tickets, but school officials, anticipating a rush, often do not announce r downplay the opening of ticket sales.

Most IU students played a sport in high chool, and many continue on at some vel in college, either at the intramural or ie varsity level. The campus has two ain athletic facilities: "HPER is a big arehouse . . . that's where all the noonsense people work out. The SRSC is here all the sorority and frat people go work out . . . so they look really good in eir matching workout outfits."

Extracurriculars are also important to udents. *The Indiana Students* is a fullze student-run paper that most students ead. Also, community service organizaons abound. The IU Student Organizaon is recognized by the administration the most important on-campus organi-

zation, "But no one knows exactly what they have their hands into."

Whether they come for the noteworthy academics, the Big Ten experience, or the closeness to home, the Hoosiers are happy with their school. Freshmen should be warned that the sheer size of IU can be overwhelming, however, and the transition from high school to college can often be difficult. Everyone finds their niche though, and once settled in, students can expect four years of work, fun, and basketball galore.—*Sarah DeBergalis and Staff*

ie three best things about attending IU are "the open-mindedness everywhere, the Greek system, and HPER classes."
ie three worst things about attending IU are "the language requirement, The Greeks, and being in a small town."
ie three things every student should do before graduating from IU are "to bike in the 'Little 500,' to figure out what a Hoosier is, and to take an HPER class for credit."
ie thing I'd like to have known before coming here is "all the rules of basketball . . . I had to learn fairly quickly."

Purdue University

Address: 1080 Schleman Hall, West Lafayett, IN 47907
Phone: 765-494-1776
E-mail address: admissions@adms.purdue.edu
Web site URL: www.purdue.edu
Location: suburban
Founded: 1869
Private or Public: public
Religious affiliation: none
Undergraduate enrollment: 30,159
Total enrollment: 35,715
Percent Male/Female: 57%/43%
Percent Minority: 11.0%

Percent African-American: 4.0%
Percent Hispanic: 2.0%
Percent Asian: 4.0%
Percent in-state/out-of-state: 74%/26%
Percent Pub HS: NA
Fraternities: 20%
Sororities: 18%
Number of Applicants: 18,343
Percent Accepted: 87%
Percent Accepted who enroll: 41%
Entering: 6,543
Transfers: 1,966
Application Deadline: rolling
Mean SAT: 540 V, 568 M

Middle 50% SAT range: 470–580 V, 490–630 M
Middle 50% ACT range: NA
Mean ACT: 25
3 Most popular majors: electrical and computing engineering, elementary education, communications
Retention: 87.0%
Graduation rate: 64.0%
Library: 2.2 million volumes
Tuition and Fees: $3,500 in; $11,720 out
Room and Board: $5,260
On-campus housing: 43%
Financial aid, first-year: 41%

Purdue is more than just a great engineering school. While its reputation for academic excellence in engineering draws some of the most promising prospects from all over the world, Purdue also boasts a campus teeming with school spirit, a friendly, down-to-earth student body, and a vibrant social scene.

Excellent Academics

It is in academics that Purdue sets itself apart. The school's tradition of educational excellence, especially in engineering, has produced famous alumni such as Neil Armstrong and other astronauts. "It was the reputation of the engineering department that brought me here," said one undergrad. Students are almost universally proud of Purdue's high position on national engineering rankings, and they also report that management and pharmacology are particularly strong programs.

While undergrads find their workloads "manageable," course requirements are stringent. "It can easily take four and a half or five years to graduate, with all the courses you have to take," said one student. Class sizes, especially in beginning lecture courses, can be as big as 800 students, but this does not bother most

people. "The large lectures break up into small recitations led by a TA," explained one undergrad. "That makes it very easy to ask questions and get individual help." While some students say they have problems with the accents of their foreign-born TAs, most find the quality of teaching quite high. Professors, specifically, draw rave reviews. "The professors here are world-class," said one student. "They're excellent across the board."

Midwestern Greeks

Socially, Purdue is considered one of the biggest Greek schools in the Midwest. With over 40 fraternities and 20 sororities, the Greek scene is certainly strong, but non-Greeks have no reason to feel left out. "The social life here is so big that it does not really matter whether you rush a frat or not," explained one undergrad. Students report that frat parties are generally closed. "You have to know someone to get your name on the list," said one student. "If you're on the list, they'll let you into all the parties." As an alternative to the Greek scene, many students go to less-selective apartment parties or hang out in dorms. Students said that there is a fair amount of alcohol on campus, despite the conservative administration's dry campus policies. RAs are generally quick to uphold the rules, writing up students—especially freshmen—who are caught with alcohol. Students said that non-drinkers do not feel left out of the social life: "You always see plenty of non-drinkers at parties." Many undergrads report that drug use on campus is low. As far as romantic life, students report a mix of random hookups and traditional dating. "There's one thing you can say about Purdue," said one undergrad. "There are certainly a lot of beautiful people on campus."

Life in Indiana

Dorm rooms at Purdue are standard college fare: small doubles with two beds, two desks, two closets, and two sets of shelves. Most students make lofts for their beds, creating extra floor space for a TV and couch. Freshmen live in dorms, but most sophomores move into apartments or fraternity/sorority houses. Dining halls are located in the dorms, and students can choose to eat at any dorm's dining hall. Meal plan options include 10, 15, and 20 meals a week, with "dining dollars" providing extra options at university-owned convenience stores. Food is described as "not great, but not that bad."

As a large university, Purdue attracts a diverse student body. "There's lots of diversity here, but there's still a Purdue stereotype—it's some kind of conservative preppie frat boy," said one undergrad. Even with its diversity, students noticed a lack of integration among different ethnic groups. "You'll often see groups of African-American students or groups of Asian students not mixing with other groups," explained one student. With around three-fourths of the student body hailing from within Indiana, social groups tend to form quickly. "People already knew each other before they came here," said one undergrad, "but it still seemed very easy to meet people. You meet new people every single week."

Purdue's campus is large, but nothing is too far away. "All the classes are close to each other," said one student. "I never have more than a five-minute walk to class." Students enjoy the aesthetic aspects of the campus, as well. "It's very pretty," said one undergrad. "All the buildings are made of red brick, and there are lots of trees." Many students frequent the CO-REC, a large gym and sports center located on campus and open to all students.

Outside of Class

Extracurricular activities are a large part of many students' lives at Purdue. The *Exponent*, Purdue's student newspaper, draws many budding journalists to its staff. Academically inclined organizations, especially engineering groups, also flourish. For the athletic-minded, Purdue runs a large intramural sports program that pits dorm floors against one another. Students compete for bragging rights in a number of different intramural sports throughout the year.

Sports play a large role in campus life. Not only do intramurals bring many participants to the playing field, but Purdue's membership in the Big Ten Conference also ensures a high level of competition in varsity athletics. Purdue has a long tradition of athletic excellence, and the students stand behind their teams. One football game that always draws student interest is the battle against archrival Indiana University. The winner of the game keeps the Oaken Bucket, a traveling trophy signifying the schools' strong rivalry.

> **"The professors here are world-class...excellent across the board."**

Men's basketball is always popular at Purdue, with the Boilermakers consistently in pursuit of the Big Ten championships and a place in the NCAA tournament. Students pile into Mackey Arena to cheer on their team. Getting a ticket can be difficult, as the games are almost always sold out. These sporting events draw the large student body together. Face paint and other visible signs of school spirit are always present at sporting events, along with a number of cheers and chants unique to Purdue.

Purdue provides an intricate mix of focused academics, varied social scene, and diverse student body. Within its beautiful campus are more opportunities than any student could take advantage of, and more important, a student body that is prepared for the challenge these opportunities present. "If there's one thing that differentiates Purdue from other universities," said one undergrad, "it's the students. We're proud to be Boilermakers, and the school spirit here reflects that." —*Jeff Kaplow and Staff*

FYI

The three best things about attending Purdue are "the wide variety of options and the opportunity to explore many different areas, the beautiful campus in a great town, and the friendly people and knowledgeable faculty."

The three worst things about attending Purdue are "the parking, the libraries are not very user friendly, and the amount of annoying construction going on."

The three things every student should do before graduating from Purdue are "to make a fountain run (run through one of Purdue's many fountains), go to 'Breakfast Club,' and visit the bar known as Harry's Chocolate Shop."

One thing I wish I knew before coming here is "never pursue a major you don't really like—especially at Purdue."

Rose-Hulman Institute of Technology

Address: 5500 Wabash Ave, Terre Haute, IN 47803
Phone: 812-877-8213
E-mail address: admis.ofc@rose-hulman.edu
Web site URL: www.rose-hulman.edu
Location: suburban
Founded: 1874
Private or Public: private
Religious affiliation: none
Undergraduate enrollment: 1,545
Total enrollment: 1,678
Percent Male/Female: 83%/17%
Percent Minority: 6.0%

Percent African-American: 1.0%
Percent Hispanic: 3.0%
Percent Asian: 1.0%
Percent in-state/out-of-state: 48%/52%
Percent Pub HS: 85%
Fraternities: 45%
Sororities: 35%
Number of Applicants: 3,295
Percent Accepted: 67%
Percent Accepted who enroll: 12%
Entering: 395
Transfers: 18
Application Deadline: 1 Mar
Mean SAT: 650 V, 700 M

Middle 50% SAT range: 590–700 V, 667–740 M
Middle 50% ACT range: 22–36
Mean ACT: 30
3 Most popular majors: mech eng, elec eng, chemistry
Retention: 96.0%
Graduation rate: 69.0%
Library: 74,205 volumes
Tuition and Fees: $20,135 in; $20,135 out
Room and Board: $5,751
On-campus housing: 98%
Financial aid, first-year: 90%

Located in sleepy Terre Haute, Rose-Hulman Institute of Technology may not have the same recognition that rivals MIT and Caltech can claim, but Rose can certainly hold its own among the big schools. If you are looking for a topnotch engineering program at one of the best technology specialty schools in the nation, this is the place for you.

Big Changes, Small School

For such a small school, Rose has had a lot of changes in the past few years. Most notable was the 1995 decision to go coed and admit women to the traditionally all-male school. Students and faculty have welcomed the change, and today over 10 percent of Rose students are female.

The campus is also currently undergoing a massive facelift. A multimillion-dollar Sports and Recreation Center is the newest addition, along with the addition of state-of-the-art classrooms in Olin Hall, the creation of Cook Stadium, new tennis courts, the construction of Hulman Union (the cafeteria), CTRI (Center for Technological Research with Industry), and the establishment of a new dorm. The school has also announced the construction of a fine arts building (Hatfield Hall), expected to be completed by the fall of 2001.

Nothing Comes Easy

Academics are the number one priority at Rose, and the quiet campus allows students to take on challenging course loads. There are no easy majors—Rose keeps its students constantly busy. "We joke that civil engineers don't work because they're always outside in the sun during labs, but there are no slackers . . . they just won't survive four years." Another joke about the school's difficulty tells of a Rose student who failed out, transferred to Purdue (a rival school), and subsequently got a 4.0 GPA. Despite such challenging course work, Rose-Hulman offers a learning center, which offers tutoring by appointment. Students do complain about some of the academic requirements, such as College and Life Skills, a course that "supposedly helps freshmen make the transition to college."

> "Rose is awesome if you're willing to work your ass off for four years."

The advantage of being at a small school is readily apparent in class sizes—over 30 students in a class is almost unheard of, and the norm is between 10 and 20. Students are also quick to point out the absence of TAs on campus: "There are none. Every class is taught by a professor." Teachers are always available for students to talk to and often go out of their way to help. One student told of a professor who hand-delivered a film to his dorm room one night because it was not available for rental.

Is There a Social Scene?

In contrast to the rave reviews about academics, students say the social scene at Rose leaves much to be desired. Despite the presence of two additional colleges, Terre Haute has little to offer students looking for off-campus fun. As one student bluntly said, "It sucks." Instead, frat parties are more common options on

weekends. Almost half of Rose's student population goes Greek, with eight fraternities and two sororities to choose from. With regard to alcohol, students say that the administration takes a lenient position. Kegs are not allowed on campus, but students say officials do not go looking for violations. As far as the dating scene goes, most students with a significant other are seeing someone off-campus, but the odds definitely favor the women at Rose. One student summed up the social scene by saying that "there aren't a lot of alternatives, but I don't think people even have time to notice, we're all too busy working."

Living at Rose

Dorms at Rose are pretty typical, and freshmen have first priority. The new dorm will help with the recent housing shortage, which had forced many upperclassmen to live off-campus. All residence halls have RAs, and freshmen dorms are also assigned sophomore advisors to help with the adjustment to college. Students praise this support system, but complain about the visitation regulations: guys have to be off girls' floors (and vice versa) by 2 A.M. There are not many options for on-campus eating; Rose has only two dining halls and another eatery called the Worx. The food, though, is described as "decent."

Life at Rose

Often mentioned is the lack of diversity in the Rose student body. Most students are white, middle-class, and from Indiana. Rose's athletic department is Division III, and while academics come first, intramurals are very popular. Many students agree that they "wouldn't go anywhere else." One tradition they love is the annual homecoming bonfire, for which "they have to redirect air traffic" because of its enormous size.

For those considering Rose, students advise you to be absolutely sure that you want to study engineering or science before coming. If you do, remember that this school is difficult, but worth it. Rose-Hulman is quickly gaining the national attention and praise it deserves. As one student said, "Rose is awesome if you're willing to work your ass off for four years."—*Sarah DeBergalis and Staff*

FYI

The three best things about attending Rose-Hulman are "the small size of the school, the family atmosphere combined with the educational environment, and the Greek life (which is unlike the Greek life at any other school)."

The three worst things about attending Rose-Hulman are "the work load, the apparent lack of school spirit, and the male-to-female ratio."

The three things every student should do before graduating from Rose-Hulman are "to go to homecoming, have a talk with Dr. Hulbert, and live on campus for a year."

One thing I wish I knew before coming here is "that the Integrated Curriculum is way too stressful to take here at Rose-Hulman."

St. Mary's College

Address: Office of Admissions, LeMans Hall, Notre Dame, IN 46556
Phone: 800-551-7621
E-mail address: admissions@saintmarys.edu
Web site URL: www.saintmarys.edu
Location: suburban
Founded: 1844
Private or Public: private
Religious affiliation: Roman Catholic
Undergraduate enrollment: 1,355
Total enrollment: 1,355
Percent Male/Female: 0%/100%

Percent Minority: 6.0%
Percent African-American: 1.0%
Percent Hispanic: 4.0%
Percent Asian: 1.0%
Percent in-state/out-of-state: 24%/76%
Percent Pub HS: 54%
Fraternities: 0%
Sororities: 0%
Number of Applicants: 920
Percent Accepted: 85%
Percent Accepted who enroll: 52%
Entering: 406
Transfers: 75
Application Deadline: 1 Mar

Mean SAT: 560 V, 550 M
Middle 50% SAT range: 500–610 V, 500–600 M
Middle 50% ACT range: NA
Mean ACT: 25
3 Most popular majors: business administration, communication, nursing
Retention: 88.0%
Graduation rate: 72.0%
Library: 198,729 volumes
Tuition and Fees: $16,184 in; $16,184 out
Room and Board: $5,632
On-campus housing: 82%
Financial aid, first-year: 77%

A student at this small Catholic women's college can be assured that she will not get lost in the crowd. At St. Mary's College in Notre Dame, Indiana, one can have the best of both worlds: the intimacy of a small single-sex campus, with the facilities of the large University of Notre Dame just across the street.

Liberal Arts Curriculum

Academically, St. Mary's "belles," as they're known, pursue one of five degrees: bachelor of arts, bachelor of business administration, bachelor of fine arts, bachelor of music, or bachelor of science. All students are required to declare a major at the beginning of their sophomore year. Through the core curriculum at St. Mary's, students are encouraged to pursue a broad-based liberal arts education. Most students fulfill all of the core requirements, along with the foreign-language requirement, by the end of their sophomore year, after which they take more specialized classes suited to their major. One first-year student who had not yet decided on her major said that "the core requirements are a relief. They give me some direction."

Students at St. Mary's can take classes at Notre Dame, and many do. Notre Dame students take St. Mary's courses as well. St. Mary's courses have a great advantage because of their small size: one frosh said each of her five classes had fewer than 20 students. The largest classes on campus are the introductory science classes, which are still remarkably small—around 50 students. In addition, at St. Mary's there are no teaching assistants, so students say a professor "with the highest degree in the field" will be teaching your courses. The student-teacher interactions are also excellent. In addition to having her professors' home phone numbers, one student even attended a Halloween party given by her philosophy professor.

Registration takes place over the summer. First-year students are sent a guidebook of courses, from which they select 10. A schedule is then sent home, usually including the student's top five classes. Upperclasswomen generally do not have difficulty enrolling in their first-choice courses.

Academics at St. Mary's are rigorous but manageable. "The classes are small enough so all my questions are answered and I understand the material, which makes the classes seem easier," one student said. Undergrads claim that there are no true "gut" courses, although Beginning Acting is an easy class according to some.

An Integrated Campus

St. Mary's has its own library, named Cushwa-Leighton, which is separate from the Notre Dame facilities. To study quietly, many students go to Cushwa, which reportedly is so conducive to studying that Notre Dame students like it, too. For social studying, and for simply socializing, most St. Mary's students go to the larger library at Notre Dame.

> "The classes are small enough so all my questions are answered and I understand the material, which makes the classes seem easier."

The majority of St. Mary's students live on campus in four residential halls. McCandless, the most modern of the four, provides each student with a small study carrel space across the hall from her bedroom. According to one student, "Each dorm has its own personal character." Each small study room is equipped with air-conditioning, which helps beat the hot Indiana weather at the beginning and end of the year. Students also live in Le Mans Hall, which is relatively old, but beautiful;

Holy Cross Hall, which has larger rooms and big suites; and Regina Hall, which has only singles. All of the dorms (with the exception of McCandless) as well as the computer clusters and various other facilities across campus are connected via underground tunnels.

There are stringent rules, called parietals, dictating when members of the opposite sex are allowed in the dorms. Males have to be out of the dorms by midnight during the week, and by 2 A.M. on weekends. The same rules apply at Notre Dame.

There is one main cafeteria on campus, and the food there is reasonably tasty. Students can frequent the dining hall as many times a day as they like (it's open from 7 A.M. to 7 P.M.). Vegetarian options are always available, as are a salad bar and a grill. Most students eat on campus because there are few options in the local town of South Bend. When the women of St. Mary's do leave campus for a meal, their choices "tend to be limited to fast food."

Midwestern Belles

Because South Bend has little to offer a college crowd socially and culturally, much of what happens at St. Mary's centers on life at Notre Dame. Since neither has a Greek system, the schools are interrelated through clubs and extracurriculars. One student claimed that "going back and forth to Notre Dame is an extracurricular activity." However, "some people have a love-hate relationship with Notre Dame," another student added. St. Mary's undergrads participate in a wide range of activities from student government to intramural sports to writing for the *Observer*, the daily paper. The main connection between the two schools is athletics. St. Mary's has its own, recently built athletics center (the Angela Fitness Center) and Belles play competitively in basketball, volleyball, and tennis, yet their true allegiance is to Notre Dame. One frosh said, "People try to rile up some school spirit, but it's just not there. Mainly, it's for Notre Dame."

In addition to Notre Dame sports, St. Mary's students take part in Notre Dame social events. St. Mary's itself is a dry campus, but that does not stop undergrads from busing over to Notre Dame to drink (a shuttle runs between the two schools almost 24 hours a day). Popular events on campus also include "screw your room-mate" dances. At these events, room-mates fix each other up on blind dates, using the "Dog Book," a book with photos of all the freshmen. Although St. Mary's does offer some social venues, the major-ity of St. Mary's students spend their free time socializing at Notre Dame.

Students at St. Mary's date, but random hookups also occur, despite the strong Catholic overtones at the school. General, informed discussions on safe sex are rare, and the administration has something of a

"don't ask, don't tell" policy, according to students.

The campus is politically conservative, and while the college is not as diverse as larger institutions, it makes a concerted effort to attract women from different backgrounds and geographic areas. Cur-rently, the majority of the students at St. Mary's are from the Midwest.

St. Mary's is a small Catholic college with all the resources of a large university (as a result of its proximity to Notre Dame)—and St. Mary's students rely on their neighboring university for so-cial, athletic, and academic enrichment. —*Heather Topel*

FYI

The three best things about attending St. Mary's College are that you get the benefits of both single-sex education and co-educational, great professors, underground tunnels (who wants to walk in the rain?).

The three worst things about attending St. Mary's College are how everyone spends all of their time at Notre Dame, parietals, the lack of restaurants in town.

The three things that every student should do before graduating from St. Mary's College are setting up your roommate for the "screw your roommate" dance, go to a sporting event, take a class that you had never considered taking before.

One thing I'd like to have known before coming here is "that the picture I sent them before freshman year was going to be put into something called the 'Dog Book'—how insulting."

University of Notre Dame

Address: 1 Grace Hall Notre Dame, IN 46556
Phone: 219-631-7505
E-mail address: admissio.1@nd.edu
Web site URL: www.nd.edu
Location: suburban
Founded: 1842
Private or Public: private
Religious affiliation: Roman Catholic
Undergraduate enrollment: 7,875
Total enrollment: 10,275
Percent Male/Female: 45%/55%
Percent Minority: 14.0%

Percent African-American: 3.0%
Percent Hispanic: 7.0%
Percent Asian: 4.0%
Percent in-state/out-of-state: 91%/9%
Percent Pub HS: 52%
Fraternities: 0%
Sororities: 0%
Number of Applicants: 8,578
Percent Accepted: 42%
Percent Accepted who enroll: 54%
Entering: 1,945
Transfers: 131
Application Deadline: 9 Jan

Mean SAT: 650 V, 668 M
Middle 50% SAT range: 610–710 V, 630–720 M
Middle 50% ACT range: NA
Mean ACT: 29
3 Most popular majors: accounting, political science, finance
Retention: 97.0%
Graduation rate: 86.0%
Library: 2.6 million volumes
Tuition and Fees: $22,200 in; $22,200 out
Room and Board: $5,750
On-campus housing: 79%
Financial aid, first-year: 52%

Not far off the interstate in South Bend, Indiana, a statue of a bearded man in flowing robes

stands atop the library of the University of Notre Dame. "Touchdown Jesus," as he is known to students, is representative of all that Notre Dame stands for—Catholic ethics, a rigorous education, and football.

Serious Academics

Notre Dame offers four different schools for undergraduates—Business Administration, Engineering, Science, and Arts & Letters—with differing requirements within the specific colleges. In the College of Arts & Letters, which includes the largest number of undergrads, students must take two each of philosophy, theology, math, and natural science, as well as one class each in the social sciences and in fine art/literature. There are approximately 50 majors to choose from. ND's academic offerings are described as a broad spectrum of everything, "except communications, which is a bit lacking." Otherwise, "they offer everything I might ever want to take," said one student. In the College of Arts & Letters students said that philosophy and English are both known as tough majors, and theology and government are both strong departments. Intro philosophy is a favorite class, but if you are looking for guts, students recommended intro sociology, intro government, some arts classes, and the math and science classes for non-majors. Intro to biology enrolls approximately 300 students, which is one of the largest classes undergrads ever encounter. Most average about 30, with some class sizes slightly higher.

The most popular majors are government and finance. Students say that engineering and science majors are set apart from others by the intense number of hours they find themselves consumed with work. Many come to Notre Dame already having decided on a major but find they want to change their minds after the first year; most notably, many students who enter as business majors transfer into the College of Arts & Letters, a relatively easy process.

Students praise the school's emphasis on undergraduate education: "Grad students don't really have a presence, except for some TAs in big lab classes. The administration is actually trying to recruit more heavily and spend more on the grad schools." ND professors are generally accessible and approachable, especially those who teach small classes. As students move up within their individual majors, they tend to get to know their professors better. "Most people have good working relationships with their professors," said one student. Getting good grades is not overly difficult, "if you do the work," of which there always seems to be a lot. "Sometimes the workload interferes with the social setting," said one undergrad. "We spend so much time related to academics." Another student said, "There are lots of motivated students here and lots of pressure, but most of it is self-imposed."

God in the Classroom?

"Religion and God definitely do come up a lot," said one student. "Religion is continually around you on a day-to-day basis, but it's not oppressive." Crucifixes hang in every classroom and building on campus, and all students at Notre Dame are required to take theology, "but the theology which is taught is not specifically Catholic," pointed out one non-religious undergrad. The student went on to say "taking theology is really good for a lot of students who have never been exposed to religion in this way."

Students say that lots of people at Notre Dame are religious, but label their peers as "fairly open" and the school's priests as "fairly liberal." Approximately 85 percent of the ND population is Catholic, with about 60 percent actively practicing. There is a chapel in every dorm where mass is held five days a week. One student warned that incoming freshmen might be put off by the prominence of their classmates' religious faith, but "the majority of students are not gung-ho about religion." Nevertheless, students say that the non-religious or non-Catholics miss out on certain aspects of ND culture, such as going to mass in the dorms on Sunday—they "have to find other ways to participate in the ND family."

The South Bend Social Scene

Like at many colleges, the weekend at Notre Dame begins on Thursday, when many students head out to bars. Friday night usually brings dorm parties with beer and friends, in anticipation of the next day's football game. About half the undergraduate population hits the tailgate before the game on Saturday, after which students usually spend a low-key evening hanging out with friends or studying, even after victories. "Everyone stands the whole game, so we get really tired by the end," explained one student. Sunday is a day for homework, inter-hall sports, and mass in the evening. Students said they actually drink more during the non–football seasons, "but [drinking] isn't a big deal and there's not a lot of pressure to drink," said one undergrad. Those students whose "crappy fakes" cannot get them into bars tend to hit off-campus parties or drink in the dorms (there are no frats). Although students report that the administration is rather lenient regarding alcohol, it is apparently not so lax about visiting hours. ND's parietals dictate that students cannot be in the room of members of the opposite sex after midnight Sunday to Thursday and 2 A.M. Friday to Saturday. Students caught breaking the rules are sentenced to community service or kicked off-campus; expulsion is the punishment if one is caught having sex. "That's where you see the strict adherence to Catholic tradition," said one student. "It's not forced down your throat, but this place is definitely a Catholic institution."

Students admitted that beyond partying, there is really "not that much to do . . . South Bend leaves a little to be desired." The Student Union Board organizes movies and barbecues on a regular basis and plans major events like An Tostal, ND's spring festival. There are two or three school-sponsored concerts each semester with bands such as Third Eye Blind and Aerosmith.

A superficial look around the Notre Dame campus would give the impression that the school is populated by yuppies, according to one undergrad. "But once you get to know people you see that there's more diversity," said another student. "There are a lot of hidden talents you'd never know people had just by looking at all the North Face and Abercrombie & Fitch." Another student said, "Everyone gets homogenized . . . you just need to peel back the layers." But students said there definitely is an identifiable stereotype: "white, suburban, conservative, Midwestern, and preppy," listed one undergrad. Some people are more vocally dissatisfied with ND's lack of diversity. "Yes, all the different races are represented, but the large majority is Catholic and white, and I would like to see more of a mix."

> **"Religion is continually around you on a day-to-day basis, but it's not oppressive."**

Gay and lesbian rights have recently become a huge issue on campus, as the administration "struggles with how to treat everybody equally and still retain the school's Catholic nature," according to one student. The issue is whether to add sexual orientation to Notre Dame's legal nondiscrimination clause. There is only a handful of openly gay people on campus, which is not surprising given the level of homophobia that students notice pervades the campus atmosphere. In general, the student body is "fairly conservative . . . most people yearn for the Reagan years." But the campus rarely gets politicized over national issues, as immediate campus concerns tend to take precedence.

Dorm Community

Eighty-five percent of Notre Dame students live on campus. Dorm unity abounds, adding to the strong sense of community with regular social functions and inter-hall sports. "It becomes almost like a frat," said one student. "Dorm life is the source of all my close friends." Everyone is randomly assigned to roommates and dorms (which are single-sex) at the beginning of freshman year, and most end up living in doubles. Approximately half of the senior class moves off-campus into apartment complexes, and those who don't all get singles. The competition to be one of the six RAs in every dorm is stiff because these select seniors become the leaders of the dorm community. Although social life seems to revolve around the dorms, students said that the dining hall is "the place to go to see and to be seen." Undergrads can choose a 14- or 21-meal plan option with $200 for the other food outlets—such as the Burger King—located all over campus. Generally, the dining hall food is "not bad, although it gets repetitive."

Life Outside of Class

Notre Dame students have plenty of activities and clubs to join, ranging from the College Democrats to the "Right to Life" group to various service clubs. But above all, sports seem to dominate students' free time. About 90 percent of ND students were varsity athletes in high school, according to one undergrad. Thus they come out in full force to join the inter-hall contact football league, as well as the lacrosse, soccer, baseball, hockey, and boxing teams. "Recreation sports are overarching," said one student. "Exercise in general is big . . . lots of people work out." A recently finished sports center houses three basketball courts and a weight-suspended track for student use.

In addition to inter-hall leagues and personal training, sports occupy the time of a large majority of the student body off the playing field, as well. An estimated 95 percent of students hold season tickets to ND football games, which are a huge source of unity and pride. "People here really love [football]," said one student. "Going to games is one way to demonstrate your love for the university, and it's a big rallying point for the community." Other varsity sports are well recognized, too; men's basketball, hockey, women's basketball, and women's soccer—a national powerhouse—all bring out crowds for their games. But, the general feeling is that football traditionally overshadows everything else at Notre Dame. "A lot of kids work really hard, and sometimes that just gets swept under the rug," said one undergrad. Regardless, students have enormous pride in the historic success of the football program, a pride that manifests itself in an array of traditions, including well-attended pep rallies. "It's appealing to me," said one student, "because people here have a really strong sense of the school. This translates into an enormous sense of unity and pride."—*Liz Kukura and Staff*

FYI

The three best things about attending Notre Dame are "the tailgates before every football game is the perfect combination of absolute chaos and the best party of your life, the breaks during the semester right when you are really starting to burn out, and the incredibly close community created in the dorms which leads to really close events like dorm masses and dances."

The three worst things about attending Notre Dame are "the competition, the lack of diversity, and the sweeping under the rug of real issues and problems on campus."

The three things every student should do before graduating from Notre Dame are "to streak through the second floor of the library during exam week, party nonstop from Friday afternoon until Saturday afternoon after the football game, and tour the Golden Dome."

One thing I wish I knew before coming here is "people should know that Notre Dame football games (home games) only happen six weekends out of the year. They are fun while they last but no one should come here simply because of them."

Valparaiso University

Address: Kretzmann Hall, Valparaiso, IN 46383-6493
Phone: 888-GO-VALPO
E-mail address: undergrad_admissions@valpo.edu
Web site URL: www.valpo.edu
Location: small city
Founded: 1859
Private or Public: private
Religious affiliation: Lutheran
Undergraduate enrollment: 2,986
Total enrollment: 3,650
Percent Male/Female: 47%/53%

Percent Minority: 8.0%
Percent African-American: 3.0%
Percent Hispanic: 2.0%
Percent Asian: 2.0%
Percent in-state/out-of-state: 35%/65%
Percent Pub HS: 80%
Fraternities: 29%
Sororities: 32%
Number of Applicants: 3,494
Percent Accepted: 78%
Percent Accepted who enroll: 33%
Entering: 886
Transfers: 72
Application Deadline: rolling

Mean SAT: 592 V, 601 M
Middle 50% SAT range: 530–660 V, 530–660 M
Middle 50% ACT range: 24–29
Mean ACT: 26.4
3 Most popular majors: nursing, education, English
Retention: 86%
Graduation rate: 68%
Library: 673,800 volumes
Tuition and Fees: $17,636 in; $17,636 out
Room and Board: $4,660
On-campus housing: 93%
Financial aid, first-year: 85%

Until a few years ago, when its basketball team catapulted into the Sweet Sixteen of the NCAA playoffs, few people outside the Midwest knew about Valparaiso University. Valpo, as it is affectionately called by students, is a small private Lutheran school in northeastern Indiana.

VU prides itself on the absence of TAs. The students are overwhelmingly pleased with the dedication of their professors who teach all undergraduate classes, including labs and language sections. One student reported that the "faculty tend to be very receptive to individual pursuits and are very welcoming." Students must take 124 credits, including three theology classes, and in their opinion, too many general education requirements. The average class size is 20 students with some classes made up of as little as 10 or 15 people. Christ College was established as an honors program for the humanities that focuses on writing skills. One complaint about Valpo's curriculum is that many theology classes tend to be focused on Christian doctrine and echo the administration's position on certain issues. Except for some engineering classes, which are known to be difficult, the workload at Valpo is not considered very demanding.

To Party or Not to Party
Officially, Valpo is a dry campus, although non-drinkers mentioned that they often feel left out of the social scene. With few exceptions, only fraternities are allowed to live off campus while sororities are housed in dorms. Freshman dorms are considered "decent" and RAs are available for help and advice in all dorms. Most dorms are single-sex by floor. An extremely unpopular university regulation is the enforcement of visiting hours for all members of the opposite sex, which mandates that no visitors are allowed in the dorms after midnight on weekdays and 2 in the morning on weekends.

Students report that frat parties draw sizable crowds on the weekends, but undergrads also like to hang out at the Student Center. Many complain about the lack of alternatives in town, but one student suggested that a lot of people are simply unaware of all the resources Valparaiso, Indiana, has to offer since the university does not encourage interaction with the community. The most obvious example of that interaction is that though VU students are required to have a meal plan for six semesters, students often frequent local restaurants. Two popular places nearby are Al's Diner and the Night

Owl coffee shop. In addition, many freshmen go home for weekends—and, as one student pointed out, Chicago is not too far away.

Extracurricular activities flourish at Valpo. They range from traditional newspapers, Student Senate, a student-run radio station, community service organizations, to the more bizarre Jonathan Rivera Fan Club. Founded a couple of years ago by Jonathan's roommate, Jonathan's fan club has become an official organization complete with buttons and T-shirts.

Basketball is definitely the most popular sport at Valpo, and student-only sections make for easy access to games. Other varsity sports are not as popular but intramural sports remain a great alternative for most students.

Incoming freshmen be warned: VU undergraduates report that they are part of an extremely homogenous student body. The stereotypical Valpo student is Christian, white, from the Midwest, and middle to upper-class. In addition, the university has a reputation for being homophobic and not very receptive to interracial dating.

> **"Faculty tend to be very receptive to individual pursuits and are very welcoming."**

The majority of students are satisfied with the academic and social life at Valpo. If you are looking for a small university with an extraordinarily dedicated faculty, be sure to give Valpo a closer look.
—*Sarah DeBergalis and Staff*

FYI

The three best things about attending Valparaiso University are "the faculty, the frats, and the classes."

The three worst things about attending Valparaiso University are "Valparaiso, Indiana; the diversity; and the requirements."

The three things every student should do before graduating from Valparaiso University are "to attend a basketball game, to join an organization, and to go to Chicago for the weekend."

One thing I'd like to have known before coming here is "what life is like in rural Indiana."

Wabash College

Address: P. O. Box 352, Crawfordsville, IN 47933-0352
Phone: 800-345-5385
E-mail address: admissions@wabash.edu
Web site URL: www.wabash.edu
Location: small city
Founded: 1832
Private or Public: private
Religious affiliation: NA
Undergraduate enrollment: 868
Total enrollment: 868
Percent Male/Female: 100%/0%
Percent Minority: 14.0%

Percent African-American: 5.0%
Percent Hispanic: 5.0%
Percent Asian: 4.0%
Percent in-state/out-of-state: 71%/29%
Percent Pub HS: 91%
Fraternities: 70%
Sororities: NA
Number of Applicants: 924
Percent Accepted: 73%
Percent Accepted who enroll: 32%
Entering: 297
Transfers: 5
Application Deadline: 1 Mar

Mean SAT: 576 V, 598 M
Middle 50% SAT range: 520–630 V, 540–650 M
Middle 50% ACT range: NA
Mean ACT: 25
3 Most popular majors: history, economics, psychology
Retention: 81
Graduation rate: 69
Library: 253,024 volumes
Tuition and Fees: $16,975 in; NA out
Room and Board: $5,435
On-campus housing: 99%
Financial aid, first-year: 100%

Wabash College is rich in history, tradition, and financial endowments. As one of the few remaining all-male colleges in the United States, Wabash thrives on spirited students and exceptionally loyal alumni. "People who come here support it until they die," claimed one Wabash student.

Hard-Core Curriculum

Based on a strong core curriculum, academics are rigorous at Wabash. "There are not many classes that you can blow off," one student reported. Undergraduates must take courses in the natural sciences, math, a foreign language, English composition, literature, and fine arts, regardless of their major. Sophomores must take Cultures and Traditions, a course that studies the philosophies and political ideas of various cultures in the same period in history. "It's quite politically correct, but you learn a lot," one student said. To graduate, all Wabash seniors must pass "comps," a daylong series of oral and written exams administered by professors in the student's major.

Students report that the religion and economics departments are particularly strong. The philosophy department benefits from a prestigious faculty that includes well-known philosopher William Placher. English majors say their department has a particularly cohesive faculty that works well together as a team. Art and music, however, do not fare as well in students' opinions. Many Wabash students are on a pre-professional track and hope to enroll in law or medical school after graduation; as a result, the college is reportedly strong in the premed sciences such as biology and chemistry.

In addition to strong academics in the classroom, Wabash also offers its students the chance to study abroad or obtain various internship positions through a wide range of off-campus study opportunities and an extensive alumni network.

Super-Small Classes

Wabash's size allows not only for small classes (the largest class, a popular classics lecture, enrolls about 110), but also for maximum student-faculty interaction. Most Wabash professors live within walking distance of the campus and often eat lunch or talk informally with their students. Professors routinely give out their home phone numbers to their classes, and students say they are comfortable calling them at home for help. Students cite this open communication and sense of friendship with faculty as one of the best aspects of Wabash. The sense of community often endures long after graduation.

Wabash students also benefit from the new fine arts center on campus, which includes a large art gallery, a new auditorium, classrooms equipped with modern audiovisual equipment, and practice rooms with pianos. Salter Hall, located in the arts center, is reportedly one of the most acoustically sound halls in the state of Indiana. The recently renovated Detchon Center houses the classics and foreign-language departments, a computer center, and several new classrooms. According to students, Detchon is "a good place to study." For serious study, students go to the Lilly Library, also recently modernized, where "it is always quiet, no matter what," according to one sophomore.

No Woman, No Cry?— The Social Scene

Although Wabash is an all-male school, most students say they find no shortage of female company. Many attend social events at Purdue and Indiana University, both less than 90 minutes away. One student, however, pointed out that the lack of women, combined with the un-happening surroundings of Crawfordsville (a town of 15,000 in which "Wal-Mart serves as the social epicenter"), can make the Wabash experience socially isolating in relation to the outside world. In his assessment of the social situation at Wabash, he continued, "We are encapsulated in this tiny microcosm filled with testosterone, and the result is a return to the primordial instincts of aggression and survival." But the capsule also serves as a social safe haven, a tightly knit community where "all students feel somewhat connected to one another." In this sense, Wabash can resemble a "huge male-bonding fest."

Nowhere is this more apparent than in Wabash's fraternities, which dominate the campus social scene. Rush starts during spring visitation for high school seniors and resumes as soon as freshmen arrive on campus. Beer drinking is a central activity on Greek Row and throughout Wabash, despite the college's "Gentleman Rule" that says each Wabash undergrad must "behave like a gentleman on- and off-campus at all times." One student warned that this is a "very wet campus, one of the wettest I've seen."

The largest campus-wide event happens each fall when the Wabash Little Giants and their archrival DePauw University compete for the Monon Bell in the oldest football rivalry west of the Allegheny Mountains. In 1993, the 100th anniversary game was nationally televised and covered in *Sports Illustrated*. Homecoming week features special events such as the Chapel Sing, in which pledge brothers assemble in front of the chapel to sing the school song. Whichever group yells and sings the loudest wins the competition, as judged by the Sphinx Club, an exclusive club whose members perform community service, promote school spirit, and symbolize "the essence of a Wabash man." The competition is more tiring than it sounds, for Wabash has the longest school song in the nation; pledges must exercise their vocal cords for over 45 minutes!

Other sports events take place in a somewhat more subdued manner, although student participation in sports remains high. "It's really hard to be cut [from a team] here, so lots of people can participate no matter what their skill or experience level," explained one junior. The swim team and the football team usually draw the most student support, as does the well-ranked cross-country team. Other teams, however, have less impressive records, and in the words of one student, "This is definitely not a jock school." Wabash students also participate in intramural sports ranging from touch football to bowling. The athletic facilities are "in need of an upgrade," according to one student, although another allows that the facilities are "not bad for Division III."

Students also participate in extracurriculars from the *Bachelor*, a widely read weekly newspaper, to the student-run radio station WNDY—the Giant. There is also a strong theater program that produces many plays throughout the year.

Food Fights

Despite the administration's reported efforts to "diversify the food scene," Wabash students report that the food, while edible, is certainly not what you would eat if you had a choice. Although each of the many fraternity houses has its own in-house cook, food in the houses is reportedly not much better than in the cafeterias. The required plan of 19 meals per week has been a recent point of contention between students and the administration, and many students want a more flexible (and less expensive) plan. Nonetheless, off-campus restaurants and bars offer a break from dining hall food. The Silver Dollar Bar currently reigns as students' favorite local bar. Little Mexico and Joe's, a bar and grill, also draw many away from dining halls.

Living Arrangements

The large majority of Wabash students live in fraternity houses during their four years at the college. But among the campus dorms, students cite the recently renovated Martindale and the quiet Wolcott Hall as most desirable, while dorms such as Grant are less coveted. One floor in Morris Hall was recently designated as dry in an effort to reduce peer pressure and provide a quiet haven for nondrinkers. Space reportedly abounds in all Wabash dorms except those with single rooms.

The campus is self-contained, with a mix of architectural styles. Despite the mix, however, one student said, "The buildings here are very square; they really all look the same." With generous funding from graduates, Wabash is able to maintain first-rate facilities and provide financial aid to a large percentage of students, a major draw for out-of-staters in need of financial assistance.

> **"People who come here support it until they die."**

Although about three-fourths of the student body hails from Indiana, many different nationalities and races comprise the student population. Many students feel, however, that the campus is not diverse enough. The administration has reportedly stepped up its minority and international recruitment efforts. One student described the campus as filled with "lots of liberals in search of a well-rounded education." Others, however, say the prevailing conservative political climate can, at times, lead to closed-mindedness and stereotyping, especially in relation to such issues as feminism and homosexuality.

In spite of these complaints about the lack of diversity at Wabash, many are proud of the solid education, strong heritage, and fierce loyalty that come with being a Wabash man. "It's hard to explain, but after coming here, I wouldn't go back to a coed university," one Wabash transfer student said.—*Susanna Chu and Staff*

FYI

The three best things about attending Wabash are "great financial aid, spacious dorm rooms, and not having to worry about what girls think of you every second."

The three worst things about attending Wabash are "how large an Indiana student body population there is, the Gentlemen Rule, the lack of female company."

The three things that every student should do before graduating from Wabash are "hang out at the Silver Dollar Bar, attend the Wabash/DePauw game, branch out and go to a social event of some sort at another nearby school."

One thing I'd like to have known before coming here is "how easy it is to get stuck in the tiny world of Wabash and forget about what happens outside."

Iowa

Cornell College

Address: 600 First Street, West Mount Vernon, IA 52341-1098
Phone: 319-895-4477
E-mail address: admissions@cornell-iowa.edu
Web site URL: www.cornell-iowa.edu
Location: rural
Founded: 1853
Private or Public: private
Religious affiliation: none
Undergraduate enrollment: 1,024
Total enrollment: 1,024
Percent Male/Female: 43%/57%
Percent Minority: 9.0%

Percent African-American: 3.0%
Percent Hispanic: 3.0%
Percent Asian: 2.0%
Percent in-state/out-of-state: 26%/74%
Percent Pub HS: 85%
Fraternities: 35%
Sororities: 35%
Number of Applicants: 1,075
Percent Accepted: 83%
Percent Accepted who enroll: 27%
Entering: 241
Transfers: 0
Application Deadline: 1 Feb

Mean SAT: 565 V, 579 M
Middle 50% SAT range: 500–630 V, 520–630 M
Middle 50% ACT range: NA
Mean ACT: 25
3 Most popular majors: psychology, economics, English
Retention: 82.0%
Graduation rate: 56.0%
Library: 172,000 volumes
Tuition and Fees: $18,836 in; $18,835 out
Room and Board: $5,140
On-campus housing: 86%
Financial aid, first-year: 90%

Imagine starting and ending a class in just one month. It sounds impossible, but for Cornell College students, month-long classes are a reality. The small Mount Vernon, Iowa, college operates on a block system whereby students enroll in just one class at a time. While many other colleges and universities divide their academic years into fall and spring semesters, Cornell's system is comprised of nine blocks, each for three and a half weeks. Many students describe the short class periods as "intense," but insist that they are "manageable."

Block Scheduling

The nine blocks are spread from late August until early May. Students typically enroll in a class for eight of the nine blocks, with the leftover block becoming three and a half weeks of vacation time. However, particularly ambitious students can enroll in courses throughout all nine blocks. In such cases, the ninth block course can be taken for free. Because the winter recess is currently just one week and students do not have a spring vacation, there has been a call on campus to change the system to eight blocks, adding a spring break and lengthening the winter vacation.

All students must take four blocks of a foreign language (although testing out is possible), one of fine arts, one of math, two of physical science, and three of humanities. There are also requirements in writing and physical education. Students who choose to double major try to fulfill the requirements in the first two years through introductory-level courses, leaving their final two years for more intense and upper-level study in their chosen fields. Although many students bubble with delight over the block system, some undergrads admit that it is difficult to fit a year's worth of a language into less than a month, and that a more "conventional" approach for teaching foreign languages would be more effective.

Not having to plan a semester full of classes in advance allows students much more time to decide on a major. In the past, many students have chosen to become triple or quadruple majors. However, this past year Cornell limited students to two majors, with the hope of fostering a basic liberal arts education while requiring its graduates to have a sharper focus.

All of the block courses are taught for five days a week, some meeting twice a day. Classes begin on the first Monday of each month and continue until the final Wednesday of that month. According to one sophomore, "The block system lets you focus on one thing. Some nights you have a lot of stuff to do, but other nights you won't have a damn thing, which is nice." Another student described the average amount of homework per night as "around one hour."

Besides the unique block system, many students choose Cornell because of its impressive student-faculty interaction. Enrollment in most classes is capped at 25, the average class size is just 15, and all courses are taught by professors. Many students express a high level of comfort with all of their professors; home visits with profs are not uncommon.

Special Programs

Students name the sciences, especially biology, as the best departments. Cornell's special 3-2 engineering program allows students to complete three years of selected courses at Cornell and then transfer to Washington University in St. Louis to earn a joint B.A.-M.S. degree from the two schools. Cornell also has an early-acceptance pre-dental program associated with the nearby University of Iowa. After completing their sophomore year and taking the Dental Achievement Test, students who are accepted into the program are assured a place in the U of I School of Dentistry after graduation. Another popular area of study is religion. Many students cited such religion courses as Epistles of Paul, The Idea of God, and The Question of Faith as some of the more stimulating courses at the college.

Many students choose to study abroad during their time at Cornell. One of the most popular Cornell-sponsored programs occurs during the fifth block, which begins after New Year's. The program consists of a trip to England for the entire length of the block to study and travel. Many students praise the creative nature of the program, calling it a "very good trip." Students may also study abroad for a year or a semester through programs of the Associated Colleges of the Midwest or by joining an approved program from another university.

Social Associations

Although the college has no Greek system, it has local groups called associations. One such association is Phi Beta Kappa, the nation's oldest scholastic honorary society. The groups are referred to by their shortened names, often Greek letters, such as the "Gammas." The associations sponsor most of the on-campus parties, including the Axetoberfest put on by the "Axes" at a farm just outside Mount Vernon in the middle of October. Pledging for the associations (six men's and six women's) occurs in the spring for freshmen and in the fall for sophomores, climaxing during the four-day break between the first and second (fall) or seventh and eighth (spring) blocks.

> "Not having to plan a semester full of classes in advance allows students much more time to decide on a major."

Besides participating in the social associations, many students choose to visit one of the two local bars or go to the University of Iowa campus in Iowa City. One student described both of the bars as "cool," but "very different from each other; Joe's is more for the athletic types and the more social-life conscious, while Randall's crowd is more mixed." Both of the bars allow anyone 19 years of age and older to enter, but you must be 21 to drink.

Although Cornell is situated in the small town of Mount Vernon, few students seem to mind the quiet setting. One student from Chicago said, "Coming to Mount Vernon was a big change in that it was more rural, but once you get yourself a group of friends, you're pretty much set." Another student complained that "it takes more effort to find stuff to do on the weekends," but overall students are happy with the friendly town. According to one student, "The campus makes up the town. We keep a lot of the businesses running and they really suffer during the summer."

Moreover, Cornell is within 20 miles of both Cedar Rapids and Iowa City. The University of Iowa provides added resources, such as library materials. One ju-

nior explained that although there "is not much microfilm or microfiche at the Cornell library, students can go to Iowa City for a lot of their research."

Cornell continues to make its mark among the numerous small Midwestern colleges because of the block system. This system allows undergrads to study subjects with a degree of attention unmatched at other schools, yet still be exposed to many different people and their ideas due to the constant change-over of classes. According to students, the constant change at Cornell provides for a stimulating and exciting four years.
—*William Chen and Staff*

FYI

The three best things about attending Cornell are "the block system, the student-faculty interaction, and our social associations."

The three worst things about attending Cornell are "our locale, the emphasis on one course for an entire block, and our less than okay research facilities."

The three things every student should do before graduating from Cornell are "go biking in Mount Vernon, pledge an association, and study abroad."

One thing I'd like to have known before coming here is "how much I like Mount Vernon."

Grinnell College

Address: P.O. Box 805, Grinnell, IA 50112
Phone: 515-269-3600
E-mail address: askgrin@grinnell.edu
Web site URL: www.grinnell.edu
Location: small town
Founded: 1846
Private or Public: private
Religious affiliation: none
Undergraduate enrollment: 1,335
Total enrollment: 1,335
Percent Male/Female: 45%/55%
Percent Minority: 12.3%

Percent African-American: 3.0%
Percent Hispanic: 4.0%
Percent Asian: 5.0%
Percent in-state/out-of-state: 16%/84%
Percent Pub HS: 78%
Fraternities: 0%
Sororities: 0%
Number of Applicants: 1,757
Percent Accepted: 67%
Percent Accepted who enroll: 28%
Entering: 325
Transfers: 28
Application Deadline: 20 Jan

Mean SAT: 669 V, 659 M
Middle 50% SAT range: 620–730 V, 610–710 M
Middle 50% ACT range: 27–31
Mean ACT: 29
3 Most popular majors: anthropology, biology, economics
Retention: 92.0%
Graduation rate: 82.0%
Library: 393,583 volumes
Tuition and Fees: $18,990 in; $18,990 out
Room and Board: $5,600
On-campus housing: 100%
Financial aid, first-year: 91%

Nestled between the bridges of Madison County and baseball's field of dreams lies Grinnell, Iowa, a rural, "not exactly Manhattan," town that boasts rows of corn and a gas station

that, although once called Always Open, has been renamed Almost Always Open. Don't let the town's obscure location and small size fool you, however; it's in this town that you can find Grinnell College, a liberal arts college that 1,300 Birkenstock-clad students call home. Despite its remote geography, these laid-back but dedicated Grinnellians flock to Grinnell because it offers challenging academics, eccentric opportunities, hard-core partying, and yeah . . . the six-week winter vacation.

A Recipe for Sleep Deprivation

This six-week vacation serves as a respite from the intense academic load that Grinnell's students endure. Students claim that Grinnell has "the second highest workload in the country." The 100 pages of reading that some classes demand per night has convinced one Grinnellian that "the workload is like the third level of hell." Despite the massive amount of work, students enjoy their academic experiences.

One defining mark of this academic experience is the freshman tutorial. All freshmen enroll in a tutorial in which they can hone their writing. Past tutorials have surveyed topics like "Inside *Star Trek*" and "Music & Nature." With class sizes limited to 12 students, the tutorials provide freshmen a lot of advice on how to improve their writing and analytical skills.

The class sizes don't increase after the freshman tutorial, however. While some classes like Intro to Psychology have 60–100 students, students report that most of their classes range between 2 and 25 students. They also promise that as topics narrow and levels advance, class size decreases.

> **"The workload is like the third level of hell."**

In addition to small classes, students enjoy close contact with great faculty. One student proclaimed that her professor was a "goddess," yet the professors are approachable and considerate. "I had to drop one of my classes because I was having health problems. The professor was incredibly kind to me and said he hoped I'd be able to retake the class next year." There are no TAs, but there are "mentors" who have taken the class before and help grade and tutor.

Students insist that no slacker major exists at Grinnell. All majors require dedicated work, but bio/chem and other science majors are especially challenging. Students claim that education concentrators and theater majors put in some serious hours, too. But not all classes are as intense as organic chemistry. Students can choose to take Exco classes, noncredit courses in which members of the Grinnell community or Grinnell students teach on random subjects. One student was delighted to have taken Yoing for Pleasure, a class that uncovered the secrets of yo-yos.

Where Have All the Grinnellians Gone?

Although one student announced, "We are the *royalty* of procrastination," students eventually have to hit the books and find a place to study. If you live in a single, the quiet of your room may be ideal. Burling Library offers a "really cozy" place to study. An added incentive to Burling is the opportunity to take a study break and contribute graffiti on the basement's bathroom walls. Students say that "not only does the administration not care about the graffiti, they actually encourage it."

For those who prefer background noise and a social atmosphere, the Forum Grill is a good place to whip out the books. The Forum Grill is located in one of the campus' two student centers: the Forum and the Harris Center. Students can go to the Forum to buy food ("you can get Ben and Jerry's nearly any time of day"), peruse the art gallery, play the grand piano, have a small meeting in the reserved rooms, or visit the student government offices. Harris provides students with a concert hall for parties and musicians, a TV lounge with couches, and a game room with pool and foosball tables.

Other notable areas on campus are the recently completed Robert Noyce Science Center and a Bucksbaum Center for the Arts, which students consider "two great additions." Students love the fact that "no two buildings really match." The Fine Arts building, for example, is shaped in a circular pattern "reminiscent of a nautilus shell" while the Goodnow building looks more like "a stone castle from the European Middle Ages." The architectural diversity is welcome since otherwise "you feel trapped in the middle of cornfields."

While off-campus housing is cheaper, most students opt to live on campus. While there's "no exposed plumbing, no dripping asbestos," the suites are "not exactly hotel quality." Students can choose from Cleveland, "the smoking dorm"; Read, "the nonsmokers' dorm"; Loose, the dorm with the coziest main lounge; Younker, "the party place"; and Norris, the air-conditioned building. The campus is divided into two areas: "jocks live on North campus" and "alternatives live on South campus." Between the two areas are the ever-popular Bob's Underground Café, an enclosed loggia, and a dining hall.

The dining hall is "nothing to write home about," but students say that the food is getting better ever since Hungarian Noodlebake has been removed from the menu. Students also recommend avoiding the mozzarella sticks. Bob's Underground, the Pub, Pizza Hut, Pag's (an Italian eatery), Saint Rest's (a coffee house), and Café Phoeniz (the ritzy restaurant) are more popular places to dine.

When They're Not Studying

Despite the inordinate amount of reading and work required of the average Grinnell student, extracurriculars are popular and eccentric. Students can join SCA (Society for Creative Anachronism), Free the Planet (an environmental group), Dagorhir (a blue foam sword-fighting group), the Campus Monarchists (the group that proposed building a moat around North Campus . . . their project was denied funding), and the Vegan Co-op. Traditional extracurricular activities are available, too: community service, the literary magazine, a comic magazine, a weekly paper, and the symphonic band, to name a few. The Grinnell Singers, an audition-only group, is also popular. All these groups tend to

take the place of a Greek system, and students appreciate the absence of fraternities and sororities.

Grinnell students are generally stereotyped as "liberal, gay, pot-smoking activists." The liberal attitude, students say, is a stark contrast to the conservative Midwestern town that surrounds the campus. Passionate liberalism makes for a charged political environment, and the Campus Democrats is a popular club. Students attest to the fact that there are "no out of the closet Republicans."

Sports don't draw huge crowds. While the intramural football, ultimate Frisbee, and rugby teams are relatively popular on campus, the varsity football team went undefeated last year, but few people knew about it or celebrated it. Spectators at varsity events tend to be friends of the athletes.

After grueling weeks of activities and schoolwork, students relieve stress by partying hard on the weekends. Due to a lax alcohol and drug policy and the free beer at Harris parties, drinking is quite pervasive. It's not uncommon to spot a "Has anyone seen my bong?" sign drifting around campus. Other activities are also available, thanks to the yearly activity fee required of each student. This fee funds free performances of groups like the Russian National Ballet and Second City. Other campus activities include house parties that are off campus, Waltz (the semester formal), Disco (the yearly disco dance), the Drunken Titular Head Festival (an independent movie festival), Mary B. James (the annual cross-dressing party), Alice in Wonderland (a music festival with live bands), and the 10/10 progressive drinking party.

"Intense!" best describes this liberal college in Iowa. Whether it's the grueling academic life, the offbeat clubs, the creative organizations, the political aura that surrounds campus, or the big-time partying, Grinnell offers an educational experience of the utmost caliber. —*Marti Page*

FYI:
The three best things about attending Grinnell are "the people, the freedom students are given, and the great academics."
The three worst things about attending Grinnell are "the stress, the pseudo-openmindness, and the dining hall food."

The three things that every student should do before graduating from Grinnell are "contribute to the graffiti in Burling Library, explore the steam tunnels, and go to a Mary B. James cross-dressing dance."

One thing I'd like to have known before coming here is "that you really need a car to get out of these cornfields."

Iowa State University

Address: 100 Alumni Hall, Ames, IA 50011-2011
Phone: 515-294-5836
E-mail address: admissions@iastate.edu
Web site URL: www.iastate.edu
Location: suburban
Founded: 1858
Private or Public: public
Religious affiliation: none
Undergraduate enrollment: 21,035
Total enrollment: 25,384
Percent Male/Female: 56%/44%
Percent Minority: 8.0%
Percent African-American: 3.0%

Percent Hispanic: 2.0%
Percent Asian: 3.0%
Percent in-state/out-of-state: 83%/17%
Percent Pub HS: NA
Fraternities: 6%
Sororities: 6%
Number of Applicants: 8,914
Percent Accepted: 91%
Percent Accepted who enroll: 47%
Entering: 4,812
Transfers: 2,262
Application Deadline: rolling
Mean SAT: 590 V, 610 M

Middle 50% SAT range: 520–670 V, 540–690 M
Middle 50% ACT range: 22–27
Mean ACT: 25
3 Most popular majors: elementary education, mechanical engineering, civil engineering
Retention: 84.0%
Graduation rate: 62.0%
Library: 2 million volumes
Tuition and Fees: $2,786 in; $9,346 out
Room and Board: $3,958
On-campus housing: 34%
Financial aid, first-year: 75%

Squirrels scamper across the copper roofs, leaves float between Greco-Roman pillars, and students steal kisses as the campanile (clock tower) begins to strike 12. In the 1920s, traditions such as kissing under the clock tower, or "campaniling," were sacred, the fraternity and sorority systems were strong, and most of the students had similar backgrounds and came from Iowa. Today, traditions such as campaniling and the friendly midwestern atmosphere remain, but Iowa State has changed with the times. The popularity of fraternities and sororities has steadily declined, and the administration is making a concerted effort to create a more diverse student body on a campus already known for strong academic and extracurricular activities.

Across the Board

Iowa State's undergrads are divided into seven different colleges: agriculture, business, design, education, engineering, family and consumer sciences, and liberal arts and sciences. Those who have already made career decisions can apply to the college of their choice. Those who are undecided are welcome as well; they simply apply and sort out their plans with an advisor after they arrive on campus. Although most students at Iowa State take academics seriously, they admit that the workload, course requirements, and academic experience vary greatly depending on the college and the individual. Classes can range in size from 8 to 400, and in subject from introductory theater to soil management to poultry nutrition.

The engineering and architecture programs are popular, and one student said, "the agriculture program here is as good as it gets." Many in-staters come to the university to learn how to manage the vast farms that fill some of the most fertile land in the nation. With hog and cattle management facilities and genetic research farms located throughout the state and the fact that farming is big business in Iowa, there's little doubt why students give it such high marks.

Where to Lay Your Head

Most freshmen live in residence halls on campus. Friley reportedly is the second-largest college dorm in the country, and the modern Towers is said to be comfortable but distant from the center of campus. Some complain about the extra blocks in their early-morning dazed rush to class. Despite the availability of campus housing, a large portion of the student body lives off-campus with the more lax regulations and greater privacy that the Greek system offers.

> "Iowa has more to offer than just corn."

Students in the residence halls and the Greek system are the most involved in the campus social scene. Although the fraternities host many of the campus parties, students report that "pressure to rush remains within the Greek system." Those not interested in the fraternities or sororities have other options. Memorial Union offers not only reading rooms for quiet study but also a bowling alley, pool tables, and video games. It also houses the Maintenance Shop, a campus bar that sponsors concerts ranging from blues to alternative rock, along with comedy shows and poetry readings.

The shopping area (known as Campus Town), restaurants and bars of Ames (population 47,200) offer students some off-campus entertainment. Café Baudelaire tempts many students with Middle Eastern and Indian food, unusual drinks, and bands who perform in the window. Establishments like People's Bar and Grille and Underwhere attract the 21-and-over crowd.

Sports and Fun

Athletic contests at Iowa State are social occasions for both Iowa State students and the Ames community. The basketball team, a success in the Big Eight athletic conference, draws the widest student and community support. The future of Cyclone basketball did look shaky when Hilton Coliseum, like much of Iowa, lay submerged under 14 feet of floodwater in the summer of 1993, but with strong community support, the stadium and other water-damaged buildings were repaired.

Students rave about the new recreation center, which offers extensive aerobic and weight lifting facilities as well as basketball courts and playing field for club and intramural sports. The recreation center even organizes trips for students interested in activities such as rock climbing or horseback riding.

VEISHEA is HUGE

VEISHEA (pronounced "vee-sha"), one of the largest student-run festivals in the nation, is also one of the most popular annual events on campus. About 400 students work together to plan and organize this campus and community celebration that includes a musical production, food fair, and a battle of the bands, and culminates in a parade with floats, balloons, and athletic events. The average Iowa State student is from small-town Iowa, but the universtiy also attracts many students from midwestern cities such as Chicago and Minneapolis. The administration has recently made efforts to attract more minority and international students. As the minority population at Iowa State has begun to grow, some tension has developed; according to undergrads, some members of the community and student body were never really prepared for diversity. Some minority students say they sometimes feel invisible and that they "only want equality." After a recent boycott of an African-American history class whose professor made what some students felt were racist remarks, many organizations and departments implemented changes designed to improve race relations. The student government, for example, planned an international student week with cultural activities, lectures, dancing, and Global Food Fest.

An Administration that's Truly in Touch

One of the best aspects of Iowa State, students say, is the university's flexibility. According to one student, there's no better example of this than the school's agriculture program, which manages to stay up to date in its research and in giving hands-on experience to its students. But whether you're looking for an education integrated seamlessly into the practicality of farming, or you're challenged by the abstract fundamentals of mathematics, students say their school has it all. As one student quipped, "Iowa has more to offer than just corn."—*Madhu Pocha and Staff*

FYI

The three best things about Iowa State are "how many people are involved in extracurriculars, the agriculture program is awesome, and the people here are friendly."

The three worst things about Iowa State are"the Greeks are in decline, it's too homogeneous, and some classes are too huge."

The three things that every student should do before graduating from Iowa State are "participate in VEISHEA, attend a basketball game, and do intramurals."

One thing I wish I knew before coming here is "how often people make fun of us about corn!"

University of Iowa

Address: 107 Calvin Hall, Iowa City, IA 52242-1396
Phone: 800-553-4692
E-mail address: admissions@uiowa.edu
Web site URL: www.uiowa.edu
Location: small city
Founded: 1847
Private or Public: public
Religious affiliation: none
Undergraduate enrollment: 19,537
Total enrollment: 28,846
Percent Male/Female: 46%/54%
Percent Minority: 8.1%
Percent African-American: 2.3%

Percent Hispanic: 2.1%
Percent Asian: 3.3%
Percent in-state/out-of-state: 70%/30%
Percent Pub HS: 89%
Fraternities: 11%
Sororities: 12%
Number of Applicants: 11,358
Percent Accepted: 83%
Percent Accepted who enroll: 41%
Entering: 3,859
Transfers: 1,318
Application Deadline: rolling
Mean SAT: NA V, NA M

Middle 50% SAT range: 520–660 V, 540–660 M
Middle 50% ACT range: 22–27
Mean ACT: NA
3 Most popular majors: psychology, communications studies, English
Retention: 82.0%
Graduation rate: 63.5%
Library: NA
Tuition and Fees: $2,906 in; $10,668 out
Room and Board: $4,594
On-campus housing: NA
Financial aid, first-year: NA

Set in the relatively small college town of Iowa City, the University of Iowa provides a quality Big Ten education at a "surprisingly nice tuition bill," according to one pleased student. The home of the Hawkeyes combines a thriving social scene with strong academics. When asked what set the University of Iowa apart from other schools, a senior simply replied, "We're the best!" and expressed his sympathies for those who did not have the good fortune or foresight to attend the university themselves.

No Corn and a Huge Mall?

"The biggest myth about our school is that it's in the middle of the cornfields," said a senior marketing major. "If you drive out ten minutes, you can see cornfields, but there are no farms on campus. Nobody believes it until they see it, and then they're like, 'Wow, cool town.'" While most students expressed positive feelings about Iowa City, which is home to many movie theaters, restaurants, pizza places, coffee shops, bars, and is just two miles from Coral Ridge Mall, the third-largest in the Midwest, one student complained that "after four years here, you certainly realize this town is pretty boring."

The reason for boredom among a minority of students is the widespread drinking on campus; U of I students are typically known as "educated drinkers." While many school-organized activities are available, such as frequent lectures (recent lecturers include Maya Angelou and Adam Carolla and Dr. Drew from MTV's *Loveline*), rock concerts, and special pre-screening of movies such as *The Game*, the typical weekend involves "drinking it alive and well in the binge-drinking capital of the Midwest. There is a bar for everyone in Iowa City," described one student. He went on to explain that 19-and-over bars and dance clubs such as The Field House and The Union Bar give students their "first taste of barstool subculture" while sports bars such as the Sports Column or Mondo's are great for "cheering on the Hawks with buddies." The liberal and pot-smoking crowd tend to hang out at places such as The Sanctuary or The Mill. And while the Hawkeye wrestling team has won almost every national title for the past twenty years, tailgates associated with the football team play the important role on weekends. In some cases, the tailgates have even overshadowed the sport. One freshman reported seeing "many drunk and hungover people sitting outside and drinking near where a football game was many hours after a game."

Stepping Up

A few years ago, the university received an $800,000 federal grant from the Robert Wood Johnson Foundation for their Stepping Up University/Community Action Partnership to Reduce High-Risk Drinking Project. In recent years the entire campus has maintained a campaign against binge drinking. In response to an alcohol-related student death a few years ago during a Greek rush, the administration has put the frats under heavy pressure, while "most sororities went dry years ago," according to the university president. Parties are still prevalent, however; popular ones include the Beta Blue Hawaii, '70s parties, and margarita party nights.

What's Wrong with Chicago Suburbans?

Many students joke that their school should be called the University of Illinois at Iowa because of the large number of students from suburban Chicago. Some find that the mixing between these students and those from rural Iowa as well as the large percentage of gays and lesbians in Iowa City creates a great deal of school diversity. But others complain about the lack of racial diversity. But students agree that everyone from students to professors to residents of Iowa City are very friendly. "Everyone says hi whether you know them or not," said one senior.

Don't Hate Us 'Cuz We're Beautiful

U of I's campus is gorgeous, as the school is built around the beautiful gold-domed former Iowa capital building. The Iowa River runs through the middle of campus, splitting the graduate and undergraduate buildings; the west side contains the university hospital, the third-largest teaching hospital in the nation. While this causes a severe shortage in parking spaces, as one senior put it, "those are the sacrifices you make for beauty." As for the size of campus, one student praised its compactness, stating that "everything is within walking distance," while another praised the three different bus lines linking the different parts of campus. Many students sit in the Pentacrest, the center of campus, to study or meet people, and even in the middle of the night, students feel safe walking alone.

Most students live off campus in privately owned apartment buildings, but the dorms are almost all air-conditioned and have nice, large rooms. Each residential hall has its own personality, ranging from Burge, David Letterman's number one party dorm, to Rienow and Slater, the jock dorms, to Stanley, the quiet dorm. An RA system is in effect, but "if you don't tick them off, they won't mess with you," said one student. Dining hall food is generally considered decent, although a freshman recalled asking an upperclassman how dinner was and receiving the response, "It was good, but I feel sick."

Streaking and Religious Studies

U of I has relatively small classes (most are under 50 students, with large lectures split into 20-person discussion sections). Students also benefit from professor and TA attention during office hours. One student mentioned that the business classes utilize advanced technology and multimedia to make learning interesting. U of I boasts one of the nation's best writing programs, while the graduate students who attend the highly reputed Writer's Workshop where Kurt Vonnegut once worked "pass much of their knowledge to undergrads." Students also cite the physics, Russian, astronomy, and political science departments as amazing. The political science, English, and creative writing TAs are reportedly awesome, while the science TAs are known to be a bit lacking. However, that may stem from the fact that most U of I students are humanities-oriented. When asked to name the most heinous thing about classes, most students mentioned "waking up for morning classes." Some U of I classes begin as early as 7:30 A.M.

When asked about professors, students praised such interesting and humorous teachers as Judeo-Christian Tradition professor Jay Holstein, who once claimed that he would retire if a student streaked during his class (a male student did precisely that a few months later, and Holstein explained that he had meant a female student).

Almost everyone is involved in at least one of the 350-plus student organizations, which include Habitat for Humanity, African American World Studies Association, American Medical Women's Association, Gay Lesbian Bisexual Transgender Union, and Campus Crusade for Christ. Most students are athletic, and "almost every athletic team is in the hunt for the Big Ten title," raved one senior. Aside from the reputedly strong club and intramural teams, students also go in droves to play pickup basketball games in the Field House; alums who have visited campus recently include NBA point guard B. J. Armstrong, formerly of the world-champion Chicago Bulls. Many students also have jobs or volunteer.

> "Everyone says hi whether you know him or not."

All in all, the University of Iowa is a happy, thriving community. Most students find the friendly, open environment, great bargain education, and charming college town and campus a comfortable and interesting place to spend four years.
—*Jennifer Wang and Staff*

FYI
The three best things about attending U of Iowa are "you get to meet a lot of different kinds of people, the wide selection of things to study, the friendly atmosphere."
The three worst things about attending U of Iowa are "bad parking, huge classes, science TAs."
The three things every student should do before graduating from U of Iowa are "study, party, then party some more."
One thing I'd like to have known before coming here is "how much students here drink and have sex."

Kansas

Kansas State University

Address: Anderson Hall, Room 1, Manhattan, KS 66506
Phone: 785-532-6250
E-mail address: kstate@ksu.edu
Web site URL: www.ksu.edu
Location: suburban
Founded: 1863
Private or Public: public
Religious affiliation: none
Undergraduate enrollment: 16,936
Total enrollment: 20,306
Percent Male/Female: 53%/47%
Percent Minority: 8.0%

Percent African-American: 3.0%
Percent Hispanic: 2.0%
Percent Asian: 2.0%
Percent in-state/out-of-state: 91%/9%
Percent Pub HS: NA
Fraternities: 21%
Sororities: 20%
Number of Applicants: 6,398
Percent Accepted: 66%
Percent Accepted who enroll: 73%
Entering: 3,085
Transfers: 1,771
Application Deadline: rolling

Mean SAT: NA V, NA M
Middle 50% SAT range: NA V, NA M
Middle 50% ACT range: NA
Mean ACT: 22.8
3 Most popular majors: animal science, journalism, mechanical engineering
Retention: 77.0%
Graduation rate: 45.0%
Library: 1.4 million volumes
Tuition and Fees: $2,467 in; $8,772 out
Room and Board: $3,640
On-campus housing: 28%
Financial aid, first-year: NA

Known to its fans as the "Happy Purple Place," K-State overflows with school spirit. One student summed up the energy by saying, "Everyone here has at least six purple shirts, and they're not afraid to wear them!" Kansas State University has a centralized campus about 1.5 miles long, set amid the Flint Hills of northeast Kansas. Consisting largely of limestone buildings covered with ivy, students are quick to point out the beauty and variety of the gardens and shrubbery around campus that are largely due to the extensive horticultural program. True to its location in the American heartland, KSU exemplifies the typical all-American college.

K-State is located in Manhattan, Kansas, a town that thrives on the vitality and the business the students bring. When students leave for the summer, a large number of pizza places and other college oriented businesses close. Manhattan is very supportive of the school and its students, and the residents proudly display K-State's colors and symbols. In fact, the town firetrucks are emblazoned with three foot tall Powercats in honor of the school mascot, Willy the Wildcat. However, due to the town's relatively small size, many students often travel as often as once a week to Lawrence (45 minutes away) to shop, and at least twice a month to Kansas City (2 hours away).

Not Just Farmers and Country Music

K-State was originally an agricultural college, and while some students complain that the school retains an unfair image as being filled with "farmers, hicks, and country music," others are proud of the distinction that the agricultural programs have brought to the university. The academic programs are divided into nine colleges, and while the College of Agriculture is just one of these, it provides some of the most distinctive majors that K-State offers. Among these are baking and milling (officially known as grain science and industry), which prepares its students for jobs with grain processing companies, such as Kellogg's. Leadership Studies, another unique program created in 1997, deals with the theory and practical application of leadership abilities and skills.

Another prestigious program at K-State is the Architectural College, to which students must apply to directly upon entering the university. According to one architecture major, students in the program are expected to put in at least 20 hours a week in the studio. Many report that they virtually live in the studio, which is equipped with strategically placed vending machines for microwaveable meals. Architecture, along with milling, veterinary science, and engineering are known as "weed-out majors" in which the first two years of study are particularly demanding and time consuming in order to limit the enrollment.

Nuclear Engineering 501: Atomic Gut

K-State actually runs its own small nuclear reactor. Located on campus, this unit is used to power the campus. It is also used to show how nuclear power works as part of an infamous gut class: Introduction to Nuclear Engineering, a course some students say is graded purely on attendance. Other reportedly easy classes include Music Literature Lab, Introduction to Applied Architecture, and Impact of Technology on Society.

Kansas State freshmen find that their first semester schedule is largely predetermined by a set of mandatory core classes. Because the registration process is based on seniority, upperclassmen report few problems getting into the classes they want, while sophomores and second-semester freshmen have a much harder time. Students find the advising system cumbersome and unhelpful and the advisors uninformative and inflexible, and thus the academic advising system is not well liked. Some students even choose to circumvent the advising system, claiming "it's easier to guide yourself."

Groovin' with the Profs

Professors at K-State get rave reviews for being "very open, accessible, and friendly," often distributing their home phone numbers in class. "You're just as likely to see your professor in a bar on Saturday night as on campus," one student claimed. Another student dubbed many of the professors "closet hippies." "They talk to you like human beings. We've got 27-year-old professors; you cannot beat that!" said one undergrad. Many professors reportedly also have a sense of humor. One freshman remembered when her professor, who always wore jeans and a white shirt, came to the last day of class "wearing plaid pants, a polka-dot shirt, and showed slides of David Hasselhoff (of *Baywatch* fame) and himself in a play from his days in college."

Teaching assistants are common in math and science, but rare in other subjects. One textiles major claimed that in four years she had only one TA, although an engineering major had them in about half of his classes. The TAs assist, rather than lead, classes, serving primarily as lab facilitators. Some TAs received poor reviews by students, largely based on their poor grasp of the English language. Running on a semester system, K-State academic requirements include two English composition classes, psychology and sociology, college algebra, history, macro and micro economics, and human development. There is no language requirement, and a physical education requirement was dropped in 1997. Class size varies by college, but the average lecture consists of about 250 students while discussion classes enroll from 20 to 40 students.

While most students find a car unnecessary on campus, those who live off campus complain about the parking situation. Some drivers report at least an hour's wait for a space in the student parking lots, although the faculty lots have "plenty of empty spaces." Students often park instead at their fraternity or sorority houses and then walk to class from there. Bicycles are very popular, but can be ridden only around the periphery of campus.

Study Habits

Students cite Turtle Creek as a favorite spot to hit the books, or just spend a lazy Sunday afternoon. Located about 10 minutes from campus by car, this large lake is where the crew team rows. Students also use the creek to swim and water ski, and some hike on the extensive trail system surrounding it. Many students study at the Manhattan City Park, or in the shade of the large trees on campus. The campus libraries close at midnight, so late-night studiers crowd coffee shops in Manhattan, as well as the Village Inn, the only 24-hour restaurant in Manhattan known for its comfy booths, milk shakes, and fried chicken for the sleep-deprived.

Life on Campus

While a large portion of K-State upperclassmen prefer to live in apartments off campus, few students complain about the dorms. Most dorms are L-shaped buildings with two wings of double rooms. Each floor determines its own quiet hours and rules, although the top floor of each building is designated as an "intensive study" floor with longer quiet hours. Each building is about eight stories high, with an elevator at the apex of the "L." There is 24-hour visitation on single-sex floors, but males must always be escorted when on female floors.

Dorm rooms are fairly large, with air conditioning and a three-panel window. One freshman reported that she and her roommate fit a loft, two desks, a couch, and a coffee table into their room. The lighting is more than sufficient—as one student said, "Turn that puppy on and you're blind!"

Students say they feel safe on campus, and additional outdoor lighting was recently installed. Safety phones are located throughout campus and an escort service will walk students home upon request.

Undergrads are less enthusiastic about campus food, although a salad bar, a grill, vegetarian, and vegan options are available. Students can choose between a standard meal plan or a debit system that deducts the cost of each meal from an account. Some favorite eateries off-campus include Rock-a-Belly Deli, Habachi Head (Cajun), and Pizza Shuttle.

Kabillion Activities

On-campus activities are extensive. "There are kabillions of them!" one student professed. *The Collegian*, the school newspaper, and the marching band are both popular. Societies based on interests and majors also abound. Although it rarely snows in Kansas, the university has a ski clubs as well as a rock-climbing club. The Landane Lecture Series brings one speaker to campus each month: recent speakers have included Henry Kissinger and Colin Powell.

The university recently renovated Farrell Library, the Student Union, and the sports complexes. The library, previously criticized for its small size, is now "huge." Study space abounds in a modern, comfortable environment. The Student Union, a.k.a. the Onion, houses a bowling alley in the basement, places to study, to watch TV, arcades, a pool table, a cafeteria-style restaurant, and a sit-down restaurant. Every other Tuesday a large crowd gathers in the Onion to watch *South Park*. *Jerry Springer* is also popular, as are *The Simpsons* and *The X-Files*.

Working Out the Wildcat Way

Athletics are very popular at K-State. Athletes and non-athletes alike call the recreational center the "Taj Mahal" of sports complexes. Even the football stadium has recently been expanded to increase seating. "Everyone attends football games," said one fan. At games, Willy the Wildcat often spells KSU with his body, while fans scream the letters. At every touchdown or field goal, the fans point to the end zone and scream, "Good for another wildcat!"

A large number of students are involved in the intramural sports program. Frisbee and golf are extremely popular. "Powder puff" football (women's flag football) is also a favorite, as is wallyball (a variation of volleyball played in a racquetball court).

After Hours

Kansas State University is officially a dry campus, but some students say drinking is popular. While most claim that being underage is no problem, security officers hand out many citations for MIPs (Minor in Possession) each week, and this deters a significant portion of the under-21 crowd. The social life for most students revolves around Aggieville, an off-campus strip that houses 37 bars in a two block radius. Underclassmen tend to congregate at the dance bars, particularly a club nicknamed "Kiddie Junction." Upperclassmen find seclusion in the quieter jazz bars, particularly Auntie Mae's. "Everyone in the bars are smoking Marlboro or Camel Lights," one student said. Although chain smoking is popular, students rarely light up on campus. Some students report that marijuana is present on campus, but others claim it is rare or underground.

> "The Greek system is very strong at K-State, but students agree that participation is far from essential."

K-State is one of the few schools where traditional dating is common, especially "Coke-date" (an informal study session over Cokes at a coffee shop). These low-key dates relieve the pressure of a "first date" environment, but provide an alternative to Aggieville. Most students feel that the gay population is not visible on campus, but homosexuality is generally accepted. Ethnic diversity on campus has improved over recent years, but is still behind when compared to other universities. Students seem unconcerned, saying the school is remarkably diverse for its location.

The Greek Life

The Greek system is very strong at K-State, but students agree that participation is far from essential. While undergrads tend to move in either Greek or non-Greek circles, there exists no hostility between the groups. First-year sorority members live in dorms, while men live in their fraternity houses all four years. Annual theme parties include: the Festival of Gluttony, where students ride a waterslide from a barn roof; Patty Murphy (a party named after a fraternity member who allegedly drank himself to death during prohibition), which features tombstones and hot tubs as decorations; and the Mud Bowl, a beach volleyball tournament to raise money for Alzheimer's research. The largest event of the year, however, is homecoming. Planning begins in the spring for the following year's game. Fraternities and sororities team up to compete in float building, body pyramid building, parade, and chanting contests, and winners are announced at the homecoming football game.

K-State Is...

Students report that their classmates generally have a "happy-go-lucky" attitude and a "polite and social" demeanor. The dress is preppy and casual, the mood is friendly. "People that I've never met before open doors for me," recounted one student. Others echo this sentiment by saying that school spirit and friendliness are the two attributes that most clearly define Kansas State University's personality.—*Cynthia Matthews and Staff*

FYI

The three best things about attending K-State are "the professors, the sports, and the people."

The three worst things about attending K-State are "the city (or lack thereof), the bureaucracy, and the escorts on the women's floors."

The three things that every student should do before graduating from K-State are "to go to the Festival of Gluttony, to play IMs, and to go to Turtle Creek."

One thing I'd like to have known before coming here is "that cars were so important. If you don't have one, you need to know someone who does!"

University of Kansas

Address: Office of Admissions and Scholarships, 1502 Iowa Street, Lawrence, KS 66045
Phone: 785-864-3911
E-mail address: adm@ukans.edu
Web site URL: www.ukans.edu
Location: suburban
Founded: 1866
Private or Public: public
Religious affiliation: none
Undergraduate enrollment: 19,183
Total enrollment: 27,567
Percent Male/Female: 48%/52%

Percent Minority: 7.0%
Percent African-American: 2.0%
Percent Hispanic: 3.0%
Percent Asian: 2.0%
Percent in-state/out-of-state: 68%/32%
Percent Pub HS: NA
Fraternities: 20%
Sororities: 22%
Number of Applicants: 8,518
Percent Accepted: 61%
Percent Accepted who enroll: 75%
Entering: 3,901
Transfers: 2,190
Application Deadline: rolling
Mean SAT: NA V, NA M

Middle 50% SAT range: NA V, NA M
Middle 50% ACT range: 20–26
Mean ACT: 24
3 Most popular majors: biological sciences, psychology, business
Retention: 78.0%
Graduation rate: 50.0%
Library: 3.5 million volumes
Tuition and Fees: $2,092 in; $8,693 out
Room and Board: $3,941
On-campus housing: 48%
Financial aid, first-year: 39%

Built into the side of a mountain, the University of Kansas gives its students plenty of exercise trekking to classes. As one student put it, "You can tell what year students are by the size of their calves." "KU calves" are only one of many characteristics that distinguish this public, Midwestern school, well-known for its nationally ranked basketball team.

The University of Kansas is generally considered "easy to get into, but hard to stay in." While not as selective as such state schools as the University of Michigan, Ann Arbor or the University of North Carolina, Chapel Hill, KU provides a top-quality education at a reasonable price. The university some students describe as a "good deal" is notable for its strong commitment to the liberal arts, mirrored by the large percentage of students enrolled in the program. All students in the school of liberal arts must meet a core group of requirements that include Western and non-Western civilization classes as well as prove proficiency in a foreign language. Outside of liberal arts, the requirements vary dramatically from program to program. The fine arts school, for example, has musical performance requirements. Recently, the university increased its ef-

forts to recruit more academically talented students. The school's Honors College offers selected undergrads small seminar classes taught by actual professors. Class sizes are limited to 30 students and even freshmen in the Honors College have access to these classes. The Honors College professors earn higher reviews on average than the majority of university faculty. As one freshman raved, "My history teacher is the bomb!" Overall, students are pleased with the range of majors and classes available under the liberal arts program. Introductory classes tend to be large and taught by graduate teaching assistants (GTAs), especially in math and science, while upper-level courses are smaller and taught by professors. Several teachers and classes received great reviews. In particular, Dr. Dennis Dailey's class on human sexuality is very popular. Academics are seen as challenging, but never overwhelming. Foreign languages have a reputation for being difficult. "Some people avoid liberal arts just to avoid the foreign language requirement," one student said. But, students report that many easy, "gut" classes can be found in the art history and child development departments. Some students have grievances with the grading scale used by professors. "The grading scale is not uniform at all. A 94 percent can be an A in one class or a B in another." Despite this, undergrads generally find professors friendly and accessible, although it can take some effort to get to know them.

What is the typical KU student like? While there is no predominant stereotype, students describe their classmates as attractive and fairly preppy or alternative in style. The school is rather homogeneous: students are mainly Caucasian, Christian, heterosexual Midwesterners. However, the university has a fairly tolerant and liberal reputation. Nicknamed "Gay U." by some, the university has a substantial gay and lesbian community. Overall, racial diversity is improving at the school due to the concerted effort of undergraduate admissions in recruiting minority students.

Party School

Ranked as the number eight party school in the nation by the Princeton Review, KU has a social life one student described as "very happening." Rush, or "going Greek," is a popular and painless but fairly competitive process. With a large Greek scene, a party can always be found, the majority of them open to non-Greeks as well. For many freshmen experiencing freedom for the first time, drinking is a popular weekend activity. Though KU is a dry campus, some students say alcohol is easy to find, the drink of choice being "whatever you can get your hands on." However, many options exist for non-drinkers at KU. Kansas City is a popular weekend destination for upperclassmen, and several good dance clubs, such as Bleachers, surround the campus. The "Day on the Hill" music festival held every spring attracts big-name bands like They Might Be Giants. Another popular pastime is dating, which students unanimously described as "big," along with casual sex. On a related note, legend has it that the large, bronze Jayhawk statue in the center of campus will fly away if a virgin ever graduates from KU.

Kansas Livin'

Undergrads describe the tree-filled KU campus as "gorgeous." The buildings are an eclectic mix of collegiate-style architecture and modern structures like Wesco Hall, where many English classes are held. Situated in the heart of the campus, the patio and stairs that surround Wesco Hall are known as "Wesco Beach," a popular hangout before, after, or even during classes. Overall, students say they feel very safe on campus. Security does not seem to be much of an issue in the quiet town of Lawrence.

Campus facilities, for the most part, are in excellent condition. Although some students complained that the dorms are "old and crappy," renovations of all the dorms are underway. The university is moving toward "suite" style dorms like Templin, which contain suites of four or more students who share a common living room and bathroom. Many upperclassmen choose to live off campus, but one senior described the renovated dorms as "the best place to live." Naismith Hall, run by Holiday Inn, is considered very nice, as are the scholarship halls reserved for Honors College students. Described as "a community within a community," the scholarship halls require students to share the responsibilities of chores and cooking.

> **"The drink of choice is 'whatever you can get your hands on.'"**

Most students at KU do not make their own food, but instead eat their meals in the dining halls. Many rate the dining hall food average to below-average, with "recycled menus" being the major complaint. The most variety and the best food reportedly is available at "Mrs. E's", the largest dining hall on campus. Vegan and vegetarian options are always available. For those tired of dining hall food, popular restaurants await in Lawrence, including Papa Keno's ("pizza to die for"), La Familia (Mexican), and Java Break (coffee shop).

"Something for Everyone"

With more than 400 campus organizations, "there's something for everyone here," one student said. KU even has a Dr. Seuss Club, whose members proudly affirm their affinity for green eggs and ham.

Writing for the *University Daily Kansas*, the campus newspaper, is a popular extracurricular for many aspiring journalists.

By far the greatest pastime for KU students is watching their beloved Jayhawks basketball team on the court. KU b-ball games are an event in themselves. To kick off the season, KU coach Roy Williams organizes a midnight pep rally and exhibition for the fans, affectionately termed "Late Night with Roy Williams." Students demonstrate their KU spirit by camping out days in advance to get prime seats for the games, held in the always-packed Allen Field House. Chants of "Rock Chalk, Jayhawk, KU" can be heard at any sporting event, showing the ever-present spirit of KU fans.

KU fans love not only their team but also their school. When asked if they would pick KU again as their college choice, a number of students responded with an enthusiastic "Yes!" Quality academics combined with exciting sports and an active Greek scene make KU an attractive choice.—*Madhu Pocha and Staff*

FYI
The three best things about attending the University of Kansas are "the bars, the hottie frat boys, and the basketball team."
The three worst things about attending the University of Kansas are "the bars, the hottie frat boys with attitudes, and the hills that smokers can't walk up."
The three things that every student should do before graduating from the University of Kansas are "attend a KU game, dance/wade in the Chi Omega Fountain, go to O Street."
One thing I'd like to have known before coming here is "everyone has a significant other!"

Kentucky

Centre College

Address: 600 West Walnut Street, Danville, KY 40422
Phone: 606-238-5350
E-mail address: admission@centre.edu
Web site URL: www.centre.edu
Location: rural
Founded: 1819
Private or Public: private
Religious affiliation: none
Undergraduate enrollment: 1,052
Total enrollment: 1,052
Percent Male/Female: 50%/50%
Percent Minority: 4.0%

Percent African-American: 3.0%
Percent Hispanic: 1.0%
Percent Asian: 0.0%
Percent in-state/out-of-state: 64%/36%
Percent Pub HS: 80%
Fraternities: 61%
Sororities: 68%
Number of Applicants: 1,219
Percent Accepted: 86%
Percent Accepted who enroll: 28%
Entering: 294
Transfers: 29
Application Deadline: 1 Feb

Mean SAT: 608 V, 602 M
Middle 50% SAT range: 590–670 V, 570–670 M
Middle 50% ACT range: 25–29
Mean ACT: 27
3 Most popular majors: English, economics, history
Retention: 87.0%
Graduation rate: 64.0%
Library: 270,000 volumes
Tuition and Fees: $20,350 in; $20,350 out
Room and Board: $5,300
On-campus housing: 100%
Financial aid, first-year: 61%

Although Centre is in a small town in the heart of Kentucky, its students seek expansion, not isolation. The first thing they learn, and the lesson they never tire of teaching others, is the meaning of a liberal arts education.

The Main Course

Instead of feeling limited by Centre's rigorous commitment to the liberal arts, most students defend and praise it, saying they enjoy a well-rounded education. Many talk of interests they never would have developed (a dreaded art class often ends up a favorite) or knowledge they never would have acquired (the humanities cores are crucial for educated travel in Europe, one student noted) without the general education requirements. Students must complete 115 course hours in areas outside their major, which include such subjects as religion, anthropology, economics, philosophy, and the humanities. In addition to general education courses,

Centre students must complete the Convocation program, which requires attendance at 12 arts performances (from Broadway shows to renowned lecturers) at the Norton Center for the Arts on campus, or at the recently completed visual arts center.

Students resist naming one department as the strongest, claiming that each has excellent faculty and resources; past limitations in science the recently renovated Olin Center has compensated for facilities for the physical sciences. Small classes—none with more than 30 to 35 students and some with as few as 8—and uncommonly accessible professors who give out their home phone numbers, invite students to dinner, and chat with them in dining halls are universally appreciated.

Almost everyone lives on-campus, and students generally are pleased with their housing, noting that it is fairly easy to choose their living arrangements. Dorm rooms were recently connected to the computer network. A number of upper-class dorms are coed; freshmen live in single-sex dorms, with men and women on opposite sides of the campus and no visitation hours allowed until the second semester (until midnight on weekdays, 2 A.M. on weekends). One student reported that while the RAs on each floor act more as figures of authority than friends, some do relax the rules as long as students are discreet about their visitors.

A less popular development is the recent turning of "Frat Quad"—once the hub of social life on campus—into regular dorms. Six fraternity and three sorority houses now constitute Greek Park, whose more peripheral (and dangerous, due to the traffic) location on a public street and reduced size (housing 8 to 10 members instead of 28) has left many students disgruntled. Some worry that the administration is attempting to phase out Greek life, or at least minimize its importance, and predict that such efforts will make Centre more of a suitcase college.

Side Dishes

Besides ensuring personal attention, Centre's small size translates into both extensive and intensive extracurricular opportunities. "Everyone wears a lot of hats," explained one student; one senior said he is captain of the baseball team, frat rush chair, a peer counselor, and member of the College Council, which is involved in instituting academic changes such as the addition of minuses to the grading scale last spring. Most students are involved in sports, often on a varsity level. The Centre Colonels make traditionally strong showings in football and basketball against rivals Trinity and Rhodes Colleges, and field a nationally competitive soccer team. Renovated weight room facilities and a proliferation of intramurals keep students active. In addition, students can write for the campus paper, the *Cento*, work on the yearbook, or join the outdoor club.

Centre has the social hazards of many other small colleges: it tends to split into cliques, "flinging" takes the place of dating, and "if you do something stupid the whole campus knows it." Students describe their classmates as "very diverse,"

yet the standards are relative; while minority groups such as BGLAD (sponsoring bisexual, gay, and lesbian awareness days) and the Black Student Union are active, they are small. One student said that despite the presence of opposing political views, conservatism seems to prevail, and Confederate flags pop up in a number of rooms on campus without causing conflicts. In general, political activism takes the form of private discussions or involvement in student government.

Students agree that outsiders stereotype Centre as a "smart, rich school" and cite strained relations with the residents of Danville. While one student explained that it is not fair to assume all Centre students are upper-middle class, since the majority receive some sort of financial aid, she added that Centre can be "pretty materialistic;" it is rumored to be the college with "the highest ratio of packages per person from J. Crew."

Some students see the attrition rate as fairly high. In spite of the upperclass peer counselors for freshman orientation and peer mentors for freshmen with academic adjustment problems, the transition from high school to college can be difficult here. Students caution freshmen about becoming too easily demoralized: many are used to being at the top of their high school class with little work, and then are shocked when they cannot get straight A's at Centre.

Dessert

While Danville's movie theater shows new releases for only two dollars, one student quipped, "The height of excitement in town is a visit to the supermarket." Yet opportunities to pursue different social avenues abound.

Alternative entertainment is provided by the Student Activities Council (SAC), which brings in popular bands and sponsors dances, although these have not been widely attended in the past. The Warehouse, renovated last year, is the student recreational center. The Centre Grille's fast-food offerings are included in an alternative flex-dollar plan, in which students can supplement 14 meals from the main Cowen Dining Hall with $200 for snacks (on-campus students are required to be on a meal plan). Tightened security has put a damper on the tradition of "running the Flame," in which students streak from their dorms around the central campus statue and back.

Fortunately, the college's central location and the prevalence of cars on campus compensate for any limitations in the immediate surroundings. Since Boyle County is dry, students must drive half an hour to buy alcohol: a nuisance to some, but for others "going on a run" is a welcome excuse to get off-campus. Undergrads can also stop at a Taco Bell (lacking in Danville) or shop at a mall in the nearby city of Lexington, where the University of Kentucky serves as a supplement to Centre's library resources and course offerings. Most liberating and most widely hailed, however, are the semester-abroad opportunities. Each fall and spring trimester (each 12 weeks long), Centre sends 20 students to Regent's College in London and 20 others to study in Strasbourg, France. While science students have a harder time leaving campus, due to sequential courses (many required classes are offered in alternate years and must be taken in a prescribed order), with extra summer classes and by planning ahead they too can take advantage of the study-abroad program. During the short winter term, biology majors can embark on trips to the Bahamas or Ecuador with their professors and earn their two credits there; some history majors study in Vietnam during these six weeks.

> "Everyone wears a lot of hats," explained one student.

Without sacrificing the advantages of a small college, Centre seeks out ways to diversify college life. Students follow the many roads that lead from Centre, but are glad to find the close community intact when they return.—*Seung Lee and Staff*

FYI

The three best things about attending Centre are "the chance to study abroad, the Convocation requirement, and the personal investment students make in this place."

The three worst things about attending Centre are "the clique tendency, being named the Colonels, and the attempt to phase out Greek life."

The three things that every student should do before graduating from Centre are "run the Flame, use winter term to travel, and go to the Danville movie theater."

One thing I'd like to have known before coming here is "you need a car to have any kind of social existence."

University of Kentucky

Address: 100 Funkhouser Building, Lexington, KY 40506
Phone: 606-257-9000
E-mail address: admissio@pop.uky.edu
Web site URL: www.uky.edu
Location: urban
Founded: 1865
Private or Public: public
Religious affiliation: none
Undergraduate enrollment: 17,155
Total enrollment: 23,540
Percent Male/Female: 48%/52%
Percent Minority: 9.0%

Percent African-American: 6.0%
Percent Hispanic: 1.0%
Percent Asian: 2.0%
Percent in-state/out-of-state: 87.0%/13.0%
Percent Pub HS: NA
Fraternities: 14%
Sororities: 16%
Number of Applicants: 7,789
Percent Accepted: 78%
Percent Accepted who enroll: 43%
Entering: 2,626
Transfers: 2,202
Application Deadline: rolling

Mean SAT: NA V, NA M
Middle 50% SAT range: NA V, NA M
Middle 50% ACT range: 22–27
Mean ACT: 25
3 Most popular majors: accounting, biology, psychology
Retention: 78.0%
Graduation rate: 48.0%
Library: 2.8 million volumes
Tuition and Fees: $2,680 in; $8,040 out
Room and Board: $3,470
On-campus housing: 30%
Financial aid, first-year: 53%

Recently, the University of Kentucky set an ambitious goal for itself: to become a top twenty research university. This goal has noticeably reshaped the campus: renovating buildings, reshaping the attitudes of the students, and even restructuring entire departments, causing considerable and often difficult transitions. Yet students seem optimistic about the future of UK. "They are finally getting their act together. Instead of just talking about progress, we're actually seeing some."

Quest for Excellence

The academics of UK have been a major issue, and a major motivator for the University's goal to become a top 20 institution. Since the University stated its goal, students have reported an increase in professor-undergraduate interaction. "Before, the professors only cared about working with graduate students . . . now it seems like professors and undergraduates really work together." UK is divided into five colleges, to which students apply directly: architecture; engineering; arts and sciences; business and economics; and communications. Students say the programs in agriculture, architecture and the sciences are top-notch, and the phar-

macy program is also one of the best in the nation. Students reported that the strongest departments are Communications and Health Sciences, while math and the "hard sciences" like physics and chemistry are the toughest classes. UK has introductory courses ranging in size from 50 to 150 people.

Students from Lexington Community College also take classes at UK, and this is beneficial for many students living in the Lexington area. Students can take general instruction courses at L.C.C. where there is "better interaction with the instructors" and then move on to UK. Many undergraduates also choose UK because of their strong financial aid program. Freshmen who do well on the PSAT and become National Merit Finalists can earn a full ride. As a result, more and more eligible students are choosing to accept UK's offer to pay for tuition, room, and board.

There is very little difference between freshmen and upperclassmen on-campus housing at UK. "Upperclassmen are less likely to be in one of the Towers on South campus, but all the dorms are about the same." Still, some students complained that although the housing is about equal for upperclassmen and freshmen, it's all pretty bad. The campus dorms are either single-sex or coed by floor and regulations regarding opposite-sex visitation are strictly enforced

Construction, Construction, Everywhere

In order to achieve their goal to become a top research university, UK has embarked on a spree of construction on campus, to the point where it seems like "someone dropped a construction crew and told them to fix everything and build everywhere." Recently completed was the $50 million construction of the WT Young Library, which is one of the "best networked libraries in the entire U.S." However, the construction can be a "nuisance." Some students also complain that certain projects are "really a waste of money." For example, UK has recently started using expensive brick signs that say "University of Kentucky" at all intersections which some students find pointless and annoying.

But the main reason to move off campus, according to students, is the food. "A lot of students complain that they could never possibly eat the amount of food they're charged for on their meal cards," one undergraduate said. Some don't bother with the meal plan at all. Popular off-campus eating options include mostly fast-food restaurants, such as Kentucky Fried Chicken and Long John Silver's. "It's really hard to eat healthy," one student complained.

Not Entirely Greek

The University of Kentucky draws students from over one hundred countries and students feel that the University is very open to diversity. Although some students reported that a Greek stereotype dominates the image of the average student—"the standard frat boys, sorority chicks, jocks, etc."—most students believe that this is not exactly the truth. Most non-Greek students do not feel left out at all, and in fact, "some of the office bearers of the Student Body don't belong to any Greek houses."

Backwoods Kind of Guys

Although there is always a Greek event every weekend on campus, there are plenty of other things to do. The party scene is just as big on campus as it is off campus, and very popular. It's also diverse. "Some people are really into drinking and partying every weekend day, but others do it sparingly, or don't drink at all. There is a wide band of attitudes and beliefs." Still, the cult of moonshine isn't entirely dead, and "lots of backwoods kinda guys go here . . . there is a lot of drinking and drugs."

The surroundings offer other options for use of free time. Many students noted the sharp contrast between the city of Lexington and the surrounding hills. "It's more city than country," one junior said of Lexington, "but one of the best things about UK is being able to go just ten miles off campus and end up on a beautiful hillside or horse farm." Yet, some students rarely leave campus except to go home— "most everything is within three miles of campus. People go to malls, parks, libraries, etc." But for the adventure-seekers, greater Kentucky offers plenty of escapes from campus: "Louisville for cool night life, Beckley for skiing, Cumberland for water sports." Students even go to Cincinnati to see the Bengals and the Reds. "They are all pretty near and quite inexpensive."

And, of Course, Basketball

Even outside basketball, UK has a strong athletic tradition. One student commented that "not only are students and faculty fans, but most of the state is fanatical about UK athletics." Though there may be other sports at the University of Kentucky (there are 22 Division I sports) the sport that excites the campus and state the most is, obviously, basketball. The UK Wildcats have "the best (record) of all the NCAA basketball teams." Spirits at these games are high. Tickets to basketball and football games are free to students, and the games always have huge attendance. Even though many go to the games, one student complained that "we don't have pep rallies very often which is another issue."

Within the shadow of the basketball team, UK's football is really starting to make a name for itself. In 1998, the sophomore quarterback Tim Couch won the Heisman Trophy and was then recruited to play for the Cleveland Browns. Plus, in line with the recent construction on campus, twenty thousand seats have been added to the stadium, making it a circular stadium that seats almost fifty thousand.

> "Still, the cult of moonshine isn't entirely dead, and 'lots of backwoods kinda guys go here.'"

When extracurricular energy at UK isn't devoted entirely to basketball, students manage to get involved in other activities. The school newspaper, the *Kentucky Colonel*, covers life both at UK and in Lexington. Political activity among UK students is relatively low except during campus or national elections, when the Young Republicans and Young Democrats hold rallies on campus for their candidates. Other Activities range from waterskiing to UKLUG (Linux Users Group) to outreach programs. Although there are over two hundred organizations on campus, one student complained that community service is not very popular on campus. "That really bothers me. [There is a] lot of apathy here."

Oh the Places You'll Go

Change is really apparent at UK. "It is really growing," said one student, "and with the new mission to be a top 20 research school, lots of world class research is being done here. You can really go far here if you try." So as UK gets closer and closer to reaching its goal, the question is: What next?—*Nicole Jabaily*

FYI

The three best things about attending the University of Kentucky are "girls . . . man . . . awesome girls; inexpensive living; and the feeling of belonging to UK basketball religion."

The three worst things about attending the University of Kentucky are "no skiing resort nearby even though you see a lot of snow; people prefering Stanford students over you at your job just because you're from UK; and being thought a redneck or hillbilly."

The three things that every student should do before graduating the University of Kentucky are "get drunk on bourbon, get bankrupt at Keeneland, and go rafting at Cumberland."

One thing I'd like to have known before coming here is that "the rest of my high school, which is also in Lexington, Kentucky would also be here."

Louisiana

Louisiana State University

Address: 110 Thomas Boyd Hall, Baton Rouge, LA 70803
Phone: 225-388-3202
E-mail address: lsuadmit@lsu.edu
Web site URL: www.lsu.edu
Location: urban
Founded: 1855
Private or Public: public
Religious affiliation: none
Undergraduate enrollment: 22,714
Total enrollment: NA
Percent Male/Female: 48%/52%
Percent Minority: 19.0%

Percent African-American: 9.0%
Percent Hispanic: 2.0%
Percent Asian: 4.0%
Percent in-state/out-of-state: 91%/9%
Percent Pub HS: NA
Fraternities: 12%
Sororities: 15%
Number of Applicants: 9,752
Percent Accepted: 81%
Percent Accepted who enroll: 64%
Entering: 5,083
Transfers: 1,322
Application Deadline: 1 May

Mean SAT: NA V, NA M
Middle 50% SAT range: NA V, NA M
Middle 50% ACT range: 21–26
Mean ACT: NA
3 Most popular majors: business management, engineering, education
Retention: 83.0%
Graduation rate: 48.0%
Library: NA
Tuition and Fees: $2,721 in; $6,621 out
Room and Board: $3,910
On-campus housing: NA
Financial aid, first-year: NA

L SU students say that when it comes to their school and sports, they bleed purple and gold. In the words of one student—"Football is king here!" Last season when rumors spread that not all students would be guaranteed tickets to home games, there were mini-riots, protests, and demonstrations. Said one student, "Maybe it's a Southern thing, maybe it's a Louisiana thing, but that's just how it is."

Academics: Not Always First Priority

Like most big schools, Louisiana offers its students a great deal of academic diversity, with majors spanning the humanities and the sciences. But as many students are quick to say, "Yeah, academics are a priority, but they're not always first priority." Indeed, some students resent what they feel are the school's overly lax academic standards—"It's way too easy to get into LSU. A lot of people come in that just want to screw around, and that makes

it hard for the rest of us." Many hard-core studiers can be found among the ranks of engineering majors, reportedly among the hardest discipline LSU has to offer. Graphic design and photography were described as "considerably less challenging."

But for all students, getting into classes is reportedly a big problem. One senior called the registration process "painful . . . involving lots of time wasted standing in line." Another student exclaimed, "Thank God we only do it twice a year!" Once registered, however, students generally have few complaints. Class sizes were described as "decent," requirements "doable," and grading "fair—though not uniform throughout majors."

In light of the student body's mammoth proportions, however, one student did lament that it was all too easy for students to slip through the cracks. "TAs do most of the grading so the teacher doesn't really learn how you do work, and the TA doesn't associate a face with the name," he complained. Indeed, in attending such a large school, students commonly complain that the administration is often inefficient and seldom very helpful. Concerning LSU bureaucracy, one student said, "It's hell, as evidenced by the joke told to every arriving freshman who's been given the LSU runaround—you've just taken and passed LSU 1001."

Another student was quick to counter, however, that "professors are genuinely concerned about you and what you learn, if you take the time to approach them." LSU reportedly has an overabundance of instructors from foreign countries, however, which, as one student commented, makes for some "interesting classroom experiences." One senior recommended that students should "just ask around and find out who speaks plainly."

The Sophomore Run from Residential Life

One student reported that "the dorms tend to have a high turnover rate." And based on what students say about on-campus housing, it is not hard to see why. An average freshman dorm room was described by one student as "small, ugly," and resembling a "mental institution." Strict visitation restrictions and "crazy card-access rules" also contributed to students' overall dissatisfaction with residential life; visitors of the opposite sex are not allowed after a certain time, and they must be checked in and escorted by a resident at all times. In spite of the downside to dorm life, however, most students would agree that living on campus the first year is important for forging friendships and getting a little taste of the typical college experience. But as one student was quick to add—"After first year run—just run away from residential life."

First years can choose from a variety of dorms, which students say all have distinct personalities. One student broke them down into four categories—"There are the honor's dorms, the slacker dorms, the freak dorms, and the frat and sorority dorms." Another student characterized them by gender. "The girl dorms are a bit snobby. Guy dorms are laid back." For girls, East Laville and Evangeline are said to be "awesome"; for guys, top picks include McVoy and West Laville, both "surrounded by all-girls' dorms." About Kirby-Smith, a notoriously bad guy dorm, one student commented, "Apparently the inhabitants don't know much about personal hygiene."

Many upperclassmen move into apartments on campus after their first year. Typical accommodations are described as "nice, but small and very expensive." Each comes equipped with its own kitchen, washer/dryer, and living area. Several apartment complexes near campus are also popular options, especially because many of them fall on a city bus route. Buses run every 8 minutes or so, and off-campus dwellers report using them quite frequently in order to get back to campus. One student praised the setup as "very convenient."

"Tiger Town"

Students say that Baton Rouge, or "Tiger Town," as it is affectionately called, "looks more like a town than a city." One sophomore complained, "It's not like Boston or Seattle where it has a huge downtown area and you can walk everywhere. You've got to have a car here—everything's 10 minutes away." And with the dearth of adequate campus parking, owning a car can prove problematic. The school has been making efforts to improve the situation, but as one student pointed out, even this new parking is not always accessible. "They're building new lots all the time, but the lots are out in Egypt compared to where your classes are."

School food was described as "awful." Students out looking for alternatives can find them at any one of the numerous local eateries. Don's Seafood, Nympha's, and Pasttimes (pizza) are among the more popular student choices. The student union also offers a variety of fast-food places as well, with everything from McDonald's to Chick Fil-A and Pizza Hut.

"Getting Sloppy"

Drinking is a popular pastime at LSU, especially on weekends when "getting sloppy" is the thing to do. "It's involved in about 75 percent of what we do," said one student. Popular local bars include the Caterie and the Varsity. On campus as well, alcohol abounds at parties thrown by frats and in the dorms. Students also rave about street parties, when everyone living on a certain street "closes off this street just off campus, and everyone from LSU is invited to party out in the street all night." One such street party, traditionally held around Halloween, is especially fun, students say. During the fall, students spend their time hopping from tailgate party to tailgate party before and after football games. In fact, football game days are the only days when students are allowed to drink openly on campus. All other days of the year, students say, on-campus drinkers risk the wrath of the administration. But generally, the school tends to be "tougher on the frats because of a high-profile student death related to alcohol a couple years ago."

When asked, LSU students agree that their school merits its reputation as a party school. Interestingly though, in light of this school-wide penchant to party and drink, it is surprising to note that most students would also agree that non-drinkers "don't really feel so out-of-it on campus." Many students would say that you don't have to drink at parties— "there's only pressure to drink within the Greek system—otherwise those who don't want to drink don't have to." Another student added, "I don't drink, and I have lots of fun. You can go out or not go out. It's all about the crowd you prefer."

Certainly the Greeks do dominate aspects of campus life, but those students who don't care much for the party or frat scene can find their kicks in any number of other areas. People with cars will often take road trips to New Orleans, a massive "breeding ground of culture," only an hour's drive away. Locally, the music scene is a major draw. Many nearby hangouts feature live bands 7 nights a week. "That good old grunge sound tends to be pretty popular here," said one student. "This is one city rebelling against the mainstream."

But closer to the mainstream is where most LSU students would fall, politically. The student body tends to be very conservative. Said one student, "Sure we have our crazies and left-wing nuts, but overall, we're pretty conventional and tradition-oriented." In accordance with the school's very political atmosphere, recent campus visitors have included former president George Bush, Sr. and William F. Buckley, Jr. One student even recalled that in his political science classes, three former state governors delivered guest lectures in the time frame of one semester. The typical student was described as a white, middle to upper-class Republican, from the state. One senior described the typical student wardrobe—"Most people are from Louisiana, so odds are they are wearing Structure or Abercrombie. And girls love those black pants."

Rooting for the Home Team

But politically conservative or not, one area in which all LSU students can stand united is in the sports arena. Students will often rave about their Saturday nights in Death Valley, a popular nickname for Tiger Stadium, where students go to watch football games en masse. One senior described the atmosphere at games—"LSU fans are the craziest I have ever seen. Anytime we score a touchdown, the student section throws their cups in the air whether they're full or empty. The band sits by the student section and plays and dances with the students—it's insane!" Before every football game, the cheerleaders parade Mike the Tiger, the school mascot, around the stadium in his cage and try to make him growl. All students agree he is the symbol of school unity, a sentiment that moved one student to exclaim, "Everybody loves Mike the Tiger. And if you ask every person, you'll get 30,000 different opinions on everything except that."

> **"Everybody loves Mike the Tiger."**

Football is undoubtedly the dominant sport, but other team sports enjoy their own measures of success as well. The basketball and baseball teams are particularly popular and generally perform very well at the national level. The LSU basketball team was ranked 15th in the nation last year, and the baseball team, after winning 4 national titles in the 1990s, ranked third.

Sports are definitely a high priority for students at this school. Most report that their free time is spent either going to the various games or playing in games themselves. School intramurals enjoy high student participation, with rugby and flag football being especially popular. Other school extracurriculars with mass appeal include the LSU student government and the school's daily newspaper, the *Daily Reveille*. Many students report working part-time on the side as well.

And as at most large schools, students can find a niche virtually anywhere, and no two students will have the same college experience. This variety is what appealed most to one student, who praised LSU's "multitude of atmospheres." "You can find virtually any type of environment on campus—a study environment, a social one, quiet, loud, fun, serious—it's all there at the same time. That's what makes LSU such a great place." Prospectives looking for their own niches would undoubtedly be able to find one at LSU. —*Jane H. Hong*

FYI

The three best things about attending Louisiana State are "the school spirit, the beautiful campus, and the support from the Baton Rouge community."

The three worst things about attending Louisiana State are "the parking lots that get taken over by football fans, the gross dorms, how registration is a hassle."

The three things every student should do before graduating from Louisiana State are "eat at the Chimes, sit on the Parade Grounds at night, go to at least one football game."

One thing I wish I had known before coming here is "you're just a number—no one is going to help you find out all the rules and regulations."

Tulane University

Address: 6823 St. Charles Avenue, New Orleans, LA 70118-5680
Phone: 504-865-5731
E-mail address: undergrad.admission@tulane.edu
Web site URL: www.tulane.edu/admission
Location: urban
Founded: 1834
Private or Public: private
Religious affiliation: none
Undergraduate enrollment: 7,163
Total enrollment: 11,438
Percent Male/Female: 47%/53%
Percent Minority: 25.0%

Percent African-American: 5.0%
Percent Hispanic: 4.0%
Percent Asian: 6.0%
Percent in-state/out-of-state: NA
Percent Pub HS: 65%
Fraternities: 19%
Sororities: 33%
Number of Applicants: NA
Percent Accepted: 78%
Percent Accepted who enroll: 19%
Entering: 1,620
Transfers: 164
Application Deadline: 15 Jan
Mean SAT: 651 V, 640 M

Middle 50% SAT range: 600–700 V, 590–690 M
Middle 50% ACT range: 27–31
Mean ACT: 29
3 Most popular majors: social sciences, engineering, business
Retention: 0.9%
Graduation rate: 72.0%
Library: 1,300,050 volumes
Tuition and Fees: $25,390 in; $25,390 out
Room and Board: $6,908
On-campus housing: 90%
Financial aid, first-year: 62%

When Tulane University initially built its library, there was one slight miscalculation. The engineers did not account for the fact that there were going to be books in the library. As a result, the building has sunk somewhat with the weight of the books.

Although their library now leans slightly, Tulane students are still able to take advantage of the space to study. Tulane students work hard to meet tough academic standards, but they also take plenty of time to enjoy their community in New Orleans.

The Curriculum

Academically, Tulane has several colleges to suit the academic needs of its undergraduates. These include the University College, designed to accommodate older students returning to school; Tulane College for men; and Newcomb College for women. Although male and female students apply to different colleges within the university, this separation only applies to the registration process. All academic classes are open to all students regardless of their particular college. Students interested in more specialized programs can also apply to the engineering school or architecture schools.

Students are required to fulfill numerous general education requirements. One undergrad noted that "despite these requirements, many students are able to use AP credits to get out of them." Those in the specialized schools at Tulane are required to take core classes within their respective colleges along with electives, which are taken alongside classmates in Tulane-Newcomb. Students declare majors in their sophomore year. In terms of class size, some introductory classes can be large, but most classes enroll about 20 students. As one student noted, "the administration is good about keeping classes small." Tulane students say they generally are content with their professors, although some dislike the stringent attendance policy enforced in class. Of her foreign-language class, one student said, "you are allowed three misses, and I've already missed five. For every miss after those first three, one point gets taken off your final grade!" Although some students feel "bogged down by the work," many report that the academic program at Tulane is "conquerable."

Swinging Social Scene

Although Tulane is often considered one of the best universities, academically, in the Southeast, some students believe that the social life is "much more important." According to one student, "In New Orleans and on campus, drinking rules the social activities here." At Tulane, students are allowed to drink in their dorm rooms. One undergrad reported that the legal drinking age is not always an obstacle because "fake IDs are easy to get and the

bars usually don't care. I went to a bar with the ID of someone who looked nothing like me and I got in, no problem."

The Greek tradition is strong at Tulane. "Frat parties are open to whoever wants to go, although I think they are pretty lame," said one undergrad. Social activities, such as those planned by the Tulane University Campus Productions (TUCP), an organization that sponsors large screenings of movies and live shows, gets rave reviews from students. Students can also head over to the University Center (UC), which houses a pub, arcade, radio and TV stations, and various restaurants. Recently, Kevin Spacey and Spike Lee came to speak on-campus.

New Orleans Fun

Of course, many students are quick to point out that there is always New Orleans itself "if you want to have a good time." For $1.25, students can take the St. Charles streetcar right into the city. Many students find themselves "drinking the night away" in the French Quarter ("the Quarter") on famous Bourbon Street. Restaurants abound in New Orleans, although some tend to be expensive. Students on a tighter budget, "can always chow some food from Cucos," explained one undergrad. Some upperclassmen have cars, but the high cost of a parking permit and the cheap trolley fare into town deters most students from keeping a car on campus. One cannot talk about New Orleans and not mention Mardi Gras. The celebrations last about two weeks. There are daily parades before Mardi Gras and nine of them on Mardi Gras. People from all over the country come to New Orleans to try to collect beads, which is "almost always accomplished by stripping." "Alcohol flows freely and people go wild."

Tulane students agree that dating is prevalent on campus. As one student reported, "There are some brutally hot people here!" New Orleans also offers plenty for romantics to do, like taking "a carriage ride around the French Quarter." One student added that, "all of the dorms had sex orientation, but they ran out of free condoms."

Several students complained that Tulane lacks a diverse student body. According to one student, "it looks like all the guys just walked out of Structure, and all the girls just came out of Express." Another student noted that "there seems to be a lack of African-American students and it bothers me more and more."

Nightmare Housing

Housing at Tulane draws mixed reviews. Freshman living is reportedly the worst. Upon seeing her freshman dorm, one student said, "No way! No! I'm not living here." The two primary freshman dorms are Sharp and Monroe. Just mentioning these names provoked one student to exclaim, "Nightmare!" Collectively, the two dorms are labeled "the projects" and complaints center on the age and poor maintenance of the buildings. Specific complaints about the current state of these dorms include "experiencing projectile vomit on the walls" and "calcium deposits in the showers that causes them to flood." In addition, one student reported that "the elevators are always broken and I live on the twelfth floor!"

> "Tulane students work hard to meet tough academic standards, but they also takes plenty of time to enjoy their community in New Orleans."

There are, however, some popular dorms on-campus. The honors dorm, Butler, is considered quite "respectable," and the all-women's dorm, Josephine Louise, is "just beautiful." Mayer Residences consist of suites and some super singles and students refer to Mayer as being "superb." Willow Hall, which includes two special projects, was opened this year. These projects are the Urban Village and Leadership Village. Students get into these "villages" by application and once a member, they can benefit from classes that are offered specifically for them. "Some people have two-story rooms" in Willow that are "incredibly luxurious and beautiful." Students report sophomore dorms are much cleaner and more expansive. The dorms have air-conditioning, although one student said that in some cases, it was "not functional." RAs live on each hall, although students report that "RAs are not very strict" and the regulations are "fairly relaxed." Despite the poor quality of freshman dorms, social life is much better compared to upperclassmen dorms. Many upperclassmen choose to live off campus, and often find cheaper rates than the cost of university housing.

Food at Tulane is reportedly "low quality, though they try hard," said one undergrad. Another added that the dining services at Tulane are run by the Marriott, "so it's respectable." There are currently five campus dining facilities: the UC, der Rathskeller, Bruff Commons, the Drawing Board and TU Deli. UC has Taco Bell, Subway and Pizza Hut and Bruff Commons has Sbarro among the options they present. All freshmen must purchase a meal plan through the university. Though one student noted that, "the dining halls are on par with the best high school cafeterias in the nation," others complain about the cost of the meal plan. Meals are purchased before school starts and "food is really pricey." The dining hall hours have become a lot more flexible in the recent years. Deli and Taco Bell are open until 11 P.M. and Bruff Commons serves a Late Night Meal from 10.30 P.M. till midnight which is popular among students. There are vegetarian options, but "it seems to be the same veggie thing every day," said one undergrad. Though the dining halls are clean, one upperclassman said the dining hall "is definitely not someplace you could sit in all day and hang out because it is a very enclosed and drab sort of atmosphere."

The Garden District

The Tulane campus is not situated in the heart of New Orleans, but in the neighboring Garden District. The Garden District is "the wealthy, beautiful part of the city" and home to famed author Anne Rice, whom Tulane students often report seeing on campus. The campus is divided into two different areas: "The front half is pretty, with open grassy areas and Romanesque and Gothic architecture. The back half, though, looks like trashy '70s." Many undergrads consider the campus beautiful, but some feel "there is too much construction going on." "Bring a bike," suggested one undergrad. "Roller blades are not the best here because the sidewalks are all torn up." Students say that they feel moderately safe on campus. As one student said, "You can't go out by yourself at night. You go five blocks and you are in the ghetto. It's as if the Garden District is a facade of mansions hiding what is really there."

Tulane students also find some time to get involved in extracurricular activities. Students cite the service organization CACTUS, as well as various religious organizations, particularly Jewish groups, as very strong and active.

Sporting events are fairly popular. Although Tulane usually has "sucky teams," according to one student, the recent emergence of Tulane football, which capped an undefeated season in 1998 with a Liberty Bowl victory, has drawn notice around the country. Football games themselves are quite an event. The games are played in the New Orleans Superdome and "according to some Southern tradi-

tion, everybody dresses up for them." The football games are popular, with tickets included in Tulane's tuition. School spirit runs high, with the new school mascot, Riptide, the pelican, leading the way. For those who do not want to commit to varsity sports, there are plenty of club sports and intramurals for students. Reilly Recreation Center offers students a variety of choices including yoga and dance classes, indoor and outdoor pools, squash and tennis courts, and a fitness center.

Tulane definitely holds up its reputation as a party school, but students also stress strong academics. Students from the North are particularly struck by Tulane's Southern charm. As one senior reflected, "My years have been truly awesome and I have met a lot of really great people from all over the world. I don't know what makes one college better than another, but Tulane has a great mix of being in a really cool city, yet having its own campus at the same time."—*Jeff Kaplow and Staff*

FYI

The three best things about attending Tulane are "the location, excellent faculty who give personal attention, and Mardi Gras."

The three worst things about attending Tulane are "freshman dorms, the Greek system is emphasized too much, and lack of student community/camaraderie."

The three things that every student should do before graduating from Tulane are "attend Mardi Gras celebrations, get involved in All-nighter events, explore New Orleans' restaurants."

One thing I would like to have known before coming here is "how bad and unpredictable the weather is."

Maine

Bates College

Address: 23 Campus Ave, Lewiston, ME 04240
Phone: 207-786-6000
E-mail address: admissions@bates.edu
Web site URL: www.bates.edu
Location: small city
Founded: 1855
Private or Public: private
Religious affiliation: none
Undergraduate enrollment: 1,650
Total enrollment: 1,650
Percent Male/Female: 48%/52%
Percent Minority: 8.0%

Percent African-American: 3.0%
Percent Hispanic: 1.0%
Percent Asian: 4.0%
Percent in-state/out-of-state: 10%/90%
Percent Pub HS: 60%
Fraternities: 0%
Sororities: 0%
Number of Applicants: 3,950
Percent Accepted: 32%
Percent Accepted who enroll: 38%
Entering: 479
Transfers: 1
Application Deadline: 15 Jan

Mean SAT: 660 V, 660 M
Middle 50% SAT range: 630–700 V, 630–700 M
Middle 50% ACT range: NA
Mean ACT: NA
3 Most popular majors: psychology, biology, English
Retention: 93%
Graduation rate: 87%
Library: 499,777 volumes
Tuition and Fees: $31,400 in; $NA out
Room and Board: included in tuition
On-campus housing: 100%
Financial aid, first-year: 44%

"The professors are more available than most students' parents," said one undergrad, "we get to see more snow than the Olympic ski team," added another, and "you can see the world, travelling to a different country every year, and make up a major for it," noted a third. All three are referring to the opportunities they have at Bates College in Lewiston, Maine.

Tons of Options

Students cite "professors' commitment to each individual regardless of class size" as the most exciting aspect of Bates academics. Professors teach all classes and there are no TAs. "I love seeing professors outside of class who know me by name and being able to discuss topics other than class with them," said one sophomore. Biology, English, and political science are regarded among the strongest departments. Most students agree that neuroscience and biochemistry are the hardest majors.

Students can also choose to have a secondary concentration, the Bates name for a minor. Although secondary concentrations are not yet available in all departments, students are happy with this aspect of the curriculum, which was added several years ago. The toughest classes are organic chemistry and "Math Camp," whereas intro-level geology and psychology are the popular gut courses. Most classes tend to enroll between 15 and 25 although their sizes can vary, according to major. One senior said, "I've had theater classes with 8 people, and intro psych with over 100." Students report that Bates offers "tons" of special programs. "Go away to a foreign country your freshman year! I went to Japan, with no prior study in Japanese," recommended one sophomore. Finally, Bates offers a "3-2" program in which students get their B.A.s in engineering in three years at Bates, and go on to get their master's in two years at either Dartmouth or Columbia.

Bates students are required to take five

humanities courses, with three of the five relating to each other in a "cluster." Three social science courses are also required along with three science classes, two of which must be related and one in quantitative reasoning. Students can use AP credits to fulfill some of these requirements. There is also a four-credit physical education requirement that can be fulfilled by playing a varsity sport or with classes such as Scuba Diving, Swing Dancing or Bowling. Students refer to these requirements as "pretty easy to fulfill, important and not so strict." With regard to grading, "most professors have forgotten the first letter of the alphabet," said one student. Another one added that "there's this fairy tale about someone graduating with a 4.0 long long ago, but that is all it is, a fairy tale."

The Best Idea Since Sliced Bread

As one student defined it, Bates's Short Term program, which occurs during the last week in April and the month of May, is the "best thing since sliced bread." Bates students choose from a wide array of opportunities in selecting and planning Short Terms. Students must attend two short terms during their time at Bates, in which they take one class that meets three to five times a week. Some majors have required short term classes such as "Cell Hell" for biology majors. This is a cellular molecular biology class that meets four times a week and has two lab periods. Most students, however, get to leave campus for Short Term. Last year, students went to Jamaica for African-American studies, to Sri Lanka for an anthropology class, to Utah to study Native American art, and to Mexico to study women in Mexican nationalism. Others stayed in Lewiston for International Debt Negotiations or Perspectives on Education. Batseys refer to the Short Term as "the best thing about Bates academically." One junior adds "the class offerings *rock* and it's *such* a fun 5 weeks—reward for all the hard work over the year."

Food and Sleep: The Necessities of Life

Most Bates students choose to live on campus, where they have guaranteed housing for four years. They can choose to live in dorms or in one of the thirteen on-campus Victorian "houses." Houses are quieter and smaller than dorms and they provide a more intimate and family-like atmosphere. Freshmen are grouped in Freshman Centers, clusters of usually 12 freshmen and their Junior Advisor (JA) who live in the same section in a house or dorm and share a faculty advisor. "JAs definitely want to be your friend; mine is now one of my closest friends," said one sophomore. The many housing options available after freshman year are "coed, single-sex, chem-free dorms/houses, theme houses, mixed with freshmen or not mixed with freshmen." It's "almost exclusively seniors who live off campus." The Village is the newest dorm built in 1994 and it's "like a hotel." It consists of three separate buildings and a social hall in the center and has "awesome" rooms, some of which even have lofts.

Students are really happy with dining hall food. You can be either on or off the meal plan and "if you're on, you can go as often as you want and eat as much as you want." Many refer to it as "the best college food I've had; huge selection and good quality." Commons, the main dining hall, is the center of campus life and a "great place to socialize." One problem is that there is not enough space for all the students, so it is "way overcrowded." "Just don't go on peak hours and things are fine," recommends one student. The Den is a campus restaurant that hosts "Terrace Parties" sponsored by various student groups. The student-run on-campus coffeehouse, the Ronj, named for its orange walls, is a popular hangout at late night hours and on Saturday afternoons. Although students usually don't leave campus to eat, Chopsticks receives credit as a great restaurant off campus.

Paul Newman and St. Patrick

The administration "tries not to get involved with alcohol but encourages non-alcohol related activities." Party hosts need to have permission from the administration in the form of "blue slips" and they are also required to check IDs. "Underage people still drink all the time, but they do have to be slightly more smart about it." Drug use on campus consists mostly of marijuana. Some popular parties of the school year are the Halloween Party, the '80s Party, and "Lick-It" which is sponsored by the GLBA—the Gay Lesbian Bisexual Alliance. Most students' comments on Lick-It are along the lines of "it's *crazy*" and "it is a must every year." Random hookups are quite common at Bates. "You're either randomly hooking up or you are married," says one senior. "It's cold, people need to stay warm," notes another. The President's Gala, a formal dinner-dance held by the college president for students and faculty, is another popular event. "The concert series are also great: free jazz, classical, and types of music you've never heard before," says one sophomore. Recent performers at Bates have included Indigo Girls, Wyclef Jean, Dar Williams, and Ani DiFranco. On Paul Newman Day, students try to drink 24 beers in 24 hours and carry on their normal activities, usually unsuccessfully. This tradition is derived from the movie *Cool Hand Luke*, in which Paul Newman had to eat 50 eggs in one hour. On St. Patrick's Day, the rugby team sponsors the "Puddle Jump," which involves getting dunked in the ice-covered Lake Andrews.

Outside of Class

Everyone does something at Bates. The most popular extracurricular activities are the Outing Club, which has "a ton of members" and various sports. "Debate is elite" and volunteering opportunities are made possible through the community service house and several school-sponsored organizations. Some of the more unusual extracurricular groups are Strange Bedfellows, an improv comedy group, and Club Meat, a meat appreciation club to counter the vocal vegetarian population. Writing for the weekly *Bates Student* or hosting a radio show on WRBC, the campus radio station, are among the other possibilities. "You can really do anything, and if it's not here yet, it's easy to start it and get funding."

In its first years as a varsity sport, crew is one of this year's most popular teams. There are 92 people on it, making it the largest team on campus with 5.7 percent of the student population. People also enjoy soccer games because the soccer team buys beer for the fans before games.

A historical event took place last year when the football team won a game. Students are generally proud of Bates athletics. Besides varsity sports, a lot of people enjoy the laid-back atmosphere of intramurals. "Everybody is working out all the time," one student said. The Underhill Ice Arena, completed in 1995, includes an ice rink and the Davis Fitness Center with new cardiovascular equipment. Merrill Gym has weights, squash and racquetball courts, and a "great" indoor pool.

> **"Short-term is the best idea since sliced bread."**

Students think the Bates campus is "really pretty, with red-brick buildings and lots of trees." In the center lies "the Puddle" (Lake Andrews), the scene for the famous Puddle Jump. Pettingill Hall, the new building for the social sciences, is "gorgeous with waterfalls in the 3-story glass atrium overlooking Lake Andrews and state-of-the-art, with tons of computers and comfy places to study." One student referred to it as the "most incredible building I've seen on any college campus." Contrary to students' positive feelings about their campus, many believe that the area around campus *sucks*. "There is *no* reason to do *anything* in Lewiston, besides go to CVS or Walmart." Most students refer to Lewiston as "the worst aspect of Bates." Portland and Freeport, both 40 minutes away, "are a blast but they are somewhat of a commitment." Students agree that it helps to have a car or know someone who does; a lot of upperclassmen have cars.

Although the Bates student mostly consists of "fit, preppy, friendly kids looking like models in the L.L. Bean catalog," diversity has been increasing in the recent years. Regardless of background, Bates students share a similar trait. "Everyone's friendly here, you can walk through the dorms, find an open door and go meet people," noted one junior. Most Batseys agree that this friendly atmosphere, various academic offerings, and fun traditions such as the Puddle Jump and Paul Newman Day "make the trip up to Lewiston, Maine worthwhile."—*Engin Yenidunya*

FYI

The three best things about attending Bates are "academic calendar (so many vacations, Short Term), friendly atmosphere on campus, there's always someone I can bum a cigarette off."

The three worst things about attending Bates are "New Englanders that can't find Texas on a map, we see more snow than the Olympic ski team, and Lewiston."

The three things that every student should do before graduating from Bates are "try the Puddle Jump, complete Newman Day, attend Lick-It."

One thing I would like to have known before coming here is "small schools are small and although it can be a huge benefit, there are also some consequences."

B o w d o i n   C o l l e g e

Address: 5000 College Station, Brunswick, ME 04011-8441
Phone: 207-725-3100
E-mail address: admissions-lit@polar.bowdoin.edu
Web site URL: www.bowdoin.edu
Location: suburban
Founded: 1794
Private or Public: private
Religious affiliation: none
Undergraduate enrollment: 1,583
Total enrollment: 1,583
Percent Male/Female: 50%/50%
Percent Minority: 13.0%

Percent African-American: 2.0%
Percent Hispanic: 3.0%
Percent Asian: 8.0%
Percent in-state/out-of-state: 14%/86%
Percent Pub HS: 59%
Fraternities: 0%
Sororities: 0%
Number of Applicants: 3,821
Percent Accepted: 31%
Percent Accepted who enroll: 36%
Entering: 473
Transfers: 33
Application Deadline: 1 Jan
Mean SAT: 670 V, 670 M

Middle 50% SAT range: 620–710 V, 620–710 M
Middle 50% ACT range: NA
Mean ACT: NA
3 Most popular majors: government/legal studies, biology, history
Retention: 92.0%
Graduation rate: 84.0%
Library: 870,000 volumes
Tuition and Fees: $23,395 in; $23,395 out
Room and Board: $6,285
On-campus housing: 100%
Financial aid, first-year: 40%

With trees that change color during the fall, old-brick architecture, and a quaint chapel peeking out from its secluded location, Bowdoin College is a hamlet of pristine beauty, an archetype of a small New England liberal arts college. Students hang out around the quad at the center of campus, and a laid-back atmosphere prevails. As one student said, "Everyone's a slacker at Bowdoin, or at least pretends to be."

Distribution Requirements

This is not to say that academics are by any means second-tier. Behind the laid-back facade, the academics are rigorous. Many come to Bowdoin to participate in its renowned science classes, including the popular premed and environmental science tracks. Undergraduate require-ments include two classes in each of four distribution groups: natural sciences, social sciences, humanities, and non-Eurocentric studies. Students describe these requirements as "not hard to fulfill," and explain that the requirements for some of the majors provide a lot more structure and challenge than the distribution requirements.

Students at Bowdoin generally feel that they get a lot of academic guidance and that it is not easy to get lost in the crowd. One freshman explained, "My faculty advisor made sure picking my courses went smoothly, and helped a lot with everything. I had no idea what I was doing. He got me started in figuring it all out." It is not unusual for students at Bowdoin to receive regular phone calls and e-mails from their professors. Some even baby-sit for their professors or join them for dinner. For the most part, men and women at Bowdoin believe that teachers are happy to help, especially those who are genuinely interested in learning. Although introductory classes—especially in the natural sciences—can be large, with some lecture classes averaging 80 people, most classes are much smaller and emphasize individual attention. All courses are taught by professors; teaching assistants help with discussion sections and labs. According to one student, "TAs are really out there to help you. You feel like they're there because they really want you to understand what's going on in class."

Popular Activities

Outside of classes, Bowdoin students have numerous extracurricular and social opportunities. Many are involved in the popular Outing Club, which sponsors hiking and camping trips and exposes students to the vast resources of their surroundings. Skiing is also a favorite activity during the long, cold winter months. Most undergrads play sports at levels ranging from varsity intercollegiate to intramural. "Almost everybody I know is on some kind of team," one student observed. "And if you're not playing, you're watching games." Many, however, complain about the quality of the sports teams, with the exception of a few sports such as men's hockey, touted as "the big thing on-campus." Hockey games are often the central focus of Bowdoin winter weekends.

Bowdoin's large fraternity system is being phased out and replaced by a system of "social houses." The class of 2001 was the first class not allowed to pledge a fraternity, which means frats will no longer exist by the fall of 2000. This has been a source of growing tension between students and administrators for a number of years. Frats used to provide a large part of the social life on campus, and the popular frat parties open to all offered large quantities of free beer every weekend. The newly developed social houses—coed nonresidential associations that "throw good parties"—are replacing the function of the frats. The school is generally pretty relaxed about drinking, according to one student who described the school's attitude as follows: "Drinking makes you drunk, and don't get in trouble with the law, but what we don't know cannot hurt us."

Aside from the frats and social houses, other social activities include regular movies on campus, as well as school-sponsored events such as funk and disco parties, and the '80s bash. Off-campus activities include trips to Portland bars and clubs, local bowling alleys, and strip malls. Students at Bowdoin are also known for traditional "late-night Bean runs" to the Freeport L. L. Bean store, which is open 24 hours a day. Many students prefer to stay on-campus and have little contact with the small Brunswick community, despite the availability of a shuttle system and the short walking distance into town. Several people say it is essential to have a car on-campus, because "Brunswick, Maine, is the most boring town in the entire universe." Parking is readily available on-campus, and some recommend four-wheel drive for the harsh Maine winters.

Housing Options

Students consider housing at Bowdoin adequate and comfortable, but "nothing special." All freshmen live in one of the "Bricks"—six brick dorms located around the Quad. By virtue of this first-year dorm assignment, all freshmen belong to one of the five houses, and can eat meals and participate in activities there. Freshman housing is coed, with single-sex and mixed halls. Residential advisors are generally easygoing, and as one freshman said, "We're all just kids here in the dorm, including the RA, and he's just another guy on the floor." Freshmen spend a lot of time just "hanging out" in the dorms. One student says, "my whole dorm gets together to watch *The Simpsons* and the Patriots."

> "Everyone's a slacker at Bowdoin, or at least pretends to be."

Options for upperclassmen include theme houses, such as the Wellness House, which does not allow smoking, drugs, or alcohol in the dorm and enforces quiet hours; the international house; 16-story Coles Tower, with suite-style living; and apartment-style housing with a kitchen, bathroom, and common room. Apartments are located farther from campus than other housing options, but many feel that the improved living conditions are worth the walk. Students are generally very happy with the housing situation, and most live on campus all four years.

Bowdoin men and women are pleased with the flexible hours and meal plans of the two dining halls. The Smith Student Union, Bowdoin's student center, is considered a "great place to hang out." The center has a state-of-the-art gym, a cafe, a convenience store, Ping-Pong and pool tables, and a comfortable area to lounge. The atmosphere on-campus is friendly, and students notice little segregation between underclassmen and older students.

Tradition is valued at Bowdoin. The university is proud of its historical graduates, including Nathaniel Hawthorne and Henry Wadsworth Longfellow. Overall, students at Bowdoin praise the friendly rural environment and the tradition and personal attention of the college. Despite some complaints about the isolation and cold New England setting, Bowdoin undergrads feel a genuine attachment to their school.—*Abby Taylor and Rachel Grand*

FYI

The three best things about attending Bowdoin are "professors, housing, free beer."

The three worst things about attending Bowdoin are "workload, narrow social life, too small size."

The three things that every student should do before graduating from Bowdoin are "go camping in Maine, take a variety of courses outside your discipline, get alcohol poisoning."

One thing I would like to have known before coming here is "how limited the social scene is."

C o l b y   C o l l e g e

Address: 4800 Mayflower Hill, Waterville, ME 04904-8848

Phone: 207-872-3168

E-mail address: admissions@colby.edu

Web site URL: www.colby.edu

Location: small city

Founded: 1813

Private or Public: private

Religious affiliation: none

Undergraduate enrollment: 1,764

Total enrollment: 1,764

Percent Male/Female: 48%/52%

Percent Minority: 10.0%

Percent African-American: 2.6%

Percent Hispanic: 2.4%

Percent Asian: 4.8%

Percent in-state/out-of-state: 11%/89%

Percent Pub HS: 61%

Fraternities: 0%

Sororities: 0%

Number of Applicants: 4,503

Percent Accepted: 33%

Percent Accepted who enroll: 34%

Entering: 489

Transfers: 10

Application Deadline: 15 Jan

Mean SAT: 660 V, 660 M

Middle 50% SAT range: 610–690 V, 610–700 M

Middle 50% ACT range: 26–30

Mean ACT: 28

3 Most popular majors: biology, English, economics

Retention: 91

Graduation rate: 89

Library: 924,900 volumes

Tuition and Fees: $31,580 in; NA out

Room and Board: NA

On-campus housing: 100%

Financial aid, first-year: 39%

"Maine—the Way Life Should Be." It's a popular T-shirt slogan in the state of Maine, and students at Colby seem to agree. Colby kids speak with enthusiasm about lots of things: their professors, their campus, and most of all, their fellow students. "I have never felt more at home than I do here," raves one sophomore. "I actually get homesick for Colby when I'm on vacation at my real home." What is it about Colby that inspires such affection? There seem to be several answers to this question.

Despite chilly winters and perpetual student consumption of hot chocolate, this small liberal arts college is known for providing, as one student explains, a "warm, comfortable atmosphere for students who are serious about learning how to think and learning how to live." Colby's small size (about 450–500 a class) encourages students to form a close-knit community, which allows "tons of opportunities to not only get involved, but take on positions of leadership," and intimate class settings with professors described as "both personal and personable." The secluded campus in Waterville, Maine, is "one of Colby's best attributes," featuring redbrick Georgian architecture, duck ponds, and sprawling lawns that "look beautiful in every season." Another student pointed out that, "from the leaf-pile frolicking in the fall, to the first snowball fight of the winter, to the pickup Frisbee games in spring, you cannot help but love this New England atmosphere." Even those from the West Coast find the Maine appeal hard to deny.

Getting the Job Done

While some report that "it's definitely possible to slack off here and still get by," most Colby students are committed to making the most of their learning opportunities. One junior noted that "if you're not self-motivated, which most people here are, then the professors will motivate you. They have a way of doing that—it's almost eerie." Academics in general at Colby, like the students, are described as "fairly well-rounded." Students give the English, political science, and psychology departments particularly high marks, and developments in the science curriculum have many students talking. Colby also has the Olin Science Center, which boasts state-of-the-art laboratories equipped with the latest technology, a research greenhouse, computer classrooms, a new science library, and laboratories designed for collaborative student-faculty research.

The biology department has also enjoyed a long-standing tradition of excellence.

Colby has a somewhat unique set of course requirements that draws comments ranging from "no big deal—it's stuff you'd take anyway" to "confusing and a pain in the butt." Courses are divided into six "Areas," and students must complete one credit in all but Area V, in which two credits are required. Area I encompasses the arts; Area II, historical studies; Area III, literature; Area IV consists of classes in quantitative reasoning; Area V, the natural sciences, and one of the two required credits must be a class that involves laboratory work; and Area VI covers the social sciences. Other requirements include one course that covers issues of diversity, and some feel that this requirement is a "lame attempt on the part of the administration to compensate for the fact that our school is rather homogeneous." The physical education requirement has been recently revised, and now involves students participating in Colby's "Wellness Program." This program requires students to complete four credits, which can be met by participating in wellness seminars, fitness classes, varsity athletics, or club sports. Starting with the class of 2002, students have to fulfill their wellness requirement in their freshman year. "Rumor has it if you don't, then you set up chairs for graduation but I am not sure if that is actually true."

Students are expected to declare a major by the end of freshman year, but a sophomore cautions that "this stresses too many people out unnecessarily—it's really easy just to fill out 'Undeclared.'" Unique to Colby is the "Jan Plan," which gets very high marks among the student body. The Jan Plan is a break from the traditional semester system during the month of January, when students can pursue personal projects of interest, take classes for full credit, intern with local businesses, and even travel nationally or abroad. While the school offers a wide range of courses, some students complain that the offerings are "too traditional." But most feel that what they sacrifice in terms of class diversity by attending a small school pales in comparison to the benefits: intimate classes, individual attention, and a strong sense of belonging in an academic community.

A Winter Wonderland

While the strong academic program is certainly a draw, most students would agree that the campus life is the best part of Colby. Students describe their peers as "friendly and outgoing," and "fun-seeking, rugged types." Most Colby kids are fond of the outdoors, and are thrilled to take advantage of their location by going skiing, sledding, or hiking. Prior to the start of freshman year, many students participate in COOT (Colby Outdoor Outing Trips), which are described as a great way to meet people and assimilate into the Colby community. The Outing Club is one of Colby's largest and most popular organizations; it offers expeditions such as backpacking along the scenic Maine coast, loans equipment to all interested students, and even maintains a 17-mile stretch of the Appalachian Trail. One junior remarked gratefully that, "if I didn't have the Outing Club, I don't know what I'd do. It keeps me sane." Indeed, it appears that to be truly happy at Colby, one must appreciate the natural part of the outdoors and not expect too much else from outside the campus borders.

Waterville does inspire some affection for its "quaint country stores" and "New England charm," but received generally low marks for catering to student needs and providing nighttime recreation. "You can buy beer in town," noted one student, "but that's about as far as the town's contribution to the social life goes."

Social life on-campus centers on the housing program, which follows the "Commons" system. The campus is divided into four Commons, each one containing several residence halls, dining halls, and student lounges. At the intersection of the four Commons lies the student union, which contains the post office, snack bars, and space for speakers and parties. Each Commons has its own Commons Council and budget to sponsor activities for residents, and this also creates good leadership opportunities for those interested in self-government.

Dorms were given decent reviews on the whole. Most rooms in the Commons are two-room doubles with one bedroom and a common area. There are some singles, but as one student points out, "would you rather share a bedroom and living room with a friend, or live in a two-by-nothing cubicle alone? Singles are not in very high demand here." Housing has undergone some improvement. After fraternities were abolished in 1984, the frat houses were converted into on-campus housing with larger rooms and central locations. Also, the school recently constructed three new dorms, which feature larger suites. The most recent addition to the housing options is the "Senior Apartments" that are only available to seniors. They are "absolutely amazing by normal standards—not just by campus living standards." Each apartment has a fully equipped kitchen, a living room, at least one bathroom, and bedrooms.

Most students stay on campus all four years, if nothing else because the administration requires them to apply to live off campus, and off-campus housing is in short supply. But because nearly all social life revolves around the campus, most find living at Colby more desirable anyway. "At first I was disappointed and annoyed that I couldn't live off campus senior year," recalls one student. "But now I realize that I spend all my time here anyway, so it probably would have been more of an inconvenience than anything else!"

Cutting Through the Red Tape

Off-campus housing policy isn't the only problem students have with the Colby administration. One issue frequently mentioned is difficulty with financial aid. "The financial aid office is abysmal," griped one student. "They seem to thrive on alienating and confusing us." Some point to the school's problems with financial aid as one reason the student body has remained so homogeneous. "Why does it seem like almost everyone here is an L. L. Bean–wearing, Jeep Cherokee–driving, well-to-do preppy northeastern WASP?" wondered one freshman. Not all students agree that the student body is so extremely uniform, however. Two-thirds of students come from public schools, and an increasing amount are beginning to arrive from areas outside the Northeast. It also appears that the administration is pushing for more diversity, though "somewhat unsuccessfully," according to a few. One noteworthy step Colby has taken is ts huge capital campaign called the Campaign for Colby, which aimed to raise 100 million dollars by the end of 1999, but actually exceeded its goals and raised more than 150 million dollars. The money raised will be focused on improving financial-aid packages for students. "Colby has a long way to go," reasoned one student, "but is definitely moving in the right direction."

"White Mules Rule!"

While Colby's mascot, the white mule, may be puzzling to some, the enthusiasm for school athletics is definitely clear. Nearly all students participate in some form of athletics, be it varsity teams, intramural sports (called I-plays), or working out in the recently renovated athletic center. School spirit abounds, especially when major teams go head-to-head with rivals Bates or Bowdoin.

> **"Every so often there are benefits to the cold weather, like when the boilers break and classes are canceled!"**

Administration tightened its alcohol policy last year. "Alcohol no longer seems to flow freely." "Since the hosts are held responsible for all the incidents occurring at their parties, seniors really don't want to host parties. So the campus has engaged in all-school events." There is a party in the student center every weekend sponsored by the school. Usually, there are parties on both Friday and Saturday nights every weekend. At these parties, people of legal drinking age can usually buy alcohol from kegs once they show their ID's. "As a result in the crackdown on alcohol, drinking is mainly done in rooms." "One thing though—people really do go to the school parties . . ."

For those not wishing to engage in "mass alcohol consumption," Colby does have a couple of "chem-free" dorms, which are much appreciated by their residents. The school has also begun to sponsor better and more frequent campuswide events, although the traditional ones remain the most popular. Such traditions include Homecoming weekend and the Junior/Senior formal, which are always big draws. And only Colby students get to look forward to the First Night of Loudness, which takes place in the fall, and the Last Night of Loudness, occurring in the spring. Both are immensely popular parties that feature hit singers or bands. Previous guests include Jewel, the Indigo Girls, and the Beastie Boys.

"If you're thinking about Colby," one student offered, "you can't ignore the snow factor, you just can't. It's a surprisingly large part of life here." True, Maine winters are not for everyone, but "every so often there are benefits, like when the boilers break and classes are canceled!" Weather conditions aside, most students find Colby College to be a tremendously rewarding place to spend four years. Perhaps most important, they feel like they are truly part of a community. "When I was sick and had to spend a few days in the health center," one student recalls, "my professor actually came and visited me to fill me in on what had taken place in our class discussions. I think it was at that moment that I knew I had really come to the right place." —*Rachel Grand*

FYI

The three best things about attending Colby are "beautiful campus, close-knit community, we have a funny mascot."

The three worst things about attending Colby are "no real diversity, pretty far from a major city, the administration."

The three things that every student should do before graduating from Colby are "go backpacking, play on a team and beat Bowdoin and Bates at least once, take a wild challenge during Jan Plan."

One thing I would like to have known before coming here is "when they say people work hard and party hard, they really mean it."

College of the Atlantic

Address: 105 Eden Street, Bar Harbor, ME 04609
Phone: 800-528-0025
E-mail address: inquiry@ecology.coa.edu
Web site URL: www.coa.edu
Location: suburban
Founded: 1969
Private or Public: private
Religious affiliation: none
Undergraduate enrollment: 283
Total enrollment: 283
Percent Male/Female: 34%/66%
Percent Minority: 1.0%

Percent African-American: 0.0%
Percent Hispanic: 1.0%
Percent Asian: 0.0%
Percent in-state/out-of-state: NA
Percent Pub HS: 75%
Fraternities: 0%
Sororities: 0%
Number of Applicants: 233
Percent Accepted: 55%
Percent Accepted who enroll: 43%
Entering: NA
Transfers: 0
Application Deadline: 1 Mar

Mean SAT: 650 V, 630 M
Middle 50% SAT range: NA V, NA M
Middle 50% ACT range: NA
Mean ACT: 28
3 Most popular majors: human ecology, marine biology, arts and design
Retention: 75.0%
Graduation rate: 58.0%
Library: 0
Tuition and Fees: $19,248 in; $19,248 out
Room and Board: $5,220
On-campus housing: NA
Financial aid, first-year: 71%

"Before COA was COA, it was a mission dedicated to teaching people how to make the world a better place. When the college was founded in 1969, its original name was going to be "Acadia Peace College." COA's idealistic roots are still apparent today.

A Single Degree

College of the Atlantic awards one undergraduate degree: the Bachelor of Arts in Human Ecology. Within this degree, students create their own curricula by concentrating in one or more of the following: public policy, marine studies, environmental science, natural history museum studies, design, teacher education, landscape and building architecture, and selected humanities studies. "Each of the 275 students here has a different definition of human ecology," according to several students. Academic offerings are divided into the three areas of Environmental Science, Arts and Design, and Human Studies. COA has the trimester academic calendar: there are three terms of 10 weeks during which students usually take three classes. They are not allowed to take more than four classes each term. A common feeling is that the term is "six weeks of a fine workload and four of hell where all the final projects are due." COA has a "loooooong" winter break that

starts with Thanksgiving and goes until the first week of January.

During their time at COA, each student is required to take two courses in each of three areas—Environmental Sciences, Arts and Design, and Human Studies—along with a Human Ecology Core course, one Quantitative Reasoning course, and one Writing course. Students also have to write a Human Ecology essay, do an internship, participate in 40 hours of community service, and complete a Final Project. Most students agree that the requirements are "pretty lenient."

For the required internship, which is usually done junior year, students forfeit regular classes for a term, and instead do an internship for three course credits. "Some people live on campus and intern at a nearby organization, whereas others travel to other parts of the U.S. and the world for different opportunities." "Wherever you want to go, whatever you want to do, it's up to you," said one student. "The Yucatan Term" that runs from December to March is an option, "popular with some students." In this program, a group of COA students and professors travel to the city of Meridan in Mexico's Yucatan region and hold three classes there. COA has established exchange programs with two universities, one in Uruguay and the other in the Czech Republic.

Students can also transfer credits from other colleges' transfer programs. COA students also get ample research opportunities. "We have two field houses and our own farm. Tell me which other school has these?" Mount Desert Rock and Great Duck Islands are "popular hangouts" for various land and sea bird species as well as for seals, dolphins, porpoises, and whales. Beech Hill Farm offers activities such as organic farming, winter gardening, soil maintenance, seed and plant collections.

COA students have nothing but praise for their professors. "We are extremely lucky to have a faculty so devoted to the idea of human ecology," said one senior. "They are really good about meeting with students outside of class, and allowing room for the integration of courses," added another student. Most professors are well published and respected in their fields. A few visiting professors also teach classes each term. COA's small size has its pluses—"you're not just a faceless number lost among the hoards." It also has its minuses, a major one being its course offerings: "There are many terms when I feel that there aren't enough classes being taught. But there is usually some amazing class I love to take." Another student complained that, "getting into classes can be a problem, a lot of the courses are limited to a very small size." "There are sometimes really cool classes, like photography, that everyone wants to take," but due to size limitations, they cannot.

Substance-free and Meat-free

The five dorms at COA are Blair-Tyson, Seafox, Ryles, Cottage House, and Peach House. Seafox, which is the substance-free form, is right next to the ocean and has the best view. Its neighbor, Ryles, is the party dorm. Ryles and Peach House are also known as the "hippie houses." Blair-Tyson is very new, has a "modern look overall" and mostly has singles. In the dorms, floors and bathrooms are usually coed and RAs are "cool as long as you clean up after yourself." "Different students like different houses or dorms for their particular needs, wants and likes," one junior explained. Overall, students are happy with their dorms. Compared to

other schools, "rooms are considerably larger and most have furniture that is in good condition." Only first-year students are guaranteed on-campus housing. International students and transfers have priority for on-campus housing among upperclassmen but usually the dorms fill up before they get a chance. Therefore, living in off-campus apartments or houses is a "necessity" for almost all upperclassmen. Almost all students agree that they like living in town.

The meal plan is "expensive" but the food is reputed to be "the best of the best." Students refer to the food as "very new-age and phoo-phooish" and agree that there is "definitely something for vegans and veggies, not always for normal meat guys." A meat-lover noted that, "people in the kitchen probably use tweezers when handling the meat." Another student added, "meat: they give an honest effort, but if you are afraid of eating meat, how can you prepare it?" The only on-campus dining facility is the cafeteria named "Take A Break" referred to as "Tab" in everyday COA language. "Tab is open 5 days a week, otherwise all of the dorms have kitchens and students feed themselves on the weekend." Some students voice concerns about the short dining hall hours: "the cafeteria is only open for two and a half hours for breakfast and lunch and an hour and a half for dinner." Several explicitly stated that the hours are "kind of lame" or that "they suck."

Social Life! Love Life?

"Usually a student meets people within their first term here, and they can meet a lot of people, but after the first term the social circles tighten, and it is rare to become friends with someone you weren't friends with in the beginning," acknowledged one student. COA "tries for organized activities but it is not always successful with such a small student body." Still, not all students complained about the social life. One sophomore explained that there are often "neat people speaking on campus, movies and dances" and a few local bands "play here every once in a while." "I heard that Phish played here before they were huge," added one student. The campus-wide organized activities are "okay, they usually don't pull a huge crowd, but those that go enjoy them." The Tab also serves as the venue for contra dancing classes after dinner and yoga classes are offered in the student lounge.

Parties usually take place in people's houses in town where under and upperclassmen mix "as there aren't enough people for too many parties anyway." This means that, "sometimes there are different parties, but for the most part you will find the same people at the same parties." However, there have been some cool theme parties such as the "'80s party and the disco night." Another student felt that the smallness served to bring people together, "since there are not a tremendous amount of people on the island, different groups mix more here than they might elsewhere." Kegs are not allowed on campus. The administration's alcohol policy is "it's fine as long as we don't see the bottle or smell the alcohol." Students repot that marijuana is "the dominant drug on campus."

Besides attending parties, COA students fill their weekends with a variety of activities. Reel Pizza in town is a place that "a lot of COA students frequent." Run by former COA students, Reel Pizza has frequent independent movie screenings and offers a "cozy atmosphere" with reclining couches and beanbags. In order to escape the isolation of COA, students recommend a car "if you want to go anywhere." They warn that public transportation is not available. Students especially find cars handy, "when it's cold in the winter, so you can leave campus." If you don't have a car, you will most certainly have a friend with one since, "probably about half the people have cars." On the other hand, "another ⅕ don't know how to drive."

The love life at COA varies. Most people have significant others instead of random hookups. "We're too small a college for one-night stands," noted one student. Furthermore, "rumor spreads incredibly fast and you'd end up in the same classes as the other person anyway." One thing that almost everyone mentioned is that "there are not enough males on this campus." There are "more than twice as many girls as there are guys." This could benefit COA men. However, one student pointed out that although "there are plenty of attractive women, they're usually dating each other." Lesbian couples are visible at COA, but "I don't know of any gay males here." The general consensus seemed to be that, "there isn't a lot of sex at COA, the few people who have sex have it a lot, but there just aren't that many people who get action." So, many students turn to long-distance relationships to cope.

COA Active

Hiking is the most popular activity among COA students. All students get a free membership to the local YMCA where they go to swim, play basketball, or use the fitness center. Volleyball and soccer become popular sports when the weather conditions improve. Men and women's soccer teams are called "the Black Flies because we don't stink, we suck." However, one student reported that with "the coldest days of winter comes a strong wave of knitting mania. Most people start going around campus with knitting needles and yarn in their hands. It lasts a couple of weeks and then flies away." Free Tibet is one of the popular activist organizations on campus: "There are more Tibetan prayer flags on campus than there are American ones." Social Environmental Action (SEA) is another one of them. Allied Whale is an organization that catalogs all humpback whales that live in the North Atlantic and are also involved with seal stranding.

Pot-smoking Crunchy Tree-huggers

"I hate to say it, but the stereotypical COA student is a hippie," admitted one junior. Some phrases that students used to describe the stereotypical COA student are "crunchy tree-hugger, vegan/vegetarian, middle class, white, overly idealistic, pot-smoking, usually female, spiritual person." Some students said that there is "a real sense of community." However, they also mentioned that the student body is "too homogenous." There is "very little ethnic or cultural diversity." Several students complained about "students being prejudiced towards people taking opposite stances even though most of them desperately try not to seem or sound like t." Another one added, "There is nontraditional segregation. If you are somehow not environmentally conscious or friendly, or if you throw a bottle in the trash and don't recycle, you are evil and treated accordingly." Fashion at COA is stereotypical of tree-huggers: "Most people here wear Carharts. To class, they wear whatever they have on, or have had on for the last week. There are some "mainstream" people here this year, who dress semi-trendy, but most of them are leaving next year." Although students expressed interest in diversity, one student felt that such a population just wasn't "attracted to COA."

Mount, Desert, and Island

COA is located on Mount Desert Island, in the resort town of Bar Harbor, Maine. The location speaks for itself; how can you get more isolated than a place that combines "mount," "desert," and "island?" However, this is only the case in the cold months of Maine. The island becomes a haven for tourists in the summer and, especially, in the fall. Reflecting the resort atmosphere of the town, a number of restaurants close at the end of the season, although "some good places stay open." Many recommend Jordan's, "an awesome breakfast place that has award-winning blueberry pancakes." One student warned, if you like big movie theaters and city life, stay away from Bar Harbor."

Almost all students "love" campus because it is "pretty, unique, small, cozy, and right by the ocean." One student praised that, "there are a bunch of great spots to get away, do some work, or whatever. Having the ocean border one side of campus is a definite plus." One student described the bay as "the biggest eye-catcher, along with trees and lobster boats." Acadia National Park, located next to the school, "definitely adds to the campus life." One student said that "the surrounding area is the campus life, without it COA wouldn't be special." Turrets, an administrative office building with two large classrooms, is a gorgeous old stone building with wooden hand carved stair banisters and lavishly detailed ceilings. A new building was recently constructed for the Natural History Museum. Safety on campus is not an issue at all: "There is nowhere safer. At night the campus is like an empty city where everyone left their lights on."

> **"We're too small a college for one-night stands."**

COA's unique location on Mount Desert Island provides incredible opportunities for the study of human ecology. Interdisciplinary studies flourish at COA due to its academic flexibility and professors' willingness to integrate courses. If the idea of studying human ecology excites you, why not consider coming to COA and sharing your enthusiasm with fellow students and brilliant professors?—*Engin Yenidunya*

The three best things about attending COA are "the students, your closeness to your professors, self-directed curriculum."

The three worst things about attending COA are "the lack of diversity among students, a lack of needed (or wanted) courses, and the fact that Bar Harbor isn't much of a town during the winter."

The three things that every student should do before graduating from COA are "hike every square inch of Mount Desert Island, complete the Bar Island Swim (a 1/3 mile swim to the closest island in the fall, find something to be an activist for, and send a school wide e-mail vouching for your cause."

One thing I would like to have known before coming here is "how negatively people who are the opposite of crunchy would be received."

University of Maine / Orono

Address: Admissions Office, 5713 Chadbourne Hall, Orono, ME 04469-5713
Phone: 207-581-1591
E-mail address: umadmit@maine.edu
Web site URL: www.umaine.edu
Location: NA
Founded: 1865
Private or Public: public
Religious affiliation: none
Undergraduate enrollment: 7,882
Total enrollment: 9,945
Percent Male / Female: 49%/51%
Percent Minority: 7.0%

Percent African-American: 1.0%
Percent Hispanic: 1.0%
Percent Asian: 1.0%
Percent in-state / out-of-state: 85%/15%
Percent Pub HS: NA
Fraternities: 14%
Sororities: 6%
Number of Applicants: 4,568
Percent Accepted: 85%
Percent Accepted who enroll: 42%
Entering: 1,611
Transfers: 477
Application Deadline: NA

Mean SAT: 539 V, 542 M
Middle 50% SAT range: 480–590 V, 480–600 M
Middle 50% ACT range: 20–23
Mean ACT: 21
3 Most popular majors: el. education, business, nursing
Retention: 80
Graduation rate: 53
Library: 792,402 volumes
Tuition and Fees: $4,656 in; $11,946 out
Room and Board: $5,256
On-campus housing: 84

Best-selling horror author and University of Maine at Orono alum Stephen King probably didn't get his ideas from the four years he spent at the school's campus, which students described as idyllic. Both the campus and the surrounding area are "beautiful," while somewhat isolated, students said, and even during winter hikes "across the mall"—a central green resembling a football field—they still often pause to admire the beauty of the forested landscape. Because the nearest metropolitan center, Boston, is four hours away by car, the university offers many on-campus social events and sponsors extremely popular yearly trips to Montreal and Quebec, where students bond, in one upperclassman's words, "by club-hopping, intoxication (legal drinking age in Canada is 18), and the intense ignorance of the French language." Nearby Arcadia National Park and Baxter State Park also topped the list of "must-sees," especially for wilderness-loving students.

It's a Small World After All
Although more than 7,000 undergraduates and almost 2,000 graduate students are enrolled at the University of Maine, many students find the campus community tight-knit and extremely friendly. One said

the size is just right, "large enough that never get bored but small enough that don't feel like just a number." That sense community results from a shared sen of school spirit that pervades every aspe of life at the University of Maine, insi and outside the classroom. Students reg larly join the school's mascot, Banan the black bear, in enthusiastically chee ing at the "incredible" hockey game where five students, campus celebriti known as the "Naked Five," paint MAI on their chests and run around the are when the team scores. In 2000, a group women joined them for the first tim spelling BEARS, inaugurating what one the participants hopes will become a ne tradition. "Even the most timid stude will get swept up in the excitement school rivalries, especially while watchi the University of Maine's hockey, bask ball and football teams," one uppercla man promised, adding that he atten most games even though he is not a spor enthusiast.

Students uninterested in sports can st find plenty to do on and around campu Celebrities visit the University of Mai frequently, and some recent guests ha been Stephen King, Hillary Clinton, the \olent Femmes, and the Dave Matthew Band. Honor societies and clubs cater almost every interest, including environmental and outing clubs, cheering clubs, a marching band and more eclectic groups like a campus branch of the Society for Creative Anachronism—dedicated to reenacting medieval and Renaissance celebrations. A popular freshman carnival held every fall prepares students for dorm theme parties marking events like Mardi Gras and Halloween, charity balls and the spring "Bumstock" celebration, a weeklong concert of local bands modeled on the legendary Woodstock. Another popular communitybuilding event is the "Ritual of the Boot," a rite of passage at the popular in-town Oronoka restaurant for Maine students turning 21. The ceremony involves drinking beer from a bootshaped pitcher and posing for snapshots that are posted on the Oronka's walls. Students who break the boot while drinking, though, have to pay for it, prompting one to make the sage suggestion, "Bring your credit cards for insurance." One student did caution, though, that those who do not enjoy parties will sometimes find their on-campus social options limited.

A Hard Day's Work

Life at Orono isn't all fun and games, though. In fact, the University of Maine, one of New England's best-kept academic secrets, boasts several widely esteemed academic programs, offers a wide range of honors classes and is particularly strong in engineering and music. Physics and math programs are extremely competitive, and the school is a national center for sensor research. One student did complain, though, that some prominent professors are at the University of Maine primarily to research and regard "teaching only as a side requirement."

Students applying to University of Maine must choose between its five colleges: liberal arts and sciences; engineering; education, public policy and health; education and human development; and natural sciences, forestry and agriculture. Because each school has its own specific academic requirements, transferring between colleges is difficult, although all have share university-wide core requirements mandating classes in arts and humanities, math, science and ethics. A wide range of small honors classes and labs complement the large introductory lectures, and all students develop individual courses of study in their senior year as part of the required "Senior Capstone Experience." Students in the honors program must write a senior thesis. The campus's "huge" Fogler library, the largest in Maine, boasts 950,000 volumes and owns a specialized collection, housed in a separate branch in nearby Walpole, of 12,000 volumes dealing with marine studies. Other special collections include the library's "Canadiana" and lumbering and logging archives. Convenient networking services in almost every room also make research easier.

Urban Legends

Opened in 1868 as State College of Agriculture and the Mechanic Arts with only 12 students and two faculty members, the University of Maine has enjoyed a long and colorful history. Legend has it that three dead construction workers from early in the century remain beneath the concrete of one building's steps, but students differed on which building. Another popular story states that the original mascot, a live black bear cub kept in one of the fraternity house's basements most of the year, had to be replaced by a costumed performer after it attacked the University of Connecticut husky at a basketball game. Students said they did not know whether Stephen King heard—or invented—these stories as an undergraduate. Many students believe the school's greatest legend is King himself, who graduated in 1970 with a B.A. in English, three years before the publication of *Carrie* made him famous, and still attends basketball games and visits campus frequently. King met his wife, Tabitha, in the stacks of the Fogler Library, where they both worked as students.

Bon Appétit

Many students said the quality of the school's dining hall food pleasantly surprised them and expressed satisfaction with campus meal plans. Popular features include a full "beans and greens" vegetarian program and the ability to transfer meal plan funds to campus snack bars, markets and convenience stores and local restaurants, including pizzerias that deliver as well as the school-owned Bears' Den and M.C. Fernald's. Different meal plans allow students to have from 7 to 19 dining hall meals a week and from $50 to $500 in transferable meal funding. Special meal plans are also available for commuters. Some students also said they appreciate the flexibility of a "grab-'n-go" dining hall policy that allows them to eat their meals on the run.

> "Even the most timid student will get swept up in the excitement of school rivalries, especially while watching the University of Maine's hockey, basketball, and football teams."

But dining halls are hardly the only haunts of hungry University of Maine students, as a number of inexpensive restaurants are on or near the campus. Students with cars frequently visit the mall in nearby Bangor, home to a variety of restaurants, while others take advantage of the oncampus Taco Bell and Pizza Hut. Numerous pizza houses, almost all of which deliver, are in Orono, and students said two of the most popular are Pat's Pizza and Pizza Dome. Two clubs, Jeddy's and Margarita's, were also highly recommended. For students who prefer to stay in, individual dorms sometimes provide extra food, giving out snacks during finals and on other occasions throughout the year.

Home, Sweet Home

Some students did remark on the lack of diversity among the student body, less than four percent of which is made up of ethnic minorities, but most were not perturbed by it. Theme housing, including a "chem-free dorm" where no drugs and alcohol are served, an all-female dorm and the "S-cubed" dorm for science students, as well as the availability of on-campus apartments, mean that most students end up happy with their living arrangements. "The community is close-knit enough that meeting people with your general interests is never a problem," one student said. Freshmen are mixed with upperclassmen in the dorms, which many students think is a good thing, saying it broadens their social horizons. Students must live on-campus as freshmen and are free to commute or move off-campus afterward, but most don't. "I never thought that I would choose to spend four years in a dorm," one senior remarked. For most, the strong campus-wide sense of community and school spirit is enough to keep them in Orono. Besides, no one wants to miss the chance to see Stephen King if he happens to turn up.—*Erik Johnson*

FYI
The three best things about attending the University of Maine at Orono are "the beautiful location, strong academic programs, and tight-knit campus community."
The three worst things about attending the University of Maine are "frigid winters, remote location, and lack of cultural diversity."
The three things that every student should do before graduating from the University of Maine are "visit as many parts of Maine as you can; go on the seven hour sojourn to Quebec and Montreal; and attend a hockey game."
One thing I'd like to have known before coming here is "how cold 10 below really is!"

Maryland

Goucher College

Address: 1021 Dulaney Valey Road, Baltimore, MD, 21204-2794
Phone: 410-337-6100
E-mail address: edmission@goucher.edu
Web site URL: www.goucher.edu
Location: suburban
Founded: 1885
Private or Public: private
Religious affiliation: none
Undergraduate enrollment: 1,137
Total enrollment: 1,303
Percent Male/Female: 27%/73%
Percent Minority: 14.0%

Percent African-American: 8.0%
Percent Hispanic: 3.0%
Percent Asian: 3.0%
Percent in-state/out-of-state: 40%/60%
Percent Pub HS: 64%
Fraternities: 0%
Sororities: 0%
Number of Applicants: 1,951
Percent Accepted: 79%
Percent Accepted who enroll: 20%
Entering: 270
Transfers: 31
Application Deadline: 1 Feb

Mean SAT: 600 V, 570 M
Middle 50% SAT range: 540–650 V, 520–630 M
Middle 50% ACT range: NA
Mean ACT: 26
3 Most popular majors: psychology, biological sciences, English
Retention: 82.0%
Graduation rate: 58.0%
Library: 290,000 volumes
Tuition and Fees: $20,200 in; $20,200 out
Room and Board: $7,380
On-campus housing: 85%
Financial aid, first-year: 64%

Panthers, Bears, Jackrabbits, these are all common names for mascots, but a gopher? But, students love their Goucher Gopher and its small size and friendly attitude makes it a perfect symbol for the small, close-knit community of the campus. Goucher College is a small liberal arts school in Baltimore, Maryland. According to one student, the size of the student body, presently 1,200 students, is an advantage. For students who may be overwhelmed by large student bodies, one feels a sense of belonging at Goucher, a place where everybody knows each other.

Freshman year is a huge focus at Goucher, with many programs and classes designed to help students adjust to college life and become acquainted with other freshmen. Freshmen are required to participate in the Exploring New Frontiers, (until 1997 called, Common Intellectual Experience) program, in which they are to choose a class from a list of English, sociology, and history offerings.

According to one student, all ENF classes meet at the same time, all papers are due at the same time, and it is a way for freshmen to bond and offer support to each other. That way, everybody is going through the same thing, and everybody understands and can help each other out with academics, said one student.

There are also other classes that freshmen are required to take to ease their adjustment to college life. One unpopular requirement is "Wellness," a seven-week-long course that freshmen must take although it is worth no course credits. It is more of a discussion course than a class, and topics include alcohol, sex, date rape, and other major issues on-campus. Consisting of about 15 to 20 freshman, the class meets three times a week for 50-minute intervals. Though some students complain about this requirement, many have found it beneficial in the end because it allows for student bonding and student awareness.

Across the board, Goucher seeks highly

qualified students and, as an added incentive, provides merit-based scholarships in addition to need-based awards. Under the Trustee Scholarship Program, five exceptional students receive full tuition and room and board for four years.

Hittin' the Books

There are a lot of academic requirements at Goucher, but rather than limiting their choices, students find that they expand their academic opportunites. One student commented that requirements are a good thing because students can get a well-rounded education. It allows students to take classes they would not have taken otherwise. Many students found that they enjoyed these classes and ended up taking more within the field. "You learn to have an open mind and try new things," said one student. Students are required to take one class in each of the following departments: humanities, social sciences, natural science, mathematics, and the arts as well as two computer classes and two different physical education classes. Students typically take about four or five classes a semester, equivalent to about thirty credits a school year. And class size is small, typically enrolling about 15 to 20 students, with the larger lecture classes enrolling 50 students at most.

One popular and advantageous requirement is the "off-campus experience," which allows students in their junior or senior years to intern or study abroad. Students have the opportunity to participate in an exchange program with Exeter, a university in England, and one student can win a scholarship to study at Oxford for a year. Students also intern in Washington or Baltimore as well as in the local community. For example, one student majoring in elementary education is required to be a student-teacher at a local elementary school her senior year. Students find this to be a rewarding opportunity beyond the gates of Goucher.

Goucher Social Scene

The academic environment is stressful, which is normal for a college campus. Academics are demanding and may be intense, but the social atmosphere is not lacking. Hanging out together on campus is popular, and Towson, a suburb eight miles away from Baltimore, is a popular hangout as well. There is a huge mall and movie theaters for students to spend their free time. Neighboring schools such as John Hopkins University, Towson State, Loyola, and Morgan State provide social opportunites for students as well. Many of these schools invite Goucher students to their major parties and mixers.

A popular campus hangout is the Pearlstone Student Center, which recently underwent renovation to make it more spacious and open. The Student Center is always full of activity; all the club offices are located there, as well as the bookstore, post office, cafe, and the famous Gopher Hole. One student described the Gopher Hole as a "non-alcohol pub" that is a popular hangout at night for students and serves as a snack bar and coffeehouse complete with a TV and dartboard.

Social events are easy to find at Goucher. The Student Activites Association organizes campus-wide parties and events. There are usually major social events every month. In October, all the "houses" or residential halls compete in the Pumpkin Bowl, complete with many silly, but fun games. The water-balloon toss is one of the popular ones, and the house that wins the most games wins a prize for its residential hall. The prizes usually consist of a VCR or TV for the common room. However, the main objective of the event is to have a goofy time. In November, everybody gets fixed up on blind dates for the annual blind date formal ball. There is a Mardi Gras celebration in the spring and the carnival and dancing are events students look forward to. Kegs are not allowed on-campus, yet most say that this rule is not strictly enforced. One student reported that alcohol is readily available to all students, including freshmen.

As for the dating scene, one student warns others to be careful. Since Goucher is a small school, word gets around fast. This includes information regarding who is exclusively dating whom as well as with whom somebody randomly hooked up the other night. The male/female ratio is 30/70, because Goucher only became coeducational in 1989. Yet, females do not find that there is a lack of male companionship. For those who aren't satisfied with the selection, many go off-campus to other nearby colleges in their pursuit of love.

Activities

Student involvement in extracurricular and community activities is gaining momentum. There are many community service opportunities under the umbrella organization CAUSE, Community Auxiliary Service. CAUSE volunteers for Habitat for Humanity, in soup kitchens, as well as Parents Anonymous, a child abuse prevention program. The campus offers a variety of extracurricular activities to be involved in, including the Hispanic Club, UMOJA, the African American Students Alliance, and the Student Activities Association, which organizes monthly social events. Students interested in journalism can work for the campus paper, the *Q*.

Most students live on-campus, since the school only allows about 10 percent of juniors, and 15 percent of seniors to live off-campus. However, most students are satisfied with their residential halls. Freshmen are scattered around campus; they are not concentrated in certain areas. This is an advantage for freshmen; they have the opportunity to live with upperclassmen, who serve as sources of advice and support.

> **The male/female ratio is 30/70, because Goucher only became co-educational in 1989.**

Students describe their campus as beautiful and, depending on the season, green grass and fresh flowers are abundant. In the center of the campus lies a gazebo, chapel, and the student center.

Freshman entering Goucher campus are told that Goucher's founders are very close by. Rumor has it that the founder John Goucher and his wife are buried under the front gates of the school. Their unrelenting dedication to the school is mirrored by that of the students.—*Sathya Oum and Staff*

FYI
The three best things about attending Goucher are "the attractive campus, the attention paid to freshmen, and intense but not overwhelming academics."
The three worst things about attending Goucher are "the lack of faculty diversity, the lack of student diversity, and the smallness."
The three things that every student should do before graduating are "go to Gator's (a dance club), volunteer for Habitat for Humanity, and hang out at the Gopher Hole."
One thing I'd like to have known before coming here is "how useful a car would be."

Johns Hopkins University

Address: 3400 North Charles Street, 140 Garland, Baltimore, MD 21218
Phone: 410-516-8171
E-mail address: gotojhu@jhu.edu
Web site URL: www.jhu.edu
Location: urban
Founded: 1876
Private or Public: private
Religious affiliation: none
Undergraduate enrollment: 3,743
Total enrollment: 5,022
Percent Male/Female: 59%/41%
Percent Minority: 32.0%

Percent African-American: 7.0%
Percent Hispanic: 3.0%
Percent Asian: 22.0%
Percent in-state/out-of-state: 13%/87%
Percent Pub HS: 61%
Fraternities: 30%
Sororities: 25%
Number of Applicants: 8,578
Percent Accepted: 41%
Percent Accepted who enroll: 28%
Entering: 945
Transfers: 98
Application Deadline: 1 Jan

Mean SAT: 670 V, 700 M
Middle 50% SAT range: 620–720 V, 670–740 M
Middle 50% ACT range: NA
Mean ACT: 31
3 Most popular majors: biology, biomedical engineering, international relations
Retention: 95.0%
Graduation rate: 83.0%
Library: 3.2 million volumes
Tuition and Fees: $17,440 in; $17,440 out
Room and Board: $8,730
On-campus housing: 99%
Financial aid, first-year: 50%

Contrary to its reputation as a pre-med haven, Johns Hopkins, located in Baltimore, Maryland, has a place for all types of students, from artists to athletes to—yes, pre-meds.

First-Rate Academics

Hopkins students are proud to be at a university "which really feels like it's the ninth Ivy [League school]." Hopkins is a place for those who want to learn. Students find that there really are no majors for those who "want to slack off." Undergraduates are split into two schools: the School of Arts and Sciences and the George William Carlyle Whiting School of Engineering. Every undergrad must take both humanities and science courses and, while there are no official "cores," two to three semesters of writing-intensive courses are required. Perennially popular majors include English, international relations, chemistry, physics, and biology.

With the exception of a few large lecture and introductory courses that can have enrollments in the hundreds (but break down into smaller sections), class sizes are relatively small and foster lively debate and discussion. Students say that they love their professors and feel comfortable talking to their peers and asking for notes. "Grading is tough, but people

are not as cutthroat as the reputation of Hopkins might imply," one student noted. "Students are willing to help each other learn." At Hopkins, all freshmen take their first-semester courses pass/fail, which encourages students to take challenging courses without having to fear poor grades.

While students praise the strong English and science departments, some feel that Hopkins could be more committed to the fine arts as there are few art or theater courses. Through a cross-registration program with the world-renowned Peabody Institute, however, Hopkins students can take music courses and attend all kinds of recitals. Many music majors even take the majority of their courses at Peabody because the program is "so excellent."

A Common Misconception

A common misconception about social life at Hopkins is that there is hardly any partying on-campus. Drinking and Greek life make up a significant part of the social scene. While kegs are officially illegal on-campus, some students say that the administration tends to look the other way when it comes to underage drinking. When students are not drinking at the campus pub or on a grassy hill affectionately coined "the beach," they drink at fraternities. Many freshmen spend their first weekends at frat parties. However, Hopkins has a policy against letting freshmen rush during their first semester on-campus, and because most Greek parties are open to all students, only a small percentage of students end up joining fraternities.

Non-Greeks and non-drinkers alike certainly do not feel left out at Hopkins. There are many exciting things happening on-campus each weekend. Students are uniformly impressed with Hopkins's conscious efforts to provide an alternative to studying or drinking on-campus by hosting dances and movie nights.

Dating has also carved a smaller, but noticeable presence for itself on-campus. However, while Hopkins students are very quick to point out that they consider themselves a liberal student body and boast a plethora of gay and ethnic student organizations, they do admit that many gay and interracial couples are not necessarily "out in the open yet."

In terms of other weekend events, students also enthusiastically anticipate the Milton S. Eisenhower Symposium, which draws "brilliant and famous" speakers to campus all year round to address the subject of the year, such as "Religion in America," on weekends. This lecture series is open to all students, and recent speakers have included Ralph Reed, Alan Dershowitz, Michael Dukakis, George Bush, and Jesse Jackson.

Extracurricular Variety

Hopkins students are active in all aspects of campus life. Over half of the student body participates in some sort of extracurricular activity, the most popular being a cappella singing groups, community service, and cultural organizations.

You cannot discuss sports at Hopkins without mentioning the stellar lacrosse team. The focus of school pride, the men's lacrosse team is the college's sole Division I team (the rest are Division III). While teams other than lacrosse do not draw many spectators, sports are a popular pastime, as many students play intramural sports, particularly Ultimate Frisbee.

Baltimore and Beyond

When freshmen first arrive on-campus for orientation, they report that two things usually strike them. First, students notice that all the buildings have the same architectural style. Second, students comment that "all these bedrooms are tiny." Many students live in triples that are "not very luxurious." But within these cramped surroundings, freshmen get a chance to be highly social, often making friends for the next four years on their floor or in the courtyards.

> In terms of other weekend events, students also enthusiastically anticipate the Milton S. Eisenhower Symposium, which draws "brilliant and famous" speakers to campus all year round to address the subject of the year.

Sophomore lives across the street from campus in recently renovated dorms (McCoy, Wolman, and Bradford), that are "especially nice," according to one student. Upperclassmen can choose to live in off-campus apartment buildings (Homewood and Ivy) but most choose private housing.

Even though some dorms might be short on elegance, the campus itself reportedly "more than makes up for it." Students like to sit on the grassy fields in the middle of campus surrounded by the beautiful red-brick and masonry university buildings. Two popular resources on-campus are the Baltimore Museum of Art, which includes works by Matisse and Degas, and the Milton S. Eisenhower Library, which becomes "a second home" for many undergraduates during their tenure at Hopkins.

While Baltimore holds its share of attractions for students, it is an urban area with its share of drug and crime problems. Some do not feel safe venturing off-campus and always use the van service when they need to leave the plush grounds of Hopkins. Others heatedly refute others' assessment of Baltimore as being a dangerous city, remarking that some "ultra-sheltered suburbanites" are only experiencing culture shock at being in an urban environment.

The Nitty Gritty

Many students dread meals almost as much as studying for finals. Their reactions to on-campus eating ranges from disgust to utter disbelief at the amount of food "that cannot easily be identified." While there are options for vegetarians, one student complained that the primary food option of choice is salad: "Salad for breakfast, salad for lunch, salad for dinner, seven days a week, nine months of the year . . . yucky and boring."

Some students flee off-campus to the various ethnic restaurants and small eateries. Remarking that there are no McDonald's or Burger Kings within walking distance, one student described the Baltimore restaurant scene as, "No big, national, crappy, freeze-dried franchise chains, but rather smaller, family-owned, good food."

In general, students find it very hard to complain and truly appreciate all the academic opportunities available to them. While the area surrounding campus is admittedly not a highlight of undergraduate life here, undergraduates warn that not choosing Hopkins because of Baltimore would be a "huge mistake" as students are continually "thrilled to be learning from superb professors and talented peers."
—*Alex Timbers, Susanna Chu, and Staff*

FYI

The three best things about Johns Hopkins are "being able to study music and be pre-med, the Baltimore Museum of Art, and watching quality lacrosse."

The three worst things about Johns Hopkins are "the reputation that we are lame and obsessed with studying, all the work, and having to watch yourself in Baltimore."

The three things that every student should do before graduating from Johns Hopkins are "go to lectures—we get great people to speak here, hang out at the 'beach,' and avoid eating on campus as often as you can."

One thing I'd like to have know before coming here is "how you don't just have to be a pre-med to come here."

St. John's College

Address: P. O. Box 2800, Annapolis, MD 21404
Phone: 800-727-9238
E-mail address: admissions@sjca.edu
Web site URL: www.sjca.edu
Location: small city
Founded: 1696
Private or Public: private
Religious affiliation: none
Undergraduate enrollment: 452
Total enrollment: 516
Percent Male / Female: 54% / 46%
Percent Minority: 5.0%

Percent African-American: 1.0%
Percent Hispanic: 2.0%
Percent Asian: 2.0%
Percent in-state / out-of-state: 17% / 83%
Percent Pub HS: 65%
Fraternities: 0%
Sororities: 0%
Number of Applicants: 446
Percent Accepted: 78%
Percent Accepted who enroll: 38%
Entering: 134
Transfers: 11
Application Deadline: 1 Mar

Mean SAT: NA V, NA M
Middle 50% SAT range: 660–750 V, 580–680 M
Middle 50% ACT range: NA
Mean ACT: NA
3 Most popular majors: liberal arts only major
Retention: 80%
Graduation rate: 77%
Library: 100,000 volumes
Tuition and Fees: $23,290 in; NA out
Room and Board: $6,360
On-campus housing: 100
Financial aid, first-year: 45%

"This school is a legend by itself. It is distinctly different," is how one student describes St. John's. With its unique approach to education, St. John's, the third oldest college in the United States, has been teaching its students through the "St. John's method" since 1696.

Tutors and Fellow Students

St. John's has a different approach to education. The curriculum is "the Program," and the professors are "tutors." "We call our professors here "tutors" because they guide us along a path as opposed to instructing us," explains a student. The Program, based on the Great Books of Western Society. Music, math and science also constitute a major part of students' curricula, and even math is taught through Great Books: "Reading Newton in the original text is how we learn calculus," explains a student. The Great Books Program doesn't have any electives, and all courses are required: four years of mathematics, one and a half years of Greek, one half year of French, one half year of Shakespearean poetry, one half year of modern poetry, three years of Laboratory Science, one year of Music, four years of Seminar, one major essay at the end of each year, and one year of freshman chorus, in which freshmen gather weekly to sing. However, there are also Preceptorials, or specialized classes on one particular subject. Preceptorials can only be taken in junior and senior years, and include subjects ranging from Aristotle, to Joyce, to Faulkner, to William James.

No Grading

There are no tests and students' papers aren't graded. Instead students receive a grade for their work in a semester, calculated from a combination of papers and class participation. Class participation is considered "the quality and caliber of what one says, its tone, and how one treats confusion, difficulty in understanding himself and in others." Tutorials and labs have around 14 students with one tutor, and seminars average about 20 students and two tutors. Students enjoy this method of education, though the reading load can be tremendous.

Everyone is called Mr. or Ms. in class, including the tutor. A student describes the classes as "egalitarian," even with world-renowned tutors such as Eva Brann, Laurence Berns, A. P. David, and Joe Sachs. Also, the weekly Friday night lectures host visitors from philosophy departments of other schools such as Stanly Fish, Robert Pinsky, and Robert Fagles.

Students have a close relationship with their tutors: they play sports together, tutors are invited to student parties, and they have dinners together regularly. Students find the tutors interesting and "cool." Even though all the classes have a tutor, some science and music courses also have assistants who help with the technical setup.

Older Students, Less Underage Problems

Parties are regularly organized and attended. The average St John's student is older than the college mean; therefore, underage drinking is less of a problem than elsewhere. However, underage drinking isn't tolerated. Coffee-shop parties, which take place twice a month at the basement of McDowell hall, are very popular. The Great Hall, an 18th century ballroom that doubles as the main classroom, hosts formal balls every month. Swing-dances, the Pink Triangle Society cross-dress parties, and the annual Seducers and Corrupters party, make up a colorful social life for students. However, Lola's is probably the greatest theme party: a casino night. "There's live music, gambling (blackjack, poker, and roulette), dancing, and a couple of bars. It's a great time. Some of our tutors will deal blackjack. It's a lot of fun," a student describes Lola's, adding, "We are allowed to hold this event because our school charter is older than that of the state of Maryland." Kegs are allowed on campus. The Senior Prank, which is based on kidnapping students from class and spending the evening drinking, is popular among students.

Reality Bites

Croquet Weekend, of *Sports Illustrated* and National Public Radio fame, is the weekend of the annual croquet match against the Naval Academy. A coffee-shop party takes place the previous night. The day of the match itself is ". . . an all day lawn party with people wearing sundresses and linen suits." A cotillion dance takes place after the match where Godiva chocolates with the St. John's seal on them are served with champagne. A student-run group, Reality, whose central activity is

Reality Weekend, organizes Lola's, Croquet Day, and the coffee-shop parties. Juniors organize Reality Weekend as a celebration for graduating seniors. Beer, live music, a three-day film festival, beer, and Spartan Madball are the key features of the Reality Weekend. Rules of Spartan Madball are having no shoes, no weapons, and no vehicles. The goal is to run the ball through the goal on a field with no boundaries. Spartan Madball, played once a year, resembles rugby.

Ideas Are What Counts

Even though there are some drawbacks of having a small community, St. John's students enjoy it. It is easy to get to know people since everyone is open and eager to discuss and share opinions. But, racially and ethnically, the student body is very homogeneous. "Our joke is that you can describe a third of the student body by saying 'oh, he's a tall, skinny, white guy.' But that matters very little, since the ideas are what count, and there is a huge range of ideas people here hold," is how one student describes his peers. Another student relates that even when they are drunk, their discussion subject is most probably Aristotle.

Most upperclassmen live off campus. All freshmen are required to live on campus, and the floors are single-sex except for two dorms on campus. "The Resident Assistant's main goal is to take care of you, not be a policeman." Humphreys, a freshman dorm, is well-liked and Chase-Stone, an upperclassman dorm, with its hardwood floors and high ceilings, is also highly desirable. Another freshman dorm is Randall—famous for its clanking pipes and small rooms. Paca-Carroll is the "quiet dorm."

Historic Grounds

McDowell Hall, the main classroom building, is an 18th century colonial Governor's mansion. Lafayette danced in the Great Hall of McDowell Hall when he visited Annapolis after the American Revolution. The Liberty Tree on front campus, which was cut down after Hurricane Floyd, was the meeting place for the Sons of Liberty of Maryland of the American Revolution. Humphreys Hall was a hospital and a morgue, and Pinkney Hall was a barracks during the Civil War. The newly built gym features a suspended track around the ceiling.

Overall, the campus is small and is characterized by its colonial red-brick buildings. It is a safe campus situated in a safe city, Annapolis. The quad is the place to meet on lazy Sundays. Even though there are some eating-out options in Annapolis, D.C., and Baltimore offer superior restaurants.

Students find the food on campus mediocre. There are 3 meal plans: 5, 14, or 21 meals per week and it is mandatory to be enrolled in one of them. The dining hall offers many options to vegetarian students. The Little Campus, which recently closed down, was students' eat-out choice for over 30 years. Now, Harry Browne's is their new preference. Student also enjoy sushi at Nikko or Joss.

The Sports Triangle

People are engaged in many activities on campus; therefore, most stay in Annapolis rather than going to D.C. or to Baltimore. Students in Project Politae work for Habitat for Humanity; St. John's Chorus sings; the elected Delegate Council distributes funds to student activities; and the Student Committee on Instruction discusses Program issues. Mabel the Swimming Wonder Monkey is a different organization that "watches and heckles bad movies." In Melee, students are involved with medieval arts and crafts as well as rubber sword-fighting.

> **"Reading Newton in the original text is how we learn calculus."**

Fencing, crew, and croquet are the only three varsity sports of the college, and students are proud of their success: "We hold the proud honor of being the National Intercollegiate Croquet Champions for the third year in a row this year." All other sports are played as intramurals. Nearby golf courts and a swimming pool are available to students.

Students are proud to be a part of the St. John's tradition and are happy to study in a unique educational environment. "St. Johns is totally incomparable. This place is unique, and it is what I always wanted." —*Yakut Seyhanli*

FYI

The three best things about attending St. John's are "the Program, the thinking, and discussing."

The three worst things about attending St. John's are "news traveling fast, the Program—makes one realize how many more books s/he wants to read, and how little time one has."

The three things that every student should do before graduating from St. John's are "going to a coffee-shop party, picking a fight in Melee Club, and listen to a senior oral."

One thing I'd like to have known before coming to St. John's is "its math and lab programs are intense."

United States Naval Academy

Address: 117 Decatur Road, Annapolis, MD 21402
Phone: 410-293-4361
E-mail address: NA
Web site URL: www.usna.edu
Location: suburban
Founded: 1845
Private or Public: public
Religious affiliation: none
Undergraduate enrollment: 4,020
Total enrollment: 4,021
Percent Male / Female: 85% / 15%
Percent Minority: 17.0%

Percent African-American: 6.0%
Percent Hispanic: 7.0%
Percent Asian: 4.0%
Percent in-state / out-of-state: 6% / 94%
Percent Pub HS: 60%
Fraternities: 0%
Sororities: 0%
Number of Applicants: 9,813
Percent Accepted: 16%
Percent Accepted who enroll: 79%
Entering: 1,165
Transfers: 0
Application Deadline: 28 Feb

Mean SAT: 638 V, 666 M
Middle 50% SAT range: 500–600 V, 625–675 M
Middle 50% ACT range: NA
Mean ACT: NA
3 Most popular majors: political science, economics, oceanography
Retention: 86.0%
Graduation rate: 80.0%
Library: 470,000 volumes
Tuition and Fees: $0
Room and Board: $0
On-campus housing: 100%
Financial aid, first-year: 0%

Sink or swim? In one of the Physical Readiness Tests (PRTs) that United States Naval Academy students must pass, students must jump off of a ten-meter platform into a diving well. The situation is analogous to the leap that these same students made in deciding to attend the Naval Academy: it is a difficult decision to make, and, once your toes are lined up at the edge of a platform 30 feet above water, the move to commit follows with a precipitous descent into the watery world of the midshipman, or "middie" as Naval Academy students refer to themselves.

One of the major enticements to take the plunge at one of the government service academies is the promise of a salary of almost $550 a month from the time you matriculate—i.e., free education. As with most government offers, however, there is a hook: in obtaining a degree from the United States Naval Academy you are promising at least five years of your life to active duty in either the United States Navy or Marine Corps.

Plebe Life

First-year students, or "plebes" (shortened from the word "plebeian"), are immersed completely in the spartan lifestyle of the academy. The requirements in every spectrum of plebe life are numerous. One student remarked, "This place is all about requirements." Plebes are expected to take two semesters of chemistry and calculus, as well as classes dealing with naval history and ethics. Students are also expected to maintain certain body-weight standards and participate in a rigorous physical regimen including either varsity athletics or intramural competition in one of the following: swimming, boxing, wrestling, judo, weight training, hand-to-hand combat, and other activities.

The students generally see these requirements as providing them with a "base for any Academy grad to pursue virtually any graduate work regardless of the degree you receive here." However, some students say that the requisites also can be a pain, because they "don't leave you with many options." There is a strict honor code that all students must adhere to regarding their academic and personal lives. Students say it works well and everyone follows it.

Free Time
The social options are often as rigid as the academic options, as plebes are only allowed "liberty" (free time) between Saturday's noon formation and 11 P.M. that evening. Many plebes choose to spend this time "sleeping, sleeping, sleeping," while others choose to visit their sponsor families (Annapolis families that provide surrogate homes to middies) or watch television.

As middies move up in the ranks from plebe year, they begin to enjoy extended liberty. Hours are extended on the weekends, and gradually, by the time students reach fourth-year status, life reaches the normalcy of "a student at most any other undergraduate institution."

The limits imposed on socializing are numerous, however. Middies are not allowed to "fraternize" or have sex with other students and there is definitely "a stigma attached to dating other mids." Since the male-female ratio at the USNA is better than five to one "you basically have to go into town for any kind of relationship." A student must also be "sat" or satisfactory in the area of academics in order to have liberty. Those students with a sub-2.0 GPA, or more than two D grades in any classes, lose their liberty privileges and must spend their weekends studying.

Those who must hit the books usually go to the sole library on-campus, Nimitz, which has over half a million volumes, or for the more socially inclined, Dahgren Hall at the Drydock Restaurant. Academics at the academy are intense, but students generally have a lot of cooperative help to offer one another. One student remarked, "There's a real strong sense of 'let's get each other through this purgatory.'"

Dorm Details
When evening studies in Nimitz have drawn to a close, students return to Bancroft Hall, the huge dormitory that houses all of the academy's 4,000-plus students, and which is also known as "Mother B." Bancroft hall is currently undergoing renovation, which is expected to be completed by 2008. The current rooms were described as either "saunas" or "meat lockers" since the facility lacks air-conditioning. The rooming options were also described as "nonexistent." Every student has a personal computer, and is connected to the campus-wide data network, but phones are allowed only "in rare cases." "Shoes gotta be shiny, clothes folded, beds made, and doors kept open so that inspectors can spot-check us with their white gloves." The dorms are coed "like an apartment building," and "learning to live in close quarters with both sexes can be a challenge, but it works . . . of course there are strict rules of decency," one middie reported.

> "Shoes gotta be shiny, clothes folded, beds made, and doors kept open so that inspectors can spot-check us with their white gloves."

With the strict honor code of the Naval Academy, theft of property is "never a problem," and with Marines and Department of Defense police patrolling the campus, students agreed that the campus is very safe.

A major facet of the USNA is the school spirit that the administration helps foster with "spontaneous, but mandatory" pep rallies. During "Army Week," the week before the big football game against their

West Point archrivals, "chaos, pandemonium, and stress relief" are the results of massive school spirit.

Overall, students at the United States Naval Academy are well aware of the fact that they lead a "non-traditional college life" in a "none too diverse" and "extremely conservative" setting, but they balance the current situation with the eventual payoff. Said one third-year student, when asked what advice he would give to high school seniors, "Be sure it is what you want, and be prepared to make many sacrifices. But, oh, is it worth it when you get that diploma."—*Vladimir Cole and Staff*

FYI

The three best things about attending USNA are "the discipline, the free education, and the physical regime."

The three worst things about attending USNA are "the lack of personal space, lack of personal time, and lack of personal choice."

The three things that every student should do before graduating are "live up Army Week, make sure your room is ready for inspection, and don't get caught with another middie."

One thing I'd like to have known before coming is "how rigorous training can be."

University of Maryland / College Park

Address: Mitchell Building, College Park, MD 20742-5235
Phone: 301-314-8385
E-mail address: um-admit@uga.umd.edu
Web site URL: www.maryland.edu
Location: suburban
Founded: 1856
Private or Public: public
Religious affiliation: none
Undergraduate enrollment: 24,776
Total enrollment: 33,006
Percent Male/Female: 58%/42%
Percent Minority: 57.0%

Percent African-American: 49.0%
Percent Hispanic: 1.0%
Percent Asian: 6.0%
Percent in-state/out-of-state: 79%/21%
Percent Pub HS: 0%
Fraternities: 11%
Sororities: 13%
Number of Applicants: 16,837
Percent Accepted: 64%
Percent Accepted who enroll: 38%
Entering: 4,056
Transfers: 0
Application Deadline: 1 Feb

Mean SAT: NA V, NA M
Middle 50% SAT range: 540–640 V, 560–670 M
Middle 50% ACT range: NA
Mean ACT: NA
3 Most popular majors: criminology and criminal justice, psychology, accounting
Retention: 88.0%
Graduation rate: 31.0%
Library: 3.5 million volumes
Tuition and Fees: $4,050 in; $10,938 out
Room and Board: $6,216
On-campus housing: 80%
Financial aid, first-year: 46%

As it moves up in national rankings, University of Maryland has become one of the most highly respected state schools in the country. With improvements in academic departments, further development of honors programs, proximity to Washington, D.C., (nine short miles away) and a lively social scene, Maryland offers its students "a good time and a great education."

Academics

University of Maryland prides itself in offering a liberal arts education, having extensive core requirements in addition to requirements for one's major. These include two writing courses, one math class, and a "diversity" course, in addition to twelve distributional courses in the humanities, math and sciences, and social sciences and history. Most find taking classes in a variety of disciplines to be a great experience, especially if "you don't know what you want to major in."

The preprofessional departments are extremely respected at Maryland, particularly engineering, life sciences, journalism, and business, while the humanities tend to be weaker. Many students find class sizes to decrease as one begins to take upper level courses. "It doesn't really matter if there are 100–1500 students in the intro classes, but in my advanced courses there are only 10–20 students in them, one with several professors working with us; it's really amazing," one student explained. Maryland offers everything from gut courses like Bowling and Sex Education to more challenging honors seminars. However, Business 110 with Professor Nickels attracts quite a following: "It's practically a requirement for the diploma," one student joked. Voted Professor of the Year for the past 3 years, Nickels offers his legendary "happiness speech" on how to be happy in this course, and consistently gets incredible reviews from his students.

Incoming freshmen have a variety of honors programs available to them. In the College Scholars Program, a 2-year program specific to a particular subject, Scholars live with others in their program and enjoy smaller classes. However, depending on the particular subject the programs vary in strength. "I didn't get that much out of it," said one student who participated in the Government College Scholars Program, "though I know others who really enjoyed their program." The University Honors Program, which is more difficult to get into, has gotten great reviews from a majority of students as a way to get a challenging curriculum for the first two years of college. "It could not be better. The classes were small and the professors were really motivated and interested in teaching," one honors student said about the program.

Facilities

Maryland offers two major libraries for studying: McKeldin (the graduate library) and Hornbake (the undergraduate library). More serious studiers choose McKeldin, while the upper levels of Hornbake are usually suitable as well. However, the basement of Hornbake tends to be more social.

Other facilities include the Maryland Center for Performing Arts, which just opened in 1999, and the Recreation Center, a $125 million athletic complex that has "everything" and is open for all students. In addition to the new plant life building and Computer Science building, there are plans to build a new Student Center.

Residential areas at Maryland are separated into North and South Campus. Although living on campus is never compulsory, the majority does live on campus. There has been an increase in the amount of juniors and seniors who opt to live on campus, causing a housing shortage for freshmen, who mostly live in North campus, often in triples, due to the housing problem. The dorms on North Campus, which are considered "not too bad but a little on the small side," are a great social environment for freshmen to meet fellow classmates. The majority of upperclassmen live in the apartments and suites of South Campus, often enjoying single bedrooms and spacious living space. While most dorms are coed, other living options include athletic housing, language housing, special honors housing, and substance-free housing.

Food

While one student described the food as "terrible," another said that it "could be worse." Most students do recommend "North Woods" eatery on North campus, an all-you-can-eat buffet, which offers food that is "more healthy and much less greasy." There is always the option of eating out at Papa John's, Taco Bell, Denny's, Wa Wa, the Bagel Place, or other late-night spots around campus.

College Park

"College Park isn't really a college town but we really don't need one with D.C. so close and everything else happening on campus," one student noted, summing up the role of College Park in the lives of Maryland students. Although the town offers Cornerstone, Bentley's and Santa Fe

Café, three popular bars, most go to Washington, D.C., on the weekends or stay on campus. Security around campus is said to be very good, with a solid police presence and good lighting.

Outside of Academics

Although its students tend to be from Maryland, New Jersey, and New York, that does not mean they are not diverse. Coming from all parts of the political spectrum, students are known to be tolerant, making minorities and the gay and lesbian community feel generally comfortable and supported.

The variety of extracurricular activities includes a juggling club, a Baha'i Club, a healthy intramural sports program, a skydiving club, and a wide variety of ethnic organizations are just a few of the many organizations that are on campus. "Habitat for Humanity has been one of the greatest things I have been a part of here. We have been doing demolition and reconstruction on rundown housing in a low income Baltimore neighborhood," one student said. He continued, "I feel like I'm really helping out the community." The daily newspaper, the *Diamondback*, has wide readership among Maryland students as does the literary magazine, *Stylist*, and various ethnic magazines. While the Greek scene is present on campus, and involves 10 percent of the student population, it is no longer the major force on campus that it used to be. Students find that "Maryland is big enough for everybody to find a niche and people they like." One thing that does unify the student body is athletics, particularly football and basketball. With both teams having extremely strong records in the past few years, school spirit and student participation have been overwhelming.

Events such as "Midnight Madness," an evening in October when students sleep over at the gym to celebrate the beginning of basketball season, and Homecoming further foster school pride. Soccer, lacrosse, and field hockey events are also well-attended by students. Besides athletic events, Maryland students have the "All Niter," a fall festival at the Student Union and "Art Attack," an all day music event in the spring, where bands like George Clinton's P-Funk play. Besides these school-sponsored events, there are always parties going on, particularly, between Thursday and Saturday night. While drinking can be heavy on campus, the administration has continued its no-keg policies in an attempt to crack down on excessive drinking, though "the actual implementation of the policies is really pretty lax." Marijuana, the most popular drug on campus, is "present, but not overly so."

> "Habitat for Humanity has been one of the greatest things I have been a part of here. We have been doing demolition and reconstruction on rundown housing in a low income Baltimore neighborhood."

As the University of Maryland is consistently improving its image as a nationally respected university, "it is still the only place I know where you can have amazing school spirit, (my buddies and I are always waiting for basketball tickets a couple hours before the game), a great social life (there's always something to do) and still get a solid diploma at the end, too."
—*Jessica Morgan*

FYI
The three best things about the University of Maryland are "the beautiful campus, honors program, and being close to Washington, D.C."
The three worst things about the University of Maryland are "parking, College Park, and bureaucracy. "
The three things that every student should do before graduating are "attend *every* basketball game, go to 'Art Attack,' and rub Testodoe's [a turtle] nose before an exam."
One thing I'd like to have known before coming to the University of Maryland is "how amazing watching basketball can be."

Massachusetts

Amherst College

Address: P.O. Box 5000, Wilson Admission Center, Amherst, MA 01002
Phone: 413-542-2328
E-mail address: admission@amherst.edu
Web site URL: www.amherst.edu
Location: small city
Founded: 1821
Private or Public: private
Religious affiliation: none
Undergraduate enrollment: 1,664
Total enrollment: 1,664
Percent Male/Female: 52%/48%
Percent Minority: 25.3%

Percent African-American: 6.4%
Percent Hispanic: 6.6%
Percent Asian: 12.0%
Percent in-state/out-of-state: 14%/86%
Percent Pub HS: 57%
Fraternities: 0%
Sororities: 0%
Number of Applicants: 5,194
Percent Accepted: 19%
Percent Accepted who enroll: 43%
Entering: 422
Transfers: 5
Application Deadline: 31 Dec
Mean SAT: 700 V, 697 M

Middle 50% SAT range: 650–760 V, 650–740 M
Middle 50% ACT range: 27–33
Mean ACT: 30
3 Most popular majors: English, pol. science, psychology
Retention: 97
Graduation rate: 96
Library: 889,989 volumes
Tuition and Fees: $25,259 in; $25,259 out
Room and Board: $6,560
On-campus housing: 100%
Financial aid, first-year: 43%

The squirrels at Amherst College have been known to throw acorns at students with terrifyingly accurate precision. Fortunately, they are the one and only hazard of the Amherst campus. Set in the quaint, picturesque, friendly town of Amherst, Massachusetts, Amherst College has a familial quality to it. With a total enrollment of only about 1,600, students know the face, if not the name, of almost every other student at the school.

Intimate Academics

"Overall, the thing that satisfies me most about Amherst is the professors," says one sophomore. Professors at Amherst are generally extremely approachable and described as "inspiring and very dedicated to making you a better student." Students say profs are "very eager to help you and encourage you." Since Amherst does not have graduate students, profes-sors teach all of the classes and most of the discussion sections.

Class sizes are also learning-conducive. Most sections have between 20 and 25 people, and lecture classes normally enroll about 45 students. When 70 students crowd into a class, students complain about it being too large.

Because of the intimate academic atmosphere, many students are able to build close relationships with their professors, even going out to dinner or taking trips to Boston with them. Professors are known to befriend their students. (Of course, professors may not always be so beloved. Rumor has it that the Amherst grad who wrote the screenplay for the movie *Dead Poets Society* included the name of his English professor as the author of a particularly disagreeable and pompous introduction to a textbook.)

The only required class for all Amherst students is a semester-long freshman seminar. Freshmen choose from a list of 15 interdisciplinary classes such as Reading Paris and Imagining Landscape. Otherwise, students are free to choose whichever classes they wish—as long as their faculty advisor approves the schedule. Students preregister for classes and have two weeks at the beginning of the semester to make changes to their schedules. A faculty advisor is assigned to each freshman, but students can choose their own advisors once they declare their major. Classes also can be taken with the pass-fail option, although few choose to use it.

Students can design their own interdisciplinary majors and cross-register for courses in the Five-College consortium, which includes neighbors Smith College, University of Massachusetts at Amherst, Mount Holyoke, and Hampshire College. Students from any of these five colleges can take classes offered at the other schools for credit. Some male students have been known to take classes at the two women's colleges, Smith and Mount Holyoke, for nonacademic reasons.

> **Some male students have been known to take classes at the two women's colleges, Smith and Mount Holyoke, for nonacademic reasons.**

"The amount of reading and the expectations of the professors are huge," said one English major. Amherst is a reading-and-writing-oriented school. No matter what your major, you will have to write papers. Even science classes require them.

Tales of Beer

According to students, the Amherst social life revolves mainly around drinking. "The administration turns a blind eye to underage drinking, just as long as you're not in Amherst town and don't make the school look bad," said one sophomore. "Getting drunk turns into a status thing. People brag about getting drunk in class. People do it because everyone else does." Another student agreed: "Hanging out at Amherst means getting together and drinking." Although there are non-drinkers, "the niche is very small," one student said.

Especially for Amherst women, dating can present something of a problem. Everyone agrees that it is much easier for the guys to find available girls due to the proximity of Smith and Mount Holyoke. Many Amherst guys seem to believe the saying, "Smith to bed, Mount Holyoke to wed, Amherst girls to talk to." "We're [the guys'] lab partners," complained one Amherst female. "People don't date much. There are lots more random hookups," an Amherst male added.

Even for those who don't drink or date, there is plenty to do at Amherst on the weekends besides catch up on reading and admire the scenery. Amherst is a college town, and the surrounding area caters to college students. An abundance of restaurants, movie theaters, fast-food restaurants, pharmacy stores, bookstores, and other shops along with a nearby mall and supermarket, are accessible on foot or by bus. A free bus system links the five colleges in the consortium.

Life in the Dorms

The administration allows only 50 seniors to live off-campus each year. All other students must live on-campus, where housing is quite plentiful. Freshman year is spent in the freshman dorms, the only housing with single-sex floors and single-sex bathrooms. Each floor has a resident counselor to perform such duties as giving study-break parties. After freshman year, students choose their own roommates and, through a draw, pick their own rooms. There are no dorms designated specifically for sophomores, juniors, or seniors, but many dorms primarily house members of a particular class. Residents say dorm rooms are in decent, livable condition, but they are by no means luxurious or new.

Other housing options include "social dorms" and theme houses for various cultures such as the Asian-American house. All Amherst students buy a meal plan for the school's dining hall. Students are satisfied, but not thrilled, about the quality of their food. Vegetarian dishes and a salad bar are offered at every meal. However, even a nonvegetarian agreed that "there are no decent vegetarian options."

Outside the Classroom

Almost everyone at Amherst participates in one or two extracurricular activities. Faculty advisors encourage their students to get involved by making sure their class schedules are not so time-consuming that they prevent them from having outside interests. Among the activities available are five a cappella singing groups, underground fraternities and sororities (officially banned by the administration), and various religious and ethnic groups. Though some students participate in community-service activities, such activities are not extremely popular.

Complaints about the Amherst admin-istration by various student groups are not uncommon. "The administration, especially the president, neither listens to nor respects students, especially minority students. They want to make Amherst into one unified, unrealistic, colorblind society. But it's not just the minorities; most kids on-campus feel the administration does not listen to them," said one Asian sophomore.

Amherst students from every background, though, agree that their classmates are on the whole very friendly. While some complain about the school's academically intense atmosphere, competitiveness is not pervasive; instead students tend to be "closet grade-hounds" who describe Amherst as a warm and caring place.—*Sherry Tsai and Staff*

FYI

The three best things about attending Amherst are "the helpful professors, the small science courses, and the relaxed social scene."
The three worst things about attending Amherst are "the fact that you've met everyone by sophomore year, the cold, how busy most people are."
The three things that every student should do before graduating are "get a slice at Antonio's, get a cup of coffee at The Black Sheep, make a friend at one of the other colleges nearby."
One thing I'd like to have known before coming here is "that everybody knows everybody else's business."

Babson College

Address: Mustard Hall, Babson Park, MA 02157-0310
Phone: 781-239-5522
E-mail address: ugradmission@babson.edu
Web site URL: www.babson.edu
Location: suburban
Founded: 1919
Private or Public: private
Religious affiliation: none
Undergraduate enrollment: 1,685
Total enrollment: 1,685
Percent Male/Female: 63%/37%

Percent Minority: 14.0%
Percent African-American: 2.0%
Percent Hispanic: 5.0%
Percent Asian: 7.0%
Percent in-state/out-of-state: 42%/58%
Percent Pub HS: 50%
Fraternities: 20%
Sororities: 10%
Number of Applicants: 2,316
Percent Accepted: 46%
Percent Accepted who enroll: 37%
Entering: 443
Transfers: 47
Application Deadline: 1 Feb

Mean SAT: 566 V, 608 M
Middle 50% SAT range: 540–630 V, 570–660 M
Middle 50% ACT range: NA
Mean ACT: NA
3 Most popular majors: finance, marketing, economics
Retention: 91.0%
Graduation rate: 62.0%
Library: 130,000 volumes
Tuition and Fees: $21,072 in; $20,172 out
Room and Board: $8,392
On-campus housing: 96%
Financial aid, first-year: 45%

Babson College students often say, "If you want to go into business, it's an excellent school, the best," and the real world agrees. Babson is consistently rated one of the best business schools in the country, and students say that if you know what you want to do, it's the place for you.

Born into Money

Most of the students complain about the heavy workload they face from the start of their freshman year. Students start their business education with foundations classes. FME, Foundation through Management Experience, the special program for freshmen, includes introductions to accounting, marketing, business and information systems. After these introductory level courses, which are also known as the "boot camp," second-term freshmen actually lay their hands on money and start a small business of their own. After devising different plans for forming a business during the first semester, the class chooses from these plans and proceeds to enact some in the second term. With the use of a loan from the school, students in the past have set up calendar and cookie companies and even a "flow glow" company, which did special-event decorating. In their second year, students get to choose a company like Tommy Hilfiger, Timberland, or Royal Caribbean and analyze the firm in detail. During this "Intermediate Management" they go to the plant and prepare a presentation of the company. In their last two years, they specialize in one area of study. Internships during these years help the students get acquainted with the business world. While the library provides good research resources, students also use the VAX computer network for online information about jobs and internships.

Marketing is one of the most popular majors and students note that "finance is coming up strong." Entrepreneurial studies is another strong major and is ranked high nationally. Babson also has an arrangement with Wellesley College, by which students can take Russian and Italian classes at Wellesley.

Students are impressed and satisfied with the faculty. Since the number of students in class usually varies between 20 and 25, undergrads interact with professors in almost all of their classes. "The professors care about you," says one student, pointing out their accessibility as an especially strong point. Even though there are no TAs in classes, students have mentors who help them with questions they have about classes and serve as advisors. Starting freshman year, when students participate in the Freshman Year Experience, faculty advisors and advisees meet for a movie or dinner to get to know each other better.

The Suites and the City

Social life in Babson is mostly described as "the Suites and the City." Suites, which are larger and more comfortable compared to dormitories, are mostly occupied by fraternity members and sports players. Five dormitories out of fourteen are air-conditioned; many have single-sex floors. Each dorm has a common lounge where students relax on comfortable couches and play air hockey or foosball. All dorms have laundry rooms and kitchens and are all centrally located. Seniors have priority for singles and suites.

Students say the parties in the suites are the best parties at Babson. There are also 3 semiformal parties every year, as well as theme parties including fall weekend, Oktoberfest, and Harvest. There are also weekly parties sponsored by CAB, Campus Activities Board and by the Knight Auditorium. Even though drinking is not a problem in suite parties the school is very strict about the drinking age. As long as you are not seen by an RA (one of whom lives on every floor of the dorms), students say there aren't any real problems with drinking. Many students party at Boston College and Boston University, as well. This involvement with other colleges is also a result of the male to female ratio, which is roughly 7:3. The lower ratio of females to males on campus makes it "a challenge for men to get laid," students complained.

Students enjoy the location of the college. Boston is easily accessible with the T, commuter rail, and buses. Still many have cars since they find the hours of the public transportation inconvenient on weekends. The preponderance of cars on campus creates a parking problem, and for the freshmen, the situation is even worse; their parking lot is farther away from the center of campus.

The area where Babson is located is one of the richest areas of the country; the expense of going out explains why students find it "easy not to be social." Off-campus housing is available, but the rents of nearby apartments are high. Therefore some students end up finding apartments far away from school, which requires them to get cars.

Student Body on Safe Grounds

Students say the Babson population is segregated. The percentage of foreign students is not high and foreigners mostly associate with themselves. The same holds true for athletes and Greeks. Some have complained about the cliques within the student body.

Students socialize in Reynold, a popular spot for lunch, where cold and hot dishes as well as fast food from restaurants like Pizza Hut can be purchased. For dinner, however, many prefer going to Trim, the dining hall of the college. Students appreciate the variety of the dishes served there. Of course, you can always go to Wellesley to eat out—or have coffee at Starbucks. Another popular place on campus is Roger's Pub, which is named after Roger Babson, the founder of the college. Roger Babson was a prohibitionist and many students say he must have "rolled over in his grave when his name was given to the pub."

Although the number of student organizations is not very high, many work efficiently and are popular among the students. These include Student Board, Campus Activity Board (CAB), Entrepreneurship Club, Marketing and Philosophy Clubs and sports clubs like men's soccer and basketball, and women's field hockey and lacrosse. Particularly popular, CAB not only plans the weekly dances, but also arranges for speakers to come to Babson, and most students are pleased with their choices, pining only for their hero—"if they could get Bill Gates!"

Students also enjoy the safety of the campus. They don't report any concerns about going out at any time during the night. Most say they have no problem walking to Sorenson Center, the center for theater and fine arts, or returning from Wellesley or from the PepsiCo Pavilion Gym—which provides students with an indoor pool, track, squash, racquetball courts, a weight room, three basketball courts, and a dance/aerobics center.

Babson's Effort

"Babson is trying to differentiate itself from other business schools," commented one student. Students observe that the college is changing its curriculum and its methods every year. In the last few years, students have been concentrating more on team-teaching and enjoy learning how accounting, business, and team-teaching fit together.

> **"Babson is trying to differentiate itself from other business schools."**

Also, each freshman class now chooses a council, made up of respresentatives from their class, who prepare certain resolutions for their year. Students find this useful and believe these resolutions also add to the improvement of the college, the social life, and their year.

Besides the city, students are here for one reason: getting into the real world fast. Even though the business world is competitive, they know that their Babson education is a great advantage. "It's the best, and is still going strong."—*Yakut Seyhanli.*

FYI
The three best things about attending Babson are "specialized education, preparing for the real world, proximity to the city."
The three worst things about attending Babson are "female to male ratio, an expensive environment, the sports."

The three things that every student should do before graduating from Babson are "go to the city, take road trips, live in a suite."
One thing I'd like to have known before coming here is "the heavy workload of the freshman year."

Boston College

Address: 140 Commonwealth Avenue, Devlin Hall 208, Chestnut Hill, MA 02467
Phone: 617-552-3100
E-mail address: ugadmis@bc.edu
Web site URL: www.bc.edu
Location: suburban
Founded: 1863
Private or Public: private
Religious affiliation: Roman Catholic
Undergraduate enrollment: 8,925
Total enrollment: 9,079
Percent Male/Female: 47%/53%
Percent Minority: 18.0%

Percent African-American: 5.0%
Percent Hispanic: 5.0%
Percent Asian: 8.0%
Percent in-state/out-of-state: 28%/72%
Percent Pub HS: 58%
Fraternities: 0%
Sororities: 0%
Number of Applicants: 16,373
Percent Accepted: 40%
Percent Accepted who enroll: 35%
Entering: 2,250
Transfers: 507
Application Deadline: 15 Jan
Mean SAT: NA

Middle 50% SAT range: 590–680 V, 610–690 M
Middle 50% ACT range: NA
Mean ACT: NA
3 Most popular majors: English, finance, psychology
Retention: 94.0%
Graduation rate: 81.0%
Library: 1.4 million volumes
Tuition and Fees: $21,700 in; $21,700 out
Room and Board: $7,270
On-campus housing: 98%
Financial aid, first-year: 48%

At night during exam week, most colleges are silent as their students bury themselves in books. Not so at Boston College, where every night during finals, at exactly 11 o'clock, each member of the undergraduate population of 9,000-plus leans out of his or her window and . . . screams. This tradition, which lasts anywhere from 15 to 30 minutes, is described by one junior as "what unites the entire student body."

That's not, fortunately, the only thing that brings the students together on the campus of this Jesuit university in suburban Boston. Classes, extracurriculars, and an active social scene also unite the fun-loving undergraduates who always find a way to combine hard work and play.

Hitting Those BC Books

The university contains four undergraduate schools: Management, Nursing, Education, and Art and Sciences. All of the schools share a core curriculum of introductory classes. Students have to take courses in math and natural sciences, two semesters of a language, two semesters of theology, and a writing seminar. There is also a cultural diversity requirement, ensuring that every Boston College graduate has not only a detailed knowledge of his or her major field of concentration, but also a solid liberal-arts base, in keeping with the Jesuit tradition. Students seem divided on the core curriculum. While some like the liberal attitude and wide selection of classes, others feel that there are too many requirements. Most students spend their first two years fulfilling the cores, which have large, impersonal lectures with sections taught by graduate student TAs.

The most popular departments in the School of Arts and Sciences are political science, philosophy, and English, all of which students say are excellent. Some of the smaller departments, like film studies, are, according to some undergrads, not as well maintained by the university. The School of Nursing requires students to work at hospitals in the community, an experience described by one student as "incredible, incomparable to any amount of class time." The five-year joint bachelor/master's degree offered by the School of Education provides students with many opportunities to work in the Boston community while studying closely with professors. The very selective School of Management is said to be the most demanding and competitive.

Students can take classes in any one of the departments, and have access to a wide variety of programs. One of these is PULSE, which requires four classes a year and 12 hours of volunteer work a week, and which satisfies the theology and philosophy core. There are also many university-run foreign-exchange and Immersion programs, in which undergrads can experience a different culture.

> "Every night during finals, everyone leans out of his or her window and . . . screams."

All of the classes are said to be challenging. According to one student, "in order to do well, you have to learn something, both about the subject and about yourself." The specialized classes within the majors are reportedly small and personal; many of the courses are taught by priests who, in the words of one sophomore, "reach out to students. Everyone is encouraged to think for themselves, to find out who they are." Many students were surprised by the dedication of the professors. "The faculty takes care of you," said one undergrad.

Busy Days, Busier Nights
Don't get the impression that Boston College is all about academics, however. There are tons of extracurricular activities for undergraduates, most of which are showcased at Activities Day. (Where else in the Northeast can you find a Surf Club?) Since there are so many activities, everyone pretty much does something. Intramural and club sports are very big, as is student government. The college also sponsors several events. In the last year, guest speakers to Boston College have included Cornell West, Oliver Stone, and Danny Glover. There are also dances, such as the formal Spring Fest, and "Who's on First," a freshman/sophomore semiformal. The student government also puts on concerts and movies.

Sports are also a very big part of college life. During football season, according to one sophomore fan, life revolves around the games. The two biggest events of the year are homecoming and the Notre Dame football game. Football is not the be all and end all of sports at BC, however; the basketball and hockey teams draw almost as much support and revelry.

Boston College has a well-developed social scene, although as one female junior lamented, "nobody dates." BC students claim to have the best of both worlds: they can stay on-campus or venture into downtown Boston, easily accessible by public transportation (BC has its own subway stop). The city is their playground and its stores, restaurants, museums, and nightclubs are at their fingertips.

Naturally, there are also a lot of parties, both on-campus and off. The administration's strictly enforced zero-tolerance policy of no kegs on-campus does not prevent underage BCers from having a good time. Students are quick to point out that both people who drink and people who don't will be able to fit in and have fun. According to one junior, "There is always a party, even on weeknights. You will not be bored." Major sporting events are also calls for celebration at BC. Seniors and juniors, at least those over twenty-one, frequent Boston bars such as Mary Ann's and Great Scott's, while freshmen and sophomores go to private events or Harvard Square. There are no visible hard drugs on-campus, although "weed is big and so are 'shrooms." There are no fraternities or sororities, a detail praised by students who prefer the "nonexclusive way this place works."

Undergrads describe the typical BC student as "preppie." In recent years the ethnic minority population is increasing, but the campus is still predominantly white. Several ethnicity-oriented clubs exist and are active on-campus.

Life In A Big City

Most Boston College students agree that the campus is beautiful. Located on Chestnut Hill, the campus consists of four divisions: Upper Campus, Lower Campus, Middle Campus, and Newton-campus. All are close to one another with the exception of Newton, which is about a mile-and-a-half shuttle ride away. Students say the third of the entering freshman class who live on Newton may feel isolated, but they have "much much much nicer rooms." In general, the freshman dorms at BC are "average." Sophomores have a lottery for apartment-rooms in one of two new dorm buildings, while lucky seniors live in the "Mods," which "look like cottages." According to one hopeful junior, "That's where all the action is." Since only School of Nursing students and privileged members of the School of Arts and Sciences, namely athletes and honors students, are guaranteed on-campus housing for all four years, most juniors live off-campus. The undergraduate rooms range from "a hole in the wall" to luxury accommodations complete with air-conditioning, carpeting, and kitchenettes. It all depends on the luck of the draw.

Surprisingly enough, BCers actually like the campus food. The dining halls are described as being clean and comfortable, and the food is rumored to be very good (some food, like that of Upper Campus, seem to be the exception). Freshmen are usually surprised to find so much variety in the cafeterias. Undergrads say there is everything a person could want, from hamburgers and fries to gourmet dishes.

Like many urban and suburban campuses, Boston College has a well-designed security system that, although described as "very tight," is appreciated by students, who feel safe and taken care of. That feeling of being looked after may come in part from the presence of the Jesuit fathers. The priests not only teach, but also live in the dorms with the students. Students agree that the fathers are normal people, and that "they care about what happens to every student" without seeming overbearing or intrusive.

Most Boston College undergrads love their school's mix of academic work and play. BC is a place for people who want to learn about everything and who want to have fun. A word of advice: When you ask BC students if they like their school, or if they would choose it again if they could start over, don't expect anything but an emphatic YES!—*Tamara Whalen and Staff*

FYI

The three best things about attending BC are "location, parties, extracurriculars"

The three worst things about attending BC are "jocks, preppie students, large lectures."

The three things that every student should do before graduating from BC are "participate in extracurriculars, take advantage of professors' office hours, visit the Doug Flutie tribute in the gym."

One thing I'd like to have known before coming here is "at times, social situations can be cliquey, like in high school."

B o s t o n   U n i v e r s i t y

Address: 121 Bay State Road, Boston, MA 02215
Phone: 617-353-2300
E-mail address: admissions@bu.edu
Web site URL: www.bu.edu
Location: urban
Founded: 1839
Private or Public: private
Religious affiliation: none
Undergraduate enrollment: 15,873
Total enrollment: 28,487
Percent Male / Female: 42% / 58%
Percent Minority: 24.0%
Percent African-American: 4.0%

Percent Hispanic: 6.0%
Percent Asian: 14.0%
Percent in-state / out-of-state: 23% / 77%
Percent Pub HS: 72%
Fraternities: 30%
Sororities: 40%
Number of Applicants: 28,090
Percent Accepted: 55%
Percent Accepted who enroll: 27%
Entering: 4,225
Transfers: 557
Application Deadline: 1 Jan
Mean SAT: 636 V, 640 M

Middle 50% SAT range: 590–680 V, 680–690 M
Middle 50% ACT range: 26–29
Mean ACT: 28
3 Most popular majors: soc sciences, bus adm. / commerce / mgmt., mass communications
Retention: 85
Graduation rate: 66
Library: 2.1 million
Tuition and Fees: $25,044 in; $25,044 out
Room and Board: $8,450
On-campus housing: 100%
Financial aid, first-year: 58%

Located in one of the country's best college towns, Boston University prides itself on its location. In fact, it's often a key factor in many students' college choice. Not only do students love and enjoy Boston and the variety it offers, but they also enjoy the variety at BU itself. With 25 different schools of study, BU caters to a range of academic appetites. And with a population of nearly 30,000 students, the size of the student body affords everyone an opportunity to find a niche.

25 Choices!

Even before freshmen arrive on-campus, they are placed in one of BU's 25 schools. The most popular choice is the College of Arts and Sciences. With its recently built facilities, BU's School of Management is considered one the university's strongest schools. Also, the College of Communications has its own radio and television stations to give students hands-on experience in media. Students seeking a greater challenge have the opportunity to participate in the University Professors Program, which allows a small number of students to work one-on-one with a professor in a specific field for their four years. Students are also able to broaden their educational horizons through many study-abroad programs. However, those whose academic interests are not well defined can enter the College of General Studies, which gives students an opportunity to figure out which interest they would like to pursue.

When undergrads really need to study, they head to Mugar Memorial Library, the campus's main library. According to students, the higher you go at Mugar, the less social and more intense the atmosphere. Other libraries include the Martin Luther King Library, Beebe Library, and the Science Library.

"Prison" Living

When it comes to housing, BU underclassmen get the short end of the stick. Students complain about power failures and slow elevators. Because it is an urban campus, security is rather tight, as well. "It's like we're in prison or something," one student said. The slightly more comfortable upperclassmen dorms are arranged in suites, some with private bathrooms. One dorm, Warren Towers, is home to more than 1,700 students and is the largest dorm facility in the United States. "Although someone on the outside may think that it is overwhelming, I love it," one freshman said. "There are always new people to meet in addition to your closest friends, some of whom are bound to live near you." The food at BU was ranked second in the nation, and students applaud the dining facilities for offering diverse dining options. Meal plans vary as much as the food selections. Different plans allow students to eat at George Sherman Union, order from Domino's Pizza, visit the Late Night Cafe at the GSU, and put these purchases on their meal card. In addition to campus dining, there is no shortage of local restaurants at BU. Students can eat at nearby places such as Pizzeria Uno and Taco Bell or at myriad restaurants in Boston.

Metropolitan Campus
Because BU is in the city, security is an important issue. Police officers patrol the campus, and well-lit walkways are posted with blue-light emergency phones. Security is also enforced in the dorms, where students are governed by strict rules. When guests visit at night they must sign in and leave before midnight. Students often complain about this rule, but on this open campus, they also are very concerned with safety. As one student said, "My dorm is right smack in the middle of the city, homeless people live right outside." Many students also noted the importance of choosing to live near the particular college in which you are enrolled. By living within walking distance, it makes things more safe and convenient. The social scene at BU is very diverse. Students feel a connection with both the university and the surrounding city. "When someone asks me if they would fit in at BU, the only response I could honestly give is that I strongly feel that anyone can fit in at BU because it is a big school in a big city, and it offers a wide and varied student body and social scene," said one student. In addition, the student government and administration have been working hard in the recent past to promote student unity and connection to the school community. They have planned barbeques, luaus, outdoor movie

screenings, and formals, among others activities.

BU students participate in a number of extracurricular activities. Many work on the student newspaper, the *Daily Free Press*, which is a popular publication circulated on-campus and throughout Boston. Support groups such as the African-American Association also attract an active membership. Intramural sports also appeal to students, who find them enjoyable yet low-key, requiring no great time commitment.

> "Anyone can fit in at BU because it's a big school in a big city."

BU students like watching their nationally acclaimed hockey team, the Terriers, during the winter months, especially when they play against rival Boston College. BU has a fraternity system, but it has minimal impact on the social scene. In an attempt to dodge the campus's strict drinking rules and host many parties, most frat houses are off-campus. Drinking is a large part of the scene at Boston University. Despite the recent alcohol ban in all Massachusetts state schools, students say alcohol can be found off-campus. Those who don't drink can find plenty to occupy their time socially in the city. Boston's transit system, the T, provides quick, cheap access to all areas of Boston, and cultural offerings like theater and art museums are free of charge to BU students. Clubs are popular, as are Red Sox games and many other city activities. "At some schools, social life revolves solely around frat parties or something else," one student said. "At BU, I have gone to clubs, bars, fraternity parties, cultural events, and sporting events. I never get bored."

Boston University is one of the largest private schools in the country. Its location and size present students with numerous opportunities for both academic and social growth. Career and internship opportunities abound. Students love their city, but some find the BU scene large and difficult to break into. It is up to each student to pursue his or her own interests at BU.
—*Ellen Moskowitz and Staff*

Brandeis University

Address: 415 South St., MS003, Waltham, MA 02254
Phone: 781-736-3500
E-mail address: sendinfo@brandeis.edu
Web site URL: www.brandeis.edu
Location: suburban
Founded: 1948
Private or Public: private
Religious affiliation: none
Undergraduate enrollment: 3,112
Total enrollment: 4,527
Percent Male/Female: 44%/56%
Percent Minority: 14.2%

Percent African-American: 2.0%
Percent Hispanic: 2.5%
Percent Asian: 9.7%
Percent in-state/out-of-state: 26%/74%
Percent Pub HS: 70%
Fraternities: 0%
Sororities: 0%
Number of Applicants: 5,792
Percent Accepted: 52%
Percent Accepted who enroll: 27%
Entering: 793
Transfers: 51
Application Deadline: 31 Jan

Mean SAT: 660 V, 660 M
Middle 50% SAT range: 610–710 V, 610–710 M
Middle 50% ACT range: NA
Mean ACT: NA
3 Most popular majors: psychology, biology, economics
Retention: 89.0%
Graduation rate: 73.0%
Library: 1 million volumes
Tuition and Fees: $24,421 in; $24,421 out
Room and Board: $7,040
On-campus housing: 99%
Financial aid, first-year: 45%

When people think of academic excellence in the Boston area, the names Harvard and MIT automatically come to mind. However, not far from those two schools, in Waltham, Massachusetts, is Brandeis University, a comparatively young university well known for its academic intensity, driven students, and renowned faculty. While its reputation may not be as tremendous as its neighbors, Brandeis refuses to be overshadowed by any of its competitors.

Classes

Classes at Brandeis are universally described as difficult, although students agree that professors are fair and "generous with the grading." Although one senior glibly remarked that the "grading is too easy. . . . I cannot respect professors who do not fail at least half of the class," many students find the workload extremely heavy.

Brandeis, an institution with a great deal of liberal arts focus as well as one with a devotion to research, does not claim to be easy. Although some students call American studies, history, and philosophy easy majors, sciences and mathematics are considered difficult and outstanding areas of study. Computer science also is a popular department. Academic requirements for all students include three semesters of language training, a writing course, classes in quantitative reasoning, a physical education requirement, and 32 hours of credits chosen from clusters, including Medicine and Social Policy. "There isn't an exceptional amount of flexibility in the core, but the school has done a good job of picking out the stuff that we really need to learn," said one student.

Class sizes vary widely at Brandeis. Some introductory classes such as chemistry and biology enroll as many as 300 students, but most seminars are capped at 20 to 30. Students praise the small classes for their academic rigor as well as for the professors' willingness to allow even non-majors into some advanced sections. Some undergrads praised professors Jacob Cohen in American Studies and Ira Gessel and Paul Monsky in mathematics for close rapport with students. Most of all, commented one senior, "they make you think."

With so much focus on academics, however, some students don't have much time for other activities. Campus extracurricular activities tend to be "diffuse" and "diverse," with organizations as varied as the Green Club, a social- and community-service organization, to "a revolutionary Maoist organization whose members hate greens . . . and get together to eat cookies."

Coffee in the Castle?

For weekend amusement Brandeis students generally find themselves on a quest to popular nearby spots in Waltham and farther away, such as Harvard Square, Faneuil Hall, and the clubs of Boston. "At least one night each weekend is spent in Boston," said one student. "Campus activities are very hard to find, and people from other schools mingle in Boston, so it's a nice way to meet other people." The fraternities, which are not recognized by the university and appeal to a very limited number of Brandeis students, throw theme parties, such as Hawaiian night, for all students and occasional formals for their members. On-campus, a group called Student Events organizes weekend social activities such as a "Screw-Your-Roommate" dance, but attendance tends to be minimal. "On-campus events tend not to be very popular," said one student. "Brandeis is the kind of school where you have to make your own social life. You really have to search for things to do." Campus hangouts, such as The Castle and Cholmondley's, a coffee spot inside the Castle, are popular for socializing as well as study

breaks among students resting their eyes after visits to the main Golfarb-Farber Library or the Gerstenzang Science Library.

The social scene at Brandeis is cliquey, according to students, and one senior joked that although "people who cannot pronounce 'shibboleth' are impaled . . . otherwise, we get along fine." The school is quite diverse, but the student population is predominantly Jewish. "There really isn't any religious or ethnic tension, but if you're Jewish, you are more likely to fit in." One junior praised his schoolmates for what he described as a very healthy ability to harmonize. Dating at Brandeis does not receive high marks, although this was not thought to stem from a lack of places for students to go out together. The academic intensity also spreads to the weekends. "There are a lot of Ivy League rejects here who think that graduate school is a second chance to make it there, so they spend all of their weekends studying," said one student.

> "There really isn't any religious or ethnic tension, but if you're Jewish, you are more likely to fit in."

Students report that although the two dining halls at Brandeis are very nice, the food is not. However, improvements in the diversity and quality of offerings make students optimistic about the future of their dining hall food. Kosher meals are available in a separate cafeteria, but some students complain about limited vegetarian offerings. Food in Waltham and in Boston is better but more expensive.

Most Brandeis students live on-campus, but dorm rooms are guaranteed only for freshmen and sophomores. Residents describe the rooms as "pretty good," and some have kitchens. Freshmen live in coed dorms and generally share double rooms. Upperclass dorms are also coed. There are multiculturally themed houses as well. RAs live in every dorm, but students don't find them "an oppressive form of authority." Students who live off-campus generally rent nearby apartments, primarily populated by graduate students. Security is praised, and students say they feel safe on-campus.

Have Fun—But No Contact Sports

Varsity sports do not play a large role at Brandeis, and the university has no football team, but varsity basketball draws quite a bit of support from the student body. The Gosman Center is a new athletic complex frequented by varsity sports teams and the popular intramural groups alike. This facility has doubled in recent years as a practice venue for the Boston Celtics. The school mascot is the owl, and the teams are named the Judges. "The owl mascot is more valid for the academics than the athletics here," said one student.

Many Brandeis students describe their classmates as "definitely wealthy." Neither predominantly conservative nor liberal, Brandeis is a politically active school. While there is a large Jewish community on-campus, students say the school is far more diverse than many think.

Surrounded by older, prestigious institutions, Brandeis holds its own as a center for intellectual thought. Attaining its stature within the context of a diverse community of students dedicated to academic challenge has created a powerful research university where undergrads can learn and thrive.—*Erik Weiss and Staff*

FYI

The three best things about attending Brandeis are "range of courses offered, small class size, number of student organizations."

The three worst things about attending Brandeis are "interaction between different groups is somewhat limited, bureaucracy, cost."

The three things that every student should do before graduating are "explore the Castle, go to Trisk Dance, chat with Alwina Bennett (Coordinator of Peer Counseling and a personality on campus)."

One thing I'd like to have known before coming here is "there is a segment of the population that is filled with apathy."

Clark University

Address: 950 Main Street, Worcester, MA 01610
Phone: 508-793-7431
E-mail address: admissions@clarku.edu
Web site URL: www.clarku.edu
Location: urban
Founded: 1887
Private or Public: private
Religious affiliation: none
Undergraduate enrollment: 1,928
Total enrollment: 3,003
Percent Male/Female: 41%/59%
Percent Minority: 12.0%

Percent African-American: 4.0%
Percent Hispanic: 4.0%
Percent Asian: 4.0%
Percent in-state/out-of-state: 41%/59%
Percent Pub HS: 80%
Fraternities: 0%
Sororities: 0%
Number of Applicants: 3,236
Percent Accepted: 73%
Percent Accepted who enroll: 21%
Entering: 487
Transfers: 43
Application Deadline: 1 Feb

Mean SAT: 574 V, 566 M
Middle 50% SAT range: 520–630 V, 520–620 M
Middle 50% ACT range: 22–28
Mean ACT: 25
3 Most popular majors: psychology, government, biology
Retention: 87.0%
Graduation rate: 65.0%
Library: 560,836 volumes
Tuition and Fees: $23,300 in; $23,300 out
Room and Board: $4,350
On-campus housing: 95%
Financial aid, first-year: 79%

Cluttering the Clark University campus are posters that display a large pea pod with different colored peas inside. Underneath it reads, "Categorizing people isn't something we do here." This diversity is what draws many students, 14 percent of whom hail from foreign countries, to Clark.

Freudian Slip

Last year, a statue of Freud erected in Red Square, the center of campus, was the subject of heated debate among students. The sculpture commemorates Freud's visit to Clark, the only campus where Freud ever spoke. His presence on campus put Clark's psychology department in the spotlight, and it has traditionally been a popular department with the students. Students also have the opportunity to explore many other departments, because they are required to fulfill a program consisting of classes in eight perspectives: aesthetic, historical, values, language, science, formal analysis, verbal expression, and comparative.

Other popular departments include the new Center for Holocaust Studies, and the interdisciplinary communications and culture major. Professor Bowden, one of the geography department's most respected faculty members, is a favorite among students. One of Bowden's students said, "He is a big part of the reason I chose to minor in geography. Everyone should take a class with him." Students also gave good reviews to the Creative Actor and Medical Ethics classes. Although many regard art as a slacker major, one art student reported that "art classes are much more time consuming and demanding than any other classes I've taken."

Some students claim that academic variety is sacrificed to Clark's small size. This small size, however, allows students to interact more intimately with their professors, who, undergrads say, are down to earth, very understanding, and incredibly approachable. Some professors even incorporate dinners into their classes. TAs do not teach classes, but they are there to help.

Given Clark's sense of internationalism, it's no surprise that the Study Abroad Department is very popular; most students go away during their spring semester of junior year. Popular destinations include Scotland, London, Spain, Africa, and Japan. For those who want to try out being abroad for a shorter amount of time, Clark also participates with The College of the Holy Cross in a month-long May term in Luxembourg.

You Can Do What You Want to Do

Clark's social life is what you make of it. The weekend begins on Thursday since many students don't have class on Fridays. The Clark Student Activities Board lures to campus entertainment acts ranging from bands and comedians to hypnotists. The Clark University Film Society shows second-run movies, and Clark University Players Society puts on theater productions. One of the newest and most popular groups on campus is the improv troupe called the "Peapod Squad." Their popularity has soared and good seats at shows are a hot commodity. Also worth noting are the two a cappella groups, the Counterpoints (all female) and the Clark Bars (coed).

For such an academically motivated school, Clark has an inviting party scene. On weekends, underclassmen flock to crowded parties at upperclassmen's, off-campus houses. Kegs are very common at these parties. Of-age and resourceful underage students frequent the local bars, such as Scarlet O'Hara's. One underclassman admits, "my social life is limited because I do not have a fake ID."

Students maintain that Clark's alcohol policy is pretty lenient. Freshman dorms are dry and no kegs are allowed in campus housing. Students who are 21 are free to drink but no open containers are permitted in public. While campus police enforce this policy, they are not as strict as the Worcester Police. One student said, "Due to the school's location, the school police seem to focus more on safety and less on alcohol policies."

Alcohol's presence at Clark is magnified on Spree Day, which is usually held in April as a celebration of the coming of spring. The date is selected and kept secret by a committee of upperclassmen until that day when they interrupt students' slumber by banging on garbage cans and yelling. Classes are canceled that day as students and staff flock to the Campus Green, which transforms into a carnival. Musical groups like Parliament Funkadelic have played in the past. By five o' clock, most students retire to their rooms to pass out.

Dorms

Campus housing is mandatory for freshmen and sophomores, but decent on-campus options are available. Freshmen have the choice of living in an upperclassman hall or a freshman hall. Freshman halls are louder and more open to socializing than their counterparts. Rooms in the freshman halls, Wright and Bullock, are reportedly small but acceptable, and some say the better social life is worth the cramped living. A senior commented that living in a freshman hall was "the highlight of my four years." Resident Advisors (RAs) in freshman halls try to be your friend, according to one student, but often seem more like police who strictly enforce quiet hours.

Maywood Hall, the newest residence hall, seems to be the most desirable of the upperclassman dorms. It features apartment-style living, with 4 to 6 person suites that consist of bedrooms, a common room, and private bathroom. Unfortunately for freshmen, they are not allowed in Maywood. In addition to the traditional dorms, students can live in theme houses like the Quiet House, the Year-Round House, and the Substance-Free House.

Freshmen and sophomores must be on a meal plan, which consists of boards (individual meals) and flex dollars that give students an account to spend as they choose. Students can eat either in the dining hall or at the Bistro, a deli that offers sandwiches, salads, and grilled food made to order. Some say that food in the dining hall is mediocre, but always suspiciously better when parents and prospective students are around. However, the variety of choices are good, and there is a special vegetarian/vegan section. The sandwich counter is a favorite of many students. The draw of the dining halls is not necessarily the food however; it's a great place to "sit with friends and talk and laugh a lot." Students are not rushed in and out, and mealtimes are considered a social gathering.

Little "Brick" Different

Clark's campus is very compact: a "far" walk on campus takes less than 10 minutes. Most of the buildings are fairly modern and constructed of brick. The Goddard Library (named after Robert Goddard, creator of the rocket) was built to look like an open book from an aerial view. The library's strange shape makes for many interesting hiding places. According to

Rolling Stone magazine, the Goddard Library was Jerry Garcia's favorite place to trip. At the center of campus is Red Square that, due to reconstruction, is no longer red. Right next to Red Square is the Campus Green, a very social place in warm weather where people read, lay out, or play Frisbee.

Dana Commons is the student union and offers a place to e-mail, play Ping-Pong, shoot pool, watch movies, hold meetings, or eat at the Midnight Cafe. The University Center (UC) is home to meeting rooms, the dining hall and Bistro, the mailroom, and the general store. The UC is at the center of campus and is a popular meeting place.

Wormtown

Worcester, is a sizeable industrial city in the middle of Massachusetts, and unfortunately, Clark sits in one of its less desirable areas. As in any big city, safety is a concern at Clark and thus students are encouraged to stay in groups and take advantage of the foot- and car-escort services. The key to staying safe at Clark is to use common sense and lots of caution.

While many students complain about Worcester, the city has its attractive points. The Worcester Centrum is a large concert arena, which hosts shows ranging from Phish to WWF. Worcester has many bars, a few dance clubs, and interesting international restaurants like Thai Cha Da, Dalat, House of India, Cactus Pete's and Tortilla Sam's. No trip to Clark would be complete without a trip to Tatnuck Bookseller and a meal at Wendy's Clark Brunch. Wendy's is a popular Clarkie hangout and is very social. Breakfast is served all day and Annie, the owner and cook, knows the students by names and loves to talk with them.

Worcester's location is close to nature trails, skiing, and Boston. Although Clark provides a shuttle to and from Boston, many students feel that cars are a necessity. Those without cars often borrow friends' cars or resort to begging for rides.

Extracurricular Activities

Clark prides itself on its abundance of clubs and extracurricular activities. Groups range from the Bisexual, Lesbian, and Gay Association (BILAGA), Caribbean American Students Association, the Animal Rights Group, and MASSPIRG (an environmental group). Some clubs sponsor activities such as speakers and discussions. Religion on campus is not overly visible, but Hillel and the Clark Christian Fellowship do exist and help to create a religious community. Also, Clark students are fairly community service oriented. MASSPIRG works closely with the community in environmental contexts and a newly formed group, Rotoract, is based solely on community service.

> According to *Rolling Stone* magazine, the Goddard Library was Jerry Garcia's favorite place to trip.

Many student athletes said that the Clark athletics are under-appreciated and under-funded. Clark is a Division III university that actively recruits athletes, but it does not offer sports scholarships. The men's basketball team and women's soccer teams are the most popular among fans. The softball team, the women's soccer team, and the men's soccer team have all received NCAA tournament bids. Clark has no football team, which tends to prevent any swelling of school spirit. Despite lack of outside appreciation, however, one junior athlete says that "among athletes, everyone is very close and dedicated and driven by a sincere love of the game."

Intramurals are popular, and sometimes become competitive. Pick-up sports like basketball, soccer and Frisbee bring out lots of Clarkies. The student body is fairly health conscious, making the fitness center (with cardiovascular equipment and weights) often very crowded.

Good Things Come in Small Packages

Whether it's a chat with Annie the cook at Wendy's, a quiet evening hidden in Goddard Library, or a frolic on Spree day, Clark provides a small, but delightful, community. While sometimes the town of Worcester can be daunting, Clarkies find that their little peapod is a great place to spend their four years of college.
—*Jessica Bondell*

FYI
The three best things about attending Clark are "the diversity of students, small classes, and great professors."
The three worst things about attending Clark are "the high costs, Worcester, and lack of school spirit."
The three things every student should do before graduating from Clark are "get something pierced, eat at Wendy's Clark Brunch, and take a nap on the green."
One thing I'd like to have known before coming here is "how small the school feels after a few short years."

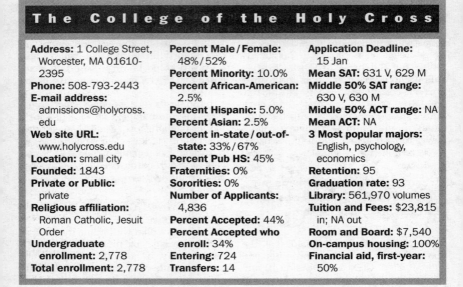

The College of the Holy Cross

Address: 1 College Street, Worcester, MA 01610-2395
Phone: 508-793-2443
E-mail address: admissions@holycross.edu
Web site URL: www.holycross.edu
Location: small city
Founded: 1843
Private or Public: private
Religious affiliation: Roman Catholic, Jesuit Order
Undergraduate enrollment: 2,778
Total enrollment: 2,778

Percent Male/Female: 48%/52%
Percent Minority: 10.0%
Percent African-American: 2.5%
Percent Hispanic: 5.0%
Percent Asian: 2.5%
Percent in-state/out-of-state: 33%/67%
Percent Pub HS: 45%
Fraternities: 0%
Sororities: 0%
Number of Applicants: 4,836
Percent Accepted: 44%
Percent Accepted who enroll: 34%
Entering: 724
Transfers: 14

Application Deadline: 15 Jan
Mean SAT: 631 V, 629 M
Middle 50% SAT range: 630 V, 630 M
Middle 50% ACT range: NA
Mean ACT: NA
3 Most popular majors: English, psychology, economics
Retention: 95
Graduation rate: 93
Library: 561,970 volumes
Tuition and Fees: $23,815 in; NA out
Room and Board: $7,540
On-campus housing: 100%
Financial aid, first-year: 50%

Steeped in tradition and Jesuit ideals, the College of the Holy Cross offers students a strong liberal arts education in a close-knit, nurturing setting.

Intense Academics

Holy Cross offers students a rigorous liberal arts education, grounded in competition between students and close interaction with professors. Through its distributional requirements, the school makes students as well-rounded as possible: everyone must take one class in religion, history, philosophy, literature, the arts, math, science (or two classes in either math or science), and two classes in the social sciences. Students generally find the requirements beneficial, and many take advantage of AP credit to wave survey courses. Most students at Holy Cross take their classes very seriously, and competition for good grades is intense. On top of this, grading is extremely difficult. According to one freshman, "There are no easy majors, and there is no grade inflation at all. I heard that there hasn't been a 4.0 in ten years." The competition is balanced by open access to professors, who tend to be genuinely interested in students' academic careers and active in helping them to do well. One student raves that "I have yet to meet a professor who wasn't interested in the success of his students." Furthermore, TAs never teach classes, and the small class size (usually between 12 and 24 students) provides an intimate, more engaging learning environment.

Incoming students interested in a course of study concentrated in the humanities can apply to the First Year Program. Every year, 160 students enroll in the program, which includes a 15-person seminar and an emphasis on philosophy and the pursuit of truth and knowledge. Participants report developing a sense of family with their fellow students and 8 professors that comes from living together in the same dorm, Hanselman Hall, and involvement in extra meetings and extracurricular activities. Of FYPpers, as student in the program are called, one student says, "I have yet to meet one who's normal; they are really quirky people." Holy Cross's other special program is a highly selective honors program in which students enroll beginning junior year. Under the guidance of two faculty advisors, fourth-year students in the program devote a quarter of their time to a research project in their major field. In addition to the special academic programs, the administration supplements the educational experience by bringing in guest speakers and lecturers. As one student put it, "there's a different lecture every night."

Student Body: Homogenous but Connected

While for many, the student body is the most attractive aspect of Holy Cross, for others it is the most in need of diversification. The student population is predominantly white, Irish-Catholic, and many feel that this adds to the closeness of the students: ". . . we all have a lot in common in the way of previous experiences. Students can relate to each other pretty well." Other students regret "how homogenous it is," citing the overwhelming presence of white students clad in Abercrombie & Fitch clothing. "If you love hanging around with white, Irish Catholics," remarked one student, "come on down." These students maintain that most at Holy Cross cannot relate to minorities. Generally, however, students feel comfortable and are not bothered by the seeming lack of diversity. They say that there is more racial diversity on campus than one would think, given the stereotype, and they recognize that the administration is taking steps to diversify the student body.

Beyond racial uniformity, students have other problems with the lack of diversity. "There is a problem with homophobia here," said one student. In response to this problem, students have started three support and activist groups for gay students. Other students complain of the lack of creative diversity: "Artists and creative writers would make life a little more interesting."

The unifying and most noticeable quality of the students, however, is not their ethnicity, but rather their personal drive and their intense motivation in all of their pursuits. A universal quality of the students is that they seem to thrive under stress. "I don't really know any slackers," says one student. Whether it's academics, athletics, or extracurriculars, Holy Cross students truly strive for excellence in achievement.

Social Scene

Despite the administration's efforts to curb drinking on campus, it is still "the major part of social life" at Holy Cross. A typical Saturday night for students begins with having a couple of beers in someone's dorm room and then going to Caro Street to hit one off-campus drinking party after another. Students do not see drinking as a problem, but rather as a good balance to the overwhelming workload. "There is a lot of partying," says a freshman at Holy Cross, "but we do a ridiculous amount of work as well." The school is cracking down on drinking, however, and students complain of strict regulations and intrusive police intervention: "The administration is by far the worst part of HC. Their alcohol policies include hiring off-duty police officers to arrest students who party off campus." The regulations have done little to stop students from spending their weekend as they want. Still, upperclassmen warn that "the partying culture can fool a naive freshman into thinking that HC is only about drinking."

For those not intrigued by off-campus parties, the school provides events every weekend to keep campus life fun. "Students can always find something to do," emphasized one undergrad. Movies, guest speakers, shows, and concerts are almost always weekend options. The school has an annual Opportunity Knocks dance, in which students set their roommates up on blind dates. The student Center, Hogan, boasts a bookstore, a popular coffee spot, Cool Beans, and a deli, Crossroads, where students often gather to study or just hang out. Next to Crossroads is the campus pub, where good bands often play. The pub is limited to those over 21, and they are very strict about having ID. Another big part of the social life is the ultimate Frisbee league, which students take very seriously. Every night, two teams square off on the fields; as one spectator stated, "it's a big deal." Students stress that it is generally easy to meet people if you get involved in sports or extracurriculars, and social groups are pretty flexible, although "it gets kind of cliquey around activity groups." Students note that there is no permanent dating scene, "just random one-night stand hookups." There are also no fraternities or sororities, but sports teams fill the role of a Greek System—there are, for example, a soccer house and a rugby house that throw parties and hold events.

Though Worcester is by no means a college town, venturing into the city can expand students' social options. Some students complain of the lack of a bar scene and say flat out that "Worcester sucks, there is no night life at all," while others praise the vast array of restaurants and shopping malls. One student calls Worcester "the diner capital of the Northeast." Worcester also has some good clubs such as The Source, which is especially fun on Thursday nights. The Palladium is reportedly "a great place to check out some great bands," and the Centrum is a larger venue for bigger concerts and events. Without a car, however, it is difficult to get off campus and into Worcester. The problems that students have with Worcester often pertain to being portrayed as party animals and the police, who "exist only to nail HC students."

Campus Life

The most striking aspect of the campus at Holy Cross is how "pristine" it looks, according to students. On the outskirts of Worcester and separated from the city by a large iron fence, the campus is set on a hill, with the dorms, administration buildings, classroom buildings, and the Hart Center (the athletic center) rising respectively above one another. The campus greenery is impressive, and "it seems that the grass is cut every other day." One student remarked that "the physical plant guys must be obsessive-compulsive." The Hart Center was recently remodeled to include a Wellness Center with state-of-the-art fitness equipment. The athletic facilities also include an Olympic-size swimming pool, a basketball court, and a hockey rink which most Holy Cross students make use of. Beyond 25 varsity sports such as the championship level women's basketball team, students can participate in one of 17 club sports or work out in the gym. Most people do some kind of physical activity at Holy Cross.

Overall students agree that the dormitories are comfortable. Freshmen and sophomores get doubles with two desks, two beds which can be beds, Ethernet, and cable television. Wheeler is the oldest dorm on campus and is known as the party dorm. "Kids are really friendly there," said one student. Students in the First Year Program all live in Hanselman Hall, one of the nicest "hill" dorms. Juniors and seniors have the option of moving off campus, but most stay on campus and live in Alumni and Carlin, dorms with all quads—with two big bedrooms and a large common room. Students can choose in any year to enter substance-free housing in Loyola, which "has really nice rooms and facilities." Dorms are coed, with alternating male and female floors. For safety purposes, a key-card is required to get into the dorm buildings and into the hallways. That is, guys cannot get into female floors without the permission of the girls on the floor. As one student notes, however, "the doors are often propped open, and if they're not, you just wait a few minutes until someone goes out the door."

Dining at Holy Cross is decent, and there is one gigantic dining hall—Kimball. Students choose between all-you-can-eat dining hall food upstairs in Kimball and a food court downstairs. There is also a campus restaurant, but a good reason is usually needed for meal transfer. Students can also go off campus to eat in one of the city's many restaurants.

> "There is a lot of partying, but we do a ridiculous amount of work as well."

Campus life at Holy Cross is made complete by student involvement in extracurricular activities. Beyond academics and athletic activities, students are active in everything from the campus newspaper—the *Crusader*—to a mock trial team and Model United Nations. "Pretty much everyone is involved in extracurriculars," said one student. As with their studies, students are "really dedicated" to their outside activities, and they are often defined by what they participate in. Their friends become those whom they associate with in these activities. While there is not much political activism at the college, volunteering and outreach to the city are very popular. There are several community programs, and "the Jesuit ideal of service really does live in the hearts of HC students." With an education and philosophy rooted in Jesuit ideals and the closeness between students, "HC is a place where you can get very involved," a setting in which determined and talented students will undoubtedly thrive.—*Chiraag Bains*

FYI

The three best things about attending Holy Cross are "the professors, the beautiful campus, and the connection with my classmates."

The three worst things about attending Holy Cross are "Worcester residents, Worcester, and Mount St. James."

The three things that every student should do before graduating are "check out Caro Street on a Saturday night, go to the Opportunity Knocks dance, and play a good game of dorm Assassins."

One thing I'd like to have known before coming here is "you are stuck on campus freshman and sophomore year unless you know someone with a car."

Hampshire College

Address: Admissions Office, 893 West Street, Amherst, MA 01002

Phone: 413-559-5471

E-mail address: admissions@hampshire.edu

Web site URL: www.hampshire.edu

Location: rural

Founded: 1965

Private or Public: private

Religious affiliation: none

Undergraduate enrollment: 1,160

Total enrollment: 1,160

Percent Male/Female: 44%/56%

Percent Minority: 11.0%

Percent African-American: 4.0%

Percent Hispanic: 3.0%

Percent Asian: 4.0%

Percent in-state/out-of-state: 21%/79%

Percent Pub HS: 54%

Fraternities: 0%

Sororities: 0%

Number of Applicants: 1,854

Percent Accepted: 65%

Percent Accepted who enroll: 25%

Entering: 335

Transfers: 111

Application Deadline: 1 Feb

Mean SAT: 647 V, 592 M

Middle 50% SAT range: NA

Middle 50% ACT range: NA

Mean ACT: NA

3 Most popular majors: art, theater, creative writing

Retention: 77.0%

Graduation rate: 38.0%

Library: 110,000 volumes

Tuition and Fees: $24,984 in; $24,984 out

Room and Board: $6,622

On-campus housing: 99%

Financial aid, first-year: 53%

If you ever thought that you were born in the wrong era, that you would have been better off growing up in the liberal days of the 1960s, then Hampshire College is likely for you. Hampshire and its students defy classification and are as liberal as can be imagined. However, underlying this environment of seemingly little responsibility is an academic plan that requires an immense amount of individual care and attention.

A Unique Education

Hampshire students benefit from several unique features of the college; namely, its focus on individual learning, the absence of tests and grades, and the college's membership in the Massachusetts Five College Consortium. Hampshire students engage in an individualized course of study as soon as they arrive on-campus. The academic structure of Hampshire consists of three divisions. Students must complete work in each division to graduate. First, students must complete coursework in the four schools of Division 1: humanities and arts, natural science, social science, and cognitive science. In those four schools, students can complete coursework either through formal classes or by doing projects. "It's possible to graduate Hampshire without ever taking a class," said one student.

Division 2 requirements constitute the coursework that makes up a students major. Students pick an advisor with whom they work on a portfolio of their projects and research. Projects can take the form of internships, artistic creations, classwork, or study abroad. Once a student has completed Division 2, he moves on to Division 3, in which the student completes the equivalent of a senior thesis or project in his or her concentration. Students normally work on their Division 3 project for an entire year, consulting constantly with faculty members. One student noted that "all the professors here are very willing to work and they know their fields of study incredibly well." In place of grades, students at Hampshire receive detailed critiques of their work.

Hampshire's small size and liberal bent on academia creates an environment in which individual learning is encouraged. As a result, however, departments are scattered and often lack focus and resources. To compensate, Hampshire is a member of the Five College Consortium, and shares resources with Smith College, Mount Holyoke College, Amherst College, and the University of Massachusetts at Amherst. "Hampshire might not have the depth of the fields, but the Five College system makes up for it. We have access to their classes, resources, and professors, and a bus runs through the Five College circuit every half hour," said one student; another student found that most Hampshire students take advantage of the consortium.

The uniqueness of Hampshire's academic structure has received both praise and criticism from students. "It takes a really unique kid to do well here, because it's so easy to do nothing and stick around for eight years, as a lot of kids do," said one student. "You have to have an immense drive and take a real responsibility for getting an education. No one here is going to hand anything to you." For those students who do take that responsibility, however, the experience can be very rewarding. "It's the best educational idea I've ever heard," said one student. "It's basically laissez-faire applied to a college. I've never seen anyplace like it, and you learn so much more here about everything academic and nonacademic than at a conventional school because you design your entire education."

Social Life

The social scene at Hampshire is just as liberal as the academic scene. According to one student's estimate, half the Hampshire population is made up of "hippies," meaning "they don't bathe, they have dreadlocks and listen to the Grateful Dead." Vegetarians and vegans make up a majority of the population, and recreational drug use is not unheard of. Students at Hampshire get along incredibly well and, according to one student, "everything here is okay as long as you believe in it. No one is unapproachable." The campus is increasingly diverse, and there is little to no racial or sexual-orientation tension. Minorities feel very comfortable on-campus. "Everyone at Hampshire seems to be bisexual. It's a running joke," said one student. Religion is not very big at Hampshire, but there is a predominance of Jews. "The Yiddish Book Center is based at Hampshire," said one student, "I suppose that draws a lot of Jews here. It's really the only active religion. Atheism is second to Judaism."

The Hampshire administration contributes to this cooperative, permissive atmosphere. "The administration really does not comment. If it does not harm anyone, then they think it's okay," said one student. "Officially they would have to condemn it, but we don't really have rules. We go by community standards and campus norms."

Some of those norms would not be norms at any other school. The most popular club on-campus is the Bondage and S&M club, and the most popular event each year is the Drag Ball, for which students dress in drag and local drag queens come and perform. And Hampshire Halloween was named by *Rolling Stone* as one of the best parties of the year.

Student interests range from the mainstream to the fringe. "This might be the only place that you'll hear the Grateful Dead, Miles Davis, and hardcore Gothic music simultaneously while watching *Dawson's Creek* and obscure German art films in one night," said one student.

Living it Up

Housing at Hampshire offers a large number of options. Students can live in dorms or modular housing. Dorms have mostly singles, and students are guaranteed rooms there. In the dorms, there are several theme halls, including lesbian and gay, clothing-optional, substance-free, and study-intensive options. Mods offer greater diversity. There are five mods, each of which has its own characteristic population. For example, the hippies on-campus live in Endfield while the more academically oriented students stay in Greenwich. All students must live on-campus for the entirety of their Hampshire education. "The dorms are very social. All the bathrooms and halls are co-ed," said one student. "People love living in dorms." There are residential assistants in the two dorms who, according to one student, "are supposed to carry out the policies of the housing office, but don't really care what you do."

The housing buildings like the other buildings on-campus, are described by students as "ugly." However, the setting of the school is idyllic. Hampshire is situated on what used to be an apple orchard and is surrounded by woods. The administration is currently building a student center, and is constantly improving classroom and academic work space. The building for which Hampshire is known, however, is its "Yurt," a Mongolian shack made of animal skins. The building, which started out as a former Hampshire student's Division 3 project, currently boasts heat and an Internet connection.

All students in dorms and many students living in mods eat at Saga, the large cafeteria on-campus, whose food is provided by Marriott. The food gets poor ratings from students: "The motto here is, Saga: where food goes to die." However, Saga does offer a large array of options, including many vegetarian and vegan dishes. "They know their audience well," said one student. The nearby presence of the other member colleges of the consortium led to an abundance of restaurants

catering to college students, so there are a large number of businesses that deliver food until 3 or 4 in the morning.

On weekends, Hampshire students often split their time between Hampshire proper and the nearby towns of Northampton, Amherst, and, two hours away, Boston. On-campus, students often go to the Ash Auditorium, a large cultural center that has hosted the likes of Blonde Redhead and Lou Barlow of Sebadoh in the recent past. Mods also throw parties almost every weekend. Students often go into Amherst, Northampton, and Boston for a wider offering of social options. However, there is little social mingling between the Consortium colleges. "You have your friends from the classes you take at other schools, but that's about it," said one student. "Most of the time, you'll just see them in Amherst or Boston on the weekends anyway." There are often fraternity parties at UMass, but Hampshire students "would never even think of going."

> According to one student's estimate, half the Hampshire population is made up of "hippies," meaning "they don't bathe, they have dreadlocks, and listen to the Grateful Dead."

Since the fraternity scene is obviously not an option at Hampshire, students have to find other ways to keep themselves busy. Two campus newspapers, *Omen* and *Foreword*, are well-read on-campus, and the Hampshire Community Council works to "determine policy as much as student organizations can." The most popular activities on-campus are theater and music. Theater students tend to stick together and hang out on weekends. Musicians, however, wander from group to group. "There are some pretty amazing musicians here, and everyone is willing to play with everyone else," said one student. "There are no organized, formal bands. You make your own, put up a poster, and get a lot of responses." Musicians frequently play in four or five groups simultaneously.

The focus on arts leaves little room for athletics on-campus. "Athletics are sort of looked down upon here, but, as with everything else, no one really cares," said one student. Hampshire is part of the New England Small Schools League and competes against other schools with less than 1,500 students in Ultimate Frisbee and basketball. "Ultimate is immense here, our basketball team is a joke, and football is nonexistent," said one student. "But watch out as you walk on-campus. I've gotten hit by at least 100 Frisbees in my two years here."

Students at Hampshire revel in their freedom and uniqueness. They are able to create an idiosyncratic social and academic scene while drawing on the academic offerings of four other schools and the cultural offerings of two nearby towns and one nearby city. If you are self-motivated and interested in learning more outside the classroom than inside, Hampshire is likely for you.—*Alan Schoenfeld and Staff*

FYI

The three best things about attending Hampshire are "very understanding professors, 850 acre campus yet nothing is farther than a 2.5 minute walk, Yiddish Book Center."

The three worst things about attending Hampshire are "optional showering and optional smell, excessive pot smoking, and (relatedly) lack of Visine in school book store, which happens to sell lesbian and gay porn but no straight porn."

The three things that every student should do before graduating from Hampshire are "spend a lot of time at the Hampshire Tree, fall asleep in Franklin-Patterson Hall, sample the delicate fare of Saga."

One thing I'd like to have known before coming here is "despite the fact that Amherst is close, civilization is far, far away."

Harvard University

Address: Byerly Hall, 8 Garden Street, Cambridge, MA 02318

Phone: 617-495-1551

E-mail address: college@fas.harvard.edu

Web site URL: www.fas.harvard.edu

Location: urban

Founded: 1636

Private or Public: private

Religious affiliation: none

Undergraduate enrollment: 6,704

Total enrollment: 18,103

Percent Male/Female: 54%/46%

Percent Minority: 36.0%

Percent African-American: 9.0%

Percent Hispanic: 8.0%

Percent Asian: 19.0%

Percent in-state/out-of-state: 16%/84%

Percent Pub HS: 65%

Fraternities: 0%

Sororities: 0%

Number of Applicants: 16,818

Percent Accepted: 12%

Percent Accepted who enroll: 79%

Entering: 1,643

Transfers: 79

Application Deadline: 1 Jan

Mean SAT: NA

Middle 50% SAT range: 700–790 V, 690–790 M

Middle 50% ACT range: NA

Mean ACT: NA

3 Most popular majors: government, economics, biology

Retention: 96.0%

Graduation rate: 97.0%

Library: 13 million volumes

Tuition and Fees: $21,342 in; $21,342 out

Room and Board: $7,514

On-campus housing: 100%

Financial aid, first-year: 52%

It is 3 A.M., and the snow is piling on your bedroom window ledge. You are exhausted and frustrated. You only have five more hours before lab, and you still have not cracked your chem problem set. You would like to ask your roommate for help, but she is constantly trembling from her caffeine addiction, and besides, she might reset your alarm clock for 9:30 A.M. if you seem distracted.

While one undergrad laughed at the ludicrousness of this scenario, she sighed and admitted that "there is some truth to the piling snow and the hour of night." Although Harvard often gets the reputation of having a cutthroat, intellectual-elitist environment, one undergrad said that "the competition is really with yourself. All pressure is self-inflicted; I guess we're all cursed with the desire to do well." But it's this "curse" among students that upholds and strengthens Harvard's outstanding academic reputation, which attracts notables such as Nelson Mandela and the UN secretary general to speak on-campus. And celebrities aren't the only ones drawn to the Harvard name; every year an extremely high percentage of accepted students decide to matriculate there, and undergrads say that "the 'I'm going to Harvard' thing is a pretty big deal." However, besides the "Harvard name," the achievements of Harvard's world-renowned faculty and alumni as well as its honored traditions continue to woo prospective students into prestigious Harvard Yard.

Professors and Grad Students

Undergrads rarely complain about the illustrious Harvard faculty, and most are quick to praise Harvard's academics, but benefiting from Harvard's academics largely depends on self-motivation and your teaching fellows (TFs), graduate students pursuing their Ph.D.s. One student noted that "while TFs are meant only as a supplementary resource to professors' lectures, all one-on-one interaction happens with them. So, it's really important that you find enthusiastic TFs." Lectures are where "professors speak; you listen," one undergrad said, "and discussion sections are where you work through the material."

However, at Harvard, when professors speak, students always listen, because they are nearly always renowned in their field. As an undergrad, students can take African-American studies from Henry Louis Gates or Introductory Economics from former presidential economic advisor Martin Feldstein. Lectures might enroll "several hundred students or only 17;

the numbers really depend on the level of the course and the popularity of the professor," noted an undergrad. The smaller classes are mandatory freshman expository writing courses, seminars, and language classes. These "smaller courses are harder to get in to, and sometimes people get locked out," one student said. After undergrads declare their concentration (Harvard's term for the major), "it's easier to get into smaller classes within your concentration," one sophomore noted. During sophomore year students usually take a "tutorial," which is a seminar that brings students and professors closer together within each department. If a student wants to graduate with honors, and most do, taking these "tutorials" in addition to writing a senior thesis is required.

Before graduating, Harvard students must complete a core curriculum. Students must take courses in 8 out of 10 core disciplines, including courses in literature and humanities, natural sciences, foreign cultures, and social analysis. Generally, students "enjoy fulfilling the core requirements," noted an undergraduate, "because it gives you an opportunity to take a class you'd never really take unless you had to." Many students respect the theory behind the core curriculum, which is to introduce students to intellectual prospectives of a variety of departments. "Overall, people don't really gripe about the required courses," one student said, "a course on listening to classical music has been one of my favorites." Harvard also requires students to demonstrate proficiency in a foreign language, pass a statistics exam, and complete a freshman expository writing course.

In order to help students find the "fun classes," Harvard has the "Q-Guide" and "Shopping Period." The "Q-Guide," officially the Harvard University Course Evaluation Guide, is a catalog compiled by students that rates different characteristics of a course, such as the professor, readings, lectures, and overall competitive atmosphere. "It's a respected guide, and most students use it to choose courses," one undergrad said. Students can also determine which classes they want to add to their schedules by "shopping" for courses. "Shopping Period" is a week at the beginning of each semester during which students can sit in on different classes before deciding on what to take.

Perhaps the most common gripe from Harvard students is the school's final exam schedule. Instead of taking place before winter break in December, final exams do not occur until students return in January. Thus, each year undergrads leave campus for the holidays with unfinished papers and final exams hanging over them. This may seem like a nightmare, but one student noted that "it's really not that bad. We have a two-week reading period after break, and that's usually enough time to catch up on reading, so you don't feel burdened over break."

Out in the Yard

While Harvard may focus on its academics, undergraduate life is not necessarily centered only in the classroom. Students claim that the classroom is just one arena for their education. "About half of our time is spent on academics and the other half is for extracurricular activities," one undergrad remarked. The list of Harvard student organizations is extensive, and students can do anything from writing for a travel guidebook to acting in a theater troupe. One student reported. "There's so much stuff you can do that it would be a waste not to pursue some of it." Students also noted the range of students' interests; "you can pretty much find someone with an interest in anything," a student observed, "and usually an 'interest' means they've written a book or something." Getting involved in Harvard's organizations, publications in particular, can require "comping," the application process students complete to demonstrate their skill and commitment to an organization. Other extracurricular activities include a cappella groups, crew (particularly for freshmen), and community service. Most service groups work under Phillips Brooks House, where "there are a hundred different projects that constantly are looking for eager volunteers."

Other attractions of student life can be found outside of Harvard's gates. Students often take the twenty-minute T (subway) ride to Boston's museums, symphonies, restaurants, and clubs. A freshman acknowledged that "whether or not you go into Boston a lot, it's great to know that it's there." Students who don't want to venture as far can also find plenty to do around Cambridge. Harvard Square is home to various shops, bookstores, cafes, and restaurants, in addition to the "many interesting entertainers that frequent the newsstand," one student said, referring to the center of Harvard Square. Although most bars near Harvard are strict on IDs, on-campus parties usually offer an outlet for beer-drinking and socializing. Each residential house also hosts several dances and parties throughout the year. Generally, though, one student stressed that "Harvard is not a party school at all. There are some who probably never go out," and students looking for a party scene tend to seek it "in nearby Boston and at MIT." Also on-campus, Harvard's "finals clubs," that are upscale fraternities, host social events. However, these all-male clubs, such as the Fly, throw weekend keg parties that are often invitation-only for males and open to all females.

Despite remnants of the old-boy, aristocratic Harvard, such as the finals clubs, Harvard's student body is made up of people from all over the world with varied and fascinating backgrounds. One freshman was surprised at the number of attractive and "cool" people he met at Harvard; another commented that "maybe you don't see the people you thought Harvard was made up of, because they're all in their rooms studying all the time."

Building Blocks

After most freshmen spend their first year living in suites on Harvard Yard, students form "blocking groups" with up to 16 friends. Each group is randomly assigned to one of 12 houses, where the students live for their remaining three years, except for the few students who live off-campus. Each house, which ranges architecturally from traditional to modern, has its own dining room, library, computer room, and special facilities like dark rooms or recording studios. Dining options at Harvard also include Annenberg (where most freshmen eat) and several cafes around campus, such as William James Hall Cafe, the Greenhouse (which now delivers pizza), and Conroy Commons. Freshmen often socialize at Loker Commons, located downstairs from Annenberg at the heart of Harvard Yard, where there is a food court, pool tables, and cable TV. At these cafes and at various campus stores, students can purchase items with Crimson Cash, a debit account set up using students' Harvard IDs.

> **"If you get in to Harvard, why would you ever go anywhere else?"**

Outside of Loker Commons and dining halls, students run into friends at Harvard's libraries. Most study at Lamont Library because it is seen as a study library, while Widener is "more of a research place." Students also often study together and "do a lot of group work for economic, statistics, and science courses;" one freshman noted that "everyone works really hard, and group work is encouraged in certain courses."

There is no question that a Harvard diploma can lead to many opportunities. However, one alumna stressed that graduates still must prove themselves just like everyone else; though an undergrad who works hard at Harvard usually has the skills to succeed in any field. While students report that it is easy to become isolated in such an intense, intellectual atmosphere, students still appreciate the benefits of the Harvard experience. One freshman said Harvard "has been the best experience of my life—the tradition, the education, the people—it has been incredible so far." The talented student body, exciting metropolitan location, and inspiring faculty, imbues Harvard with unsurpassable intellectual excitement and energy. One proud student understandably asked, "If you get in to Harvard, why would you ever go anywhere else?"
—*Leslie Kane and Staff*

FYI

The three best things about Harvard are "the diversity among students, living in the Boston area, the amazing academic resources."

The three worst things about Harvard are "the limited social scene, the food, and the highly stressful atmosphere."

The three things that every student should do before graduating from Harvard are "go to the Harvard-Yale game, sit in on a lecture by Dr. Cornell West, and visit the Grille."

One thing I'd like to have known before coming here is that "I would meet some of the most amazing people I've ever encountered, but that the dating/social scene is like being in high school again—awkward and inept."

Massachusetts Institute of Technology

Address: 77 Massachusetts Avenue, Communications Office, Cambridge, MA 02139
Phone: 617-253-4791
E-mail address: admissions@mit.edu
Web site URL: www.mit.edu
Location: urban
Founded: 1861
Private or Public: private
Religious affiliation: none
Undergraduate enrollment: 4,372
Total enrollment: 9,947
Percent Male/Female: 59%/41%
Percent Minority: 49.0%

Percent African-American: 7.0%
Percent Hispanic: 11.0%
Percent Asian: 31.0%
Percent in-state/out-of-state: 11%/89%
Percent Pub HS: 70%
Fraternities: 50%
Sororities: 30%
Number of Applicants: 8,250
Percent Accepted: 23%
Percent Accepted who enroll: 55%
Entering: 1,068
Transfers: 37
Application Deadline: 1 Jan

Mean SAT: 706 V, 753 M
Middle 50% SAT range: 650–750 V, 720–790 M
Middle 50% ACT range: NA
Mean ACT: 31
3 Most popular majors: electrical engineering, computer science, mechanical engineering
Retention: 97.0%
Graduation rate: 81.0%
Library: 2.4 million volumes
Tuition and Fees: $25,000 in; $25,000 out
Room and Board: $6,900
On-campus housing: 99%
Financial aid, first-year: 60%

Imagine dropping a carton of Coffee-mate from a fifth-floor stairway and then lighting it as it nearly hits the ground floor and watching it turn into a fireball that whooshes back up to the top. Or consider spending the average week-night downing endless streams of Mountain Dew, Jolt, coffee, or anything caffeinated as you slave over hellishly long problem sets. Picture sitting next to published research scientists at dinner, the same people that you went out and played ultimate Frisbee with the day before. This is MIT. MIT runs the gamut of students—from "total tech-geek to normal-cool to smart jock," but the common traits that run through all MIT students are creativity, intensity, and focus.

Academic Firehoses

A common description on-campus of an MIT education is that it's like drinking from a fire hose. MIT is an intense academic environment where students "live, breathe, and eat math-science." All Techies share a common appreciation for the "beauty of math and science," but the intense course load of MIT students leaves them feeling "perpetually hosed." (Hosed being slang for exhausted, that is,

being very, very exhausted and still needing to finish two more problem sets for the next day.) MIT, as students advise, is not a school for slackers, and it's not uncommon for some students to pull all-nighters and stay in on the weekend to study. To help freshmen adjust to this intense environment where they are forced to balance academics, extracurriculars, and friends, first-year grades are given out on the basis of pass-fail. This is regarded by students as a "truly great thing." While not all students have a 'good time' while at MIT, when Techies graduate, "all the hard work becomes worth it. By coming to MIT, we're trained to endure the extremes of intensive work and no sleep—and learn to love it."

All Techies are required to fulfill extensive science and laboratory requirements as part of their rigorous MIT education. As freshmen, MIT students are required to take two terms of math, two terms of physics, one term of chemistry, and one term of biology. Students can obtain advanced placement for any of these subjects, but MIT recommends that Techies "get the 'core' down, as these subjects are essential for virtually every major at MIT." Even within the science requirements, though, there is some choice available to students. One student explained that there are three "flavors" of the required one-year physics sequence so that people who either hate or love the subject can "find their happy niche here."

The other academic requirements are a physical-education course (including a swimming test), eight HASS (humanities, arts, and social sciences) courses, and three writing-intensive courses. MIT does a good job of presenting humanities classes (which can be very unpalatable to some hard-core math/science students) in an interesting way. For example, MIT offers classes such as Technology and Culture, Modern Science Fiction, and a new history class called "Erasmus to E-Mail: Technologies of the Word, 1450–2000."

While few students major in humanities subjects at MIT, many are highly interested in them. Musical groups, theatrical performances, and literary publications abound on-campus. Most humanities classes are relatively small (usually 25 people or less) and humanities teachers usually receive higher ratings than science teachers on class evaluation forms. However, some undergraduates say that it's a daily fight for professors to get students interested in these classes.

Students report all academic departments to be strong, and across the board, professors tend to be exceptional, with Nobel laureates and prize-winning scholars in many departments (for example, Noam Chomsky in the linguistics department). While TAs do teach a few courses, full professors teach all freshman-year courses. TAs are usually restricted to heading recitation and tutorial sections. TAs are generally good, but departments are very sympathetic to students and allow students to switch recitation sections so that they can have better TAs.

Most introductory classes enroll 300–400 students. However if students prefer more individual attention, they can choose among several special programs for freshmen. One such program, the Experimental Study Group (ESG), allows students with advanced standing to take courses with two or three people and move at their own pace with the supervision of a professor or older ESG student. Students in these programs have easy ac-

cess to tutoring. ESG, one student said, "was the best choice I could have ever made academically." As freshmen, Techies can also cross-register, with permission, at nearby Harvard and Wellesley in classes that MIT does not offer. Other options for upperclassmen include studying for a combined B.S. and master's in five years, and the Undergraduate Research Opportunity Program, which connects students with paid research jobs in some of the best labs in the country.

"No major here is easy," students say. Electrical engineering combined with computer science (called Course 6) is considered notoriously hard. Course 6 doubled with astrophysics is considered suicide. However, civil engineering and oceanography are comparatively easy by MIT standards.

Although MIT students have a "ridiculous amount of work sometimes," it's partly because everyone here wants to do a lot—"they're involved in extracurricular activities, they want to take some hard classes in things that they're interested in, and most people also want to have a social life; so the natural instinct for MIT students is to go out and do a lot because the school has so much to offer."

Energy

On the whole, MIT students are a different brand of students altogether. The MIT student's brain functions more technically. For example, Techies describe themselves as the type of people who would "go into a store like the World of Science and question the clerk how a particular gadget functions, forget about the price." One student insists that there is an "energy or excitement that's hard to describe, but that can be pretty inspiring sometimes." Students all share a passion for what they do and don't mind expressing it. It's rare to find one-dimensional people at MIT; and whether you're into playing varsity Ultimate Frisbee, reading up on quantum mechanics, or watching *Dawson's Creek*, "you're accepted for what your passions are." And students say that "since the campus is so diverse, you can find people who are interested in pretty much anything you can think of. You don't have to give up your individualism when you come here."

The Party Scene

MIT students "study hard and party hard." In fact, MIT has gained the reputation of a party school. At any given MIT frat party, people from Wellesley, Tufts, Boston University, Boston College, and sometimes Harvard are visible trying to join in the fun. Considering the 60/40 male/female ratio, Wellesely women are almost a given at any MIT party.

Greek letters are visible everywhere. Sororities and fraternities account for about a third of MIT's student body and are pretty active socially. During rush and orientation, frats try to recruit rushees by offering free steak and lobster to all who visit. Sorority rush is a bit more like interviewing for a job or joining a discussion group, with not as much free stuff, but "still quite fun." Because of the recent drinking death of a freshman pledge and the administration's new, strictly dry policy on drinking, rush was slightly less successful this year than in past years. Since many parties don't have alcohol anymore, attendance at those parties has dropped to approximately two-thirds of what it used to be. But students claim that now, "there's no longer the pressure to drink." Frats have come up with creative alternatives to parties centered around alcohol—for example, they've held "bubble basement" parties where they fill the basement of the frat house with soap bubbles.

For those that don't like the party scene, there is nearby Boston, which is just across the Charles River, and Harvard Square, only two stops away on the T (Boston's subway system), to offer plenty of diversions. There's shopping, coffee bars, clubs, Toscanini's ice cream, and plenty of cultural events including the philharmonic, the Boston Museum of Fine Arts, and the theater. Boston, many students say, was one of the reasons that they decided to come to MIT. However, Boston's nightlife is dampened a little bit by the fact that the T stops running not long after midnight, so it's difficult to do things in the city much after that without a car or a taxi.

MIT Dorms: Personality

"One of the best things about MIT is the housing system." Unlike many other colleges, during the first two weeks of freshman orientation, Techies are allowed to choose the dorms they want to live in, as well as their roommates (if they wish). This year, "virtually every freshman got his/her first-choice dorm and roommate," thanks to an improved computer housing assignment program. As a result, each dorm has it's own personality and most people are very happy with their housing. Generally, students choose to spend all four years in the same dorm and since most dorms house less than a hundred people, they're very tight-knit communities where upperclassmen are close to their underclassmen neighbors. East Campus is known for its generally quiet dorms, but some have some floors with "personality" (for example, the fifth floor that does the Coffee-mate fireballs.) On another end of the spectrum is McCormick, the only all-female dorm on-campus. It has grand pianos on the first floor and is extremely convenient to everything on-campus. While there are no all-male dorms, within each of the different dorms, suites and floors may be single-sex.

As the "premiere technical institution in the world," MIT also fittingly has the facilities to accompany it." MIT, as a cutting-edge university, invests a lot of money to make sure that its facilities stay modern. Computers are certainly state of the art and are a way of life on-campus. On Athena, MIT's computer network, students can find not only their e-mail, but also their course work on the Web and certain types of modeling software. Also, one of the most "fun things on the network is zephyring," which is a form of instant messaging sent across the network. MIT students would "suffer withdrawal symptoms without e-mail and zephyring." In addition to the money that MIT spends on its facilities, students themselves sometimes take on projects to build new and better computer interfaces and equipment.

Life After Science

"Half the football team is absent from practice when there's a huge organic chem test the next day." Academics may come first at MIT, but sports are still a big part of students' lives; nearly 80 percent of students are involved in sports (at least at the intramural level), and MIT has approximately 40 varsity sports teams (one of the most of any college in the United States). Varsity sports teams include basketball, crew, fencing, sailing, tennis, soccer, and the coed pistol and rifle teams. One of the most popular intramural sports is the D-league Hockey team (no experience necessary). As one frat described, "Our D-league hockey team has just mastered the intricacies of skating forward." MIT's policy of not recruiting athletes is generally regarded by students as a good thing 'because it shows that MIT's not willing to compromise the quality of its student body for athletics."

MIT students are also known for their mischievousness. "Hacking"—pulling off amusing and clever pranks—is a big tradition at MIT. There are a few hacking groups on-campus, and the administration does not actively discourage it. A good MIT hacker pulls off a slick and harmless prank that demonstrates his or her ability to think of such a thing. "We know how to have fun with our intellect." Some of the most famous hacks always seem to involve decorating the MIT dome (Building 10) as a pumpkin, putting a pay phone that rings on the dome, building a snowman on the dome, and putting a police car with flashing lights on that dome. At a Harvard-Yale football game a few years ago, MIT hackers trained pigeons to flock toward the sound of a whistle and let them fly to the referee at the start of the game. Clearly, "this isn't the work of your every-day nerd."

The one "everyone's done it" thing at MIT is the Orange Tour, during which hackers come out on popular weekends, especially during orientation, and take hundreds of people onto the rooftops of MIT in the middle of the night until the early morning. Advised to dress in dark clothing and sneakers, students get to follow "Jacks" around taboo places (underground, roofs, ventilation ducts, and hidden corridors). "It's a thrilling experience, perhaps something of an initiation rite to welcome students to MIT."

> **"We know how to have fun with our intellect."**

MIT students seem to have a love-hate relationship with their school. Although a favorite MIT slogan among students is "IHTFP," translated "I Hate This (expletive) Place," because of the immense amount of work that students are bombarded with, they usually rave about the school to others. One student described it as "Awesome Hell . . . nowhere but MIT could I find the combo of great and rigorous academics, hard partying, athletics, and diversity, all in the city of Boston." —*Melissa Lau and Staff*

FYI

The three best things about attending MIT are "you get to choose where and who you live with, incredible minds to meet, classes for freshmen are pass/no credit."

The three worst things about attending MIT are "problem sets, the fact that MIT is so spread out, stress."

The three things that every student should do before graduating from MIT are "UROP (undergraduate research opportunity program), climb on top of one of the domes, take wine tasting."

One thing I'd like to have known before coming here is "the benefit of taking as many AP exams as possible to pass out of intros."

Mount Holyoke College

Address: 50 College Street, South Hadley, MA 01075
Phone: 413-538-2023
E-mail address: admission@mtholyoke.edu
Web site URL: www.mtholyoke.edu
Location: suburban
Founded: 1837
Private or Public: private
Religious affiliation: none
Undergraduate enrollment: 1,979
Total enrollment: 1,982
Percent Male / Female: 1% / 99%
Percent Minority: 19.7%

Percent African-American: 5.2%
Percent Hispanic: 5.0%
Percent Asian: 8.8%
Percent in-state / out-of-state: NA
Percent Pub HS: 62%
Fraternities: 0%
Sororities: 0%
Number of Applicants: 2,435
Percent Accepted: 60%
Percent Accepted who enroll: 38%
Entering: 563
Transfers: 59
Application Deadline: 15 Jan

Mean SAT: 626 V, 602 M
Middle 50% SAT range: 600–660 V, 570–650 M
Middle 50% ACT range: 25–29
Mean ACT: 27
3 Most popular majors: biology, English, social sciences
Retention: 94%
Graduation rate: 79%
Library: 653,613 volumes
Tuition and Fees: $24,200 in; NA out
Room and Board: $7,110
On-campus housing: 99%
Financial aid, first-year: 66%

Picture a small, liberal arts college for women, dedicated to excellence, and tucked into the small, picturesque New England town of South Hadley, Massachusetts. The close-knit community allows the women of Mount Holyoke to build lasting, meaningful relationships with professors and peers as well as strengthen their independence and individuality. However, this quaint and peaceful community exists within the broader world of the Five-College Consortium that unites Mount Holyoke with Smith College, the University of Massachusetts/Amherst, Amherst College, and Hampshire College. The consortium gives the Mount Holyoke students access to the academic resources and social activities of five colleges.

Small but Intense

Academics at Mount Holyoke are almost universally described as extremely rigorous. Students are required to take distribution requirements consisting of three classes in the humanities, two in math or science (one with lab), two in social science, one in foreign language, one "multicultural" course, and six credits of physical education. The amount of time that the requirements take up, particularly the hefty PE requirement, is some-

times a hassle, but on the whole, most Mount Holyoke women enjoy the diverse requirements; one student explained that they "got me to think harder about what I was doing before I declared my major."

Some of the most popular majors at Mount Holyoke are reportedly psychology, English, chemistry, and biology. While one student claimed that "all of the departments are strong," some claim that the classics major is the least popular. Students say that class size varies a lot, and large classes tend to be science lectures, Intro Psych, and other introductory classes that fulfill distribution requirements. However, most of these larger classes only enroll 50 to 60 students, while most upper-level classes have less than 20. One student said that "the classes are tiny, and students participate (whether they want to or not) in class."

Professors at Mount Holyoke are "fun, accessible, and just generally awesome." There are a few TAs, but students say that all of the teaching is done by professors. TAs may aid in labs or lead help sections, or language fellows may teach the discussion part of language classes and leave the teaching of the class to a professor. Some famous faculty include prizewinning poet Mary Jo Salter, National Security Advisor Tony Lake, author Beverly Tatum (*Why*

Are All the Black Kids Sitting Together in the Cafeteria?), and statistician George Cobb. Even high-profile professors are described as extremely friendly and accommodating, a factor to which many students attribute their decision in choosing Mount Holyoke.

In addition to everything that Mount Holyoke has to offer its students academically, students also have access to everything that the Five-College Consortium has to offer. The consortium forms a larger collegiate grouping in which all of the members benefit from the resources of the others. Any student at Mount Holyoke can take classes at these other institutions and get credit for them, and students also can use any of the other four colleges' library systems and benefit from other academic offerings such as lectures and special programs.

Living Among Women

One student summed up the visual appearance of the Mount Holyoke campus by saying "This is what I grew up thinking colleges were supposed to look like." Women at Mount Holyoke consistently rave about their campus, dubbing it the "most beautiful campus in the country." It has trees, grass, two lakes, a waterfall on the north end of campus, and old redbrick buildings with ivy on them everywhere. Students describe the campus as fairly self-contained, and very safe, because of its location in tiny South Hadley. One of the most distinctive buildings on-campus is the library, which students admire both for its impressive architecture and for how conducive it is to getting work done; students can choose either to hide away in the silence of the stacks and study on comfy sofas, or they can sit together in meeting rooms for more informal, group studying.

Since students are required to live on-campus for all four years unless they have special permission, most live in the dorms, which are reportedly quite nice. Most students prefer the older dorms, such as Pearsons and the Rockies, because they are more beautiful and have unique features, like windowseats; newer dorms, though, are often more spacious. Dorms consist of mainly double and single rooms, and all seniors and most

juniors get singles. Every dorm is single-sex, since Mount Holyoke is an all-women's school, but there are no restricted hours for guests, male or female, in the dorms. The only rule is that guests must be escorted up and down the stairs or the escalators by a resident student. Each floor has one single-sex bathroom on it, and each dorm has a nonsmoking floor or two. There are also "quiet hours" between 11 P.M. and 8 A.M. on weekdays, and there are two floors on-campus that are official "quiet floors" for "people who want peace 24 hours a day."

Every dorm also has a dining hall, and a full meal plan is included in tuition. Students say that, although the same menu is served at each location, the smaller the dorm, the better the food tends to be. There are vegetarian and vegan options at every meal, which are reportedly tastier than the nonvegetarian dishes. Students like to order in pizza or eat at some of the many restaurants and delis in South Hadley or in nearby Amherst or Northampton. However, since all meals have already been paid for with tuition, students generally only go out on weekends or when they have an off-campus class in Amherst or Northampton.

Outside of Class

Mount Holyoke women "do an amazing amount of extracurricular work, whether it be community service, college government, or campus organizations." Despite the heavy academic workload, most students reportedly find a lot of time to spend on the vast number of groups open to them. There are lots of political organizations to become involved in, several publications, including a student newspaper called the *Mount Holyoke News* and a variety of literary magazines, and a very active Student Government Association. Musically inclined students can join the Glee Club, or one of two English Handbell Choirs. Mount Holyoke also has a program called Free Theater that allows students to produce shows independent from the theater department and thus encourages experimental works and participation by nontheater majors. A more unusual, though popular, group on-campus is the Lunar Howling Society, in which a group of women "go out and hoot at the full moon once a month." One student said that she had "never heard anyone complain about the lack of organizations to join!"

Sports are also an option for athletic Mount Holyoke students. Reportedly the biggest rival school is nearby Smith. Students say that the two schools have a "great relationship and a healthy competition." The most popular and competitive varsity teams are said to be field hockey, crew, lacrosse, and basketball. In addition to these, there is also a very successful rugby team; the team, though only a club team, is currently undefeated, and has "a huge cult following." There are also a number of intramural sports in which any student can participate, and the athletic facilities—including the gym, pool, dance studios, workout rooms, weight machines, tennis courts, and a huge equestrian center—are open to anyone and reportedly very extensive.

Social life at Mount Holyoke is a bit more low-key than at many colleges, but nonetheless can be very satisfying. Some students claim that to have any fun at all, students must either own a car to get off-campus to parties at Amherst or UMass, or else have enough patience to wait for the free bus service that runs between campuses and neighboring towns. However, others say that Mount Holyoke is such a close-knit community that its students have fun with their friends at smaller gatherings on weekends in the dorms, or at larger, campus parties such as Vegas Night and the Sophomore Semi-Formal. There is no Greek system at Mount Holyoke, which most students appreciate. Students say that the small size of their campus is enough to bring people together.

The Mount Holyoke administration is extremely anti-drinking, with stringent rules against having kegs in the dorms. One student claimed that Mount Holyoke could be "the driest campus in the nation." But others reported that, while the drinking scene might not be comparable to that of *Animal House*, it is not totally nonexistent, and if people want to drink, they would be able to obtain alcohol, and many frequently do. Mount Holyoke students throw parties, like most college stu-

dents, which often attract students from the other schools in the surrounding area. Not all students party or drink by any means, but those who want to have big parties do. They just have to be very discreet about their alcohol consumption, due to the strict regulations.

Students report that the campus is fairly open to sexual or romantic relationships of any kind. One student summed it up by saying "lots of women have boyfriends elsewhere. Others have girlfriends here. Some have both." While there are obviously no guys in classes, they are in no short supply, since there are several large coed colleges nearby, and there are always lots of male visitors around, especially on weekends. Students are quite accepting of the lesbian or bisexual students, and the LBTA (Lesbian/ Bisexual/Transgendered Alliance) has a very strong presence on campus.

Students at Mount Holyoke are fairly liberal in general, and described as extremely politically active, but the campus admittedly does house some more conservative types as well, including the College Republicans organization. The student body is also described as incredibly diverse, hailing from all over the U.S. and the rest of the world, although most do come from the Northeast.

> **"Lots of women have boyfriends elsewhere. Others have girlfriends here. Some have both."**

Students at Mount Holyoke love their school for the great balance it gives them. At Mount Holyoke, they find an extremely rigorous academic program with a lot of outlets for extracurricular activity. They also find a small, supportive community of women that is right near a large population of other college-age men and women. Lastly, they find a contained college in a small town but have access to the social and academic resources of the Amherst/ Northampton area. At Mount Holyoke, many women feel that they truly have the best of both worlds.—*Lisa E. Smith and Staff*

FYI

The three best things about attending Mount Holyoke are "the professors, the campus, and the way people are really committed to their activities."

The three worst things about attending Mount Holyoke are "the size, the girls who have money and flaunt it, the self-righteousness of some people."

The three things that every student should do before graduating are "watch a rugby game, talk to Tony Lake about military stuff, play an IM."

One thing I'd like to have known before coming here is "how funky-smelling girls bathrooms can be."

Northeastern University

Address: 360 Huntington Avenue, 150 Richards Hall, Boston, MA 02115
Phone: 617-373-2200
E-mail address: admissions@neu.edu
Web site URL: www.neu.edu
Location: urban
Founded: 1898
Private or Public: private
Religious affiliation: none
Undergraduate enrollment: 19,447
Total enrollment: 26,869
Percent Male/Female: 50%/50%
Percent Minority: 14.0%

Percent African-American: 5.0%
Percent Hispanic: 3.0%
Percent Asian: 6.0%
Percent in-state/out-of-state: 71%/29%
Percent Pub HS: NA
Fraternities: 4%
Sororities: 4%
Number of Applicants: 16,979
Percent Accepted: 66%
Percent Accepted who enroll: 25%
Entering: 2,802
Transfers: 1,334
Application Deadline: rolling

Mean SAT: 540 V, 552 M
Middle 50% SAT range: 480–590 V, 490–600 M
Middle 50% ACT range: NA
Mean ACT: 23
3 Most popular majors: busniess, engineering, criminal justice
Retention: 81.0%
Graduation rate: 44.0%
Library: 1.1 million volumes
Tuition and Fees: $14,830 in; $14,830 out
Room and Board: $5,680
On-campus housing: 75%
Financial aid, first-year: 73%

Looking for a school that combines fast paced academics with real-life experience—all located in metropolitan Boston? If so, then Northeastern, with its unique co-op program may be the school for you. But, as students warn, this program is not for everyone even "if the school can be."

The Trimester System

Students who attend Northeastern can usually plan on being in school for an average of five years since about 95 percent of the undergraduate population take advantage of the co-op program. Although the program differs for each major, students take either a 3 or 6 month co-op paid internship each year in their field of interest and work instead of attending classes during those months. Freshmen who choose not to participate in the co-op take a freshman English class and other introductory courses. Students say that the co-op program is one of the best and most unique things about Northeastern, but one freshman warns, "If you don't wanna take co-op, then don't come here."

Because of the way the co-op program is structured, classes are set up in a trimester system. This can be both an advantage to those students who like to take a variety of courses, but also a disadvantage because "the classes move at a really fast pace." This calendar will most likely be replaced by the semester system in either 2001 or 2002, a possibility which has caused jubilation among some students and drawn complaints from others who are worried about how it will affect their co-op experience. Most likely, the new system will make for fewer, but longer co-op experiences.

Majors that can be directly applied to post-grad careers are popular at Northeastern. It is no surprise that both the business and criminal justice programs are considered strong. Some students report that they offer the most interesting and most well-paid internship opportunities. Comparatively, the English and math departments tend not to be so strong. Class sizes range from about 20 to over 200, but the majority of classes reportedly have only 25 to 30 people. Students say that professors are friendly and helpful. "They know me," says one student. Another offered a tip for dealing with professors and the administration at large schools like Northeastern: "Get your point across and be actively involved."

Big City Living

Most students agree that one of the best things about Northeastern is living in the city. Located in downtown Boston, the campus is in close proximity to just about everything you could need. However, that is not to say that there is not enough happening on Northeastern's campus students have to leave it to find excitement. The Carl S. Ell Student Center is a popular hangout for upperclassmen and freshmen alike. The school bookstore is connected to the Center, which houses the offices of many campus organizations in addition to offering a cafeteria, a study room, and a lounge. For more serious studying, there is the Snell Library, which is described as "huge" and "great."

As far as campus living goes, freshmen generally live in one of three dorms, although on-campus housing is optional due to the large number of commuter students. Dorm rooms are "like prison cells," according to one student. Stetson East and Stetson West are considered to be the worst, while Kennedy Hall, the honors dorm, is considered one of the best. Students may also opt to live in Coe Hall, a wellness dorm, or Rothman, an international dorm. Most dorms are coed by hall with single-sex bathrooms. There is currently a new dorm under construction.

Upperclassman housing is determined through a lottery system and "if you don't get housing have fun finding a place in Boston for a reasonable price," said one student. One of the downsides of city living is that dorm residents must have their cards swiped by an attendant and sign in guests 24/7, even if their visitors are just students from another dorm. All campus dorms are also staffed with residential advisors. According to students, the RAs are generally a mixed bag of upperclassmen who are willing to let rules slide and others who are strict about alcohol policies.

Again, because of the university's urban location, there are innumerable food options around campus. Undergraduates can choose from 3 different meal plans, but freshmen must have at least 10 meals per week. Students may also choose to have money put on their Husky Card, which allows them to eat at many local establishments—something that makes many cafeteria-weary students happy. Local favorites include Pizzeria Uno, Chicken Lou's, and Au Bon Pain, as well as Marche's at the nearby Prudential Center and numerous take-out and fast-food restaurants on adjoining Huntington Avenue.

Uh, Football Team?

When asked about the Husky football team, one student giggled and innocently asked, "Do we even have a football team?" Undoubtedly, the football team has a less than illustrious record, finishing 10th in the Atlantic 10 conference in 1999. Hockey reportedly receives more support, especially at the annual game against the University of New Hampshire and at the Bean Pot Tournament against across-town rivals Boston College, Boston University, and Harvard. Men's and women's crew have also posted strong seasons in the past. Still, students say that school spirit at Northeastern is not incredibly strong, partly due to the popularity of the co-op program, which detracts attention from other aspects of Northeastern including their often lackluster sports teams.

Intramural sports are popular, however, and varsity athletes and non-varsity athletes alike use the facilities at the Marino and Cabot Centers. Non-athletes can also participate in various cultural clubs, dramatic and musical events, or write for various publications, including Northeastern's literary magazine, *The Spectrum*.

Boston Night Life

Weekends at Northeastern start on Thursday nights, and there is no end to the variety of entertainment options available in Boston. Most freshmen frequent nearby clubs and parties, while upperclassmen attend apartment parties and bars. Underclassmen agree that while being underage does pose a problem, it does not stop them from drinking, though the university is stepping up its efforts to crack down on underage drinking with a stronger campus police presence. Though dating isn't all that common, students say that "there are a ton of random hookups mostly because kids from BC, BU, and Emerson all mix at clubs."

In addition to parties, the city of Boston also offers alternatives such as theater, dance and symphony concerts by such acclaimed orchestras as the Boston Pops. Cambridge and Harvard Square are other popular destinations. When students just want to hang out, they tend to "hang out with friends in dorm rooms," and when the weather is nice people can lounge on the "beautifully landscaped campus" or hop on the T, which runs right through the middle of campus. The T is Boston's subway system and goes just about everywhere in Boston.

At Northeastern, "There is no stereotype. Everything goes." It is a relatively diverse campus, ethnically and culturally, although some feel that it is not as diverse geographically. The majority of students come from the Northeast, and as one Ohio resident griped, "People wonder why I don't have a southern accent. When I meet other people from the Midwest, we have an automatic bond." According to one student, though "the school is diverse as a whole, you don't see as much mixing as you should." Many students feel that there are lots of cliques on campus. Nevertheless, the atmosphere tends to be liberal, and the gay and lesbian population is generally accepted by students and the administration alike. Most students come from middle-class backgrounds, and work-study is a popular form of employment on campus.

"If you don't wanna take co-op, don't come here."

Northeastern is a fast-paced career-oriented university, and with its innovative co-op program, students get cutting edge work experience combined with a rigorous education. The city of Boston offers unlimited opportunities in work, cuisine, and entertainment, and the proximity of the university to the T is invaluable. But prospective students should be warned that Northeastern is a university for those who know what they want and are not afraid to go after it, since it may be easy for the less determined to become lost in the fast shuffle of city and university life.—*Melissa Merritt*

FYI
The three best things about attending Northeastern are "the city, the co-op program, and lots of offerings in every field."
The three worst things about attending Northeastern are "the size, the poorly organized administration, and the trimester system."
The three things that every student should do before graduating from Northeastern are "do the co-op, explore Boston, and voice your opinion to the administration."
One thing I'd like to have known before coming here is "how the trimester system really works."

Simmons College

Address: 300 The Fenway, Boston, MA 02115
Phone: 800-345-8468
E-mail address: ugadm@simmons.edu
Web site URL: www.simmons.edu
Location: urban
Founded: 1899
Private or Public: private
Religious affiliation: none
Undergraduate enrollment: NA
Total enrollment: NA
Percent Male/Female: 0%/100%
Percent Minority: 25.0%

Percent African-American: 16.0%
Percent Hispanic: 3.0%
Percent Asian: 6.0%
Percent in-state/out-of-state: 45%/55%
Percent Pub HS: NA
Fraternities: 0%
Sororities: 0%
Number of Applicants: 1,184
Percent Accepted: 85%
Percent Accepted who enroll: 72%
Entering: 271
Transfers: 52
Application Deadline: 1 Feb

Mean SAT: 546 V, 537 M
Middle 50% SAT range: NA
Middle 50% ACT range: NA
Mean ACT: 24
3 Most popular majors: education, communications, business
Retention: 82%
Graduation rate: 71%
Library: NA
Tuition and Fees: $20,134 in; NA out
Room and Board: $8,046
On-campus housing: 90%
Financial aid, first-year: 85%

The 1999–2000 school year marks the 100th anniversary of Simmons College. To celebrate the event, the faculty has compiled a CD-ROM, which they will take on the Centennial Road Show, bringing the anniversary to all of those alumni who would otherwise be unable to make the celebration. The Road Show is an indication of just how far Simmons has come, and how far its alumnae have gone. The anniversary provides a good opportunity for Simmons to marvel at one hundred years of giving young women the preparation needed for success in this world.

Heavy on the Science

Simmons's greatest academic strength lies in its science departments. The physical therapy department offers a six-year doctorate program. Nursing majors benefit from internships at area hospitals, including one that is across the street from the college. Some majors require a hospital internship to graduate. The abundance of student interns reflects the preprofessional goals of the women here. Many students describe themselves as pre-something, including a fair share of premeds. Unfortunately, some students find that the strength of the science departments is balanced by a weakness in other areas. "If you are coming to Simmons to be a science or management major, great. If you are coming to Simmons for a liberal arts education, not so great." In addition to management, students also consider communications and education to be strong nonscience majors.

The small size of Simmons makes it easy to get small classes. As freshmen, students might find themselves in a Spanish class with just four other people, including the professor. If a large lecture course is more up their alley, introductory courses—particularly in the sciences—often enroll more than one hundred women. In large lectures and small seminars alike, students find the professors to be personable and accessible. One professor "took [her] entire class out to a movie and a nice dinner—all expenses paid."

Simmons's small size also makes it possible for underclassmen to get into upperclassmen seminars. "Classes are fairly easy to get into if you are willing to go find a teacher and make some requests." On the flip side, a Simmons curriculum also includes several required courses. Students must attain intermediate skill in a foreign language by taking three semester of language, and all freshmen are required to take a multicultural English course. By graduation, all students will also have been in seven "modes of inquiry" and in four physical education classes of their choice, ranging from yoga to tennis.

Simmons offers several term abroad programs, including a course of study in say Córdoba, Spain which draws many Simmons students for both semester long and short-term courses. A photography course in Paris and Marine Biology in Puerto Rico are offered, as well.

Living in Beantown

The city of Boston has become the playground for the women of Simmons College. The college campus consists of two buildings for classes and a residence area comprised of redbrick dorms surrounding a grassy courtyard. Another college campus sits between the residential and academic buildings and the city of Boston fills up the rest of the surrounding space.

"One of the best things about Simmons is the residents campus: it is beautiful." The quadrangle "makes you feel like you're not in the city." Inside the dorms, the rooms can be small, but nice. One student divides the dorms into two groups: "hotel dorms" and "ghetto dorms." The moniker "hotel dorm" is usually reserved for those dorms that have been recently been renovated, like Dix and South Halls. The college plans on eventually renovating all nine of its dormitories. All of the dorms have RAs that keep the peace and, although none of the dorms are known as quiet dorms, each has quiet areas. Bartol, one of two dining halls, is conveniently located near the residence halls.

A seven-minute walk separates the academic buildings from the residential buildings. The two main classroom buildings—the recently renovated Main College Building and the Science Building—have nice lecture halls. The school's other dining hall, The Fens cafeteria, is located in the MCB. The Beatley library is also situated in the academic part of the campus. Beatley provides a nice place to work on group projects and to study, although some describe it as "scary." The construction of a new student recreation center is nearing completion.

The location of the campus puts it in close proximity to all of the happening places in Beantown. Only a few blocks separate the MCB from Fenway Park and Kenmore Square. The T takes students almost anywhere in Boston (making the daunting task of "pahking the cah" unnecessary); the T stop is only a hop, skip, and a jump away from the MCB.

Social Life?

The weekend plans of most Simmons' students depend on what is happening in Boston. Due to a lack of men and strict alcohol/noise regulations, parties on Simmons campus are rare occurrences. If students stay in on the weekend, they'll usually rent a movie. When they want to go out, they look to Boston. "There's a lot of stuff to do in Boston: go to coffee houses with friends, shop on Newbury or at the Cambridgeside Galleria Mall, go to the science museum and catch a planatarium show, go to the aquarium, or just go see a movie." When looking for a little bit more debauchery, the women of Simmons often go to parties at "larger schools like MIT, BU, Wentworth, and, sometimes, Harvard."

> One student describes the dining hall food as "good, actually, I've had much worse."

The few social events that happen on Simmons's campus are more appreciated because of their scarcity. Each dorm holds mixers, and students look forward to the Mr. Simmons pageant each spring. Students can cut a rug at the Sadie Hawkins Dance and the Valentine's Day Dance. And after four years of college, seniors get to bring their parents in for the Father/Daughter and Mother/Daughter weekends.

Happenings On Campus

Every week, the Campus Activities Board brings to campus special acts, including "everything from hypnotists to a cappella singing groups. Usually they are free and provide some entertainment on campus." Student groups range from the usual—the Colleges of the Fenway Orchestra, student government, and hall council—to the unusual. In addition, the college requires students to perform community service.

For the athletes who don't play a varsity sport, intramurals become an outlet for athletic enthusiasm. The school has a program called Leap, in which many different sports and other classes are offered, like aerobics, dance, learning to dive, and Alaskan dog sledding. Nonvarsity athletes will also find that they have easy access to gym facilities, which are described as nice. The gym, which is located in the residential area, contains Nautilus equipment, a "gorgeous" pool, and a suspended track for student use.

Wining and Dining

Even with the luxury of living in America's seafood Mecca, students don't find their dining hall food to be all that bad. One student describes the food as "good, actually, I've had much worse." Of course, even the best dormitory food gets a little old after a while; luckily, students at Simmons have the culinary delights of Boston right at their fingertips. The city boasts such popular restaurants as the Cheese Cake Factory, Brown Sugar, Vinny Testa's, and Bertucci's. On campus, Quadside café offers "yummy junk food" and doubles as a popular late night hangout.

The lack of male students on campus provides a unique experience for the ladies of Simmons. "It is definitely a different experience than coed. You become much more independent and head strong, and you receive a better education because your degree is not compared with a male's." Students also note that the absence of the male gender results in a student body that does not have to worry about competition for guys. "It's pretty comfortable in the sense that you don't really have to worry about what you look like hanging around the dorms or even going to class for that matter." Most importantly, this small school in the heart of Boston provides a nurturing environment where women can learn, grow, and experience life. Simmons is just the first stop for these women who will be prepared to go out and make a difference in this world.—*Kenneth Tseng*

FYI
The three best things about attending Simmons are "Boston, the friendly people, and the Physical Therapy Doctorates Program."
The three worst things about attending Simmons are "all girls, all girls, all girls."
The three things that every student should do before graduating from Simmons are "see a Red Sox game, visit the Museum of Fine Arts, and go to the Valentine's Day Ball at the top of the Prudential Building."
One thing I'd like to have known before coming here is "save more money, especially quarters."

Smith College

Address: 7 College Lane, Northampton, MA 01063
Phone: 413-585-2500
E-mail address: admissions@smith.edu
Web site URL: www.smith.edu
Location: suburban
Founded: 1871
Private or Public: private
Religious affiliation: none
Undergraduate enrollment: 2,655
Total enrollment: 2,778
Percent Male / Female: 0% / 100%
Percent Minority: 17.0%

Percent African-American: 4.0%
Percent Hispanic: 3.0%
Percent Asian: 9.0%
Percent in-state / out-of-state: 21% / 79%
Percent Pub HS: 68%
Fraternities: 0%
Sororities: 0%
Number of Applicants: 3,125
Percent Accepted: 56%
Percent Accepted who enroll: 39%
Entering: 643
Transfers: 110
Application Deadline: 15 Jan

Mean SAT: NA
Middle 50% SAT range: 620–720 V, 590–670 M
Middle 50% ACT range: NA
Mean ACT: NA
3 Most popular majors: government, psychology, English
Retention: 88.0%
Graduation rate: 77.0%
Library: 1.2 million volumes
Tuition and Fees: $21,680 in; $21,680 out
Room and Board: $7,560
On-campus housing: 100%
Financial aid, first-year: 59%

Walk around the picturesque town of Northampton, Massachusetts, and you will inevitably spot a proud Smithie wearing a T-shirt that reads, "It's not a girls' school without men—it's a women's school without boys." While some treasure the experience of college without men, students inevitably questioned why she decided to "condemn herself to life without the opposite sex." While the value of an all-women's college will always be debated among Smithies, there is no doubt that Smith's inspiring academic program and involved community provide an incomparable college experience.

Academics

Academic life at Smith is marked by a great degree of freedom. Having no distribution requirements allows for much exploration, but it also puts much responsibility on undergraduates to chart and plan their own education. Opinions vary on how challenging courses are at Smith. One student guaranteed that "every course is difficult—this is Smith." Other students, however, said that each class is what each student makes of it. One senior commented that "how much useful information you learn has nothing to do with

the difficulty of the course," and that the difficulty of a class "depends entirely on the professor."

Students applaud the teachers for their accessibility, explaining that the accessibility of professors "really adds to Smith's close-knit feel." One student explained how she meets with professors: "I e-mail them, call them, or go to their office hours. I sometimes drop in on my favorite profs, Kiki Smith (costume design) and Ernie Alleva (philosophy), just to say hi." Part of this personal attention can be attributed to the intimate class settings. All classes are taught by professors, and most of the classes are very small. The few larger classes are very uncommon, according to one sophomore who said that "when one of my classes had 150 students, people were surprised."

Smith boasts particularly strong English, government, women's studies, and art history departments, but also because of its involvement in the Pioneer Valley's Five-College Consortium. Students from Smith College, Hampshire College, Mount Holyoke College, Amherst College, and the University of Massachusetts at Amherst can hop on one of the consortium's complimentary buses and attend classes at any of the five schools. Students appreciate the broad spectrum of classes that this cooperative of schools offers, and "almost everybody" has "thoroughly explored the entire Five College area," making friends at the other four schools. This program is especially appreciated because of the opportunity to pursue the sciences, one of Smith's weaker programs, at other schools that have more developed facilities.

Northampton Life

Life in Northampton provides a refuge from the tedium of studying. Downtown "NoHo" is within a three-minute walk from campus. The proximity to town allows students to frequent Pearl Street, where there are many little shops and restaurants. Fun retreats in NoHo include the Fire and Water Vegetarian Cafe, Bart's Ice Cream, the Haymarket coffeehouse, and local bars. For a great meal, students often choose Jake's No Frills Dining and Spaghetti Freddy's. One student commented that "Northampton is an interesting place to walk around, but it's frustrating to shop unless you have a lot of money." Also accessible to students at Smith is adventure in Amherst, where students can take buses. Because movies are shown in Amherst every weekend, many students enjoy making the quick trip.

Students say that they feel safe in the area around Smith, possibly a result of a great campus security. One student commented that "they're nice and respond pretty quickly, and they will give you a ride across campus if you don't feel safe walking home at night." Another student noted how "walking home at night, I've often seen campus security pass me two or three times."

Smithies are currently observing changes to their 125-acre campus. A new student center is under construction, but one student complained that to build the new facility, "they had to tear down two houses, and housing is getting really cramped." Other highlights on-campus are the Lyman Plant House, complete with Botanic Gardens, an art museum complete with more than 24,000 works, a new Bass Science Building, the Young Science Laboratory, and the Nielson Library. Students interested in using the school's athletic facilities can enjoy 25 acres of

playing fields, an all-weather track, crew facilities and a boathouse, lighted tennis courts, riding facilities, and a three-building complex called the Ainsworth Gymnasium.

Utilizing these facilities are 14 varsity sports, which are "pretty popular, but not to the point of fanaticism." Crew, rugby, and lacrosse attract a surprising number of participants, one student said, and large crowds gather to watch competitions against rivals like Wellesley and Mount Holyoke.

Housing and Social Life

The Smith housing situation is unique. Instead of huge dorms, Smithies live in houses, each one with access to a kitchen and dining room. These houses coordinate social activities, ranging from formal dinners to afternoon teas. When in such close quarters, students cement close friendships. One student noted that "your house becomes like a big extended family, even if there are 90 or 100 students living there!" Because of the enthusiasm for the house system, very few Smithies live off-campus. Each house also has its own dining hall, or shares one with another house.

> According to several students' estimates, as high as 50% of the students have had some lesbian experience by the time they graduate.

Opportunities for activities abound at Smith. One student boasted that "everybody at Smith is involved in something, whether it is sports or community service or ethnic or identity groups or music or theater or art." In each of these categories there is some sort of organization, ranging from the Nosotras for Latina students to the Korean-American Students of Smith to the Service Organizations of Smith (SOS) to the Sazanami Club to the Smiffenpoofs, the oldest female a cappella group in the nation. Basically, "if you can think of it, there's probably a club for it at Smith." Smithies are characterized by their great political awareness and activism, according to one student who also said that "Smithies are really enthusiastic about feminism and gay rights." According to several students' estimates, as high as 50% of the students have had some lesbian experience by the time they graduate. Students cite both the environment and the self-selected student body. Students are also interested in race issues, and marking their desire for a diverse student body was the inauguration of Ruth J. Simmons, the college's first African-American president.

There is always something for people to do at Smith. For the politically minded, there are frequent lectures and debates. For those interested in fine arts, there is always a movie or play or dance or concert. A concert hall attracts names like Fiona Apple, Squirrel Nut Zippers, and Ladysmith Black Mambazo. Smith also, despite the fact that it is an all-women's school, has a party scene like most coed schools; the typical weekend at Smith includes parties, "almost every Friday and Saturday involving beer, deafening music, blinding lights, smoke, and drunk UMass frat boys."

Traditions

When it comes to traditions, one student commented that "you'd be surprised at what some of those Smithies have thought up over the years!!!" Students celebrate Otelia Cromwell Day, the birthday of the first black student to graduate from Smith, by organizing various lectures and workshops that address minority issues. Mountain Day, a day that the president spontaneously announces in October, is also an appreciated Smith tradition. Quad Riot elicits excitement among students who emerge from their rooms and launch a barrage of attacks using personal-hygiene products.

Despite the absence of men on-campus, Smithies have a great time. Their activities, clubs, sports, organizations, and classes provide innumerable opportunities to explore. Going to Smith is all about exploration, and it is a great place to pursue new things while securing close-knit friendships.—*Marti Page and Staff*

FYI

The three best things about attending Smith College are "its housing experience and tradition, its support for international students, and having no curriculum."

The three worst things about attending Smith College are "the small bar and club scene, having no men, and its not much flavored food."

The three things you should do before graduating from Smith College are "join the quad riot, attend the immorality ball, and study in the island."

One thing students would like to have known before coming to Smith College is "how strenuous the workload is."

Tufts University

Address: Bendetson Hall, Medford, MA 02155
Phone: 617-627-3170
E-mail address: uadmiss_inquiry@infonet.tufts.edu
Web site URL: www.tufts.edu
Location: suburban
Founded: 1852
Private or Public: private
Religious affiliation: none
Undergraduate enrollment: 4,791
Total enrollment: 8,742
Percent Male/Female: 48%/52%
Percent Minority: 27.0%

Percent African-American: 6.0%
Percent Hispanic: 6.0%
Percent Asian: 15.0%
Percent in-state/out-of-state: 26%/74%
Percent Pub HS: 59%
Fraternities: 14%
Sororities: 7%
Number of Applicants: 12,366
Percent Accepted: 33%
Percent Accepted who enroll: 30%
Entering: 1,267
Transfers: 134
Application Deadline: 1 Jan

Mean SAT: NA
Middle 50% SAT range: 610–700 V, 630–710 M
Middle 50% ACT range: NA
Mean ACT: NA
3 Most popular majors: international relations, English, biology
Retention: 95.0%
Graduation rate: 76.0%
Library: 900,000 volumes
Tuition and Fees: $23,106 in; $23,106 out
Room and Board: $7,108
On-campus housing: 99%
Financial aid, first-year: 37%

Tufts University, situated on a suburban hilltop overlooking Boston, in many ways has the best of both worlds. Only a few miles outside of the city, students can take advantage of Boston's theaters, restaurants, nightclubs, stores, and concerts by taking the T, Boston's subway system. But while Tufts benefits from its proximity to Boston, it remains a contained and almost secluded campus in the suburb of Medford. The campus itself has open lawns and trees, and is quiet, since no major roads cut through it. Tufts students experience the richness of a big city in a quiet, suburban community.

Academics

Academics at Tufts are tough, but most students feel that they are up to the challenge. Undergrads apply to either the School of Engineering or the School of Liberal Arts, both of which mandate very stringent "distribution" requirements. Students in the liberal arts program must take two courses in each of five areas: natural sciences, mathematics, fine arts, humanities, and social sciences; six semesters of foreign language or culture; and also one class that completes the World Civilizations requirement, which is a class in a non-Western discipline. Engineering

students must take the language and World Civilizations requirement, as well as two semesters of English composition and writing. Many students find these requirements excessive and "a pain in the neck." However, standardized test scores may be used to waive some of these requirements, which "gives us a little more freedom," and some students report that it's easy to find courses that fulfill more than one requirement.

Class sizes at Tufts are large for introductory lectures, around 100 to 200 students, but more specific courses, such as upper-level courses for your major, generally enroll around 20 people. Classes are always taught by professors; TAs often lead recitations sections and labs for the larger courses. Classes like English, foreign languages, and philosophy are reported to be kept small in order to encourage "interaction and discussion." Sometimes students can get closed out of classes during registration, when students are assigned registration times and classes fill on a first come, first served basis. Students say they get into most of their top-choice classes with no problem, and even if you are closed out, "speaking to the professor and showing genuine enthusiasm generally gets you in." Freshmen also go through a weeklong orientation, which helps them to choose classes for the upcoming fall.

Some of the most popular majors at Tufts are international relations, economics, biology, and psychology. Many students who major in international relations go on to Tufts' world-renowned graduate school, the Fletcher School of International Law and Diplomacy. International relations majors, as well as language majors, have the opportunity to go abroad their junior year to places like Ghana, England, France, and Spain, and about a third of all juniors end up taking advantage of these programs. Since there is no major for pre-med students at Tufts, many who wish to go on to medical school major in biology. Pre-meds are reported to be "hard-core competitive," not only in academics, but in terms of "anything else they think that med schools might look at." People in other areas of study also may foster this sense of competition, but in general "people aren't competitive with anyone but themselves," said one undergrad. Students say that there are times when people will study on Friday nights, but those same people might end up going out and partying on a weeknight. Tufts students tend to think that although "academics are definitely the prevailing concern," they have found a balance between intense, never-ending studying and complete abandon.

Uphill and Downhill

Freshmen at Tufts are required to live on-campus, and generally sophomores also live in the dorms. Some of the dorms are large buildings with long hallways of double and single rooms, while others are smaller and organized into suites. Housing is divided into two campus areas, Uphill and Downhill, with Uphill nearer to classes and Downhill nearer the Campus Center. Some students criticize the dorms for their "lack of maintenance," but say that they "each have their charm." West Hall, a big Gothic-style dorm in the middle of campus, is considered one of the best due to its prime location and nice rooms. Wren Hall, one of the dorms arranged into suites, is described as "maze-like and antisocial," and is said to have very small rooms. Dorms are coed, but floors are divided into single-sex sections. In addition,

there is one all-female dorm on-campus, but it does not restrict visiting hours for males.

Other rooming options include off-campus housing, Greek housing, or cultural houses. A large number of juniors and seniors choose to live off-campus, often in group houses near campus. These houses often throw good parties, and although rent is expensive, one student said she liked "being part of a neighborhood and having our own little community." There are also several Greek houses, and cultural houses such as the Russian house, Asian-American house, and African-American house. Students like the atmosphere of these cultural houses, but claim that the "worst thing about them is the distance to the Campus Center."

Dining options at Tufts are quite good. Freshmen are required to purchase a full meal plan, which they sometimes "aren't too thrilled about," but after that, the options include a full meal plan or partial plans of 14 meals per week, 150 or 95 meals per semester, or the "point system." Points can be used in any of the campus dining halls, in the Campus Center, and in several restaurants and coffee shops off-campus. Since there is so much choice, students say they are quite satisfied with their options, "especially after you visit your friends at other colleges." The two large dining halls on-campus, Carmichael and Dewick MacPhie, serve traditional dining hall fare, and generally have a lot of different options at each meal, even though "from week to week you find the same meals being served over and over." Hodgdon, also small, is praised for its stir-fry and rotisserie chicken and allows students to order food to go. The Campus Center has several shops for sandwiches, subs, pizza, and snacks. Students almost universally praise campus food, both in quality and variety, but they also tend to eat out a lot. Some students say they order take-out "all the time," and also go into Harvard Square or the North End in Boston for meals on the weekends.

Busy and Content

When asked how much time Tufts students spend on extracurriculars, one student enthusiastically responded, "Most!" Undergraduates produce a variety of publications, including the *Tufts Daily*; the *Observer*, Tufts' oldest paper, which comes out every Thursday; and *Zamboni*, a humorous paper that satirizes the other two more serious papers and is published about once a month. There are also several literary journals, such as *Queen's Head*, and literary magazines for specific ethnic groups, such as the *Asian-American Voices*. Tufts also offers extensive opportunities for students to get involved in traditional activities such as singing groups, ballroom dance, and student government, as well as some more unusual groups like the Monty Python Society. In addition, the Leonard Carmichael Society is an umbrella organization for over 30 community service groups on-campus, and is entirely student-run. As one student reported, "Most students are actively involved in at least one extracurricular activity, if not more."

Sports at Tufts are not such a big deal, since the school competes in Division III (except for the sailing team that is the top-ranked national team), and students say that the school is "not that great in sports at all." Students do muster up a lot of school spirit at times, though, particularly when the situation involves basketball or their mascot, Jumbo the elephant. Tufts varsity basketball games always draw a large crowd, especially when the team makes the championships, where Tufts pride is at its highest. As for Jumbo, one student said "it seems that the mascot being an elephant had a lot to do with swinging some students' preference toward Tufts." Intramurals are fairly extensive at Tufts, involving "every sport you could possibly hope for!" Facilities are not large, but there is a new intramural gym, Chase gymnasium, and undergrads say the facilities are always open for the entire student body. In addition to traditional sports, the Tufts Mountain Club, which owns a lodge in New Hampshire, is also a popular activity, offering outings in rock climbing, kayaking, hiking, and camping.

Social life at Tufts offers a wide variety of options. On weeknights, students who want a break from their studying can find others to go out to coffee shops or the Campus Center, just to hang out. On weekends, there are always parties and dances, often held by student organiza-tions. The Programming Board is in charge of big social events on-campus, and fraternities, while not particularly a large force, do organize house parties every weekend. The T and buses make transportation into Boston so easy that many students, especially upperclassmen, wander off-campus for weekend entertainment at clubs, theaters, restaurants, and other attractions. In Medford itself, which "used to be pretty dead, but is now coming into its own," there are a lot of CD and clothing stores, restaurants, and bars.

Officially, the Tufts administration has designated the campus drug-free, and kegs are not allowed. In reality, though, some students say there is a small, but quiet, drug scene, and beer is plentiful at frat parties and on-campus parties alike. Undergrads say that most of their peers drink, and that "people who drink tend to drink a lot." Some students harshly criticize Tufts' dating scene, which many regard as practically nonexistent. Relation- ships are nearly always "short and sex-oriented," or long-distance; "a lot of people have girl/boyfriends from home, so if you are looking for anything long-term . . . forget it!"

> **Tufts also has a large population of international students, but one student said undergrads tend to be "very cliquey in terms of geographic origin."**

The Tufts student body contains a healthy mix of ethnic backgrounds, though some students criticize its lack of diversity. The majority of students are from New England and New York, but there is representation from all 50 states. Tufts also has a large population of international students, but one student said undergrads tend to be "very cliquey in terms of geographic origin." Some also feel that Tufts is lacking in economic diversity and in African-American students. Tufts has many organizations and cultural houses for minority students to help foster a strong community. The student body tends to be "mostly politically liberal, and almost completely socially liberal," although there are a small number of active conservatives. Although students tend not to show their school spirit in huge outbursts of support at giant sporting events, and may criticize things about their school, "most students enjoy being here at Tufts and would be proud to say they are a student here."

Students find Tufts to be a school with very high academic standards and a plethora of outside activities. In addition, Tufts is ideally located for "people who like to have access to the big-city activities that Boston offers, but still like to come home to a quiet place in a neighborhood with families living in houses all around."—*Lisa E. Smith*

FYI

The three best things about attending Tufts are "its being close to Boston, the intercultural week and the study abroad opportunities."

The three worst things about attending Tufts are "lack of housing options, its small size, and lack of computers."

The three things you should do before graduating from Tufts are "participating in the Naked Quad run, watching the city from the library's roof at night, and going abroad."

One thing students would like to have known before coming to Tufts is "the prominent place of the Greek system in social life."

University of Massachusetts / Amherst

Address: University Admissions Center, Amherst, MA 01003
Phone: 413-545-0222
E-mail address: mail@admissions.umass.edu
Web site URL: www.umass.edu
Location: suburban
Founded: 1863
Private or Public: public
Religious affiliation: none
Undergraduate enrollment: 18,752
Total enrollment: 23,932
Percent Male/Female: 50%/50%
Percent Minority: 15.0%

Percent African-American: 5.0%
Percent Hispanic: 4.0%
Percent Asian: 6.0%
Percent in-state/out-of-state: 75%/25%
Percent Pub HS: 89%
Fraternities: 6%
Sororities: 6%
Number of Applicants: 17,691
Percent Accepted: 74%
Percent Accepted who enroll: 29%
Entering: 3,737
Transfers: 1,794
Application Deadline: 1 Feb
Mean SAT: 558 V, 566 M

Middle 50% SAT range: 510–610 V, 510–620 M
Middle 50% ACT range: NA
Mean ACT: NA
3 Most popular majors: communications, psychology, hotel/restaurant/travel administration
Retention: 79.0%
Graduation rate: 34.0%
Library: 2.8 million volumes
Tuition and Fees: $1,714 in; $9,756 out
Room and Board: $4,790
On-campus housing: 96%
Financial aid, first-year: 60%

Nestled in the pleasant college town of Amherst is a public university that was once labeled "ZooMass." True to its label, the campus was marked by extended party weekends, great basketball, and a reputation as New England's party school. While life at the UMass now has increasing academic prestige, vestiges of this reputation remain: its basketball and football teams still enjoy national prestige, and it maintains its party-school image. UMass today boasts an award-winning faculty and updated facilities, enabling it to attract students who want both fun and academic promise.

Academics

UMass academics provide opportunities for every interest. With bachelors degrees offered in over 90 areas, students enjoy a selection of every conceivable major, ranging from building materials and wood technology to sports management to business writing. Those students who desire to pursue an uncovered subject are free to explore a self-designed major.

Whatever their major, students must fulfill some graduation requirements, most notably the Social World requirements. The Social World requirements entail classes in six disciplines including literature, the arts, history, the social and behavioral sciences, and the natural sciences. Students must also fulfill certain writing requirements. They are required to enroll in a "College Writing" class freshman and junior years. Students benefit from the small, seminar-style writing courses that are limited to 25 students. The writing class taken junior year must be specific to the student's elected major. Many students complain about these requirements, but others acknowledge that the class requirements are "stuff you'd be taking, or at least should know anyway."

Students affirm the difficulty of many of the courses offered at UMass. While students report that slacker classes exist (especially in the physical education courses and "those courses that cover stuff you already know"), the general opinion about classes is that they are tough. One freshman declared that "all my classes are impossible" while another complained that "any course toward your major is hard." Despite these reports, many students feel that classes are "tough enough to keep you on your toes, but not always tough enough to fail you."

Earning particularly high ratings from students is the English department where the faculty stars include John Edgar Wideman (a two-time winner of the PEN Faulkner Award and a recipient of a MacArthur Genius Award) and James Tate (the 1992 Pulitzer Prize winner for American poetry). Students also give favorable marks to the economics department, the School of Management, the School of Food and Natural Resources, and the School for Humanities and Fine Arts.

The science departments have expanded rapidly, thanks to new building facilities like the recently constructed Knowles Engineering Building, the Silvio Conte Center for Polymer Research, and the University Marine Station at Glouces-ter. UMass has it all, from the classic chemistry lab to the unique Agricultural Experimental Station at Waltham.

For the student who desires to explore another subject in which UMass does not specialize, students have a varied selection of classes from other institutions. UMass is a member of the Five-College Consortium, an intercollegiate academic program that permits students from UMass, Smith, Mount Holyoke, Amherst, and Hampshire to take classes at any of the other schools. Students also have the option to enroll in international exchange programs and join in various internships for credit. Students who graduate from high school with high SAT scores and class ranks are invited into the UMass honors program. Ultimately, students say that UMass provides them with opportunities that "can typically be found only at private schools."

The College Town

Undergrads speak highly of Amherst, a "bustling college town" in the historic Pioneer Valley of western Massachusetts. Students report that they feel safe when walking around campus, but security still provides a bus that circles the 1,400-acre campus every 15 minutes. For no cost, the bus provides transportation to the neighboring schools, the mall, and distant parts of the campus. The northern portion of campus is characterized by its Georgian and colonial architectural styles while the southern part is more modern. All freshmen and sophomores are guaranteed on-campus housing. Freshmen like the fact that there is no distinct or separate freshman dorm because they can learn from the upperclassmen with whom they intermingle. Most floors are coed, but there are special floors like the 24-hour quiet floor and some single-sex floors for women. Students do warn against dorms in the "Sylvan Area," and are confident that dorms will be even better "as soon as the new furniture is put in." Once students reach their junior year, many choose to live off-campus.

In these dorms are DCs (Dining Commons) where students enjoy a varied palette of foods. The food "isn't actually that bad," and there are options even for the vegetarian and vegan. The DCs are close and convenient, especially those that have the extended eating hours. Many students enjoy the food at the school's most popular hangout, the Blue Wall.

Social Life

UMass was not given the title "ZooMass" for no reason, any weekend invariably includes parties at one of the 20 fraternities or sororities located on or near campus. Underage drinking, however, is strictly regulated by campus police and the administration's hard-line approach. One of the things that makes UMass so exciting are other creative opportunities on the weekends. The campus center has a program called SEV (Something Every Friday) that offers, of course, something every Friday. Recent "somethings" have included hypnosis, improv comedy, ice skating, and movies. Movie selection is good, students claim. One weekend, for example, the campus center played *Armageddon* and *There's Something About Mary*. UMass has frequent concerts with such famous names as Korn, U2, Tori Amos, Natalie Merchant, and Bob Dylan. Weekends include some sleep and some study, too; and with study comes the need for study breaks. One student related one creative study break: "Sixty of us were sledding down the hill behind my building last night. We stayed there going crazy until 1 A.M."

Athletics and other extracurricular activities make UMass even more exciting. Sports have traditionally played a key role on the UMass campus. Their particularly strong basketball and football teams are popular, and games are well attended. There are plenty of unique organizations, according to a freshman who claimed, "We have [an organization] for everything you can think of, and if there isn't one, you can start one!" One student noted that she and her friends were starting a "frato-sorority."

> There are plenty of unique organizations, according to a freshman who claimed, "We have [an organization] for everything you can think of, and if there isn't one, you can start one!"

Students attend the university to take advantage of both the excitement and the academic rigor of the school. Academic opportunity, a variety of extracurricular activities, the symbiotic relationship of the Five-College Consortium, and a legacy for partying combine to make UMass at Amherst a great school.—*Marti Page and Staff*

FYI

The three best things about attending Umass at Amherst are "being a part of the 5 college consortium, Durfee Gardens, and a diverse student body."

The three worst things about attending Umass at Amherst are "drinking policies, the food, and too many TA's for classes."

The three things that every student should do before graduating from Umass at Amherst are "visiting the Durfee conservatory, riding the elevators in the library without getting sick, and taking a class from one of the four other colleges."

One thing I'd like to have known before coming to Umass at Amherst is "the school has very high standards."

Wellesley College

Address: 106 Central St., Wellesley, MA 02481
Phone: 781-283-2270
E-mail address: admission@wellesley.edu
Web site URL: www.wellesley.edu
Location: suburban
Founded: 1870
Private or Public: private
Religious affiliation: none
Undergraduate enrollment: 2,240
Total enrollment: 2,240
Percent Male/Female: 0%/100%
Percent Minority: 37.0%

Percent African-American: 7.0%
Percent Hispanic: 6.0%
Percent Asian: 23.0%
Percent in-state/out-of-state: 17%/83%
Percent Pub HS: 60%
Fraternities: 0%
Sororities: 0%
Number of Applicants: 2,862
Percent Accepted: 46%
Percent Accepted who enroll: 46%
Entering: 603
Transfers: 23
Application Deadline: 15 Jan

Mean SAT: 678 V, 671 M
Middle 50% SAT range: 680 V, 670 M
Middle 50% ACT range: 29
Mean ACT: 29
3 Most popular majors: econ, psych, English
Retention: 95%
Graduation rate: 90%
Library: 728,000 volumes
Tuition and Fees: $23,320 in; NA out
Room and Board: $7,234
On-campus housing: 100%
Financial aid, first-year: 51%

On the Sunday before the first day of classes, Wellesley women come together on this "Flower Sunday" in the Wellesley chapel and have a day of reflection. On a beautiful day in the middle of the fall semester, all of the Wellesley women gather for a college-wide picnic. Wellesley College is a tradition-filled school whose traditions are not kept merely for the sake of tradition, but rather, because they are examples of the sense of community that the women of Wellesley share. Located in the relaxed, tightly-knit, suburban town of Wellesley, Massachusetts, an even stronger community rests within the walls of the college. Wellesley women are united by their common sense of drive. At Wellesley, the women know what they want and are driven to achieve it.

The Wellesley Voice

Wellesley is unusual not only because it is an all-women's college, but also because of the women who go there. Its student body is described as "intense, intelligent, beautiful, and international." As a women's college, students feel encouraged to find their own voice. Their professors want them to really find themselves in everything they do—from the outside activities that they pursue to their coursework. As one freshman commented, "It's nothing like high school. My professors really want to know what I think, how I express those thoughts, and how I can develop myself as a person."

Although the academic environment at Wellesley is very intense, the students there are supportive of each other; "Wellesley is very much a community." Thanks to the way the school is organized, Wellesley women become a part of an extensive nurturing network. For instance, frosh can talk to their "big sister" (an upperclasswoman who helps first-years adjust), the head of their dorm floor, the dorm house president, a first-coordinator, or a head of their dorm.

Wellesley is a very liberal and "politically correct" place. Although all of its students are very accepting of one another's differences, some say that the political correctness can get a bit ridiculous. One student complained that her dorm was not able to call a dance the "Holiday Ball" in order not to offend those who don't celebrate any of the December holidays.

Intensity

Wellesley is not a place to kick back. "'Slackers at Wellesley' is a total oxymoron." According to students, the hool's women are all "intensely driven." everything they do, Wellesley women sh themselves, not because they are rced to, but because they want to. Most e actively involved in two, three, four, d even five activities at one time, saying e want to make the most of our time re."

The administration has recently im- sed some new academic regulations to ighen the academic rigor of the school. idents entering after the fall of 1997 are iuired to fulfill a new set of distribution iuirements. They must take one class m each of the following areas: lan- iage and literature; the arts (visual arts, isic, theater, film, and video); social and havioral analysis; natural or physical ience, with lab; and mathematical mod- ng/problem solving. For those students it are not oriented toward math and the iences, there are courses available that e intended for non-majors. But some ience and math majors complain that ere are not enough nonmajor humani- s and social sciences classes. Although e strict requirements have earned the iool a nickname "HELLesley," most say iey aren't too hard to fulfill." In addition the new distribution policy, students ist now take 34 instead of 32 credits in ier to graduate.

Academic life is rigorous and "some- ies you feel like the endless stream of rk will never end, but in the end, it's en- ily worth it." Although there is "tons of rk, it's manageable." The rigors of llesley, most students say, is worth the crifices that they must make. One fresh- in noted, "I look at some of the seniors d see how articulately they relay ideas. what Wellesley does to a timid and iewhat quiet first-year student like my- f." Further, to lessen the stress on stu- ints around final exam time, Wellesley ows students to schedule their own ex- is to ensure that they aren't too over- ielmed.

Students are generally very satisfied th their courses. They love the small e of the classes, many of which are typ- lly under 25 people, because they en- urage students to become articulate, d discussion is especially lively in the per-level classes. Only a few introduc- y classes are taught in large lectures.

Touted departments include economics, political science, and art history, while African studies, women's studies, and so- ciology are reportedly less popular. Pro- fessors are said to be generally very "supportive and nurturing" while pushing students "to develop our ideas and selves." One senior raved, "Some profes- sors will have the class over for dinner. They are so considerate and sincere."

While Wellesley College itself is small and limited in the number of classes that it can offer, the number of classes available to its students is immense. As part of a 12- college consortium with nearby schools such as MIT, Harvard, and Mount Holyoke, students are able to take classes that are not offered on-campus at any one of the other consortium schools. One upper-class science major said, "It's great. I can take advanced science classes that aren't offered by Wellesley and have the resources of all the other schools open to me."

Total Freedom?

As an all-women's school, the absence of "boys" makes the Wellesley experience drastically different from most other col- leges. For many, it's "theoretically a bless- ing" not having to worry about what we wear or how to act to attract a guy's atten- tions. "I chose Wellesley because it'd let me concentrate on my education rather than what I look like at two in the morn- ing." Many consider it to be "Total Free- dom" because there aren't any guys around.

Many Wellesley women believe that at- tending an all-women's college trans- forms them and their education. "I marvel at how confident and articulate the upper- class women are," one first year student said. "They know their stuff and have no trouble and no qualms in stating their opinion." Discussion and debate were cited to be at a very high level. One student explained, "I think that at coed institutions, women don't have the same opportunit- ies to develop this self-consciousness about their abilities as women. The most important thing I'm getting out of my Wellesley education is the knowledge that as a woman, I have the opportunity and ability to do whatever I put my mind to. Period. It's what the Welesley experience is."

Social Scene

The social scene at Wellesley generates the greatest number of complaints by students. To have a social life "takes a lot of effort at Wellesley." One student explained that "Wellesley is self-contained except for the town of Wellesley, where the only thing most students go for is the CVS pharmacy there." It is popular for women to go off-campus on weekend, since reportedly "campus parties are usually rather sad." Boston is one popular and easily accessible destination. The college runs a bus or "Love Truck" between Boston and Wellesley that leaves every hour from both destinations and costs only a few dollars. It makes stops at Harvard Square, MIT's "Frat Row," and, at scheduled times, the Museum of Fine Arts in Boston. "First-years cannot have cars, and without the bus, we'd be stranded here," one frosh emphasized. Some Wellesley women felt that it was difficult to meet "decent" non-Wellesley students because the only chance they have to mix with others is at off-campus parties on the weekends.

However, many students do enjoy staying on campus. One frosh's roommate was "shocked about the fact that there are plenty of people who stay in on the weekends." On weekend nights, a lot of people hang out in their friends' rooms; "there's no pressure to go out and party if you don't want to." Also many people have friends from other schools stay over with them during the weekends, to such an extent that the "campus looks coed on weekends."

Wellesley's own social scene currently includes four social clubs that each have a theme: TZE (art and music), ZA (literary), Phi Sigma (lectures), and the Shakespeare Society, which puts on two of the Bard's plays each year.

The basic unit of social and residential life at Wellesley, though, is the dorms—whether they are old and Gothic or modern. The three modern dorms, though seemingly out of place on the Wellesley campus, feature rooms with built-in dressers, shelves, and closets, although some students prefer the exterior beauty and spacious rooms of the older dorms. The dorms all house members of every class, which students say makes campus life more cohesive, since freshmen and seniors live side by side in the residences.

> "It's nothing like high school. My professors really want to know what I think, how I express those thoughts, and how I can develop myself as a person."

The food at Wellesley generally gets high marks. One upperclasswoman noted that she had been to several other colleges and "their food was not nearly as good as ours." In addition, the dining halls have very flexible hours; they are open continuously from 7 A.M. to 8 P.M., and are located in each dorm complex. There are also no restrictions on how much one can eat. "The food system here is great!" said one student. "I can get food whenever want it."

The Tradition of Wellesley

Wellesley women say that the school's famous alumnae have inspired them. Hillary Clinton, Nora Ephron, Lynn Shurr, Cokie Roberts, Diane Sawyer, and Madeline Albright are just a few of the women that got their start at Wellesley. "It's intimidating but also inspiring to know that I'm carrying on the tradition that these women have established. But I know that I have everything available to get to the same places that these women have."—*Melissa Lau and Staff*

FYI

The three best things about attending Wellesley are "the professors, the prestige, and the educational atmosphere."

The three worst things about attending Wellesley are "an all female environment which encourages cattiness (competition and anal-retentiveness), preprofessional atmosphere, an administration that gets out of touch for such a small school."

the three things that every student should do before graduating from Wellesley are "go to the dyke ball, skinny dip in Lake Waban, go to a volleyball game."

One thing I'd like to have known before coming here is "you have to work harder than they tell you to find some sort of social life that you can fit into."

Wheaton College

Address: Norton, MA 02766
Phone: 800-394-6003
E-mail address: admission@wheatonma. edu
Web site URL: www.wheatoncollege.edu
Location: suburban
Founded: 1834
Private or Public: private
Religious affiliation: none
Undergraduate enrollment: 1,500
Total enrollment: 1,500
Percent Male/Female: 34%/66%
Percent Minority: 11.0%

Percent African-American: 4.0%
Percent Hispanic: 3.0%
Percent Asian: 3.0%
Percent in-state/out-of-state: 38%/62%
Percent Pub HS: 61%
Fraternities: N/A
Sororities: N/A
Number of Applicants: 2,463
Percent Accepted: 71%
Percent Accepted who enroll: 25%
Entering: 427
Transfers: 21
Application Deadline: 1 Feb

Mean SAT: 610 V, 590 M
Middle 50% SAT range: 570–640 V, 550–630 M
Middle 50% ACT range: 22–28
Mean ACT: 26
3 Most popular majors: psychology, economics, sociology
Retention: 85%
Graduation rate: 70%
Library: 371,071 volumes
Tuition and Fees: $24,450 in; $24,450 out
Room and Board: $6,920
On-campus housing: 100%
Financial aid, first-year: 63%

Since 1921, Wheaton students have observed the school's Honor Code. First-year students arrive on-campus and are led into the college's chapel for a discussion of the policy—which allows tests to be taken unproctored and relies on each individual to be completely truthful. At the end of four years, seniors again convene in the chapel—this time just before graduation—to sign out of the Honor Code. Wheaton's small size allows such advantages as the Honor Code as well as personal relationships with professors. However, it also prevents students from getting lost in the crowd or preserving their anonymity.

Wheaton College is a focal point of the sleepy town of Norton. "We would like our own town," said a senior. Thirty-five minutes from Boston and twenty minutes from Providence, Wheaton appears to be too isolated and picturesque to be situated between two thriving urban centers. Only 1,400 students populate Wheaton's campus—which resembles an overgrown prep school.

The college is divided into New and Old campuses by Peacock Pond. New Campus was developed ten years ago when Wheaton, formerly an all-girls school, became co-educational. New Campus features dining halls Chase Square (which has a saute line and a variety of hot meals) and Chase Round (which has fast-food offerings such as grilled cheese, pizza, and fried foods). Old Campus invites diners to Emerson.

Real-World Academics

Academic departments at Wheaton adopt a supportive approach. Professors' offices are often located directly across from their classrooms, and class sizes allow for individual attention. Students say that the sciences have a good reputation and are known for doing a large amount of fieldwork. The average upper-level class in any subject has from 17 to 22 students, while introductory classes usually top off at 70. "All classes are taught by professors," said a student. "There are TAs, but they simply help the professors." The school is also making a push toward technology-oriented classrooms.

Popular majors are psychology, Hispanic studies, political science, English, and biology. Students do not have to declare a major until junior year. Wheaton requires a general education program beginning with a first-year seminar to aquaint freshmen with each other and orient them toward their liberal arts education. Additionally, the college requires students to take a semester each of a lab science, natural science, physical education (unless involved in a competitive sport), English, and a year of a foreign language. To fulfill the rest of the general education requirement, students choose from a variety of courses including multicultural and math and logic offerings. Wheaton also requires students to have a "second transcript," detailing real-world work experience earned while at the school. The college pushes the value of internships constantly, students say. Students can also design their own majors. "It lets people focus more on their interests," said a senior. "It's good for people who want to go to grad school."

Playing Around

Outside classes, sports are a big focus. Wheaton boasts the Haas Center, completed in 1992, which features an indoor track, a swimming pool with underwater speakers for the synchronized swimming team, and other state-of-the-art facilities. Varsity games—especially against rivals Brandeis and Babson—are often well-attended. A sophomore said that a recent game against Brandeis' soccer team was played in the pouring rain "but there were tons of people who just came anyway. It was a mudfest." There are also intramural sports ranging from Ultimate Frisbee to flag football and club sports such as golf and rugby that compete against area schools.

The various sports teams are the most popular extracurricular activities at Wheaton, although other groups draw strong followings. Student government is said to be competitive; a senior noted that "it gets pretty heated around election time." There are also two a cappella groups, the Whims and the Wheatones, and such far-ranging activities as Students for a Free Tibet.

Residential Life

The Wheaton community maintains its intimacy in part because 98 percent of the 1,400 students live on-campus. There is little alternative housing in Norton, and the school limits the number of seniors who may live off-campus. The dorm rooms are generally small, though students say it is better to live on Old, rather than New, Campus. The jewel among the dorms is Keefe Hall, located near an old favorite, Gebbie Hall. Keefe features spacious three-to-six-person suites and an elevator.

> "All classes are taught by professors," said a student. "There are TAs, but they simply help the professors."

Floors in most dorms are single-sex by room. However, there is an all-male floor and an all-female dorm as well as a substance-free dorm and a twenty-four hour quiet dorm. Eight to ten people can also create theme houses, such as "Athletes Against Alcohol," which might be based on a community service program. A panel chooses the best theme ideas and awards the houses to the chosen groups of students.

Where's the Party?

Students commonly mingle in the Balfour-Hood Center, which contains a dance studio, cafe, mailboxes, weight room, video arcade, and Ping-Pong table. School dances or performances are often held in the Center's Atrium. Wheaton weekends tend to be quiet. The school has adopted a policy that students cannot be seen with alcohol or it will be confiscated. Most of the big parties are given by the school, since there are no fraternities or sororities, and people are carefully carded. "It's not a drastic policy," said one student. "Parties tend to be small and quiet. It's a mature atmosphere." Students who are over 21 can have a beer at the Loft, the school's bar, and others come to see comedians or various performances. According to one student, "there's also a great student-run coffee shop called the Lyon's Den," where musicians and comedians perform. Many Wheaton students use the weekends to catch up on work or hang out with friends.

In nearly all aspects of campus life, Wheaton students maintain that "how much you get involved is how much you get out of it," said a sophomore. Academics, sports, and extracurricular activities are encouraged by the school community. Students say that professors are often seen cheering on soccer teams and that the president of the school often takes strolls around campus. —*Kara Miller and staff*

FYI

The three best things about attending Wheaton are "sautes, accessible professors, and pleasant peers."

The three worst things about attending Wheaton are "more and more dorm-crowding, the female/male ratio, and the price."

The three things that every student should do before graduating from Wheaton are "build a boat for the Build-Your-Own-Boat Race, find something fun to do in Norton, and take a psychology class."

One thing I'd like to have known before coming here is "how important it is to develop a taste for coffee."

Williams College

Address: 988 Main Street, Williamstown, MA 01267
Phone: 413-597-2211
E-mail address: admission2williams.edu
Web site URL: www.williams.edu/admissions.edu
Location: small city
Founded: 1793
Private or Public: private
Religious affiliation: none
Undergraduate enrollment: 2,113
Total enrollment: 2,162
Percent Male/Female: 51%/49%
Percent Minority: 22.2%

Percent African-American: 7.0%
Percent Hispanic: 6.0%
Percent Asian: 9.0%
Percent in-state/out-of-state: 14%/86%
Percent Pub HS: 57%
Fraternities: 0%
Sororities: 0%
Number of Applicants: 5,007
Percent Accepted: 23%
Percent Accepted who enroll: 47%
Entering: 544
Transfers: 9
Application Deadline: 1 Jan

Mean SAT: 701 V, 700 M
Middle 50% SAT range: 650–760 V, 660–750 M
Middle 50% ACT range: NA
Mean ACT: NA
3 Most popular majors: economics, history, English
Retention: 98%
Graduation rate: 94%
Library: 934,755 volumes
Tuition and Fees: $24,790 in; $24,790 out
Room and Board: $6,730
On-campus housing: 100%
Financial aid, first-year: 44%

Does the idea of enjoying doughnuts and apple cider on a mountaintop with friends on a beautiful fall day appeal to you? When you picture the ideal college setting in your mind, does it encompass intimate and lively class discussions led by brilliant yet accessible professors? Could you learn to become fervently enthusiastic at the sight of a purple cow? If your answers to the above questions are yes, you may want to give Williams College a closer look.

A World of Opportunity

"Williams is so amazing, I cannot imagine myself anywhere else," gushed one freshman. Indeed, Williams does seem to have so much to offer its students. It is undoubtedly a top-notch academic institution, and students rave about the accessibility of the professors and the benefits of the small class sizes. The school takes its role as a leading liberal arts college quite seriously, and "values the student-faculty relationships excessively." Professors are described as "easy to get to know," and even make an effort to learn all of their students' names so they can greet them in passing outside of class. Professors often give students their home phone numbers as well. Students point out that "the difference between Williams and your average research university is that instead of being concerned with fitting in everything they want to talk about, the professors here make sure that you are getting everything you want out of the class." Nearly all intro-level lectures, such as Psychology 101, have under 150 students, and upper-level classes range from about 30 in a class to fewer than 10. Lively class discussion is encouraged; as one student said: "The professors love it when a good fight breaks out."

There is also an excellent support system for those feeling they need a bit of help on the side. Each department has its own peer tutoring program, and Teaching Assistants, although few in number, do exist. They do not teach any courses, but rather assist the professors and are present at every class. Each student is also assigned an academic advisor, who is a good resource throughout the four years. For a school of such small size, Williams has a good deal to offer in the way of academics. The English, economics, and history departments are reputedly strong, and the natural sciences are also given good reviews, with the caveat that they require a lot of lab time. Williams does have its share of gut courses, especially in the sciences: Physics 100 ("Funhundred") and Geology 166: Climates through Time (the classic "Rocks for Jocks") are perennial favorites. But even these courses offer challenge, and the typical Williams student will seek it. Most students seem to be "academically well-rounded; you see a lot of double-majors."

To fulfill the distribution requirement, students must obtain at least three credits in each of three divisions. Division One is comprised of languages, including English, and the arts; Division Two includes history, philosophy, religion, and the social sciences; Division Three covers mathematics and the natural sciences. The requirement is generally thought of as "painless," and "the courses are ones that you would want to take anyway." Williams does maintain its swimming test and PE requirement, but these too are fairly easy to fulfill, as is the "Peoples and Cultures" one-course requirement, which is usually met by taking an anthropology course. One benefit of attending a small college is the lack of competition to enroll in certain courses. Students report that it is rare to be closed out of a class, although some courses do give preferential status to upperclassmen. Registration has been made simple through Williams' computerized UNIX "self-reg" program, which is reportedly convenient and easy to use. The college calendar is designed on a 4-1-4 system, meaning that students take four courses in the fall and the spring, but engage in Winter Study for the month of January. During Winter Study, students have the option of taking a single course (for credit or for fun), working at an internship, or creating an independent-study program of their own. Many look forward to Winter Study as a break from the academic routine and a chance to devote themselves to one thing in a way they don't otherwise have time to do. Other study options available to Williams students are the Williams-Mystic program, which allows students to pursue American maritime studies in Mystic, Connecticut, for a semester; the Williams-Oxford exchange with Exeter College in Oxford, England, for a year; or the 12-College Exchange, where students can spend a semester or a year at one of the other schools in the program.

Size Does Matter

While the academic offerings at Williams are comparable to those at larger institutions, this school's small student body sets it apart in a number of ways. Many students find that they can recognize almost everyone in their class by the end of freshman year, and this has its ups and downs. One female student explained that "being in such a small class does have its drawbacks, but none that I didn't expect when I chose to come here." Frequently mentioned gripes include limited social options, lack of privacy, and a good deal of gossip. "Gossip here is inevitable because everyone knows whom everyone else is talking about," remarked one student. "You may have heard of Six Degrees of Separation . . . at Williams, we have one degree," commented another.

However, the intimate atmosphere fosters a sense of community that indeed drew many students to Williams in the first place. There are several annual events that students always look forward to: Mountain Day, where the entire student body treks up to a mountain and then gets apple cider and doughnuts; a barbecue on Convocation, and a couple of semiformal dances. Being in a graduating class of about 500 also makes for an interesting dating scene. There is not much formal dating at Williams; as is common in other colleges, people tend either to engage in random hookups, or to settle into longlasting relationships. Unique to Williams, however, seems to be the phenomenon of students being incredibly eager to jump to conclusions about the relationships of others. One sophomore lamented that "you walk across the street with someone, and all of a sudden, you're thought of as a couple!"

Living in Style

The housing at Williams was given high marks across the board. Freshmen generally live in either Frosh Quad or Berkshire Quad, and are split into entryways of about 20 freshman each with two Junior Advisors (JAs). Because the JAs are not given any benefits by the school for their services, they are more eager to become friends with their advisees than to crack down on rules in the dorms, and are described as "awesome" and "great to have around." Housing definitely serves as a big social unit freshman year. Most frosh live in doubles, but some do get singles. Upperclassmen can often secure singles off of small hallways with a large common room at the end, an arrangement whose success can be measured by the overwhelming majority of students who choose to live on-campus all four years. While some of the housing is spread out or

a bit removed from the center of campus, students feel that "making the walk is never a chore, because it is so beautiful here!" And whatever dorm one is in, the view from the window is sure to be a gorgeous one.

Work Hard, Play Hard

The old college cliché still seems to thrive at Williams. While devoted to challenging academics during the week, Ephs (named for school founder Colonel Ephrain Williams) waste no time in having fun when Thursday night rolls around. Thursday is usually dance night at the Log, a Williams-owned multipurpose space close to central campus. Since the abolition of fraternities in the 1970s, students have been left to their own devices to find parties on the weekends, but "there always seems to be something going on." Sports teams often provide social units and hold parties, so being on a team has its advantages. However, it seems that "most parties open to everyone at around 11:00." Alcohol is often a presence, but there is little report of drugs or even cigarettes. And there are a fair amount of students who don't drink; "the campus is very accepting of that." Many students pointed to the fact that Williams is a very "health-conscious" campus, perhaps stemming from the large percentage of undergraduates who participate in athletics. Sports are very popular, and football and basketball games are always well attended, especially if against archrival Amherst College. Purple Cow fanatics will cheer on their teams in the worst of New England weather. The school spirit at Williams is hard to ignore, and often lasts long after graduation. This leads to a strong alumni network that has proved very helpful to recent graduates of the school searching for jobs beyond the "Purple Bubble."

For those not interested in sports, Williams also has a lot to offer in the way of extracurriculars. Said one sophomore, "the school really wants everyone to become involved, so they give the students every opportunity to become leaders." Aspiring thespians can take part in one of the ten theatrical productions each year, or join the Cap and Bells dramatic society, whose alumni roster includes Stephen Sondheim. A cappella singing groups are popular, as are dance troupes. Williams has an excellent outdoor club, which offers trips to the nearby Berkshire Mountains. The college council is also active and well respected. As one freshman put it, "Everyone here does some form of something." Once a student finds his or her niche, the small student body allows for many leadership opportunities: "Williams creates an environment where the individual can really shine." The school seems to have struck an important balance between emphasis on the individual and a strong sense of community.

Looking Ahead

Williams seems to be constantly looking for ways to improve student life, and this has led to some renovations and constructions that students believe will add a lot to the campus. Goodrich, a new student center, has just been completed and includes a coffee bar and performance space. Alumni have also recently donated $20 million that will be used over the next four years to refurbish performing arts facilities.

> "You may have heard of Six Degrees of Separation . . . at Williams, we have one degree."

Of course, there is still room for improvement. The campus is not as diverse as many would like, although students remark that the administration does seem to be trying to remedy this. The image of the preppy athlete still dominates, and walking around the campus, one notices a "preponderance of J. Crew model lookalikes." However, the political scene is described as slightly left of the center, and alternate lifestyles, while not the norm, are generally accepted with ease.

"Williams is an amazing place, but I think some people are disappointed when they realize the location isn't exactly a hub of excitement and culture," pointed out one freshman. The largest student dissatisfaction appears to be with Williamstown itself, a sleepy New England town with only two commercial streets. Some students wish that there were more off-campus dining options, as Pappa Charlie's deli is the "only place suited to a student's budget." The college has a couple of art museums, including the highly reputed Clark Art Institute. There is also a movie theater on Spring Street, although students note that it plays mostly "random independent flicks." The students who are happiest at Williams seem to be the ones who are content to have their lives revolve around the campus. But with all the sports, arts, and other diversions, you would be hard-pressed to claim that there is nothing to do. And most Ephs would agree that the best part of Williams is the people: "Everyone here can surprise you in some way." Perhaps most important of all, Williams students are happy. "I cannot always pin a reason on it," said one junior, "but I don't think a day goes by when I don't stop, look around, and smile."—*Rachel Grand and Staff*

FYI

The three best things about attending Williams are "quaint Williamstown, sports life, and personal attention on all levels."

The three worst things about attending Williams are "the rumor mill, not having enough time to spend taking advantage of everything Williams offers, and the 'health-conscious' attitudes."

The three things that every student should do before graduating from Williams are "have a huge snowball fight, visit the Berkshires, and start ordering from the J. Crew catalog."

One thing I'd like to have known before coming here is "how much of an advantage you get by way of personal attention at a smaller school."

Worchester Polytechnic Institute

Address: 100 Institute Road, Worcester, MA 01609
Phone: 508-831-5286
E-mail address: admissions@wpi.edu
Web site URL: www.wpi.edu
Location: suburban
Founded: 1865
Private or Public: private
Religious affiliation: none
Undergraduate enrollment: 2,783
Total enrollment: 3,742
Percent Male/Female: 87%/13%
Percent Minority: 11.0%

Percent African-American: 2.0%
Percent Hispanic: 3.0%
Percent Asian: 6.0%
Percent in-state/out-of-state: 50%/50%
Percent Pub HS: 79%
Fraternities: 30%
Sororities: 30%
Number of Applicants: 3,158
Percent Accepted: 78%
Percent Accepted who enroll: 28%
Entering: 688
Transfers: 114
Application Deadline: 15 Feb

Mean SAT: 620 V, 660 M
Middle 50% SAT range: 570–670 V, 620–710 M
Middle 50% ACT range: NA
Mean ACT: NA
3 Most popular majors: mechanical engineering, electrical engineering, computer science
Retention: 91.0%
Graduation rate: 58.0%
Library: 350,000 volumes
Tuition and Fees: $21,770 in; $21,770 out
Room and Board: $6,912
On-campus housing: 96%
Financial aid, first-year: 73%

Where can a serious science or engineering student get lots of hands-on project experience, jump into vibrant campus extra-curriculars and really get a taste for the fun-filled scenic Northeast? Worcester Polytechnic Institute, of course. Founded in 1865 at Worcester, Massachusetts, WPI is the nation's third oldest engineering school and emphasizes a hands-on, practical approach to learning.

Learn By Doing
The WPI academic calendar consists of four seven-week quarters and a summer quarter. Students will take three courses per quarter, giving them a more intense focus on the subject matter. This quarter system draws mixed reviews, with some students convinced that "it allows you to concentrate more on each class" and others citing it as one of the worst features of WPI.

Mechanical Engineering remains the number one major at WPI. Web-minded Bill Gates wannabes are filling up the Electrical and Computer Engineering and Computer Science departments, making them the second and third most popular

majors. Students at WPI enjoy their courses—"My favorite class was Anatomy. The professor was so cool, he'd just do all sorts of things, like make up songs about the bones!"— and class size is "perfect, IMHO (In My Humble Opinion)!" Introductory level courses, particularly in biology, are generally large lectures (around 200 students). Students say advanced courses can have as few as 8 per class, however.

The great personalities of professors come up several times as a WPI plus, "The professors are wicked nice!" gushed one student. Still, students better beware of "whole departments that basically don't speak English," laughed one biotechnology major. Students warn especially of teaching assistants in the Russian department and teaching assistants *and* professors in the Math department who may be English-challenged.

As members of the Worcester Consortium, WPI students can take classes at nine other area colleges including Holy Cross, Assumption, Clark, and Worcester State. Although it is not common to do so, WPI students who have elected to dual-enroll find the humanities classes at neighboring schools "rewarding" and "very good."

All undergraduates at WPI participate in WPI Plan. The WPI Plan involves three comprehensive projects, each combining classroom learning with hands-on experience off campus. The first, the Sufficiency, focuses on the humanities and arts. WPIers choose a sequence of five humanities courses and complete a project on a theme arising from the five. Topics have ranged from the love affair between Antony and Cleopatra to the impact of radio astronomy on the development of cosmology. Students generally finish twenty to twenty-five page long Sufficiency papers in their sophomore year.

Part two of the Plan, the Interdisciplinary Qualifying Project (IQP), puts multidisciplinary teams of students to work with professionals for a seven-week quarter. Teams solve thought-provoking technology and society problems. With project centers in London, Bangkok, Venice, Australia, and Puerto Rico, many WPI students elect to go abroad during their IQP term. In the past, IQP projects have examined tourism in Puerto Rico or the biological effects of marine organisms in Venetian canals.

Part Three, the Major Qualifying Project (MQP) is the longest and most intense; students devote their time to research or problems directly related to their major.

Girls and Greeks
With twelve fraternities and two sororities, WPI has a strong Greek system, which students admit dominate the social scene. Thirty-five percent of the undergraduate men and forty percent of the women undergraduates at WPI are Greek members. But even those who are part of some of the major mixing find it tiresome. Laments one sorority girl, "I wish I had known how strained the social scene was—how much it would revolve around Greek life." WPI students concede that in a heavily male-dominated population (78 percent male, 22 percent female) not being Greek may leave the guys feeling more left out than the gals.

Still, many insist, "Greek life is important if you want to have a really active social life." The rush process is traditional and brief, lasting for a few weeks before Thanksgiving break in November. Fraternities tend to build their membership around "common interests," and WPIers consistently refer to "the soccer frat," "the football frat," and "the drug frat." Speaking of drugs and alcohol, this is not a campus where "serious" drugs have a presence. Students report the occasional recreational use of marijuana, 'shrooms, and speed, but they are not a centerpiece of the social action. As for alcohol, WPI is a place where "people can party like crazy on weekends and still pass all their classes," says one student. Most underclassmen head to off-campus apartment parties, or frat parties (if they know someone and can get on the "list"). However, most say the pressure to drink is fairly relaxed. "I know a lot of guys in frats who don't drink, and it's cool," one student said. "People respect that."

> "My favorite class was Anatomy. The professor was so cool, he'd just do all sorts of things, like make up songs about the bones!"

Friendships are strong at WPI. Some students credit the nature of their project-based schoolwork and shared common interests ("engineering!") for bringing this student body together. "More than friends," however, is a different issue altogether. Guys don't like the 80:20 percent guy:girl ratio. This leads many of the male population to go a-hunting elsewhere on weekends, particularly at Holy Cross or Assumption where the ratio favors them instead.

Living Large
Virtually all freshmen at WPI live on campus in dorms. Although WPI began a five-year program to fully renovate the majority of its residence halls in 1996, the food that they serve is still "really bad!" Poor food convinces many students to live off campus. Rent is reasonable, and "some apartments are closer than the dorms!" Owning a car is "useful, but not necessary" since WPI maintains a free late-night escort service, SNAPS, for stu-

dents' safety in not-so-safe Worcester. Limited availability of parking spaces is a complaint.

Those legitimately over twenty-one ("if you're not over twenty-one, don't even try") enjoy the bar scene in downtown Worcester, a fifteen minute walk from campus. Especially popular are The Leatrim on Thursday nights ("Everybody goes. It's like a club/bar on Thursday nights, but every other night of the week, it's just a dive bar,"), The Irish Stein, and The Firehouse.

Finding Friends

When asked to enumerate the student stereotype at WPI, responses were: "Smart kids, big egos, somewhat geeky." Students don't become so engrossed in their work, however, that they don't have time to join one of WPI's 130 organizations. Students at WPI love being involved because it offers a great way to make friends.

Students also enjoy their school traditions. One tradition, The Skull, is alive and well. Skull is a senior honor society, which "taps" 10–15 juniors every spring. Activities of the organization are highly secretive, but students are very aware of their presence and prestige. When asked what its like, one WPI student responded, " . . . a couple of my best friends are members, yet they swear secrecy and don't tell much about it." Another student confirmed that "Skull is top secret. Details are hard to come by." So, what is clear? We do know Skull owns and meets in an old windowless building on the corner of campus and pledges "wear long yellow ribbons every day like pledge pins, and they get shorter and shorter as they get closer to being initiated." Hey, isn't this a movie? —*Ann Sun*

FYI

The three best things about attending WPI are "pretty good campus, good reputation, great travel and project opportunities."

The three worst things about attending WPI are "incompetent math instructors, $10 for a parking decal but there are no places to park after 9 A.M., and no liberal arts."

The three things every student should do before graduating from WPI are "see Bancroft tower, join a club . . . or several, and take classes not directly related to your major (at Holy Cross, etc.)."

One thing I wish I had known before coming to WPI is "how strained the social scene really is."

Michigan

Albion College

Address: 211 E. Porter,
Albion, MI 49224
Phone: 517-629-0321
E-mail address:
admissions@albion.edu
Web site URL:
www.albion.edu
Location: urban
Founded: 1835
Private or Public: private
Religious affiliation:
Methodist
**Undergraduate
enrollment:** 1,425
Total enrollment: 1,425
Percent Male / Female:
47% / 53%
Percent Minority: 8.0%
Percent African-American:
3.0%

Percent Hispanic:
1.0%
Percent Asian: 3.0%
**Percent in-state / out-of-
state:** NA
Percent Pub HS: NA
Fraternities: 45%
Sororities: 50%
Number of Applicants:
1,421
Percent Accepted:
85%
**Percent Accepted who
enroll:** 35%
Entering: 412
Transfers: 25
Application Deadline:
1 Apr
Mean SAT: 579.36 V,
588.5 M

Middle 50% SAT range:
520–630 V,
530–640 M
Middle 50% ACT range:
22–28
Mean ACT: 24.95
3 Most popular majors:
bus. / marketing;biological /
life sciences;social
sciences / history
Retention: 84%
Graduation rate: 71%
Library: 316,335 volumes
Tuition and Fees: $23,454
in; $23,454 out
Room and Board: $5,220
On-campus housing:
100%
Financial aid, first-year:
64%

How do students describe Albion?
"Well, it's small," one undergrad
said. "It's old—1880s; it's like any
other college," another added. And about
the sports teams, students say "anyone
can play." It seems safe to say that Albion
College attracts students from Michigan
and the surrounding states for reasons
other than a unique exterior.

Tightly Knit Courses

One thing that is unique about Albion is
the student-faculty interaction. Class size
averages around 20, and even some of the
introductory-level classes are no larger
than 40 or 50. There is no need for TAs at
Albion, and although undergraduate student assistants sometimes lead discussions, students can direct any questions to
the professors who teach their classes.

The curriculum at Albion has always
been strong, designed to produce well-
rounded students. Undergrads are required to take core courses in the following categories: social sciences, math, natural sciences, humanities, fine arts,
gender studies, ethnicity, and interdisciplinary studies. Many students do not like
this system; one undergrad called the requirements "way too harsh" and "going
out of control." Some students feel the requirements take up too much time if they
want to do anything more complicated
than a simple major. "It gets to the point
where you're scrounging to take courses
that fulfill your major. It distracts you
from focusing on things that you are genuinely interested in," said one student.

The Departments

According to students, economics is a
strong department, and pre-med courses
are popular as well. The Gerstacker Program in Professional Management and the
Gerald R. Ford Institute for Public Service
offer internships for political science and

business majors. These internships, which take place throughout the nation, not only give students a brief escape into the "real" world but also build valuable resume experience; some students form relationships with companies that result in jobs after graduation. Students majoring in other areas can elect to go off-campus for a semester, usually with an international program through the Great Lakes Association of Colleges or with internship programs that offer experience in fields other than business.

Albion has a wide variety of extracurricular activities, including roughly 95 student groups. Students report that "almost everyone is active in something," from the student senate to the newspaper to a campus political group. The activities these groups offer provide much of the action that would otherwise be missing on such a small campus and allow students to take leadership positions in nearly any area they choose.

A Sports Boost

Sports also enhance campus life. Since Albion is a Division III school, almost anyone who's interested can join a team. "There's less pressure from the administration for a team to have a winning record," said one student, and consequently a large percentage of the student body is involved in sports; the facilities are reportedly top-notch. School spirit runs high as students cheer various Briton teams to victory. In recent years the football team has won the MIAA championship and has even reached the Division III national tournament.

The town of Albion has little to attract a student crowd aside from a couple of 21-and-over bars including Casseralli's, a student favorite. Students who have cars often choose to "get out when they can" and visit friends (and parties) at one of the nearby universities; Michigan State and the University of Michigan are less than an hour away. Students without the luxury of private transportation usually occupy themselves with parties or fraternity functions on-campus. The Greek system at Albion is powerful, which some students attribute to the "lack of a better option." Despite Albion's ban on kegs, frat parties take place nearly every weekend

and are well attended. A student committee provides other entertainment such as concerts and dances, but these are not much competition for the Greeks. As one junior put it, "If a sorority or fraternity isn't your thing, it can get a little boring." A new student center has just been completed and the college hopes it will broaden student social options.

Making the Arrangements

All Albion students must live on-campus. Some feel that this leaves "no escape from institutional living," but admit they "knew this was the deal when we enrolled." Freshmen live together in Wesley Hall. For the remaining three years, students can choose to live in one of the three main coed dorms (Seaton, Twin Towers, and Whitehouse Hall), the campus fraternity houses (few sorority members choose the live-in option), some "slightly off-campus" college-owned apartments, or all-female dorms.

> Students report that "almost everyone is active in something," from the student senate to the newspaper to a campus political group.

Aside from community service groups, students have minimal interaction with the town, which is racially diverse and economically depressed in contrast to the largely white and upper-middle-class college population. Some students feel that town-gown relations might improve since the admission committee recently increased minority recruitment.

Undergrads who seem most comfortable at Albion are those who have grown up in a small town. Many students have trouble making the adjustment, and one said that most seniors he knows are "ready to leave after four years." The small environment reportedly "weeds out" students who are interested only in a social life, leaving behind the academically inclined.

It is not surprising that more than one student used the phrase "make your own fun" to describe the social scene at Albion. Many said that they meant it more as a challenge than a criticism. There is no question that Albion is not for everyone, but perhaps the best thing about it is that it does not claim to be.—*Heather Topel and Staff*

FYI

The three best things about attending Albion are "the internship opportunities, the strong student-faculty relationship, and how active people are here."

The three worst things about attending Albion are "the extensive academic requirements, living in Albion itself, and the small-town mentality."

The three things that every student should do before graduating from Albion are "get involved, drink lots of coffee, and procrastinate long and often."

One thing I'd like to have known before coming here is "how small this place can be."

Alma College

Address: 614 W. Superior Street, Alma, MI 48801
Phone: 800-321-ALMA
E-mail address: admission@alma.edu
Web site URL: www.alma.edu
Location: small city
Founded: 1886
Private or Public: Private
Religious affiliation: Presbyterian
Undergraduate enrollment: 1,383
Total enrollment: 1,383
Percent Male/Female: 42%/58%
Percent Minority: 10.2%

Percent African-American: 1.9%
Percent Hispanic: 1.7%
Percent Asian: 6.0%
Percent in-state/out-of-state: 95%/5%
Percent Pub HS: 93%
Fraternities: 23%
Sororities: 23%
Number of Applicants: 1,439
Percent Accepted: 82%
Percent Accepted who enroll: 32%
Entering: 377
Transfers: 38
Application Deadline: NA

Mean SAT: NA
Middle 50% SAT range: NA
Middle 50% ACT range: 25
Mean ACT: 24.93
3 Most popular majors: bus. adm, biology, education
Retention: 89%
Graduation rate: 70%
Library: 230,398 volumes
Tuition and Fees: $14,998 in; NA out
Room and Board: $5,460
On-campus housing: 90%
Financial aid, first-year: 97%

The Alma College campus is a pleasant place—"The buildings are red and white brick, not Gothic or modern" and have "a nice feel." The MacIntyre Plaza has a garden and chairs, and there are trees and flowers everywhere. Both the beauty and the idyllic solitude of the campus reflect what students describe as an isolated, cozy place to receive a liberal arts education.

A Well-Rounded Education

Students at Alma take 168 credits, normally 46 courses, to earn a degree, and along with selecting an area of concentration, they must complete a range of general-education requirements. These include courses in Basic Skills, a year of English and one semester of mathematics, and courses fulfilling requirements in Historical Perspectives, Fine Arts and Humanities, Social Sciences, and Life and Physical Sciences. Before finishing these courses, students must do lab work in the sciences, and take courses in creative or performing arts, religion or philosophy, and literature. Creative and performing arts classes take advantage of the extensive and beautiful Heritage Center and the "theater and dance departments, which are strong for a school of Alma's size." The performing arts requirement can be accomplished with anything from piano lessons, to highland dance classes, a reflection of the school's Scottish heritage.

The academic calendar includes a month-long spring term after the traditional spring semester. Everyone must complete two spring terms, usually after sophomore and junior years. One course must be a designated "S" course, which usually involves travel. Classes meet every day and can be "highly intense," but one junior noted that the homework load is usually about the same as that of four courses during the regular semester. Offerings are generally creative: one student's rhetoric class traveled to Detroit to help prisoners write essays, while another class visited African-American churches throughout the area. Some students spend the term interning in journalism in Washington, D.C., traveling with the education department to London schools, or going to Australia with the business club.

"No Easy Way Out"

Student opinions on the level of academic intensity vary. One sophomore said that the workload was comparable to other schools, while a junior said that everyone has "a ton of work." All students agree that professors push the students, who are generally from the top of their high school classes. "Students are at college because they want to go, not [because they] have to go. Everyone is academically-oriented and career driven," said one senior. "Everyone is used to being the best and tries to do it again," although no one feels that the school is dog-eat-dog or has unfriendly competition. Grading is "tough, but not impossible," and some of the toughest work happens in introductory courses because "every department has weeder courses . . . to keep classes small."

Alma's strongest programs include the sciences (especially biology), education, and business. Exercise and Health Science (EHS) is a popular option, especially for those aspiring to medical school. A new wing, which includes a cadaver lab, opened in the physical education building in December 1997 to accommodate the growing interest in EHS. Students have few complaints about any one department, although traditional majors such as philosophy and mathematics are quite small.

Class size at Alma usually averages around 20 students, and the largest course on-campus has about 65 students. Most professors "work to facilitate discussion" and "work really hard to know students." They give out e-mail addresses, home phone numbers, and hold office hours. One junior reported that students could even send e-mail to the college president and expect an answer. Students had no problems getting into classes (a talk with the professor of a closed class usually does the trick,) but one undergrad explained that at a school as small as Alma not every course is offered every semester. Another noted the need for greater diversity in the curriculum, citing the limited course offerings in areas such as Jewish religion and women's studies.

"Cheers"

Alma college is a small college in a small town, and students report that they know almost everyone. The students have nicknamed the school Cheers, "because everyone knows everyone's name." Students even said that they have specific spots in the dining hall where everyone knows they sit. Cliques are "inevitable" and the school is sometimes "too small," but most students are happy with this atmosphere, and picked Alma because of it. "It is a big, friendly, teddy-bear place," said one junior.

The students within the "Alma Bubble" are fairly homogenous, mostly white, middle class, and from suburbs north of Detroit, or from small towns surrounding Alma. Few students are from other states or ethnic groups, and the school is working hard to recruit a more diverse student body. Although the student body has a reputation for being conservative, one student reported that he was "not looked down on for being liberal." The Young Republicans are active on-campus, but "if you come in right wing and uptight, you cannot leave that way." Although minority recruitment is a somewhat touchy issue, "most people realize that the campus would be more interesting and have more flair [if it were more diverse]." Homosexuality is also fairly accepted; a popular female art professor is openly married to another woman.

Quiet Campus

Students describe Alma as very quiet on the weekends. Alma is "an hour away from everything, and once you're on campus you have to study because there's nothing else to do." Although the college has a sizable number of Greeks, and though there are parties most weekends, students feel little pressure to rush or drink. Fraternity parties are small affairs compared to those at nearby Central Michigan University or Michigan State, partially because the administration owns the houses, and "the dean of students will go to every fraternity party more than once [to check it out]." Dorm parties occur, but students are careful "not to draw attention to it."

Many students leave campus for socializing, partially because "they want a change of environment from studying so hard." One senior estimated that she left campus two weekends out of every month. Popular destinations include CMU and MSU, along with Mount Pleasant, which has "better restaurants," a casino, and several popular bars, including Wayside, which features swing dancing.

On weekends, a main force on-campus is ACUB, or Alma College Union Board. ACUB sponsors coffeehouses with live music on Friday nights, and brings concerts, films, and other events to campus, which are generally "very well-attended." Sororities throw formals throughout the year, and homecoming involves a week of celebration and draws many alums back to campus.

Comfortable Living

Alma dorms earn few complaints. Freshmen and sophomores usually live on main campus, in one of four dorms, two all-male and two all-female. All of the rooms are fairly similar, and "bigger than a lot of schools." The administration is in the process of upgrading all of the rooms, wiring them for the Internet, and adding new furniture and carpeting. Juniors and seniors can move to South Complex, which is further from the classroom buildings and "more like an apartment complex." Theme housing is also available, and fraternities and sororities have limited residential space.

Marriot provides all of Alma's meals, although the main dining hall, Hamilton Commons, retains the nickname Saga, after the company that once provided food. The food is described as very good, with hot food, a grill, a salad bar, deserts, vegetarian items, and a deli at every meal. Students can also take Munch Money to Scottie's, a convenience store, or Joe's, a popular hangout that serves hamburgers. Also, the dining hall staff is very "nutrition-oriented" and displays nutritional information above all the foods served.

Sports and Honors Societies

Almost everyone at Alma is involved in extracurricular activities, and students point out that they have a large number of organizations for the school's size, probably more than 100. Of that number, only 20 to 25 are social, and most of the others are connected with some academic discipline. "Most people strive to be a part of [honorary] societies," said one senior. There is also a strong Model UN team and several popular Christian organizations.

> **"Once you are on campus you have to study because there's nothing else to do."**

Almost half of the student body is involved in varsity athletics. Because most athletes can be on full teams, intramurals are less popular, although the school plans to build a new IM facility beginning in the spring of 2000. School spirit runs high at Alma, and football and soccer games are well attended. One cheerleader said, "Our away-game crowd is often bigger than [the opposing team's] home crowd."

Alma College is admittedly a small college in a very small town. But the isolation of the "Alma Bubble" is not necessarily a turnoff. Students feel that their education is well-rounded and solid, and that their community is friendly. One spirited junior even said, "It's a bubble because it's so perfect!" —*Bethany Lacina*

YI

he three best things about attending Alma are, "the accessibility of the administration, the academics, especially the dance and theater departments, and the Spring Term."
he three worst things about attending Alma are, "the Alma Bubble, the prevalence of cliques, and the lack of social activities/opportunities at Alma and its towns."
he three things that every student should do before graduating Alma are "trying to stay on campus for some weekends, revel in the school's athletic spirit, and get involved in a honorary society."
ne thing I'd like to have known before coming here is "how small it really is!"

Kalamazoo College

Address: Office of Admission, 1200 Academy Street, Kalamazoo, MI 49006
Phone: 800-253-3602
E-mail address: admission@kzoo.3eu
Web site URL: www.k200.edu
Location: small city
Founded: 1833
Private or Public: Private
Religious affiliation: none
Undergraduate enrollment: 1,367
Total enrollment: 1,367
Percent Male/Female: 44%/56%
Percent Minority: 9.4%

Percent African-American: 3.3%
Percent Hispanic: 1.5%
Percent Asian: 4.5%
Percent in-state/out-of-state: 70%/30%
Percent Pub HS: 85%
Fraternities: 0%
Sororities: 0%
Number of Applicants: 1,410
Percent Accepted: 77%
Percent Accepted who enroll: 34%
Entering: 370
Transfers: 18
Application Deadline: 1 Feb
Mean SAT: 640 V, 622 M

Middle 50% SAT range: 590–690 V, 570–670 M
Middle 50% ACT range: 26–29
Mean ACT: 27.6
3 Most popular majors: economics, biology, political science
Retention: 89%
Graduation rate: 71%
Library: 300,978 volumes
Tuition and Fees: $19,188 in; $19,188 out
Room and Board: $5,787
On-campus housing: 99%
Financial aid, first-year: 97%

What is an ideal liberal arts school? Maybe it is one that would offer more than the generic promise of small class size and a well-rounded education. Students at Kalamazoo College in western Michigan think their K-Plan does just that. Before graduation, they will be exposed to traditional, experiential, and foreign education, in a friendly environment.

Special K

Under Kalamazoo's K-Plan, students are required to take courses across the liberal arts and sciences, including emphasis on the "K" Foundations of written expression, oral expression, quantitative reasoning, and information and computer literacy. Also, five quarters of physical education are mandatory. Few students are bothered by these requirements because, as one junior said, "You can go Rollerblading three times a week and call it PE."

Students are also encouraged to complete a quarter of Career Development, usually as an off-campus internship. Course credit is not granted, but 85 percent of students still participate. They keep a journal for the school, and the work experience is recorded on their transcript. Also optional, but very common among juniors, is foreign study, taken during either both the fall and winter quarters, or over the spring quarter. While students can travel to every continent and innumerable countries, the most popular program is in Madrid, "where the school sends all the Spanish students who don't really speak Spanish." Seniors complete a SIP (Senior Individualized Project), an original thesis that must be defended before a panel of faculty from the student's major.

In addition to all of this, a freshmen writing seminar is mandatory, as well as 25 LAC (liberal arts colloquium) credits, which can be fulfilled through attendance of on-campus cultural events, such as Kalamazoo Symphony Chamber Orchestra concerts, scholarly lectures, and professional theater productions. Students enjoy the LAC credit requirement, and one student said, "I had them done before the end of sophomore year. Lots [of the events] are really interesting." There are some recent modifications to the K-Plan. All graduates will now be completing a Web portfolio, which is an online record of school and work experiences, which one student sees as a "fairly simple" requirement. The administration has also eliminated on-campus classes in the summer, and Career Development now usually happens the summer after sophomore year, instead of in the spring. Motivating factors for this change included the chance to allow more continual involvement in extracurricular activities. Other students have pointed out that the new calendar has made class scheduling, especially in the sciences, more difficult.

Academically Intense

Kalamazoo academics are generally described as "very intense." One chemistry major said, "You can just go to class and get B's, but you really have to put work in to get A's." "Stress levels are high here," noted another student, partially because classes move quickly to fit material into a quarter rather than a semester. Foreign languages are especially difficult to master in the limited time frame. Kalamazoo is well-known for its biological sciences, and pre-med, pre-law and the natural science majors are the "hard-core stressed-out people." Pre-meds also have the largest classes, with introductory science courses averaging around 60 students. According to some students, the administration favors the science programs. "They have the most spending and the most scholarships available," said one biology

major. A sociology major complained that his department is understaffed by comparison.

Faculty in Flux

Most students like their professors, and say they are "cool people," but are concerned with the administration's handling of faculty, particularly with the high faculty turnover in recent years. This turnover is due partially to administrative initiatives, and partially to lower-than-average faculty salaries. A senior chemistry major noted that the department has been dismantled except for one teacher, and is now made up of temporary faculty. Despite these difficulties, however, teaching assistants exist only to oversee introductory labs, and native speakers are used as TAs in language labs. A French major, with a German and Chinese double minor, exclaimed about the TAs: "I cannot tell you how helpful it is [to have a native speaker]."

Still Liberal Heaven?

Kalamazoo's community has long been marked by its liberality, though its population remains fairly homogenous. Most of the students are white, upper-middle-class Michigan residents. Although, one senior said, there are two groups, "one that pays full tuition, and the other receives a whole lot of aid." The school is working to bring more minorities to both the student body and the faculty through a new staff position devoted to diversity initiatives and the student organization CORD (Coalition on Race and Diversity).

Politically, most students lean to the left. "Lots of people wear gay pride rainbows on their backpacks and everyone wears a ribbon on AIDS Day." The most popular extracurricular activities on-campus are those related to liberal causes. Respected groups include the Black Student Organization (BSO), Envirorg (the Environmental Organization), and the Non-Violent Students Association. Students celebrate "Coming Out Day," and "Pentagon Day," when the military and war in general are protested with slogans such as "Beer, not bombs." Community service is also popular, with a strong Habitat for Humanity chapter. Students also participate in a wide range of non-social action groups in the performing arts, various academic groups, and even a Society for Creative Anachronism, a group that celebrates all things medieval. One student said, "Most people are involved in at least a couple of things.".

A Varied Social Life

Social life at Kalamazoo is not that of a typical party school. One junior said, "Freshmen tend to party, while upperclassmen chill out a bit more and have dinner parties with wine." School sponsored formals, held about once a quarter, are poorly attended and "are most fun if you get drunk before you go—most people go that way." In the absence of fraternities, most parties are held by students who live off-campus, by some of the sports teams, or as small gatherings in dorm rooms. Students report little pressure to drink, especially after freshmen year, and there are always alternative cultural activities on-campus. The quarterly theater productions and the improvisational group Monkapult, for example, are very popular. The city of Kalamazoo adds little to the school's social life and students tend to live in "the K Bubble," venturing out only for road trips to Chicago or Detroit.

Although Kalamazoo is small, few are willing to characterize it as cliquey. "People have their own groups of friends, but I've met new people even into my senior year," said one student. Athletic teams, especially the men's and women's swim teams, are known for being elitist, but few other extracurricular activities dominate a person's social life. One sophomore said she would be "comfortable asking anyone to do something for her." Another student was more cautious, saying, "If you survive the smallness of Kalamazoo the first year, you'll love it."

Students tend to be unenthusiastic about athletics. Few people attend sporting events, even for successful teams like swimming and tennis, both the male and female squads. Pickup soccer and Ultimate Frisbee games ("the most popular sport on-campus") dot the Quad. Kalamazoo alums are even known to bring their disks back to campus over homecoming to play the school's long-standing Frisbee golf course.

Ghet-Trow and the Great Dorms

The housing policy at Kalamazoo has just undergone a major change; recently, for the first time, seniors could live off-campus. Many seniors have taken advantage of relatively inexpensive apartments in historical homes surrounding campus. One senior said, "I walk into the dining hall and see only 10 people I know [because so many are off-campus]." Students living on-campus are fairly enthusiastic about the dorms, all of which are coed. One junior said that they are "the best thing at K. They're socially conducive, because you live, work, and play with the same people." Two dormitories contain suites, and the others have a mixture of doubles, quads, and some singles. All the dorms have been remodeled in the last two years, including the replacement of carpets with bare tile floors. Harmon is "a good size and social," while Trowbridge, the oldest of the dormitories, earns the nickname Ghet-Trow (from "ghetto") for its large size and convoluted layout.

> "Lots of people wear gay pride rainbows on their backpack and everyone wears a ribbon on AIDS day."

The K meal plan ranges from ten meals a week to a carte blanche, and includes money that can be used at Quadstop, a '50s-style restaurant in the student center, "which is good for studying when you don't really want to study." The one dining hall on-campus, Hicks Center, has been recently remodeled, and students are pleased with the facilities, though the food is "all the same . . . normal dining hall food."

Kalamazoo College naturally stands out among many small schools, with its uniquely close-knit community and the K-Plan. It offers a strong, thorough academic experience with a comfortable college lifestyle. —*Bethany Lacina*

FYI

The three best things about attending Kalamazoo are, "its academic K-Plan, CORD, and the close-knit community."

The three worst things about attending Kalamazoo are, "the intensity of academics because of the quarter system, the high faculty turn-over, and the smallness of the school."

The three things that every student should do before graduating Kalamazoo are "participate in Career Development, go abroad, and participate in social activism or community work."

One thing I'd like to have known before coming here is "that I would rarely see a professor twice over the years because they come and go so quickly."

Michigan State University

Address: 250 Hannah Administration Building, East Lansing, MI 48824
Phone: 517-355-8332
E-mail address: admis@msu.edu
Web site URL: www.msu.edu
Location: small city
Founded: 1855
Private or Public: public
Religious affiliation: none
Undergraduate enrollment: 33,571
Total enrollment: 43,571
Percent Male/Female: 47%/53%
Percent Minority: 15.5%

Percent African-American: 8.7%
Percent Hispanic: 2.3%
Percent Asian: 3.9%
Percent in-state/out-of-state: 91%/9%
Percent Pub HS: NA
Fraternities: 5%
Sororities: 5%
Number of Applicants: 22,751
Percent Accepted: 72%
Percent Accepted who enroll: 41%
Entering: 6,650
Transfers: 2,596
Application Deadline: rolling

Mean SAT: 563 V, 547 M
Middle 50% SAT range: NA
Middle 50% ACT range: NA
Mean ACT: 23.7
3 Most popular majors: business-marketing, psychology, accounting
Retention: 88.0%
Graduation rate: 69.0%
Library: 4,200,000 volumes
Tuition and Fees: $4,418 in; $11,820 out
Room and Board: $4,298
On-campus housing: 98%
Financial aid, first-year: 42%

Michigan State University, located in East Lansing, Michigan, is a large university with a friendly, inviting personality. Students at MSU work hard, party often, and enjoy the numerous benefits that Michigan State offers them.

Lots of Choices

Academically, Michigan State provides a varied and challenging program. All freshmen must take several required classes, including precalculus, English, and an integrated arts and humanities class called American Thought and Language. In addition to the standard MSU undergraduate curriculum, students can apply to specialized honors colleges within the university, including the general honors college, a science honors college called Lyman Briggs, and the James Madison Honors Arts and Letters program. These colleges

have specific requirements, including set living arrangements in certain dorms, and often have separate classes reserved for their students.

No matter the college, students generally find MSU's academics challenging. "I never feel like I'm totally caught up," explained one undergrad. "Sometimes I just wish I could stop the clock, catch up on all my work, then press play again." Introductory courses specifically are often more difficult than students expect. "They use the huge intro courses to weed out students who aren't really committed to the subject," said one student. "You really have to work hard to stay afloat."

Among academic disciplines, students complain that the math department is by far the worst on-campus. "Math here is absolutely horrendous," said one undergrad. "Horrible, just horrible," echoed another student. "Math is all taught by TAs, at least in the lower-level courses." The teaching assistants also faced criticism. "One of my TAs can barely speak a word of English, and another one couldn't teach a math class to kindergartners," said one student. "They simply don't know enough about teaching," explained another undergrad. "They might know all the math or science in the world, but if they cannot bring it down to our level, they're not doing their job."

However, large class sizes make TAs essential to the learning process at MSU. Huge lecture classes have small TA-led discussion sections so that students can participate in class. Most students expressed satisfaction with the mix of small and large classes, but some complained of downsides to large lecture sections. "It limits what the professor can do," said one undergrad. "It can make it difficult to get individual help and nearly impossible for the professor to give anything but multiple-choice tests. The professor and TAs would never have enough time to grade 500 essays." Overall, students say they are happy with their academic regimen. "It can be difficult, but we have great professors working to help us understand really hard material," said one student.

The Social Side

As for social life, MSU lives up to its party school reputation. The Greek system is very strong in East Lansing, and frat parties provide a large part of the social scene. Open parties are rare, with students struggling to get their names added to lists of potential partygoers. "Women have a much easier time getting into frat parties," said one undergrad. "If you don't know someone in the frat, guys are out of luck, but girls can just go and ask nicely and they'll be let in." House parties are also common, and much less discriminating. "Anyone willing to pay the $3, or whatever, is welcome at most house parties," explained one student. Undergrads claim that random hookups make for the majority of romance on-campus. But dating couples, while in the minority, do have a presence as well.

Drinking constitutes a large part of MSU social life. "Alcohol here is free-flowing," said one student. Non-drinkers do not seem to feel left out of the party scene, however. "You can go to the party, dance and talk to friends, and have a great time, all without drinking," said one undergrad. Though marijuana use is relatively common, students report that other illegal drugs are rare on campus. Simply hanging out in dorms or houses is another common pastime for Michigan State students. The campus has no shortage of entertainment possibilities, with many movie theaters and popular concert venues, like the Breslin Center.

Living It Up?

Freshmen at MSU are required to live in dorms, with the option to move off-campus starting sophomore year. Most, however, spend sophomore year in dorms, only moving to a house, apartment, sorority, or fraternity their junior year. Students generally complain about the quality of dorm rooms. "They're like a closet," said one student. Because of the small size of the rooms, lofts, which elevate the students' beds and leave more space to relax in the room, are very common. About half of the dorm rooms are suites, with two doubles sharing a bathroom. Other dorm rooms are mostly doubles, and students share a bathroom with other residents of the floor. One dorm, Mason Abbot, recently underwent renovations, and its central location makes it popular among undergrads.

Students have a variety of choices for meal plans. They can eat at any of the 14 undergraduate dining halls with a choice of 10, 15, 20, or an unlimited number of meals per week included in the plan. In addition, students can open a Spartan Cash account, which allows them to purchase items at Sparty's Convenience stores, Owen Cafe, Lafayette Squire, Hungry Howie's Pizza, and can also be used for laundry.

Bringing It All Together

Students praise MSU's sprawling campus. "It's huge," said one undergrad. "We've got beautiful parks, wide-open spaces, and even nature trails." But despite its great size, students claim that the campus brings the student body together. "Even though it's a really big campus it feels much more like a small town," explained one student. "It's the people that make the place, and the people here are nicer than any group I've ever seen." Students at MSU tend to see the university's main asset as the students themselves. "The people here are just incredible," said one underclassman. "When I moved in I thought that it would be really hard to meet people, but everyone is so nice. If you run into someone you don't know on the street, you can just start up a conversation and meet someone new."

Beyond Spartan Academia

As can be expected at such a large university, opportunities for extracurricular activities abound. Popular organizations range from campus wide political groups all the way down to dorm hallway organizational units. Students find there is no lack of involvement on-campus. Whether it's with the Aerospace Club, the African-American Film Association, Gospel Chorale, or the East Lansing Progressives, "Everyone I know is involved in some kind of group," said one undergrad.

One extracurricular that draws attention from all parts of campus is varsity sports. As a member of the Big Ten Conference, MSU faces some of the toughest athletic competition around. A nationally ranked football team continually draws crowds of more than 75,000 fans to cheer them on, and basketball and hockey also have a large student following. Non-varsity athletes can take part in intramurals.

> **"Everyone you meet at this place is proud to be a Spartan."**

Students consider school spirit to be very high on campus, and they take great pride in MSU's long tradition of excellence, which carries all the way back to 1855 when it was founded as the first land-grant school in the country. Said one student, "If there's one thing you can generalize about almost all the students here, and that's hard at such a big school, it's that everyone you meet at this place is really proud to be a Spartan."—*Jeff Kaplow and Staff*

FYI

The three best things about attending MSU are, "that it is the ultimate party school, that it has a strong Greek system, and that you can still get a good education."

The three worst things about attending MSU are, "the math department, the abundance of terrible TAs, and the enormous class sizes."

The three things that every student should do before graduating MSU are "rush—it makes your social life much more easy, live in an apartment—dorm life is nothing to write home about, and take pride in being a Spartan."

One thing I'd like to have known before coming here is "that I should not worry about the size because the people are so nice and friendly. There is always the opportunity to meet new people."

University of Michigan

Address: 1220 Student Activities Building, Ann Arbor, MI 48109-1316
Phone: 734-764-7433
E-mail address: ugadmiss@umich.edu
Web site URL: www.umich.edu
Location: urban
Founded: 1817
Private or Public: public
Religious affiliation: none
Undergraduate enrollment: 24,015
Total enrollment: 36,450
Percent Male/Female: 50%/50%
Percent Minority: 26.0%

Percent African-American: 9.0%
Percent Hispanic: 4.0%
Percent Asian: 12.0%
Percent in-state/out-of-state: 71%/29%
Percent Pub HS: 80%
Fraternities: 20%
Sororities: 20%
Number of Applicants: 19,114
Percent Accepted: 69%
Percent Accepted who enroll: 42%
Entering: 5,327
Transfers: 1,074
Application Deadline: 1 Feb

Mean SAT: NA
Middle 50% SAT range: 560–660 V, 590–700 M
Middle 50% ACT range: NA
Mean ACT: NA
3 Most popular majors: psychology, business administration, mechanical engineering
Retention: 95.0%
Graduation rate: 57.0%
Library: 6.5 million volumes
Tuition and Fees: $6,070 in; $18,910 out
Room and Board: $5,486
On-campus housing: 97%
Financial aid, first-year: 36%

Thousands of fans and alumni wake up every morning with Michigan banners on their walls and the fading sounds of the "Victors" fight song ringing in their ears. With more alumni than any other school and a huge fan base due to the most successful college sports program in history, Michigan students cannot go anywhere without finding a friendly Wolverine connection. "Even when I was traveling in Kenya," said one undergrad, "I could swear that one of the Masai tribesmen was wearing a Michigan hat."

The Leaders and Best

The University of Michigan is known for excellence in many areas and, following closely to the words of its fight song, many of its academic departments are "the leaders and best" in their fields. "There's no such thing as a bad major at Michigan," said one student. "We know we really cannot go wrong, even at such a large school with so many choices." U of M consists of 13 colleges, including nursing, dental, drama, engineering, and business, among others; the largest is the College of Literature, Science and the Arts (LSA). Each school has different admissions options, with some admitting undergrads directly from high school and others admitting students only after sophomore year.

Popular majors include psychology, political science, biology, and English. While graduation requirements vary across majors, undergrads must fulfill distributional requirements in foreign languages, quantitative reasoning, humanities, social science, natural science, and writing. There are many special programs for Michigan undergrads. Inteflex is an elite 8-year combined B.A. and M.D. program. The Honors program gives students' access to specific honors classes and increased access to professors. The Residential College (RC) program is designed to make a large university much smaller by placing all RC students in the same dorm. RC classes (which can also be taken by students not in the Residential College) are small, and students receive evaluations rather than grades. In addition, many dorms have special academic programs associated with them. Mary Markley Residence Hall hosts the 21st Century Program, which helps students adjust to the college experience, and the Lloyd Scholars program—for those living in Alice Lloyd Residence Hall—houses teachers in close proximity to students.

Weekend Fun

Underclassmen report that their social lives revolve around sororities and fraternities. "There's a lot of pressure to rush," explained one sophomore, "because fraternity parties are the only game in town before you turn 21 and can get into bars." Recently, there has been a crackdown on underage drinking, however, and frat parties are no longer such a guaranteed good time. "They've never had lists to get into parties before, but now you definitely have to know someone to get into a frat party," said one student.

Upperclassmen reportedly move away from the Greek scene. "Bars are very popular if you're of age. Ann Arbor has a fantastic bar scene," said one undergrad. Popular drinking spots include Rick's, Touchdown's, and Scorekeeper's. For non-drinkers, Ann Arbor offers a number of movie theaters, concerts, and coffee shops. "Sure, most people drink," said one student, "but that does not mean that those who don't can't have a good time, too." Students said that while drugs are prevalent on-campus, there's no real pressure to participate. "Lots of my friends smoke pot, but I never feel like I have to join in," said one undergrad. Common drugs include pot and "lemons" (also known as GHB), which enhance the effects of alcohol.

Students say that while there seem to be more than enough attractive students on-campus, finding that significant other can be a difficult process. "For underclassmen, hooking up at parties is the norm," explained one student, "but as you get older, you tend to move away from that. Maybe it's because you're going to less crazy frat parties, and more just hanging out with your friends." Some students bemoaned the lack of dating at U of M. "Nobody seems to date here—either you hook up, or you're engaged; there's nowhere in between," said one undergrad.

Home Sweet Home

Students overwhelmingly praised Ann Arbor as a "great college town." The streets of the small city boast an eclectic mix of shops, with many music stores, bookstores, cafes, and restaurants. There are movie theaters, clubs, and bars for entertainment, and the busy streets remain crowded with students until very late at night. "I feel very safe and comfortable in downtown Ann Arbor." Still, some students warn against complacency: "No matter how safe you may feel, you should always walk home in groups," cautioned one undergrad.

Students generally move off campus after freshman year, living in a private house or apartments in Ann Arbor, or moving into a fraternity or sorority house. Although some sophomores choose to live in dorms, the on-campus residence halls are made up of mostly freshmen. Incoming students choose their housing by ranking three locations: North Campus, Central Campus, and the Hill. From their rankings, they are assigned to individual dorms in one of these areas. Students say that Central Campus has the best location and the Hill has the best social life, but North Campus is very undesirable. "Only engineering and art students want to live there because it's close to their classes," explained one student. "For everyone else, it's so far away that you almost feel like you're at a different school." Students also make use of the special residential programs (the 21st Century Program and Lloyd Scholars Program) to guarantee themselves a place in a certain residence hall. Once admitted to the program, students must live in the designated dorm. "I applied to Lloyd Scholars," said one undergrad, "because there's no way I'm getting stuck on North Campus."

Wolverine Pride

U of M students love their sports teams. The fantastic success of the entire athletic program ensures that students and local fans alike will continue packing into sports venues and cheering on their teams. Among the many great programs, the highlight of Michigan sports is football. A perennial contender for Big Ten Conference champion, the maize and blue often find themselves in the hunt for the national championship. Every year culminates in their final game: a battle against archrival Ohio State. Explained one student, "It's like a fight between good and evil. The Wolverines represent all that we stand for, and the Buckeyes [of Ohio

State] are a threat to our very way of life!" Other notable football rivals include Michigan State, which prompts wild parties as high school friends at the two schools are reunited, and Minnesota, which plays Michigan every year for the Brown Jug, the oldest trophy in college football. U of M basketball and hockey garner huge support from the student body, as well—students have been known to camp out for two days to secure the best hockey tickets.

For non-varsity athletes, Michigan offers numerous club sports and intramurals. Club sports at Michigan are reportedly "taken very seriously," and often rank with other schools' varsity programs. Intramurals allow fraternities, sororities, and dorm hallways to compete in such classics as ice hockey and such innovative contests as broomball. "The sports facilities here are really great," said one undergrad. "They have everything you need."

With more than 650 registered student organizations, U of M offers many options for extracurricular life. Popular activities include writing for the Michigan Daily, singing in a cappella groups, performing in numerous theater groups, and joining pre-professional societies, depending on one's major. "Anything you want to do, there's an organization for you," said one student. In addition, Michigan's extracurricular activities system is very decentralized and makes it easy for students to start a new club or society. "If you cannot find it, you can make it," said one undergrad.

U of M combines all the resources of a large university with a top-notch academic environment and immense school spirit. Just attending an average football game or walking down the streets of Ann Arbor offers a glimpse of the Michigan experience. Students warn not to fit U of M into the mold of the average state school. "We're better than the rest," one student explained, "in sports and academics, and even in our little idiosyncrasies." One such tradition takes place every spring during finals. Students take a break from studying and run in the Midnight Naked Mile: "First you see a thousand people, and you think that's the most naked people you've ever seen," said one undergrad. "Then you see another thousand run past you. It's simply amazing."—*Jeff Kaplow*

FYI

The three best things about attending U of M are, "its school pride, a great college town, and top-notch academics."

The three worst things about attending U of M are, "the pressure to rush, the normalcy of hook-ups, and the overwhelmingly large scale of everything."

The three things that every student should do before graduating U of M are "take advantage of Wolverine connections, enjoy Ann Arbor's great bar scene, and run in the Midnight Naked Mile!"

One thing I'd like to have known before coming here is "to avoid living in North Campus like the plague your freshman year."

Minnesota

Carleton College

Address: 100 South College Street, Northfield, MN 55057
Phone: 507-646-4190
E-mail address: admissions@acs.carleton.edu
Web site URL: www.carleton.edu
Location: rural
Founded: 1866
Private or Public: private
Religious affiliation: none
Undergraduate enrollment: 1,881
Total enrollment: 1,881
Percent Male/Female: 47%/53%
Percent Minority: 17.0%

Percent African-American: 3.0%
Percent Hispanic: 4.0%
Percent Asian: 9.0%
Percent in-state/out-of-state: 23%/77%
Percent Pub HS: 76%
Fraternities: 0%
Sororities: 0%
Number of Applicants: 2,871
Percent Accepted: 56%
Percent Accepted who enroll: 33%
Entering: 484
Transfers: 29
Application Deadline: 15 Jan
Mean SAT: NA

Middle 50% SAT range: 630–730 V, 630–710 M
Middle 50% ACT range: NA
Mean ACT: NA
3 Most popular majors: biology, English, economics
Retention: 95.0%
Graduation rate: 81.0%
Library: 530,000 volumes
Tuition and Fees: $22,470 in; $22,470 out
Room and Board: $4,584
On-campus housing: 100%
Financial aid, first-year: 54%

For a small liberal arts college in rural Minnesota, Carleton College has been doing some moving and shaking. In the surprising admissions turnout for the class of 2002, no one from the waitlist was admitted and therefore, 1998–99 campus housing was filled to capacity. The school combines high-powered academics with a friendly Midwestern atmosphere to give it a character uniquely its own. As one student says, "I never walk anywhere without having someone smiling at me." A sophomore also commented, "At Carleton, I have worked harder than I ever thought I could and played harder than I ever thought was humanly possible."

Academics

Carls take their academics very seriously. They must fulfill requirements in each of four distributional groups (arts and literature, math and science, humanities, and social sciences) in order to graduate. On top of this, students must also fulfill a physical education requirement, a language requirement, and a writing requirement, which is described as particularly difficult by students. Finally, every student is required to take a cultural awareness class, where each student chooses to focus on a culture other than his or her own. While many students welcome this opportunity, others complain that it is simply a way of making a student body lacking in ethnic diversity seem more politically correct. A sophomore said, "The distributional requirements push me to think in ways I thought I wouldn't be comfortable doing." Some of the more popular majors include biology and English. The geology department is also recognized as one of the best in the country.

Carleton students have a very special relationship with their professors. Most students go on a first-name basis, and it isn't uncommon for students to be invited to a professor's house for dinner. Such openness between students and faculty facilitates a very casual atmosphere and an excellent support system. Carleton also has a number of studying facilities that include the Math Skills Center and the "Write Place," both offering tutors 24 hours a day. Classes are taught solely by professors and are kept very small. In fact, the average class size is 17, with 35 percent of the classes having 10 or fewer students. There are TAs, but they are used only as a supplement to the professors.

Home, Sweet Home

Carleton is divided into East and West campus, with West known as the rowdy side. Individual dorms are coed and are not separated by year, allowing freshmen to quickly form close bonds with upperclassmen. There is particularly strong camaraderie within floors. As a sophomore said, "It's all about seeing friends first thing in the morning with messy hair and pajamas!" Besides dorms, upperclassmen have the choice of living in one of 30 theme houses, which include things like language houses and an outdoors clubhouse. In many ways, theme houses take the place of Greek life, which does not exist on-campus. Another popular option is off-campus housing. In fact, half of seniors live in off-campus housing, and much of the upperclassmen party scene is off-campus due to the recent administration crackdown on kegs.

Let the Party Begin

The social life at Carleton is best summarized by a student who said, "You do what you want to do." There are many popular weekend activities including SUMO—the Student Union Movie Organization—and the Cave, a club that attracts many bands and is free to students. Both drinking and pot smoking are fairly widespread, but there is little pressure to participate in either activity. Most of the parties are small private parties, but there are some big yearly all-campus bashes including Spring Fling and the Screw-Your-Roommate

dance where roommates are responsible for finding dates for each other. Recently the administration had made an effort to curb alcohol on-campus, which has prompted several people to move their parties off-campus, but for the most part, the party scene remains the same. For those who seek the excitement of the big city, Carleton has a regular shuttle that takes students between the Twin Cities and the Mall of America, which are forty miles away.

Beyond the Books

Because Carleton is a Division III school, varsity athletics are not the primary interest of many students. Women's rugby, soccer, and basketball are among the more popular varsity teams. However, none of these sports can claim a place in the hearts of students like Ultimate Frisbee. It is played on every level and every floor has its own team, which is a source of great pride. Currently, students claim that there are 1.797 Frisbees per capita. This spirit has helped the women's varsity team to become one of the top three in the nation.

> Currently, students claim that there are 1.797 Frisbees per capita.

There are several other activities besides sports. The student newspaper, the *Carltonian*, is published once a week. Community service is popular, with one-third of the student body participating. Another activity that draws crowds is the modern dance group Ebony, which boasts participation by 1 out of every 10 women on-campus. Even if an activity isn't offered, it is easy to start a new club by signing up a few people.

Academically, Carleton is unbeatable in terms of liberal arts education. Socially, it offers the time of your life.—*Stephanie C. Manson*

FYI
The three best things about attending Carleton are "the small classes, that it's easy to form close relationships with professors, and the laid back atmosphere that allows you to do your own thing."

The three worst things about attending Carleton are "it can get claustrophobic, not much school wide spirit, and the snow in Minnesota."

The three things that every student should do before graduating from Carleton are "learn to really play Frisbee, make frequent trips to Minneapolis–St. Paul, and shop all day at the Mall of America!"

One thing I'd like to have known before coming here is "that people from Minnesota really do talk like the people in that movie, *Fargo*."

Gustavus Adolphus College

Address: 800 W. College Avenue, St. Peter, MN 56082-1498

Phone: 507-933-7676

E-mail address: admission@gustavus.edu

Web site URL: www.gustavus.edu

Location: suburban

Founded: 1862

Private or Public: private

Religious affiliation: Lutheran

Undergraduate enrollment: 2,543

Total enrollment: 2,543

Percent Male / Female: 44%/56%

Percent Minority: 6.0%

Percent African-American: 2.0%

Percent Hispanic: 1.0%

Percent Asian: 3.0%

Percent in-state / out-of-state: 76%/24%

Percent Pub HS: 92%

Fraternities: 26%

Sororities: 20%

Number of Applicants: 1,993

Percent Accepted: 79%

Percent Accepted who enroll: 42%

Entering: 659

Transfers: 25

Application Deadline: 1 Apr

Mean SAT: 610 V, 613 M

Middle 50% SAT range: 560–670 V, 560–670 M

Middle 50% ACT range: 23–29

Mean ACT: 26

3 Most popular majors: biology, psychology, communication studies

Retention: 91%

Graduation rate: 76%

Library: 260,758 volumes

Tuition and Fees: $18,250 in; NA out

Room and Board: $4,605

On-campus housing: 100%

Financial aid, first-year: 90%

The infamous winters of Minnesota might be expected to engender equally cold social environments, yet nothing could be farther from the truth about Gustavus Adolphus College. With excellent academics and a high rate of extracurricular participation, this liberal arts school has a lot to offer its Gustie population—not the least of which is an invitation to the Nobel Conferences held at the college each year.

Unique Curriculum

Gustavus requirements include a personal fitness credit, two human behavior/sociology credits, three writing credits, and one credit in religious studies. Students find the requirements one of the strong points of their college. The school runs on a 4-1-4 schedule, with four classes taken in the fall, one class during a short winter session called J-term, and four more classes during the spring semester. Incoming frosh select a first-semester class, described as a seminar-style "first step into college" course reserved strictly for first-year students. The professor of a student's seminar serves as his or her freshman faculty advisor.

Biology is reportedly the strongest and most popular major at Gustavus. Political science and psychology are popular as well. The biology department guards against overcrowding in introductory courses by splitting classes into two sections of approximately 80 people each (chemistry and psychology do the same). TAs assist students in lab classes, but professors do most of the formal teaching. Students relish the relationships with their professors, who often invite students over for dinner or organize opportunities to conduct research. Professors are also known to have saved students "out registered" from a class. Registration usually works out for most people, althoug one undergrad said, "you may have to do a bit of finagling here and there." Frosh register over the phone before they arrive at school, while other students (with priority to upperclassmen) do so during a four-day period at the beginning of the semester. Academics are definitely competitive at Gustavus, but the "really good balance" that exists makes success an "achievable goal," one student said.

A Hilltop Campus

The self-contained campus is situated on top of a hill within the small town of St. Peter and includes a blend of older buildings and newer ones erected in the 1960s. Students in certain dorms enjoy a view of the Minnesota River Valley. The Arboretum, located on the west side of campus, attracts students looking for a "neat place to go watch the stars at night." St. Peter provides some off-campus housing but is "not much of a metropolis by any means," according to one student. Larger nearby cities include Mankato, a 10-minute drive away, and Minneapolis–St. Paul, less than two hours away. The Safety and Security department provides effective 24-hour security, Night Hosts guard the entryways from the hours of 8 P.M. to 3 A.M., and an escort service is available for students walking through campus at late hours. "I've never felt unsafe on campus," one female student said.

All first-year students are required to live on-campus. The North End is a reputed center for jocks and major party life, while those more interested in a quiet, academic, and artsy environment prefer the South End. The nine campus dorms are coed by floor or, in some cases, by section. Norelius Hall houses frosh and sophomores, and Wahlstrom includes students from all four classes. Dorms have "a lot of community to them," and are often the site of casual socializing or studying. The International House attracts international students and those interested in foreign studies. Collegiate Fellows and Head Residents (similar to RAs) offer a peer-support network. Off-campus houses are available in St. Peter and are close enough so that "off-campus students don't feel isolated."

The College Dining Room (CDR) is the central cafeteria on-campus. According to one student, "When you get the chicken strips, you realize someone loves you. When you get the tuna melt, you know Domino's is always a phone call away." The meal plan is mandatory for first- and second-year students, most of whom live on-campus. An additional option includes the flex plan, which gives students either $75, $100, or $200 to spend as they wish. Students looking for snacks find them at the campus Canteen shop.

The three-floor Gustavus Adolphus campus library, Folke Bernadette, is equipped with computer labs, audio-visual resources, a relatively broad selection of research materials, and an interlibrary loan connection with Mankato State University. Conference rooms also are available for social studying. The newly constructed Olin Hall is a center for math, computer science, and physics, and also has an observatory. The Nobel Hall of Science was renovated just a few years ago, and the King and Queen of Sweden were present during the opening of a new wing.

Golden Gusties

A large number of students participate in intramurals and form teams according to dorm or social group affiliations. Choirs and bands also draw large numbers of students. Future journalists and publishers write for the *Gustavian Weekly*, the primary school newspaper released every Friday, and the biannual *Fire Thorne* literary magazine. A number of students also support the Gustavian college yearbook. While students here generally shy away from political activism, they often engage in community service through the Meaningful Activities for Gusties in Community (MAGIC) student group, which connects undergrads with various community programs. Some students have worked with mental health patients, and the Study Buddies Program allows undergrads the opportunity to tutor area high school students. Less traditional groups include the Gustavus Sauna Society, which meets regularly in the athletic center saunas.

Gustavus Adolphus athletes maintain especially strong traditions in gymnastics and hockey, with the former team winning the national championship four out of the last five years. The new Lund Athletic Center houses all the athletic facilities, such as an ice arena, five racquetball courts, and an indoor track. One student mentioned how "people joke that Lund looks like a country club." The Golden Gustie mascot, Gus the Lion, inspires devoted fans (especially during hockey games) to dress in gold and black, including wigs. Many alumni return during homecoming, which features a dancing debut by the first-year hockey players during the football halftime.

The Campus Activities Board and the Student Activities Office organize most of the social activities on-campus, and the Peer Assistance group promotes parties that advocate "healthy lifestyles." Two big parties are the President's Ball, a formal held each year in a rented hall in the Twin Cities, and Earth Jam, a spring festival featuring multiple bands, which one student called "a very small version of Lollapalooza." Christmas in Christ Chapel attracts people interested in hearing seasonal music from the student choirs and orchestras. Gustavus provides a DJ in the Dive student center every Friday and Saturday night, and the Campus Activities Board also sponsors one or two concerts a year.

Greek participation increases during rush time, but few students describe the Greeks as especially influential in campus social life, although they hold many of the parties on campus. In keeping with the casual social scene, dating is said to be fairly low-key and usually in the context of friendships. According to one student,

"People would like to see dating happen more often."

> According to one student, "People would like to see dating happen more often."

Most Gusties are natives of either Minnesota or the greater Midwest. Students describe their classmates as "not terribly diverse" and feel that a population of white, midwestern students "can get a little frustrating at times." In response to the limited diversity, the Diversity and Affirmation Committee recently held a "Building Bridges" conference aimed at developing a more minority-friendly environment at Gustavus. The college has support groups for Asian and African-American students, but some report that the Hispanic support network is weak. The gay, lesbian, and bisexual students on-campus strongly promote Coming Out Week and dedicate time to increasing student awareness on-campus.

"Everyone has a lot of Gusty pride," one student said. Gusties proudly speak of their academic standing, competitive sports teams, congenial atmosphere, and prime access to the annual Nobel Conferences. Future Gustavus students not only need winter coats and flannel sheets, but also a "get-involved attitude" to maintain the strong Gusty tradition.—*Tahia Reynaga*

FYI
The three best things about attending Gustavus Adolphus are "cool people, winter session, and professors who are on your side."
The three worst things about attending Gustavus Adolphus are "sometimes unrecognizable food, a few cocky athletes, and frostbite."
The three things that every student should do before graduating from Gustavus Adolphus are "go to the President's Ball, go to earth Jam, and go to the Nobel Conferences."
One thing I'd like to have known before coming here is "that you need to talk your way into some classes."

Macalester College

Address: 1600 Grand Ave.,
St. Paul, MN 55105
Phone: 651-696-6357
E-mail address:
admissions@macalester.
edu
Web site URL:
www.macalester.edu
Location: urban
Founded: 1874
Private or Public: private
Religious affiliation:
Presbyterian
**Undergraduate
enrollment:** 1,794
Total enrollment: 1,794
Percent Male / Female:
42%/58%
Percent Minority: 12.4%

Percent African-American:
4.0%
Percent Hispanic: 3.0%
Percent Asian: 5.0%
**Percent in-state / out-of-
state:** 26%/74%
Percent Pub HS: 67%
Fraternities: 0%
Sororities: 0%
Number of Applicants:
3,162
Percent Accepted: 53%
**Percent Accepted who
enroll:** 27%
Entering: 460
Transfers: 31
Application Deadline:
13 Jan
Mean SAT: 664 V, 650 M

Middle 50% SAT range:
610–720 V,
610–690 M
Middle 50% ACT range:
27–31
Mean ACT: 29
3 Most popular majors:
psychology, biology,
economics
Retention: 90.0%
Graduation rate: 77.0%
Library: 477,908 volumes
Tuition and Fees: $21,614
in; $21,614 out
Room and Board: $5,932
On-campus housing:
100%
Financial aid, first-year:
74%

Leave no stone unturned, leave no establishment unquestioned. Macalester students are wickedly proud of their uncanny knack for questioning, injecting, inspecting, detecting, and dissecting every possible establishment in society. Almost every course, from economics to Spanish to history, is taught with a race, class, gender, or sexuality spin. As one student said, "even in the hard sciences, there are classes like 'Biology and the Female Body/Reproduction.'"

Small Class Sizes

Macalester uses its small size of 1,600 students to its advantage in the classroom. All the classes are small and one junior noted that her largest class ever had twenty-seven students in it. Most classes have less than twenty students, and it is not uncommon to have less than ten. This small population fosters close teacher student relationships, though the class size can be a problem for freshmen, who often get shut out.

Until very recently, Macalester offered a J-term: a time to take an exploratory class during the month of January in between the two semesters. During this time, students could take anti-establishment courses like "Cursing and Swearing." Two years ago it was eliminated, and now it is a shade of its former self. The dorms are still open, if the students make arrangements in advance, but no classes are offered directly through Macalester. Now students can use the time to pursue internships, conduct independent studies, or take courses at some of the other schools in the Twin Cities.

As with many colleges and universities around the country, Macalester has its fair share of grade inflation. As and Bs abound, while Cs are "reserved for personal vendettas or total slackers." As one student said, "There's a few crusaders trying to curb it [grade inflation] but everyone just ends up hating them."

From Kosovo to Rothko

The Macalester campus does not remain faithful to a set building type. Situated over four blocks, it sports both red-brick buildings with white trim, and modern, glassy structures, which create an impressive skyline to compliment the fall colors. The newest architectural dilemma on campus is the student union. A new one will be ready by April 2001, but in the meantime, Macs are without a formal student union building. Students are able to make do, though, as the chapel has been turned into a student lounge at lunch and dances are held in the field house in socks—shoes are forbidden. One student complained that, "the place where our union used to be looks like Kosovo. When it is finished, it will look like Rothko." Yet some are excited about the new building and its advertised amenities, like a post office, lecture hall, and innovative dining facilities.

Currently, all students on the meal plan dine at Kagin Commons. Non–first-year students can choose between 12 and 19 meals per week. Vegetarian and vegan options come with every meal, and the Hebrew House in Kirk Hall offers biweekly Shabbat dinners. The food drew poor marks from the students. Unfortunately, it is not even a matter of getting used to the Macalester cuisine: "The food was great my first year, but I detest it now because it is always the same," explained one student.

Macalester has a variety of housing options, ranging from the six-story Dupre Hall to the charming, antiquated Wallace to the aptly named (or unnamed, rather) New Hall, the newest and nameless building on campus. All freshmen and sophomores must live on campus. However, Macalester does not have enough housing for everyone. Seniors get first dibs on the remaining space and many juniors are left to fend for themselves in off-campus housing. Finding apartments is often difficult, and some people end up living far from campus.

One of the Twin Cities's wealthiest residential neighborhoods surrounds Macalester. A small shopping area with a mix of eclectic shops and cafés is conveniently situated right off campus. Transportation is made easy with an excellent and inexpensive bus system. Since Macalester is located directly between Minneapolis and St. Paul, students can experience the best of both cities. The Twin Cities have no lack of clubs and shows, and they are home to nationally renowned icons like the Walker Museum and Prairie Home Companion.

Internationalism

Macalester students say they're known for being "smart, but badly dressed" and are generally proud of this distinction. Because of the trend at Macalester to question everything that has to do with the establishment, women are often stereotyped as ultrafeminist: no makeup, no dresses. And everyone who is politically verbal is considered liberal. The few conservative students on campus are generally quiet, and socialism is the accepted ideal. Macalester currently enrolls students from 76 different countries despite its small size. One famous alumnus includes Secretary General of the United Nations Kofi Annan.

The student body is small and intimate, but some feel that this can get cliquish at times. Others disagree, saying the small atmosphere is a great way to get to know people well. Because of the size of the student body, news travels quickly. One student mourned that this "can be a real molestation when you do something stupid or get a bad reputation."

Hippie Holdout

Macalester students pride themselves in their political and social awareness. In many ways, said one student, Macalester is a "hippie holdout because students hold protests and vigils for darn near everything." Community service is especially big at Macalester, where MACTION maintains its status as a popular community service group. MACTION organizes one-time community service events, but no continuing projects. The Queer Union (QU) is a "really awesome and high profile" group for gays, lesbians, and bisexuals. QU is involved with promoting HIV and AIDS awareness on campus. It reportedly used to organize a mass coming-out party on Parents' Weekend, but the administration convinced its members to change this tradition. Regardless of the group, people usually join some organization that focuses on issues they care about. Other popular groups on campus include Macnaked, a group that holds random Frisbee tournaments in the buff at midnight, and Fresh Concepts, the "funniest improv group on campus."

Although most people participate in activities, varsity sports are not as popular here as elsewhere. The football team rarely wins, and football players in general have a bad reputation. Students equate them with bad high school memories: "We were all oppressed by them in high school, and the tables are definitely turned here." The most popular team on campus is a toss up between men's soccer and women's soccer. At soccer games, bagpipes sound every time the soccer team scores a goal. Women's soccer made headlines when it won the NCAAIII championship in 1998.

For students who do not play sports or the bagpipes, there are plenty of "fun athletic cheers" to urge their team on and upset their opponents. Several students mentioned the cheer, "Drink blood, smoke crack, worship Satan . . . GO MAC!"

Colonial Rematch

Aside from varsity sports, intramurals abound. Soccer seems to be the most popular sport intramural. A favorite non-varsity event is the annual Colonial Rematch. Every fall at Macalester, the European students take on the African students in the ultimate payback for imperialism. The European students, varsity players from Denmark, Germany, or Spain gather in earnest, while the African team shows up, having never practiced, and delay the game half an hour while they "run around the field with flags, take pictures, yell a lot and practice other forms of quite amusing intimidation."

The Greek system has been banished from the Macalester campus, but students generally agree that the Greeks would feel left out anyway. For the Greek-seeker, sports teams often have houses off campus that act as similar communities. But for most students, the parties are quite

sufficient without Greeks. Students rave about the biannual QU dances. One senior claims, "people get naked and dance on the tables long after the lights come on. Nothing like it." Another phenomenon on campus is the "progressive" floor-wide party, where each room offers a different kind of drink. Students go from one room to the next drinking, partying, and dancing in the various ambiences.

> "Macalester students are wickedly proud of their uncanny knack for questioning, injecting, inspecting, detecting, and dissecting every possible establishment in society."

Drinking is big on campus, and visible, but most people feel that it is done in moderation. Alcohol is permitted, provided it is in a private room, but rumors now circulate that the administration wants to make Macalester a dry campus. Pot is the drug of choice, and harder drugs are not accepted. Still, as one student put it, choosing not to drink is "generally respected." The same applies for other drugs. Still, Macalester is not a party school. For better or worse, many people spend the entire weekend studying in the libraries.

Yet despite this, Macalester students are overwhelmingly happy with their college selection. When asked whether, knowing what she knows now, she would choose Macalester again, one senior said, "I would choose this school in a heartbeat."—*Nicole Jabaily*

FYI
The three best things about attending Macalester are "internationalism, small class sizes, and guys in kilts."
The three worst things about attending Macalester are "the career development center, the rate at which gossip travels, and the Minnesota winter."
The three things every student should do before graduating from Macalester are "ring the sex bell, study abroad, and attend the Queer Union dances."
One thing I'd like to have known before coming here is that "students are extremely politically active."

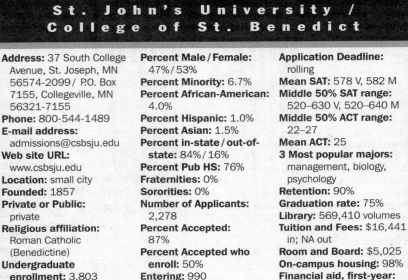

St. John's University / College of St. Benedict

Address: 37 South College Avenue, St. Joseph, MN 56574-2099/ P.O. Box 7155, Collegeville, MN 56321-7155
Phone: 800-544-1489
E-mail address: admissions@csbsju.edu
Web site URL: www.csbsju.edu
Location: small city
Founded: 1857
Private or Public: private
Religious affiliation: Roman Catholic (Benedictine)
Undergraduate enrollment: 3,803
Total enrollment: 3,932

Percent Male/Female: 47%/53%
Percent Minority: 6.7%
Percent African-American: 4.0%
Percent Hispanic: 1.0%
Percent Asian: 1.5%
Percent in-state/out-of-state: 84%/16%
Percent Pub HS: 76%
Fraternities: 0%
Sororities: 0%
Number of Applicants: 2,278
Percent Accepted: 87%
Percent Accepted who enroll: 50%
Entering: 990
Transfers: 100

Application Deadline: rolling
Mean SAT: 578 V, 582 M
Middle 50% SAT range: 520–630 V, 520–640 M
Middle 50% ACT range: 22–27
Mean ACT: 25
3 Most popular majors: management, biology, psychology
Retention: 90%
Graduation rate: 75%
Library: 569,410 volumes
Tuition and Fees: $16,441 in; NA out
Room and Board: $5,025
On-campus housing: 98%
Financial aid, first-year: 92%

St. John's University for men, and its sister campus, the College of St. Benedict for women, give the word "teamwork" a new meaning. Located in northern Minnesota, these two campuses are four miles apart, but are close in every other aspect. "Community" is the byword at St. John's/St. Ben's, beginning with academics. The faculty is approachable, and professors get to know students on a personal level. "If you are having a bad day, the professor will ask you why you're not being yourself," one St. Ben's sophomore said.

To graduate, students must satisfy many liberal arts requirements, including fine arts classes. In addition, all undergrads must take at least six "flagged" courses, which emphasize either writing, discussion, quantitative analysis, gender issues, or global topics. The theology department earns student praise, and courses emphasizing gender development and differences are also popular. The school enjoys a lofty reputation in Minnesota: "Not that money's everything, but you see a lot of their graduates doing

really well around here," one student proudly proclaimed.

The Benefits of the J-Term

Students are also quick to praise the "J-term," a three-week January semester during which they enroll in a single class. "It's a nice transition period, instead of jumping right back into things after Christmas break," one Johnnie said. Many use the J-term to study in other parts of the world. St. John's and St. Ben's offer programs in a broad range of locations, including Cairo, Rome, London, Spain, Greece, China, El Paso, and New York City. Those who opt to stay on-campus for J-term can choose from any number of unconventional courses, including Detective Fiction and Books You've Always Wanted to Read.

The town of "St. Joe" contains a number of popular bars, including Sal's and Loso's (aka "The Middie"). The current favorite of most Johnnies is the LaPlayette (affectionately dubbed "The La"), known for its Taco Tuesday nights. For movies or a good meal, students usually head to the small city of St. Cloud, about a ten-minute drive from either campus. A car is not necessary for a social life; the "great" busing system, which runs until 2 A.M. every night, connects the campuses to St. Joe. Campus hangouts including the pub in the Sexton Commons, a huge new student center on the St. John's campus. The St. Ben's library is also quite a social scene on weeknights—a sharp contrast to the studious atmosphere of the St. John's library.

The Watab Mixer and Pine Stock

Both campuses are large, scenic, and secluded. With a definite sense of privacy, a small island in the middle of Lake Watab is host to the year's two biggest parties: the Watab mixer and Pine Stock. The Joint Events Council, which sets up guest speakers and other campus programs, arranges for a band to play at these parties. Notable guests have included Soul Asylum, Blues Traveler, and the Jayhawks.

Unlike the celebrated *Dead Poets Society* look" of St. John's, St. Benedict has modern architecture—with the noticeable exception of the library. "It sticks out like a sore thumb," said one Bennie, which is not to say Gothic architecture does not have its place on-campus; students affirm that Abbey Church at St. John's is "a beautiful, beautiful building. It's just breathtaking, really."

Catholic Influence, Not Rule

St. Ben's students say there is not a bad dorm to be found on their relatively young campus. Lucky seniors end up in the West Apartments, whose units feature a kitchen, large living room, and two spacious double bedrooms. Johnnies usually vie in the annual housing lottery for the Menton Court, site of 11 luxurious suites of four singles and a large bathroom. Dorms are the only place where Bennies and Johnnies live separate lives—but according to one Johnnie, "They don't do bed checks or anything." Students who live on-campus have a full meal plan, which allows them to eat in either the large commons or a smaller dining hall. Those who live off-campus or in the West Apartments can charge meals on a dining hall account if they wish.

A large portion of the students are children of St. John's/St. Ben's alumni, which some say enhances the sense of community. Most students hail from Minnesota, and an overwhelming majority are Roman Catholic. Out-of-staters and non-Catholics are nonetheless welcome. "It's a very warm, supportive place—people readily accept you for who you are," one New Yorker said.

St. John's and St. Ben's are private schools in the middle of small college towns, and townsfolk repeatedly stereotype the students as "rich and preppy." Locals have griped about the late-night partying, but town-gown relations are reportedly "just fine. We don't have more quibbles than the next college town." If anything, they are on the upswing: VISTO, a student volunteer group, does a lot of charity work in the town, particularly around Christmastime. A core council consisting of town residents and students also works to improve community relations.

> "It's a very warm, supportive place—people readily accept you for who you are," one New Yorker said.

VISTO is one of many strong extracurricular clubs and organizations at St. John's and St. Ben's. Both campuses have active student governments, and the Joint Events Council has members from both colleges. The schools support chapters of Greenpeace and ROTC, along with several bands, a cappella groups, and choirs. The radio station, KJNB, is popular among students and locals and often has listener call-in shows. Campus publications include the *Record* at St. John's and the *Independent* at St. Benedict's; both are biweeklies and they come out on alternate weeks. The brand-new Haehn Campus Center at St. Ben's boosts extracurricular life even more with its restaurants, intramural and varsity gyms, conference/banquet rooms, and a dance floor. Students consider themselves politically active, and although a sizeable liberal contingent exists, the majority of students at both schools have a conservative slant.

Football Fever

The most popular activities, in terms of sheer numbers and spirit, are without a doubt home football games. A perennial Division III powerhouse led by coach John Gagliardi (who made the cover of Sports Illustrated this year), the Johnnies finished the season undefeated, going 9–0. Students usually pack each game, but biggest is the game against the archrival college of St. Thomas. "The St. Thomas games can be violent affairs," a senior quipped. Intramural sports, some of which take place in Warner Palaestra, are also popular. The Palaestra gym features an eight-lane pool, an indoor track, racquetball courts, and a sauna. Also the new facilities at the Haehn Center are available to students.

Tradition thrives at St. John's and St. Benedict's. The week before Thanksgiving break, the campus sits down for a large turkey meal together, and before Christmas, students gather for the lighting of an enormous tree in the Great Hall. With generation after generation of families attending the schools, along with close interaction between the two campuses and a friendly face everywhere you turn, it's no wonder St. John's and St. Benedict's are a team to be reckoned with. Said one student, "Life here actually is a cliche—it's community-oriented, everyone really looks out for each other, and I cannot imagine going to school anywhere else."—*William Chen and Staff*

FYI

The three best things about attending St. John's/St. Benedict are "caring professors, great dorms, fun football."

The three worst things about attending St. John's/St. Benedict are "town-gown problems, boring weekends, and snow."

The three things that every student should do before graduating St. John's/St. Benedict are "go to the Watab mixer, take a religion course, and drink at The La."

One thing I'd like to have known before coming here is "classes that others consider interesting I find dull."

St. Olaf College

Address: 1520 St., Olaf Ave, Northfield, MN 55087

Phone: 800-800-3025

E-mail address: admissions@stolaf.edu

Web site URL: www.stolaf.edu

Location: small city

Founded: 1874

Private or Public: private

Religious affiliation: Evangelical Lutheran Church of America

Undergraduate enrollment: 2,868

Total enrollment: 2,998

Percent Male/Female: 43%/57%

Percent Minority: 8.0%

Percent African-American: 1.0%

Percent Hispanic: 3.0%

Percent Asian: 1.0%

Percent in-state/out-of-state: 49%/51%

Percent Pub HS: 87%

Fraternities: NA

Sororities: NA

Number of Applicants: 2,359

Percent Accepted: 76%

Percent Accepted who enroll: 43%

Entering: 767

Transfers: 37

Application Deadline: 1 Feb

Mean SAT: 635 V, 634 M

Middle 50% SAT range: 580–680 V, 580–680 M

Middle 50% ACT range: 24–29

Mean ACT: 26.7

3 Most popular majors: bio, eng, econ

Retention: 94.0%

Graduation rate: 77.0%

Library: 502,954 volumes

Tuition and Fees: $18,250 in; NA out

Room and Board: $4,320

On-campus housing: 100%

Financial aid, first-year: 61%

St. Olaf students say that they draw from their college both quality academics and opportunities for growth. Situated in the hills above the small town of Northfield, Minnesota, St. Olaf may be isolated, but this isolation creates a sense of community that seems to permeate every aspect of college life.

Academic Environment

Academics at St. Olaf are excellent and intense. Students have to fulfill a wide variety of distribution requirements, including courses in language, religion, multiculturalism, math, and writing. "Professors expect a lot of their students," said one Ole. "It depends on how seriously you want to take it," said another. Close relationships with professors make students eager to live up to their teacher's expectations, but professors also try to help students do well. "I've never had a professor that I didn't feel free to call at home," a student said. "Profs always have their doors open, and you can always stop by," said another. St. Olaf also makes an effort to provide its students with any academic help they may need. A writing center and a tutoring program are set up to help any students who are having difficulty.

Popular majors at St. Olaf include biology, chemistry, and English. Music and math are both highly respected majors, expecially music, an intense and excellent program. The small size of the school translates into fairly small classes for most Oles—introductory science classes have 50 to 60 students, and most classes have 15 to 30. The January Interim gives Oles a chance to explore a single class in more depth, and the subjects offered are more interdisciplinary and unusual, ranging from classes on the Philosophy of Poetry to American Technologies to Masterpieces of Mathematics.

Ole Livin'

St. Olaf is located on a hill about a mile outside of Northfield. The small campus and the distance from town make some students feel like thay are "in a bubble." "We're very safe and protected here, but also very isolated," said one junior. Most Oles love their campus, which is spread across 350 acres and filled with trees. Students gather to study in Rolvaag Library,

to eat at the cafeteria, to attend chapel services at Boe Memorial Chapel, and to listen to bands or watch movies.

Almost all St. Olaf students live on-campus. First-year students are housed in one of five dorms, three of which house only first-years. Upperclass students can live in one of six other houses, including Manitou, a popular dorm that has "pods," which are suites with a common room. Upperclass students can also live in one of 14 special houses. Some of these are language houses, while others, known as Honor Houses, are granted by application to groups of students who carry out service projects over the course of the year. Most rooms are "standard dorm style," students say. "The dorms are nothing special," said one student. "It's the people living in them that provide the atmosphere." All dorms are coed by floor. First-year students have junior counselors to help guide tham through the year, while upperclass dorms have resident advisors.

St. Olaf changed food-service companies in 1996, a change that most students welcomed. "The food is so good now," one student said. Others, however, think that the new food service needs work. "It's too gourmet," one student complained. "They use too many spices." Most students agree, however, that the new food service has brought more flavor and less repetition to the school's only cafeteria. All students who live on-campus are required to have a full meal plan, so meals are a good way to run into nearly everyone on-campus. "It's a great way to see everyone," said one student. "It's a very important part of life at St. Olaf."

The administration at St. Olaf makes it difficult to get a car—although "if you can think of a good reason they'll usually let you"—so most students spend their weekends on-campus. St. Olaf is officially a dry school, forbidding the consumption of alcohol anywhere on-campus, but students say that this rule is regularly violated. "The dry campus policy keeps it from becoming an all-encompassing thing," one student said. "There's not the pressure to drink that you find at other schools." On the weekend, students can choose from a variety of plays, concerts, and movies put on by the school. "The school provides a lot of things, but if you're not interested, you have to make your own social life," said one Ole. Many students choose merely to hang out in their rooms with friends. "Social life here can be really casual," said one student.

Students who have cars or who can beg a ride from a friend often travel to Northfield or up to the Twin Cities of St. Paul and Minneapolis for the weekend. In Northfield, students eat at Reub n' Stein or dance at the Grand, a small nightclub that brings in bands. During the day, some students enjoy shopping on Norhtfield's main street and soaking up the "classic small-town atmosphere." Students also can choose to make the 45-minute trip to "the Cities." First Avenue, a Minneapolis nightclub, is a popular destination, as is the Mall of America, the country's largest shopping mall.

Student Life

When they are not studying, St. Olaf students seem to find plenty to do to occupy their time. "Everyone I know is busy all of the time," said one student. Student organizations cover every interest, from juggling to fly-fishing. Music organizations are among the most popular and excellent groups at St. Olaf, with 22 registered on-campus. The St. Olaf orchestra and choir are both highly regarded. The St. Olaf Choir Christmas concert is broadcast on national television, and the groups tour the world. The Student Activities Committee is popular, as is the volunteer program, which draws many students to help out in Northfield and the surrounding communities. Intramural sports are "a really big deal" and have widespread participation, especially in broomball.

Varsity sports also draw a large segment of the St. Olaf population. The coed swim team is a perennial conference champion, and one swimmer said "the team is like a family to me." Although students say "sports aren't a really big deal at Olaf," the athletes feel a great deal of support from their teammates. "There isn't a huge amount of school spirit about the athletic teams," one student said. "The sports are mainly for the athletes."

Relogous groups also add a lot to extracurricular life at St. Olaf. St. Olaf is affiliated with the Lutheran church, and almost half of St. Olaf students are

Lutheran, while many of the rest belong to other Christian denominations. The Christian Activities Network, an umbrella group, has large student participation, as do the Fellowship of Christian Athletes and numerous Bible-study groups. A half-hour chapel service is held every day, during which there are no classes. "It's by no means required, and there is no pressure to go, but it's a large part of many people's days," said on student.

According to one undergrad, the student body at St. Olaf is "overwhelmingly white, middle-class, and Midwestern." Over half of the students are from Minnesota. "There's very little diversity here," said one student. "St. Olaf just does not draw a variety of ethnic groups." Most students are from the Midwest, although a significant number come from the West Coast. "Students are basically ignorant about issues of multiculturalism," said one student. The political climate tends toward conservatism. "Even though some of the professors and the courses are liberal, most of the studetns come from strong conservative backgrounds, and school policy is conservative," said one Ole.

> Perhaps because of its limitations in the area of multiculturalism, St. Olaf has an extremely strong and important study-abroad program.

Perhaps because of its limitations in the area of multiculturalism, St. Olaf has an extremely strong and important study-abroad program. "For some people, it's the heart of the St. Olaf curriculum," said one student. Many students study abroad in such popular programs as the Global Semester, with terms in Asia or the Middle East. Students also have many options for studying off-campus within the United States, such as the Urban Studies program in Chicago or the term in the Boundary Waters of Minnesota.

For students who want the support and comfort of a college "that really cares about its students" while providing a strong liberal arts education, St. Olaf is a place to look. "Although we are all very different people, we share many common ideals and beliefs," one student said of himself and his classmates. The unity of ideals that many students at St. Olaf share may create a slightly homogenous envi-ronment, but it also creates a place that nearly 3,000 talanted and dedicated students are proud to call home.—*Kathryn Eigen and Staff*

FYI

The three best things about attending St. Olaf are "our curriculum rocks, the social scene is casual, and we are in the Midwest!"

The three worst things about attending St. Olaf are "its white middle-class student body, community service is practically a must, and we are a dry campus."

The three things that every student should do before graduating from St. Olaf are "partici-pate in Global Semester, attend bible study, and don't forget to play broomball."

One thing I'd like to have known before coming here are "that religious extracurricular activi-ties are a really big deal."

University of Minnesota / Twin Cities

Address: 240 Williamson Hall, 231 Pillsbury Dr. SE, Minneapolis, MN 55455-0115
Phone: 800-752-1000
E-mail address: admissions@tc.umn.edu
Web site URL: www.umn.edu/tc
Location: urban
Founded: 1851
Private or Public: public
Religious affiliation: none
Undergraduate enrollment: 26,968
Total enrollment: 45,361
Percent Male/Female: 47%/53%
Percent Minority: 15.0%

Percent African-American: 4.0%
Percent Hispanic: 2.0%
Percent Asian: 8.0%
Percent in-state/out-of-state: 72%/28%
Percent Pub HS: NA
Fraternities: 6%
Sororities: 6%
Number of Applicants: 15,319
Percent Accepted: 73%
Percent Accepted who enroll: 46%
Entering: 5,141
Transfers: 2,107
Application Deadline: rolling
Mean SAT: NA

Middle 50% SAT range: NA
Middle 50% ACT range: 22–27
Mean ACT: 24.5
3 Most popular majors: engineering, social sciences, business
Retention: 82.0%
Graduation rate: 51.0%
Library: 6,000,000 volumes
Tuition and Fees: $4,649 in; $12,789 out
Room and Board: $4,494
On-campus housing: NA
Financial aid, first-year: NA

Located on the banks of the Missis-sippi River, under the shadows of Minneapolis skyscrapers, is the University of Minnesota. The Twin Cities campus is the largest of Minnesota's state universities. With nearly 23,000 under-graduate students and a total enrollment of about 37,000, the U of M can be over-whelming at times. According to students, the size of this university is both its great-est strength and its greatest weakness.

Lots of Options

Such a large university affords a multi-tude of academic options. There are six undergraduate colleges: the College of Agriculture, College of Liberal Arts, Col-lege of Human Ecology, College of Nat-ural Resources, General College, and the Institute of Technology. Students cite many programs in each college as particu-larly strong, including economics, politi-cal science, history, journalism, and engineering. Engineering provides a unique opportunity for its majors, who have the option of alternating three months of classwork with three months of real-world work experience. Students say this special program is an example of the university's attempt to give them an edge in the competitive job market. In ad-dition, an Honors College offers highly motivated and talented students smaller classes and more interaction with professors. Those in the Honors College cite class size as their primary reason for choosing the special program. Classes in the rest of the university have a reputation for being notoriously large. Some are so big that they use television monitors. But introductory courses are the largest, so as classes become more specialized, the average class size drops.

Classes are organized around a trimester system, and students have both cheers and jeers for this schedule. Several undergrads complained that they cannot always cover material in enough depth under the trimester system. According to one student, "Classes feel scrunched together at times." The accelerated pace of the calendar, however, allows students to take more classes than a semester system allows. For some students, the opportunity to explore unfamiliar subjects and new areas of study more than make up for any flaws in the current system.

Huge U of M

The huge student population of the U of M is also reflected in the expanse of the campus. Located in the heart of Minneapolis, the university is separated into East and West Banks. The East Bank is the main campus, while the West Bank is home to the university's business school. The agriculture school is in nearby St. Paul. Commenting on the spread-out campus, one freshman said, "I've been here two quarters and I've only seen probably a third of the school." The main downtown campus (East Bank) is an eclectic mix of old and new buildings that span a wide range of architectural styles. The Mall, a centrally located grassy area, is a prized spot for meeting and people-watching, and a green escape from the concrete jungle that comprises much of the university. The large number of campus parking lots is a necessity at a university where nearly 90 percent of the students live off-campus.

The small percentage of students who live on-campus describe dorm life as "fun" and "a great place to meet people and make friends." The average freshman dorm room is quite large with single beds, no bunking necessary. Students on each floor must share a common bathroom. Besides the eight residential dorms, students have a plentiful supply of off-campus housing to choose from. The most popular locales include Dinkytown and Stadium Village. Many students find that off-campus living is generally cheaper, and the money saved by living off-campus is very important to cash-strapped undergrads.

On or Off?

The high percentage of off-campus students does affect U of M social life, which can feel "fragmented." Most of the excitement on weekends centers on frat parties, sporting events, and bar-hopping. For most freshmen, the Greek scene is where the fun is. The percentage of U of M undergrads involved with the Greek system is small, but the actual number of students who belong to frats and sororities is quite large. As a result, frat parties dominate weekends at the U of M.

> **"I've only seen probably a third of the school."**

All sorority houses are now dry and many of the fraternity houses are following suit. This new policy has met with mixed reviews from students, Greek and non-Greek alike. Upperclassmen tend to prefer local bars and clubs like Bullwinkles', Foul Play, the Gopher Hole, Sally's, and Sgt. Preston's. Students of all classes can be found at basketball and hockey games. Both sports are extremely popular and strong at this Big Ten school. Basketball and hockey are also the most popular intramurals at the school, but intramural sports make up only a small fraction of the more than 500 undergraduate organizations. Overall, students report that it's hard not to find a group to join among the hundreds on-campus.

U of M students find plenty of entertainment in the city of Minneapolis. Common destinations include the Walker Art Gallery designed by the famous architect Frank Gehry; the Metrodome, home of the Minnesota Twins baseball team; and the Target Center, site of Timberwolves NBA games. The Mall of America, the nation's largest enclosed shopping center, is in nearby Bloomington. For intrepid U of M shoppers, this gargantuan mall is a regular weekend destination.

Like the Mall of America, the University of Minnesota's size is its most distinguishing characteristic. It gives the university an economically and ethnically diverse student body, an extensive choice of majors, courses, and extracurricular activities, and a varied social scene. Students agree that the University of Minnesota is both exciting and overwhelming, but if you choose to come here, do not forget to pack a parka—Minnesota winters are vicious.—*William Chen and Staff*

FYI
The three best things about attending U of M are "the picturesque surroundings; the people; and the student center."
The three worst things about attending U of M are "the size of the campus; the split between campuses; and the stench around the farm."
The three things that every student should do before graduating from U of M are "visit the Mall of America; eat cheese, we've got a lot of it; and go out on one of the thousand lakes."
One thing I'd like to have known before coming here is "how incredibly big this place is."

Mississippi

Millsaps College

Address: P. O. Box 151192
Phone: 601-974-1050
E-mail address:
www.admissions@millsaps
.edu
Web site URL:
www.millsaps.edu
Location: urban
Founded: 1890
Private or Public: private
Religious affiliation:
methodist
**Undergraduate
enrollment:** 1,191
Total enrollment: 1,314
Percent Male / Female:
45% / 55%
Percent Minority: 13.0%

Percent African-American:
9.0%
Percent Hispanic: 1.0%
Percent Asian: 3.0%
**Percent in-state / out-of-
state:** 57% / 43%
Percent Pub HS: 64%
Fraternities: 55%
Sororities: 56%
Number of Applicants:
912
Percent Accepted: 87%
**Percent Accepted who
enroll:** 36%
Entering: 284
Transfers: NA
Application Deadline:
1 Jul

Mean SAT: 600 V, 580 M
Middle 50% SAT range:
550–650 V, 530–620 M
Middle 50% ACT range:
24–29
Mean ACT: 27
3 Most popular majors:
business administration,
English, biology
Retention: 85%
Graduation rate: 62%
Library: 200,302 volumes
Tuition and Fees: $15,029
in; NA out
Room and Board: $6,106
On-campus housing: 96%
Financial aid, first-year:
98%

Entrenched Ivy League–style behind a sturdy iron fence, manned gates, and a conservative history, Millsaps College seems an incongruity in the middle of Mississippi's bustling political and social capital, Jackson. All around the college, the city of Jackson tempts students to enjoy its concerts, plays, shopping, and fertile work environment, but within the iron gates the campus life is busily quiet and beautifully serene.

Jackson, Mississippi

Truth be told, Millsaps is not in one of Jackson's most prestigious or beautiful neighborhoods, but some students see their proximity to the problems of a big city as "a real opportunity for community service work. Jackson's only as much as you make of it, and luckily, there is a lot of opportunity to do good in the city." The Mississippi Opera Association, Mississippi Symphony Orchestra, New Stage Theater, Jackson Zoo, and a planetarium add to the incentive to explore beyond the comfortable confines of the college. Jack son also hosts an international ballet com petition every four years (the next scheduled for 2002).

Within the iron fence, students enjo the amenities of an impeccably sculpte campus, which one student described a "spotless," another as "small, nice, iso lated," and another as "distractingly r mantic." A valley-like depression, calle the bowl, is in the center of this Greek R vival campus; students flock to the bov on nice days (the average annual tempe ture in Jackson is 64 degrees) and in b tween classes to socialize, toss Frisbee sit and chat, eat lunch, and chill on th manicured lawn.

Old Southern Competition

The laid-back look of the campus can b misleading, however. Students at Millsap study more than they will casually admi "Actually, this place is hard as hell—son of us study all the time just to survive The founders of this Methodist Churcl affiliated college may not have intended a study environment of hellish intensity, but the students must be able to handle the competitive pressures of a small community and a liberal arts education, where students tend to agree that academics are first, and extracurriculars an afterthought.

Students cite the life sciences as the most popular majors, with biology topping the popularity and difficulty lists. A large number of Millsaps students are pre-med, and many others study business administration. Registration is a painless process at Millsaps, and classes generally enroll fewer than 20 students. Teaching is done mostly by doctorate-holding professors, although Millsaps does have a teaching apprenticeship program that allows students interested in education to assist in some teaching duties. Professors are "extremely accessible," said one student, and other students remarked that professors sometimes invite their classes to dinner.

Students must satisfy a core curriculum consisting of one mandatory first-year class, Introduction to Liberal Studies, and one fourth-year mandatory class, Reflections on Liberal Studies. The other eight courses can be taken from a range of disciplines, all of them focusing on a high degree of cross-relevancy. More than half of Millsaps freshmen opt for the challenging Heritage Program, a four-course series stressing interdisciplinary learning.

When students need to cram, they head to Millsaps's main library, the Millsaps-Wilson Library, or to Olin Hall, the science building. Dorm rooms, which are typically doubles (with a limited number of singles) are also favorite study spots, since many of them have views overlooking the beautiful bowl.

Greek or Geek

Despite the intense academics, Millsaps students find plenty outside of the academic sphere to keep them busy. Over half of the campus decides to go Greek, explaining why one student felt "there's too much pressure to rush." Since all freshmen and sophomores must live on-campus (with the exception of married students and those who commute from home), Greek activity draws students from the center of campus to Frat Row, where the weeknight party scene is the biggest. Millsaps has six fraternities and six sororities, but no theme, athletic, or special language houses. In addition to the Greek scene, students often involve themselves in extracurricular activities related to their major. Popular options include the Millsaps chapter of the American Chemical Society for pre-meds, and the Millsaps Computer Club for computer science majors. Other popular organizations are Habitat and Circle K, a community service group.

Students who live close by (most students are from Mississipi and the surrounding states) usually go home for the weekend, and others seek out private parties, frat parties, and activities in Jackson. In recent years, however, the student affairs office has brought free concerts to campus and organized other activities in an effort to keep students at Millsaps on weekends. Another major social activity is Major Madness, a weeklong spring festival of bands, Greek events, and general good times.

> **Over half of the campus decides to go Greek, explaining why one student felt "there's too much pressure to rush."**

The obvious alternative to the outdoor and social Greek life is the dorms. Millsaps has both coed and single-sex dorms, which residents generally describe as sufficient, although some complained about communal showers.

Millsaps Dining Hall Services offers 21- and 14-meal plans that can be used both at the main cafeteria, or "the Caf," as students call it, and at Acy's Place, a campus institution where students have enjoyed traditional college sandwich-and-fries fare for almost 40 years now. Student satisfaction with Millsaps food seems low: one student remarked, "the spicy beef pie is the hard way out of final exams." To satisfy their late-night junk-food cravings, students head to the Waffle House, or that other center of fine southern fast food dining, Krystal, both of which are open 24 hours.

Millsaps sports don't generate a lot of student support, even though the Division III football team is very successful against rivals Trinity, Sewanee, and Rhodes. To promote student athleticism and boost school spirit, the administration has spent over $17 million on a new student center that will include an indoor workout facility, a basketball court, and an indoor track, as well as a student plaza for outdoor events such as concerts and parties. The new facility is scheduled to be completed by January 2000.

Overall, students say they are satisfie with their choice of Millsaps, and th value of the education they are getting Millsaps accepts the common applicatio and follows a need-blind admissions po icy. One student specifically mentione that the generous scholarship aid pack ages Millsaps offers were a major incer tive to admission, and others appreciat the proximity of their homes in the Sout Said one student, "Sure, you could pa more for worse weather and more stres but why?" —*Jeff Kaplow and staff*

FYI

The three best things about attending Millsaps are "our pretty campus, the friendly professors, and the financial aid."

The three worst things about attending Millsaps are "ridiculously hard work, low quality area, and odd housing policy."

The three things that every student should do before graduating from Millsaps are "take a road-trip to New Orleans, laugh at your premed friends (assuming you're not premed), an hand in a paper on time."

One thing I'd like to have known before coming here is "to avoid anything that sounds fancy in the dining hall."

M i s s i s s i p p i   S t a t e   U n i v e r s i t y

Address: P.O. Box 6305, Mississippi State, MS 39762

Phone: 662-325-2224

E-mail address: admit@admissions.msstate.edu

Web site URL: www.msuinfo.ur.msstate.edu/admissons

Location: rural

Founded: 1878

Private or Public: public

Religious affiliation: none

Undergraduate enrollment: 12,879

Total enrollment: 16,076

Percent Male/Female: 56%/45%

Percent Minority: 21%

Percent African-American: 17.8%

Percent Hispanic: 1.0%

Percent Asian: 1.0%

Percent in-state/out-of-state: 78%/22%

Percent Pub HS: NA

Fraternities: 17%

Sororities: 18%

Number of Applicants: 5,949

Percent Accepted: 80%

Percent Accepted who enroll: 34%

Entering: 1,928

Transfers: 1,453

Application Deadline: rolling

Mean SAT: NA

Middle 50% SAT range: NA

Middle 50% ACT range: NA

Mean ACT: 24

3 Most popular majors: elementary education, marketing, business administration

Retention: 78.2%

Graduation rate: 41.0%

Library: 1,422,763 volumes

Tuition and Fees: $3,017 in; $6,119 out

Room and Board: $4,835

On-campus housing: 85%

Financial aid, first-year: 81%

Longtime rivals of Mississippi State University like to stereotype it as an institution filled with country bumpkins, but MSU is a far cry from its rivals' slander. MSU's unusual academic programs and warmhearted students attract a diverse population from all over th country.

The Programs

Students report that academics at MS are strong, with architecture, veterina science, agriculture, and engineering among the most notable departments. Yet, in addition to these majors, MSU offers smaller, more unusual programs. The professional golf management (PGM), retail floristry, turf-grass management, and landscape architecture programs attract focused students from across the nation. Students also make use of MSU's large co-op program to get "real life" training or job experience. Although certain majors require a co-op experience, many students take co-op jobs to earn extra money or simply to get away from the classroom for a while.

Most MSU undergrads spend their first two years fulfilling a core curriculum, which includes courses in the natural sciences, English composition, humanities, and social sciences, in addition to three hours in computer literacy, a junior or senior writing class, and speech. Students generally agree that the core is not a burden, although one student said speech is unpopular. "Many students are terrified to speak in public," she explained. Upperclassmen report that overall, MSU academics are not too demanding and that plenty of "blow-off" and fun courses, in areas such as military science, floral design, arts and crafts, horseback riding, tennis, and aerobics, ease the academic load. One highly recommended course is Dr. Hank Flick's interviewing and communications class, which has been known to involve such activities as reading a Dr. Seuss book on a fountain in the middle of campus to fulfill a "social norm violation" assignment. Dr. Sandra Harpole's physics class is also popular for its outstanding, "magic show–like" demonstrations.

Dynamics of the Class

Introductory classes tend to be large (around 250 students), while upper-level courses are small (around 15 students). Professors teach most courses, while TAs lead discussion sections and labs. In general, professors are eager to get to know their students if students take the initiative: many undergrads describe student-faculty relations as "great." One student recalled that all of her professors sent her get-well cards when she had her tonsils removed.

Registration occurs during the preced-

ing term for upperclassmen and during the summer for incoming freshmen, and students agree that in most cases they have no trouble registering for desired classes. Dedicated students with either a high GPA or high ACT scores not only get preference during registration but also may qualify for the honors program, which offers smaller, more intense, and occasionally more unusual classes (for example, wine-tasting, for students 21 and over). Honors students rave about the program, claiming that they enjoy MSU's best dorms, professors, and facilities. Honors courses and honors forum discussions are not completely exclusive; regular students who avidly want to enroll in them can do so with permission from the honors director. As one student explained, "Accommodations are often made."

Extracurricular Activities

Outside of the classroom, students participate in a number of extracurricular activities. One student explained that the easiest way to get involved is to join one of the Student Association committees, which plan the majority of the school-affiliated social events. Other groups include the Black Friars theater group, an association for players of Dungeon and Dragons–style role-playing games, and pre-professional fraternities for students in such fields as music and engineering. Students with journalistic aspirations can work on the biweekly student newspaper, *The Reflector*. The administration also encourages students to help out with freshman orientation and recruitment. When the weather is warm, students play Frisbee on the Drill Field. Another campus hangout is the student center, which has a movie theater, a bowling alley, and numerous video games.

When students want to hit the books, they often go to Mitchell Memorial Library for quiet studying. Students describe the structure as "massive," containing almost everything they could ever need academically. When undergrads prefer to study in groups, they usually go to each other's rooms, apartments, Allen Hall, or McCool Hall.

Dorms are in good condition at MSU, yet only about one-third of the student body, mostly freshmen, lives on-campus. The two honors dorms, one for freshmen and one for upperclassmen, are coed by wing and are considered the best. MSU also has 12 single-sex non-honors dorms. Most freshmen live on campus because, as one student explained, "living on-campus your first year allows you to meet your social crowd."

Instead of purchasing a meal plan, MSU students buy a Money Mate card, from which they deduct the cost of each meal they eat. Students can use their Money Mate cards at either the cafeteria, which serves only breakfast and lunch, or the food court, which houses various fast-food restaurants like Taco Bell and Great Wall of China. When students want variety, they go off-campus to the popular Bulldog Deli, Oby's, and the Cotton District Grill.

The Social Scene

Because in-state students often go home on weekends, campus parties are more common during the week. About one-fifth of MSU students belong to the Greek system, but independents say that there is no pressure to rush: because the school is relatively small, almost everyone knows a fraternity member, so invitations to Greek parties are easy to get. Since the administration enacted a dry-campus policy, drinking has become less prevalent at campus parties. "It doesn't matter if you are 19, 21, or 50—you can't have alcohol on-campus," one student explained. Any frat caught with alcohol at one of its parties will be put on probation. Even with this stringent policy, however, students report that MSU still has its share of drinkers at Greek "swaps" or mixers, and private parties given by students living off-campus. Most MSU students also have cars, so nearby bars such as Doug's, Rick's, and Mulligan's are also easily accessible. On-campus, the main social event of the year is the Super Bulldog Weekend, which involves homecoming-type festivities and a weekend of parties centered on the baseball team. All students, as well as many alumni and town-folk, join this campus celebration.

Sports, both varsity and intramural, are popular at MSU. Students are filled with pride for their nationally ranked baseball team, and because MSU has the largest campus baseball facility in the United States, the school hosts divisional championships every year. Football and basketball games are also well attended, especially against archrival University of Mississippi. (Until recently, students substituted "Go to Hell, Ole Miss" for the "amen" at the end of the prayer at every football game.) During varsity games, Bulldogs fans try to sneak cowbells into the stadium and ring them while rooting for their team, even though the bells have been outlawed by the Southeastern Conference. Sports teams garner so much support that motor homes filled with fans roll into town on home-game Thursdays. The Sanderson Center, a 150,000-square-foot recreational facility that houses state-of-the-art athletic facilities for student and administrative use, is at the heart of MSU's large intramural sports program.

> During varsity games, Bulldogs fans try to sneak cowbells into the stadium and ring them while rooting for their team, even though the bells have been outlawed by the Southeastern Conference.

The majority of MSU students come from Mississippi, and according to undergrads, the general political climate is conservative. Fraternities and sororities are racially segregated and the campus has no active gay or lesbian groups, which some students attribute to the school's location in the Bible Belt. As one student explained, "We'll be nice to gays, but they will not be accepted." Furthermore, drugs and pre-marital sex are generally not discussed on-campus. Some students are active in campus and state politics, although they say they tend to hold conservative views regardless of their party affiliation. As one student explained, "If you're from the North, it's culture shock."

MSU is located in Starkville, Mississippi, which students described as "not a very happening place." Starkville is a quiet, conservative town, yet Starkville residents often attend MSU athletic games and campus activities. The undergrads call the campus beautiful and feel that it is generally safe. University police and a student escort service ensure security on-campus.

Recently, MSU has grown increasingly serious about its academics, boosting its efforts to recruit the brightest students in Mississippi. Yet undergrads report that the greatest asset of their university is the friendliness of the student body. According to one student, many undergrads go on to attend MSU graduate school simply because they don't want to leave the students and teachers of their undergraduate years. "You must visit the campus and discover the great southern hospitality for yourself," she said, "for nowhere else except at MSU will you always find a smiling stranger who readily says 'hi' to all."—*Jeff Kaplow and Staff*

FYI

The three best things about attending MSU are "intramural play, Money Mate cards, and the co-op opportunities."

The three worst things about attending MSU are "Starkville, partying only during the week, and Northern culture shock."

The three things that every student should do before graduating from MSU are "enjoy Super Bulldog Weekend, ring a cowbell, and appreciate southern hospitality."

One thing I'd like to have known before coming here is "how strange it is that we party during the week."

University of Mississippi

Address: 145 Martindale University, MS 38677
Phone: 601-232-7226
E-mail address: admissions@olemiss.edu
Web site URL: www.olemiss.edu
Location: rural
Founded: 1844
Private or Public: public
Religious affiliation: none
Undergraduate enrollment: 8,888
Total enrollment: 10,280
Percent Male/Female: 47%/53%
Percent Minority: 13.0%

Percent African-American: 11.0%
Percent Hispanic: 1.0%
Percent Asian: 1.0%
Percent in-state/out-of-state: 66%/34%
Percent Pub HS: 70%
Fraternities: 33%
Sororities: 35%
Number of Applicants: 4,067
Percent Accepted: 78%
Percent Accepted who enroll: 59%
Entering: 1,838
Transfers: 983
Application Deadline: 16 Aug

Mean SAT: NA
Middle 50% SAT range: NA
Middle 50% ACT range: NA
Mean ACT: 23
3 Most popular majors: general business, biological science, accounting
Retention: 76.0%
Graduation rate: 28.0%
Library: 1 million volumes
Tuition and Fees: $3,053 in; $6,155 out
Room and Board: $3,360
On-campus housing: 95%
Financial aid, first-year: 33%

A s visitors step onto the campus of the university affectionately known as "Ole Miss," they cannot help but be reminded of a historical tradition that include belles, chivalry, and classic southern hospitality that many students on-campus praise with enthusiasm.

A Stronger Academic Program?

In addition to a nationally ranked pharmacy program and the recent addition of an extensive acoustics lab, Ole Miss offers strong humanities departments. One English major reported, "I haven't had an English class I didn't enjoy." The university has invested a "ton of money to make the academic program here stronger." Such investments include revamping the science departments, and so far students say the engineering program has seen the most marked improvement. Although business is a popular major at Ole Miss, some students say the program could be more challenging.

For undergrads "seeking a greater academic challenge," Ole Miss has also opened a new honors college, thanks to a sizable donation from alumnus James Barkdale, the CEO and president of Netscape. Undergraduates praised the McDonnell-Barkdale Honors College for its academic rigor, small class sizes of 15, and the enthusiasm of its professors. One student noted that "most importantly, this program also creates a close knit community among the students, because certain dorm floors are devoted to students within the Honors College."

One of the biggest complaints from students is the "excessive class size" at Ole Miss. Many required classes are "simply too big." Although most classes enroll fewer than 30 students, one senior reported that his seminar, which he felt should have had no more than 20 students, had around 50. In these situations, professors are helped by TAs, which "helps a little in curbing class size."

Ole Miss is one of three schools in the nation to offer a department of Southern Region Studies, which includes such classes as Southern Fiction, Folk Art, and the History of the Blues. Undergrads even have access to B. B. King's blues record collection, which was recently donated to the university. Another popular resource is the Sarah Isom Center for Women's Studies, which conducts classes and seminars that focus on women's issues.

Rebel Tradition

The University of Mississippi is keenly influenced by long-standing southern traditions and a lively sense of community that encompasses the surrounding town of Oxford in northern Mississippi. The school band still plays "Dixie" and students still wave the "Rebel" flag at sporting events. Ole Miss students see such traditions as evidence, not of intolerance,

but of strong school spirit. As one student said, "We are just incredibly excited to be a part of traditional school pride here." In fact, the university is attempting to distance itself from its history of prejudice.

One example of this effort was the decision to revamp the school mascot, replacing the image of Colonel Reb as a southern plantation owner with a new Colonel Reb decked out in school colors with a football jersey and helmet. Undergrads at the University of Mississippi enjoy "hollering for our teams!" Before most football games, students reportedly partake in "grove-ing," a practice of extensive mingling during tailgate parties.

Afraid to "jinx" their teams, fans stand during all four quarters of home football games, sitting only during halftime. Huge crowds attended "the Game" against the university's ultimate rival, Mississippi State. As one student said, "For the bigger games, people start parking their trailer homes on Thursday in anticipation for game Saturday!"

Ole Miss students sometimes complain that from sports to religious associations, "it is hard to get involved with other organizations as people tend to form cliques quickly and introductions are made more difficult." Another student added, "I only know two or three people in a few random groups, largely because they tend to hang out only by themselves."

Party, Party, Party!

Students at the University of Mississippi pride themselves in being able to have a good time "no matter the circumstances. We may lose a game, but we never lose a party. Our football might not be best in the (SEC) division, but we can party harder than you can," one undergrad said. Greek life at the University of Mississippi is an "integral part of life here." As one student reported, "Greeks basically run the school." Fraternities and sororities are very large organizations, and it is not uncommon to see alumni return for weekend Greek parties. Another student particularly noted that "husbands bring their wives and you see forty-year-olds passed out on the floor! It gets a bit ridiculous."

Although kegs are not "technically allowed on-campus," students report that "they are prevalent in many social situations." Fraternity houses are off-campus so they do not have to worry about such regulations. As one student pointed out, "It's supposed to be a dry campus, but the last party I went to had 12 kegs." While Ole Miss does not publicly condone drinking, one student said that drinking "goes on, they know it, we know it . . . we just have an understanding, that's all."

Students who do not join fraternities are not left out of social interaction. As one student explained, "There are so many frat boys here that it's not hard to find a friend that'll get you into a party or invite you to go hang with the guys." For students not interested in Greek life or the party scene, the university sponsors lectures and trips on weekends. Other opportunities range from hearing visitors like comedian Adam Sandler speak, visiting William Faulkner's house, or playing pickup basketball games with professors "as long as you are willing to participate." If Greek life gets old, Memphis is only a 45-minute drive from campus and, as one undergrad explained, "it is not totally unheard of for students to head out of town for a weekend getaway."

Conservative Housing Policy
The University of Mississippi abides by Mississippi state law forbidding coed housing in state dormitories. According to one student, "This is just a prime example of the conservative bent on-campus." On weekdays, visiting hours for the opposite sex end at midnight, while weekend hours are extended to "only 1 A.M." Although students have clamored for an open 24-hour visiting policy, they say the proposal has been "quickly shot down" by campus administration.

While dorm restrictions reduce opportunities for both sexes to intermingle, students generally are content with housing options. Dorm residents say the rooms are "ample for the number of people living in them." For the most part, only freshmen live in the dorms because "sophomore year, everyone migrates to the frat houses. Most upper-class students rent apartments close to campus," one undergrad said. Cars are reportedly not essential for students living on (or close to) campus. One student said, "You can usually hitch a ride from a friend who has a car, so there isn't really a problem getting around unless you want to go somewhere without your friend or you have no friends at all!"

> **"This is just a prime example of the conservative bent on-campus."**

Undergrads at the University of Mississippi are attracted to a vibrant tradition of school spirit and southern pride. Students receive a solid education in both academics and social interaction. As one student said, "This place is what college should be . . . you work hard and play a thousand times harder."—*Jeff Kaplow and Staff*

FYI:
The three best things about attending Ole Miss are "the school's tradition and spirit, a friendly student body, and the off-campus party scene."
The three worst things about attending Ole Miss are "the conservative housing policies, the Rebel Burgers in the dining halls, and overcrowded classrooms."
The three things every student should do before graduating from Ole Miss are "work out at Ole Miss Fit, the student rec center; go to The Game; and 'grove' at as many tailgates as possible."
One thing I wish I'd known before coming to Ole Miss is "the administrations overly conservative policies."

Missouri

University of Missouri / Kansas City

Address: 120 Administrative Center, 5100 Rockhill Road, Kansas City, MO 64114-2499
Phone: 816-235-1111
E-mail address: admit@umkc.edu
Web site URL: www.umkc.edu
Location: urban
Founded: 1929
Private or Public: public
Religious affiliation: none
Undergraduate enrollment: 6,108
Total enrollment: NA
Percent Male / Female: 42% / 58%

Percent Minority: 23.0%
Percent African-American: 12.0%
Percent Hispanic: 4.0%
Percent Asian: 6.0%
Percent in-state / out-of-state: 87% / 13%
Percent Pub HS: NA
Fraternities: 0%
Sororities: 0%
Number of Applicants: 2,695
Percent Accepted: 63%
Percent Accepted who enroll: 39%
Entering: NA
Transfers: 0
Application Deadline: rolling

Mean SAT: NA
Middle 50% SAT range: NA
Middle 50% ACT range: NA
Mean ACT: 24
3 Most popular majors: psychology, computer science, liberal arts
Retention: 73%
Graduation rate: 19% (within 5 years)
Library: NA
Tuition and Fees: $4,560 in; $12,476 out
Room and Board: $5,600
On-campus housing: 6%
Financial aid, first-year: 54%

Ignore the stereotype. "The University of Missouri at Kansas City is not a hick school." In fact, Kansas City is one of the fastest growing cities in America. Located in the heartland of America, UMKC offers an affordable education in an urban setting.

Known as the "artsy" member of the UM system, UMKC may not draw as many out-of-state students as some other state schools, but it still offers a diverse student body. What it lacks in geographical diversity, it makes up for in its students' wide-ranging backgrounds and interests. A large percentage of UMKC students are part-time or returning students, many of them having to balance their studies with jobs or families.

Ambitious Academics
As can be expected with a older student body, UMKC is known for its excellent preprofessional programs and tends to at-

tract students who are career-oriented. Specifically, the dual-degree programs that offer a B.A. or B.S. degree in conjunction with a degree in medicine, law, dentistry, or education, cater to ambitious and focused students.

The College of Arts and Sciences is comprised of fifteen departments ranging from traditional majors such as English and History to more unusual departments such as Military Science. Computer Science and Psychology are two of the most popular departments. Requirements vary according to major. Overall, the requirements for B.S. and B.A. degrees are similar except that a B.S. degree requires a total of 60 hours in math and science credits. In general, students must complete a minimum of 26 total semester hours and a minimum of 12 semester hours in their respective majors to graduates. Double and combined majors are also available.

UMKC students must comply with a

unique Missouri law that requires students to complete courses about the U.S. Constitution and the Missouri State Constitution. Though most appreciate the former requirement, some out-of-staters complain about the latter.

Students who wish to intensify their academic experience can participate in a special honors program that encompasses much more than their requisite honors classes. Honors students have their own publications—*The Undergraduate Review* and *The Onner's Gazette*—and have access to special honors facilities. The program itself centers on a weekly one-hour colloquium offered every semester. Honors in all classes meet with the faculty and distinguished guest lecturers to discuss a wide range of subjects.

With a student to professor ratio of 12:1, UMKC prides itself on its small class sizes. Hence, though UMKC is a research institution, students are not bogged down in huge classes with little student-professor interaction. "At UMKC you don't feel like a number. The professors I have encountered are extremely accessible," one student said. The one complaint students did have concerned the intensity of work. "I didn't expect my American Studies course to be so intensive. I am enjoying it though," one freshman said.

Kasey the Kangaroo

How UMKC came to have a kangaroo as its mascot is a question that has been pondered for years. Although UMKC officially got the idea for its mascot from two kangaroos adopted by the Kansas City Zoo back in 1936–37, the kangaroo was probably adopted largely because of Disney's "Kasey the Kangaroo's" popularity. Apparently, "Kasey" seemed the perfect mascot for a school called "KC."

The kangaroo is a prominent symbol. First-years arriving in the fall are greeted by organizations at the Roo Fair, a one-day activities fair that introduces students to UMKC's more than 200 organizations. Some of the many organizations range from *U-News*, the weekly student newspaper, to *KCUR*, UMKC's public radio station, one of the first educational radio stations in the state. But even with the wide range of activities, students wishing to start new organizations will find the Student Life Office extremely helpful. With over a dozen fraternities and sororities, Greek life undoubtedly plays a role on campus as well. But, according to students, "if Greek is not your thing, that's okay too."

For the athletically inclined, UMKC is a NCAA Division I affiliate. Part of the Mid-Continent Conference, the school offers a wide range of varsity teams for both men and women. Women participate in basketball, golf, tennis, volleyball, cross-country, track and field, and softball. Men compete in basketball, golf, tennis, cross-country, track and field, rifle, and soccer.

> "Coming to UMKC from New York City, I was shocked to see how friendly Kansas City is. People on the street will stop to say hello or good morning."

Even if they don't take part in varsity athletics, most students come out to cheer for their favorite teams. Among the biggest events of the year is the basketball game against Kansas State University, one of UMKC's traditional rivals. During this game, the UMKC stands are often packed, and the Kangaroos go wild. For less hard-core athletes, UMKC offers a wide range of intramural sports at Swinney Recreational Center.

Campus Living or Apartment Style?

Despite the bustling on-campus extracurricular life, less than 10 percent of students actually live on campus. The one on-campus dorm is "Residence Hall" with approximately 330 students living within its walls. The rest of the student masses live off campus. For non-Missouri natives, the availability of cheap local housing is one of UMKC's greatest draws. "Coming from out of state I was worried at first about finding a place. It turned out to be the easiest part of coming to college," one student said.

To facilitate student searches for off-campus housing, UMKC has its own real estate office. It helps students find nearby university-owned rentals while the Welcome Center has listings of non-University-owned property. Students describe the rentals as relatively inexpensive and extremely convenient. The Twin Oaks Apartment complex is popular among students. Located on the west side of campus, its proximity to UMKC make it a favorite.

Small-Town Friendliness

Contrary to popular belief, Kansas City is truly a bustling city with the friendly atmosphere of a small town. "Coming to UMKC from New York City, I was shocked to see how friendly Kansas City is. People on the street will stop to say hello or good morning," one student said. Located in one of Kansas City's most happening neighborhoods, UMKC offers its students a lively off-campus social life. Close by are the popular 51st Street Coffeehouse, Main Street eateries, and area parks and museums. Less than a fifteen-minute walk from campus is the Country Club Plaza shopping and restaurant district. With its Mexican architecture and numerous fountains, the Plaza area is quite a "site." For students wishing to splurge, the Plaza houses such upscale stores as Ralph Lauren and Tiffany's. Lots of students also frequent Abercrombie & Fitch, the Gap, and The Limited. Also nearby is the Cheesecake Factory, a popular restaurant among UMKC students. Within minutes of campus, Westport has many bars featuring live bands, and is the place to be for nightlife. Students would agree that social life in Kansas City is great because it is safe as well as relatively inexpensive. Unlike students at other urban schools, UMKC students report that they don't have to worry so much about safety during a night out on the town.

With its abundance of activities on and off campus, it's no wonder UMKC students have so much school spirit. They rave about UMKC life both inside the classroom and out. As one student said, "I just hate the thought of graduation." —*Alyssa Blair Greenwald*

FYI
The three best things about attending UMKC are "Kansas City, affordable living, and the arts department."
The three worst things about attending UMKC are "Kansas City, requirements, and the intense work."
The three things that every student should do before graduating from UMKC are "to explore haunted Epperson House Hall, be Kasey the Kangaroo, attend a UMKC-KSU game."
One thing I'd like to have known before coming here is "that there are so many local students."

University of Missouri / Columbia

Address: 230 Jesse Hall, Columbia, MO 65211
Phone: 573-882-7786
E-mail address: admissions@missouri.edu
Web site URL: www.missouri.edu
Location: suburban
Founded: 1839
Private or Public: public
Religious affiliation: none
Undergraduate enrollment: 17,346
Total enrollment: 22,483
Percent Male/Female: 47%/53%
Percent Minority: 11.0%
Percent African-American: 7.0%

Percent Hispanic: 1.0%
Percent Asian: 3.0%
Percent in-state/out-of-state: 89%/11%
Percent Pub HS: NA
Fraternities: 25%
Sororities: 23%
Number of Applicants: 8,092
Percent Accepted: 80%
Percent Accepted who enroll: 55%
Entering: 3,737
Transfers: 1,592
Application Deadline: rolling
Mean SAT: NA
Middle 50% SAT range: NA

Middle 50% ACT range: 23–29
Mean ACT: 25
3 Most popular majors: business administration, biological sciences, psychology
Retention: 83.0%
Graduation rate: 28.0%
Library: 4.5 million volumes
Tuition and Fees: $4,299 in; $11,685 out
Room and Board: $466
On-campus housing: 83%
Financial aid, first-year: 57%

Like many large state schools, the University of Missouri is defined by an active frat life and a relatively loose attitude toward academic life. At the same time, the sheer immensity of a state institution guarantees that students can find something to fit their interests. A closer look reveals some local color peeping through the State U mask.

Mizzou Curriculum

Students consider academics at Mizzou "average to moderately difficult." The undergraduate core curriculum includes a three-year language requirement and two writing-intensive courses, the hardest of the requirements to fill. Two of the more prominent academic programs are the Minority Achievement Program, which offers workshops to promote further education and teach effective study habits, and the extensive study-abroad program. The journalism school is the most recognized department that the university has to offer and is the main source of the small out-of-state diversity on-campus. Undergrads report that along with the psychology department, the journalism school is the most popular. Some of the hardest classes are in the sciences, including University Physics, "the roughest course they offer here," one student said. One of the more popular courses is Human Sexuality, which has a more laid-back reputation. Professors teach lecture classes and TAs teach the smaller sections, but as one student explained, "many of the TAs are foreign and hard to understand, so you end up learning the most from books."

Academics are not a great source of stress for many Mizzou students. As one undergrad said, "Even during finals week, people don't seem very flipped out." People study in the two main libraries on-campus, the law library and Ellis, which are some of the biggest libraries in the state. Several new campus facilities are in the works, including a new wing for the chemistry building and a new cafeteria. The athletic facilities are particularly popular. One student called them "excellent, with at least six basketball courts and even a climbing wall."

Landscapes, Frats, Food

"The prettiest part of campus has to be the main quad with the pillars. There are always students out there having fun," another undergrad reported. The University of Missouri's huge campus is a big part of the surrounding town of Columbia. Students say it is a safe environment with "enough to offer," including a mall, restaurants, and the Blue Note, a local dance club and bar. The residents of this college town are friendly and take advantage of the facilities on-campus. The town also plays an important role in student housing.

According to students, off-campus living is cheaper than staying in the dorms, and shuttles connect off-campus apartment buildings to different parts of campus. Off-campus residents say it is not necessary to have a car, although it is convenient for trips to the nearest big cities.

On-campus living is more convenient, with doubles and singles and community bathrooms. Suites of two bedrooms with a shared bathroom are also available, but these go mainly to the juniors and seniors. One student explained, "The rooms are boring, with thin cement walls and lofts or cots, but at least there aren't any bunk beds." Juniors and seniors get the best housing, and the best dorm is one of the only all-women dorms on-campus—Johnston Wolpers—which one student said "looks like a hotel" and has air-conditioning. Most of the other dorms are coed with single-sex floors. Each floor of the residential halls has a residential advisor as part of a bigger advising system that first-year students find particularly helpful.

> There is a lot of spirit behind the Tigers, especially the men's basketball team, which draws a full crowd for every game.

Other housing options include theme houses, language houses, and fraternity and sorority houses. The campus has a large Greek community, and their housing is, as one student described, "mansion-like."

Students who live on-campus choose a meal plan of 7, 14, or 21 meals a week. Food can also be charged on student ID cards at the Brady Commons student union, which has Chik-Fil-A, Taco Bell, Pizza Hut, and Burger King outlets. The dining hall food does not get rave reviews, but is generally considered "acceptable," and there are always vegetarian options. Most students eat off-campus in town a couple of times a week, with options from the cheapest and favorite Taco Bell to the nicer and popular El Maguay Mexican restaurant. Some students find local coffee shops also offer a good place to study.

The university also offers an "E-Z Charge" to its students, which gives each student $400 of credit to spend each month. It is accepted at the bookstore, dining halls, campus convenience stores, Brady Food Court, and Memorial Union Food Court. "You end up buying everything you want on it at an extremely over inflated price. Don't get it—it's very addictive," one student advised.

Athletics and Associations

Athletics play a big role in Mizzou life. There is a lot of spirit behind the Tigers, especially the men's basketball team, which draws a full crowd for every game. Kansas University is the rival that draws the most student animosity on-campus. Intramural sports are popular among extracurriculars. Options range from volleyball and basketball—which are some of the more popular—to the rock-climbing club that makes use of the climbing wall in the campus athletic complex. The meteorology club, the roller hockey club, and Peaceworks, an environmental awareness group, attract interest, as do many minority groups on-campus, from the Asian American Association (AAA) to the Romanian Student Association to LUBRASA for Luso Brazilian students. Students do not consider Mizzou's undergraduate population diverse, although support networks for minority students include the ethnic clubs and other groups such as the Black Culture Center and the Black Collegiates. Another significant and controversial minority group on-campus is the Triangle Coalition for gay and lesbian students. Most student groups are funded by the Missouri Student Association, MSA, the student government. The MSA, however, is "known as a joke rather than as an important student force," according to one student.

Campus Events

Students involved with the MSA work to organize movies, concerts, speakers, tutoring, rides, and advice opportunities. It has brought in such celebrities as George Stephanopoulos, and organized barn dances—including its own version of the popular MTV program *Singled Out* for Valentine's Day. Other big social events revolve around basketball games, such as big pep rallies before the games and other parties put on by the fraternities. One of the biggest events of the year is homecoming for the big football game each fall. The university has rules against kegs on-campus, but the administration has a reputation for being relatively lax with the frat houses. There are also rules about drug use on-campus, but some students say they are not well enforced. Other activities include the yearbook, the *Savi-tar*, and the *Maneater*, the bi-weekly newspaper. Performance opportunities on-campus also abound, with theater, singing, and orchestral student performing groups.

The student body is considered rather conservative by many undergrads, more so than the surrounding town. Diversity continues to be an issue for students on-campus, as the majority are white Missouri natives. Different programs have been introduced to promote diversity and raise the academic level of the school. The Bright Flight program and the Curator Scholarships both offer opportunities to students with good ACT scores and class rank. The Conley Scholars Program is also a unique academic opportunity for incoming students. It guarantees four years in the University of Missouri Medical school without taking the MCATs. In general, the campus, while large, is full of what students agree are "friendly" people.—*William Chen and Staff*

FYI
The three best things about attending the University of Missouri are "tons of opportunities to perform, the journalism school, and the Tigers."
The three worst things about attending the University of Missouri are "E-Z Charge system, Missouri natives are everywhere, and how expensive on-campus living is."
The three things that every student should do before graduating from the University of Missouri are "go to MSA events, go Greek, and drive to St. Louis to party."
One thing I'd like to have known before coming here is "that people don't stress too much about their academics."

W a s h i n g t o n   U n i v e r s i t y

Address: Campus Box 1089, One Brookings Drive, St. Louis, MO 63130
Phone: 800-638-0700
E-mail address: admisions@wustl.edu
Web site URL: www.admissions.wustl.edu
Location: suburban
Founded: 1853
Private or Public: private
Religious affiliation: none
Undergraduate enrollment: 5,689
Total enrollment: 12,088
Percent Male/Female: 50%/50%
Percent Minority: 22.0%

Percent African-American: 7.0%
Percent Hispanic: 2.0%
Percent Asian: 12.0%
Percent in-state/out-of-state: 13%/87%
Percent Pub HS: 67%
Fraternities: 22%
Sororities: 21%
Number of Applicants: 17,109
Percent Accepted: 34%
Percent Accepted who enroll: 24%
Entering: 1,384
Transfers: 187
Application Deadline: 15 Jan
Mean SAT: NA

Middle 50% SAT range: 620–710 V, 650–730 M
Middle 50% ACT range: 28–32
Mean ACT: NA
3 Most popular majors: psycology + biology, engineering, buiness
Retention: 96%
Graduation rate: 86%
Library: 3,350,122 volumes
Tuition and Fees: $24,745 in; NA out
Room and Board: $7,724
On-campus housing: 99%
Financial aid, first-year: 58%

"**M**eet me in St. Louis," sang Judy Garland. And so says Washington University, a private liberal arts institution, to prospective students. Contrary to its misleading name, this university is not located in the Pacific Northwest but in the heart of the Midwest. Like the city which it calls home, Washington University is a surprisingly energetic and dynamic place, combining midwestern values with sophistication and culture.

W.I.L.D. at Wash U.

Wash U, as it is called by students, begins to endear itself to most freshmen upon their arrival. Incoming students are welcomed by a multitude of social activities. Freshman orientation is consistently described as excellent. "I was in love with Wash U from the beginning," said one student. A junior vividly remembers her freshman orientation: more than a thousand freshman waving Glow Sticks on a dark and sticky St. Louis summer night. Not coincidentally, the university's chancellor happens to be the inventor of the Glow Stick. For freshmen, there is also the lure of Frat Row, where parties are always to be found. These parties are preceded by

Thursday nights at the Rat (a bar), which kick off the weekend for fun-seekers.

Some of the best parties, however, are sponsored by the school. The beginning and end of each year is marked by W.I.L.D. (Walk In Lay Down), a campus-wide party and musical festival. Usually the lineup for W.I.L.D. includes a few campus and local bands, along with a big-name group (the Spin Doctors have performed in the past). Another huge party held biannually is Bauhaus, hosted by the School of Architecture, in which students dress in black and white and attempt to capture the spirit of the architectural movement of the same name. However, do not be scared off by the seemingly intellectual nature of this party, for as one architecture student put it, "We're just a bunch of wannabes having fun."

After freshman year, Wash U students begin to discover the allure of off-campus attractions. "The Loop," a trendy St. Louis shopping/entertainment district close to campus, is one of the gems that students soon discover. According to one Midwestern student, it is here where east and west coasters begin to lose their stereotypes of provincial Midwestern life. The Loop is famous for its offbeat stores, like

Vintage Vinyl (CDs, records, tapes), and its diversity of eating establishments.

Restaurants range from the St. Louis Bread Company (a local chain restaurant famous for its sourdough bread) to the Red Sea (Ethiopian). There is also diversity in the people who populate this eclectic neighborhood. Families, corporate executives, yuppies, tourists, teenyboppers, young suburbanites, ravers, punks, hipsters, and of course preppy college students all congregate in the Loop.

Meet Me in St. Louis

Wash U students often venture into St. Louis to enjoy the many attractions including Laclede's Landing (a fashionable and hip entertainment district on the riverfront). The Landing is home to Planet Hollywood, Mississippi Nights (considered the best nightclub in St. Louis), and even a celebrity wax museum. Nearby the Cardinals (baseball), the Blues (hockey), and the Rams (football) play.

Closer to campus is the St. Louis Galleria (one of the region's largest shopping malls) and Forest Park (one of the largest municipal parks in the country). Inside Forest Park await not only jogging paths and golf courses, but also museums, a zoo, and an outdoor theater, all free to residents of St. Louis.

Out-of-state students happily discover that Midwesterners are indeed friendly and warm people. Nearly 90 percent of the student body comes from outside of Missouri. "Most people really come to like the school and are pleasantly surprised by the friendly atmosphere," said one student. However, some negative stereotypes persist. "The school is a little uppity," stated one student. This student went on to say, "At times, there's a certain swank atmosphere. I went to a party once where grilled crawfish and portabello mushrooms were served." However, the school is committed to attracting a diverse student body, ethnically and economically, with a commitment to meeting 100 percent of financial need.

In general, Wash U students appreciate the diversity that already exists on-campus but have differing opinions over the effects of that diversity. One sophomore stated that "some of the minority groups segregate themselves from the rest of the school." The observance of this phenomenon has led to nicknames like "The Asian Mafia." Other Wash U students passionately disagree and contend that the ethnic groups are very open and inclusive.

Pre-med Anyone?

Students say that academics at Wash U are "amazing" and "challenging." Across the board, departments are strong, with biology consistently ranking as one of the best departments of its kind in the country. Among pre-med students (who tend to be biology majors), the atmosphere is extremely intense and competitive, but rarely cutthroat. "You will definitely run into some psycho pre-meds here," assured one student. Indeed, Wash U med school is considered one of the best in the country.

Outside the sciences, however, the "learning climate is very comfortable" and a little more laid-back. Students consider the business school to be the most relaxed of all. Although highly ranked, students have nicknamed it "baby school (B-school)" for its comparatively lax schedule (there are no classes on Fridays, for example).

Scheduling has recently become easier for all students with online registration and an "awesome" advising system. There are no specifically required classes at Wash U, but undergraduates must fulfill distributional requirements in the natural sciences, social and behavioral sciences, history and literature, and cultural studies. For the latter, two courses dealing with multicultural and gender issues must be taken. No students expressed any ill will toward the distributional courses, and most gushed about classes like African-American Religion. This course, like many introductory courses, numbers in the hundreds. However, class size varies by subject and by level.

To provide support throughout the process of choosing classes, a strong advising system begins freshman year. Every frosh meets with his or her advisor during the first weeks of school.

Living on the *Titanic*

During those first few weeks, freshman also get situated with their new home. All freshman (except commuter students) are required to live on-campus. Unfortunately, housing is in higher demand now due to rising matriculation rates and larger freshman classes. The university is even offering incentives (like free telephone and ethernet) for upperclassmen to live off-campus. For many, this is an offer too good to refuse: "I'm looking forward to living off-campus next year because it's become so crowded."

As a result of this housing pinch, the university has gone on a building boom to meet the demand for student housing. The reaction to the new dorms has been mixed. According to an upperclassman, the lobby of one building "looks like you just stepped on-board the *Titanic*." Though attractive, the new dorms have brought complaints. Many students have observed that the walls in the buildings are not insulated well and are too thin, allowing sound to travel easily.

Despite these minor grievances, students like both the old and new dorms. The rooms are best described as institutional and uniform, with space at a premium for those living in triples (doubles and singles are also available).

With the new dormitories has come a new food-service provider and students could not be happier. All students raved about the variety and quality of the food. "The food was OK before, but it's really good now," said one student. The flexible meal plans allow students to eat at any of the many dining halls that dot the campus and several fast-food restaurants. With "yummy" dining hall food, Wash U again bucks stereotypes.

Brains and Braun

Though consistently ranked as one of the best undergraduate institutions in the country, this seemingly "nerdy" school is, in fact, quite athletically inclined. Washington University's teams often rank among the best in the nation in Division III. The women's basketball team is the reigning national champion and women's volleyball has won ten national titles. However, according to one student "sports don't really bring students together."

Fun on Frat Row

Joining fraternities or sororities becomes a way of connecting with the school. Non-Greeks and Greeks seem to get along well at Wash U and "there is no stigma against or for fraternities or sororities." Fraternities have houses along Frat Row, but sororities do not. The administration's recent crackdown on underage drinking is of concern to both Greek and non-Greeks. Wash U is a wet campus, but the university is in the process of reconsidering its alcohol policies (considered very lax in the past). Alcohol still can be had by those underage without too much struggle, students report.

Those not into the drinking or partying scenes can amuse themselves with an array of extracurricular activities. The range of possibilities is endless and encompasses everything from student publications (*Student Life* and *Cadenza*) to improv performance and comedy (INPO—In No Particular Order). In addition to campus activities, St. Louis provides many opportunities for internships, work, and community service.

Stop and Smell the Roses

Despite the numerous enticements that surround them, Wash U students do take time to relax amid the beauty of their campus. As one student relates, "Even when I'm down, the beauty of this school uplifts me." The collegiate Gothic architecture was described as "gorgeous" by many students. However, the campus does contain an eclectic mix of architectural styles, ranging from the aforementioned Gothic to the postmodern.

> **"With 'yummy' dining hall food, Wash U again bucks stereotypes."**

Washington University in St. Louis often gets confused with the University of Washington, but there is no confusion when it comes to the overall quality of this institution. Academic departments are strong, most notably biology, and extracurriculars are numerous. In addition to the Greek system, St. Louis provides constant diversion. Even so, the living environment of Wash U manages to keep most students happy on-campus. As one senior stated emphatically, "Wash U has given me a remarkable college experience." Four years at Washington University provides an experience full of opportunities, and many memories of glow sticks, of course.—*Madhu Pocha and Staff*

FYI

The three best things about attending Wash U are "the vibrant off-campus attractions, the excellent academic offerings, and the gorgeous campus."

The three worst things about attending Wash U are "people misunderstanding which school you're from, overcrowded dorms, and the cost of tuition."

The three things every student should do before graduating from Wash U are "hang out in Laclede's Landing, watch the Wash U Symphony Orchestra (or any other musical group) perform, and party during W.I.L.D."

One thing I wish I'd known before coming to Wash U "is what an awesome city St. Louis is!"

Montana

University of Montana

Address: Admissions & New Student Services, University of Montana, Missoula, MT 59812-2016
Phone: 406-243-6266
E-mail address: admiss@selway.umt.edu
Web site URL: www.umt.edu
Location: small city
Founded: 1893
Private or Public: NA
Religious affiliation: none
Undergraduate enrollment: 10,035
Total enrollment: 12,208
Percent Male/Female: 49%/51%

Percent Minority: 6.0%
Percent African-American: 1.0%
Percent Hispanic: 1.0%
Percent Asian: 1.0%
Percent in-state/out-of-state: 75%/25%
Percent Pub HS: 70%
Fraternities: 60%
Sororities: 60%
Number of Applicants: 4,506
Percent Accepted: 85%
Percent Accepted who enroll: 52%
Entering: 2,060
Transfers: 1,019
Application Deadline: 1 Mar

Mean SAT: NA
Middle 50% SAT range: 480–590 V, 470–590 M
Middle 50% ACT range: 20–25
Mean ACT: 22.6 composite
3 Most popular majors: business, education, medical sciences
Retention: 77%
Graduation rate: 39%
Library: 570,287 volumes
Tuition and Fees: $1,967 in; $8,076 out
Room and Board: $4,000
On-campus housing: 80%
Financial aid, first-year: 45%

If a large, open green the size of two football fields, filled with ardent Frisbee players and engaged artists, is your idea of college life, perhaps a closer look at Big Sky country is in order. At one end of the "oval," as the campus green is called, stands stately Main Hall. Directly behind the tower of Main Hall, the peak of Mt. Sentinel reminds one of the natural beauty of the area. This mix of academic buildings and untouched natural wonders is what makes the University of Montana special.

A Montana Education

While the varied callings of their beautiful environment tempt Montana students, undergrads here are serious about their academics. The university features a general education requirement for all liberal arts students. Everyone must graduate with "competency" in three major areas: writing composition, math, and foreign language. Luckily, there are approximately 75 classes to choose from in each category. Students must also take two classes in each of six categories: expressive studies, such as studio art, dance, or music; literary/artistic studies, such as English or art history; historical/cultural studies; social sciences, ethical and human values; and natural sciences. Students have mostly positive attitudes toward the general education requirements, although some say they already learned the material in high school. One student said, "The requirements are beneficial. I came to school with one major in mind and the General Education Program opened my eyes to the fact that I could take other classes and not get hindered." Popular majors include business, education, forestry, wildlife biology, environmental studies, and creative writing. Some of these majors may be pursued by taking classes at other schools in the university besides the liberal arts school. Students can apply to these schools separately during the admissions process. Montana's schools include the School of Pharmacy, the School of Education, the School of Allied Health, the School of Journalism, and the School of Business. In addition, the Davidson Honors College is a small liberal arts college within the university. To be accepted and remain a member of the honors college, a student must have finished freshman year, maintain a certain GPA, and participate in volunteer service. All classes in the honors college are small, with no more than 20 to 25 people.

As many sometimes tire of the long and cold Montana winters, studying abroad is a popular option. Students can travel with University of Montana faculty to such countries as France, Spain, Germany, Australia, Mexico, New Zealand, and many East Asian countries while living in the homes of native families.

Men and women at the University of Montana say that their classes range from 300-person introductory lectures to smaller classes of up to 25 students. "The difficulty of the course work depends on how much you apply yourself," said one student. Those who wish to study intensely do so in Mansfield Library or the study rooms in the University Center, while anyone who wants an atmosphere more conducive to socializing can study in the first floor of the library or the study lounges in each residence hall.

Students find faculty to be relatively accessible, although their approachability varies with professors and programs. Almost all classes are taught by professors, although some introductory classes such as math, English, and psychology are sometimes taught by teaching assistants. While registering for classes at large state universities can be a hassle, the university has moved to make the process easier for students. In order to register for their classes, Montana Grizzlies find the Dial-a-Bear Registration system very satisfactory. It is "definitely a positive," said one student. The system dictates that students meet with their appointed advisors prior to registering, then call up the system to see if they've gotten into the classes they wanted. Registration goes smoothly, with

27 phone lines allocated to the process. Each semester, priority switches from those with last names in the first half of the alphabet to those in the last half so that registration is fair. Students said they often get their first picks, regardless.

Life at UM

On-campus living is mandatory for all freshmen. All of the dorms at the University of Montana are located within a ten-minute walk, at most, of major classroom buildings. Students say the main difference between the dorms is that some have been renovated and some not. Even the nonrenovated dorms are reputed to be "not bad" by students familiar with the typical college dormitory. The most recently renovated dorm is an upperclassman dorm, Panzer Hall—to live in this dorm students must have a GPA of at least 3.0. Panzer consists of suites in an almost apartment-like setting. Turner Hall (an all-female dorm), Elrod (an all-male dorm), Jesse and Aber (the two high-rise dorms), and a dorm for married students are also available for on-campus living. Some dorms have substance-free floors or floors reserved for students in the Honors College.

All dorms include a laundry room, game room, and lounge in which students can come together to study, watch TV, or just hang out. Each floor has an RA, who can be a sophomore, junior, or senior. The RA serves as a liaison to University administration, an enforcer of rules, a counselor, and a resource for information in campus life. RAs, in conjunction with the student organization Peers Reaching Out, present information on sex, drugs, drinking, assault, stress management, and other pertinent topics at the beginning of the year. The degree to which underage drinking rules are enforced depends on the individual RA, although students generally feel the alcohol policy on-campus is relatively strict. Students also said that there is a definite drug scene on-campus, including marijuana.

Many upperclassmen move off-campus to apartments in Missoula, which are accessible to campus by walking or bicycling, or by public buses, which are free to all students with their university ID. Many bring cars to campus, which allows them to find apartments farther from central campus. These apartments have the advantage of being cheaper than those in the heart of Missoula. Students can also live in the fraternity and sorority houses—although these houses are not very large and are not the most popular housing option on-campus, according to students.

Students who live on-campus are required to purchase the meal plan, and many say the food isn't bad. "While the cooking isn't like Mom's, overall it's by far the best college food I've had," said one transfer student. The university has one main dining hall, nicknamed "the Zoo." Students can also use their meal plan at Mama Zula's Pizzeria and the Country Store, or use "Bear Bucks" at Copper Commons cafeteria or Cafe Bristo in the University Center. For off-campus eating and coffee students frequent eateries and fast-food outlets in Missoula. Favorite coffee places include BoJangle's, which has live entertainment and poetry readings, and Cybershack, where you can enjoy a cup of joe while e-mailing your best friend from home. Popular Missoula restaurants include the Depot (for fancy fare), Food for Thought, Finnigan's, and Pizza Pipeline.

On weekends students tend to spend their days either engaged in outdoor activity, indoor sports, or studying. With the amazing natural environment, students always have something to do. The nearest ski area is 15 to 30 minutes by car, and those enrolled at the university are given special discounts. In the fall and spring, students enjoy hiking, biking, jogging. Besides skiing, winter activities include trips to the indoor gym facilities of the Harry Adams Field House, Shriver Gymnasium, or the Rec Annex to use climbing walls, weight rooms, basketball courts, racquetball courts, exercise rooms, wrestling rooms, and more.

Besides these weekend activities, other sports activities are also actively pursued. Intramurals are popular, especially softball, soccer, and basketball. Varsity sports are also a big deal at the university. The women's soccer team is very successful, women's basketball has gone to the league tournament for the past three years, and the football team recently won the championship.

Having Fun

One big event of the year is the Montana/Montana State football game. For this game and for all others the newly renovated 20,000-person football arena is packed—this is a pretty amazing feat considering that the whole university has less than 15,000 students and the town of Missoula only 50,000 residents. Homecoming weekend, with floats and all draws a crowd. The Forrester's Ball, in which the gym is changed into a mining town, is also popular; party-goers enter the ball through a mine shaft and all drinks or food must be purchased for the price of a kiss.

Other extracurricular activities include Peers Reaching Out, Advocates (a group of student ambassadors to the University), ASUM (the student government), the choir, the band, Greek activities, dance and theater productions, and writing for the *Kaimon* (the university paper that comes out Tuesday through Friday).

> The nearest ski area is 15 to 30 minutes by car, and those enrolled at the university are given special discounts.

On weekend evenings students either go out to bars, go to parties off-campus, or go to the alcohol-free Nite Kourt events sponsored by a student organization, Residence Life. These events usually take place once a month and can include free use of the game room, a comedian, a Velcro obstacle course, or a mix and mingle event. University Productions also sponsors small concerts twice a month. Fraternities used to be more of a force at U of M, but since the campus went dry in October of 1996, their parties have died down.

Many other changes are also in the works or have recently taken place, although these are more structural in nature. A new business school building was recently completed, the Panzer Residence Hall and the Miller Residence Hall were renovated, and a new Honors College building was built. In addition, the Student Health Center was expanded, and University Center was remodeled to include more eateries, study lounges, student organization offices, a game room, the women's center, a bank, a post office, a hair salon, a computer store, a travel agency, and a ballroom. Remodeling of the University Theater is scheduled to start soon and both the university and the Missoula community will benefit.

Big Sky, Small Town

The university and the town of Missoula are very connected and, as students attest, have an "excellent" relationship. Students see shows at the Montana Repertory Theater or visit the Southgate Mall, while Missoula residents come and see theater and dance productions at the university theater or sporting events at the field house. Many students enjoy Missoula so much that they spend the summer there rafting, kayaking, and hiking.

While most of the undergrads are from Montana, many students come from other parts of the country as well as other parts of the world. The atmosphere is described as liberal, yet diverse, ranging from "cowboys to tree-huggers." The campus has a small minority population and a small but active lesbian/gay population as well. All students interviewed said that the school possessed a great deal of spirit and, as one student said, "You'll see the same student at a sporting event and at an art show. The environment is one of 'pat me on the back, [and I'll] pat you on the back.'" —*Staff*

FYI

The three best things about attending Montana are, "big mountains, laid back people, lots of trails to run on."

The three worst things about attending Montana are "lousy weather, the traffic downtown, loud train whistle."

The three things that every student should do before graduating from Montana are, "smell the fresh air, especially if you're from the east coast, travel abroad, and try the velcro obstacle course."

One thing I'd like to have known before coming here is "how anti-fraternity the administration is."

Nebraska

Creighton University

Address: 2500 California Plaza, Omaha, NE 68178
Phone: 402-280-2703
E-mail address: admissions@creighton.edu
Web site URL: www.creighton.edu
Location: urban
Founded: 1878
Private or Public: private
Religious affiliation: Roman Catholic (Jesuit)
Undergraduate enrollment: 3,917
Total enrollment: 6,292
Percent Male / Female: 41% / 59%
Percent Minority: 19.0%

Percent African-American: 3.0%
Percent Hispanic: 3.0%
Percent Asian: 12.0%
Percent in-state / out-of-state: 43% / 57%
Percent Pub HS: 53%
Fraternities: 29%
Sororities: 30%
Number of Applicants: 3,268
Percent Accepted: 89%
Percent Accepted who enroll: 27%
Entering: 802
Transfers: 147
Application Deadline: 1 Aug
Mean SAT: NA

Middle 50% SAT range: 520–640 V, 520–650 M
Middle 50% ACT range: 23–28
Mean ACT: 25
3 Most popular majors: health professions, business, biological sciences
Retention: 85.0%
Graduation rate: 57.0%
Library: 780,000 volumes
Tuition and Fees: $12,858 in; NA out
Room and Board: $5,190
On-campus housing: 100%
Financial aid, first-year: 60%

When asked to name their favorite aspect of Creighton, students agree on one: the size of the school. They say the small size of the campus and classes make it "easy to get to know your professors and people around you." One student remarked, "When you're in a smaller situation, you're more apt to work in teams." Thanks to its size, a student choosing Creighton can expect a warm atmosphere to go along with a rigorous academic program.

Close Interaction

The relatively small enrollment at Creighton makes small classes and close faculty-student interaction possible. Freshman introductory classes like chemistry and psychology hold between 40 and 60 students, while upper-level classes rarely enroll more than 20. Students say the abundance of personal attention from the faculty is one of Creighton's strong points

and many delight in the fact that their professors actually know their names.

Creighton has three undergraduate schools: the College of Arts and Sciences, the business school, and the nursing school. The business school attracts many students, and the nursing school is said to be "excellent and pretty demanding." Within the College of Arts and Sciences, biology, chemistry, psychology, and education are the most popular majors—each gets high praise. Students have a hard time naming "worst departments," and besides complaints about the lack of a music program, they say they are generally "pretty satisfied" with Creighton's existing majors and departments.

Those interested in the health fields are particularly satisfied at Creighton. According to one student, "If you're interested in health professions, this is the school for you." A great number of students are interested in medicine, den istry, and nursing. One student praised the concentration of the student body in the sciences, saying that it allowed him to be "surrounded by people with the same focus, which is important." Many of those who don't go on to medical or dentistry school do graduate work in the sciences.

Academics are described as "competitive" and "challenging, but nothing overly demanding." One student said there are definitely not any [guts] in the sciences, and most classes are writing-intensive anyway." Another mentioned a gymnastics class as a gut, but on the whole students seem to agree that there are few easy courses.

A Demanding Core Curriculum

A rigid core curriculum exists in the arts and sciences school, which one student said provides "a good base in just about anything." One drawback is that "you're not going to like all the classes you're going to take." To graduate, students must complete 128 credit hours, with 64 of them going toward the core. The core itself is comprised of six classes in theology/philosophy/ethics; six in Culture, Ideas, and Civilizations; two in the natural sciences; two in the behavioral sciences; and five in Skills (English, math, communications). In addition, two intro-level language classes or one higher-level language class is required. The business and nursing schools have different requirements, but all Creighton students, regardless of school, must complete the theology requirement. Some students felt six classes devoted to religion is "a little excessive," while others criticized some of the views taught as "really biased and lame." Defenders of the requirement pointed out that other religions besides Catholicism are covered and maintained that "religion is never forced on anyone."

One disadvantage of Creighton's small size is its small library. A frustrated student complained that "for major research, you have to go elsewhere." To supplement its limited collection, the three-story Reinhart Library participates in an interlibrary loan system, allowing students to gain access to any book in any college within a week or two. Students also praised the librarians for going out of their way to help.

All freshmen and sophomores must live on campus. Of the four dorms, three are coed by floor and the fourth, Deglman, is all-female. One student recommended Deglman to incoming first-year women because "people really get to know each other there." Swanson, "the loudest and dirtiest" dorm, is also the biggest and is known as the party dorm. Another housing option is the small Creighton House, where everyone has his or her own room and takes turns cooking meals. Students also can request to live in specified floors known as the Wellness Community or the Study Community. Study Community floors are meant to be quieter than normal floors, while Wellness Community floors are supposedly substance-free. One freshman living there described the policy as a "joke," however, "because people have beers in their fridges."

For the first two years, undergrads must buy a meal plan. Students eat either in the two main cafeterias or in the Student Center, which houses some fast-food places such as Taco Bell and Godfather's Pizza. When Creighton students want to escape what some feel is the "gross" on-campus food, they frequent such off-campus eateries as Austin's Steakhouse, the Garden Cafe, and TGI Friday's.

Filling Those Extra Hours

Also at the Student Center are fireside chats held weekly by school president Father Morrison, and Java Joint, coffeehouse sessions where students play blues and drink coffee. On warmer days the grassy mall in the center of campus replaces the Student Center as the main hangout. The mall, which still has train tracks on it from the days trains ran through the campus, is the site of one of the biggest parties of the year. During the first week of the fall term, a stage is set up and a reggae band is brought in for Jamaican Jam. Another popular event is called Dim Wand, the name of a hypnotist who comes to hypnotize the students in his audience. Another unusual, popular activity is The Price Is Right, for which Creighton buses students to the nearby Civic Center to compete in their own version of the television game show. Prizes include trips to New York City, mountain bikes, and color TVs.

Regarding social life, one student reported that "there is always something to do," while another added the corollary that "there's not much to do if you're under 21." Off campus, students like to frequent the historic part of Omaha known as Old Market, where bars, restaurants, and shops line quaint cobblestone streets. Other things to do on a weekend include going to the movies, the bowling alley, or frat parties.

About one-third of Creighton students participate in the Greek system, but students report there is no pressure to join and no stigma against the non-Greek. Most frat parties are open to all, so independents do not feel excluded. Although some students say Omaha has a high underage drinking rate, the school administration upholds a strict alcohol policy.

Many students also participate in community service activities, especially Habitat for Humanity. With organizations such as Habitat, students take service trips across the country during their vacations. Students also go on weekend spiritual retreats. Those interested in journalism write for the weekly newspaper, the *Creightonian*, or work for JTV, the student-run television station. Those with a literary bent work on *Windows*, a quarterly literary magazine.

Students also participate in Division I sports and intramurals. Creighton has no football team, but as one student said, "soccer and baseball rock here." The women's softball team also does well, and the tennis team is nationally ranked. Creighton Blue Jay athletes practice and play in the Kiewit Athletic Center, while nonathletes use the Fitness Center connected to the Student Center. "Practically everyone does intramurals," said one undergrad, with volleyball, basketball, and soccer among the most popular.

Many undergrads do not consider Creighton's student body diverse; most people come from the Midwest and only a small percentage come from foreign countries. One student saw the homogeneity as a boost for campus clubs: Multicultural activities are a "big thing just because the school is not very diverse." Regarding the political scene, one undergrad said the campus is "not a political hotbed," adding that views were largely right-leaning. The lack of a pronounced lesbian/gay community at Creighton is consistent with this assessment.

> **"Students felt six classes devoted to religion is 'a little excessive,' while others criticized some of the views taught as 'really biased and lame.'"**

When asked what they would tell high school students thinking of applying to Creighton, students advised a visit to the campus, "because if you don't like Omaha, you will be miserable for a while." Undergrads say the city is boring, and some lament that the campus is "not really pretty because it's in downtown." One good thing about the campus is that it's safe. Students say they feel very safe on campus because "Creighton spares no expense" on security. Guards are said to be "always driving around looking for things to do," and will even drive students anywhere within reason at night. In general, however, students said they would tell high school seniors to apply to Creighton simply because "you get your money's worth" through its tough academic program and lots of personal attention.
—*Santosh Aravind and Staff*

FYI

The three best things about attending Creighton are "it's easy to get to know your professors, it's the place to be if you're interested in service to others, and we get cool Spring Fling performers like Third Eye Blind, Smashmouth, Goo Goo Dolls, New Radicals, and this year, Bush and Moby."

The three worst things about attending Creighton are "rumors spread quickly, people are cliquish, and lack of school spirit."

The three things that every student should do before graduating from Creighton are "go to the Henry Doorly Zoo (*very* cool rainforest exhibit), go see a Huskers game, and experience a tornado."

One thing I'd like to have known before coming here is "that there's basically no nightlife. Everything closes before midnight."

University of Nebraska / Lincoln

Address: 1410 Q Street, Alexander Bldg-East, Lincoln, NE 68588-0417
Phone: 402-472-2023
E-mail address: nuhusker@unl.edu
Web site URL: www.unl.edu
Location: small city
Founded: 1869
Private or Public: public
Religious affiliation: none
Undergraduate enrollment: 17,804
Total enrollment: 22,142
Percent Male/Female: 53%/47%
Percent Minority: 6.1%

Percent African-American: 2.0%
Percent Hispanic: 1.6%
Percent Asian: 2.1%
Percent in-state/out-of-state: 71%/29%
Percent Pub HS: NA
Fraternities: 16%
Sororities: 17%
Number of Applicants: 7,500
Percent Accepted: 92%
Percent Accepted who enroll: 53%
Entering: 3,658
Transfers: NA
Application Deadline: rolling

Mean SAT: NA
Middle 50% SAT range: NA
Middle 50% ACT range: NA
Mean ACT: NA
3 Most popular majors: NA
Retention: 79.0%
Graduation rate: 45.0%
Library: 2,278,154 volumes
Tuition and Fees: $3,338 in; $7,845 out
Room and Board: $4,070
On-campus housing: NA
Financial aid, first-year: 61%

With three national titles in the past ten years, University of Nebraska at Lincoln Cornhuskers pride themselves on their football dynasty. While many other large state universities boast of powerhouse programs and dedicated fans, those unfamiliar with Nebraska cannot fully appreciate the magnitude of Husker spirit. Said one student "It's like religion here, on game days Memorial Stadium becomes the third largest city in Nebraska, and if by chance we lose the entire state needs antidepressants!" Another noted that "at Nebraska there are four seasons of sport. In the fall is football season. The winter is football recruiting season, followed by spring football practice. Lastly comes summer and general anticipation of the coming fall! Isn't it great?"

Colleges, TAs, and Honors

While most UNL students will tell you that the football team is close to perfection, many feel that university academics are in need of some more coaching. Nebraska is divided into nine different academic colleges: the College of Agricultural Sciences & Natural Resources, the College of Architecture, the College of Arts & Sci-

ences, the College of Business Administration, the College of Engineering & Technology, the College of Fine & Performing Arts, the College of Human Resources & Family Sciences, the College of Journalism & Mass Communication, and the Teacher's College. Each college offers a variety of majors totaling 149 in all, and ranging from Grazing Livestock Systems to Pre-Nuclear Medicine. Students feel that the large selection of majors encourages everyone to find a course of study they enjoy, but also note that overly easy majors abound. Slackers avoid any hard sciences, but find refuge in the Communication Studies, Business Administration, and Fishery and Wildlife departments. Grading is known to be "a little too nice to the student," and one student summed up the workload by saying, "It's definitely harder than high-school, but never unreasonable."

Big lecture classes at UNL seldom exceed an enrollment of 150, and students seem content with class sizes. Said one junior, "at the lower levels the classes are small enough to get to know the teacher but too big to know everybody in the class; but as you get more into your major the numbers go down." Students report that professors are friendly and accessible, but only to students who make the effort to meet them. Conversely, students are critical of TAs, many of whom cannot speak English. One sophomore estimated that 10 percent of Nebraska's TAs aren't capable of teaching class, and two others mentioned that they are failing classes specifically because their TAs do not understand English. Said one: "If my TA didn't understand a word on my exam he would count it wrong."

On the upside, Huskers seeking a more challenging academic environment may choose to participate in the University Honors Program. Incoming freshmen are considered for the program based on their ACT/SAT scores, and their high school grades and curriculum. Once enrolled, they enjoy smaller classes and work directly with top faculty members. The program culminates in a senior thesis, and along the way honors students have access to special housing in Neihardt Hall and exclusive honors computer centers.

Dry? Who's Dry?

Because most UNL students live in Nebraska, many report going home on weekends to visit with high school friends and to get laundry done. Others caution that this does not mean UNL is a boring place to be once classes end. On the contrary, Huskers find each other extremely friendly and enjoy their social scene. Officially, UNL is a dry campus, but students report that they don't have much difficulty in finding alcohol. Because of the dry campus rule, most underclassmen choose to party in off-campus apartments or at the fraternity houses, while upperclassmen frequent the bars of downtown Lincoln. The Greek system maintains such a strong presence on campus that many students consider the campus stereotype to be that everyone is Greek. Fraternities host many of the year's biggest parties, with themes such as *Gilligan's Island* and *Grease*. Those who aren't members of a fraternity or sorority don't seem to mind the social alternatives however, and the Greek system isn't considered exclusive by non-Greeks.

Nebraska's size affords students with a wealth of clubs and extracurricular organizations in which to participate. Governmental and political organizations, ethnic clubs, and sports and recreational teams provide Huskers with outlets for every kind of creative, athletic or community service oriented student.

Once again, football's role in the social scene at UNL cannot be understated. Nothing brings out the Nebraska faithful in greater numbers than a Saturday morning tailgate, as Huskers of all ages intermingle in support of their common cause. As one female student noted, "I don't even especially like football, but going to a Husker home game is an experience not to be missed."

Dorming and Dining

UNL requires its freshmen to live in one of the 12 university residence halls, but students don't have many complaints about dorm room quality. All residence halls are either single-sex or coed by floor, and provide students with amenities such as high-speed Internet access, cable, and air-conditioning. Different residence halls make up larger communities, which feature dining and laundry facilities, computer labs, and recreational areas. Halls are staffed by RAs, who help younger students with academic questions and encourage dorm residents to get involved in different campus activities. Different halls cater to different groups of students and hold somewhat different reputations. Abel and Sandoz accommodate mostly freshman students. Sandoz is all female, while Abel is coed and known as the party dorm. Cather and Pound are coed halls reserved for upperclassmen, and offer their residents laundry and computer facilities on every floor. Love Hall offers its 46 female residents a co-op atmosphere in which they share household responsibilities and costs.

One student summed up dining at Nebraska by saying "to be honest, it's a far cry from mom's home-cooking, but it's bearable." Dining hall food is labeled as "boring," and students make comments like "how many times in a week do they expect us to eat spaghetti?" On the plus side, Huskers on a meal plan have the option of eating at any one of the campus' dining halls, and their Student ID cards double as charge cards for between-meal snacks. Vegetarian options are plentiful, yet equally unimaginative. For those who wish to eat out, downtown Lincoln offers virtually every type of fare, from fast food to popular restaurants like Old Chicago and Carlos O'Kelley's. One particular section of the city, known as the Haymarket, is especially liked by students, who mention it as a great place to take a date on a stroll or for a cup of coffee at The Mill.

Two Campuses, One Union

UNL's campus is divided into two sections. Most departments reside on City Campus, while the agriculture and home economics schools inhabit East Campus. Shuttle buses run between the two sections, but students are often labeled as either "frat boys or sorority girls" on City and "hicks" on East. Active students enjoy the Lee Sapp Recreational Center for its indoor climbing wall, racquetball and basketball courts, weight room and two indoor tracks. They can also watch the men's and women's varsity basketball teams take on their Big 12 rivals in the Devaney Sports Center. Students looking for a cultural experience can also benefit from the Lied Center for Performing Arts, a 150,000 square foot performance house that has hosted such notables as the Philadelphia Orchestra and the Broadway musical *Les Misérables*.

The university's social center is undoubtedly the Nebraska Union, which contains the University Bookstore and the offices of the school paper the *Daily Ne-braskan*. Renovated and expanded in 1998, the Union now contains a convenience store, big-screen television lounge and game room in its basement, and an art lounge, computer room, copy shop and large auditorium on its first and second floors. These new additions combined with a popular food court make the Union one of UNL's most popular attractions.

Cornhusker Spirit!

When asked what building on their campus is most impressive, Huskers routinely answer "Memorial Stadium, of course!" With the addition of $40 million worth of skyboxes for the 1999 football season, Memorial Stadium is the pride of many a Nebraskan, just like the team itself. While football may be a rallying point for school spirit, Huskers are quick to add that "Pride in this school comes from living in such a clean, safe, and beautiful environment . . . football just helps us express our feelings!" If enjoying their football prowess is truly an indication of how Huskers delight in their school, then the University of Nebraska is certainly a great place to be.—*Robert Berschinski*

> "I don't even especially like football, but going to a Husker home game is an experience not to be missed."

FYI

The three best things about attending the University of Nebraska are "Husker Spirit, small town students, and the student to teacher ratio."

The three worst things about attending the University of Nebraska are "Cold Nebraska winters, the parking situation, and the separate campuses."

The three things that every student should do before graduating from the University of Nebraska are "go to a Husker game, meet new people, and realize that the greatest days of your life will be spent at UNL."

One thing I'd like to have known before coming here is "I would have liked to have seen more of the dorms before I had to choose one."

Nevada

Address: MS 120, Reno, NV 89557
Phone: 775-784-6865
E-mail address: unrug@unr.edu
Web site URL: www.unr.edu
Location: small city
Founded: 1874
Private or Public: Public
Religious affiliation: none
Undergraduate enrollment: 8,816
Total enrollment: 12,532
Percent Male/Female: 46%/54%
Percent Minority: 13.9%

Percent African-American: 2.0%
Percent Hispanic: 5.0%
Percent Asian: 5.7%
Percent in-state/out-of-state: 78%/22%
Percent Pub HS: 93%
Fraternities: 11%
Sororities: 5%
Number of Applicants: 8,546
Percent Accepted: 85%
Percent Accepted who enroll: 51%
Entering: 2,498
Transfers: 953
Application Deadline: 1 Mar

Mean SAT: 518 V, 525 M
Middle 50% SAT range: 515 V, 525 M
Middle 50% ACT range: 22
Mean ACT: 22
3 Most popular majors: elementary education, psychology, biology
Retention: 78%
Graduation rate: 44%
Library: 956,282 volumes
Tuition and Fees: $2,327 in; $5,500 out
Room and Board: $5,100
On-campus housing: 49%
Financial aid, first-year: 70%

Picture a university with a low-key atmosphere and very reasonable tuition set against the mountains of Nevada. This is UNR, a Nevada state university that educates both fraternity brothers and senior citizens alike.

Oodles of Colleges

Ten colleges comprise UNR: agriculture, arts and sciences, business administration, education, engineering, human and community sciences, business administration, journalism, mining, and nursing. Students select their college as sophomores, but they can take classes in any field regardless of their year. The School of Journalism, among the strongest of all the colleges, maintains a faculty including Pulitzer Prize-winning alumni. The School of Engineering also draws raves from students: "Engineering, especially mechanical engineering, is just great. All of my teachers have been really interesting."

A newly implemented core curriculum includes "Western Traditions." All students must complete classes that, together, present a broad overview of Western history, philosophy, and literature. One student complained that Western Tradition classes demand "way too much reading, sometimes 200 or 300 plus pages a week." Another student believed that "understanding our Western tradition is important for anyone living in a Western society like ours." Aside from Western traditions, students must take two to three upper-level, interdisciplinary "Capstone" courses.

Students herald the UNR Honors Program. Honors students have smaller classes; one student said that her psychology honors class had only 30 students, as opposed to the typical 150. Honors students may choose to live in honors housing, which lodges men and women in different buildings, claims 24-hour quiet periods, and offers restored buildings with "very comfortable" suites. Only honors students can graduate with Greek distinction of either magna cum laude or summa cum laude.

An Older Student Body

The average age of the UNR student is 26, and the undergraduate population includes a large number of people from the community, including senior citizens and those who have returned to school several years after high school. Many UNR students work during the day and commute at night. Older undergrads reportedly "make other students work harder because they tend to ruin class curves." However, older students "have real-world knowledge of what we're only seeing in the classroom," explains one engineering major. "I mostly benefit from having them here."

Despite its proximity to many strip clubs only one county away, UNR attracts a rather conservative student body. "Most of the people who have political interests are Republicans," explains one junior. Students at UNR are also ethnically and racially homogeneous. "My high school was more diverse," complained one student. Most students are Nevada natives or Californians looking to "escape the UC system," as one said. (Through a "good neighbor" policy, Californians can attend UNR for a lower tuition than they would pay at a University of California school). Regardless of age, most UNR students choose to live off campus; even freshmen are not required to live on campus. Those who stay on campus live in the Manzanita, Juniper, Canada, Nye, White Pine, or Lincoln dorms.

Students describe the campus as "pretty and clean." The redbrick buildings and bell tower on the main quad draw praise from students: "The older brick buildings are a refreshing change from the '70s and '80s concrete you see everywhere else."

'Thletes and Greeks

Huge, beer-laden tailgates and rowdiness accompany football games, which are always well attended. The swim team usually wins its conference, and the boxing team is nationally recognized. UNR has recently joined the Big West division, home of archrival University of Nevada/Las Vegas. Intramural sports are popular as well.

> "Engineering, especially mechanical engineering, is just great. All of my teachers have been really interesting."

Despite small membership, fraternities and sororities maintain a strong social presence. Greek parties are popular, and non-Greeks can attain invitations easily. Because of alcohol regulations, dorm parties are rare, but parties in apartments around campus are common. The campus coffeehouse and local bowling alleys offer non-drinking options. However, commuters tend to participate in life less than those living at UNR, and older students normally avoid the UNR party scene. Many students believe that "a fake ID is a must." Local bars like the Beer Barrel and Little Waldorf are popular hangouts, while casinos attract student gamblers. Concerts with local bands always bring in large numbers, while some students frequent nearby Lake Tahoe and its ski slopes.

UNR has an exciting social scene, and its reputation is growing as its low tuition brings out-of-staters to the campus. Students say they're pleased to be getting such a well-rounded education in a relaxed setting.—*Brian Abaluck and Staff*

FYI

The three best things about attending UNR are "the low cost of tuition, the flexibility of class scheduling, and the many colleges."

The three worst things about attending UNR are "the disunited student body, the lack of diversity, and the lack of campus-sponsored activity."

The three things every student should do before graduating from UNR are "go to Lake Tahoe for a weekend, go to a football game against the University of Nevada/Las Vegas, and get some real-world experience."

One thing I wish I'd known before coming to UNR is "the strongly Republican bent of the student body."

New Hampshire

Dartmouth College

Address: 6016 McNutt Hall, Hanover, NH 03755
Phone: 603-646-2875
E-mail address: admissions@dartmouth.edu
Web site URL: www.dartmouth.edu
Location: rural
Founded: 1769
Private or Public: private
Religious affiliation: none
Undergraduate enrollment: 4,021
Total enrollment: 5,308
Percent Male/Female: 52%/48%
Percent Minority: 24.0%

Percent African-American: 6.0%
Percent Hispanic: 6.0%
Percent Asian: 10.0%
Percent in-state/out-of-state: NA
Percent Pub HS: 66%
Fraternities: NA
Sororities: NA
Number of Applicants: 10,259
Percent Accepted: 20%
Percent Accepted who enroll: 49%
Entering: 1,054
Transfers: 25
Application Deadline: 1 Jan
Mean SAT: 713 V, 713 M

Middle 50% SAT range: 670–770 V, 680–760 M
Middle 50% ACT range: NA
Mean ACT: NA
3 Most popular majors: biology, government, economics
Retention: NA
Graduation rate: 94%
Library: NA
Tuition and Fees: $26,424 in; NA out
Room and Board: $7,209
On-campus housing: 100%
Financial aid, first-year: NA

The joke goes like this: "How many Dartmouth students does it take to change a light bulb? None. Hanover doesn't have electricity!" Dartmouth's Ivy brethrens like to poke fun at this ambient, picturesque college town in New Hampshire as being desolate and barren. Others call the town "Hangover" in reference to scenes from Animal House, a movie inspired by life at Dartmouth. While Hanover is relatively removed from major cities and the drinking party scene represents much of Dartmouth's social atmosphere, such generalizations cannot accurately characterize life at this prestigious and spirited university. Instead, enthusiastic Dartmouth students describe it as a school "steeped in history and tradition, yet moving forward and advancing academically, socially, and technologically."

Academics

Unique to Dartmouth is its innovative Dartmouth Plan. The academic calendar includes four 10-week terms each year, one of which is in the summer. Students choose three of the four terms and are expected to remain on campus for three terms during their freshman and senior years and during the summer term of their sophomore year. While students rarely take more than three courses each term, "the consequence of this system is that Dartmouth's courses are more compact and intense, ordinarily covering in 10 weeks what similar courses would cover in 13 or 14 weeks." One junior complained that the D-plan makes it difficult to maintain friendships, saying "sometimes my friends are off while I am on campus." Still, most undergrads appreciate the flexibility it offers. Students can land internships in the unconventional, and therefore less competitive, seasons like fall or spring. The D-Plan is also conducive to studying abroad in Dartmouth's popular Language Study Abroad (LSA) or Foreign Study Program (FSP). These programs allow undergrads to study the language, literature, culture, and politics of another country.

On campus, Dartmouth's classes are intense and reputable. Some students report that Intro to Geology ("Rocks for Jocks"), Music 4 ("Clap for Credit"), and Computer Science 4 ("HTML for Dummies") are slacker classes, though. Tough classes include Econ 1, considered to be "the most frequently failed class at Dartmouth," organic chemistry, physics, and biochemistry. Each class is what you make it, one senior said, because "students compete against themselves and not each other."

The Dartmouth mandatory distribution requires that freshmen take 10 classes in 8 intellectual groups: arts, social analysis, literature, quantitative or deductive science, philosophy, religious or historical analysis, national science, technological or applied science, and international or comparative studies. In addition, students must take one course each in U.S., European, and non-Western society. Each freshman is required to take an intensive seminar that focuses on written expression, and students must demonstrate proficiency in one foreign language. The culminating senior exercise comes in many forms: the thesis, paper, exhibition, or performance.

Dartmouth may include three professional schools, the Amos Tuck School of Business Administration, the Thayer School of Engineering, and the Dartmouth Medical School, but its commitment to undergraduates remains strong. Undergraduates all commend the classes for their small sizes. The report of this student is not uncommon: "The only large (enrollment above 100) classes I have been in are the intro-level premed classes and Econ 1. Freshman year, most of my classes had enrollments of 15 or less and that has been the trend of my Dartmouth experience ever since. I have had classes with enrollments of three. I have really had the opportunity to get to know my professors." Another senior boasted that she had "never had a TA, and most of my professors are renowned in their fields of study." Students list such professors as the French professor Rassais, the art history professor Kenseth, Greek and Roman Studies professor Bradley, biochemistry professor Sloboda, chemistry professor Stockmeyer, philosophy professor Sinott-Armstrong, philosophy professor Masters, and others as notable faculty.

While some students commented on the relative weakness of Dartmouth's social sciences, economics, and education departments, there was a tremendously high rating for its computer science, biology, chemistry, geology, dance, and foreign language departments. Computers play a significant role at Dartmouth. One student emphasized their significance by saying "all freshman must buy (or come with) their own computers." These computers, mostly Macintosh, are a primary source of communication because of Dartmouth's e-mail program, nicknamed "blitz-mail." Before classes, at the gym, after meals, or in the library, students can check and compose blitzes. One student noted that "if people want to make dinner plans, they don't call, they blitz." Blitzmail also serves to update students on the many campus activities and provides instant communication between students and teachers. One student mentioned, "my art history professor blitzed me just to say hello and see how I was doing because I was a freshman in her class."

Social Atmosphere

Dartmouth's social scene is marked by its activities, organization, athletics, Greek system, and alcohol. The Dartmouth Outing Club is one of Dartmouth's most popular clubs, providing the outdoor enthusiasts with opportunities to backpack, canoe, bike, and hike before classes start. Meeting people on the DOC trips is, according to one freshman, "the easiest thing to do when you're stuck in the middle of the Upper Valley for four days singing crazy songs and doing weird dances."

"Schmen," Dartmouth's fond nickname for freshmen, gather in "schmobs" (groups of schmen) and enter the Dartmouth Forest for four days of bonding and fun. Another notable organization is the Tucker Foundation, a group on campus that provides funds and guidance in student-organized international charity projects. Dance, a cappella singing groups, the Dartmouth Review, and Dartmouth's radio station are also popular.

Sports play a defining role at Dartmouth. While some students praise the Big Green spirit at each sporting event, others say the sports are "too popular" and those who do not play are "automatically marginalized." One student estimated that 80 percent of the students are involved in some athletic program and most students attend the games. Dartmouth's soccer, ice hockey, and other varsity sports have traditionally been strong. Intramural sports are incredibly popular, although they can get competitive. Those who do not choose to participate in varsity of intramural sports can go to the gym which has recently installed more exercise equipment to meet the demands of students.

Students say that drinking is very prevalent at Dartmouth. According to one freshman, "Dartmouth is a big drinking school and there's no way around it. If you go out, you pretty much have to [drink] to have a good time." Several students described the typical weekend schedule: "drink, dance, and drink some more." Such a carefree attitude toward alcohol raises concern about rape and sexual assault, which students worry often go "unreported." While there has been an effort to create nonalcoholic alternatives to Dartmouth's traditional frat parties, "many of the events are not very well attended." Still, some students believe that "there are lots of other things to do besides going to parties and getting drunk."

The prevalence of alcohol can perhaps be attributed to Dartmouth's strong Greek system. At least 50 percent of the students are in a fraternity or sorority, and the Greek influence is "getting bigger." Some students complain that the Greek system "tends to dominate much of the typical Dartmouth student's life." Others say that Greek parties are open to anyone, so they

are both entertaining and a great way to meet upperclassmen. Students appreciate the fact that rush is during sophomore year because it enables them to "see what the Greek scene is all about without having the pressure of joining."

However, all of this may be changing. Just before the 1999 annual Winter Carnival weekend, the president of Dartmouth College announced that all the Greek system would "end as we know it." This naturally caused a great deal of discontent among the student body, since the traditional Greek system is such an integral part of student life, and the Winter Carnival in particular. In reaction to this news, the council of Fraternities and Sororities at Dartmouth voted to cancel all 21 parties planned for the Winter Carnival weekend, as one student said to "show the administration what life is like up here without the Greek system." Immediately following the announcement, there were protests at the president's house, and there were also protests during the Winter Carnival itself. Nearly a year late in January, 2000, the final proposal was released. It include implementing a comprehensive residential "cluster" system and stricter alcohol regulations. The rules on existing "Coed Fraternity Sorority" organizations would become stringent, effectively forcing some of them to be no longer recognized by the College.The reforms will be implemented over the next five to seven years, subject to approval by Dartmouth's board of trustees at a vote in the spring. In the interim, Dartmouth will consult students, alumni and faculty for feedback on the recommendations, which the trustees will take into consideration when voting on the report's findings. In addition, the new system would be subject to a full review in 2005.

Student Life

Students disagree on whether or not there is a typical Dartmouth student. Some exclaim that "Dartmouth is the most diverse place I have ever lived!" Others describe the typical Dartmouth student as a "government or economics major, upper-middle-class, dresses well, wants to be an investment banker, and belongs to a frat/sorority." Many students have wardrobes that are compilations of fleece, J. Crew, and Gap. Dartmouth has had a bad reputation in the past for being a bastion of white male students, but students agree that such is no longer entirely true. The influx of females, a new, more generous financial-aid program, and an increasing percentage of minorities have all contributed to a more diverse student body. There is a "modest gay and lesbian population on campus, and homophobia is not as rampant as it has been in the college's past."

Students rave about the Dartmouth campus. Its brick buildings are described as "very New Englandish," "typically Ivy League," and "well maintained." Some of its notable structures are the gym; the Thompson Arena, the new Special Collections Library; Kiewit, a nine-story underground bomb shelter and computer center; the Roth Center for Jewish Studies, which includes a kosher kitchen and Judaic library; and new psychology and chemistry buildings. In addition to this construction, Bradley (also known as the ugly Shower Tower) is being demolished and the library is being updated.

The beauty of the Dartmouth campus is captured in its miles of trails, mountains, ski resorts, golf course, lake, and river. One junior explained the beauty of the nature on the Dartmouth campus. "In the fall, the leaves change into beautiful colors. In the winter, the white of the snow is blinding. Spring, when the mud finally disappears, is always worth the time it takes to arrive." Hanover winters can be harsh, but students celebrate the cold with Winter Carnival, where students participate in ski and skating races and make ice sculptures. Not only is the campus picturesque, but it is also safe. One student reported that it was not uncommon to see a jogger at midnight. Another student illustrated how safe the campus was with a story of one late night at Food-Stop, a local hangout. "A cop car turned on its sirens and pulled over a car. Suddenly another one came from the other direction with its lights on and boxed in the car. Since it's rare to see so much activity in Hanover, I strained to hear the cops as they were talking to the driver of the car. The girl had been pulled over because she had a broken taillight."

Reportedly, freshmen receive the best dorms—centrally located doubles or triples that occasionally have a fireplace or bathroom. "My freshman-year dorm was great. All of my classes were right across a parking lot (which was particularly nice in the middle of the winter). We had two rooms for three people—one for beds, one for computers—and a bathroom with a sink and a toilet. The showers were just down the hall. Our dorm was one of the only ones that was coed by floor, as most are coed by room." Each freshman is assigned to a UGA group, and the UGA (Undergraduate Advisor) "helps you out if you have a problem, and coordinates events to bring your group closer together." Sophomores do not have such good luck. Because upperclass housing is based on seniority, sophomores tend to receive the smallest dorms in the most distant locations. Students consider the River Dorms and the Choates the worst dorms because of their distance from central campus. Students rate Mass Row, Gold Coast, Topliff, and Fayers highly because of their convenient locations.

> There is a "modest gay and lesbian population on campus, and homophobia is not as rampant as it has been in the college's past."

Students almost unanimously praise Dartmouth's food for its variety and great taste. The dining halls have convenient hours and healthy food options. The five full-service dining halls operate on an a la carte system, and students deduct each item from their debit account. Students complain that the food is extremely overpriced and are especially exasperated that there are no free refills on soda. Another complaint is that money remaining in an account at the end of the term does not roll over. Still, students enjoy the healthy food options, including vegetarian alternatives, in Collis Cafe and Home Plate as well as the "greasy but good stuff" in the Courtyard Cafe. Students also appreciate the convenient hours of operation of the Food Court, the main cafeteria. For those who want a change from the cafeterias, there are the local hangouts. A zoning ordinance has excluded fast-food chains from coming onto campus, but students can frequent EBA's (Everything But Anchovies), the Dirt Cowboy Cafe, Ramunto's Pizza, and the Ben & Jerry's ice cream parlor.

Rich Traditions

Dartmouth students enjoy the spirited, long-lasting traditions that have captured the experience of all students, from the freshman to noted alumni like Daniel Webster, Theodore Geisel (Dr. Seuss), and C. Everett Koop. Alumni return for the homecoming weekend during the fall term and gather around a huge bonfire on the Dartmouth Green, watching the freshmen run around the blazing mound the number of times that correlates with their class year. The Class of '03 will endure 103 circles around the bonfire after the they parade through the streets of Hanover proudly sporting their "Big-D" hats, bracelets, T-shirts, sweatshirts, and other Dartmouth paraphernalia for the annual Freshman Sweep. Moosilauke Weekend involves a 50-mile hike along the Appalachian Trail to Dartmouth's Raving Lodge at Mt. Moosilauke. Students listed the Disco Inferno (a '70s party), the Polar Bear Swim (a midwinter dive into the frigid Occum Pond), eating green eggs and ham in commemoration of Dr. Seuss, the Ledyard Challenge (which involves "canoeing to the bridge crossing to Vermont, running across it, and swimming back, all naked without getting caught"), and the ice sculptures of Winter Carnival. All of these traditions exemplify life at Dartmouth; they capture the school's passion for the outdoors, for constant activity, and for a great education.—*Marti Page*

FYI
The three best things about attending Dartmouth are "the small intimate classes, the proximity to ski slopes, and the contagious school spirit."
The three worst things about attending Dartmouth are "social life revolving around alcohol, being isolated in New Hampshire, and occasionally the stiflingly small and homogeneous student body."
The three things that every student should do before graduating from Dartmouth are "boot-n-rally at a party (throw-up and then drink some more), do more dating and less hooking up, and participate in Freshman Sweep."
One thing I'd like to have known before coming here is "a foot of snow only looks pretty in pictures, not when you have to walk in it."

University of New Hampshire

Address: 4 Garrison Avenue, Durham, NH 03824

Phone: 603-862-1360

E-mail address: admissions@unh.edu

Web site URL: www.unh.edu

Location: rural

Founded: 1866

Private or Public: public

Religious affiliation: none

Undergraduate enrollment: 10,765

Total enrollment: 12,454

Percent Male/Female: 42%/58%

Percent Minority: 4.0%

Percent African-American: 1.0%

Percent Hispanic: 1.0%

Percent Asian: 2.0%

Percent in-state/out-of-state: 63%/37%

Percent Pub HS: 84%

Fraternities: 10%

Sororities: 10%

Number of Applicants: 8,514

Percent Accepted: 78%

Percent Accepted who enroll: 32%

Entering: 2,321

Transfers: 702

Application Deadline: 1 Feb

Mean SAT: 554 V, 560 M

Middle 50% SAT range: 510–610 V, 510–610 M

Middle 50% ACT range: NA

Mean ACT: NA

3 Most popular majors: psychology, business, biology

Retention: 82.0%

Graduation rate: 49.0%

Library: 1,000,000 volumes

Tuition and Fees: $6,555 in; $14,340 out

Room and Board: $4,798

On-campus housing: NA

Financial aid, first-year: 35%

Set in the beautiful White Mountains, the University of New Hampshire boasts a "laid-back and casual atmosphere." Professors are approachable and students praise campus life. "There are a ton of different people here so everyone can find a group that they fit in with," explained one undergrad. But UNH isn't just peaceful mountain vistas. "The students go crazy for hockey," said one student. "We put on curly wigs and face paint. Every time a goal is scored for us, a song starts overhead, and people wave their hands in the air; it's a real fun time." UNH provides a dynamic balance between a laid-back environment in a rural New England town with warm, passionate people, and a lot of fun.

Another Business Major?

Students at UNH agreed that classes are "what you make of them." Business is the most popular major on campus. "Many business majors at UNH either chose business because they couldn't think of anything else, or because they dropped their first major and ended up in business," explained one undergrad. Students also praised the English department, and said the engineering department is "one of the world's best kept secrets." Students who do choose engineering find that the major is incredibly demanding. "They do a really thorough job teaching—you are initially told that it may take you five years to complete the major," said one undergrad.

Regardless of which major students choose, General Education (GenEd) requirements force undergrads to take classes in eight specific knowledge areas. One sophomore complained, "Personally, I feel they're stupid, and I'd rather not deal with them. I'm taking a mythology course I'll never use." But some students do feel that GenEds serve their intended purpose. "They can be a pain in the butt to schedule, but they break the monotony of taking major classes. I would have perished if I were stuck doing only math and computer science classes at UNH and not taken other interesting classes, like theater and English," acknowledged one undergrad. Introductory GenEd classes are usually the largest on campus, but class size wasn't viewed as a problem by most, since more advanced courses are generally quite small.

Students consider their instructors very approachable. Professors encourage their students to get to know them better, making themselves available in person and through e-mail. "I am in some pretty big classes, but you can still get to know the professors," said one undergrad. UNH has other resources for academic help, including a writing center, where graduate students assist undergrads with essays and other assignments.

Students study mostly in libraries and their dorm rooms. In 1998, UNH opened the newly renovated multimillion dollar Diamond Library, which is "so nice, it makes you want to study." In addition, there are a number of specialized branch libraries, such as the Bio-Sciences Library in Kendall Hall, which offer good places to study if the dorm gets too loud.

Eating and Sleeping

UNH sprawls over nearly 200 acres of land, featuring courtyards, grassy areas, and a traditional New England feel. The campus is split into four regions with three dorm areas and one area of on-campus apartments. Underclassmen usually live in the dorms, where there are two Residential Advisors (RAs) per floor. RAs are not disciplinarians, but they enforce some rules and seek help when students are in trouble. "My RA is strict when she needs to be," said one undergrad, "but she definitely has time to be our friend." The largest dorm on campus is Stoke Hall, housing nearly 600 students. Stoke, like other dorms, has outdoor volleyball and basketball courts, a new recreation room with a Ping-Pong table, a snack bar, and a 24-hour quiet study lounge. Minidorms, 6 small themed houses in a circular drive, offer an alternative housing option. Students apply for minidorms based on special interests such as the creative and performing arts, outdoor experience, academic awareness, or science and engineering. The themes allow students to immerse themselves in a particular interest and get to know others with similar ideas.

Many upperclassmen choose not to live in the dorms. The school owns three on-campus apartment buildings: Gabbs, Woodside, and Forest Park Apartments. Students can also choose to move off campus, either to a fraternity or sorority house or to apartments in Durham and nearby towns. However, those who bring cars warn of "Parking Services and their psycho ticket-giving lackeys" and the difficulty in finding parking. Explained one undergrad, "the parking situation for commuters has almost come down to a blood sport!"

Students love chickwiches, which are available at one of the 3 dining halls on campus. One student explained, "It's like a hamburger, except with chicken." The food is described as "pretty fattening," but students admit there is a decent variety, and vegetarians say they have plenty of choice in the dining hall. Freshmen are required to have a meal plan, which includes 19 meals per week. Students can also use their meal plan to get up to $5 toward food at the Memorial Union Building (MUB), the student union center, instead of eating a meal in one of the dining halls. MUB has some classic fast food chains, such as Papa Gino's Pizza, Taco Bell, and DeAngelo's Subs. During lunch and prime time, transfer meals can be eaten at the Wildcattesen, a food court under one of the dining halls. There, students can eat pizza, subs, or even made-to-order Asian food.

Small Town Living

UNH is located in Durham, a typical New England small town with a non-student population of around 13,000. "Durham is a small 'main street' town," explained one undergrad. "There are two bars, a few take out-pizza places, two restaurants, two coffee shops, one grocery store . . . you get the picture." There are some common student hangouts in Durham, including Mike Libby's bar, where every Tuesday night is nickel draft night. "Vegetarians should definitely try a falafel at Aladdin's Pocket, located inside the Laundromat," said one undergrad. The Licker Store, an ice cream and coffee shop, is also popular with students, featuring "really good iced coffee shakes," and a day-old bin full of muffins and pastries for the student on a budget. Students who find the town dull have many other options. Undergrads hang out at the MUB, and an on-campus movie theater plays 3 or 4 movies a week. They also enjoy the newly renovated Whittenmore Center, a sports complex with basketball courts, indoor running tracks, and exercise equipment.

UNH students pride themselves on being active, and with regard to extracurricular activities, "there is something for everyone." Clubs range from singing groups and community service, to an Outing Club, which takes trips white water rafting and hiking. The student-run radio station, WUNH, is a 6,000-watt noncommercial radio station that plays music before it hits the mainstream. And, thanks to the Internet, WUNH has "listeners in Australia, Finland, Florida, and Boston." For live entertainment, students turn to the Paul Creative Arts Center, where student theater and music groups frequently perform.

> "The whole campus turns into a pack of animals clutching beers and running all over the town of Durham."

For those who still want to get off campus, the school provides a free bus service, Wildcat Transit, which takes students to the city of Portsmouth, only 10 minutes away. In the warm months, students go hiking or head to the beach, and in the winter, UNH is perfectly located for the weekend skier. There are numerous local ski resorts, and Killington, one of the country's best ski resorts, is less than 3 hours away.

Weekends start on Thursday nights. UNH tries to maintain a dry campus, so parties involving alcohol are at fraternities or off-campus apartments. "The authorities are pretty strict about drugs and alcohol in the dorms," said one student, "but no one gets caught if it's at a party." The frat scene is loud with music and dancing, and those who want to go to a "chill party," head to house parties in Newmarket or hang out in the Gables, the on-campus apartments. School sponsored activities, such as hypnotists, outdoor movies, game shows, and swing dancing lessons, are popular, and national bands often stop at UNH arena, including such headliners as the Dave Matthews Band.

Hockey is a great unifier on campus. Quite simply, "hockey rules." Even those who hate the sport admit that everyone at UNH gets involved during hockey season. "The whole campus turns into a pack of animals clutching beers and running all over the town of Durham," explained one undergrad. "They have huge bonfires and go insane. It's interesting to watch." In recent years, the Wildcats have contended for the NCAA title, and UNH fans often lead the Hockey East Conference in attendance. Bizarre traditions accompany the general pandemonium during the games. "During every game, after our first goal, someone throws a big fish on the ice," explained one student.

The flying fish at hockey games might seem out of place in a peaceful New England town like Durham, but UNH is more than just a laid-back atmosphere and great skiing. Students pursue their academic and social lives with the same spirit they throw at the opposing hockey team. In and out of the classroom, UNH offers exciting opportunities which the student body, a spirited and friendly group, take full advantage of. —*Ashleigh Hegedus*

FYI
The three best things about attending University of New Hampshire are "small classes with lots of individual attention and instruction, fifteen minutes from the ocean and forty-five minutes from the mountains, and chickwiches."
The three worst things about attending University of New Hampshire are "not enough parking, the price of tuition, and crazy weather."
The three things that every student should do before graduating from University of New Hampshire are "nickel draft night at Libby's Bar, sex on Wagon Hill, at least one hockey game."
One thing I'd liked to have known before coming here is "that knowing your way around Windows will not prepare you for computer science classes."

New Jersey

The College of New Jersey

Address: Office of Admissions, P.O. Box 7718, Ewing, NJ 08628-0718
Phone: 609-771-2131
E-mail address: admiss@vm.tcnj.edu
Web site URL: www.tcnj.edu
Location: suburban
Founded: 1855
Private or Public: public
Religious affiliation: none
Undergraduate enrollment: 5,853
Total enrollment: 6,711
Percent Male / Female: 40% / 60%
Percent Minority: 16.2%

Percent African-American: 6.0%
Percent Hispanic: 5.0%
Percent Asian: 5.0%
Percent in-state / out-of-state: 95% / 5%
Percent Pub HS: 65%
Fraternities: 17%
Sororities: 17%
Number of Applicants: 5,755
Percent Accepted: 55%
Percent Accepted who enroll: 38%
Entering: 1,207
Transfers: 94
Application Deadline: 15 Feb
Mean SAT: NA

Middle 50% SAT range: 560–660 V, 580–670 M
Middle 50% ACT range: NA
Mean ACT: NA
3 Most popular majors: business, elementary education, English
Retention: 93%
Graduation rate: 76.0%
Library: 0
Tuition and Fees: $4,168 in; $7,278 out
Room and Board: $6,161
On-campus housing: 0%
Financial aid, first-year: 94%

The name has changed from Trenton State College to The College of New Jersey, but the school's academics and affordability have remained the same. The first public college founded in New Jersey continues to impress its students with its strong academics and variety of opportunities.

No Babying Here

TCNJ students are quick to praise the academics and stress that expectations are high. "They don't baby you, even though it is a state school," one student said. Undergraduates call the curriculum "rigorous," "thorough," and "highly competitive," although one student admitted that academics are not everyone's top priority. Qualified students seeking an extra challenge can enroll in TCNJ's honors program. One student warned, however, that "the honors students are separated from the general student population as fresh-

men and thus are never fully integrated into campus life." Other educational opportunities include the International and National Exchange Programs for those wishing to travel and learn in different settings. For students interested in pursuing a career in medicine, TCNJ offers a seven-year medical program that includes three years at TCNJ and four years at UMDNJ (the University of Medicine and Dentistry of New Jersey). A similar program for law and justice students is offered in conjunction with the Rutgers School of Criminal Justice.

TCNJ is known for its education department. "The college was founded on making teachers," said one student. Other popular majors include biology and English. Several students remarked that the art department is among the least popular. Regardless of their major, all students must complete several requirements, including interdisciplinary courses, English/public speaking classes, and math. One student described the requirements as "bearable," but another complained that the required three semesters of a foreign language "just add to the workload." Students also note that the mandatory classes fill up quickly, making it hard to fulfill the requirements.

Classes, even at the intro level, are small at TCNJ; few undergrads have classes larger than 30 students, and higher-level courses are even smaller. Although intro classes are small, one student said that the entry-level courses are not among the most exciting. "Math 101— lots of people I know have composed the most wonderful poetry during such classes." Students praise the fact that only "quality" professors teach undergraduates, and say that student-faculty interaction is good due to the size of the classes.

The Campus
The students commend the facilities as well, describing them as "really clean" and "well kept." Undergrads study (or write poetry, as the case may be) in the Roscoe L. West Library, a multilevel research facility described as "expansive." The campus has a variety of architectural styles that one student called "a mismatch of architectural trends. The original structures are really quite beautiful, but some of the later buildings are just mistakes." Many students mentioned the prevalence of construction around campus. In the next few years, the college reportedly has plans to build a new science building and expand the training and recreation center.

Students describe the campus, located in suburban Ewing, New Jersey, as "self-contained." The trees, large lawns, and lakes (complete with "tons of geese") on campus create an environment that is much different from urban Trenton. The security measures on campus, which include the student security patrol, emergency police phones, and pedestrian escort service, remind the students that they are not isolated in suburbia. Students describe the security measures as "effective" and note that they "keep problems to a minimum." Nearly all freshmen and sophomores live on campus because they are guaranteed housing. Many upperclass-

men decide to live off campus in affordable apartments a short drive away. The fraternities and sororities also have off-campus housing for upperclassmen.

How We're Livin'
All freshmen are housed in Travers-Wolfe Towers, while most seniors on campus live in Community Commons, which offers carpeted doubles with private bathrooms. Several students mentioned that the worst dorm is Centennial because it is old. TCNJ also offers special-interest housing, such as honors and music dorms. Some dorms are coed by floor; others have mixed halls. CAs (Community Advisors) live on every floor. Along with the Ambassadors (who help organize some activities), the CAs make up the counseling system at TCNJ.

Two of the three campus dining areas are in Travers-Wolfe Towers and the Commons. The Student Center offers a variety of meal choices as well; it contains a Taco Bell, a salad bar, a deli, and a snack bar. The dining halls offer vegetarian options, but one student described them simply as "pasta, dry and stale." Another student complained that there is little variety, especially on weekends, when the Student Center is closed. Undergrads often eat off campus at chain restaurants such as the Olive Garden, Ground Round, and Burger King, as well as the diners on nearby Route 1.

Abounding Activities
Extracurricularly, TCNJ has a lot to offer. Because many people come to TCNJ to study music, there are many small music ensembles on campus, as well as the symphony, the concert band, and the TCNJ Chorale. Students can join over 140 clubs, including the fencing club and the Frisbee club. They can also write for the Signal, the weekly campus newspaper. For those interested in intramural sports, volleyball and football are among the most popular.

TCNJ does not disappoint serious athletes, either. The college has 21 varsity sports, many of which are among the best in the NCAA Division III. Women's field hockey, softball, and cross-country are consistently strong teams, while the men's wrestling and tennis teams also have impressive records. Students describe the athletic facilities as "outstanding": Packer Hall houses the pool and basketball courts, while the football team plays in the lighted, Astroturf-surfaced stadium.

> **Students describe the campus, located in suburban Ewing, New Jersey, as "self-contained."**

On the social side, some students feel that opportunities at TCNJ are narrow. Students hang out in the Student Center or in the lounges in their residential buildings. The big social events on campus include homecoming and the semiformal. On other weekends, students can go to frat parties, which are all off campus. Since most Greek parties are open to all, students feel that the Greek system at TCNJ is "a good way to meet people." Another option on the weekends is the "Rat" (short for Rathskeller), the campus bar that often hosts live bands and serves beer to those with valid IDs. Although one student described TCNJ as "definitely not a dry campus," students generally don't feel that drinking is a large problem. For variety, some students make the relatively short drives to Princeton or Rutgers Universities, while others make the roughly hour-long drive to New York City or Philadelphia. TCNJ's location makes it helpful, if not necessary, to have a car. Since students are not guaranteed parking until their junior year, many depend on upperclassmen for transportation off campus.

Who We Are

Many undergrads notice a lack of diversity within the student population. Although there are some minority fraternities and other minority clubs, the actual minority population is small. One student said that there is "absolutely no diversity, although the administration would have you believe so." Another student commented that "there is talk about diversity, but the people don't really mix." Over 90 percent of the students come from New Jersey. With TCNJ's continued high rankings in various publications, however, students from nearby states (such as Pennsylvania and New York) have begun to take advantage of TCNJ's opportunities.

any students cited TCNJ's value and affordability as reasons to attend the college. "It's a great school . . . a great opportunity, and it provides students with a lasting education," said one TCNJ advocate. Realistically, TCNJ students know that they will not find "the culture of New York" in suburban Ewing, New Jersey, but they believe that the quality of the academics and the "friendly, close-knit" campus make the experience worthwhile.—*Abby Rubin and Staff*

FYI

The three best things about attending TCNJ are "it's close to my home, the chance to live with all your classmates freshman year, and the education department."

The three worst things about attending TCNJ are "the fact that we can't have cars till we are juniors, the New Jersey heavy student population, and there is not that much to do on Friday nights."

The three things that every student should do before graduating from TCNJ are "head into either New York or Philly, shoot some hoops at Packer, and go to the Rat."

One thing I'd like to have known before coming here is "Ewing isn't the greatest place to spend four years."

Drew University

Address: 36 Madison Avenue, Madison, NJ 07940-1493
Phone: 973-408-DREW
E-mail address: cadm@drew.edu
Web site URL: www.drew.edu
Location: suburban
Founded: 1866
Private or Public: private
Religious affiliation: none
Undergraduate enrollment: 1,526
Total enrollment: 2,127
Percent Male / Female: 41% / 59%
Percent Minority: 15.0%

Percent African-American: 4.0%
Percent Hispanic: 5.0%
Percent Asian: 6.0%
Percent in-state / out-of-state: 96% / 4%
Percent Pub HS: 64%
Fraternities: 0%
Sororities: 0%
Number of Applicants: 2,361
Percent Accepted: 74%
Percent Accepted who enroll: 20%
Entering: 340
Transfers: 11
Application Deadline: 15 Feb
Mean SAT: 625 V, 617 M

Middle 50% SAT range: 550–670 V, 540–650 M
Middle 50% ACT range: NA
Mean ACT: NA
3 Most popular majors: political science, psychology, English
Retention: 87.0%
Graduation rate: 74.0%
Library: 420,000 volumes
Tuition and Fees: $21,702 in; $NA out
Room and Board: $6,372
On-campus housing: 96%
Financial aid, first-year: 65%

Hailed more than once by the Princeton Review as one of America's "Top Ten Most Beautiful College Campuses," Drew University breaks the stereotype of "ugly New Jersey and its turnpike." With its majestic trees and winding paths, the school has earned the nickname "University in the Forest." Students say stepping on campus is like entering a different world, leaving all types of urban ugliness and commercial eyesores behind. Yet, Drew offers the best of both worlds, occupying a prime location in Madison, New Jersey, just 30 minutes from the skyscrapers of New York City and less than an hour from the sands of the Jersey shore.

Academic Breadth and Depth

In an effort to ensure both "breadth and depth" in education, Drew University requires its students to complete both a major and a minor. General requirements include two courses in four distribution groups: natural and mathematical sciences; social sciences; humanities; and arts and literature. In addition, there is a writing and foreign language requirement. Most students agree that fulfilling them is "not too much of a chore." Another stu-

dent remarked with regret, "At first they [the requirements] seem really annoying, but now that I'm done with them, I wish I had taken the time to enjoy them more."

True to the school's liberal arts roots, popular majors at Drew include theater, psychology, and English, but students refrain from sticking their school into a mold. "It's a good mix of arts and sciences, not just a science or English school." Indeed, science majors report "excellent facilities," and one physics major went so far as to say "Drew's physics department is the reason I came here."

Students of all majors praise their school's "warm and caring" faculty. As one student boasted, "Here the professors are concerned about each student—they care about you instead of their master's degree or their book publishing. You're a name to them, not a number." Another student simply said, "Academically, I have no complaints."

Special Stuff

Although the majority of students do come from the New York/New Jersey area, Drew offers a number of special academic programs that draw students from beyond the bounds of metro New York.

Particularly popular is the school's 7-year accelerated medical program, conducted in conjunction with the University of Medicine and Dentistry School of New Jersey. Students accepted to this program complete college in three years and proceed directly onto medical school without having to relive the application process. Other similar pre-professional programs are available in the fields of law, business, and teaching. The school has a highly developed study abroad program, as well. One student estimated that roughly half of the student population participates in these international seminars, month-long programs in January and June that allow students to study in places such as Ireland, Egypt, and France.

Specifically for freshmen, the First-Year Seminar Program offers students the opportunity to study a topic in depth with small classes consisting of 12 to 16 people. The professors leading these seminars also serve as the students' faculty advisors, providing frosh with an early chance to establish relationships with their instructors. Student feedback on the seminars ranged from good to bad: one first-year described the selection of topics as "anything a kid would ever want to know," while another grumbled that they "only seem interesting until you get to class." In recent years, seminar topics have included the History of New York City, the NCAA and the Student Athlete, and Images of Women in Quebec Literature.

Another very popular Drew program is the Computer and Knowledge Initiative Program through which all students receive a free personal computer, software, and printer upon entering Drew as a freshman. Students praise the free stuff as "awesome—the best!"—an enthusiasm added to by the fact that these computers are theirs to keep even post-graduation. Network access in the dorms adds convenience to students' lives and makes for a well-connected student body.

Small School Living

Most students live on campus for all four years, since decent housing in surrounding Madison tends to be expensive and hard to find. There are few complaints, however, since dorms are generally livable. Housing options range from single-sex suites to coed floors that house only singles. Every dorm has a Residential Adviser (RA) on each floor (usually an undergraduate), and a Residential Director (RD) in charge of everything (usually a graduate student). The situation for freshmen is slated to improve as well, since freshmen dorms are scheduled for renovation next summer. Students can also opt to live in one of seven theme houses. Among the more popular are La Casa, a Latino dorm; The Earth House, concentrating on environmental concerns; and Umoja House, the African-American house.

Campus food is described as "pretty good." The vegan line, though repetitive, is edible, and there is a grill room and stir-fry bar for students tired of the regular lunch-line fare. Students can either eat at Commons, the only campus dining hall, or use "points" to buy munchies at the snack bar or The Space, both located in the University Center. The Other End is another frequented campus eatery. On weekends, the coffee shop–type establishment hosts bands, and students can sit, sip coffee, and enjoy the mellow ambiance.

"More than Its Fair Share of Weirdos"

Students count their school's small size as both a blessing and a curse. As one student explained, "It's great because you get to know people, but it's ridiculous—if there's someone new on campus, you'll know." Though small, however, the student body reportedly does not lack variety. Said one student, "It is a liberal arts school, so you get more than your fair share of weirdos, but it's still a college so you get every type of person." Apparently the variety works though—different types of people are generally said to "mix pretty well." "There are definite groups, but they're not really exclusive," observed one student. One area in which the school's size can hurt, however, is the dating scene. "There are so few people, so there's not much choice," complained one sophomore male.

The school's small size takes its toll on the social life in other ways, as well.

"There's always something happening—it's just hard to find it sometimes," said one student. Since the school has no fraternities and sororities, upperclassman dorms are the primary sites for bacchanalian blowouts. Recent changes in the administration's alcohol policy are reportedly hindering dorm party success, however, as the school cracks down on campus drinking. Thus far, it seems its attempts are working. Many students report that nowadays, parties are often moved to off-campus venues in efforts to dodge the new university regulations.

The Roads of Jersey

Students describe Madison, New Jersey, as "not a college town at all." "Small and quaintly residential," it offers students little more than basic necessities, like a supermarket, a movie theater, and a CVS Pharmacy. Sweet Dreams coffee shop is a notable exception, named by student after student as the best place to take a date near campus. Nearby Morristown, with its wider selection of eateries and bigger movie theater, is a fast five-minute drive for students with cars or friends with cars. On weekends, too, many students with cars will head for New York City, 30 miles west of campus. But since only juniors and seniors are allowed to have cars on campus, underclassmen often have to find their own fun around campus.

> **"Drew University breaks the stereotype of 'ugly New Jersey and its turnpike.'"**

Drew students report that there is no shortage of school-sponsored events. Drama tends to be very popular, and student productions are well-attended. Most non-student plays are held at the recently rebuilt S. M . Kirby Shakespeare Theater, while most student performances take place in the Commons theater. Drew is also home to the annual New Jersey Shakespeare festival, which celebrates the Bard and his greatest works. Visitors flock from all over the state to attend this May event, and students take a lot of joy in the prestige the event brings to their school. "It's great because a lot of times students can get really involved in planning and preparations for it," said one student.

There's More to Life . . .

Drew athletics are a popular extracurricular activity, thanks to what one student called the school's "phenomenal" facilities. Although Drew has no football team, other sports like soccer and those on the intramural level draw considerable student support and substantial participation. For the not-so-athletically inclined, Drew offers a host of musical, literary, and service groups. Popular a cappella singing groups include On a Different Note and 36 Madison Avenue, also known as "MadAv." Campus publications like the literary magazine, *Insanity's Force*, and the weekly newspaper, the *Acorn*, give students the opportunity to display their journalistic talents. Community service organizations, especially environmental concerns groups, enjoy high student participation.

As one student concluded, "Many people are here because they have to be—they don't really think about it and just go through the motions, and because Drew's a very liberal school with lots of freedom, it's easy to just stay that way. But I'd warn everyone not to squander the experience—there's just too much out there to waste time. And what better place to spend your four short college years than Drew?" —*Jane H. Hong*

FYI
The three best things about attending Drew are "the small classes, the personalized attention, and the gorgeous campus."
The three worst things about attending Drew are "there's not much to do on the weekends, the fact that you need to be a junior to have a car, and there's no Greek life."
The three things that every student should do before graduating from Drew are "to take a road trip to the city, to study abroad, and to go to Sweet Dreams Café with a date."
One thing I'd like to have known before coming here is "how small the school is."

Princeton University

Address: P.O. Box 430,
Admission Office,
Princeton, NJ 08544
Phone: 609-258-3060
E-mail address: 0
Web site URL:
www.princeton.edu
Location: suburban
Founded: 1746
Private or Public: private
Religious affiliation: none
**Undergraduate
enrollment:** 4,624
Total enrollment: 6,200
Percent Male / Female:
53% / 47%
Percent Minority: 30.0%
Percent African-American:
8.0%

Percent Hispanic:
7.0%
Percent Asian: 14.0%
**Percent in-state / out-of-
state:** 12% / 88%
Percent Pub HS: 60%
Fraternities: 0%
Sororities: 0%
Number of Applicants:
13,006
Percent Accepted:
13%
**Percent Accepted who
enroll:** 69%
Entering: 1,171
Transfers: 0
Application Deadline:
3 Jan
Mean SAT: NA

Middle 50% SAT range:
680–780 V,
690–780 M
Middle 50% ACT range:
NA
Mean ACT: NA
3 Most popular majors:
history, economics,
politics
Retention: 98%
Graduation rate: 90%
Library: 5,000,000
volumes
Tuition and Fees: $24,630
in; NA out
Room and Board: $6,969
On-campus housing: 97%
Financial aid, first-year:
NA

A "Gothic paradise," Princeton University has one of the most striking campuses in the nation. Manicured lawns, stone buildings bedecked with ivy—the way one might envision Princeton is not so far from the reality. Located in an upscale New Jersey suburb, the enclosed campus is hailed by students as exceptionally safe. "I feel comfortable walking by myself nearly everywhere," one student reported. Although the surrounding town of Princeton is not especially lively, the university's prime location is ideal. New York City and Philadelphia, two favorite destinations among Princetonians, are each less than an hour's train ride away. There is much more to Princeton, however, than a pretty facade. Students agree that the school's real gem lies in the wealth of its academic offerings.

World-Class Academics

At the center of the university's reputation for excellence is its distinguished faculty. Absolutely amazing scholars teach here," said one junior. "Virtually every professor is a forerunner in his or her field." Lecturers include Nobel Prize winners, prominent politicians, cutting-edge journalists, and even a former president of France. Literary masters Toni Morrison and Joyce

Carol Oates head the university's outstanding creative writing program. In addition to being accomplished, professors are also extremely accessible. Princetonians in all departments have close relationships with faculty. Because the university's graduate program is relatively small (there are approximately double the number of undergrads as grads), professors actively and energetically delve into undergraduate teaching. An economics major said, "Unlike at many other Ivy Leagues, undergrads here are number one in the eyes of the faculty, and the professors make you feel it." Another student agreed: "The professors here don't want to just be lecturers. They want to interact with us, hear our viewpoints, and learn from us as well."

Even first-year students enjoy the advantages of close student-faculty relations. Freshman Seminars offer students the opportunity to work in a small group setting (roughly 12 to 15 students) on innovative topics. Of the 50 or so seminars offered each year, recent topics have included Blasphemy and Pornography as well as Extraterrestrial Life and Literature. Princetonians agree that although academics are rigorous, competition is far from cutthroat. A comparative literature major explains, "Students here are surprisingly laid-back—everyone has a thousand interests outside of studying. But if you're not careful, the workload can really creep up behind you and give you a swift kick in the ass."

To graduate, all students must take a minimum of 30 courses in seven distributional areas: Epistemology and Cognition, Ethical Thought and Moral Values, Historical Values, Literature and the Arts, Social Analysis, Quantitative Reasoning, and Science and Technology. Much to the dismay of humanities students, two semesters of a lab science as well as a semester of math are also mandatory. Those who dread the hard sciences, however, can take "softer," statistics-oriented social science courses such as Election Statistics. Further requirements include a one-semester writing class, a junior essay, a senior thesis, and proficiency in a foreign language.

Although the quality of academics is high across the board, students praise the highly selective Woodrow Wilson School of Public and International Affairs as exceptional. Providing participants with hands-on experience in government and policy-making, the "Woody Woo" program, as it is commonly called, culminates in a project in which students propose a solution to a global problem. Other popular majors (or "concentrations") include economics, English, history, politics, and engineering. For those whose interests lie beyond a single field, "certificate" programs (similar to minors) are offered. Students agree that the most strenuous majors are those in the School of Engineering (SE). In addition to taking rigorous upper-level science courses in their first year, SE students, approximately one-sixth of the student body, must complete 36 courses to graduate as opposed to the standard 30. "You hardly run into engineering students," one junior said. "They're almost always locked up in a library or a laboratory."

Courses at Princeton range from elementary to overwhelming. "Shake and Bake" (Earthquakes and Volcanoes) and "Nuts and Sluts" (Abnormal Psychology) are notorious guts, while a course on "The Divine Comedy" is described by one sophomore as "Dante's next level of Hell." Virtually all courses, however, are reading-intensive. "Professors assign more pages to read than there are seconds in a day," one sophomore joked. Dedicated Princetonians from all academic backgrounds may also opt for the Humanities Cycle, an intensive yearlong sequence (begun in the second semester of freshman year) that covers the great works of Western thought. Consisting of three seminars and two lectures, the cycle was hailed by one participant as "an amazing experience. It provides you with one-on-one interaction with the best professors on campus." However, students warn that the program is not for the faint at heart; it is "a massive time commitment" and "definitely limits your opportunities to explore other fields and activities."

Learning at Princeton reaches far beyond the classroom. Not-for-credit sophomore workshops offer second-year students the opportunity to explore such unconventional topics as Architecture and Ethnicity and Transvestitism and Performance. These classes meet three to five times per semester and frequently involve field trips throughout the Northeast (all expenses are covered by the university). Also popular are college-sponsored Meistro dinners in which students dine with prominent artists and scholars.

Talent Reaches Beyond the Classroom

"The most wonderful thing about Princeton students," one politics major reflected, "is that each person is amazingly talented as well as intelligent. I'm constantly being surprised by the depth of people's interests—it's really cool to discover that my next-door neighbor is not only a Westinghouse scholar, but also an amazing poet or that a girl in my history class used to dance with a professional ballet company." Students can express these diverse talents through over 200 student-run organizations ranging from intramural sports and student government to science fiction discussion groups. With the largest membership of any association on campus, the Student Volunteer Council connects students with community service projects in neighboring Trenton and Newark. Performance opportunities also abound. For the musically inclined, there are twelve a cappella groups (which take advantage of the campus's Gothic architecture each weekend by hosting mini-performances known as "arch sings"), a glee club, a variety of bands, and an orchestra. All of these groups benefit from the luxurious new practice spaces provided by the recently completed Woolworth complex. On a more dramatic note, favorites among thespians and audiences alike include the Triangle Club, a one-of-a-kind musical comedy ensemble, "side-splitting" improv comedians Quipfire!, and the Princeton Shakespeare Company. Dance companies Body Hype and Expressions similarly draw sold-out crowds.

Although some students say support for Princeton varsity teams is "pathetic" (partially due to the fact that Palmer Stadium is "literally crumbling at the seams"), students grab their furniture to fuel the bonfire traditionally lit after the Tiger football team defeats both Yale and Harvard. Another annual ritual is the Cane Spree, a day of competition between freshmen and sophomores that culminates in mud wrestling.

Where We Live, Eat, and Other Important Details . . .

Princeton freshmen and sophomores live in one of five residential colleges—Rockefeller, Mathey, Butler, Wilson, and Forbes. Although slightly removed from the other colleges, Forbes is said to have the best double rooms as well as the best food on campus. However, getting good housing in this college is simply the luck of the draw: a number of first-year students in Forbes are housed in "the most run-down rooms on campus," known as "Freshman Slums."

Overall, students report that the food served in the college dining halls is "pretty decent," featuring grill items and many vegetarian options at every meal. Juniors and seniors can choose to remain in the residential colleges and act as mentors for younger students, but the majority choose to move to upperclassmen housing ("Almost no one moves off campus," one junior said). Upperclassmen, however, do not eat in the college dining halls. They may join one of 12 "eating clubs" (by far the most popular option), join a co-op in which students prepare meals for each

other, or declare themselves "independent" and cook for themselves.

Although the eating clubs exist for the functional purpose of feeding juniors and seniors, they also dominate Princeton's social scene. Prospect Avenue, the site of all 12 clubs, simply called the "Street" by students, is the heart of the school's social life. The clubs are in former mansions and are all equipped with dining rooms, computer labs, and areas for large social events (only officers are permitted to live in the clubs). Meals are prepared by chefs, and the food is reported to be "exceptional." The more ritzy clubs, such as the Ivy, even have waiters.

> **"Virtually every professor is a fore-runner in his or her field."**

PClub membership begins the second semester of sophomore year. Each club has a distinct identity. Cap and Gown is athletic, Tairus is "artsy," Ivy is "exclusive," while Tiger Inn is "all about alcohol." Due to these generalizations, said one sophomore, "people tend to identify you by your club." Seven of the clubs are non-selective; students simply "sign in" with a group of friends and are assigned to a particular club by lottery. The other five clubs select members through "bicker," a process similar to Greek rush ("It's basically a lot of interviews and a lot of beer," one student said). For those who choose to undergo this process, bicker can be a source of stress. According to one junior, "If you aren't in the same eating club as your friends, you basically can't spend time with them at any meals." Those who have their heart set on one particular club can bicker multiple times. "You can usually get in the second or third time around," one undergrad reported.

Let the Weekend Begin

Weekends at Princeton begin Thursday nights at the "Street" and center on parties at the eating clubs. The majority of these events are not restricted to members, although some clubs distribute a limited number of passes when featuring particularly popular bands or DJs in order to prevent overcrowding. "Even if you can't get into a particular party, you'll still see everyone you know and have a good time. It's the Street that people go to rather than a specific club," one student insisted. Alcohol is readily available and is a central feature of these parties, but students report little pressure to drink. Beer is served in the basement or "tap room," of each club and is removed from the dancing and socializing that takes place on the main level. "It's great," declared one student. "If you want, you can just go to a party and dance and have a wonderful time without coming into contact with alcohol. On the dance floor, you can't tell who has been drinking and who hasn't." Friday nights at Princeton are much tamer, known across campus as "culture night." Students take a break from partying to enjoy the university's numerous student productions and concerts. The more adventurous travel to nearby New York City to visit friends, go clubbing, or join college-sponsored excursions to Broadway shows. Among the biggest events of the year are the House parties, a three-day-long extravaganza hosted by the eating clubs. One student explained, "It's like a three-day-long prom," involving a semiformal, a formal, and a day of lawn parties. "People take it really seriously because you have the same date for three days straight. You can feel the tension mount about five weeks beforehand."

Population Breakdown

Although over half of Princeton students receive some form of financial aid, many students insist that the university has a very upper-middle-class feel. "People have preconceived notions about Princeton—that it's exclusive and run by some ole' boys network. It's not like that at all," said one student. "There are people here from every class and every background." Other students find the campus to be lacking in ethnic diversity. One sophomore said, "The student body tends to be more diverse with regards to nationality than to race." But Princetonians tend to agree that the breadth of student interests and talents helps diminish whatever homogeneity exists among the campus's socioeconomic population.

rinceton offers students the opportunity to learn from some of today's most prominent scholars in a secluded environment that can sometimes feel more like a community than a world-class institution. Students are encouraged to consider the Princeton experience for themselves.
—*Lauren Rivera and Staff*

FYI

The three best things about attending Princeton are "the school's focus on undergraduates, the 'Street,' eating clubs where people drink every Thursday and Saturday night, and the residential college system."

The three worst things about attending Princeton are "the not-so-diverse student body; some dorms are really old and gross; the oh-so-boring residential town of Princeton."

The three things every student should do before graduating from Princeton are "to go to the 'Street' on dean's date (the day before finals start), to take a class with Professor Uwe Reinhardt, and to eat dinner at the Ivy Eating Club."

One thing I'd like to have known before coming here is "how homogeneous the student body can sometimes be."

Rutgers, The State University of New Jersey

Address: 65 Davidson Road, Piscataway, NJ 08854-8097
Phone: 732-932-INFO
E-mail address: admissions@asb-ugam.rutgers.edu
Web site URL: www.rutgers.edu
Location: suburban
Founded: 1766
Private or Public: public
Religious affiliation: none
Undergraduate enrollment: 27,086
Total enrollment: 48,341
Percent Male / Female: 47% / 53%
Percent Minority: 34.0%

Percent African-American: 8.0%
Percent Hispanic: 8.0%
Percent Asian: 18.0%
Percent in-state / out-of-state: 91% / 9%
Percent Pub HS: NA
Fraternities: 8%
Sororities: 5%
Number of Applicants: 23,183
Percent Accepted: 63%
Percent Accepted who enroll: 35%
Entering: 5,112
Transfers: 6,546
Application Deadline: rolling
Mean SAT: NA

Middle 50% SAT range: 510–630 V, 540–650 M
Middle 50% ACT range: NA
Mean ACT: NA
3 Most popular majors: psychology, biology, economics
Retention: 89.0%
Graduation rate: 42.0%
Library: 6,200,000 volumes
Tuition and Fees: $4,732 in; $9,626 out
Room and Board: $5,314
On-campus housing: 52%
Financial aid, first-year: 52%

Study nerds. Partiers. Slackers. Jocks. Every type of student is to be found at Rutgers, where diversity is key. Said one student, "Don't believe it when someone tells you that he's the typical Rutgers student because there is no such thing."

Rutgers University encompasses ten undergraduate colleges: Rutgers; Cook; Douglass; Livingston; the College of Pharmacy; Mason Gross School of Arts; the College of Engineering; the School of Business; the School of Communication, Information, and Library Studies (SCILS); and University College.

Each college maintains a distinctive personality within the larger university. Rutgers College, the largest and most competitive school, focuses on liberal arts. Its colonial College Avenue campus is said to be the social center of the university. Cook College, known for its many "wide open spaces," centers on the agricultural and life sciences. Only females reside on Douglass' beautifully bucolic campus, home of the nation's largest all-women's college. Austerely-styled Livingston, the newest college, offers liberal arts with a social-issues focus while University College accommodates the non-traditional returning and adult students. The university's five remaining schools offer specialized programs in fine arts, pharmacy, engineering, business, and communications.

Despite its notorious reputation as an "easy school," Rutgers succeeds in luring some of New Jersey's best students with generous scholarships, special honors, and pre-professional programs. And many Rutgers students would agree that "state school or not, Rutgers shouldn't be anyone's back-up college."

Rutgers—Not a BS School

Students agree that doing well at Rutgers requires a fair amount of work. One freshman lamented that the school's academic program is "vastly underestimated." "You can't just fool around here. A lot of people don't realize that and are rudely awakened freshman year when they get all Ds," added another student. General academic requirements vary from college to college. Rutgers College is generally considered the most rigorous, requiring students to complete both a major and a minor. Other requisites for Rutgers College include two expository writing classes, commonly called "Expos," and two courses in each of six academic disciplines. Other colleges typically demand less of their enrollees. Livingston, in particular, is known as the "easiest college to get into and graduate from."

Across the board, most students say that Rutgers sciences are more difficult than the humanities. Engineering was commonly named the hardest major with one student commenting on the unusually high dropout rate of engineering majors from the program. "It seems like everyone who starts out as an engineering major ends up switching after freshman year." So-called gut majors include psychology and communications.

Size Does Matter

Students love Rutgers' big-school atmosphere. "Nothing beats big schools. You just have so much to choose from—so many classes, friends, clubs and things to join." Still, most students would also agree that attending a large school has its disadvantages. One student complained that Rutgers' enormous size made her feel like "just another number" among the ranks of the near-25,000 undergraduate population. "I just don't feel like anyone really cares about the individual student. I barely even know my own professors, much less the administration." Other student grievances include jam-packed introductory lecture courses and "an annoying time trying to get into the classes that you want."

At Rutgers, students register for classes over the phone. Many would agree that although this system adds convenience to the harrowing process, it can also be a nuisance. One freshman complained, "The whole automated thing is great and all, but you have to call at like 6 A.M. to ensure that the classes you want are still open." As a last-ditch resort, though, many students opt to get into closed classes by obtaining special permission. "It's a hassle, but it's worth it," noted one student.

In the words of one Rutgers senior, "Your Rutgers academic experience all depends on how you approach it. If you have motivation and a thirst for knowledge, you'll learn a lot. If you don't care and choose to sleep during classes, then you won't. It's as simple as that."

The Alcohol Culture

In line with Rutgers's reputation as a major party school, many students admit that partying is definitely a priority. Frosh are particularly notorious, typically spending their weekends "looking for parties and trying to get drunk." After dark, they flock to frat houses lured by the promise of free beer. Indeed despite the administration's strong efforts to reduce the campus alcohol presence, drinking remains a popular student pastime. For those who choose not to take part in the alcohol scene, both the university and downtown New Brunswick offer a host of fun alternatives.

Students with access to cars can find their kicks off-campus, journeying to either New York City or Philadelphia or trekking downtown to enjoy the cultural nightlife there. A short walk from College Avenue campus, lower New Brunswick is the quintessential college town, attracting students with its variety of cafés, restaurants, and theaters. Off-campus wanderers are warned not to wander too far, though, since parts of downtown can be dangerous.

Campus Life

Students agree that life on campus can be a lot of fun. "There are so many people here—it's wonderful!" gushed one student. Most freshmen live on campus their first year, supervised by dorm preceptors (residential advisors) who have been called everything from "awesome" to "anal."

Depending on their college affiliations, students can live in a variety of dorms ranging from the College Avenue river dorms to the Livingston quads, which one student called "reminiscent of the Projects." Other residential options include off-campus and university-sponsored special-interest housing. The average dorm room was described as "small and plain—pretty much what you would expect." The Easton Avenue apartments, housing a modern gym and parking garage, are a notable exception. "Everyone drools over them," said one student.

One thing that few Rutgers students would not salivate over, however, is the school food. "The cafeterias may be sanitary, but the food's just no good," complained one student. The ever-popular "grease trucks" perennially circling campus offer hungry students an alternative, serving up fat-filled favorites like greasy hamburgers and oily onion rings. "I feel my arteries close up every time I see a truck drive by," joked one student.

Students can also find other fast food fare at the student center, a popular hangout with ATMS, computer labs, and places for groups to socialize and study. For more quiet study sessions, many students opt for the multi-level Alexander Library, also located on the College Avenue campus. "It's absolutely huge and scary—I love it," said one frequent visitor.

There's More to Life . . .

Offering a variety of activities from a cappella singing groups to competitive ballroom dance teams, Rutgers boasts a seemingly endless list of extracurricular offerings. "Although at first a lot of people feel overwhelmed by all the choices, everyone seems to find their place eventually in at least one campus group," said one student. Among the university's better-known organizations are the college's daily newspaper, *The Targum*, the weekly *Rutgers Review*, and the Rutgers College Program Council, the group (RCPC) responsible for bringing a lot of bands and speakers to campus.

The university's plethora of racial and ethnic groups also enjoys mass involvement, representing various elements of the eclectic minority population. But they remain controversial in many students' eyes. According to one ex-member, they "perpetuate racially segregated groups" at a school infamous for its racially divided atmosphere." "The idea behind the groups is great, but in practice, they're little more than social groups," observed one student. "Rutgers would be better without them."

Sports, on the other hand, make few waves among the Rutgers student population. "No one even seems to care about them," remarked one student. A fair number of students regularly attend varsity games, but according to one student, they only go "to laugh at the athletes for being as bad as they are." In spite of the school teams' normally less-than-stellar playing, Rutgers has its share of noteworthy athletes in certain areas with members of the track and men's soccer teams regularly achieving recognition on the national level.

> **"We're not just a bunch of NYU rejects."**

No doubt, students can still find excellent athletic facilities at Rutgers. The Sonny Werblin Recreational Center is particularly popular among students from all over the campus. Oftentimes, students will opt out on their own gyms and make the long trek to Busch campus just to use the Center's modern equipment. Complete with two swimming pools, an impressive weight room, and modern courts, the Center is like a "Jack La Lanne times two."

State School? So What?

Rutgers students are proud to be part of such a large, diverse, and stimulating environment. Said one student, "Yeah, Rutgers is a state school. Yeah, Rutgers is a public school. So what? That doesn't make it a bad school." Another student put it more sarcastically, "A lot of people don't realize that you actually have to study here. We're not just a bunch of NYU rejects." So, what does that mean to prospectives? As one senior advised, "Before visiting Rutgers, remind your potentially misinformed self that people who go to state schools aren't necessarily second-rate students."—*Jane H Hong*

FYI
The three best things about attending Rutgers are "the school's location between New York City and Philadelphia, the diversity of the student body, it's inexpensive."
The three worst things about attending Rutgers are "it's in Jersey!, having to ride buses to classes because they're so far away, R.U. Screw—getting caught up in administrative red-

tape, getting lost on the huge campus, being treated like a number rather than a person—basically all the bad things that come with attending a really big school."

The three things that every student should do before graduating from Rutgers are "take Theater Appreciation, visit all the different campuses, have a 'fat-cat' (i.e. a double cheeseburger with french fries on top) from a grease truck."

One thing I'd like to have known before coming here is "how impossible parking is . . ."

Seton Hall University

Address: Bayley Hall, 400 South Orange Avenue, South Orange, NJ 07079-2697
Phone: 973-761-9332
E-mail address: thehall@shu.edu
Web site URL: www.shu.edu
Location: suburban
Founded: 1856
Private or Public: private
Religious affiliation: Catholic
Undergraduate enrollment: 4,700
Total enrollment: NA
Percent Male/Female: 46%/54%

Percent Minority: 28.0%
Percent African-American: 13.0%
Percent Hispanic: 1.0%
Percent Asian: 6.0%
Percent in-state/out-of-state: 70%/30%
Percent Pub HS: 68%
Fraternities: 11%
Sororities: 9%
Number of Applicants: 6,000
Percent Accepted: 70%
Percent Accepted who enroll: 25%
Entering: 1,050
Transfers: 287
Application Deadline: 1 Mar

Mean SAT: 522 V, 530 M
Middle 50% SAT range: 460–560 V, 450–560 M
Middle 50% ACT range: 19–24
Mean ACT: 23
3 Most popular majors: communications, biology, criminal justice
Retention: 84.0%
Graduation rate: 38.0%
Library: 459,458 volumes
Tuition and Fees: $18,000 in; $18,000 out
Room and Board: $7,000
On-campus housing: 60%
Financial aid, first-year: 72%

At Seton Hall University, two traditions dominate the school: Catholicism and men's basketball. Despite the large number of commuters, students at the Hall enjoy a sense of community and a busy social life with active fraternity and sorority life. Between hanging out on the campus green, satisfying late-night munchies at the Maplewood Diner, and spending weekends in New York City, students combine the best of both worlds with a small campus in suburbia located near a major metropolitan city.

Academic Life

The Seton Hall academic program retains its religious foundation. Although the core curricula vary among the five different schools—the College of Arts and Sciences, the W. Paul Stillman School of Business, the College of Education and Human Services, the College of Nursing, and the School of Theology—they all include six credits in religion. In addition, all freshmen take a course in time management and study skills. Students comment that the core curriculum requirements are not difficult to fulfill and provide a nice academic sampler. "I didn't have any problems taking my requirements and major classes. I'm going to graduate in four years and I only had to take 18 credits one semester," said one student.

Classes are generally kept very small. Although some freshman intro classes approach 100 students, most classes enroll approximately 20 to 40. Because many classes have a size limit, students trying to register for popular classes encounter some difficulties. Registration is by class in order of seniority, in random alphabetical order for each class. "If you're a freshman whose last name is at the bottom of the registration, a lot of times you won't get the classes you need," remarked one student. However, students toward the top of the waiting list usually get into the class within the first week. In extreme cases, deans ask the professors to increase class sizes to allow more students from the waiting lists into the courses.

Despite these efforts, students sometimes remain shut out of required classes. As one student explained, "A lot of times people are here more than four years because they can't get the classes they need, and some are only offered in spring or in fall." Students also complain about a shortage of teachers for the popular communication classes.

In addition to communications, business-related subjects, nursing, and secondary education are also very popular majors. The sciences are not. "Seton Hall University is not really a science school. If you want to be a doctor, you don't come here. We are known for our law and business schools," said one student.

Classes are taught by professors, although some teaching assistants help run science labs. Priests teach classes with a religious base. Students are relatively satisfied with the interaction with faculty, noting that most professors keep accessible office hours and will give students their home phone numbers.

Location, Location, Location

Seton Hall's location in South Orange, New Jersey (except the Law School, which is in Newark), is a major factor in some students' decision to attend. A majority of students are from the Northeast and like the school's closeness to home, especially since approximately 40 percent of the students are commuters. Furthermore, students can enjoy a taste of the cultural offerings of the Big Apple with SHU's close proximity to New York City. Although students feel safe on the actual campus, students noted that while the adjacent village of South Orange is also safe, the other side of campus goes into Newark, which can be dangerous. Despite the feeling of safety in South Orange, one student remarked that South Orange "doesn't like the fact that it is a college town." Campus security is extremely effective, according to students. There are pedestrian escorts, gatekeepers at the

two entrances, and constant patrols. In addition, due to a rape three years ago in a dorm, dorm security measures have been beefed up. Students carry ID badges that they must show at the front desk of any dorm, and must sign in any visitors.

A Mix of Old and New

The campus is enclosed by a fence and contains a mix of old and new buildings. Since the campus is small and self-contained, students feel it fosters a sense of community. Said one, "You won't get lost in the shuffle here." Students enjoy the benefits of a small campus, such as not having to wake up too early to get to classes. The main buildings are centered on a green where many parties are held in the spring. Spring is a favorite time for students because the campus is abloom with flowers and people migrate outdoors. "People live and sleep on the green in spring," said one student. Throughout the year, undergrads can also be found hanging out in the student center with its organizational offices, the cafeteria, and the fraternity and sorority Greek room.

When it comes to studying, students prefer the $20 million Walsh Library. The third and fourth floors of the library contain over 400 study carrels and many group-study rooms, providing students with plenty of space for hard-core and social studying.

A new business and education building that is home to the psychology department opened recently. An addition to the Brennan Recreation Center is currently under way, although students are reportedly satisfied with the current gym facilities. All Seton Hall students have free access to its weight room, Olympic-size swimming pool, indoor track, weight and exercise equipment, and many aerobic classes such as step, slide, and abdominals.

Although many people commute from home, the majority of students opt to live in campus residential halls. Freshmen live together in a freshman dorm that is coed by wing. Upperclassmen live in dorms that are coed by hall. Students report that the best dorm is Xavier, which features private bathrooms (shared by two doubles) and wall-to-wall carpeting. Older halls, such as the freshman dorm and Aquinas Hall, are the least popular. There are many options in dormitory living, such as nonsmoking floors, substance-free floors, single rooms, modern-language floors, all-female Neumann Hall, and Ora Manor—university-owned apartments for upperclassmen. Although the university does not permit official fraternity houses, many Greeks opt to live together in off-campus housing.

Students report that the RAs are active with the freshmen to help them in their adjustment to SHU. All underclassmen except freshmen can serve as RAs. RAs hold monthly meetings and sponsor different events like pizza and ice cream parties.

SHU has only one cafeteria, but it resembles a mall food court with its stands for Carvel, Kentucky Fried Chicken, Pizza Hut, Taco Bell, a bagel place, and Healthy Food Choice. "When I first started out, there were no franchises. Since I've been here, it's gotten better. But some people complain because it's fattening," one student said. Students can opt to enter varying amounts of money into their declining balances for meal plans, and commuters have special options as well. Vegetarian options are available. Although the cafeteria is open until 1 A.M., students are more likely to satisfy their late-night munchie attacks by visiting the Maplewood Diner or by ordering take-out from Village Pizza, El Greco's, a Chinese restaurant, or Cluck U. chicken.

The Social Scene
The large number of commuters affects SHU in its extracurricular and social activities. One commuter reported that she felt somewhat isolated at first and found it difficult to get involved in activities since club meetings are conducted at night. However, the university has made efforts to accommodate the commuters by establishing a commuter lounge and a commuter council. Each month, the commuter council raffles off a great parking spot—a coveted item at a school notorious for inadequate parking facilities.

Despite the occasional difficulties, both commuters and residents get involved in a wide array of activities. Extracurriculars include intramural sports; the weekly student newspaper the *Setonian*; the yearbook, the *Galleon*; gospel choir; the radio station; the Student Government Association (SGA); and a pep band for basketball games. The diverse student body of Seton Hall has many special-interest organizations like the Women's Resource Center, Black Student Union, African Student Leadership Coalition, Latino organizations Adelante and Caribe, and a Filipino group. A Student Activities Board sponsors movies and other campus events and the university SHUttle van provides transportation to local malls and movie theaters.

Community service is an important aspect of Seton Hall campus life. Entering freshmen even have a community service requirement for graduation. Students can be found providing gifts and putting on a Christmas show for underprivileged children in events like "Joy to the Children" and "Deck the Halls."

Sports and More
With Division I status for teams, SHU Pirates events are a popular spectator sport. Since there is no football team, fall sports are dominated by the men's and women's soccer games. Come winter, students are off to the Continental Airlines Arena to watch the men's basketball team face off against big rival Rutgers and out-of-state competition like St. John's and Georgetown. Basketball season is a social time, with the Midnight Madness pep rally before the first game. Many students attend the games and can be found painting their faces blue and white in support of the Pirates, but support for the team reportedly varies with the team's record.

Beyond basketball, Greek life is a dominant social force. "For the size of the campus, we have a pretty high percentage of students who are Greek," observed one student. Big events include formals and the fall Greek Week competition between the fraternities and sororities. Although the Greek parties and activities are not exclusive events, one student admitted that it is difficult to know where and when these events are if you are not part of Greek life. According to another student, the administration is not too friendly toward the

Greeks because "they are the biggest suppliers of alcohol." Last year, a dean called the South Orange police to warn them about a fraternity party being planned, which the cops subsequently busted.

> Between hanging out on the campus green, satisfying late-night munchies at the Maplewood Diner, and spending weekends in New York City, students combine the best of both worlds with a small campus in suburbia located near a major metropolitan city.

As a response to the Greek system, the university has been trying to sponsor other no-alcohol campus events such as a weekly coffeehouse with poetry readings, bands, or comedians. Other popular campus events include the Pirate Queen and King Contest, the SGA Halloween Party, Parents Weekend in March, the Senior Formal, and University Day in the fall with booths on the green and a university mass.

The fact that SHU is a Catholic university affects the school: priests teach classes and there are religion course requirements. As one student said, "When morals come into question, Catholic standards are applied." One student reported that a roommate was fined for cohabitation because the visitor logs revealed that a member of the opposite sex had spent the night. Furthermore, the administration refuses to recognize a proposed gay and lesbian organization. However, if you are looking for a sound education to supplement your religious background, Seton Hall could be just the choice for you.
—*Katie Lindgren and Staff*

FYI

The three best things about attending Seton Hall are "the commuter lounge, SGA Halloween Party, and watching the Pirates in action."

The three worst things about attending Seton Hall are "commuter school issues, no football team, and a sometimes stifling Catholic tradition."

The three things that every student should do before graduating from Seton Hall are "go clubbing in New York City, participate in Greek Week, and get psyched for Midnight Madness."

One thing I'd like to have known before coming here is "how much of an effort the SHU administration makes to keep students happy."

Stevens Institute of Technology

Address: Office of Undergraduate Admissions, Castle-Point-on-Hudson, Hoboken, NJ 07030
Phone: 201-216-5194
E-mail address: admissions@stevens-tech.edu
Web site URL: www.stevens-tech.edu
Location: small city
Founded: 1870
Private or Public: private
Religious affiliation: none
Undergraduate enrollment: 1,533
Total enrollment: 3,248
Percent Male/Female: 78%/22%

Percent Minority: 42.0%
Percent African-American: 5.0%
Percent Hispanic: 13.0%
Percent Asian: 24.0%
Percent in-state/out-of-state: 66%/34%
Percent Pub HS: NA
Fraternities: 35%
Sororities: 35%
Number of Applicants: 1,990
Percent Accepted: 67%
Percent Accepted who enroll: 29%
Entering: 428
Transfers: 94
Application Deadline: 1 Mar
Mean SAT: 620 V, 680 M

Middle 50% SAT range: 550–650 V, 600–720 M
Middle 50% ACT range: NA
Mean ACT: NA
3 Most popular majors: engineering, computer science, chemical biology
Retention: 85%
Graduation rate: 27.0%
Library: 0
Tuition and Fees: $20,890 in; $NA out
Room and Board: $7,280
On-campus housing: 76%
Financial aid, first-year: 60%

W hat makes Stevens different from other science and technology schools? In the words of one student—"the city of course!" Situated along the Hudson River, the Stevens campus maintains its 55-acre presence in Hoboken, New Jersey, just across the river from the wonders of New York City's downtown Manhattan. This metropolitan location affords Stevens students unparalleled opportunities through easy access to the city and its numerous resources.

Just for Engineers?

Stevens offers a variety of majors ranging from physics to American history, but as one student quipped, "you don't come here to study English." Most students consider Stevens a school mainly for wanna-be engineers where the vast majority of students opt to major and ultimately pursue careers in engineering-related fields. Other popular majors include computer science and chemical biology, programs that most students would describe as "pretty good."

Not surprisingly, the Stevens curriculum aims primarily to accommodate engineering majors, requiring all students to complete courses typically expected of engineers-in-training. While this works out well for would-be engineers, those students outside the majority field are not always so happy about their school's seemingly narrow focus. As one non-engineering major complained, "I'm getting an engineering education when I should be getting a chem-bio education. What chem-bio major needs four semesters of calculus?"

Indeed many students would agree that Stevens has some stiff requirements. Unlike freshmen at most other schools, Stevens freshmen are not allowed to choose their own classes. Instead, they follow a schedule of required courses in calculus, computer science, physics, general chemistry, humanities, and physical education with honors students typically allowed some class choice. After first year, students have a great deal more freedom, but are still expected to meet other general academic requirements, which include four semesters of calculus, six semesters of physical education, and eight semesters of humanities.

Students often joke about Stevens's humanities courses, commonly referred to as "Hum." "The whole range of humanities here falls under a one-syllable title— kinda tells you something, doesn't it?" remarked one student. Even so, most students would agree that while humanities classes at Stevens are not-all-that-challenging, they are likewise not easy-As. "They're not hard as long as you do the work," said one student. Stevens students also have the option of taking humanities classes at New York University through the NYU-Stevens cross-registration program. Because of their hectic schedules, however, some students find it difficult to take advantage of the program. "It's just too big a hassle," one student put it bluntly.

In addition to its regular academic programs, Stevens offers a number of accelerated pre-professional programs that enable students interested in medicine, dentistry, and law to earn both a Bachelor's and a professional degree in seven years. Another popular program is the "Co-op," a five-year plan that allows students to spend three to six semesters working at such global companies as Lucent and General Electric as well as at a number of local companies. Participation proves advantageous to students in that it reduces one's courseload without costing an extra year of tuition and gives them a chance to earn pay ($7,000 a year on average) while gaining valuable work experience. Stevens places 100% of its Co-op applicants, and about 40% of students are currently involved in the program.

Overall, most students would agree that academics at Stevens are "pretty demanding," a rigor compounded by heavy courseloads. The graduation requirement of 135 to 150 credits (which differs with major) results in students taking an average of 19 to 21 credits, the equivalent of 5 or 6 classes, per semester. "Everyone studies. You can't do well otherwise," warned one student.

A lot of students choose to do their work in the Stevens library, which one freshman described as "a nice, quiet place to study." It apparently lacks the resources needed for research, however. "It

has like 3 books—all from the 1970s or before," complained one student. The situation has gotten better, though, with a new program available on-line that, for a fee, allows students to request needed publications directly from publishing companies. "It's really convenient," said one frequent user.

A Room with a View

Residential students can live in one of the school's five dorms or, if involved with one of the twelve Greek groups on campus, in a house on Fraternity Row. Frosh usually live in single-sex dorms, made up mostly of doubles. After their first year, students can request dorms with housing assignments made on a first-come, first-serve basis. Upperclassmen have their choice of dorms and room set-ups with many opting to double-up in Technology Hall, the only dorm with amenities like air-conditioning, carpeting, and private bathrooms. Many rooms facing the river offer beautiful views of the New York City skyline, but as one student said, "No one really cares about rooms with views. It's sad—we probably have the best view of any college in the world, and we totally take it for granted."

Although Stevens is primarily a residential school, the campus can look pretty empty on weekends as many New Jersey students head home. For some of the weekend campus-dwellers, the Stevens social life "revolves around New York City," just a $1 PATH train ride away. Typical activities for city-goers include shopping, clubbing, and "just wandering around the city streets." For those students who prefer to stay closer to campus, fraternity parties are always an option. Currently, about one-third of students are involved in Greek life, but as one non-member explained, "Parties are a lot of fun even if you're not in a frat, and there's no pressure to drink if you don't like that sort of thing."

Another popular destination any day of the week is Washington Street, just a two-block walk from campus. Students can choose from a wide variety of eatables with everything from Chinese take-out to "pizza places out-the-wazoo." "Every other place is a food joint," said one frequent visitor, "and everything else is a bar." Indeed Hoboken is notorious for its abundance of pubs. One student claimed that Hoboken was known for having the "highest density of bars in the country." "It's great if you're 21 or have a fake ID, but only if you're into that kind of thing," added another student.

Out-of-Class

Most students would agree that Stevens has a "fairly social atmosphere, but only for those who choose to take part in it." Women reportedly have an easier time getting dates, which is not surprising in light of the lopsided male-female ratio. One female student protested however, "The guys here snag us the minute we arrive—we don't even have time to breathe." Faced with a dearth of females, Stevens men tend to find dates at other colleges or back in their hometowns. A typical date entails "eating out—it always beats campus food," remarked one student. In general, students describe the food at Stevens as "just plain nasty," a situation ameliorated by the many dorm kitchens available for student use. "A lot of us make our own food," said one student.

> "We probably have the best view of any college in the world, and we totally take it for granted."

As for extracurricular involvement, many students call it "limited" with those "students who get involved tending to get very involved." More than 50 student organizations are registered at Stevens. The more popular ones among them are WCPR, Stevens's own radio station; the *Stute*, Stevens's weekly newspaper; the Black Student Union (BSU) and the Indian Undergraduate Association (IUA), two of the more vocal ethnic groups on campus.

Although Stevens has no football team, varsity and intramural sports remain popular. The $13 million Charles V. Schaefer Jr. Athletic Center offers sports aficionados and dilettantes alike access to a fitness center, pool, squash court, and four-court gymnasium.

Students on Stevens

Stevens students agree that their school lacks school spirit, a chronic condition that led to their inclusion in the Princeton Review's ranking of the top-ten "unhappiest college students in the United States." Many students would dispute this title, however, with one student emphatically declaring "I love it here, and if I had to go back and do it all again, I'd definitely come to Stevens." Student feelings vary overall, ranging from an intense hatred to a passionate love for Stevens.

So, in light of such conflicting messages, what advice would current students give to prospectives? As in the words of one wise senior, "What else can you do? You should visit the campus, of course, but when you do, close your eyes to how pretty Hoboken is, ignore the view, forget what everybody else tells you, and really ask yourself, '*Would I be happy here?*' Do that and I guarantee you'll find your answer."—*Jane H Hong*

FYI

The three best things about attending Stevens are "free laptops for freshmen, small classes, the integration of computers into classroom learning."

The three worst things about attending Stevens are "it's so small you can't avoid people you don't like, administrative red-tape, poor lab equipment."

The three things that every student should do before graduating from Stevens are "go to New York City, go to Castle Point and look at the NYC skyline, watch the lights of the Empire State Building go out at 12 midnight."

One thing I'd like to have known before coming here is "just how bad the Humanities department is."

New Mexico

New Mexico State University

Address: Box 30001, MSC 3A, Las Cruces, NM 88003-8001
Phone: 505-646-3121
E-mail address: admissions@nmsu. edu
Web site URL: www.nmsu.edu
Location: urban
Founded: 1888
Private or Public: public
Religious affiliation: none
Undergraduate enrollment: 12,831
Total enrollment: 15,449
Percent Male / Female: 47% / 53%
Percent Minority: 50.0%

Percent African-American: 3.0%
Percent Hispanic: 42.0%
Percent Asian: 2.0%
Percent in-state / out-of-state: 80% / 20%
Percent Pub HS: NA
Fraternities: 8%
Sororities: 5%
Number of Applicants: 6,624
Percent Accepted: 68%
Percent Accepted who enroll: 51%
Entering: 2,266
Transfers: 670
Application Deadline: rolling
Mean SAT: NA

Middle 50% SAT range: NA
Middle 50% ACT range: 18–24
Mean ACT: 21
3 Most popular majors: elementary teacher education, marketing, hotel management
Retention: 72.0%
Graduation rate: 44.0%
Library: 1,032,970 volumes
Tuition and Fees: $2,502 in; $8,166 out
Room and Board: $3,726
On-campus housing: 50%
Financial aid, first-year: NA

While the rest of the country braves the winter cold, students at New Mexico State University sunbathe on the well-kept, palm-tree-lined lawn of a spacious compus that provides an oasis in the middle of the desert. Located in the southern part of the state, and only 45 minutes from the Mexican border, NMSU attracts students looking for quality education and a relaxed atmosphere.

The six undergraduate colleges at NMSU (business administration, education, human and community services, arts and sciences, agriculture, and engineering) offer an abundance of academic programs. A number of students attend NMSU for the highly respected agriculture department, but the engineering program also receives attention for its research in geothermal and wind energy. "NMSU is not known as the liberal arts school in the state; that credit goes to University of New Mexico," said one senior. "We're more known for our ag and applied sciences schools." Not surprisingly, NMSU ranks high in the volume of engineering research and development that goes on there, compared to other schools of its size. The engineering college consists of several facilities, including a brand-new $15 million research complex and the soon to be completed Center of Sustainable Arid Land, appropriate for the dry New Mexico climate.

The limited use of graduate students as TAs contributes to a stong level of interaction between undergrads and professors. Most upper-level courses average 20 to 30 students. Instead of giving preference during registration, the university uses a lottery based on the first letter of the student's last name, so that all students have a fair shot at obtaining the courses they want. (Crimson Scholar honor students and disabled students, however, have priority over all other undergrads.) One student described NMSU academics as taxing, but not overwhelming. For those who do find the course load too arduous, physical education classes are known for their easy requirements.

Southwest Charm

The campus architecture, with slanted flat-top roofs, red tile, and Navajo white stucco, accentuates the southwestern atmosphere at NMSU. Students agree that the campus looks attractive except in February, when a lot of the grass looks dead. Favorite places to study include campus lawns and the two university libraries. The New Library, completed a few years ago, houses the arts, education, and humanities resources. The older Branson Library includes information on business, agriculture, and the sciences. It's usually not hard to find a quiet place to study, one student said.

Because of the wide range of university housing, a high percentage of students live on campus. Several apartment buildings are open to students with at least sophomore status. To accommodate nontraditional students with spouses and/or children, NMSU also offers family student housing units with two bedrooms, a bath, kitchen, and indoor/outdoor living space. The majority of undergrads, however, choose the standard university dorms. Rules forbid drinking in all of the dorms except for Alumni, which is reportedly the party dorm.

Better Dine Out

University dining receives less than favorable reviews. Out of approximately 13,000 undergrads, only about 1,300 purchase a meal plan. One student government representative said that the administration may bring in outside companies once the present food service contract expires. Currently, the dining system consists of one dining hall serving standard cafeteria fare and eight satellite stations that serve snack foods and drinks.

A number of campus groups work to generate a social scene at NMSU. The Corbett Center, a popular hangout during the day, includes a small art gallery, a movie theater, and the campus bookstore as well as a dining hall and a game room. Several student organizations such as the student

government and the biweekly *Round-Up* newspaper use the recently expanded center as a meeting area. The Association of Students—New Mexico State University (ASNMSU) organizes a book swap at the beginning of each semester and screens current movies on Sundays, among other activities. Recent entertainers to visit the campus have included Garth Brooks, Pearl Jam, and Salt 'n' Pepa. Fraternities organize parties on most weekends, but students say that only a very small portion of NMSU undergrads join the Greek system.

Sports Haven

Aggie athletics receive enthusiastic support from the NMSU community. Men's basketball remains the number one draw as the team consistently fights for the top spot in the NCAA. The women's volleyball team has seen similar success in intercollegiate competition. NMSU football also gets a lot of hype, one student said. Once named *Sports Illustrated's* worst college football team, the program has grown with a change in coaching staff. Now, the program challenges rival University of Texas/El Paso in the annual football showdown. Besides intercollegiate sports, NMSU offers intramural volleyball, soccer, touch football, and other outdoor sports. At the Activities Center, students oftern borrow sporting equipment (such as canoes, tents, bicycles, and rock-climbing gear) to experience the New Mexico landscape on their own.

> **"We're more known for our ag and applied sciences schools."**

Undergrads generally agree that Las Cruces is a great college town. Students frequent its night spots, especially Cowboys, a country-western dance club. On Mondays, disco night at the Rock Island Bar usually attracts a number of partygoers. Some favorite restaurants include Little Nellie's and Chopi's, both restaurants in Old Mesilla along the Rio Grande.

Although students report a low crime rate in Las Cruces, NMSU stresses the need for continued safety and provides a dependable security system that includes emergency phones and security patrols around the area. When Las Cruces starts to seem stifling, students often escape to dance clubs in El Paso or to bars across the border in Mexico.

The friendly attitude pervasive at New Mexico State distinguishes this school from other universities. You don't have to walk around with your head down. You can't help meeting people here, one student said. The beautiful weather allows students to roam the campus, and as another student said, this makes the dating scene pretty happening.

Regardless of the stifling heat of the New Mexico desert surrounding Las Cruces, students say NMSU's combination of work and leisure makes the climate just perfect.—*Brian Abaluck and Staff*

FYI

The three best things about attending NMSU are "sunny weather, the awesome party scene, and the hot girls."

The three worst things about attending NMSU are "a social scene that depends on alcohol too much, no major cities nearby, and its not being well known."

The three things every student should do before graduating is "make the trip to Lake Havasu for spring break, head down to Mexico for a tequila party, and go country line dancing at Cowboys if you've never done it."

One thing that I'd like to have known before coming here is "the non-tech areas are not very strong and most people are very pre-professional."

University of New Mexico

Address: Admissions Office, Student Services Center, Room 150, Albuquerque, NM 87131	**Percent African-American:** 3.0%	**Middle 50% SAT range:** 480–610 V, 470–590 M
Phone: 505-277-2446	**Percent Hispanic:** 31.0%	**Middle 50% ACT range:** 19–25
E-mail address: apply@unm.edu	**Percent Asian:** 3.0%	**Mean ACT:** 22
Web site URL: www.unm.edu	**Percent in-state / out-of-state:** 83% / 17%	**3 Most popular majors:** university studies, elementary teacher education, psychology
Location: urban	**Percent Pub HS:** NA	
Founded: 1889	**Fraternities:** 5%	
Private or Public: public	**Sororities:** 4%	**Retention:** 70.0%
Religious affiliation: none	**Number of Applicants:** 4,171	**Graduation rate:** 0.0%
Undergraduate enrollment: 16,295	**Percent Accepted:** 191%	**Library:** 2,200,000 volumes
Total enrollment: 23,770	**Percent Accepted who enroll:** 68%	**Tuition and Fees:** $2,242 in; $8,461 out
Percent Male / Female: 42% / 58%	**Entering:** 2,586	**Room and Board:** $4,300
Percent Minority: 43.0%	**Transfers:** 1,481	**On-campus housing:** NA
	Application Deadline: 1 July	**Financial aid, first-year:** 41%
	Mean SAT: 543 V, 533 M	

S ituated in the center of Albuquerque, the University of New Mexico is a different kind of state school. Most members of the student body live off campus, and many are returning students who have full-time jobs. The school has a cul-

tural and social diversity that almost any university would be hard-pressed to rival.

Light Academics

One student described UNM academics as "fairly easy," but another said, "It depends on what you want to get of it." The biology, geology, and photography departments have earned the most praise from undergrads, while some report that the math and music departments need improvement. Students can take courses in the university graduate schools, but priority for all classes goes to graduate students and upperclassmen, making it a problem sometimes to get the classes you want, according to a sophomore. Although pre-professionalism abounds at UNM, undergraduates agree that the college still has a strong liberal arts program.

Monster Courses

Students sometimes complain about class sizes, which can be as big as 500 students in introductory classes. Most courses are taught by professors, but graduate students teach some introductory-level courses. Undergrads report that faculty-student interaction can be very good when the student takes the initiative. The academic environment is quite laid-back and not intensely competitive, according to one senior. Qualified students with high GPAs are eligible for enrollment in an honors program that offers special seminars that emphasize reading, discusstion, and writing.

UNM students seem satisfied with the university facilities. The six libraries, especially Zimmerman Library and the technical libraries, are the best places for quiet study. A grassy area under the trees by the duck pond is another relaxing place to get work done. A favorite spot for social study is the Cellar, a pizza place located in the basement of one of the dorms, where there's also a game room. Another popular UNM hangout is the Student Union Building (SUB), which has a courtyard and a ballroom. In town, students enjoy hanging out in several of Albuquerque's cafés, including the Double Rainbow, and in various bookstore-cafes.

Social Events? Go Greek

Since few UNM students live on campus, most parties happen in off-campus houses. Only a small number join fraternities, but frat parties are extremely popular. The biggest fraternity party of the year, the Can You Bring bash, requires all guests to bring a can of food to be given to the Albu-

querque poor. On campus, UNM offers at least 600 clubs, according to one student, including theater, music groups, community service, and the *Daily Lobo*, a highly praised student newspaper.

A Place to Hang My Hat

Campus housing is said to be quite good. The best (and most expensive) dorms are the Student Residence Centers (SRCs), which are apartments with private bathrooms and kitchens. In contrast, in the Eldorado dorm, 100 women share two communal bathrooms. One student stated, Even though Eldorado isn't the greatest dorm, it's still a place to hang my hat.

The architecture is typical New Mexico–style, and students emphasize that the school's setting in the Sandia Mountains is simply gorgeous. Safety is a growing concern on UNM's compus, but escorts are available 24 hours a day. UNM has one central cafeteria, and students report that the food is unpopular. Many students choose to cook for themselves, and there is no scarcity of alternative off-campus eateries. Frontier, a 24-hour food shop, is one of the favorite places to eat off campus, and Albuquerque also offers a wide variety of Mexican restaurants.

Howling Lobos

Sports are big at UNM, whose mascot is El Lobo, Spanish for the wolf. Students are especially proud of their basketball team, which won the Western Athletic Conference championship in 1994. The Lobos' biggest rival is neighboring New Mexico State University, and it is a tradition for the Lobos to howl at their opponents before every basketball game. The volleyball and tennis teams have also had successful seasons recently. UNM's athletic facilities include the on-campus Johnson Center, which has, according to one student, everything you can imagine in terms of sports equipment, as well as the football stadium and another recently built gym in downtown Albuquerque. Club sports and intramurals are popular, particularly skiing. In fact, one undergraduate said that many people make their schedules around the time they can go skiing.

Some students call life in Albuquerque slow, but another praised the town's good theaters, which host symphony concerts, dance shows, and Broadway productions. Since most students live in town or grew up in the community, town-gown relations are warm and friendly. For students who feel the need to escape, beautiful and culturally rich Santa Fe is only two hours away, as is the famous Taos ski resort.

Diversity University

The UNM student body is a diverse ethnic mix. The number of minority students, particularly Latinos, gave one sophomore the impression that here, whites are a minority, although another student said he had expected the Latino population to be even larger. UNM is, in fact, a bilingual school, and many courses are taught in Spanish as well as in English. One international student said that there is a strong minority support network, and that the campus has centers for all minorities, including gay and lesbian students, who reportedly are accepted by the rest of the student body. Undergrads also seem to have an open attitude toward drugs. According to one, you can freqently smell people smoking pot on campus. Many UNM undergrads study part-time and are older than the average college age; the average age of freshmen is 20.

Size: Asset or Problem?

The size of the university is a problem for some and an asset for others. On the one hand, a student complained, in a large university like this you end up being a number. On the other hand, UNM's size puts many resources at students' disposal. The key to the University of New Mexico, as one student remarked, is that it has a lot to offer, and you have to decide what you want to get out of it. The university's relaxed atmosphere, its extensive resources, and the socially and culturally diverse student body give undergrads great freedom to shape their education according to their interests, and provide them with great opportunities for a solid education.—*Kurtland Ma and Staff*

> **Many UNM undergrads study part-time and are older than the average college age; the average age of the freshman class is 20.**

FYI
The three best thing about attending UNM are "the awesome cultural diversity, all the hard partying that goes on here during the weekends, and the pretty campus."

The three worst things about attending UNM are "the town of Albuquerque, feeling like this place is too big, and many people's focus on life after college instead of life during it (many older and off-campus students)."

The three things every student should do before graduating are "go skiing at Taos as often as you can (it's so cheap as a student), go drive through the desert at 100 mph, and you gotta go to the UNM vs. NMSU football game."

One thing that I'd like to have known before coming here is "how easy it is to get the bad habits of slacking and sleeping really late here."

New York

Adelphi University

Address: 1 South Avenue, Garden City, NY 11530
Phone: 516-877-3050
E-mail address: admissions@adlibv.adelphi.edu
Web site URL: www.adelphi.edu
Location: urban
Founded: 1896
Private or Public: private
Religious affiliation: none
Undergraduate enrollment: 2,774
Total enrollment: 7,003
Percent Male / Female: 33% / 67%
Percent Minority: 21.0%

Percent African-American: 12.0%
Percent Hispanic: 6.0%
Percent Asian: 3.0%
Percent in-state / out-of-state: 93% / 7%
Percent Pub HS: 83%
Fraternities: NA
Sororities: NA
Number of Applicants: 1,420
Percent Accepted: 78%
Percent Accepted who enroll: 29%
Entering: 321
Transfers: NA
Application Deadline: rolling

Mean SAT: 490 V, 490 M
Middle 50% SAT range: 410–540 V, 460–588 M
Middle 50% ACT range: NA
Mean ACT: NA
3 Most popular majors: business-management, education, nursing
Retention: 74.0%
Graduation rate: 34.0%
Library: 480,000 volumes
Tuition and Fees: $14,000 in; NA out
Room and Board: $6,850
On-campus housing: 41%
Financial aid, first-year: 87%

After years of complaints about the administration from faculty and students at this Long Island school, heads finally rolled in the spring of 1997: all but one member of the board of trustees were ousted by the state, and the new trustees removed university president Dr. Peter Diamondopoulos from office. While Diamandopoulos's few fans praised his work in putting the university back in the black and attempting to improve the school's reputation, his critics pointed to his generous salary and benefits, the school's precipitously decreasing enrollment, and its soaring tuition—especially for a predominantly middle-class, commuter school—as proof that financial responsibility is more than just balancing the books. Despite the opportunity afforded by recent events for great student-faculty bonding, all are glad that Adelphi is right on track and credit the university for fostering a spirit of openness and community.

Personalized Academics

Undergrads consider classes at Adelphi "intimate." The average class has 20 students, and one student said this fosters "great group discussions." Professors are "extremely accessible and willing to help with academic or personal problems," said one undergrad; another added, "The profs here really know what they are talking about." Students generally find lectures entertaining and informative. "I have not dozed off in class yet," one student claimed. The classrooms reportedly are "clean and well-lit."

Adelphi has three main schools: business, nursing, and arts and sciences. The core curriculum requires all students to take courses in three classifications: Modern Conditions (humanities), "Core Comp" (English), and Origins (arts and sciences). Academically, many students feel that the core requirement is a waste of time. "It is boring, unnecessary, and is wreaking havoc with my GPA," one undergrad said.

Another student complained that the core credits are "made up by Adelphi—you can't transfer them to any other school." Some students, however, like the fact that core classes allow them to meet people majoring in the other divisions: "I met my best friend in our core comp class," one undergrad said.

Students consider psychology, nursing, business management, and biology among Adelphi's best departments, although some feel that the psychology department does not have enough professors. The science departments, especially biology, are dominated by prospective pre-med majors and offer what undergrads generally believe to be the toughest classes on campus. Students describe the level of competition on campus as "moderate," with workloads that are "hard, but not impossible." The university's Honor College, however, which has smaller classes, has a reputation among students as being "fiercely competitive and almost impossible to get into." Adelphi has a number of tutoring programs to aid students having difficulty in their classes, including writing, math, and science tutors. The Learning Disability program entitles participants to extra tutoring and untimed tests. There is also an English as a Second Language program for international students that one undergrad said "needs work, but does help a little."

Safe Dorms, Safe Food

The majority of Adelphi students live off campus, either with their parents or in apartment complexes. For students who do live on campus, there are four dorms: Chapman, Earle, Linen, and Waldow. Waldow is a women's dorm (the others are coed) and "has the biggest rooms on campus," one resident said. Chapman is centrally located and students often call it the best dorm because of its modern facilities and convenient location. Earle is a popular meeting place for students, but some complain that the noise can get out of hand at times. Next year, the school will reopen Eddy Hall, while this year it closed St. Paul's Apartments.

Adelphi provides an escort service at night and has installed emergency telephones throughout the campus to increase student safety. Visitors must leave their IDs with the dorm guards. Although many students say they have "never felt uncomfortable on campus," others find the security measures excessive and often "a hassle."

Most Adelphi students are pleasantly surprised by the campus food, which includes ever-popular pizza, hamburgers, salads, and frozen yogurt. "I couldn't believe it. It is not that bad," one undergrad said. Not all students share this enthusiasm, but the University Center (UC), deli, and Sbarro's pizzeria are campus alternatives to the dining halls. The UC is also a popular hangout for studying and socializing, despite some student complaints that it closes "too early."

Social Dynamics

The majority of Adelphi students come from the tri-state region (New York, New Jersey, and Connecticut), particularly from Long Island. Despite efforts to increase Adelphi's international and minority population, some minority students claim the old administration was "unsympathetic" to their calls for increased student diversity. Many students feel Adelphi has a problem with diversity; the campus is primarily white, and some minority students say they feel "out of place" and uncomfortable. Despite this, the university supports several clubs for students of color, including the NAACP and APO (African People's Organization).

Extracurricular activities at Adelphi are plentiful. School publications include the *Delphian*, the weekly newspaper; *Ascent*, the literary magazine; and the *Oracle*, the student yearbook. The Student Activities Board plans trips into Manhattan and other activities. Other popular campus groups include the Student Political Association and student government.

Sports are a key part of life at Adelphi, and produce the only visible displays of school spirit on campus. Adelphians take sports very seriously and take immense pride in their Division I Panthers lacrosse and women's soccer teams. Adelphi has no varsity football team; instead, students rally around the men's basketball team. "They're awesome," exclaimed one spirited fan.

> Adelphi combines small classes with an intense academic environment that fosters a sense of camaraderie.

Officially, Adelphi is a dry campus, but according to students, alcohol is plentiful. The local bar scene includes a popular hangout called the Rat as well as Rhythm and Bruise, the Corner Bar, 007, and Bucano Bean. Fraternity and sorority parties draw large crowds of revelers on Thursdays. On weekends, Adelphi generally becomes a "ghost town" because most students leave to go home.

Adelphi combines small classes with an intense academic environment that fosters a sense of camaraderie. While students like the intimate academic environment, their life outside of class often is not closely connected to the school, especially if they live off campus. Still, students are sure that things can only get better at Adelphi.—*Susanna Chu and Staff*

FYI

The three best things about attending Adelphi are "small classes, a close-knit community, and the energy of the student body."

The three worst things about attending Adelphi are "we are a dry campus, core class work, and a sad party scene on weekends."

The three things that every student should do before graduating from Adelphi are "watch the Panthers in action, get involved, and live off campus for a year."

One thing I'd like to have known before coming here is "that this place gets awfully quiet when people head home for the weekends."

Alfred University

Address: One Saxon Drive, Alfred, NY 14802	**Percent African-American:** 3.4%	**Middle 50% SAT range:** 530–620 V, 520–630 M
Phone: 800-541-9229	**Percent Hispanic:** 3.9%	
E-mail address: admwww@alfred.edu	**Percent Asian:** 1.7%	**Middle 50% ACT range:** 23–28
Web site URL: www.alfred.edu	**Percent in-state/out-of-state:** 67%/33%	**Mean ACT:** 23
Location: rural	**Percent Pub HS:** NA	**3 Most popular majors:** art and design, ceramic engineering, materials science
Founded: 1836	**Fraternities:** 15%	
Private or Public: private	**Sororities:** 8%	
Religious affiliation: none	**Number of Applicants:** 1,954	**Retention:** 83%
Undergraduate enrollment: 2,112	**Percent Accepted:** 82%	**Graduation rate:** 65%
Total enrollment: 2,435	**Percent Accepted who enroll:** 35%	**Library:** 231,629 volumes
Percent Male/Female: 50%/50%	**Entering:** 556	**Tuition and Fees:** $18,498 in; $18,498 out
Percent Minority: 9.4%	**Transfers:** 110	**Room and Board:** $3,740
	Application Deadline: 1 Feb	**On-campus housing:** 95%
	Mean SAT: 567 V, 564 M	**Financial aid, first-year:** 83%

"If you want a bustling city life, Alfred University is not the place to be. But for everything else a college student needs, it's great," boasted one Alfred student. True to his words, Alfred University, located in upstate New York, is a small-town school. Yet, what it lacks in big city glamour it makes up for in rolling pastures and a close-knit community. Its nationally recognized ceramic engineering department doesn't hurt, either.

Not Your Typical Curriculum

Academics at Alfred are truly unique and diverse. Popular majors range from the less common, athletic training, to more typical offerings such as computer science and mechanical engineering. Students at Alfred tend to have a wide array of academic interests. Classes are described as challenging, and students agree good grades are not so easy to come by, although requirements and difficulty do vary by major. The only course all students are required to take is physical education. "I guess they want us all to be fit," one student said.

One of the strongest and most popular majors at Alfred is ceramic engineering. Not only is Alfred nationally recognized for its faculty in this department, but the school also makes available many co-op opportunities for students who want to pursue this field. Indeed, the program is so good many students say they came to Alfred because of it. Other strong departments include the arts, computer science, business, English, and history. The music department, on the other hand, does not receive such rave reviews due to its limited course selection.

In addition to its regular academic programs, Alfred offers a special honors program for qualified students. This program provides academically ambitious students more access to the best professors at the university. Honors students have the opportunity to delve into certain fields in more depth than they would studying under the normal program.

As a small school in a small town, it is not surprising that Alfred gets good reviews for its class sizes. The average class enrolls only about 15 students, and professors not only teach all lectures, but conduct all discussion sections as well. The small course size fosters a supportive environment, and many students note that they feel close to their professors. The close-knit community also proves advantageous in that it allows students to participate more actively in their own education. In fact, it is not unusual to find professor-student interactions even out-side the classroom. Professors and students are often seen meeting for a meal or coffee in a local eatery. At Alfred, learning is not confined to the classroom.

The two libraries on campus also receive acclaim from students. Of the two, Herrick Memorial tends to be the more popular study place, and is often crowded. The other library, Scholes, has the largest ceramic engineering research collection in the world.

In addition to these excellent libraries, Alfred boasts many new classroom buildings. Olin is a fairly recent business building, and the Miller Performing Arts Center and Glass Science Laboratory are both new additions to the campus. This is not unusual for Alfred, which tends always to be on the cutting edge. "Our campus is constantly being remodeled—it's great!" boasted one student.

Northern Exposure

First-year students live in special freshman dorms, usually in doubles, coed by floor. Barresi is one popular freshman dorm, whereas Tefft tends to be less popular. Upperclassmen select rooms by lottery and have a wide array of choices open to them, ranging from suites to campus apartments with full-size kitchens. In addition, a large number of students live off campus in sorority or fraternity houses.

Food is reportedly not horrible, and students may eat in either of the campus's two dining halls—Powell, located in the campus center, or Ade. Alfred changed dining services a few years ago, and students say they are benefiting from it. Many students opt to eat at off-campus eateries as well. Popular spots include the Collegiate, The Dill Pickle, Little Sicily's, and Alfred Pizza and Sub Shop.

Extracurricular Life in the Boonies

Alfred University is an extremely health conscious school, so it is no surprise that sports are very popular. Alfred is a Division III school and cannot offer athletic scholarships, but the school still manages to have great athletic competition. The lacrosse team is very good, having made the Division III Championships twice in the last four years.

School spirit at athletic events is extremely high, as many an Alfred student comes out to support the Saxon Warriors. The school's athletic facilities are described as "fairly good" and are open to all students, free of charge. These include squash courts, basketball courts, a swimming pool, and a weight room. For those not as athletically inclined, intramurals are popular, including everything from squash to basketball.

In addition to sports, other popular campus activities include participating in the college newspaper, the *Fiatlux*, which is distributed biweekly. Other journalistic venues include literary magazines such as the *Alfred Review* and the *Poasis*. Students describe both of these magazines as "bizarre but interesting." Other popular extracurriculars include the school radio station and a jazz band that has performed around the world. Greek life also holds a strong presence on campus, and according to students, is the "be-all-and-end-all" of campus social life. Alcohol is also big, and binge drinking is perceived as a problem by some. However, despite the pre-dominance of alcohol, students say they do not feel pressure to drink.

> **"If you want a bustling city life, Alfred University is not the place to be. Yet for everything else a college student needs, it's great."**

Located in such a rural community, Alfred sponsors many on-campus activities. One in particular is Hot Dog Day, the campus's biggest weekend of the year, featuring parades, nonstop partying, live bands, and "a lot of fun."

Although many of the students come from New York, Alfred draws in a wide range of students from all sorts of backgrounds. In this small town, these students band together and experience what has been described as "a great four years." Said one student, "Although Alfred isn't for everyone, if you can handle small town life, do give it a try. You won't be disappointed."—*Alyssa Blair Greenwald*

FYI

The three best things about attending Alfred are "the small classes, the parties, and the ceramic engineering department."

The three worst things about attending Alfred are "the bad weather, the binge drinking, and the fact that SUNY Alfred is right across the street."

The three things every student should do before graduating from Alfred are "hang out in Hornell, get pizza from Alex's, and go to the Collegiate Restaurant."

One thing I'd like to have known before coming to Alfred is "how small a town Alfred really is."

Bard College

Address: Office of Admissions, Annandale-on-Hudson, NY 12504

Phone: 914-758-7472

E-mail address: admission@bard.edu

Web site URL: www.bard.edu

Location: rural

Founded: 1860

Private or Public: private

Religious affiliation: none

Undergraduate enrollment: 1,233

Total enrollment: 1,427

Percent Male / Female: 42% / 58%

Percent Minority: 12.0%

Percent African-American: 4.0%

Percent Hispanic: 4.0%

Percent Asian: 3.0%

Percent in-state / out-of-state: 76% / 24%

Percent Pub HS: 60%

Fraternities: 0%

Sororities: 0%

Number of Applicants: 2,508

Percent Accepted: 47%

Percent Accepted who enroll: 30%

Entering: 349

Transfers: 36

Application Deadline: 15 Jan

Mean SAT: 650 V, 610 M

Middle 50% SAT range: 530–700 V, 540–670 M

Middle 50% ACT range: NA

Mean ACT: NA

3 Most popular majors: literature, fine arts, social sciences

Retention: 83.0%

Graduation rate: 65.0%

Library: 260,000 volumes

Tuition and Fees: $24,000 in; NA out

Room and Board: $7,200

On-campus housing: 99%

Financial aid, first-year: 58%

If an annual drag queen contest, known simply as "The Drag Race," is a must have for your future college, look no further than Bard. Set in the lush Hudson River Valley, Bard College boasts a naturally beautiful location and Bard students take advantage of this serene setting to engage in a variety of artistic, academic, and social adventures.

Arts Abound

While all Bard students have to take at least one lab course and one science/mathematics course, students are quick to get those requirements out of the way to delve into the arts and humanities. Bard students are also required to take courses in a foreign language, social and historical studies, literary texts and linguistics, and philosophy. According to one student, "the requirements are really fair and really easy to manage as long as you don't slack." While the school's majority is made of artists, it is actually the concentrations in art that are the most difficult. Majors in photography, film, painting, and sculpture find that there is simply "a lot of work and a lot of time involved."

Difficulty aside, Bard students enjoy small classes, which seem to diminish in size as students progress in their studies.

One junior reported that his largest class had 21 students. As for getting into classes themselves, students appeal to their professors, explaining why they want to take that class, in lieu of traditional registration. While it is naturally a system easiest for seniors, another student said that "it's actually pretty easy if you plan. I've rarely had difficulty in getting into my classes." Students are universally pleased with the chance to work closely with faculty in their small classes and find their professors easily accessible and willing to help. Some classes are indeed challenging, but as one student remarked on the Bard experience, "It's as hard as you make it and the professors are able to match that."

Social Life?

Although Bard makes use of its beautiful, pastoral setting, it is also quite remote and limiting to those who want an active social life. As one student said, "You either party at bars, or go to campus parties, or just hang out in the dorms." When students aren't living it up at local joints like Stony Creek or Pongo, they can be found on campus, partaking in the various movies, concerts, or lectures that are constantly happening. Bard students particularly like the annual theme parties, such as the Silk Party, an S&M Bonanza, and the annual Drag Race. Moreover, national and local bands perform quite frequently. Many students also like to use the Bard Student Center, which has a multipurpose room, a computer room, two study rooms, a post office, the bookstore, and two key features, an ATM and a room full of La-Z-Boy seats and a television.

Toga parties and *Animal House*–like behavior don't really exist at Bard, since there is no Greek system. As one junior put it, "I have some friends who drink beer and are athletic, and that's about as close as it gets." Even without a Greek system, however, the students at Bard still have enough parties to go to. Alcohol and drugs are definitely present on campus, with one student estimating that "about 70 percent of the students smoke cigarettes, you can't avoid it." Alcohol is also part of the social scene with the administrative stance being that it is their job to "protect, not enforce."

Have Wheels, Will Travel

What makes up a typical Bard student? Well, according to a sophomore, it's "impossible. We have rich hippies and lazy jocks. We're mostly middle ground; there are a lot of free spirits who are still hard-working." The Bard population is relatively diverse, although one junior commented that "Bard's small, so it can start to get homogeneous." Although most students don't fit into a general schema, it is clear that a sizeable percentage of students have cars. Cars are "very necessary. There is nothing in walking distance besides the campus, so you have to drive at least three to four miles to get to local towns."

Close Quarters

One student described his freshman dorm room as "extremely small and cramped." The housing situation at Bard is not looked on with particularly glowing eyes. The school was once so tight for housing that it actually had students living in emergency trailer housing. Despite these conditions, there are some nice living arrangements on campus. These include Super Cruger and Keen, two new and modern dorms, as well as Manor, an old mansion. Manor is definitely considered one of the best places to live, although as one resident said, "It's a little removed

from central campus." All dorms have PCs (peer counselors), who "have to enforce some rules, but usually let people do what they want." Students looking for variations on dorm housing can choose to live in quiet dorms, a co-op or a number of small two-story houses owned by Bard. Many upperclassmen move off campus because they feel housing is "mediocre. It's expensive, and you might get a good room or not. Nothing's sure." For those who do live off campus, Tivoli and Red Hook are popular complexes and, when compared to dorm housing, are either less expensive or the same price for a lot more.

> "I have some friends who drink beer and are athletic, and that's about as close [to Greek] as it gets."

The dining system at Bard is also seen as rather poor. One student simply said, "It's expensive, and it's pretty bad." However, students agree that there is a lot of food available and a lot of choice, just not very good quality. One sophomore complains, "There's lots of starch." Bard has one dining hall, Kline, where most students go. Vegetarians and vegans never feel left out as there are "plenty of options." The dining hall itself is not really a very social setting; students tend to rush in, eat, and leave. For those looking to have some stimulating dinnertime conversation, they have the choice of either going to Down the Road in the student center, or going out to eat. Within a 20 minute radius of campus, Bard students frequent a variety of restaurants, which, according to a senior, "are pretty varied for such a small place." Favorite places include Osaka, Panada, Stony Creek, The Rotisserie, and the Red Hook Diner.

Outside of Class

While it is certainly easy to get involved in extracurricular activities at Bard, few students seem to take advantage of it. One student described Bard as having "enormous amounts of small organizations, which are easy to join. But most people are just too lazy to do it." Furthermore, given the artistic inclination of its students, there is clearly little focus on athletic activities. There are a variety of clubs that engage in artistic expression as well as prominent feminist and women's rights groups. Also active are ethnic and cultural clubs such as the African Students Organization, Asian American Students Organization and Central European Students Organization. While community service is not as popular at Bard, it is the school's hope that within two years, at least 50 percent of the campus will be involved in some kind of volunteer work. Also, for a school with almost three-fourths of its students on some kind of financial aid, most Bard students have work-study jobs. For the more active students, there is a strong in-

tramural sports following, with softball, rugby, soccer, basketball, and tennis making up the most popular teams. While the school does compete intercollegiately, there is little school spirit for these events. Rugby is the only sport at Bard with a real following.

The students of Bard love the location on a "gorgeous piece of land in the Hudson Valley filled with historical sites and wonderful landscaping." At the same time, they love the hour and a half drive away from New York City, where there is a wealth of social opportunities. Bard is a truly stunning place for those geared toward the humanities. As one student put it, "Bard gives you the freedom to figure out what you need."—*Shu-Ping Shen*

FYI

The three best things about attending Bard are "freedom, the natural environment, and the faculty."

The three worst things about attending Bard are "food, housing, and expensive tuition."

The three things that every student should do before graduating from Bard are "go abroad, take advantage of famous faculty, and meet the president."

One thing I'd like to have known before coming here is "how remote Bard really is."

Barnard College

Address: 3009 Broadway, New York, NY 10027
Phone: 212-854-2014
E-mail address: admissions@barnard.edu
Web site URL: www.barnard.edu
Location: urban
Founded: 1889
Private or Public: private
Religious affiliation: none
Undergraduate enrollment: 2,270
Total enrollment: 2,270
Percent Male/Female: 0%/100%
Percent Minority: 35.0%

Percent African-American: 4.0%
Percent Hispanic: 6.0%
Percent Asian: 25.0%
Percent in-state/out-of-state: 39%/61%
Percent Pub HS: 58%
Fraternities: 0%
Sororities: 0%
Number of Applicants: 3,841
Percent Accepted: 36%
Percent Accepted who enroll: 40%
Entering: 553
Transfers: 0
Application Deadline: 15 Jan

Mean SAT: 671 V, 652 M
Middle 50% SAT range: 620–700 V, 610–680 M
Middle 50% ACT range: NA
Mean ACT: 29
3 Most popular majors: English, psychology, political science
Retention: 94.0%
Graduation rate: 65.0%
Library: 180,000 volumes
Tuition and Fees: $21,410 in; NA out
Room and Board: $9,084
On-campus housing: 95%
Financial aid, first-year: 46%

Barnard College offers its students the best of three worlds. As a women's college, it creates an environment that supports and empowers

women. As an affiliate of Columbia University, it offers all the resources and prestige of an Ivy League institution. As an urban school, it provides students with easy access to all the attractions and distractions of New York City, "the ultimate college town."

Academics

Clearly Barnard is not your typical women's college. According to one student, Barnard is only "as much of a women's college as you want it to be." Indeed, many students would agree the school has a defined coed environment though only women may matriculate. As one student explained, "Most classes have men in them, though there tend to be fewer in Barnard classes." Barnard women also have the option of cross-registering for classes at Columbia and vice versa. Depending on major, some Barnard women end up taking almost all of their classes at Columbia, while others go their whole four years without taking one. "It's so great because you have the power to choose. The decision to cross-register is all up to the individual," said one student.

Barnard's core class requirements are designed to give students a broad academic overview, and many Barnard women would agree that they do just that. According to some students, however, the requirements can get ridiculous at times. In particular, one junior called the physical education requirement "absolutely absurd because people should be able to choose whether they want to be fit and not be forced to take class" and the two required semesters of lab the "bane of my existence because lab work is so time-consuming." As a liberal arts school, students say Barnard's English and political science majors are particularly strong. Sociology is reportedly among the school's easier majors as the requirements are less intensive. But above all, as more than one student emphasized, "Barnard is by no means a slacker school—everyone here works and works hard."

Students also feel privileged to learn under the guidance of Barnard's exceptional faculty. Students raved about their "totally amazing" professors. In particular, the faculty's availability and approachability were said to foster close professor-student relationships. The school attracts its share of famous instructors, including Holocaust survivor Elie Wiesel, who has been on campus recently to give a series of lectures. Both Barnard and Columbia students alike vie for places in Professor Thurman's (actress Uma Thurman's father's) Indo-Tibetan Studies courses.

City Living

Due to exorbitantly high New York rents, most Barnard students live in dorms for all four years. Students can choose to live in either Barnard or Columbia housing and can specify how many people they want to live with. Single-sex or coed floors are also available. School dorms are described as "generally pretty clean and decently sized" with the exception of Reid and Brooks, which were both described as "really old." The majority of dorms, however, have undergone recent renovations, which has contributed to the small number of complaints about housing.

There is an RA system for freshmen. The typical RA was described as "pretty helpful," but "not all that important, to put it truthfully." First-years live in the Quad, which is comprised of four connected dorms, and they are required to be on the meal plan. Most upperclassmen live in suites with kitchens, and drop the meal plan soon after freshman year. Students generally agree that being on the meal plan and having to consume school food is not terrible. The dining services are said to offer adequate vegan and kosher options. "Food is just horrendously overpriced," added one student.

Alternative fare is easy to find. The surrounding neighborhood, Morningside Heights, offers students a host of dining options, from cheap and quick to more expensive sit-down meals. Noteworthy among the local establishments are Tom's Diner (of late *Seinfeld* fame); Ollie's, a popular Asian noodle shop; and Café Pertutti, famous for its wonderful pastas. Students looking for more authentic ethnic cuisine or just a more extensive menu can find it in New York City's Chinatown, Koreatown, or Little Italy—all just a $1.50 subway ride away.

Morningside Heights, New York City

Barnard occupies a small campus just across the street from Columbia in uptown Manhattan's Morningside Heights.

Most students would say the local area is "pretty safe" despite its location on the outskirts of Harlem. Yet, they still warn against walking alone at night. Escort services are available, though according to one student, "not too many students use it." The neighborhood was described as "calm, even kinda boring." According to one student, "It's a great place to live because everything you could possibly need can be found within a 12-block radius."

Because of Barnard's location in New York City, students agree there is never a shortage of things to do. Any day of the week, great shopping, famous sites, and great theater are minutes from campus. According to some Barnard women, a typical Friday night inevitably involves "bar-hopping or clubbing somewhere downtown." Getting alcohol is reportedly not a problem, especially since fake IDs are easily obtainable. Weekend frat and suite parties at Columbia are also popular, especially among the first-years. Drugs do not have a sizable presence on campus, though as one student said, "they're definitely there and widely used by some." Considering Barnard's prevalent alcohol culture, one junior warned that the school can be "socially difficult" for non-drinkers. Whether on campus or in the city, most students are able "to find our niches and amuse ourselves."

A Bastion of Independence
On the whole, Barnard tends to be a very self-focused environment. "It's a real fend-for-yourself kind of atmosphere," one student said. "As a result, it can sometimes be a very cold place because the city dilutes a specific Barnard campus identity." Students tend to be cliquey, which contributes to the common student complaint that the school lacks community. Cliques also tend to divide along ethnic lines.

Students are quick to identify certain causes which bring Barnard women together. Every year, the school hosts a march entitled "Take Back the Night" which seeks to empower women against violence and abuse. Started during the 1960s in the wake of the women's and sexual liberation movements, the march enjoys high participation even today as Barnard and Columbia students alike join for a common cause.

The Student Stereotype
Extracurricular life at Barnard is closely tied to Columbia. Most organizations allow potential members to join from both schools. Varsity sports are also joint enterprises. Intramural sports at Barnard, such as rugby and crew, enjoy a more modest popularity. One senior described Barnard women as "fairly apathetic" and complained that "it's hard to get people out for clubs." In addition, many students opt to join city organizations instead of school-sponsored ones, another factor in lower student participation.

> Barnard is only "as much of a women's college as you want it to be."

Among school groups, ethnic organizations like the Latino and Korean student associations are especially popular. This fact seems to contradict the stereotype of a typical Barnard student—"a Caucasian girl clad in the latest fashion, cell phone in one hand, cigarette in the other." Students are proud of their school's great ethnic diversity although one student did complain that the school seemed to have a "preponderance of Valley Girl types." Lesbian groups also have a strong presence on campus. "I don't think there are necessarily more lesbians here than at other places—they're just a lot more active and visible here," said one student.

In Columbia's Shadow?
Barnard College has been affiliated with Columbia University for more than a century. Even after all that time, however, tensions between the two schools reportedly run pretty high. Barnard undergrads report that Columbia students oftentimes begrudge them as being a "drain on Columbia's resources." According to one student, many Columbia students "think Barnard women are less intelligent and that Columbia doesn't get a higher ranking because of Barnard's lower admission standards." A well-known saying among Columbia men reflects this attitude: "Barnard women to bed, Columbia women to wed." One junior refuted this sentiment, however. "I know a lot of

Barnard girls who were accepted to both schools and chose Barnard over Columbia. And I also have friends who transferred to Barnard from Columbia." Others echo her response. "Some people think Barnard is full of dumb lesbians who want to feed off Columbia, but in actuality, only a select few ignorant people actually express that attitude."

How would Barnard students respond to accusations that their school hangs on Columbia's coattails? Said one student, "We stand in no one's shadow, including Columbia's. Barnard is a terrific school in its own right." With a campus in one of the world's most exciting cities, Barnard is as exceptional a women's school as one can get, offering its students a supportive yet challenging environment amidst the metropolitan madness.—*Jane H. Hong*

FYI
The three best things about attending Barnard are "the personal attention, the great faculty-student interaction, and its location in the city."
The three worst things about attending Barnard are "the stereotypes of Barnard students as dumb lesbians, the affiliation with Columbia, and the lack of community."
The three things that every student should do before graduating from Barnard are "take a women's history class, march in 'Take Back the Night,' and go downtown and see a Broadway show."
One thing I'd like to have known before coming here is "how independent everyone here is."

The City University of New York System

The City University of New York (CUNY—pronounced "kyoony"), underwent radical revision on November 22, 1999, that its Chancellor, Matthew Goldstein, hopes will "redefine and substantially broaden the view of the role and promise of a public urban university." On that date, New York State Board of Regents approved CUNY's Master Plan Amendment proposal to remove remedial courses from the baccalaureate curriculum and demand demonstration of basic skills through the SAT, ACT, or Regents Exams. It also revamped its intra-system transfer policies and got a $97 million boost from the 1999–2000 state budget. Through these changes, CUNY hopes to improve its academic image, the strength of its offerings, and the retention and success of its students. Whether Goldstein's plans will be successful or headed for a fall, only time will tell.

Variety and Different Focus
CUNY is the third-largest university system in the world with 200,000 students on 21 campuses (10 undergraduate, 6 community colleges, 1 technical, 4 graduate) throughout the five boroughs of New York. Additional 150,000 part-time and continuing-education adult students attend a CUNY school. Its student body reflects the city's ethnic diversity: 32% of students are black, 31% white, 25% Hispanic, and 12% Asian. Although the differences among colleges are immense, nearly all the students interviewed by the *Insider's Guide* mentioned the word "bureaucratic." As one student said, the colleges are "run by the city of New York, so basically . . . anyone you deal with at the administrative level gives you the same attitude you would expect at the Department of Motor Vehicles."

A Good Deal
Despite the dissatisfaction with the administration, however, most CUNY students feel they're getting a good education and a good deal. The huge variety of night courses attracts a large population of students who work during the day. All of this is available at a price made more reasonable by the fact that most students are from New York and can live at home, which is "a big reason" many students choose CUNY schools. According to one undergrad, "Most students I know

here work and are from families where that's necessary." Understandably, most students take up to six years to graduate and the graduation rate is low.

Each school has its individual strengths. "[Each college] has different concentrations," one student said. "Hunter has a big nursing school; at Queens, it's English; at Baruch, it's business; and The City College covers the technical areas: engineering and computer science." According to students, these individual strengths help them decide which school to attend. "If a student lives in Brooklyn, and wants to be an English major, it's not that big a commute—he'll go to Queens," one student explained.

Grab Bag

Campus environments vary as well. Students describe the colleges in Manhattan as more fast-paced and urban than those in the other boroughs; they are also considered "more liberal" and "free." According to one undergrad, some students from suburban Long Island "come to Queens and are in awe of it—if they went to Manhattan, they'd have a heart attack. The culture is different in Long Island: you really don't see anyone with a shaved head and nose ring walking around the other campuses." Students in Manhattan say, "It's Manhattan"—in the middle of everything, creating an extremely diverse and exciting environment.

Admissions criteria depend on the individual school. Spaces in the community colleges are guaranteed to New York students who have earned a high school diploma, while the four-year schools maintain more selective admissions policies. Students are required to have a cumulative academic average (CAA) of 80, a measurement that incorporates grades only from "academic" subjects such as math, English, science, foreign language, and history.

> As one student said, the colleges are "run by the city of New York, so basically . . . anyone you deal with at the administrative level gives you the same attitude you would expect at the Department of Motor Vehicles."

Overall, students praise the faculty as one of the CUNY system's greatest assets. "We have a lot of really fine teachers here," one student said. Others described their professors as "gifted people as well as gentle and giving teachers," and "excellent, and nationally renowned."

New York City serves as both CUNY's campus and its source of extracurricular activities: A CUNY ID can get a student discounts at many museums, galleries, and theaters around town. One student even claimed that "if you make arrangements, there's hardly a museum in the city that won't let you in for free." However, this does not prevent some CUNY schools from having strong extracurriculars, including newspapers, clubs, and student government.

Students generally agree that the CUNY system provides a solid education for people of all ages, interests, schedules, and backgrounds. General Colin Powell and Jerry Seinfeld are two of many distinguished alumni of the CUNY system, as is the current Chancellor Goldstein. The colleges are reportedly "malleable to the individual student's ambitions" and meet the changing needs of a remarkably diverse population. According to one student, "Overall, the administration is pretty unpopular, but the teaching is informative if you choose the right courses—it's a good education."—*Seung Lee and Staff*

City University of New York / City College

Address: 138th and Convent Avenue, New York, NY 10031
Phone: 212-650-6977
E-mail address: admissions@admin.ccny.cuny.edu
Web site URL: www.ccny.cuny.edu
Location: urban
Founded: 1847
Private or Public: public
Religious affiliation: none
Undergraduate enrollment: 8,930
Total enrollment: 12,093
Percent Male/Female: 48%/52%
Percent Minority: 87.0%

Percent African-American: 39.0%
Percent Hispanic: 35.0%
Percent Asian: 13.0%
Percent in-state/out-of-state: 85%/15%
Percent Pub HS: 85%
Fraternities: 0%
Sororities: 0%
Number of Applicants: 3,333
Percent Accepted: 68%
Percent Accepted who enroll: 43%
Entering: 988
Transfers: 0
Application Deadline: 15 Jan
Mean SAT: NA

Middle 50% SAT range: 430–570 V, 460–590 M
Middle 50% ACT range: NA
Mean ACT: NA
3 Most popular majors: electrical engineering, computer science, psychology
Retention: 83.0%
Graduation rate: 14.0% (within 5 years)
Library: 1.2 million volumes
Tuition and Fees: $3,200 in; $6,800 out
Room and Board: no dorms
On-campus housing: 0%
Financial aid, first-year: NA

Located in Harlem and intersected by busy city streets, the City College of New York (CCNY) is an institution whose assets include New York City itself. Although CCNY has no campus housing, its academic offerings are considerably more diverse than those of most other CUNY schools. CCNY provides students with a good education at a great price that attracts commuters from all five boroughs of New York City.

Academics

Undergrads report that CCNY has a number of strong departments, including English, political science, and history. One student said, "The caliber of the teaching staff is excellent." However, CCNY has not been unaffected by recent cuts to CUNY's budgets. While film, media, and music have grown recently, that has come at the expense of dance and theater. Pressed by diminishing funds, the college president, herself an anthropologist, recently threatened to eliminate the anthropology department. Only when she learned she risked losing her place in the American Association of Anthropology did she preserve the department, although one anthropology major said, "It is not a very strong department." Undergraduates and graduate students take classes together.

Most students agreed that CCNY is strongest in, and best known for, the sciences and engineering. One student said, "[CCNY] boasts about all the money it has for research."

The engineering school is separate from the school of liberal arts, and has its own building. One special engineering program is the Program for Retention of Engineering Students (the PRES Program), which provides tutoring and counseling for minority engineering students.

Another special academic program is the seven-year B.S./M.D. program in the Sophie-Davis School of Biomedical Education. Sophie-Davis has a selective admissions policy and a preset medical curriculum. Students must sacrifice the freedom to choose their classes, and must commit to working for at least a year in the community after receiving their medical degree. In exchange, they get an affordable path to an M.D.

The liberal arts school also has special programs, including the Honors Program and the Scholars Program. Students who are admitted into the Honors Program based on placement-test results have special Honors advisors and receive priority in course registration. Students in the Scholars Program, which is similar to the Honors Program, have special class sections and receive academic scholarships.

Regardless of the program they choose, all CCNY undergraduates must fulfill course requirements in the sciences, social sciences, English, a foreign language, math, art, music, and physical education. Required classes include English 110 (Freshman Composition), World Civilization, and World Humanities. Students also must pass proficiency tests in math, reading, writing, and speech. Some students report that the academic requirements are ultimately beneficial, though one science major said, "I don't want to take any of these non-science courses because they are boring." Another student complained about the required Freshman Orientation, a semester-long, pass/fail course "worth zero credits."

Many introductory courses are lecture classes of a few hundred people. However, students reported that professors teach nearly all classes. "I haven't experienced graduate students teaching classes, which is what I expected." A freshman said, "I only see the TA when the prof gives a test."

Weekly review sections called recitations supplement many large classes. More advanced classes, as well as Honors and Scholars sections, often number 20 to 25 students. While professors are usually given high marks, some are difficult to understand. One student said, "I've had professors with thick accents. Sometimes they were very hard to understand and I wished that they had slowed down."

Undergrads report that CCNY has a number of good, quiet places to study if you know where to look. Unfortunately, many consider the main library, officially called the Morris Raphael Cohen Library, too noisy for serious studying. The North Academic Center (the NAC), a central building where most classrooms are located, is said to be a better destination when it's time to really hit the books. The air-conditioned science library in the Robert E. Marshak Building and the music

library in Shepherd Hall are also generally good places to get work done. The writing center in Townshend Harris Hall, where all students can get assistance with papers from writing tutors, is quiet as well.

As one student said about CCNY, "There is such a mix of people here." Outside of class, students are involved in a variety of cultural and ethnic clubs, a major reason minority students say they feel so comfortable on campus. New York City also contributes to this feeling of comfort. A student from Sweden said, "One thing I like about New York is that no matter who you are, you fit in."

The diverse student body also has diverse interests. Although CCNY has no dorms and students live off campus, the week has designated club hours for extracurricular activities. Students participate in a number of extracurricular activities, including drama club, the Government and Law Society, the very active Day and Evening Student Governments (day and evening students have separate student governments, even though the two groups are closely affiliated), and the Frederick Douglass Society, a speech and debate club. CCNY, which is very much a "working-class school," has many political students who are inclined toward activism. Students protest rising tuition, budget cuts, and the bureaucratic administration, which "can be a pain sometimes." The Student Coalition is a prominent activist undergraduate organization that organizes demonstrations and petitions.

Some students devote their time to the three student newspapers: the *Campus*, a monthly that is the general school paper; the *Paper*, an African-American publication; and *Nightwatch*, which is aimed at evening students. The newspapers are generally "well respected," though one student expressed doubt that they are free to print what they wish. "The student newspapers have no controversy. They include things like letters from the president. When you work on the school paper, there are eyes on you."

The college has no football team, but students rally around the basketball, baseball, volleyball, and lacrosse teams instead. Popular intramural programs in soccer, swimming, volleyball, and basketball, which often are played during club hours, are "well run and easy to sign up for." The Herman Goldman Center for Sports and Recreation, a new outdoor sports complex, recently opened to student praise.

There are comparatively few campus social events, mainly because CCNY is a commuter school. One student said, "I don't even interact that much with people. They have parties here but I don't want to come back to school and then leave the area at 3 A.M." There are a few fraternities and sororities with houses, but they are focused on service more than on parties.

When they find themselves with free time, students just hang out more than anything else, one undergrad said. Popular hangout spots include a few restaurants near campus. The surrounding neighborhood has its advantages and disadvantages. One woman said, "[The neighborhood] has a bad reputation, but while I wouldn't want to walk alone there late at night, there are many things there that I like to do." Another student described the neighborhood as "very neighborhoody."

CCNY's campus, a mixture of modern and Gothic architecture, also offers students many options. The eight-story North Academic Center houses classrooms, the student center and lounge, and a ballroom. One student said, "Everything's there." Many students use the student lounge and center to study or to hang out. There is also an on-campus theater and an art building that shows exhibits. Students complained that there are not enough computers and that the gym is open at odd hours.

CCNY has the feel of a real campus in the middle of the city; as one undergrad said, "Since all buildings face inward, it seems like a real campus." Nonetheless, CCNY is in an urban location, and campus security is not lacking. The entrances of all campus buildings are well guarded, and everyone must present an ID before entering a building. A computerized door system using swipe cards was recently installed as a new safety measure. One student added "A CCNYttle is offered if you miss the last bus home, or security will personally drive you to the train station."

> "There is such a mix of people here."

Some CCNY students have part-time jobs or children and see CCNY as a place to get a college degree and a better job. However, others are there to learn; one student called CCNY "a mind-stimulating place." CCNY's lack of dorms and location in New York City have the drawback of causing a reported lack in traditional school spirit. Nevertheless, CCNY's solid academic programs and low tuition make it a bargain.—*Billy Rahm and Staff*

FYI

The three best things about attending CCNY are "the city (of course), the sciences, and the diversity of people."

The three worst things about attending CCNY are "the sense of security (the lack thereof), the outrageous living expenses, and the fact that everyone commutes."

The three things that every student should do before graduating from CCNY are "see a Yankees game, play basketball on a mid-Saturday morning, and try the local diners."

One thing I'd like to have known before coming here is "that the lack of dorms takes away from that 'college' feeling."

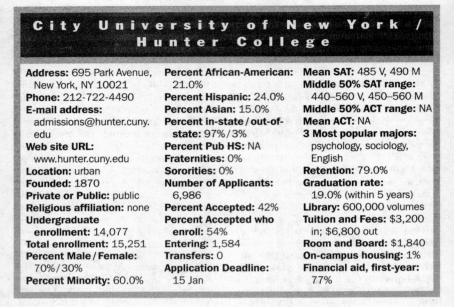

City University of New York / Hunter College

Address: 695 Park Avenue, New York, NY 10021
Phone: 212-722-4490
E-mail address: admissions@hunter.cuny.edu
Web site URL: www.hunter.cuny.edu
Location: urban
Founded: 1870
Private or Public: public
Religious affiliation: none
Undergraduate enrollment: 14,077
Total enrollment: 15,251
Percent Male / Female: 70% / 30%
Percent Minority: 60.0%

Percent African-American: 21.0%
Percent Hispanic: 24.0%
Percent Asian: 15.0%
Percent in-state / out-of-state: 97% / 3%
Percent Pub HS: NA
Fraternities: 0%
Sororities: 0%
Number of Applicants: 6,986
Percent Accepted: 42%
Percent Accepted who enroll: 54%
Entering: 1,584
Transfers: 0
Application Deadline: 15 Jan

Mean SAT: 485 V, 490 M
Middle 50% SAT range: 440–560 V, 450–560 M
Middle 50% ACT range: NA
Mean ACT: NA
3 Most popular majors: psychology, sociology, English
Retention: 79.0%
Graduation rate: 19.0% (within 5 years)
Library: 600,000 volumes
Tuition and Fees: $3,200 in; $6,800 out
Room and Board: $1,840
On-campus housing: 1%
Financial aid, first-year: 77%

Located in the heart of a great cultural center, Hunter College in New York City has an extremely diverse undergraduate community, dedicated professors at the top of their fields, and solid educational opportunities.

Academic Opportunities

Students cite nursing, education, and the performing arts as the best departments at Hunter, with English and communications also garnering high praise. The honors program offers interdisciplinary courses to qualified students, which allows them to devote less attention to core requirements and more to their majors. Hunter also offers study-abroad programs in Europe, Africa, Asia, South America, and the Caribbean, with Europe the most popular destination.

The college's distribution requirements include one lab science, several courses in the humanities, music, sociology, or economics, and four semesters of a language. Few students complain about these requirements. Classes can be as large as 300 in the sciences and introductory lectures and as small as ten in the upper-division and honors classes. Evening sessions are popular at Hunter, especially among the many students holding day jobs.

Students say professors are supportive and "treat us as human beings." At least 50 percent of the staff are adjunct professors, whom students say are outstanding. Students don't have as much access to these professors, however, because adjuncts have neither on-campus phone numbers nor offices. For the most part, students say they must make appointments to see their professors. "The professors are there but students have to make the effort to get help," claimed one undergraduate. TAs do not lead sections or teach classes.

Commuter School

Hunter's main academic buildings are uptown, on East 68th Street, but the only dorm is on 25th Street. A shuttle bus runs from the dorm to the campus every hour, and public transportation is abundant. First- and second-year students generally remain at the school for the whole day. Between classes, they hang out or study in the cafeterias, hallways, lounges, or club offices. Although Hunter is primarily a commuter school, students say it's easier to meet classmates and become involved in campus life if they live in the dorm, which houses about 400 people. Most of the dorm residents are in the nursing, physical therapy, athletics, or honors programs. With no meal plan, students are forced either to dine in the neighborhood's numerous eateries or, as most prefer, prepare food for themselves in the kitchens located on every dorm floor. Each dorm room has the added convenience of a sink. Many undergrads go to Hunter's library to study. As one sophomore put it, the quiet is "like a cemetery." Commuter students generally opt to study at home.

New York City provides students with countless options for entertainment including, but hardly limited to, world-famous theaters, restaurants, and museums. Campus parties are rare, and students say drinking is rare as well. Sororities and fraternities play a minor role in campus life, occupying no houses and performing charity work as their main activity. Cultural clubs organize some social events such as dances and rallies. RAs on each floor of the dorm sponsor activities each month, ranging from a papier-mâché night to a game night.

Politically Active

The fact that most Hunter students hail from New York, New Jersey, or Connecticut does not at all imply a homogeneous student body. According to one student, "It's incredible; everyone's completely different, yet they live together in harmony." Another student called Hunter a "mini-NYC." Many students are politically active, especially concerning issues of racism, feminism, abortion rights, the environment, gay and lesbian rights, and AIDS. The student branch of New York Public Interest Resource Group (PIRG) gets students involved in both environmental and campus issues. The active student senate represents academic departments, school interests, and students at large. One student said anyone can join the senate, although not everyone gets to vote. The teachers who are involved are said to be "top-notch."

Although sports are not a big priority on campus, both basketball games and wrestling matches are well attended. Intramurals such as volleyball are also quite popular. Hunter's athletic facilities receive positive reviews despite the complaint that, as one student put it, "they're hidden in the basement." Students read the *Hunter Envoy*, a biweekly newspaper, as well as other student publications. Ethnic organizations (such as the Asian-American, Caribbean, Greek, Puerto Rican, and African-American clubs) are very popular, as are dance groups, choir, jazz band, and theater clubs. The student-run Shakespeare Society also produces a full play and a collection of scenes once a semester. No classes are held during Dean's Hours every Tuesday from 2 to 3 P.M. and every Wednesday from 1 to 3 P.M. so that student clubs and organizations can hold meetings.

The Hunter campus is truly part of the city. According to one student, "At times it's good because you're involved with the real world, but you also miss out on the things a private university in the city can offer, like a campus and unity." One undergraduate said there's "not really a campus, just some buildings together, and the dorm is by itself." Many students work full-time and consider school a "part-time thing." The city provides easy access to work and job openings.

> **"It's incredible; everyone's completely different, yet they live together in harmony."**

"The school is involved with the community, and the community is involved with the school," one student said. The area around Hunter is a commercial district, so it's busy, and students assert that they "blend in." The school has taken measures to ensure student security, including emergency phones and guards that one undergrad reported "roam around a lot." Each dorm resident is generally allowed no more than two guests at a time.

According to one student, "The teachers are at the top of their fields and really want to teach, but they're not teaching under the best conditions." Students are managing all the same, however. As one undergraduate pointed out, "It is a city school, and the tuition is still low."

One student warned incoming freshmen to "make sure you're on top of your education and getting what you want. No one's going to help you unless you ask for help." Another student suggested that if you're looking for a structured program and lots of guidance, Hunter might not be the best choice. But Hunter students seem satisfied. "We get a much richer experience because of the huge diversity in terms of nationality and also in terms of age," one said. "This diversity gives a unique flavor to Hunter College." In fact, many undergrads see Hunter as a working model of the real world. —*Staff*

FYI

The three best things about attending Hunter are "the campus, the location, and again, the location. How can anyone top the Upper East Side?"

The three worst things about attending Hunter are "the high cost of living, the lack of school unity, and the lack of academic structure."

The three things that every student should do before graduating from Hunter are "see a student production, get out of the city at least once, and do part-time work as a street vendor or a cabbie."

One thing I'd like to have known before coming here is "that cafes are the best place to study."

City University of New York / Queens College

Address: 65-30 Kissena Blvd., Kiely 217, Flushing, NY 11367
Phone: 718-997-5608
E-mail address: NA
Web site URL: www.qc.edu/admissons
Location: urban
Founded: 1937
Private or Public: public
Religious affiliation: none
Undergraduate enrollment: 11,566
Total enrollment: 15,686
Percent Male/Female: 37%/63%
Percent Minority: 42.1%

Percent African-American: 10.0%
Percent Hispanic: 16.0%
Percent Asian: 16.0%
Percent in-state/out-of-state: 98%/2%
Percent Pub HS: 67%
Fraternities: 1%
Sororities: 1%
Number of Applicants: 4,632
Percent Accepted: 58%
Percent Accepted who enroll: 39%
Entering: 1,037
Transfers: 1,209
Application Deadline: rolling

Mean SAT: 544 V, 555 M
Middle 50% SAT range: 450–560 V, 470–580 M
Middle 50% ACT range: NA
Mean ACT: NA
3 Most popular majors: accounting, sociology, psychology
Retention: 82.0%
Graduation rate: 38.0%
Library: 489,096 volumes
Tuition and Fees: $3,393 in; $6,993 out
Room and Board: NA
On-campus housing: 0%
Financial aid, first-year: 50%

Take 76 acres of gently rolling grassy hills, plop down a handful of student-filled buildings and some fountains, roll in the spired skyline of the largest and busiest city in America, and you get Queens College. Students claim that Queens College has the finest professors and the nicest campus of any CUNY school. Just as the college uniquely accommodates itself to both city and nature lovers, it stretches to fit a wide range of academic needs, from honors seminars with renowned professors to catch-up work in algebra.

Academic Options

All Queens College undergrads must fulfill the Liberal Arts and Science Area Requirements (LASAR), which divide the college curriculum into seven areas. Students take introductory courses in each area, many of which are large lecture classes. Although the lectures generally do not break down into smaller discussion sections as they do at some other colleges, students agree that the professors are very accessible. "At the first class, one famous professor gave us his home phone number," reported one junior.

Outside of introductory courses, students can expect an average class size of 20 to 40 people. ("That's not to say all 40 show up," one junior said.) Some students complain that these small courses fill up too easily. According to one, "I knew some guys who had to take an extra year to graduate because they couldn't get what they needed for their majors." Music students enter the renowned Aaron Copland School of Music, which features a rotating staff of prominent modern composers.

Special academic programs at Queens include an honors sequence in the Western tradition comprising 16 courses centered on a selection of "Great Books," an honors sequence in math and the sciences, and honors programs in business and journalism. Students consider the latter two an especially good value, with extra-small classes, full scholarships, summer internships in New York (which help establish impressive résumés and important connections), and, in the business program, a class with the president of Queens College. One business honors student said, "The most I've ever had in a class is 20 people, and honors students can register before the rush, so I always get my courses."

Queens reaches out to everyone, however, not just the academic elite. Its SEEK program (Search for Education, Elevation, and Knowledge) is designed for students who might have missed a few essential high school courses or who aren't ready for a standard college curriculum. Available only to New Yorkers, SEEK provides personal academic counselors who help students schedule the necessary college prep classes that will enable them to begin the LASAR sequence and eventually earn a bachelor's degree. According to one student, "If it weren't for SEEK, I wouldn't be in college." Other flexible academic features at Queens include evening classes and Fresh Start, a bachelor's program for anyone who's been out of school for more than three years.

Campus Life, Commuter School

Since Queens College is a commuter school (there are no dorms; most students live with their parents), many students leave the campus after classes. To encourage undergrads to spend a little extra time on campus, however, the administration schedules "free hours" in midday, during which no classes are held. During this time, one student said, "Everyone goes to the cafeteria or the student union," which features a pizza parlor, Dunkin' Donuts, TCBY, Taco Bell Express, and a kosher kitchen. "There are a lot of cliques in the student union," one student said. "You can pretty much map out who's going to sit where." But the union also is the headquarters for more than 175 extracurricular clubs and organizations, along with Thursday night club-hosted parties, frequent guest lectures, a wide-screen TV, and a formidable collection of pool tables. Students agree that taking part in the social life at Queens requires some initiative; despite the large number of clubs, many events are poorly advertised.

> **"Queens reaches out to everyone."**

Many Queens College students laugh at the mention of athletics. The campus has a gym and playing fields; in fact, new facilities recently were built for softball, soccer, and lacrosse. Only the fans are missing. As one team member said, "If we get 20 people to come see a game, that's a great turnout." Those who use the gym say it's fine, but a little old. The biggest problem, one student reported, is that there's "no ventilation in the gym. In the hot weather, I almost passed out a few times."

Recently, articles in the *QC Quad*, the weekly campus paper, reported on the university's proposed plans to cut some of Queens's smaller departments and consolidate them with similar programs at other CUNY schools. Although students taking classes in one of these departments are concerned that they might have to commute as far as the Bronx or Staten Island, Queens is not the only school in the CUNY system that has had budget problems in recent years.

Queens offers an inexpensive, flexible education with a wealth of impressive professors, many of whom earned their degrees from the most prestigious schools in the country. Sure, traditional "school spirit" is a foreign concept at this unique school, but if you're looking for a solid education, no matter what your background, grab a subway token and take a look at Queens.—*Susanna Chu and Staff*

FYI

The three best things about attending Queens College are "the great professors, the terrific backdrop, and the laid-back atmosphere."

The three worst things about attending Queens College are "everyone commutes, so there's no sense of community, and it's harder to meet people."

The three things that every student should do before graduating from Queens College are "go bar hopping in the city, go to a Broadway play, go to a few campus parties."

One thing I'd like to have known before coming here is "how rural the place seems. Definitely not a city life."

Clarkson University

Address: Holcroft House, Potsdam, NY 13699-5605
Phone: 800-527-6577
E-mail address: admissions@clarkson.edu
Web site URL: www.clarkson.edu
Location: NA
Founded: 1896
Private or Public: private
Religious affiliation: none
Undergraduate enrollment: 2,581
Total enrollment: 2,902
Percent Male/Female: 73%/27%
Percent Minority: 7.0%

Percent African-American: 3.0%
Percent Hispanic: 1.0%
Percent Asian: 2.0%
Percent in-state/out-of-state: 60%/40%
Percent Pub HS: 91%
Fraternities: 15%
Sororities: 17%
Number of Applicants: 2,568
Percent Accepted: 83%
Percent Accepted who enroll: 33%
Entering: 707
Transfers: 143
Application Deadline: 15 Mar

Mean SAT: 575 V, 626 M
Middle 50% SAT range: 530–630 V, 570–660 M
Middle 50% ACT range: NA
Mean ACT: NA
3 Most popular majors: civ. eng., mech. eng., interdisplinary eng. & mgmt.
Retention: 84.5%
Graduation rate: 71.4%
Library: 237,251 volumes
Tuition and Fees: $20,289 in; NA out
Room and Board: $7,484
On-campus housing: 98%
Financial aid, first-year: 96%

Constant ice storms and snow fail to dampen the enthusiasm of Clarkson students in the classroom, laboratory, or their myriad other activities. Dedication to a rigorous training in engineering or business and management is what brought Clarkson students to this small and technologically developed campus in Potsdam, New York. Rising to the challenges of a demanding set of courses while taking time to enjoy college life to its fullest characterizes Clarkson students as they prepare for a definite set of goals in the field of engineering and business management.

The Workload

Although few students describe their workload as impossible, many clearly approach their undergraduate courses as a graduate training program. Students major in such diverse fields as finance, management and engineering, computer science, biology, aeronautical engineering, and civil and environmental engineering. While one student commented that the "engineering facilities are good, but as far as other majors, there are some complaints," the school does not deny that "engineering makes up the bulk of the student body." Clarkson accordingly is equipped for such technologically challenging areas of study, with a "very network-oriented" campus connecting computers at many different laboratories and work spaces, such as the new Center for Advanced Materials Processing (CAMP). The school has recently received high honors from the Accreditation Board for Engineering and Technology (ABET).

To prepare them for any major in the field of engineering or business, first-year students at Clarkson are required to take courses in inorganic chemistry, physics, calculus, and two liberal studies classes known as Great Ideas in Western Civilization. During their remaining three years, all students are required to take two more liberal studies courses in addition to mathematics electives such as statistics, linear algebra, and microeconomics. Even with these requirements, students are able to take some free electives.

Clarkson professors participate in research for government, military, and civil departments such as NASA, conduct experiments in zero gravity welding for the new international space station, and explore high-temperature deposits, aircraft structures, and even treatments for breast cancer. Students praise profs such as Jim Peploski in chemistry, Amy Zander in civil engineering, and M. Sathyamoorthy in aeronautical engineering for their teaching as well as for being "very easygoing and fun in general." Liberal studies professor Wes Craven even developed the idea for the *Nightmare on Elm Street* movies based on Elm Street in Potsdam. One senior stated, "I can't think of any professors that I didn't like" and regretted not getting to know all of his professors. While first-year classes in areas such as chemistry can have up to 200 students, after freshman year the classes get "pretty small, but still big enough to get to know people," one student said. With most classes enrolling around 30 students, the school creates "a small, intimate environment . . . with a lot to offer." Departments also host faculty-student socials to enhance contact.

What They Do

But avidly reading and exploring projects in the lab is only part of the Clarkson University experience. "Everyone's involved in something . . . anything that you can think of, we have someone doing it," one student said. The Pep Band, the Clarkson Integrator, the Flying Club, Amateur Radio, the Garage Club, the Environmental Club, and community service projects such as the Red Cross, Coed National Service Organization, Pets for People, and the Food Bank comprise some of the over 160 organizations and clubs that Clarkson students participate in, despite their challenging workloads. Jobs and research projects, however, often take the lion's share of many students' spare time.

While campus social life at Clarkson once was dominated by the Greek societies, the university has recently "toned down" the Greek system after a drinking-related fatality. The administration has installed a Greek Affairs Manager. According to one senior, students want to have fun, but "on the side of caution." Clarkson is officially a dry campus with no kegs allowed and stiff penalties for drinking among students under 21. "So freshmen can no longer place empty beer bottles in their windows," one junior joked. Another agreed that Clarkson is a "conservative school . . . taking a conservative stance." While the Greek parties are still well attended, students agree that you "don't have to be Greek to get things done."

Naturally, "come Friday, everyone wants to blow off steam," and for those who do not participate in Greek societies, the school manages to keep weekends exciting as well. Guest lecturers are invited to give talks on topics ranging from UFOs to wildlife photography to alumni networking and information about the engineering industry and management. A recent year-long series of activities with the theme "Victorian Era to *Star Trek* Era" included parties, time capsules containing CD-ROMs of student e-mails, and guest lectures. The Clarkson Union Board is a student organization that puts on non-alcoholic "midnights" with music, magicians, and comedians. The school also sponsors dances and Honor Society formal events. Many students find recreation in the vast outdoor spaces of Potsdam like hiking and skiing. "If you keep your eyes open, opportunities present themselves," one student said.

As for dating, the "ratio favors the women, but Potsdam State is not far away," one sophomore commented. Students agree that the characteristic social environment at Clarkson on the weekend is large groups of students hanging out together to watch a movie or go downtown. Potsdam has quite a few bars and coffeehouses that host jazz and blues groups. "There's more than enough to do here," one junior reported. Potsdam is close to Adirondack Park, Lake Placid, Lake Ottawa, and Montreal, a popular destination for students in search of a larger party scene. But time for excursions out of the Potsdam area is limited, and most students stay close to campus.

Food at Clarkson receives the most critical reviews. "The tacos seem to give some GI trouble. They taste good, but it's a time bomb," one senior reported. The campus has numerous dining centers. Some are cafeteria style, while others have more of a fast-food setting, such as the new Cheel Center. Potsdam has local pizza restaurants, fast food, a family restaurant, and a '50s-style diner where "it's really fun to watch them cook on the grill," said one student customer.

The school administration is reluctant, some students reported, to allow undergrads to move off campus except for economic reasons or residence in a Greek house. Most dorms are coed, except for freshman dorms. All dorms have cable TV and each room has a computer network connection. Also available are university-run apartments where students can live on campus without being on the meal plan. The campus used to be separated into Hill and Downtown halves, but current construction is aimed at consolidating the campus. From dorms, classes are generally a five- to ten-minute walk, although "some lazy bums actually drive to class! But there is no reason," said one junior. A shuttle bus connects the Clarkson campus, downtown Potsdam, and Potsdam State University. The administration recently installed blue-light security phones, and students generally walk in groups, although there have not been many crime-related incidents. "It's probably the safest place in

the world, unless the squirrels get rabies," said one city-bred student.

Sports at Clarkson centers on hockey, Clarkson's only Division I sport. "If you're not a hockey fan when you start, you are when you leave," assured one enthusiastic senior. Engaged in a prolonged rivalry with nearby St. Lawrence, the hockey team is "almost mythical on campus," according to students. Extensive recruiting has created "a little animosity" between the hockey team and the rest of the student body in terms of privileges, one student said, but school spirit seems to override these concerns, as the games at the Cheel Center are always well attended. We have "the best hockey and pep band in the East!" one band member exclaimed. Another student added, "The pep band has a high opinion of themselves." The baseball team has also performed well over the past few years. For non-varsity athletes, intramurals and gym classes are very popular at Clarkson.

The Student Body

Many Clarkson students have lower- to upper-middle-class backgrounds, and the school gives a great deal of financial aid. "I didn't expect as much as I got," said one junior. Undergrads say the student body is racially homogeneous and generally "moderate Republican." One senior found it "surprising . . . that [there] are no major rifts. Everybody gets along pretty well."

> **"The best hockey and pep band in the East!"**

Clarkson students agree that "everyone is here because they like it." The intense academic focus leads those who dislike the school or the academic orientation to leave early in their college career. "The reputation is very good, and you can get a lot out of this place if you want to . . . and we're all very proud of Clarkson," said one student. Devotion to their selected tracks of study and loyalty to their school are the hallmarks of this spirited student body as its members prepare for the real world and enjoy their college years to the fullest.—*Eric Weiss and Staff*

YI

▶he three best things about attending Clarkson are "the friends, the challenging academics, and Potsdam."

▶he three worst things about attending Clarkson are "how the teachers are difficult to understand, the weather, and Potsdam."

▶he three things every student should do before graduating from Clarkson are "go to Duffs, attend a hockey game, and pull a prank."

▶ne thing I wish I had known before coming here is "how difficult the Chemical Engineering program was."

Colgate University

Address: 13 Oak Drive, Hamilton, NY 13346
Phone: 315-228-7401
E-mail address: admissions@mail.colgate.edu
Web site URL: http://www.colgate.edu
Location: rural
Founded: 1819
Private or Public: private
Religious affiliation: none
Undergraduate enrollment: 2,868
Total enrollment: 2,876
Percent Male/Female: 48%/52%
Percent Minority: 16.0%

Percent African-American: 5.0%
Percent Hispanic: 4.0%
Percent Asian: 6.0%
Percent in-state/out-of-state: 32%/68%
Percent Pub HS: 71%
Fraternities: 33%
Sororities: 31%
Number of Applicants: 5,590
Percent Accepted: 42%
Percent Accepted who enroll: 32%
Entering: 750
Transfers: 9
Application Deadline: 15 Jan

Mean SAT: 644 V, 651 M
Middle 50% SAT range: 600–690 V, 610–700 M
Middle 50% ACT range: 28–32
Mean ACT: 29
3 Most popular majors: economics, English, history
Retention: 97%
Graduation rate: 89%
Library: 615,940 volumes
Tuition and Fees: $24,750 in; NA out
Room and Board: $6,330
On-campus housing: 100%
Financial aid, first-year: 41%

Looking for a small school with an incredible amount of choices? Colgate is probably the only school that can claim 13 as its lucky number. Thirteen Baptist men with 13 prayers and $13 founded Colgate in 1819. Located in Hamilton, New York, with close to 3,000 undergraduates, Colgate has grown from humble beginnings into a small liberal arts institution with a big reputation.

"You Have to Take the Swim Test"

With 49 concentration (major) choices, Colgate offers a very diverse academic program. All freshmen choose a seminar class for which they receive credit. The topics run the gamut from biology to global change to philosophy. Each class has roughly 20 students and the seminar professor becomes the student's faculty advisor until the spring of sophomore

year, at which point each student chooses his or her major. Freshmen are enthusiastic about the seminar program because it allows them to interact with their advisee group regularly. They also have the opportunity to create a good relationship with their advisor in and out of the classroom.

Colgate requires 32 credits to graduate. Students must take two classes in each of three distribution areas: social sciences, natural sciences, and humanities. In addition, there is a four-credit physical education requirement as well as a mandatory swim test. One student explained, "You have to take the swim test, or else they make you set up all the chairs for graduation. That's a lot of chairs."

Colgate also offers a multitude of study abroad programs, as well as unique short-term abroad opportunities. These trips apply classroom concepts in more realistic settings. If you study Japanese, you can take advantage of the one-month program in Japan called Living in the Religious Heritage of Japan; or if you are interested in the classics, Colgate offers the Material Culture of Rome and Pompeii trips for beginning classics students. There are also several other similar trips, and Colgate students find them highly accessible and enjoyable.

All in all, the students find the workload "difficult, but manageable" and average three hours of work a night. Class size is small, with most enrolling between 20 and 40 students. There is only one class with more than 100 students. Students cite economics, astrophysics, and upper-level calculus as the most painful classes at Colgate. Students reportedly "love our professors." They say that the professors are intelligent, amiable, and approachable. One student recalls an instance when her professor took her out to lunch and discussed Oprah with her. Many others have been invited over to professors' homes for dinner or study breaks.

Besides good professors, Colgate students have the chance to listen to great speakers. In the past, speakers such as Jesse Jackson, Mikhail Gorbachev, and Bill Cosby have graced the Colgate campus to speak to students.

It's Beautiful

One reason speakers might be happy to visit Colgate is that its campus is gorgeous. It is situated on top of what is fondly known as Cardiac Hill. The majority of freshmen dorms are on the top of the Hill, while the fraternities, upperclassmen housing, and restaurants are on the bottom of the Hill. Many students joke that a significant part of every student's life is negotiating the daily trek up the Hill. The picturesque landscape is full of lush greenery and the academic buildings overlook Moraine Lake. In terms of architectural beauty, students list Persson Hall and the chapel as two of the most noteworthy buildings on campus. Persson has a glass walkway that gives a magnificent view of the campus and the lake. The chapel is the most prominent building seen from the quad, and is an attractive place for students to lie out and study in the sun.

So, Where Do I Live?

There are roughly seven freshmen dorms each year. Most dorms are coed but single sex by floor with two or three people per room. One dorm, Andrews, has suites with common rooms for three to four people. The rooms come with bunk beds, dressers, desks, and either a closet or a wardrobe. East, another dorm, is substance-free, while West is considered the party dorm.

Students are sent roommate preference forms before their freshman year, and for the most part, students are happy with their first-year rooms and roommate assignments. There is also a Residential Advisor program for freshmen which pairs groups of students with an upperclassman who watches over them during their freshman year. The function of an RA is to help students move in, deal with roommates, and enforce no-alcohol-in-room policies. Reportedly, RAs are strict with regulations, but "if you leave your door closed they'll leave you alone."

After freshman year there are multiple housing options. There are special-interest houses such as the Asian Interest House, the Harlem Renaissance Center, and the Ecology House as well as dorms. Sophomores tend to stay in the dorms, while juniors often move into on-campus Colgate apartments, and seniors enter a lottery to live off campus.

"Tasty, but Dangerous"

The food at Colgate is not four-star quality, but it serves its purpose. Students advise staying away from most meat and shepherd's pie. One student commented that the cheesesteaks and pizza are "tasty, but dangerous because they come back to haunt you later." Freshmen and sophomores use a 19-meals-per-week plan, while most juniors and seniors who live in rooms with kitchenettes tend to make their own food. Students report that the dining halls are clean and welcoming, and that students can just sit in them and talk for hours over coffee. There are plenty of seats and food is served until 6:30 P.M. The dining halls also do an adequate job of providing variety and alternate options for vegetarians and vegans. Students say that there are not many off-campus restaurants, but among the most notable is Sushi Blues, while the best coffee shop is on campus and is called the Barge.

Homogeneous

Students report that the one word to describe the student body is "homogeneous." The average Colgate student is white, preppy, athletic, wealthy, and drives a Jeep Grand Cherokee. Many people drive, although parking availability is a problem. One student commented on the general economic status of the student body by describing the parking lot as "looking like a showroom." The wardrobe of choice also resembles a showroom and showcases primarily J. Crew, Banana Republic, and Abercrombie & Fitch.

In general, the students are happy with the student body. People are pretty laid back and sociable. They gather together with friends to watch *Party of Five*, *Ally McBeal*, *Friends*, *The Simpsons*, and *Dawson's Creek*. Phish, the Grateful Dead, R & B, and funk can be heard blasting out of dorm rooms. While there is not much ethnic diversity at Colgate, minorities are not complaining too heavily.

"Oh Yeah, People Can Get Play"

Colgate students go out Monday, Wednesday, Thursday, and Friday nights. Until ten years ago, there were no classes on Tuesday or Thursday, so students were able to go out and party on Monday and Wednesday nights. Though there are now classes on Tuesday and Thursday, they tend to be low-key so the tradition of weekday partying is kept alive, if in slightly modified form.

The social scene at Colgate revolves around the Greek system and bars. Since the bars tend to stringently check IDs, most freshmen spend their nights at fraternity parties. Due to the administration's newer and stricter policies on alcohol, all fraternity parties must be catered by an outside service. As a result, frats have to pay a substantial amount of money to throw a party, and consequently, the door fees for such parties have risen to around $5. Upperclassmen often spend their evenings in one of the three popular bars down the hill: the Jug, Risky Business, and the Hour Glass.

> **The social scene at Colgate revolves around the Greek system and bars.**

Although the Greek system has a large role socially at Colgate, there is no real pressure for everyone to join. Non-Greeks do not tend to feel left out, because the frat parties are open to all students. Students rush fraternities and sororities in their sophomore year. It is not hard to rush, and it does not involve hazing. The most popular frat is Sigma Chi and the most popular sorority is Kappa. Frats also throw big, annual theme parties such as Beta Beach and Derby Days. Beta Beach is a pool party in the middle of winter, and Derby Days is a week-long series of athletic and drinking events.

There is not much of a dating scene at Colgate; instead, there is a much wider occurrence of random hookups. Students say that the student body "is hot, and you can get a lot of play."

Spare Time

Colgate has many extracurricular organizations that students join in their spare time. Some of the most respected are Outdoor Ed, Student Government, the Link Program, and Sidekick. Outdoor Ed sponsors adventure trips in the area, the Link program supplies juniors and seniors work with a seminar professor to help advise groups of freshmen, and Sidekick pairs Colgate students with disadvantaged elementary school children. There is also a popular improvisational comedy group called Charred Goosebeaks and a radio show called "Sunday Night Procrastination." Few students work actual jobs.

Da Jocks

The most popular teams at Colgate are football, hockey, and basketball. The football team, the Red Raiders, won the Patriot League 2 years ago. Most students attend the football games and many alumni return for them as well. There is a strong sense of school spirit, and most students will even travel to away games in order to support their teams. The gym facilities are also excellent, and many students take advantage of the weight room and tracks. The Greek system is involved in organizing intramural games, and students are enthusiastic about these as well.

Colgate is a serious academic institution with a relaxed, party atmosphere. Students who want a gorgeous campus set in the cozy hills of Hamilton, New York, and who are up for the academic challenge, should definitely put Colgate at the top of their list.—*Dana Peck and Staff*

FYI
The three best things about attending Colgate are "the parties, the people, and the amazing faculty."
The three worst things about attending Colgate are "the 'sameness,' the amount of work, and the class size (professors always know when you're not there)."
The three things that every student should do before graduating from Colgate are "hear a famous speaker, study abroad, and get a good fake ID."
One thing I'd like to have known before coming here is "that there's a huge hill separating campus and where everyone hangs out!"

C o l u m b i a　U n i v e r s i t y

Address: 212 Hamilton Hall, 1130 Amsterdam Avenue, MC 2807, New York, NY 10027
Phone: 212-854-2522
E-mail address: ugrad-admiss@columbia.edu
Web site URL: www.columbia.edu
Location: urban
Founded: 1754
Private or Public: private
Religious affiliation: none
Undergraduate enrollment: 3,948
Total enrollment: 21,857
Percent Male/Female: 49%/51%

Percent Minority: 33.2%
Percent African-American: 9.6%
Percent Hispanic: 7.7%
Percent Asian: 15.7%
Percent in-state/out-of-state: NA
Percent Pub HS: NA
Fraternities: 8%
Sororities: 8%
Number of Applicants: 13,012
Percent Accepted: 14%
Percent Accepted who enroll: 56%
Entering: 955
Transfers: NA
Application Deadline: 1 Jan

Mean SAT: 663 V, 671.6 M
Middle 50% SAT range: 650–750 V, 640–740 M
Middle 50% ACT range: NA
Mean ACT: NA
3 Most popular majors: English, political science, history
Retention: 93.0%
Graduation rate: 88.0%
Library: 2,000,000 volumes
Tuition and Fees: $24,150 in; $24,150 out
Room and Board: $7,732
On-campus housing: 99%
Financial aid, first-year: NA

A re you bored by the idea of spending the next four years in Small Town, USA, where your college is the entire town? Would you like to live in a city where art and theater are at your fingertips and the nightlife rages into the morning hours? Check out New York's Columbia University where students have the advantages of both an Ivy League education and life in the big city.

One of the first things prospective students learn about Columbia is the school's strict core curriculum requirement, which many seem to feel is both a blessing and a curse. All students must take the yearlong Literature Humanities, and Contemporary Civilization classes, as well as Arts Humanities, Music Humanities, and Logic & Rhetoric, which are each semester-long courses. Everyone must also take at least two classes in a related subject area, which fulfill the Major Cultures requirement (for example: Latin American Civilizations and History of Harlem, or Asian Texts and Japanese Film), three classes for the science requirement (two of which must be in sequence), and pass the foreign language requirement.

Although students are not unanimous in their like or dislike of the requirements, the core is certainly something that everyone complains about. "At first I was really annoyed [by the core] because I wasn't particularly interested in some of the classes," said one student. "It sounds lame, but I really am becoming more well-rounded because of it." One concern about the core curriculum is that there are so many sections of each course being taught each semester, it is difficult to establish uniform grading policies and to regulate the quality of the teachers. Graduate students, who generally receive mixed reviews, also teach some core classes.

However, students are enthusiastic about their professors, who are reportedly very accessible. One student was disappointed with a TA for Arts Humanities who had no appreciation for the material, but said that her music professor made up for it. "He is a world-renowned musician, had written books and composed. But after I didn't do well on the exam, he spent 45 minutes humming with me in his office to help me remember a piece."

Beyond the core curriculum, students are impressed with Columbia's wide course offerings, especially considering the small size of the undergraduate population. Political science, economics, and English rank among the most popular majors, while foreign-language majors are less common. Classes at Columbia tend to be small, except for a few introductory classes such as economics. "There is generally no problem getting into classes except freshman year, when they pre-register you for your core classes," said one student. "I couldn't fit in any of the other things I wanted to take."

Unlike many colleges, students are not actually required to declare a major, but can instead choose to concentrate in a specific area or areas. Theoretically, this allows students more freedom to take advantage of the liberal arts environment, but in many departments the concentration is only two or three classes less than a major, and therefore most people—with the exception of some pre-meds—choose to declare a major anyway. One student complained about the lack of academic guidance she has received. "There are no advisors until after you declare your major, and even then the administration isn't very friendly or helpful," she said. There's also a lot of red tape."

Life in the Big City

Although location is always a factor in the college search, prospective Columbia students should think twice as hard about the school's environs. "Life at Columbia totally revolves around being a part of New York City," said one student. New York is the "city that never sleeps," and the weekends and sometimes the weekdays represent just that. A subway stop directly on campus makes it easy for people to leave the Upper West Side and venture over to the East Side or downtown. In *Time Out New York*, the *Village Voice*, and other newspapers and magazines, Columbia undergrads find huge numbers of movie, club, gallery, theater, and restaurant listings. Favorite activities include an afternoon at the Museum of Modern Art (free admission with your student ID) or a walk/ride in Central Park. "There is so much to take advantage of," said one student, "and Columbia does a good job of getting students involved in the city." One drawback to the college's location, however, is New York City's high cost of living. This is especially true for students who frequent downtown clubs and bars. But there are cheaper regularly scheduled movies, as well as concerts and plays, on campus.

Columbia's urban setting greatly influences the college social life. "There is less campus life than at other schools because we're right in the city," explained one undergrad. Students tend to drink at bars, rather than attend campus parties, which are busted pretty easily by the NYPD. Although some head to other sections of the city to party, several bars in the Columbia vicinity cater to college students, including the West End, which attracts a sporty crowd, Cannon's, the Heights, 1020, and Soha. Some say a fake ID is useful, and many students have them because the bars are really strict. Although Columbia does have a Greek system, frat life is small and often looked down upon, while sororities are even less popular.

Drugs are popular but isolated at Columbia. "If you get into drugs, it's really easy to get them," said one student. "But the drug scene is not necessarily centered on campus. It's easy to go to parties in Brooklyn or to raves downtown," said another, "and no one knows what you do when you go off campus."

Clubbing is also popular among some Columbia students ("a night at Twilo is literally an all-night experience"). Students are quick to point out, though, that drinking and drugs are by no means the only things to do.

The Typical Columbia Student

The general consensus is that there is no typical student at Columbia. One student describes a division between those who choose Columbia for New York City—they are into the scene, hit the bars every weekend, dress well, and seem really superficial—and those students who choose Columbia for its Ivy League status, lost sheep who try really hard to be sophisticated. One undergrad described the student body as cliquey, while another said more generally: "We have a diverse student body, not just ethnically or politically but also according to interests, which is not always so good because it's hard to find one thing for the student body to focus on."

Despite this seeming lack of unity, however, students said it is not hard to meet people, especially during freshman year. "Your core classes are small with all freshmen, so you know everyone," explained one undergrad, plus the communal atmosphere in dorms and the dining hall social life really helps. Freshman year is also the only year students are required to buy a university meal plan (most upperclassmen choose not to). On-campus food options include the one dining hall, John Jay, a grocery store called J.J.'s Place, and several fast-food vendors where students can arrange to have meal plan points. Dining hall food received average marks, with weekend brunches being the favorite meals.

The majority of Columbia students live on campus all four years (housing is guaranteed). "The dorms range from really good to pretty bad," said one student. The newest dorm is East Campus: twenty stories high with views of the East and West Rivers, suites for five students configured like three-bedroom apartments with a common room, bathroom, and kitchen (and fridge). This is quite a contrast to some of Columbia's older dorms, "But the worst dorms are no worse than what I've seen at other colleges," said one student. Columbia has an RA system on each floor of its dorms, but RAs are reported to be not too strict, as long as students do not abuse their privileges. The administration has restrictions on alcohol, drugs, cooking equipment, and incense, as well as scheduled quiet time in the dorms, but students say that nothing is too strictly enforced.

"There are so many things to worry about security-wise at Columbia that the students have a lot of freedom in other areas," explained one undergrad. Students said that being safe at Columbia is all about using common sense and being careful in the city, especially in the Morningside Heights area where the campus is located, running approximately from 110th to 120th Street. "Columbia is in the middle of the city, but it's closed off so there is a feeling of a campus," explained one student. The only major complaint about the physical plan was the current shortage of places for students to meet. The student center was recently torn down to make way for construction of a new center, the Alfred Lerner Hall, due for completion in the fall of 2000. It will include a more upscale restaurant, a black box theater, offices for campus organizations, study space, computer labs, a print shop, an auditorium, and a game room.

Beyond Academics

Extracurricular activity is a big part of life at Columbia. "Few people just go to school," said one undergrad. "If you have an interest in something, chances are you can find a group that you'll fit into." Visible groups on campus include a number of religious and cultural groups. Political activists are also prominent on campus with poster campaigns about issues outside Columbia, especially around election time. "You can't be on College Walk without getting accosted by the ISO [Independent Socialists Organization, one prominent political group]," joked one undergrad. Columbia's active gay and lesbian community has a big presence on campus as well. "For a campus that is fairly conservative, we have a tight-knit gay community with tons of activity," said one undergrad. "If you're comfortable with yourself, then it's totally comfortable to be out at Columbia. People don't get away with making homophobic remarks—it just doesn't fly."

Opportunities for creative students include theater and music groups, as well as literary magazines and Columbia's daily newspaper, the *Spectator*. Student editors can apply for a position as a Writing Fellow and get paid and receive credit for helping other students with their papers. "Community service is also popular because we live in a neighborhood where there are a lot of opportunities to help," explained one student. Community Impact organizes programs in which students volunteer to tutor in Harlem schools, to care for children of homeless people so they can look for jobs, or to clean parks in nearby neighborhoods. Community Outreach day is an annual event when students devote a Saturday to cleaning the city; last year over 1,000 members of the Columbia community participated.

Columbia is not known for athletics, although the student body is fairly active, both in club sports and on an individual level. Popular club sports include those for tae kwon do, Ultimate Frisbee, rugby, and archery. The fencing and swimming teams stand out as two of the most consistently successful teams, although football is the only team people actually go to watch. One student said, "There is no school spirit here, except maybe at the homecoming football game." Columbia does actively recruit, although not heavily enough, in the opinion of one athlete. However, teams do play a prominent role in the campus social life—members of a team tend to eat and hang out together a lot.

Sharing Columbia

Columbia students have the opportunity of taking classes at Barnard, which was once Columbia's sister school and still remains all-female. Students from both schools interact frequently, often living and taking classes together. Some students complained that the relationship between the colleges makes for weird tension between females at Columbia and Barnard. "Some girls at Columbia think they're superior, and some girls at Barnard antagonize Columbia students," said one undergrad. Said another student, "Classes at Barnard don't have to be all-female, but many are. I've heard that the atmosphere in some classes is sexist against men . . it's weird because there's no separate school for men, just for women."

> **"Life at Columbia totally revolves around being a part of New York City."**

Another unique characteristic of life on campus is the presence of a large number of graduate students. "There are a lot of older people around," said one student. "And there's not much interaction between grad students and undergrads outside of the classroom. There's almost some tension about it because a lot of the university is geared to the grad schools."

"I think Columbia would be ideal for grad school, when you know better what you want when you have a life established," said one undergrad. "It's rough being an undergraduate here, especially freshman year, because it's not an outright friendly environment." "[Columbia] is a very sophisticated school. You have to be driven, have a goal, and be ready to pursue your own path."—*Liz Kukura and Staff*

FYI
The three best things about attending Columbia are "the sex ratio—with Barnard, and then Columbia being half female, this is a great place to be a single guy; NEW YORK CITY; and the core curriculum."
The three worst things about attending Columbia are "the lack of on-campus social life (though this is improving), the lack of trees, and the fact that you need 124 points (5.5 classes per semester) to graduate."

The three things every student should do before graduating from Columbia are "hook up in the library stacks, go to the roof of Butler Library at night . . you can see all the way down to the World Trade Center, and do the 'Trinity' [basically, making your way from Cannon's Pub, to the West End, to the Amsterdam Cafe, local bars, all in one night]."
One thing I wish I knew before coming here is "that Columbians are rather independent people."

Cooper Union for the Advancement of Science and Art

Address: 30 Cooper Sq., New York, NY 10003
Phone: 212-353-4120
E-mail address: admissions@cooper.edu
Web site URL: www.cooper.edu
Location: urban
Founded: 1859
Private or Public: private
Religious affiliation: none
Undergraduate enrollment: 870
Total enrollment: 907
Percent Male/Female: 65%/35%
Percent Minority: 42.0%
Percent African-American: 6.0%

Percent Hispanic: 8.0%
Percent Asian: 27.0%
Percent in-state/out-of-state: 54%/46%
Percent Pub HS: 70%
Fraternities: 20%
Sororities: 10%
Number of Applicants: 2,216
Percent Accepted: 13%
Percent Accepted who enroll: 69%
Entering: 200
Transfers: 33
Application Deadline: arch-Jan 1, art-Jan 10, eng-Feb 1
Mean SAT: 690 V, 740 M

Middle 50% SAT range: 650–740 V, 750–780 M
Middle 50% ACT range: NA
Mean ACT: NA
3 Most popular majors: fine art, electrical engineering, mechanical engineering
Retention: 91.0%
Graduation rate: 78.0%
Library: 97,000 volumes
Tuition and Fees: NA in; NA out
Room and Board: $0
On-campus housing: 22%
Financial aid, first-year: 100%

Set in the fast-paced, heart-pounding Big Apple, Cooper Union (CU or Cooper) is a place where innovation and diligence are the staples of life. Graced with the legacy of historical figures such as Abraham Lincoln and Thomas Edison, Cooper is no stranger to fame or ingenuity. Its concentrated emphasis on the undergraduate experience in the areas of engineering, art, and architecture is bolstered by a rare financial advantage: full-tuition scholarship for all students.

Serious Stuff

"Academics is the number one thing at Cooper," says one senior who characterizes his peers as energetic, inquisitive intellectuals who believe that there is always more than one solution to any question. With academic requirements ranging from calculus, physics, and chemistry to engineering and the humanities, the challenging and highly structured curriculum of Cooper Union reflects a commitment to build students' analytical and problem-solving skills. Class size typically ranges from 6 to 23, and this close-knit environment demands a considerable amount of dedication, enthusiasm, and participation from the student body. One freshman said, "With almost no lecture classes, this is the place where they really work your noodle." With few "free nap" classes, students become fully absorbed, often hands-on, in original projects that ultimately yield significant rewards in broadening their thinking about the connection between real-world situations and theoretical learning.

The grading system is designed in such a way that those who devote the time and effort will get grades that "honestly reflect their perseverance through the thinking hurdles along the way." Several upperclassmen dismiss the notion that there are professors that give no As. There seems to be a consensus at CU that "the instructors are fully aware of how much time people need to spend in finding 'a different angle' of thinking." While Cooper is not a liberal arts college by any measure, students of all concentrations (majors) are required to take four years of humanities classes such as introductory courses to the plays of Shakespeare or studies in literature. This shift from solely science-centered programs to a more diverse broad-based education was the result of student action in 1997. Many undergraduates felt that their only contacts were the 20 or 30 other people in their major and that they lacked the kind of learning alternatives that other college students enjoyed. The administration's quick response in improving this situation clearly demonstrates its desire to provide Cooper students with a more integrated undergraduate experience.

Moreover, CU is consciously making an effort to highlight the importance of its bond with the surrounding community by taking full advantage of the cultural events available in New York.

Who's Teaching?

Professors, who are passionate about their areas of research, are not only approachable, but actively seek out means to stimulate their students and increase the pulse of academic life. Some leading researchers in their respective fields include Emanuel Kondopirakis (mathematics), Fred Siegel (humanities expert on American cities), John Bove (organic chemistry), Toby Cumberbatch (electronics), Irv Brazinsky (thermodynamics). "Cooper has a very interactive environment between students and professors, who are more like your contemporaries." "You really learn about what it's like to use the information they teach you in the classroom and apply it in life," says one junior. Another sophomore said, "I was really surprised when I found out last year that there is only one section offered per subject. This way, we have the opportunity to regularly communicate with even the most well-known professors. This just

doesn't happen at other technology-oriented schools where TAs lead the majority of classes." A number of upperclassmen agree that they have had a number of awe-inspiring discussions in classrooms and with professors in which all their years of learning at Cooper seemed to "just come together and fit perfectly like a jigsaw puzzle. It was amazing."

Mingling with the NYC Crowd

"Freshman year is relatively less intensive and more all-nighter oriented," remarks one junior. Compared to the progressively accumulating workloads of juniors and seniors, freshmen have relatively little work since they must first fulfill graduation requirements within well-defined schedules. Although it is great to live on campus and move to the beat of the East Village's vibrant nightlife, being underage has its disadvantages in New York City, where there is strict enforcement of the underage drinking law. Nevertheless, a freshman states that "people are always able to find their niche in club parties, fraternity/sorority gatherings, semi-formals, alumni dinners, and somewhere within the large number of other entertainment options NYC has to offer."

Since many Cooper students share the belief that its student body is pretty homogeneous, socially, they tend to mingle with the general college population in the area. As a result, relationships between Cooper and non-Cooper students are quite common. Furthermore, free parties such as the Halloween and St. Patrick's Day celebrations are wonderful opportunities to introduce oneself to the intriguingly diverse and animated 18-to-23 crowd of New York. Students also say there is very little evidence of substance abuse at Cooper besides the continuous doses of coffee that pervade every other college environment during times of stress.

Any Time to Spare?

Despite its serious focus on academics, most Cooper students are encouraged to become involved in at least one extracurricular activity. People at CU become very active beyond the classroom setting mainly because they are sincerely excited about expanding the horizon of their interests. One senior said, "It is not easy to continually devote a large part of time to extracurriculars, especially as the years go on, but everyone, even those who commute, manages to find time to take part in the Club Hour," a designated time for the meeting of undergraduate groups. The variety of organizations at CU is just as abundant as at any other college, striving to provide for interests in a number of areas. Groups such as Renaissance, the Chinese Student Association (CSA), the African-American student organization (Onyx), and the Jewish student organization (Kesher) regularly sponsor trips to concerts at the Lincoln Center, movies and lecture events, and other social activities. Professional societies in such fields as mathematics, architecture, and mechanical, chemical, and electrical engineering often host lectures and other learning opportunities outside the classroom. "A large number of people also work in industry while attending class as further study enrichment," reported one junior.

Sports at Cooper Union are very much like at other colleges. CU does actively recruit athletes, as it believes that physical competitions also enhance the mental capacity of its students while infusing the campus with a greater sense of school pride. Cooper students are equally proud of their men's tennis team as they are of their intellectual abilities. Athletes are not stereotyped in any way, although it is traditional that "freshmen athletes are covered with shaving cream, sticky sugary liquid, and paint if they fall asleep after their first road trip." Despite the inconvenience of participating in sports when one is not on a team, the Hewitt gym is always available to anyone eager for a good workout, and a pool is accessible at the Asser-Levy facility within walking distance from the center of campus.

A "Citified" Experience

Cooper's campus is what students describe as "citified." There has been continual debate about how advantageous the locale of CU really is. There are those that claim that "the city detracts from campus life, since there are so many other things

someone can do in New York." Others complain that CU really "has no campus in the sense that there is little greenery." However, one advantage is that the buildings are very close to one another, making travel from class to class a breeze. Student consensus is that security has improved considerably in recent years.

> **"If you really do know what you want, and your parents have no problems with a free education, Cooper is the place to be."**

With rental rates at a premium in the city, living arrangements at Cooper are cheap according to students and comparatively sophisticated or even luxurious. One sophomore commented, "The average freshman suite is a single-sex apartment with its own kitchen and bathroom. All the buildings and suites are air-conditioned and are pretty well kept by the Cooper custodial staff." Privacy and convenience are some notable qualities of CU's dormitories, and housing is guaranteed for all those who are not within commuting distance. "People get along very well and voluntary segregation really doesn't exist in the dorms," says one senior. On the other hand, the situation in the dining halls is not as pleasant. Although there are some satisfying vegetarian options, tasty would not usually be an honest description of the provisions "except for wrapped food, which can also be easily transported." Nonetheless, Pizzeria Uno, BBQs, Kiev, Peking Duck House, and a notable combination of other cultural cuisine are available within walking distance of the school.

On the whole, CU students advocate that "there aren't that many other places that offer one of the best undergraduate experiences in engineering, art, or architecture. If you really do know what you want, and your parents have no problem with a free education, Cooper is the place to be."—*Roletta Chen and Staff*

FYI
The three best things about attending Cooper Union are "the full-tuition scholarships for all, New York City, and the amazing professors."
The three worst things about attending Cooper Union are "the intense course load, lack of campus, and being underage in New York City."
The three things every student should do before graduating from Cooper Union are "dance at Twilo, study with world-renown researchers, and explore the Village."
One thing I'd like to have known before coming here is "how much work it would be."

Cornell University

Address: 410 Thurston Avenue, Ithaca, NY 14850
Phone: 607-255-5241
E-mail address: admissions@cornell.edu
Web site URL: www.cornell.edu
Location: rural
Founded: 1865
Private or Public: private
Religious affiliation: none
Undergraduate enrollment: 13,442
Total enrollment: 18,914
Percent Male/Female: 53%/47%
Percent Minority: 30.0%

Percent African-American: 5.0%
Percent Hispanic: 7.0%
Percent Asian: 17.0%
Percent in-state/out-of-state: 45%/55%
Percent Pub HS: NA
Fraternities: 32%
Sororities: 27%
Number of Applicants: 19,860
Percent Accepted: 34%
Percent Accepted who enroll: 44%
Entering: 2,971
Transfers: NA
Application Deadline: 1 Jan
Mean SAT: 660 V, 695 M

Middle 50% SAT range: 610–710 V, 650–740 M
Middle 50% ACT range: NA
Mean ACT: NA
3 Most popular majors: social sciences, economics/business, biological/nutritional sciences
Retention: 93.0%
Graduation rate: 81.0%
Library: 5.8 million volumes
Tuition and Fees: $18,854 in; NA out
Room and Board: $7,827
On-campus housing: 96%
Financial aid, first-year: 52%

The Pumpkin appeared in the fall of 1997. Perched precariously atop McGraw Tower, it created a stir on campus and received national attention: campus intellectuals analyzed the physics of its placement and the school Web site put up a 24-hour Pumpkin-cam; even the *New York Times* wrote a story about it. The Pumpkin has long since fallen off, but it is a fitting symbol for Cornell University: a fun school whose students never lose their intellectual curiosity.

The Pressure Is Intense

At Cornell, the academic pressure is intense. "It's a competitive atmosphere—I definitely feel the crunch," admitted one student, "although the academic opportunities are tremendous." Indeed, Cornell offers something for everyone, with seven undergraduate schools that range from agriculture to hotel management. Arts and Sciences as well as the School of Engineering are generally considered the most rigorous, while the Hotel School is known to be the least rigorous. Said one student, "Hotellies have one paper to write a semester, and spend the rest of the time getting dressed up and eating cookies."

Although the school's most popular majors are psychology, biology, and government, students are required to fulfill distribution requirements that cover all ranges of the academic spectrum. Arts and Sciences students must take nine courses: five from the social, sciences/history and humanities/arts and four from the physical and biological sciences. Each student must also be proficient in a foreign language, although most fulfill this with advanced placement credit from high school. Finally, every Cornellian must pass a swim test and take at least two PE classes. Most students end up taking a PE class every semester; Cornell offers everything from figure skating to archery in its physical education department.

With over 13,000 undergraduates, Cornell's introductory classes are huge—often with hundreds of students. One student explains, "My Intro Psych class has about 1,500 people in it—but the professor is so outstanding he keeps everyone interested." Some students find the TAs frustrating. One student complained, "Half of the time I don't think my TA speaks English." Smaller classes, however, are fairly easy to find if you put forth the effort. Said one student, "Out of my four classes, three are under twenty students, and I'm only a freshman."

Most students spend their time studying in one of Cornell's fifteen libraries. As one student said, "The Law Library is so quiet, breathing is loud." The best places to study are Uris and Olin, and many students rave about the view from the Uris lounge, described as a "good place to pretend you're studying." Regardless of where they study, students report that they feel the pressure to do well. "Sometimes, I feel like I can barely keep up," admitted one student. "The work just never stops."

Wining and Dining

Living at Cornell is as varied as the academic program it offers. Soon all freshmen will live on the quieter North Campus, which is undergoing $65 million in renovations. West Campus, where most Cornellians live, is described as "crazy." Said one student, "It's like a non-stop party. There are always people running around or screaming out their windows." Despite the reputation of West Campus, most students choose to live in a Greek house or in nearby Collegetown. Those who live off campus, however, soon begin to crave Cornell's "unbelievable" food service, which is run in part by the hotel school. Each part of campus has its own cafeteria, which offers everything from pizzerias to ice cream parlors. Sunday brunch is especially popular: raves one student, "It's probably the best meal I've ever had in my life."

Greek Chic

Cornell boasts 52 fraternities and 13 sororities. Although most students claim there is "no pressure" to rush, the presence of the Greeks pervades social life. From Delta Delta Delta and AOPi's annual "Green Eggs and Kegs" homecoming party to after-hours fiestas that do not begin until the wee hours of the morning, Cornell students are never without a party. Some of these parties, however, carry on without alcohol with a new administration policy which forces parties to be catered and students to be ID'd at the door. Despite these new regulations, many students report that drinking is available if you are interested in participating. As one student admitted, "I haven't had a problem getting drunk, although they are trying to make it a bit difficult."

For those not into Greek life, other social opportunities are plentiful, although as one student complained, "The parties . . . instigate the moral abysses into which the entire community sinks." Nevertheless, those wishing to ignore Greek life can take in a movie at the Cornell cinema, or the over-21 crowd can visit one of college town's many dance clubs, such as Republica and the Palms. The biggest party of the year, Slope Day, is an annual event replete with food and live music. It's also the "one day the administration looks the other way with regard to drinking." Indeed, as one student admits, "Cornell students do drink a lot—although I know a lot who don't. It's totally your option." Drug use is reported to be about "average in comparison to other schools," with the most popular substance being marijuana.

How We Fill Our Time

Most students at Cornell take part in at least one of the school's many extracurricular activities. The most popular are the student publications, including the *Cornell Daily Sun*, which boasts such prominent alumni as E. B. White. Theater performances are also popular, as are a cappella groups and improv comedy groups. Many students also take part in community service groups, which work with run-down sections of the Ithaca community.

Sports also take up a large part of life at Cornell. On Saturdays, "everyone goes to the football game" to cheer on Big Red. When hockey season rolls around, the fans become more rabid: one student reported that camping out overnight for tickets is not uncommon. Intramural sports are also popular, drawing a large number of students out of their rooms to play flag football, hockey, and basketball. The more daring may even try Cornell's large rock-climbing wall.

Neither Snow nor Rain . . .

Students described Cornell's campus as "beautiful, but isolated," especially during the fall, where "the trees are just magnificent." The winters, however, are less popular. They are long and cold, and as one student put it, "God's revenge on someone!" The weather is often described as "Ithacating—some sort of rain, snow, or sleet, with constantly gray skies."

Despite the ambiguity, Cornellians refuse to stay in, and they report that security is "never a problem." The university runs escort services to walk students home late at night, as well as littering the campus with emergency blue-light phones. When out, Cornellians reported that they see "mostly New Yorkers," probably because of Cornell's state-funded schools (Cornell is a half public, half private institution). One student, however, complained, "More than half of my classmates must be from Long Island!"

Cornellians take pride in their school. "I came here and fell in love with the campus," said one student. Cornell is a place where "almost anyone can find a niche." Gushed one student, "The mix of work and play here is outstanding. I couldn't imagine myself anywhere else in the world." —*Matthew Fogel and Staff*

> "It's a competitive atmosphere—I definitely feel the crunch."

FYI
The three best things about attending Cornell are "the huge variety of classes to take, it's affordable for anyone who can achieve the level of excellence required, and it's in a beautiful and natural setting."
The three worst things about attending Cornell are "the winter weather, the huge ass campus is very spread apart, and New York City is a 5-hour drive away."
The three things that every student should do before graduating from Cornell are "slide down the slope on a cafeteria tray during the winter, swim in the gorges during the summer, and get drunk on Slope Day."
One thing I'd like to have known before coming here is "how far it is from everywhere else!"

Eastman School of Music

Address: 26 Gibbs Street, Rochester, NY 14604-2599
Phone: 716-274-1060
E-mail address: esmadmit@uhura.cc.rochester.edu
Web site URL: www.rochester.edu/eastman
Location: urban
Founded: 1921
Private or Public: private
Religious affiliation: none
Undergraduate enrollment: 503
Total enrollment: 825
Percent Male/Female: 45%/55%

Percent Minority: 12.0%
Percent African-American: 3.0%
Percent Hispanic: 2.0%
Percent Asian: 7.0%
Percent in-state/out-of-state: 17%/83%
Percent Pub HS: NA
Fraternities: 13%
Sororities: 11%
Number of Applicants: 899
Percent Accepted: 29%
Percent Accepted who enroll: 47%
Entering: 122
Transfers: 0
Application Deadline: 1 Jan

Mean SAT: 600 V, 650 M
Middle 50% SAT range: NA
Middle 50% ACT range: NA
Mean ACT: NA
3 Most popular majors: music performance, music education, music composition
Retention: 89.0%
Graduation rate: 72.0%
Library: 500,000 volumes
Tuition and Fees: $20,320 in; $20,320 out
Room and Board: $7,512
On-campus housing: 98%
Financial aid, first-year: 70%

D o you love music? Not just as a hobby, but as your life? Do you love music enough to practice until you get calluses from playing your instrument for so long? Enough to sing not just in the shower, but for hours at a time? If you do, you probably already know about this world-renowned music school. At the Eastman School of Music, serious musicians can immerse themselves in an environment where everyone thinks about, listens to, or plays music 24 hours a day.

Learning about Music

Eastman provides its students with a rigorous and thorough musical education as well as a solid humanities background. Most students are performance majors (the technical name is "applied music"). The next most popular majors are music education, composition, and theory. The performance major requires three years of theory, two years of music history, covering everything from Gregorian chants to contemporary music, and, of course, weekly lessons. Performance majors must be competent piano players regardless of their chosen instrument. All performance majors must take Piano 101 and 102, or test out of this requirement. East-

man also has a humanities requirement, which can be filled with courses in literature, history, languages, philosophy, or a combination of these. Eastman students are serious about their humanities classes as well as their music, and classes are not easy. As one undergrad explained, "It seems like either you do really well or you completely fail." By senior year, most of Eastman's requirements are out of the way, and students have more flexible schedules that allow them to audition for jobs or graduate school.

Because Eastman is part of the University of Rochester, students have access to the university's libraries and other facilities. Some of the humanities classes are held on the U of R campus, although as one student said, "You can make it all four years without leaving this campus." The reason many like to stay on the Eastman campus is the 15- to 20-minute bus ride to the U of R.

Students who apply to Eastman can ask to work with a particular professor, and many apply to the school primarily to do just that. One student, for example, said he met his cello teacher at a summer music camp and decided to go to Eastman so he could continue to study with her. Some popular professors include clarinetist Kenneth Grant, pianist Barry Snyder, and flautist Bonita Boyd. The members of the Cleveland String Quartet also teach at Eastman and attract many to their classes and concerts. Students have substantial contact with faculty members, both in lessons and in other contexts like chamber groups.

Living and Breathing Music

Everything at Eastman revolves around music. The musical motif on campus is inescapable; the snack bar is called the Orchestra Pit and the newspaper is called *Clef Notes*. Students rave about their "access to music on hand anytime." They can go to concerts every night if they want to; Eastman's calendar is filled with student and faculty performances by soloists and groups in the Eastman Theater, concerts every other week by the Rochester Philharmonic Orchestra (Eastman students get free tickets), and limitless other performances. Eastman's Sibley Library also has an enormous music collection (the second-largest in the nation), including books, manuscripts, and recordings of "just about everything," one student said. Whenever undergrads want to listen to music but just can't find a concert to go to, they can always listen to their favorite symphony or opera at the library. Students who want to participate in athletics, student government, and other nonmusical extracurricular activities can journey over to the University of Rochester campus.

For those with the energy to play for more than the three to six hours they're expected to practice each day, there are plenty of opportunities to perform. Some students give several recitals a year, while others only do one in their four years at school. Many undergrads participate in chamber orchestras, quartets, or other small ensembles, either for credit or for fun. Jazz bands and string quartets are in constant demand at local restaurants and bars. Traveling Broadway shows that come to Rochester sometimes need a player to fill in and look to Eastman students for help. Students also have many chances to play at church services, weddings, and other special events.

Few Distractions

The Eastman campus is small, with just three buildings located in the heart of downtown Rochester: Eastman Commons, a classroom building, and Sibley Library. The food at the cafeteria is "pretty normal," according to one student. "You know, it's got a salad and pasta bar, burgers and fries, and a frozen yogurt machine." In the dorm, freshmen live in doubles, and all upperclassmen have singles. Moving off campus is a popular option for juniors and seniors, but freshmen and sophomores are required to live on campus. Many students prefer the dorm because the surrounding neighborhood reportedly "isn't the greatest." Dorm life exposes students to an environment where everyone knows everyone else and has the same interests, so life can get a little boring. For those who need to get away, popular options include the Rochester Club, which features jazz every Friday night, and the Spaghetti Warehouse. Students also like to hang out and "go crazy" at nearby dance clubs in downtown Rochester.

> **"It's not like a big old party school."**

Campus social life is somewhat limited. As one student explained, "It's not like a big old party school." For those who favor the Greek scene, there is one all-male fraternity, one sorority, and one coed fraternity. The all-male and all-female groups each have a floor of the 14-story Eastman Commons to themselves. The all-male fraternity sponsors most of the parties, while the other Greek groups focus on community service work. Eastman has two annual formals, one in the fall and one in the spring. Small parties in the dorm are common; one student remarked that the delivery truck from a local liquor store is frequently spotted outside the dorm. Students don't seem to mind the low-key social scene; as one sophomore pointed out, "The fewer distractions, the easier it is to concentrate on practicing—which is good, I guess."

Freshmen typically arrive at Eastman

from all corners of the world with visions of their names in lights. Each dreams of being the next great viola player, soprano soloist, or jazz pianist. These dreams become transformed over the next few years into more realistic aspirations. One junior explained that it doesn't matter to her whether she ends up as the soloist with a major symphony or a player in a community orchestra: "As long as I'm playing, that's cool with me."—*Susanna Chu and Staff*

FYI

The three best things about attending Eastman are "the faculty, the caliber of the students, and the connections you build."

The three worst things about attending Eastman are "Rochester, the competitiveness, and the gloomy weather."

The three things that every student should do before graduating from Eastman are "attend a seminar by a world-famous musician, play every instrument once, and go see Niagara Falls."

One thing I'd like to have known before coming here is "how competitive people are."

Eugene Lang College of the New School University

Address: 65 W. 11th Street, New York, NY 10011
Phone: 212-229-5665
E-mail address: LANG@newschool.edu
Web site URL: www.lang.edu
Location: urban
Founded: 1919 Univ;1978 college
Private or Public: private
Religious affiliation: none
Undergraduate enrollment: 520
Total enrollment: 520
Percent Male/Female: 32%/68%
Percent Minority: 23.0%

Percent African-American: 7.0%
Percent Hispanic: 11.0%
Percent Asian: 5.0%
Percent in-state/out-of-state: 41%/59%
Percent Pub HS: 40%
Fraternities: 0%
Sororities: 0%
Number of Applicants: 718
Percent Accepted: 54%
Percent Accepted who enroll: 31%
Entering: 120
Transfers: 84
Application Deadline: 1 Feb

Mean SAT: 610 V, 580 M
Middle 50% SAT range: NA
Middle 50% ACT range: NA
Mean ACT: 27
3 Most popular majors: writing, cultural studies, psychology
Retention: 73.0%
Graduation rate: NA
Library: NA
Tuition and Fees: $19,915 in; NA out
Room and Board: $9,000
On-campus housing: 80%
Financial aid, first-year: 72%

Situated in the heart of New York City, Eugene Lang College is the undergraduate, liberal arts college of New School University, formerly known as the New School for Social Research. Founded in 1973 as the Seminar College of the New School for Social Research, Lang acquired its current name when philanthropist Eugene Lang and his family donated $5 million to the school in 1985. Despite the name change, seminars that range in size from 5 to 15 students remain the basis of the educational experience at Lang.

It's All Up to You

Lang is a small college, which enrolls about 500 students and offers a strong liberal arts education. The New School University is comprised of Actors Studio Drama School, Eugene Lang College, Graduate Faculty, Mannes College of Music, Milano Graduate School, The New

School, and Parsons School of Design. It also has affiliated programs with Benjamin N. Cardozo School of Law, Dial Cyberspace Campus, Educated Citizen Project, Jazz & Contemporary Music/New School University BFA Program, and Joffrey Ballet School/New School University BFA Program in Dance. It is obviously a bit confusing to try to make sense of how all these schools interact, but students can take classes at the other schools to a certain extent.

Courses at Lang itself are divided into five broad areas of concentration: literature, writing, and the arts; social and historical inquiry; mind, nature, and value; urban studies; and cultural studies. Students use these areas as the basis for designing their own majors. "You don't actually design your major all by yourself; there are certain paths you can take like gender studies, queer theory, or education under cultural studies," said one student. Since most classes at Lang are interdisciplinary, students say that they get exposed to many different subjects rather than sticking with a single one.

Lang's strength is in the social sciences. Students looking for hard-core science courses and lab facilities have to enroll in courses at Cooper Union and transfer their credits. Many students also take classes at Parsons School of Design, and juniors and seniors can take graduate classes at the Milano Graduate School. Seminars, often taught by famous professors or by published authors, can be very demanding and usually involve several writing assignments. Although, in the past, students could have a casual attitude about attending classes, this year the administration has started enforcing an attendance policy: the professor has the right to fail students who miss more than three classes throughout the semester. However, one student commented, "This is not the way it works in practice. The professor usually lowers your grade instead of failing you."

Students complain about the small number of full-time faculty members and the big "turnover of professors." Since most professors are only "visiting" they are "here for one term and disappear the next." Overall, students have praise for their professors: "I have had some incredible professors who have helped me make important decisions affecting my life." Students see their interactions with professors as one of the major benefits of attending Lang. "I can call all of my professors at home," one student exclaimed. Students are also positive about the advising system: "My advisors did really advise me—about academic issues as well as about my personal life." One student went as far to say, "I probably would not be in New York right now if it wasn't for my advisors. That's how close you can get to them." Lang has a study-abroad program with the University of Amsterdam, but that is the "only official study-abroad option." Many students still go to different countries for a term or an entire year.

Registration is the "biggest pain!" There is no phone or online system for registration. One senior explained, "Starting with the seniors, each class meets in a big room and registers for classes. It is total chaos." Since all courses are capped at 15 students, "you may end up registering for classes totally different from the ones you had in mind if you are unlucky in the registration draw." Students can add and drop classes after registration, which usually brings them "closer to their initial set of desired courses." Administrators, however, usually known to students on a first-name basis, receive very good overall reviews for their responsiveness and willingness to help.

New York, New York

Most Lang students are self-defined urbanites. For those who aren't, adjusting to life in New York City is the biggest challenge. Social life centers on clubs and cafés in Greenwich Village as well as other parts of the city. "Parks are also great in the spring," said one enthusiastic junior. Most students agree that "you can either fall through the cracks or benefit from everything the area has to offer."

Students think of their classmates as a reflection of New York City: diverse, liberal, and individualistic. "One thing we don't have at Lang are conservatives—we are a fairly progressive bunch," noted one sophomore. However, despite the progressiveness, "the political activism of the Seminar College days has faded away."

Formal extracurricular activities and sports programs do not exist at Lang. "There are not many sports fans here." Those who are into sports can participate in Cooper Union's small intramural sports program. Lang in the city is a college-sponsored program that offers students discounted tickets to performances, movies and art events, but "is not used by many students." One student explained, "You don't go through the school, you create your own independent life." Lang's Internship Coordinator helps place students in internships with employers in the city. Professors' connections also help in getting high-quality internships. "We even get credit for internships; they are an incredible experience. They allow you to bring theory and practice together," said a senior.

A Single Building

Eugene Lang is situated in a five-story building that contains classrooms, study rooms, and a small cafeteria. One student said, "We, at least, don't have to walk for miles to get from one class to the other." However, students taking classes at Parsons or at the Milano Graduate School have to walk "a couple of streets." Lang's library is part of a three-school consortium with the libraries of Cooper Union and New York University, giving students access to nearly 3.3 million volumes.

> **"Survival in New York City is a big part of the Lang experience."**

One housing option for Lang students is the three residence halls within walking distance of the school building: Loeb Hall, Marlton House, and Union Square. Rooms vary in size and type depending on the building. The dorms do not belong entirely to Lang; students share them with students from Parsons School of Design and Mannes College of Music, which are also schools under the New School University. Space is guaranteed to freshmen and first-year transfer students but others are often forced to enter the painful search for apartments in New York City. "I would not recommend the dorms, but then, I would not recommend looking for an apartment in your first year in New York either," noted one student. "The moment you move to an apartment, your social life is totally independent from the school." These "New Yorkers" have to commute to school.

Lang combines a strong liberal arts education and small seminars with the opportunities of the most urban setting possible. This combination leads Lang students to build their potential in their time here and leave Lang as independent thinkers and as individuals.—*Engin Yenidunya*

FYI
The three best things about attending Eugene Lang are "your close relationship to your professors, being in the city, and very small class sizes."
The three worst things about attending Eugene Lang are "the registration process, the terrible dorms, and you can get lost in New York."
The three things that every student should do before graduating from Eugene Lang are "enjoy New York City, do an internship, and study abroad."
One thing I would like to have known before coming here is "that dining halls are almost nonexistent."

Fordham University

Address: 441 East Fordham Road, Thebaud Hall, New York, NY 10458
Phone: 800-FORDHAM
E-mail address: enroll@fordham.edu
Web site URL: www.fordham.edu
Location: urban
Founded: 1841
Private or Public: private
Religious affiliation: Roman Catholic (Jesuit)
Undergraduate enrollment: 6,358
Total enrollment: 5,740
Percent Male / Female: 41% / 59%

Percent Minority: 24.0%
Percent African-American: 6.0%
Percent Hispanic: 14.0%
Percent Asian: 4.0%
Percent in-state / out-of-state: 67% / 33%
Percent Pub HS: 34%
Fraternities: 0%
Sororities: 0%
Number of Applicants: 7,630
Percent Accepted: 65%
Percent Accepted who enroll: 33%
Entering: 1,636
Transfers: 0
Application Deadline: 1 Feb

Mean SAT: 589 V, 574 M
Middle 50% SAT range: 530–630 V, 520–620 M
Middle 50% ACT range: NA
Mean ACT: 25
3 Most popular majors: business administration, psychology, communications
Retention: 88.0%
Graduation rate: 59.0%
Library: 1.6 million volumes
Tuition and Fees: $18,295 in; $18,295 out
Room and Board: $7,810
On-campus housing: 50%
Financial aid, first-year: 73%

Be it the wide lawns and Gothic architecture in the Bronx, or the towering 20-floor complex in the heart of Manhattan, the two campuses of Fordham University give its students both the rushed atmosphere and rare calmness that only New York City can offer.

Two Campuses, Like Curriculums

Students at Fordham University attend either Fordham College at Rose Hill, which is the College of Business Administration, or Fordham College at Lincoln Center. While the two campuses, Rose Hill and Lincoln Center, are both physically and characteristically separate, the schools share a core curriculum. The Core is an extensive list of requirements of courses ranging from rhetoric, theology, and philosophy to social and natural sciences. While many students see the curriculum as a good basis for the study of liberal arts, more than one student described the program as having too great "an emphasis on what's Western. The philosophy classes can be very dogmatic." Fordham is a Jesuit school and thus has a theology requirement. While the study of religion is not the school's driving force, one junior said that "some theology classes, such as

'Faith and Critical Reasoning', seem to be attempts to convert you to Christianity. I'm not such a fan of that." Advanced students may choose to join the Honors program, which is made up of a group of specific classes of very interdisciplinary material, including a junior term abroad, an internship, or directed reading. For all students, a Fordham education is topped off with a senior seminar in Values and Moral Choices. Despite the program's Western leanings, Fordham students must also take at least one class in global studies, and one in American pluralism, which emphasizes ethnicity, race, and class in the United States. The Lincoln Center campus also offers a unique Bachelor of Fine Arts in Dance in combination with the Alvin Ailey Dance Center.

Classes are reportedly easy to get into and are generally small. One student said that "I've been lucky enough to never have more than 25 students in my classes." Humanities-based classes are popular, and many major in English. Science classes are reportedly tough, and are almost exclusively taught at the Rose Hill campus, which, according to one Lincoln Center student, "is extremely aggravating." Whatever inconveniences there may be, Fordham students are extremely happy with their professors. TAs are rare except in laboratory settings, and often teach only in conjunction with another professor. What some students find upsetting about their classes is the fact that "a lot of students aren't interested. They see class as something they have to get over." Regardless, Fordham boasts an excellent academic reputation rooted in Jesuit tradition.

Social Life?

Perhaps because of its location in a city where there are almost too many things to do, students report that "social life on campus is pretty scant. We're in New York, after all." Regardless, there is a Weekend Activities Committee which has brought musical groups like the Indigo Girls to campus and shows movies on Tuesdays and Thursdays. As a result of this lack of campus life, one on-campus student stated, "You better make friends right in the beginning. Those friends are the ones who you'll end up hanging out with all the time." One sophomore stated that "a lot of kids at Fordham are from around here, so they already have friends and don't bother too much with social life here." Fordham students make the most of their location, often going to theater and museums in the city and participating in the bar and club scene both in the Bronx and in Manhattan.

> "Social life on campus is pretty scant. We're in New York, after all."

The student body itself is statistically diverse, but many students see diversity only in the numbers. Fordham attracts many commuter students, and according to one student, "A lot of the commuters are the minority students and, as a result, there's not always a lot of racial interaction." Perhaps social lifestyle most differentiates the two campuses of Fordham. Students at Rose Hill claim that there is little sex on campus, while the students in Manhattan simply say, "There is a lot of sex, and not always within the student body." Additionally, while the lesbian and gay community of Rose Hill is quite small,

one student described Lincoln Center as "just exuding gayness." Thus, depending on the campus, the lifestyle at Fordham can be either calm or wild.

A Dee-luxe Apartment in the Sky

Rose Hill students who choose to live on campus usually aim for Alumni Court North and South, the two newer dorms on campus. Students also have the option of living in the Residential College of Queen's Court. Many students, though, do choose to live off campus. Meanwhile, in Manhattan, students live in a 20-floor apartment building with large suites containing bathrooms and kitchens. According to one sophomore, though, "it gets pretty tight because lots of people like it." At both campuses, the major grievance with housing is the enforced restrictions. There is a strict sign-in policy, and students may not have guests of the opposite sex stay in their rooms. Additionally, any guests who do come to stay must look for a new place soon, because they are allowed a two-night maximum. All residence halls have RAs, whom the students describe as very active. As one student put it, "The RAs are great. They monitor the building and make the dorms a good living situation."

Gothic and Modern

The greatest physical difference between the Rose Hill and Lincoln Center campuses is their distinct architectural styles. While Rose Hill boasts sprawling lawns and traditional Gothic architecture, Lincoln Center is comprised of three buildings, all very modern. Within these different buildings, however, the same goals are met at the two campuses. In the Bronx, there is the Vince T. Lombardi Athletic Center and McGinley Hall, the student union, which houses two cafeterias and Dagger John's Pub. In Manhattan, students take advantage of the aptly named Fitness and Exercise Center, and frequent the Lowenstein Center for food, which includes going to bar Blarney's. As for food, students often purchase a meal plan, although opinions on the campus food range from "good" to "very bad, except on turkey night." Of course, the area provides a wealth of restaurants and students often cook for themselves as well.

Outside of Class

Fordham students, when not in class, can often be found doing community service, ranging from organized activity through Kiwanis-sponsored Circle K, the POTS Soup Kitchen, or finding such opportunities independently, be it at one of New York's hospitals or the Red Cross. There are a number of clubs at both campuses, ranging from ethnic clubs such as Molino, which emphasizes African culture, to academically related groups, such as the Pre-Law Society. Varsity sports are on campus, but, according to one student, "There's not a whole lot of support for the

Rams." For students in need of physical activity, without the rigor of varsity level athletics, there are both intramural and club sports, ranging from lacrosse to an intramural screaming contest.

Fordham University and New York City provide students with a solid liberal arts education as well as a lot of real world experience. As one student said, "Sometimes I feel more real when I go into the city. I see a lot more than when I'm cooped up studying all the time." With a range of academic and extracurricular possibilities, students at Fordham love their school and enjoy their status as "New York City's Jesuit University."
—*Shu-Ping Shen*

FYI

The three best things about attending Fordham are "location, small size, and teacher-student relation."

The three worst things about attending Fordham are "no campus life, slightly oppressive Jesuit atmosphere, and small size."

The three things that every student should do before graduation from Fordham are "work in New York City, live on top floor, get in touch with your club kid side."

One thing I'd like to have known before coming here is "most of the campus is female."

Hamilton College

Address: 198 College Hill Road, Clinton, NY 13323	**Percent African-American:** 3.0%	**Mean SAT:** NA
Phone: 800-843-2655	**Percent Hispanic:** 4.0%	**Middle 50% SAT range:** 600–690 V, 590–690 M
E-mail address: admission@hamilton.edu	**Percent Asian:** 4.0%	
	Percent in-state / out-of-state: 57% / 43%	**Middle 50% ACT range:** NA
Web site URL: www.hamilton.edu	**Percent Pub HS:** 62%	**Mean ACT:** NA
Location: rural	**Fraternities:** 29%	**3 Most popular majors:** economics, government, English
Founded: 1812	**Sororities:** 12%	
Private or Public: private	**Number of Applicants:** 3,909	**Retention:** 92%
Religious affiliation: none	**Percent Accepted:** 42%	**Graduation rate:** 85%
Undergraduate enrollment: 1,740	**Percent Accepted who enroll:** 30%	**Library:** 538,377 volumes
		Tuition and Fees: $25,050 in; NA out
Total enrollment: 1,740	**Entering:** 500	**Room and Board:** $6,200
Percent Male / Female: 51% / 49%	**Transfers:** 17	**On-campus housing:** 100%
Percent Minority: 11.0%	**Application Deadline:** 15 Jan	**Financial aid, first-year:** 62%

Imagine yourself on an intimate campus, in the middle of green grassy hills, where everyone knows your name and TAs do not exist. Nestled in quiet upstate

New York, Hamilton sits on top of a hill with countryside views that stretch for miles. But beauty is not the only thing that distinguishes Hamilton. Students extol their educational experience at this prestigious liberal arts college as well.

Small Classes with Energetic Professors

When students enter Hamilton as freshmen, they are required to take two classes in four different distributional groups: mathematics and science, the arts, historical studies and social sciences, and humanities and languages. A course in ethical issues is also required, and students must take either a language or a class on culture to fulfill the cultural diversity requirement. Students must also take three six-week PE classes (varsity athletes only take two), ranging from scuba diving to badminton.

Students praise both their teachers and small classes. "The biggest class I have ever been in is 70 students, and that was only because it was an introductory class." Classes as large as that are broken down into weekly discussion sections of no more than 20. Most classes are capped at 25, however, with a given quantity of freshmen, sophomores, juniors, and seniors allowed in each section. Although classes fill up quickly, students report that if they go and talk with the professor, they will probably be admitted. Every class is taught by a full-fledged professor. "At Hamilton there are no TAs, and every professor on the faculty has a Ph.D." Since Hamilton has no graduate students, the professors focus all their time on undergraduate teaching, and they are said to be very accessible. "I even had one professor who brought doughnuts and coffee to class for our 8:30 A.M. class."

When it comes to majors, chemistry, history, and public policy are notorious for keeping students up late at nights. If you want the easy way out, major in communications. Popular majors include economics, English, history, and psychology, and students love the anthropology and sociology departments. If you are a geology major, Hamilton has a program that takes students to Antarctica. "Chemistry classes, especially organic, are impossible here." But there are some "gut" classes available to fulfill the mathematics/science requirement, one being "A Physicist's View of Nature." As one student puts it, "You can definitely make it through without doing a ton of work. It's up to you." Most Hamilton students are happy with their educational experience.

A Dazzling, Isolated Campus

All Hamilton students laud their beautiful campus, which is split into two parts: North Campus (nicknamed "the white side") and South Campus (nicknamed "the dark side"). The North Campus hosts beautiful traditional buildings described by one student as "more Ivy League than the Ivy League itself." Between the buildings are expansive green lawns, where many students play Frisbee. The not so popular South Campus, formerly the women's college, is home to the "artsy" population and is known for its "hideous" 60s style buildings made out of gray cement.

Although Hamilton students love the beauty of their school, many complain about its isolation. "We are in the middle of nowhere." The town of Clinton has few shops, and only two bars. Many students travel to Syracuse, 45 minutes away, to fulfill their shopping needs, or to the small mall and movie theater 10 minutes away. Freshmen are not allowed to have cars, but after the first year about 70 percent of the students drive. Most students see having a car as essential to escaping the tiny town of Clinton. The weather is another factor that Hamilton students complain about. Winter in Clinton begins in October and ends in May. "If you aren't into cold weather, then you will not dig the conditions here."

Students at Hamilton are very happy with their living accommodations. Five years ago, fraternity houses were banned and the school bought the houses from the fraternities, renovating them and making them into dorms. Although it created upheaval in the years following, students from all classes now live together in the same dorms, and the upperclassmen singles are huge. Students can live on single-sex floors if they wish, although the coed floors are known to be much cooler. Freshmen, sophomores, and most juniors are required to live on campus and rooms are assigned by a lottery system. Seniors and juniors who pull a low lottery number can live off campus. Freshmen are assigned resident advisors, who help them adjust to college life.

The most popular places to live include Saunders House and DKE, both of which are old frat houses. Many students who live in Dunham complain about its location and the trek to classes in the cold weather, as the dorm is situated at the bottom of the hill.

Homogeneous Hamilton

Hamilton definitely lives up to its reputation as being a very homogenous, white, upper-middle-class school. One student states, "Everyone here is wealthy, wears Patagonia, J. Crew, North Face and Abercrombie, and drives a Jeep Grand Cherokee. There is a little underlying granola as well." Although the administration is trying to recruit minorities, they still constitute a very small percentage of the student body, and many students note the lack of diversity on campus. Some say there is also racial segregation, especially noticeable in the dining halls. Interracial couples on campus are not common, and there is not a large homosexual population either. As far as the rest of the dating scene is concerned, students report there are not many long-term relationships at Hamilton, "just a lot of random hookups." Another common characteristic students note is "how nice everyone is here." One thing that Hamilton does have is good financial aid. There are merit scholarships as well as purely financial grants. One student remarked, "If you need the money and are qualified to come, Hamilton will give it to you."

Dining and Nightlife

All Hamilton students living on campus must be on the meal plan. Freshmen and sophomores are required to take the full meal plan, and juniors and seniors can opt for the 14 meal a week plan. The Diner, one campus spot that accepts the meal plan, has a jukebox and good food. They make fresh cheeseburgers and let students place personalized orders. The other dining halls are said to be clean, but the food is not too appealing, although they do have a stir fry bar in which chefs cook the food in front of you. Many noted that the vegetarian options "could be a lot better."

When dining off campus, many go to Zebb's for hamburgers or to the Adirondack coffee shop. The VT (Village Tavern) is the most popular bar in town, and a major hangout for upperclassmen and underclassmen with ID. Otherwise, students party in their rooms or go to fraternity parties, which have to be held in students' rooms since there are no frat houses anymore. There are some theme parties, such as "Mardi Gras," and "Heaven and Hell," that have huge turnouts. There are also some sororities on campus, though none of them are national, and they have never had separate housing. Greek life is more key to the guys on campus, but people in general do not feel excluded if they are not a part of Greek life.

Hamilton also lives up to its reputation as a party school. Many claim that getting alcohol is definitely not a problem, and some students report that people who don't drink sometimes feel uncomfortable. The administration is said to be pretty relaxed on its alcohol policy, although it does require that anyone who plans to throw a party with mass quantities of alcohol attend a two-hour lecture about abusing alcohol. After the lecture, the hosts are given a pass that allows them to serve alcohol. Students say that pot is also fairly easy to find on campus, though most reject more hard-core drugs.

> **"If you aren't into cold weather, then you will not dig the conditions here."**

"Most of the weekend life is on campus, as there is not much to do off, and the school does a great job at providing entertainment." This year the band Dispatch has visited the campus, as well as other groups such as an African drumming group. The five a cappella singing groups at Hamilton also have huge turnouts for their shows. The school even provides popular free movies on the weekends. In the realm of extracurriculars, one of the most popular organizations on campus is The Outdoor Club, which has climbing and backpacking trips. Community service and writing for the weekly newspaper, *The Spectator*, are popular activities as well. Every Sunday night in the winter is "Sunday Night Skiing" night, and many students board buses to go. Several participate in intramural and varsity athletics, and the turnout for varsity events is said to be fair. The biggest game of the year is the first ice hockey game against Colgate. In keeping with tradition, all Hamilton students throw oranges onto the ice before the game.

Overall, Hamilton students are very content with their educational experience. The small student body and rural setting can be both very intimate and at times isolating. However, most students seem to be happy with the academic and social opportunities available to them and equally happy with their choice to attend Hamilton. Just remember to bring a good winter coat for the cold winters and good hiking boots. —*Carolyn Grace*

FYI
The three best things about attending Hamilton are "great professors, huge beautiful campus, and the variety of extracurriculars."
The three worst things about attending Hamilton are "Clinton, no frat houses, snow in October."
The three things that every student should do before graduating Hamilton are "Sunday Night Skiing, go to Antarctica, go to Turning Stone Casino."
One thing I'd like to have known before coming here is "how cold winters really can be."

Hobart and William Smith College

Address: 629 South Main St., Geneva, NY 14454
Phone: 315-781-3472
E-mail address: HOADM@HWS.edu
Web site URL: www.hws.edu
Location: small city
Founded: 1822
Private or Public: private
Religious affiliation: none
Undergraduate enrollment: 1,850
Total enrollment: 1,850
Percent Male/Female: 48%/52%
Percent Minority: 14.0%

Percent African-American: 6.0%
Percent Hispanic: 4.0%
Percent Asian: 3.0%
Percent in-state/out-of-state: 50%/50%
Percent Pub HS: 65%
Fraternities: 0%
Sororities: 0%
Number of Applicants: 2,597
Percent Accepted: 75%
Percent Accepted who enroll: 25%
Entering: 500
Transfers: 35
Application Deadline: 1 Feb

Mean SAT: NA
Middle 50% SAT range: 530–620 V, 530–620 M
Middle 50% ACT range: NA
Mean ACT: NA
3 Most popular majors: English, economics, psychology
Retention: 87%
Graduation rate: 83%
Library: 350,000 volumes
Tuition and Fees: $24,342 in; $24,342 out
Room and Board: $6,882
On-campus housing: 100%
Financial aid, first-year: 66%

Located on exquisite Seneca Lake, Hobart and William Smith Colleges (HWS) offer students a unique package of comfort and academics. Both Hobart, the men's college, and William Smith, the women's college, have their own deans, masters, athletic teams, student governments, and admissions staffs, but the two colleges share a single campus, faculty, classes, and dorm system.

Together but Apart
This "coordinate system" of different administrations but common experience mainly draws praise from students. Many women consider the numerous support

groups, the women's studies program, and the general focus on women's issues "empowering." However, some males feel that the coordinate system benefits only women, and some are convinced that HWS should place "more emphasis on the coming together of the sexes than on each sex finding its own strength." But regardless, Hobart men leave college sensitive to women's issues and problems.

A Carefully Groomed Campus

Nature has endowed HWS well with Seneca Lake, and HWS administrators have carefully built and maintained the campus. The appearance of Hobart and William Smith Colleges is "addictive" and "breathtaking." One student explained, "I knew I was coming here as soon as I set foot on campus." Not only is the campus beautiful, but it is also "incredibly well kept."

How picturesque is Seneca Lake? According to legend, all the buildings that have been built between the "Lady of the Lake" statue and Seneca Lake have burned to the ground because the Lady of the Lake will not allow any object to obscure her gorgeous view.

Geneva, New York, home of HWS, is not a college town. One student joked, "Hobart would be perfect if it were in Ithaca." The Seneca Lake area does, however, have its benefits: there are numerous wineries in the area that offer wine tasting to those who are of age.

Living

In general, students like their dorms. Yet, one senior complains that "the housing situation sucks" because of Hobart and William Smith's strict limitations for off-campus living. But students are generally happy with on-campus options. Freshmen live in standard, comfortable dorms. But upperclassmen can now live in luxurious condominiums. According to one pleased student, "The condos are nicer than my house." Other options such as theme houses and the field house, where students till their own land, offer unique living arrangements.

Hobart and William Smith students like their dining hall food in general. The quality is mediocre, but "the variety is amazing," said one senior. Outside of the dining halls, students can snack at The Cellar, Cafe Cabana (downtown), or Just Cookies and Pies (which, paradoxically, serves top-notch sandwiches also). Spinnakers and Ports offer more upscale, gourmet meals.

Typical Students?

Two traits characterize the typical student at Hobart and William Smith: "well-off" and "friendly." Yes, "80 percent of the campus dresses in J. Crew," said one student, but the other 20 percent feel little pressure to conform. Most of the students are Caucasian and hail from New England and the Mid-Atlantic suburbs. Some feel that "Hobart is not as diverse as it could be," but Hobart is now making a large-scale effort to attract and support minority students. The fact that minorities comprise 20 percent of the class of 2001 indicates that minority-recruiting efforts have succeeded. While some say that students still segregate themselves to some degree, one senior said, "Your group changes from where you come from [and what ethnic group you are] to where you are or where you are going." However, one Hispanic freshman believes, "Some people here can be so close-minded at times it is not even funny." The gay and lesbian population is small, but accepted. The Gay, Lesbian, Bisexual Friends Network provides support to homosexual students and awareness to others

Greek life at Hobart plays a major role in social life. Also, the condos provide more than enough space for room parties. In general, alcohol is readily available, and HWS can be "a real weed-fest," though most feel that drugs are no more or less prevalent at HWS than at other colleges. Random hookups are common, but "long-term relationships are difficult."

Extracurriculars

In extracurriculars, students range from "apathetic" to "fanatical," with the mean skewed towards the "apathetic" end of the spectrum. However, student government, especially William Smith's Congress, affects life directly and powerfully. "Geneva Heroes" brings Hobart and William Smith students together with area eighth graders to perform community service.

> **"Each student does something deviant. Last year, one girl ate an earthworm, lots of people did stripteases, and some guy stole a fire hydrant and brought it to class."**

Academics at Hobart are what one makes of them. The year is divided into three trimesters, allowing students to take few classes at once. In political science, English, women's studies, and biology, Hobart and William Smith excel. Hobart students rave about the accessibility and excellence of their professors. Jack Harris, one well-loved professor, spices his sociology class with "Deviance Day," where "each student does something deviant. Last year, one girl ate an earthworm, lots of people did stripteases, and some guy stole a fire hydrant and brought it to class."

A new science building provides science majors with excellent facilities. Physics, however, is a weak point. Additionally, Hobart and William Smith send hundreds of students abroad each trimester. The destination list is huge for such a small school, and professors accompany students to some foreign locations.

Still, Hobart and William Smith seem to attract "a lot of kids who had all the opportunities in the world in high school, but only took advantages of a few of them." HWS changes most of these people, but nevertheless fails to inspire some.—*Brian Abaluck and Staff*

FYI
The three best things about attending HWS are "that it's two different schools, but they're really together, so it's coed."
The three worst things about attending HWS are "Geneva, the lack of anything constructive to do, and the apathy of the student body."
The three things that every student should do before graduating from HWS are "piss off someone of the 'opposing' gender, tell a tourist the 'Lady of the Lake' legend, and throw a party in your condo."
One thing I'd like to have known before coming here is "how much emphasis there would be on gender differences."

H o f s t r a   U n i v e r s i t y

Address: Admissions Center, Bernon Hall, Hempstead, NY 11549
Phone: 516-463-6700
E-mail address: hofstra@hofstra.edu
Web site URL: www.hofstra.edu
Location: suburban
Founded: 1935
Private or Public: private
Religious affiliation: none
Undergraduate enrollment: 8,915
Total enrollment: 12,439
Percent Male/Female: 47%/53%
Percent Minority: 18.0%

Percent African-American: 8.0%
Percent Hispanic: 6.0%
Percent Asian: 4.0%
Percent in-state/out-of-state: 85%/15%
Percent Pub HS: 70%
Fraternities: 10%
Sororities: 10%
Number of Applicants: 8,086
Percent Accepted: 83%
Percent Accepted who enroll: 30%
Entering: 1,775
Transfers: 1,447
Application Deadline: rolling
Mean SAT: 543 V, 549 M

Middle 50% SAT range: 490–580 V, 490–590 M
Middle 50% ACT range: NA
Mean ACT: 24
3 Most popular majors: psychology, accounting, marketing,
Retention: 78%
Graduation rate: 42%
Library: 1.4 million volumes
Tuition and Fees: $13,238 in; $13,328 out
Room and Board: $6,880
On-campus housing: 37%
Financial aid, first-year: 71%

Nestled in the flower-filled city of Hempstead, New York, home of the annual Daffodil Festival, is a campus that students guarantee is "incredibly gorgeous." Its campus, coupled with its "comparably affordable" tuition, draws both local and international students.

Hitting the Books

Hofstra offers classes that span the spectrum of subjects and levels of difficulty. As long as students meet the foreign language requirement and the core requirements in math, social science, humanities, cross-cultural studies, and natural science, they may participate in an academic honors program or one of several study abroad programs. Students find that computer science, engineering, biochemistry, business, and math are more difficult than "*the* slacker major": physical education. While PE majors' "backpacks aren't always full," other classes generate workloads that range from "one hour per week per class to a couple hours per day per class."

Regardless of their major, however, students can have free time "if you're efficient with your time." Many find that the best place to study is the Axinn library, but others opt for their rooms, the student center, dorm lounges, or, for the half of the student body that commutes, home. Recently, students are sticking around campus a little more, thanks in part to the new modern chemistry building and modern business building.

In addition to Hofstra's great class offerings, students rave about their school's small classes. Class sizes range from a couple of people to a maximum of 65. While the small class size increases contact and fosters conversation with the professors, some students complain that the limited class size forces the administration to cap certain classes based on seniority. Sometimes, however, students who personally speak with professors manage to "weasel" their way into classes.

Life On and Off Campus

While half of Hofstra's student body commute, the other half live in dorms that "aren't too bad." While eagerly awaiting the completion of the "New Complex," students can choose to live in singles or suites. While most rooms in the fifteen-story Tower are singles, students complain that the bathroomss "aren't that clean" and that the singles "are closets!" Larger rooms in Nassau, Suffolk, Colonial Square, and The Netherlands are slightly more distant from campus. Students generally prefer Nassau and Suffolk over the other two options. These dorms are all equipped with a kitchen, a TV lounge, and laundry rooms. Students have the choice of living on single-sex floors, smoke-free floors, and alcohol-free floors in the dorms. The administration's alcohol policy is supposedly enforced by each dorm's Resident Advisor (RA), but RAs are reputed to let some things slide.

Nearby are a variety of restaurants that are included in students' meal plans. Students are free to choose from seven restaurants on campus, including Bits 'n' Bites, the Hofstra Deli, and the cafeteria in the student center that stays open until 2 A.M. Students who want to venture off campus to eat can choose from "quick food" places like McDonald's, Checker's, Friendly's, Burger King, Subway, and 7-Eleven, or from restaurants like Hooters or TGI Friday's, or the "excellent cuisine" of Vincent's Italian Restaurant. For an even greater selection, students can make the 15 minute trek into New York City. Coffee shops, like the popular Witch's Brew, also provide a mellow place for students to hang out.

The off-campus scene in the city of Hempstead isn't something students rave about. While safety "isn't really a problem," most learn not to walk into downtown Hempstead at night. Most students have cars which make shopping at the Roosevelt Field Mall and off-campus partying popular. One student claimed that "if you meet someone from Hofstra, it's usually not on campus."

The administration does make an effort to offer fun on-campus events. In addition to the on-campus movie theater, there are often special events like lectures and seminars. Students enjoy the selection of movies that the on-campus theatre offers, but they complain that the screen is too small and that the sound quality is poor. The administration brings in quite a few bands and performers as well, including

Billy Joel, George Clinton, Eve 6, Mighty Mighty Boss Tones, Busta Rhymes, and Third-Eye-Blind. Off-campus parties are popular, and students enjoy such on-campus parties as the Freak Formal on Halloween, the Scrufest, the basketball team's Midnight Madness, and Homecoming. Because "Greek life dominates," there are always frat parties to choose from as well.

The Student Body

While students generally consider their classmates to be "pretty friendly," impressions of the diversity on campus seem to differ. One student claimed, "We have students of every race, religion and color;" another thought that "there's a little more diversity than my high school, but that's not saying much"; and another student criticized the fact that "everyone here is rich." Diversity, he claimed, was hindered by the fact that "everyone here drives a beamer or a Mercedes in his Polo or Hilfiger outfit."

Students certainly have a diverse selection of extracurricular activities to choose from. Hofstra is the nation's only school to have a ROYGBIV (acronym for the colors of the rainbow) club, where students color in coloring books. More demanding commitments include the symphonic band, the accounting club, the school newspaper, *The Chronicle*, theater groups, student government, and intramural sports. Students frequent the Hofstra Recreation Center to stay in shape and

have fun. The Rec Center houses basketball courts, a track, a pool, classrooms for karate and an "increasing number" of classes, and "basically, all your gym stuff."

> **"Everyone here drives a beamer or a Mercedes in his or her Polo or Hilfiger outfit."**

Sports teams are "becoming" more popular, thanks to the new 5,000-seat basketball arena. In addition to the solid basketball team, Hofstra's men's lacrosse and football are popular. Women's athletics are becoming increasingly popular as well. Also popular on campus is the Hofstra Greek life. Social life at Hofstra is shaped by fraternity and sorority parties and events. There's no great pressure to join a frat or sorority, and students regard the pledging process as "fun." Students claim that these parties are better than those at Hofstra USA—the school's own nightclub. Carding is strictly enforced at Hofstra USA, but when frats or sororities host parties at neighboring bars, students say the carding policies tend to be more lenient.

Hofstra students, whether commuting or residing in the dorms, enjoy their school. Its small campus and friendly student body make this university a fun place to "get a great education but not for a lot of money."—*Marti Page*

FYI
The three best things about attending Hofstra are "the price, the atmosphere, and its great reputation."
The three worst things about attending Hofstra are "the Tower, the fact that you need a car, and the commute."
The three things that everyone must do before graduating from Hofstra are "*actually learn what you're majoring in*, go to the Freak Formal, and go to Vincent's Italian Restaurant."
One thing I'd like to have known before coming here is "that you need a car."

The Julliard School

Address: 60 Lincoln Center Plaza, New York, NY 10023
Phone: 212-799-5000
E-mail address: news@juilliard.edu
Web site URL: www.juilliard.edu
Location: urban
Founded: 1905
Private or Public: private
Religious affiliation: none
Undergraduate enrollment: 474
Total enrollment: 770
Percent Male / Female: 50% / 50%

Percent Minority: 24.8%
Percent African-American: 8.2%
Percent Hispanic: 3.1%
Percent Asian: 13.5%
Percent in-state / out-of-state: NA
Percent Pub HS: NA
Fraternities: NA
Sororities: NA
Number of Applicants: 1,755
Percent Accepted: 8%
Percent Accepted who enroll: NA
Entering: NA
Transfers: NA

Application Deadline: 1 Dec
Mean SAT: NA
Middle 50% SAT range: NA
Middle 50% ACT range: NA
Mean ACT: NA
3 Most popular majors: music, dance, drama
Retention: NA
Graduation rate: NA
Library: 73,000 volumes
Tuition and Fees: $16,000 in; $16,000 out
Room and Board: $6,850
On-campus housing: 100%
Financial aid, first-year: 91%

High above the taxi-lined streets of midtown Manhattan stand two buildings where the sounds of violins, singing, and clarinets drown out the noise of automobiles down below. The buildings belong to Julliard—you might have heard of it. The buildings once housed Robin Williams, Patti Lupone, and Wynton Marsalis—you might have heard of them. The buildings now house the next generation of performers—you will hear of them someday.

Twentieth Floor. Please Exit the Elevator Now For...

One of the school's towers at Lincoln Center houses classrooms, libraries, practice rooms, performance spaces, and the administration of the school. Inside these walls, students train with premier teachers—and they train hard. They're out from early in the morning until at least ten at night training, practicing, rehearsing, attending classes, and trying to grab a meal in between.

Julliard students are enrolled in one of three programs: music, drama, or dance. Within each area of concentration, the faculty is made up of respected professionals and experts in their field. "If you're good," one student noted, "you can get a good professor. It doesn't matter how old you are." Students are not just taught their skill; they are driven to master it. "The training is so beneficial. They have a lot of money, so they can offer a lot," said one sophomore. Students within each of the programs are a community unto themselves, an arrangement not without its disadvantages. "Especially with casting," a drama student complained. "The directors already know who they want before the audition. It's not based on your ability in the audition, it's already predetermined."

In addition to classes in their concentration, students are required to take one humanities course per term. A musician praised the humanities course as a break from the music that taught her to "open her mind to new ideas" instead of "worrying about her concerto." But one dancer described the courses as "poorly thought up." He continued: "They are trying to get you to look inside yourself, and it doesn't work." Julliard students desiring a more diverse curriculum are permitted to enroll in classes at Columbia. However, few students take advantage of this opportunity because, as one musician pointed out, "it takes a lot of time!" Most students simply cannot fit the time-consuming uptown commute into their busy schedules.

Inside the Community of Artists

There is nothing ordinary about living in Lincoln Center. Students praise the hotel-like atmosphere with two great views of the Hudson River and Broadway. First year students are required to live in the residence hall, and this helps to foster a sense of community within the school. "We're like a family," one musician said. All of the accommodations in the high rise are suites shared by up to seven students. Some students complained about the reliability of the phone system within these suites, noting that "at certain times in the night you try to call out and you can't—it just happens randomly." Regardless of the occasional communication glitch, students were enthusiastic about living with their talented peers. One musician remembers: "I played a Bach piece and my roommate choreographed a dance to it. It was really beautiful." Life in the residence hall inspires creativity in many.

And what about New York City? Some students wanted to escape the city and complained that they did not have "a real campus," while others appreciated Lincoln Center's "prime location." The Center's proximity to Central Park and the Metropolitan Opera Company provides students with the opportunity to escape into nature and attend a world-class production in the same evening. Attending professional performances inspires the students. One student remembers a particularly moving musical performance: "The way that they performed, it made me forget that I was at a performance. It made me think of my own performance and how I can make audiences feel the same." Even though the students embrace professional performances for inspiration, some lament their twenty-four-hour days, which does not allow for much time to take full advantage of Manhattan. When students are not recovering from their tiring weekdays or trying to learn from master performers, they frequent local restaurants and bars where, one drama student noted, "ID is not a problem." Inside the residence tower, there are "community assistants" to help plan events for the floor and the entire building from Sushi Night to a St. Patrick's Day party.

Julliard students believe that there is a misconception that their school is cut-throat. "Before coming here there were all these horror stories like razor blades between piano keys," one musician noted. "Actually," another musician continued, "people here are pretty normal. Ultimately it is a great place—people are really nice." The students are supportive of one another, and they have great respect for one another's talents. Because they spend so much time practicing and training, "it's kind of hard to meet people outside of your department. There isn't much time. It's pretty closed off." Students on campus are accepting of interracial and same sex relationships, but some girls complained that there are "not enough straight guys to go around for all of the girls."

Despite the Manhattan backdrop and Lincoln Center accommodations, Julliard stills falls victim to the ills of institutional food. One student warned: "Stick to the salad bar—it's safe. Veggie burgers and sandwiches are fine. But any of the cooked food . . ." The students' busy lifestyle makes it hard to eat healthy. When "they give you half an hour to eat, all you can do is grab a slice of pizza and a Coke." Students are concerned that eating disorders are not addressed, particularly among the dancers. One student called for a "class on nutrition."

Above and Beyond Lincoln Center

Does everyone at Julliard become a celebrity? Well, that depends on whether or not you want to be famous. One dancer noted, "There are some people who say, 'I'm going to make it.' But I don't consider them artists. They are not here to do what they love, but to be a star." Certainly, the name Julliard will open doors after graduation, and the extensive alumni network provides great opportunities to graduates. One drama student claimed, "We know each and every person who has graduated: what they are doing, if they've got a job, if they don't have a job, even how long their contracts are for." If nothing else, students are prepared to fight their way to the top through mastery and application of their talents.

When Julliard showcases its talent, New York listens. Students feel that the school puts an emphasis on "getting into a company" after graduation. They are encouraged to excel as individual performers in the context of a supportive community. In addition to being able to present themselves effectively, graduates are equipped with skills to teach their art to aspiring students. "There is no pressure on becoming famous. There is immense pressure on becoming an artist, and artists aren't famous until they're dead," one student said.

> **"The emphasis here is on the process—how to do it properly, not just whether you can do it."**

Julliard recently renovated its Lila Acheson Wallace Library. The collection now includes more than 50,000 scores; 20,000 books on music, dance, and drama; 15,000 sound recordings; and 500 videocassettes. And last spring, The Campaign for Julliard was announced: Over the next five years, one hundred million dollars will be spent on a wide range of projects to better prepare Julliard students for the demands of the new century. These include efforts to expand and enrich the curriculum, increases in scholarship aid and faculty salaries, commissions to produce new artistic works, and the renovation and enhancement of the school's Lincoln Center buildings.

Julliard's focus is intense. Students warn prospectives "you need to know what you're doing before you go into a school that is so one dimensional." But it is precisely this focus which allows students to turn their talent into mastery.
—*Jason Friedrichs*

FYI
The three best things about attending Julliard are "the city, being surrounded by really talented peers, and the faculty."
The three worst things about attending Julliard are "the incredibly fast pace, lack of straight guys, and favoritism."
The three things that every student should do before graduating from Julliard are "go to the Metropolitan Opera, go to another division's performance, and walk through Central Park."
One thing I'd like to have known before coming here is "that everything was going to be a surprise."

Manhattanville College

Address: 2900 Purchase Street, Purchase, NY 10577
Phone: 800-32-VILLE
E-mail address: admissions@mville.edu
Web site URL: www.manhattanville.edu
Location: suburban
Founded: 1841
Private or Public: private
Religious affiliation: none
Undergraduate enrollment: 1,145
Total enrollment: 1,895
Percent Male / Female: 31%/69%
Percent Minority: 28.0%

Percent African-American: 8.0%
Percent Hispanic: 14.0%
Percent Asian: 6.0%
Percent in-state / out-of-state: 66%/34%
Percent Pub HS: NA
Fraternities: 0%
Sororities: 0%
Number of Applicants: 1,143
Percent Accepted: 70%
Percent Accepted who enroll: 37%
Entering: 296
Transfers: 200
Application Deadline: rolling

Mean SAT: 510 V, 520 M
Middle 50% SAT range: 510–760 V, 520–700 M
Middle 50% ACT range: NA
Mean ACT: NA
3 Most popular majors: psychology, management, political science
Retention: 80%
Graduation rate: 53%
Library: 280,000 volumes
Tuition and Fees: $16,760 in; $16,760 out
Room and Board: $8,000
On-campus housing: 68%
Financial aid, first-year: 88%

Situated in the town of Purchase in the suburbs of New York City, Manhattanville College combines solid academics with a small, personal atmosphere of learning. The prevailing philosophy of Manhattanville is to offer the utmost challenge to its students in an environment that is enjoyable and personal, to prepare them for life beyond college.

Manhattanville's Departments

Students report that the strongest departments are psychology, political science, English, history, music, and dance, while the weakest are chemistry and physics. According to one undergrad, "Some students have to go to SUNY/Purchase to take physics." Classes usually average 15 to 20 students, and rarely exceed 35. Professors are readily accessible and are reportedly eager to talk with their students. All lecture classes are taught by professors, while student instructors, or SIs, lead review sessions. Manhattanville offers study-abroad programs in Florence, Paris, London, and other cities. A new program called CSTEP (Collegiate Science and Technology Entrance Program) offers qualified high school seniors and Manhattanville students lectures in scientific and technological areas, as well as field trips and conventions that offer opportunities to speak with business representatives. Students can also apply for internships with nearby companies such as Pepsico, IBM, and the Nestlé Corporation. Students say these internships sometimes result in full-time employment after graduation. Many undergrads, however, aspire to continue their education in graduate programs in law, medicine, and other fields.

Manhattanville students are required to take a writing course, eight credits in math and science, six credits in the arts, three credits each in humanities and the social sciences, and six credits in "global perspectives." Classes in Western and non-Western culture can be waived if a student majors or minors in a foreign language. All freshmen take a yearlong preceptorial class, in which they read and write about a wide range of classical literature. Students generally agree that at first these requirements seem to be a "has-sle," but say that in the end they expand their knowledge and contribute to a strong liberal arts education.

Manhattanville also has a unique "portfolio system" designed to track students' progress through their college years. Students meet with their individual faculty advisors in the beginning of their freshman year to create a four-year course list. Each subsequent spring, students then place a written self-examination and an example of the work they have accomplished during that school year in their portfolios, where it will later be reviewed by a committee of faculty members and administrators.

Campus Life

Manhattanville dorms are reportedly comfortable and well-kept. Two of the most popular dorms, Tenney and Spellman, were recently renovated, and even Damman, generally regarded as the worst dorm, has undergone renovation. All four dorms are coed by suite or room. Spellman houses predominantly freshmen, while Founders houses juniors and seniors. A portion of Tenney Hall is an intercultural center that is home to many of the international students on campus. The center offers multicultural meetings, lectures, and events. Most students live on campus, and those who do not usually commute.

For those who live on campus, the college meal plan allows them to get food at the cafeteria or the Cafe. The cafeteria serves everything from stir-fry, salad, and vegetarian food to hot entrees like chicken and pasta. The Cafe offers more opportunities for snacking, with such choices as grilled sandwiches, pizzas, and burgers. Students use a meal card to "charge" food during designated "equivalency hours."

Most Manhattanville students come from the tristate area of New York, New Jersey, and Connecticut, and many go home on weekends. There is no Greek system at Manhattanville, and campus social life on the weekends is traditionally slow. Some students are trying to compensate for this with a Clubs Council, which meets every week to organize weekend events. Also, students regularly hold parties in their rooms. One student joked that, if worse comes to worst, "you can follow the rugby team, and there is a party around them all the time."

Although the reportedly conservative administration has a strict policy against kegs on campus, in recent years students have been allowed to organize registered "pub nights" in response to the growing popularity of the nearby bars in town like O'Henry's and JB's. The newly formed Monday Night Football pub night keeps students on campus to watch televised football games and to drink at the Pavillion, the student center. The best parties of the year are the Fall and Spring formals and the Quad Jam. Following the Spring Formal, the Quad Jam is a daylong party where students can "drink, dance, and play games" to the music of up to ten bands. Entertainment on campus also includes occasional movie marathons and Sunday nights at the Coffee House, where people read poetry, play the guitar, or listen to performances given by visiting bands. During the week, students socialize at the Pavillion while picking up their mail or going to the bookstore.

> **"The personal attention we get is sometimes overwhelming."**

Sports-minded students can find outlets in club and intramural sports. The most popular club sport is rugby, while football, soccer, and lacrosse dominate in intramurals. Other students get involved in clubs such as LASO (the Latin American Student Organization) and the BSU (the Black Students' Union). Students also write for Touchstone, the campus newspaper, or the student literary magazine. Undergrads report that there is not much interaction between the students and the surrounding community, and community service is not popular at Manhattanville. According to one student, the college and the town "try to stay out of each other's way." Once a semester, however, a campuswide drive collects clothes, books, and toys for the needy in the area.

Students report that the administration is generally responsive to their complaints and needs. After a recent incident involving racially motivated vandalism, the administration immediately tightened campus security and also organized a discussion forum to address students' feelings and proposed solutions. Some undergrads believe the college should install a new outdoor lighting system for improved safety.

The student body is fairly diverse and politically liberal. Many students describe their classmates as politically aware without being very politically active.

According to students, Manhattanville College is an excellent place to receive a good education and lots of personal attention. Undergrads can find both tranquility and excitement by dividing their time between suburban campus life and visits to nearby New York City. This excitement will soon be added to. The New York Rangers are building their practice arena on campus, and the school is starting a hockey team. Students enjoy the quality of life at Manhattanville and the opportunities it provides. As one student remarked, "If you want to be in control of your future, come to Manhattanville."—*Ann Zeidner and Staff*

FYI

The three best things about attending Manhattanville are "the people, the location, and the personal attention."

The three worst things about attending Manhattanville are "the sparsity of classes, the lack of weekend social events, and the strict administration."

The three things that every student should do before graduating from Manhattanville are "watch the Super Bowl at the Pavillion, figure out if anyone else likes the portfolio system, and meet a hockey player."

One thing I'd like to have known before coming here is "just how much attention one gets."

New York University

Address: 22 Washington Square North, New York, NY 10011	**Percent African-American:** 7.0%	**Mean SAT:** NA
Phone: 212-998-4500	**Percent Hispanic:** 8.0%	**Middle 50% SAT range:** 620–710 V, 610–710 M
E-mail address: none	**Percent Asian:** 16.0%	
Web site URL: www.nyu.edu/ugadmissions or www.nyu.edu	**Percent in-state / out-of-state:** 31%/69%	**Middle 50% ACT range:** NA
	Percent Pub HS: 71%	**Mean ACT:** NA
Location: urban	**Fraternities:** 7%	**3 Most popular majors:** visual and performing arts, business, social sciences
Founded: 1861	**Sororities:** 6%	
Private or Public: private	**Number of Applicants:** 28,794	**Retention:** 88%
Religious affiliation: none	**Percent Accepted:** 31%	**Graduation rate:** 72%
Undergraduate enrollment: 18,204	**Percent Accepted who enroll:** 40%	**Library:** 3 mil +
		Tuition and Fees: $23,456 in; $23,456 out
Total enrollment: 37,124	**Entering:** 3,642	**Room and Board:** $8,676
Percent Male / Female: 41%/59%	**Transfers:** 904	**On-campus housing:** 84%
Percent Minority: 31.1%	**Application Deadline:** 15 Jan	**Financial aid, first-year:** 63%

Located near New York City's Greenwich Village, NYU provides students the opportunity to frequent myriad nightclubs and cafés, walk right through a movie shoot, or just hang out and listen to music in Washington Square Park. "The City is within us," one student proudly proclaimed.

Diversity Sums It All Up

Mention NYU, and instantly you hear NYC, which everyone simply refers to as "the City." Often regarded as the college's best feature, the City is about as diverse as they come. Anything you're looking for, it's got. NYU dorms and class buildings are integrated into the City—providing easy access to theater, the arts, the world's leading business center (Wall Street), and hundreds of restaurants. "It's the real world, with all types of people with various backgrounds and interests," remarked one student. Added another, "New York City will challenge the way you think and view the world. As they say, 'If you can make it here, you can make it anywhere.'"

NYU has a student body representative of the City's diversity. Students come from all over the U.S. and the world. With six separate undergraduate schools, ranging from traditional academic areas to colleges devoted to the arts, social work, or music, NYU reflects the multitude of cultures represented in the Village. Each maintains its own personality and academic requirements. NYU's version of the small liberal arts college, the College of Arts and Sciences, requires students to take courses under the Morse Academic Plan (MAP) with the intention of providing a well-rounded liberal arts education. Requirements are not universally loved. "They take a long time to wade through," remarked one undergrad. "And with the amount of money we're paying, we should be able to take what we want."

The Gallatin Division of NYU takes a different approach, however. Referred to as the "create your own major" division, work is self-paced and credits are earned as academic work is completed. Professional schools include the Stern School of Business; the School of Education, Health, Nursing, and Arts Professions; and the School of Social Work. Among these, the most selective are the Tisch School of the Arts and the Film School. As one student put it, "They have excellent education in drama, film, and dancing. They have Academy Award winners working there."

As one of the largest private universities in the nation, NYU is inundated with inordinately large lecture courses. Little personal attention is provided "unless you *really* make an effort to track someone down" and graduate students teach many classes, including most of the freshmen writing courses. The close-knit, pleasant atmosphere of smaller, enclosed campuses is absent here. "You can get lost in such a large university," said one student.

Living in the City

While NYU is concentrated in one of the nicer and safer areas of New York, there is no clear delineation between campus and Greenwich Village. The quality of dorms varies, but residents are generally pleased. Some are apartment-style and have private bathrooms, and "although you have to clean them, they are a huge advantage." Many are renovated apartment buildings and residential hotels. Others—including Rubin, Weinstein, and Hayden—are more traditional, and house many freshmen. The Weinstein cafeteria has interative televisions—students just touch the TV screen to request a video from the NYU music video station. Hayden Hall is located right on Washington Square Park and is known as a bit of a "creepy dorm" because it is so old. Third Avenue North is a dorm that is considered "in between" the good and the bad, though its dining hall "kind of has a fifties twist to it." Carlyle is considered good because of the apartment-style rooms, but it is a bit of a walk from campus. Although Goddard is traditional, many students like it for its proximity to most classes. Broome Street is "supposed to be huge in terms of space, but 10 or 11 people share one kitchen and two bathrooms." One of the noisier dorms is Brittany, which houses many students from Tisch.

Regarding food, one freshman admitted, "It started off great, but now it gets kind of boring." At meals, cereal, a salad bar, hamburgers, hot dogs, turkey burgers, and three entrées are always offered. But whatever cuisine you crave that the dining halls can't provide, you can find in the city. "There's at *least* a couple eateries anywhere you walk." One area, referred to as "the Four corners," has a café at each corner, including the Café Figgaro—a vegetarian place known for its falafels. Though admittedly, "it can be very, very expensive to attend NYU—there are numerous forms of financial aid, merit scholarships, and work-study programs, but living in the city can put a hole in your pocket."

Events Actually *on* Campus

There are many activities on campus, but like the academics, "it's easy to get lost in the shuffle here." Students said that being part of an organization can help to ease the feeling. Popular on campus are the Political Spectrum, Peers' Ears, and the Sexual Health Advisory. A daily newspaper, the *Washington Square News* is also continually seeking writers, as are literary magazines and cultural publications. Students for Social Equality, a political based group, is also popular among dents. But if none of the existing or tions particularly strike one's creating a new one is not reg difficult task. "If you have an idea an have people willing to do it, NYU will give you a budget," one undergrad pointed out.

> "It's the real world, with all types of people with various backgrounds and interests. Anything you're looking for, it's got."

Despite all the efforts to bring activities on campus, NYU's social life revolves around the City. Students frequent local night spots, from jazz clubs like Boo Radley to dance clubs like the Wetlands. With no major Greek life, few parties are actually held on campus grounds. In fact, no place on campus is really large enough to throw a traditional dance or party. However, the offerings are plentiful off campus, and many students choose to spend much of their leisure time there. You can find parties with nonstop action 'til 4 A.M. You can find quaint little coffee shops dimly lit. You can find comfortable outdoor cafés with views of the New York masses walking by.

With no clear definition of a campus and undergraduate students spread far apart, there is little school spirit. There is very little focus on organized athletics, though club sports, including ballroom dancing and racquetball, are popular. "Just look at the name," one student pointed out, referring to NYU Violets, "and you can tell why." For those who want to work out, the Jerome S. Coles Sports Center maintains stellar facilities, including an Olympic-size pool, an additional dive pool, a track, and tennis courts.

Given its location, security is tight in campus buildings. Students use their ID cards to get into campus buildings, and 24-hour security guards monitor all dorms. But most feel safe in Greenwich Village and the East Village. The increased activity at night around the NYU neighborhood also provides security in anonymity, giving the impression that the areas around campus are a safe place to walk. "The lights come alive at night," one student remarked. Although undergrads sometimes complain about losing IDs and consequently being locked out of their own dorms, one explained that "it's just important to be alert and to use common sense when living in New York City as in any place!" Doing so opens many doors—the City is at the students' fingertips, and all recommend that good use be made of this opportunity to melt into the country's most populous and most vibrant city.

—*William Chen*

ee best things about attending NYU are "New York City, the diversity of student body, rich environment that allows for hands-on learning, and a dynamic social life." orst things about attending NYU are "no clear delineation of a campus, the large er of students, the hefty price tag on education."
The three things that every student should do before graduating from NYU are "take advantage of the City and have fun, get work experience, and decide for yourself what's important for you to do before graduating!"
One thing I'd like to have known before coming here is "that the City is not as dangerous and 'scary' as many believe it to be."

Parsons School of Design

Address: 66 Fifth Avenue, New York, NY 10011
Phone: 212-229-8910
E-mail address: parsadm@newschool.edu
Web site URL: www.parsons.edu
Location: urban
Founded: 1896
Private or Public: private
Religious affiliation: none
Undergraduate enrollment: 1,800
Total enrollment: 2,600
Percent Male/Female: 30%/70%
Percent Minority: 41.5%

Percent African-American: 6.0%
Percent Hispanic: 12.0%
Percent Asian: 23.0%
Percent in-state/out-of-state: NA
Percent Pub HS: NA
Fraternities: 0%
Sororities: 0%
Number of Applicants: 2,827
Percent Accepted: 46%
Percent Accepted who enroll: 50%
Entering: 658
Transfers: 327
Application Deadline: NA

Mean SAT: NA
Middle 50% SAT range: NA
Middle 50% ACT range: NA
Mean ACT: NA
3 Most popular majors: communication design, fashion, illustration
Retention: NA
Graduation rate: NA
Library: 17,700 volumes
Tuition and Fees: $20,470 in; NA out
Room and Board: $8,900
On-campus housing: NA
Financial aid, first-year: 85%

In the heart of New York, in downtown Greenwich Village, students are finding their way through the challenge of Parsons and the excitement of the city.

One student says, "We have access to all kinds of facilities and events in the city that has offerings from all over the world. Even beyond what the city can give us, the university offers information and facilities for the ones who are interested in learning."

The City as Campus

New York City is one of the most dynamic cities of the world, offering many centers for culture, design, communications, architecture, and business. The campus, located in Greenwich Village, is at the heart of Manhattan's artistic life. There is one main campus building at Parsons and three residence halls in walking distance of the Village campus. Loeb Residence hall is mostly provided to freshmen. It provides access to an art studio, a reading room, a lounge and laundry room. The other two residence halls, The Marlton House and Union Square, are for those above 19. These two offer singles, doubles, and some suites.

As for other resources, Parsons provides its students with links to New York University's and Cooper Union's libraries. In addition, many students take advantage of Parson's study abroad programs. Israel, the Netherlands, Great Britain, and Sweden are popular destinations for students, and many choose to go to Paris.

Students who enroll in the Paris program take French Language classes, a part of the core curriculum. The aim of this core curriculum, which also entails Liberal Studies courses that offer classes on the intellectual and historical aspects of France, is to help students become more independent in their environment.

Not Only Fashion Design

Parsons New York offers three four-year undergraduate art and design options: B.F.A., a Bachelor of Fine Arts, B.B.A., a Bachelor of Business Administration, and a five-year B.A./B.F.A. The Bachelor of Business Administration requires the completion of a specific curriculum in design marketing. The five-year dual degree offers students a complete studio art or design major along with a liberal arts education.

Since Parsons is a part of the New School program, students always have the option of choosing electives from the New School for Social Research. The first year is the "Foundation Year" and the courses offered, which are basics of drawing and design, are the "Foundation Courses." The Foundation program is also offered as a part of nondegree programs. Freshmen take classes in small sections, with 15 to 20 students, often taught by professionals in the field of the class.

> **"The workload is too much. Many of the people usually drop out the first year and some more drop out the following years."**

Parsons challenges all students and weeds out slackers. "The workload is too much. Many of the people usually drop out the first year and some more drop out the following years," comments a student. Fashion and product design are considered the hardest majors, whereas design marketing isn't considered as challenging.

Four affiliate schools send graduates to Parsons, where they complete their bachelor's degree. These two-year schools are located in Paris, the Dominican Republic, Kanazawa, Japan, and Seoul, South Korea.

It Takes Two to Tango

The students enjoy their time in the city, but many have money issues. "You have to pay a lot to either rent an apartment or live outside Manhattan and take the subway. Parsons is a very expensive school," one student says. This common observation may have some correlation to Parsons's emphasis on marketing your designs and making money. Students say that it is a "School of Design" and not a "School of Art." One student explains, "Anyone who doesn't like to make money when they graduate or anyone that is really interested in fine arts and learning skills and crafts should stay away!"

Also, social life doesn't really exist on campus or in school but in the city. Being underage can cause great problems since it narrows down the clubbing options for going out. However, almost all have found ways to solve the problem. Because so much of student life takes place out of school, "I feel like a working adult here, because I live in an apartment and go to school every day like my office and come home and I have a completely different social life."

Designers Lead the Way

Many famous and successful designers, artists, and employers at large corporations visit Parsons frequently. The teachers are all professionals in their fields and many are working designers in Manhattan. "They just teach part-time, which is very cool." Students have great connections through their savvy teachers. Therefore,

many obtain outstanding and competitive internships.

As long as they can manage to find a balance between New York City life and schoolwork, students are happy to be a part of a lively, energetic city. And since art has been said to imitate life, New York and Parsons are guaranteed to produce many complex masterpieces.—*Yakut Seyhanli*

FYI

The three best things about attending Parsons are "being in the city, having great internship options, and the study abroad in Paris."

The three worst things about attending Parsons are "having great expenses, many people around you doing drugs, and the city."

The three things you should do before graduating from Parsons are "do a great internship, take advantage of all the city has to offer to you, and study abroad."

One thing students would like to have known before coming to Parsons is "how important it is to manage your time."

Rensselaer Polytechnic Institute

Address: 110 Eighth Street, Troy, NY 12180-3590
Phone: 518-276-6216
E-mail address: admissions@rpi.edu
Web site URL: www.rpi.edu
Location: suburban
Founded: 1824
Private or Public: private
Religious affiliation: none
Undergraduate enrollment: 4,591
Total enrollment: 6,560
Percent Male/Female: 75%/25%
Percent Minority: 20.0%
Percent African-American: 4.0%

Percent Hispanic: 4.0%
Percent Asian: 12.0%
Percent in-state/out-of-state: 51%/49%
Percent Pub HS: 79%
Fraternities: 37%
Sororities: 26%
Number of Applicants: 4,664
Percent Accepted: 81%
Percent Accepted who enroll: 30%
Entering: 1,133
Transfers: 0
Application Deadline: 1 Jan
Mean SAT: 607 V, 659 M

Middle 50% SAT range: 480–600 V, 620–710 M
Middle 50% ACT range: 23–30
Mean ACT: 27
3 Most popular majors: general engineering, management, computer science
Retention: 92.0%
Graduation rate: 44.0%
Library: 440,000 volumes
Tuition and Fees: $22,300 in; $22,300 out
Room and Board: $7,692
On-campus housing: 57%
Financial aid, first-year: 76%

Looking for a great technology school that excels in sports extracurriculars? A line of hundreds, if not thousands, of students wraps around the Student Union and school has not even started yet. Why are they out there? The answer: these students in RPI's "hockey line" are competing with one another to get the best seats for this year's hockey season. "People live outside day and night

until the tickets are officially on sale," says one undergraduate. The hockey team forms the basis for school spirit at RPI, a school that offers strong academic programs and a great view of Troy and Albany, New York.

They Have a Ton of Work

At RPI, undergraduates can choose to major in one of five schools: Engineering,

Humanities and Social Sciences, Management and Technology, Architecture, and Science. Although these five schools cover a wide range of areas, students agree that "RPI is primarily focused on Engineering," which sometimes annoys students in the other schools. Students are generally excited about RPI's attention to "teamwork and hands-on activities, which allows you to dive right into your major." Most think that management is an easy major, described by one as requiring "some pretty basic classes, as well as some leadership classes." The toughest courses depend on the major, but the two most commonly cited are Differential Equations ("Diffy-Q") and Introduction to Engineering Analysis. Regardless of major, all students must fulfill distribution requirements that include courses in humanities and social sciences. Opinions on the distribution requirements vary from "they are great because you get exposed to the material outside your major" to "they are a waste of time and effort." Class size varies between 30 and 40, although there are some larger intro classes. By senior year classes can be as small as 5 or 6 people. Most students find the grading fair; some complain that "the curve usually ends up being one or two points that don't really help." Professors teach most classes, and TAs, who are usually grad students, lead all sections. Professors receive good reviews overall; however there are some "that everyone dislikes." Many students also complain that they have difficulty understanding their TAs' foreign accents. Students always feel that they have "a ton of work," but they also say that "it's worth it because we're learning stuff that we'll actually use."

Livin' It Up

"Most people here, of all ages, drink," said one student. Fraternity houses and the downtown bars and clubs are popular hangouts for both under- and upperclassmen. Underage drinking is not allowed on campus, although for most students, "drinking is the norm." Fraternities and sororities are popular on campus, although several students think that "this year's incoming class was not very thrilled about rushing." There is no pressure to rush. As one student put it, "nothing pushes the frat/sorority thing." The best parties of the year are SAE's "Red Death," Phi Kappa Alpha's "Shoot the Dog," and Phi Mu Delta's "Kamikaze." Some people smoke pot, but that is reportedly the extent of drug use on campus.

Although most students do drink, students say that there is no pressure to drink and there are many "dry activities" going on as well. The Student Union is in between the dorms and the lecture halls and is a popular hangout. A lot of students also do work there during the day. There is always something going on at the Union, from second-hand clothing and CD sales to musicians' performances and movie nights. Mother's Wine Emporium is a Student Union–funded coffee house run by undergrads and brings acoustic music to the campus. Those interested in theater can go to the Playhouse to see plays while those eager to see famous performers head to the Field. Bob Dylan, Korn, and Offspring are among the performers scheduled for the spring of '99. Students agree that cars are "extremely useful" for going off campus and some even refer to them as a "must." Students report that "about half" of the student body have cars.

Beds and Plates

Freshmen are required to live in the dorms, and most are satisfied there. After freshman year students choose among moving to upperclassmen dorms, becoming an RA, living off campus, and moving into a frat house. Most RAs are "pretty easygoing" and get along well with the students. All dorms are now coed except Cary Hall. Upperclassmen dorms are nicer than the freshman dorms and they have air-conditioning, which freshman dorms don't have.

There are various meal plans that the students can choose from. Based on the plan they choose, they also get RADs or MADs (Rennselaer or Marriott Advantage Dollars) on their cards. Students are happy with the dining options and say that "there are plenty of places to eat around. Almost every building has something." The Commons, Bar-H, and Russell-Sage are the three largest dining halls. In addition to these, there are many fast-food options at the Student Union. Finally, off-campus restaurants offer a wide price range and "definitely something for everyone," and plenty of students choose to dine out on weekends.

The Ratio Says It All

According to female freshmen, the student stereotype is "that we are all male and all dorks," which is, in fact, not true. Students have different opinions about the diversity on campus. Some talk about a "good racial/ethnic mix" while others say that the student body is "not diverse enough: too many normal people." However, all men agree that the 3:1 male to female ratio "sucks." Females, on the other hand, take advantage of this ratio: "We females love it." Another related complaint is that there is not enough sex. An interesting T-shirt on campus says, "Sex Kills—Come to RPI and Live Forever." The all-female Russell Sage College across the street helps to improve the unequal male-female ratio.

Besides Classes and Parties

Most students are involved in extracurriculars or sports at RPI. This involvement comes in different forms, ranging from writing for the *Poly*, the daily, to driving for the RPI ambulance, from joining the Ballroom Dance Club to joining the *X-Files* Club. Students get involved in community service through APO and Circle K, whereas ethnic groups unite in organizations such as the Black Students' Alliance and Alianza Latina.

> **"People live outside day and night until the tickets are officially on sale."**

Hockey is the most popular sport at RPI and "Big Red Freakout" is the biggest hockey game of the year, followed by wild parties and "lots of alcohol." This year, Dartmouth will be RPI's guest at this game. Besides the hockey team, "most teams have been doing exceptionally well this year." RPI recruits mainly for hockey, football, and basketball. Frats form teams to compete in the intramurals. "You either have to be in a frat or play for one," says one student. Pickup ultimate Frisbee is also fairly popular.

If technical education is your first priority and the idea of shouting "Go RED!" for one of the nation's best hockey teams sounds exciting to you, then RPI may be a great choice.—*Engin Yenidunya and Staff*

FYI

The three best things about attending RPI are "the first-rate faculty, the high-quality resources for research and learning, and being able to interact with a high-caliber student body."

The three worst things about attending RPI are "surviving the terrain, surviving the winter storms, and climbing all those damn stairs!"

The three things every student should do before graduating are "attend at least one hockey game, go to at least one event in Troy Music Hall, and attend one production in the Playhouse."

The one thing I wish I'd known before coming here is "the nature of RPI's relationship with industrial giants like Microsoft and IBM."

Rochester Institute of Technology

Address: 60 Lomb Memorial Drive, Rochester, NY 14623
Phone: 716-475-6631
E-mail address: admissions@rit.edu
Web site URL: www.rit.edu
Location: rural
Founded: 1829
Private or Public: private
Religious affiliation: none
Undergraduate enrollment: 10,626
Total enrollment: 15,000
Percent Male / Female: 65% / 35%
Percent Minority: 13.0%

Percent African-American: 5.0%
Percent Hispanic: 3.0%
Percent Asian: 5.0%
Percent in-state / out-of-state: 65% / 35%
Percent Pub HS: 80%
Fraternities: 10%
Sororities: 10%
Number of Applicants: 7,151
Percent Accepted: 78%
Percent Accepted who enroll: 40%
Entering: 2,231
Transfers: 0
Application Deadline: 15 Mar
Mean SAT: NA

Middle 50% SAT range: 520–620 V, 540–650 M
Middle 50% ACT range: NA
Mean ACT: NA
3 Most popular majors: photography, information technology, mechanical engineering
Retention: 84.0%
Graduation rate: NA
Library: 360,000 volumes
Tuition and Fees: $17,328 in; $17,328 out
Room and Board: $6,852
On-campus housing: 60%
Financial aid, first-year: 80%

B rick, brick, brick, brick, lots of brick. That is how most students describe RIT's campus. No wonder why the family, alumni, and student weekend is known as the Brick City Festival. Every building is made of red brick at this university, which offers a strong education combined with valuable training for the workplace.

Academics You Can Actually Use

The single word that describes RIT academics best is "pre-professional." The main focus here is on life after graduation. As one student describes it, "We actually learn stuff that we'll use later on in life." Upon application, students choose to enroll in one of the six colleges that focus on applied science and technology, business, science, engineering, imaging arts and sciences, and liberal arts. Students may also choose to enroll in the National Technical Institute for the Deaf (NTID). Because they must make this commitment so early on, "most freshmen arrive with their majors and even careers in their minds."

Both the photography department and the engineering programs receive high praise from students, while NTID is the world's largest mainstream college program for the deaf and hearing-impaired. This institute provides sign-language interpreters in every classroom and in laboratories to give 1,100 students with impaired hearing a first-rate, fully integrated college experience.

The academic requirements at RIT consist of "a general core of classes and a core of classes inside the major." Although some engineering and science majors say that "liberal arts is an easy major," in general most agree that "no major is particularly easy." Class size varies depending on the level of the course. Students say the majority of classes tend to be 40 students or less, with some larger introductory classes. Laboratory classes are "usually around 10 or so." Although the majority of students seem to be happy with most professors and describe them as "extremely knowledgeable in their subject areas" and "more than willing to help out their students," one student did confess that "there are always a few not-so-good ones around." Most professors are "easy to contact and get along with." There are "hardly any TAs, and they are "used primarily for grading."

RIT's quarterly system creates a fast-paced schedule. Generally, undergraduates think that "RIT provides great academic instruction." In most majors, students combine classroom education and work experience through RIT's very popular cooperative education program (Co-op). These students take five years to complete their degrees, and in their last two years they spend four of the eight quarters working full-time in a firm. Students describe the benefits of Co-op as "gaining valuable experience in the workplace, being able to apply what you learn in your courses, having an advantage over other job candidates, and helping finance your education." The company assignments for Co-op are based on students' interests and career choices with companies ranging from AT&T, General Motors, Texas Instruments, and Xerox to IBM as employers.

Residential Life—Many Options to Choose From

Freshmen are required to live in the dorms, which students say are "in good shape" and are coed either by floor or by door. Most have doubles, and some have singles. The renovation of five dorms has been recently completed and five others are currently being renovated, one at a time. The new rooms will have full air-conditioning and heating, more closets and floor space, and jacks for phone, cable, and network connections. After freshman year, the three housing options are living in the dorms, living in on-campus apartments, and going off campus. A number of hearing-impaired students also choose to live in the "NTID dorms," specifically designed for the deaf and hearing impaired. Four on-campus apartment complexes all have the convenience of bus service and the advantage of an active social scene. RIT also has special-interest housing options consisting of Art, Community Service, Computer Science, Engineering, Photo, Unity and International Houses, where students with similar interests live together on a designated floor. The Greeks also live together in ei-

ther the dorms, the apartments, or their own houses.

Where Do They Eat?

There are three places to eat on campus. Gracie's, the "all-you-can-eat buffet-style dining hall" with a wide range of options; the Commons, a restaurant-style dining hall; and the Student Alumni Center cafeteria. The RITskeller, beneath the cafeteria, has a full bar that serves alcoholic drinks to staff, faculty, and students who are over 21. Not long ago, a new coffee stop was added in the Commons called the College Grind. When going off campus, Nick Tahoe's in Rochester, which is open 24 hours, is a student favorite. The restaurant is known as "the home of the original Garbage Plate." As one student says, these plates make "a good 2 A.M. I-need-to-study meal." There are also "corner stores" in the tunnels under the dorms where students can buy snacks. These tunnels are also favorite places to socialize because they have pool tables and arcade games.

Who Are These People?

"Deaf, hearing, white, black, Asian, Indian, foreign, musician, artist, engineer—we've got it all," commented an undergraduate about the student body. "The only stereotype is that we don't have any school spirit," another one adds. There is a wide enough variety of students on campus that anyone should be able to find plenty of people with similar interests. While some groups form right away and remain constant, most students find their groups changing throughout their four years at RIT. One point that all students agree on is that the student body "needs more women," although they admit the male-female ratio has recently been improving, though slowly. Despite these extremes in the student body, one student claims that "people start to look and act alike at the end of senior year, as if they were coming from the same factory."

Which Way Is the Party?

The Greeks throw parties, and there are smaller parties in the dorms in addition to apartment parties. Alcohol is completely banned from dorms and frat houses and may only be served in apartments. But non-drinkers say they do not feel excluded at any of the parties. Fraternities and sororities are not dominant in the social scene and their parties are open to nonmembers. Their houses are located on the "Quarter Mile," the famous path from the dorms to the academic buildings. One student referred to how there are "lots of random hookups among frats and sororities."

Most other social events are held at the Student Alumni Union. The College Activities Board shows current movies on the weekends; "concerts and lectures are also common." As one student said, "You do have to know where to look, but the events are out there." Upperclassmen also go off campus to local bars like the Creek. About ten minutes from campus, Rochester offers bars, clubs, restaurants, concerts, and movies. Having a car or knowing someone with a car helps a lot when someone wants to go off campus. Although many students consider cars essential, "they are by no means required to have fun at RIT."

When They Are Not Studying!

The Rochester Wargamers Association and Guild (RWAG) is the largest student club on campus "because they count anyone who comes to their meetings as members." The members play role-playing games and different card games. The RIT Formula SAE Team is another popular organization that designs, builds, and races its own cars. In 1998, the Rochester Cannabis Coalition was a controversial club—they were denied official recognition and use of student government funds because they supported education about cannabis. Although some students use soft drugs, the drug scene is not extremely popular at Rochester.

> "Deaf, hearing, white, black, Asian, Indian, foreign, musician, artist, engineer—we've got it all."

RIT's varsity teams do not attract huge crowds. Men's and women's hockey are the most popular teams, with "very, very enthusiastic fans." The basketball teams follow the hockey teams in terms of popularity. One student stated that "the general RIT population couldn't care less about how the sports teams are doing." Another undergraduate said, "We are good at grades, not sports." Despite this lack of support for varsity sports, intramural sports are often played and attract large participation.

RIT is for the career-oriented student who has already made certain decisions about the future. And this planning reportedly pays off. Firms are ready to grab RIT students upon graduation because of the high quality of their education and their workplace experience that they have already gained through Co-op. What most of these career-oriented students discover, though, after four or five years, is that "they didn't actually expect to enjoy RIT so much!"—*Engin Yenidunya and Staff*

FYI

The three best things about attending Rochester Institute of Technology are "the student diversity, the practical academics, and the Co-op education program."

The three worst things about attending Rochester Institute of Technology are "the workload, the lack of school spirit, and the dining hall hamburgers."

The three things every student should do before graduating from Rochester Institute of Technology are "party like nuts, study hard, and go to Nick Tahoe's."

One thing I'd like to have known before coming here is "how much brick there is—it's everywhere."

Sarah Lawrence College

Address: 1 Mead Way, Broxville, NY 10708-5999
Phone: 800-888-2858
E-mail address: slcadmit@slc.edu
Web site URL: www.slc.edu
Location: suburban
Founded: 1926
Private or Public: private
Religious affiliation: none
Undergraduate enrollment: 1,178
Total enrollment: 1,495
Percent Male/Female: 27%/73%
Percent Minority: 16.4%
Percent African-American: 6.0%

Percent Hispanic: 5.0%
Percent Asian: 5.0%
Percent in-state/out-of-state: 21%/79%
Percent Pub HS: 65%
Fraternities: 0%
Sororities: 0%
Number of Applicants: 2,070
Percent Accepted: 43%
Percent Accepted who enroll: 31%
Entering: 278
Transfers: 28
Application Deadline: 1 Feb
Mean SAT: 640 V, 570 M

Middle 50% SAT range: 590–700 V, 520–610 M
Middle 50% ACT range: 23–28
Mean ACT: 25
3 Most popular majors: writing, theater, literature
Retention: 92.0%
Graduation rate: 63.0%
Library: 288,000 volumes
Tuition and Fees: $25,256 in; $25,256 out
Room and Board: $8,000
On-campus housing: 95%
Financial aid, first-year: 48%

For those who dare to take the road less traveled, Sarah Lawrence offers a supportive learning environment. In a peaceful suburb of New York City, this small liberal arts college caters to students interested in shaping their own educational experience.

Serious Students

The curriculum at Sarah Lawrence College consists of three courses per semester, each of which requires an independent project. Course registration requires an interview process: students interview teachers to find out about the course material and expectations, while professors decide whether the students are right for their class. According to one student, the process is "not too difficult, but can sometimes be a problem with very popular classes." All first-year students must take a freshman studies course, and individual meetings with the professor of this course take place weekly. By graduation, all students must have taken one course in three of the following four disciplines: humanities, creative arts, social sciences/history, and natural sciences/math. Aside from these requirements, students are free to choose from a diverse course list. Art courses are especially popular, but one student reported that the art facilities

don't measure up to the level of student interest. Writing and psychology are also popular departments.

In their first two years at Sarah Lawrence, students choose a faculty advisor to help them design their program of study. Students meet with their advisor, or "don," once a week during their freshman year and biweekly thereafter. Student-faculty relations extend beyond these routine meetings and classes, however. Many students say they even "hang out with their teachers." This strong relationship is bolstered by the small seminar courses that dominate the departments at Sarah Lawrence. Seminar sizes generally range from 12 to 18 students. The college offers some lecture courses, however. While they are taught by professors, there are some TAs, who are available primarily for students who need extra help.

Students at Sarah Lawrence say they are "passionate about learning," and they appreciate the college's emphasis on the learning process instead of on grades. Unless students ask for letter grades in their courses, they receive only written evaluations detailing their performance. The de-emphasis on grades makes the academic atmosphere "not competitive at all," one student said. Special academic programs at Sarah Lawrence include independent-study projects, study abroad, and a continuing education program for students of nontraditional age.

Outside Involvement

Research for classes can be done at the college's Esther Raushenbush Library, although one student said, "It doesn't have a great selection of anything . . . students do research there because there isn't anywhere else." Despite its reportedly limited resources, the library is a comfortable place for quiet study, especially the "pillow room," which is so comfortable that some students can barely stop themselves from falling asleep in it. One of the reasons cited for this is the building's poor lighting. For better lighting, some people choose to study in their dorm rooms or in empty classrooms.

Some students live off campus, but most choose to live on campus because off-campus housing tends to be expensive. Housing options at Sarah Lawrence range from single-sex and coed dormitories to quiet houses where no one is allowed to make any noise that can be heard outside the door. Much of the student housing shares building space with offices and classrooms; campus residents recommend living in one of the newer, more standard dorms "if you want to have a social life." Some of the rooms are considered "very pretty," while others are categorized as "generic dorm rooms." Dining options are not quite as varied. First-year students are required to eat on the school's meal plan, in either the school's main cafeteria or the health-food bar. The third dining option is a fast-food restaurant, the Pub. Dinner is also a good time for socializing, since many students hang out at the dining halls. Students also praise the dining halls for offering ample vegetarian options, and they say that "it's much easier to be a vegetarian than an omnivore at SLC."

One undergrad described the Sarah Lawrence student body as "diverse in every way I can possibly think of." Many students come from the East and West Coasts, although demographics are fairly scattered. While students admit there is some truth to the Sarah Lawrence stereotype of the "radical, black-clad lesbian," they agree that this is not an accurate portrait of the entire student body. Originally a women's college, Sarah Lawrence went coed in 1968, and has even attracted a few conservatives into its fold. In general, however, students lean toward the political left. Sarah Lawrence has a fairly large and accepted gay and lesbian population, and gay issues are at the forefront of discussion. Ethnic minorities are also well represented on campus with active minority-student groups such as the Black Student Union.

Extracurricular Activities

Extracurricular activities at Sarah Lawrence reflect a wide range of student interests. Despite one student's negative appraisal ("there's not much to do ever, and a lot less on weeknights"), there does seem to be a lot going on. Student government is very big. Improvisational comedy groups are available for the more lighthearted; one student described them as a group of people "who think they're humorous." Many of the activities at Sarah Lawrence have artistic themes—writing is one of the major modes of expression. The *Sarah Lawrence Review* and *Dark Phrases* are student-written literary and poetic compilations. Another is a semiregular newspaper called the *Phoenix*. Student-run concerts are fertile ground for aspiring musicians. Throughout the week, guest lecturers and poetry readings are held by student organizations. Although "there aren't lot of places to hang out on campus," one student said, undergrads congregate in dorm rooms or the student-run coffee house, Javahouse, which raises money for scholarships.

On weekends, students go into New York City or to local bars like the Spinning Wheel. On campus, there are movies and a dance every Saturday night. All campus parties are initiated by students and must be registered with college administrators. According to one student, the administration takes a position on alcohol that is "officially discouraging, but in actual practice doesn't care." Some students say that the administration has been taking a stricter stance recently, but that room searches are not allowed unless they receive a complaint. The students themselves have quite lenient attitudes toward alcohol and drug consumption. Even if they do not spend their free time "drinking or doing some kind of chemicals," one student said, they are tolerant of those who do.

Some other activities that students rate highly are gay/lesbian/bisexual Coming Out Week and the Deb Ball, which began as a debutante ball for the prim Sarah Lawrence women of decades past, but has since become a less "proper" tradition. The annual Bacchanalia, a spring festival of bands, beer, and dancing, also earns student praise.

Campus response to sports varies. Some students claim that "a few people do them, but they're no big deal for the rest of campus," while others enthusiastically support varsity sports, particularly hockey. Students have enjoyed the new Campbell Sports Center and the announced construction of Leckonby Football Stadium. Sarah Lawrence also has varsity men's and women's tennis, crew, cross-country, and equestrian teams, and it sponsors a number of intramural sports.

The Sarah Lawrence campus is self-contained and situated within a quiet suburb of New York. Students call the campus "very beautiful"; it's surrounded by trees, rocks, lots of hills, and, strangely enough, skunks. The relationship between the college and the affluent, rather conservative community of Bronxville, however, is "a bit of a conflicting situation," according to one undergrad, who felt that local residents "aren't too pleased with the students who go here." The benefit of living in such a wealthy enclave is that crime is minimal. Security guards patrol the area, but security measures are generally unobtrusive. The school also provides emergency phones and escort services. Students keep their doors and windows locked to guard against theft, but one student reported that the crime is "nothing comparable to other schools I've seen or been to."

For students entering Sarah Lawrence, advice from those on the inside is "if you're a very curious person, then Sarah Lawrence would probably be a good place." Students are generally independent in their academic pursuits, so if that is what you have in mind, Sarah Lawrence can make all the difference. —*Billy Rahm and Staff*

> **Originally a women's college, Sarah Lawrence went coed in 1968, and has even attracted a few conservatives into its fold.**

FYI
The three best things about attending Sarah Lawrence are "the contact with the professors, the de-emphasis on grades, and the diverse student body."
The three worst things about attending Sarah Lawrence are "the cold winters, occasional housing problems, and the lack of choices for places to study."
The three things that every student should do before graduating from Sarah Lawrence are "check out Javahouse, go to a hockey game, and explore New York City."
One thing I'd like to have known before coming to Sarah Lawrence is "that school spirit is so low."

Skidmore College

Address: 815 North Broadway, Saratoga Springs, NY 12866-1632
Phone: 518-580-5570
E-mail address: admissions@skidmore.edu
Web site URL: www.skidmore.edu
Location: suburban
Founded: 1802
Private or Public: private
Religious affiliation: none
Undergraduate enrollment: 2,184
Total enrollment: 2,198
Percent Male/Female: 39%/61%
Percent Minority: 10.0%

Percent African-American: 2.0%
Percent Hispanic: 5.0%
Percent Asian: 3.0%
Percent in-state/out-of-state: 93%/7%
Percent Pub HS: 60%
Fraternities: 0%
Sororities: 0%
Number of Applicants: 5,431
Percent Accepted: 48%
Percent Accepted who enroll: 23%
Entering: 599
Transfers: NA
Application Deadline: 1 Feb

Mean SAT: 606 V, 605 M
Middle 50% SAT range: 560–640 V, 560–640 M
Middle 50% ACT range: NA
Mean ACT: 23
3 Most popular majors: English, business, psychology
Retention: 89%
Graduation rate: 69.0%
Library: 410,000 volumes
Tuition and Fees: $24,000 in; $24,000 out
Room and Board: $6,950
On-campus housing: 80%
Financial aid, first-year: 39%

About half a mile from downtown Saratoga, on the peak of a hill lies "a beautiful campus" despite its "somewhat ugly '60s style buildings." Skidmore College offers a fine liberal arts education for its small population. However, academics are far from the only thing on its students' minds. They also rave about the attractiveness of the student body, the town's great social scene, and thriving extracurricular organizations.

Academics

Skidmore is definitely a school for humanities-oriented students. In addition to the requirements of their respective majors, all Skidmore students have core course requirements, including two Liberal Studies classes, two society classes, two arts courses, two science courses, and one non-Western course. One junior praised the core requirements, saying, "They allow for a broad range of study in many disciplines before specializing in a major." Another junior said that though "the LS1 course encompassed everything" and was "useful," it was "a little boring." More bluntly, explained a senior, "the core requirements are fairly easy and the major requirements are all intense. Most people do a double major or a major and minor in two unrelated fields. Slackers only have one major so they don't have to do as much."

Classes are small, averaging about 15 students a class, and there aren't any TAs. "If you have a group of people who love what they're doing, it can be really stimulating," said a computer science major. One senior said that "grading is very easy, and all in all, classes are fairly laid back and students get involved." However, business classes are known to be quite intense and demanding. Study abroad programs, summer programs, and co-ops with other schools are also available for students to participate in.

Skidmore professors are great, say students. "I firmly believe that the Skidmore faculty are some of the most inspiring and hard-working professors in higher education. The best part is seeing how much every professor loves what he or she does, and seeing students get really involved in a great discussion," said one student. Popular teachers include English professor Tom Lewis, who won an Emmy award for a documentary on American highways, English professor Stephen Millhauser, who recently won a Pulitzer Prize, and Sheldon Solomon, who among other habits, drinks tons of coffee, wears shorts in the dead of winter, and "is a genius." Raved a junior, "We have several notable professors in virtually every department. You don't realize how many important people teach at Skidmore until you look around. It's pretty amazing." Best of all, "there's a close relationship between faculty and students. Faculty often make themselves available outside of their office hours," said a pleased sophomore.

Social Life

Despite the lack of Greek life at Skidmore, these kids know how to party come the weekend. Explained a senior, "Freshmen tend to stay in the dorms with small parties or they head on down to the campus housing where juniors and seniors live." As for the upperclassmen, a junior joked that they, in turn, go and look for the freshmen, in addition to parties, bars, and concerts. One popular party is Diva Night. "There are plenty of social alternatives, but people usually just want to get drunk," said one student. It's too bad, because "there is a ridiculous amount of organized activities on campus. If you can make it to every campus activity, you'll end up failing out of school and going broke. But at least you'll have a great time in the process," a junior quipped. Discounting the on-campus bar, most claim that being underage is not a problem. Despite the fact that kegs are not allowed on campus, one student boasted, that it "very rarely stops us." Indeed, students report that there is quite a bit of drug and alcohol use on campus.

"There are more random hookups than there are bricks in this school—the hookups usually lead to relationships, so I have no objections to that," said one student. This isn't a problem for male students, as one raved, "the female population is gorgeous, I've had friends come up and visit, then declare they are transferring after seeing the wildlife at one party." Females also agreed that the student population is plenty attractive at their school. Furthermore, students all said that it is very easy to meet people at Skidmore, and while there are quite a few cliques, they are easy to get into and change often.

There are plenty of places for students to take dates and to chow in general.

While dining hall food isn't too bad and Skidmore offers quite a few vegetarian options, the multitude of great restaurants in Saratoga are a much better option. Students mentioned The Saratoga Brew Pub and Maestro's as great date restaurants. Summed up one senior expertly, "Esperanto, the Brew Pub, and The Parting Glass are all good places to bet a quick bite, and the latter two serve great pints. Great food is found at Scallions, Wheatfields, and Lillian's." A Skidmore professor owns Esperanto, and one junior recommended the doughboys there as being particularly scrumptious.

90210-esque?

As for the students themselves, as one junior put it, the population is filled with "rich, spoiled brats." A little less scathingly, one senior said, "the student stereotype is that everyone is rich. Most people wear designer casual wear to class. People are shunned for wearing Gap. Even the school bus is white. Everyone is very into looking good, so there is a good amount of working out and staying in shape." The general consensus was that the student body is "way too homogeneous," and that "more internationalism and racial diversity" is needed at Skidmore. One junior said that the stereotypical student is a "pretty, shallow, rich, white girl from Long Island." However, another student countered that there are many homosexual and interracial couples, and that "everything is accepted at Skidmore."

Especially popular on campus are the a cappella singing groups. One senior said "Everyone loves the music groups. The Bandersnatchers are gods in the eyes of some people." Most students, if not in a cappella groups, are involved with other forms of performance art. Students mentioned The Wombats, Skidmore's official Ultimate Frisbee club, Sketchies, a sketch comedy troupe, and the orchestra as popular organizations. Community service is "not super popular, but a lot of people do volunteer." The school is quite community oriented, said one sophomore, "Most concerts are open to the public for free and volunteering clubs often get involved with local children and local issues."

Intramurals are also big, although varsity sports are not popular—probably be cause Skidmore does not have a football team. "The school does not support the athletic teams, and therefore they don't play well. It's a shame," lamented one student. Athletes all live on South Campus because it is closer to the gym. One junior complained about frequently malfunctioning treadmills at the gym, but mentioned that there is a pool, tennis courts, and a public golf course in town.

Campus and Dorms

Aside from problems finding parking, students love the campus and town, which they say is gorgeous, though not exactly hopping. On the flip side, students always feel safe and have no security issues. "The campus is right up against a forest and the outskirts of the city are on the other side," explained one student. One senior did complain, however, that the school needed more "open grass space."

Students love their dorms, even describing freshman year housing fondly. "There are only two bad dorms, and they are Moore and Skidmore halls. Skidmore Hall is as far south on campus as possible," said one student. However, warned a junior, "Your sophomore year can be bad if you get a bad lottery number—you could end up in Moore Hall, an off-campus dorm." A senior said that Moore is about a five-minute ride by car and that "pretty much you are stuck there sophomore year unless you have a good room

number." Students tend to prefer North Campus to South, "but all the dorms are far more accommodating than anywhere else I've been," praised one student.

> "The campus is right up against a forest and the outskirts of the city are on the other side."

Nonetheless, many students live off campus, especially seniors, "though there are some juniors and a handful of sophomores. Usually people want to be close to the heart of the campus to know what's going on," said a senior. The dorms have a great many restrictions, but most of them are enforced with an "if-the-RA-didn't-see-it-I-didn't-do-it" state of mind, said one student. Other buildings of note are the music building, which was funded by the Filenes family, and a "gigantic" art museum being built near the gym. All in all, Skidmore is a fun place that provides a complete education for students who don't mind a small school atmosphere. As one senior summed up, "I would choose Skidmore again any day, the education is good and the people are all really chill. The atmosphere is great on campus and if you can't get laid here you need to seek professional help."—*Jennifer Wang*

FYI
The three best things about attending Skidmore College are "that the male to female ratio is 40:60, the small classes, and the fun professors."
The three worst things about attending Skidmore College are "the small town, how you can't do much without a car, and the small selection of guys."
The three things that every student should do before graduating from Skidmore College are "go bar-hopping in Saratoga, get involved in as much as you can without killing yourself, have sex in the north woods."
One thing I'd like to have known before coming here is "the right way to pick up a woman."

St. Bonaventure University

Address: PO Box D, St. Bonaventure, NY 14778
Phone: 716-375-2400
E-mail address: admissions@sbu.edu
Web site URL: www.sbu.edu
Location: rural
Founded: 1858
Private or Public: private
Religious affiliation: none
Undergraduate enrollment: 2,209
Total enrollment: 2,822
Percent Male / Female: 49%/51%
Percent Minority: 3.0%

Percent African-American: 1.0%
Percent Hispanic: 1.0%
Percent Asian: 1.0%
Percent in-state / out-of-state: 78%/22%
Percent Pub HS: 68%
Fraternities: 0%
Sororities: 0%
Number of Applicants: 1,618
Percent Accepted: 93%
Percent Accepted who enroll: 38%
Entering: 572
Transfers: 0
Application Deadline: rolling

Mean SAT: 532 V, 532 M
Middle 50% SAT range: 480–590 V, 470–580 M
Middle 50% ACT range: NA
Mean ACT: 23
3 Most popular majors: education, journalism, accounting
Retention: 83%
Graduation rate: 51.0%
Library: 270,000 volumes
Tuition and Fees: $13,280 in; $13,280 out
Room and Board: $5,400
On-campus housing: 98%
Financial aid, first-year: 75%

One student at St. Bonaventure University described both the advantages and the disadvantages of attending this small, liberal arts–oriented, Catholic university when he said, "Everyone knows everybody else. You go out on the town on a Friday night and you'll probably see one of the priests wherever you are. It's no big deal to see him at a bar. You just say, 'Hey, Father,' and then you go on with whatever you're doing. He might even come over and join you."

Out of necessity, St. Bonaventure is a fairly self-contained and close-knit community. Set in the Allegheny Mountains, the campus is quite isolated. The nearby working-class town of Olean (population 25,000) has few attractions for the college crowd. As one student said, "You see a lot of trees." Buffalo, the nearest big city, is an hour away and easily accessible if your friend owns a car.

St. Bonaventure undergrads enroll in one of four schools: arts, sciences, business, or education. Students consider education and accounting among the strongest and most popular majors. The philosophy and English departments also earn praise, but some describe the science departments as merely "adequate."

Know Your Profs

In keeping with its liberal arts emphasis, St. Bonaventure requires undergrads to take a large number of core courses, including three theology courses, three philosophy courses, and additional courses in English, math, and science. Enrollment in these required classes usually exceeds 50, but students report that overall the average class size is closer to 20. Some upper-level courses even have as few as 2 to 5 students.

Undergraduates generally consider their professors accessible. Because of the small class sizes, professors know their students by name. To give motivated students a wider range of academic options, St. Bonaventure allows undergrads who qualify to take supplementary seminars as part of an honors program.

The Saints and the Spooks

One of the most popular courses at St. Bonaventure deals with theology and the occult. Detached observers can speculate all they want about why demonic possession and exorcism hold such fascination for St. Bonaventure students, but the students themselves simply flock to the "Spooks" class. Only so many can flock at once, however, because Father Trabold requests that the front row of seats be reserved for visiting "spirits."

St. Bonaventure recently started a four-year Environmental Studies program with course work in environmental ecology, chemistry, biology, and engineering in addition to liberal arts course work. A program requires its students to participate in an internship in the field. The school's proximity to Allegheny State Park aids student research and hands-on experience. The biochemistry program is quite popular as well. The fine arts are now more appealing thanks to the new $7 million Quick Fine Arts Center.

Life and Dorms

Housing at St. Bonaventure ranges from dorms to campus apartments to off-campus accommodations. Undergrads agree that Devereux is the dorm best suited for partying and least conducive to studying, despite the small, attractive rooms. Doyle offers a quieter atmosphere. Most of the dorms are coed by floor. Newly built are the Townhouses, the first phase of a three-part project. The Townhouses offer seniors and grad students modern facilities for a more independent lifestyle. Freshmen are concentrated in single-sex dorms.

St. Bonaventure students have a new outlook on the food. The Reilly Center, the recently remodeled student center, provides them with a more attractive dining atmosphere. In addition, they can charge everything in the Reilly Center on their meal cards, including food at the Taco Bell. When undergrads need a break, they run either to S&G, considered the best and cheapest place to eat off campus, or the recently remodeled New Moon Cafe, a coffee shop where acoustic musicians set the mood.

Sports Crazy

Sports, especially intramurals, are some of the most popular extracurriculars on campus. Basketball fans are thrilled about the improvement in the Bonnies' current record; basketball is reportedly "a big to-do" at St. Bonaventure. Spirited fans are often spotted "acting like animals," dressing up like the visiting team's coaches and

throwing newspapers on the court. The baseball team has a new coach and an improving record. Hockey is another popular sport, but watch out: after the first goal of every game, St. Bonaventure fans reportedly throw seafood onto the ice. In addition, skiing and snowboarding are "a good way to get rid of those mid-semester blues," since the Holiday Valley Ski Resort in the Allegheny Mountains is just a 15-minute drive from campus and the campus ski club receives student discounts. In fact, St. Bonaventure students are so interested in sports that courses are offered in both basketball and tennis coaching.

Aside from sports, St. Bonaventure students can get involved with the weekly newspaper, the *BonaVenture*; a literary magazine; a theater group; and various other clubs. The Campus Ministry is one of the largest student organizations, and its popular Big Brother/Big Sister program allows students to volunteer in the surrounding low-income community.

The Party Places

St. Bonaventure has no Greek system, but the weekend parties still have defined admission. The on-campus parties are generally held by upperclassmen and are limited to their friends and sports teams. Off-campus parties, though less frequent, feature open admission and wild and crazy fun for all. The most popular annual event is the school-sponsored Spring Weekend, which features outdoor concerts by bands such as Blues Traveler, and accompanying parties. Off campus, students frequent the bars in Olean, such as Mad Dogs, the Burton, the Other Place, and the Hickey. During the week, movies, bands, and Wednesday-night comedians who "aren't that funny" are some of the on-campus nighttime social options.

Some students describe St. Bonaventure as "a mostly white, middle-class, Catholic university" and complain of the relatively homogeneous student body.

Some students describe St. Bonaventure as "a mostly white, middle-class,

Catholic university" and complain of the relatively homogeneous student body. Most undergrads come from New York or the New England area.

St. Bonaventure undergrads readily admit that they are part of a small community in less-than-cosmopolitan surroundings, but most are quick to say how satisfied they are. Students praise St. Bonaventure's open, accepting community. As one student said, "Friends of mine who come and visit from other colleges can't believe how easygoing and friendly everyone is here. Colleges with fraternities don't have the same open-door policy we have. Knowing everyone, since it's such a small school, really makes school comfortable and easy." St. Bonaventure is a fine choice for anyone seeking a small, reasonably priced liberal arts college with a Catholic emphasis and a close-knit atmosphere.—*Neel Gandhi and Staff*

FYI

The three best things about attending St. Bonaventure are "the close friendships, the faculty, and the intramurals"

The three worst things about attending St. Bonaventure are "the poor science department, its isolated location, and the cold."

The three things that every student should do before graduating from St. Bonaventure are "play on an intramural team, go skiing, and have fun on Spring Weekend!"

One thing I'd like to have known before coming here is "that you really need a car to go anywhere off campus."

St. Lawrence University

Address: Payson Hall, Canton, NY 14618-3597
Phone: 315-229-5261
E-mail address: admiss@music.stlawu.edu
Web site URL: www.stlawu.edu
Location: rural
Founded: 1856
Private or Public: private
Religious affiliation: none
Undergraduate enrollment: 1,921
Total enrollment: 2,031
Percent Male/Female: 51%/49%
Percent Minority: 6.0%

Percent African-American: 2.0%
Percent Hispanic: 2.0%
Percent Asian: 2.0%
Percent in-state/out-of-state: 47%/53%
Percent Pub HS: 68%
Fraternities: 17%
Sororities: 30%
Number of Applicants: 2,499
Percent Accepted: 71%
Percent Accepted who enroll: 27%
Entering: 479
Transfers: 58
Application Deadline: 15 Feb

Mean SAT: 557 V, 561 M
Middle 50% SAT range: 510–620 V, 520–610 M
Middle 50% ACT range: NA
Mean ACT: 24
3 Most popular majors: English, psychology, economics
Retention: 83.0%
Graduation rate: 75.0%
Library: 470,000 volumes
Tuition and Fees: $21,175 in; $21,175 out
Room and Board: $6,340
On-campus housing: 94%
Financial aid, first-year: 85%

Tucked into a corner of the Adirondacks, in a small town in New York near the Canadian border, sits St. Lawrence University, just small enough to fit into the little town, but big enough for its students to call home. The relatively small size of SLU allows the formation of a close-knit community, both within the student body and between the students and faculty. The rural location affords opportunities for outdoor activities and gives the campus its beautiful backdrop, the pride of many an SLU student. Even though many students complain about the huge piles of snow in the cold winter months, most agree that the warmth of the friendly people around them more than makes up for the weather.

Studying at SLU

Academics at St. Lawrence are described as difficult at times, but, as one student said, "You don't have to be doing work ALL the time." Some of the most popular departments include economics, psychology, and biology—with geology cited as a less popular subject. Because of the small size of SLU, students benefit from small class sizes and they enjoy close contact with professors right from the start of their freshman year; students reported that essentially all classes enroll between 20 and 25 students, are taught exclusively by professors, and have a TA or two to give extra help to students that need it. Small class size rarely results in students being shut out of classes they want to take, though. One student said, "Registration usually is pretty hectic . . . students line in front of the registrar's office and wait for hours to get classes, but then everybody usually gets the ones they want in the end."

St. Lawrence's academic program includes a fair number of required courses: undergrads must take courses in two out of three groups: modern languages, math- or computer-related courses, and fine arts or music. They also are required to take at least one class each in the humanities, social sciences, and lab sciences, and one class which relates to a non-Western culture. Opinions of these requirements vary from "a hassle" to "a good way to get us to start exploring different departments." In addition, freshmen participate in First Year Program, a year-long course devoted to developing oral and written communication skills, taken with other students from the same dorm. While many students acknowledge the benefits of FYP, others complain about how the course runs the whole year and often conflicts with other desired courses.

When students at St. Lawrence want to study, they often head for Owen D. Young Library, the main library on campus. ODY is a fairly modern building; and although its aesthetic merits are often debated, most agree that the recent renovation has made the atmosphere on the inside cheerful and stimulating. However, the lively atmosphere also frequently inspires conversation, and many students describe ODY as more of a social place than a studious one.

For hard-core, serious studying, Madill, the science library, is the best bet.

Living and Eating

Housing at SLU is mainly in dorms, although there are also off-campus options such as Greek and theme housing and athletic suites. The dorms are mostly set up in traditional singles and doubles, and are coed, but some dorms also offer the option of suites with kitchens, mostly for upperclassmen. Students cite Sykes as one of the best dorms, with Whitman as the best dorm for freshmen. On the other hand, Lee and Rebert halls are said to be the worst, although even in those less desirable dorms, rooms are reportedly spacious and nicely furnished. Almost universally, students praise their dorms, whether they live in the best or worst location, for the sense of community fostered there.

As upperclassmen, students at St. Lawrence have more housing options, although finding an off-campus apartment isn't really one of them, since available apartments are extremely scarce in Canton. However, many upperclassmen choose to live in Greek houses, which lie just at the edge of campus; one student living in her sorority house described her experience by saying it is "very homelike, and there is always something to do." Theme housing is another alternative to dorms available after freshman year, and such houses include a house for environmentalists, for people who enjoy outdoor activities, and for cultural groups and international students.

SLU students tend to give their meal plan and dining options high ratings. There are three on-campus eating establishments: Dana Dining Hall (a traditional cafeteria), Northstar Pub, and Jack's Snack Shop (a deli). The pub has more of a relaxed atmosphere where students go to hang out and relax, and the food there is considered the best of the options on campus, particularly the chicken wrap sandwiches. Jack's Snack Shop, on the other hand, is the place to go if you need to pick up a quick bite, and is frequented by students in between classes. There are two meal plans available to students, the 21-meal plan, which is only accepted at Dana, and a declining-balance plan which is accepted at all three on-campus locations. While students favor the declining-balance plan because of its flexibility, most agree that it is impossible not to run out of money before the end of the semester, and so that plan is better for students who are not eating all of their meals on campus.

When students get tired of the places to eat on campus, or just want to treat themselves, they look to the restaurants in the town of Canton. For quick meals, there are the standard chains: McDonald's, Burger King, and Pizza Hut. There is also A-1 Oriental Kitchen, which is a popular delivery choice. Other restaurants in Canton include Sergie's Pizza, which has pizza and Italian food, Jerek Subs, and The Lobster House. The Cactus Grill, a Mexican restaurant located in nearby Potsdam, is also frequented by many St. Lawrence students.

Life after Studying

Students at St. Lawrence spend a lot of time on extracurricular activities, and there is "always something to get involved in." One of the most active groups on campus seems to be the Outing Club, which goes on lots of trips and does other activities together. A recently founded karate club, which is student-run and student-taught, is growing rapidly, an example of the ample opportunity to start new organizations if you are interested. Many students also spend their time working for *The Hill*, the main weekly publication of St. Lawrence.

Sports are also an option at St. Lawrence, for both fans and athletes. Varsity soccer and hockey are the most popular, with rugby and lacrosse games also drawing crowds. School spirit peaks at the time of the Clarkson-SLU hockey game, and the longtime rivalry draws huge crowds. Students say that you have to get tickets at least a week in advance if you don't want to stand up to watch the game, but that it is one of the highlights of the year that cannot be missed. Sports are not limited only to varsity athletes, though, as St. Lawrence has a wide variety of intramural teams which allow people of all levels the opportunity to play. In addition, the athletic facilities are described as "great, and always available to

everybody." Recently the hockey rink was renovated, and a new outdoor track and football stadium were built, and with a new recreation complex in the works, facilities at SLU are in tip-top shape.

> **Students complain that campus security and Canton police strongly frown upon student alcohol use, which is not allowed on campus.**

Unfortunately, the social life and weekend plans are definitely limited by the small student body and Canton. Some things that students do when they are hanging out or partying include shooting pool, going to see a movie (with a discount for showing a student ID), going to see a band playing at Java House, and going to a frat party. However, students complain that campus security and Canton police strongly frown upon student alcohol use, which is not allowed on campus. On top of that, on and off-campus parties alike tend to get shut down soon after they begin. Thus, most students say that they spend a lot of time hanging out in bars in Canton with their friends, or taking trips on the weekend to Ottawa, the capital of Canada, or to Syracuse, both of which are within a few hours' driving distance.

Even though there may be downsides to living in a remote, rural town, students at St. Lawrence agree that the beauty of their campus and the surrounding area is worth it. The architecture of the university, a mixture of old and modern buildings, the quaintness of the town of Canton, and the beauty of the mountains and forests make St. Lawrence a scenic and pleasant place. If you are looking for a school with a fast-paced, urban environment and a restaurant and club for every night of the week, SLU may not be for you; however, if you want a school with a tightly knit community of professors and students, set in a beautiful landscape offering a place to hike or just sit and contemplate, St. Lawrence University is the one.—*Lisa Smith*

State University of New York System

Comprising more than 64 schools, the State University of New York is one of the largest state university programs in the nation. One of the greatest benefits of SUNY, according to students, is its diversity. With undergraduate populations ranging from 9,000 to 16,000, the four university centers—Albany, Binghamton, Buffalo, and Stony Brook—are the largest and wealthiest SUNY campuses. SUNY's 13 smaller university colleges focus on the arts and sciences. They include locations in Brockport, Buffalo College, Cortland, Empire State, Fredonia, Geneseo, New Paltz, Old Westbury, Oneonta, Oswego, Plattsburgh, Potsdam, and Purchase, New York. Thirty SUNY schools are community colleges and various other colleges which specialize in different areas. There are six colleges of technology, four health science centers, five statutory colleges associated with private schools like Alfred and Cornell Universities, as well as several schools offering special programs in technology, optometry, maritime science, environmental science, and forestry.

The Different Flavors of SUNY Schools

Besides offering a wide variety of academic programs, SUNY schools differ greatly in size, location, and competitive flavor. Considering the many choices available, some students may find it difficult to decide which school is right for them, but SUNY has responded to this concern by simplifying the application process. Forty-nine schools use SUNY's common application, allowing students to apply to several schools with just one form.

The SUNY schools are diverse in many ways, but SUNY students share a common bond as over 90 percent of them come from New York. One reason for the high percentage of in-state students is the low in-state tuition cost. Economical as it is, however, some students nevertheless find that it is becoming more and more difficult to pay for tuition. In recent years especially, tuition assistance programs (TAPs) have been significantly reduced as a result of state budget cuts. These cuts have affected not only the cost of a SUNY education, but, in some cases, also the size and quality of various academic programs within the system.

Despite rising costs, though, students still agree that, with their wide range of affordable educational options, SUNY schools are a great deal for New York residents. The following four articles describe SUNY's centers in Albany, Binghamton, Buffalo, and Stony Brook, New York.—*Steven Hayhurst and Staff*

State University of New York / Albany

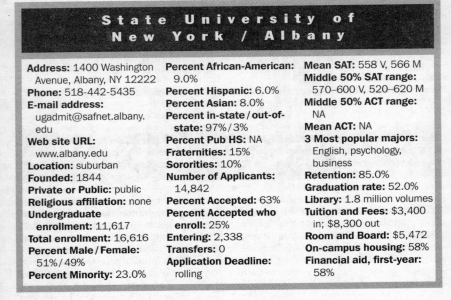

Address: 1400 Washington Avenue, Albany, NY 12222
Phone: 518-442-5435
E-mail address: ugadmit@safnet.albany.edu
Web site URL: www.albany.edu
Location: suburban
Founded: 1844
Private or Public: public
Religious affiliation: none
Undergraduate enrollment: 11,617
Total enrollment: 16,616
Percent Male / Female: 51% / 49%
Percent Minority: 23.0%

Percent African-American: 9.0%
Percent Hispanic: 6.0%
Percent Asian: 8.0%
Percent in-state / out-of-state: 97% / 3%
Percent Pub HS: NA
Fraternities: 15%
Sororities: 10%
Number of Applicants: 14,842
Percent Accepted: 63%
Percent Accepted who enroll: 25%
Entering: 2,338
Transfers: 0
Application Deadline: rolling

Mean SAT: 558 V, 566 M
Middle 50% SAT range: 570–600 V, 520–620 M
Middle 50% ACT range: NA
Mean ACT: NA
3 Most popular majors: English, psychology, business
Retention: 85.0%
Graduation rate: 52.0%
Library: 1.8 million volumes
Tuition and Fees: $3,400 in; $8,300 out
Room and Board: $5,472
On-campus housing: 58%
Financial aid, first-year: 58%

SUNY Albany lies at the heart of the state's SUNY system. Located in New York's bustling capital city, the school provides a sound academic environment that will not strain the student budget.

Unforgiving Requirements

Strict course requirements, however, do strain students' schedules. All undergraduates must take two courses each in humanities and arts, social science, and natural science, as well as two writing-intensive classes. "It's those writing classes that are particularly annoying," one junior said, complaining about the number of assignments. Other requirements include a cultural and historical perspective class and a class in human diversity. These interdisciplinary classes combine the social sciences and the humanities. Particularly driven students can also participate in the General Education Honors Program, which centers on small discussion sections with professors.

Although upper-level courses usually enroll around 30 students, introductory lectures max out at 400. Professors are not inaccessible, however, and undergraduates remain the school's focus. Students apply to a particular school after their freshman year. The schools of business and criminal justice tend to be the most selective. Applicants must take a placement test, submit a writing sample, and meet a minimum grade-point average. Albany features many strong academic departments, most notably in psychology and English. Students also say the political science program, assisted by the backdrop of the state government scene in Albany, is excellent.

A Divided Campus

"Campus" is a misnomer of sorts for SUNY Albany. The university actually has two campuses, one uptown, one downtown. The uptown campus is the school's true center, containing most of the student housing and academic buildings. Four quads—Dutch, Colonial, State, and Indian—form the corners of the uptown campus's square design, enclosing an open area around a fountain known as "The Podium." Various dorms and special-interest halls are contained within the quads.

Students insist that despite the dorms' identical appearance, each has its distinct personality. Perhaps this is because students are free to live with peers who share their interests. Wellness Hall, for example, stresses health and exercise and has Nautilus machines. One of the quads is reserved for first-year students only. "It's comforting knowing that everyone you live with is entering the same situation," one freshman said. Other special-interest options include Math Hall, Science Hall, and Substance-Free Hall. Those few undergraduates living on the uptown campus often complain about the accommodations, which generally take the form of either suites with private bathrooms or doubles with hall bathrooms. Downtown campus, about a ten-minute walk away, wins in the looks category with ivy-covered brick buildings as opposed to the "gray and dreary" structures of uptown. Many students move off campus after their first or second year. The school owns off-campus housing called Freedom Quad, where many graduate students reside.

A New York Crowd

So many New Yorkers make the trek upstate for school that a Long Island–based rock radio station, WDRE, now broadcasts its signal in Albany. Because a large portion of the undergraduate population comes from the melting pots of New York City and Long Island, the campus is ethnically if not geographically diverse.

> Albany offers much more than a great educational bang for your tuition buck.

According to students, the nearly 30 frats and sororities are a significant force at SUNY Albany. Rushing is a popular undergraduate activity, although students generally do not feel pressured to participate. The Greeks are the primary campus source of parties and alcohol. "I'm glad you don't have to be a full-fledged member to attend their parties," said one sophomore. Albany's several bars and pubs provide an alternative to the Greek night life for the 21-and-over crowd—the Lamp Post, Peabody's, and Washington's Tavern are perennial student favorites.

Albany students report feeling content with the school's food policy—mainly because they can charge purchases at Taco Bell, Nathan's, and Pizza Hut to their meal accounts. When students spend time in the city, it is mainly for food or to socialize at the bars.

Despite the popularity of political science as a major, the school student government reportedly lacks mass student appeal. The Student Association organizes some annual social events, such as the year-end "Party in the Park" and Fallfest, both of which feature live music, dancing, and plenty of food. The student newspaper, the *Albany Student Press*, comes out twice a week and draws enthusiastic undergraduate participation. Unfortunately, the same cannot be said for varsity sports, but students have glowing praise for the school's recently built "tremendous" sports complex, where many work out in their spare time. Students also have no complaints about the security and safety of the school. An escort service and shuttle van serve as alternatives to late-night walking. Abundant emergency phones throughout campus also work to put students at ease.

All things considered, Albany offers much more than a great educational bang for your tuition buck. Its satisfied student body and sound academics would make it a great deal in any state of the union.
—*Ann Zeidner and Staff*

FYI
The three best things about attending SUNY Albany are "the dorms are all really close to one another, it's easy to meet people here, and the variety of night life—there are lots of clubs and bars in the area."
The three worst things about attending SUNY Albany are "the coed bathrooms in some dorms, the SNOW, and sometimes it's hard to get all the classes you want."
The three things every student should do before graduating from SUNY Albany are "take a road trip to Canada, visit Lake George, and go out and experience the Albany night life."
One thing I'd like to have known before coming here is "it's TOO easy to have fun here—which makes it hard to do much else."

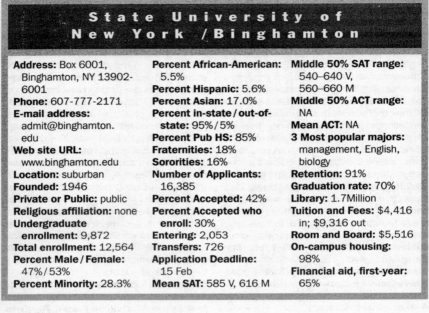

State University of New York / Binghamton

Address: Box 6001, Binghamton, NY 13902-6001
Phone: 607-777-2171
E-mail address: admit@binghamton.edu
Web site URL: www.binghamton.edu
Location: suburban
Founded: 1946
Private or Public: public
Religious affiliation: none
Undergraduate enrollment: 9,872
Total enrollment: 12,564
Percent Male/Female: 47%/53%
Percent Minority: 28.3%

Percent African-American: 5.5%
Percent Hispanic: 5.6%
Percent Asian: 17.0%
Percent in-state/out-of-state: 95%/5%
Percent Pub HS: 85%
Fraternities: 18%
Sororities: 16%
Number of Applicants: 16,385
Percent Accepted: 42%
Percent Accepted who enroll: 30%
Entering: 2,053
Transfers: 726
Application Deadline: 15 Feb
Mean SAT: 585 V, 616 M

Middle 50% SAT range: 540–640 V, 560–660 M
Middle 50% ACT range: NA
Mean ACT: NA
3 Most popular majors: management, English, biology
Retention: 91%
Graduation rate: 70%
Library: 1.7 Million
Tuition and Fees: $4,416 in; $9,316 out
Room and Board: $5,516
On-campus housing: 98%
Financial aid, first-year: 65%

Over their college years, SUNY Binghamton students learn to appreciate life's small pleasures—jaunts through the rain, midnight food runs, good movies on free cable. And although many upperclassmen admit their school can get pretty monotonous—"there's nothing to do out here in the middle of nowhere!"—most would agree that it gets better as it goes. Even those students who reported loathing the school their freshman year now offer this caution to their successors: "If you want to transfer out of this place, transfer out quick because this school really grows on you. Everything—the place, the people, even the never-ending rain—it all gets better as time goes on. Trust me, if you stay here, you'll hate your first year but love the rest."

The Ivy of the SUNYs

Binghamton is widely recognized as one of the most academically competitive SUNYs, attracting many of New York's best with its affordable quality education. The university comprises five undergraduate schools catering to a wide range of interests: the Harpur College of Arts and Sciences, the Decker School of Nursing,

the School of Management, the School of Education and Human Development, and the Thomas J. Watson School of Engineering and Applied Science.

Graduation requirements vary with school and program. Generally, though, most majors have to fulfill one course credit in each of four core areas: the arts, pluralism, global studies, and communications. In addition, all students must earn two phys ed credits and satisfy a writing requirement. Many can appreciate the general education requirements and think them great in theory but typically hate them in practice. Said one senior, "Requirements are good in the sense that they encourage students to get a broad view of things, but they're kind of a waste of time, too."

And if there's one thing Binghamton students lack, it's enough time in the day. One student emphasized, "Binghamton may be easy enough to get into, but it's really hard to stay in." Students of all majors claim to grapple with "substantial" workloads, but engineering, management, and science (especially pre-med) majors reportedly suffer the heaviest loads.

Class sizes at Binghamton follow traditional college patterns—huge introductory courses of up to several hundred students with numbers generally shrinking as classes become more specialized in the upper levels. Teaching is generally rated as average. One student remarked, "Some professors don't even really seem to like teaching, but then there are those that make you really love your classes. I guess it's that way at most schools." TAs often co-teach and lead discussion sections for lower-level courses, becoming fewer and far between at the higher levels.

Students conveniently register for classes via computer, a process which one sophomore described as "very easy and great in that I can register from home if I want to." Because class availability follows a pecking order dictated by seniority and major, frosh sometimes find themselves having a hard time getting into the classes they want. But, according to one experienced senior, "If you know what you're doing, you can pretty much petition and beg your way into any class." In several instances, though, the classrooms themselves have lacked the space to accommodate enrollees. Faced with a shortage of seats, many students ended up sitting through class without desks or chairs. One student voiced his concern: "It's like you're paying money to sit on the floor. That's just not right."

In years past as well, students have had to deal with similar shortages in housing. One year, in fact, the situation was so bad that some freshmen were forced to take up temporary quarters in TV common rooms because there were no permanent rooms available. Despite occasional problems, however, most students seem pretty content with their on-campus housing. One student described the dorms as "totally decent" with "relatively big and clean" rooms.

Community Life
Undergrads live in one of five "communities," each of which includes several coed dorms and a central building that houses a dining hall. Each community has a distinctive character and stereotype attached to it. Newing College is the Greek-dominated party dorm. Hinman is the quiet haven for hardcore studiers. Dickinson is racially

and ethnically diverse, while College-in-the-Woods (CIW) is notorious for abundant drug use. The fifth dorm, the graduate community, is restricted to juniors and seniors. The summer before freshman year, incoming frosh are asked to indicate their first and second community choices on a preference sheet, and in most cases, they are assigned to one of the two. After freshman year, students can choose to remain in their communities, move to another, or move off campus. Apartments are generally "cheap and easy to find," but students without cars may find transportation a problem.

Most communities have libraries where students can do work, but the main Bartle Library is also a popular study spot. Late-night studiers seeking a quiet atmosphere can find it in the "tombs," a popular nickname for a scary tomblike section of Bartle's main lobby.

In Pursuit of the Freshman
After stressful study sessions, Binghamton students grab much needed sustenance at Snax or the Night Owl, open until midnight and 1 A.M. respectively. Students can charge these purchases to their meal plans.

At mealtimes, Bing students have the option to eat in the community dining halls or at the minimall, which sells typical food-court fare like Taco Bell, Chinese food, pasta, and char-grilled items. School food was described as "decent but pretty repetitive" with the same entrees offered again and again. "How many ways are there to prepare chicken?" wondered one student. "And amazingly, no matter how they make it, it all tastes *exactly the same.*"

For students looking to escape campus food, Binghamton's main throughway, Bethel Parkway, is a hungry man's heaven. Dozens of eateries ranging from dirt-cheap grease to pricier four-star cuisine dot this long asphalt strip. Perenially popular options include TGI Friday's, Olive Garden, Denny's, and Tony's—great food at a bargain. No. 5 was said to be a good place to take a date. Local Binghamton also lures students with sports bars and a handful of clubs. Some clubs will periodically hold "SUNY nights," which one student described as "a good way to meet other people in the university."

The Self-Contained Brain

Seen from the air, the Binghamton campus is arranged in a circle, which students have affectionately dubbed "the Brain." Wooded mountains enclose the campus, creating a valley of sorts; this valley tends to keep clouds in, resulting in lots of rain and snow. "Don't forget to bring an umbrella," advised one student.

Just a short walk from campus is a nature preserve spanning 117 acres. "It's a great place to take a date," said one sophomore guy. Other students flock there to escape the noisy campus construction currently in process. "I mean, it'll be great when the campus union is renovated and those new dorms are done, but for now, I'm just looking to get away from the racket," said one student.

Because Binghamton's campus is so isolated and self-contained, most students agree that cars are a necessary evil for off-campus treks. "Cars are great because of the freedom they give, but parking is a drag," said one car owner. Not only are parking spaces on campus limited, but the lots are often inconveniently located. Newing College's three parking lots are commonly referred to as "heaven," "purgatory," and "hell," with hell being the farthest from campus and heaven the closest.

Cars also prove convenient when Bing students just want some "away time." While New York City, a three-hour drive, may be a bit far for a road trip, major college towns Syracuse and Ithaca are both less than an hour away, making for a good day or weekend getaway.

Weekend Fun

Back on campus, Greeks tend to dominate social life. The party scene revolves around the frats, which regularly throw weekend bashes. Alcohol abounds at these events; for $3, attendees can drink as much as they want. Considering the abundance of inebriated guys and girls in attendance at these parties, it is not surprising that here are where most random hookups occur. Some people will go with dates, but it's less common.

For students not into the partying and drinking scenes, the university offers a host of other social options. Movies, student productions, guest lectures, and dances are just a few of the alternatives. The campus pub is also another fun hangout, with a bowling alley, arcade, and billiards.

Surprising Diversity

Binghamton has no football team, a reality that undoubtedly contributes to the general absence of school spirit among the student body. Despite that empty pocket, however, intramurals or "co-recs" are pretty popular, especially soccer and rugby. The university athletic facilities are divided between the East and West Gymnasiums. East Gym is generally considered the better of the two, but unlike West Gym, is not free. Remarked one student, "For a school without a football team, we have a ton of really big and buff guys."

> **"For a school without a football team, we have a ton of really big and buff guys."**

In addition to intramurals and recreational sports, lots of students report heavy involvement in campus extracurricular groups. The student association, Binghamton's answer to student government, is generally recognized as pretty popular. Cultural organizations also enjoy high student participation, not surprising in light of the school's diverse student makeup. Music-minded students can perform in school musical groups like the orchestra and wind ensemble, and journalistic or literary minds can write for one of several campus publications. Binghamton students hold a variety of interests, and club offerings reflect this wide range.

Indeed Binghamton's student body can be surprisingly diverse and eclectic considering Binghamton is a state school full of mostly New Yorkers. Even within the state, though, certain regions are said to be over-represented—Long Island in particular. For some this can be a drawback, as one student complained, "There are too many students from Long Island, Westchester, and New York City. There aren't even that many from upstate New York!" But all things considered, Binghamton qualifies as a wise college choice for Yan-kee and non-Yankee alike, offering an excellent education for the money and a diversity rarely found at state institutions. —*Jane H. Hong*

FYI

The three best things about attending SUNY/Binghamton are "the people—they're awesome!—the cost, and the beautiful scenery."

The three worst things about attending SUNY/Binghamton are "the administration—it's disorganized and has some poorly trained staff—the lack of parking, and the apathetic professors."

The three things that every student should do before graduating from SUNY/Binghamton are "go to the Highest Point with that special someone, go to Denny's at 3:30 A.M., get lost at the nature preserve."

One thing I'd like to have known before coming here is "that I would need a car. Oh, and to bring an umbrella because it never stops raining here!"

State University of New York / Buffalo

Address: 17 Capen Hall, Buffalo, NY 14260
Phone: 716-645-6900
E-mail address: ub-admissions@admissions.buffalo.edu
Web site URL: www.buffalo.edu
Location: suburban
Founded: 1,846
Private or Public: public
Religious affiliation: none
Undergraduate enrollment: 15,663
Total enrollment: 23,429
Percent Male/Female: 53%/47%
Percent Minority: 25.0%

Percent African-American: 8.0%
Percent Hispanic: 4.0%
Percent Asian: 12.0%
Percent in-state/out-of-state: 98%/2%
Percent Pub HS: NA
Fraternities: 1%
Sororities: 1%
Number of Applicants: 14,108
Percent Accepted: 71%
Percent Accepted who enroll: 29%
Entering: 2,871
Transfers: 0
Application Deadline: rolling
Mean SAT: 561 V, 584 M

Middle 50% SAT range: 500–600 V, 520–630 M
Middle 50% ACT range: NA
Mean ACT: 25
3 Most popular majors: psychology, business administration, health-related professions
Retention: 82.0%
Graduation rate: 31.0%
Library: 3 million volumes
Tuition and Fees: $3,400 in; $8,300 out
Room and Board: $5,804
On-campus housing: 22%
Financial aid, first-year: 55%

In 1846, University at Buffalo was a private medical school consisting of a few lecture rooms in an old church. As the years went by, the university slowly expanded by adding a pharmacy school, a law school, a dental school, a school of arts and science, a school of management, and numerous other offerings. After becoming part of the SUNY system in 1962, the college grew rapidly and split into North Campus and South Campus. Today's Buffalo students have the pleasure of attending the largest public university in New York. Size is one of the school's most unique characteristics; SUNY Buffalo boasts the largest faculty in the SUNY system and the greatest number of degree programs.

Big Options

"This school has just about every single major you can think of." Buffalo offers a wide variety of majors as well as the option of double majoring or minoring in a subject. As one student notes, "Having a second major or a minor can be pretty common." Those who do not wish to follow a traditional major program have the freedom of designing their own major. One sophomore gladly noted, "Although the requirements for graduation vary by major, there is no physical education requirement." When asked about the academic environment at Buffalo, one student replied by saying, "It is a big engineering and science school." Some of the strongest programs at Buffalo include the engineering and pharmacy departments, which rank among the best in the SUNY system.

Students agreed that the science, engineering, and computer science courses, as well as pre-med classes, tend to be on the more difficult side. One student commented, "Your workload depends on which classes you take. If you are pre-med, prepare to lose some sleep." For those who are searching for classes that do not require too much work, several recommended courses are Methods of Inquiry and Psychology 101.

According to one student, "Registration is primarily done through a phone system called BIRD, while some people take advantage of the newly introduced online registration." The large student body creates some difficulties during registration period. As one student complained, "The Internet becomes very slow and classes fill up quickly. It is extremely hard to get the class you want, or when you want it." Priority is given to students who have received more credits, so in general seniors get first pick while freshmen hope there will still be empty slots when it is their turn. "Getting into some classes can be real tough for freshmen," said one student. There is a broad range in class size, ranging from small seminars of about ten students to introductory lectures with over five hundred students.

Although developing a relationship with the professor is harder in the lecture classes, students can get to know them by visiting during weekly office hours, which every teacher holds. Students can also receive help by attending the smaller recitations led by graduate-student TAs. Students are happy with the majority of their professors. As one student said, "My English teacher played the guitar and sang to us." However, "Sometimes you will find a teacher that is hard to understand or does not really know English, especially in the math department." As a response to the general academic environment, one student replied, "I hate work, but I love to learn."

Social Life

When the week of classes is over, students have fun by doing almost whatever they want. Fraternities on South Campus, bars on Main Street, and dorms are popular sites for those looking for parties. Although alcohol is allowed for those above 21, "it is usually consumed by minors." For non-drinkers, there are plenty of other options, such as a movie theater, a symphony orchestra, concerts, or just hanging out with friends. During Fall Fest and Spring Fest, popular bands perform at North Campus for the students. After attending one of the on-campus concerts, one student proudly exclaimed, "I saw Busta Rhymes!" Students can easily attend local Buffalo Bills or Sabres games or travel about twenty minutes north to Canada. As one student commented, "UB has a ton of organized activities from clubs to specific dorm-arranged activities. There is always something to do."

At Buffalo, the large student body makes it possible for almost anyone to find a group of friends that share their interests. As one student put it, "I found it very easy to meet people. There is always room for one more in a group. Most of my friends were made through friends, dorm, and classes." One negative aspect of the size of UB is that people must make a conscious effort to keep up contacts. With many students, "groups form right away, but can change in an instant."

Quality of Life on Campus

Since UB is part of the SUNY system, nearly all of the students are New York State residents. The school is in large part comprised of middle-class people from Rochester and Long Island, but there is a great amount of ethnic and religious diversity. Although there were mixed opinions among students about the necessity of a car, there was a general consensus that they were helpful. While one student claimed, "You need one like you need air to breathe," another stated that they "aren't needed but are a big bonus."

Buffalo is the only SUNY school that does not require freshmen to live on campus, so those who live nearby often commute. With such a large student body, a good number of people also choose to stay off campus. One student commented, "The rent is decent, and proximity is not bad either." There are RAs for everyone living in dorms, regardless of their year. They are generally nice but "won't hesitate to turn you in if they have to." Students live on coed floors with single-sex bathrooms. UB helps bring together people of similar interests by offering theme housing, which in turn creates different personalities for different dorms. The living situations have been improving recently with the addition of the Hadley Village Undergraduate Apartments, the Flickinger Court Graduate Apartments, and South Lake Village Apartments.

I'm Getting Hungry . . .

Students feel safe while on Buffalo's large campus and often visit the surrounding areas for entertainment. Many places are within walking distance, and several malls are less than a twenty-minute drive away. UB students enjoy eating out once in a while and can pick from a large number of choices, including Starbucks, Red Lobster, and Olive Garden. Students with a tongue for fast food enjoy visiting Taco Bell, Burger King, and Campus Pizza & Italian Specialties. Duffs, a local restaurant where chicken wings are served, cannot be missed according to several students. "While in Buffalo," one student said, "you must eat the Buffalo wings! You just have to eat them, they *are that* good."

While eating under the university's meal plan, students have several places they can enjoy all-you-can-eat dining hall food. Although some students have complained about the inconvenient designated meal times, there are plenty of vegetarian options and meal plans can be used at other locations. There are definitely noticeable cliques in the dining halls, where people can often be found chatting long after they have finished their meals.

How About a Pick-up Game?

Basketball and football are big sports at UB. Even though the Division IA football team does not have a winning reputation, one spirited student remarked, "I don't miss a home game." On campus, there is much more to sports than the varsity teams. The athletic facilities include a new football stadium and a natatorium that has hosted the World University Games and the Empire State Games in the past. For people who do not play varsity sports, it is easy to find a pick-up game. Each year, over 9,000 UB students take a break from their work and participate in club sports or intramurals.

> **"My English teacher played the guitar and sang to us."**

The city of Buffalo has much to offer to the university and its students. The size of the school allows people to choose their own education and have a great time along the way. When approached with the idea of going back and choosing a college again, one undergraduate enthusiastically replied, "I would definitely choose UB. I love it!"—*Robert Wong*

FYI
The three best things about attending UB are "the size of the school, the freedom, and always having something to do."
The three worst things about attending UB are "the size of the school, the weather, and early classes."
The three things that every student should do before graduating from UB are "have Buffalo wings at Duffs, keep in touch with their friends, and do their homework and learn something."
One thing I'd like to have known before coming here is "how useful a car is here."

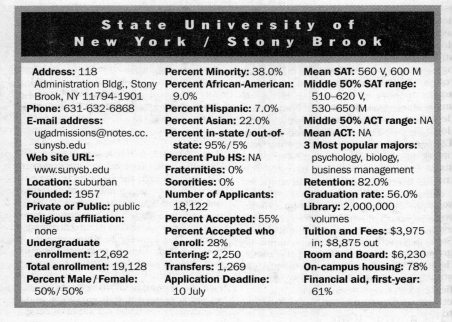

State University of New York / Stony Brook

Address: 118 Administration Bldg., Stony Brook, NY 11794-1901
Phone: 631-632-6868
E-mail address: ugadmissions@notes.cc.sunysb.edu
Web site URL: www.sunysb.edu
Location: suburban
Founded: 1957
Private or Public: public
Religious affiliation: none
Undergraduate enrollment: 12,692
Total enrollment: 19,128
Percent Male/Female: 50%/50%

Percent Minority: 38.0%
Percent African-American: 9.0%
Percent Hispanic: 7.0%
Percent Asian: 22.0%
Percent in-state/out-of-state: 95%/5%
Percent Pub HS: NA
Fraternities: 0%
Sororities: 0%
Number of Applicants: 18,122
Percent Accepted: 55%
Percent Accepted who enroll: 28%
Entering: 2,250
Transfers: 1,269
Application Deadline: 10 July

Mean SAT: 560 V, 600 M
Middle 50% SAT range: 510–620 V, 530–650 M
Middle 50% ACT range: NA
Mean ACT: NA
3 Most popular majors: psychology, biology, business management
Retention: 82.0%
Graduation rate: 56.0%
Library: 2,000,000 volumes
Tuition and Fees: $3,975 in; $8,875 out
Room and Board: $6,230
On-campus housing: 78%
Financial aid, first-year: 61%

Nearly half a century ago, SUNY Stony Brook was founded to produce math and science teachers and become one of the finest research universities in the nation. Although initially located in Oyster Bay, Long Island, in 1962 the university was relocated to a 480-acre area in Stony Brook, approximately 60 miles outside of Manhattan. The university has grown to include a College of Arts and Sciences, a College of Engineering and Applied Sciences, a school of management, a medical school, a dental school, and a hospital. The university has greatly increased the quality of its reputation, and the Carnegie Foundation now considers Stony Brook one of the top 70 research schools in the United States. With over 1,100 acres and 70 academic departments, Stony Brook is one of the few major nationally ranked schools situated on Long Island.

Dedicated Students

Stony Brook students are happy with their academic environment. In the words of one student, "I'm extremely satisfied at a university like Stony Brook." Running on the semester system, Stony Brook requires students to take their Diversified Education Curriculum. In order to satisfy this, students must take one course each in American pluralism, European history, non-Western history, fine arts, humanities, math, technology, and writing. In addition, two courses must be completed in the natural sciences and the social and behavioral sciences. The one-year foreign language requirement can be satisfied with a score of 75 or higher on the appropriate New York State Regents examination.

Students describe the university as having excellent professors and a good working environment. All school faculty members are involved in teaching, as well as research. Some of the more notable members of the faculty include Nobel laureate physics professor C. N. Yang and mathematics professor John Milnor, winner of the prestigious Fields Medal. Another important resource for Stony Brook students to take advantage of is the seminars offered by professors on field studies and the environment of jobs in their field.

At Stony Brook, students can expect to find large lectures in introductory courses, but the professors keep the class interested in the material. One student recalled how his physics professor performed entertaining experiments in class that demonstrated the principles they were studying. Although the introductory biology and psychology classes may each enroll nearly five hundred students, more advanced seminars tend to be much smaller with approximately twenty students per class. Each lecture is broken down into much smaller recitations led by TAs that facilitate learning through more one-on-one interaction. The only problem students noted was that several TAs have trouble with their English.

Students agree that the engineering and science classes tend to offer the greatest workload and most competition. However, this does not pose a problem for Stony Brook students since the school is great in those areas and "everyone seems dedicated to their work." Although more students choose to major in the technical fields, a large number of people study liberal arts. This can be partially attributed to the DEC, which allows students to explore different areas of study. Another option that students make use of is majoring in a second subject. In the words of one student, "I couldn't be more satisfied with this school's academics."

Living at Stony Brook

With 26 residential halls, Stony Brook is the largest residential campus in the SUNY system. Students have the choice of living in corridor-style dorms or suite-style dorms. The corridor dorms allow students to live in singles or doubles along a hallway and share common areas, bathrooms, and cooking areas. In suites, four to six students share two to three bedrooms, a common area, and a private bathroom. The university offers special living options, such as 24-hour quiet hour dorms and substance-free rooms for students who wish to live in areas without alcohol or tobacco. Aside from the residential halls, two different on-campus apartment complexes are available for graduate students, families, and married couples. Six computing centers are provided for the convenience of students. More athletically inclined students can attend the seven athletic centers at Stony Brook, which are open seven days a week. At the

athletic centers, Stony Brook residents have the option of taking aerobics classes, lifting weights, using Nautilus equipment, or training on state-of-the-art Cybex circuit machines.

Each year, the Department of Residential Programs holds hundreds of educational and social events for Stony Brook students. Some of the more popular annual events include Roth Quad Regatta (students, faculty, and staff design their own boats and race them across Roth Pond), Spirit Night (music, fireworks, and a skit to show school pride), Homecoming (a parade, football game, and crowning of the King and Queen), and Ultimate Spring Blast (a week of carnivals, shows, fireworks, food, and fun). The school also sponsors diversity themed months, during which cultural, social and educational activities are used to celebrate a different group each month.

Outside of the Classroom

Security is important at Stony Brook, and the university does a good job of making students feel safe on campus. University police officers patrol the campus at all hours and check IDs at the main gate after midnight, when the campus is closed to students who do not have Stony Brook identification or prior permission. All residence halls are locked 24 hours a day, and only students who live in a hall have the access card to get in. The campus is well-lit at night and "blue-light phones" placed throughout the campus allow students to call for help from anywhere. Another useful option is the free Walk Service Program, which lets students call for two people with walkie-talkies to escort them to their destination.

Stony Brook offers twenty intercollegiate varsity sports for its students, ten for men and ten for women. The Stony Brook Seawolves' athletic success can be seen by their rise from NCAA Division III. After a ten-year process that began in 1989, Stony Brook has recently completed a full upgrade of its athletic program to Division I level. The most popular teams on campus are the basketball and soccer teams, which both draw large crowds as they begin making their name in Division I.

For students who wish to have some fun off campus, public transportation is a popular option. The Stony Brook station of the Long Island Railroad is on campus, allowing students to travel to other parts of Long Island, as well as into New York City. On-campus and off-campus buses can be used to get to nearby malls and towns, such as Port Jefferson, the Smithhaven Mall, and Stony Brook Village. The Port Jefferson Ferry lies just a few minutes away, giving students the ability to travel across Long Island Sound to Bridgeport, Connecticut.

The school is known for being a "suitcase" college, as many students choose to go home over the weekend However, the students who stick around campus do not have any trouble finding ways to have fun. The student union has planned activities every night, and school-organized movies and concerts give students even more options to choose from. Other hangouts include fraternities, sororities, bars, clubs, and "The Spot" (a nightclub where bands come and play). Most students are satisfied with the social alternatives and can almost always find something amusing to do either on or off campus.

What's for Dinner?
Stony Brook's meal plan received positive reviews from its students, who felt that "the school has a good selection of just about everything." Students can choose from over 25 options, including a Pizza Hut, Burger King, Deng Lee's Chinese, Wrap-a-bles, and a made-to-order grill. A Kosher-dining hall is available, as well as low-sodium, low-fat, and cholesterol-free selections. The meal plan is required for first-year students, except for those living in cooking suites. For students who want a change of taste, there are also many nearby places to find something good to eat. Some campus favorites include local diners, Red Lobster, and Boulder Creek.

"You can find it ALL."

Although the majority of Stony Brook students are from the southern portion of New York State, the student body still offers a wide range of diversity. Many different ethnic groups are well-represented; however, there is some tendency for groups to self-segregate. When asked if any particular style of clothing or genre of music stood out at the school, one student replied, "You can find it ALL." The strong academic program and public school tuition combine to make Stony Brook a school that no one should skip over.
—*Robert Wong*

FYI
The three best things about attending Stony Brook are "the professors, the working environment, and the science and engineering departments."
The three worst things about attending Stony Brook are "the campus, too many commuters, and nonscience departments could be stronger."
The three things that every student should do before graduating from Stony Brook are "take advantage of professors' seminars, go to Spirit Night, and make some close friendships."
One thing I'd like to have known before coming here is "that there would be so many Long Islanders here."

Syracuse University

Address: 201 Tolley
Administration Building,
Syracuse, NY 13244
Phone: 315-443-3611
E-mail address:
orange@syr.edu
Web site URL:
www.syracuse.edu
Location: urban
Founded: 1870
Private or Public: private
Religious affiliation:
none
**Undergraduate
enrollment:** 10,491
Total enrollment: 14,557
Percent Male / Female:
47% / 53%
Percent Minority: 18.0%

Percent African-American:
8.0%
Percent Hispanic: 5.0%
Percent Asian: 5.0%
**Percent in-state / out-of-
state:** 48% / 52%
Percent Pub HS: 80%
Fraternities: 17%
Sororities: 23%
Number of Applicants:
12,115
Percent Accepted: 58%
**Percent Accepted who
enroll:** 37%
Entering: 2,600
Transfers: 0
Application Deadline:
15 Jan
Mean SAT: NA

Middle 50% SAT range:
530–630 V,
540–640 M
Middle 50% ACT range:
NA
Mean ACT: NA
3 Most popular majors:
information management
and technology,
architecture, psychology
Retention: NA
Graduation rate: 56.0%
Library: 3.1 million volumes
Tuition and Fees: $19,360
in; $19,360 out
Room and Board: $8,400
On-campus housing: 72%
Financial aid, first-year:
62%

Snow on Commencement Day? Sounds like a fantasy, huh? Well, not at Syracuse. Members of Syracuse University's Class of 1997 witnessed snow on their Commencement Day. Snow that starts in November and continues through March or April does not seem to change the undergrads' studying or partying patterns. And certainly, snow does not keep hard-core fans of the nationally ranked football team from filling up the Dome to see the Orangemen play.

Academics: So Many Options

The academic experiences of Syracuse students vary a lot due to Syracuse's twelve different undergraduate schools and colleges. These separate schools specialize in education, architecture, arts and sciences, engineering and computer science, social work, management, nursing, human development, visual and performing arts, information studies, law, and public communications; and each has its own requirements. In particular, the Newhouse School of Public Communications is considered one of the best communications schools in the U.S., and it is the most prestigious school of the university.

Many students, though, are enrolled in the College of Arts and Sciences, which provides a basic liberal arts education. The distribution requirements in this college consist of four courses in both of the social science groups, natural sciences and math, and humanities. Students can also take classes from other schools within the university. For this reason, coming to Syracuse undecided in major is not a problem; students can enter one of the schools after developing an interest in that area in the introductory classes. Transferring to Newhouse, though, is more difficult compared to the other schools and requires a higher GPA.

In each of the schools at Syracuse, professors teach most of the classes, and students seem happy with the professors overall. Opinions on professors vary from "I haven't had any professors I didn't like" to "I have had amazing professors and not so exciting ones." Students also report that professors are usually accessible, although one student added that "it is sometimes hard to get to know them on an individual basis." Also, TAs who teach the sections generally receive good reviews from the students. As students report: "They know what they are doing" and "it is easier for them to relate to the students because of the small age difference." Some students, though, have had problems with a few of their TAs' accents.

Class size varies among the schools. The largest class at Newhouse consists of 75 people, while some intro classes in the Arts and Sciences can reach 200. Classes that enroll more than 100 students meet in smaller groups of 20 for discussions. The upper-level classes, in contrast, are smaller in size. Most students consider engineering and architecture the most difficult majors. Several students identify science, calculus, and management courses as "pretty tough for non-majors." One favorite class among students is the half-semester course called Freshman Forum, which consists of 15 freshmen meeting with an advisor and "provides an opportunity to get to know the campus and the things going on."

To Drink or Not to Drink

Partying is a major "concern" for many undergraduates at Syracuse. As one student said, "You could call Syracuse a party school, but there is the other side as well." The non-alcoholic and non-partying social options have been improving. A senior commented that "there were not so many social alternatives before as there are now." Those who are not into partying choose to hang out in one of the numerous coffee houses in the surrounding area or attend events sponsored by different school organizations.

One thing that all students agree on is that "the parties are there if you want it." Greek and house parties are the two main options, although the Greeks are becoming more and more exclusive because of the university's banning of alcohol on campus. One student reported that there are "rumors that the chancellor is trying to get rid of all the Greeks." And there is evidence to support that claim. Fourteen fraternities and sororities "are gone" for various reasons since he assumed his position. Since the Greeks are limiting access of non-members, a student advises, "If you want alcohol, go to the houses." Walking down Euclid Street en route to the house parties is a "big freshman thing." For some, "the best parties are the house swing parties, where there is swing music and the atmosphere is great." Syracuse

also has tons of entertainment beside parties. The School of Music organize concerts on a regular basis. There are als famous bands and musicians who ha concerts on campus. Cherry Poppin' Da dies, A Tribe Called Quest, and Billy Jo all appeared in the fall of 1998. Differe events draw interesting speakers to car pus. Some recent interesting guests we the cast of *Real World: Seattle* and Al Keyes.

For entertainment or other purpose everyone seems to agree that cars are e tremely useful at Syracuse. As one st dent reports, "You can get off-campu jobs and you can get around much easie Buses operate between the campus an downtown, but cars are definitely "bette "Having a car allows you to do more inte esting things and have more fun." Hov ever, students warn that parking is serious problem.

No Stereotypes

Although almost half of the students Syracuse are from New York State, ever one here mentions the diversity. Th agree that "there is no stereotypical Syr cuse student." There is a mix of uppe class and middle-class, and althou different ethnicities are represented, st dents report that people from the groups tend to stick together. "General cliques are evident [on campus]," said o student. Cliques also form among grou of students who share majors becau "they see each other all the time and sha common interests."

According to several people, Comi Out Week was a time when "the homose uals' voices were heard a little louder th people would like to hear." A lot of peop are "very close-minded about this issue Others find it "great that gays and lesbia have formed a union to educate people The fraternity brothers and sorority s ters also tend to stick together all t time, and freshmen that live in the sar dorm usually hang out with one anothe as well.

Bed and Breakfast: Living and Food

There are several living options at Syr cuse. All freshmen and sophomores ha to live on campus. On-campus options include dorms and university-owned apartments on South Campus. Dorm rooms can be singles, open doubles, or split doubles, and for the most part students have the opportunity to choose the dorm and the type of room that they want to stay in. The dorms differ in that some are coed by floor, others by wing and by door. There are also quiet lifestyle and wellness floors that are alcohol- and drug-free. Each floor sets its own standards, which can concern anything from quiet hours to bathroom rules. Students are assigned RAs, and they report that most RAs are "friendly and want to be your friend." In some cases, "juniors and seniors get a sophomore RA, which creates strange situations." After sophomore year, many students choose to live off campus.

Syracuse students offer different opinions on food. "Food sucks," say some while others say, "Food is pretty good overall." The quality of food differs depending on the dining hall. Most dorms or their neighboring dorms have dining halls. There are two food courts on campus with favorite options such as Burger King, Taco Bell, Sbarro's and Dunkin' Donuts. Marshall Street, which is right beside the campus, is also popular during lunch breaks, with several pizza places, cafés, and ethnic restaurants.

And onto the Campus

The university is located on a hill that overlooks downtown Syracuse, a medium-sized city that is a twenty-minute walk away. As one student said, "It is not urban, it is not suburban. It is somewhere in between." Students cite the "huge" mall nearby as popular because it includes a large-screen movie theater. On campus, the "Mount" is an area where several freshman dorms are located. Students report that the 120 stairs from the main quad to the Mount create a serious challenge in icy winter conditions. At the center of campus is the "beautiful" Quad surrounded by academic buildings that are a part of the College of Arts and Sciences. The other schools are pretty separated from one another, but no distance requires "more than a fifteen-minute walk."

Not long ago, a new law school building was added that now serves as the main building of the College of Law.

The Schine Student Center is also a popular hangout for students. They pass through there during the day, stop by to quickly check their e-mail, or enjoy lunch in the food court. It includes a large auditorium, a gallery, a food court, a game room, and several lounges and meeting rooms. The university bookstore and offices of several student organizations are also in this building. For the studious, the main library, Bird, has more than 2 million volumes. Those who find "studying in the dorm difficult" often visit the Carnegie Library or the Moon Library. Some students also enjoy spending time in the Lowe Art Gallery and the Sculpture Court. Interested students can see both amateur and professional theater productions year-round at the Syracuse Stage.

The Orangemen

Sports are really big at Syracuse. All women's and men's varsity teams are NCAA Division I, and many are nationally ranked. The 50,000-seat Carrier Dome is home for the football, basketball, soccer, and lacrosse teams and is the largest domed stadium on a college campus. Football, basketball, and lacrosse are the three most popular sports that also attract local crowds.

> **"There is no stereotypical Syracuse student."**

This year, women's varsity softball joined the ranks of Syracuse's acclaimed varsity sports. But even if varsity sports are not your thing, Archbold and Flanagan Gymnasiums provide plenty of opportunities to be involved in sports. Intramurals are "well organized and attract many people," and floors usually form their own teams or students sign up in the gym to join other teams. If you have been looking for just the right combination of sports, academics, and fun, consider Syracuse. It may be the perfect school for you!
—*Engin Yenidunya and Staff*

FYI
The three best things about attending Syracuse University are "the great sports, it's tons of fun, and all the snow."
The three worst things about attending Syracuse University are "the cold, the need for a car, and the cliques."
The three things every student should do before graduating are "paint yourself orange, party like mad on the weekends, and watch a game in the Carrier Dome."
One thing I'd like to have known before coming here is "how much snow Syracuse gets."

Union College

Address: Becker Hall, Schenectady, NY 12308
Phone: 518-388-6112
E-mail address: admissions@union.edu
Web site URL: www.union.edu
Location: small city
Founded: 1795
Private or Public: private
Religious affiliation: none
Undergraduate enrollment: 2,084
Total enrollment: 2,191
Percent Male / Female: 52% / 48%
Percent Minority: 13.0%

Percent African-American: 4.0%
Percent Hispanic: 4.0%
Percent Asian: 5.0%
Percent in-state / out-of-state: 49% / 51%
Percent Pub HS: 69%
Fraternities: 31%
Sororities: 26%
Number of Applicants: 3,761
Percent Accepted: 46%
Percent Accepted who enroll: 31%
Entering: 535
Transfers: 34
Application Deadline: 1 Feb

Mean SAT: NA
Middle 50% SAT range: 560–650 V, 580–670 M
Middle 50% ACT range: NA
Mean ACT: NA
3 Most popular majors: psychology, economics, political science
Retention: 94.0%
Graduation rate: 83.0%
Library: 293,253 volumes
Tuition and Fees: $24,963 in; $24,963 out
Room and Board: $6,639
On-campus housing: 99%
Financial aid, first-year: 58%

The Idol, a Chinese sculpture of lions and cubs, was donated by a Union alumnus who wanted to give something back to his alma mater. The administration did not find the Idol so aesthetically pleasing and relegated it to the basement of a building on campus. Upon receiving the news that the donor would be visiting, the university prominently displayed the sculpture in front of West Dorm. After the alumnus left, some students took it upon themselves to improve the Idol by painting it. The Idol has since moved several times, but the tradition of painting this sculpture has remained at Union. A sports team, a fraternity, or just a group of boisterous students can paint the Idol with their names, letters of their Greek organization, or just about any other decoration imaginable. In the spring, the Idol tends to change color more than once an evening.

Three Times Fun

Academic life is intense at Union. One freshman claimed, "I've never worked so hard just to keep up," while a sophomore said, "It's difficult to get an A, but a B or C is no problem." Union keeps class sizes small, with approximately 40 students in an introductory course, and as little as 10 or fewer in upper-level classes. This type of educational setting allows students to have extensive contact with professors and get to know them well. Students find their instructors quite accessible, a necessity at an institution like Union where there are no teaching assistants.

Union runs on a trimester system. Students have three separate segments of study as opposed to two in the traditional semester system. School starts two weeks later than most colleges, includes a Christmas break of six or seven weeks, and does not end till the middle of June. Students generally take three classes per trimester and are usually in class only on Monday, Wednesday, and Friday. Most students are in favor of this system because "it allows us to really concentrate and spread out our work." But the trimester system also means that at times there are only 10 weeks to complete a course that usually requires 15 weeks. The administration is considering a change to a semester schedule in the future just for this reason.

In addition to completing 36 classes, Union students also need to fulfill the General Education Curriculum (GenEd), which includes two history courses, two sciences with labs, one introductory course in the social sciences, and either demonstration of foreign-language proficiency or a term abroad. All freshmen must take the Freshman Preceptorial, a class that includes a lot of reading and "basically teaches you how to write." Union also requires a number of Writing Across the Curriculum courses (WACs), which emphasize writing in several departments. Because class registration is done by person instead of with computers, it can be time-consuming and difficult to get into a class. Undergrads in different majors experience a range of academic expectations. Those interested in engineering reportedly have a more difficult and heavier course load than psychology or political science majors do, which can be for "slackers." Some of the most common majors are biology, psychology, and engineering. The engineering school has a well-respected program in conjunction with General Electric that offers students access to the latest technology. One of the most popular classes is a study of the Holocaust taught by Professor Berg, an expert in the field. Most students try to take this course before they graduate, making it one of Union's largest classes, enrolling approximately 200 students. Professor Baker, a world-famous biomedical ethicist, is another distinguished member of the Union faculty.

There are a number of special academic opportunities at Union. Students can study in York, England, through a program sponsored by the English department, learn about various medical systems of the world while traveling to Europe and East Asia, or participate in a marine biology program in Maine. In addition, Union offers a seven-year combined medical school degree in conjunction with Albany Medical School as well as a five-year MBA program. Undergrads also have the opportunity to create their own major within a department.

Greek Life and Alcohol

Two things dominate the social life at Union: Greek life and alcohol. This aspect of Union hits first-year students particularly hard. One sophomore summed up the situation, "If you like to drink and party, Union is the place for you. If you don't like to drink, you could be bored." Another student said, "I spent my first semester drunk three or four nights a week." Union is "the mother of all fraternities." Considering the 26 fraternities and 6 sororities that exist in a school of only 2,000 people, it is safe to say that Union's Greek system is huge. The Greek scene "rules the social life at Union." One unofficial Union graduation requirement is the "campus crawl," which involves stopping by all the fraternities in one night and having a beer at each one. For the most part, fraternity parties are free and are open to everyone, which prevents non-Greeks from feeling alienated. Freshmen are not allowed to rush until the second trimester. Some Hellenic organizations are more selective than others, although anyone who wants to join will be able to at least get into one of the "nerd frats."

The university recognizes the drinking problem on campus and is trying to crack down on alcohol consumption. One moderately successful solution attempted was an alcohol awareness week during which a semiformal dance was held and all the fraternities were closed for the week. But non-drinkers say they can fit in at Union. According to one such student, "There are so many social alternatives on campus, especially since the Student Activities Office is creating more options."

Preppy Is Popular

When walking around campus, students often feel as if they have stepped into a

J. Crew catalog. Dressing well is important to most Union students, and preppy is definitely the popular look. Most students come from wealthy backgrounds. Jeep Grand Cherokees and BMWs fill Union's parking lots. One student was amazed by how many "really smart people" there are at Union and how everyone "has something intriguing about him or her." However, there is not much geographical or ethnic diversity among its largely conservative students. Most students are from the Northeast, especially New York and Massachusetts. Few students come from outside the Mid-Atlantic and New England states, and even fewer are internationals. Minority students often self-segregate, a tendency that is especially apparent in the dining hall, where different ethnic groups cluster at separate tables. Interracial as well as homosexual couples are rare at Union. Union can be difficult for those on financial aid because most scholarships do not cover the expenses of the academic materials, which carry inflated price tags due to a monopoly of the book market.

After a hard day of work and play, students head home to dorms that students find satisfactory. The university consistently tries to improve the living conditions through renovations, and there are many options available. Several large, coed dormitories such as West, Fox, and Davidson have the reputation as party dorms. Webster, the coed, substance-free dorm; Richmond, the all-female dorm equipped with night security; and South, the all-male dorm, reportedly provide quieter living arrangements for those who like sleep. Many dorms have alternating smoke-free floors at every other level. Members of fraternities or sororities can live in their respective houses. Non-Greeks who seek a sense of camaraderie can choose to live in a theme house, where residents share similar interests. Housing is guaranteed only through junior year, leading some seniors to find accommodation off campus.

Union students unanimously describe their ivy-covered walls, French-style architecture buildings, and arched doorways as "beautiful." Many admit that Union's striking, 204-year-old campus is what drew them to the school. However,

its location in Schenectady, New York, does not provide much choice in entertainment. Without access to a car, the selection of off-campus activities is meager. Although freshmen cannot have cars, an estimated 85 percent of upperclassmen have their own transportation in order to take advantage of the bars, clubs, and shopping in Albany, which is about a half-hour drive from campus. Students generally feel secure on the campus, although some express concern while off campus. One undergrad commented, "You don't want to go off campus alone." Many students take an active stance in trying to improve the community. They get involved in various community service programs such as Big Brothers, Big Sisters, and tutoring for elementary schoolchildren.

There are many places to study, including North Colonnade, an all-night study facility, and the Nott Memorial, the only 16-sided figure in the Western Hemisphere, which contains an art gallery and a huge study lounge where "you can hear a pin drop." Few students utilize the Schaeffer Library for studying. Union students who do not require silence for their studies can go to the Reamer Campus Center, where they will always to be able to find an empty room for group studying among the number of study lounges that the facility houses. One student cannot even imagine Union without the always busy campus center. Jackson Gardens is a great hiding spot to spend a lazy Sunday either reading or just hanging out.

Most students agree that the dining hall fare leaves something to be desired. There are two main dining halls on campus, West Dining Hall and Upperclass Dining Hall. The reportedly "horrible" West Dining Hall caters to freshmen while Upperclass has a much better reputation among the students and is exclusively for those who have completed their first year. One student recommends "sticking to the staples like the salad, sandwich, or bagel bars." The meal plan, which can range from 7 to 15 meals per week, also includes a Validine card, a debit card with a $200 balance that can be used to buy food at a number of on-campus eateries with options such as deli, pizza, and grill. Since Marriott runs all dining options, there are no chain restaurants on campus, forcing students off campus to get their fast-food fill. The university recently implemented a common lunch period so that all students are out of class for lunch at the same time. This has caused some controversy because of the crowding it causes in dining halls.

Pucks Flying

Union students are quite busy during the week participating in over 70 clubs and activities. There is something for everyone. Activities include the Ballroom Dance Club, a cappella singing groups, an Outing Club for those who like to hike and ski, and even a Skydiving Club for those adventurous students who want to add excitement to their college experience. Writing for the *Concordiensis*, a weekly newspaper, or the *Idol*, a popular literary magazine, are two other alternatives. Drama students are attracted to the Mountebacks, the longest continually run college theater troupe. Hockey, Union's only Division I sport, is also the only sport to draw a large following of spectators and fans. The Flying Dutchmen get the biggest turnout for their rowdy games against rivals Rochester Polytechnic Institute and Hamilton College. The team usually does well, until they play "the big teams, like some of the Ivies." The football team, although it does not garner the following of the hockey team, has been quite successful recently, along with the swim team and the crew team, a club sport hoping to gain varsity status. Intramurals are not hugely popular among Union students, despite several interesting choices including squash, broomball, and tennis. The facilities for athletes are more than adequate. The newly renovated Alumni Gym has a huge drawing, and many students work out there New weight-lifting equipment, tennis and squash courts, as well as a pool combine to make the gym a top-notch exercise facility.

> **When walking around campus, students often feel as if they have stepped into a J. Crew catalog.**

Union students display their uniquely fun-loving side through an on-campus tradition that "everyone must do at least once before graduating." The Naked Nott Run requires a student, most likely drunk, to disrobe and run nude around the Nott Memorial Building, usually while it is snowing. Spirited students as well as serious academics and an active party scene combine to make Union College a unique institution of higher learning. And students would agree that Union is an amazing place.—*Naomi Schoenbaum and Staff*

FYI
The three best things about attending Union College are "Jackson Gardens, the small size, and it has good places to study."
The two worst things about attending Union College are "walking around the Nott, which is like a wind tunnel in the winter, and the lack of a variety of things to do."
The three things that every student should do before graduating from Union College are "take an art class, paint the Idol, and take a term abroad."
One thing I'd like to have known before coming here is "the town is really dead. You have to find your own way of doing things."

United States Military Academy

Address: Directorate of Admissions, 606 Thayer Road, West Point, NY 10996-1797
Phone: 914-938-4041
E-mail address: admissions@www.usma.edu
Web site URL: www.usma.edu
Location: rural
Founded: 1802
Private or Public: public
Religious affiliation: none
Undergraduate enrollment: 4,165
Total enrollment: 4,165
Percent Male/Female: 82%/18%

Percent Minority: 19.0%
Percent African-American: 7.0%
Percent Hispanic: 4.0%
Percent Asian: 7.2%
Percent in-state/out-of-state: NA
Percent Pub HS: NA
Fraternities: 0%
Sororities: 0%
Number of Applicants: 11,491
Percent Accepted: 10%
Percent Accepted who enroll: 99%
Entering: 1,134
Transfers: NA
Application Deadline: NA
Mean SAT: 627 V, 641 M

Middle 50% SAT range: 570–660 V, 590–680 M
Middle 50% ACT range: NA
Mean ACT: NA
3 Most popular majors: economics, political science–international politics, mechanical engineering–general mechanics
Retention: NA
Graduation rate: 78%
Library: 500,000 volumes
Tuition and Fees: 0%
Room and Board: $0
On-campus housing: 100%
Financial aid, first-year: 0%

There is no wussy orientation program for incoming "college" freshmen of the United States Military Academy. The opening weeks of training for cadets, affectionately known as the "Beast," are mandatory for all incoming students and future military officers. Students endure long hikes, target practice, and the gas chamber. One student reminisced, "The Beast was the most intense six weeks of my life." It is during this time that the most cadets are apt to drop out. For the 90 percent or so who do survive, the United States Military Academy, known as West Point, is four years of free "education with a purpose" that ultimately requires the cadet to pledge allegiance to the flag for several years after graduation in exchange for this world-class training.

GI Joe Hits the Books

Academics, above all else, are the top priority for cadets at West Point. The course load, while including such traditional subjects as writing skills, psychology, foreign language, economics, politics, and geography, also gives third- and fourth-year cadets a bit more leeway in terms of electives.

Far and away the most popular major on campus is engineering. Engineering math courses are rigorous in terms of both workload and grading. Civil and mechanical engineering top the list as the most popular of the engineering subspecialties and earned high marks from the cadets. Slacker majors at West Point are nearly nonexistent. While the political science and history departments are routinely praised, science and engineering, being the main focus of study, cause the most consternation and exasperation. One cadet stated that his physics and chemistry courses were "ludicrously hard." Some of the least favorite of West Point's requirements are the physical education classes that include such fear-inspiring disciplines as "boxing." According to one cadet, who put it quite succinctly, "PE just sucks."

But fear not, future cadets, for the academy provides a Center for Enhanced Performance that improves cadets' reading skills, speaking abilities, and study habits. Professors are also readily available to help upon request. One student recalls meeting with a physics professor for a late night study session the night before an exam.

Class sizes, ranging from 16 and 20 students, are as small and accommodating as the most prestigious American liberal arts institutions. Smaller class sizes facilitate open discussion and help encourage cadets to ask questions when the material presented is particularly difficult.

The library, although disparaged by some students, is currently undergoing renovations that are scheduled to be complete in 2002, just in time for West Point's Bicentennial.

This Ain't No Party, Soldier

Perhaps the most drastic change that comes with military life is the alteration in the social lives of the cadets. The main credo of any nascent cadet is, "Get the hell away from Post," Post being the affectionate term for the academy. Life at the academy is strictly regimented with designated times for everything from extracurriculars to movies. Intramurals are popular options with most cadets, since the campus is chock-full of sports enthusiasts. However, waking up at 6 A.M. every day for roll call tends to drain most.

Dining hall food at this verdant redoubt on the Hudson tends to draw mediocre reviews from most students. A perk of the experience, at least for upperclassmen, is the fact that first-years, a.k.a. plebes, must serve their elders. The first two meals of the day can be nerve-wracking for plebes as they are generally expected, at these meals, to remain at the beck and call of the other cadets. Dinner is generally more relaxed (and is optional), allowing cadets time to kick back and gossip about the day's events. The potentially angst-ridden plebe will be happy to know that breakfast and lunch are optional on weekends, providing a brief respite from the upperclassmen. There has been a recent push on campus and by the administration to reduce the level of hazing that occurs at the academy.

On-campus dating is sparse thanks in part to the fact that strict regulations exist concerning male–female interactions. Another possible factor contributing to this paucity of "lovin'" may be the fact that, according to one cadet, the women at West Point "ain't nothing to rave about." However, according to some female cadets, being in the minority, they can always find a date on campus. Unfortunately for the sexually deprived senior, West Point forbids seniors from dating plebes. Some cadets attempt to maintain their relationships from high school. The other cadets provide them with the moniker, "2 Percent Club." Simply put, of those who attempt to maintain their relationships from high school, only about 2 percent are successful.

At West Point, no Greek system exists. The camaraderie provided for students by the Greek system at other universities is fulfilled by the military regimentation—"training, sleeping, eating, learning together"—the sense that everyone is in it together.

Character development and education are what inspires most cadets. "Not everything about this place is great, but everything helps to make us better leaders, no matter how much it may suck. I'm glad I'm here." While this may sound a bit contrived, West Pointers insist that they are not brainwashed. "You just have to accept the fact that this lifestyle is nothing like that of the typical college student."

The typical college lifestyle? We all know that means raucous binge drinking, right? Not at West Point. The administration keeps a tight ship allowing only those legally able to drink to do so on Post. So those 18-year-olds that love "alky shoot" or the "beer funnel," you'd best stay away.

Dorm lifestyle at West Point is also somewhat different from the typical college experience. The rooms are small and all basically look alike. Cadets must keep their rooms in tiptop condition, owing to the frequent inspections that occur throughout the year. Companies, a military-type unit, are comprised of around 120 cadets. Throughout the year these cadets work to overcome and adapt to the hardships of military lifestyle. As a result, close friendships are formed. One cadet's advice is to "quickly adapt." Those slow to adapt to the military lifestyle are often left feeling lonely and abandoned.

Leaving Post is a popular option for

cadets. Only seniors can leave on week-days but everyone, with permission, can head into town on the weekends. Popular destinations, outside of the local region, include Boston, New York City, and, in some isolated instances, Washington, D.C. However, the majority of cadets remain on campus during the weekends. Frequently, movies are shown in academy halls throughout the weekend at specified times.

Sports are also extraordinarily popular on campus. Varsity games are frequently attended by cadets and pick-up games can always be found on campus. Attendance at football games is mandatory. The Academy has a 40,000-seat stadium. Mandatory attendance is not a problem for cadets because, simply put, everyone is into athletics. Personal fitness is a virtue on this campus and encouraged by the administration—hence the popularity of sports. The Army, in fact, requires that cadets participate in intramural activities. Clubs are also popular on campus and range from martial arts to film forums.

The campus itself is dominated by Gothic architecture with a smattering of recently renovated buildings. Renovations continue in preparation for West Point's 200th birthday in 2002. Construction has dominated campus in recent years, but most cadets are not fazed, believing the renovations will greatly improve the efficiency of the campus.

Nach der Schule

During the first two summers of their West Point Careers, cadets must attend Camp Buckner. The level of training is intense and prepares them well for future combat. After that, they may be stationed at any location within the United States. Again, adjustment and adaptation is the key to success at West Point.

After graduation, West Point cadets are required to serve six years in the United States Army. Many graduates generally look forward to this period of growth and maturation, calling it an incredible learning experience. The cadets are commissioned into the army as 2nd Lieutenants.

"PE just sucks."

Overall, the benefits of a West Point education are tremendous but the adjustments numerous. Graduates wax romantic about their days at "The Point." This institution forever changes the hearts and minds of its graduates.—*Sean McBride*

FYI
The three best things about attending West Point are "the camaraderie, the regimentation, and the sports."
The three worst things about attending West Point are "the 6 A.M. wake-up call, the regimentation, and physics."
The three things that every student should do before graduating from West Point are "go bar-hopping in town, attend an Army-Navy game, and get an awesome post."
One thing I'd like to have known before coming here is "the difficulty of adapting to the military lifestyle."

University of Rochester

Address: Box 270251, Rochester, NY 14627-0251
Phone: 716-275-3221
E-mail address: admit@admissions.rochester.edu
Web site URL: www.rochester.edu/eastman
Location: suburban
Founded: 1850
Private or Public: private
Religious affiliation: none
Undergraduate enrollment: 4,452
Total enrollment: 8,451
Percent Male/Female: 51%/49%

Percent Minority: 23.0%
Percent African-American: 6.0%
Percent Hispanic: 5.0%
Percent Asian: 12.0%
Percent in-state/out-of-state: 50%/50%
Percent Pub HS: NA
Fraternities: 20%
Sororities: 14%
Number of Applicants: 8,869
Percent Accepted: 62%
Percent Accepted who enroll: 17%
Entering: 935
Transfers: 242
Application Deadline: 31 Jan

Mean SAT: 638 V, 688 M
Middle 50% SAT range: 590–680 V, 620–700 M
Middle 50% ACT range: 26–30
Mean ACT: 28
3 Most popular majors: biological sciences, engineering, psychology
Retention: 93%
Graduation rate: 65.0%
Library: 2.8 million volumes
Tuition and Fees: $20,540 in; $20,540 out
Room and Board: $7,160
On-campus housing: 100%
Financial aid, first-year: 66%

G raffiti is not really against school regulations. You do not always have to trudge through snow to get to class in the Northeast. It is not really that frosty during the winter in upstate New York—in fact, sometimes it gets pretty hot. How could all of this be true in the dead of winter at the University of Rochester, an academically exceptional school, on ice? The Tunnel that connects numerous academic buildings on campus underground becomes the primary route of choice during snowy winter months on campus. The Tunnel also pays a price for its popularity as students often leave their mark upon its walls.

Academics Win Out

Academics are reportedly a high priority among UR students. As one sophomore reflected, "If it is ever a choice of academics versus participating in extracurricular activities of any sort, academics will always win out." Special programs at the University of Rochester attract students from across the nation. One of the most popular programs is the Rochester Early Medical Scholars (REMS), a program that guarantees talented students a place in the university's medical school upon completion of their undergraduate education at Rochester. Students at the Eastman School of Music within the university boast about superb performance facilities and one of North America's most comprehensive academic music libraries.

The University of Rochester offers undergraduates the option to participate in either the regular curriculum of the school or the Honors program. Some subjects such as Philosophy, History, and the Practice of Non-Violence are offered at the "Quest" level, meaning that they are intense courses that strongly emphasize collaboration between students and professors. Students apply for these classes, and take no more than one per term. Personal interaction between students and professors is fostered in a smaller class setting. However, students who want to take advantage of these courses are required to apply in order to take classes at this level. Additionally, the University of Rochester offers the "Take Five" Scholars Program. This program grants undergraduates the opportunity to stay at Rochester for a fifth year, tuition-free, in order to take courses that supplement their regular course requirements.

The housing system at Rochester is

highly specialized. Incoming freshmen are given very long, "often tedious," questionnaires to complete. Students have the option to apply for special-interest housing. The possibilities for special-interest housing are numerous, including medieval houses, drama houses, community service dorms, and athletic dorms. Within such diverse housing options, students may also select international floors, language floors, computer interest floors, music floors, or even quiet study floors. While many of the dorm buildings have been newly renovated, many students seem to agree that single-sex dorms still remain the worst. As one freshman female asked, "Can you just imagine a bunch of guys grouped together? It is so sloppy and awful!" Despite these specific housing options, students at Rochester do not believe that they miss out on meeting people of diverse backgrounds and tastes even though the University of Rochester draws a large percentage of students from New York State.

The social scene at the University of Rochester reportedly "revolves around alcohol—drinking underage here is never a problem." The campus has a Greek system whose fraternities and sororities are the scene of many weekend social functions. One student noted that "they've got lots of brick and ivy, which I always thought a proper college should have. But, more importantly, they have that and plenty of beer." Parties can be "either quiet drinking parties or lively dances." In terms of the university's response to underage drinking, many students believe that "UR has more of a 'don't ask, don't see, don't tell' policy." The university does sponsor movies on the weekends, albeit not first-run. Still other students simply opt to "just hang out" in the student center designed by master architect I. M. Pei (perhaps best known for his pyramid sculpture at the Grand Louvre in Paris). Though some students find the immediate area surrounding the campus "dull and gray," recent concerts by Jewel and the

Verve Pipe are "testimony to the fact that Rochester is what you make it."

> **"They've got lots of brick and ivy, which I always thought a proper college should have. But, more importantly, they have that and plenty of beer."**

Students at Rochester participate in numerous extracurricular organizations on campus. There are over 100 student organizations registered at Rochester, ranging from cultural associations to gaming clubs, gay/lesbian coalitions to conservative unions, literary magazines to newspaper publications. The a cappella singing groups such as the Yellowjackets and SWINGSHOT!? are also very popular. Students say that undergraduates take advantage of numerous community service opportunities on campus, which draw over 70 percent of the UR student body. During the annual Wilson Day, the freshman class gather together to go out into the city of Rochester and volunteer their time for the day.

Athletics at UR do not seem to draw much student support. In fact, many athletes themselves grumble at the lack of enthusiasm and school spirit, stating, "It would be great if once in a while fans would actually come to root for our side!" What does draw student involvement are the intramural games on campus. Undergraduates reportedly "flock to the fields to compete against one another." Some of the most popular intramural sports include soccer, Ultimate Frisbee, and even crew.

Though it may get cold in the winter, students at the University of Rochester keep warm together in the Tunnel beneath the campus. With strong academics and an active student body, Rochester provides an environment where students feel comfortable sharing their talents, thoughts, and ideas, and learning from one another.—*Melissa Chan and Staff*

FYI
The three best things about attending Rochester are "the snow (assuming you love snow), a beautiful campus, and top-notch academics."
The three worst things about attending Rochester are "the food, the cold, and the athletic facilities (though renovations will be complete in August of 2000), and all the rain."

The three things every student should do before graduating from Rochester are "sled with the food trays, play snow touch football, and lick the flagpoles."
One thing I'd like to have known before coming here is "it's really, really cold."

Vassar College

Address: 124 Raymond Avenue, Poughkeepsie, NY 12604-0010
Phone: 914-437-7300
E-mail address: admissions@vassar.edu
Web site URL: www.vassar.edu
Location: suburban
Founded: 1861
Private or Public: private
Religious affiliation: none
Undergraduate enrollment: 2,350
Total enrollment: 2,350
Percent Male/Female: 40%/60%
Percent Minority: 22.0%

Percent African-American: 6.0%
Percent Hispanic: 5.0%
Percent Asian: 10.0%
Percent in-state/out-of-state: 28%/72%
Percent Pub HS: 60%
Fraternities: 0%
Sororities: 0%
Number of Applicants: 4,777
Percent Accepted: 42%
Percent Accepted who enroll: 32%
Entering: 640
Transfers: 25
Application Deadline: 1 Jan

Mean SAT: 677 V, 654 M
Middle 50% SAT range: 730–640 V, 700–610 M
Middle 50% ACT range: NA
Mean ACT: 30
3 Most popular majors: English, psychology, political science
Retention: 96%
Graduation rate: 87%
Library: 900,000 volumes
Tuition and Fees: $24,030 in; NA out
Room and Board: $6,700
On-campus housing: 98%
Financial aid, first-year: 53%

Vassar College is eclectic. Once a women's college where pearls and gloves were required at daily tea, Vassar has come a long way. It became co-ed in 1968, but traces of its early days can still be found in the hallways of the original dorms, which were originally built seven feet wide to accommodate the hoop skirts characteristic of 19th-century women's fashion. Throughout the years, Vassar's strong commitment not only to academics but also to the idea of open-mindedness and tolerance has endured. Its atmosphere is distinct, composed of liberals and conservatives, homosexuals and hippies, aesthetes and scientists, feminists and communists, interest and apathy.

Academics

Students give their professors uniformly high marks. A philosophy major said that the "quality of the professors is the most attractive feature of Vassar." Given the small size of the school, there is a great deal of student-faculty interaction, and almost all professors are highly accessible; in fact, the majority of them live on campus. Often faculty go out of their way to demonstrate their devotion to students—a sophomore noted that his professor once invited him to dinner to continue a discussion. Another student was excited about the fact that Maya Angelou was a visiting professor.

Classes at Vassar are small and intense: most enroll fewer than 25 students. TAs do not teach any classes, and most people feel there is a genuine focus on the individual student. Registration is done on the Internet, and most students feel it is a breeze. Some do complain, however, that because many classes have capped enrollments, it becomes difficult and often impossible to get into them.

While Vassar has some basic requirements, students describe the curriculum as "open," "self-structured," and "empowering." First-year students must take a small, writing-intensive course, but have the freedom to choose from a wide range of possibilities in several departments. Students must also fulfill a quantitative (natural or social science) requirement and demonstrate proficiency in a foreign language, through either two semesters of language at Vassar or high scores on placement, SAT II, or AP tests.

English, cognitive science, and art history are named among the best departments at Vassar, and one student said the film and drama departments are on the rise. In addition to standard majors, Vassar has several interdisciplinary majors and also the option to design your own area of concentration. In general, chemistry courses are reputed to be unusually difficult, and most believe there are no standout gut courses. An extremely popular class that "almost every Vassar student has taken," according to one undergrad, is Drugs, Culture and Society.

Vassar offers a number of unique academic programs. One opportunity that students take advantage of is field work, an internship arranged through a specific academic department; the four-hour weekly time commitment is worth half a credit per semester. The choice of internships is unlimited, many of them are local, and transportation is often provided. Junior Year Abroad is another popular program, with approximately one-third of juniors participating. Candidates for study abroad face strict GPA and language requirements, which do not discourage students with strong interest. Established Vassar programs are located in many European countries, such as France, England, Spain, and Germany, but students have the option to choose their own (often exotic) destination and create an individualized program of study.

Facilities

Ranging from Gothic to modern, even the architecture at Vassar is eclectic. Students are generally happy with Vassar's facilities and describe Thompson Library as "beautiful and amazing—it looks like a cathedral." With a collection of about 750,000 volumes, sizeable for a small liberal arts college, the library is more than adequate for most people's needs. Hardworking Vassar students can find a great place to study in the quiet nooks of the library that "are nice places to work where you can't be disturbed." The library recently reopened after a 2-year renovation project.

Almost all Vassar students spend their four years living on campus in one of the nine dorms. After their first year living in a double, students are guaranteed singles. The most popular dorms are Cushing and Jewitt, the largest dorm, known for its distinctive tower. Main has wide hallways, large windows, and an ideal central location, according to residents. The most unpopular dorm, Noyes, which one student said "is really a Motel Fifty," is said to be less comfortable and ugly. All dorms are coed save one: Strong, in keeping with Vassar tradition, is an all-female dorm. Many juniors and seniors live in the coveted Terrace Apartments (TAs) or Town Houses (THs), which can be either single-sex or coed. Each dorm is equipped with a parlor, TV room, game room, and laundry room. In addition, because a member of the famous Steinway family was once a student at Vassar, a Steinway grand piano can be found in every dorm. "There is definitely a sense of community within each dorm," reported one student. This community, which includes Student Fellows (advisors to freshmen who provide support rather than discipline) and House Fellows (professors who live in dorms, offer advice and guidance, and organize occasional study breaks), makes it easy for the Vassar student to build lasting relationships and complete the transition from high school to college.

Vassar's All-Campus Dining Center, known as AC/DC, garners criticism from the student body. Despite the fact that "there are a lot of options, especially for vegetarians and vegans," many students either don't really care about the food ("It's okay—nothing special") or dislike it ("It's kinda gross"). One student noted that improvements are being made to dining fare. The Retreat, an on-campus snack bar, is more popular, offering a wide variety of food and a convenient location. All students living on campus (except those in Terrace Apartments or Town Houses) are required to be on the meal plan, and most don't venture into Poughkeepsie to eat out. When they do, favorite eateries include the Mill House Panda (good Chinese food), Saigon Cafe, and Pizzeria Uno.

Trashed and Bashed

Despite the absence of Greek organizations, students say alcohol is both accessible and widely consumed. After all, Vassar was founded in 1861 by a brewer. Keg parties are commonly held in dorms, and must be registered with the university. Students generally agree that the administration's enforcement of the drug and alcohol policy is, in a word, "lax." Matthew's Mug, the on-campus bar, is open all week and is extremely popular. Aula, the campus dance club, is also a hot spot with students. Social nightlife at Vassar is often said to "revolve around the Mug and Aula." The Campus Activities Office, Vassar Student Association (VSA), and Vassar Campus Entertainment (VICE) organize many campuswide events, as do various student organizations and clubs. Also, each dorm throws a "campus party" during the year—another indication of the strong residential community at Vassar. The Homo Hop, the biggest and most popular dance of the year, is sponsored by one of the most vocal groups on campus, BiGaLa (the bisexual, gay, and lesbian organization). Teetotalers and nonpartyers can go to the weekend Blodgett film series, a play or concert on campus, a movie in town, or take the train to New York City, less than two hours away.

Passionate About Their Beliefs

Athletics definitely are not the first thing that comes to mind when thinking of Vassar College. While students do participate in an extensive intramural system, varsity athletes and school spirit are in short supply. The exceptions to this are excellent men's and women's volleyball teams, and competitive field hockey and lacrosse. Popular intramurals include rugby and ultimate Frisbee. The mascot, not surprisingly, is the Brewer.

If athletics are not Vassar's strong suit, the arts certainly are. According to one student, "There is a new production almost every weekend—theater at Vassar is intense." A strong interest in the dramatic arts isn't where it ends. Other arts-related campus activities include several bands, a gospel choir, more a cappella singing groups than any other college its size, improvisational theater groups, and a widely admired radio station. In addition, Vassar has an active outing club, the Black Student Union, Asian Student Alliance, Korean Student Alliance, a literary magazine, and BiGaLa, among myriad other activities.

While Vassar students generally are active, one junior said that before she came to Vassar, students appeared to be genuinely interested in the community. "Now that I'm here," she lamented, "I don't think so anymore." Political activism is virtually nonexistent. A senior film studies major attributed the absence of activism to the lack of ideological tension: "Vassar is a place where most students share common beliefs—there is little tension here." Nevertheless, there is definitely a strong sense of social activism: students are concerned about such topics as gay rights, reproductive rights, and women's issues. The campus weekly, the *Miscellany News*, often publishes politically oriented articles, and students can keep up with national headlines in a small-scale daily newspaper, the *Vassar Daily*.

> In general, Vassar students are extremely tolerant and decidedly liberal.

Vassar's campus is "beautiful," with two lakes and a golf course on the grounds. It is self-contained, separated from Poughkeepsie by a guarded gate, which creates a highly isolated atmosphere. Security is not a problem: all buildings are locked and an ID is required for entrance. There is a campus patrol, and emergency phones can be found all over the campus. Many students feel that Poughkeepsie is basically dead: "There's not much to do, there's no culture; all you can do is go to the mall." One student mentioned that "it's easy to get away—you just need a car." Town-gown relations are severely strained, and there is "resentment in the Poughkeepsie community," one student said. A junior psychology major mentioned the efforts of a select few Vassar students in their attempt to foster a positive relationship between the school and town, but expressed discouragement due to the "general sense of apathy at this place."

Vassar students hail from almost every state and several foreign countries, but the majority are from New York and California. Many students also noted the lack of cultural diversity. While one senior said the student body was "pretty homogeneous," he added that the "administration is working hard" to recruit minorities. Minority students at Vassar have a strong support network in the campus ethnic organizations and the Multicultural Center. A common complaint is that the male to female ratio is a bit unbalanced: approximately 40 percent male, 60 percent female. Again, the administration is making efforts to attract more males, and based on recent matriculation rates, its initiatives have been successful. Students say the Vassar stereotype encompasses "freaks, homosexuals, eccentrics, and Deadheads," and the fashion prototype is "long hair, vintage clothing, and body piercings." In general, Vassar students are extremely tolerant and decidedly liberal.

"People here are passionate not only about their classes but about their beliefs," reported one student. "That's what I love about this place." Vassar students are proud of their school's genuine commitment to academics, the beauty of their secluded campus in Poughkeepsie, and the feeling of acceptance and freedom that pervades their environment. "It's empowering," one sophomore asserted. Vassar College is eclectic. In step with Vassar's lasting sense of tradition, afternoon tea is still served in Rose Parlor, only pearls and gloves are no longer required. *—Siddhartha Shukla and Staff*

FYI

The three best things about attending Vassar are "the small classes, the beautiful campus, and the liberal attitude of the students."

The three worst things about attending Vassar are "there's very little to do on campus after 10 P.M., Poughkeepsie is the armpit of the world, and it's hard to find men to date (but easy to find women to date)."

The three things every student should do before graduating are "spend a weekend in New York City, eat at the Acropolis diner, go to the Mug—our one and only dance club."

One thing I'd like to have known before coming here is "how hard it is to keep yourself entertained in Poughkeepsie."

Wells College

Address: 170 Main St, Aurora, NY 13026
Phone: 800-952-9355
E-mail address: admissions@wells.edu
Web site URL: www.wells.edu
Location: rural
Founded: 1868
Private or Public: private
Religious affiliation: none
Undergraduate enrollment: 404
Total enrollment: 404
Percent Male / Female: 0% / 100%
Percent Minority: 13.0%

Percent African-American: 4.0%
Percent Hispanic: 2.0%
Percent Asian: 6.0%
Percent in-state / out-of-state: 65% / 35%
Percent Pub HS: 92%
Fraternities: 0%
Sororities: 0%
Number of Applicants: 410
Percent Accepted: 90%
Percent Accepted who enroll: 37%
Entering: 135
Transfers: 32
Application Deadline: 1 Mar
Mean SAT: 580 V, 540 M

Middle 50% SAT range: 520–630 V, 490–600 M
Middle 50% ACT range: 22–27
Mean ACT: 24
3 Most popular majors: biological & chemical sciences, English, visual & performing arts
Retention: 79.8%
Graduation rate: 68.0%
Library: 248,130 volumes
Tuition and Fees: $12,300 in; NA out
Room and Board: $6,100
On-campus housing: 99%
Financial aid, first-year: 88%

Wells students are enthusiastic about their small community in Aurora, New York. Fairly compact and surrounded by Cayuga Lake and rolling hills, the rural campus boasts waterfalls, hiking trails, and small gardens. Students describe the campus as "wooded and peaceful." They rave about their interaction with professors, the history and traditions of Wells women, and the strong alumnae support.

Stellar Interaction

Students cite interaction with faculty as one of the best things about Wells. "They teach brilliantly and interactively. The faculty make the college experience worthwhile," one senior said. Students describe Wells as a tight-knit community where students are treated "with respect and understanding by professors." Undergrads report that they get to know their professors quite well, and it is not uncommon to go over to their houses for dinner or to baby-sit or just hang out in their offices.

The range of academic possibilities is extensive and students have the option to create their own class or major. All students must fulfill distribution requirements by enrolling in courses in foreign language, formal reasoning, arts and humanities, natural and social sciences, wellness, and physical education. In addition, as part of the liberal arts curriculum, students must take a group of courses whose theme is "Learning for the 21st Century." Priority for registration is given by class, beginning with seniors. With the exception of creative writing and computer classes, students report that there is usually no problem getting into classes. Notoriously popular classes include Human Sexuality and Women and Sex in Early Modern Europe. Courses are described as rigorous, and one senior said, "Classes are rough and getting As is getting tougher." Another student called the grading "tough, but fair."

Small-town Living

The town of Aurora is about 25 minutes north of Ithaca, and students wanting a change from the typical Wells social scene generally go to Cornell University or Ithaca College on weekends. Students also go to Syracuse for women's studies lectures or other campus events. "Many first-years start at Wells thinking that it's going to be like a huge school. They see all the images of what a college is like and when Wells doesn't fit all that, they freak out," said one student. As one student explained, the people that Wells are right for are the ones who see that, in fact, Wells is different—a small, all-female community, who "because of our location in the middle of nowhere are forced to come up with our own fun, thus creating very strong friendship bonds." Some activities Wells students create includes organizing dances such as Mainly '80s and Disco Dodge, playing sports on campus, and going to the Morgan Opera House in Aurora for plays. There are no sororities on campus and while students say alcohol is not hard to obtain, they also advocate there is no pressure to drink.

A Place for Self-Expression

Students describe Wells as a great place for self-expression and exploration. In speaking of student support for the lesbian and bisexual students on campus, one undergrad described the campus community as "very supportive of people's lives." Wells's minority population is small. Many students at Wells are from instate or the Northeast. Further, there are minority clubs and cultural activities on campus for support and learning, such as the United Women of Color and the American Indians in Science.

Home Is Where the Heart Is

Many dorms are actually old homes, each with their own unique feel. There are four residence halls, and a fifth is currently being renovated. Glen Park is the old home of Henry Wells, who founded Wells Seminary in 1868 for the "gift of female education." Students say it has a "homey feel," with a large, central kitchen, three floors of rooms, and a spiral staircase winding through the middle. Each room is different, but many have high ceilings and wooden floors. Leach is a more typical dorm, with three floors of rooms and a large central lounge. Dodge, a dorm built in the '60s, draws the most complaints for its age, but also inspires fierce loyalty from those that live there. Although it has smaller rooms, upperclasswomen can obtain singles in rooms meant to be doubles. Dodge hosts one of the biggest campus events, the Disco Dodge, in the fall.

Almost all students live on campus, since they need special permission to live off campus. First-year students are assigned "sisters" from each of the three other classes to provide guidance and friendship. There is also an RA system in the dorms. Recent renovations to the ever popular Weld House, a dorm used by students of all years, has provided Wells students with expanded Internet access, two 24-hour computing labs, and a network connection in every room. The renovations to Weld are part of a general $2.4 million technology upgrade currently going on around the campus. Wells's students, by the end of the renovations, will possess the most up-to-date computer software and hardware with a student-computer ratio of 3:1.

Students must buy a meal plan of 19 meals per week. During the week, meals are served in one dining hall, though the Somner Student Center provides weekend brunch and Saturday dinner. Somner Center is open daily until midnight and the meal plan allots each student $50 a semester to spend there (they can also pay cash). Students say the dining hall has a huge salad bar, a deli bar, and for hot food a meat line and a wellness/vegetarian line. Undergrads report that vegetarians usually have no problem finding something to eat.

Active Women

Sports at Wells have been improving. Wells recently joined the All Women's College Conference (AWCC) and now offers students the opportunity to participate on the field hockey, lacrosse, swimming, and soccer teams among others. Other athletic options include intramural basketball and volleyball, and there is a golf course on campus for student use, as well.

Rife with Tradition

Wells is famous for its traditions. Students are divided into odd/even classes depending on year of graduation for such events as the Odd/Even basketball game. Other traditions include the Junior Blast, where first-years hide the juniors' beds and leave clues about where to find them. Fall and spring weekend festivities feature bonfires and concerts, which in the past have drawn such acts as the SpinDoctors Other traditions include a countdown the last hundred days of senior year; seniors mark the first day of the countdown with a champagne breakfast and wear their graduation robes. Bells are rung from Main tower to celebrate everything from the first snowfall to the marriage of a Wells woman.

> **Students describe Wells as a great place for self-expression and exploration.**

Wells is noted for its consistent and strong alumnae support, and students praise the opportunities this support provides for leadership and internships Wells offers a leadership week where alumnae help match students with internships in January for credit. One student said, "Our alumnae network is really amazing and it's one of the things that think makes Wells women so successful Alumnae feel indebted to the school and give by way of internships, which I think is one of the reasons why Wells women have such high graduate school acceptance rates."

Wells is not right for everyone, but for the student who seeks a school with strong academic roots and many opportunities to participate in tradition and form lasting friendships, Wells is a strong community. One student said, "This tiny school has a unique all-female environment. The atmosphere on campus is supportive and open—people can be who they want to be. I wouldn't trade my Wells experience for the world!"—*Laura Chaukin and Staff*

FYI
The three best things about attending Wells are "the small class sizes, the personal relationship with professors, and the internship opportunities."

The three worst things about attending Wells are "the weather—'I slid to class today,' the relative isolation, and the small library."

The three things that every student should do before graduating from Wells are "take a women's studies class, study abroad (popular destinations include England, Italy, Spain, and the Dominican Republic), and JUMP IN THE LAKE."

One thing I'd like to have known before coming here is " the rich history of the area."

Yeshiva University

Address: 500 West 185th Street, New York, NY 10033
Phone: 212-960-5277
E-mail address: 0
Web site URL: 0
Location: urban
Founded: 1886
Private or Public: private
Religious affiliation: none
Undergraduate enrollment: 1,990
Total enrollment: 4,989
Percent Male / Female: 53%/47%
Percent Minority: 0.0%
Percent African-American: 0.0%

Percent Hispanic: 0.0%
Percent Asian: 0.0%
Percent in-state / out-of-state: 39%/61%
Percent Pub HS: 3%
Fraternities: 0%
Sororities: 0%
Number of Applicants: 1,374
Percent Accepted: 84%
Percent Accepted who enroll: 70%
Entering: 610
Transfers: 71
Application Deadline: 15 Feb
Mean SAT: NA
Middle 50% SAT range:

510–630 V, 560–675 M
Middle 50% ACT range: NA
Mean ACT: NA
3 Most popular majors: psychology, accounting, pre-med
Retention: 84%
Graduation rate: 49%
Library: 960,000 volumes
Tuition and Fees: $12,834 in; $12,834 out
Room and Board: $4,212
On-campus housing: 100%
Financial aid, first-year: 75%

Yeshiva University stands at the junction where the religious meets the secular, uptown meets downtown, and tradition meets the modern day. For students who are interested in Judaism and willing to work hard, Yeshiva just might provide the best of all of these worlds—along with a terrific education.

The university consists of two undergraduate schools: Yeshiva College for men and Stern College for women. Stern, located just a few blocks from the Empire State Building in midtown Manhattan, is a 30-minute subway ride from the Yeshiva College campus in Manhattan's Washington Heights section. Because of the university's strong religious commitment, all classes and facilities are separate for women and men.

Academics

The academic program at Yeshiva is twofold, as students must satisfy both religious and secular course requirements.

All men enroll in one of three religious studies programs, depending on religious background and interest. Students in the Mazer Yeshiva Program, the most rigorous, spend three hours every weekday morning studying the day's lesson, then two hours each afternoon at a lecture given by a rabbi. At 3 P.M. they begin their secular studies, a program as demanding as the typical course load at most other colleges.

Students in the other programs, Stone Beis Midrash Program, Isaac Breuer College (IBC), and James Striar School (JSS), complete their daily religious studies at 1 P.M. and then start their secular courses. (Some IBC classes are taught in Hebrew.) The demands of a dual religious-secular program mean that students often remain in class as late as 9 P.M. "It can be very rough, but you do get used to it once you get into the swing of things," said one student.

Women follow a core program of religious studies that requires them to take three Judaic studies classes for six consecutive semesters. Like its men's counterpart, Stern offers religious classes at beginning, intermediate, and advanced levels. Stern has its own faculty, although some professors teach jointly at Yeshiva and Stern. Unlike Yeshiva, Stern also has a popular "shaped major" program through which students can take classes at different local universities for majors not offered at their own college, including fashion design and marketing at the Fashion Institute of Technology. Occupational therapy and nursing are also available at NYU or Columbia. At Stern, the most popular major in the area of secular studies is psychology; at Yeshiva College, it is biology.

Most students at Yeshiva University are career-oriented. Popular majors include accounting and pre-med, and the undergraduate Sy Syms School of Business attracts many students as well. Acceptance rates to graduate schools are high, one student stating that "tons go on to Harvard Law." Most departments are considered strong, although one student said the psychology major at Stern is popular "because it's an easy way out."

Many students spend their first year studying in Israel, which means that they must satisfy the university's requirements in three years instead of four. This situation often makes an already heavy workload at Yeshiva even more intense. But while some complain about academic pressure, there are few, if any, complaints about student-faculty relationships. With few graduate TAs and many small classes, students and professors get to know each other well. "Teachers have a lot of time for students, and they know us by name," one student said.

Separate, Not Equal

Facilities at Stern and Yeshiva Colleges are separate, but not equal. Uptown at Yeshiva College, students have use of the well-equipped Max Stern Athletic Center (yes, the Stern Athletic Center is on the Yeshiva College campus) and the Schottenstein Student Union, which houses student organization offices, a theater, and the school's radio station, WYUR. An indoor swimming pool was recently completed, and a pedestrian mall runs through the center of campus.

Downtown at Stern, facilities are sparse. The campus has two buildings: one is the dorm, and the other contains everything else. The crowded location and the high cost of midtown Manhattan real estate have made expansion of existing facilities difficult. Stern administrators have been "trying to find additional space, but they don't have much room to grow," one student reported. Despite these constraints, Stern recently expanded and renovated its library and has purchased an off-campus apartment building. Moreover, with all the attractions of downtown New York City literally at their doorstep, Stern students feel their location compensates for the lack of facilities. "Midtown Manhattan is like a campus in itself. [Yeshiva] doesn't have what we have," one junior said.

Yeshiva men might agree, but for different reasons. The Washington Heights area has some crime problems. Campus security, however, is tight and effective, and a van escort service operates nightly.

The majority of undergrads live on the campus of either Stern or Yeshiva, and there are no fraternities or sororities. Some freshmen at Yeshiva College live in noisy Rubin Hall, which is located "right on top of the cafeteria," one resident complained. Other freshmen live in the quieter and less popular Muss Hall, reached by walking through the high school building in front of it. The newest dorm, Morgenstern Hall ("Morg"), is centrally located and is popular among the upperclassmen. Stern women live in Brookdale Hall or the newly acquired apartment building. In the dorm, groups of four to five students share a kitchen area and a bathroom. "It's kind of homey," said one student. Because of limited space on campus, students can choose to live in off-campus dorms for the same cost as campus housing.

All new students on campus must be on the meal plan, which functions as a debit card: students pay a flat sum at the beginning of the year and the cost of each meal they eat is deducted from that sum. Students describe the food as "not so terrible," but too expensive. All food at Yeshiva is kosher. Some students prefer to make their own meals or eat out at nearby kosher pizza places and delis. A cafeteria/grocery store is also located on the Yeshiva College campus.

A large percentage of Yeshiva students come from the New York City area, but a substantial number come from out of town as well. While many are Orthodox, students with Reform and Conservative Jewish backgrounds are also well represented. Each weekend, the campuses empty out as students go home or to friends' homes to celebrate the Sabbath. Various student organizations sponsor several weekend programs each semester that combine religious observance with discussions and student activities.

Homogeneity

Even with their heavy workload, Yeshiva and Stern students enjoy plenty of extracurricular activities. Intramural sports, especially basketball, are popular at Yeshiva. Basketball is also Yeshiva's most popular varsity sport, and Stern fields varsity teams in basketball and tennis. Campus newspapers include Yeshiva's *Commentator* and Stern's *Observer* and *Hamevaser*, a university publication that explores Jewish issues. The student government acts in campus politics and organizes student activities. The drama society produces one or two plays each semester. "It's easy to get involved in activities," one student said.

Students are politically active, particularly on issues concerning Israel, although one student bemoaned the lack of debate. "We are politically active, but in a homogeneous sense," he said.

Uptown, Downtown

The distance between Stern and Yeshiva Colleges does not prevent students from enjoying an active social life. A shuttle service runs frequently between the two campuses, but most socializing happens off campus. While the university does not sponsor dances, student-organized social events on holidays including Hanukkah, Purim, and Israeli Independence Day are popular. Thursday night is "date night," when students spend a night on the town at comedy clubs or Broadway plays. Many students are married, and engagement parties are common. "There are almost two engagement parties every week," one student estimated. Most married students live in off-campus apartments.

> **"Teachers have a lot of time for students, and they know us by name," one student said.**

Judaism is integral to campus life at both Yeshiva and Stern Colleges. Along with an impressive double curriculum comes an excellent academic program for students interested in virtually any field of study. Its less cohesive campus social life is offset by the lures of New York City. As far as students are concerned, Yeshiva has the right formula for secular learning and the development of a deeper, more appreciative understanding of the Jewish religion.—*Staff*

FYI
The three best things about Yeshiva and Stern are "the New York location, the helpful faculty, the solid academics that combine both religious and secular studies."
The three worst things about Yeshiva and Stern are "the cramped campus, the limited varsity sports teams, and the intense workload."
The three things that every student at Yeshiva and Stern should do before graduating are "go to Israel, watch a varsity basketball game, and study in a coffee shop."
One thing I wish I'd known before coming to Yeshiva and Stern is "the high price of New York and all the little expenses that living off campus entails."

North Carolina

Davidson College

Address: P.O. Box 1737, Davidson, NC 28036-1719
Phone: 704-892-2230
E-mail address: admission@davidson.edu
Web site URL: www.davidson.edu
Location: suburban
Founded: 1837
Private or Public: private
Religious affiliation: Presbyterian (USA)
Undergraduate enrollment: 658
Total enrollment: 1,623
Percent Male/Female: 44%/56%

Percent Minority: 7.0%
Percent African-American: 2.0%
Percent Hispanic: 1.0%
Percent Asian: 4.0%
Percent in-state/out-of-state: 23%/77%
Percent Pub HS: 51%
Fraternities: 50%
Sororities: NA
Number of Applicants: 3,185
Percent Accepted: 37%
Percent Accepted who enroll: 41%
Entering: 472
Transfers: 11
Application Deadline: 2 Jan

Mean SAT: 658 V, 662 M
Middle 50% SAT range: 620–710 V, 630–700 M
Middle 50% ACT range: 27–31
Mean ACT: 29
3 Most popular majors: biology, English, history
Retention: 64.0%
Graduation rate: 29.0%
Library: 440,000 volumes
Tuition and Fees: $20,658 in; $NA out
Room and Board: $6,126
On-campus housing: 100%
Financial aid, first-year: 35%

Nestled quietly in North Carolina, Davidson College offers a challenging liberal arts education with an environment that is "really tranquil and beautiful." Often considered the "Pomona of the South," Davidson, a Presbyterian school 20 miles outside of Charlotte, is a close community of dedicated students and faculty.

Challenging Academics

Describing academics, one student said, "The professors want you to do well." Although students find the academics at Davidson rigorous, they have nothing but compliments for their accessible professors. Because classes are generally 20–30 students with no lectures and no TAs, Davidson students enjoy individual attention from professors genuinely interested in teaching, not just research. "They are really personal and are always sure to learn your name. If you're not doing well in their class they'll be sure that you get all

the extra help you need," one student said.

Help from professors proves useful in tackling the challenging academics at Davidson. "The work is really tough, but doable," said one undergrad. "It can be really stressful. I work a lot more here than I did in high school." While Davidson students may be working a little harder than those at other schools, most agree that "the effort is really worth it and everyone else is working just as much so it feels like we're in it together."

Davidson prides itself in giving its students a liberal arts education. Like most schools, there are a variety of requirements in order to ensure that students, at the very least, "learn a little about a lot of different topics." With required courses in English, social science, history, religion and philosophy, mathematics, and art, most students enjoy "taking classes they really wouldn't take the time to look at." However, as one physics major stated, "I really didn't want to take the required religion course and that's one less class I could take of something else." In addition to major requirements, there are PE requirements as well. While some students feel weighed down by the large amount of required courses, the options Davidson offers make fulfilling the necessary courses much easier. "There is really a fair amount of flexibility with the academic requirements and you can do things like waterskiing to fulfill the PE requirements," one student said.

Davidson offers a wide variety of respected majors as well as minors. This small southern school is particularly known for its pre-med program with one of the most popular majors being chemistry. "It seems like everyone here is premed," one student noticed. But despite the challenges that come with the premed curriculum, "everybody is so nice, not cutthroat like at other schools." English is considered one of the easier majors, "because while we [science majors] are slaving away in the labs every afternoon, they are playing Frisbee on the grass."

A Close Community

"You can strike a conversation with anyone here and people I don't even know say hi to me all the time," said one freshman. descriptions of Davidson inevitably include the Honor Code and Southern hospitality. An integral part of the campus, the Honor Code impacts all parts of life. As one student described, "The Honor Code basically says that we must not cheat, lie, or steal and should report anybody who does. I've never seen anybody do any of that the whole time I've been here. People leave their keys in their car with the engine running, rooms are left unlocked, and twenty dollars would be left on the ground and would not be touched. That's nice to know."

There are complaints, however, about the homogeneity of the student body. "Everybody here is Christian, white, and either from North or South Carolina." While recruitment of international students and enrollment of students from other states is increasing, there is still a lack of diversity. Nevertheless, this lack of diversity does not keep the Davidson campus from having a diverse array of activities for its students. Besides writing for *The Davidsonian*, or *Libertas*, students are also involved in such organizations as Learn and Serve, a community service organization, the Dahn Hak Club, which teaches ancient Korean holistic medicine, or the Ultimate Frisbee team. Additionally, the Intervarsity Christian Fellowship is very popular. Because Davidson is a Presbyterian school, most students are religious, and Christianity plays an integral role on campus. There are also 11 varsity sports for men and 10 for women at this Division I school, with Davidson remaining very competitive. The wide variety of activities is endless. "It's not hard to find something you like to do, what is difficult is choosing among all the possibilities and if there isn't a club for what you want to do, you can just start it up yourself," said one student.

Patterson Court

Centered on Patterson Court, a semicircle of houses and fraternities are generally considered the focal point of the Davidson social scene. Greek life is still a major part of socializing, even though the administration has been deeply involved to ensure there is no hazing. "In the fraternities here you must still pledge and be chosen by the fraternity brothers in order to join, but drinking isn't really a big part of the scene. There are a lot of guys who don't drink at all, then there are others who are big party animals." For women, there are eating houses, each with its own character. Approximately 86 percent of women end up joining one of the eating houses. While the food is thought to be "less greasy than Commons, there is a lot less choice, which is annoying." Eating house membership is done by lottery, which most consider "really fair. You can also transfer easily if you want." Eating houses, fraternities, and the Black Student Coalition sponsor social functions, but nonmembers are also welcome. While some eating houses offer themed formals like "Heaven and Hell," the school administration sponsors independent social functions and formals that many students attend. The Grey College Union also sponsors performances by musicians and comedians as well as other events. Some recent performers presented by the Union include Hootie and the Blowfish, the Indigo Girls, and Chuck Davis and the African Dance Ensemble.

Davidson students certainly aren't lacking in spirit. Football games are very popular, particularly because of the team's recent good record, basketball games are also well attended. Besides going to Patterson Court, Union, or attending sports events, some students drive 20 minutes to Charlotte, which "has some good restaurants and clubs."

Posh Living

"I loved the freshman housing," one sophomore said. While the freshman rooms are rather small and most of the furniture is built-in, "you get to meet so many people and there is such hall bonding." Most freshmen live in Richardson Hall on five single-sex floors. Others live in Belk Hall, which supposedly sports even smaller rooms. Sophomores live in "Sophomore City," comprised of three identical dorms. "I like the dorms except I live down the hill in Erwin, which is a 10-minute walk to classes," one sophomore said. Ninety-five percent of students live on campus, with rooms determined by lottery. There is no special-interest housing and fraternities are nonresidential. Nevertheless, by senior year, "you get these great suites with a living room and a kitchen."

The Town of Davidson

There are mixed feelings about Davidson, the town. Most students find it to be spirited and cute. With places like Ben and Jerry's, Summit (a coffee shop), and a soda shop, Davidson offers a few hangouts a very short walk from campus. But having only one main street, the town "can be really boring and if you don't have a car, it can feel restrictive."

> **"The Honor Code basically says that we must not cheat, lie, or steal and should report anybody who does. I've never seen anybody do any of that the whole time I've been here."**

One student said, "I chose Davidson College for its small town atmosphere, small teacher-student ratio, its value of service, its reputation of honor, and, above all, the amazing education the college offers. The atmosphere at Davidson is like no other I've experienced." While providing students with the best in faculty, facilities, and education, Davidson fosters a caring environment where students feel comfortable trying new things and continuing on with things they enjoy. Whether that be varsity sports, intramural athletics, religious fellowship, singing groups, visual arts, or dancing wildly on Patterson Court, Davidson offers it all "Davidson is a place where you are assured to be challenged, not only academically but spiritually and socially as well."—*Jessica Morgan*

FYI
The three best things about Davidson are "the Honor Code, friendliness, and the academic challenge."
The three worst things about Davidson are "being far from a major city, lack of diversity, and lack of choice of eating house food."
The three things that every student should do before graduating from Davidson are "go to professors' office hours, go crazy on Patterson Court, and learn to throw a Frisbee."
One thing I'd like to have known before coming here is "how hard I'd be working."

Duke University

Address: 2138 Campus Drive, Box 90586, Durham, NC 27708
Phone: 919-684-3214
E-mail address: askduke@admiss.duke.edu
Web site URL: www.duke.edu
Location: urban
Founded: 1838
Private or Public: private
Religious affiliation: Methodist
Undergraduate enrollment: 6,388
Total enrollment: 11,589
Percent Male/Female: 52%/48%

Percent Minority: 30.0%
Percent African-American: 9.0%
Percent Hispanic: 4.0%
Percent Asian: 13.0%
Percent in-state/out-of-state: 12%/88%
Percent Pub HS: 66%
Fraternities: 29%
Sororities: 42%
Number of Applicants: 13,942
Percent Accepted: 28%
Percent Accepted who enroll: 43%
Entering: 1,693
Transfers: 97
Application Deadline: 2 Jan
Mean SAT: NA

Middle 50% SAT range: 640–730 V, 660–760 M
Middle 50% ACT range: 29–33
Mean ACT: 30
3 Most popular majors: biology, economics, psychology
Retention: 96.0%
Graduation rate: 87.0%
Library: 4,500,000 volumes
Tuition and Fees: $23,210 in; NA out
Room and Board: $7,088
On-campus housing: 84%
Financial aid, first-year: 44%

An excellent academic program, an excellent sports reputation, and an excellent party scene. What more could you want? Duke, the so-called "Ivy of the South," has made a name for itself both in academics and in athletics. In a school where "freshman" is synonymous with "pre-med," students study hard and play hard in order to succeed at one of the top universities in the country. According to campus legend, James Duke founded the school after trying to buy Princeton but was informed that the school would not change its name. So he left for Durham, North Carolina, and established a school comparable to the Ivies, with a Southern twang.

Academic Rigors

Despite all the pre-meds and Duke's notorious superiority in the sciences, the administration strives to maintain a liberal education program. Distribution requirements are abundant, but most students take them in stride, and as one said, "It just makes you plan your courses more efficiently."

The curriculum is divided into six different areas of study: arts and literature, natural science, social science, foreign language, quantitative reasoning, and civilization. Of the areas, students are required to take three classes from four groups; two classes from a fifth group, and may avoid one group altogether if they so choose. As one student put it, the joy of this system is that "if you don't like math, you don't have to take it."

Gut courses such as Introduction to Jazz, Introduction to Computer Science, Biological Anthropology, and Anatomy allow some students to make it through distribution requirements that would otherwise prove to be quite daunting. However, Duke is not for the faint of heart, and even the "easy" classes are full of students looking to get the most out of their education, with the best grades they can.

Choosing a major at Duke can be a difficult task, as there are so many of them. However, even if you don't find what you're looking for, Program II allows students to create their own major with the help of a professor who then becomes your major advisor. After you write a lengthy proposal, it is reviewed by senior professors and deans who hopefully allow you to continue in that direction. Ideas for majors like "cognitive neuroscience" get reviewed, and often approved, so that you can major in literally anything you like.

Freshmen also have the opportunity to participate in FOCUS, a first-semester program that allows students to take seminar classes in subjects normally reserved for juniors and seniors. One freshman mused that FOCUS "exposes you to a lot of ideas that you probably have never heard of before, it allows closer interaction with fellow students, and closer interaction with professors—things that many freshmen on other campuses miss out on until later years." These classes are capped at 15 students, but the participants warn that they are "very writing and reading intensive and are definitely more work than a regular freshman class load," but that "it is worth it in the long run."

As an "almost Ivy," Duke employs some of the best professors in the country. One of the most popular is James Bonk, who teaches Chemistry 111, and as students point out, it seems like half the freshman class has him every year, because so many are pre-med. Also notable is Professor Knut Schmidt Nielson in the biology department, who has helped biology become the most popular major on campus. A close second, however, is public policy. This fast-growing major is popular because, according to one student, "you can go into so many different things."

Students overall are extremely happy with Duke academics, though they do have a few complaints. One is the presence of undergraduate TAs. One student explained that "an undergraduate is a TA because he or she already took the class and did awesome in it, but it's still sort of weird to be learning from your peers." The other complaint is the registration system. Duke uses ACES (Automated Computer Enrollment System), allowing students to enroll over the phone. However, signing up is based on your graduating year and Social Security number, so it is possible to "get the shaft," as one student put it. "Getting into classes can sometimes be a problem for the more popular classes such as Abnormal Psychology; Biological Psychology; History of Terrorism; Drugs, Brain, and Behavior; and a slew of others." However, "you usu-

ally end up okay." There are some introductory classes that have over 50 students, but most of the intermediate-level classes have less than 30 and in the more specialized classes, there will be less than 20 students.

What the Hell is "Tenting"?

Students at Duke study hard. So, in response, they play hard as well. The choice method of "playing" is basketball. If you're not on the team, you had better be getting ready for a game, painting your face, or doing a stint as a Blue Devil—which entails painting your entire body blue and white, then doing your best to rally the crowd, distract the other team, and cause general mayhem in the stands.

But tenting? It goes like this: There are a few choice b-ball games every year that everyone wants to go to, and which tickets are almost impossible to come by. So, enthusiastic fans get into groups of ten or so, put up a tent outside the stadium, and wait. FOR WEEKS. The rule is that someone must be in the tent at all times, and so they are. Sounds like a month-long party? It is. As one student put it, "This is one of the greatest experiences you will ever have. It's just amazing. Everyone who is tenting out right now for the St. John's and UNC games is just having an awesome time. It's a completely chill atmosphere and everyone gets along with everyone else." Not to mention the large presence of alcohol in the tents . . .

To those not playing varsity sports, Duke offers tons of intramurals. Popular IMs include football, soccer, and Ultimate Frisbee. For those just looking to work out, a $20 million, 99,000-square-foot facility, named for the Northwest Airlines cochairman Gary L. Wilson, just opened in October of 1999. It nearly doubled the size of the old gym, and offers state-of-the-art equipment for all Blue Devils.

But Where Will I Live?

One student probably said it best when he stated, "Freshman Campus looks like UVA—red brick with a beautiful, domed auditorium at the end of the quad." The main campus (where most upperclassmen live) has been termed "Gothic Wonderland" and its centerpiece is the beautiful chapel. Freshman Campus includes the Student Union, a choice dining spot for frosh, the Marketplace, and Trinity Café. After a year on Freshman Campus (a.k.a. East Campus), students move to West Campus, where they choose between living in fraternity houses, selective houses (the coed alternative to frat life, with a shorter rush period), or dorms. The most talked about dorm is Trent. As one student put it, "Trent is what everybody fears. It's actually pretty nice, but it's in the middle of nowhere." However, Trent has its perks. It's quiet, it's secluded, and it gives students the opportunity to "block." In Trent one can choose to live with one's friends, whereas in other dorms one must rely on a lottery, and you could end up "next to some random people."

But, given several student responses, the people are not that random. One of Duke students' major complaints is the lack of diversity. While people hail from all over the country, they are primarily "preppy rich kids." And the small amount of diversity that does exist tends to lead to tension, not acceptance. "There's a lot of self-segregation among ethnic groups," pointed out one student. However, the administration is making efforts to change this, with such additions as the Spectrum "diversity house."

Duke has one of the best meal plans around. According to one student, almost any restaurant up to about 5 miles away delivers till about 4 in the morning. There are PLENTY of eating options. And even the dining hall food is apparently "not that bad."

The students' relationship with Durham is not all that it could be. According to one student, "Durham does not have much to offer, and safety is always a concern." It is apparently possible to go all four years without ever feeling the need to leave campus. The tight community at Duke makes for plenty of good times, though "after a few years here, the social scene can get kind of old." Fortunately, Duke offers an excellent study abroad program, and every year, approximately a quarter of the juniors escape to study anywhere from China to Europe to Australia. As one student put it, "They make it really easy to go abroad," and so many students do.

Is There Anything to Do Besides Sports?

To answer that, YES! One student put it best when he said, "You can do anything from race car driving to skiing to wind surfing to water-skiing to pretty much anything you can think of—and if we don't have it, you can make it."

Duke's library system, the Perkins libraries, contains nearly 5 million volumes, collected in different buildings, from the main library to the music library to the rare books and documents library. Duke also boasts the largest collection of prosimian primates (lemurs) anywhere in the world. As one student put it, "It's just amazing to go down there and watch them interact." One wonders if students are reminded of the Blue Devils at a UNC game.

When not studying, Duke residents enjoy a "damn good party scene." With abundant frats, it's difficult to find a night without a party. The parties range from the usual keg-in-a-frat-house genre to such events as the Reggae Jam. Because of the close-knit campus, students on West Campus claim that they can just step outside their doors and find "awesome bands playing" or something else exciting to do. Over the past few years, the college has cracked down on underage drinking, and now East Campus is completely dry. It is still, of course, possible to elude the system, but the repercussions are serious, and with West Campus a short walk away, most freshmen simply don't risk it. There is an on-campus bar, Hideaway, and according to one student, "When in doubt, go there." Also, the Kudzoo Tavern, a local hangout boasting local musicians, and some "pretty big music," also admits the under-21 set.

> "The choice method of playing is basketball. If you're not on the team, you had better get ready for a game."

Students who choose to abstain from alcohol don't find the pressure to be unbearable. There are plenty of "mellow" activities, and no one cares if you don't drink at a frat party. Some students would argue that since the crackdown on alcohol, drug use has increased. However, it remains fairly underground, and with the exception of pot, almost invisible. As one student put it, "The drugs are pretty mild."

Overall, students are happy at Duke. As one freshman exclaimed, "After about two days, it already felt like home." The people, though a bit homogeneous, are friendly, easygoing, and aware of what a gift a Duke education is. Students study hard and play hard in preparation for the real world to come.—*Kyla Dahlin*

FYI

The three best things about attending Duke are "the great people; the basketball; and the mixture between academics, athletics, and an awesome social scene."

The three worst things about attending Duke are "the bus system, Durham, and the lack of a dating scene."

The three things that every student should do before graduating from Duke are "TENT!, study abroad, and take a trip down to the primate center."

One thing I'd like to have known before coming here is that "there's no need to worry about finding normal people that don't study 24/7, they exist."

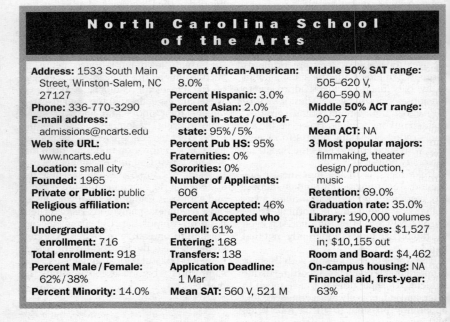

North Carolina School of the Arts

Address: 1533 South Main Street, Winston-Salem, NC 27127
Phone: 336-770-3290
E-mail address: admissions@ncarts.edu
Web site URL: www.ncarts.edu
Location: small city
Founded: 1965
Private or Public: public
Religious affiliation: none
Undergraduate enrollment: 716
Total enrollment: 918
Percent Male/Female: 62%/38%
Percent Minority: 14.0%

Percent African-American: 8.0%
Percent Hispanic: 3.0%
Percent Asian: 2.0%
Percent in-state/out-of-state: 95%/5%
Percent Pub HS: 95%
Fraternities: 0%
Sororities: 0%
Number of Applicants: 606
Percent Accepted: 46%
Percent Accepted who enroll: 61%
Entering: 168
Transfers: 138
Application Deadline: 1 Mar
Mean SAT: 560 V, 521 M

Middle 50% SAT range: 505–620 V, 460–590 M
Middle 50% ACT range: 20–27
Mean ACT: NA
3 Most popular majors: filmmaking, theater design/production, music
Retention: 69.0%
Graduation rate: 35.0%
Library: 190,000 volumes
Tuition and Fees: $1,527 in; $10,155 out
Room and Board: $4,462
On-campus housing: NA
Financial aid, first-year: 63%

At the North Carolina School of the Arts, there are roughly a thousand aspiring artists of all ages and disciplines; naturally, things work a little differently here. NCSA does have a homecoming football game, but it's a game between students and faculty, and the homecoming queen is usually a drag queen. What students love about NCSA is that they can address their instructors by their first names and develop close working relationships with professionals in their field of interest. As one student explained, "Don't come here looking for the traditional college."

Six Times the Fun

North Carolina School of the Arts (NCSA) is divided into six schools: dance, drama, filmmaking, music, theater design and production, and visual arts. Students apply to and enter only one of the six schools. Students spend the first year taking courses from a general curriculum in their specific school, after which students choose a major within that school. For example, students in theater design and production take classes such as Scenic and Lighting Design their first year, but may eventually choose to major in stage managing. NCSA attracts a wide variety of students, some who already have undergraduate degrees or work experience in their field of study, and the first-year program is designed to put everyone on an equal level. Classes are small, with multiple sections of the same class being taught by different instructors, and cover several different topics in the area of study.

Although the school encourages a relaxed work environment, the first year is not an easy one. Students are expected to dedicate themselves seriously to their art. The term "second year slaughter" comes from the school's policy of cutting students the faculty judges to be unprepared for the level of dedication required to be successful in the school. Film students are expected to work on four shoots a week, and design and production students often pull "triple crews"—working from 8 A.M. to 11 P.M. on a set. Understandably, most students describe NCSA as "intense."

In addition to work in their respective fields, students are required to take general studies (GS) classes that are more like traditional liberal arts classes. Often, professors design GS classes with connections to the students' artistic interests, such as philosophy of art or art history. One student said that these attempts can get "kind of out there" in trying to capture the students' attention, but few students seemed genuinely displeased with the course offerings. The professors "know you're here for your art," and most GS classes take the students' interests and time constraints into account. For the most part, GS courses are seen as a necessity. However, some academically oriented students find them "disappointingly unchallenging" and "not very worthwhile."

Relaxed Social Scene

NCSA is not all about work; students do have social lives. Although most complain that they just have "too little time" to do much outside of class work, weekend evenings are usually left open. According to one student, "There's always a party somewhere on campus." In addition to parties, students hang out, watch videos, or head to the college-sponsored coffee house. The week before graduation the school sponsors Beaux Arts, NCSA's version of a spring fling, including special events and bands during the week, a carnival on Saturday, and a semiformal dance at the end of the week. In addition, there are always the roughly 200 performances per year put on by the students themselves as part of their studies.

During the school year, the school organizes special events, featuring outside bands and alumni speakers, but for the most part, students provide their own entertainment. This can be somewhat difficult since, as one student put it, "NCSA isn't in the best neighborhood." For a college town, Winston-Salem tends to close down early, and security is an issue in the immediate area around campus. Another student recommended to entering students, "Try your best to bring a car."

Despite the shady neighborhood, students often venture out into the community to take advantage of alternatives to the dining hall "cuisine." Popular restaurants are usually cheap and fast. Monterrey's, a Mexican restaurant near campus, is a popular hangout. For late-night meals, which are common for theater students who often rehearse until well after the dining hall closes, there is Mr. Waffle, open 24 hours a day, as well as a Waffle House and an IHOP.

Because students spend so much time working with people in their school, they also tend to socialize primarily with their classmates. While there are plenty of stereotypes about students in each of the schools, prompting names like "film monkeys" for film students and "bun heads" for ballet dancers, students report little actual animosity or competition. Many said the separation of schools makes it difficult to meet people outside of one's own academic area. Yet, because NCSA has only about a thousand students, some students view the small size and structure as a benefit, because "you get to know people really well."

Sweet Valley High

Students have a different reaction to the presence of the NCSA high school located on campus. The high school students live in separate dorms and are generally discouraged from associating with college students, but some classes enroll both high school and college students. Although one college student said he felt sharing classes with high school students "forces you to be in a more responsible position," undergrads report some resentment of the high-schoolers on campus. NCSA has a joint high school and college graduation ceremony, and college dancers are often in competition with younger performers. In other aspects, the college and high school operate fairly independently. The college has its own student government association, cultural groups, and other student organizations. Few students have much time for extracurricular groups, but rehearsals are not scheduled Sunday evenings to give students time for other activities.

NCSA is a relatively new school and is going through structural and organizational changes. Several construction projects now in the works are slated to be completed by the year 2000. The dorms are now being renovated (some students describe the current facilities as looking like "a women's penitentiary"). A new film building has opened, complete with a large theater and soundstage. The film program itself is relatively new, causing some students to describe it as "disorganized" because the curriculum is constantly changing.

> As one student explained, "Don't come here looking for the traditional college."

Students at NCSA are expected to perform at a high level of professionalism in exchange for the experience of living and working in a creative community of talented artists. While they have the standard college complaints about dining hall food and dorm living, their dedication to their art is unique.—*Jeff Kaplow and Staff*

FYI
The three best things about attending from NCSA are "great faculty, good bunch of kids, and a good dance program."
The three worst things about attending NCSA are "the cafeteria is bogus, the weather is very overcast and rainy, and the tendency for things to get muddy everywhere."
The three things that every student should do before graduating from NCSA are "hit Ziggy's at least once (rock club downtown), hike up Pilot Mountain, and take the astronomy class."
One thing I'd like to have known before coming here is "the workload would be so intense."

North Carolina State University

Address: Campus Box 7103, Raleigh, NC 27695	**Percent African-American:** 10.4%	**Middle 50% SAT range:** 530–620 V,550–650 M
Phone: 919-515-2434	**Percent Hispanic:** 1.7%	**Middle 50% ACT range:** 21–27
E-mail address: undergrad_admissions@ncsu.edu	**Percent Asian:** 4.7%	**Mean ACT:** 25
	Percent in-state / out-of-state: 92%/8%	**3 Most popular majors:** business management, electrical engineering, communications
Web site URL: www.ncsu.edu	**Percent Pub HS:** 91%	
Location: urban	**Fraternities:** 10%	
Founded: 1887	**Sororities:** 9%	**Retention:** 88%
Private or Public: public	**Number of Applicants:** 12,227	**Graduation rate:** 65%
Religious affiliation: none	**Percent Accepted:** 61%	**Library:** 2,820,312 volumes
Undergraduate enrollment: 21,684	**Percent Accepted who enroll:** 50%	**Tuition and Fees:** $2,340 in; $11,580 out
Total enrollment: 28,011	**Entering:** 3,571	**Room and Board:** $4,560
Percent Male / Female: 59%/41%	**Transfers:** 1,085	**On-campus housing:** 75%
Percent Minority: 17.5%	**Application Deadline:** rolling	**Financial aid, first-year:** 42%
	Mean SAT: 577 V, 602 M	

North Carolina State University is a school so large that few students have trouble finding a program that suits their interests. The school is especially well-regarded for its agriculture, architecture, and engineering schools. NC State is also the single largest research institution in North Carolina. Undergraduates claim that the size of the university is not overwhelming, and that it even has a relaxed and slow-paced environment.

The campus is located in Raleigh, the capital of North Carolina, and although it is definitely not a quintessential "college town," the city contains many rich cultural offerings such as the Museum of Natural History, the State Museum of Art, a repertory theater, and a symphony. Students tend to remain close to the campus, however, and spend most of their off-campus time on Hillsborough Street, which offers a variety of clubs, bars, bookstores, cinemas, and restaurants.

Heavy Workload

Freshman and sophomores must fulfill the requirements of their individual majors. Among the range of majors, engineering,

business, and pre-med are three of the most popular. Students often find the workload to be a little heavier than they initially expected. The School of Design is heighly respected and the engineering program attracts many out-of-state students who see NC State as a bargain compared to other private technology institutes. Engineering students seem to appreciate the wide variety of classes (14 different engineering tracks) offered in this department. One undergraduate described the academic setting as "both challenging and laid-back, yet without either cutthroat intensity or total laziness."

Parties Are Out of Control

Students say the laid-back environment of the school is conducive to an extensive social life. While some students feel that there is litte else to the social scene except drinking, others opt to go bowling or take advantage of Raleigh's museums and shops. Drinking is common among undergrads, and the alcohol policy is basically "ignored," according to one student. The administration is attempting to regulate off-campus drinking, since, as another student argued, "It makes the university look bad when [the students] trash residential areas." Fraternities often are held responsible for partying gone out of control. The Greek system at NC State is fairly large, but one student said, "You don't have to be in a fraternity or sorority to have a social life." Fraternities hold many parties, including the State Lawn Party in the fall, which attracts students from neighboring colleges such as Duke and Carolina.

Students at NC State take part in many extracurricular activities as well. Intramural sports are reportedly the most popular, especially among fraternity and sorority members. Religious groups, such as the Campus Crusade for Christ, and volunteer organizations like Habitat for Humanity have chapters on campus. At the performing arts center, a number of student theater groups give an average of two performances each per year.

The Union Activities Board also sponsors programs and activities in the Union Student Center, such as musical and theater production and debates that address current political, social, and economic issues. The board is divided into roughly a dozen committees, including the Entertainment Committee, which invites outside speakers. The Union Student Center is also a general meeting place for such organizations as the student literary magazine, the *Windover* yearbook, and the radio station. The campus also has two newspapers: the *Technician* and the *Nubian Message*, an African-American publication founded recently.

Diversity?

Some students voice concerns about the limited diversity among undergraduates, as well as the fact that different ethnic groups tend to isolate themselves from one another. The university administration reportedly is attempting to increase the diversity of the student population. Presently, about more than 80 percent of undergraduates come from North Carolina, and male students outnumber females. There are, however, international students from 97 different countries and an increasing percentage of minority students. The school has a wide variety of ethnic organization, and the Black Stu-

dent Board of the Union Activities Board sponsors an annual Pan-American festival that spans several days. Nevertheless, one student remarked, "When you walk into a class or dining hall, you can definitely tell what the racial situation is."

Generally, students seem to be tolerant of differences in beliefs and ethnicity, but this tolerance is not boundless. In particular, gay and lesbian student organizations have been, in the words of one graduate, "challenged by hatred and intolerance on campus." Anti-gay slurs have been spray-painted in the "free expression tunnel," a tunnel on campus where students are allowed to express their opinions with spray paint. Although NC State reportedly is working on incorporating sexual orientation into its non-discrimination policy, the school is, according to one student, "far behind."

Students report that NC State is dominated by conservative attitudes and beliefs, although many undergrads are not politically active. Popular political groups include the Young Republicans and student government, which organizes debate forums with the Union Activities Board. One student lamented the low voter turnout for the student government elections.

Varsity sports are a vital part of life at NC State. Most NC State athletic teams consider UNC–Chapel Hill their biggest rival. Both the basketball team and the football team have often been nationally ranked in the past and enjoy widespread support from students and alumni alike. Students commonly camp out overnight for football tickets, and the games themselves, along with the tailgates, turn the athletic events into social gatherings. Students report that school spirit is abundant, expecially in the annual football game against UNC. In the case of an NC State victory, celebrating crowds of students have been known to bring traffic to a halt on Hillsborough Street.

Sick of Brick

The university houses freshmen in one of 19 coed and single-sex residence halls across campus. Freshmen are guaranteed housing, and in the last few years the university has been able to guarantee housing to all undergrads. Housing is divided into four sectors: East Campus, which is NC State's orginal campus; West Campus, considered to be the most social; Lee and Sullivan, which are coed and have what some residents call "lax" regulations; and Center Campus, which consists of single-sex dorms. There are also theme dorms, including Alex International (in which international students room with American students for a cross-cultural experience), Arts and Creative Living (for students interested in fine arts), and High Technology (with computer hookups to the university mainframe in every room). Many of the dorms across campus do not have air-conditioning, but a few have been converted from hotels.

The campus itself is dominated by colonial brick buildings, and as one student said, "You will get sick of brick very fast." There is even a quad paved in brick called Brick Yard. Incongruous to the overall architecture is Harrelson Hall, whose circular structure stands out among the rest of the campus buildings. The campus has a wooded area for hiking and a hill called Court of the Carolinas, which is a popular site for picnics, sunbathing in the spring, and sledding in the winter.

> **Generally, students seem to be tolerant of differences in beliefs and ethnicity, but this tolerance is not boundless.**

Although the NC State campus might seem intimidating to students from small towns, undergrads say that they feel safe. The university provides an escort service along with other security measures. The citizen of Raleigh also have organized groups concerned with public safety and city awareness.

Despite some prevalent political views and similar geographic orgins, the NC State student body is too large to be homogeneous. Combining academics with a lively social scene and southern hospitality, NC State is attractive, expecially for in-state students. As one undergrad put it, "The lifestyle here is perfect!"—*Reid Lerner and Staff*

FYI

The three best things about attending NC State are "the crazy parties, the huge research facilities, and the fact that I am close to home."

The three worst things about attending NC State are "how this place can swallow you up, the dependence on alcohol for a good time, and the self-segregation that takes place."

The three things that every student should do before graduating from NC State are "chant loudly for NC State against UNC–Chapel Hill at the games, write for one of the papers, and hit the frat scene."

One thing I'd like to have known before coming here is "how this place is sometimes like a scene from *Animal House*."

University of North Carolina / Chapel Hill

Address: Jackson Hall
153A, Campus Box 2200,
Chapel Hill, NC 27599
Phone: 919-966-3621
E-mail address:
uadm@email.unc.edu
Web site URL:
www.unc.edu
Location: suburban
Founded: 1789
Private or Public: public
Religious affiliation:
none
**Undergraduate
enrollment:** 15,291
Total enrollment: 24,439
Percent Male/Female:
39%/61%
Percent Minority: 18.0%

Percent African-American:
11.0%
Percent Hispanic: 1.0%
Percent Asian: 5.0%
**Percent in-state/out-of-
state:** 83%/17%
Percent Pub HS: 86%
Fraternities: 18%
Sororities: 18%
Number of Applicants:
17,236
Percent Accepted: 35%
**Percent Accepted who
enroll:** 57%
Entering: 3,436
Transfers: 1,244
Application Deadline:
15 Jan
Mean SAT: 610 V, 611 M

Middle 50% SAT range:
560–670 V,
570–670 M
Middle 50% ACT range:
NA
Mean ACT: NA
3 Most popular majors:
biology, business,
psychology
Retention: 82.0%
Graduation rate: 62.0%
Library: 4,000,000
volumes
Tuition and Fees: $1,456
in; $10,622 out
Room and Board: $5,010
On-campus housing: 40%
Financial aid, first-year:
26%

Most students at the University of North Carolina at Chapel Hill can agree on one thing: in the heart of the South, their college is a "Southern piece of heaven." The undergraduate population at America's first state university is more than 15,000 (well over half the of the total student population), but students still praise UNC/Chapel Hill for its balance of academic and athletic strengths, as well as its beautiful geography and laid-back atmosphere.

They've Got It All

Academic life begins in the General College, which demands fundamental liberal arts requirements during freshman and sophomore years. Students work with an advisor, assigned to them according to academic or professional interests, who ensures that prerequisites are completed before students declare their majors at the end of sophomore year. Those wishing to pursue a major in one of UNC's professional schools—business, education, journalism and mass communication, law, information and library science, or social work—must apply to the appropriate school at this time. Otherwise, students remain in the College of Arts and Sciences as they complete their majors. According to one undergrad, General College requirements are useful because "a college education should be more than four years of preparation for a career." UNC/Chapel Hill also offers a Division of Health Affairs, which includes five schools: dentistry, medicine, nursing, pharmacy, and public health.

Students consider the communications school and science departments to have some of the best academic offerings available, while math and classics are said to be weaker. Students cite Calculus II, Journalism 53, and the introductory chemistry and economics classes as among the hardest undergraduate courses at UNC, and suggest geology or geography for an easier course load. Standard workload depends largely on the specific classes one chooses: "Finding the right mix is key," said one undergrad. "Generally, the course work is reasonable, yet challenging." Class size varies dramatically, ranging from intro lectures of 400 to 450 to classes of 15 to 30 students taught by TAs. "There are a lot of TAs teaching classes, but everyone finds a good mix of professors and TAs," said one student. "Even though it's sometimes intimidating, students who are really eager can always seek out a professor, and usually find that it's well worth doing."

Well-known professors include Dr. George Rabinowitz and Chuck Stone, the first black nationally syndicated columnist and White House correspondent for ABC News, a particularly controversial and popular professor on campus. One transfer student said, "It's really the teachers that make the difference in the quality of education here."

The most common complaint about academic life at UNC/Chapel Hill is the frustrating registration process, not surprising for a school of its size. Each graduating class is assigned a different weekend, and students are given a specific day to register using "Caroline," the school's telephone registration system. "Freshmen at the end of registration have a really hard time getting into the classes they want," said one student, "and it doesn't get much easier until you're an upperclassman." Actually reaching Caroline can also pose a problem: "Getting through is tough—this semester I had to wait for three hours, listening to busy signals." Scheduling difficulties can also cause problems for students. One undergraduate said, "This place is so big that I've had to take classes at night—that's no fun!"

Who They Are

Students at Chapel Hill come from all types of backgrounds. One student said, "It's pretty diverse, and becoming more so." Some, however, complain that they are aware of racial tensions on campus and do not feel much is being done to alleviate them. "There is little overt racism," said one undergrad, "but people's prejudices do tend to manifest themselves quite strongly, especially among certain cliques." Another common complaint is the unbalanced undergraduate male-female ratio, which has been heavily weighted toward women in recent years. The look of a typical Tar Heel varies. "Some people are really preppy—nice sweaters and shirts all tucked in—others wear sweats," explained one student. A stranger walking past a UNC dorm might

be surprised at the different kinds of music blaring from the windows; musical tastes include country, Christian, bluegrass, rap, acoustic rock, and show tunes.

Living It Up

An average weekend at UNC/Chapel Hill includes some combination of the following: going out to dinner on Franklin St., football/basketball game on Saturday, studying, sleeping, and partying. Much of the party scene is centered around Frat Court, where underage students have no problem finding alcohol. The drug scene is described as both "typical for college" and "not nearly as popular as at other schools I visited." While Greek life plays a major role in student life, "fraternity jerks and sorority nits don't rule the campus," one undergrad said. Upperclassmen apartments are other popular party locations. Highlights of the year include big parties like Reggae Fest and Halloween, when 30,000 students from UNC and other North Carolina schools take over Franklin Street. Students also flood the main drag for huge victory celebrations, which, with a winning basketball and football program, occur often. One student described the administration's policy on alcohol as, "Don't get wasted." Recently, a greater effort has been made to organize alternative activities to discourage drinking, including alcohol-free parties.

Some non-drinkers say they feel left out of a social life so heavily focused on partying. But according to one Tar Heel, "At a school this big there's something for everyone." Some nightlife hotspots are restaurants, coffee houses, movie theaters, and a comedy club, many of which are on or near Franklin St. The Cat's Cradle is a music club within walking distance that attracts many nationally recognized bands. Going off campus is popular with some undergrads, but "it depends a lot on whether you have a car."

The scope of the dating scene at UNC/Chapel Hill draws mixed opinions. "There are a lot of random hookups, but that doesn't necessarily mean sex," said one undergrad. "And there is less dating among students than hooking up." Others said there are a lot of couples on campus.

Most students agreed, however, that while there are definitely both gay and interracial couples at UNC, there are not many, and even fewer are very visible.

Outside of Class
UNC/Chapel Hill certainly offers extracurricular opportunities, which range from honing one's journalistic skills on the *DTH* (*Daily Tar Heel*) to reaching out with community service projects, many of which are run by fraternities and sororities. Students enjoy attending plays, art exhibits, concerts, and listening to speakers. But the focus of UNC's extracurricular life is sports, in which both the athletes and the fans get heavily involved. One student estimated that three-quarters of his peers were involved in athletics, ranging from competitive intramurals to using the impressive gym. The most popular teams to follow are football, basketball, and women's soccer. UNC/Chapel Hill boasts impressive fan attendance, and games are often sold out. One student reported spending several Saturday nights camping out for basketball tickets, an example of the pride Tar Heels take in supporting their teams.

Day-to-Day Living
All UNC freshmen are offered on-campus housing. They can also choose to live in Granville Towers, paying extra money for maid service, cable TV, and good food. Dining hall offerings received mixed reviews, and many students reported heading off campus to hit local sub shops and coffee shops. Pepper's Pizza and Outback Steakhouse are two popular dinner locations.

On-campus housing is divided into the North, Middle, and South Campuses. North Campus is generally considered the best location, followed by Middle, and then South, which is a 10-minute walk from the center of campus. UNC has experienced some recent problems with overcrowding, and while some students still live in temporary housing, "It's getting better," reported one undergrad. Campus dorms vary in size and attractiveness, but dorm life is considered the easiest way to get to know people. "My closest friends are people who live near me in my dorm,"

said one undergrad. RAs do have a presence in the dorms, but, according to one student, they are "strict enough, but not really that strict."

Beautiful North Carolina
For many undergrads, the school's beautiful campus is what attracted them to UNC/Chapel Hill. The building style is predominately red brick with tall white pillars and marble accents. "There are lots of trees and flowers everywhere," said one student. "It's so easy to fall in love with the campus." One undergrad complained, however: "I don't always feel safe here . . . there have been a lot of robberies recently." In response to such concerns, the administration has implemented several systems for safe travel across campus. U-Bus, P-2-P, and Safe Escort—university-run bus and police escort programs—are three ways the university helps students get around campus and Chapel Hill itself.

Some students also complained about UNC's frequent construction projects. "The only thing that's more constant than the basketball team being in the top ten is the inconvenience of construction on campus," said one undergrad. "There is always something being built or renovated."

The Tar Heel Way
At a state university as large and spread out as UNC/Chapel Hill, it is inevitable that the administration will maintain a vigilant presence and sometimes make decisions that are disagreeable to a percentage of the population. One undergrad complained about the hierarchy of power he observes at UNC. Most prominent are the alumni who can park where they want, drink when they want, and sit wherever they want at sporting events. Among the undergrads, the instate students follow in importance. "In-staters have far less tuition to pay and many more opportunities for scholarships so they won't have to pay it," said one student. At the bottom of the totem-pole one finds the out-of-state undergraduates. "Many of us chose Chapel Hill over the wallet-breaking Ivy League, but the administration does not seem to appreciate our decision, aiming every tuition hike our way."

"The only thing that's more constant than the basketball team being in the top ten is the inconvenience of construction on campus," said one undergrad.

Transfer students are housed together in a dorm with graduate students "who don't like to socialize with undergrads," and international students, "who tend to stick together." "It's especially hard since most transfers aren't from the 'friendly and more hospitable South,'" said one converted Tar Heel, "and therefore we get the reputation of being the anti-social dorm."

Many undergrads describe going to school in "Blue Heaven" as "the quintessential college experience." One student said, "UNC may be a 'party school,' but it also concentrates on academia. We have a good balance." The culture shock that many northerners and midwesterners encounter upon moving to the South is usually overcome by the beautiful North Carolina weather. "All I know," said a spirited Tar Heel, "is that everyone who goes here loves it and doesn't want to leave."
—*Jeff Kaplow and Staff*

FYI

The three best things about attending UNC are "the libraries, the trees, and the Cultural Studies Department."

The three worst things about attending UNC are "all the kids who aren't in the Greek system who act like they are, the food, and the huge class size."

The three things that every student should do before graduating from UNC are "have sex in the study lounges of Davis, eat at the Cosmic Cantina, and go to the UNC-Duke game."

One thing I'd like to have known before coming here is "it's easy to get lost within many departments."

Wake Forest University

Address: P.O. Box 7305, Reynolda Station, Winston-Salem, NC 27109
Phone: 336-758-5201
E-mail address: admissions@wfu.edu
Web site URL: www.wfu.edu
Location: suburban
Founded: 1834
Private or Public: private
Religious affiliation: none
Undergraduate enrollment: 3,877
Total enrollment: 5,892
Percent Male/Female: 67%/33%
Percent Minority: 13.0%

Percent African-American: 9.0%
Percent Hispanic: 1.0%
Percent Asian: 2.0%
Percent in-state/out-of-state: 93%/7%
Percent Pub HS: 70%
Fraternities: 36%
Sororities: 48%
Number of Applicants: 6,132
Percent Accepted: 48%
Percent Accepted who enroll: 34%
Entering: 993
Transfers: 279
Application Deadline: 15 Jan
Mean SAT: NA

Middle 50% SAT range: 600–690 V, 620–700 M
Middle 50% ACT range: NA
Mean ACT: NA
3 Most popular majors: business, psychology, biology
Retention: 93.0%
Graduation rate: 70%
Library: 1,300,000 volumes
Tuition and Fees: $19,450 in; NA out
Room and Board: $5,450
On-campus housing: 100%
Financial aid, first-year: 25%

For its third "theme year" a committee of Wake Forest University faculty and staff declared 1998–99 "The Year of Globalization and Diversity." After years exploring the arts and religion in America through a series of campus events, Wake Forest's new theme reflects the progressive nature of a school striving to be recognized as one of the country's top colleges.

Learning at WFU

Wake Forest's rigorous academics have no doubt contributed to the school's growing prestige. "Don't expect to slack off here," said one senior. Business and premed-oriented majors like biology and chemistry are considered the school's strongest, but students are hard-pressed to name classes in any area that aren't intense. For the purpose of ensuring a liberal arts education the college requires that students complete three courses in each of four areas: literature and arts; natural sciences and math; history, philosophy, and religion; and social and behavioral sciences. In addition, all students must fulfill requirements in foreign language, health and exercise, and writing. Freshmen are required to take a First-Year Seminar, a class limited to 15 students and chosen from a wide variety of topics that change yearly. Students may also apply to the Open Curriculum program that reduces divisional requirements and allows for a more self-defined program of study. Students may participate in study-abroad programs at Wake Forest faculty–staffed "houses" in London, Venice, and a soon-to-be-completed Vienna location. Students are encouraged to participate in the popular programs at other universities, including Tokai University in Japan.

Renowned author Maya Angelou teaches at Wake Forest, though students note that due to its popularity her class is difficult to get into. In general, though, students remark on the quality of interaction with dedicated professors who are experts in their fields. The few teaching assistants at Wake Forest conduct only lab and health courses. Academic advising utilizes both faculty and upperclassmen who function as general guidance counselors until the student has chosen a major and receives an advisor specific to his or her chosen course of study.

Living at Wake

Wake Forest students have the pleasure of studying on a campus graced by splendid traditional southern architecture. Facilities include the Z. Smith Reynolds Library, open 24 hours a day, and said to be a prime socializing spot for those cracking the books. The university is also nearing completion on construction of a new psychology/ Romance languages and literature building, slated to be finished in the fall of 1999. Students catch home basketball and soccer games at the Reynolds Gym. For those who have athletic spirit themselves, the new Benson University Center houses a fitness room.

The Benson Center also contains several fast-food restaurants, including Pizza Hut, Subway, and Taco Bell. The fast-food court is open until midnight and serves as a much-appreciated alternative to Wake Forest's dining hall, which students term the "Pit." Wake uses a "food money" system in which students pay only for the meals they eat, with the value of the food being deducted from their food account. Students can also use their meal plans at "The Magnolia Room," which students say "has a great atmosphere, if you don't mind paying a little more for the pleasure of eating at a table complete with cloth napkins."

Students rave about dorm life. Freshmen are randomly assigned to singles, doubles, or triples in one of a number of residence halls, though they have the option of specifying preferences for coed, single-sex, and substance-free housing. Some freshmen rooms, especially those in Babcock, are described as more luxurious than those for the upperclassmen. The new Polo Dorm, known as the Polo Palace, is for upperclassmen and has town-house and studio-style apartments complete with kitchenettes. The university also maintains off-campus apartments and theme houses, though the majority of students choose to live on campus all four years. All rooms have ethernet connections for high-speed access to the Internet, evidence of Wake Forest's commitment to technology. Every residential hall houses at least one RTA (Residential Technical Advisor). The school's most innovative attempt at ensuring that its students are technologically proficient began with the freshmen of the Class of 2000. All students now receive laptop computers upon beginning their studies at Wake Forest. The computers can then be traded in junior year for an up-to-date model.

Demon Deacon Free Time

Characterizations of Winston-Salem, Wake Forest's home, range from "cute" to "lame." Students with cars say they primarily use the town for grocery shopping, eating out, or clubbing. Brew-ha-ha's and Ziggy's are popular clubs and have hosted performers including the Dave Matthews Band. Though students report that a large number of the many North Carolinians go home on weekends, life at Wake is very campus-oriented. The student union houses a movie theater and a diverse range of fine arts events and lectures. Parties are predominantly on campus or on Polo Road, a very close walk. Wake is a wet campus, and drinking figures prominently in weekend activities. The school maintains strict regulations against underage drinking and unregistered parties. Greek life is said to be the most influential social force at Wake, but independents are welcome at Greek parties after ten o' clock. A large percentage of freshmen rush, and note that the deferred rush allows for a transition to college life prior to the rush process. Other popular organizations and activities include *Old Gold and Black*, the campus newspaper, religious singing and fellowship organizations, and intramural athletics. One of the most prominent changes at Wake has been the reform of its Judicial Board of Investigators and Advisors, run by student prosecutors and defenders charged with enforcing the honor code, to ensure that the system is fair for all students.

A Spirited Student Body

Though the football team has not had any recent successful seasons ("I'd rather watch my high school team," said one freshman.), students consider Wake a school infused with spirit. Men's basketball at Wake is nationally renowned, and women's sports including soccer and track and field are strong. Evidence of Deacon spirit lies in the tradition of "Rolling the Quad." After team victories irreverent students run back to campus and throw rolls of toilet paper over the trees on the campus quad.

> "Slowly," said one student, "the school is becoming less and less cookie-cutter, J. Crew–like, but slowly is the operative word."

Students note that the administration is trying very hard to project an image of diversity, as evidenced in this year's theme, in an effort to compete for the top-quality students that better-recognized schools are attracting. Nevertheless, students describe themselves as predominantly preppy, white, and wealthy. "Slowly," said one student, "the school is becoming less and less cookie-cutter, J. Crew–like, but slowly is the operative word."

As Wake Forest takes strides to gain equal recognition with schools of equal academic caliber, students note that "this is a great time to be at Wake." As one senior said, "Be ready to see one of the most beautiful campuses in the Southeast, meet the most amazing people you ever will, and make the best friendships you could ever dream of."—*Ellen Lee Moskowitz and Staff*

FYI

The three best things about attending Wake Forest are "small class sizes, the beautiful campus, and the ubiquity of technology."

The three worst things about attending Wake Forest are " the not too exciting town of Winston-Salem, lack of parking, and the food service people who close early and are rude."

The three things that every student should do before graduating are "take history with Jeffrey Lerner—he's very eccentric—go down to Carowinds Amusement Park in Charlotte, and go to Reynolda Gardens in the summertime."

One thing I'd like to have known before coming here is "things on campus would be as expensive as they are."

North Dakota

Students at the University of North Dakota praise the varied offerings of their school, such as the strong aeronautics program, the Burger King in the student union, and the safe campus conditions. However, many complain about one item that even school officials would rather choose to ignore as they attempt to build a nationally diverse student body—harsh winter weather. Each year the winter months bring frigid temperatures and endless inches of snow to the UND campus. The school, according to one senior, has few underground tunnels to provide protection from the elements and only a limited number of "plug-ins" that students can use to prevent their cars from freezing in the parking lot.

Strong Technology Programs

Although UND offers a number of liberal arts majors and reputable pre-professional programs, the aeronautics and engineering departments are reportedly the most highly regarded and attract students from all over the country. One student said the nearby Center for Aerospace Science adds to the school's reputation and has helped make both aviation and aeronautical studies two of the most popular majors on campus. Other popular programs include communications, nursing, and physical therapy. All students must take courses in the humanities, social sciences, and natural sciences in order to fulfill general education requirements, which one engineering student said are "pretty easy" to fulfill.

Class size, as one student described, reaches nowhere near the size of other major state universities. Introductory courses in the sciences enroll about 150 students in each section while upper-level courses have fewer than ten students. Consequently, few students find themselves shut out of a classroom: "I sometimes might not get the particular section and time period, but I've never not gotten into a class I wanted to take," one undergrad said. Students register over the phone in order of most credit hours and highest grade point average during days specifically assigned by the registrar's office. The same phone system also allows students to change classes and check their grades and financial aid status.

As Liberal As You Can Be in North Dakota

The size of the university allows for strong interaction between professors and students. "Most professors teach a lot, but they don't bog you down with so much work; they're more concerned with students learning," one junior said. Only professors teach actual classes, but TAs do lead lab recitations and review sections. Students interested in advanced work may qualify for the general honors program of the university or for more specific honors work often found within the major. UND also offers free tutoring in all subjects as well as free counseling through the student counseling center.

Comfortable Campus

After the spring thaw each year, the groundskeepers at UND are said to plant an "awesome amount of flowers," which gives the campus a very "green" feel during the warmer months. Self-contained and located at the edge of town, UND is a small campus and includes some newer facilities intermixed with the older buildings that are prevalent. "Some buildings are very old, but they're still very clean and comfortable, and the school has been upgrading classes with multimedia equipment," one junior said. The Chester Fritz Library provides an adequate collection of publications, but one student described the online system as "hard to use" and some of the material as "outdated for some subjects like engineering." The librarians, however, are "very helpful" in addressing student requests. Many students head to the library of their particular department for serious and uninterrupted study. Other study locations include the second floor of Memorial Union Student Center, the Burger King, and the study rooms located in each dormitory.

A large percentage of students at UND choose to live off campus; many students are "older and/or married people putting themselves through college." Thus, the university offers on-campus single and married student apartments at "affordable" rates. Students can also choose to live in the regular dorms. Although it is available to only juniors and seniors, students consistently mention Swanson as the most popular and comfortable dorm. Swanson has a glass elevator, bathrooms in every room, and a system that allows residents to buzz in guests. Other students often choose to live in fraternity or sorority housing.

Wilkerson Hall houses the main cafeteria, which provides a wide variety of entrées and a salad bar. Students opting to live in campus dorms must purchase a meal plan, which they can redeem at either Wilkerson or the dining hall in the student union building. The town of Grand Forks offers limited food options as well: the 42nd Street Eatery, a deli-style place with sandwiches and coffee, and Speedway, which has cheap entrees.

Limited Social Opportunities

The University Program Council works to provide quality social activities on campus, and recently sponsored performances by country music entertainers Travis Tritt and Reba McEntire at the Chester Fritz Auditorium. Council members also sponsor movie nights and a coffee bar at the Memorial Student Center, which also includes several game and recreational rooms, the popular Burger King, and comfy chairs to "just hang out with friends." Limited social opportunities exist in Grand Forks (especially for those under 21), but many students of age frequent Bucks Down Under for cheap pitchers and the Antique bar. The university strictly enforces a "no alcohol" rule on campus, but fraternities may sponsor parties (since their houses are off campus) if they hire security guards to prevent underage drinking. Thus, many students feel the party scene at UND lags behind those at other colleges and universities.

Most students at UND are from either Canada or the northern United States. One student felt the university does not take enough measures to ensure geographic and ethnic diversity on campus, and that "students are about as liberal as you can be in North Dakota, which doesn't say very much, and most aren't politically active." A recent controversy on campus involved Native American students, who protested the school's use of the "Fighting Sioux" as the UND mascot. Negotiations are still in progress to find an alternative symbol.

The Hyslop Sports Center attracts a number of students looking to unwind after a hard day of class, and includes everything from dance and aerobics classes to an indoor track, Olympic-size swimming pool, and modern exercise equipment. The Division I hockey team usually plays to sellout crowds, since students enjoy free admission to all games. Other successful teams include those for men's and women's swimming and basketball, which attract the most spectators when playing rivals North Dakota State University or the University of Minnesota, Minneapolis. A large group of students also participate in intramural sports, such as tennis, soccer, basketball, and volleyball.

Other popular pastimes include writing for the *Dakota Student*, which is a bi-weekly campus newspaper with a weekly arts and entertainment section. Others participate in the student government or the University Program Council, which plans entertainment and social activities for students. The highest student involvement, however, reportedly occurs in the various clubs associated with majors, such as the Engineer's Council, Psychology Club, and Medical School Club. In fact, there are so many extracurricular clubs and organizations that students say they often have trouble attracting enough members to sustain themselves.

> A large percentage of students at UND choose to live off campus; many students are "older and/or married people putting themselves through college."

UND provides a police force for the school, emergency phones, and an escort service, but the hometown atmosphere that characterizes the Grand Forks community causes few students to worry about issues of safety on campus. The close-knit feel, according to several students, is one of the most attractive qualities of UND. Despite the daunting North Dakota weather, students say the academic and social environment at UND more than compensate for the discomforting winter temperatures.—*Marti Page and Staff*

FYI
The three best things about attending UND are "small class sizes, small student body, and plenty of on-campus single and married student housing."
The three worst things about attending UND are "cold winters, poor technology, and poor academic standards and expectations."
The three things that every student should do before graduating from UND are "visit Turtle River State Park, check out the Icelandic State Park, and go fishing in the Red River."
One thing I'd like to have known before coming to UND is "that the school seems to have low expectations and seems to require little from its students."

Ohio

Address: 795 Livermore Street; Yellow Spring, OH 45387
E-mail address: admissions@antiochcollege.edu
Web site URL: www.college.antioch.edu
Location: rural
Founded: 1852
Private or Public: private
Religious affiliation: none
Undergraduate enrollment: 595
Total enrollment: 624
Percent Male / Female: 34% / 66%
Percent Minority: 12.0%

Percent African-American: 6.0%
Percent Hispanic: 3.0%
Percent Asian: 2.0%
Percent in-state / out-of-state: NA
Percent Pub HS: NA
Fraternities: 0%
Sororities: 0%
Number of Applicants: 465
Percent Accepted: 85%
Percent Accepted who enroll: 30%
Entering: 119
Transfers: 0
Application Deadline: rolling
Mean SAT: 509 V, 495 M

Middle 50% SAT range: 540–670 V, 520–600 M
Middle 50% ACT range: 25–28
Mean ACT: 24
3 Most popular majors: psychology, visual arts, literature / creative writing
Retention: 74%
Graduation rate: 60%
Library: 300,000 volumes
Tuition and Fees: $21,628 in; $21,628 out
Room and Board: $4,176
On-campus housing: 100%
Financial aid, first-year: 73%

Peace studies in Tibet. Brazilian rain forest ecology. The circus. Students at Antioch regularly participate in such eclectic programs—and all for credit! Co-op credit, that is.

Interesting Academics

One of the many distinctive features of Antioch College is its co-op program, which requires students to take classes on campus for two of the four terms each year (fall, winter, spring, summer), and go on co-ops, which are similar to work-study programs, for the other two. Students have high praise for the co-op program; in fact, many cite it as their main reason for attending Antioch. "It gives me credit and experience doing real things," said one student. Antioch recently switched from a semester to a trimester system, which changes the number of course and co-op credits required of each student. First-year students generally spend the fall and winter terms on campus, and then do co-ops in the spring and

summer. After the first year, students can design their own program of work and study, choosing when they will be on campus and when they will be on co-op. The co-op office is filled with resources and information about students' experiences on co-ops from previous years. Students are assigned a co-op advisor, but many find their specific program advisor to be more helpful.

> **"What is mainstream here makes us freaks to the rest of the world."**

Students can choose to go on virtually any co-op they like, although at least one must include studying a culture other than one's own. Many students fulfill this requirement by doing a co-op overseas; however, it is possible to do a domestic field program, such as examining the African-American experience in the Deep South. Most students try to relate their co-op to their major, but this connection is not required. Undergrads can study peace processes in the Middle East, work at a center for missing children in Minnesota, or run the lights and electronics for a circus, as one student recently did. While students thoroughly enjoy the Antioch co-op experience, they warn that it is intense. "Antioch is a full-year commitment," explained one student. "You don't have summers free, because you are either studying or on co-op." Consequently, it is "easy to get off track from a four-year plan," said one second-year student. "It's common to spend five years here."

Academics at Antioch are generally strong, although students are more attracted to the co-op program than to specific departments. Nonetheless, psychology, environmental science, communications, and women's studies are all well-regarded, while the education and music departments are said to be weaker. Students must demonstrate competence in a foreign language, and either pass or place out of a quantitative reasoning course. Students can pre-register for up to three classes over the summer. The small student-faculty ratio allows for a "very personalized education," according to one second-year student. Most classes enroll 10 to 15 students. "The largest class I've heard of had 40 people," said one student.

Campus Facilities

While the co-op program receives praise, students are less enthusiastic about the facilities on campus. Most of the facilities are reportedly "old and decrepit, but still useful," said one student. The Olive Kettering Library "looks ancient and smells of old books," according to one first-year. The librarians are said to be helpful, although students agree that the library needs new resources. The periodicals holdings are extensive, but students find the collection of newer books to be rather limited, which some attribute to financial limitations. "The library has been enlarged five times and we still need another, but there is no money," one student complained. Consequently, students tend to study in their rooms, or take a 20-minute car ride to the largest nearby library at Wright State University. Other buildings on campus, however, have been renovated recently, including South Hall (home to the co-op office and library), a computer center for students with learning disabilities, and various classrooms.

The majority of Antioch students live on campus. Dorms vary widely in terms of facilities and themes. Presidents dorm has singles and hall kitchens. This dorm permits alcohol but is quiet and smoke-free. West does not have kitchens, but permits smoking. Birch is widely known as a party dorm; North houses primarily first-years and transfers; and Units is a new group of dorms supposedly "so clean they're sterile," in the words of one North resident. Spalt has different language halls, and is located in the International Building, which has classrooms downstairs from the dorm rooms. Some dorms are single-sex, and since there are more women than men at Antioch, there are more all-female than all-male dorms. Like many other buildings at Antioch, the dorms generally are "run-down, but safe," one student said. Most dorms do not have phone connections for each room; residents share one common phone per hall instead. In addition, each hall also has its own common area.

Unusual Social Life

Because of the co-op program, only half of the Antioch student population is on campus at any given time. There are no varsity sports at Antioch, but intramurals such as softball and Frisbee are popular. Politically, the student body is decidedly liberal, and extracurriculars include animal-rights and environmental organizations as well as a Winnie-the-Pooh support group, established solely as "an excuse to act silly and make people feel good," in the words of one member. Media enthusiasts can write for Antioch's weekly paper, *The Record*, or work at one of the two radio stations on campus—WYSO (the official school station) or AntiWatt (a smaller, pirate station). The Lesbian, Gay, and Bisexual Center (LGBC) is extremely popular; one student said it sometimes seems as if "about half of campus is homosexual." The center sponsors dances and potlucks, among other activities.

Frequenting the Caf

The LGBC is located in the Student Union, which also houses the women's center, a

TV and video lounge, practice rooms for bands, and a space to hold dances. The cafeteria, known as "the Caf," is also located in the Student Union, as is the C-Shop, the campus coffee shop. The food on campus is reportedly "not bad"—good news for first-years and transfers, who are required to buy a full plan of 19 meals per week. The Caf offers a plethora of options for vegans and vegetarians, including a tabbouleh and hummus bar. The C-shop is popular, but serves only snack foods. Off campus, students eat at Haha's Pizza, Sunrise Cafe, and Carol's Kitchen. The Tavern, reportedly one of the oldest standing buildings in Ohio, as well as Current Cuisine and Chill Lights, also earn student praise.

Parties happen almost every night, according to one second-year, but Friday is considered the biggest social night. A first-year described a typical weekend as "go out Friday, sleep Saturday, homework Sunday." Antioch students tend to have small get-togethers in each other's rooms, or go to dances held in the student union every Wednesday and Saturday. To get away from the small town of Yellow Springs, students can travel to Dayton for clubbing. The Wellness Center, which exists to improve students' mental and physical well-being, also sponsors dances and shows movies every Friday. Social activity at Antioch often has a political edge: the annual Drag Ball Halloween dance, for example, has led to an entire weekend focused on gender issues, with speakers brought in by the Wellness Center. Div dances, which bring together students from the on-campus and co-op divisions, take place at the end of each quarter.

Sexuality Taken Seriously

The Antioch administration made national headlines recently with its sexual harassment policy, requiring students to request permission from their partners before engaging in any sexual act. Although the policy has disappeared from the headlines, students still "joke about the hooking-up policy, though it's nice to have as a backup," said one first-year. Another student praised the sexual harassment policy for its ability to "open up the community" and make issues like safer sex more prominent. "All bathrooms now have safe-sex packages with everything you could ever need, so there is really no excuse for not having safer sex here," she said.

Regarding alcohol and other drugs, the administration is "lax, to say the least," according to one second-year. Students report that the main security issue is bike theft, and that the security guards tend to "baby-sit," rather than enforce alcohol rules.

Student Body

Antioch's Community Council, which consists of elected student and faculty members, sponsors weekly community meetings open to all staff, faculty, students, and administrators. The meetings are a time to "voice concerns, make proposals to the community government, or just hang out and eat ice cream," said one council representative.

Students at Antioch describe themselves as "radical," which is probably not an exaggeration. A liberal school tends to have liberal students, and Antioch students are "honest, if nothing else," said one first-year. While Antioch draws applicants from most of the continental U.S. and partakes in an exchange program with Kyoto-Seika University, a sister college in Japan, students reported that the majority of their classmates are white. The general opinion at Antioch, according to a second-year, is "whatever goes, goes, as long as you're cool and respectful." To put that in perspective, she added that "what is mainstream here makes us freaks to the rest of the world." Antioch students are content with their "freakish" community. While one student admitted that the constant moving between co-ops and campus is "tiring," she added that the frequent change meant that "there are always different people on campus, which is exciting." The unusual opportunity for free expression in personal life and in academics may be "too unique" for some, one student warned, but for those who can handle it, the Antioch experience is unparalleled.—*Staff*

FYI

The three best things about Antioch are "the co-op program, the opportunity to get hands-on experience, small class size."

The three worst things about Antioch are "the decrepit buildings, the poorly stocked library, and an unconventional schedule."

The three things that every student should do before graduating from Antioch are "go on some exotic co-op, go to a Div dance, and go clubbing in Dayton."

One thing I'd like to have known before coming here is "how the co-op schedule makes it hard to always be at school at the same time my friends are."

Bowling Green State University

Address: 110 McFall Center, Bowling Green, OH 43403
Phone: 419-372-2086
E-mail address: admissions@bgnet.bgsu.edu
Web site URL: www.bgsu.edu/welcome
Location: rural
Founded: 1910
Private or Public: public
Religious affiliation: none
Undergraduate enrollment: 15,040
Total enrollment: NA
Percent Male/Female: 43%/57%
Percent Minority: 7.1%

Percent African-American: 4.0%
Percent Hispanic: 2.0%
Percent Asian: 1.0%
Percent in-state/out-of-state: 92%/8%
Percent Pub HS: NA
Fraternities: 15%
Sororities: 11%
Number of Applicants: 9,483
Percent Accepted: 92%
Percent Accepted who enroll: 42%
Entering: 3,664
Transfers: NA
Application Deadline: 15 Jul
Mean SAT: 552 V, 523 M

Middle 50% SAT range: 460–570 V, 460–570 M
Middle 50% ACT range: 19–25
Mean ACT: 22
3 Most popular majors: education, business, nursing
Retention: 78%
Graduation rate: 26%
Library: 4.2 million volumes
Tuition and Fees: $3,870 in; $9,158 out
Room and Board: $4,392
On-campus housing: 41%
Financial aid, first-year: 55%

While for one weekend each year, it is the internationally revered home of the World Tractor Pulling Championships, the town of Bowling Green is perhaps better represented through its offering of a solid and dynamic liberal arts education to the students of Bowling Green State University.

An Academic Myriad

With over 160 majors including everything from glass, popular culture, and fiber/fabric to the more traditional areas of study in the humanities, arts, and sciences, it is rare to find a student who cannot find a personal course of study at BGSU. While almost all academic programs are regarded as strong and marketable, the most popular majors among undergraduates are biology, psychology, and the renowned and competitive education program. Several options are available to fulfill each student's needs, including self-designed majors, double majors, an honors program, and several pre-professional programs. Getting into classes is not typically a problem. One student noted that being shut out is particularly unlikely "if you get on waiting lists immediately and actually talk to people to get strings pulled." Another student liked the fact that he could easily take classes outside his major, such as dance and theater. Students generally praise most of their professors, even when they have problems communicating with them. "My English teacher barely speaks English," said one undergraduate. "We are always asking him to repeat what was said and say it slower, but he's a good sport about it." Another undergraduate was impressed by the fact that her professors "remembered [her] name, and who I was." Students were pleased with several creative assignments, including everything from "stand in front of a mirror naked and watch yourself" to "just relax for the weekend."

The Living Experience

The rules at BGSU dictate that freshmen and sophomores are required to either live on campus or with their parents, although the general consensus is that "everyone gets around them." Almost 60 percent of BGSU students live off campus, as apartments are widely available close to campus. Rent can be rather high, though students say the experience is worth it. For those students who live on campus, coed dorms of single and double rooms are the norm. However, special housing for honors students, musicians, and other special interest groups is available, as well as housing in any of the 35 fraternities and sororities. Every dorm has its definite set of rules, and while some halls strictly enforce these regulations, others barely acknowledge their presence. Each student living in a residence hall is required to purchase a meal plan (students in the Anderson or Bromfield halls are exempted) which can be used at any dining hall on campus, as well as at a local convenience store, where one student observed, "A box of Lucky Charms costs over five bucks!" The Sundial has been noted as "the best place to eat, but it's mass chaos at mealtime."

> "Supposedly, the ghost must be invited to every theater production or something bad will happen during the play, so every year they personally invite her."

Students tend to be pleased with the campus's appearance. The trees and landscape are frequently praised, and while the weather is notorious for being bitter cold, students note that the fall and winter seasons enhance the natural beauty of the area. The student union, a main center of activity on campus, is currently closed, and a new, improved facility will open in

two years. The renovated student union will accommodate the massive growth the school has experienced since the original building was built in 1958. An old cemetery marks the middle of campus, a landmark which most students find compelling, and a school myth says that the ghost of a woman haunts Hanna Hall. "Supposedly," one student reported, "the ghost must be invited to every theater production or something bad will happen during the play, so every year they personally invite her."

The town of Bowling Green integrates with parts of the university, and undergraduates say that relations between the town and school are comfortable and friendly. Most students work either on or off campus, which, combined with the great number of commuters, makes space in campus parking lots frustratingly scarce. One student noted that sometimes it took him over half an hour to get to his car from his residence hall. Students who work exceptionally late hours can apply for special permits which allow them to park nearer to their dorms. During the nighttime hours, some students are made wary by what they see as the lack of security and lighting, while others commented that they did indeed feel safe on campus.

When Friday Comes . . .

For BGSU students, weekends mean almost anything: partying at a frat or private apartment, clubbing in either Bowling Green or nearby Toledo, working out at the gym (a greatly acclaimed facility) or playing intramurals, going to a football or hockey game, seeing a show, going home, taking a road trip, working, or most likely, a mixture of many of the above. While Bowling Green is a dry campus and the rules are strictly enforced in residential halls, undergraduates observe that being underage isn't really a problem, with the help of a fake ID or an older friend.

The Greek system is prominent; as one student noted, "God, if I see another toga I'll scream!" But, students says that it is definitely not an overpowering social force. Many are involved in Bowling Green's 180 registered student organizations, which include everything from religious and cultural groups to honor societies, music groups, political and public speaking forums, and drama. Marching band and

Greek activities are regarded as the most popular extracurriculars. BGSU actively recruits athletes, with football, basketball, and hockey receiving the most attention. "There is a good amount of school spirit, and it's nice to see it," one undergraduate noted. "However, it's not overdone." Most students attend the annual football game against rival school University of Toledo, where one student insists "You must get your picture taken with Freddy and Freida Falcon!"

When describing the student population, most regard their peers as laid back and friendly. "There is a stereotype of the khaki wearing prep here, but honestly, no one really cares," noted one undergraduate. Diversity is "present, but very minor," although multicultural organizations on campus thrive. Bowling Green is a high quality university with a great number of opportunities in all spheres—academic, extracurricular social, and plain old every day living. "Our colors may be poop and orange," exclaimed one student, "but we're really cool, I promise!"—*Amanda Ambroza*

FYI

The three best things about attending Bowling Green are "the tree-laden landscape, the town is interesting and integrated with the campus, and the friendly people."

The three worst things about attending Bowling Green are "there's rarely enough parking, the frigid cold, and water that's much less than tasty."

The three things that every student should do before graduating from Bowling Green are "ride the elevators in University Hall and try to make it out alive, go to football and hockey games, and walk on the right side of the seal."

One thing I'd like to have known before coming here is "the legend of the ghost because it scares the bejeebers out of me."

Case Western Reserve University

Address: 10900 Euclid Avenue, Cleveland, OH 44106
Phone: 216-368-4450
E-mail address: admission@po.cwru.edu
Web site URL: www.cwru.edu
Location: urban
Founded: 1826
Private or Public: private
Religious affiliation: none
Undergraduate enrollment: 3,598
Total enrollment: 9,601
Percent Male/Female: 60%/40%

Percent Minority: 21.0%
Percent African-American: 5.0%
Percent Hispanic: 2.0%
Percent Asian: 13.0%
Percent in-state/out-of-state: 58%/42%
Percent Pub HS: 70%
Fraternities: 32%
Sororities: 16%
Number of Applicants: 4,380
Percent Accepted: 72%
Percent Accepted who enroll: 24%
Entering: 766
Transfers: 81
Application Deadline: 1 Feb

Mean SAT: NA
Middle 50% SAT range: 590–710 V, 630–730 M
Middle 50% ACT range: 26–31
Mean ACT: NA
3 Most popular majors: biology, psychology, management
Retention: 92.0%
Graduation rate: 73.0%
Library: 2,015,763 volumes
Tuition and Fees: $20,260 in; NA out
Room and Board: $5,815
On-campus housing: 85%
Financial aid, first-year: 92%

C ase Western Reserve University, the largest private research institution in Ohio, is committed to excellence in teaching, research, and scholarship. Students are enthusiastic about the ample academic resources and the welcoming social scene.

Serious About Science

At Case Western, the focus is on academics. The work is intense, and students spend most of their time just trying to keep up. Many described their courses as difficult and time-consuming. Introductory classes are often large, particularly in calculus, chemistry, and physics, which enroll over 100 students each. Despite the size of these classes, professors are described as "good and personable." Core engineering classes also tend to be large, but most arts and sciences classes enroll between 10 and 30 students. Everyone is required to take some of these smaller classes, and thus no one graduates without benefiting from the low student-to-professor ratio.

Reportedly, the toughest classes are in the math and statistics departments. Engineering and computer-science majors, as well as students in accounting and management, must fulfill a large number of requirements. All students must complete the Arts and Science Core Curriculum, which mandates a broad course base, from English to music. Some students described these general education courses as "challenging." A large number of Case Western Reserve University students major in science and engineering disciplines. Students who want to pursue a medical career can apply to the Case Western premedical/medical school program during their senior year of high school and have guaranteed admission to Case Western Medical School after they complete their undergraduate core curriculum. Engineering students can also attain a five-year B.S./M.S. Students report, however, that Case Western's humanities are not just for those who change their minds about science.

Relaxed Living in the Midwest

Case Western is only a short drive or transit ride away from the heart of Cleveland, so many students spend their weekends downtown. On campus, the social scene revolves around dorms and dorm common rooms. CWRU also has a Greek system that contributes to the social life of the university by sponsoring parties. But non-Greeks say that they definitely do not feel excluded from the campus social scene, as most Greek parties are open to nonmembers.

"CWRU students are notoriously apathetic about things like homecoming and football," one undergrad said. But the campus is friendly, and it's easy to meet people: "By the time you're here two or three years, you feel as if you know a ton of people." Dating, as in "going on dates," is not as common as hanging out in friends' suites.

Living in Cleveland

Most Case Western students dress casually for class, in "jeans and T-shirts and warm clothes in the winter—it gets cold in Cleveland." In terms of student population, one undergrad reported that the "ethnic diversity is pretty good for a Midwestern school." Freshmen usually live on the north side of campus; upperclassmen live on the south side. Most upperclassmen live in suites with six single bedrooms and a common living room and bathroom. Some students object to the housing policy, which requires students to live on campus until they are 21, a senior, or married. Most seniors remain on campus anyway. All dorms have RAs, but they are "typically easygoing and don't report minor offenses," one student said.

> "CWRU students are notoriously apathetic about things like homecoming and football."

The Case Western campus fills a long, narrow strip of urban Cleveland. It is composed of 128 acres in University Circle, a 450-acre farm in nearby Hunting Valley, two astronomy observatories, and 87 buildings. Students say that they feel safe on campus, despite the urban environment. The campus is well-lit and rarely desolate. Noteworthy campus buildings include the Kelvin Smith Macromolecular Building and the Kent Hale Smith Library. Severance Hall, which is not a university building but sits right near campus, is the home of the Cleveland Orchestra and a site where part of the movie *Air Force One* was filmed. The Thwing Center has been newly renovated to house offices of student organizations. A new master plan has been developed for campus expansion and projects like revamping the Student Center.

Students reported that campus food is not great, but the dining halls are clean and are open for all-you-can-eat anytime from 7 A.M. until 11 P.M. All students who live on campus (which is almost everyone) are required to purchase the meal plan. One complaint about the dining halls is that they are placed at the opposite ends of campus near the dorms, so it is hard to make it to the dining hall for lunch after class in the center of campus.

The Film Society and Phi Beta Kappa are two of the most respected organizations on campus. Many students take advantage of the plentiful opportunities for campus jobs. Sports are not very popular at Case Western Reserve, but the Spartans' varsity teams participate in the NCAA Division III competition.

Students searching for a school that excels in engineering and the sciences may find that Case Western Reserve University more than fits the bill. Located in downtown Cleveland, Case Western combines a national reputation for academics with a friendly urban campus.—*Roseanne Pereira and Staff*

FYI

The three best things about Case Western Reserve University are "the social scene, the science departments, the Greeks."

The three worst things about Case Western Reserve University are "the football team, any school-sponsored event like homecoming, and the name."

The three things that every student should do before graduating are "do research with a faculty member, find some gut classes, and party!"

One thing I'd like to have known before coming to Case Western Reserve University is "how hard being an engineering major was going to be."

The College of Wooster

Address: 1189 Beall Ave, Wooster, OH 44691
Phone: 800-877-9905
E-mail address: admissions@wooster.edu
Web site URL: www.wooster.edu
Location: small city
Founded: 1866
Private or Public: private
Religious affiliation: Presbyterian (USA)
Undergraduate enrollment: 1,709
Total enrollment: 1,709
Percent Male/Female: 47%/53%
Percent Minority: 6.8%

Percent African-American: 4.3%
Percent Hispanic: 0.8%
Percent Asian: 1.6%
Percent in-state/out-of-state: 44%/56%
Percent Pub HS: 77%
Fraternities: 15%
Sororities: 12%
Number of Applicants: 2,195
Percent Accepted: 79%
Percent Accepted who enroll: 30%
Entering: 517
Transfers: 17
Application Deadline: 15 Feb
Mean SAT: NA

Middle 50% SAT range: 540–650 V, 540–650 M
Middle 50% ACT range: 24–28
Mean ACT: NA
3 Most popular majors: history, English, political science
Retention: 84%
Graduation rate: 73%
Library: 410,771 volumes
Tuition and Fees: $27,200 in; $27,200 out
Room and Board: included in tuition
On-campus housing: 98%
Financial aid, first-year: 98%

D o not let the relaxed, pastoral setting of The College of Wooster fool you. At the core of this idyllic campus is an intense academic program featuring small classes and professors "who rock." Located in the rural northern Ohio town of Wooster, the college seems to have something unique to offer just about everyone—from its Bagpipe Band representing Wooster's rich Scottish tradition to the independent study program required of juniors and seniors.

Gettin' Tough

The College of Wooster requires its students to take a fairly extensive set of core courses, but they are generally described as easy to complete. "You just have to remember to do them!" Students need three courses in the social sciences and/or history, three courses in math and/or science, and three courses in literature, philosophy, and/or the arts. Students must also take a first-year seminar, pass a writing requirement, complete two courses in a foreign language, and do a religion course, as well. The sciences are reportedly the hardest majors, while communications and history are supposedly the easiest. English, music, biology, and chemistry all receive good reviews. Chemistry majors can enjoy a newly renovated building, and all science majors can take advantage of the two-year-old science library. Students interested in engineering also have the option of participating in Wooster's 3+2 program, in which students finish their last two years at another school.

Both juniors and seniors take part in Wooster's independent study (IS) program within their majors. During junior year, students spend one semester fulfilling the requirements of the program, while seniors spend their entire year doing so. Getting into classes is generally not a problem, though one freshman warned that getting into lower-level language courses and nonlab science classes can sometimes be challenging. Most students also seem very happy with their professors and cite the small class sizes of about 15–20 students as a huge asset. Overall the workload is said to be "tolerable," with students describing themselves as "well-worked."

Student Life

Generally people at Wooster study in their rooms, but some take advantage of the library, Andrews, to study. Lowry, the student center is reportedly busy as well, but the snack bar area is said to "need a major face lift." Dorms were described as "pretty nice." Freshmen live in all but four of the dorms, which house solely upperclassmen. Some of the more popular freshmen dorms include Armington, Stevenson, and Bissman—but they're all fairly loud and are considered party dorms. Nicer dorms include Luce and Kenarden for sophomores, juniors, and seniors because they are newer and have carpeting and air-conditioning. Program dorms are also popular. After freshman year, students have to enter a room draw or apply to the special program dorms, which include languages, smoke-free, chemical-free (no alcohol), and a quiet dorm. Students can also move off campus or into one of the small houses owned by the university, although housing is guaranteed all four years.

Students generally go to Lowry, the main dining hall, for meals, or try and find some better food off campus. The on-campus meal plan is a 21-meal per week plan, and the dining hall offers open hours from 7 A.M. to 7 P.M. However, the food is "not great" ("the cookies are good"), so many students look elsewhere to find better food. Matsos, a Greek restaurant, The Old Jaol, and Woogle's, a bagel shop, all offer a change of menu. Wooster, being a small town, does not offer much in the way of late-night hangouts. "We need a Starbucks or something that can stay open until 12 A.M. or 1."

Social scene

One of the big social scenes on campus is the Greek system. The Greeks throw many of the weekend parties and being underage is not perceived as a problem for most students. Generally, there is much to do on campus over the weekend from "seeing plays and going to concerts to dancing and drinking." Campus-wide parties include the '70s/'80s Dance, '20s Prohibition Party, Bacchanalia, and Spring Fest. The latter two are considered to be the biggest social events of the year, and students camp out in the cornfields to party and listen to various bands.

However, partying is not the only thing going at Wooster on the weekends. There are many active extracurricular clubs such as Let's Dance—a swing dance club—the Art Club, and numerous others, including club sports. Students seem to agree that what the town of Wooster lacks in things to do, the college seems to make up for with movies, seminars, and productions over the weekends.

While they don't play a huge role at

Wooster, athletics are nonetheless well-respected, with both the football and baseball teams consistently posting winning seasons. Perhaps one of Wooster's most unique traditions is the Bagpipe Band, which, fully clad in kilts and knee socks, accompanies the football team onto the field and plays during the games. In addition, the college has its very own 18-hole golf course and boasts a new weight room "with state-of-the-art Cybex weights, treadmills, bikes, and stairmasters. It's really nice." One thing that the school lacks, however, is an adequate field house, and many students express hope that a new one will be built in the near future.

Little Diversity

Most students at Wooster hail from Ohio and the Northeast, but there is also a significant international contingent. This is about where the diversity at Wooster ends though, as most students are white and come from a middle-class background. The student body tends to be self-segregating with students sitting with their own groups in dining halls. Although the school is fairly homogenous, one student commented that "our largest minorities are Indians and Pakistanis, and

not much else." However, diversity is improving. Minorities actively participate in various cultural clubs such as the Black Students Association and Student Allies of Sexual Minorities. Other campus-wide organizations include *The Voice*, the student newspaper, the Outdoor Club, and the Wooster Volunteer Network.

> "We don't worship jocks or fraternities, and we aren't all tree-huggers. I guess we defy some of the stereotypes and that differentiates us from a lot of schools."

In general, The College of Wooster provides an intense academic experience for students who know how to get what they want and who are not afraid to work hard to get it. A typical Wooster student stereotype is hard to describe. Perhaps one student said it best when he explained, "We don't worship jocks or fraternities, and we aren't all tree-huggers. I guess we defy some of the stereotypes and that differentiates us from a lot of schools."—*Melissa J. Merritt*

FYI
The three best things about attending The College of Wooster are "the faculty, the students, and the community."
The three worst things about attending The College of Wooster are "its location, the academic registration process, and the food."
The three things that every student should do before graduating from The College of Wooster are "use the bathroom at the Underground, eat at the Old Jaol, and study abroad."
One thing I'd like to have known before coming here is "how the registration process works."

Denison University

Address: Box H, Granville, OH 43023	**Percent African-American:** 4.5%	**Middle 50% SAT range:** 560–650 V,
Phone: 800-DENISON	**Percent Hispanic:** 4.4%	560–660 M
E-mail address: admissions@denison.edu	**Percent Asian:** 1.6%	**Middle 50% ACT range:** 25–29
Web site URL: www.denison.edu	**Percent in-state / out-of-state:** 41%/59%	**Mean ACT:** 27
Location: suburban	**Percent Pub HS:** 70%	**3 Most popular majors:** economics, English,
Founded: 1831	**Fraternities:** 30%	psychology
Private or Public: private	**Sororities:** 32%	**Retention:** 84.3%
Religious affiliation: none	**Number of Applicants:** 2,991	**Graduation rate:** 74.0%
Undergraduate enrollment: 2,176	**Percent Accepted:** 69%	**Library:** 347,624 volumes
Total enrollment: 2,176	**Percent Accepted who enroll:** 29%	**Tuition and Fees:** $22,210 in; $22,210 out
Percent Male / Female: 45%/55%	**Entering:** 587	**Room and Board:** $6,300
Percent Minority: 10.8%	**Transfers:** 15	**On-campus housing:** 99%
	Application Deadline: 1 Feb	**Financial aid, first-year:** 99%
	Mean SAT: 602 V, 609 M	

Located on a hill in the middle of Ohio, surrounded by hills and big trees, full of squirrels running about, harboring a bioreserve, Denison inspires descriptions of "peaceful" and "beautiful." Aside from their spectacular surroundings, Denison students describe a demanding courseload and a social life dominated by Greeks.

Broadening Horizons

Students say Denison offers a broad but comprehensive liberal arts education. The General Education Requirements (GER) include two years of a foreign language and distribution courses that span a range of categories including philosophy, math, and science. "The requirements can be a burden, especially if you want to have a double major," a student commented. Environmental studies, biochemistry, computer science, and biology are considered to be the hardest majors, while political science, music, and economics are relatively easy. Still, many students find themselves overwhelmed with work and don't report any lazy Sundays. Even though pre-professional students don't have their own majors, programs are offered to these students that include special advi-

sors and related clubs. These include the pre-med, pre-vet, and pre-law clubs. Students usually find it easy to get into classes, even though most classes are capped at 15 to 20 people, but "some studio art classes are hard to get in," one student complained.

Pleasing Professors

Students are pleased with their professors, noting that many of them are well-known in their fields: "The microbiology professor worked on the Viking program to determine if there was life on Mars." "I had a class of ten people and toward the middle of the semester, people stopped participating and the discussions weren't very good, so the professor had us over to his house for dinner and a 'therapy session' so we could make the class better," recalled a student. Another said, "We had a medieval feast in my Anglo-Saxon English class. An English professor invited our class to his house for a movie and dinner." Students emphasize that professors try to make students think constantly and not memorize in "everywhere but the chemistry department." Also, the speakers that visit the school are enjoyed by many Denison students. Among recent visitors was scientist Keith Campbell, who cloned "Dolly" the sheep. TAs are useful for students in that "they add to professors' help but don't replace it." The biggest complaint about academics is that "grading is harsh."

Greeks and Their Beer

"If you are not obnoxious then being underage is not a problem," commented one student. Upperclassmen parties are common, but not as popular as the fraternity and sorority parties that take place off campus. The two bars in Granville are also popular with upperclassmen. "D-Day (Derby days) is a great activity," students say, complimenting their drinking festival. At keg parties, everyone pays for a mug and is bussed out to a field where there are many kegs waiting for them. Drugs are not as common as drinks: "Marijuana is popular, but there are strict rules against it. Beer rules here." There are two formal parties per year which are the only occasions people get dressed up for, unless you are part of the Greek system. As for relationships, "There is a lot of sex, but homosexuals and interracial couples are frowned upon," says one student.

Besides beer . . .

Nondrinkers, characterized as mostly "sports people," also find things to do. Other social activities on campus include lectures, movies, and dances. Students feel "you have to search out the fun activities but they do actually exist." Student organizations like the juggling club add color to the social life on campus. Community service is also very popular. Nevertheless, many find the life outside the university "dull." There aren't many options for dining or shopping in Granville. Pizza Hut and Taco Bell are the most common dining places to go to outside of the Denison meal plan, which students must purchase. "I would never recommend anyone attending Denison University unless you like to live in the same room eating the same horrible food for four straight years," one student said. The cafeterias are noted for their crowded lines although "the cafeteria people are some of the nicest people you have ever met." The limited public transportation to any nearby cities like Columbus makes cars a must for many.

Inn Denison?

The freshman dorms aren't a big complaint at Denison; students note that "the nightmare starts later," when you realize that you are phased out of off-campus housing. Students feel stranded by these kind of restrictions: "Their reasoning is that they believe on-campus living is a significant determinant in having a fruitful Denison career while in reality it is to force all students into paying the school for residential expenses as well as the costly meal plan." Also, a housing lottery results in many juniors staying in freshman dorms. Shorney is known as "the Ghetto" while the Sunset dorms are apartments, air-conditioned and the biggest dorms on campus. Students believe that instead of building new dorms, the administration should allow more off-campus housing.

Abercrombie, J. Crew, and North Face are the uniforms of many.

Wealthy and Homogeneous

Many complain of the cliques that form right away. However, "it's still true that a couple bottles of beer always open up the way for new friendships." The typical Denison student is characterized as rich and preppy. Abercrombie, J. Crew, and North Face are the uniforms of many. "Wealth is prevalent," is a common comment, and most of the students seem to have come from "wealthy East Coast boarding schools." Students report geographic, but not ethnic, diversity. The student body is very athletic. Swimming and lacrosse recruit heavily while "football doesn't matter that much. The lacrosse team made the final four last year and men and women's swim teams are strong competitors for the national championships."

Enjoy the Peace

Despite the difficult classwork, students seem to be happy with their choice of college. With its peaceful campus and wild Greek parties, Denison is indeed a place to be enjoyed.—*Yakut Seyhanli*

FYI

The three best things about attending Denison are "small classes, caring professors, and the May term internship program."

The three worst things about attending Denison are "limits on off-campus housing, transportation, housing lottery."

The three things that every student should do before graduating from Denison are "walk up the hill from Mitchell center in the middle of winter, get lost in the library stacks, do at least one May term internship."

One thing I'd like to have known before coming to Denison is "that there's a lack of social activities off campus around Granville."

Kent State University

Address: P.O. Box 5190, Kent OH 44242-0001
Phone: 330-672-2444
E-mail address: kentadm@admissions.kent.edu
Web site URL: www.kent.edu
Location: suburban
Founded: 1910
Private or Public: public
Religious affiliation: none
Undergraduate enrollment: 17,275
Total enrollment: 21,653
Percent Male/Female: 41%/59%
Percent Minority: 9.9%

Percent African-American: 7.7%
Percent Hispanic: 1.0%
Percent Asian: 1.0%
Percent in-state/out-of-state: NA
Percent Pub HS: NA
Fraternities: 7%
Sororities: 6%
Number of Applicants: 8,594
Percent Accepted: 93%
Percent Accepted who enroll: 44%
Entering: 3,820
Transfers: 913
Application Deadline: rolling
Mean SAT: 510 V, 503 M

Middle 50% SAT range: 460–570 V, 450–570 M
Middle 50% ACT range: NA
Mean ACT: 21
3 Most popular majors: nursing, psychology, architecture
Retention: 71.5%
Graduation rate: 43.0%
Library: 2,077,369 volumes
Tuition and Fees: $5,014 in; $9,918 out
Room and Board: $4,530
On-campus housing: NA
Financial aid, first-year: NA

Kent State University will live on forever as the site of intense Vietnam War protest, which exploded into the shooting of four students on May 4, 1970. Kent State, however, doesn't try to keep the event under wraps. In fact, the university just inaugurated a memorial for the four students. Additionally, students at Kent are able to study conflict management and dispute resolution. This nontraditional subject matter is representative of the various academic opportunities that surround the Golden Eagles.

Academics Abounds

Students at Kent State have many choices of courses of study. Aside from a traditional College of Liberal Arts and Sciences, Kent State also hosts the College of Fine and Professional Arts, the School of Nursing, a College of Education, and a College of Business Administration, among others. The College of Education and the Fine Arts program are considered quite strong. Regardless of major, however, students are allowed to take classes in any of Kent's colleges. As part of the

Kent experience, students are required to fulfill Liberal Education Requirements (LERs), which consist of courses from all fields, including humanities, fine arts, social sciences, and basic sciences. Student opinion is split on these requirements. One sophomore said that "we have to take 39 LERs, which are supposed to make us well-rounded students, but that means I have to take a lot more of these annoying classes when I really would like to delve into my major." Another student, however, said that "they can be kinda fun and relatively easy, so I don't mind them too much." Students are cautious about the nursing and architecture programs, both of which have notorious reputations for being difficult.

For those who seek a greater academic challenge, there is an Honors College, which allows students to take more advanced classes as a freshman. One freshman said, "Instead of having to go through basic English 1 and 2, I was able to jump right into a more in-depth literature class." Being part of the honors program, as another student described, "affords more attention from the professors. You're not as anonymous." Freshmen in the Honors College get to take smaller classes, although class size does not appear to be a major problem at Kent. Most classes range from 25 to 30 students, while larger classes, as one senior said, "rarely exceed 75 students or so." TAs are definitely present on campus but rarely teach classes above the introductory level, particularly in the English, Foreign Language, and some science departments. The academic options at Kent are quite varied and as one student put it, "if you choose the right classes, academics are great. There are a lot of classes offered."

Where to Go for a Good Time

Kent not only offers plenty of classes, but there are many social options as well. Though many join fraternities, one junior explained that "life is still pretty balanced. There's no real pressure to go Greek." Aside from Greek life, the Student Center serves as a social center, housing a concert hall in the basement, pool tables, and plenty of restaurants. Additionally, as one student stated, "A lot of the student orga-nizations are based there, so it can get really social." Various departments organize lectures open to students of any discipline and there is a pretty lively music scene. The university recently procured George Clinton and the Psychedelic Funk to play at its homecoming. Students on campus find it quite easy to meet each other. As a freshman said, "This school is pretty large, which can be an adjustment for some people, but it's easy to meet people from all sorts of backgrounds." As for off-campus fun, there is a "big strip one block away with bars and restaurants," described one senior. There, students profit from the food at Ray's Place and the $3 pizzas at The Loft. On the weekends, students generally stay on campus, even students from nearby Cleveland.

Why Leave?

Students have good reason to stay on campus since it is, simply put, "very beautiful." The campus covers several blocks with "hills, nice landscaping, and these wonderful trees that are naturally there. Front Campus is one the prettiest spots and is right by the fashion museum," described one freshman. The campus boasts a recently built wellness center, where students partake in aerobics, yoga, and various fitness classes. Students can get around campus very easily thanks to KSU bus service, which one student called "a very intricate and efficient system." Safety on campus is a very minor issue; students are quick to mention the security escort service, which students find particularly useful on late nights coming home from the library.

Coming home, however, does not necessarily mean returning to the lap of luxury. As one student described the dorms, "If you're in a double, it's pretty small; if you're in a single it's really, really small." Freshmen are not required to live on campus, although most do. Freshmen generally choose from Terrace Dorm, which is coed, or the single-sex dorms, Prentice and Dunbar, for women and men respectively. Students in the Honors College get to live in Honors Housing, which tends to be better. There are strict visitor policies; officials emphasize that visitors must be escorted at all times. Students who might not want to deal with these policies move off campus. There are many apartment complexes in the surrounding area, most of which are served directly by the Kent bus system, making them extremely convenient.

On-campus dining is described as "pretty good. We have a lot of options here." All students are given a Flash Card from the beginning, which then serves as a debit system for all the food establishments on campus, which include a McDonald's and Friendly's in the Student Center. For those in search of a more fancy meal, Mario's is one of the few restaurants where students can sit down and be waited on. Kent State has not been described as very vegetarian friendly, but it has, according to students, improved its selection in recent years. While on campus students rarely go off campus to eat, one student cited The Pufferbelly as "very worth going to."

Socially Conscious Students

The Kent State student body is very involved in social causes, mostly through community service. The strong Greek system recently staged a Build-a-Playground Campaign, in which they went to a local elementary school and built a playground set in one day. The school also has a strong America Reads program. Students can find pretty much anything at Kent, ranging from the Christian Coalition to the Neo-Pagan Coalition, or the more prominent chapter of Amnesty International and the Lesbian, Gay, Bisexual Union. Students can get involved in physical activity either through personal workout at the wellness center, or else join intramural and club teams, among which the Green Dragon Kung Fu Club is quite popular. Varsity sports do not play a central role in student life. As one student described it, "There is plenty of school spirit, although that doesn't mean our teams are that great. Our football team just won its first game and the season's almost over." Regardless, the male and female basketball teams are both well-regarded, especially due to recent success in NCAA tournaments.

Kent State offers its students many academic and social opportunities. Furthermore, the school strongly emphasizes diversity and has been attempting to improve its racial makeup. The school also fosters many artistic endeavors. For example, a large community of published writers live and work at Kent, a situation which one student described as being "a great opportunity if students take the initiative to do something with it." Kent, while still greatly tied to its past history, has evolved since May 4, 1970, and maintains a very dynamic and socially minded student body.—*Shu-Ping Shen*

> "If you're in a double, it's pretty small; if you're in a single, it's really, really small."

FYI
The three best things about attending Kent State are "graduating, amount of student activities available, and the computer labs."
The three worst things about attending Kent State are "parking, consistency from your advisors, and the almost too political nature of the campus."
The three things that every student should do before graduating from Kent State are "go to Brady's Café, visit the Fashion Museum, and check out some musical event."
One thing that I'd like to have known before coming here is "the variety of majors that were available."

Kenyon College

Address: Ransom Hall, Gambier, OH 43022
Phone: 740-427-5776
E-mail address: admissions@kenyon.edu
Web site URL: www.kenyon.edu
Location: rural
Founded: 1824
Private or Public: private
Religious affiliation: Episcopal
Undergraduate enrollment: 1,572
Total enrollment: 1,572
Percent Male/Female: 44%/56%
Percent Minority: 11.0%

Percent African-American: 4.0%
Percent Hispanic: 3.6%
Percent Asian: 3.4%
Percent in-state/out-of-state: 20%/80%
Percent Pub HS: 76%
Fraternities: 37%
Sororities: 30%
Number of Applicants: 2,420
Percent Accepted: 68%
Percent Accepted who enroll: 28%
Entering: 459
Transfers: 3
Application Deadline: 1 Feb
Mean SAT: 666 V, 634 M

Middle 50% SAT range: 610–710 V, 580–690 M
Middle 50% ACT range: 27–31
Mean ACT: 29
3 Most popular majors: English, psychology, political science
Retention: 92.5%
Graduation rate: 82%
Library: 1 million plus
Tuition and Fees: $24,590 in; $24,590 out
Room and Board: $4,160
On-campus housing: 100%
Financial aid, first-year: 41%

Not many colleges are located in a genuine village. With a population of just 650, however, Gambier, Ohio, home to Kenyon College, a post office, a bookstore, and a few eateries, truly is a village of distinction. Nestled in a wooded campus of more than 800 acres, Kenyon provides such a unique atmosphere that one student explained that "you forget the rest of the world exists after a while."

ABCs of Academics

Although situated in a relaxed, pastoral village, the academics at Kenyon can often be intense. Traditionally, English is known as the strongest department, and many students take advantage of this reputation. One student commented that "there are a lot of people in the English department, so it might be hard to get the classes you want." The sciences, meanwhile, also boast solid departments. One biology major said that "even the intro classes are very hard. If you're not ready, you're in big trouble!"

Most students agree that "a nice thing about Kenyon is the class size." Most classes run from just 10 to 20 students, and one student said that "intro bio is my biggest class, and while it would have

hundreds of students at other schools, my class is only 60!" With this small class size, it follows that the faculty-student interaction at Kenyon is described as "good, but only if you want it." One student said that "all my professors would recognize me." All classes at Kenyon are taught by professors, and "if you put in the effort, you can create a good relationship with them."

Academics at Kenyon are structured around a core curriculum. Students are required to take two semesters of classes in each of the following four areas: fine arts, humanities, social sciences, and natural sciences. One student explained that "even though we have these requirements, it usually happens anyway." Most students agree that the requirements are a good way to broaden your academic experience.

One Kenyon student explained that "you have to study a lot to do well, but you don't have to study a lot to stay here." Students agree, though, that most people do study a lot at Kenyon. Many study in their rooms, but they are also found cracking the books in the Olin Chalmers Library, which, according to one student, "can be social, if you are visible, but if you hide, it's good for studying." Although the library at Kenyon boasts extensive reources, if students cannot find what they re looking for, they can hop on the Kenyon shuttle to Columbus, Ohio, just an hour away, and visit the Ohio State University libraries for more in-depth research. Kenyon is in the middle of building several new facilities. One is the Robert J. Tomsich Hall, a new chemistry building, to be completed for the 2000-2001 school year. A new music building will also be completed in the future.

Livin' It Up

All students live on campus all four years, which is not such an issue, as one student explained that "you have to live on campus because there is no other place to live . . . the school is the town!" Students describe the dorm situation as "pretty good." One sophomore explained that "as a freshman, my room was kind of small, but pretty nice." All freshmen live together on the north side of campus, which helps them get to know each other. Also, RAs live in each residence hall. After freshman year, though, students are entered into a lottery system to choose their housing. One student explained that under this system "as a sophomore you can easily get screwed, but juniors and seniors usually end up with good housing."

There are "all kinds of different ways to live" at Kenyon. There are single-sex dorms, loud party dorms, quiet dorms, substance-free floors, and apartment-style living. Woodland Cottages, with contemporary apartments, is a prime residence, and the rooms even have kitchens in them for the ambitious Kenyon students. Old Kenyon, the first collegiate Gothic building in the United States, is described as a picturesque Kenyon building." The rooms are reported to be modern and beautiful, but also "loud, with frequent fire alarm pulls." Juniors and seniors can also choose to live in fraternities or sororities, or other group living arrangements.

Not Great, but Livable

One student described the food situation at Kenyon as "not great, but livable." Students use their all-you-can-eat meal cards at one of two dining halls on campus. Pierce Hall, with more of the traditional dining hall setting, is equipped with the typical dining hall food." It is designated the social dining hall, and one student explained that the long walk to get to the food through the tables of students eating is known as the "cat walk" because "all eyes are on you." The other dining hall, Gund Hall, is located on the north side of campus, and many freshmen eat there, since it is close to their dorms.

While some students agree that the culinary options are plentiful, others hasten to add that "it's always the same, and it's only good if you learn to make your own things." At Kenyon, since there are a variety of eaters, including many vegetarians and vegans, there are always different options to choose from. However, students who prefer to go out for dinner may be disappointed with the selection in Gambier. Students can either choose the Red Door, a coffee shop, or Pirate's Cove, a pizza place. Many students choose to venture to Columbus for more dining options.

Night Out in the Village

At Kenyon "the party scene is the social scene, but you do not have to drink in order to party," explained one student. Most parties at Kenyon are Greek-based, and one student said that "most people who drink rely on the Greeks." Although there are not a lot of fraternities, they do provide much of the social life on the weekends. Juniors and seniors will often host house parties as well. One student described the social options as "mediocre, but that's the way I like it." For those who prefer to stay away from the party scene, most just "hang out." There are also movies shown every weekend, which are popular alternatives. One student explained that "one time a hypnotist came. That was a big thing here." For those who yearn for more excitement than Gambier can provide, they can either travel five miles to the town of Mt. Vernon, or take the one hour ride to Columbus, which has more opportunities for dining, movies, bars, and other entertainment.

Students generally agree that while some serious dating does occur, there are mostly just "lots of hookups." One student said that "most people aren't looking for a long-term relationship right now . . . they don't have time."

On the Go

"People try to be active here [at Kenyon]. Being isolated, you have to find a way to spend your time, or you will be bored." One student described the Kenyon population as "a good balance between academic and athletic." A good portion of the Kenyon student body is athletes. Kenyon's swimming and diving team, the most accomplished, boasts 18 consecutive national titles for men, and 14 for women. The tennis, men's soccer, and cross-country teams have also had recent successes. Kenyon is a member of the NCAC, and also participates as an NCAA Division III school. Students who are not varsity athletes are often found participating in club sports or intramurals, such as rugby or Ultimate Frisbee. One student added that "a lot of people play pretty much anything."

While athletics do dominate the Kenyon extracurricular scene, many students do explore other outlets. The Kokosingers (an all-male a cappella group) and the Owl Creek Singers (an all-female group) are available for those students who are musically talented. For those who prefer the hustle and bustle of journalism, the *Collegian*, Kenyon's weekly newspaper, is an option. The *Gambier Journal* and the *Kenyon Observer* are published less frequently, and explore cultural, political, and social issues. Students can also explore student government with the Kenyon Student Council or the Senate, which is comprised of students and faculty. For the aspiring actors, the Kenyon Dramatic Club, an extremely active group, sponsors many theatrical events throughout the year.

Lack of Diversity

One student expressed the opinion that "diversity is one area definitely lacking both in faculty and students." The issue of diversity has been heating up lately, beginning with the decision a couple years ago not to rehire two minority professors, which led to a "diversity rally." Since then, many discussions and forums have been held to deal with the issue of minorities at Kenyon, with both student and faculty participation. One student described the effort so far as positive and said that "a lot of people are working on it."

A Final Glimpse

Overall, students feel very comfortable at Kenyon. One student said that "the campus is beautiful, and the village is unique, but it's a long way from anything else." While this isolation may be a deterring factor for some people, most students at Kenyon are too busy to notice, and when they do, they sit back, relax, and admire their beautiful village.—*Marissa Kantor and Staff*

> "Being isolated, you have to find a way to spend your time, or you will be bored."

FYI
The three best things about Kenyon are "small classes, high professor interaction, the really cool people here."
The three worst things about Kenyon are "it is in the middle of nowhere, there is no diversity, and sophomore housing."
One thing that every student should do before graduating from Kenyon is "go to Philander's Phling."
One thing I'd like to have known before coming to Kenyon is "how small the village really is."

Miami University

Address: 201 South Campus Avenue Bldg.; Oxford, OH 45056
Phone: 513-529-2531
E-mail address: admission@muohio.edu
Web site URL: www.muohio.edu
Location: suburban
Founded: 1809
Private or Public: public
Religious affiliation: none
Undergraduate enrollment: 14,803
Total enrollment: 16,328
Percent Male/Female: 45%/55%
Percent Minority: 8.4%

Percent African-American: 4.0%
Percent Hispanic: 2.0%
Percent Asian: 2.0%
Percent in-state/out-of-state: 73%/27%
Percent Pub HS: NA
Fraternities: 24%
Sororities: 27%
Number of Applicants: 11,862
Percent Accepted: 78%
Percent Accepted who enroll: 37%
Entering: 3,423
Transfers: NA
Application Deadline: 31 Jan
Mean SAT: NA

Middle 50% SAT range: 540–630 V, 560–650 M
Middle 50% ACT range: 27–31
Mean ACT: NA
3 Most popular majors: marketing, elementary education, zoology
Retention: 90%
Graduation rate: 62%
Library: 2.1 million volumes
Tuition and Fees: $4,766 in; $11,226 out
Room and Board: $5,070
On-campus housing: 100%
Financial aid, first-year: 34%

If your vision of college life combines serious academics with an active social scene set against a backdrop of colonial-style redbrick buildings and beautifully designed courtyards, you might want to consider a visit to Oxford, Ohio, home of Miami University of Ohio.

Oxford Academia

During the week, academics are very important to the majority of Miami students. As one student said, "Miami is filled with people who make sure they get their work done before they go out." The academic requirement for students is the Miami Plan, which aims to give students a strong liberal arts foundation and consists of foundation courses in English, humanities, social sciences, natural sciences, fine arts, and formal reasoning. In addition to this curriculum, further study must be done in an area outside of the chosen major, and a senior project or seminar must be completed. While the Miami Plan certainly gives students broad exposure to a variety of academic disciplines, many students find the requirements stifling. They feel that they take classes they do not want to take, only to fulfill a requirement. Students register for classes by phone,

and though priority for scheduling is given to upperclassmen, most students do not have problems getting the classes they want.

Miami University is divided into six schools: arts and sciences, applied science, education, business, fine arts, and allied professions. The business school in particular garners rave reviews from students, as do many science and business classes in general. One major unique to Miami University is paper science, which prepares students in the study of the production of paper. Students placed elementary education and communications as among the easier majors offered. In addition to liberal arts majors, pre-professional programs are offered in law and medicine. Among the distinctive academic programs Miami offers are the University Honors Program, which features community service projects and a seminar format of instruction; the School of Interdisciplinary Studies, which allows students to create their own majors; and a study-abroad program at the university's campus in Luxembourg. This program allows students to live with a local family, travel independently in Europe, and complete Miami requirements all at once.

Students generally seem extremely happy with academics at Miami of Ohio. While classes are said to be challenging, most students feel the level of instruction is excellent. With the exception of some introductory courses, classes are generally small, with an average range from 15 to 30, and students feel that student-faculty interaction is outstanding.

A Whole New World

Facilities on campus are in superb condition. Many students find King library, the main library, perfect for researching and studying. In addition, libraries for science, music, and art and architecture are easily accessible and well-used. Other well-maintained facilities include the Outdoor Pursuit Center, which hosts outdoor adventure trips, and the Recreational Sports Center, which as one student put it, "has everything anyone could ever want in an athletic facility, from whirlpools to climbing walls as well as an indoor soccer complex."

Students at Miami love their idyllic campus setting. One building in particular that catches their attention is Upham, where to get to classes, they can walk through a beautifully designed archway. Ancient Miami folklore also says that if two people kiss under this archway at midnight, they will undoubtedly get married. But, not all folklore is so optimistic. Many students walking on the slant walk, a particular sidewalk with the school emblem engraved in it, avoid stepping on the school seal because doing so is a precursor to failing all your exams. Students also appreciate how well-kept their campus is. "I would feel bad dropping a gum wrapper because it's so clean!" said one freshman.

Students must live in dorms during their first year, but after freshman year many Miami students choose to live off campus. Dorms are situated in different quads on campus: North, South, East, and Central. In addition there is a Western Campus, which many students feel is secluded from the rest of the university. Most dorms are coed by floor, but there are also three all-male dorms and seven all-female dorms. Among the student-rated best dorms are MacCracken and Hamilton, all-female dorms that women can move into as sophomores. Most feel that their dorms are adequate but not great. Food options abound at Miami, where most students are happy with the food quality and variety. Students seem content with eating at either the dining halls or the student center.

Pass the Feta Cheese

With over 300 student-run organizations, Miami has a lot to offer for those looking to be involved extracurricularly. Among these organizations are the *Miami Student*, a biweekly publication said to be the oldest college newspaper in the nation, and the Campus Activities Council. Students in fraternities and sororities also help in the leadership and organization of these groups. Many students are also involved with club sports and intramurals, such as flag football and rugby. However, students complain of a lack of spirit for their college varsity teams. While some attend football games, the crowd is said to be "calm" rather than loud. Students claim some of the best teams at Miami are the men's swimming and ice hockey units.

While students generally agree that they are studious during the week, the Miami weekend scene is a thriving one. The Greek system is the center of social life on campus. However, freshmen do not rush until second semester of freshman year, leaving some feeling left out during first semester. Many students feel that joining a sorority or fraternity is the key to having a vibrant social life because it is easy to meet people at fraternity-sponsored social events. Although there are many campus-run activities like concerts and lectures, most feel that these are overshadowed by the Greek scene. Some of these events include Green Beer Day, where all beer is dyed green in honor of St. Patrick's Day, and the many "Grab a Date" dances, where fraternity or sorority members scurry around to pick dates for the evening. Many students also spend their leisure time on Uptown, a brick road lined with many restaurants, bars, and dance clubs. Some popular bars in town include Mack and Joe's, First Run, and Hole in the Wall. On campus, students must live according to the administration's strict "three strikes" policy. Here, if a student receives three alcohol violations, he or she is suspended from school.

Despite administrative efforts, drinking is still quite prevalent at Miami. Students say, however, nondrinkers will not have a problem with the campus social scene provided they are comfortable with the party scene itself. In addition to all these social events on campus, some students also take occasional trips to Cincinnati or Dayton for movies, special events, or a more varied social scene.

> **"Miami is filled with people who make sure they get their work done before they go out."**

While diversity is slowly increasing at Miami, students say "that's not saying much." One student described diversity at Miami as being "diversity between what Abercrombie sweater you're wearing." Indeed, most students who attend Miami come from white, upper-middle-class, conservative families. Most students also come from Ohio or other midwestern states. Students agree that homosexual couples and interracial couples are not condoned by a large part of the student body, and students with a more liberal view than most Miami students tend to live on Western Campus. Students feel that the Miami student body is friendly overall. However, some out-of-state students find it harder to find their niche because so many in-state students already arrive with friends from home and connections at the school. Many students suggest the Greek system as the fastest way to meet friends. Also, male freshmen seem to find it more difficult to make ties with upperclassmen. One student cited a "respect factor" expected of freshmen men to male upperclassmen.

Miami students also seem to take pride in their appearance. Students wear dressy clothing pretty regularly, giving support to the description of Miami as "J. Crew U," full of "black pant girls and khaki boys." Many also put in the effort to keep fit. As one student put it, "Any time of day you'll see people running, and the Rec Center's always busy." Perhaps due to these efforts, males and females both agree that the campus is not the only thing that looks good at Miami. While there are more females than males on campus, females describe the stereotypical Miami male as a "player just looking for a good time" instead of a serious commitment.

Although student spirit for the Redhawks athletic teams is fledgling at best, students have pride in their school. Miami alumni, happy with their college experience, give large donations to the school each year. Both the alumni and the current students believe that a beautiful campus, excellent undergraduate instruction, and students who take pride in themselves all combine to create a fulfilling college experience.—*Roseanne Pereira and Staff*

FYI
The three best things about Miami are "the small classes, the Greek scene, and the beautiful campus."
The three worst things about Miami are "the lack of diversity, lack of school spirit, and conservatism."
One thing every student should do before graduating from Miami is "drink some green beer on St. Patrick's Day."
One thing I'd like to have known before coming here is "most students are from Ohio."

Oberlin College

Address: 101 N. Professor St., Oberlin, OH 44074-1075

E-mail address: college.admissions@oberlin.edu

Phone: 800-622-6243

Web site URL: www.oberlin.edu

Location: small town

Founded: 1833

Private or Public: private

Religious affiliation: none

Undergraduate enrollment: 2,951

Total enrollment: 2,973

Percent Male / Female: 41% / 59%

Percent Minority: 23.0%

Percent African-American: 8.0%

Percent Hispanic: 5.0%

Percent Asian: 9.0%

Percent in-state / out-of-state: 9% / 91%

Percent Pub HS: 67%

Fraternities: 0%

Sororities: 0%

Number of Applicants: 4,855

Percent Accepted: 50%

Percent Accepted who enroll: 30%

Entering: 729

Transfers: 91

Application Deadline: 15 Jan

Mean SAT: 685 V, 643 M

Middle 50% SAT range: 630–730 V, 600–700 M

Middle 50% ACT range: NA

Mean ACT: 28

3 Most popular majors: English, biology, history

Retention: 90%

Graduation rate: 80%

Library: 1,541,260 volumes

Tuition and Fees: $24,264 in; $24,264 out

Room and Board: $6,178

On-campus housing: 100%

Financial aid, first-year: 55%

If you are a staunch conservative and want to be surrounded by others like yourself, Oberlin may not be the place for you, according to students at this small liberal arts college. In fact, for many students, the appeal of Oberlin is that it "offers an atypical college experience, one that engages your mind in a very upbeat, dynamic way." Oberlin offers not only a rigorous academic program, but also opportunities for individuals to be assertive, politically active members of the student body.

Oberlin students are known for working very hard academically. Under the 9-9-9 requirement system, they must take nine credit hours each in the natural sciences, humanities, and cultural-diversity departments, as well as fulfilling their major requirements. Oberlin students must also complete three different January Winter Term projects over their four years. Projects range from all kinds of internships to reading Northwest poets to traveling around the Pacific Northwest to writing poetry. One of the more famous projects designed at Oberlin was the re-creation of the journey traveled by escaped slaves through the Underground Railroad. Although many students design their own

majors at Oberlin, the two most popular majors are English and politics. It is reportedly difficult to get into classes in the art department because they are so popular. Class size varies, but the average range is 20 to 25 students. Students say some of the best gut courses include Einstein and Relativity, Musical Acoustics, and Modern Japan.

The Con

Oberlin is well-known for its premier music conservatory, which attracts world-renowned musicians and conductors (students as well as professors) to the campus. The Conservatory, or "the Con," has been heralded not only as an asset to those talented enough to take part in its programs, but also as a cultural resource for the entire college community. As one student said, "Whether or not you play an instrument you benefit from the Con. Amazing musicians who love to get together and just jam surround you. We also get to attend some great concerts."

Undergrads typically study in the main campus library, which one student said is "designed to be totally seventies—it's really wacky." Some of its best features are the "womb chairs—God's gift to

Obies," which are big plastic chairs that reportedly block out sound from all directions. Students do not recommend trying to study in dorm rooms. The fluorescent lights in the rooms are not particularly well liked. One student said, "They put a sickly green tint on everyone and everything in the room. Bringing your own light source is a definite must!"

Drugs and Alcohol

Social life at Oberlin does not center on a Greek system—the school has no fraternities or sororities—and students do not seem to mind. "I am so relieved not to deal with the pressures of the rush process," said one student. Oberlin has a varied social scene. Students drink, but the drug scene is reportedly much larger. Though drugs and alcohol are reportedly prevalent on campus, most students would agree that "those who don't want to party hard-core don't feel too left out on campus." For Oberlin students, the festivities associated with a typical weekend begin on Thursday afternoon and continue until Sunday afternoon (when most "weekend warriors" actually buckle down and get working). Most of the parties on campus are hosted by co-ops, selective organizations that serve as social centers. Some of the most important social events of the year are the Kumba Party, the Drag Ball, a huge Halloween party, and a semiformal hosted by Oberlin's "hippie dorm." There is also a dance place for students at the "Sco," a campus disco that, according to one student, is "kind of lame." In terms of the dating scene, students agree that random hookups are more prevalent than actual relationships. Students report a substantial number of gay couples on campus, but interracial couples are rare.

Support for sports on campus does not seem to be a high priority for most Oberlin students. The Ultimate Frisbee team is considered one of the most "serious" of all the sports. When asked about Oberlin's sports record, one student replied, "I don't have the faintest idea, to be honest. I'm sure we may have won a game or something sometime." Another student added that "athletics here are pretty much a joke," even though Oberlin offers gym facilities for the athletically inclined.

Surrounded by Hippies

While not recognized for its tremendous school spirit, the student body at Oberlin is known for its involvement in community service activities and political organizations. In fact, the college itself has a strong reputation for its very liberal, nonconformist, and politically dynamic student body. One student noted that she was "proud to be surrounded by hippies." Another student recalled, "Within the first week of being here, I had already been to my first environmental rally." Some of the most popular extracurricular activities include various environmental groups, the Feminist Majority, an array of workers' rights organizations, the Queer Support Group, and the Socialist Students Union.

Students also enjoy just spending time with one another. It is reportedly "not odd to encounter Grateful Dead music blaring from dorm room windows, flowered tapestries hanging on the walls, or even assorted groups of people doing anything from fitting puzzle pieces together to drumming and chanting during a rainstorm!"

Housing receives lukewarm reviews from students. Though one resident called the freshman housing "okay—not good, not bad," sophomores usually get "larger rooms that are in better shape," while a large number of juniors and seniors live off campus. Some of the students' favorite campus dorms are Talcott, "aka the Magic Kingdom because it is spacious and beautiful," and Langston. Harkness, on the other hand, is considered one of the worst dorms on campus because of what one student called its "unsanitary environment, because the bathrooms are just never cleaned." An extremely popular housing option is the co-op system and the Special Program Houses, which include German, French, Spanish, Russian, Third World, Jewish, African Heritage, and Women's houses. In these systems, students share the responsibility for meals and other household chores. According to one resident, "You just can't beat 'em. I feel really like I'm part of a family here." The Special Program Houses options are so popular that they require a separate application process, but students consider them "well worth the effort—if you can get in."

Co-ops provide dining considered far superior to the dining halls. According to one student, the dining-hall fare is "absolutely disgusting! I definitely don't love this place for its food." Students who choose not to live in a co-op have a 21-meal-a-week plan that can be used at the Stevenson cafeteria or in several other co-ops located on South Campus. Other dining alternatives include the Rathskeller ("the Rat"), a restaurant located in the Student Union, and off-campus eateries such as the Java Zone, the Feve coffeehouse, Pizza Hut, and Subway.

According to some students, Oberlin's architecture and campus are "like the landscape—not really much to look at." One student noted that "if you're looking for big Gothic or colonial architecture, don't even consider Oberlin." One student also commented that most of the buildings at Oberlin were "distinctively undistinctive."

Although the campus may not be picturesque, the student body reportedly more than makes up for it. According to one student, "I have met some of the most amazing people here—along with some of the weirdest—that I will probably ever meet." Many are continually impressed by the energy and dynamism of their peers. Oberlin offers an eclectic educational experience that strives to emphasize individualism. Said one student, Oberlin has "the makings for genius, madness, and good times."—*Roseanne Pereira and Staff*

"Athletics here are pretty much a joke."

FYI

The three best things about Oberlin are "the liberal, open-minded atmosphere, outstanding music conservatory, people here tend to 'hang out' more than party."

The three worst things about attending Oberlin are "tuition, people take their politics (and themselves) too seriously, dining halls."

The three things that every student should do before graduating from Oberlin are "attend a concert at the conservatory, get involved in community service, eat at a co-op."

One thing I'd like to have known before coming here is "that there are more 'peculiar' people here, I believe, than at most other colleges."

Ohio State University

Address: Third Floor Lincoln Tower, 1800 Cannon Dr., Columbus, OH 43210
Phone: 614-292-3980
E-mail address: telecounseling@fa.adm. ohio-state.edu
Web site URL: www.osu.edu
Location: urban
Founded: 1870
Private or Public: public
Religious affiliation: none
Undergraduate enrollment: 36,092
Total enrollment: 48,003
Percent Male/Female: 52%/48%
Percent Minority: 17.0%

Percent African-American: 8.0%
Percent Hispanic: 2.0%
Percent Asian: 6.0%
Percent in-state/out-of-state: 94%/6%
Percent Pub HS: 87%
Fraternities: 6%
Sororities: 7%
Number of Applicants: 19,805
Percent Accepted: 74%
Percent Accepted who enroll: 42%
Entering: 6,105
Transfers: 1,715
Application Deadline: rolling
Mean SAT: 564 V, 581 M

Middle 50% SAT range: 500–620 V, 520–640 M
Middle 50% ACT range: 22–27
Mean ACT: 24.6
3 Most popular majors: social and behavioral sciences, business, engineering
Retention: 82.8%
Graduation rate: 55.9%
Library: 5,285,344 volumes
Tuition and Fees: $4,137 in; $12,087 out
Room and Board: $5,328
On-campus housing: 85%
Financial aid, first-year: 91%

"Botanical material or not, Brutus kicks butt," explained one Ohio State University student, referring to Brutus the Buckeye, OSU's mascot. Ohio State is one of few colleges whose mascot is not an animal, but a nut.

We're Talking Huge

Educating over 36,000 undergrads, OSU is not only an athletic powerhouse, it is a research institution and an academic force. Business, education, and engineering are among OSU's strongest departments. All students must fulfill the requirements of the General Education Curriculum (GEC), which, depending on one's major, include a number of classes in history, science, math, English, social sciences, humanities, foreign language, and physical education. All freshmen are required to enroll in an orientation course called University College, which informs students about degree requirements, dorm regulations, and how to use the libraries.

Although students sometimes find it difficult to select a schedule from over 10,000 classes, the administration attempts to facilitate the process by providing Better Registration Using Touchtone Phones for University Students (BRUTUS), a telephone registration system. "It's easy and convenient," one freshman said. Students complain, however, that it is not uncommon to get shut out of a class. Athletes and honors students get priority for class placement. Class sizes can range from over 700 students in introductory psychology to fewer than 10 in foreign-language classes. Lecture classes also have recitation sections led by teaching assistants. One freshman lamented the abundance of foreign TAs who "have problems communicating with the students." OSU is on a quarter system, but the administration recently has discussed the possibility of changing to a semester schedule.

Library resources are extensive, and most students use the libraries for research but study in dorm lounges. Honors students also have access to an honors house where they can find a quiet place to study.

An Off-Campus Environment

Most OSU students live off campus. Some complained that crime from nearby downtown Columbus has carried over into the off-campus neighborhoods, and students are concerned about the lack of security phones off campus. On campus, however, the security reportedly is satisfactory. There are three dorm clusters: North Campus, South Campus, and the Towers. According to students, North Campus dorms are quiet, the Towers are far from central campus, and South dorms are more social. "People leave their doors open here on South Campus," reported one freshman. The Towers and North Campus were renovated within the last decade and have air-conditioning, while students living on South Campus have to put up with older facilities and the uncomfortable humidity of the summer months.

Each cluster of dorms has a commons cafeteria, where students can go for a sit-down meal, and a Buckeye Express that offers takeout service. The meal contracts are reportedly "flexible." Students can purchase a set amount of meals per week and receive $100 dollars on their BuckID for the quarter, which can be spent at fast-food restaurants in the Ohio Union or in other stores close to campus. Students also can opt to have no meals and $500 on their BuckID each quarter.

High Street

When students want to get food or coffee, they usually go to one of the many shops on High Street. The Flying Tomato, BW-3's, Beekman's, and Grinders are popular, as are coffee shops such as Brenen's, Insomnia, and Idiot Boy. High Street is also home to several bars and dance clubs such as the Edge, Mr. Mustard's, and Not Al Toos.

Football and More Football

Ohio State's Greek system is strong, and there are usually several fraternity parties during the weekend. But the biggest bashes are the "all-campus" parties that occur after a home football game against Notre Dame or the University of Michigan. "It's like a riot," said one freshman. Greek Week, held during the spring, is another major social event. "It's a week of drinking and parties," one pledge reported.

However, the Greek system does not dominate OSU's social scene, and stu-

dents say it is easy to get involved in other activities. Whether you want to write for OSU's student newspaper, the *Lantern*, or perform plays for local elementary schools with the Griffin's Tale acting troupe, "OSU is so large that it offers just about everything," said one education major. OSU also attracts famous speakers, such as President Bill Clinton, former prime minister of Great Britain Margaret Thatcher, and comedian Adam Sandler. If students want to relax, many go to the Oval, located at the center of campus. "When it gets warmer, people will go to the Oval to suntan, Rollerblade, walk their dog, or even drink," one student reported.

In the Big Ten conference the buckeye is a symbol of power. The football team had a successful year in 1995 with a record of 11–2, missing a chance to go to the Rose Bowl only because of a loss against their rivals, the University of Michigan Wolverines. According to students, home football games attract several thousand undergrads who sit in a designated section. Before each game, the students paint signs and decorate their faces with OSU's colors, scarlet and gray. The gymnastics and synchronized swimming teams have also had successful records in recent years. With the new Schottenstein Arena under construction, the basketball team will have the chance to improve their record in the future. Students don't have to be recruited athletes to get involved in sports at OSU. Intramural sports are popular among undergrads, especially soccer, football, hockey, rugby, and inner-tube water polo.

> **"OSU is so large that it offers just about everything."**

Students praised the close relationship the administration, especially President Gordon Gee, maintains with them. "President Gee walked through the student section of a football game to talk with the students, and he even remembered the name of the girl sitting next to me," one freshman said. President Gee is also known to attend Greek functions and pass out cookies to students studying in their rooms. Despite OSU's large size, students agreed that with the help of their classmates and the administration, it's possible to have a personalized experience at one of the nation's largest universities.— *Jessica Morgan and Staff*

FYI

The three best things about OSU are "the football team, the Greek system, and the diversity."
The three worst things about OSU are "how hard it is to get the classes you want if you don't have priority, foreign TAs you can't understand, and inaccessible professors."
One thing every student should do before graduating from OSU is "see our football team CRUSH the University of Michigan Wolverines."
One thing I'd like to have known before coming here is "that you have to be careful, or you could get lost in such a big school."

Ohio University

Address: 120 Chubb Hall, Athens, OH 45701
Phone: 740-593-4100
E-mail address: frshinfo@ohiou.edu
Web site URL: www.ohiou.edu
Location: small city
Founded: 1804
Private or Public: public
Religious affiliation: none
Undergraduate enrollment: 16,218
Total enrollment: 19,155
Percent Male/Female: 40%/60%
Percent Minority: 7.0%
Percent African-American: 4.0%

Percent Hispanic: 1.0%
Percent Asian: 1.0%
Percent in-state/out-of-state: 84%/16%
Percent Pub HS: 81%
Fraternities: 12%
Sororities: 16%
Number of Applicants: 11,785
Percent Accepted: 80%
Percent Accepted who enroll: 36%
Entering: 3,449
Transfers: 504
Application Deadline: 15 Feb
Mean SAT: 557 V, 533 M
Middle 50% SAT range: 500–600 V, 490–600 M

Middle 50% ACT range: 22–26
Mean ACT: 23.6
3 Most popular majors: teacher education, interpersonal communications, journalism
Retention: 84.0%
Graduation rate: 70.0%
Library: 2,233,465 volumes
Tuition and Fees: $4,800 in; $10,101 out
Room and Board: $5,484
On-campus housing: 96%
Financial aid, first-year: 41%

Colorful flower beds, rolling hills, and lush trees characterize the campus of Ohio University. Many students cite the cobblestone streets, acres of green grass, and small surrounding community as factors in their decision to attend OU. This large state school has more to offer than just charming scenery, however. For many of the students roaming the picturesque campus, academics are the first consideration.

Challenging and Fast-paced

Students view OU's academic curriculum as challenging and fast-paced. In addition, most say that the choice of classes is diverse enough to satisfy almost anyone's interests. Undergrads consider the college of journalism among the best departments, and telecommunications, one of the most popular majors. To ensure a well-rounded education, the university requires all students to fulfill three "tier" requirements before graduation. Tier One consists of math and English courses taken during the first year. Tier Two requires 30 credit hours in the following five subject areas: applied sciences and technology, humanities and fine arts, natural sciences and mathematics, social sciences, and third world cultures. Students cite the third world cultures requirement as especially thought provoking, since it deals with issues beyond more traditional, Western civilization courses. The third tier consists of an English composition course taken during junior year. The most popular courses fill up quickly, so some students have to settle for their second-choice classes in order to meet the requirements on time.

Class size at OU ranges from 20 students in small seminars to about 300 in lecture courses. Professors teach the large lecture courses and reportedly are receptive to students' questions. Aside from handling the smaller lecture discussion sections, TAs teach most lower-level English courses, which students tend to enjoy. One freshman described his English course as "the most fun course I've taken yet."

Where You'll Live

Dorms at OU promote interaction among all levels of undergraduates. The seven freshman dorms allow frosh to get to know each other during their first year, while the other three classes mix in several upperclass dorms. Single-sex and coed housing are available to accommodate student preferences. Bryan Hall is especially popular for its kitchen, laundry facilities, and quiet location. Residents consider the other dorms comfortable and spacious, although some recommend bringing a carpet to avoid "cold floors in the morning."

While Alden Library is considered the best place for quiet study or research at OU, in warm weather many students take their books outside and engage in some social studying on the college green. A sort of outdoor student union, the green is also a favorite spot for organizational meetings, picnics, or just plain hanging out between classes. The Baker Student Center is another popular destination for students looking to blow off steam. It houses a bowling alley and billiard room, and is the site of social events sponsored by the University Program Council. During the winter, students relieve stress by sledding down Jefferson Hill.

With more than 20 bars and dance clubs in Athens, drinking at OU is a common weekend activity. The Athens police department guards against underage drinking, however, by placing officers in bars. Apart from off-campus drinking, there are many university-sponsored activities through out the year. OU's annual Halloween celebration is the largest campus party, attracting 30,000 students from colleges all over Ohio. To prepare for the celebration, the OU administration closes off Athens's main street, and students cover the town with Halloween decorations and posters. On Halloween night, students dress in costumes and party up and down the streets of Athens.

The Greek system at OU is strong, with most students calling it the backbone of OU's social scene. With such a large student population, fraternities and sororities provide a more personal environment conducive to socializing. "There really isn't pressure to rush," one freshman said, "but it is encouraged because it's how you meet people."

> **During the winter, students relieve stress by sledding down Jefferson Hill.**

As for sports, the OU Bobcats are traditionally strong in hockey; Bird Arena is always standing-room-only during hockey games. On the other hand, OU's football squad is not as successful. Although many fans turn out to cheer for the team in the first half of home games, the crowd usually disperses after the nationally acclaimed marching band finishes its halftime show. Even during games against the Miami University Redskins, OU's biggest football rival, crowds are scarce. Intramurals don't draw much support.

OU has earned itself a party-school reputation, but with such a large student body, there are just as many students who choose a less rigorous social scene as those who go out every night. Nevertheless, students at OU are a spirited group, and this spirit shows itself in the many activities that they engage in, from studying to partying.

No matter how students decide to

spend their four years at OU, the fact is that most are happy with their education and college experiences when they gradu-

ate. As one senior put it, "OU is a school I can be proud of."—*Santush Aravind and Staff*

FYI

The three best things about OU are "games against our rivals, freshman English, and having the Baker Student Union."

The three worst things about OU are "our crummy football team, the tier system, and our party-school rep."

The three things that every student should do before graduating from OU are "sled down Jefferson Hill, hit the Athens bar scene, and really dress up for Halloween."

One thing I'd like to have known coming here is "how much I would hate to leave this place."

Ohio Wesleyan University

Address: 61 South Sandusky Street; Delaware, OH 43015

Phone: 740-368-3020

E-mail address: owuadmit@cc.owu.edu

Web site URL: www.owu.edu

Location: suburban

Founded: 1842

Private or Public: private

Religious affiliation: Methodist

Undergraduate enrollment: 1,873

Total enrollment: 1,873

Percent Male/Female: 49%/51%

Percent Minority: 7.0%

Percent African-American: 4.0%

Percent Hispanic: 1.0%

Percent Asian: 2.0%

Percent in-state/out-of-state: 37%/63%

Percent Pub HS: 71%

Fraternities: 50%

Sororities: 30%

Number of Applicants: 2,021

Percent Accepted: 85%

Percent Accepted who enroll: 30%

Entering: 515

Transfers: NA

Application Deadline: rolling

Mean SAT: 593 V, 619 M

Middle 50% SAT range: 530–640 V, 530–660 M

Middle 50% ACT range: NA

Mean ACT: 26

3 Most popular majors: zoology, psychology, economics/management

Retention: 81%

Graduation rate: 58%

Library: 490,000 volumes

Tuition and Fees: $20,940 in; $20,940 out

Room and Board: $6,560

On-campus housing: 99%

Financial aid, first-year: 73%

Just fifteen minutes outside of Columbus, Ohio, is the small town of Delaware, which is home to the even smaller Ohio Wesleyan University. With a population of almost two thousand people, Ohio Wesleyan creates a supportive and personal environment. As one student said, "I feel like I know all of campus, if not by name, by face." These feelings of comfort and community extend into all realms of campus life.

Where Everybody Knows Your Name

Academics at OWU are highly praised by students who love their small classes and caring professors. As one sophomore put

it, the professors are "obviously here because they want to be here." Students applaud that professors know them by their first names, give out home phone numbers, entertain them at picnics or dinners, and just generally "work with you to make sure you get what you want out of a class." This creates an atmosphere where students feel supported by their professors.

The university, as a whole, is reportedly committed to helping students excel. For example, the Writing Resources Center is open Monday through Friday with the purpose of helping all students become "more confident, effective writers." One undergrad says, "The step-by-step help I received at the Writing Resource Center improved my writing dramatically." Another mentioned that while "They won't write the paper for you, they will help with any stage of the writing process." This is only one of the many academic support systems that OWU provides for its students. However, students do note that they do have problems with the administration when it comes to "implementing and supporting [other] student services."

Academically, OWU is a liberal arts college that exposes its students to a wide range of academic disciplines. To ensure a well-rounded education, the college requires Freshman English (or the equivalent in the form of standardized test scores), two semesters of a foreign language (or suitable proficiency test scores), one course in fine arts, three in the social sciences, three in the natural sciences, three in the humanities, plus at least 15 "above-110 classes." Also required are three writing-intensive courses and a course that deals with non-European culture. While students have mixed views on these requirements, as one particular student complained about the language requirement, most feel that it directs rather than limits their course schedule. They find that there are enough courses available to make it easy to find a class that you are interested in that also fulfills a requirement. While most majors are considered difficult, students cited the sciences as having the most difficult majors, and sociology as one of the easiest majors. Most students say it is easier to be admitted to Ohio Wesleyan than to stay there. As one junior put it, "I lose friends every year who just can't make the grade."

Let's Go . . .
Battling Bishops!!!

Yes it's true. The Battling Bishop was featured as one of the worst college mascots nation in *Time* magazine. However, this doesn't stop the students of OWU from competing and winning in many athletic activities. While it is said that the spirit is especially high for lacrosse and men's soccer, which has won the NCAA Division III championship in nine of the last fifteen years, no sport is without support. That also goes for club and intramural competition, as the university embraces the idea that "there's something for everyone at OWU."

And for those of us who lack certain hand-eye or foot-eye coordination, OWU has a multitude of other activities ranging from academic honor societies to service clubs to the See America Club. Student actors are able to participate through the strong theater program in numerous productions throughout the year. For the writers of the university, there is both a school newspaper, the *Transcript*, and a campus literary magazine, the *Owl*. Among the larger community service activities are the efforts of the Delaware Initiative and Columbus Initiative.

Chow and Chambers

Students at OWU describe the food as "not bad" and "edible." Students can use their meal card at any cafeteria, dining hall, and Thompson's, an on-campus grocery store that has convenience items and the all-important ice cream. Students generally eat at one of the dorm dining halls or the Campus Center, which during weekday lunchtime is reportedly extremely packed.

Students have a wide variety of options regarding their housing, including an all-female dorm (Hayes Hall), coed dorms, and Welch, which prohibits loud noise and alcohol and requires a 3.0 GPA for admittance. While Stuyvesant and Smith are named as two of the best coed dorms, students say that everyone regards their one dorm as the best, and Stuy and Smith just happen to house more students. In addition, 50 percent of men and 30 percent of women are involved in the Greek system and choose to live in their respective houses after freshman year.

The campus itself is described as having a "New Englandish" appeal with a variety of limestone, old stone, and brick buildings. It also encompasses over 200 acres of "lush landscaping and tree-lined walkways." Many of the older academic buildings' designs give hints of prior purposes. One undergraduate goes as far as to say, "Almost every building here was once something else," such as a hotel or Methodist church.

Finding a Niche

As most OWU students study hard on the weekdays, they feel proud in their ability to party come the weekend. A typical weekend schedule has been described as "Friday, party; Saturday, sleep late, maybe take in a sporting event, then party; Sunday, work." Students believe that they use the same intense focus for academics during the week as for partying on weekends. Students also like to designate Wednesday as a party night, in order to break up the workweek. However, while it may seem that drinking is prevalent on party nights, non-drinkers will not feel uncomfortable at OWU as long as they can be comfortable being around other people who do drink. Drugs, on the other hand, are not "big in the frats," as one student said, but can be found for those who are interested.

> **"It is because of the students and our social lives that Ohio Wesleyan is a school worth attending."**

While many students choose to go to the "Hill," where fraternity houses are, on weekends, there exist many alternative campus hangouts. Popular amongst the student population, the Grub Pub entertains with comedians and musical groups. And for still more comic relief, one can do no better than turning to the Battling Bishops for finely tuned improv skills. Still, there are also frequent film screenings in the Philips Auditorium as well as the Coffee House. Students also report that hanging out in the dorm rooms is a common occurrence. In addition, off-campus housing has recently become the site of many weekend parties.

Yet, while there are a multitude of options, some students are dismayed by the lack social life "because you are constantly seeing the same people." But this can also be helpful as it helps incoming students find their niche: Wherever you go, you will recognize a friendly face. The quaint town of Delaware also adds to the comfort and intimacy of the student body. It provides some small shops and restaurants, and if students want big city excitement, they need only travel as far as Columbus.

It Just Makes You All Warm and Fuzzy Inside

Students describe their peers as open-minded and accepting of both homosexual and interracial couples. While some students complain about the lack of diversity, one student said that the diversity is "good, but that the international students tend to be cliquey with one another." In fact, despite the name Ohio Wesleyan, over half the population comes from out of state. The school has even established scholarships for students from different geographical backgrounds within the United States. Although Ohio Wesleyan shares the many benefits of small schools, it does have some drawbacks. As one student noted, "Everyone you run around with socially will know lots about you," so breaking out of constricting cliques can be difficult.

However, most students attend Ohio Wesleyan because they believe that the positive aspects of a small college far outweigh the negatives. Overall, students seem to credit themselves and their peers as the reason for attending the university. One student said, "It is because of the students and our social lives that Ohio Wesleyan is a school worth attending." The students at OWU are friendly, open-minded, hardworking, and fun people who want to experience their lives to the fullest. They work hard and party hard. Moreover, they value that the same peers, who they can carry on a thoughtful discussion with during the academic week, are the same people that they can dance the night away with on the weekends.
—*Marissa Wagner*

FYI
The three best things about Ohio Wesleyan are "incredible and caring people, a unified campus, and the ability to participate in any organization."
The three worst things about Ohio Wesleyan are "no low-fat and low-sodium foods, the isolation, and the Housing Department."

The three things that every student should do before graduating from Ohio Wesleyan are "to take a semester abroad, be in the Delta Zeta Jello Tug-O-War, and live in a SLU (small living unit)."

One thing I would like to have known before coming here is "the Language requirement and the isolation."

University of Cincinnati

Address: PO Box 210063; Cincinnati, OH 45221-0091
Phone: 513-556-1100
E-mail address: admissions@uc.edu
Web site URL: www.uc.edu
Location: urban
Founded: 1819
Private or Public: public
Religious affiliation: none
Undergraduate enrollment: 20,656
Total enrollment: NA
Percent Male / Female: 52% / 48%
Percent Minority: 18.0%

Percent African-American: 14.0%
Percent Hispanic: 1.0%
Percent Asian: 3.0%
Percent in-state / out-of-state: 94% / 6%
Percent Pub HS: NA
Fraternities: 23%
Sororities: 14%
Number of Applicants: 10,704
Percent Accepted: 86%
Percent Accepted who enroll: 29%
Entering: 3,068
Transfers: NA
Application Deadline: 31 Jul
Mean SAT: 548 V, 556 M

Middle 50% SAT range: 480–600 V, 480–620 M
Middle 50% ACT range: 20–26
Mean ACT: 23
3 Most popular majors: communication arts, psychology, accounting
Retention: 70%
Graduation rate: 42% (within 5 years)
Library: 1.8 million volumes
Tuition and Fees: $4,026 in; $11,532 out
Room and Board: $5,958
On-campus housing: 29%
Financial aid, first-year: 58%

With a "very compact" campus, a majority of students living off campus, an enormous spectrum of interests, and "good school spirit at the Bearcats games," the University of Cincinnati contains many elements that combine to form the uniquely "urban but fairly quiet" atmosphere of the school.

The Social Spectrum

The wide variety that characterizes almost every aspect of the university begins with the social options facing each student at UC. On one hand, the "Greek societies lead the party scene," especially at the beginning of each quarter, when frats throw large open parties. Other popular fraternity events include the Sigma Alpha Epsilon Wedding Party, where everyone dresses in secondhand wedding clothes, and the infamous Paddy Murphy Week, which one student explained as an annual "weeklong party in honor of the SAE brother, Paddy Murphy, who tried to rid the world of alcohol during Prohibition, by drinking as much as he could, and died in the process." Aside from these large parties thrown by the Greek societies, many students shy away from the scene, saying that "there is so much else to do, I would never waste my time at a frat house" and insisting that SAE in fact stands for "Same Assholes Everywhere."

Despite some apparent tensions between social groups, UC students seem to "always unite at the Bearcats games." The men's basketball team is popular both with students and locals, especially around the time of year near the Crosstown Shootout with rival Xavier University. "You can wait in line for five days to get tickets," one student claimed. For the nonvarsity athletes, UC offers club and intramural teams, all with "excellent facilities, but better ones for the varsity teams," as well as workout rooms, indoor tracks, and other fitness facilities. Each dorm also contains a weight room.

There is extensive construction and renovations occurring on campus. The expanded and renovated 93.2 million dollar CCM Village for the Conservatory of Music has just been completed as well as the Vontz Center for Molecular Studies. In fact University of Cincinnati was designated "as one of the 20 'most distinguished campuses' in Europe and America" in 1999.

If You're Afraid of Heights, Um . . .

The five dormitories—two coed, one all-female, and two all-male—are all eleven-to-twelve-story skyscrapers. Each dorm contains a kitchenette and lounge per floor, as well as a main-lobby lounge, laundry facilities, a computer room, meeting rooms, and a weight room. Sawyer, "the best dorm on campus," goes to lucky upperclassmen who get a kitchen, bathroom, and common room in each suite. Students sound fairly happy with the living space, but they tend to complain about the height of the buildings and "the largest cockroach in the world," rumored to live in Daniels. On-campus living could get even better, students said, because "they plan to cover the campus with turf . . . someday we might actually have grass." The administration has taken action to increase the amount of "open space," by razing several building and replacing them with parks. "It's nice to look out the window and see grass instead of a big ugly building," one student said.

> Despite definite positive reviews about the co-op program, some students have criticized the academics at UC for being "frustratingly simple at lower levels."

The small percentage of on-campus residents "get pretty tight but don't explore the city as much as the off-campus livers," said one student. A common complaint is that "Cincinnati requires a car for college life." Most students wander beyond the realm of the university to frequent off-campus bars and coffeehouses, in the nearby trendy Clifton area, and the more culture-hungry students find intrigue at various theaters, concerts, symphonies, films, and art shows that the city has to offer. "Cincinnati's not so bad," claimed a second-year student from outside Ohio. "If you look hard enough, you can find stuff here, it's just a really different atmosphere from, say, New York—much smaller scale." Students inclined to disagree tend to head up to other nearby colleges, such as Ohio State or Miami, when things at UC slow down.

Academics: Divided Opinions

Students must enroll in one of the academic schools—the School of Business, School of Engineering, Cincinnati Conservatory of Music (CCM), College of Arts and Sciences, or College of Design, Art, Architecture, and Planning (DAAP). Overall, students seem happy about academic options, facilities, and instruction. "The best part is that we only have one real requirement: a year of freshman English," one undergrad said. Students who join the co-op program rave about the experience. The program provides for a work-study job that includes paid internships with local businesses, "invaluable hands-on" experience, and many future contacts. Despite definite positive reviews about the co-op program, some students have criticized the academics at UC for being "frustratingly simple at lower levels." "Registration is the worst," said one student. "I never get the classes I want." Now, students can register online, "which makes the process a lot easier." Another student explained that "if you want good classes, you have to fight for them, but it's not that hard. I think whether you get professors or TAs, though, kind of depends on what department you're in and how lucky you are."

Overall, students agree that UC is a big enough school that "you can find a little of everything." Students say the *News Record*, a triweekly newspaper, has good stories. Another place where students often reach a consensus involves the food: "It sucks." "It's disgusting." "Don't do it, man." But again, there are always a few students who insist that "it's edible."

In a school large enough for a good amount of diversity, "the personality of this school seems really schizophrenic at times, but that's just because there are so many different aspects to everything." If you are looking for it somewhere, it's probably somewhere at UC.—*Lisa Barrett and Staff*

FYI

The three best things about UC are "the co-op program, the honors program, and diversity."

The three worst things about UC are "the food, registration, and the intro classes."

The three things that every student should do before graduating from UC are "eat out, um, eat out, and eat out again."

One thing I'd like to have known before coming here is that "you are really on your own because it is such a big school."

Wittenberg University

Address: P. O. Box 720, Springfield, OH 45501
Phone: 800-677-7558
E-mail address: admission@Wittenberg.edu
Web site URL: www.wittenberg.edu
Location: small city
Founded: 1845
Private or Public: private
Religious affiliation: ELCA-Lutheran
Undergraduate enrollment: 2,028
Total enrollment: 2,105
Percent Male / Female: 45%/55%
Percent Minority: 10.0%

Percent African-American: 6.0%
Percent Hispanic: 1.0%
Percent Asian: 2.0%
Percent in-state / out-of-state: 55%/45%
Percent Pub HS: 75%
Fraternities: 15%
Sororities: 30%
Number of Applicants: 2,425
Percent Accepted: 89%
Percent Accepted who enroll: 28%
Entering: 620
Transfers: 35
Application Deadline: NA
Mean SAT: 560 V, 565 M

Middle 50% SAT range: 545–620 V, 555–640 M
Middle 50% ACT range: 24–28
Mean ACT: 25
3 Most popular majors: business, biology, education
Retention: 85%
Graduation rate: 71%
Library: 340,000 volumes
Tuition and Fees: $21,679 in; NA out
Room and Board: $5,400
On-campus housing: 98%
Financial aid, first-year: 75%

At Wittenberg University, the freedoms of a liberal arts education are combined with a conservative background based in Wittenberg's Evangelical Lutheran Church affiliation, a mix that students at Wittenberg find "supportive" and "just plain perfect."

Wittenberg's small student population is an asset in the eyes of most students. "Our size really makes it easy to get to know people. In fact, you can't escape it. From my first day on campus people I didn't know were saying hi to me," one student said. Other students were slightly less enthusiastic about the fact that their classmates knew all the details of those inevitable freshman-year mistakes. As one student put it, "Word travels fast, real fast."

Wittenberg Wisdom

Deadlines approach even more quickly. "We aren't some Ivy League, but we're no slackers either. I'd say we're as East Coast, academically, as an Ohio university can get." Wittenberg grants scholarships based on academic merit, but not athletic ability. Students whose grades fall below

2.3 are given a semester to repair their grades before the administration suspends them.

Some students describe the course offerings at Wittenberg as "run of the mill," but the individual attention students receive is "truly above average." "I've never had a teaching assistant teach any of my classes," said one student, "and I've found my professors extremely approachable when it comes to scheduling appointments." Class sizes cater to this same idea, with a class of 40 students occurring "rarely, even then only in the pre-med and intro science classes." Most classes enroll fewer than 20 students.

Pre-laws, Pre-meds, Prerequisites

Popular departments at Wittenberg include biology, geology, and psychology, with numerous pre-med and pre-law students as well. The Wittenberg education is founded on prerequisites in each of seven areas: Integrated Learning; Natural World; Social\Institutions; the Fine, Performing, and Literary Arts; Religious and Philosophical Inquiry; Western Historical Perspectives; and Non-Western Cultures. Students also have to fulfill requirements in the two co-curricular areas of physical activity (which can be fulfilled through either intercollegiate athletics or various health and fitness courses) and community service, which requires sophomores to complete 30 hours of community service over the course of one term.

The campus facilities vary from "newly renovated and modern" to "built in the sixties and seventies and definitely showing it." Myers Hall, the original Wittenberg building of 1846, still stands and today houses Wittenberg's honor students. Dorms are coed, but floors are single-sex, and students can visit the opposite-sex floors only until 12:30 A.M. Students are required to live on campus for the first two years, after which time all but a few move off campus. Students complain that the dorms are surrounded by low income housing, making the off campus housing a more attractive option.

BYOB

Fraternity and sorority members, who make up approximately one-third of the campus population, live off campus in one of Wittenberg's 11 Greek houses (6 sororities and 5 fraternities), where much of the school's nightlife is centered. Alcohol is allowed only in the rooms of students 21 and over, and fraternity parties, instead of providing kegs, are BYOB. Keg parties can be found at private student houses off campus and out of the jurisdiction of university policy. The Ringside Cafe, which has a weekly college night, is a popular student hangout and many students say they drink, on average, four times per week. The town of Springfield "kinda sucks," one candid student remarked, because "we are the fast-food mecca of America." Students who want to find some serious grub often have to hunt long and hard before they find a cool hangout like Springfield's Mike and Rosey's Restaurant.

The student union, however, with its Marriott-catered food and flexible meal plans, is a popular hangout for the social studier and hungry student. The second floor of the union has a la carte food service open until 1 A.M., as well as a bar.

Students are heavily involved in a wide range of extracurriculars. Intercollegiate sports, especially against rivals Denison, Ohio Wesleyan, and Oberlin, are popular draws, as are various intramurals, rock climbing, spelunking, and waterskiing on the nearby Springfield reservoir. To get away from campus, students often visit the "neat little hippie town" of Yellow Springs, a 15-minute drive from campus. When students want to relax on campus they head to the Hollow, a grassy vale that is filled with sledders throughout the winter. Warm weather invites sunbathing, picnicking, and Frisbee-tossing to the Hollow.

> **"From my first day on campus people I didn't know were saying hi to me."**

When spring approaches, the Hollow is also home to a weekend of music, drinking, and general stress relief called Wittstock. Past Wittstock performers have included Hootie and the Blowfish and

10,000 Maniacs, while some students "just go for the carnival aspect of it."

Recent changes to campus life have been minimal. Wittenberg switched from a trimester to semester system three years ago, and the new university president, Baird Tipson, "runs things pretty smoothly," one student said. Perhaps the homogeneity of the university is responsible for the smooth aspect of campus life. The population is predominantly Caucasian, and alternative lifestyles, such as homosexuality, are "kept on the down low . . . we don't discuss it much, and perhaps it's better that way."

Regardless of general student attitudes toward minority groups, undergrads described the atmosphere as "supportive," "intensely friendly," even "homey." Just one warning before you decide to make "Sprinklefield" your home away from home: "be prepared for the wet."—*Vladimir Cole and Staff*

FYI

The three best things about attending Wittenberg are "small class size accompanied by personal attention by professors, friendly and aesthetically pleasing campus, and off-campus housing for juniors and seniors in the immediate campus area."

The three worst things about attending Wittenberg are "the new parking lot that eliminated the Frisbee golf fields, some residence halls outdated and inadequate parking, and no paper towels in the bathrooms."

The three things that every student should do before graduating from Wittenberg are "go abroad, visit the Career Placement and Development Office, and take advantage of exit meetings."

One thing I'd like to have known before coming here is "that tuition increases 4% every year."

Oklahoma

Although outsiders tend to characterize Oklahoma State as simply an agricultural university, one student pointed out that "the Ag school is actually the fourth smallest on campus." Oklahoma State has shed its "hick" image and now boasts top-rated undergraduate business and engineering programs. In fact, *Business Week* has recently ranked the accounting program among the top 15 in the United States.

A Building Program

Not surprisingly, the administration has worked to supplement OSU's rising academic reputation with first-rate campus facilities. Willard Hall, previously an undergraduate dorm, underwent extensive renovations and now houses the education department. Since the 1997–98 school year, the new $17.3 million Food Technology Center has been in use, and in 1998 of-ficials completed the construction of a $27.5 million engineering lab. Only a few years ago, the university also celebrated the opening of an advanced telecommunications building, which NASA uses to broadcast educational programs to high schools across the country.

Open Doors, Open Arms

Students are generally satisfied with the faculty at OSU. "Our professors don't just have office hours," one junior said. "They pretty much have an open-door policy where we can go in anytime." The most significant praise, however, went to OSU president James Halligan and his administration for establishing themselves as "the most student-oriented people on campus, even more so than the professors." A number of new programs, focusing specifically on undergraduates, have improved the quality of life at OSU. For example, the administration recently increased the number of senior professors that teach introductory courses and reduced the university's traditional reliance upon graduate TAs.

OSU rewards its most gifted students by offering a strong honors program. Students have the option to enroll in either the general honors program or an honors program in their particular major. All enjoy similar privileges: special housing in Parker Honors Hall, use of a special honors study lounge and computer lab located on the fifth floor of the Edmon Low Library, priority enrollment for all courses (even before graduating seniors), and extended library checkout privileges equivalent to those of graduate students. Non-honors students report that quality attention is also paid to their needs as well–most classes enroll only about 20 to 40 students, although introductory lecture courses such as chemistry attract up to 300 undergrads. The university also sponsors study-abroad programs and internship opportunities with OSU alumni.

Academic requirements vary within each major, but all students must take introductory courses in political science, American government, English, and American history. Despite the strong focus on academic excellence at OSU, students say the wine-tasting class or "any leisure and health elective" can provide a brief respite from the rigors of academic life.

Home, Sweet Home

The frosh-dominated Kerr-Drummon dorm is said to be the most popular on campus. In addition to the special honors housing, OSU also provides a special athletic dorm, Bennett Hall, with modern amenities to appease its athletes, who must live on campus all four years at OSU. Interested students can sign up to live on special foreign language or "major" floors. Each college cafeteria also serves its own special theme food; student favorites include the Italian, Mexican, and bakery items. Strict rules concerning curfews and alcohol, however, have motivated many upperclassmen to move off campus after their mandatory freshman year on campus.

Wide World of Sports

Many students participate in intramural sports at OSU. "We have traditional sports, like football and soccer, but we also have things like Frisbee or Ping-Pong," one student said. Students can also become involved in various student government and planning committees designed to enhance the quality of academic and social life on campus. The Student Activities Board recently sponsored visits from speakers as varied as former First Lady Barbara Bush and sex therapist Dr. Ruth Westheimer.

The OSU homecoming festivities, said to be the third largest in the nation, represent the most spirited campus-wide event. Fraternities and sororities spend over a month prior to the big weekend "completely covering their houses with decorations" in a style usually reserved for parade floats. The Harvest Carnival is also an integral part of Homecoming, and several groups sponsor entertainment activities or food booths for the event.

School spirit for OSU athletics increased substantially two years ago when the men's basketball team reached the Final Four of the NCAA championship tournament. This recent boost to the athletic program only added to prior OSU victories, including the Cowboy football team's success against the University of Oklahoma Sooners for the first time in 19 years during the fall 1995 season. The women's basketball, men's baseball, and wrestling teams are reportedly successful as well. Pistol Pete, the OSU mascot, and other fans are also celebrating the renovation of Gallagher Iba Arena (formerly notorious for its limited seating capacity during basketball season), which will now accommodate 6,000 additional fans.

The focus on physical fitness extends beyond the athletic teams, however, to include all members of the OSU community. The Wellness Center is available to those who wish to follow a holistic approach to self-improvement by addressing emotional, spiritual, and physical health. For old-fashioned, heart-pumping exercise, the Colvin Center has basketball and racquetball courts, a rock climbing wall, aerobics classes, a swimming pool, weight-lifting equipment, and other fitness outlets for both the serious athlete and occasional health-minded undergraduate.

"Not Greek or Geek"

No single group dominates the campus social scene. Fraternities and sororities are popular, but students agree that the campus attitude is "not a 'Greek or geek' thing at all." Parties sponsored by Greeks are open only to members and their invited guests. Students looking for a party scene leave the dry OSU campus for Tumbleweeds, a country-western dance bar, or Eskimo Joe's, a combination bar and restaurant. Some traditional party events during the year include the campus-wide festivities over the OSU–Oklahoma University football game weekend and the more clandestine "Field of Dreams," a bash held out in the Oklahoma countryside. Alcohol is "socially accepted" as a large part of the OSU party scene, but students contend that "no one ever brags about or offers drugs and they are definitely not done in public, even at parties." For those seeking other weekend opportunities, Tulsa and Oklahoma City are just a little over an hour from the OSU campus.

Who Are We?

Students consider their classmates fairly "open-minded, considering their background," one undergrad said. Most students are white, come from in-state rural areas, and are largely conservative. The percentage of minority students is low, but these students reportedly receive the respect of other undergrads and attention from administrators hoping to increase diversity on campus. Generally, undergrads are "laid-back, not artistically expressive, and do not dress up for class." Other than

local university issues, students are described as apathetic when it comes to political activity. One senior noted how a Stillwater city proposal to completely ban open alcohol containers or alcohol consumption on the streets, even for those over 21, passed because of poor student turnout at the city polls.

This redbrick, Georgian-style campus is in the midst of the Stillwater community and has no significant problems with security or safety. OSU reportedly ranks as the safest school in the Big 12 conference. Nevertheless, well-lit, emergency phones dot the campus, and security officers patrol the area 24 hours a day. When asked about the surrounding community, one student said, "The population of Stillwater is small, so you have that hometown atmosphere, though we're still big enough for a Super Wal-Mart."

> The OSU homecoming festivities, said to be the third largest in the nation, represent the most spirited campus-wide event.

Academics and extracurriculars provide challenging opportunities without stifling the relaxed attitude of the majority of students. Undoubtedly, the small-town, country atmosphere attracts a number of students to OSU. As one student said, "Anyone interested in the university should visit the campus. We don't put on a show for visitors—all the students and staff members are friendly every day. And that just makes all the difference in the world."—*Kurtland Ma and Staff*

FYI
The three best things about attending OSU are "the friendly attitude on campus, the student-focused administration, and the Greek scene."
The three worst things about attending OSU are "living in Stillwater, sometimes tough academics, and a conservative environment."
The three things that every student should do before graduating from OSU are "participate in Homecoming, go to Tumbleweeds, and watch the Sooners."
One thing I'd like to have known before coming here is "how much school spirit there is."

Oral Roberts University

Address: 7777 South Lewis Avenue, Tulsa, OK 74171
Phone: 918-495-6518
E-mail address: admissions@oru.edu
Web site URL: www.oru.edu
Location: suburban
Founded: 1963
Private or Public: private
Religious affiliation: Christian (nondenominational)
Undergraduate enrollment: 2,788
Total enrollment: 3,682
Percent Male/Female: 42%/58%
Percent Minority: 28.0%

Percent African-American: 21.0%
Percent Hispanic: 4.0%
Percent Asian: 2.0%
Percent in-state/out-of-state: 26%/74%
Percent Pub HS: NA
Fraternities: 0%
Sororities: 0%
Number of Applicants: 1,734
Percent Accepted: 63%
Percent Accepted who enroll: 68%
Entering: 696
Transfers: 442
Application Deadline: rolling
Mean SAT: 538 V, 523 M

Middle 50% SAT range: NA
Middle 50% ACT range: NA
Mean ACT: 23
3 Most popular majors: elementary teacher education, telecommunications, business/accounting
Retention: 80%
Graduation rate: 44.0%
Library: 750,000 volumes
Tuition and Fees: $10,160 in; NA out
Room and Board: $4,728
On-campus housing: 70%
Financial aid, first-year: NA

Glistening in gold and silver, the Oral Roberts University Prayer Tower rises 250 feet toward heaven, exemplifying the school's commitment to religious excellence and perseverance. People worship inside the tower 24 hours a day, 365 days a year, and a prayer line receives telephone calls from across the nation. From the tower's observation deck, visitors behold a panorama encompassing all of ORU's other architectural wonders, including the 4,500-seat Christ Chapel and a 50-foot sculpture of praying hands.

Religious Rules

In 1963, Oral Roberts claimed to receive a vision from God calling for a university to be built in Tulsa. Roberts promptly obeyed and founded Oral Roberts University. Not surprisingly, religion influences student life, both in and out of the classroom. The university holds mandatory chapel services twice a week for all students. The campus dress code stipulates, with exceptions for Fridays and Saturdays, shirts and ties for males, and modest skirts for females. (In recent years, however, the code has relaxed to allow casual but appropriate attire for both sexes after 4 P.M.) When students apply, they must sign a statement agreeing to follow an honor code that forbids drinking, smoking, cheating, and premarital sex. All female students have a midnight curfew, and male students must observe the same curfew for their first two years.

ORU requires students who are not living with their families to live on campus, but few students see this requirement as a burden because the dorms provide pleasant accommodations. Extensive renovations of the dorms are currently under way, and a food court including fast-food restaurants is also planned. Students live in single-sex wings that serve as social substitutes for sororities and fraternities. Although dancing remains forbidden on campus, each wing hosts clambakes and other events. Most students who choose to attend ORU do not mind the rules; in fact, one undergrad explained that "living a Christian life here has made me stronger, and, frankly, I wouldn't want to live amidst the grease of secular life."

Academic Resources

Academically, many students gain communications experience by working for ORU's television station or for the national Abundant Life Prayer Group. The Learning Resource Center is the primary academic facility on campus, with 4.5

acres of libraries, classrooms, and labs. The Center, like all the dorm rooms, is hard-wired with a closed-circuit TV system so students can watch different educational programs as well as 26 channels offered on cable. The administration blocks out some channels, such as MTV, because they are deemed inconsistent with ORU's religious spirit. Sermons are also occasionally shown, which give the observer a taste of what one student called ORU's specialty—"Charismatic Christianity." Many students report that the theology program is excellent, despite one undergrad's complaint that "there's not much serious questioning or confrontation." In recent years, the education department also has earned praise from students. The business school, located in a building that one observer described as "futuristic in a sixties sense," is popular because it instructs young capitalists on how to combine morality and economics.

In pursuit of excellence in mind, body, and spirit, ORU requires all students to participate in sports. Many play intramurals, and attendance at varsity games is high. Last year, in an effort to invigorate the sports program, ORU changed the name of its teams from the Titans to the Golden Eagles. All ORU teams play in Division I, and the basketball and golf teams usually bring the most victories. The Tulsa community uses ORU's basketball arena, the Maybee Center, for everything from local sports to graduations and concerts. Major performers such as Garth Brooks have performed there in recent years.

Students generally agree that ORU has changed for the better. Four years ago, the 75-year-old Oral Roberts stepped down as president of the university and passed the post on to his son, Richard Roberts. Students describe the younger Roberts as highly approachable and popular on campus. Enrollment continues to increase, and if you are seeking a spiritual, as well as an academic, collegiate experience, you may be one of the growing number of applicants considering Oral Roberts University.—*Brian Abaluck and Staff*

> **In pursuit of excellence in mind, body, and spirit, ORU requires all students to participate in sports.**

FYI
The three best things about attending ORU are "the theology program, being a part of a group of people with a shared value system, and having to participate in the sports program."
The three worst things about attending ORU are "the censorship of television channels like MTV, mandatory chapel services, and the lack of alternative extracurricular opportunities."
The three things that every student should do before graduating from ORU are "play intramurals, go to prayer group regularly, and take advantage of the city of Tulsa."
One thing I'd like to have known before coming here is "just how little people challenge their own religious beliefs."

University of Oklahoma

Address: 1000 Asp Ave, Norman, OK 73019
Phone: 800-522-0772
E-mail address: ou-pss@ou.edu
Web site URL: www.ou.edu
Location: small city
Founded: 1890
Private or Public: public
Religious affiliation: none
Undergraduate enrollment: 17,264
Total enrollment: 21,339
Percent Male/Female: 52%/48%
Percent Minority: 24.4%
Percent African-American: 7.2%

Percent Hispanic: 5.7%
Percent Asian: 3.9%
Percent in-state/out-of-state: NA
Percent Pub HS: NA
Fraternities: 19%
Sororities: 22%
Number of Applicants: 6,384
Percent Accepted: 89%
Percent Accepted who enroll: 64%
Entering: 3,298
Transfers: 1,485
Application Deadline: 15 Jul
Mean SAT: NA
Middle 50% SAT range: NA

Middle 50% ACT range: 21–27
Mean ACT: 24.5
3 Most popular majors: management & information systems, psychology, journalism
Retention: 80.3%
Graduation rate: 48.2%
Library: 4,107,132 volumes
Tuition and Fees: $2,456 in; $6,791 out
Room and Board: $4,384
On-campus housing: 80%
Financial aid, first-year: 75%

Y ou are driving in your car with five of your best, rowdiest buddies squished into the backseat. The radio is blasting country-western music as you race along I-35 at breakneck speed. Once you arrive in Dallas, the party has just begun as you, along with over 100,000 other fans, pile into the Cotton Bowl for some good ole-fashioned Sooner Tradition. The weekend rounds out with parties destined to turn Dallas, Texas, into the party town it was meant to be, and you leave with the knowledge that the return trip is just another year away.

Sound like a description from a college admissions brochure? Not likely, since the true life of the University of Oklahoma student reaches beyond academics and university regulations and into a strong social realm. Social life is "what makes OU, OU," as one student said, and football is often the main event. The famous OU-Texas game is the high point of the season—the biggest game against the biggest rival, where the majority of Sooner fans attend and the rest watch on television as they party at home. "Our team right now isn't the best we have ever had, but we still sell the stadium out every weekend," one senior noted, and every student we spoke with named football games as one of the best weekend activities.

A New Academic Agenda

OU president David Boren has been particularly working to enhance the quality of academic instruction and the state of classroom facilities. In fact, this former senator teaches "one of the best classes at OU," a university-required course on American government in which Boren draws from his own political career. Another popular professor, "Dr. Indestructo," excites students in his Introductory Physics class by drinking liquid nitrogen, exploding objects, and "often even endangering his own well-being." Other popular majors include business, political science, and English, which draw rave reviews from many students. Humanities and social sciences have been improving, and the university launched an international and area studies program during the 1997–98 school year. As one senior noted, "These frosh are really lucky to be able to enjoy the benefits of academic improvements for the next couple of years."

President Boren has also been working to attract a growing number of National

Merit Scholars to the university. These scholars have a great deal that includes full tuition, early enrollment, smaller classes, and annual recognition at the halftime of a football game, when they line up from end zone to end zone. These honors students are also allowed to register for classes before the rest of the student body.

OU classroom facilities are praised for their "good sound systems and modern computer projection systems," indispensable in large lecture courses in a variety of areas including the sciences and art history. Students also take advantage of the Sam Noble Museum of Natural History, which displays artifacts of Oklahoma and the Midwest.

Happenings on Campus

Fraternities and sororities dominate social life at OU. Independent students can gain access to some Greek parties with friends who are members. Many view Greek life as "a great way to meet lots of people," but others criticize the Greek system as "exclusive." Drinking is common; one student said, "If you come here, you'd better bring a good liver." However, many students prefer nights of bowling or movies to drinking.

Though the administration aspires to attract minorities, OU students often consider themselves homogeneous. One student from the Midwest called Oklahoma "the Buckle of the Bible Belt" and noted the powerful Christian presence on campus. Another student lamented, "I've been looking for a drug scene all year but haven't found one."

Intramurals are the major extracurricular activities at OU. A wide range of sports are available ranging from the traditional football, basketball, softball, and baseball to the ever-interesting ooze-ball (a form of volleyball played on a muddy court hosed down by the Norman Fire Department) and "pickleball" (coed touch football).

The Sooner Tradition

The Sooner Tradition embodies a culture of strong school spirit and outstanding varsity athletics. Those who question the importance of football need only look to the 75,000-seat Memorial Stadium, home of Sooner football, located at the dead center of campus. Though the football program has struggled since the departure of shoot-from-the-hip coach Barry Switzer, outstanding facilities and strong alumni economic support "should one day restore glory" to Sooner football tradition. Students have also proven themselves to be more than fair-weather sports by making football games sell-outs.

The OU Environment

Students express overall satisfaction with the OU campus. OU architecture is a mix of stone Gothic and colonial redbrick, which one student described as "Gothic Cherokee." The addition of new sidewalks and gardens, "always well kept," have also bettered the campus in recent years. Dorms are newly renovated and modern in design. Unfortunately, to the dismay of many students, "the sculpture of a blue Mustang horse with freakish, red-glowing eyes" mars campus aesthetics. Passing by this large statue, students wonder why the "eerie and idiosyncratic" horse is present.

The city of Norman, located 20 minutes from Oklahoma City, surrounds the university and is "obviously geared toward OU students." McDonald's, Taco Bell, the Olive Garden, Don Pablo's, and a handful of coffeehouses thrive around the university. Twenty-four-hour restaurants such as Denny's and the Kettle are popular places for social studying.

On-Campus Dining Options

The only cafeteria open to all students at the University of Oklahoma is the Couch Cafeteria, which, according to one student, "looks exactly like an airline terminal—complete with flags." Students find the food mediocre, though varied. Couch offers Sooner Sports Grill's hamburgers and wings and make-your-own stir-fry as well as an assortment of daily specials. The meal plan includes "Dining Sense," which gives students a debit card to purchase food from surrounding restaurants and convenience stores.

First Come, First Served

Freshmen who choose not to live at home must live on campus. The two most desirable dorms, Walker Tower and Adams, are arranged in suites of two double bedrooms joined by a bathroom and are slightly larger than most other dorm rooms. Other residence halls have singles with communal bathrooms at each end of the hall. Housing is assigned on a first come, first served basis, so those wishing to avoid the unpopular Cross Center with its "crumbling walls and bad plumbing" must make housing decisions quickly. Dorms are coed by floor freshman year and coed by suite in upperclass dorms. The university limits coed visitation in the freshman dorms; all visitors must be out of students' rooms by midnight on weeknights and 2:00 A.M. on weekends in order to avoid citations and fines. Freshman floors also have RAs, who serve not only as academic advisors, but as social organizers.

The Wilkinson Complex is a group of dorms offering large rooms and exclusive access to the Jefferson Cafeteria and is largely available to athletes and honors students. The recent $500,000 renovation has made the Jefferson Cafeteria an "excellent facility with really gourmet fare." The Jefferson Cafeteria also hosts the popular "Seafood and Steak Night" every Wednesday night. Scholars and athletes reportedly get along "remarkably well, largely because we both get special treatment here," said one sophomore.

Students define the University of Oklahoma in terms of tradition. The majority of students are from in state or the Midwest, and many of the current undergrads were preceded at OU by their parents. The Sooner Tradition creates a culture of massive school spirit and ensures exciting sporting events. Just try not to forget that this is the "friendly South" in the fourth quarter of a close OU-Texas game!
—*Brian Abaluck and Staff*

> Scholars and athletes reportedly get along "remarkably well, largely because we both get special treatment here," said one sophomore.

FYI

The three best things about attending OU are "the football games, the charm, and warm spring afternoons outside."

The three worst things about attending OU are "fraternities, sororities, and the people who populate them."

The three things that every student should do before graduating from OU are "go to the Texas-Oklahoma football game, play pickleball, date a cheerleader."

One thing I'd like to have known before coming here is "how tough the science classes would be."

The University of Tulsa

Address: 600 South College Avenue, Tulsa, OK 74104
Phone: 918-631-2307
E-mail address: admission@utulsa.edu
Web site URL: www.utulsa.edu
Location: urban
Founded: 1884
Private or Public: private
Religious affiliation: Presbyterian (USA)
Undergraduate enrollment: 2,920
Total enrollment: 4,236
Percent Male/Female: 48%/52%
Percent Minority: 21.0%

Percent African-American: 8.0%
Percent Hispanic: 3.0%
Percent Asian: 3.0%
Percent in-state/out-of-state: 77%/23%
Percent Pub HS: 85%
Fraternities: 12%
Sororities: 13%
Number of Applicants: 1,918
Percent Accepted: 80%
Percent Accepted who enroll: 39%
Entering: 597
Transfers: 612
Application Deadline: rolling
Mean SAT: 610 V, 605 M

Middle 50% SAT range: 550–680 V, 540–670 M
Middle 50% ACT range: 23–29
Mean ACT: 25
3 Most popular majors: finance, psychology, accounting
Retention: 75.0%
Graduation rate: 32.0%
Library: 800,000 volumes
Tuition and Fees: $13,400 in; NA out
Room and Board: $4,660
On-campus housing: 100%
Financial aid, first-year: 59%

People come to the University of Tulsa for the same reason they come to Tulsa itself: TU offers diversity, beauty, and opportunity in the heartland of America. TU's relatively high rate of acceptance does not mean the curriculum lacks vigor; in fact, students say the university offers a challenging, world-class education.

A Top Priority

TU's commitment to academic excellence reaches many programs. The College of Engineering and Applied Sciences is considered preeminent worldwide, particularly for its petroleum research and chemical engineering programs. The English department is recognized nationally as a center of James Joyce scholarship. The department publishes the *James Joyce Quarterly*, an academic journal with international circulation, and the McFarlin Library houses a special collection that features Joyce's writings along with 20th-century Anglo-Irish, American, and Native American literature.

Students consider the university's commitment to a strong academic program a top priority. The university curriculum, called the Tulsa Curriculum, provides a solid foundation in the liberal arts. The Tulsa Curriculum is divided into three parts: the core curriculum, the general curriculum, and the major area of concentration. The core curriculum focuses on reasoning, writing, math, and language courses. In order to fill the general curriculum requirements, students must take two courses in each of four blocks: Artistic Imagination, which includes literature and art courses; Social Inquiry, which studies the nature and behavior of the individual and group; Comparative and Historical Interpretation, which includes classes on religion, politics, economics, and culture; and Scientific Investigation, which consists of classes in the experimental and natural sciences.

Undergraduates note the strength of many of TU's departments. The School of Business is particularly impressive, with strong programs in marketing and communication. Additionally, with the current emphasis on computers and technology, TU's Management Information Systems (MIS) program is very popular among undergraduates. Students do say, however, that programs in music, theater and economics are lacking, and the TU Honors program also gets mixed reviews: some students find it rewarding, while others believe it needs improvement. All agree, however, that the small class size and personal attention given to students by professors makes Tulsa's academic program attractive. One senior says, "I have been here for four years and have never been taught by a teaching assistant and have never been in a class with more than 35 students."

All Work and No Play?

Of course, life at TU is not all work and no play. There are a number of activities in which to get involved and meet other people. The largest organization at TU, the Student Association, is responsible for coordinating various student activities and community service projects. Undergraduates also enjoy writing for TU's newspaper, *The Collegian*, or managing the student-run radio station, the Underground. Students also spend time in many of the different ethnic organizations on campus.

Perhaps the best way to meet other people at TU is through the Greek system. Fraternities and sororities host parties almost every weekend. While drinking is officially forbidden, enforcement is lenient and most would describe TU as a wet campus. By going Greek, freshmen have an easy way to go to great parties such as Snake-in-the-Grass and Pike Fest, meet a lot of new people quickly, and make many new friends. If the Greek scene is not for you, however, don't worry. There are plenty of other alternatives. When the Student Association is not sponsoring a dance or party, you can find them throughout the dorms. As one student puts it, "TU students love to have fun. Finding a party is never a problem." Also, it is quite common to hang out with friends at JR's or at the Hut.

Students also take advantage of the city's entertainment. The city boasts a nationally renowned ballet corps, an opera company, a philharmonic, and several theater groups. The Gilcrease and Philbrook are popular museums. Reportedly, the Gilcrease Museum has the largest collection of Western American art in the world. Tulsa also boasts several festivals during the year, including Octoberfest, Reggaefest, and Mayfest.

Students take their dates out to one of the city's restaurants, such as the Metro Diner, or they frequent malls such as Woodland Hills, Promenade, and Southroads. Free university shuttle service provides transportation to all of these places as well as to movie theaters around the city. And, at the end of 1998, two 20-screen movie theaters were built in Tulsa, one of which is very close to campus.

Where We Hang

When students hang out on campus, they usually spend time in the Allen Chapman Activities Center (ACAC), one of the university's two libraries, or their dorms. ACAC features the Hurricane Hut (a restaurant that serves as a center for beer guzzling), as well as meeting halls and study rooms. Many undergraduates like to study on the green lawns surrounding the church-like McFarlin Library or inside the law library, which is open 24 hours.

Although housing is reportedly comfortable, with dorm rooms including air conditioning, cable, and computer connections, a large percentage of the student body chooses to live off campus or in fraternity or sorority houses. Many believe the food, which some diners call "unappetizing" and "monotonous," has driven students off campus.

There are five dorms on the TU campus: Lottie Jane, John Maybee, Twin Towers, Tower West, and Lafortune. Tower West and Lafortune are coed by suite, while Lottie Jane and John Maybee are single-sex. Twin Towers offers newer, smaller rooms, and is coed by floor. Housing in the area can be found cheaply, and the new University Square Apartments provide the benefits of apartment living on-campus. While most agree housing at TU is not a problem, they complain about a lack of parking. And although the new shuttle service is helpful, most students agree a car is very important.

What students at the University of Tulsa really enjoy about their school is its size. The approximately 4,200 undergraduates are just enough to establish a diverse community while keeping a family-like environment. Tulsa is also known for its commitment to athletics. Sports are popular, although some students think TU places too much emphasis and funding on the sports program. Men's basketball is thought to be the biggest sport, and a new Convocation Center is being built for the basketball games. The football team plays in Skelly Stadium and is usually heavily supported at games. TU has a wide variety of men's and women's sports in everything from tennis to golf. Students not wanting to play a varsity sport take advantage of the popular intramural program.

A small, private school in America's heartland, the University of Tulsa is proud to provide its students with a solid liberal arts education. Prospective students are encouraged to take advantage of Tulsa Time, the University's program for prospective students to visit the campus, ask questions, and experience life at TU. As one student said, "When you have a degree from TU, people pay attention." If you are looking for a beautiful, active, and fun university in a great city with a strong academic program, then the University of Tulsa is definitely for you.—*Brian Abaluck and Staff*

> **"TU students love to have fun. Finding a party is never a problem."**

FYI

The three best things about attending TU are "the quality of the faculty, the gorgeous campus, and low cost of entertainment."

The three worst things about attending TU are "the ill-equipped career services center, the cliques, and the poor equipment in the Computer Supported Writing Center."

The three things every student should do before graduating from TU are "take at least one class from Dr. Joseph Kestner, visit the Alexander Hogue Gallery, and do an internship at one of the publications."

One thing I wish I'd known before coming here is "how humid the summers are."

Oregon

Lewis and Clark College

Address: 0615 S.W. Palatine Hill Rd, Portland, OR 97219-7899
Phone: 503-768-7040
E-mail address: admissions@lclark.edu
Web site URL: www.lclark.edu
Location: suburban
Founded: 1867
Private or Public: private
Religious affiliation: none
Undergraduate enrollment: 1,742
Total enrollment: 3,203
Percent Male / Female: 40%/60%
Percent Minority: 11.0%

Percent African-American: 1.0%
Percent Hispanic: 2.0%
Percent Asian: 7.0%
Percent in-state / out-of-state: 27%/73%
Percent Pub HS: 72%
Fraternities: 0%
Sororities: 0%
Number of Applicants: 3,013
Percent Accepted: 69%
Percent Accepted who enroll: 25%
Entering: 521
Transfers: 69
Application Deadline: 1 Feb
Mean SAT: NA

Middle 50% SAT range: 580–680 V, 570–660 M
Middle 50% ACT range: 25–29
Mean ACT: NA
3 Most popular majors: English, biology, sociology
Retention: 80.0%
Graduation rate: 59.0%
Library: 175,854 volumes
Tuition and Fees: $21,520 in; $21,520 out
Room and Board: $6,100
On-campus housing: 99%
Financial aid, first-year: 85%

Not far from the city of Portland, Oregon, students at Lewis and Clark College carry on blissfully on a wooded estate with a spectacular view of Mt. Hood in the distance. Small classes, a close-knit community, and a love for the great outdoors draw a diverse student body to this oasis in the Pacific Northwest where outdoor activities are never too far away.

Attentive Academics

Lewis and Clark is known for its strong academic departments that lavish students with personal attention. Favorite majors include international affairs, biology, business, English, and sociology/anthropology. Classes generally enroll around 20 students, although some introductory courses can enroll between 40 and 60 students. Small class size allows undergraduates the opportunity to "become closer with professors," who are known to take keen interest in their stu-

dents. One student described her professors as, "approachable, friendly, and involved in the academic careers of their students." Another student added, "Professors at LC do not try to push their ideas onto you. They are well-educated and want to see you grow with the expertise they can provide in their field." There are no TAs at Lewis and Clark. Students feel that academics are "challenging." However, one undergrad explained that students "enjoy the challenge because they respect the professors and feel intellectually rewarded by their classroom experience."

As part of the liberal arts requirement, incoming freshmen are required to take Inventing America, a survey course covering American history and philosophy. The class is apparently "hated by most freshmen." However, one undergrad explained that "Inventing America can be an amazing class with the right professor, which is pure luck because all different types of professors teach it (including psychology, biology, math, etc.)."

Many students flock to Lewis and Clark for its renowned international affairs and language departments. Students also report these departments as being the "most demanding academically." Many students double major with whatever language they are taking. Students praise the extensive study-abroad programs, which allow them to travel and implement their newly acquired language skills. Over half of all Lewis and Clark undergrads go abroad before they graduate. They can choose among programs in Germany, France, and England, as well as those in more exotic places such as India and Argentina. Lewis and Clark also allows students to study in Washington, D.C., while completing an internship with a government bureau or private company. For one student, working in Washington "provided me with work experience while I went to school at the same time."

When Lewis and Clark students need to hit the books, they use the "totally awesome" Watzek Library. Watzek has a wide array of resources including an interlibrary exchange program, which allows students to borrow from other libraries if their own does not have what they need. There are study rooms for group study, long tables, and private carrels with computer hookups that allow students to check their e-mail from a laptop instead of waiting in line at the computer center. "Everyone goes" to the library, said one student, "which makes it a pretty social place."

Since the mid-1990s, a number of construction projects have revamped the Lewis and Clark campus. The size of Watzek Library was doubled and a center for the humanities and arts was finished in 1996. The Templeton Center was restructured, bringing the "headquarters for student activities closer together, which is a plus," according to one undergrad. Students also rate the weight room as "a step up." A new arts and humanities building and music building were completed in 1998.

No Greek Scene? Thank God

There is no Greek system at Lewis and Clark, but students do not seem to miss it. One student explained that it was "a big part of why people come to LC." The Greeks were removed from campus in the early 1970s with a donor's amendment. Apparently, the donor would not give the school her fortune unless they promised to prohibit Greek houses, install an all-women's dorm, and serve ice cream at every meal!

Despite the lack of a Greek scene, Lewis and Clark is not lacking in social events on the weekends. Although this is not a "major party school," many students partake in a drink or a joint or two over the weekend. Dating does occur at Lewis and Clark, though, how often depends on which student is asked. Random hookups also occur frequently; students do warn that with a small campus, the social scene can seem "filled with rumors" at times, but people are "mostly laid-back about romance here."

Lewis and Clark is technically a dry campus, but apparently this policy does not stop anyone from drinking. Although students report that campus police will "write up" students and repeat offenders may find themselves before a peer review committee, it does not happen very often. However, due to this policy, most large parties are held off campus. Lewis and Clark students are lax when it comes to drugs and alcohol. One student explained that "it is easy to drink and smoke here, though it is not done in excess too often." Marijuana is the most prevalent drug found on campus, although drugs like LSD and mushrooms are also in use to an extent.

Students report spending their weekends doing numerous activities on and off campus. Popular hangouts on campus include two student-run cafes, the Rusty Nail and the Platform, which host music events regularly. Many students enjoy the big-screen movies presented every Saturday night in Council Chambers by the Students Organized for Activities (SOFA). Many students report they enjoy just "relaxing with friends on-campus." Since Lewis and Clark's campus is located in a suburban neighborhood (which means there is nowhere to go "just off campus"), many students venture into Portland for nighttime activities. Undergrads describe Portland as "a great city where the people are always friendly despite all the rain." There are numerous clubs, pubs, bars, and restaurants that students enjoy going to, including Fulton Pub, Buffalo Gap, and Seges. In addition, Powell's is also a popular Portland gathering spot for Lewis and Clark students. It is the largest independent bookstore in America and apparently has "good readings on Friday nights." Portland also has a growing swing and rave scene as well. However, students complain that fun in Portland only lasts so long because "everything closes very early, like 10 P.M. on the weekends."

Many a Rainy Day

Fortunately or unfortunately, depending on whom one asks, there are many rainy days on the Lewis and Clark campus. The LC campus is not a place to be without an umbrella, which drives some students nuts. Yet, other students appreciate the weather because campus is like "a huge, wet garden." Green is certainly the most appropriate adjective for the campus, which has a rose garden, lots of trees and grassy lawns, and cobblestone paths, not to mention the "spectacular" view of Mt. Hood. The charm of a lush campus "makes students love Lewis and Clark despite the impossible rain."

Freshmen and sophomores are required to live on campus, although many students consider this requirement restrictive and overly expensive. Some go so far as to equate living on campus to "hell on earth." Although others feel that "it is hard to meet new people when you move off campus and you are closer to the campus facilities on campus." Students who live on campus are usually housed in dorm rooms in groups of two, four, or six (known as a "six-pack"). Room size and amenities vary from dorm to dorm. Most dorms are coed by floor (because residents of each floor share a bathroom) and some have language theme floors. While students rate Copeland as the best dorm, Platt Howard (also known as "the projects") is consistently called the worst. Copeland is known across campus for throwing parties and is generally acknowledged as the most social dorm. Hartsfeld, which offers some suites, is preferred by upperclassmen who remain on campus; the atmosphere is peaceful, which allows for better studying. For those who do not mind the walk, the luxurious Stewart dormitories, about 10 minutes from the center of campus, have walk-in closets and large rooms, although they reportedly lack the social atmosphere of Copeland. Lewis and Clark has one all-female dorm, commonly referred to as "the convent."

The main dining hall at Lewis and Clark is in the Templeton College Center, nicknamed "the Bon" (pronounced as "Bone") for the catering company, Bon Appetite. Students living on campus must purchase a meal plan that includes at least 14 meals per week. The food is considered "pretty good," for college food. Students say that Bon Appetite, which is considered the best food service in the Northwest, offers a variety of options for each meal. Pizza, salad, and sandwiches are popular choices. Several vegetarians, of whom there are many at LC, reported that they cater well to their needs. Students who have Flex points, which are purchased at the beginning of the school year, can use them at the Trail Room, a grill on the floor below the Bon. Students rarely venture off campus for a meal, as there is little choice in the residential neighborhood surrounding the school. Domino's Pizza does deliver, but most students save their money for quality meals in downtown Portland.

It is generally agreed that there is a "big schism" between people who live on and off campus after sophomore year. Since the campus is surrounded by a suburban residential area, housing is often more affordable off campus than on. A large number of upperclassmen choose to move out of the dorms and into "cheap and plentiful" apartments or houses with friends. For those who live farther away from campus there are shuttle buses run by the college. Many students have cars, but caution that one has to be careful to avoid parking tickets.

Trail Blazers

Many students fear that Lewis and Clark will soon be stereotyped by their most famous graduate, Monica Lewinsky. In reality, students say that "there are a lot of rich kids rebelling" at LC. The school does make up for its "nonexistent" racial diversity with a good number of international students and a diversity within the students' backgrounds and interests. Students feel that they are "mostly liberals, who are upstarts seeking change and newness in the world." However, others pessimistically believe that "everyone here pretends to be hippie and liberal while content to buy their Tommy gear and be apathetic to global and environmental causes." Generally, undergrads feel that "most students accept people for who they are and are supportive of people of different races, religions, and sexual orientations."

The student body of Lewis and Clark has low school spirit. What spirit there is for varsity athletics is "mostly athletes supporting their friends and other athletes." This does not mean, however, that Lewis and Clark students swear off athletics altogether. In fact, intramural sports are some of the most popular activities on campus, especially volleyball, skiing, soccer, crew, rugby, lacrosse, and sailing. Students who aren't as into school-sponsored athletics enjoy taking advantage of their natural surroundings by participating in outdoor activities. Hiking, rock climbing, mountain biking, and skiing are popular sports. One student suggested that Lewis and Clark students are passionate about "outdoorsy" activities since "the Nalgene bottle clipped onto a backpack with a carabiner is the biggest fashion statement here." Students can reach the Oregon coast in two hours and the Columbia River Gorge in about an hour's drive. Both are apparently "breathtaking, even on a drizzly day." For the nonathletes, there is the campus TV station, LCTV, and radio station, KLC. Various green clubs are also reportedly popular. Aspiring writers can join either the *Pioneer Log* or *Sacajawea's Voice*, the two campus newspapers.

Even at a college without tremendous school spirit, the Lewis and Clark mascot, the Pioneer, is an appropriate representative of the school. An attitude typical of Lewis and Clark is apparent in one of the school's mottoes: "Do not follow where the path may lead, go instead where there is no path and blaze a trail." Although students rally around the fact that their school is actually a close-knit community, "people here like to do their own things, and Lewis and Clark's free-minded attitude encourages this." Students at Lewis and Clark are individuals who "blaze their own trails," but who will come together to support their community. Many students believe that Lewis and Clark offers them the best of all worlds—a solid liberal arts education in a community of outdoors lovers.—*Alison Pulaski and Staff*

> Students feel that they are "mostly liberals, who are upstarts seeking change and newness in the world."

FYI

The three best things about attending Lewis and Clark are "the small classes, the fact that professors listen to you, and that everything is green."

The three worst things about attending Lewis and Clark are "the isolation of being off campus, that everyone thinks that kids here are like Monica Lewinsky (alumnus), that Monica Lewinsky no longer attends."

The three things that every student should do before graduating from LC are "go to Portland, hike around Mt. Hood, and go somewhere weird to study abroad."

One thing I'd like to have known before coming here is "how many inches ice cream can add to your waistline."

Oregon State University

Address: 104 Kerr Administration, Corvallis, OR, 97331-2106
Phone: 541-737-4411
E-mail address: osuadmit@orst.edu
Web site URL: www.orst.edu
Location: suburban
Founded: 1868
Private or Public: public
Religious affiliation: none
Undergraduate enrollment: 12,194
Total enrollment: 14,336
Percent Male / Female: 54% / 46%
Percent Minority: 13.0%

Percent African-American: 1.0%
Percent Hispanic: 3.0%
Percent Asian: 8.0%
Percent in-state / out-of-state: 84% / 16%
Percent Pub HS: NA
Fraternities: 25%
Sororities: 22%
Number of Applicants: 6,946
Percent Accepted: 80%
Percent Accepted who enroll: 54%
Entering: 3,020
Transfers: 1,373
Application Deadline: rolling

Mean SAT: 534 V, 551 M
Middle 50% SAT range: 480–590 V, 490–610 M
Middle 50% ACT range: NA
Mean ACT: 23
3 Most popular majors: business administration, liberal studies, exercise and sport science
Retention: 79.0%
Graduation rate: 28.0%
Library: 1 million volumes
Tuition and Fees: $3,549 in; $11,817 out
Room and Board: $5,064
On-campus housing: 95%
Financial aid, first-year: 65%

When Oregonians think of Oregon State University, many classify it as a fraternity-dominated party school. Although the school recognizes a whopping 26 fraternities and 13 sororities, students there will quickly point out that OSU has much more to offer than just frat parties, including the small-town environment of Corvallis, the beautiful setting of the campus, a strong academic curriculum, and an active student body.

Small Town Life

Corvallis, Oregon, is a town of about 30,000 people situated 15 miles off Oregon's main freeway, Interstate 5. A few students describe Corvallis as "quiet and a little boring," but most undergrads love the town's slow pace and quaint feel. Corvallis really caters to the students and their needs, with "a little downtown surrounding the campus," one undergrad noted. Indeed, there are enough pizza joints, coffee shops, and bars just off campus to satisfy any college student. Because of the university and technology/computer firms in the area, Corvallis attracts a large number of educated professionals and is definitely "not a hick town" as some people might think. One town spot that all students are familiar with is "the Ette," a grocery store some say is

known for its cheap prices and high volume sales of Busch Light.

Oregon is famous for its outdoor opportunities, and Corvallis doesn't disappoint. Many students go camping on long weekends in the spring and fall, make frequent trips to the Cascades for downhill skiing, or take off for the scenic Oregon coast, which is only 45 minutes away. When students miss the action of the big city, many travel to the lively club and bar scene of Portland, just an hour and a half to the north. Lots of students have cars, so transportation usually is not a problem, even for those who don't own a car.

Another benefit to small-town life is safety. Car break-ins and other petty thefts are almost unheard of in Corvallis, and most students report feeling "completely safe." One female undergraduate, however, said that she feels secure during the day on campus, but around the off-campus houses and fraternities at night is "a little more sketchy."

"Bac Core"

Oregon State's Baccalaureate Curriculum (Bac Core) requires all students to take classes in a variety of fields before burying themselves in their major. One engineering student admitted that the core's emphasis on writing and liberal arts "is actually pretty good stuff." Other students agreed that the course requirements are "fair," although possibly a bit too easy. According to one student, "If you passed fourth grade, you'll get an A."

Outside of the core, students have rave reviews for their classes and programs. Despite a student body of almost 15,000, undergrads rarely have problems getting in to the classes they want to take. Some departments, such as English and the arts, offer many small classes, (20 people or fewer). One student said it's easy to "get involved in your classes, outside of class" through such activities as plays and art shows. Oregon State is known for its top-notch engineering and agriculture departments, but the other majors get their share of attention. One forestry student praised his department, noting that the TAs and professors were knowledgeable and the location of the classrooms near a forest helps in learning. Undergrads call the workload "decent," although it can pile up and become a burden just like at any other college. Classes are challenging, but not impossible: one student suggested that "if you go to class and do some reading, then you're fine." Common complaints about the occasional unhelpful TA or professor with a thick foreign accent exist here, but students say they are satisfied overall.

To Rush or Not to Rush, That Is the Question

So just how big is the frat scene at Oregon State? Twenty-six fraternities and 13 sororities are a lot, but only about 25 percent of students actually pledge. Different houses hold functions from Thursday through Saturday, and these parties (some of them are themed) reportedly are "creative, well-decorated, and pretty fun," even for non-frat types. As a result, people up and down Oregon know OSU for its lively party scene and big bashes. These parties can get pretty wild: one female undergrad reported seeing "naked guys running around at parties all the time." Non-Greeks say they "associate, but don't totally hang out" with the fraternities, and usually no friction occurs between these two groups. Because the fraternities tend to be a bit choosy, pledges describe the rushing process as "somewhat difficult,"

but well worth it once they're accepted into the frat of their choice.

Although not everybody participates in the fraternity circuit, it can seem as if all students partake in heavy drinking. Stores around campus card regularly, but a large number of students are over 21 or have fake IDs. One student described many of her classmates as "drunks," and others agreed that the unofficial mascot of OSU would be a beer mug. Unfortunately, non-drinkers can feel out of place in this environment. But breathe easy, fearful parents: according to students, OSU is "definitely more of a drinking school than a drug school," and drug usage is considered peripheral.

As an alternative to the drinking and fraternity scene, the Student Council keeps activities running for students' enjoyment, including formal dances, tailgates, and special events like Dad's Weekend. Students at OSU are "very friendly," and most have an easy time meeting other people and making new friends. Not many students join clubs or other extracurricular activities, however, claiming that they are plenty busy with jobs, academics, and partying. Formal dating does not have a strong presence here, and one student described the dating scene as, "People do it, but they're not in the majority."

Beaver Believers

Sports and athletics are a major part of life at OSU. The grassy fields and state-of-the-art gyms provide venues for intramural sports or just working out. Students form their own IM teams, so often the competition is between numerous fraternities and a few "GDIs" (independents).

Despite the perennial losing records of many OSU varsity teams, students still have school spirit. "People are way more into women's sports," one undergrad reported, "especially women's basketball." Football games are a fun place to socialize, but students consider basketball the most popular sport. The biggest sports event of the year is the football "Civil War" game against archrival University of Oregon, when thousands of "Beaver Believers" (OSU alumnus) descend upon Parker Stadium for a game that's always packed and competitive. But throughout the year, whenever OSU gets that occasional win, "the school goes nuts."

Photogenic Campus

All students at OSU have great things to say about the physical campus. It is large and spread out with "old, beautiful brick buildings" and plenty of open spaces. Careful attention is paid to the landscaping, with thick grassy fields, bushes, flowers, lamps, and benches to highlight the grounds.

Reviews of the campus housing, however, are less enthusiastic. Freshmen who choose to live on campus are housed in dorm rooms with two people per room and about 40 per floor, which are described as "old and a little crowded." Students can choose to live in single-sex, coed, or "quiet" dorms. Upperclassmen, whose dorms are traditionally bigger, also have the option of "wellness" dorms like Sackett that prohibit drinking, smoking, and other drugs. After freshman year, many students move off campus, choosing to rent houses and apartments in town. Dining hall food does not elicit rave reviews, so many students opt for the mall-style food courts in the Memorial Union, where fast-food joints such as Burger King, Taco Bell, and Subway accept points from the meal system.

The student center, better known as Memorial Union, or "MU," to students, is a popular and beloved hangout. Students go there "all the time" to use its rooms for napping, studying, or meeting people. The building, which adjoins the campus bookstore and cafeteria, also contains the student agencies and even a bowling alley and game room in the basement.

Overall, students agree that Oregon State is much more than just a typical fraternity party school. Among the challenging academics, beautiful location and campus, and a hearty and sometimes wild social life, undergrads find their niche easily. As a result, one said, "most students love it here."—*Johnny Swagerty and Staff*

Classes are challenging, but not impossible: one student suggested that "if you go to class and do some reading, then you're fine."

FYI

The three best things about attending OSU are "the parties, the people, and the beauty of the place."

The three worst things about attending OSU are "the housing, people drinking way too much, and the required classes."

The three things that every student should do before graduating from OSU are "bring your father to campus for Dad's Weekend, especially if he's an alum, take a road-trip, weak sports teams."

One thing I'd like to have known before coming here is "that it rains all the time in Oregon."

Reed College

Address: 2303 SE Woodstock Blvd, Portland, OR 97202
Phone: 800-547-4750
E-mail address: admission@reed.edu
Web site URL: www.reed.edu
Location: suburban
Founded: 1909
Private or Public: private
Religious affiliation: none
Undergraduate enrollment: 1,353
Total enrollment: 1,353
Percent Male/Female: 46%/54%
Percent Minority: 12.0%

Percent African-American: 1.0%
Percent Hispanic: 4.0%
Percent Asian: 6.0%
Percent in-state/out-of-state: 8%/92%
Percent Pub HS: 62%
Fraternities: 0%
Sororities: 0%
Number of Applicants: 2,018
Percent Accepted: 68%
Percent Accepted who enroll: 24%
Entering: 337
Transfers: 45
Application Deadline: 15 Jan

Mean SAT: 690 V, 654 M
Middle 50% SAT range: 640–730 V, 610–700 M
Middle 50% ACT range: NA
Mean ACT: 29
3 Most popular majors: biology, English, psychology
Retention: 88.0%
Graduation rate: 65.0%
Library: 450,000 volumes
Tuition and Fees: $24,050 in; NA out
Room and Board: $6,650
On-campus housing: 98%
Financial aid, first-year: 48%

When asked to describe the typical Reedie, many students come up with one word: "strange." "People who wouldn't fit in anywhere else fit in at Reed," said one student. "Everyone's wacky here—and most people are wonderful." Many students at Reed say that they can't believe that they would love another school nearly as well. "Reed is as unique as its students. Actually, that is probably because the students make the school."

Amazing Academics

Academics at Reed are excellent, intense, and "amazing." "Don't come here if you want lots of free time, or if you're not serious about learning," said one student. Every student's academic career at Reed begins with "Hume 110," a required freshman intensive reading and writing course. All sections have 18 or fewer students, and the swift pace and high standards set the tone for the rest of a student's time at Reed. "It gives us all a common experience, and it's a great introduction to college," one sophomore said. In order to complete a Reed degree, students are also required to take two courses in each of four distribution groups and one year of a lab science. "The requirements are pretty easy, although the science part is hard on us humanities majors," said one student. Popular majors include biology, English, and psychology. Reed's commitment to academic freedom includes allowing students to design their own course of study, and interdisciplinary majors are also very popular. Students can be even more creative with their coursework during "Paideia," a 10-day period before spring semester where students take noncredit courses in such areas as bagel-making and underwater basket-weaving. Academics at Reed become even more difficult junior year, when students are required to pass qualifying exams in their major, although students report that few fail. Senior year, Reedies must complete a thesis and defend it in front of their advisor and three other professors from their department. "It's probably the hardest thing I've ever had to do," said one student. "But it was also incredibly rewarding." Even in the midst of their toughest classes, however, Reed students have the help of their excellent faculty. "The professors here are amazing," said a senior. "They're always willing to help." "Professors are personable and open-minded," said another. Classes at Reed are fairly small and always taught by professors, and classes with more than 30 students are considered large. "Classes are hard, but no one really cares," said one student. "Everyone has the same amount of work." Students say that academics form such a large part of life at Reed that "studying all the time isn't all that bad."

Time to Relax

Despite all their work, students at Reed still find time to relax. "People say they study all the time, but no one really does," said one student. Students say that the college cliche that "students study hard and party hard" is doubly true at Reed. "It's hard for some students to handle," said one Reedie. "Everything is intense here." One of the school's nicknames is "Weed," and students report that marijuana use is fairly common. "People can't do too much and keep up with their classes, but a lot of people dabble," one student said. Other drugs are also common, as is drinking, but students say that there is little pressure to partake: "Reed is a very 'do your own thing' school." The social life is generally fairly casual. Students report that there is not a lot of dating. "People either hang out or have sex," said one undergrad. Downtown Portland is nearby, and many students who need a break from life at Reed go to the city for dinner or dancing. "Portland's great," said one student. "It has everything." Another student complained, however, that "everything seems to close at 10 P.M."

> "We have a great assortment of hippies, goths, punks, skaters, skids, and just plain weirdos."

Even with everything else that they have to do, Reedies still seem to find time for extracurricular activities. Students say participation is "irregular." Some people are really into it, and some could care less. "Academics are the first priority for pretty much everyone," said one junior. For students who choose to participate, there are many campus groups, and if they don't find what they want, they can "just start it themselves." Community service through SEEDS (Students for Education Empowerment and Direct Service) and other organizations is very popular. Students can also choose to work for the newspaper, the *Quest*, or for the campus radio station. Other activities are as unusual as the students who participate in them, and range from the Fetish Student Union and the wine-tasting club to more conventional choices such as the Feminist Student Union and the French Club. Sports at Reed are played "the Reed way"—for fun, not for competition. "Few people are very serious about sports, but lots of people enjoy them," said one student. "It's a great way to relax," said another.

The Reed Campus

Reed students describe their campus as "lovely." "Most of it's right out of *Dead Poets Society*," said one sophomore. The 28 dorms are "generally nice." Old Dorm Block is described as "beautiful," and Anna Mann House as "luxurious." Even the notorious Asylum Block was recently renovated, and now it is "very livable if you can stand the aesthetic ugliness." One sophomore, however, found Asylum Block so unattractive that she chose to move off campus rather than live there. "I've seen asylum rooms, and these are worse," she said. Students generally live in suites. Other living options include the Woodstock language houses and student-chosen theme houses. Students are not required to live on campus after their freshman year, and many choose to move off. "The dorms are kind of shabby. It's just not worth it," said one student. Housing around campus is reasonably priced and not difficult to find. Campus residents are required to have a meal plan. Students say that the dining hall has a variety of foods with plentiful vegetarian and vegan entrees but "it's mostly really gross." "They try, and it keeps getting better, but it will take a lot of improvement," one student said. "Most people stick to the Ben & Jerry's Ice Cream and a few other selected items." Reed students are liberal and politically active. "Our unofficial slogan is 'communism, atheism, and free love,'" said one sophomore. "There is just a little communism, a whole lot of atheism, and hardly any free love unless you get lucky at the winter formal." "A lot of people here were considered different in high school," said another. "We have a great assortment of hippies, goths, punks, skaters, skids, and just plain weirdos." In this diverse community, students are united by their dedication to academics and by their "open minds." Students say, however, that they would like to see more ethnic and cultural diversity at Reed, which many think is lacking, despite the school's dedication to academic diversity.

Students warn that "Reed isn't for everyone." Although most Reedies are dedicated to their school, they realize that the very characteristics that make them love it might turn others off. Therefore, they advise high school students looking at Reed to be careful. "Be sure to visit first," said one senior. "If you love it on sight, like I did, you'll probably never lose that love." For those who take the plunge, Reed provides a "supportive environment, both academically and emotionally." "School is life and life is school here," said one student. For those who feel at home at Reed, however, both school and life are challenging and satisfying.—*Kathryn Eigen and Staff*

FYI

The three best things about attending Reed are "small classes, senior theses, and really chill people."

The three worst things about attending Reed are "potheads, people who seem to think they're in the sixties and the Man is out to get them, and food that only tastes good to potheads."

The three things that every student should do before graduating from Reed are "go to the Winter Formal, talk to lots of people about politics, and read on your own."

One thing I'd like to have known before coming here is "strange people are cool."

University of Oregon

Address: 1217 University of Oregon, Eugene, OR, 97403-1217
Phone: 541-346-3201
E-mail address: uoadmit@oregon.uoregon.edu
Web site URL: www.uoregon.edu
Location: urban
Founded: 1876
Private or Public: public
Religious affiliation: none
Undergraduate enrollment: 13,426
Total enrollment: 16,716
Percent Male/Female: 47%/53%
Percent Minority: 14.0%

Percent African-American: 2.0%
Percent Hispanic: 3.0%
Percent Asian: 6.0%
Percent in-state/out-of-state: 73%/27%
Percent Pub HS: 80%
Fraternities: 11%
Sororities: 11%
Number of Applicants: 7,157
Percent Accepted: 90%
Percent Accepted who enroll: 38%
Entering: 2,422
Transfers: 1,371
Application Deadline: 1 Feb
Mean SAT: 558 V, 552 M

Middle 50% SAT range: 500–620 V, 500–610 M
Middle 50% ACT range: NA
Mean ACT: NA
3 Most popular majors: business, journalism, psychology
Retention: 82.0%
Graduation rate: 59.0%
Library: 2,366,626 volumes
Tuition and Fees: $3,810 in; $13,197 out
Room and Board: $5,350
On-campus housing: 64%
Financial aid, first-year: 45%

Located near the Willamette River and the Cascade Mountains, the University of Oregon's 250-acre campus offers its students the vast resources of a public university along with the individual attention given by a midsize institution.

The combination of well-regarded academics, diverse extracurricular opportunities, and lush, green surroundings make Oregon an amazing place to spend the college years.

Academics

In addition to major requirements, most students find the general distribution requirements, or academic "clusters," to be very rewarding. By taking classes outside his major to fulfill the requirement, one student said, "I never would have taken some of the classes I ended up really enjoying." Although most introductory courses are large, students say that professors are very accessible. "You just need to make an effort and the professor would be happy to meet with you," said one freshman. To contrast this large size, all English and math courses are capped at 30 students per class. Classes become much smaller in upper division courses; some classes have no more than four students. Although the majority of majors offered at UO are respected, the pre-professional programs are particularly well-regarded; Business, Journalism, and Architecture boast superb faculty and strong reputations. One academic option for freshmen is the Clarks Honors College, a liberal arts program for first-year students, which offers small classes, individual attention from top-notch professors, and a work load emphasizing writing, verbal skills, and critical thinking. With the best professors of the university at their disposal (including UO's president), honors students say it is most definitely worth the work.

Extracurriculars Abound

With ferocious spirit, the Ducks are a force to be reckoned with on the track, field, or elsewhere. Varsity athletics play an important role for students, with track and field, basketball, and football teams drawing the biggest crowds. Besides going to the soon to be renovated Autzen Stadium to see the Ducks fight it out against archrival Oregon State, students are heavily involved in intramural sports, community service, and political action. "We don't just talk, we do something," one student said about activism on campus. As the sixth largest source of Peace Corps volunteers, UO also boasts over 250 active student organizations ranging from the *Oregon Daily Emerald*, the daily newspaper, to a variety of political interest groups heavily involved in local and national politics. The community internship program, which entails working in Eugene for academic credit, is a combination of community service and work experience. "There is something here for everyone. It is just a matter of finding your thing," one student noted, demonstrating the diversity of the UO campus.

A Social Niche for Everyone

Besides extracurricular activities, UO students like to party. The Greek scene is prominent, and includes 15 fraternities and 11 sororities. In contrast to the Greeks, there is a high contingency of alternative or hippie crowds, sometimes referred to as the granolas. Drug use isn't unheard of, and although marijuana is predominant, mushrooms and LSD are present as well. Many students, however, have no problem finding a niche between these two extremes and, in the end, everyone has a group of friends. Sometimes students go to Eugene for the weekend because it is a "fun, liberal place." Others say it's "dead" at night, and tend to stay on campus. Students are extremely happy with campus security; good lighting, call boxes, and a Safe Rides program all combine to ensure students have no problem walking around late at night.

Dorms and Dining

Freshmen who choose to live on campus stay in Bean Hall, Hamilton, or Walton dorms. Bean, known for being "small and dark," exclusively houses freshmen, while Hamilton and Walton house a mixture of freshmen and upperclassmen. Students have the choice of single-sex, coed, athletic, or "academic pursuit" dorms. In addition to meeting fellow students through dorms and classes, Freshman Interest Groups (FIG) led by upperclassmen bring students together in groups of 15 to 30 people who share the same academic interests. "It was a great way to meet people and see if other people are going through the same thing you are, academically or otherwise," one student said.

Many sophomores remain on campus

and live in Hamilton, Walton, or Carson. Because Carson also houses graduate students, undergraduates claim it is a much quieter area of campus. Another option is Riley dorm, where 75 percent of the residents are international students. "It's a great place to live. You get to meet and hang out with people from all over the world," one American student said. While those who live on campus must have a meal plan, the variety of places to get food makes it "doable." As junior year rolls around, the majority of students move off campus to nearby apartments. Rather than having a meal plan, many upperclassmen eat at the Erb Memorial Union (EMU), the student center, between classes. There, students can use their meal plan to purchase food from Subway, Jamba Juice, and Pizza Hut, or specialty food at the Market Place, which offers different types of food every day. "Without fail, I go the EMU on Tuesdays for Indian and Wednesdays for Mexican," one student said.

Getting a Face Lift

While UO is already a well-respected institution, its campus is still changing for the better. The science research buildings, home to two American Cancer Researchers, were recently renovated, while the gym has just undergone the first phase of remodeling. Now equipped with a new fitness center, an indoor rock climbing wall, and an AstroTurf field, the facilities are open for intramural and physical classes. In addition, more renovations of the gym will soon be completed, as well as the stadium and Gilbert Hall in the near future. Great strides are also being made with the computer system on campus. With the purchase of new Internet servers and Internet connections in every classroom and dorm, it will not be long before UO reclaims its rank in Yahoo! as the most wired college. By bringing together a great faculty, developing facilities, and a smaller student body in comparison to other public institutions, UO makes itself a well-regarded school that offers a solid liberal arts education.—*Jessica Morgan*

> "It will not be long before UO reclaims its rank in Yahoo! as the most wired college."

FYI

The three best things about attending University of Oregon are "the Ducks, the tolerance, and the EMU."

The three worst things about attending University of Oregon are "rain, um, rain, and, um, rain."

The three things that every student should do before graduating from UO are "go to a football game, listen to your parents, and buy an umbrella."

One thing I'd like to have known before coming here is "how much you can get out of any class if you just show some initiative and talk to the professor."

Willamette University

Address: 900 State Street, Salem, OR 97301
Phone: 877-LIB-ARTS
E-mail address: undergrad-admission@williamette.edu
Web site URL: www.willamette.edu
Location: small city
Founded: 1842
Private or Public: private
Religious affiliation: United Methodist
Undergraduate enrollment: 1,725
Total enrollment: 2,365
Percent Male / Female: 45%/55%
Percent Minority: 13.1%

Percent African-American: 1.6%
Percent Hispanic: 4.0%
Percent Asian: 6.4%
Percent in-state / out-of-state: 37%/63%
Percent Pub HS: 81%
Fraternities: 25%
Sororities: 21%
Number of Applicants: 1,541
Percent Accepted: 89%
Percent Accepted who enroll: 26%
Entering: 375
Transfers: 68
Application Deadline: 1 Feb
Mean SAT: 600 V, 610 M

Middle 50% SAT range: 560–670 V, 560–670 M
Middle 50% ACT range: 24–29
Mean ACT: 27
3 Most popular majors: biology, business economics, English
Retention: 88%
Graduation rate: 74%
Library: 280,000 volumes
Tuition and Fees: $21,700 in; NA out
Room and Board: $5,700
On-campus housing: 98%
Financial aid, first-year: 85%

In the heart of downtown Salem, Oregon, surrounded by office and state government buildings, one finds the oasis of Willamette University. The campus, with lush greenery, historic redbrick structures, and a stream crossing through it, complements a unique university where academic fervor mixes with an intimate, friendly, and fun student body.

Professors Who Care

Willamette University, the oldest university west of the Mississippi, has a reputation for strong academics. With Oregon's seat of government right across the street, it's no surprise that political science is one of the most popular majors. Following the recent completion of the Olin Science Center, more and more students are choosing to specialize in the natural sciences, especially biology and chemistry. In addition, strong departments at this liberal arts institution include economics, psychology, and English.

Students across the board rave about the quality of the academic experience here. The average class size consists of about 25 students, and one undergraduate commented that a 35-student lecture constitutes "a really big class." As many seminars and upper division classes only enroll eight to ten students, undergraduates report that "we can do so much more within our classes," such as long discussions, special projects, guest speakers, and even field trips. Classes are challenging but not overwhelming, and students are able to adjust to the rigorous atmosphere after their first year. For a university of its size, Willamette offers an incredible number of courses, and students can only complain that they don't have time to take all the classes they would like.

One of the most remarkable features of the university is the degree to which professors care about and are involved with their students. For better or worse, professors keep track of undergrads and follow their progress. As one student explained, "If the professor notices you have missed a few classes, or that your grade is slipping, he will definitely take you aside to talk about what's going on with you and try to find a solution." Professors reportedly "know their stuff well," and one student reverently referred to his history professor as "ferocious—the smartest guy I've ever met." In general, professors are both very well respected and well-liked.

"Drying Out" the Campus

Dominating the social scene recently is the administration's move to make Willamette a completely dry campus. Suddenly, alcohol is no longer served at on-campus functions, and students risk punishment if they are caught with alcoholic beverages. Even the fraternities, which are located on campus, now host dry parties.

However, this administrative action has not halted the social life at Willamette. More parties are now thrown off campus, in the apartments or houses of students, and upperclassmen frequent the handful of bars in close proximity. Occasionally, undergraduates will make the trek to Portland, 45 minutes away, to hit the bar and club scene there. On campus, the University sponsors one to two formal dances per semester, new release films played in school auditoriums, and events such as Art Attack, a weeklong celebration of the arts, and WUstock, a popular homecoming celebration. Five fraternities and three sororities are located at Willamette, but non-Greeks report that they do not feel excluded. Salem, a town of about 90,000, is not known for a "bumpin'" weekend scene. Besides the few bars immediately around campus, students say entertainment in Salem is limited to the movies and bowling but praise the quality of nearby movie theaters and bowling alleys.

Students at Willamette are serious about their extracurricular activities as well. At such a small school, almost every student plays some kind of sport, with a surprising number involved at the varsity level. Football, soccer, basketball, and track are popular among undergraduates, but a wide range of varsity sports are available. School spirit "depends on the season," although the men's basketball team recently won an NAIA division championship. At every basketball game, fans fill the auditorium to sing the favorite "Ooh ah Bearcats" song. A plethora of other extracurricular activities are also available, with most students participating in some club or group. The debate team, outdoors groups, and volunteer organizations are most popular, and students speculate that sports or volunteering is the most commonly participated activity.

Campus and Facilities

Students say it's easy to get hooked on what many people consider Willamette's greatest attribute: its "picturesque," "stunning," "quaint and beautiful" campus. Some undergrads also describe the campus as "red and green—there are red bricks and green trees and lawns." The grounds are so well kept that students wonder just how much money the University spends on groundskeeping. Squirrels abound, and ducks paddle around Mill Stream, which runs right through campus.

> "If the professor notices you have missed a few classes, or that your grade is slipping, he will definitely take you aside to talk about what's going on."

The other University buildings and facilities are a source of pride for students and administration alike. Students hit the books in 24-hour study rooms at the Mark O. Hatfield Library or in open classrooms around campus. When they feel like taking a study break, they drag their books to the Bistro, a student-run coffee shop. Many students, especially those who live in the West Campus, "away from the frats," find it quiet enough to study in their dorm rooms or in the student lounges.

Students name Doney the best dorm because it's quiet, but other dorms are considered comfortable as well. Kaneko, a new dorm built by Willamette's sister school, the nearby Tokyo International University of America, is equipped with tennis courts, a swimming pool, air-conditioning, and tinted windows; the dorm is a "regular Hilton." Freshman and sophomores are required to live on campus, but about half of juniors and seniors choose to move off campus to nearby West Salem. Of them, most are very satisfied with the apartments and houses available, the safety of the neighborhood, and the increased op-portunities "to find something to do."

Willamette students are from mostly conservative, white, upper-middle class backgrounds, although in recent years the campus has become increasingly diverse.

Students realize that the student body is fairly homogenous but do not report that this takes away from their overall experience there. One undergraduate reported that the campus was "pretty diverse" compared to the state of Oregon itself, but Japanese students from TIUA add an international perspective both in and out of the classroom.

How Do You Say "Willamette"?

Students all agree that the intimacy between students, the faculty, and the administration distinguishes Willamette from other universities. There is a "close camaraderie" between students in the small school, and everyone feels like they know a lot of their classmates, "but in a good way." Professors genuinely care about the students in their classes, and even the administration exudes a feeling of intimacy and compassion toward undergraduates.

Willamette students generally are very content with their college choice. Students only really complain about the price of attending the school, which indicates something of the happiness of students there. Just listen to a Willamette student's spirited cry when an outsider mispronounces the school's name: "It's Wil-*lam*-ette, dammit!"—*Johnny Swagerty*

FYI
The three best things about attending Williamette are "small and intimate classes, the attractiveness of the main campus, and the friendships formed on campus."
The three worst things about attending Williamette are "high cost of attending, lack of party/social oppurtunities, and the rain in Oregon."
The three things that every student should do before graduating are "visit the Star Trees, take rhetoric class, and be 'Mill-Streamed,' when you are thrown in the Mill Stream fully clothed on a special occasion."
One thing I'd like to have known before coming here is "that there is a much higher percentage of girls to guys."

Pennsylvania

Allegheny College

Address: Office of Admissions; Allegheny College; Meadville, PA 16335
Phone: 814-332-4351
E-mail address: admiss@admin.alleg.edu
Web site URL: www.alleg.edu
Location: rural
Founded: 1815
Private or Public: private
Religious affiliation: United Methodist
Undergraduate enrollment: 1,897
Total enrollment: 1,897
Percent Male/Female: 47%/53%

Percent Minority: 5.4%
Percent African-American: 2.0%
Percent Hispanic: 1.0%
Percent Asian: 2.0%
Percent in-state/out-of-state: 58%/42%
Percent Pub HS: 80%
Fraternities: 14%
Sororities: 22%
Number of Applicants: 2,947
Percent Accepted: 82%
Percent Accepted who enroll: 22%
Entering: 532
Transfers: 0
Application Deadline: 15 Feb

Mean SAT: 591 V, 589 M
Middle 50% SAT range: 545–640 V, 540–630 M
Middle 50% ACT range: 23–28
Mean ACT: 25
3 Most popular majors: psychology, biology, English
Retention: 87%
Graduation rate: 62%
Library: 650,000 volumes
Tuition and Fees: $20,410 in; $20,410 out
Room and Board: $4,970
On-campus housing: 100%
Financial aid, first-year: 83%

Walking through the 72 acres of western Pennsylvania that form Allegheny College, a visitor would be likely to first notice the sheer beauty of the campus. One student described Allegheny as "beautiful . . . picturesque, very distinguished . . . very much like out of a movie," with its grass, walkways, and old buildings. But the college's setting is definitely not its only source of appeal. Students agree that Allegheny's carefully tailored liberal arts curriculum and scientific and athletic excellence are among its major draws.

Academics: Liberal Arts and a Common Bond

In addition to the demands of individual departments, Allegheny has a unique sequence of graduation requirements. All freshmen choose a "Freshman Seminar" from among the more than 30 offered each year. Past options have included Creativity and Problem Solving, Anthropology and Dance, and Biotechnology. Each student's seminar professor becomes his or her advisor for at least two years. All sophomores take Writing in the Liberal Arts seminars. The more than 20 annual section choices in this program have included Films of Ingmar Bergman and Woody Allen, Political Economy, and The Revolutionary Mind. During their junior and senior years, students pursue a major, a minor, and a Senior Project in their major field. The project, or "Comp," must include a Junior Seminar, independent research, and an oral defense. Students' majors must be in one of three divisions (Humanities/Arts, Natural Sciences, and Social Sciences), accompanied by a minor in another area, and at least two courses completed in a third. With all of these requirements, plus a physical education requirement, students are left with about 13 to 15 free course slots for electives. Students generally do not mind Allegheny's requirements: "It's a liberal arts school," one sophomore pointed out, "so you expect to do that when you come here." According to students, the hardest and often the best classes are in the sciences, and one of the college's proudest recent achievements is a new science building. Concerns about a pro-science bias came to the forefront recently when, in budget cuts, the college merged the philosophy and religious studies departments and eliminated several humanities majors and minors including classics, Greek, and sociology/anthropology. Not everyone agrees with the student who complained, "The facilities for the humanities are really run-down." However, many students feel that it is a better college for science majors than people who want to focus on the humanities.

Some of Allegheny's academic features, however, cut across departmental lines. Besides the special requirements, Allegheny academics features small class sizes, close student-professor relationships, and an almost complete absence of graduate student teaching assistants. Classes usually are not difficult to get into, and students tend to participate in class. Allegheny students report that the college is academically intense. "I have time to myself on the weekends a little," says one junior communication arts major, "but I don't think I could ever have one day and not do any work."

Student Life

In addition to the beauty of the campus, a typical visitor to Allegheny would notice rap music booming out of dorm room windows and students walking to class in jeans and baseball caps. One student described the typical Allegheny student as "WASP, very J. Crew, loafers, well dressed, good socioeconomic background, bio or chem major, partier," and from Pennsylvania or the surrounding states. Most students are socially conservative, and some students see a link between Allegheny's small number of minority students and

students' attitudes about race and sexual orientation.

"You need to get involved to really experience Allegheny," reported one junior. "There is a group for every interest and if you don't find one, you can start your own." Many student groups are housed in the student center, which is also a popular hangout. Most people are involved in at least one activity, with sports being a particularly major focus. Allegheny does not give sports scholarships, but "for a Division III small, private school," one student said, "they're among the best on the East Coast," particularly in football and women's soccer. The new gym offers excellent facilities and many students participate in intramurals.

When asked what freshmen do on the weekends, one junior replied, "hope that they can get beer, and drink in their rooms without the RAs catching them, or go out to house parties and stand around a keg in a crowded basement hoping to get drunk, while being grossly overcharged for their cup." Upperclassmen tend to socialize at bars and invitation-only parties. Drinking and rowdiness are not permitted in dorms, and kegs are allowed only with a party permit. Fraternity parties, which do not serve alcohol and are usually open to all students, are also a big draw. While there is some hostility between Greeks and non-Greeks, students say the year-long rush process is open and friendly. School-sponsored events such as the annual Springfest and weekly movies and lectures are also major activities. These, along with plays and cultural events, are among the options for those who choose not to drink, a choice that one student reports is possible, and even common, but can be difficult.

> "You're friends with everybody, you walk down the street and say hi to people. . . . It's like a family," one student said.

Students report a certain amount of apathy toward social events at Allegheny. One sophomore said "People are more into just getting their degrees," while one junior said that most people are not particularly thrilled with the social alternatives "but no one has any clue how to make it better." Small-town Meadville, Pennsylvania, offers movie theaters and restaurants, but not much else for the college crowd. Students often go home or to Pittsburgh (an hour and a half away and home to many students) on the weekends. Some students also report a certain "cliquey" quality to the Allegheny community, and some complain about the "gossip mill." One sophomore called Allegheny's social scene "high schoolish."

Allegheny students cite the school's size as one of its major assets and flaws. "I never expected to know everyone either by name or face on campus," reported one junior. Its size limits students' options, but encourages student-professor interaction. "You're friends with everybody, you walk down the street and say hi to people. . . . It's like a family," one student said. Depending on the student, four years at Allegheny can seem a long time to spend in such a closed-in environment or can provide a challenging, exciting experience in a picturesque setting. —*Jessica Champagne and Staff*

FYI

The three best things about attending Allegheny are "small classes, nice campus, good science programs."

The three worst things about attending Allegheny are "low access to alcohol, sometimes slow social scene, budget cutting."

The three things that every student should do before graduating from Allegheny are "go tube-sledding, visit Philadelphia, come up with a false rumor about yourself and see how far it travels."

One thing I'd like to have known before coming here is "that I wouldn't be going and getting trashed very often."

Bryn Mawr College

Address: 101 North Merion Avenue, Bryn Mawr, PA 19010-2899
Phone: 610-526-5152
E-mail address: admissions@brynmawr.edu
Web site URL: www.brynmawr.edu
Location: suburban
Founded: 1885
Private or Public: private
Religious affiliation: none
Undergraduate enrollment: 1,242
Total enrollment: 1,779
Percent Male / Female: 0% / 100%
Percent Minority: 26.4%

Percent African-American: 5.4%
Percent Hispanic: 3.0%
Percent Asian: 17.0%
Percent in-state / out-of-state: 18% / 82%
Percent Pub HS: 73%
Fraternities: NA
Sororities: 0%
Number of Applicants: 1,596
Percent Accepted: 59%
Percent Accepted who enroll: 20%
Entering: 344
Transfers: 8
Application Deadline: 15 Jan
Mean SAT: 670 V, 640 M

Middle 50% SAT range: 610–710 V, 600–680 M
Middle 50% ACT range: NA
Mean ACT: NA
3 Most popular majors: English, math, biology
Retention: 95%
Graduation rate: 81.2%
Library: 1,062,594 volumes
Tuition and Fees: $22,730 in; NA out
Room and Board: $8,100
On-campus housing: 99%
Financial aid, first-year: 56%

Right outside of Philly there are easily available profs that actually care about undergrads, a party scene that covers four colleges, and traditions to boot. There's only one college that fits this description: Bryn Mawr. Located on

Philly's swanky Main Line, Bryn Mawr College combines a healthy social life with an incredibly intense intellectual life. Being a single-sex university doesn't faze Bryn Mawr women: "At Bryn Mawr we're a community of women—empowered, beautiful, and intelligent."

No Slackers

Academics at Bryn Mawr are described by one sophomore as a "ton of work"and are the number one priority for Byrn Mawr students. The school stresses a core set of academic standards that include a Freshman Liberal Studies Seminar sponsored by the English department, three humanities requirements, two social science courses, and three courses in the natural sciences. Unfortunately for students not inclined toward the sciences, this includes two labs. Like introductory courses at similar institutions, the Freshman Seminar focuses on the students' writing. According to one student, there are no "gut" majors. Every field of study is challenging in its own unique way. But those classes with particularly mean reputations include organic chemistry and elementary Greek and Latin. Greek students, according to student legend, "eat, sleep, and dream Greek."

Class size at Bryn Mawr is generally small. The intro courses tend to be larger, but, generally, class size runs between 20–50 students. Classes also include some students from surrounding schools such as Haverford. Pre-registration is key and students have a 10-day shopping period during which they decide their upcoming semester schedule. Upperclassmen are not given preference in registration. Bryn Mawr uses a lottery system to determine whether or not students make it into the class of their choice. Registrars try to accommodate students and are generally described as "helpful, courteous, and accommodating." Seniors, however, do receive preference if the course is a requirement for their major.

Professors here are "awesome." "I once had a major test coming up. I didn't feel prepared at all so I called up my professor. She sat down with me and went over the work. It was wonderful." This kind of faculty dedication is not uncommon at a small school such as Bryn Mawr. Professors readily hand out their home phone numbers and E-mail addresses. Often, they burn the midnight oil long past office hours to accommodate a student in need. Lucky students have even set up lunch dates with their professors to discuss the latest math theorem or that Byron poem that was difficult to understand. As for the TAs, so often feared by students at large research universities, they are present on campus and do assist in teaching. All classes are, however, taught by professors.

With such stress placed on academics at Bryn Mawr, one would think that there is an intense feeling of competition. According to one student, "Competition is not a problem at Bryn Mawr. We're all in this together." The honor code also helps to discourage competition by preventing students from discussing tests and grades outside of class. The code also allows for unproctored exams and plays an integral role within the school community.

Slackers, although lacking at Bryn Mawr, will be happy to know that grades are not sent home to parents. Every student's academic file is kept confidential. This adds to the feeling of "independence" that many freshmen say, "they absolutely love."

Social Life: Crazy, Sexy, Cool

Thanks to brother school Haverford, Bryn Mawr women do enjoy the "traditional" college experience. Although there are some parties at Bryn Mawr, Bryn Mawrians often head into Philly, where UPenn and Drexel are located, or Swarthmore and Haverford to party on the weekends. Haverford, the main party locale, is a mere mile away. It is easily within walking distance of the campus and a bus runs between the two schools every fifteen minutes. A lot of individuals head into Philly for "College Day," which is sponsored by Philadelphia area colleges and includes parties, concerts, and general merriment.

Bryn Mawr's alcohol policy follows Pennsylvania law. If you're 21 you can have a wet party or alcohol in the room. Nevertheless, most at Bryn agree that underage students who desire alcohol can easily aquire it. In general, Bryn Mawr students are fairly responsible drinkers. As for the non-drinkers, the school sponsors several bashes annually including the Fall Bash and the semiformal Pallas Athena.

Beyond the normal party scene, Philadelphia offers myriad activities for the culturally minded student. The Ben Franklin Parkway in Philadelphia has a ton of museums and other cosmopolitan activities for the burgeoning aesthete. The Society Hill Area, including South Street, is also a popular destination for the Bryn Mawr student. The Hill offers several artsy movie theaters and South Street is known for its trendy shops and restaurants.

On campus hangouts include the "Campus Center." The Center boasts a small café where students frequently congregate. It also sponsors a Performing Arts Series along with dances and little concerts.

Dating at Bryn Mawr received mixed responses. While dating certainly isn't the dominant form of social activity, students do "see" other students from neighboring Haverford and Penn. Some girls have serious boyfriends off campus and at home. There is also an active Rainbow Alliance on campus and issues of sexuality are freely discussed at Bryn Mawr. As one student puts it, "single sex doesn't mean no sex."

Incoming students to the college are welcomed at the beginning of the term with freshman orientation. Each freshman is assigned to a Customs Group during "Customs Week," known at other colleges as Orientation Week. Two sophomores lead these inchoate Bryn Mawr groups and act as valuable resources for the new students. The Customs Groups established during the first week provide a social foundation for the incoming class. Freshmen can often be seen with their group heading to meals or other activities.

Living It and Loving It

Living arrangements at college are probably one of the major concerns of incoming students. Bryn Mawr's campus is full of beautiful old Gothic dorms, in a style that rivals Princeton and Yale. Rhodes Dorm was just recently renovated over the summer of '99. All dorms are also, thanks to technology savvy administrators, wired to the Ethernet.

The rooms themselves are fairly large by college standards and 70 percent of them are singles that are "greatly appreciated" by freshmen looking for a nap after a particularly trying test. The school guarantees housing for all four years. Nevertheless, some upperclassmen choose to live off campus. A recently rebuilt facility known as Glen Meade was once a house owned by the school and now serves as student housing. Although the majority of students do live on or near campus, Bryn Mawr also has a few commuters.

What about the individuals whom you'll be sharing your lives with for the next four years? Students at Bryn Mawr, unlike other schools, are not cliquish. While some in the country characterize Bryn Mawr as a bastion of liberalism and feminism most students are quick to discount that myth. There is a definite ethnic and geographical diversity present on campus that helps to combat stereotypes.

Bringing guys into this community, specifically the dorms, has never been a problem. Male visitors are expected to abide by the honor code and students are, of course, responsible for the behavior of their guests. It is expected that roommates will notify each other when a guy spends the night. Students themselves decide on the coed status of the bathroom on their floor at the beginning of the year. In other words, many choose to have coed bathrooms to accommodate boyfriends and friends.

The social lives in the dorms are enhanced by the presence of upperclassmen in all dorms. No dorms at Bryn Mawr are specifically reserved for freshmen. Hall Advisors help to monitor the girls but are there only in an advisory capacity.

The campus itself is verdant and quaint. Everything is confined to a large rectangular area and all buildings are contained within this area. Bryn Mawr, the town, is a wealthy suburb of Philadelphia that contains numerous coffee shops and small commercial outlets. Town-gown relations are positive as the town actively supports Bryn Mawr students in their social outreach efforts.

Students are apt to hang out in their dorm rooms but often venture into the town proper to socialize at Starbucks or Xando. During most weekdays students are either studying or shopping in the city. While some students do dine off campus, the food on campus is "really good, especially the all beef hamburgers." There are four dining halls on campus, including one in Brecken Dorm. A lot of Haverford boys also eat at Byrn Mawr. On weekends, however, students tend to venture into Philadelphia to eat or they can easily order pizza and Chinese food from local restaurants.

Extracurriculars and Traditions

Students are often dedicated to extracurriculars and Byrn Mawr is no exception. The Student Self-Government Association is a popular and well-respected organization on campus. Students also actively participate in Christian Fellowship, Jewish Fellowship, as well as cultural and academic groups.

> **"Students at Bryn Mawr, unlike other schools, are not cliquish."**

But perhaps what makes Bryn Mawr what it is today are its Traditions; Traditions with a capital "T." The Traditions are four events conducted each year. They are mostly for the freshmen but are heavily attended by upperclassmen as well. Parade Night is the first of these traditions, designed to welcome freshmen into the Bryn Mawr community. Lantern Night is also an all-school extravaganza. Each class holds up a lantern of a distinct color used to identify the class. Rumor has it that the girl whose lantern burns out first will be the first in the class to earn her Ph.D. Hell Week, a time-honored parody of sorority rushes, is also wildly popular among sophomores and freshmen. "The Hellers" (the sophomores), are each assigned a freshman. For the remainder of the week the freshman must do the every bidding of the sophomore. Luckily for the freshman, sympathetic juniors rescue them from the nefarious grip of the sophomores by providing them with little treats and respites during the week. Lastly in May, the college president rides into campus on a horse to open up May Day celebrations. The president then delivers a speech, which is then followed by a Maypole Dance. The girls then proceed to buckle down for final exams.

A Final Word

Students rave about the benefits of having a single-sex education. Single-sex education "provides girls with an opportunity to gain confidence" and students tend to "feel a lot more confident in [their] academic abilities" after only a year.—*Sean McBride*

FYI
The three best things about attending Bryn Mawr are "the Traditions, friends, and the professors."
The three worst things about attending Bryn Mawr are "the massive amount work, the lab requirements for science courses, and the stress."
The three things every student should do before graduating from Bryn Mawr are "to ring the Taylor Bell, go abroad, and party in Philly."
One thing I wish I knew before coming here is "there are so many vegan dishes in the dining hall!"

Bucknell University

Address: Office of Admissions, Bucknell University, Lewisburg, PA 17837
Phone: 570-577-1101
E-mail address: admissions@bucknell.edu
Web site URL: www.bucknell.edu
Location: rural
Founded: 1846
Private or Public: private
Religious affiliation: none
Undergraduate enrollment: 3,403
Total enrollment: 3,506
Percent Male/Female: 52%/49%
Percent Minority: 10.4%

Percent African-American: 3.2%
Percent Hispanic: 2.8%
Percent Asian: 4.1%
Percent in-state/out-of-state: 33%/67%
Percent Pub HS: NA
Fraternities: 38%
Sororities: 43%
Number of Applicants: 7,011
Percent Accepted: 44%
Percent Accepted who enroll: 29%
Entering: 889
Transfers: 22
Application Deadline: 1 Jan
Mean SAT: 614 V, 637 M

Middle 50% SAT range: 570–650 V, 590–680 M
Middle 50% ACT range: 26–29
Mean ACT: NA
3 Most popular majors: business admin., biology, economics
Retention: 94%
Graduation rate: 88.5%
Library: 670,000 volumes
Tuition and Fees: $23,839 in; NA out
Room and Board: $5,596
On-campus housing: 100%
Financial aid, first-year: 50%

Situated in the rustic setting of Pennsylvania in the small town of Lewisburg, which one student described as the epitome of small town America, lies Bucknell University. Although Bucknell is isolated from the hustle and bustle of a city, students find plenty to do on campus, and remark that the lack of off-campus activities actually adds to the university's strong feeling of community. One sophomore said, "Yeah, Bucknell is small, but I don't think it's ever constricting."

Work Hard

Bucknell has strong engineering and business programs. Other popular majors include psychology, biology, and political science, and many students choose to double-minor. The only large classes, enrolling up to 100 people, tend to be introductory ones that range in difficulty; a junior said, "It completely depends on your major: Intro to Sociology is an easy A, but Intro to Psych is hard because they try to weed people out for the major." The majority of classes are small, with the average size around 20 to 30 students; some classes may have as few as 8 students.

As for the liberal arts requirements students have to meet, one student remarked, "I love them—we have a very diverse curriculum," while another sophomore felt that "the requirements are too easy," especially since they do not include foreign language. First-year students must complete an English and a math course, and sophomores must take two lab sciences; other requirements outside of those for departmental majors include four courses in the humanities, two in the social sciences, and the completion of three writing courses. First-year students also take a seminar to work on foundational skills, which "introduce you to a higher way of thinking, writing, analyzing, and arguing," and which they will need in the coming years at Bucknell.

> "Yeah, Bucknell is small. But I don't think it's ever constricting."

First-year students can apply to a special Residential College seminar program in which they live in Smith Hall, recognized as one of the nicer dorms on campus, on a floor with others in the same program: the Environmental College; the International College; the Arts College;

the Social Justice College; and the Humanities College.

As far as getting the classes you want, one student said, "It's not a problem except for the last 10 percent who register; everyone else pretty much gets their first choice of classes and first choice time slots." All classes are taught by professors, with TAs available for extra help and discussion sections. Most students are happy with their professors, and find that many go out of their way for undergrads. One sophomore reported, "One professor came up to my room one day and just hung out and talked about my paper. Most of the profs will meet you over lunch if you need help; I haven't had a professor yet who was opposed to helping out."

Play Even Harder

The weekend starts on Wednesday for Bucknell students and lasts all the way through Sunday, with the main focus on the Greek system. Recently, the administration has begun enforcing a strict policy against underage and excessive drinking. One student explained, "You get fined $50 if you're found drunk. The second time it's a $100 fine and a year of probation. The third time you lose off-campus privileges, you have to write letters to the administration, and go to a class; there's also a fine of $150 per person in a house hosting a party with underage drinking." Despite the steep penalties, some students find ways of getting around the rules and describe the weekend as "the partying time."

The Greek system plays a large part of social life at Bucknell. Students are not allowed to rush until their sophomore year, which most Greek members feel is a good thing, since they get to look around more, and aren't "just thrown in somewhere." One student described bid day, the day when students find out which fraternities or sororities have accepted them, as "the best day of my life here." Students consider the annual House Party at the end of the spring the best party of the year; one student said, "They basically block the campus off from the outside world for two days at the end of April and every frat holds a party." One student not involved with the Greek system said, "It's tough not to be [in a fraternity/sorority], it depends on your personality, but if you're strong enough, you can do it." The administration provides social alternatives to those not involved with Greek life, such as movies every Wednesday and Saturday, concerts, comedians, and drama shows. The university also sponsors two big concerts each year, one in the fall and one in the spring.

Your New Home

Bucknell students are satisfied with their living situations on the whole, and most stay on campus all four years. Smith Hall, home of the residential college programs, is considered one of the best first-year dorms, while juniors seek out rooms in Hunt Hall. Students generally are satisfied with freshman housing, and after that, as one student commented, "If you're lucky, and you are one of 200 out of 900 that get good room pick numbers, the rooms are big and pretty nice. Otherwise you get stuck in a dingle (a single with two people), which has about an 8' x 15' floor space after all of the immobile [built in] furniture."

About half of the dorms are air-conditioned and all except one are coed. Dorms have mixed and single-sex halls, but as one sophomore remarked, "the closest you'll get to same-sex housing is a wing [of a dorm]." The "sorority dorm" is the only all-female dorm, and sorority members are usually required to live there for a semester or a year, since the sororities don't have official houses. There are also special housing options such as the residential colleges, one substance-free house, called "Calvin and Hobbes," and Bucknell West, also called the mods, which "look like trailer houses" and have kitchens and family rooms; one junior said of the mods, "they're nice but far away."

Bucknell students have four places to eat on campus: the Bison, an a la carte grill, a sub shop, Larison Dining Hall, the Terrace Room, which serves sandwiches and grilled items, and the "Caf," the main dining hall. One student remarked that the atmosphere of the dining hall is "somewhat cliquey, frosh all sit on one side; all the minorities sit in the same spot; the sororities sit in the middle." According to one senior, "They require you to have a meal plan if you live on campus, but they have many different packages, so you can usually find one that suits your eating habits. Freshmen are automatically given a 19-meals-a-week plan." What does one do when the dining hall just doesn't cut it? "There are some great little delis in town; there's this one called Five Points, they have the weirdest combinations of food, the Champion [sandwich] is the best!" said one student. Other popular eateries are Vinari's, the Italian Terrace, BJ's, 7th St. Cafe, and the Bison.

Outside of Class

Bucknell offers a wide range of activities for students, from student government to community service clubs. Bucknell is a very athletic campus, with many students participating in club and varsity sports, as well as intramurals. One student said, "The gym has very nice athletic facilities, but the pool is kind of crummy. We also have a golf course." The most popular teams are the well-supported men's and women's basketball teams and the football team. While the administration is trying to get more students out to the football games by offering free season passes to all students, many already have a lot of team spirit for their Bisons.

What makes a Bucknell student? "There are two kinds, there are all the J. Crew junkies and the rest are the pocket-protector boys," one student said. The campus has a very small minority population that is reportedly not very well integrated into campus life. According to one junior the minority situation is "okay, but we definitely should increase it." Bucknell does provide a student resource center that includes a minority affairs division, and a cultural house for students who choose to live with other minorities.

Walking by the dorms on any given day, you would probably hear the Dave Matthews Band blaring from the radio and see *Friends* on the tube. Although students agree that the campus is pretty uniform, they find that the "sense of community makes the school really close." One sophomore remarked of her classmates, "Everyone's really really friendly; it's not even funny."

Despite its remote location Bucknell students are happy there, finding that the secluded and enclosed nature of the school helps foster the sense of community that makes Bucknell an exciting and enriching place to live and learn.—*Katherina Payne and Staff*

FYI

The three best things about attending Bucknell are "class size, social scene, and the excellent professors."

The three worst things about attending Bucknell are "sometimes too small of a campus, registering for classes is inefficient, location."

The three things that every student shoud do before graduating from Bucknell are "get drunk and hook up, utilize the alumni and professors to make connections in your field, and live off-campus so you know what the responsibility is like."

One thing I'd like to have known before coming here is "that the social scene was so Greek-dominated!"

Carnegie Mellon University

Address: 5000 Forbes Ave, Pittsburgh, PA 15213
Phone: 412-268-2082
E-mail address: undergraduate-admission@andrew.cmu.edu
Web site URL: www.cmu.edu/enrollment/admission
Location: urban
Founded: 1900
Private or Public: private
Religious affiliation: none
Undergraduate enrollment: 5,136
Total enrollment: 8,436
Percent Male/Female: 64%/36%
Percent Minority: 29.0%

Percent African-American: 3.0%
Percent Hispanic: 5.0%
Percent Asian: 20.0%
Percent in-state/out-of-state: NA
Percent Pub HS: NA
Fraternities: 23%
Sororities: 9%
Number of Applicants: 14,130
Percent Accepted: 38%
Percent Accepted who enroll: 23%
Entering: 1,254
Transfers: 49
Application Deadline: 1 Jan
Mean SAT: 651 V, 710 M

Middle 50% SAT range: 600–700 V, 650–750 M
Middle 50% ACT range: 27–31
Mean ACT: 29
3 Most popular majors: elec and computer engineering, computer science, business administration
Retention: 91.8%
Graduation rate: 77.7%
Library: 935,888 volumes
Tuition and Fees: $22,300 in; $22,300 out
Room and Board: $6,810
On-campus housing: 99%
Financial aid, first-year: 56%

Carnegie Mellon students are sometimes affectionately referred to as "the freaks and geeks," according to one sophomore, because the school is known for its unusually strong fine arts, computer science, and engineering programs. This is not surprising considering that it is the first university in the world to have its own wireless computing network (which began in October 1999 in partnership with Lucent Technologies), as well as the first to award an undergraduate degree in drama (1917). The expression "freaks and geeks" isn't necessarily a bad thing—"everybody here is really nice. Even when they're studying their [butts] off, they're all really civil and there's never academic competition," said one freshman. In any case, students agree that the academics at their Pittsburgh-located school are challenging but incredible, that the social life is good if you know where to look, and most importantly—if it floats your boat, you can major in bagpipes.

Computers, Art, and More Computers

CMU is very computer-oriented; it's "a techie school all the way," said a sophomore, but he added that "there are many wonderful arts programs." Just keep i mind that "no matter what field you are i you *will* be a computer addict before yo leave," warned a business ethics and hi tory and public policy double major. Th academic requirements differ betwee the five undergraduate schools—the Me lon College of Science, the Carnegie Inst tute of Technology, the College of Fir Arts, the College of Humanities and Soci Sciences, and the School of Computer Sc ence. "Each school has a different 'co curriculum,' as does every major," e plained a German and business doub major. These core classes are not the mo enjoyable: "I have always hated GenE classes—I think they're boring and eas presenting no challenge to anyone and o fering only a little information," explaine a sophomore. Students agreed that th workload was quite heavy, especial in computer science, math, and enginee ing classes, but that slacker majo and classes did exist. Some cited mus performance, psychology, English, an modern languages as the easiest major Some of the specialized majors, especial the robotics minor in computer scienc and human-computer interactions, earne praise from students. Also mentioned wa the five-year master's program where "you start prepping for your master's while you're still an undergrad, and then [in the fifth year] you student-teach and do other master's classes. Then you graduate with a master's in your field *and* with a teaching certification," explained one student.

Class size tends toward extremes, from as small as 5 to 15 people in discussion sections and recitations, but with lecture courses ranging up to the 300s. However, lecture classes are still small enough that students can ask questions of the professors, if necessary. One student said that "a lot of professors are famous for research in their fields, but to us unenlightened, we wouldn't know the difference." Students did agree that the computer science and history profs are superb. In particular, Peter Stearns, who is the head of the History Department and Dean of Humanities and Social Sciences, "is an awesome historian—he knows so much and can put it in language that is easily understood," gushed one sophomore.

Student participation in classes, however, is not the best—"People here tend to be pretty apathetic," described a chemical engineering major. "In recitations, most people go just because they feel that they would be wasting their money should they not go. In lectures, half the class is asleep." Indeed, "profs who randomly call students from the roll tend to discover just how many people are asleep," said an electrical and computer engineering and computer science double major. Also, "there aren't enough TAs that speak English," complained a sophomore. Grading tends to be "pretty tough," but most professors grade on a curve, and will only curve students' grades up but not down. Student opinion on academics could be best summed up by one student's rave: "Rigorous, interesting, and just what I was looking for when I came here. Overall thumbs *way up*."

The Girls Got It Good

One legend at CMU exemplifies the imbalance between males and females at CMU: "A few years back—the number of years ranges—there was supposedly a survey done of all students in Computer Science. It was found that there were more Dave's enrolled than females," one sophomore

said. And despite the prevalence of wealthy kids, students all mentioned the diversity of the student population. An architecture student gushed, "we have students that dress, act, and have totally different personalities! That's what makes CMU so great!" Students pointed out that CMU is especially diverse in terms of sexuality—"It's a fairly gay-positive campus, with huge support from the administration," explained a member of cmuOUT. He also said that "there are also great deal of Asian—including Indian—and white interracial couples."

Unfortunately, mourned one sophomore who voiced the opinion of many CMU students, "In terms of attractive people, our campus is pretty limited. There's not really enough girls to go around, but, if I were a girl, I probably wouldn't want to date most of the freaky and dorky guys here either. So, in general, not many of us get play. It sucks to be us." It seems that most students definitely put academics above social life.

Furthermore, students said that social groups that formed during freshman orientation never quite seemed to break apart. One junior said that CMU "is very, very cliquish—especially among ethnic groups." Indeed, at dining halls (which serve awful meals—students warn future freshmen to get as small a dining plan as possible), tables are comprised either of "cliques or loners," said a sophomore. Not much dating goes on, and one information decision systems major said that "all of the sex is casual and fleeting."

However, frats and sororities are not hard to rush—"Rush is mainly going to the different houses and playing games," explained one freshman. Cool frats and sororities mentioned were Kappa Kappa Gamma, Phi Kappa Theta, and Theta Xi. Unfortunately, "parties suck . . . crappy beer, bad music," complained a student. Most freshmen only have the option of frat parties on weekends, explained one upperclassman, because they don't know enough people to go to other parties. Another junior said that upperclassmen tend to go to private parties or clubs and bars, while a sophomore concurred and added that they also go to raves. One student said that "There is a lot of binge drinking and a good bit of drug use, mostly weed."

Kegs are allowed on campus into the non-dry frat houses, but no alcohol is allowed in students' rooms. Cool theme parties include the jungle party, the swing party, and the beach party.

Most students who wish to stay sober on the weekends "watch movies in McConomy, the campus auditorium/movie theater with a kick-butt sound system." Other students opt to "go off-campus or simply play computer games," said a computer science major. Campus-organized activities are widely attended when they do occur. One sophomore mentioned the Spring Carnival in particular: "For three days the entire campus goes nuts with an actual carnival on one of the big parking lots. There are many activities, the highlights being carnival booths, buggy, and the mobot (mobile robot) competition." Buggy, explained an activites coordinator, involves the following: "Take a five-foot long bullet, cut it in half. Put it on wheels, put a person inside. Attach a bar at a sixty-degree angle from the ground, and push it around campus along a course that goes both uphill and downhill, around sharp turns. Make it a race."

Safe, Beautiful, and Good Eating

"I love Pittsburgh, this is a beautiful and safe campus," declared one pleased freshman. Added another student, "the campus is small, which is nice, because you can walk everywhere. It's very pleasant and has beautiful yellow brick buildings. However, unless it's a really nice day, you won't see anyone hanging out outside—we're notorious for hanging out in computer clusters!"

Despite the beautiful campus, most students move off campus after freshman year, even though many thought freshman year dorms were fine. Specifically, students say that Mudge, a converted mansion, is the best dorm, with suite–style, spacious rooms, and a gorgeous courtyard. Donner is "a dungeon, with small dingy rooms and shared bathrooms." One reason for the migration to off-campus housing, as one sophomore explained it, is that "it's difficult to get any unless you know people already there, at least sophomore year." Another sophomore said of off-campus housing, "It's usually cheaper than living in the dorms, and you get *way* more space and freedom." Dorms have RAs, but they're "cool." However, one major complaint made by a junior was that "there is no place to study here! You'd think they would have more open spaces!"

Good places to eat off campus include the Pirmanti Brothers, Lu-Lu's House Of Noodles, and The Union Grill Mad-Mex—there are plenty of great low-price restaurants on Craig Street, right near campus. For dates, students head over to Station Square, an area with nice restaurants.

Apathy Prevails

Varsity sports are definitely not a big thing at CMU—"People are too lazy. Only about five people go to football games," said a freshman. However, intramurals are pretty popular among students. Also well liked are the comedic organizations, KGB and CIA, which compete against one another. A sophomore mentioned that "there are quite a few hard-core community service organizations on campus." Also well respected is the International Relations Organization, Mayur (the Southeast Asian organization), and the campus newspaper. Most people participate in extracurricular activities, but people are identified more by their majors, especially the computer science majors, who, according to a junior, are known to play Quake 24/7.

> **"APATHY! APATHY! A-P-A- . . . nevermind . . ."**

A common cheer heard at the school that might reflect CMU and its students' wits and interests best is "APATHY! APATHY! A-P-A- . . . nevermind . . ." If building robots beats football, if being on the cutting-edge of incredible technology is as important as being in a great arts program for you, then CMU is definitely the place to go. As one student put it, "I have several friends who are double majoring in art and computer science and are amazingly talented in both. It makes for an interesting mix to have some of the most creative and some of the most boring people all in the same school."— *Jennifer Wang*

FYI

The three best things about attending Carnegie Mellon are "the weird relationship between the fine arts and engineers, living in Pittsburgh, and 24-hour computer clusters."

The three worst things about attending Carnegie Mellon are "the shortage of available women, the food on campus sucks, and student apathy."

The three things that every student should do before graduating from Carnegie Mellon are "to get away from the computer, sneak into the steam tunnels one night, participate in buggy and Spring Carnival."

One thing that I'd like to have known before coming here is "how boring, unimaginative and apathetic so many people are—there are a lot of cool people, but there are a lot of people who just love to code all day and have no social life or social skills."

Dickinson College

Address: P. O. Box 1773, Carlisle, PA 17013-2896
Phone: 717-245-1231
E-mail address: admit@dickinson.edu
Web site URL: www.dickinson.edu
Location: suburban
Founded: 1773
Private or Public: private
Religious affiliation: none
Undergraduate enrollment: 2,067
Total enrollment: 2,067
Percent Male/Female: 40%/60%
Percent Minority: 6.0%

Percent African-American: 1.0%
Percent Hispanic: 2.0%
Percent Asian: 3.0%
Percent in-state/out-of-state: 44%/56%
Percent Pub HS: 75%
Fraternities: 45%
Sororities: 39%
Number of Applicants: 3,434
Percent Accepted: 64%
Percent Accepted who enroll: 28%
Entering: 620
Transfers: 10
Application Deadline: 1 Feb

Mean SAT: NA
Middle 50% SAT range: 560–650 V, 550–640 M
Middle 50% ACT range: NA
Mean ACT: NA
3 Most popular majors: modern languages, political science, English
Retention: 89%
Graduation rate: 75%
Library: 452,632 volumes
Tuition and Fees: $23,505 in; NA out
Room and Board: $6,230
On-campus housing: 100%
Financial aid, first-year: 84%

Dickinson, a small liberal arts college located in suburban Pennsylvania, has much more to offer than its pastoral campus suggests. It provides students with an atmosphere of hard work and partying and a diverse educational background.

Dickinson is known for its foreign-language and political science departments. Many students opt to major in political science with the hope of eventual admission to the college's highly ranked law school.

Small, Intimate Classes

Students praise Dickinson's student-faculty ratio. The average class size is 15 to 30 students, except for several popular introductory-level courses in the science departments. All classes are taught by professors. These professors all live on Dickinson's campus and frequently invite students to their homes for meals. One student reported that some professors can even be spotted at college parties.

Students must fulfill distribution requirements outside their majors. Undergrads must take courses in philosophy, religion or environmental studies, the social sciences, the natural sciences (including lab courses), a foreign language, comparative civilizations, physical education, and a literature course in English or a foreign language. To help fulfill these requirements, some students seek out the rare "easy-A" courses such as introductory courses in psychology, lighting, and art history. While some students find these requirements "a hassle because you have to take courses you wouldn't ordinarily take," most students agree that the requirements end up making them "well-rounded." One student reported, "You have to work hard in all your classes. Dickinson has a lot more course work than a lot of other schools." All freshmen take the Freshman Seminar, an introduction to all aspects of college life, from improving one's writing to learning to make full use of the university's facilities. To further supplement the variety of classes, Dickinson allows students to design their own majors under supervision of an academic panel that reviews their course schedules every semester. Two new majors, environmental studies and environmental sciences, were added last year.

In addition to the programs offered on the campus, students can choose to spend a semester or year abroad at a wide variety of affiliated programs around the world. Programs in most European countries, Africa, Asia, and South and Central America offer the opportunity either to take classes pertaining to the student's major, or to "integrate themselves into an entirely different culture by means of host families and internship programs." Students nearly universally praised the study-abroad options at Dickinson, one going so far as to deem study-abroad "the shining jewel in Dickinson's crown."

For quiet study on campus, some students recommend the Spahr Library, although one senior called it the center of "the campus social scene." With the recent addition of the Waidner wing, the library is much larger, brighter, and more comfortable, with new furniture, computer facilities, and outlets and internet ports to accomodate laptop users. In addition, the library is also more research-friendly, since the stacks were enlarged making more materials easily accessible to students.

When they are not in the mood for the library, students opt to study in their dorm rooms or the lounge areas in academic buildings; for group studying, comfortable chairs in the spacious basement of the student union are popular.

"The Hub" of Social Life

The student union building houses the Hub cafeteria, a place to eat, study, and socialize. As one student said, "Everyone at Dickinson eats at exactly the same time, so you can find anyone at the Hub at noon." The food is largely praised, and recent renovations that shortened lines and lessened crowding in the cafeteria have improved students' opinions. A flex plan, allowing students to purchase 16 meals a week with extra points for the cafeteria and snack bar, is an alternative to the traditional required 21-meal-a-week plan. Those students looking for a break from the cafeteria turn to the Backdoor Cafe, a small local restaurant within walking distance of the campus, which is popular for its pizza and lasagna. Another area restaurant and bar frequented by students is the Gingerbread Man.

Fun Stuff

According to one senior, "everyone is involved" in several extracurricular activities, ranging from the choir and drama club to the student senate. Each foreign-language department has its own club. Concerts and plays are held in the auditorium, where renovations are under way to improve acoustics. Student publications include the yearbook, the *Microcosm*, and the weekly *Dickinsonian* newspaper. Literary magazines come and go; as one student explained, many times the magazines "fizzle out" after several issues. One junior reported that due to Dickinson's small size, there is only "a limited amount of talent and leadership" in the student body and frequently, activities are run by "the same people over and over again, just like it was in high school."

The Kline Athletic Center is a top-notch fitness center that, according to one student, has "all the resources, if you want them." The Kline Center has a new wing which houses all-new aerobic equipment and a huge Nautilus and free-weight system. Students also praise the gym for the extensive aerobics schedule and impressive track.

The most popular varsity teams are football and swimming. Except for homecoming (when alumni return) there is not a lot of support or school spirit for the teams. Intramural teams are quite popular and can be used to fulfill the physical education requirement. Soccer, basketball, and volleyball draw the most participants, especially those athletes who "don't feel like putting in all the time required for a varsity sport," one student said.

Where Sleeping Options Abound

Dorm life is "decent," according to Dickinson residents. The campus is divided into quads and traditional dorms. While the dorms have kitchens and are coed, quads are smaller and have new carpeting. The latter, as Student Directed Learning Centers, allow for theme housing including multicultural and equality groups, language houses, volunteer groups, ROTC members, and fraternities and sororities. The traditional residential halls "give more sense of community. They're louder and more fun," according to one undergrad. Another student praised Adams Hall for its large halls and secluded nature. Some criticize Morgan for its "maze-like quality." Most students live on campus for four years, an advantage one student praised because it "allows me to focus on my work alone. I don't have to deal with rent and apartments this early on."

Drink Until You Puke

Social life at Dickinson revolves around drinking. As one student said, "They don't call it 'Drinkinson' for nothing." Greek life at Dickinson is quite prevalent. Although some independents feel the Greeks are condescending, the Greeks themselves "don't see independents as losers or anything," said one student. There is reportedly a great deal of tension, however, between the administration and the Greeks. Since the administration's crackdown due to the death of a student during rush week several years ago, Greek life is seen as "going downhill." According to one student, "The fraternities and sororities do positive things for the community, too. We're not like *Animal House* or anything."

For those not interested in Greek life, there are several popular bars in Carlisle. The G-man, Fast Eddie's, and the Blessed Oliver Plunckett attract a student crowd.

To provide alternatives to alcohol-centered social events, the Campus Activities Board sponsors concerts, shows movies, and brings in performers ranging from hypnotists and magicians to comedians and singers such as Harry Connick, Jr. However, some students report that, despite the plethora of non-Greek activites available on- and off-campus, a large number of students leave Carlisle and "head for more fertile cultural areas on the weekends."

Town-Gown Blues

Carlisle, the quaint neighboring town, has "two bad malls and a bowling alley that closes at 5 P.M.," reported one undergrad. Some students sense a strong anti-Dickinson sentiment among the residents of Carlisle. As one student explained, "A lot of the people see us as 'little rich kids,' but they don't realize how much business we pull for them." While many students complain that "there's nothing to do" at Dickinson, one advised that "there actually is a lot to do if you know where to look." Students occasionally travel to Harrisburg and the factory outlets in Reading. As one student said, "If you want to do stuff, you really need a car."

> The traditional residential halls "give more sense of community. They're louder and more fun," according to one undergrad.

Dickinson's campus of limestone buildings is considered safe, an attribute the college takes measures to maintain. Dickinson requires keys and electronic key tags for entry into the dorms and provides a student patrol system. Dickinson even provides a shuttle from the campus to and from one of the most popular bars to "make sure all the drunk kids make it home safely," said one student. Although some students complain about the small size, suburban atmosphere, and upper-middle-class white-student stereotype at Dickinson, others find the size an advantage. "Even though I know a lot of people at this school, I'm constantly meeting new people," one junior remarked.

Upon graduating, Dickinson students traditionally march through the front door of the oldest building on campus. Students see this as a sign that Dickinson has opened the door to the world for them. In that world, Dickinson graduates can reminisce about four years at a college with minimal diversity but rich in a friendly, small-school atmosphere. —*Alexandra Rethore*

FYI

The three best things about attending Dickinson are "the beautiful limestone buildings and the landscape, the approachable professors, and the people you meet here."

The three worst things about attending Dickinson are "strict rules on partying, lack of housing, the town of Carlisle."

The three things that everyone should do before graduating from Dickinson are "study in front of the warm fireplace in the library, take a professor out to eat, lay out on Morgan Field during a sunny spring day."

One thing I'd like to have known before coming here is "how much you need a car."

Drexel University

Address: 3141 Chestnut Street; Philadelphia, PA 19104
Phone: 215-895-2400
E-mail address: undergrad-admissions@mail.drexel.edu
Web site URL: www.drexel.edu
Location: urban
Founded: 1891
Private or Public: private
Religious affiliation: none
Undergraduate enrollment: 8,902
Total enrollment: 10,455
Percent Male / Female: 64% / 36%
Percent Minority: 15.3%

Percent African-American: 1.0%
Percent Hispanic: 2.0%
Percent Asian: 12.0%
Percent in-state / out-of-state: 56% / 46%
Percent Pub HS: NA
Fraternities: 8%
Sororities: 5%
Number of Applicants: 9,303
Percent Accepted: 69%
Percent Accepted who enroll: 33%
Entering: 2,118
Transfers: 0
Application Deadline: 1 Mar
Mean SAT: 553 V, 578 M

Middle 50% SAT range: 500–600 V, 520–630 M
Middle 50% ACT range: NA
Mean ACT: NA
3 Most popular majors: electrical engineering, mechanical engineering, finance
Retention: 84%
Graduation rate: 50%
Library: 500,000 volumes
Tuition and Fees: $24,280 in; $24,280 out
Room and Board: $7,950
On-campus housing: 100%
Financial aid, first-year: 79%

The word students most commonly use to describe a Drexel education is "practical." Drexel students alternate classroom learning with full-time jobs and internships during their co-op semesters.

The Curriculum

"When you're comparing Drexel to other schools, think of the real-world experience Drexel offers," one senior advised. For up to three semesters during their sophomore and junior years, Drexel students leave the classroom for internships at various companies. Each internship lasts about six months and pays, on average, about $10,000. The largest co-op employers include SmithKline Beecham, Lockheed Martin, ARCO Chemical Company, PECO Energy Company, and E. I. DuPont de Nemours & Co., Inc. One senior business major who spent a semester at a steel company and two semesters at an investment banking firm explained, "It gives you good exposure at a very young age." According to students, many internships lead to employment offers.

Drexel is divided into six colleges: the College of Arts and Sciences, the College of Business and Administration, the College of Design Art, the College of Engineering, the College of Information Science and Technology, and the College of Evening and Professional Studies. However, the engineering school predominates and offers better facilities than the other schools. One freshman complained, "Ninety percent of my money goes to the engineering school even though I am not an engineering student." However, many feel that the school derives its reputation from engineering and therefore benefits all students by maintaining excellence in engineering.

And all fields of engineering, from computer to civil, are highly regarded. The architecture program draws raves from most who participate. As a result of the co-op program, business majors report satisfaction with their learning experience at Drexel. However, humanities majors often feel they have been given the "Drexel Shaft" and find the overly technical library content useless.

Campus and People

The Drexel campus itself is at best "functional" and at worst "ugly," students report. Drexel houses students in five dorms. However, many undergrads commute or choose to live off campus. The living arrangements are generally "livable but unspectacular." Yet, students writhe at the mention of dining hall food. Several students suggest that just going to the dining hall is a hopeless endeavor. One student argued, "Don't buy a meal plan. You'll regret it." Philadelphia offers plenty of eating options for the student who does not use Drexel's cafeteria.

> **"When you're comparing Drexel to other schools, think of the real-world experience Drexel offers,"** one senior advised.

The campus has a diverse population, but compared to surrounding areas of Philadelphia, the African-American population on campus is small. Drinking is common, but one student complained that "Drexel parties are lame."

Philadelphia

Drexel offers both the risks and opportunities of urban living. More than one non-Philadelphia native bemoaned Drexel's location and even the city of Philadelphia itself. One student quoted the Sherman Edwards musical *1776* to describe the city and his experience at Drexel: "Nothing's ever solved in foul, fetid, fuming, foggy, filthy Philadelphia." However, the consensus is that Philadelphia is a net positive. There is crime on campus, but emergency phones and an escort service have increased safety at Drexel, and crime has declined citywide over the past few years. The city offers a huge spectrum of recreational activities. One student frequents the Hindi music clubs, while another takes a noncredit class offered at the Philadelphia Art Museum. Many Drexel students attend fraternity parties at Temple and the University of Pennsylvania, while others party at the city's many clubs. South Street, only a few blocks from campus, offers a strong alternative scene.

For the focused pre-professional, Drexel can be a firm stepping-stone into well-paying and satisfying employment.
—*Brian Abaluck and Staff*

FYI
The three best things about attending Drexel are "Philadelphia, the internships, and the facilities."
The three worst things about attending Drexel are "the workload, those oh-so-exciting parties, and humanities classes."
The three things that every student should do before graduating are "visit the Art Museum, go to Independence Mall, dance at the clubs on Delaware Avenue."
One thing I'd like to have known before coming here is "that you need ID if you're under 21 to do a bunch of things."

Franklin and Marshall College

Address: PO Box 3003;
Lancaster, PA 17604-
3003
Phone: 717-295-3953
E-mail address:
admission@fandm.edu
Web site URL:
www.fandm.edu
Location: suburban
Founded: 1787
Private or Public: private
Religious affiliation:
none
**Undergraduate
enrollment:** 1,862
Total enrollment: 1,862
Percent Male / Female:
50%/50%
Percent Minority: 11.2%

Percent African-American:
3.0%
Percent Hispanic: 3.0%
Percent Asian: 5.0%
**Percent in-state / out-of-
state:** 36%/64%
Percent Pub HS: NA
Fraternities: 40%
Sororities: 30%
Number of Applicants:
3,926
Percent Accepted: 54%
**Percent Accepted who
enroll:** 24%
Entering: 509
Transfers: 0
Application Deadline:
1 Feb
Mean SAT: 623 V, 635 M

Middle 50% SAT range:
570–670 V,
590–680 M
Middle 50% ACT range:
24–31
Mean ACT: 27
3 Most popular majors:
government, biology,
business
Retention: 95%
Graduation rate: 73%
Library: 390,000 volumes
Tuition and Fees: $23,720
in; $23,720 out
Room and Board: $5,730
On-campus housing:
100%
Financial aid, first-year:
47%

If enthusiasm is what you are looking for, Franklin and Marshall is the place to find it. Students dedicate themselves to all aspects of college life. Many chose the college for a challenging course load, and that is what the school delivers. But their dedication extends far beyond the classroom. From helping in the community to enjoying themselves on the weekends, F&M students enjoy keeping themselves busy. Nestled in the picturesque town of Lancaster, this small liberal arts college prides itself on both academic excellence and rigor, combined with a healthy taste for amusement.

STUDY, STUDY, STUDY!

"Classes are hard," F&M students unanimously chime. When asked what an easy major is at F&M, one senior replied "I don't think that there is one." But, F&M is a college designed to be tough, and the students rise to the challenge posed by their inspiring professors. "I have tons of reading to do every night. Some people don't do all of the reading . . . but those are the students who only get average grades."

A self-proclaimed liberal arts college, F&M's focus has long been on the sciences. "The school has pretty good facili-

ties for being [so] small," one senior reported. Students say F&M's computer facilities are excellent, with Ethernet connections available in all public areas, such as libraries and classrooms, and in most of the dorms—"my whole life is on the Web," one student boasted. While the science complex was renovated recently, the school is currently trying to help the arts programs with renovations and expansions. The arts "deserve better," one student said.

Many students choose F&M for the premed program. Students "don't always survive the pre-med program, but that's what they come for," said one undergrad. "I have sympathy for the pre-meds," one junior commented. "They hammer themselves." Departments such as English, classics, and psychology are also quite strong.

Distribution requirements consist of courses in at least three different areas, such as Knowledge and Belief, Foreign Study, and Social Science. Two semesters of foreign language also are required.

Class sizes are small at F&M, topping off at around 20 to 25 students, so some freshmen have trouble getting into the classes they want. Many feel that the close rapport with professors and the small, discussion-intensive sections far outweigh any problems with registration. F&M professors, including Howard Kaye and Carol Auster in sociology, Sanford Pinsker in English, and Curtis Bentzel in German, earn student praise for their dedication and desire to teach. They "seem to want to be here [and] . . . treat you like you're smart," one student said. By the time you graduate, one student was happy to report, you're "close to one if not close to a bunch." It is not unusual for students to eat dinner or baby-sit at their professors' houses. Many students remain in close contact with professors even after graduation. One junior exclaimed in praise of his profs, "If you give them an inch, they'll give you a ton!"

Franklin and Marshall students are quick to point out that their college is not entirely a machine that grinds their faces into the books. Instead, they characterize the college as a place "that is really academically rigorous and then parties like at any other school." Extracurriculars provide the main chance to meet other people, and if "one is not involved, it makes it harder," one student reported. Popular activities to which students devote a great deal of time and energy include the drama society, known as the Green Room; the weekly newspaper, the *College Reporter*; the radio station, WFNM; the Student Congress; Minority Integration Program; and the College Entertainment Committee. Various community service programs connected with F&M's new Community and Public Service Institute and the America Reads Program also attract wide participation. Students involved in these campus activities, as well as in work study programs, consider themselves "some really dedicated individuals."

Outside the Classroom . . .

Much of the F&M social scene is dominated by Greek societies, which although not officially recognized by the college, involve the majority of the student body. Weekends consist of "frat parties, frats, and more frats," according to one senior. Although much town-gown tension stems from the Greek houses' loud parties and initiation rituals, which one member said get "pretty rough," students seem to find

that the independence of the Greek societies from the college has pulled a lot of the tension away from the school. At the same time, students agree that membership or non-membership defines them. Campus cliques center on Greek membership and reportedly turn the dining hall experience into a "Dining Hall Culture." One student warned, "You don't just sit anywhere . . . like high school."

For those who dislike the Greek system and the many parties dominated by drinking, "there really isn't much left to do [but] . . . sit around and complain," one senior groaned. Another summarized the F&M college work ethic as "kill yourself working during the week and kill yourself drinking on the weekend."

To provide an alternative for those uninterested in Greek activities, the school sponsors parties, such as the Blizzard Bash and Around the World, movies, lectures, and an occasional comedian. Recent guests include Kwaisi Infume, Maya Angelou, John Updike, Newt Gingrich, Billy Joel, and the Dave Matthews Band. A popular campus hangout is Ben's Underground, which has a pub-like atmosphere where students can eat snacks and play pool or versions of supermarket bingo and *The Dating Game*.

As for real dating, one experienced senior reported that "there isn't really much to do in Lancaster, so the dating scene is very limited." Frat parties are the center of social life on weekends, and "the parties are a lot of drinking and some dancing and hooking up. That's about it." Another student agreed that the social scene was "hookup central," with very few steady couples populating the campus.

The town of Lancaster gets mixed reviews from students. Some like its quaint affability while others lament that "Lancaster sucks . . . nothing to do." The town has a dance club for students over 18, a 24-hour bowling alley, as well as many restaurants and coffeehouses, such as the popular Fred and Mary's and the Cafe Angst. Philadelphia and Baltimore, as well as the closer malls and outlets, offer more excitement for students who have cars, but some claimed that there was too much work to allow frequent excursions.

Food at F&M gets the same sort of tempered criticism as it does everywhere. In the dining hall, suggested one grumpy student, avoid everything. Another exclaimed, "Some of their creations are just amazing!" such as the orange cheese sauce and "ratatouille." The options for vegetarians are mainly salad and pasta, and according to one student "it's bad, it's bad pasta." But, students gladly use their meal credit for snacks and sandwiches at the college Common Ground, and food in Lancaster is rated highly, with many pizza spots, chain and local restaurants, and a Farmer's Market for fresh vegetables.

Dorm life at F&M is almost universally praised. First-year students and sophomores are required to live in the dorms, with mostly coed floors, although students can request single-sex housing. Dorm life is supervised by RAs—residents call them "tools of the administration"—but this does not seriously hamper social life. The dorms are reported to be very spacious and convenient, with phone and Internet connections, but many juniors and seniors move off campus, where the housing is "pretty good," although security is less tight outside the perimeters of the campus security patrols. As for safety, walking at night "could be dangerous if people are stupid," but students generally walk in groups, especially to and from off-campus locales.

Enthusiastic participation in athletics or attendance at sporting events are not priorities at F&M. The football and basketball teams are popular and their games are fairly well attended, especially by certain Fummers who paint their faces blue and do push-ups for every Diplomat touchdown. But overall, the teams are not a central rallying point for school spirit, which, on the whole, is rated very low—"people are really negative about the school . . . very cynical in general."

F&M is a Division III college and does not give athletic scholarships. For those not on teams, club sports and intramurals are popular. The new Athletic Sports and Fitness Center (ASFC) is good for many exercise-hungry students.

While F&M students generally think of themselves as nonpolitical and "pretty apathetic," many are also fairly conservative in their views on social issues. The student population is "more diverse than people give it credit for," but one student admitted that racial minorities are seldom fully integrated into the mainstream of the student body. However, the small minority groups are active and outspoken, with the Black Student Union acclaimed for being the only really politically active forum on campus.

> Frat parties are the center of social life on weekends, and "the parties are a lot of drinking and some dancing and hooking up. That's about it."

While the challenges of the social environment make some F&M students "a little bitter," the intelligent cynicism of the student body seems to fit well with the mission of the school as a place of devotion to rigorous academics. Franklin and Marshall is a perfect fit for those students with an enthusiastic desire to educate themselves, to better their community, and to make time for a healthy social life as well. The requirements for students both in and out of the classroom are intense, and the process of rising to meet these challenges breeds a healthy dedication to all aspects of college life.—*Erik Weiss and Staff*

FYI
The three best things about attending Franklin and Marshall are "good classes, crazy partying, and air-conditioned dorms."
The three worst things about attending Franklin and Marshall are "you can't touch the trees, there's not much to do except drink, and Lancaster is not so exciting."
The three things that every student should do before graduating from Franklin and Marshall are "have Chinese food at that place in the student center, go to the Farmer's Market, and make a stir-fry."
One thing I'd like to have known before coming here is "that people judge you by your fraternity."

Gettysburg College

Address: Admissions Office; Eisenhower House; Gettysburg College; Gettysburg, PA 17325-1484
Phone: 717-337-6100
E-mail address: admiss@gettysburg.edu
Web site URL: www.gettysburg.edu
Location: rural
Founded: 1832
Private or Public: private
Religious affiliation: Lutheran
Undergraduate enrollment: 2,123
Total enrollment: 2,123
Percent Male/Female: 48%/52%

Percent Minority: 3.2%
Percent African-American: 1.0%
Percent Hispanic: 1.0%
Percent Asian: 1.0%
Percent in-state/out-of-state: 26%/74%
Percent Pub HS: 76%
Fraternities: 31%
Sororities: 25%
Number of Applicants: 3,641
Percent Accepted: 73%
Percent Accepted who enroll: 24%
Entering: 638
Transfers: 0
Application Deadline: 15 Feb
Mean SAT: 595 V, 600 M

Middle 50% SAT range: 550–630 V, 560–645 M
Middle 50% ACT range: 24-28
Mean ACT: 25
3 Most popular majors: business administration/management, psychology, political science
Retention: 87%
Graduation rate: 74%
Library: 340,000 volumes
Tuition and Fees: $23,112 in; $23,112 out
Room and Board: $5,346
On-campus housing: 100%
Financial aid, first-year: 59%

Six score and sixteen years ago, President Abraham Lincoln issued his famous address in Gettysburg, Pennsylvania. Today, the town is the site of Gettysburg College, a top-notch, small liberal arts school. Gettysburg has a student population committed to learning and a devoted faculty adept at its facilitation.

Academics at Gettysburg are centered on a traditional liberal arts core. While the school frequently adjusts the core requirements, one student compared them to the distribution requirements he had in high school, including math, English, hard science, and social science. Students also stressed that the requirements still leave them with ample room to form their schedules. As one student summed up, "Some [required classes] are eye-openers, but others are a pain."

The most popular majors at Gettysburg according to students are history, management, and psychology. All of these departments have strong faculty, according to students. Some consider management the least difficult major.

Individual Attention

Whatever one's major, one sure thing at Gettysburg College is small classes. Even popular introductory courses seldom have more than 50 students, and most upper-level courses have between 10 and 15 students. Classes of this size make it easy for student-faculty interaction. One student said, "My professors have even called me to see how things were going." Another added, "When I was in freshman year, some of my professors invited our class to her house for a cookout. It was a lot of fun and made us feel less homesick." Since Gettysburg is a small school, courses are also small, but few students report being shut out of any class. For courses with capped enrollments, seniors and majors get priority.

The Gettysburg campus itself presents students with a panoply of architectural styles. One of the oldest buildings, Pennsylvania Hall, was built in 1837, while the newest, a residential complex known as the Quarry Suites, is brand new for the year 2000. In addition, a new science building is also currently under construction. The most notable building is Glatfelter Hall, a liberal arts classroom building built like a medieval castle. Like many small colleges set apart from urban areas, the Gettysburg campus is self-contained. Students consider Gettysburg one of the safest campuses in America. The main drawback is the dearth of off-campus attractions within walking distance.

Musselman Library, built just a little over a decade ago, is universally praised by students as both a place to find materials and a place to study. As one student said, "Everyone goes to the library." Another added, "I also have my own personal 'hiding' place to do work. . . . I won't reveal it 'cause then others will realize how quiet it is and it won't be quiet anymore!" The other advantage of campus facilities is that almost all buildings are air-conditioned.

Housing at Gettysburg is based on seniority. While not everyone lives on campus, almost all students live in Gettysburg housing—either dorms or apartments in town owned by the university. Freshmen are all required to live on campus, and generally receive the smallest rooms. All dorms have live-in residential assistants, usually juniors and seniors, who serve both as counselors and disciplinarians. In addition, upperclassmen have the option of fraternity or sorority housing, choosing from approximately 11 fraternities and 5 sororities.

Fantastic Food

There is a central dining hall at Gettysburg, called Servo, as well as a fast-food take-out service called Cafe 101, more popularly referred to as The Bullet Hole. Students are upbeat about the food. "In all honesty, the food here is really great. Honest!" one student said. Freshmen must purchase a 20-meal-per-week plan; upperclassmen can choose fewer meals per week or go off the plan altogether. Students also frequent Mamma Venturi's Pizzeria (often called Mamma V's) and the Pizza House.

Intramural sports are popular at Gettysburg, as are choirs, political organizations, and community-service organizations. Aspiring writers can join the weekly news-

paper, the *Gettysburgian*, a biannual literary magazine, the *Mercury*, or the yearbook, the *Spectrum*.

Facets of Social Life

According to students, the social scene at Gettysburg truly has two faces. On the one hand, approximately half the students are involved in the Greek system, and reportedly rely heavily on fraternity and sorority houses to provide them with social activities. Independent students spend time at the Junction, a campus social center that features live bands, and a number of off-campus hangouts such as the Lincoln Diner, known for its ice cream, and the local movie theater. Regarding the alcohol policy, one student responded, "The college's policy toward alcohol is similar to that of other colleges: they do not support underage drinking and will not allow kegs on campus, but they realize what goes on in the world of college."

Regarding the alcohol policy, one student responded, "The college's policy toward alcohol is similar to that of other colleges: they do not support underage drinking and will not allow kegs on campus, but they realize what goes on in the world of college."

In general, Gettysburg students classify themselves as middle- and upper-class, clean-cut, conservative, but not politically active, and from the East Coast. However, one student hastened to point out that there is some economic diversity: "About half of us are on work-study programs, [and] not wealthy; that's just the stereotype." Students claim their peers are generally laid-back and tolerant—one of the reasons many are glad they chose Gettysburg College.—*David Oppenheim and Staff*

FYI

The three best things about attending Gettysburg are "extensive extracurricular opportunities, small classes, and the small-town environment."

The three worst things about attending Gettysburg are "high cost, the relative lack of things to do in the town of Gettysburg, and Safety and Security are really strict, even about little things like parking tickets."

The three things every student should do before graduating from Gettysburg are "visit the battlefields and learn at least a little bit about the battle, attend the Don't Break the Seal party at Mamma V's (free drinks until someone goes to the bathroom), and attend a sporting event and cheer on the Bullets."

The one thing I'd have liked to know before coming here is "how big the Greek system is."

Haverford College

Address: 370 Lancaster Avenue, Haverford, PA 19041-1392
Phone: 610-896-1350
E-mail address: admitme@haverford.edu
Web site URL: http://www.haverford.edu
Location: suburban
Founded: 1833
Private or Public: private
Religious affiliation: none
Undergraduate enrollment: 1,118
Total enrollment: 1,118
Percent Male/Female: 47%/53%
Percent Minority: 21.0%

Percent African-American: 6.0%
Percent Hispanic: 5.0%
Percent Asian: 10.0%
Percent in-state/out-of-state: 17%/83%
Percent Pub HS: 54%
Fraternities: 0%
Sororities: 0%
Number of Applicants: 2,650
Percent Accepted: 33%
Percent Accepted who enroll: 35%
Entering: 302
Transfers: 3
Application Deadline: 15 Jan

Mean SAT: 640–750 V, 640–720 M
Middle 50% SAT range: 640–740 V, 630–720 M
Middle 50% ACT range: NA
Mean ACT: NA
3 Most popular majors: biology, English, psychology
Retention: 97%
Graduation rate: 88%
Library: 513,500 volumes
Tuition and Fees: $24,940 in; NA out
Room and Board: $7,910
On-campus housing: 100%
Financial aid, first-year: 34%

Imagine a top-ranked college where the professors know your name. At Haverford, instructors not only know your name, but have "baked bread, held class in their houses, and come to my soccer games," explained one student. Professors who invite students into their homes only reflect the cohesiveness of the college as a whole. Haverford's honor code is another reflection of close-knit college life. Under the code, a student may arrange with his teacher to take an exam in his own room, and hand it in later. Undergrads say that the honor code attracts a certain type of student who wants the responsibility and respect that comes along with the code. One student said, "I was doing laundry, and I noticed a dollar bill taped on to a washing machine with a little note that said, 'If you put quarters in this machine and forgot to run it, here's your dollar back.' This is the type of behavior that often occurs at Haverford. Everyone respects each other so much that no one even considers taking money if it's not theirs."

Academic Intimacy

Students cited Haverford's small size (only about 1,200 students) as one of its most attractive features. "I think I'm getting a better education here than I would at a bigger school," said one undergrad. "I like learning from someone who knows who I am." Students said, "Classes are generally small—but not as small as they tell you on the tours." The largest classes might have up to 100 students in them, and the smallest range from 7–12 students. One undergrad said her 65-person introductory chemistry course "doesn't even feel like a huge class—the teacher knows and remembers everyone's names." Students also praised the responsiveness of their professors outside the classroom. "I've always been able to schedule an appointment with my professor," explained one student, "either by speaking to him after class or by e-mail—I've never had to wait more than a day to meet with him."

Many "fords," as students call themselves, were also attracted to the school because of its academic reputation. Remarkably, though, the honor code prohibits students from discussing their grades. Competition is "taboo," but students are "constantly challenged." "People are stressed," explained one senior, "they often think and talk about work. It's easy to lose perspective and become unaware of the outside world."

Haverford offers students the opportunity to try out classes at the beginning of each term. During a two-week-long "shopping period" at the start of the semester, students are encouraged to attend any classes in which they are interested. One student praised the system saying, "It gives us a chance to sample courses, and it helps to prevent students from getting stuck taking courses they hate." English and biology are the most popular majors, and both involve a heavy workload. According to one bio major, "Haverford earns its reputation of being a top-notch intensive biology program. The workload can be overwhelming, and is designed to drill the knowledge and understanding of concepts into you."

Haverford's small size doesn't affect its class offerings—students have the option of taking classes at Bryn Mawr, the University of Pennsylvania, or Swarthmore. Haverford and Bryn Mawr are especially close, and "before graduating, every student should take at least one class at Bryn Mawr." Additionally, Haverford offers a large study abroad program. "There are programs on all continents (excluding Antarctica)," said one student. "If you want to go there and are an average Haverford student, the college will help you get there."

Welcome Freshmen

According to one freshman, "Haverford is the perfect place to get over homesickness." Their customs group immediately integrates students into the Haverford community. Led by two upperclassmen, called "customs people," the customs group consists of about 12 "frosh" in the same hall and helps ease the transition into Haverford life. Because freshmen live with their customs group, they often go to meals and other events together, sometimes becoming so close that students describe the group as their "family" and their customs people as their "surrogate parents." Freshmen also have an upper class advisor (UCA) and faculty advisors, who help them in choosing classes each semester, but one student said, "it's generally easier to meet with your UCA because his door is always open."

Freshmen live in one of three dorms: Gunmere, "made of cinder block, so it is kind of like a jail cell"; Barclay, with many doubles and a few singles; or the HCA, Haverford College Apartments, where four students share a two-bedroom apartment. The apartments have the advantage of a kitchen and living room, although they are nearly a half-mile from campus. A student in one of the dorms reported, "I'm at most 400 feet from my farthest class." Most upperclassmen opt to live in the on-campus apartments or in themed houses.

The meal plan (20 meals per week) is required for freshmen only. The dining center (DC) is being redone, and students said it is a lot more aesthetically pleasing. Students also praised the dining options available to them, including their new Edy's ice cream machines. On Fridays, students enjoy Pastabilities, where 6 chefs cook made-to-order pasta.

Sports and the Social Scene

"People at Haverford seem pretty apathetic about sports unless they happen to play one," one student remarked. "The stands at the soccer games normally don't have more than 30 students in them, usually less, and often a good number of them are from the other school. The school doesn't have a football team, let alone a suitable stadium. My high school's football field had more bleacher space, and our team was awful." Haverford competes in NCAA Division III sports, and each student must complete a requirement of 6 half-semesters of sports by the end of their sophomore year.

Weekends start on Thursday nights, although some students complained, "Friday nights are dull." One student explained, "the student body would fall down in exhaustion if there were big parties on Thursday, Friday, and Saturday nights, so the social committee decided not to plan parties on Friday nights." There is always a campus-wide dance on Saturday night, and most students stop by after attending smaller get-togethers. Popular theme dances include La Fiesta, featuring Spanish and Mexican music, and the Drag Ball sponsored by the Gay and Lesbian Organization. "It's really interesting to see how many students actually do dress up for them," commented one student.

At Haverford, JSAAPP, the Joint Student-Administration Alcohol Policy Panel is a representative body of students and administration who meet to discuss violations of the alcohol policy. "The alcohol policy pretty much trusts us to drink responsibly," explained one student. "The college will not bust anyone for drinking, regardless of their age."

Haverford itself is located in a small town; however, there is plenty to do off campus. Students travel to Philadelphia, which is 20 minutes away by train, and visit a number of other nearby colleges, including Bryn Mawr, St. Joseph's, and Villanova. Freshmen aren't allowed to have cars, but restaurants, such as Ruby's diner and Peace O' Pizza, as well as ice cream parlors and a minimall, lie within a 10–15 minute walk from campus.

Haver-bubble

Students admitted that Haverford students tend to look very similar. "Haverford is not especially diverse," explained one student. "There has been an effort to recruit minority students, but it is still not totally effective. There isn't a wide showing of international students, and that explains why there are only two major ethnic clubs—the Asian Association and the African-American/Latino Club." A large proportion of the school is "white, upper-middle class, and from the east coast," although one undergrad argued that "Haverford students are not racially diverse, but they have diverse interests like sports, the arts and community service." Most Haverford students identified themselves as "politically liberal."

> "People are stressed. They often think and talk about work. It's easy to lose perspective and be unaware of the outside world."

Regardless of their interests and background, students felt that the honor code leads to greater respect between members of the community. "Everyone's nice," said one undergrad. "They say 'hi' to you even if you don't know them." The Haverford community is sometimes nicknamed the "Haver-bubble" since "it is such an honest place, it doesn't seem like the real world." One freshman said, "People ask me if I will be ready for the real world when I leave Haverford. I don't know, but I'm just going to enjoy my four years here."—*Ashleigh Hegedus*

FYI

The three best things about attending Haverford are "the great professors, they really get to know you; the honor code; and the beautiful campus, close to Philadelphia."

The three worst things about attending Haverford are "lack of public recognition; homogeneous student body; and its small size and limited choices of classes and extracurricular activities."

The three things that every student should do before graduating from Haverford are "get locked in the library and play dark tag; eat breadsticks at Skeeter's, the student run, on-campus pizza joint; and climb on the field house tin roof."

One thing I'd like to have known before coming here is "Friday nights are sooo dead here."

Lafayette College

Address: 118 Markle Hall; Easton, PA 18042
Phone: 610-330-5100
E-mail address: admissions@lafayette.edu
Web site URL: www.lafayette.edu
Location: suburban
Founded: 1826
Private or Public: private
Religious affiliation: Presbyterian
Undergraduate enrollment: 2,244
Total enrollment: 2,244
Percent Male/Female: 54%/46%
Percent Minority: 7.2%

Percent African-American: 4.0%
Percent Hispanic: 2.0%
Percent Asian: 1.0%
Percent in-state/out-of-state: 28%/72%
Percent Pub HS: NA
Fraternities: 38%
Sororities: 45%
Number of Applicants: 4,478
Percent Accepted: 54%
Percent Accepted who enroll: 25%
Entering: 605
Transfers: 0
Application Deadline: 1 Jan
Mean SAT: 600 V, 623 M

Middle 50% SAT range: 550–640 V, 570–670 M
Middle 50% ACT range: NA
Mean ACT: 25
3 Most popular majors: engineering, economics/business, government/law
Retention: 91%
Graduation rate: 78%
Library: 480,000 volumes
Tuition and Fees: $22,844 in; $22,844 out
Room and Board: $7,106
On-campus housing: 100%
Financial aid, first-year: 49%

Imagine spending a week attending jazz concerts in New York City as homework! That is exactly what one group of Lafayette students had to do for a jazz class they took. After their romp in New York, the students returned home to their park-like campus in Easton, Pennsylvania. Students at Lafayette are an enthusiastic bunch who always enjoy a good time and, more than anything else, value the "family atmosphere" their school offers.

The Core Curriculum

Academics at Lafayette are by no means a free-for-all. Students are required to meet distribution requirements in a wide variety of disciplines: mathematics, natural sciences, social sciences, foreign languages, and humanities. In addition, students must complete a core class called the First-Year Seminar (FYS), a writing-intensive class for freshmen. FYS topics cover a wide and untraditional variety of subjects, including one on the music industry. Students report that meeting these requirements and taking the required courses within their major is challenging, but manageable, although one science major said that it can take more than four years to meet distribution and major re-

quirements, and take any desired electives.

The administration at Lafayette recently lowered the required number of classes per semester from five to four; the new schedule has not received much support from students, who, for the most part, feel that this makes their classes at Lafayette even more precious. In general, undergrads are excited about their classes and they want to take more classes than they have time to take. This policy only makes it more difficult for students to choose their classes.

Academic Optimism

Perhaps the aspect of academics that students at Lafayette College value most is the small class size and close contact with approachable, supportive professors. Most classes enroll around 15 to 20 students, while popular introductory-level classes can enroll 60 or 70. Professors teach all classes; TAs only supervise labs. As for getting into the classes you want, one student had this to say: "Getting into classes is no problem—even as a frosh—as long as you don't mind a few 8:00 A.M.'s." The college also offers study-abroad programs in Europe for qualified students. Most generally think that grading at Lafayette is fair, although one student said that she thinks grade inflation is common in English and a few science classes.

Economics and business are among the most popular majors at Lafayette, and students consider these departments stronger than some of the others, such as history and foreign languages. Lafayette administrators are reportedly trying to improve all academic departments at Lafayette. New hirings and the expansion of many departments have boosted students' optimism about the future.

Campus Distractions

Students describe the Lafayette College campus, sitting atop a hill overlooking the convergence of two rivers, as "incredibly picturesque." Many of the dorms and academic buildings have been renovated in the last few years, so students are taking advantage of the new, modern facilities. Some of the minor perks include kitchens within the dorms, tablecloths on tables in the common dining halls, and the compact size of the campus. For those with junk-food cravings, the snack bar in Farinon, Lafayette's student center, is a popular hangout during the week. Farinon also houses the post office, the main cafeteria (popular among freshmen), and several activity rooms. Golbert's, a popular new coffeehouse, features a game room and hosts open-mike nights, outside performers, and TV nights.

The main library on campus, Skillman Library, is a serious place for everything from nightly course work (which students say averages about 2 to 4 hours) to cramming for finals. Skillman does, however, close at midnight, and some think the campus needs a place for late-night study.

For those who wander off campus for food, Pino's, a moderately priced Italian restaurant, Hill of Beans, a coffeehouse with bagels, and WaWa, a convenience store, draw a large crowd. For the many students at Lafayette who have cars, the Lehigh Valley Mall, a 20-minute drive from campus, offers more shopping and restaurants. Steak and Ale, a steakhouse, and the Olive Garden (recommended for dates) are reportedly worth the drive. Students who don't have cars don't seem to mind, though, because "a lot of people have cars, so if you walk down the hall, finding a car is a sure bet," one undergrad reported.

The Leopards at Play

Sports and other extracurricular activities at Lafayette are as important to students as academics. Both varsity and intramural sports are popular at Lafayette and several undergrads described the student body as "athletic." Intramurals are taken very seriously, especially flag football. These games take place not only among rival dorms, but also among fraternities. The varsity soccer team is often ranked among the top 25 college teams in the nation, but students say the football and men's basketball teams draw the most support. Football is by far the most popular spectator sport, but not all students necessarily get swept up in the spirit of the game, or in any sports for that matter: some do not even know whether or not Lafayette recruits athletes for its teams (it does).

The big football game of the year pits the Lafayette Leopards against their in-state rivals at Lehigh University. On the day of the game, many students rise early and drink until the kickoff. Students rate the Lafayette-Lehigh game as the second-biggest annual party, behind All-College Weekend, which brings various bands to campus each spring. Students now enjoy a multimillion-dollar sports complex at Lafayette, which just opened last year.

With so much energy spent on academics and social activities, Lafayette students have little left over for extracurriculars. The Investment Club, reportedly the most popular undergraduate organization, is responsible for investing over $100,000, given by the school and alumni. The considerable gain that has resulted has even earned the club mention in the *New York Times*. The *Lafayette*, the weekly newspaper, also enjoys strong student support, as does the student government. Many join political and religious organizations.

Cocktails, Parties, and Football

The Lafayette Leopards certainly enjoy partying: according to one student, "it would be kind of stressful to be here if you didn't want to party." The Leopards regularly get dressed up for cocktail parties held frequently during football season.

A few years ago, fraternities were responsible for the majority of social activities at Lafayette; however, this has been slowly changing. Lafayette students say that while there is still an active Greek life, fewer students are rushing fraternities and there are more school-sponsored social events. One student praised this slow move away from the Greek party scene because she said that it has made students, especially freshmen, "enjoy the school-sponsored events without alcohol more than they did in past years." Still, many social events do center on alcohol and some students say that being underage is not always an obstacle to obtaining alcohol.

The fraternities figure prominently in other areas of student life, such as housing and dining. After spending freshman and sophomore years in college housing and on a meal plan, most male students move into fraternity houses and onto their frats' own meal plans. Another popular option is college-sponsored off-campus housing, which reportedly is in high demand. Of the dorms, South College is known as the big party hall, while the all-male Blair Hall, located above the gymnasium and "a little bit out of the way," gets the worst reviews.

A Lafayette policy prevents freshmen from rushing fraternities until November. Some say they still feel considerable pressure to rush, if only because of limited social alternatives, but others expect the role of frats to diminish in the next five years. According to one junior, "If you're an independent, it's kind of rough, but most frats are open to independents coming to their parties." Another junior praised the Greek system: "There's not much else to do in Easton."

In 1996 the administration instituted a BYOB policy for parties, and prohibited kegs on campus. Currently, a new alcohol policy is being implemented that threatens to make Lafayette an even dryer campus, leaving some students to yearn for the days (just five years ago!) when *Playboy* magazine rated Lafayette one of the nation's top party schools.

Monday Night Football, Wednesday nights at Campus Pizza (a popular off-campus pizza place by day and beer joint by night), and the round of Thursday, Friday, and Saturday night parties have all become frat traditions. These parties are usually open to Greeks and non-Greeks alike. The Lafayette Activities Forum (LAF) also organizes film screenings, concerts, and other performances throughout the year. In recent years, the Dave Matthews Band, Coolio, and comedian Adam Sandler have made their way to tiny Easton to perform at Lafayette.

Both men and women at Lafayette agree that while it is said that they don't date, it is not entirely true. As one student said, "There are nearly as many people dating as there are people who are just hooking up on a one-time, no-relationship basis. . . . I think we're pretty big into committed relationships." One disadvantage of the small student body is that there just are not that many new people to meet and date after a while.

The Student Body

Lafayette students describe their classmates as generally white, Christian, straight, conservative, middle-class preppies from either Pennsylvania, New Jersey, or New York. Students also report that they tend to wear clothes from J. Crew, the Gap, and Abercrombie & Fitch. There are reportedly few minority students at Lafayette; however, the African Black Cultural Club (ABC) and the Hillel House attract many students. Many students say that the lack of diversity is their main complaint about Lafayette.

According to one undergrad, "Lafayette's small size really made the transition from high school a lot easier. It's so easy to meet people here, and soon, everybody knows each other." One junior complained, however, that "the small size of the student body and the campus make it so that you can never get away. There is always someone you know anywhere you go and everyone knows everything about everyone else." Other students believe the homogeneity and size of the college allows for extraordinary school spirit and a solid foundation for its academics and social life.—*Sevra Davis and Staff*

Lehigh University

Address: 27 Memorial Drive West, Bethlehem, PA 18015
Phone: 610-758-3100
E-mail address: inadmiss@lehigh.edu
Web site URL: www.lehigh.edu
Location: suburban
Founded: 1865
Private or Public: private
Religious affiliation: none
Undergraduate enrollment: 4,400
Total enrollment: 6,000
Percent Male/Female: 55%/45%
Percent Minority: 13.0%

Percent African-American: 3.0%
Percent Hispanic: 3.0%
Percent Asian: 6.0%
Percent in-state/out-of-state: 30%/70%
Percent Pub HS: NA
Fraternities: 42%
Sororities: 41%
Number of Applicants: 9,000
Percent Accepted: 48%
Percent Accepted who enroll: 26%
Entering: 1,080
Transfers: 130
Application Deadline: 1 Jan
Mean SAT: 607 V, 643 M

Middle 50% SAT range: 559–651 V, 592–688 M
Middle 50% ACT range: NA
Mean ACT: NA
3 Most popular majors: mech engineering, finance, industrial engineering
Retention: 92.7%
Graduation rate: 81.6%
Library: 1,100,000 volumes
Tuition and Fees: $23,150 in; $23,150 out
Room and Board: $3,680
On-campus housing: 100%
Financial aid, first-year: 53%

On the side of a mountain in the town of Bethlehem lies Lehigh University, with the fraternities at the top of the hill and the classrooms at the bottom. Some students wonder if this configuration says something about their priorities. Although Lehigh has a very active Greek system, students are more than satisfied with the academics as well. According to one student, "The most unique quality of Lehigh is that students party hard and study hard."

Academics

Lehigh, whose team name changed recently from the Engineers to the Hawks, is known for its excellent engineering school; however, the university also has fine schools of business and arts and sciences. Each school has its own set of requirements, but all first-year students are required to take English 1 and English 2. First-year students in the engineering school also must take physics, chemistry, and one elective. Class size ranges from 200 to 300 people in introductory lecture courses to around 30 people in upper-level classes. All courses are taught by professors, with TAs leading only weekly recitation sections. For an "easy A," some students recommend "religion courses" and Human Sexuality.

For students looking for a challenge, Lehigh offers special programs such as the Five-Year Plan, in which engineering students can earn a bachelor's and a master's degree in five years. In addition to this opportunity, any undergraduate may take classes in the graduate school by petitioning the graduate committee and gaining permission from the instructor.

Dorms and Surroundings

Students at Lehigh say they are quite satisfied with their housing options. Only freshmen are required to live on campus, but the majority of undergraduates remain on campus all four years. The most desirable places to live include campus apartments in Trembley and the freshman dorm known as "M&M" (McClinton and Marshall). Most dorms are coed by floor. For upperclassmen who do choose to live off campus, fraternity and sorority houses are popular options.

As for the food, students are as satisfied as they can be with food that isn't home cooking. Lehigh has five dining halls, including three traditional cafeterias, a food court with a Burger King and a deli, and a shop where students can take out bag lunches. For breakfast they can make their own omelets or waffles every day of the week. When dinner rolls around, many students would suggest forgoing the meat in favor of the safer pasta.

Social Life and Student Body

"When you are not studying, you are drinking. And when you drink, you drink a lot," said one Lehigh student. Undergrads say Greek life is basically the be-all and end-all at Lehigh; about half of them join one of the 26 fraternities and 8 sororities. Students look forward to the annual Greek Week, which occurs in the spring, and is a week filled with toga races, eating contests, and other competitions. The Lehigh/Lafayette game is one of the biggest rivalries, providing the occasion for some of the best parties. "During Lehigh/Lafayette they have sunrise cocktails every morning before classes; even the teachers are trashed the whole week. There are huge parties every night," one student said. The administration has recently made an unpopular move to regulate the size of parties. One freshman explained, "There is a new regulation limiting the number of people attending parties. Before 12:00 you must be on the 50-person guest list, an then an extra 50 people are allowed to enter after 12:00, but they have to sign an 'uninvited' guest list."

When life on the Hill becomes monotonous, students attend campus comedy acts, movies, and concerts. If students need to get away, they do not have far to go to find the big city; New York is only a two-hour drive, and Philadelphia is just 90 minutes away.

Lehigh students participate in all sorts of extracurriculars, ranging from varsity sports to community service to drama. Popular sports include football, wrestling, crew, and basketball. Students say that football is not only the dominant sport, but also dominates the social atmosphere. Games prompt an array of tailgates and early morning cocktail parties, and foster healthy school spirit.

For students who are less athletically inclined, intramurals offer competition without the pressure of organized varsity sports. Beyond the sports fields, Lehigh offers choir, drama, the *Brown and White* (a biweekly newspaper), an orchestra, and many opportunities for community service.

Through its community service programs Lehigh has been making an attempt to improve relations with the neighboring towns of Bethlehem and Allentown. For example, with STAR Academy, a popular tutoring program, Lehigh students act as mentors for local middle school and high school students. Although the programs are slowly making progress, students say that they don't go to town much and still yearn for more to do outside of the university.

> **For an "easy A," some students recommend "religion courses" and Human Sexuality.**

Most Lehigh undergrads come from the tristate region of Pennsylvania, New Jersey, and Delaware, and some students feel that the student body could be more diverse—geographically, racially, and economically. One sophomore said, "I wish it were more diversified. There are very few minorities and very few 'different-looking' people. It is very much of a 'clone campus,' I think." Yet Lehigh students are a very satisfied bunch who enjoy the university's close-knit, self-contained community.

Lehigh is a school with a lot of pride and spirit, and its students enjoy the strong academics and social life. As one student said, "My friends at other schools think I always have about 10 times more work than they ever do, but I also have 20 times more fun than they do!"—*Katherina Payne and Staff*

FYI

The three best things about attending Lehigh are "closeness to Philly, the red and orange hues of the hills in the fall, engineering."

The three worst things about attending Lehigh are "homogeneity, party size limits, and fraternities if you're not in one."

The three things that every student should do before gradating from Lehigh are "take Human Sexuality, party like a madman/madwoman, and take a day trip to Philadelphia or New York."

One thing I wish I'd known before coming here is "how so many things revolve around alcohol."

Muhlenberg College

Address: 2400 W. Chew St., Allentown, PA 18104-5586

Phone: 484-664-3200

E-mail address: admissions@muhlenberg.edu

Web site URL: www.muhlenberg.edu

Location: suburban

Founded: 1848

Private or Public: private

Religious affiliation: Lutheran (ELCA)

Undergraduate enrollment: 1,950

Total enrollment: 1,950

Percent Male/Female: 43%/57%

Percent Minority: 9.0%

Percent African-American: 2.0%

Percent Hispanic: 2.0%

Percent Asian: 4.5%

Percent in-state/out-of-state: 33%/67%

Percent Pub HS: 70%

Fraternities: 36%

Sororities: 36%

Number of Applicants: 3,274

Percent Accepted: 55%

Percent Accepted who enroll: 31%

Entering: 551

Transfers: 8

Application Deadline: 15 Feb

Mean SAT: 591 V, 596 M

Middle 50% SAT range: 546–636 V, 551–641 M

Middle 50% ACT range: NA

Mean ACT: NA

3 Most popular majors: biology, psychology, business/accounting

Retention: 93%

Graduation rate: 77%

Library: 200,000 volumes

Tuition and Fees: $21,050 in; $NA out

Room and Board: $5,650

On-campus housing: 98%

Financial aid, first-year: 65%

Muhlenberg students may complain about their course load, but most enjoy the challenge. Students are eager to learn. One says, "I like going to class each day. I have interesting courses and like to learn from them." Through many renovations, Muhlenberg is improving resources for its students.

Inside Victorian Academic Buildings

Students must take 34 courses before they graduate. The core requirements are literature, religion, philosophy, three semesters of language, two sciences, history, two courses in behavioral science (psychology, anthropology, sociology etc.), culture, art, and first year seminar. Many students are pleased with these required courses, adding that they wouldn't have taken such classes if not required. However there are some who find some of the requirements too much. "Religion and philosophy should be electives, regardless that it is a Lutheran campus," believes a student, whereas another says "we have to take two sciences which is very disturbing to us nonscience people." Every major has a set curriculum, which fills up most of the schedules. Students face some problems with the times of classes while trying to form their schedules. Also, they feel that some courses being offered only once a year causes more scheduling problems for them.

Biology, premed, chemistry, and theater arts are considered the toughest and the most competitive majors. Philosophy and especially communications are "very popular" among students and considered less rigorous than other majors. Muhlenberg sponsors many combined undergraduate/graduate programs: a 3 year undergrad/4 year grad dental program with University of Pennsylvania, 3/2 forestry and environmental studies program with Duke University, 3/2 engineering program with Columbia and Washington University as well as a 4/4 medical school admission with MCP/Hahnemann University. Students may also participate in honor programs such as the Dana and the Muhlenberg Scholar's program, create their own majors, or take courses at other schools.

Few classes have over 25 students, except for labs, and students are fond of the "personalization and attention" this brings. However, some complain that the small number of classes also makes it harder to get into them, especially in freshman and sophomore years. This problem decreases as students declare their major because then professors sign the students into classes. Students are pleased with the proficiency of the faculty and believe that they are "accommodating and care a lot about their students." A student says "I run into them [my professors] at the grocery store and it's like running into a friend." Since there are no teaching assistants teaching classes, students have the opportunity to work in classes instructed by professors who are eminent in their fields like Dr. Marjory Hardy, a professor in psychology or like Dr. Daniel Klem, "a world leader on why birds fly into windows. People from all over call him up for help in designing bird-safe buildings," is how one of his students describes Dr. Klem.

Smashmouth Isn't the Only One

Besides well-known professors, students also benefit from and enjoy the guest speakers that come to campus. Chie Abad, who was on a national tour about

sweat shops, stopped at Muhlenberg with the help of student organizations such as Amnesty International and PAT. Smashmouth also visited campus and gave a spectacular concert. Besides Smashmouth, Citizen King, Jim Breuer, the Wallflowers, George Clinton, Blues Traveler, Bob Cat have come to Muhlenberg.

Being underage has not prevented students from drinking since fraternity parties offer alcohol to all. But, the administration has become stricter about alcohol, students report, and forces students to sign in when they enter certain parties. Kegs are not allowed on campus, and students say, "frats have been temporarily closed down because of alcohol problems." Many over 21 prefer going to the bars in Allentown.

The nondrinkers also find a lot of things to do. Dances like the *West Side Story* dance, senior balls, semiformals, and fraternity or sorority formals have an important role in the social life. The shuttle running to the malls, shopping centers, and theaters are useful for freshmen since they cannot have cars on campus usually. Besides Activities Council which provides most of the programs on campus, other popular and respected student organizations are the radio station, Hillel, and APO (community service).

Prevalent Homogenity

A typical Muhlenberg student is chic, wears J. Crew, Gap, and Abercrombie, and drives a nice car. Students say that there are cliques, and even though groups aren't formed right away, people do tend to stick with those whom they meet during the first months of school through dormlife or organizations. Students find their peers homogeneous and also classify a typical Muhlenberg student as a "white, preppy student."

Renovations Revive Campus Life

The renovated gym offers a great weightlifting room and new equipment. There are also tennis courts and a pool available for students. Football, men and women's soccer, and basketball are among the popular sports. There are some traditions like the Greek Week where sororities and fraternities compete against each other. Another tradition is the annual Scotty Wood Basketball tournament. Intramurals are very popular.

> "I run into them [my professors] at the grocery store and it's like running into a friend."

Freshman dorms Prosser and New West have also undergone recent renovations. However, the worst dorm, East Hall, remains unchanged and continues to experience bug problems. Last year, a turf field and a stadium were built, and the press box and soccer fields were redone. Students are now waiting for the completion of the second Center for the Arts building. Also, a new academic building will be finished in January 2000. The Union, which includes the cafeteria, mailboxes, and meeting rooms has been renovated to provide a greater space. All dorms except Brown are coed; however, all have single-sex bathrooms. Brown, the all-girls dorm, has higher ceilings and larger rooms compared to others. Quiet hours exist during the week to help those who are studying or sleeping. Off-campus housing is not very popular. After freshman year, a lottery settles rooming, and most upperclassman rooms are quite nice.

There are two meal plans in school, and students prefer the larger one. Banana flambé is a specialty of the dining halls. Chefs cook in front of students to assure them of the hygiene of the kitchen. There is always a pasta bar and decent vegetarian options. The two dining halls, one for grab-and-go, the other for sit and talk, offer a variety for students.

Safe and Sound in Allentown

Students enjoy the beauty of their safe campus. Victorian, stone buildings make up the majority of the small, green campus. The campus is close to parks and forests. Students have to satisfy themselves with the squirrels running around on campus because pets aren't allowed anywhere on campus, including campus apartments. A couple of call boxes for emergencies and a security staff, with members on foot, bicycle, and car, enhance security. Near campus are the Katherine P. Taylor Mall, several bars, a couple of coffee shops like Perks, and restaurants: Parma Pizza, Outback, Mi-Chongs Chinese, TGI Fridays, Rudy Tuesday, Arby's, Perkinds, and the more upscale Olive Garden, King George Inn, and Carabas.

Away from Problems

On lazy Sundays, or in spring, whenever the weather is nice, students don't bother about what to do, or where to go. They take a blanket, their radio, and their tons of reading, head to a nearby park or to the center of the campus, and enjoy the feeling of learning and being challenged.
—*Yakut Seyhanli*

FYI
The three best things about attending Muhlenberg are "its friendly atmosphere, the small-sized classes, and the attention paid to students."
The three worst things about attending Muhlenberg are "the limited offerings of Allentown; everybody knowing everything about each other because of the small community; and not having anonymity."
The three things that every student should do before graduating from Muhlenberg are "walk through the rose garden of the campus, go to a candlelight carol, and go to a soccer game."
One thing I'd like to have known before coming to Mulhenberg is "that the social life's major component is frat parties."

Pennsylvania State University

Address: 201 Shields Building, Box 3000; University Park, PA 16802-3000

Phone: 814-865-5471

E-mail address: admissions@psu.edu

Web site URL: www.psu.edu

Location: suburban

Founded: 1855

Private or Public: public

Religious affiliation: none

Undergraduate enrollment: 34,264

Total enrollment: 40,471

Percent Male/Female: 54%/46%

Percent Minority: 11.1%

Percent African-American: 3.0%

Percent Hispanic: 3.0%

Percent Asian: 5.0%

Percent in-state/out-of-state: 79%/21%

Percent Pub HS: NA

Fraternities: 15%

Sororities: 15%

Number of Applicants: 23,262

Percent Accepted: 47%

Percent Accepted who enroll: 38%

Entering: 4,101

Transfers: 0

Application Deadline: 31 Jan

Mean SAT: 593 V, 617 M

Middle 50% SAT range: 540–640 V, 561–670 M

Middle 50% ACT range: NA

Mean ACT: NA

3 Most popular majors: elementary education, accounting, marketing

Retention: 93%

Graduation rate: 77%

Tuition and Fees: $5,832 in; $12,306 out

Room and Board: $4,338

On-campus housing: 100%

Financial aid, first-year: 61%

"Y**ou** haven't lived until you've experienced Penn State football." Each game day, over 97,000 fans cram into Beaver Stadium to watch the Nittany Lions ravage their opponents. "Saturdays are the greatest. I don't even like football, but the spirit here is very catching," said another fan. From the pre-game tailgate parties, to the virtually guaranteed postgame victory celebrations, the football season is a highlight for most Penn Staters. In fact, the football games are one of very few bonding forces at "Dear Old State." With over 31,000 undergrads and another 10,000 grad students, Penn State is really a small city all unto its own. But that is what the students love about their school. Sometimes, it may be even overwhelming. "It's not a matter of apathy, but the school is really huge and it's impossible to know about everything that goes on," remarked one student.

A Respected Tradition

At the heart of the Penn State system is the University Park campus. Only about 5,000 academically superior freshmen are enrolled directly at the Main Campus with about two-thirds of the students spending their first two years at one of Penn State's 22 smaller commonwealth campuses. (Don't call them branch campuses, students don't like it!) Many believe that time spent at the smaller commonwealth campuses (some smaller than 2,000) helps in the transition from high school to Penn State's colossal main campus.

Thanks to its football program, Penn State is one of the best-known state schools in the country. Although at times football seems like the only presence at Penn State, the school boasts several worthy academic departments. Students rate the engineering, agriculture, and business departments as the strongest. Also, the journalism program at the University Park campus draws many aspiring Pulitzer Prize winners, not to mention future NFL players. The university's 10 undergraduate colleges offer over 180 baccalaureate programs to satisfy anyone's appetite for learning.

In addition to the requirements of each major, students must take general education requirement classes as well as both physical education and a cultural diversity class. In general, most students find these classes a hassle and detracting from their focused areas of major. "The gym requirement is ridiculous," said one junior.

Students also complain about class size; with several introductory classes enrolling nearly 1,000 students, it is hard to find access to professors. According to one senior, "You really have to make an effort to get to know [your] professors." Fortunately, TAs hold sections for most large lectures. "Overall, I have found the TAs to be very helpful. However, the math and science TAs are usually foreign and hard to understand," said one student.

Freshmen and sophomores often feel frustrated during the registration period. Some classes are capped after upperclassmen register. "I couldn't get into four classes this semester. But one of them was required for my major, so they made an exception for me," said one sophomore. In order to get preference for classes, students with strong SAT scores and a distinguished high school record can apply to Penn State's University Scholars Program. The top-rated program allows for independent study, graduate work, and honors options in regular courses.

Beware Greeks Bearing Gifts

Although only about 16 percent of the student population joins fraternities or sororities, considering that there are 31,000 undergraduate students, that's almost 5,000 Greeks. Understandably, much of the social life at Penn State revolves around the Greek system. "Drinking at frat parties is much easier than on campus," said one junior. Another student added that "although drinking certainly doesn't define the entire frat experience here, it fills the time between football games quite well." Many independent students complain that campus life is structured around the Greeks and that their influence is "pervasive, if not total." That is not to say that there is no independent scene. Apartment parties and tailgates are just as, if not more, common as frat parties. "People tend to make friends through their extracurricular activities and their classes." Because the school is so big, cliques are common.

Undergrads can also socialize at the Hetzel Union Building (HUB), a student center with eateries, game and TV rooms, and a mammoth lawn where students can throw Frisbees and play sports. Those students who want to get involved in extracurricular activities can choose from over 400 campus clubs and organizations. From the Shakespeare Company to Penn's daily, the *Collegian*, there is something for everyone. Freshmen often have trouble deciding what to join first. "You have to be careful not to spread yourself too thin," warned one junior. Many undergrads also contribute their time to community service.

A popular event is the Dance Marathon, known to its fervid participants simply as the "Thon." It is a charity event where students raise money for cancer research at the Hershey Medical Center. To describe it as gigantic is an understatement. Each year couples from each campus organization as well as alumni dancers from all over the nation boogie, jitterbug, and country line dance for 48 hours for this great cause. It rivals even the football games as the most important social function of the year.

Another institution of large scale is the dorm system. The main campus has six clusters of dorms, with over 40 individual buildings, each housing anywhere from 300 to 700 or more students. Most freshmen are assigned to dorms in East Hall, where rooms consist mostly of two-person doubles and a few suites. Juniors and seniors who want campus housing try their luck in a lottery system. Winners can live at the spacious Nittany Apartments. However, most upperclassmen move off campus, either to apartments or frat houses. "Penn State has a strict alcohol policy and I think that pushes some people off campus," explained one senior. Students describe the dining hall food as "not bad" and "sometimes surprisingly delicious."

More than three-quarters of Penn State students are from Pennsylvania, hailing mostly from Philadelphia and Pittsburgh. Most attended public high schools, and undergrads report that their classmates generally are politically conservative and preprofessional. Some students complain that close-mindedness and "political apathy" abound at Penn State. One undergrad reported hearing a campus visitor "making these really insulting and derogatory remarks about homosexuals. He was standing near a lot of people and no one was saying anything." According to one sophomore, "There is no big student atmosphere outside of the football season. I feel that once you find a clique, you are forced to stick with it because you feel that you will get lost in the horde outside it."

Football and Penn State are synonymous for many undergrads. Ohio State and the University of Michigan are the Nittany Lions' Big Ten rivals. Tickets for the season are so popular that students must buy tickets over the summer to be guaranteed seats for games. According to one student, "it cost me $85 for 6 home games!" Other big campus events include homecoming and the mid-July arts festival. According to one student, "Stuff like

this can unify the campus, which otherwise is just too big to get a handle on."

> **"You haven't lived until you've experienced Penn State football."**

Although Penn State might seem like a faceless giant, its students often gush about how much they are enjoying their college experience. In a changing and uncertain world, Penn State's three main traditions of football, fraternities, and academics are as vibrant as ever. Undergrads agree that Penn State is what it has always been: the paragon—and stereotype—of the "all-American university."
—*Seung Lee and Staff*

FYI

The three best things about attending Penn State are "good reputation, Thon (a 48-hour dance marathon), and a kick-ass football team."

The three worst things about attending Penn State are "clickism, Greeks rule all, becoming a number."

The three things that every student should do before graduating are "check out Thon, go to at least one football game, and get a picture taken at the Lion Shrine."

One thing I'd like to have known before coming here is "that even though there are so many people, it's hard to find really good friends."

S u s q u e h a n n a   U n i v e r s i t y

Address: 514 University Avenue; Selinsgrove, PA 17870
Phone: 570-372-4260
E-mail address: suadmiss@susqu.edu
Web site URL: www.susqu.edu
Location: rural
Founded: 1858
Private or Public: private
Religious affiliation: Lutheran
Undergraduate enrollment: 1,765
Total enrollment: 1,765
Percent Male/Female: 42%/58%
Percent Minority: 5.3%

Percent African-American: 2.0%
Percent Hispanic: 2.0%
Percent Asian: 1.0%
Percent in-state/out-of-state: 64%/36%
Percent Pub HS: 85%
Fraternities: 25%
Sororities: 25%
Number of Applicants: 2,003
Percent Accepted: 79%
Percent Accepted who enroll: 30%
Entering: 475
Transfers: NA
Application Deadline: 1 Mar
Mean SAT: NA

Middle 50% SAT range: 520–620 V, 510–630 M
Middle 50% ACT range: NA
Mean ACT: NA
3 Most popular majors: business administration, communication/theater arts, psychology
Retention: 87%
Graduation rate: 67%
Library: 260,000 volumes
Tuition and Fees: $19,380 in; $19,380 out
Room and Board: $5,500
On-campus housing: 100%
Financial aid, first-year: 72%

Located in rural Pennsylvania, Susquehanna University can be easy to overlook. Prospective students who find out about it will see, however, that Susquehanna provides a close-knit atmosphere with small classes and quality education.

The school attracts many of its students from the Northeast, especially New Jersey, Pennsylvania, and New York. While the student population once consisted mainly of white middle- and upper-class undergrads, recent outreach efforts and scholarship programs have increased the number of minority students and programs.

A recently initiated merit aid program called Assistantships offers promising incoming freshmen an annual scholarship as well as an opportunity to obtain work experience under the supervision of a faculty or staff member. Another unique program is the Write Option: students in the top one-fifth of their class and enrolled in a college-preparatory program at their high school are allowed to submit two graded writing samples in place of SAT or ACT scores.

Name Games

Although the name of the school implies otherwise, there are no graduate students at Susquehanna. Many undergraduates are attracted to Susquehanna's highly rated biology and music programs. The business department, accredited by the American Assembly of Collegiate Schools of Business, is also popular; acknowledged as outstanding by business and non-business students alike, it is one of only a few schools of its size to be accredited.

The school's curriculum requires students to take courses from three broad categories: perspectives on the world (history, literature, and fine arts), intellectual skills (math, logic, writing seminars, and foreign languages), and contemporary world (social science, hard science, and technology). Few students complain about the requirements; many say that this diverse grounding adds to their educational experiences at Susquehanna. Special programs enhance Susquehanna's standard curriculum. Students can create their own major with the help of a faculty member, or can elect to travel abroad. Students seem pleased in general with the student-faculty interaction as well as the small class sizes. Classes usually have about 20 to 25 students, and the teaching is done by professors rather than TAs, who are "practically unheard of."

Service

Community service is a popular option at Susquehanna. In recent years, over half the student body has participated in volunteer services, including the Habitat for Humanity program, the Student Association for Cultural Awareness (SACA), the university's Study Buddy program with students from local schools, the Ronald McDonald House for hospitalized children, and the Pennsylvania Service Corps. Other extracurricular activities are popular as well, and the university's Degenstein Center Theater and Lore Degenstein Gallery, both with state-of-the-art equipment, provide major new showcases for student musicians, artists, and actors.

Susquehanna has a lot of school spirit, as many of the athletic teams are nationally ranked in NCAA Division III. Students frequently show support not only for their football team but also for the basketball, volleyball, and soccer teams. Intramural sports are also important at Susquehanna, and many students take advantage of the newly remodeled gymnasium. Because of Susquehanna's location in Selinsgrove, Pennsylvania, where "there's practically no downtown," social life is limited to campus activities sponsored by SAC (Student Activities Committee) and the Greek system. Most upperclassmen also own cars for trips to nearby cities for shopping, clubbing, and other diversions.

Greek Life and Beyond

Some students feel that the Greeks divide the campus, but most Greek activities are open to everyone. The two biggest social events of the year are Greek Week, which consists mostly of fraternity- and sorority-sponsored partying, and Spring Weekend, a festival held before final exams. Students report that while both events are widely attended, Greek Week is more exclusive to Greeks, and Spring Weekend better involves the entire campus. Another popular campus event is the annual

Thanksgiving dinner, where professors serve students special holiday food in the cafeteria, which is decorated with candles.

> **Classes usually have about 20 to 25 students, and the teaching is done by professors rather than TAs, who are "practically unheard of."**

While everyone at Susquehanna University is guaranteed campus housing, incoming students have complained in the past about the crowded freshman dorms, which consisted of mostly triples. The recent construction of three new residence halls, the renovation of a fourth hall, and new apartment-like dorms and suites, however, has made housing more spacious. Students can also choose to live in the University Scholars House, which includes study areas, a seminar room, a resident assistant's quarters, and a visitor's apartment that allows special university guests to interact informally with students. Some of the most popular dorms include Hassinger Hall, which features newly installed air-conditioning; also known as "Hotel Hassinger," it houses a small theater and several computer labs.

Students report that security is "good and reliable" on the Susquehanna campus, due in part to such security measures as the Walk Safe escort service.

Susquehanna offers intimate classes, a strong sense of community, and great athletics. "You can walk across campus and know everybody's face," one senior said, "but you can also go away from everyone you know and be by yourself for a while."—*Seung Lee and Staff*

FYI

The three best things about attending Susquehanna are "friendly professors and staff, the opportunity to be a scholar, athlete, musician, and leader at the same time, a beautiful campus."

The three worst things about attending Susquehanna are "the athletic facilities, not enough parking for students, limited choice for electives."

The three things every student should do before graduating from Susquehanna are "swim in the Susquehanna River, go to the Lewisburg Theater, and take Rock Music and Society."

One thing I'd like to have known before coming here is "how hard I would have to work on academics."

Swarthmore College

Address: 500 College Ave.
Swarthmore, PA 19081
Phone: 610-328-8300
E-mail address:
admissions@swarthmore.edu
Web site URL:
www.swarthmore.edu
Location: suburban
Founded: 1864
Private or Public: private
Religious affiliation:
none
**Undergraduate
enrollment:** 1,467
Total enrollment: 1,467
Percent Male / Female:
47% / 53%
Percent Minority: 32.0%

Percent African-American:
9.0%
Percent Hispanic: 9.0%
Percent Asian: 13.0%
**Percent in-state / out-of-
state:** 12% / 88%
Percent Pub HS: 64%
Fraternities: 4%
Sororities: 0%
Number of Applicants:
4,163
Percent Accepted: 22%
**Percent Accepted who
enroll:** 41%
Entering: 368
Transfers: 5
Application Deadline:
1 Jan
Mean SAT: 707 V, 700 M

Middle 50% SAT range:
655–770 V,
660–750 M
Middle 50% ACT range:
NA
Mean ACT: NA
3 Most popular majors:
biology, economics,
political science
Retention: 95%
Graduation rate: 92%
Library: 748,810 volumes
Tuition and Fees: $24,190
in; $24,190 out
Room and Board: $7,500
On-campus housing:
100%
Financial aid, first-year:
51%

Described as "idyllic and intense," "weird and diverse," Swarthmore College in Pennsylvania is absolutely one of a kind. Consider, for instance, the fact that the campus itself is situated on the 330-acre Scott Arboretum, which one student, waxing poetic, described as "a lush, wooded Arcadia." Or the tradition of the "Primal Scream," when on the evening before finals everyone opens the window and screams for several minutes simultaneously into the dark night, so that "there's this eerie howl all across campus." With a student body of just over 1,400, classes are small and the community tight, which allows for connections in the classroom and the dorm room, on the sports field and the party floor.

Kiss Your Sleep Good-bye

Academically, Swarthmore is unusually rigorous. With a normal course load of four classes a semester, it is common to have over a thousand pages of reading per week, plus a paper or two. (But don't let that intimidate you; one student promises that "you'll find yourself growing to love sleep-deprivation—it's the Swattie way.") Disciplines are grouped into three broad distributions: Humanities, Natural Sciences & Engineering, and Social Sciences. Three courses are taken in each, two of which must be Primary Distribution Courses (PDCs)—basically writing-intensive intro classes. Those who pass one year of a foreign language at Swarthmore—or three years of a language in high school—are not bound to do more. Few complain about the requirements, attesting that they are "pretty loose" and that "you end up fulfilling them without even knowing it."

During the spring of sophomore year, each student chooses a major from a wide range of traditional disciplines (English and biology are the most popular) and newer interdisciplinary fields, such as Peace & Conflict Studies and Interpretation Theory. Several often opt to design their own major. Many also apply for the selective External Examination/Honors Program for which the college is renowned. Participating students take two double-credit seminars per semester, working closely with professors and engaging in massive amounts of reading, writing, and independent research. At the end of senior year, those in the program take the External Examination—a process of both written and oral exams that are evaluated by a panel of professors and scholars from outside institutions.

In an age of ubiquitous TAs, all classes at Swat are taught by professors, who in general are described as being "cool, competent, approachable" and "willing to talk about class and about life." And because virtually all professors live in the town of Swarthmore, many hold classes in their own homes, providing snacks and tea as well as a good discussion. Not all classes are tiny (the average runs between 15 and 25 people), but anything with over 90 people (Intro Bio and Chem classes are the biggest) is unheard of, and even as a freshman you may find yourself in several classes of 10 people or less.

In a popular policy, freshmen for their first semester take all their classes pass/fail, so that there is less pressure and more adjustment time. Four more pass/fail classes are allowed for the remaining three years also. The Tri-Co setup allows Swatties to take other classes at nearby Bryn Mawr and Haverford for free. For those eager to venture farther from campus, there is an extensive study-abroad/foreign-exchange network (Swat's own programs in Grenoble and Madrid are very popular).

Even a Club for Knitters . . .

The range of extracurricular opportunities is just as broad. Musicians have numerous orchestral, chamber, and choral groups to pick from, as well as a Jazz Ensemble and even a Balinese percussion ensemble. There is a deep commitment to community service among Swatties; Co-operative Involvement and Volunteers in Committees, or CIVIC, is an umbrella organization overseeing projects, and the Swarthmore Foundation endows grants for new proposals from students. Other popular activities include the debate team, the *Phoenix* student newspaper, *Spike*, the humor magazine, Earthlust (an environmental organization), and Swat's own WSRN radio station. For the more eclectic, there are other groups like the Opera Club, Yggdrasill (the Scandinavian Society), the KnitWits (a society of knitters), and even a volunteer fire brigade. Most freshmen are amazed "how easy it is

to get involved in stuff and to do fairly significant things fairly fast."

Swatties compete in Division III athletics, and about 30 percent of the student body plays on varsity. (But "it's true that the football team sucks," a student admits rather casually.) Intramurals and club sports teams include water polo, rugby, aikido, ice hockey (the Mother Puckers), and Ultimate Frisbee (the Swarming Earthworms). To raise money, teams hold parties and other events—the men's and women's rugby players, for instance, streak and grab donations from spectators in their annual Dash for Cash. Classes in such activities as folk dancing, scuba diving, and fencing are also offered. Despite the enthusiastic participation in many sports, however, attendance at weekend games is low for the most part. "We have a lot of superb athletes, but sports simply aren't prioritized."

There are two frats (the members of which tend to be football and basketball players), but neither has a notable presence on campus except through their weekend parties. Their parties are no different from other non-frat parties—"everyone goes, but the beer is worse." Students say that the administration is fairly lax when it comes to enforcing drinking laws. The Student Affairs Committee often funds the alcohol at some social events. Most people do drink, but "there is no pressure, and drinking is definitely not the focus" of the social scene. "Parties are safe," adds another student, "people look out for one another." Nor have drugs been a significant issue—although weed is quite prevalent.

Despite the close proximity to Philadelphia, relatively few people actually go out into the city, simply because there's always so much to do on campus. Since every event at Swat, Bryn Mawr, and Haverford is free for any Tri-Co student, there are chances to meet people beyond the immediate campus. But when in need of clubs, movie theaters, restaurants, and in general a wider range of options, the city is a mere 20 minutes away by train—there's a stop right on campus.

People have "pretty healthy love/sex lives," and while hookups are constant, most relationships are serious. "It's not really dating as it is just spending lots of time with each other," according to a sophomore. A recent insider's game involves the "Swarthmore Six Degrees of Separation" phenomenon. Theoretically, any Swattie can be linked to any other Swattie via people who have hooked up with each other. There's not much privacy, and in what's known as the infamous Walk of Shame, Swatties who walk across campus back to their rooms on the morning after often are seen by everyone else from their windows.

Escaping It All

Whether for more privacy or for new diversions, moments definitely come when the Swattie will want to get away. Food and hangout places feel limited after a while, and except for the frequented Bean Bag Cafe, the town of Swarthmore doesn't have much to offer. Students usually take their meals at Sharples Dining Hall—the only cafeteria on campus (continuing a Quaker tradition of sharing meals under the same roof). The Tarble Social Center also contains a snack/coffee hangout, lounge, student activities offices, performance spaces, and the bookstore. As for the dining-hall food, students warn against the meat—or meat-like—products as well as anything fried. But other than those sketchy items, there are plenty of edible options: a huge salad bar, a deli, a grill (where burgers are custom-made), a vegetarian bar, and a self-stir-fry wok; for the truly desperate, waffles and yogurt/ice cream are available at every meal.

Housing is guaranteed for all four years, and most students—over 90 percent—choose to remain on campus in the dorms, which "vary but are overall pretty acceptable." After freshman year, students select housing by lottery and many upperclassmen get singles. There is no theme housing, but residential halls do occasionally develop their own character. One dorm, for instance, is known for its "spontaneous wrestling matches" in the corridors.

Among the more eccentric Swattie traditions is Genderfuck—supposedly a cross-dressing dance but described more vividly as "a dance/party where guys dress as girls and girls dress as sluts." Another

dance, Screw-Your-Roommate, involves roommates setting each other up on blind dates, and then each paired couple dressing up in thematic costumes or performing skits in order to find each other. Members of the Dip-of-the-Month Club meet regularly for skinny-dipping sessions in Crum Creek—a freezing, two-foot-deep stream running through campus. And then there's the McCabe Mile, a "mile-long race around the stacks in the library, started by slamming a scholarly book and rewarded with a roll of toilet paper."

Comfortable, Supportive Atmosphere

Swat is extremely diverse in every way; in general people are open and friendly, and everyone tends to have a wide range of friends—"it's the very opposite of cliquey," remarked a junior. There are a variety of support networks, such as the Black Cultural Center, Swarthmore Asian Organization, Hispanic Organization for Latino/a Awareness, Swarthmore Queer Union, and the Women's Resource Center. But the real diversity extends beyond these formations. As one student said: "Earthy-types hang out with goth-girls who are friends with the basketball player who's going out with the violinist who is the best friend of the kilt-wearer." Nor is there much real division between freshmen and upperclassmen. The stereotypical Swattie is "hardworking, PC, vegetarian, and trendy without trying to be," and the school as a whole is "definitely on the liberal side, but there is no such thing as a typical Swattie."

One thing that does seem intrinsic to every Swattie is a passion for something—or, often, for many things. "People come to Swarthmore because they really care about something, whether it's engineering, art, or literature," a sophomore declared. "I've had wonderful conversations about everything from situation comedy to semiotics, even once with a friend about whose translation of Gabriel Garcia Marquez we each preferred—and all on my own time rather than just in class." Another student agrees: "You can't help but learn here, from classes, extracurricular opportunities, or from your peers—people will get drunk here and then go play chess or have an intellectual discussion in their dorm after the party ends."

"People will get drunk here and then go play chess or have an intellectual discussion in their dorm after the party ends."

Although virtually all tend to acknowledge the uniqueness of their Swat experience, not everyone is completely happy here. The smallness of the college that fosters closeness for some translates into a sometimes stifling lack of anonymity. That "every face is a familiar one" could be both a good and bad thing, as "reputations are easily gotten, rarely forgotten," and "if you get raving drunk you can't hide the next day and have people forget." Some also perceive that students' ambitiousness occasionally leads to a self-involvement that puts work before friends. "Egos are not that huge," however, and "people are relatively modest." And while there is "a kind of playful, joking intellectual elitism here," a freshman observes, "no internal elitism exists in terms of social structures."

The college T-shirt declaring, "Anywhere else it would've been an A—really" does not exaggerate—Swatties probably do work harder than anyone else. But what makes Swat particularly special for most Swatties, as one student said, is how the school "self-selects for a kind of intellectual sensibility—it can be an incredibly total experience; I've found the people that I want to spend my time with, and Swarthmore has been wonderful because of that."—*Chinnie Ding and Staff*

FYI

The three best things about attending Swarthmore are "the individual attention from small classes, all activities and parties are free, and school has a LOT of money (top ten in endowment per student) and they use the money to fund a lot of student-run organizations."

The three worst things about attending Swarthmore are "bad or lack of sports teams, annoying to every tree with a name plate (the school is an arboretum), and sometimes the tiny student body gets to you."

The three things that every student should do before graduating from Swarthmore are "have lunch in the Rose garden, do the 'McCabe Mile', go to the 'Screw your roomate' dance where you roomates set up each other with blind dates."

One thing I'd like to have known before coming here is "that the weather in the Mid-Atlantic really does suck."

Temple University

Address: 1801 N. Broad St. Philadelphia, PA 19122
Phone: 888-340-2222
E-mail address: TUADM@VM.TEMPLE.edu
Web site URL: www.temple.edu
Location: urban
Founded: 1884
Private or Public: public
Religious affiliation: none
Undergraduate enrollment: 18,175
Total enrollment: 28,126
Percent Male / Female: 42% / 58%
Percent Minority: 41.0%

Percent African-American: 28.0%
Percent Hispanic: 3.0%
Percent Asian: 10.0%
Percent in-state / out-of-state: 80% / 20%
Percent Pub HS: NA
Fraternities: 3%
Sororities: 4%
Number of Applicants: 12,400
Percent Accepted: 64%
Percent Accepted who enroll: 23%
Entering: 2,849
Transfers: 2,037
Application Deadline: 1 Apr
Mean SAT: 518 V, 509 M

Middle 50% SAT range: 470–580 V, 460–570 M
Middle 50% ACT range: NA
Mean ACT: NA
3 Most popular majors: elementary ed, computer & info sciences, psych
Retention: 79%
Graduation rate: 42%
Library: 5,086,211 volumes
Tuition and Fees: $6,622 in; $11,740 out
Room and Board: $6,302
On-campus housing: 56%
Financial aid, first-year: 72%

If your childhood dreams have ever included becoming the star of one of America's top-rated family situation comedies, perhaps you should consider Temple University. After all, Bill Cosby is an alumnus of this Philadelphia school. But if making people laugh isn't your primary concern, Temple still might be the place for you. Indeed, Temple University has a very structured academic program with Philadelphia as its playground.

The Core

Although requirements may be different for certain majors, all students are required to fulfill core requirements. These include mathematics, lab sciences, composition, American culture, art, and social sciences. Additionally, all students must become proficient in a foreign language, or take classes in international studies. To round off their courses, all students must take a class in race studies and a year known as "intellectual heritage," which covers Western civilization from the ancient world to the modern. While many students are happy that these requirements encourage experimentation in different subjects, some students feel the core is actually quite weak. In regards to the race requirement, one student commented, "Goodness, I'm putting it off 'til senior year. It's a really PC class that professors are not keen on teaching, so it's of very low quality." Within the subject requirements, Temple students must also take a number of writing-intensive classes. According to one junior, "I sometimes think this reduces the quality of classes because people are out to take classes that fall under race and writing-intensive at the same time just to get rid of requirements."

As for actual classes, students agree that the sciences are pretty rigorous, while American studies offers many manageable classes. Students looking for a more intense atmosphere can take honors classes. Upon successful completion of eight honors course, students receive an honors certificate at graduation. Getting into classes itself is not a problem provided the student registers early enough through the school's automated telephone system. "The system is really great and convenient, but it does sometimes leave students unadvised," said one student. Class sizes rarely exceed 30 students and all students agree that there is an extraordinary amount of individual attention from professors.

To Philadelphia and Beyond

Weekends on the Temple campus are pretty low-key. "This is very much a local school," said one student, "so people leave school on the weekends and after 4:30 in the afternoon, the campus is pretty empty." However, the school is in the process of building new dorms to lure students back on campus and to augment campus life. Being in Philadelphia, though, there is a reasonable excuse for escaping from the campus. Temple students have myriad possibilities within the city. Philadelphia boasts one of the best art museums and a rich theater life—students can attend shows at the Wilma Theater and the Walnut Street Theater. Temple often arranges free or reduced tickets for students to attend special shows. For those with less of a penchant for cultural activities, there are plenty of bars and restaurants on South Street. Students like going to diners, including Oak Lane Diner and the Melrose Diner. For a night at an Irish pub, Temple students often frequent Moriarty's and Sassafrass in the Old City.

Despite the low-key campus social scene, there is a large student center, simply known as the SAC. With a food court, movie theater, and arcade, students are often found lounging or studying. "Since there are a lot of commuters, they need places to hang out." However, the newest hot spot on campus is the Tuttleman Learning Center, which just recently opened and houses 500 brand new computers complete with Ethernet access.

Living in a Hotel

For on-campus students, Temple offers a variety of dorms, and is in the process of erecting new ones. Most rooms are standard doubles with just enough room for a small fridge. Peabody, the oldest dorm on campus, has the smallest rooms. The new buildings, White and New Residence Hall are cited as the best dorms on campus, composed of suites with shared bathrooms for four people. Also popular are the Temple Towers, university-owned apartments which support a pool. However, one junior mentioned, "they have some problems with roaches and rats." As campus life is beginning to grow, the demand for dorms has gone up, causing the

school to have purchased a number of rooms in a local Best Western for roughly 130 kids. Most students, though, choose to live off campus. "In the long run, it was actually cheaper for me to live off anyway," said one student. There is no requirement that freshmen live on campus, so students of all years live in local apartments. "Also, the dorms shut down for every break, even the four day Thanksgiving holiday, so you're forced to leave if you're not a local. This means a train ticket at best, and quite possibly a plane ticket," said one junior who lives off campus.

On-campus students choose to eat in Johnson-Hardwick Dining Hall, affectionately called "the Caf." The food is described as "above par for a cafeteria, but you can't eat it for too long." The dining hall is a very social setting. As one freshman said, "dinner is a big production." In the evening, the dining hall becomes quite crowded, where one can find a number of people dressed up for a night in the cafeteria. For those on the run, there is a food court in the SAC and a café in the Tuttleman Learning Center—Fresh Bytes. While the dining options on campus are pretty good, students unanimously cite the lunch trucks as the "staple and highlight" of dining at Temple. From 11:30 to 12:30, independent food stands line the streets serving everything from soul food, all types of Asian foods, and pizza. Of course, many of the lunch trucks serve philly cheesesteaks.

The People

The lunch trucks seem to reflect the diversity of the students themselves. Temple is a tremendously diverse school with a very large African-American population. Moreover, there are a number of Indians and Asians and international students. "I've met people from Australia, Ireland, Russia, even Argentina," said one student. "Diversity truly abounds." Temple manages to bring all these students together in various extracurricular activities, such as Student Government, fraternities, and academic fraternities (which act like honor societies). However, as one junior said, "Temple is very much a working class school so almost all of the students work jobs as their major extracurricular activity." Additionally, included among Temple students are returning adult students who may have families and little time to devote to Temple extracurriculars. Regardless, "there are no idle Temple students."

> While the dining options on campus are pretty good, students unanimously cite the lunch trucks as the "staple and highlight" of dining at Temple.

When they get a break from their various activities, Temple students really enjoy basketball games. The new Apollo arena provides a world-class venue. Nationally renowned coach and defensive guru, John Chaney, provides a basketball team frequently among the nation's best. Although most students don't really have time to devote to athletics, there is the Independence Blue Cross work-out center. There, students profit from a full-service work-out club with everything from Nautilus machines to freeweights. Additionally, the Student Pavilion has both indoor and outdoor basketball and tennis courts. Other students sign up in teams to play intramural sports or take part in aerobics.

Temple, set in a lively and historic city, provides a solid education. Some students choose to spend semesters at Temple's campuses in Rome and Japan, adding an international flair to the university. "I like being here a lot and it really was the perfect choice for me," said one student. "I've learned a lot about myself and love living in a city with all sorts of people."—*Shu-Ping Shen*

FYI

The three best things about attending Temple are "being in a city, the honors program, and the lunch trucks."

The three worst things about attending Temple are "financial aid, politically correct humanities core, the faulty transcript system."

The three things that every student should do before graduating from Temple are "go to the Rodin museum, see a Temple play, see a Temple basketball game."

One thing I'd like to have known before coming here is "that the language departments were so lacking."

University of Pennsylvania

Address: 1 College Hall, Philadelphia, PA 19104
Phone: 215-898-7507
E-mail address: NA
Web site URL: www.upenn.edu
Location: urban
Founded: 1740
Private or Public: private
Religious affiliation: NA
Undergraduate enrollment: 9,692
Total enrollment: 22,148
Percent Male/Female: 52%/48%
Percent Minority: 33%
Percent African-American: 7%

Percent Hispanic: 5%
Percent Asian: 21%
Percent in-state/out-of-state: 21%/79%
Percent Pub HS: 62%
Fraternities: 30%
Sororities: 30%
Number of Applicants: 15,074
Percent Accepted: 33%
Percent Accepted who enroll: 48%
Entering: 2,384
Transfers: 254
Application Deadline: 1 Jan
Mean SAT: 598 V, 686 M

Middle 50% SAT range: 550–650 V, 650–730 M
3 Most popular majors: Banking/finance, history, psychology
Retention: NA
Graduation rate: 87% within 6 years
Library: 4.2 million volumes
Public Computers: NA
Tuition and Fees: $21,130
Room and Board: $7,500
On-campus housing: 96%
Financial aid, first-year: 46%

"What does Benjamin Franklin have to do with the University of Pennsylvania?" a prospective student recently asked when visiting the campus. Her tour guide answered, "Everything—in every UPenn student, there remains some of the innovation of the founding father, Benjamin Franklin. His creativity lives on in each of us, and the University of Pennsylvania remains one of his greatest legacies." Most students would agree with this tour guide. From the original campus tour to commencement, the community spirit and innovation that Benjamin Franklin embodied is such a part of the UPenn experience that the two are virtually inseparable.

Preprofessional Academics

"UPenn is great for those who know what they want to do," one current undergrad said. Specifically, the School of Nursing and Wharton (the business school) are geared toward those with specific careers in mind. In addition, other undergraduate schools include the School of Engineering and Applied Science and the College of Arts and Sciences. Prospective students must apply directly to the college of their choice.

Academics are usually described as "tough." Some of the strongest departments, especially the engineering programs, are particularly loaded with work. And of course, with Wharton and its international prestige, the University of Pennsylvania's business and economics departments are cited as excellent. Similarly, the Museum of Archaeology and Anthropology makes for particularly prestigious archaeology and anthropology departments, as well. Traditionally weaker departments include political science and communications. According to a prospective communications major, "the department tends to attract less ambitious students."

Introductory courses in the sciences are not favorites among many students. But students in the special Ben Franklin Scholars Honors Program can take specialized seminars in their freshman and sophomore years with top professors. The Wharton School also has specialized programs in addition to its traditional business track. These programs include the Health Care Management Nursing Program, which is a joint program with the School of Nursing, and the Jerome Fisher Program in management and technology, an interdisciplinary track combining economics and engineering or applied science. The third specialized Wharton program is the International Studies and Business program. An extremely rigorous program, it requires that students take 40 courses in business, language, and liberal arts. Admission to any of these programs is highly selective.

Living the Quaker Way

True to the communal Quaker spirit embodied in the city of Philadelphia, the University of Pennsylvania strives to foster a community atmosphere using the housing system. Not long ago, UPenn adopted the college system in which students live in one of 12 "college houses." Each college has a faculty master, a dean, graduate associates, and residential advisors. This system enables students to feel a closer bond to their community because the colleges encompass more than just living space. Each college has its own intramural teams, social events, and dining hall. Additionally, academic support is focused at the college level, and each college offers its own study groups and lectures. "I love the college system. My college is a tight-knit community," one undergraduate raved.

Dining halls received mixed reviews. Although one student warned prospective students of most meat products, other students said the dining halls were quite adequate. In addition to the dining halls in each college and in the professional schools, the campus also has coffee shops and many late night eateries options. Chats is UPenn's late night eating place, and students can charge on their accounts food from over ten vendors. In addition, Café Bon Appétit, located in the international house, offers students quality food at reasonable prices.

City of Brotherly Love

"Although Philadelphia isn't the reason I came to UPenn, it did have a big part in my decision," one undergraduate said. Many students agree that the school's urban setting is one of UPenn's greatest assets. Despite many students who prefer to remain on campus, the local area is often bustling with students. Popular nightspots include Murph's Tavern and Smokey Joe's as well as clubs on South Street, Delaware Avenue, and Center City. Great shopping areas include Liberty Place or the funkier South Street.

The city is a cultural haven, as well. The plethora of ethnic neighborhoods boasts amazing restaurants including Le Bec-Fin, a renowned French restaurant, as well as Susanna Foo, an acclaimed Chinese eatery. The Pennsylvania Ballet and Philadelphia Philharmonic are two of many world-famous artistic companies based in Philadelphia. Abounding in museums, Philadelphia offers students a true cultural experience. Sports also play a big role, and UPenn students are known to frequent Flyers, Sixers, Phillies, or Eagles games. And for those history-minded students, the Liberty Bell and Independence Hall are two of Philadelphia's many historical icons.

Of course, the urban setting also has its drawbacks, such as tightened security. With past incidences of violence in mind, the administration has been working with the mayor to ensure a safe atmosphere for the students. Their efforts have been largely successful. Crime has declined over the years not only on campus, but also in the surrounding areas. Increased lighting and escort services have helped to make it a safer place to be. In addition, the University sponsors development programs to help build and improve the neighborhoods. In short, unlike some other urban schools, UPenn doesn't just ignore the problems of its host city by shutting itself off from it—rather, the UPenn administration works hard to make Philadelphia safer for its students.

Study Hard and Play Hard

Life at the University of Pennsylvania is not just about studying. Students are known to do Ivy-caliber work but then party hard. In their words, UPenn is "Ivy League with a fun twist." The Greek system is a big part of UPenn life. With eight sororities, and over 30 fraternities, Greek life is naturally quite visible around campus. UPenn even has its own Office of Fraternity and Sorority Affairs. One UPenn student spoke about her sorority, "I love my sorority sisters. They have helped me

to find a niche here at UPenn." However, although being Greek is a common UPenn hobby, if Greek is not your thing, that's okay, too. The student body is large enough to provide a more than adequate social scene for those not interested in Greek life.

Athletics at Penn also boast a lot of participants. Football and soccer, particularly, brings out lots of fans and athletes alike. Sports games have a lot of fun and unique traditions that Penn students love to carry on. One example is the Toast throwing. After the third quarter of football games, spirited Quakers sing "Drink a Highball," and as the last line is sung "Here's a toast to dear old Penn," the fans throw toast down to the sidelines.

However, as popular as athletics and Greek life are, other extracurricular activities don't always boast as many participants. For those students that do participate, though, UPenn offers a wide variety of extracurricular activities ranging from ethnic and political groups to just plain wacky organizations. Some traditional offerings include the College Republicans and Hillel at UPenn, while Children of the Eighties, a club dedicated to the 1980s, is among the more unusual. UPenn boasts a daily newspaper, the *Daily Pennsylvanian*, and a laundry list of other literary venues. Remarking on the apathy of some students toward extracurricular life, one student said, "So many students here are preprofessional that they don't have time or don't care. Especially Wharton students, with a direct path to success, who focus more on postcollege life than what is currently surrounding them."

> **"We are as driven as our Ivy League neighbors, but we also know how to have fun."**

And without a doubt, UPenn students are driven. But as one student pointed out, "We are as driven as our Ivy League neighbors, but we also know how to have fun." Sure enough, UPenn students report being happy overall with the social scene. In the words of one UPenn freshman, "UPenn is a fun place to be. I wouldn't want to be anywhere else."—*Alyssa Blair Greenwald*

University of Pittsburgh

Address: 2nd Floor Bruce Hall, Pittsburgh, PA 15260
Phone: 412-624-PITT
E-mail address: oafat@pitt.edu
Web site URL: www.pitt.edu
Location: urban
Founded: 1787
Private or Public: public
Religious affiliation: none
Undergraduate enrollment: 14,600
Total enrollment: 26,162
Percent Male / Female: 47%/53%
Percent Minority: 17.0%
Percent African-American: 11.0%

Percent Hispanic: 1.5%
Percent Asian: 0.0%
Percent in-state / out-of-state: 86%/14%
Percent Pub HS: NA
Fraternities: 22%
Sororities: 15%
Number of Applicants: 12,863
Percent Accepted: 60%
Percent Accepted who enroll: 36%
Entering: 3,110
Transfers: 688
Application Deadline: rolling
Mean SAT: 581 V, 584 M

Middle 50% SAT range: 530–630 V, 530–630 M
Middle 50% ACT range: 23–28
Mean ACT: 25
3 Most popular majors: psychology, business, engineering
Retention: 85%
Graduation rate: 64%
Library: 4,000,000 volumes
Tuition and Fees: $6,118 in; $13,434 out
Room and Board: $5,766
On-campus housing: 34%
Financial aid, first-year: 70%

T he University of Pittsburgh, perched on a hill a few miles from downtown Pittsburgh, combines a challenging academic program with an active social scene. The Gothic traditional urban architecture that dominates the campus reflects the school's traditional focus on a liberal arts education. Its curriculum is "challenging," according to students at Pitt, with small classes and a list of requirements that account for about one-third of a student's classes.

Strong Sciences

Although these requirements seem overwhelming at first, students report that the required classes provide for a balanced education. The History of Jazz, one of the courses that fulfills the music requirement, is one of the most popular classes at Pitt and is taught by Nathan Davis, a fa-mous jazz musician. "Everyone wants to take it before they graduate," one student said. Students are required to preregister, but during add/drop period, schedules are flexible. Despite the varied class size, there is "not too much trouble getting into a class," one student said. Another added, "If a student registers early enough, he or she should be able to get into whatever class he chooses." The majority of undergrads at Pitt pursue science majors, even though Organic Chemistry is reputed to be one of the most difficult courses offered. On the other hand, "Rocks for Jocks," or Introductory Geology, is considered one of the easiest courses. Grading is easier during freshman and sophomore years, with "forgiving curves, in introductory courses. The curve becomes tougher in upper-level classes. Professors teach all courses, while recitations, which are small sections that complement the class meetings, are taught by graduate students.

Relaxed but Active Social Scene

On the weekends, Pitt students pursue a variety of activities, from attending fraternity parties and house parties to traveling to the city to watching films near campus. However, the Student Center closes at 10 P.M., so there is no central place for students to congregate on campus at night. A small percentage of Pitt men are members of fraternities. Frats are "big and visible," but "not alienating," and according to one student, they never charge admission to parties. Most students do not formally date at Pitt, although some students say serious relationships are more likely to develop as they approach senior year.

> There are dangerous areas near the urban campus, but students say they feel safe because of the "extremely active police force."

Freshman live in doubles within a circular dorm complex called the Towers. Each room is air-conditioned and shaped "like a piece of pie." After freshman year, most students have the opportunity to live in suites. About half of the upperclassmen move off campus. Most seniors live in the apartments that surround Pitt. In addition, new on-campus housing is also being added this year. Few students have cars, but the city transportation is free with a student ID, making travel into downtown convenient and accessible. Most Pitt students get involved in an extracurricular activity, such as student government, the Greek system, or sports. Notable organi-

zations include the Pitt Pathfinders, a student group that leads campus tours and works with the admissions office, and the Pitt Program Council, which organizes trips and activities for Pitt students, such as group excursions downtown. Service activities and athletics are particularly popular on campus, but one student described the campus atmosphere as "apathetic and laid-back." The cliques that form at Pitt reportedly are not exclusive, and often students are involved with many different social groups.

Pitt students say the dining hall food is "good." The meal plan provides meals and dining dollars, which can be redeemed at campus food eateries like Dunkin' Donuts and Starbucks. The area surrounding campus also has several popular restaurants within walking distance.

Pride in Learning and Sports

The campus of the University of Pittsburgh is dominated by the Cathedral of Learning, a 42-story classroom building shaped like a giant tower. Students see the Cathedral of Learning as a symbol of Pitt's commitment to academics. There are dangerous areas near the urban campus, but students say they feel safe because of the "extremely active police force." Pitt's pride and joy is a brand-new sports center that accommodates both students interested in fitness and members of the Pitt athletic teams. The Pitt Panthers compete in Division I-A. The basketball, diving, and swimming teams are especially well supported.

With the addition of the new sports complex, free transportation to the city, diverse and rich food offerings, and a strong academic program, Pitt encourages a rich college experience.—*Rebecca Pace and Staff*

FYI

The three best things about attending Pitt are "the Cathedral of Learning, the Communications major, and the hip area around campus."

The three worst things about attending Pitt are "Scaife (lecture hall), walking up a hill to get to many classes, and the Towers."

The three things that every student should do before graduating from Pitt are "eat a sandwich with french fries inside (at Pirmanti Brothers), go to a varsity sports event, and take the History of Jazz."

One thing I'd like to have known before coming here is "how confusing fraternity parties are, especially when you're not entirely sober."

Villanova University

Address: 800 Lancaster Avenue, Villanova, PA 19085-1672
Phone: 610-519-4000
E-mail address: gotovu@email.villanova.edu
Web site URL: www.villanova.edu
Location: suburban
Founded: 1842
Private or Public: private
Religious affiliation: Roman Catholic
Undergraduate enrollment: 7,130
Total enrollment: 1,019
Percent Male / Female: 49% / 51%

Percent Minority: 9.2%
Percent African-American: 3.0%
Percent Hispanic: 3.0%
Percent Asian: 3.0%
Percent in-state / out-of-state: 31% / 69%
Percent Pub HS: 50%
Fraternities: 29%
Sororities: 40%
Number of Applicants: 9,278
Percent Accepted: 62%
Percent Accepted who enroll: 28%
Entering: 1,611
Transfers: NA
Application Deadline: 15 Jan

Mean SAT: 600 V, 620 M
Middle 50% SAT range: 560–640 V, 580–660 M
Middle 50% ACT range: NA
Mean ACT: NA
3 Most popular majors: finance, biology, nursing
Retention: 92%
Graduation rate: 75%
Library: 680,000 volumes
Tuition and Fees: $20,555 in; $20,555 out
Room and Board: $3,040
On-campus housing: 61%
Financial aid, first-year: 52%

Looking for a good combination of great basketball and the Catholic tradition? If so, then Villanova University is probably the place to be. Students at Villanova are wildly supportive of their Wildcats basketball team. During basketball season, "the games are sold out all the time. People get painted up. And *everyone* is wearing their 'V' shirts," said one student. But while Villanova offers basketball thrills, students can gain much more.

The Academics

Regardless of academic department—be it nursing, engineering, or business—all Villanova students are required to take core humanities requirements, including courses in theology and philosophy. Normally taken in the freshman year, these core classes explore different themes and time periods, from the ancient and medieval all the way up to the modern. According to one student, "I think our basic requirements are pretty good, but it really was a lot of work." Aside from these core classes, students are allowed to explore the various options offered within the respective departments. According to most students, engineering and nursing are probably the most difficult departments.

One sophomore described how her friend "has really long days. Sometimes I don't see her for more than a few minutes." The departments in the liberal arts are not deemed quite as difficult and many students, in fact, feel the need to strengthen those departments.

Still, students have few complaints about their class experiences. One junior mentioned that "even for my general lecture courses, I don't think there's ever been more than 60 people." Furthermore, the professors are reportedly very accessible. One engineering major commented that "the professors don't have problems helping you after class is over or even calling them at their houses. They're really great." Another student gave a more mixed review: "I've had a few professors grossly underprepared," she said, "but, still, the teachers here are great." Villanova does not have large numbers of TAs teaching undergraduates, although they do help to grade and provide help in certain laboratory courses. While registration may often be difficult for freshmen, who sit lowest on the priority ladder, Villanova students are extremely happy with academics. "I really think I'm getting more than I'm paying for," declared one freshman.

Chugging Along . . .

Alcohol is quite present on the Villanova campus, but the administration is very adamant about restricting alcohol to students of age. Generally, to drink, Wildcats attend fraternity parties. The Greek system is very big, although those who don't rush can still attend the numerous Greek parties. For those interested in calmer activities, movies are shown every weekend in the student center and there are plenty of concerts throughout the semester. Additionally, for those in pursuit of more intellectual activities, "there are lots of forums, colloquiums, and the like—everyday. So you can definitely find one of those if you want." Other on-campus activities can be found at Connelly, the student center. There students can play pool, Foosball, board games, use the Internet, and take advantage of a huge lounge. Many juniors and seniors have cars, although freshmen are not allowed to bring cars to campus. "It's okay though," said another student, "freshmen will find plenty to do on campus." While freshmen generally stay on campus, upperclassmen do mention that they enjoy going into nearby Philadelphia often. Favorite hangouts include Club Egypt, Fels Planetarium with their Laser Light show, and South Street.

"I Like Girls that Wear Abercrombie & Fitch . . ."

One freshman described the general Villanova student to be "a really well off, white, Abercrombie & Fitch–wearing, business type." Aside from the somewhat preppy atmosphere, "people here are really friendly," said one junior. Still, students generally agree that the school could use a little more ethnic diversity.

Villanova "Wildcats" can be found participating in various extracurricular activities. Fraternities are the most popular groups, and they often carry out service projects. Other service organizations include Habitat for Humanity, and Project Sunshine, where students can devote just an hour of their time each week to helping poor children in the inner city. Student government is prevalent on campus and well-respected, as is the *Villanovan*, the school newspaper, which, reportedly, "everyone loves." Additionally, for those

who absolutely love Villanova, there is the Blue Key Society, in which students lead outside tours of the campus.

As mentioned earlier, basketball is the most attended sporting event of the year. Football, apparently, "is good, but doesn't attract a lot of people." Students in search of physical activity outside of varsity athletics can participate in intramurals, of which basketball, flag football, soccer, and softball are the most popular. Furthermore, there are two weight rooms which while in constant use, are never packed. "It's nice because the athletes have their own facilities, so the rest of us can have access to the gyms," said one student. Other sports facilities include indoor and outdoor basketball courts, as well as tennis courts, all easily accessible by foot.

Beautiful Surroundings

Due to its Catholic attachment, one of the most noticeable buildings on the Villanova campus is their Roman Catholic church. "The building is absolutely lovely, and it's a nice contrast to the new buildings on campus," said one sophomore. One of these more recent buildings is the new Center for Engineering Education and Research, while a new business school is soon to be erected. The campus is quite small; a 15 minute walk is all that's necessary for a walk from corner to corner.

Dorm life is "very nice, actually," said one freshman. "The freshmen get treated really well here, and their dorms are all basically new." Aside from comfortable pads, Villanova dorms observe quiet hours and enforce visitation policies. For first year students, visitation goes up until midnight during the week, while upperclassmen get 24-hour visitation rights. One upperclassman commented on his freshman room, "I was very happy with it—I even had a room with a sink." After freshman year, students are put into a general lottery, although everyone hopes to live in either Sheehan, Sullivan, or Good Council, which reportedly have the largest rooms and act as big social hangouts. Since Villanova only guarantees three years of on-campus housing, most seniors move off, although there are some junior apartments, sponsored by the school, which are always in high demand. Unfortunately, many students find residence hall staff rather negligent in fixing things. "I really think they don't like kids," said one student. As for safety issues, one student commented that "it's pretty good. They check the dorms every night and there's a guard sitting at every dorm after 11." While some students sometimes find the guards and dorm policies restricting, they are generally happy with the security system at Villanova.

On this lovely campus are a number of places to eat. All students living on campus must purchase a meal plan, ranging from 19 meals per week, to the "new alternative," which provides a set number of meals during the semester, or an unlimited plan. There are three dining halls, and about eight "à la carte" dining areas. As one upperclassman described, "the dining halls are fun, especially for freshmen, who inevitably spend too many hours just chatting away." Additionally, two of the dining halls remain open until two in the morning. While no food is served at this

late hour, "it's a really nice place to go and study." When seeking the excitement of restaurant food, students enjoy going off campus to local favorites such as Bertucci's, Marble's, and Minella's.

> **"[The typical Villanova student is] a really well off, white, Abercrombie & Fitch–wearing, business type."**

Clearly, Villanova is a school with a solid academic tradition where students still find time to be socially and physically active. While set in suburbia, the students also have access to a nearby city, where they can leave any worries of school behind. For the students of Villanova, a Catholic tradition is all part of the academic experience. But as a result, there is a clear sense of family at Villanova, something with which the Wildcats are very happy.—*Shu-Ping Shen*

FYI
The three best things about attending Villanova are "good schools, basketball, really great faculty."
The three worst things about attending Villanova are "fighting with management, the general courses, and the sheer amount of alcohol."
The three things that every student should do before graduating from Villanova are "do an abroad program, take a minor in something technical, go to a Nova basketball game."
One thing I'd like to have known before coming here is "that sometimes you have to leave the campus in order to have fun."

Rhode Island

Brown University

Address: Box 1876, 45 Prospect St., Providence, RI 02912
Phone: 401-863-2378
E-mail address: admission_undergraduate@brown.edu
Web site URL: www.brown.edu
Location: small city
Founded: 1764
Private or Public: private
Religious affiliation: none
Undergraduate enrollment: 5,777
Total enrollment: 7,758
Percent Male/Female: 47%/53%
Percent Minority: 27.0%

Percent African-American: 6.0%
Percent Hispanic: 6.0%
Percent Asian: 14.0%
Percent in-state/out-of-state: 3%/97%
Percent Pub HS: 60%
Fraternities: 10%
Sororities: 3%
Number of Applicants: 14,756
Percent Accepted: 17%
Percent Accepted who enroll: 56%
Entering: 1,414
Transfers: 57
Application Deadline: 1 Jan
Mean SAT: 690 V, 690 M

Middle 50% SAT range: 640–750 V, 650–740 M
Middle 50% ACT range: 26–31
Mean ACT: 29
3 Most popular majors: biology, history, English lit
Retention: 97.0%
Graduation rate: 93.0%
Library: 3,000,000 volumes
Tuition and Fees: $25,372 in; $25,372 out
Room and Board: $7,094
On-campus housing: 100%
Financial aid, first-year: 38%

"Don't you know? They're talkin' bout a revolution. It sounds like a whisper." Tracy Chapman is onstage at Brown. Buronians have filled up the Main Green, leaving their bodies to the rhythm of the music. You can tell people are enjoying themselves and see the happiness in their faces. It arises from the vast and diverse opportunities that Brown offers them.

Academics

Academics at Brown are, in a single word, unique. There are no core requirements. Students need to obtain 30 course credits for graduation. The grading system at Brown is different than most other schools: "You either get an A, a B, a C or no credit—you can't fail classes (no F's)." "You can however fail enough not to reach the graduation requirement," added another student. Students are allowed to create their own majors. Special programs include combined B.A. and B.S., and B.A. and master's programs. Program in Liberal Medical Education (PLME) is an eight-year program that accepts students into Brown University and Brown Medical School at the same time. Brown students can also take classes at Rhode Island School of Design, which is "next door."

"Classes should be picked on the basis of professor more than on the topic of the class," said a sophomore. Most students say that they have been "very happy with their professors." Most professors have "great charisma and personality that they use to spice up lectures." "They structure classes in a way that keeps you engaged." Since Brown does not have a big graduate program, "all professors are here for undergraduates and they seem to enjoy it." "We have lunch and dinner together and they hold functions at their houses since they live close to campus." They are "very available through e-mail and phone, you can always get in touch with them." Students had mixed reviews about the TAs. A student described them as "a very valuable resource and acting to supplement the lecture classes," whereas others complained that most TAs in economics, math, and computer science have accents that are difficult to understand. "TAs write NO comments on my papers when they grade them, which is really frustrating" was another complaint. However, students recommend that, "Shopping period allows you to avoid TAs altogether if you want to and to find the very best professors for you."

People tend to agree that Russian Lit is the biggest gut—"people only go to class for the exams"—and Geo 5 also known as "Rocks for Jocks" is a close second. Intro to Software Engineering (it ends up taking about 100 hrs/week by the end) and Orgo are among the hardest classes. Class size usually varies from 10 to 400 with most classes being small and medium, under 40 people. "I've had a class that was over 200 and a class that was 3 people, but most average 10–20," said one student. Getting into small seminars, English workshops, and comparative lit and art classes can be a problem. Overall, the academic environment is "cooperative, not competitive, which is great." Many students summed up their feelings about academics at Brown in three words: "I love it."

Who Are Buronians?

Several students mentioned that "although people here call themselves liberal, they get pissed if you don't agree with them" and that "excessive political correctness can get annoying at times." "Conservatives are too scared to make themselves a presence here but they are certainly in the minority." One student noted that the student body is "pretty diverse but has a tendency to enclave off, which is annoying." Another one disagreed: "I never feel like groups are exclusive." "Although we are mostly a middle-class or upper middle-class school, a sense of pretension does not exist," explained another student. Unlike most schools, Buronians (usually referred to as Brownies by themselves) tend to agree they have "enough attractive people

around." One girl noted, "I haven't met a nonattractive guy yet." Another guy added, "One thing I'll say about Brown, it is a HOT campus. Mmmmm . . . when spring rolls around, and the layers of clothing come off, it's a happy happy time of year." Most students agree that there is "a lot of sex" at Brown, but "you wouldn't know about it; it's pretty discreet and no one brags." Homophobia does not have much following: "Sexual preference is something which most people seem to be comfortable with." "It's a very friendly campus once you put yourself out there to be friendly as well," added one junior. Another summed up Buronians as "some of the nicest, most good-hearted people I've ever met. It's amazing. Good souls go to Brown." Buronians seem to be impressed with one another: "The majority blow you away with their bright minds and lists of accomplishments kept tucked away. It becomes inspiring to be surrounded by all these people with ambition and compassion."

Shelter and Food

Students are required to live on campus during their first three years at Brown. All freshmen live in doubles; singles are easy to get sophomore year. "Freshman dorms are freshman dorms—they're big and have lots of people." That is "unless you're in Andrews—that place is like a gorgeous hotel—you even have your own sinks in your rooms!" Freshman doubles are "usually the same size and they are very roomy and comfortable." Freshmen are organized into "units" that are consist of about twenty students that "you are introduced to as soon as you get to Brown and usually you share the same dorm, corridor, or whatever it is you're living in." One student explained that, "most friend groups are based on freshman unit mates. But then you branch out and meet friends of friends, etc." Students agree that dorms in general are "pretty nice." After freshman year, students can choose among a variety of living options such as frats, special interest housing, or go into the housing lottery. Greek housing at Brown is no different than dorms: frat brothers and sorority sisters live together in a certain part of the dorm. "The lottery is awful, avoid it," said several students. A senior referred to the housing lottery as "a hugely impersonal machine that arbitrarily dumps undergraduates into any of the concrete monsters littered throughout the campus." Some of the special interest houses are Buxton International House, Harambee House for those interested in African culture, West House, which is the environmental house, the Multinational and Tech Houses. There are also two co-op houses where students share cooking, cleaning, and maintenance duties and a no-substance house. Floors are almost always coed but bathrooms are not. Some students complain about "rooms and suites not being coed."

Freshmen have to stay on the meal plan but "most students go off meal plan after two years." 7, 10, 14, and 20 meal options are available. Several students mentioned that "dinner is too early—it ends at 6:45." Ratty and Verney-Woolley are the two main dining halls on campus. Food is "hardly inspiring." Besides the dining halls, students can use their meal plan credit at the Blue Room, the Ivy Room, the Gate, and the Campus Market or at Josiah's to have hot and cold snacks and beverages. The chicken specialty at Josiah's is called Carberry. The combination of these two names led to a Brown tradition several years ago: Josiah Carberry is an invented professor of psychoceramics, and is responsible for mischief on campus. His psychoceramics course was reviewed in the course critique and he has his own active Brown e-mail address.

Those who are not satisfied with the food offerings on campus have a wide variety to choose from in Providence. Providence has "lots of good restaurants for a small city." "You can come to Providence to taste a wide variety of ethnic food." The "really good food" around campus includes the cookies at Meeting Street Café, Maximilian's ice cream, the cake at Gregg's, falafels at East Side Pockets, the Italian food on Federal Hill and everything at Louie's. Louie's on Brook Street is "the great greasy spoon diner that's a Brown tradition." One student advised that, "You should go there at 5 A.M. and have breakfast with the truckers."

Social Life

Most Brown students are pretty active in their social lives and party as hard as they study. Freshmen party with their units "until they break out and go to other parties on campus." Upperclassmen usually go off campus to private parties. They also hang out in bars and clubs downtown or make the 45-minute trip up to Boston. Viva on Thayer Street is crowded on Friday and Saturday nights, although "it draws a certain kind of crowd." Most parties on campus are theme parties. The two LGBTA parties, Starf*ck and Sex, Power, God, have the reputation of being the best parties of the year with St. Anthony Hall, Buxton House, and Machado House also renowned for throwing "incredible" parties. Some students refer to frat parties as "boring keg fests" and say that "most Buronians are not into that." One student described the Greek system as being "weird—not many people are into it, but lots of people go to the parties." The Greeks are "not well-respected around campus, though individually many of them are perfectly nice people." One student summarized Greek life as "It's there, and it thrives, but it's not pervasive. You can avoid it if you want."

Non-drinkers do not feel left out of it on campus. "Even frat parties and other alcohol-based parties involve fun stuff like dancing and you can enjoy it sober." Kegs are not allowed on campus. Every party is also required to have nonalcoholic drinks, which students refer to as "a good system." "People do seem to respect the choice to not drink here more than I've seen on other campuses," commented one sophomore. About drug use, most students agreed that, "we do have our own nice hippie drug subculture dominated by pot smoking." The Presidential Gala and the Spring Ball are two of the occasions to get dressed up for. Students agree that, "you don't really need a car" but then add, "they could be useful to go Boston, get groceries, or go downtown." Parking is a major problem at Brown, which makes cars less attractive. Most people do not have cars but most people "have a friend with a car and that person gets asked a lot of favors."

"Almost everyone" at Brown engages in extracurriculars and usually "in way more than one." The Lesbian, Gay, Bisexual, and Transgendered Alliance (LGBTA) and Brown Outdoor Leadership Training (BOLT) are among the well-respected organizations. There are also some funny ones like Arrr!, which is an a cappella group founded in 1999 "dedicated to the singing of sea shanties in the style which we call *a capirate*." Third World Action (TWA) and Student Labor Alliance (SLA) are among the most vocal activist groups. Improvisational comedy groups such as Improvidence and humor magazines such as the *Brown Jug*, formerly *Exit 20*, "have a good sense of humor." *Brown Daily Herald* is the college daily whereas *George Street Journal* and the *Independent* are the weekly publications. The *Independent* is reputed to be "more intellectual, thought-provoking, and better" than the other two. *Brown Journal of International Affairs* is "one of the best, if not the best, publication of its kind." Brown students operate a TV station, BTV, and two radio stations, WNSR and WBRU. WBRU is reputed to be one of the best student radios in Rhode Island.

Most students hold jobs in addition to being involved in extracurriculars. University Food Services is a "huge employer." Other students either work in outside firms as consultants, publishers, etc., or have already formed their own businesses. Community service is popular among students and arranged through Swearer Hall. Most students agree that, "Brown isn't big on sports." One student remarked, "We did win the Ivy League Football Championship last year but most people don't care. Alums do, but not undergrads." "The Brown Band always picks fights with the Harvard Band—it's glorious," added another student. Brownies form their teams and join the intramurals in a variety of sports such as football, basketball, soccer, softball, Frisbee, and tennis. Pick-up games in lacrosse and basketball are easy to come across in the warmer months. "You can also grab your skates and go to the hockey rink." Students agree that, "there is no Brown spirit in sports." "Poor attendance at sporting events and attempted pep rallies" are evidence of this.

On and Around Campus

One student described the campus as having the "looks of an Ivy League school: nice old buildings, quaint." Another said, "a crazy mishmash of architecture; something for everyone." In the middle of campus is the Main Green, "a large lawn with classrooms, dorms, the administration building, and Faunce House." Most students agree that, "on a lazy sunny Sunday, the Green is the happiest place on Earth." University Hall, built in early 1700s, is a notable building on campus: "The cool thing is that George Washington himself stayed in University Hall during the revolution." The Duncan MacMillan Building was recently built for chemistry and geological sciences. Construction is currently going on for an addition to the engineering building, Barus & Holley. The Sciences Library, referred to as SciLi in Brown lingo, is a 14-story building with every floor painted one color of the pH scale. The thirteenth floor of this library is "famous nationwide as a hot sex spot." Rockefeller Library, known as "the Rock," holds humanities and social sciences collections in addition to John Hay, Art Slide, Music, and Demography Libraries. The newly renovated Sayles Gym is reported to be "terrible for nonathletes." The public weightroom is pathetic. Even my school had a better one," said a senior.

> "On a lazy sunny Sunday, the Green is the happiest place on Earth."

Students reported feeling safe on campus: "The school is very safe, as is Providence in general. The police are excellent here." The surrounding area "definitely adds to campus life." Thayer Street is very lively with lots of cafés, restaurants, and small independent shops and is a popular student hangout. A new mall also just opened up downtown, which is an attempt at developing Providence's social scene.

At Brown, "you have a freedom to make your own decisions, and a freedom to screw up royally and pay royal consequences." Brown's liberal approach to ed-

ucation allows students to discover their potentials and to further explore a variety of different disciplines. The open-mindedness of the student body and the emphasis on academic cooperation rather than competition allows Buronians to enjoy their four years here by making the most of their academic and social lives."
—*Engin Yenidunya*

FYI

The three best things about attending Brown are "freedom to make your education what you want it to be; cooperative, not competitive, academic environment; the politically and socially open atmosphere."

The three worst things about attending Brown are "PC hysteria, library collection not large enough, and administration policies."

The three things that every student should do before graduating from Brown are "go to the naked party at one of the co-ops, get off the Hill, and eat breakfast at Louie's at 5 A.M. with the truckers."

One thing I would like to have known before coming here is "we have such a small localized campus and a central dining hall where everyone eats, while fun, makes it feel a little bit more like high school."

Rhode Island School of Design

Address: 2 College St., Providence, RI 02903
Phone: 401-454-6300
E-mail address: admissions@risd.edu
Web site URL: www.risd.edu
Location: small city
Founded: NA
Private or Public: private
Religious affiliation: none
Undergraduate enrollment: 1,847
Total enrollment: NA
Percent Male/Female: 40%/60%
Percent Minority: 31.0%

Percent African-American: 2.0%
Percent Hispanic: 4.0%
Percent Asian: 11.0%
Percent in-state/out-of-state: 9%/91%
Percent Pub HS: NA
Fraternities: NA
Sororities: NA
Number of Applicants: 2,366
Percent Accepted: 38%
Percent Accepted who enroll: 43%
Entering: 385
Transfers: NA
Application Deadline: 15 Feb

Mean SAT: NA V, NA M
Middle 50% SAT range: NA V, NA M
Middle 50% ACT range: NA
Mean ACT: NA
3 Most popular majors: fine arts, graphic design and commercial art, industrial design
Retention: 94.0%
Graduation rate: 89.0%
Library: NA
Tuition and Fees: $20,210 in; $20,210 out
Room and Board: $6,490
On-campus housing: NA
Financial aid, first-year: 95%

Students at more traditional liberal arts schools often stereotype art school students as strange idlers who don't do any real work. This is far from the truth at the Rhode Island School of Design. With a reputation as one of the premier art schools in the country, RISD (affectionately known as "rizdee") combines a rigorous art curriculum with traditional academic requirements.

Students are required to take three English classes, four art and architectural history classes, three courses in history, politics, or social science, and four liberal arts electives—in addition to the demanding studio courses required for the fine or applied arts majors. Because students can cross-register at Brown University after freshman year, the course selections are practically endless. However, only a handful of students actually take advantage of the resources at the neighboring university, and the number of cross-registered courses for which a student can receive credit are limited. The largest departments at RISD are industrial design, graphic design, and architecture. The fine arts "suffer a little" because of this, but there is still a waiting list for all the fine arts departments.

Frosh Boot Camp

All RISD freshmen take the same foundation classes. The course load is heaviest during this first year, and as a result many feel that they have "no time to do anything social." As one undergrad put it, "All of Freshman Foundation is hell . . . like boot camp, so after freshman year anything is a breeze." A deep sense of community develops as all freshmen collectively slave over their 2-D and 3-D drawing, art history, and English courses. One student said, "Since freshmen take all the same classes and live in the same dorm complex, we are all one big happy family."

All freshmen must live in one of four halls in the quad. Each hall is coed by floor, and each floor accommodates 15 to 30 freshmen and an RA. Students have drafting tables in their rooms, and each floor also has a well-ventilated work room, TV room, and lounge. Residents say the work rooms are especially valued, since freshmen are not eligible for campus studio space. The South Hall is notable because it is equipped with air-conditioning. East Hall is reserved for people who agree not to smoke and to observe quiet hours; some students call this dorm the "hippie haven." However, designated smoking rooms are more difficult to obtain as a result of their popularity. Overworked freshmen find that their main social activity involves "just hanging out in the dorm."

RISD students are required to declare their major at the beginning of the second semester freshman year, which some feel is "way too soon." One student elaborated, "You have to choose before you have any substantial experience in your potential major."

Life After Freshman Year

Most students agree that RISD gets less intense after the grueling freshman year. Depending on their major, upperclassmen spend two to four afternoons per week in the studio and divide their mornings and evenings between academic and technical classes. Although a demanding five-year program requires architecture students to "sleep in the studio," most other students work at home. "I always read in the guidebooks that RISD students don't go out, they only work," one student said. "To a certain extent, that is actually very true. But artwork is different from academic work in that you can talk with people while you do it, and you need to. It's essential to get feedback from people while you are working."

Professors serve as harsh critics at RISD. Although students acknowledge that professors must view their work not only as teachers but as professional artists, their criticism can be discouraging. "My photography professor was so harsh during his critiques," one photography major confided, "that I haven't picked up my camera in a week. I am going to start my final project soon and do it for me, not for him." Intensive studio settings in which students aren't fond of their professors can be frustrating, but students say they generally admire their professors and point out that the small classes foster strong relationships with faculty.

Breaks from the Routine

RISD undergrads rave about the six-week-long winter session between semesters, which allows them a greater degree of freedom. "You get to take classes that have nothing to do with your major," one student explained. "Plus, it gives you a little bit of breathing room—you're only in class three times a week, so it's a relief from the usual high pressure of RISD classes." Students also use these six weeks for more independent study, often traveling internationally.

RISD prides itself on exhibiting student work, and the campus art museum has added a wing to display its modern art collection. When it comes to libraries and athletics, however, most students rely upon Brown University's resources. RISD does have its own library, and the modest student center offers occasional student-taught dance and self-defense classes, but Brown's facilities are more extensive. RISD students are proud of their hockey team, however. Known for their losing record each season, the RISD Nads attract fans who love to shout, "Go Nads! Go Nads!"

Providence Provides

Most upperclassmen live off campus. The historic houses on Benefit Street are popular, but can be expensive—students who don't want to spend as much money live closer to the Brown campus in the Fox Point neighborhood. Although this area is closer to the less affluent sections of Providence, students say they feel very safe. However, students may take advantage of the coordinated Brown and RISD shuttle buses that run until 3 A.M., or the 24-hour Brown escort service.

> "Some people like RISD but realize they need more variety. People need to be very dedicated to feel happy here. But if you are interested in getting an education in art, then RISD is an amazing place."

A student described Providence as "too big to be small-towny, but too small to be exciting." Restaurants in the Thayer Street section of town offer a more palatable alternative to RISD cafeteria fare, which many students call bland and expensive. Freshmen are required to purchase $1,500 worth of meal points a semester, with 40 percent of it refundable. RISD lets students transfer leftover meal points to the Pit, a snack bar that specializes in hamburgers and french fries. Another popular option is the Carrhaus, a student-run coffee shop with an eclectic menu including coffee, bagels, hummus, and ice cream.

Many RISD students report that their main extracurricular activities involve "working and smoking a lot of cigarettes." However, some students find time to participate in a broad range of activities outside of class, from teaching children's art classes in the Providence community to writing for RISD's fiction magazine, *Clerestory*, or for the joint Brown-RISD newspaper, the *College Hill*. More adventurous students join the daredevil Street Luging Club and roll downhill through town lying on skateboards.

Despite the low-key social scene, RISD students insist that there is always something to do. Providence is teeming with college students, and shops and restaurants thrive on student business. Boston and New York are both accessible by train or bus when students need a change of scene.

Not So Strange After All

While geographical backgrounds at RISD are diverse, socioeconomic ones are not. "Everyone comes from rich homes!" one student exclaimed. Another undergrad pointed out, "RISD divides all the money it gets from alumni among all the students and studio costs," so there isn't much left over for scholarships. Many students feel that this leads to a certain homogeneity on campus. "I thought an art school would be more accepting of an out-of-the-ordinary attitude," one undergrad said, "but I was surprised at how conservative the people I met were. People look weird and act liberal, but if you dug deeper, they probably would all be Republicans." However, it is generally agreed that the RISD students are "a neat crowd of people."

Students feel a deep connection to their school and are proud of how respected a RISD education is in the art community. Quite a few students transfer out each year, however, so students have this advice for prospectives: "Some people like RISD but realize they need more variety. People need to be very dedicated to feel happy here. But if you are interested in getting an education in art, then RISD is an amazing place."—*Siddhartha Shukla and Staff*

FYI

The three best things about attending RISD are "fun people, professors with experience in the real world, and small classes."

The three worst things about attending RISD are "Freshman Foundation, no RISD library, hard work."

The three things that every student should do before graduating from RISD are "take a class at Brown, write for the paper, and go to a hockey game."

One thing I'd like to have known before coming here is "most people here have money."

University of Rhode Island

Address: 8 Ranger Rd., Suite 1, Kingston, RI 02881-2020
Phone: 401-874-7000
E-mail address: uriadmit@uriacc.uri.edu
Web site URL: www.uri.edu
Location: rural
Founded: 1892
Private or Public: public
Religious affiliation: none
Undergraduate enrollment: 10,483
Total enrollment: NA
Percent Male / Female: 44% / 56%
Percent Minority: 9.0%

Percent African-American: 3.0%
Percent Hispanic: 3.0%
Percent Asian: 3.0%
Percent in-state / out-of-state: 69% / 31%
Percent Pub HS: NA
Fraternities: 6%
Sororities: 7%
Number of Applicants: 9,110
Percent Accepted: 79%
Percent Accepted who enroll: 30%
Entering: 2,177
Transfers: NA

Application Deadline: 1 Mar
Mean SAT: NA V, NA M
Middle 50% SAT range: 480–590 V, 480–590 M
Middle 50% ACT range: NA
Mean ACT: NA
3 Most popular majors: NA
Retention: 77%
Graduation rate: 50% (within 5 years)
Library: NA
Tuition and Fees: $4,242 in; $11,568 out
Room and Board: $6,378
On-campus housing: 42%
Financial aid, first-year: NA

D id someone say *par-tay*? At URI everyone seems to be saying "party." However, the once top-ranked party school apparently has started to lose some of its party animal charm. According to one student "URI isn't the party school it used to be." That is welcome news to an administration that has tried, in recent years, to quell the *Animal House* and focus more intently upon academics.

Hard-Core Curriculum

Party animals, don't pack your bags just yet. The University of Rhode Island does require its students to meet graduation requirements by taking courses in the natural sciences, fine arts, mathematics, languages, and social sciences. While this subject load may seem daunting, prospective students should not despair. The requirements, according to one sophomore, are "fairly easy if you pay attention in class and take semi-decent notes."

But be forewarned, introductory classes, especially at big state universities, can be ridiculously large. Some courses at URI enroll as many as 500 students. However, according to students, the average class size is 40–50 students. Certain majors also require participants to take specific classes. Students rave about the Chemical Engineering and German departments in particular, and URI has long been known for its marine biology programs.

Again, a common problem at major universities is the glut of TAs teaching classes. While URI does try to ensure that courses are taught by professors, some students complained about the high number of TA-taught lecture courses. However, when the professors are present, and that is the majority of the time, they are easily approachable if students make the effort.

For the more academically inclined graduate of the Rhode Island public school system, the university offers a rather impressive and prestigious honors program. The class sizes are generally smaller and the course load more rigorous. Students can apply directly after high school or after their freshman or sophomore years. Like most other universities, URI extends to its students the possibility of study abroad that, for some Rhode Island weary scholars, is a great chance to "escape and have a blast." URI also offers a "Centennial Scholarship" that can provide the lucky few motivated and qualified students with a full ride. You know what that means, freshmen? More disposable income and leeway with the parents!

In terms of academic upgrades, the University of Rhode Island recently committed itself to building a new $9 million environmental studies center on the Kingston campus. The price tag includes a whopping $1 million federal grant.

URI also sponsors numerous academic lectures. Recent talks have centered on such topics as "Genetic Diversity of Life," "Global Youth Cultures," and "Vietnam." Lectures are popular options for intellectual students.

Home Sweet Home

The campus of URI is a random smattering of Gothic, colonial, and modern architecture. The Quad, at the center of campus, is picturesque and, at least according to one student, a great place to "do homework or have sex." The Quad is surrounded by academic buildings, while the Greek houses are relegated to the outskirts of the sprawling campus. Campus dorms, the student center, and the library were recently renovated. "The campus feels like it's brand spankin' new!! I absolute love it!!"

> **"I'm already dreading having to leave here."**

The dorms at Rhode Island get mixed reviews. However, one enthusiastic student stated that her dorm "had a large common room, which we can easily veg out in." All dorms, save one, are coed by floor. There is an all female dorm for those interested. For the non-substance using students there is a "Wellness Dorm" that prohibits smoking and drinking. Sorority and frat houses are also popular options for upperclassmen. Many upperclassmen complain about the inadequacy of on-campus housing. However, one of the best options available for upperclassmen housing is the apartments along the nearby beach. Surf's up!

After a hard day's night in the library students can chow down at one of URI's three main dining rooms or the oft-praised "Ram's Den." Several meal plans are available to URI students, including a

10, 15, or 20 meal plan. At the Ram's Den students use food points purchased at the beginning of the semester to buy the delectable goodies offered at "by far the best food joint on campus." The other dining halls vary, with some serving fast food and others serving traditional entrées. The Den offers some well-liked grilled entrées. The university has made strides recently in helping to provide for the needs of its vegetarian students. Despite the improvements in dining, students still complain about the lack of weekend service.

One student described the town of Kingston as being "like Disney World without the rides and wonderful Florida climate." Drinking is the only thing that seems to dull the monotony of this one-horse town nestled in the vast wilderness of Rhode Island. Yet, some students relish in the small town setting, describing it as "the ideal little college town!" But where do students crash after a hearty night of hard drinking and wild fun?

Getting Soaked
on a Dry Campus

The official administration policy is one of "no alcohol." But according to most students on campus the university is wet to the point of deluge. As with most large state universities, Greek life is the dominant form of social activity on campus. All parties must be registered with the university police but this has not drastically altered the availability of alcohol. One student loudly exclaimed, "Rams party more than study." This, of course, results in the non-drinkers feeling ostracized from the mainstream and has spurred animosity between Greek and non-Greek students. Luckily for those not interested in the frat scene, the University does have an entertainment committee that brings in speakers, theatrical productions, and concerts to campus. G Love and Special Sauce recently performed on campus.

Extracurricular activities are also major parts of students' lives here on campus. Basketball and football games are particularly popular draws, especially when URI is playing cross-state rival Providence College. Other notable sports teams are the baseball, volleyball, soccer, and sailing teams. The sailing team has earned numerous national and international distinctions.

Student senate and the student run newspaper, *The Five Cent Cigar*, also garner favorable attention on campus. One of the more fascinating clubs at URI includes the Experimental Art Society that sponsors such activities as film production and instrument production. The perennial favorite Surf Club also holds September lessons for surfing novices.

The political atmosphere on URI's campus is one of liberal tolerance. Racial issues do occasionally surface on campus as a result of several racially self-segregated dorms. Student groups are attempting to combat this problem. A large part of the student body is also comprised of commuters who live nearby and drive to school.

Overall, despite academics playing second fiddle to social life, many students say that URI offers its motivated students a healthy learning experience. "As a sophomore, I'm already dreading having to leave here. I *love* this place—and it was actually my last choice in high school. Give URI a chance, you won't regret it." —*Sean McBride*

FYI

The three best things about attending URI are "the friendly and diverse student body, inexpensive cost of living, and the professors who are willing to help with just about anything."

The three worst things about attending URI are "the lack of student involvement, there's nothing to do on weekends (except drink), and the majority of students commute."

The three things everyone should do before graduating from URI are "to take part in homecoming, to run naked across the Quad, and to change their major at least once."

One thing I'd like to have known before coming here is "that URI ain't as much a party school anymore!"

South Carolina

Clemson University

Address: 105 Sikes Hall, Box 345124, Clemson, SC 29634-5124
Phone: 864-656-2287
E-mail address: cuadmissions@clemson.edu
Web site URL: www.clemson.edu
Location: rural
Founded: 1889
Private or Public: public
Religious affiliation: none
Undergraduate enrollment: 13,053
Total enrollment: 16,396
Percent Male/Female: 54%/46%
Percent Minority: 10.0%

Percent African-American: 8.0%
Percent Hispanic: 1.0%
Percent Asian: 1.0%
Percent in-state/out-of-state: 66%/34%
Percent Pub HS: 90%
Fraternities: 15%
Sororities: 26%
Number of Applicants: 9,539
Percent Accepted: 69%
Percent Accepted who enroll: 42%
Entering: 2,589
Transfers: 1,151
Application Deadline: rolling
Mean SAT: 564 V, 581 M

Middle 50% SAT range: 510–610 V, 520–630 M
Middle 50% ACT range: NA
Mean ACT: NA
3 Most popular majors: mech engineering, marketing, elementary education
Retention: 84.0%
Graduation rate: 71.0%
Library: 1,400,000 volumes
Tuition and Fees: $3,472 in; $9,372 out
Room and Board: $4,130
On-campus housing: 96%
Financial aid, first-year: 19%

Located in the rolling green hills outside of Greenville, South Carolina, Clemson University was founded a little over a hundred years ago as an agricultural institution. Oh, how times have changed! Today's Tigers are proud to boast of their perennially powerful football team and their status as one of the Southeast's emerging centers for engineering and technological studies. While it is easily apparent that the Tigers have left their mark on the Atlantic Coast Conference, there's more to Clemson than just a great football team.

Not What It Used to Be

As any student will tell you, the evidence rests in many of Clemson's academic departments, especially the College of Engineering and Sciences. Resulting from a merger of the engineering and computer science departments in 1996, the College of Engineering has developed a strong faculty and loyal student following. Students describe the college as "definitely catering to math-oriented people." On the other end of the scholastic spectrum at are the throwbacks to the school's earlier times. Agriculture and PRTM (officially for Parks, Recreation, and Tourism Management but more commonly known as Party Right Through May) are particular favorites of the slacker crowd, students report. Beginning with the class of 1996, students in all colleges are also required to complete general education requirements in order to graduate. Oral communication, writing-intensive, and computer skills classes are some of the types of general requirements.

The majority of Clemson students are happy with their classroom situation, although not everything always goes smoothly. One senior noted that "getting into classes can sometimes be a problem, but a lot of the professors will eventually give in—persistence is key!" Students are also happy with class sizes, most of which don't exceed 40 students and can be as small as 15. Like most other large universities, students have quite a bit of interaction with TAs, although some students do sometimes complain about a "language barrier." The upside to the TA situation is that many TAs attended Clemson as undergrads and, as one student put it "can relate exactly to what you are going through."

We're Gonna Party Like It's 1999

Ask any Clemson student and he or she will tell you that Tigers are a very sociable bunch. Daytime activities revolve around sports, especially football, which garners the attention of the entire campus in the fall. The aptly named "First Friday" before the home opener features a huge pep rally and parade around town. Other major gridiron-related events occur before archrival University of South Carolina comes to town and also during Tigerama, the fireworks-crazed culmination to the homecoming week.

Besides football, Clemson plays host to a full roster of varsity sports. Both men's and women's basketball enjoyed successful 1999 seasons as the former barely missed winning the NIT championship and the latter competed in the NCAA tournament. Clemson's men's golf team finished 1998 as the top-ranked team in the nation and the women's rowing team competed in its inaugural varsity season. For those a little less serious about their sports, Clemson also hosts many intramural sports, and informal games of basketball and ultimate Frisbee are common occurrences.

Nighttime activities coalesce into a happening party scene in this college town. Fraternities and sororities have a noticeable presence on campus, but Greek parties aren't exclusive and non-Greeks have ample opportunity to party on their own. Upperclassmen often spend weekend nights hanging out at the bars downtown, but underclassmen beware: it is widely understood that local clubs are cracking down on underage patrons.

Those who want to engage in clubs and activities at Clemson are met with an abundance of opportunities. Gamma Sigma Sigma and Alpha Phi Omega are two highly regarded community service organizations, and student government is well-respected. Religious groups abound on the conservative campus and students can choose to participate in many groups including the Baptist Student Union and Federation of Christian Athletes. The Edgar Allen Brown University Union is responsible for bringing in activities for Clemson students, and most Tigers share the view that "the Union rocks!" That is probably a pretty safe assumption, given that "the Union" has recently brought in acts ranging from the Rolling Stones and the Beach Boys to Adam and Dr. Drew from MTV's *Loveline*.

> "On the one hand you have the conservative, rich, Abercrombie & Fitch–wearing fraternity brother, and on the other you have the good ole Southern country folks."

Students say that friends are easily made on the Clemson campus. This idea is summed up by one junior who mentioned that "I met my entire freshman floor of 40-plus in two weeks, and I still hang out with a good deal of them." Perhaps this phenomenon can be explained by the fact that, as a group, Tigers admit to being pretty homogeneous. "There are basically two groups here," explained one female student. "On the one hand you have the conservative, rich, Abercrombie & Fitch–wearing fraternity brother, and on the other you have the good ole Southern country folks." Students report that there is little tension among the different groups and the large size of the school has led many to believe that any type of person would fit in here.

Eat, Drink, and Be Merry

Clemson undergrads have about as many good things to say about dining hall food as they do about rival USC. The recently renovated Harcombe Cafeteria draws rave reviews for its atmosphere, yet the word most associated with the fare is simply "terrible." Tigers do have other options, however. Those on the meal plan can use it to eat at one of the many local fast-food restaurants, and many students elect to cook their own meals at home. Few students choose to live in university-provided housing more than two years, and apartments and houses line the avenues surrounding the campus.

Harcombe is not the only building that impresses undergrads, though. Death Valley (the famed football stadium), Little-john Coliseum, and the Flour-Daniel Engineering Building are noted as a few outstanding examples of great Tiger architecture. The well air-conditioned ("this is the South, we would die in our sleep without them") dorms receive high marks, especially Holmes Hall, a converted hotel of four-person suites complete with two bedrooms, a kitchenette, and a bathroom. Holmes hosts many of Clemson's honors students as a perk for their scholastic achievements, but other dorms also draw high marks. The large

men's dorm Johnstone was recently renovated to better serve its inhabitants and might soon shake off its nickname as the "tin can." McCabe and Clemson House offer coed housing by the suite in the same layout as Holmes Hall, as do the profuse number of on-campus apartments. One student described the campus itself as "a paradise, with lots of beautiful trees," yet all that green has its drawbacks: many students complain that there aren't enough parking spaces for the large number of Clemson undergrads with cars.

Begun as an agriculture and farming school, Clemson has matured into a major state university that offers undergrads a comprehensive education. But, students say that oftentimes they are too busy having a great time cheering on the football team to notice. We will keep their secret.—*Robbie Berschinski and Staff*

FYI

The three best things about attending Clemson are "parties, people, excitement about sporting events."

The three worst things about attending Clemson are "location, not enough parking, over-crowded on campus dorms."

The three things that every student should do before graduating from Clemson are "go to parties, ride "Roller Coaster Road" (a wild road outside of the town), meet tons of people."

One thing I'd like to have known before coming here is "how nice the student body is."

Furman University

Address: 3300 Poinsett Highway, Greenville, SC 29613

Phone: 864-294-2034

E-mail address: admissions@furman.edu

Web site URL: www.furman.edu

Location: small city

Founded: 1826

Private or Public: private

Religious affiliation: none

Undergraduate enrollment: 2,643

Total enrollment: 2,840

Percent Male/Female: 45%/55%

Percent Minority: 9.0%

Percent African-American: 5.0%

Percent Hispanic: 2.0%

Percent Asian: 2.0%

Percent in-state/out-of-state: 30%/70%

Percent Pub HS: 75%

Fraternities: 30%

Sororities: 35%

Number of Applicants: 3,270

Percent Accepted: 67%

Percent Accepted who enroll: 32%

Entering: 748

Transfers: 56

Application Deadline: 1 Feb

Mean SAT: 622 V, 626 M

Middle 50% SAT range: 560–670 V, 570–670 M

Middle 50% ACT range: NA

Mean ACT: NA

3 Most popular majors: political science, business admin, biology

Retention: 91.0%

Graduation rate: 76.0%

Library: 390,000 volumes

Tuition and Fees: $18,266 in; NA out

Room and Board: $4,848

On-campus housing: 98%

Financial aid, first-year: 42%

Few universities give their students the opportunity to receive a top-notch education on a campus recognized by the American Society of Landscape Architects as one of the most beautifully landscaped areas in the country. Located on a spacious 750-acres campus nearby Greenville, South Carolina, Furman University offers just this. Furman students will tell you that their campus is truly remarkable, but they will also be quick to note that their challenging course load doesn't leave them too much time to stop and smell the roses.

The Secret of My Success

The campus might be a park, but classes at Furman are no picnic. Academics are a "top priority" here. Paladins take pride in the high quality and challenging nature of their academic program. The stress put on academics has its downside though, as many feel that grading is overly harsh. Students commonly expressed feelings like "I am here to get a better than average education, so the work is something I expect, but I feel like the professors are a little too hard on students at times when it comes to papers and tests." Indeed, Furman professors are notorious for limiting the amount of As given out in their classes, but are otherwise highly praised. Students like the fact that professors teach all classes and TAs only hold tutoring sessions. Just to emphasize this point, one student retorted, "What's a TA look like? I've never even seen one around." Under this system, classes average around 20 students—"nice and small, so everyone can get to know everyone else"—and students can generally get into any class they want to take.

Furman ensures that each of its students receive a well-rounded liberal arts education by requiring a large dose of general-education classes. Ranging from English Composition and Intro to Biblical Literature to Principles of Biology, the wide scope of the General Education Requirement, or GER, lays a solid foundation of learning for each and every Paladin. For the most part, students do not seem to mind this program and take advantage of their required classes to figure out exactly what they want to study. Integrated into the gen-ed curriculum is

the Cultural Life Program, which seeks to expose each and every Paladin to a broad range of cultural events throughout the school year. Students can choose to attend events ranging from lectures on the crisis in Kosovo to a performance by the Furman Symphony Orchestra. They must attend 9 CLPs per year, for a total of 36, in order to graduate.

The academic year at Furman is split into an uneven trimester system that students either love or hate. During the three-month-long fall and spring sessions each student takes three 50-minute classes that meet every day. Between the fall and spring, there is a two-month winter session during which students take only two classes, but meet every day for 75 minutes. This "wacko trimester system," as described by one student, "is really a blessing in disguise. Having so few classes at a time really lets me concentrate on the ones I'm taking, and the transition in schedule between the three trimesters keeps things new and fresh." One student exclaimed, "I can't even imagine taking more than three classes at a time!"

However, for every happy comment about the course load, there is a complaint about the way in which this system affects vacation time. "Yeah, spring break is always a blast when you get let out in mid-February," griped one student. Another student grumbled, "Whenever I'm out of class, my non-Furman friends are in, and vice versa. It's really a pain."

A Place in the Sun

Furman students do not have any problem finding activities to keep them busy in their spare time. In fact, the only complaint you might hear around campus is that they have too many things going on at once. Two of the most popular groups on campus are Furman University Student Activities Boards (FUSAB) and Collegiate Educational Service Corp. (CESC). FUSAB act to coordinate different social, cultural, recreational, and educational activities for students. Events planned by FUSAB include Homecoming, Parent's Day, and the annual music-filled bacchanalia, the Spring Weekend. Also, the body is in charge of attracting local and national performers to the campus. FUSAB was extremely proud to host Dave Matthews and Tim Reynolds last year. Prospective FUSAB members must apply to join. Still, the organization continually keeps its ear to the ground by asking any and all students for suggestions.

CESC is the campus's major community service organization, with an emphasis on the word "major." With over 1,500 members active in some capacity on the campus, 70 percent of the Furman population has worked for the CESC on one project or another. Under the large CESC umbrella, there are more than 80 agencies that serve the public. These programs range from Child Enrichment and Book Buddies to Big Brother/Big Sister and Church Ministries. The organization also hosts workshops on subjects such as child management and working with the elderly at its yearly High Rocks conference. Plus, the CESC puts on the annual May Day Play when Furman volunteers invite all the kids and adults that participate in CESC programs come to the campus for a day of fun, food, and games.

With more than one third of students involved in a fraternity or sorority, the Greek scene on campus is large, though nonintrusive—"going Greek at Furman is good for those who want it, but not a big deal for those who don't." Furman has no fraternity or sorority houses, and since students must live on campus for at least three years, it's impossible for Greeks to self-segregate. As one female student explained, "my dorm hall has about the same number of sorority and nonsorority girls, and all but one of the sororities are represented, so that shows you just how mixed the population is." This commingling helps make the Greek scene at Furman inclusive, and results in annual parties like Biker Bash and Beach Weekend that are open to all students.

However, because the campus is dry, most parties occur off campus. Students also frequently head to dance clubs in Greenville. Although putting a damper on the social lives of some students, the dry campus rule is not looked at as a major obstacle by most. "For drinkers, where there's a will there's a way" was the claim of one upperclassman, "and we also have a relatively high percentage of nondrinkers who aren't affected anyway." Said another, "Nondrinkers do not feel out of place. If anything, drinkers feel out of place when first introduced to Furman. The great thing is that many people who do not drink party just as hard as those who do!"

What, Me Play Sports?

Football season at Furman does not receive as much attention as at some of the bigger southeastern universities, but the student population at this Division I-AA school is still very involved in athletics. The university's 17 varsity teams attract recruits in most major sports, while club and intramural teams satisfy those with a hunger for sports like rugby, Ultimate Frisbee, and lacrosse. Students rate each other as "very fit and health conscious," and joggers and Rollerbladers can be seen cruising around the scenic campus at all hours of the day.

> "[Furman is] just like that *Cheers* song where 'everybody knows your name.'"

Being health conscious is just one way in which the average Paladin blends in with his or her peers. "There is definitely a lack of diversity in the student body," noted one sophomore, "upper middle-class conservative white kids walking around in North Face jackets are pretty much the norm." Another joked that "Everyone here has a car, although you don't need one since everyone here has a car . . . and fitting in is as simple as these three words: sport utility vehicle." Students also consider one another attractive, yet for some mysterious reason there is little dating on the campus. One student noted that "some people might have significant others, but I never see anyone holding hands or anything like that," while another commented that "it seems like people are only married or totally single, with nothing in between."

Life Is Beautiful

When comments like "this is the most beautiful place you will ever spend four years of your life" are so common, it can only mean that students are happy with their campus. Students love Furman's exquisite park-like environment and the atmosphere it creates. Visitors are greeted by a row of huge oak trees separating the main road from acres of well-manicured grass lawns. Once through the front gates, two large fountains and groups of students studying or playing Frisbee mark the center of campus between Daniel Chapel and Duke Library. Red brick colonial–style buildings dot a landscape that's centered on a small lake that is famous for birthday dunkings. Nearby, visitors can take in the beauty of the campus rose garden and quaint Japanese teahouse.

Living Single

For those who do spend four years of their life at Furman, dorming and dining are a top priority. Many seniors take advantage of off-campus apartments, but all other students must live in university provided housing. With two exceptions, all dorms are single sex. Most men live in the five buildings of South Housing, while the women live in Lakeside Housing. All freshman halls have at least four upperclassman RAs and freshman advisors. Most dorms have community bathrooms, although some buildings are arranged in suites with one bathroom for every two rooms. Juniors and seniors have the option of residing in the highly regarded North Village Apartments, which provide on-campus living with an off-campus feel. Here, roommates share newly built apartments that contain four singles and two baths. All dorms have visitation rules that many students consider harsh. No one is allowed in an opposite sex building past midnight on weekdays and two in the morning on weekends, and though the rule is enforced, one student confided that "people break it all the time and are never caught."

The word most often used by students to describe their dining hall is "decent." "You know, I've seen much worse, but for some reason the cooks think that everything has to be fried," was how one student depicted the situation at Charles E. Daniel Dining Hall. Overall though, students consider their food selection pretty diverse. Meal plans come with a points system allowing students the alternative of eating at the food court instead of the dining hall, and there are plenty of fast food options around campus. Additionally, those willing to make the 15-minute drive into Greenville can visit either the mall or the "strip" for a great assortment of local and national restaurants.

The Furman Show

If your college-shopping list includes high academic standards and immaculate scenery, Furman might be just what you're looking for. Small enrollment and intimate classes make for an environment that's "just like that *Cheers* song where 'everybody knows your name,'" remarked one satisfied sophomore. Those who do choose to spend their college years at Furman try not to let the breathtaking campus keep them from their studies, but in such an outgoing and friendly atmosphere, even these high-achievers have their work cut out for them.—*Robert Berschinski*

FYI
The three best things about attending Furman are that "the people are so nice, the campus is beautiful, and the students are very involved."
The three worst things about attending Furman are "students have to live on campus for three years, getting an A in a class is overly hard, and it is so pretty visitors use it as a park."
The three things that every student should do before graduating from Furman are "get thrown in the lake on their birthday, fountain hop, and work for the CESC."
One thing I'd like to have known before coming here is "there is so much to do that a lot of people over-commit and stress out."

University of South Carolina

Address: Columbia, SC 29208

Phone: 803-777-7700

E-mail address: admissions-ugrad@sc.edu

Web site URL: www.sc.edu

Location: small city

Founded: 1801

Private or Public: public

Religious affiliation: none

Undergraduate enrollment: 15,551

Total enrollment: 23,430

Percent Male/Female: 45%/55%

Percent Minority: 23.7%

Percent African-American: 19.3%

Percent Hispanic: 1.4%

Percent Asian: 2.7%

Percent in-state/out-of-state: 72%/28%

Percent Pub HS: NA

Fraternities: 13%

Sororities: 14%

Number of Applicants: 14,032

Percent Accepted: 62%

Percent Accepted who enroll: NA

Entering: 3,894

Transfers: 983

Application Deadline: rolling

Mean SAT: 550 V, 548 M

Middle 50% SAT range: 540 V, 550 M

Middle 50% ACT range: 23

Mean ACT: 24

3 Most popular majors: experimental psychology, engineering, biology

Retention: 80.9%

Graduation rate: 60.2%

Library: 3,143,505 volumes

Tuition and Fees: $3,740 in; $9,814 out

Room and Board: $4,167

On-campus housing: 82%

Financial aid, first-year: 41%

If you were asked to find a cocky student at the University of South Carolina, you would probably be hard-pressed to do so. You would, however, certainly find "Cocky," the big red mascot that leads the South Carolina Gamecocks in spirit at the football games. Football is, without doubt, the most popular sport on campus, with near full attendance at each game. And though Williams Brice Stadium is packed every weekend in the fall, students at the University of South Carolina are also busily engaged in extremely diverse studies.

Varied Studies

One of South Carolina's greatest assets is the range of course options it offers. While most students lean toward the study of traditional subjects in the College of Liberal Arts or the College of Science and Mathematics, they can also pursue degrees in more unique fields by attending the School of Applied Professions, which includes hotel, restaurant, and tourism administration, or the School of Library and Information Sciences. Students unanimously agree that the College of Business is probably the strongest program. "International business is especially strong; it was ranked number one in the country," said one freshman. Another student stated that "the journalism school is also pretty good for our region." Regardless of the school chosen, all students at USC have a number of requirements to complete. Each student must have a complete year of basic science and must take English 101 and 102, although these requirements may be waved through AP work. They must also study a year's worth of social sciences and humanities. For many majors, another required class is University 101. This class for freshmen is an introduction to college life, covering such topics as sex and how to study effectively. Although not reported to be a difficult class, one freshman said that many students "have lots of complaints about it. It's a cheesy waste of time and you have to do a lot of mindless work." After these requirements, it is necessary to begin taking classes in the major.

For the most part, students are happy with their professors, although they are not always so pleased with the classes themselves. This disappointment is an outcome of the school's registration system, which sometimes precludes students from getting into the classes they want. One freshman exclaimed that the registration system "is a pain! It's a frustrating time because so many of the classes fill up fast, and if you miss your appointment time, it's a mess." The only redeeming aspect of the registration process, according to another student, is that "you can do it over the computer, so that's kind of helpful." Aside from scheduling difficulties, the major grievance regarding classes is the size. "Sometimes they are just too large," said one junior. Introductory classes generally run about 150 to 200 students at minimum. Past the introductory level, however, many students said that smaller classes are available. Nevertheless, students are enthusiastic about their studies and, according to one freshman, so are the professors. "A lot of my professors are very enthusiastic about what they do. They want to make the class interesting because they know a lot of nonmajors end up taking their class." While there appears to be an overabundance of TAs, one student said, "There may be a lot, but they're good TAs. I haven't really run into any bad ones." Most TAs are older graduate students rather than those just having received their bachelor's degree. TAs rarely teach classes, but lead discussion groups for larger classes or facilitate laboratory work. In general, USC students assert that academics are very strong and any course of study is worthwhile.

So-So Social Options

While the view of academics is rather universal, the view of social life is not. Regarding USC, a junior stated that "academics is fine, but social life stinks," while one freshman said, "There's something for everyone here." Most students find that social options are adequate. One student said that "Columbia is a nice place. You can go see plays, movies, and the like." A popular hangout is Five Points, an area with lots of bars and eating establishments. Some students enjoy going to Tombstone, a local country dance club, but as one student said, "that's very South Carolina." Other students, many of whom live in South Carolina, choose to leave Columbia over the weekend, preferring the social life in their respective hometowns.

On campus, there do not seem to be as many options. Most campus activities are

limited to guest lecturers, ranging from Spike Lee to various academics. The university also recently hosted an academic conference on the Civil War. Students looking for less academically geared activities take advantage of a campus cable channel that shows movies every day. Greek life is rather prevalent on campus, but, as one non-Greek freshman said, "I don't feel at all like I'm out of the loop. It's not a school where you have to fit in to have a social life." As for drugs on campus, one student said, "It's such a big campus that I'm sure there's some of it going on, but I've never seen it myself."

Because USC is located in a southern state, most students joke that the school is full of "a lot of sweet, hospitable southern people." Even so, South Carolina also plays home to many international students and northeners. One freshman commented that USC is "made up of all different kinds of people." However, another student complained that "there always seems to be a black/white kind of thing. It's bothersome that our society hasn't moved on from that. It seems the people always move their own ways." Even so, one student said that "my next-door neighbors are from Philadelphia and South Carolina. Being with them has expanded my horizon by getting to know people I would have never met."

Living Arrangements

Regardless of home state or ethnicity, most South Carolina students make on-campus dormitories their home. One student simply commented that "the dorms aren't bad, depending on the building. Some of them have high ceilings so you can install lofts." Another plus is that all the dorms have air conditioning, so that the muggy South Carolina air is bearable during the spring and summer. Most freshmen live in the Towers, a group of coed dorms, though there is also one all-male dorm. The rooms there were described as "less than stellar" by one freshman, but bearable. Women searching for all-female housing can be placed in McClintock, Simms, or Wade-Hampton dorms. Coed dorms have men living on one side, while the women live on the other. Most dorms have a strict policy restricting visitors of the opposite sex to the hours of 10 A.M. to

2 A.M. "That's plenty of time to visit, but in the coed dorms, it's usually pretty easy to sneak visitors in," said one upperclassman. The best on-campus housing is reportedly the apartment complex called the South Quad or the Horseshoe apartments, usually reserved for upperclassmen.

While most students are pretty satisfied with their living arrangements, there are still complaints. Some students have also had problems with bugs in their rooms, but as another student aptly pointed out, "Don't come to the South if you don't like roaches!" To avoid hassles like these, many students move off campus, although "you don't feel a need to move off campus. It's not dorky to live on campus at all," said one sophomore. Students living off campus, though, usually invest in a car as many apartment complexes are not within walking distance of the campus. Be forewarned, however, that "parking is the biggest pain in the butt!" as one student put it. A car is also a must for off-campus students because "Columbia has a horrible public transportation system."

Good Food on a Great Campus

Though many students gripe about housing, few complain about campus food. USC has many places to eat, the most frequented being the Grand Market Place. "It's cafeteria-style, but you can get sandwiches and other hot food. It is a little expensive, though," said one student. Students in a rush usually find the food court below the Grand Market Place extremely helpful, where they can dine at Taco Bell, Sub City, and Freshen's Yogurt. Other dining options on campus include the Roost, the Bates, and the Patio, although for some students it is a long hike to get to these facilities. Students do have a few complaints about the dining system hours. "For anyplace that's all-you-can-eat, there's only a two-hour window when it's open," said one freshman. Another source of discontent is the meal plan, in which each student purchases a specific number of meals each week, ranging from 10 to 21. But, as one sophomore complained, "If you don't use a meal, it goes to waste." There are decent vegetarian options, but one student said "the dining halls don't really cater to vegetarians." Students do go off campus to eat occasionally, but as one student said, "There's really a variety on campus. Why spend money?"

> "It's a nice mix between a secluded campus, but with the advantages of a city," said one student.

The campus itself is in the middle of downtown Columbia. However, according to one student, "It's really it's own little place. It's very defined, even though it's spread out." The heart of the campus is called the Horseshoe; it is a big open courtyard-like area where "people come and jog, lay out in the sun, and just relax," reported one undergrad. USC will soon boast a new state-of-the-art physical education center as well as a new science building. Recent additions have included a new law center and the South Quad dorm. As for safety, one student said, "it's really safe as far as big schools go." Most students claim to feel safe knowing that there are call stations all over campus in case trouble should arise. One freshman said, "Use common sense and you'll be fine." Most USC students enjoy being on campus and find that while the campus is in the city, it does not exude a big-city feel. "It's a nice mix between a secluded campus, but with the advantages of a city," said one student.

Clubs and Sports

South Carolina is a very active campus. The Greek system is strong, and so are a number of ethnic clubs, including a chapter of the NAACP. Community service is extremely popular, exemplified by such clubs as Carolina for Kids, in which students go into local schools to tutor and play with local children. "Everyone is involved to a point. Many people pick one club to do on campus that they really enjoy," said one student. Other clubs include those concerned with athletics, including aerobics, bodybuilding, and fencing.

As for sports, football is, without question, the most anticipated sport of the year. USC students regularly attend football games, starting with tailgating hours before a game begins. Describing the weekly ritual, one student said, "everyone gets dressed up and then it's like a migration to Williams Brice Stadium. There's a lot of school spirit." After football, students say basketball is probably the most followed sport on campus. The USC basketball team has traditionally performed well in its conference. For non-varsity athletics, students participate in intramurals or go to the Blatt Center, where "you have your choice of treadmills, stair-climber machines, and a pool, too."

The University of South Carolina is an extremely large school, which sometimes serves as a point of criticism for many students. However, with a large school also comes numerous educational and extracurricular activities. A freshman who thought going to a big school would be a problem said, "I haven't found that to be true. You find your own little niche in a group of people. You don't have to belong to a certain group. You find your own way."—*Shu-Ping Shen and Staff*

FYI

The three best things about attending USC are "the mascot, good cafeteria food, and surprising diversity."

The three worst things about attending USC are "bugs, parking, and registration."

The three things that every student should do before graduating from USC are "paint a letter on your chest for a football game, dance at Tombstone, and tan on the quad."

One thing I'd like to have known before coming here is "how useful a car would be."

W o f f o r d   C o l l e g e

Address: 429 N. Church Street, Spartanburg, SC 29303-3663

Phone: 864-597-4130

E-mail address: admissions@wofford.edu

Web site URL: www.wofford.edu

Location: small city

Founded: 1854

Private or Public: private

Religious affiliation: United Methodist

Undergraduate enrollment: 1,100

Total enrollment: 1,100

Percent Male/Female: 53%/47%

Percent Minority: 10.0%

Percent African-American: 9.0%

Percent Hispanic: 0.0%

Percent Asian: 1.0%

Percent in-state/out-of-state: 65%/35%

Percent Pub HS: 75%

Fraternities: 50%

Sororities: 58%

Number of Applicants: 1,592

Percent Accepted: 85%

Percent Accepted who enroll: 28%

Entering: 307

Transfers: 15

Application Deadline: 1 Feb

Mean SAT: 590 V, 600 M

Middle 50% SAT range: 530–630 V, 540–650 M

Middle 50% ACT range: NA

Mean ACT: 24

3 Most popular majors: biology, finance, business economics

Retention: 89.7%

Graduation rate: 82.4%

Library: 192,776 volumes

Tuition and Fees: $16,975 in; NA out

Room and Board: $5,015

On-campus housing: 96%

Financial aid, first-year: 55%

When the Rev. Benjamin Wofford of Spartanburg, South Carolina, passed away, he left money to found a college "for literary, classical and scientific education." One hundred and fifty years later, Wofford College still stands as a bastion of solid education in an environment designed to nurture personal growth and experience.

A Select Education

Founded in 1854 and still affiliated with the United Methodist Church, Wofford has remained small by choice. The administration reportedly has no plans to expand enrollment but instead plans to concentrate on providing a select group of students with a strong education in the humanities, arts, and sciences. Professors are accessible and maintain an "open-door policy," according to students. Undergrads are required to take courses in the humanities, English, fine arts, foreign language, science, history, philosophy, math, physical education, and religion. These general education requirements are meant to ensure that by the end of their first two years, students have taken classes they normally would not have considered. Students are also required to complete four interim projects. The month of January is Interim, when students can research, travel, take an internship, or work on an independent project. Among the most popular majors at Wofford are biology, business, chemistry, English, and history. The science department is reported to be particularly strong, with "most students getting into their first or second choice of medical schools," according to one undergrad. Students also recommend the philosophy and zoology introductory courses.

Wofford's active student body puts their full support behind their impressive athletics program. As part of the deal, Wofford built a brand-new athletic complex, the Richardson Physical Activities Building, which opened in the summer of 1995. Wofford basketball, football, and soccer games already draw crowds, especially when the Terriers play rivals Citadel or Presbyterian College. "Student interest tends to drop off a bit when one of the teams is not performing well," one student said, "but overall, we are very proud of our sports teams."

Using New Technology

The F. W. Olin Building is one of Wofford's most prized possessions. Designed as a model for integrating technology in teaching the liberal arts, this state-of-the-art academic building houses high-tech audiovisual equipment, ultramodern language labs, computer science facilities (including the computer center for the school's network), and classrooms. Plans for a new science building are also in the works. "The older buildings on campus

are always kept in good shape," one student said.

Students seem content with Wofford's living conditions, and few of them choose to live off campus. A new all-female dorm gets good reviews for its two-room suites, and Dupree is considered one of the best and most social dorms for upperclassmen. Many students consider Marsh dormitory to be Wofford's least popular: it houses first-year male students, and the lack of privacy (especially in the huge bathrooms) is the biggest complaint. "The guys who live there get rowdy a lot and the place usually ends up getting trashed after a while," one student said. The fraternity houses are not residential.

Social Life

The Greek system is strong at Wofford, although kegs are banned from campus. Students say they usually have no problem finding parties off campus if there isn't anything happening on fraternity row. "There is some pressure to join a frat, but that's only because rush period starts three weeks into the fall semester," one student said. Pressure to rush is reportedly heavier among Wofford men than women.

> **"No one here is just a number."**

Wofford students tend to describe their classmates as "interesting and colorful." Although the majority of Wofford students are from South Carolina, a large percentage come from other southeastern states. Before the school went coed, its name brought to mind the image of the "Wofford Man," which one student said was a "cultured, well-liked individual—a southern gentleman." Today Wofford students preserve their traditions, but they point out that the school now "prides itself on progressive thinking." Not too progressive, however: Wofford students and administrators alike tend to be politically conservative, although one undergrad said the administration is "liberal enough to let the students do what they want." "Clashes at Wofford don't last very long. There isn't a lot of activism here," one senior reported. Life at Wofford is best described as "mellow"; life moves a bit slower than in big cities, and the atmosphere on campus is relaxed. "Wofford students are not afraid to look a campus visitor in the eye and say hello," one student said. "The school is small enough so that you know almost everyone. No one here is just a number." One student reported that it is not unusual for undergrads to "give the president of the college a high-five as he walks by."

Living in the South

The city of Spartanburg, which students describe as a "blue-collar town," offers a reasonable variety of restaurants and entertainment at low prices. It is a place where you can "find a Kmart very easily, but not a Banana Republic," one student said. The city is no bustling metropolis, but one student predicted that a new BMW manufacturing plant has the potential to "turn Spartanburg into another Raleigh."

According to undergrads, Wofford offers a friendly southern environment and a solid education, particularly for those considering a career in law, medicine, or the ministry. "Wofford transcends the classroom in many ways," one student said. "It does have the potential to be too personal due to its atmosphere and size, but I'd have to say that the positive effects outweigh the negative ones." Another student added, "If you want an outstanding overall college experience, come to Wofford, but if you want to spend four years with your nose buried in a textbook, don't."—*Jeff Kaplow and Staff*

FYI
The three best things about attending Wofford are "small classes, excellent frat parties, and mellow students."
The three worst things about attending Wofford are "no kegs on campus, crappy salad bar, and nothing to do in Spartanburg."
The three things every student should do before graduating from Wofford are "go to a frat party, attend a basketball game against Citadel, and take a road trip to the beach."
One thing I'd like to have known before coming here is "how claustrophobic campus can sometimes get."

South Dakota

Address: 414 East Clark St, Vermillion, SD 57069
Phone: 605-677-5434
E-mail address: admiss@usd.edu
Web site URL: www.usd.edu
Location: rural
Founded: 1862
Private or Public: public
Religious affiliation: none
Undergraduate enrollment: 7,232
Total enrollment: 10,119
Percent Male/Female: 43%/57%
Percent Minority: 6.0%

Percent African-American: 1.0%
Percent Hispanic: 1.0%
Percent Asian: 1.0%
Percent in-state/out-of-state: 79%/21%
Percent Pub HS: 91%
Fraternities: 9%
Sororities: 5%
Number of Applicants: 2,500
Percent Accepted: 88%
Percent Accepted who enroll: 43%
Entering: 962
Transfers: 778
Application Deadline: rolling

Mean SAT: NA V, NA M
Middle 50% SAT range: NA V, NA M
Middle 50% ACT range: 19–25
Mean ACT: 21
3 Most popular majors: business, psychology, biology
Retention: NA
Graduation rate: 46.0%
Library: NA
Tuition and Fees: $3,461 in; $7,534 out
Room and Board: $3,234
On-campus housing: NA
Financial aid, first-year: 33%

O ne might say that the University of South Dakota has a split personality: Monday through Friday the college whirls and bustles, while over the weekend it seems like a ghost town that dawdles and yawns. During the week the college offers exotic extracurricular activities, small classes led by attentive professors, and a thriving Greek scene. But on the weekends, you will find that most of the students have either gone home or to nearby Sioux Falls, South Dakota, and Sioux City, Iowa.

Premeds Study Together

Most students at USD are enrolled in the College of Arts and Sciences, which features traditional majors, including chemistry, mathematics, and English. Core requirements here usually account for about 10 of the courses that the students take. Among the requirements are at least one course in the humanities, one in the social sciences, one in math or computer science, and one in health and wellness. Students identified the biology department of the College of Arts and Sciences as particularly strong. Many of those who major in biology go on to med school at the University of South Dakota. According to several students, the pre-meds are grade-conscious, but not deathly competitive; in spite of their desire to succeed, said one student, most of "the pre-meds still study together."

Undergrads at the university may enroll in other colleges, including the School of Business, the School of Education, and the College of Fine Arts. Students cited the nationally accredited School of Business as especially good, and many involved in campus media find advisors in the Mass Communications department of the College of Fine Arts.

USD offers few colossal-sized classes. Even the lectures are tiny by state-school standards. The largest lectures might enroll about 250 students, but lectures average about 100. By junior year, classes range from about 20 to 30 students. Lectures and seminars alike are usually led by professors; TAs are a rare sight at the university. "Just about all my classes have been taught by professors," said one student, "and just about all my professors have known my name." Students work reasonably hard at USD, with many claiming to spend upward of 20 hours a week on their studies, but conceded that it is possible to get by with as little as six. The business, mathematics, and education majors were cited as burdening their students with much work.

Weekday Fun, Weekend Boredom?

Social opportunities abound Mondays through Thursdays. On Tuesdays, a local movie theater (one of two in Vermillion) offers discount movie night. Thursdays, the student association brings in a comedian to perform at Charlie's After Dark, an on-campus club. Famous speakers also appear during the week; recent speakers have included Larry King and Tom Brokaw. Promised one student, "There's a lot going on, if you pay attention to the posters." There are also plays put on through the theater department, which offers cheaper tickets to students, and several art galleries both on campus and downtown.

Thursday evenings also feature frat parties, widely attended in part because the campus is dry. You cannot miss the Greek presence on campus. According to one independent student, people in frats and sororities are often invited to more parties and make more friends. The benefits of being in one of them are not just social; one independent student lamented that students in Greek organizations seemed to have more leadership opportunities, as they have an identity and a network in campus organizations. However, not every independent student complained about the Greek scene; one student commented that she never felt at all hindered by being independent. While Greeks may have an edge in terms of leadership opportunities and social connections, other

networks like residential life, student government, and activities run through the Student Activities Center are equally open to all students.

Vermillion, according to students, has little to offer in way of fun. While there are a few bowling alleys, two movie theaters, and fast-food restaurants, most students see Vermillion as little more than a place to live, shop, and drink. There are a fair number of bars, and during Dakota Days, the annual homecoming game, which is often against South Dakota State, they may open as early as 6:30 A.M. Housing is plentiful, although students must stay on campus for at least two years before they can move into an apartment off campus. There are only a few stores in town, so finding what you want can be difficult. Complained one student, "Vermillion doesn't even have a Wal-Mart nearby," although another claimed that there was one 25 miles away in Yankton, which "to a South Dakotan is 'nearby,'" in part due to South Dakota's higher speed limit of 75 miles per hour on the highway.

And so on the weekends, students leave campus. Many go home to work and earn money for college, even if home is many hours away. "To people here, every city in South Dakota is close," explained one student. But many also go to Sioux Falls, Sioux City, or even Minneapolis, to find the kind of fun that most college students take for granted: plays, rocks concerts, and exotic restaurants, to name a few. This weekly exodus is not a very widely advertised fact; said one a USDer, "I was really surprised to see how quiet it is here on the weekends." Other students, however, say that despite the number of students who leave campus on the weekends, "If one is creative, it really isn't that hard to find something fun to do" and can find "many activities to fill the weekends."

Getting Involved

Extracurricular opportunities for students abound at USD. Students can work at the *Volante*, the weekly paper founded by *USA Today* creator Al Neuharth, and KAOR, an alternative radio station that broadcasts 24 hours a day. Those who choose to major in mass communications can also work for the campus television station, KYOT, Monday through Friday. News broadcasts are watched in homes and dorm rooms all around Vermillion. Cherry Street Promotions, a student-run advertising agency, handles marketing for campus and local businesses.

The Coyote (pronounced "Cah-yoat" here) Student Center is a popular hangout for students during the day, and also houses the Program Council, an umbrella organization of student agencies, and a student film society that shows free films on campus once a week. Community service opportunities abound in Vermillion, and many students are very proud of how much their time can be used to aid those in the surrounding areas. In fact, there are so many service options at USD that an umbrella organization called SERVE (Students Enriching the Vermillion Environment) broke away from the Program Council, and now includes programs like Adopt-a-grandparent, Big Pal/Little Pal, Into the Streets, Vermillion Heroes, and Adopt-a-school.

For the more athletically inclined, USD offers a vibrant intramural program. Students form their own teams; games are played once or twice a week. Among the more popular intramural sports are flag football, softball, and volleyball.

The dorms at USD receive praise from many students. Four of the dorms on the north side of campus, Beede, Mickelson, Olson, and Richardson, are attached to one another, and the complex has its own dining facility. The dorms on the south side, including Julian, are reputed to be more party-oriented. Students can also request to live on a quiet floor, where loud music and socialization are strictly forbidden, or a single-sex, smoke-free, or substance-free floor. Most rooms are one-room doubles, with the occasional quad and triple. Rooms are not spacious, but certainly adequate and are generally in good repair. Still, many students choose to move off campus as soon as they are allowed, in large part due to the dry-campus policy and in order to have kitchens.

Dining hall facilities were recently privatized, and one student swears the food has vastly improved as a result. Another student appreciated the dining halls' attempts to make food healthier and less greasy, but wished for greater variety in the dishes offered. Off-campus options include The Silver Dollar for steak and Chae's Chinese food.

Leaning Left

Stepping onto the University of South Dakota's three-square-block campus is a bit like dropping down the rabbit hole; the Vermillion university is not your typical state school. The classes are small. The professors get to know you personally. There is no alcohol on campus. And on the weekends, the university is desolate. But if taken full advantage of, the academic and extracurricular opportunities just might be to one's liking.—*William Chen and Staff*

FYI
The three best things about attending the University of South Dakota are "that Vermillion is a bastion of liberal thought, even in such a conservative state, friendly Midwesterners, and opportunities for academic excellence through an honors program, a Phi Beta Kappa chapter, and study-abroad opportunities."
The three worst things about attending the University of South Dakota are "the freezing cold winters, the constant threats to cutting funding that come from the state government, and the difficulty overcoming negative opinions of on-campus weekends to find something fun to do."
The three things that every student should do before graduating from the University of South Dakota are "visit a reservation and learn about the Native American tribes who live there, find the river and walk the trails, and stay on-campus at least one weekend and discover how many things there are to do, contrary to popular belief."
One thing I'd like to have known before coming here is "how fast the time would go."

Tennessee

Rhodes College

Address: 2000 North Parkway, Memphis, TN 38112-1690
Phone: 800-844-5969
E-mail address: adminfo@rhodes.edu
Web site URL: www.rhodes.edu
Location: urban
Founded: 1848
Private or Public: private
Religious affiliation: Presbyterian
Undergraduate enrollment: 1,452
Total enrollment: 1,452
Percent Male/Female: 45%/55%
Percent Minority: 8.0%

Percent African-American: 4.0%
Percent Hispanic: 1.0%
Percent Asian: 3.0%
Percent in-state/out-of-state: 25%/75%
Percent Pub HS: 64%
Fraternities: 58%
Sororities: 50%
Number of Applicants: 2,374
Percent Accepted: 76%
Percent Accepted who enroll: 23%
Entering: 411
Transfers: 48
Application Deadline: 1 Feb
Mean SAT: NA V, NA M

Middle 50% SAT range: 590–690 V, 590–690 M
Middle 50% ACT range: 26–30
Mean ACT: NA
3 Most popular majors: biology, business administration, English
Retention: 86.0%
Graduation rate: 73.0%
Library: NA
Tuition and Fees: $18,719 in; NA out
Room and Board: $5,454
On-campus housing: NA
Financial aid, first-year: 45%

Many colleges brag about their sense of community, but Rhodes students say their school takes this notion to an entirely new level. Even the iron gates and ivy-draped walls that surround the college seem to emphasize the importance of drawing students into a connected campus. While there are downsides to a close-knit environment, students say they are willing to overlook them for all the advantages that come with being a part of the "Rhodes community."

Bigger Isn't Always Better

Rhodes has all the advantages that one expects from a small liberal arts school—small student body, intimate class size, and personal interaction with faculty. The college is small enough, with 1,447 full-time students, for undergrads to get to know many of their classmates and see familiar faces when walking across campus. Some students feel restricted by this familiarity and regret that they are not always meeting new people. Others complain that the campus can be a "rumor mill, kind of like high school when everyone knew what everyone else did." Despite these grumblings, many students said they enjoy the opportunity to get to know their classmates so well.

Most classes have less than thirty students, and, typically, class size is about fifteen. The only exceptions are introductory science classes, like freshman year biology. Students stress, though, that large lecture courses are rare, and no class enrolls more than one hundred students. This personal attention requires a higher level of preparation by students. "Coming in to Rhodes, I didn't know I'd be so involved in my classes," explained one undergrad. "Professors expect everyone to participate in discussion and offer theories—and who's to say your ideas aren't better than the professor's?"

Not surprisingly, small classes lead to

greater student-faculty interaction. Students rave about the easy access to professors on campus. Many professors give out home telephone numbers and encourage calls at home. "One professor told us to call her at home at any time," said one student. "One catch, though—if we woke her baby, we failed the class. Luckily, that didn't happen!" Professors are willing to meet with students outside of class, to answer questions or to shoot the breeze, and students often see their professors around campus, at the school-wide Rites of Spring festival, or even auditing a class.

Like many liberal arts colleges, Rhodes has a core curriculum, structured so that students are exposed to a wide range of academic fields. Undergrads take classes in each of four divisions: social sciences, natural sciences (including a lab), humanities, and fine arts, as well as required physical education and religion classes. Despite the school's affiliation with the Presbyterian Church (U.S.A.), students do not detect a religious bias. The religion requirement can be filled by taking one of two tracks: Search or Life. Search focuses on the integration of history and its values within religion, and Life looks at particular religious traditions, examining sacred literature and practices. Students say Search is more inclusive of different religious traditions, but Life is considered easier.

Most departments at Rhodes are well-regarded, although students say the engineering program is weak. International studies and biology are popular majors. The small size of the school limits the choice of courses and professors in some departments, but students seem willing to sacrifice some variety for close fellowship with the faculty. Rhodes supplements its offerings with exchange programs, such as engineering exchanges with Washington University in St. Louis and Maymester foreign study programs. Rhodes also allows students to study abroad through programs sponsored by other schools.

"Walking in Memphis"

Rhodes students find far more to do with their time than just study. The Greek system sets the scene for much of the social activity around campus, with more than half of all students belonging to fraternities and sororities. Rush for fraternities and sororities envelop freshmen as soon as they arrive on campus, and new members are tapped by the end of the first week of classes. Students, even Greeks themselves, are ambivalent about this setup. "It's a great opportunity to meet people, but rush and the Greek system can shut doors and cause divisions on campus," commented one fraternity member. Generally, though, choosing not to rush does not restrict anyone from Greek parties and is not perceived as a barrier to having a thriving social life. Greeks tend to see fraternity and sorority life as one of few options on campus, while independents downplay the prominence of Greek life. Greek ties are significant, but students say they do not negate one's connections to the college as a whole.

Beyond Greek activities, social opportunities on campus can be lacking. Many students head into Memphis, home to the famed Beale Street, a haven for blues music. The renowned musical atmosphere—captured in song by Marc Cohn's "Walking in Memphis" and Bob Dylan's "Stuck Inside of Mobile with the Memphis Blues Again"—attracts students to clubs and restaurants. Having a fake ID is usually necessary to get in, although one student claims developing friendships with bouncers is just as effective. With the monopoly that the Greek system can exert over social life on campus, downtown spots are often prime gathering places for Rhodes students—don't be surprised to run into classmates when wandering around the city. Greek or not, drinking is a large part of Rhodes social life. Students say there's no pressure to drink, but alcohol is present at most social events. A new Dean of Student Affairs has shown signs of tightening alcohol use on campus, but students report that drinking practices haven't been affected yet.

Beyond Parties

Community service draws even more participants than the Greek system. Students rave about volunteer opportunities in Memphis, a typical big city with problems. Working at soup kitchens, building with Habitat for Humanity, and mentoring

Memphis kids are some of the more popular choices. Most of these groups are encompassed within the Kinney Volunteer Program, which includes all kinds of options for community service. The small campus is instrumental in getting word out about different causes. "It's hard not to know what's going on," explained one volunteer. The administration places great emphasis on volunteerism, rewarding dedicated students with special housing and scholarships in exchange for commitments to particular projects. The sense of community at Rhodes does not stop at its gates but includes the city of Memphis as well.

Students are involved in bettering Rhodes, too. In addition to traditional student government, which has poor student participation, the Honor Code Council and Students Regulations Council allow for student direction. Upon entering Rhodes, all students commit to following the Honor Code, an agreement to respect others in the Rhodes community. While it is believed that it is not universally followed, most say they like the atmosphere of trust that it creates. The Student Regulations Council is responsible for punishing students who have violated the rules, rather than having the issue brought up before a faculty committee. In essence, students are allowed to uphold the values and rules important to their community.

Student groups cater to a myriad of interests. The drama department puts on several productions each year, and there are numerous musical groups. Despite the prevailing opinion that the student body is moderate to conservative politically, multicultural groups are active on campus in promoting understanding of various cultures. While religious fellowships, Christian and non-Christian, are common, Rhodes's location in the Bible Belt and its church affiliation do not translate into an aggressive religious atmosphere on campus.

The emphasis on community does not always manifest itself in activity. Students note the lack of school spirit and consider their classmates to be "apathetic" in supporting athletic teams, which compete in the Southern Collegiate Athletic Conference. Students tend to see themselves as homogenous. "There are a lot of preppy Southern white kids around," admitted one undergrad. Minorities exist only in small numbers. While recent classes show growth in representing different backgrounds, students question how a liberal arts school can expose students to a broad range of perspectives with such underrepresentation of many ethnic groups. Still, minorities feel quite comfortable among their peers, and these concerns do not seem to dampen the affection that students have for their classmates.

> **"One professor told us to call her at home at any time. One catch, though—if we woke her baby, we failed the class. Luckily, that didn't happen!"**

Living in dorms is a further extension of the Rhodes community. Suites are common in freshmen dorms and most dorms have only fifty residents each. A new rule requires freshmen and sophomores to live on campus, and many upperclassmen do as well, which has led to a housing crunch in recent years. Students living off campus reportedly feel less connected to Rhodes, particularly since many of the neighborhoods surrounding the school are not the safest or most affluent. On campus meal opportunities are limited to the cafeteria, affectionately titled the Rat, and the Lynx Lair, a fast food–style alternative, both of which are included in the meal equivalency plan. The Rat does not garner rave reviews for its food, but students do appreciate the study breaks that it sponsors at exam time.

From small classes that facilitate involved discussions to coaching a basketball team of inner city Memphis teenagers, the focus at Rhodes is on community and getting to know those around you—students, professors, and Memphis residents. Positioned on a beautiful campus replete with Gothic style buildings made of stone, there is a sense that Rhodes is its own world, set apart from its midtown location. The emphasis on personal interaction is Rhodes's strongest drawing point, and students are not disappointed.—*Alexa Frankenberg*

FYI

The three best things about attending Rhodes are "the size of the school, being in Memphis, and close interaction with the faculty."

The three worst things about attending Rhodes are "everyone knowing what's going on with everyone else, the homogenous student body, and the unsafe neighborhoods surrounding campus."

The three things every student should do before graduating from Rhodes are "ride the Lynx, visit Graceland, and spend an afternoon in Fischer Gardens."

One thing I'd like to have known before coming here is "the participation that teachers demand of the students."

University of Tennessee / Knoxville

Address: 320 Student Services Building, Knoxville, TN 37996-4122
Phone: 865-974-2184
E-mail address: admissions@utk.edu
Web site URL: www.utk.edu
Location: urban
Founded: 1794
Private or Public: public
Religious affiliation: none
Undergraduate enrollment: 20,259
Total enrollment: 26,437
Percent Male/Female: 49%/51%
Percent Minority: 9.0%
Percent African-American: 6.0%

Percent Hispanic: 1.0%
Percent Asian: 2.0%
Percent in-state/out-of-state: 81%/19%
Percent Pub HS: NA
Fraternities: 8%
Sororities: 8%
Number of Applicants: 10,634
Percent Accepted: 67%
Percent Accepted who enroll: 39%
Entering: 4,155
Transfers: 1,427
Application Deadline: 15 Jan
Mean SAT: 550 V, 553 M
Middle 50% SAT range: 500–600 V, 490–610 M

Middle 50% ACT range: 21–26
Mean ACT: 23.8
3 Most popular majors: business/marketing, social sciences/history, engineering
Retention: 79.0%
Graduation rate: 57.0%
Library: 1,846,695 volumes
Tuition and Fees: $3,104 in; $9,172 out
Room and Board: $4,430
On-campus housing: 86%
Financial aid, first-year: 34%

I s there such a thing as too much school spirit? If there is, do not tell any members of the University of Tennessee's Volunteer Nudists society. These fans of Big Orange football are not ashamed to bare their fannies for Smokey (a hound) the mascot to almost 20,000 undergraduates at this stronghold of southern spirit.

"Heh, heh. Yeah, we're pretty good at sports" is how one "Vol" explained another's mantra that "football is life here!" UT's newly expanded Neyland Stadium, the largest collegiate football arena in the nation, seats as many as 107,000 fans. When the big game against either Florida or Alabama hits town, true UT fans gather on Yale Avenue two hours before kickoff to cheer the players on as they walk to the locker room. If the band's performance of "Rocky Top" "doesn't get you excited about UT football," says one student, "nothing will!"

Student spirit, however, is all downhill from Neyland Stadium. At this large state school, there is a small group of involved students, but in general student apathy toward campus issues runs high. As one student government participant complained, "Getting student input on any topic, political or otherwise, is like pulling teeth."

Concrete City

Another student concern is the necessity of having a vehicle, despite the perennial parking problems (a campus permit costs about $175 per year). A few daredevils try biking on campus (one student calls it "bicycle lacrosse"), but most find that they can walk from one end of campus to the other in less than 20 minutes.

In the words of one undergrad, the UT campus is "a pad of concrete set between the river and downtown." Others, however, recommend several spots with a view to kill for: the top of the Hill, where one can see from downtown Knoxville to Ayers Hall, and the view from high in McClung Tower, where the Great Smoky Mountains can be seen in the distance. Some dorm rooms enjoy a view of the Tennessee River, where the Labor Day fireworks festival, Boomsday, is held.

Dorm Dilemmas

And where can you enjoy the fireworks with that special someone? Not in your dorm room. UT's dorms are mostly single-sex, which some students cited as a good reason to move off campus, although some are coed by floor. Beds are "very narrow," and only one dorm has unlimited visitation hours; all of the others having varying rules on opposite-sex visitation that are enforced by RAs (usually upperclassmen), so romance can be quite a feat.

One student described the drinking scene on UT's officially dry campus as "pretty big for some people, but there is a growing majority who don't participate." The dating is considered "a definite plus," although one student said that "there is a large Christian element, so some people are definitely against premarital sex."

With all of these distractions, Vols (as all UT students and Tennesseans in general refer to themselves) still manage to find time not only to register but also to attend classes. Registration is done by phone, with priority given to seniors.

Prerequisites vary by major and by college. UT frosh must choose to enter one of the vocational colleges (education, nursing, agricultural sciences), or can choose to enter the College of Arts and Sciences if they are unsure about their projected major. Depending on the college, prerequisites might include languages and always include some humanities courses, but most students see the prerequisites as beneficial to their education, not a hassle. Through a petitioning system, "if you take a course you think should fulfill a requirement, you can petition it by talking to the professor, who has the ultimate say in whether you get in," one student said.

Class sizes are not in proportion to the large university. Introductory classes of close to 200 students are not uncommon, but between 20 and 30 students is a closer approximation of average class size. Students found professors approachable, although the large size of the university makes the classic "lunch with the prof" meeting of small liberal arts schools a rarity.

Spaces to Study

Undergrads who are serious about studying recommend the John C. Hodges Library (UT's main library with 2 million volumes) over the smaller Hoskins, Taylor Law, and Ag-Vet libraries. Hard-core studying is done in the stacks on the fourth through sixth floors of Hodges. Social studying is popular in the library study rooms, the Golden Roast (a coffee shop within a few minutes' walk), the Daily Grind (another coffee shop), and on the steps of Glocker, a building in the center of campus. Freshmen tend to congregate around the Presidential courtyard while upperclassmen hang out on the Humanities Plaza. The Waffle House and the International House of Pancakes (IHOP) are the 24-hour restaurants of choice for those burning the orange candle at both ends.

> **"If you take a course you think should fulfill a requirement, you can petition it by talking to the professor, who has the ultimate say in whether you get in."**

With many students commuting from home, extracurriculars do not play the role at UT that they would at a smaller, more close-knit university, but the sheer size of UT guarantees that certain activities will be popular. The Greek scene is large and students feel some pressure to rush, although some non-Greeks are completely happy with their status: "Yuck! [They're] a waste of time and money."

Is UT worth the time and money? Students say yes. Many cite UT's value as the strongest factor in their decision to attend. As one student said: "I could have gone to GA Tech or MIT, where the school was everything I wanted, and graduate in debt. Or I could come to UT, change the school to fit my needs, and graduate with no debt."—*Vladimir Cole and Staff*

FYI

The three best things about attending UT are "awesome football program, awesome basketball program, and the school spirit."

The three worst things about attending UT are "getting used to living in Tennessee, a very homogenous social scene, and it's hard to get a sense of community here, you have to find your little niche fast."

The three things that every student should do before graduating from UT are "attend as many football and basketball games as you can, visit Dolly World, and casually date as often as you can."

One thing I'd like to have known before coming here is "that as a non-Southerner, getting into the country music culture isn't as hard or as bad as I thought."

University of the South (Sewanee)

Address: 735 University Avenue, Sewanee, TN 37383
Phone: 800-522-2234
E-mail address: admiss@sewanee.edu
Web site URL: www.sewanee.edu
Location: rural
Founded: 1857
Private or Public: private
Religious affiliation: Episcopal
Undergraduate enrollment: 1,326
Total enrollment: NA
Percent Male/Female: 50%/50%
Percent Minority: 5.0%

Percent African-American: 3.0%
Percent Hispanic: 1.0%
Percent Asian: 1.0%
Percent in-state/out-of-state: 20%/80%
Percent Pub HS: 54%
Fraternities: 65%
Sororities: 55%
Number of Applicants: 1,792
Percent Accepted: 69%
Percent Accepted who enroll: 31%
Entering: 389
Transfers: NA
Application Deadline: 1 Mar
Mean SAT: NA V, NA M

Middle 50% SAT range: 570–670 V, 580–660 M
Middle 50% ACT range: 25–29
Mean ACT: NA
3 Most popular majors: English, history, psychology
Retention: 88.0%
Graduation rate: 82.0%
Library: NA
Tuition and Fees: $19,080 in; NA out
Room and Board: $5,230
On-campus housing: NA
Financial aid, first-year: 42%

What do you do when you are on top of a mountain on a 10,000-acre campus and the closest cities, Chattanooga and Nashville, are hours away? Make sure you have a car. Such are the lessons that students learn at the University of the South (called Sewanee nearly universally) along with the more traditional ones inherent to a liberal arts education.

A Work Hard Kind of School

"During the week, I would say that Sewanee students are intense about studying. The library is packed until it closes at 1:00 A.M.," said one sophomore. "If you are accepted into the school in the first place, it should never be impossible to do well in your classes. You can't be lazy here. You have to put forth a true, concentrated effort in order to succeed," commented another student. Sewanee students say that attending classes is important: "People go to class probably 90 to 95 percent of the time. . . . Every test I have ever taken here requires your presence and participation in class as well as preparation by reading the assignments," said one upperclassman. However, if a student is unable to make class, a southern sense of common courtesy and respect prevails and he or she will be sure to tell the professor ahead of time. This same attitude is taken in personal relationships with teachers outside of class. "At Sewanee it is unheard of to pass a professor on the street and not say hello," one student explained.

Students with high GPAs are invited to join the Order of the Gownsmen, an honor that gives students special privileges, like the right to pick their classes before others and to leave a class if the professor doesn't arrive after fifteen minutes.

Picking classes early can sometimes be important. Because classes are so small (the largest being the freshman premed classes, which have only 60–70 students), students say they can sometimes get closed out of a class. However, persistent students can ask special permission from the professor and often get into an otherwise closed class. Students report that a typical class load is four classes a semester. Such a schedule gives them time to complete graduation requirements, which include a choice of classes from a series of subject-divided lists.

A common complaint about classes is the repetition of professors. History is a "big department," consisting of ten professors. According to students, most other departments' faculty can be counted on one hand. Some students enjoy this, though. Having so few professors means that they can get the attention they need. In fact, students say it's common for students to talk of going to their professors' houses for dinner and having department-wide parties.

A Play Hard Kind of School

"It is Sewanee," one student said. "Of course there's a lot of drinking." If stu-

dents work through Thursday, they party hard through the weekend. Students admit that frats make up a large part of the social scene, but nonmembers are invited to every party, with the exception of some formals. Beer is plentiful and easily attainable, and students say that many drink often and to excess. According to students, there was an effort made by the administration to make alcohol less readily available on campus. However, the measure was defeated for fear that Sewanee students would drive off the mountain to do their drinking, forcing them to drive back while drunk.

A nonchalant attitude toward strict rules marks other parts of campus life. According to the university rule book, "Dormitories (or, with regard to coed dormitories, the individual dormitory rooms) are open to visitors of the opposite sex from 9:00 A.M. until 12:00 P.M. Sundays through Thursdays, and from 9:00 A.M. until 1:00 A.M. Friday and Saturday nights." Violators can face penalties ranging from a reprimand or a fine to eviction from campus. Nonetheless, students report that the rule is seldom, if ever, enforced. "As long as your roommate is not complaining, and you're not making too much noise, nobody looks twice," one sophomore explained.

The fact that Sewanee social life is based around drinking can reportedly create problems for nondrinkers. "Sewanee is a wonderful school if you find your niche right off the bat. If you don't drink and don't have a car, you could have problems if you don't find friends that support you in your decisions and interests," a light-drinking senior complained.

However, one sophomore who described herself as less of a drinker than her schoolmates said that a happy balance is easy to find. "The frats have great bands, and everybody dances like fools. I think that the rest of the campus is pretty liquored up for most of the weekend, though. . . . However, my social life is a testament that you don't have to drink to have a great time at Sewanee."

Students can also take advantage of "drier" activities on the college's location on 10,000 acres of Cumberland plateau. The Domain, as it's called, is "a dream for people who like to hike," so the school attracts "Thoreau people" interested in spending time outdoors. Without even leaving the property of the school, students can hike and go spelunking. Tennessee Williams endowed a theater on campus, and students describe the theater studies department as strong both for education and performances. During the week, students can hang out at "BC," the Bishop's Commons student union.

Leave Them in the Dust!

Sewanee is over 50 percent southern and overwhelmingly white. Said one senior, "You've got your Sewanee student running around in the woods with their hiking boots on, and then you've got your Sewanee student who's suburban and running around in his Jeep." Another student pointed out, "the campus is pretty homogeneous. We are mostly upper-class white kids who come from two-parent homes." Others stress the Episcopalian affiliation of Sewanee and note the overwhelmingly Christian nature of the student body but argue that students interpret their Christianity to mean that they should focus on openness. "We have traditions," said one senior, "but we don't cling to the unhelpful ones."

Living in a Hospital

Students generally laud Sewanee housing, and 98 percent of the student body lives on campus. Seniors, who get priority, can nearly always get singles, as do many juniors. The favorite dorm for upperclassmen used to be a hospital, and local students have stories of their parents being patients in the very rooms in which they are now living. There is widespread approval for freshman housing, as well. The newer dorms are divided into suites of two bedrooms, two common rooms, and a bathroom, shared among four people; other freshmen live in more traditional hall-based dorms. Fraternities and sororities do not have their own housing. Each freshman dorm has a group of senior Assistant Proctors living among the underclassmen and one Head Proctor, also a student. While the APs, as they're called, are ostensibly there to enforce rules, "they're students, so they're not going to go out of their way to get someone in trouble," a freshman stressed. "APs are more or less our friends."

Sewanee students say they strike a balance between their Greek partying and Greek studying. A clear line is drawn between the extensive drinking of the weekend and the hard work of the school week. Said one student, "At Sewanee we work hard and play just about as hard. During the week the focus is almost religiously centered on classwork and by the weekend everyone is ready to have a good time at the many open frat parties on campus."—*Jacob Remes and Staff*

FYI

The three best things about attending Sewanee are "the hiking opportunities, awesome dorms, faculty are friendly and available."

The three worst things about attending Sewanee are the "the limited number of faculty, Greek-centered social life, and the amount of studying we have to do."

The three things every student should do before graduating from Sewanee are "go to the Mountain Top Ball, participate in the Sewanee Outing Program, hang out at Stirling's Coffee House."

One thing I wish I'd known before coming to Sewanee is "how small the departments are."

Vanderbilt University

Address: Admissions Office, Nashville, TN 37240
Phone: 615-322-7311
E-mail address: admissions@vanderbilt.edu
Web site URL: www.vanderbilt.edu
Location: urban
Founded: 1873
Private or Public: private
Religious affiliation: none
Undergraduate enrollment: 5,780
Total enrollment: 10,022
Percent Male/Female: 47%/53%
Percent Minority: 14.0%

Percent African-American: 4.5%
Percent Hispanic: 3.4%
Percent Asian: 5.8%
Percent in-state/out-of-state: 14%/86%
Percent Pub HS: 58%
Fraternities: 31%
Sororities: 47%
Number of Applicants: 8,494
Percent Accepted: 61%
Percent Accepted who enroll: 31%
Entering: 1,633
Transfers: 69
Application Deadline: 7 Jan
Mean SAT: NA V, NA M

Middle 50% SAT range: 600–690 V, 620–710 M
Middle 50% ACT range: 27–31
Mean ACT: NA
3 Most popular majors: social sciences, engineering, psychology
Retention: 92.0%
Graduation rate: 81.3%
Library: 2,568,190 volumes
Tuition and Fees: $22,990 in; NA out
Room and Board: $8,032
On-campus housing: 100%
Financial aid, first-year: 42%

"It rocks!" This peppy student, like so many of her classmates, is raving about Vanderbilt, one of the top universities in the South, and meriting national attention as a first-rate private university. With the blend of challenging academics and a social life that receives "two very enthusiastic thumbs up," it is easy to see why so many have become so enamored with "Vandy."

Classes at Vandy

A school that prides itself on academic excellence, Vanderbilt has a top-notch undergraduate program that boasts a faculty dedicated to the intellectual pursuits of its students. TAs rarely teach except for the occasional lab or discussion section, and class sizes are small, allowing the professors to have close contact with their students. In fact, one freshman is the only student in her French literature class. It is this individual attention that sets Vandy apart from other universities. Though the students admit that academics are definitely challenging, there is no cutthroat competition for grades. This relaxed atmosphere lends an incredible environment for the undergraduate to explore and grow intellectually. The most popular

departments include economics, engineering, English, and education. Students are hard-pressed to name a weak department.

All freshman choose from among four undergraduate schools: arts and sciences, engineering, George Peabody College for Education and Human Development, or the Blaire School of Music. While a majority of the students are in the school of arts and sciences, the other schools receive good reviews from students as well. One freshman in the music school said that students particularly like it because it allows them the freedom to decide their own level of commitment, and the core curriculum includes courses that music majors would want to take anyway.

Students in the School of Arts and Sciences must complete a core curriculum called Core Program for Liberal Education (CPLE), which includes courses in the humanities, natural and social sciences, and history. Proficiency in a foreign language is also required. This curriculum receives mixed reviews from students. Some praise it for its intellectual variety and depth: "It certainly gives an excellent background in the liberal arts and really helped me decide on my major," said one student. Others don't share this enthusiasm. One freshman described the program as "a necessary evil." Another student complained, "I expected college to be a place where I could explore those subjects that interested me the most, but it [CPLE] doesn't allow me to do that." One upperclassman believes that the program tends to result in classes that students take only to fulfill the requirements, not for learning's sake. This can also affect the professor's attitude toward the class and create an unsatisfying experience.

While academics are an integral part of Vandy life, these students really know how to have a good time. The social scene is dominated by the Greek system, and every weekend at least one fraternity is having a party. Because the sororities and fraternities offer the main weekend entertainment, non-drinkers and those students not interested in pledging complain that there are very few alternatives. One senior said that if you didn't have a car and are not into the Greek scene, your options are pretty limited. Other students, however, say that if you take the initiative, you can find other things to do, although organized, campus-wide activities are limited. In fact, some undergrads complain that the administration does not do enough to organize more social activities, but others say such events would be poorly attended. But do not worry if the concept of the Greek lifestyle doesn't float your boat. Most agree that there isn't any pressure to join and all students can attend the parties whether they are a member of the frat or not. Independents say they do sometimes feel isolated in the spring when there are a number of fraternity and sorority formals.

After Class

One of the biggest campus-wide parties of the year is the Rites of Spring, a three-day festival that has featured music from the Dave Matthews Band and the Violent Femmes in recent years. Accolade, a black-tie homecoming dance, is popular with juniors and seniors, and the proceeds go toward scholarships for minority students. Vandy is in the heart of Nashville, and some students use the opportunities

that the city has to offer to their advantage. Some students go to area restaurants such as Chili's, Houston's, and the Cooker, while others head to the city to dance and hang out at the many local bars that receive rave reviews from the upperclassmen. Such popular clubs include the Exit Inn, the Underground (for those with alternative music tastes), Mickey Gilley's (not to be missed for all y'all country music fans), and the Mix Factory. One upperclassman, however, notes that the "Vanderbubble" keeps most on campus and therefore holds students back from taking advantage of the opportunities in their own backyard.

The most unpopular administration regulation by far is the new policy on alcohol, although many students agree that something had to be done. Three alcohol-related deaths in recent years have led the administration to take every effort to stop underage drinking. The first time an underage student is caught drinking (or even holding an unopened container), he or she will be put on probation, which goes on the student's permanent record; with the second offense, the student is suspended for six months; with the third offense the student is expelled. This policy is on the whole strictly enforced both by the freshman RAs (seniors who live on the freshman halls) and the Inter-fraternity Council, although one RA admitted that the policy is not enforced fairly all the time. Most students agree that the system is working. In fact, one freshman said that a tenth of her hall is already on probation. This year, before going into any frat party, each student must sign in if he/she is underage. Some say this policy has created problems because now many students are going off campus to drink and then have to drive back to campus.

Athletics are a big deal at Vandy. Though in the past few years the football team has "sucked," a new football coach has arrived recently and the Commodores are hoping to turn things around. "Woodyball," as it is affectionately called, has become huge, and the games are packed. Football games are also major social events, where many students get dressed up and go with a date. Men's and women's basketball and soccer teams have had strong seasons lately. Students are also in-volved in many club and intramural sports. The intramural sports are sponsored by fraternities, dorm floors, and student associations. Soccer, basketball, and softball are especially popular. Don't hold your breath—yes, they do have inner-tube water polo.

Community service keeps many students busy. A popular community-service project is the Alternative Spring Break Program in which students spend their spring breaks building houses in inner cities. Others become Vanderbuddies and tutor local children. Students who participate in a similar program, Culture Shock, once a month adopt an inner-city kid and entertain him or her on campus. The university has several a cappella singing groups, the most popular being the Dodecaphonics, and student publications such as the *Hustler*, the campus newspaper, and *Slightly Amusing*, a humor magazine, are other popular activities that claim the time of many students.

> **The social scene is dominated by the Greek system, and every weekend at least one fraternity is having a party.**

As for the comforts of home, housing at Vandy earns high marks from students. In fact, one claims that the dorms are like "hotels" compared with those of other schools. Freshmen live in one of three dorms: Vanderbilt-Barnard Hall, the Kissam Quadrangle, or the Branscomb Quadrangle. These living arrangements seem to be enjoyed by the freshmen as they get a chance to meet and bond with their classmates. The Kissam Quad is known as the quiet dorm, primarily because it contains only single rooms; the best rooms are said to be in Branscomb. The four dorms in Charmichael Towers are considered to be the best place for upperclassmen to live. In those residence halls, students share six-person suites and have a food court on the first floor which includes Alpine Bagel (recently replacing the Dairy Queen and Taco Bell), a pizza parlor, a deli, and a grocery store. Seniors can apply for off-campus housing, but in an attempt to maintain community spirit, the administration reportedly discourages students from living off campus.

Unlike Vanderbilt housing, the cafeteria food is pretty sketchy. In fact, some say the meals in Rand Dining Hall are downright nasty. It may not be a bad idea to have your mother stick around and cook for you. Yes, things move in the food and often you're not really sure whether you are having tapioca pudding or grits, but as one student optimistically puts it, "there is always the salad bar." Freshmen are required to be on a meal plan, but that only covers dinners six days a week. The other meals can be purchased at other places around campus that are worlds more appetizing than Rand Dining Hall. The Over Cup Oak Pub receives amazing reviews from students, and you can even get sweet tea there (it is a Southern thing). You can get all this and much more with the Commodore Card, a unique Vandy invention. In essence, each student has his or her own personal credit card to buy anything on campus, from meals to books to laundry or a midnight snack at the Mini-mart.

The Vanderbilt Student

Students definitely do not go to Vandy for a diverse student body. Recent classes have been the least diverse in a decade, though the administration recently spent more time and money than they ever have before in recruiting a diverse class. Why this lack of diversity? "Imagine lots and lots of people from J. Crew catalogs multiplying," replies one student. Another student agreed: "White, upperclass, and conservative, that's Vanderbilt." The homogeneity is one of the things that many Vandy students wish they could change about their school.

Vandy is definitely a Southern school, and it is this distinctive Southern feel that attracts many students to Vandy. Combine this with friendly students who like to have fun, a dedicated faculty, challenging academics, a beautiful campus, and a wide selection of extracurricular activities, and you have a top-notch university.
—*Melissa Droller and Staff*

FYI

The three best things about attending Vanderbilt are "the Greek life, the small class size, and the location."

The three worst things about attending Vanderbilt are "the administration's super-strict alcohol policy, the homogeneous student body, and the cafeteria food."

The three things every student should do before graduating from Vanderbilt are "be a Vanderbuddy, watch a campus band at the Rites of Spring, go to the Accolade formal."

One thing I wish I'd known before coming to Vanderbilt is "how strong the Greek influence is here."

Texas

Address: P.O. Box 97056, Waco, TX 76798-7058
Phone: 800-BAYLOR-U
E-mail address: admission_serv_office@baylor.edu
Web site URL: www.baylor.edu
Location: small city
Founded: 1845
Private or Public: private
Religious affiliation: Baptist
Undergraduate enrollment: 11,124
Total enrollment: 12,472
Percent Male/Female: 43%/57%
Percent Minority: 22.0%

Percent African-American: 6.0%
Percent Hispanic: 8.0%
Percent Asian: 7.0%
Percent in-state/out-of-state: 82%/18%
Percent Pub HS: NA
Fraternities: 20%
Sororities: 30%
Number of Applicants: 7,525
Percent Accepted: 88%
Percent Accepted who enroll: 36%
Entering: 2,938
Transfers: NA
Application Deadline: rolling
Mean SAT: NA V, NA M

Middle 50% SAT range: 520–620 V, 530–640 M
Middle 50% ACT range: 21–27
Mean ACT: NA
3 Most popular majors: teacher education, biology, business marketing
Retention: 82.0%
Graduation rate: 69.0%
Library: 1,500,000 volumes
Tuition and Fees: $11,132 in; NA out
Room and Board: $5,008
On-campus housing: 96%
Financial aid, first-year: 41%

Baylor is not only the oldest university in Texas, it is also the largest Baptist-affiliated university in the world. As a result, this university, set in Waco, has a strong Christian atmosphere that students believe makes Baylor a "very united school." As one student said, "We take pride in the traditions, and also the memories that four years at Baylor offer." In fact, the university is so central to lives of the students here that they often refer to their campus as "the Baylor Bubble."

A Solid Educational Background

Academics at Baylor are competitive, but "not overwhelming." There are only a handful of required courses at Baylor. All students must take two semesters of Chapel Forum, a seminar course where students listen to guest speakers twice a week. Several undergraduates noted that this requirement is "ridiculous" and "boring." Additionally, students must take classes in the political science and religious studies departments as well as pass physical education tests. Despite these core courses, students reportedly have a lot of freedom to take "a mish-mosh of other disciplines."

Classes are fairly small with roughly 15 students per seminar, and teaching assistants are "few and far between." The professors directly interact with the students, and seem to "really engage with us and care about our academic progress." Many undergraduates indicated that the toughest courses can be found in the biology department, as the university is nationally known for its premed program. These biology classes enable professors quickly to "weed out" the students who "can't take the heat." Aside from the occasional academic pressure, undergraduates at Baylor believe that they leave the university "with a good, solid educational background."

Visiting Hours Are a Drag

Undergraduates at Baylor are enthusiastic about the "look of our campus" with its huge trees and redbrick buildings. One Baylor student raved that the university has "one of the most beautiful campuses in America." Buildings that get the highest reviews include the golden-domed Ferrell Special Events Center and the new baseball complex, which is still in the process of being built.

Students report that dormitory housing is adequate, though most students live off campus after freshman year. It is generally agreed that the dorms on campus each have their own personalities. North and South Russell tend to be the most quiet, while Collins and Penland (for girls and for guys, respectively) are known to be the "wilder ones." All dorms are single-sex, have community showers and a Resident Advisor to enforce coed visiting hours. Members of the opposite sex are allowed into dorms only on Saturdays and Sundays from 1 to 6 P.M. Many undergraduates report that "the regulation is a drag."

An Upper-Middle-Class Baylor

Students at Baylor describe themselves as being typically upper-middle class Caucasians. Students have strong opinions about the look of their student body, as one student stated, "The student stereotype is all about a preppie blond girl with only the latest in fashion in her closet." In describing other undergraduates, "snobby" and "stuck-up" are mentioned as frequently as "friendly" and "accepting." As the school newspaper mentions, "The colors of Baylor are not green and gold, but white and khaki." One senior in particular stated that "it's pretty easy to enter this institution, especially if you fit the Baylor mold: average grades, Christian, and sporty."

Road Trips vs. the "Baylor Bubble"

Students often complain about the dearth of things to do in Waco. As one student said, "We pass time by renting movies." The Bill Daniel Student Center and the nearby International House of Pancakes, Denny's, and Common Grounds have become student hangouts. Undergrads also dine at local eateries such as Chili's or Applebee's on Valley Mill Street. Many students choose to leave campus during the weekends in order to "salvage our social lives." Trips to Austin or Dallas are frequent, and many have cars on campus for that purpose.

Those undergraduates who do decide to remain in the "Baylor Bubble," usually attend either fraternity or sorority parties. One junior noted that "Greek life at Baylor dominates campus social life." Many students indicate that the "Greeks here exude Southern hospitality, which makes it very easy to meet people." The parties on campus are "great," despite the administration's semi-strict alcohol policy. Underage drinking is by no means universal as there are many students who choose not to drink and find themselves "almost appreciated" for their decision.

> "It's pretty easy to enter this institution, especially if you fit the Baylor mold: average grades, Christian, and sporty."

The dating scene at Baylor receives mixed reviews. Some students claim that many people have boyfriends or girlfriends while others argue that dates mean very little commitment. Many students believe that it is hard to get a good sense of dating at Baylor because of the strict coed visitation policy that forces couples to stay off campus as much as possible.

The Bears and Why They Care

Sports are huge at Baylor. So huge, in fact, that the administration even includes football tickets in every student's tuition package regardless of whether the student wants them! School spirit flies high. Last year students tore down the goal post and carried it back five miles to campus after Baylor defeated the University of Texas. The Baylor Bears represent the lone private university that participates in the Big 12 Conference. Last year, the Lady Bears basketball team fought for the championship in the Women's National Invitational Tournament. The soccer teams and the tennis teams at Baylor were also ranked nationally last year. Besides team sports, many students avidly participate in the intramurals.

Student Life Beyond Sports

The Bears do not concentrate solely on sports activities, though. With over 250 official organizations on campus, the Baylor community offers a wide variety of clubs for so many interests. Organizations run the gamut from the Baylor Amateur Radio Club to the Baylor Billiards Club. Community service is also very important at this religiously affiliated university. The majority of the student body rally particularly for the special, campuswide event known as Steppin' Out where students gather together to help clean up the community for one day.

Despite the fact that Baylor is often considered simply a conservative, upper-middle-class, white, Christian university, some of the university traditions reveal that Baylor has a free-spirited side to it. For example, members of a secret society known as the Noze Brothers, who don funny glasses with plastic noses and mustaches, often show up during Chapel Forum and other popular classes to "raise a little hell once in a while." In this way, Baylor is a "great place where we not only get an education, but we learn to laugh at ourselves as well."—*Melissa Chan and Staff*

FYI

The three best things about attending Baylor are "the medium size of the school, good professors, and the student life center."

The three worst things about attending Baylor are "students are too religiously oriented, Waco, and the tuition goes up every year."

The three things that every student should do before graduating from Baylor are "go to the Dr Pepper museum, jump in the fountain, and go to the Branch Davidian compound."

One thing I'd like to have known before coming here is "how boring Waco is."

Rice University

Address: P.O. Box 1892, Houston, TX 77251
Phone: 713-348-4036
E-mail address: admission@rice.edu
Web site URL: www.rice.edu
Location: urban
Founded: 1912
Private or Public: private
Religious affiliation: none
Undergraduate enrollment: 2,807
Total enrollment: 4,062
Percent Male/Female: 53%/47%
Percent Minority: 43.0%
Percent African-American: 7.0%

Percent Hispanic: 10.0%
Percent Asian: 16.0%
Percent in-state/out-of-state: 55%/45%
Percent Pub HS: NA
Fraternities: 0%
Sororities: 0%
Number of Applicants: 7,487
Percent Accepted: 19%
Percent Accepted who enroll: 43%
Entering: 609
Transfers: 54
Application Deadline: 2 Jan
Mean SAT: NA V, NA M
Middle 50% SAT range: 640–760 V, 670–770 M

Middle 50% ACT range: 28–34
Mean ACT: NA
3 Most popular majors: economics, English, electrical engineering
Retention: 95.0%
Graduation rate: 90.0%
Library: 1,600,000 volumes
Tuition and Fees: $15,350 in; NA out
Room and Board: $6,600
On-campus housing: 100%
Financial aid, first-year: 34%

Rice University in Houston, Texas, offers an Ivy League-quality experience, a manageable tuition, a perpetually warm climate, and an up-scale urban location. And, students say, the quality of academic and campus resources of Rice matches that of any Ivy.

Academic Excellence

Students claim that academic competition between peers is minimized at Rice. "Students here are driven but not cutthroat," says one senior English major. Instead, Rice students strictly adhere to an honor code, violations of which are punishable by suspension. As one student advises, "Don't $%^& with the honor code."

Despite the tame level of competition, students say Rice academics are intense. Especially demanding majors are biology and engineering (particularly chemical engineering). Though traditionally Rice has excelled in engineering and science, the English and history departments have made great strides in recent years. The establishment of the Baker Institute for Public Policy, which funds scholars and provides a forum for public policy debate, has strengthened the political science department as well. Students say that managerial studies and sports medicine are less intense than other majors.

The core curriculum demands that students take courses in three areas: the humanities, the social sciences, and the natural sciences. With the exception of introductory lectures, classes are generally small. Students select courses during "shopping period," the first two weeks of each semester. One student explains, "You can sit in on as many courses as interest you and leave if you don't like the professor, syllabus, or course." Favorite courses include "Sex with Chad," or "Sexuality and the Social Order" taught by Professor Chad Gordon. Environmental and energy economics draws raves, and "students sleep in the hall outside his office the night before registration" to get into Professor Dennis Huston's public speaking class. Students also recommend Professor John Zamito's class on European intellectual history. For the many Rice students who aspire to careers in medicine, engineering, or science, introductory physics and chemistry are "notoriously difficult."

Residential Colleges: Centers of Life

Upon matriculation, all students become residents of one of eight colleges (a new college is under construction, and a tenth college may soon be added as well). Offering such facilities as a TV room, a game room, and weight room, colleges serve as dorms and social centers. Most students develop strong college affiliations and close friendships within their colleges. One student says, "the dorm setup at Jones College is the best." Another claims, "Will Rice College is the college of Gods and Goddesses," while Baker students bond during a naked (except for strategically placed whip cream), drunken run through campus known as the "Baker 13." In addition, each college has its own master and staff of associates. The master, a tenured professor, lives and eats with students, organizes activities, and settles personal and academic problems among students. The associates, comprised of faculty members, community members, and Rice employees advise students on classes and careers; the great majority of associates live outside of Rice, but each college houses two associates, who reportedly interact frequently with students.

Aesthetic Excellence

Rice boasts a beautiful, architecturally eclectic campus. One student gushes, "Rice's campus is gorgeous. Legend has it that the university charter requires area with wild strawberries, violets, and rabbits." Another says, "We don't even have sidewalks. The founder insisted on Pebble Paths." The buildings themselves receive mixed comments; Duncan Hall "is like Willy Wonka's magic factory or landing in the *Wizard of Oz*—people at Rice either love it or hate it." Also, the campus has many large quadrangles which provide room for frequent games of ultimate Frisbee and touch football. However, students criticize the form of the colleges: "The college buildings are the least attractive. Weiss was originally built as temporary army barracks, and looks like it. Lovett is somehow a cross between a toaster and a prison."

Constant Stimulation

Students say that life at Rice provides constant stimulation; activities abound and fun is usually available. The Cabinet, the university's student government, and the *Thresher*, Rice's newspaper, are extremely popular. The Campus Crusade for

Christ (CCC) maintains a large membership but draws criticism for excessive zeal in trying to convert non-Christians. The Residential colleges offer great extracurricular opportunities in the arts and intramural athletics; Frisbee is especially popular, and because of the warm and sun-drenched setting, students can play any outdoor sport in any season.

Chilling

Students often spend much of their time "chilling" with friends. Students talk about "normal college things—you know, sex, gossip, funny events, football," but people at Rice often extend classroom discussions into their college dining halls or into their suites through the early morning hours. Rice students describe each other as "open, with lots of J. Crew Junkies."

Colleges and various campus organizations hold frequent parties. Students say the drinking policy is "extremely lax," and "you just won't get in trouble for underage drinking." Alcohol is "an option for everyone," many claim, but those who do not drink feel little pressure to do so. Esperanza in the fall and Rondolet in the spring are the two major formals. The "Screw-yer-Roommate" dance involves finding one's roommate a blind date for a night and formulating a unique way for the roommate to find his or her date. One junior explains, " I had to gallop around the main academic quad with a stick horse and a cowboy hat and my date had to come bucking out of one of the archways with horns—I had to rope him." Students attend the Night of Decadence (NOD) dressed as minimally as possible; one student says, "It's all about plastic wrap—lots of plastic wrap." For such reasons, *Playboy* magazine has named NOD one of the top college parties.

Beer Bike, held in the spring, may be the largest social event of the year. Each college picks a theme and marches in a huge parade to the track where a nontraditional bike race is held. After a team member rides around the track twice, another team member chugs either 24 ounces (for males) or 12 ounces (for females and alumni) of beer. Most colleges "start chug practices at the beginning of the year."

One campus hangout is the Coffeehouse, "a student-run organization that donates its profits to charity and provides a forum for student performers. Further, students seem to love the two campus bars: "You gotta love Willy's Pub and Val Halla." On Thursdays, students congregate at Willy's Pub and naked Baker 13 runners receive free beer from Val Halla. For Mexican food aficionados, there are the popular Taco Cabana and Mission Burrito restaurants. House of Pies, "known as 'House of Guys' because of the transvestites who frequent it at 3 A.M.," also attracts many students.

Outside of Rice, Lai-Lai's in Chinatown offers " tantalizing, authentic, and cheap" Chinese food to groups of Rice students. Mai's and Van Loc serve excellent Vietnamese fare.

> **Most students develop strong college loyalty and close friendships within their colleges.**

Venturing beyond the boundaries of Rice, students can visit art gallery openings and festivals in the cosmopolitan city of Houston. The Westheimer Street Festival, which showcases musicians, jewelry, dancing, and crafts, also draws some Rice students. However, most Rice students say they tend to stay within campus bounds: "The hedges that surround Rice are a flimsy physical barrier but are almost impossible to penetrate mentally. There is a zoo, a free theater, and half a dozen museums across the street from Rice, but almost no one leaves campus. Although Rice is completely surrounded by Houston, it is also completely separate from it."

A warm climate, a close-knit community within each residential college, outstanding academics, and pleasant people define Rice University in order to make their college experience satisfying.
—*Conor Knighton*

The three best things about attending Rice are "the very friendly, comfortable social atmosphere, the spacious, immaculate campus, and 0-week, an orientation program to help freshmen adjust to college life."

The three worst things about attending Rice are "lack of food options on campus—there's nothing except the college cafeterias and Sammy's (which is over-priced), that you have to have a car to get around and live comfortably after freshman year (most sophomores got booted out of campus housing for a year), and the rampant political apathy on campus."

The three things that every student should do before graduating are "Run the Baker 13—it's not just a little group of exhibitionists, swim in President Gillis's personal pool (without permission, of course), and go Steamtunnelling—again, blatantly illegal, this involves breaking into the underground tunnel system beneath the campus and exploring."

One thing I wish I would have known before coming here is "there is a TON of work it doesn't matter what you're majoring in—you'll be bustin' your butt."

Southern Methodist University

Address: PO Box 750296, Dallas, TX 75275-0296
Phone: 214-768-2000
E-mail address: ugadmission@smu.edu
Web site URL: www.smu.edu
Location: suburban
Founded: 1911
Private or Public: private
Religious affiliation: United Methodist
Undergraduate enrollment: 5,620
Total enrollment: 9,464
Percent Male/Female: 46%/54%
Percent Minority: 21.0%

Percent African-American: 6.0%
Percent Hispanic: 9.0%
Percent Asian: 6.0%
Percent in-state/out-of-state: 63%/37%
Percent Pub HS: 71%
Fraternities: 36%
Sororities: 37%
Number of Applicants: 4,133
Percent Accepted: 90%
Percent Accepted who enroll: 35%
Entering: 1,218
Transfers: 452
Application Deadline: 1 Apr
Mean SAT: NA V, NA M

Middle 50% SAT range: 510–630 V, 520–640 M
Middle 50% ACT range: 21–27
Mean ACT: NA
3 Most popular majors: business administration, finance, psychology
Retention: 85.0%
Graduation rate: 71.0%
Library: 2,300,000 volumes
Tuition and Fees: $18,510 in; NA out
Room and Board: $6,901
On-campus housing: 95%
Financial aid, first-year: 35%

Located in the ritzy Highland Park section of Dallas, outsiders think of Southern Methodist University (SMU) as a college in country club clothing. Despite the student body's reputation as Beamer-driving, Gap-wearing preprofessional elites, the university is equally known for its academic pressure and commitment to excellence.

The Road to Moola

The course requirements at SMU include rhetoric, two science labs, two PE courses (generally more like health education, not gym class), one math class, and one class dealing with computers or technology. Students must also take at least five "Perspectives" courses, from the following six categories: arts, literature, religious and philosophical thought, history, politics and economics, and behavioral sciences. In addition two "Cultural Formations" courses, or CFs are required, which are "designed to be in-depth interdisciplinary approaches to knowledge within the humanities and the social sciences," and are generally taken in the second year at SMU. Students describe the requirements as "more flexible than they appear. There are quite a few choices."

Popular majors at SMU include business, communications, psychology, and

English. Students also cite theater as one of SMU's finest departments. Less popular programs include the engineering, geology, and chemistry departments. Many SMU students have pre-professional aspirations, hoping "to make a lot of money after graduation," according to one undergrad.

Class sizes at SMU vary, but students generally agree that the average course is not "gigantic." A typical introductory class ranges in size from 25 to 100 students, but most are fewer than 50, and are generally broken into discussion sections of 15–20 students. It is not unusual even for freshmen to have classes with fewer than 30 students, and class size decreases as students move into higher-level courses, with 14 to 20 students about the average size. These relatively small classes allow students and professors to interact daily. Students say that "professors are very eager to help," providing office hours in order to increase their accessibility. Teaching assistants do not play a large role at SMU, and are most commonly found in the math, science, and occasionally business departments, where they lead sections and help out in labs.

Students say that gut or "booster" classes, such as Modern Electrical Technology and Wellness exist in the hidden nooks of the SMU course book. Recently, the administration improved the registration process by allowing students to register by computer and to add and drop classes online. Students applaud this step, as it enables them to avoid the long registration lines that once marked the beginning of each semester. However, students still must go in person at the end of the semester to confirm their class registration, and lines for that can be very long.

Greek or Geek?

SMU is officially a dry campus, which translates into a harsh crackdown on underage drinking. Students say that unless you are "21 and in your room," drinking can be very risky. The administration has imposed a series of penalties for those caught violating school policy. Upon the first infraction, students are required to go to counseling. Future infractions of the policy involve fines as well as more counseling.

This strict policy reportedly is freely ignored on the sacrosanct grounds of the fraternity and sorority houses, although "you will rarely find anything stronger than cheap beer," one student said. SMU fraternities are getting stricter with drinking, and the Phi Delt fraternity has gone alcohol-free. Approximately half of SMU students are affiliated with the Greek system, and students agree that it plays a large role in campus social life. It is possible to remain independent and still enjoy the Greek party scene, though, since most Greek parties are "easy to get invitations to." However, due to the "cliquishness" of groups, undergrads say there is a "definite pressure to rush" in order to avoid the "Greek-or-geek" syndrome. Besides SMU's campuswide block party, the biggest festivities of the year are overwhelmingly Greek events such as the Shrimp Fest, the Fiji Island Party, Phi Delt's Casino Party, SAE's Guys and Dolls, and Lagnaf weekend.

Students unaffiliated with the Greek system still find plenty to do both on and off campus. Besides frat parties, students enjoy hanging out in Deep Ellum, an eclectic area of Dallas replete with bars and clubs. Although the drinking age is 21, many of the dance clubs—like Eden 2000 and Arcadia—do admit those 18 and older (still 21 to drink, of course). Downtown Dallas's West End, with such upscale hot spots as Planet Hollywood, is another popular rendezvous for students as well as tourists. In order to get around Dallas, though, a car is almost a necessity, since the city is so spread out and public transportation is limited. Students without cars say that an abundant selection of campus eateries and coffeehouses within walking distance of campus keep them busy. For socializing, the Student Center is the destination of choice.

Campus Facilities

Many of the dorms at SMU have recently undergone renovations, and have been converted to spacious, suite-style rooms. Suites in Virginia-Snider, Morrison-McGinnis, and Cockrell-McIntosh consist of bedrooms connected by their own bathroom with bathtub, counter, and sink, and also connected to a common study room big enough for four desks and shelving units. McElvaney is the most popular dorm for freshman, which boasts spacious and bright rooms, despite the fact that it is not one of the renovated dorms. Housing is all coed, except in dorms where bathrooms are in the hallways rather than within suites, in which case they are coed by either wing or floor. SMU requires freshmen to live on campus unless they commute from home, but some upperclassmen prefer off-campus housing in apartments.

Eating options include Mac's Place, which is located on the southern end of campus, and Umphrey Lee, which is located on the northern end of campus. Students generally eat at the location closer to them, but since Mac's Place is in one of the more common freshman dorms, more freshman eat there. Some students claim that Umphrey Lee is "better by far," and thus more upperclassmen opt to eat there. Other options for food on the SMU campus include a Blimpie's, a Burger King, Pangeos Wraps, and a restaurant called the Mane Course which is located in the student center.

Surrounded by the upscale suburban neighborhood of Highland Park, SMU students have few concerns about security. Nevertheless, undergrads describe campus security as tight. Campus police patrol the grounds, and emergency phones are widely accessible. At night, a student escort service will accompany anyone who does not want to walk alone from one campus building to another.

SMU students take advantage of the school's numerous extracurricular opportunities. A wide variety of cultural and religious groups sponsor meetings and campus activities. The Student Foundation, a university service organization, and the Program Council, made up of planning committees, are two popular student activities. SMU's wide variety of club and intramural sports, such as lacrosse, flag football, and volleyball, have gained tremendous appeal. Aspiring journalists can write for the *Daily Campus*.

SMU's football team recently won the Western Athletic Conference Championship against Eastern Tennessee under the leadership of Coach Mike Cavin. Although traditionally known to have a weaker football program than many in Texas, SMU is definitely on the rise.

> **SMU is officially a dry campus, which translates into a harsh crackdown on underage drinking.**

Roughly half of the students at SMU are Texans, born and bred. That does not mean that an equally large number wear cowboy boots and six-shot revolvers. According to students, SMU is "definitely a very wealthy school," but it is also "more down-to-earth than you might think." While some students fit the SMU stereotype-white, upper-class, Texan—they have increasingly reflected more economic diversity, and students report that approximately 70% of the student body receive some financial assistance.

In addition to the warm climate, students especially appreciate how SMU's picturesque, colonial, "Ivy League–looking" campus provides the best of two worlds: a tranquil setting within a cosmopolitan academic environment.—*Brian Abaluck and Staff*

FYI
The three best things about attending Southern Methodist University are "small classes, caring and enthusiastic professors, and the opportunities for educational enrichment (lectures, exhibits, performances, seminars, fairs, etc.)."
The three worst things about attending Southern Methodist University are "the heavy emphasis on Greek life, the focus of the administration on politics and the appearance of the school, and the food."

The three things every student should do before graduating from Southern Methodist University are "get cheese fries from Snuffer's on Greenville Avenue, get to know your professors on a first-name basis, and go to Deep Ellum for some sort of cultural experience." One thing I'd like to have known before coming here is "that money and politics could get you further than brains."

Texas A&M University

Address: Mail Stop 0100, College Station, TX 77843-0100	**Percent African-American:** 3.0%	**Middle 50% SAT range:** 520–620 V, 550–650 M
Phone: 409-845-1031	**Percent Hispanic:** 9.0%	**Middle 50% ACT range:** NA
E-mail address: admissions@tamu.edu	**Percent Asian:** 3.0%	**Mean ACT:** 25
Web site URL: www.tamu.edu	**Percent in-state / out-of-state:** 94% / 6%	**3 Most popular majors:** biomedical sciences, interdiciplinary studies, marketing
Location: small city	**Percent Pub HS:** NA	
Founded: 1876	**Fraternities:** 6%	
Private or Public: public	**Sororities:** 14%	**Retention:** 87.9%
Religious affiliation: none	**Number of Applicants:** 14,453	**Graduation rate:** 72%
Undergraduate enrollment: 36,082	**Percent Accepted:** 74%	**Library:** 1,506,107 volumes
	Percent Accepted who enroll: 62%	**Tuition and Fees:** $2,639 in; $7,823 out
Total enrollment: 43,442	**Entering:** 6,695	**Room and Board:** $4,898
Percent Male / Female: 52% / 48%	**Transfers:** 2,174	**On-campus housing:** 64%
Percent Minority: 15.0%	**Application Deadline:** 1 Mar	**Financial aid, first-year:** 29%
	Mean SAT: 577 V, 603 M	

The first word that should come to mind when thinking about Texas A&M is "tradition." Events such as the Bonfire, Yell Practice, and the Core Cadets are only a few of the numerous traditions that this university was built upon and that are still very much alive today. Founded in 1876 as the Agricultural and Mechanical (hence the A&M) College of Texas, the university was originally an all-male military school. Nowadays, Texas A&M is comprised of roughly 43,000 students divided into 10 academic areas. The one thing that unifies this immense student body, with its students from all 50 states and 113 other nations, is the "Aggie Spirit."

Traditions

The first thing that new Aggies must learn are the many traditions that enhance student life. Each year, for the infamous and spirited football game against the archrival University of Texas Longhorns, Aggies express their "burning desire" for triumph by constructing a massive 55-foot-high bonfire. To replace trees felled for the bonfire, students gather each spring to "replant" seedlings. During the games, students chant, cheer, and sing their fight songs proudly, directed by Yell Leaders, juniors and seniors elected by the student body to foster school spirit. One student noted that "just about everybody" goes to the games, because "if you go once, you want to go back over and over again."

Not all of the Aggie traditions are as festive. Since 1898, students have honored and recognized the Texas A&M students who have died while enrolled by congregating on the first Tuesday of every month. Students gather in front of the Academic Building and solemnly listen to the honor guard from the Corps fire a 21-gun salute. The atmosphere is so hushed and "dead silent" that "the only thing you hear are the pigeons taking off and, once it's over, the Core Cadets' boots on the gravel." Students attest to the fact that "it's one of those moments you never forget."

Hitting the Books

The undergraduate education at Texas A&M is divided into colleges that each represent a particular major. Students can enroll in the general studies program for two years, but must eventually choose a college that specializes in their major. Academic requirements, mostly described as "fair" or "not too bad," largely depend on the major. Generally, students must maintain a 2.0–2.5 GPA to stay in the college, change majors, or avoid Scholastic Probation, called "Scho Pro." Some majors such as engineering require "particularly brutal" classes. One student said that chemistry majors are known to take Math 151-Calculus three times: "Everyone's dropped out once, failed once, and gotten a B or C on the third time."

In general, class sizes for introductory or required courses, or "everything in the first two years," range from 300 to 500 students. Most students report that the large class size "doesn't pose much of a problem." Many students are comfortable with these large classes and feel that they are "adequate [and] not too bad because there is a guaranteed curve with so many people." However, as students reach upper-level courses, class sizes tend to slim down to 50 students or less while honors classes commonly enroll less than 20.

While students appreciate that professors teach most of the classes, contentment with the level of instruction varies greatly. One student characterized her professors as "very caring, you can always go to them if you have a problem. They're always very approachable—you feel welcome when you start talking to them." But another student complained that he "hardly interacts with the professors. You can if you want to, but they [have] other things on their minds." Other complaints include "my profs don't cover anything regarding the tests and don't care if you fail," and "my TA fell asleep during physics lab, sprawled across the desk." On the whole, the faculty was deemed "okay, but certainly not the highlight of academics here."

The Students

Though the university is unquestionably large, students often complain that it is "mostly white—there are minorities here, but not a lot." Other students characterize the student body as "mostly cowboys" and "conservative." Regardless of the student mix, Aggies often praise the friendliness of their peers: "If anything happens to you, you can count on anyone here to help you out." In fact, many students reported that they often receive a "howdy" from friends and strangers alike.

The most prominent student group on campus is the Core Cadets. Each year, over 800 freshmen ("Fish") join the Core Cadets; a program most often compared to ROTC, but without the national military requirement. One Core member said that "you live it, you love it. Everyone else looks up to you, though the physical training and harassment are tough to handle." Cadets not only wear their uniforms daily, but they live and eat together.

Parties and Rodeos

Texas A&M is located in College Station, a small college town that provides Aggies with many opportunities to get off campus once in a while. There are many restaurants, bars, a movie theater, and a mall in the area. The most famous off-campus eatery, the Dixie Chicken, is home to the Aggie tradition of senior "dunking," an event that gives seniors the same number of seconds as the year of their graduation to drink a pitcher of beer.

On-campus, many of the organizations such as the Aggie Angels and the Howdy Ags coordinate social activities. Because of the prominence of the Core Cadets, there is only a small Greek scene. Though alcohol at parties is prevalent, "there are virtually no drugs." Students claim that the party scene is good "most of the time, but every now and then, it can get quite dull."

Unique to the social scene at Texas A&M is "its quality." One student said that "there are plenty of beautiful girls here; and not only are they beautiful, they have class." There are reportedly some Aggie girls, called Bootchasers, who fawn over the Senior Core Cadets that wear "expensive, big, brown boots with spurs—girls think it's great." Contributing to this "great dating scene" is another Aggie football tradition. Tradition mandates that guys must kiss their dates after each A&M touchdown, extra point, or field goal.

Living Arrangements

Students of Texas A&M complain that campus housing is not the school's strong point. Though students describe dorms as "adequate" overall, the university is "famous for overbooking dorms." One student had to live in temporary housing for a week in a tripled-up dorm room while another reportedly was forced to live in a converted study lounge for an entire semester.

Once accepted, students apply for on-campus housing depending on size, facilities, and cost of particular dorms. All students suggest applying early to have a better chance of getting the dorm that you want. Kreuger Hall, one of the better dorms, was lauded for its locking doors, nice interior, and large rooms. Meanwhile, Crocker Hall was described as being "weird: they have their own traditions, and it's in its own little part of campus." Resident advisors are available freshman year for those students who need advice about academics or social issues.

Sports and Activities

For most Aggies, sports shape and enhance the college experience. Texas A&M University plays at the Division I level as a member of the Big 12 Conference. The school has 19 varsity sports: 9 for men and

10 for women. Club and intramural sports are also popular on campus. The university offers intramural competition in events including preseason basketball, outdoor soccer, team bowling, racquetball, and sand volleyball.

> Tradition mandates that guys must kiss their dates after each A&M touchdown, extra point, or field goal.

Aggies attribute the numerous and diverse extracurricular activities to the school's large student population. Students guarantee that "if there is something you are interested in, there is a club here for you." Student organizations range from academic and pre-professional to cultural and political. Various opportunities for involvement range from the Fade to Black Dance Ensemble to the Students for a Free Tibet or the Aggie Wranglers. Community service is also popular, particularly among students in groups such as Circle K International and Aggie Habitat for Humanity.

Thanks to the variety of activities, many students report that the "sense of belonging is overwhelming." Indeed, it seems that the energy of the A&M student body is manifest in the school's traditions, school spirit, and enthusiasm for their community.—*Kurtland Ma and Staff*

FYI
The three best things about attending Texas A&M are "the Aggie school spirit, the opportunities of a large school, and the athletics."
The three worst things about attending Texas A&M are "the huge student body, the housing, and some of the TAs."
The three things that every student should do before graduating from Texas A&M are "make the bonfire, go to the Dixie Chicken for 'dunking,' and experience the silent remembrance of students who have died while enrolled here."
One thing I'd like to have known before coming here is "that I couldn't keep all the stuff I'd brought in my tiny dorm room!"

Texas Christian University

Address: TCU Box 297013, Fort Worth, TX 76129
Phone: 800-TCU-FROG
E-mail address: frogmail@tcu.edu
Web site URL: www.tcu.edu
Location: urban
Founded: 1873
Private or Public: private
Religious affiliation: Disciples of Christ
Undergraduate enrollment: 6,456
Total enrollment: 7,551
Percent Male / Female: 41%/59%
Percent Minority: 12.0%
Percent African-American: 4.0%

Percent Hispanic: 5.0%
Percent Asian: 2.0%
Percent in-state / out-of-state: NA
Percent Pub HS: 91%
Fraternities: 26%
Sororities: 35%
Number of Applicants: 5,028
Percent Accepted: 75%
Percent Accepted who enroll: 38%
Entering: 1,426
Transfers: 376
Application Deadline: rolling
Mean SAT: NA V, NA M
Middle 50% SAT range: 520–620 V, 520–640 M

Middle 50% ACT range: 23–28
Mean ACT: NA
3 Most popular majors: nursing, finance, marketing
Retention: 82.0%
Graduation rate: 63.0%
Library: 1,885,702 volumes
Tuition and Fees: $13,125 in; $13,125 out
Room and Board: $4,240
On-campus housing: 91%
Financial aid, first-year: NA

Texas Christian University has long enjoyed a fine reputation in the Southwest, and especially in Texas. Yet, the administration does not use this as an excuse for inaction. In fact, one senior says that the best thing about TCU is that the school is constantly striving to improve every aspect of undergraduate life. Indeed, TCU offers the undergraduate numerous opportunities to excel both in and out of the classroom.

Academics

Most students agree that TCU provides an academically stimulating environment thanks in large part to the faculty, which includes former Speaker of the House Jim Wright. Students praise their professors for their dedication to their students and their love of teaching. The professors are extremely accessible, and they do all the teaching. One upperclassman said she approached a professor that she had never had in the classroom about a summer internship, and the next day he called her back with a job that turned out to be one of the best experiences of her life. It is this kind of individual attention that draws students to TCU.

TCU's core curriculum requires students to take classes in many disciplines. All students must complete nine hours of Foundation courses (six hours of writing workshops and three hours of math), six hours of Languages and Literature, two hours of physical education (one of which must be nutrition), and 36 hours of Exploration classes (physical sciences, life sciences, religion, history, philosophy, and fine arts). For students who wish to take a more advanced curriculum, TCU offers two honors programs. One is the general honors program consisting of two parts: the lower part requires students to take a specific curriculum of six classes, and once these are completed, the student may enter the upper level, in which he or she spends a semester doing independent research under the guidance of a professor. Though the program is challenging, students admit that the extra effort is worth it. In exchange for their hard work, they get classes that are really interesting and the chance to work one on one with a professor and to explore topics that are of interest to the student. The second honors program deals exclusively with history and is affectionately known by students as "Hell-Hit." It explores all facets of historical and cultural thought of a particular country or period of history. Outside of the honors programs, the most popular majors are nursing, psychology, business, and communications.

Student Life

Housing at TCU receives mixed reviews from students. Most freshmen and sophomores live on campus, yet the majority of upperclassmen choose to live off campus. One freshman says that the three freshman dorms are "loud and distracting," yet another believes that these living arrangements allow for an "awesome environment that is a lot of fun." Most students agree that Moncrief, reserved for varsity athletes, is the nicest dorm. Brachman is the only coed dorm on campus. The administration is in the process of renovating the dorms, and the entire campus is supposed to be completely renovated in ten years. The upperclassmen either live in apartments that are within a three-mile radius of the school or with their fraternity or sorority.

Students are required to purchase a meal card with a value of at least $350. Most students eat at the Main, the large student cafeteria which serves decent college food and has a Pizza Hut and Taco Bell. Other options include the Pit and the Hut, two campus grills, and Eden's Green, which opens for lunch only, and reportedly has a lot better food with only slightly higher prices.

The Greek system is definitely visible (over 35 percent of the campus is Greek), especially the sororities (there are ten), but it doesn't dominate the social scene. The administration does not allow any parties on campus, so the majority of them are held off campus. The drinking scene is alive and healthy, but not on campus. Both TCU and Fort Worth have adopted a new zero-tolerance policy with alcohol that one student said is "crazy enforced." If a student is underage and is caught by the "Froggy-Five-O" (campus police) at a party where alcohol is being served, he or she receives an MIP (Minor in Possession), which includes fines and the suspension of your license. Some students report that the party scene is a lot like high school. Several underclassmen said that every party they had been to had been busted by the cops. Yet one senior

explained, "If you know where to go, you don't have to worry about getting caught." One upperclassman says that the pressure to drink is not there. "After all, if you're not drinking it's more beer for me!" said one enthusiastic partygoer. Most students like having the parties off campus because there is more space and it offers a welcome change of scenery. Local hangouts include the Pub and the Hop, two clubs long associated with TCU social life. The saying goes that you don't go to TCU to find your husband. The dating scene, one senior says, "sucks eggs! NO ONE dates!" Of course, the three-to-one ratio of girls to guys does not help matters either.

The City!

TCU is only one exit from downtown Fort Worth, and for this reason nearly all students take advantage of the city life. Fort Worth has been totally revamped in the last 10 years, and students say it's the perfect way to escape the campus for a few hours. Two huge movie theaters have been built, and the clubs and bars are enjoyed by many upperclassmen. Dallas is a 30-minute drive from campus and, as one upperclassman says, "is one of the coolest cities in the country!" For students not into the party scene, Dallas-Fort Worth has its fair share of cultural attractions including Fort Worth's Museum of Natural Science and History, the Kimball Museum, the Dallas Museum of Art, the Fair Park Museum, and the Meyerson Music Center. To reach all of these destinations, students report that a car is "a must."

Lamentable Lack of Diversity

Most students admit that the lack of diversity is a big drawback at TCU. Though TCU boasts the largest percentage of minority students of any school in Texas, most students agree there is still a long way to go before significant improvements are made. One student explained, "Everybody is the same. They dress the same, look the same, and come from the same background." TCU seems a happy haven for sororities, fraternities, Republicans, and conservative, upper-middle-class students who, according to one upperclassman, drive "little red Beamers."

The word "Christian" might lead many outsiders to believe that religion is a big factor of academic and social life, but students disagree. The core curriculum includes only one religion course, Religion and Human Experience, which explores Christianity along with Buddhism, Judaism, and other faiths. There are 50 religious organizations on campus, yet students agree they aren't fanatical, and most are just a social activity for those interested.

Athletics are a big part of life at TCU, and there are a lot of neat traditions associated with sports. First of all, the mascot is a horned frog, and, as one enthusiastic student stated, "what could be cooler than having a frog as your school's mascot?" Students resort to the time-honored tradition of kissing the university's stone statue of a horned frog to earn an A, and the students throw their lucky pennies in the Frog Fountain. TCU has strong teams in basketball, baseball, tennis, and golf, but "because everyone in Texas thinks that football is the only sport," football attracts the most crowds and is still the school's most popular sport.

TCU has an impressive 160 different organizations that one senior boasts is the heartbeat of TCU. Another upperclassman said that these groups are what keep the students at the school. They offer students great opportunities for leadership, and almost all students find an activity and pursue it wholeheartedly. Many students report that these organizations enable them to form their strongest friendships at TCU. Students with an interest in journalism can write for the *Daily Skiff*, TCU's undergraduate publication, or *The Image* magazine. The TCU radio station, which broadcasts over the Dallas-Fort Worth airwaves, is another popular student activity. The music group Carral is popular among students as well. TCU is also home to many dance and theater groups that enjoy excellent reputations. Student government is popular and, unlike other schools, "actually has influence over how the school is run." In fact, 15 representatives go to the Board of Directors each semester with suggestions on how to improve the school. Recent topics of discussion have included changing the physical education requirement, adding classes on technology, and the possibility of a new student center.

> **TCU seems a happy haven for sororities, fraternities, Republicans, and conservative, upper-middle-class students who, according to one upperclassman, drive "little red Beamers."**

TCU definitely has the feel of the beautiful Southwest, as the buildings are made of southwestern brick with red Spanish-tile roofs. This scenic paradise combined with the city life of Fort Worth gives the undergraduate a great atmosphere for learning and socializing with friends. Together with a fine faculty, numerous extracurricular opportunities, a fun-filled social life, and one of the friendliest student bodies around, TCU affords the undergraduate with a rewarding college experience.—*Brian Abaluck and Staff*

FYI
The three best things about attending TCU are "Dallas/Ft. Worth, the Greek system, and the great people."
The three worst things about attending TCU are "the guy/girl ratio, the small sports department, and the cliquish nature."
The three things that every student should do before graduating from TCU are "go to Billy Bob's, swim in Frog Fountain, and ride in the back of a Froggy Five-O."
One thing I'd like to have known before coming here is "to have plenty of Rees sandals."

Texas Technology University

Address: P.O. Box 45005, Lubbock, TX 79409-5005
Phone: 806-742-1480
E-mail address: nsr@ttu.edu
Web site URL: www.texastech.edu
Location: small city
Founded: 1923
Private or Public: public
Religious affiliation: none
Undergraduate enrollment: 20,227
Total enrollment: 24,249
Percent Male/Female: 54%/46%
Percent Minority: 16.0%
Percent African-American: 3.2%

Percent Hispanic: 10.2%
Percent Asian: 2.0%
Percent in-state/out-of-state: 85%/15%
Percent Pub HS: NA
Fraternities: 14%
Sororities: 20%
Number of Applicants: 8,100
Percent Accepted: 75%
Percent Accepted who enroll: 44%
Entering: 3,372
Transfers: 1,676
Application Deadline: rolling
Mean SAT: 541 V, 554 M
Middle 50% SAT range: 490–590 V, 500–600 M

Middle 50% ACT range: 21–26
Mean ACT: 23
3 Most popular majors: marketing, management info systems, psychology
Retention: 79.0%
Graduation rate: 46.0%
Library: 4,245,818 volumes
Tuition and Fees: $3,107 in; $9,587 out
Room and Board: $4,787
On-campus housing: 82%
Financial aid, first-year: 47%

L ocated in the High Plains of West Texas, Texas Tech benefits from the nurturing environment of a medium-sized city without the congestion and stress of a major metropolis. Most buildings on campus, with clay roofs and red and beige brick walls, resemble Spanish-style fortresses. In fact, campus planner William Ward Watkin chose Spanish architecture as the model for Texas Tech's buildings because of the geographic similarity of Western Texas and central Spain. As one student said, "If you can't afford a trip to Spain, bring a banjo, go to the Tech campus, and eat at Taco Cabana. It's the closest you'll get to the real thing."

More Than Agriculture

Texas Tech's academics live up to its impressive campus. Although Texas Tech once functioned primarily as an institute for agriculture and technology, education at Tech no longer revolves around computer chips and corn. The university's core curriculum includes courses in the humanities in an effort to better prepare students to meet the challenges of the future. Most of the academic departments are expanding their curricula to become more liberal arts oriented.

With an undergraduate school, several graduate schools, a law school, and a medical school all on one campus, Texas Tech University is the most comprehensive public university in the state. The undergraduate side of the campus is split up into eight academic colleges: Agricultural Sciences and Natural Resources, Architecture, Arts and Sciences, Business Administration, Education, Engineering, Human Sciences, and the Honors College. Most students consider engineering, education, business, and architecture the strongest and most popular majors. The education program is well known because a good number of Tech students go on to become teachers. Less popular majors include fine arts and theater. For the most part, each college sets its own requirements in addition to the mandated writing courses.

Class sizes range from 300 to 400 students at the introductory level in such fields as astronomy, political science, and other science courses to as few as 20 students in English seminars and higher-level courses. The chief complaint of many students is that the majority of freshmen and sophomore classes are taught by TAs instead of professors, though many undergrads report that the student-faculty interactions during junior and senior years make up for this drawback.

Campus Facilities

Tech's vast campus offers a wealth of places where students can study, especially the recently renovated and very quiet main library, which reportedly resembles a stack of books turned on its side, the "B.A. Rotunda" of the business administration building, which is reportedly shaped like a calculator, and various dorm lounges. Texas Tech also has a Student Union and a Student Recreation Center, both about to be renovated, which offer more options for students to get together and study or just hang out.

Opinions of campus housing range from "much better than most state schools" to "mediocre." According to one sophomore RA, "The residence hall staff takes pride in providing students with the best possible environment for living and studying by organizing dorm activities and study breaks." Once a year, the residence hall administration sponsors a campus wide event featuring country singers like Tim McGraw. The freshman residence hall Chitwood/Weymouth is considered by some students the worst dorm because of its location, although others claim that it is the "place to live when you are a freshman," because it is the only high-rise dorm available for frehsman and it is very social. The Strangel/Murdough residence hall is often praised for its convenient location and "chillin'" courtyard. Most Tech dorms consist of two buildings—one for men and one for women—connected by offices, lounges, and a common cafeteria. Each dorm has its own cafeteria offering diverse cuisine including southwestern, Italian, and the "sometimes risky" Chinese entrees. While most dining hall food is considered "boring" or "old," Tech has earned the reputation for having "the best dining halls of any school in Texas." Most dorm rooms are doubles with built-in furniture and are generally considered comfortable. Although the Tech campus is not crime ridden, campus security is tight and there are security guards at dorm entrances and surveillance cameras in various parts of the campus.

Although Tech students are happy with the residence halls, many upperclassmen prefer to move off campus, and one cited a figure as high a 70% of upperclassmen living off. "Living off campus is more convenient because I can cook my own food and I don't have to deal with the noise," one junior said.

Class. Beer. Bed.

One student said social life at Tech "revolves around fraternity parties and the beer keg," since the town of Lubbock has little to offer beside a few movie theaters and a minor league hockey team, the Cotton Kings, which draws many student fans since their games are played at the Coliseum, a sporting arena right on campus. One student described Lubbock as having "enough to do to keep you occupied, but not enough to get you into trouble." However, recently a new concert venue called the United Spirit Arena was built in town, and several popular bands, including Kiss and Elton John, have played there.

Nonetheless, most students say that the Greek scene is the primary way of socializing, drinking, and meeting people at Tech. And there are numerous opportunities to do so, particularly during weekly parties. One student summarized his typical week as "going to class, then getting wasted, then going to bed." The campus and Lubbock are dry (the largest dry town in the nation), so some students obtain their alcohol from "the Strip," a row of liquor stores just outside the city which are designed to look just like Las Vegas. Some students also hang out at off-campus dance clubs such as the Warehouse, which is the most fun when local bands play there, and Midnight Rodeo. Sports bars such as the Conference Cafe are also popular, as is Liquid 2000 for techno aficionados. Other popular hangouts include Cricket's, which boasts of a full bar, over 100 beers to choose from, pool tables and several TVs, and bars like Tom's Daquaris, Clousseau's Martini bar, Bleacher's Sports Cafe, and Athens. Those looking to satisfy their midnight cravings can do so at Spanky's, IHOP, Taco Cabana, Jazz Louisiana Kitchen, or One Guy's Pizza.

The Mighty Raiders

Athletics are definitely a major part of Tech student life. In 1996, both the men's and women's basketball teams qualified for the "Sweet 16" round of the NCAA tournament. Now in the Big 12 conference, Tech battles athletic powerhouses like UT/Austin, Oklahoma, and its ultimate rival, Texas A&M. The Red Raider football team consistently ranks among the top 25 nationally, and has beaten Texas A&M 4 out of the past 5 years. Football games are usually well attended, and the spirited crowd keeps traditions alive, including "tortilla tossing," in which students toss tortillas every time the team scores. The Saddle Tramps, a group of male students, also decorate the campus with red and black streamers before games. The Lady Raiders basketball team is consistantly ranked in the top 25, and baseball games are also popular, as the team is usually in the running for the conference championship. Tech administrators also show their spirit by ringing the bells in the administration building for 30 minutes each time an athletic team wins a conference championship.

Aside from varsity athletics, Tech offers many opportunities to compete in intramural sports. Students say that IM competition at Tech is more fierce than most varsity sports. Undergrads may form their own teams or compete with different organizations on campus. One sophomore said that over 260 different teams registered to compete in the IM flag football tournament. Tech houses state-of-the-art fitness equipment, tennis courts, and swimming pools for non-varsity athletes, and a local corporation recently donated $10 million for construction of a new basketball arena.

The Heartland Ethos

Although Greek life and athletics are dominant, student life at Tech is not limited to them, since there are over 300 student organizations to choose from. Texas Tech reportedly has the second-largest College Republicans Club in the U.S. There are also political groups for more liberal students, the University Democrats and the Campus Libertarians, but students report that these groups "barely" have a presence at Tech due to the more conservative nature of the student body. Other popular organizations include Student Senate, Campus Crusade for Christ, the Marching Band, and the Future Farmers/Ranchers of America. Many students also write for the *University Daily*, Texas Tech's free daily newspaper.

Texas Tech is a conservative school that primarily fits what some students call the "Christian, white, Texan, Republican" stereotype. Although the university is trying to recruit more minority students, there is a definite lack of diversity on campus. Regardless, Tech students are very happy with their school selection, which is evident in their spirit and unity. As one student said, "We have the school spirit and traditions of Texas A&M, but with half the people." Texas Tech is a school where students can learn in a friendly, supportive Texan atmosphere for a not so Texas-sized price.—*Brian Abaluck and Staff*

FYI
The three best things about attending Texas Tech are "the school spirit, the friendliness of West Texans, and the football fever."
The three worst things about attending Texas Tech are "waiting in long lines (3 hours or more) for financial aid checks, the bovine emanations from the cattle farms, and the lesser recognition than UT or A&M."
The three things that every student should do before graduating from Texas Tech are "attend a football game, play IMs, and try to drink all the different beers at Crickets."
One thing I'd like to have known before coming here is "that there is very little diversity."

Trinity University

Address: 715 Stadium Drive, San Antonio, TX 78212-7200
Phone: 207-736-7207
E-mail address: admissions@trinity.edu
Web site URL: www.trinity.edu
Location: urban
Founded: 1869
Private or Public: private
Religious affiliation: Presbyterian
Undergraduate enrollment: 2,264
Total enrollment: NA
Percent Male/Female:
Percent Minority: 22%

Percent African-American: 2%
Percent Hispanic: 9%
Percent Asian: 9%
Percent in-state/out-of-state: 72%/28%
Percent Pub HS: NA
Fraternities: 28%
Sororities: 26%
Number of Applicants: 2,811
Percent Accepted: 75%
Percent Accepted who enroll: 31%
Entering: 649
Transfers: NA
Application Deadline: 1 Feb

Mean SAT: NA V, NA M
Middle 50% SAT range: 580–680 V, 590–690 M
Middle 50% ACT range: 26–30
Mean ACT: NA
3 Most popular majors: business administration, biology, English
Retention: 86.0%
Graduation rate: 76.0%
Library: NA
Tuition and Fees: $15,264 in; $15,264 out
Room and Board: $6,180
On-campus housing: NA
Financial aid, first-year: 44%

Trinity University is one exception to the proverb, "The grass is always greener on the other side"; grass simply does not get any greener at this small liberal arts school. With what undergrads claim is the highest gardener-to-student ratio of any school in the country and a special endowment for the upkeep of the grounds, Trinity keeps its lawns as finely manicured as any country club fairway. Students report that the "country club atmosphere" extends to other facets of campus life, from their own conservative but laid-back dispositions to the weekly housekeeping service in the dorms.

Academics and Understandings

Trinity's similarity to a country club ends, however, with academics. With its large endowment, Trinity has attracted top-rate professors to teach small classes. As a result, Trinity continually receives high rankings from *U.S. News & World Report and Money* magazine as one of the top small liberal arts universities west of the Mississippi. In classes that rarely enroll more than 50 students and sometimes as few as 8, interaction with what undergrads called the "energetic and personable" faculty is extraordinary. To help matters, all professors are required to schedule 10 office hours a week, and students say they keep them. All classes are taught by Ph.D.s, and TAs are almost nonexistent. One undergraduate remarked that he had never even had a TA during his career at Trinity. "The best thing about Trinity is the mentoring from the faculty," added Trinity's first-ever Rhodes scholar. "I was able to work on research with professors right off the bat, which later put me in a position to get accepted into some prestigious summer programs."

The core of Trinity's curriculum is the six "understandings," including such fields as Judeo-Christian culture and cognitive thinking. Students warn prospectives not to be scared off by the strange names. Undergrads must take one course in each understanding, which gives them a preview of many departments, and helps them "make a mature choice of a major," one student said. The English, political science, and history departments all are highly recommended, and the sciences, most notably chemistry, geology, and engineering have particularly good facilities, according to students. Thus, it is no surprise that biology, engineering, sociology, and business are counted among the best majors. On the flip side, some students feel the communications department is weak. As one undergrad explained, "It has no specialties, such as journalism or broadcasting, and academically it's a blow-off." A sophomore communications major admitted that "communications is not exactly a high-risk major."

The "Country Club" Setting

The Trinity campus, carved out of a limestone quarry in an affluent residential San Antonio neighborhood, was modeled after an Italian villa, and is lushly landscaped with oak trees. The buildings are constructed with the widely recognized "Trinity red" brick. "It's like all the buildings are in the midst of one big garden," said one student. Many of the dorms have balconies overlooking the athletic fields below, and the air-conditioned dorm rooms can be inviting on a hot and humid Texas day. Thanks to weekly housekeeping service, the fairly spacious rooms are kept tidy. "Unfortunately," lamented one student, "there is no butler service."

Not all students have it so good: first-year students living in Herdon, a dorm that's part of the freshman Quad, complain about square rooms, an isolated location, and the poor condition of the walls. The Quad, which is behind the campus cafeteria, is also known as "the Ghetto" by upperclassmen. Plans to wire all dormitory rooms with computer and cable connections were completed in 1996.

The university's luxurious and secluded setting is a factor in the low crime rate on campus. Students pointed to the appointment of a new security director, the creation of bicycle patrols, and an increase in the number of campus phones as signs of the administration's commitment to security on campus. An attempt to end round-the-clock access to the university computer center, however, generated criticism from a number of undergrads. As one student said, "True, the center is the farthest building from the residence halls, but there have been no major incidents and security offers an escort service for people who don't want to walk alone."

Social Life?

Aside from frat parties, Trinity does not offer much of a social life, and students often describe their campus as "dead." One student said, "If you're not in a frat or rushing, then there isn't as much to do." Local bars are tough about carding because they're not out to attract college students. St. Mary's Strip, one block from campus, offers a selection of 10 to 15 different bars, from the Crazy Horse Saloon to Joey's and Tycoon Flats. Other hangouts include Bombay's, which attracts an upscale crowd, and Sonny's. Underclassmen congregate at Nell's for pool and darts. Beyond the bar scene, San Antonio is known for its blues clubs and country-western dancing. The famous Riverwalk, a mall complex with a plethora of restaurants, is bustling every weekend, and nearby tourist attractions such as Hemisfair Park, Sea World, the Alamo, and the Tower of the Americas are also popular with Trinity students.

Food Insanity

Undergrads agree, however, that food is the main reason to go off campus. Only three hours north of the border, San Antonio is famous for its Mexican fare. While students maintain that the food on campus isn't that bad, "if I didn't eat out twice a week, I'd go insane," said one sophomore. All campus residents are required to purchase a meal plan, but have a choice between a heavy-, moderate-, or light-eater plan. Students charge meals on a credit card–like ID that moonlights as a library card.

Tigers in Sports

Trinity sports teams are undergoing something of a renaissance. In fact, Trinity has become a powerhouse in the SCAC (Southern Collegiate Athletic Conference). Students have rallied their team and games usually draw about 2,500 fans. "But no matter how big Trinity football gets, it won't be a quarter as big as high school football here," one student said, noting that the high school stadium next door dwarfs Trinity's by more than 10,000 seats. Trinity has always been known for its tennis team, which was the last team to make the divisional switch. Women's volleyball and soccer also have strong programs, and the baseball team recently had its first winning record in 20 years. "Our teams are doing better than they have historically and attendance has increased," one student said. "But I don't think it's had that big of an impact on actually generating campus-wide school spirit."

The Trinity campus, carved out of a limestone quarry in an affluent residential San Antonio neighborhood, was modeled after an Italian villa, and is lushly landscaped with oak trees.

Intramural sports get a lot of support at Trinity. The all-school flag football tournament is covered in the school paper, the *Trinitonian*, and soccer and softball are also popular. Said one student, "almost everyone is in IMs." All intramural warriors enjoy pristine playing conditions on the finely manicured fields. The crown jewel of the athletic department is the newly renovated Bell Center, featuring equipment donated by the NFL Oilers, who used to train there in the preseason.

Most Trinity students hail from Texas, and the majority come from Houston. Although the administration is making a concerted effort to attract more minority students, Trinity undergrads describe their classmates as homogeneous and a little aloof. "It's not too diverse here," one student said. "a large portion of the population is affluent and white. However, there's no discrimination here." While activity picks up slightly during major election years, the campus is "not at all politically charged," another student said. As for political designations, one northeasterner reported, "It's liberal for Texas, but really conservative compared to the Northeast." The political apathy seems to carry over to extracurricular activities as well. Many clubs are pretty "deficient" in numbers, especially organizations that promote minority awareness, but members nonetheless actively work to promote their cause.

While some students lament that the athletics and social life are better to the north at UT/Austin, the fact is that Trinity undergrads receive a top-notch education in an intimate setting. Students feel that the campus is "close-knit—like a giant family." And the grass is always green.
—*Brian Abaluck and Staff*

FYI

The three best things about attending Trinity are "the gorgeous trees, the affluence, and the family feel of the place."

The three worst things about attending Trinity are "the general lack of interest in anything, the chilly social scene, and the lack of spirit."

The three things that every student should do before graduating from Trinity are "play intramural sports, watch football, visit UT/Austin."

One thing I'd like to have known before coming here is "how much alike we are."

University of Dallas

Address: 1845 E. Northgate, Irving, TX 75062

Phone: 972-721-5000

E-mail address: undadmis@acad.udallas.edu

Web site URL: www.udallas.edu

Location: suburban

Founded: 1956

Private or Public: private

Religious affiliation: Roman Catholic

Undergraduate enrollment: 1,157

Total enrollment: 2,897

Percent Male/Female: 42%/58%

Percent Minority: 20.0%

Percent African-American: 1.0%

Percent Hispanic: 12.0%

Percent Asian: 6.0%

Percent in-state/out-of-state: 61%/39%

Percent Pub HS: 58%

Fraternities: 0%

Sororities: 0%

Number of Applicants: 902

Percent Accepted: 82%

Percent Accepted who enroll: 40%

Entering: 263

Transfers: 122

Application Deadline: rolling

Mean SAT: 613 V, 590 M

Middle 50% SAT range: 570–680 V, 540–660 M

Middle 50% ACT range: 24–30

Mean ACT: NA

3 Most popular majors: biology, English, history

Retention: 83.0%

Graduation rate: 59.0%

Library: 300,000 volumes

Tuition and Fees: $14,450 in; $14,450 out

Room and Board: $5,416

On-campus housing: 95%

Financial aid, first-year: 48%

Students often dream of visiting foreign cities such as Athens and Rome. While others dream, students at the University of Dallas, commonly known as UD, enjoy the opportunity to travel and study in these cities easily for a semester. The emphasis that the university puts on foreign exchange distinguishes this Catholic liberal arts university from many others in its league.

"Baby-sitting" Plus

Located on the outskirts of Dallas in Irving, Texas, the University of Dallas offers a core curriculum reflecting its Catholic religious tradition—all students, for example, must take two theology courses as part of their liberal arts distribution requirements. Undergrads agree that classes at UD are challenging, but not overwhelming, while "'guts' are few and far between;" many students said they would never take a class simply to raise their GPA. English is considered one of UD's strongest departments as well as one of the most popular majors. Philosophy and politics offer strong programs as well, and the sciences, particularly the premed track, are considered to be excellent. One student reported that 85% of premed students with a 3.3 GPA or higher get into their top-choice medical school.

While undergrads claim that there are no "bad" departments, some claim that UD's non-premed science departments are a bit weaker. Others complain about UD's research facilities; the university has only one small library, forcing many students to use the libraries at nearby Southern Methodist University. Professors teach all classes at UD. Small class sizes allow for frequent interaction between students and faculty, and professors often join students for dinner in the cafeteria.

UD has an attendance policy that allows students to miss no more than three classes during a semester; violators must report to the dean. Students have mixed reactions to the policy: some find it effective in making them learn, but others call it a "bureaucratic baby-sitting mechanism." One student complained, "I can't sleep in and recover from hangovers because of the mandatory attendance."

Exchange Programs

Many undergrads choose the University of Dallas for its foreign-exchange program in Rome. Participants (almost 100 percent of UD students!) spend one semester of their sophomore year on a newly built UD campus 10 minutes outside of Rome. Professors accompany students on trips and teach classes just as they would on the Texas campus. On weekends, the architecture and art classes take tours of the city. Students in the program also get 10 days off to travel "wherever they can make it," one participant said. During this break, many students go to Russia, Spain, Greece, England, or Ireland. Many participants enjoy the trip immensely, and find that it helps them gain a more intimate understanding of the Western Tradition courses they took during the prior year.

UD's main campus is a 20-minute drive from Dallas, making the city a popular weekend destination for students with cars. Undergrads describe the hillside campus as small and fairly isolated. The university has little contact with the surrounding community, although some students tutor children at nearby schools.

The university requires students to live on campus unless they live with their families in the Dallas area or are at least 21 years old. Some feel that coed dorms are in the highest demand, because the single-sex dorms have strict limits on visits by members of the opposite sex. However, others point out the fact that the opposite-sex limitations are just as severe in the coed dorms, and to the fact that student demand resulted in only one single-sex dorm in the 1999–2000 school year as evidence that students prefer single-sex living. Students also say the noisiest and rowdiest dorm is the all-female Jerome. After their first year, students can choose their dorms and their roommates. O'Connell Hall, which houses mainly upperclassmen, reportedly is one of the most popular dorms, and is harder to get into, although many recently renovated dorms which offer even more perks are quickly taking its place. Most students share double rooms. About half of UD's upperclassmen move off campus, usually to Tower Village Apartments right across the street, for cheaper housing and the possibility of keg parties on weekends.

Campus residents must be on the meal plan (either 14 or 19 meals), and students report that the food is less than appetizing. The Rat, a recreation center in the basement of the student center, is an alternative food source that also houses pool tables and a jukebox. Many students prefer the Rat's hamburgers, french fries, and pizza to the cafeteria food, although another student claimed that the food had gotten much better over her four years, and the amount of variety made meals satisfying.

Fun and Games

UD students describe their classmates as mostly white, religiously conservative Texans. There are few minority students, and even fewer openly gay men or lesbians. The general attitude toward drugs and sex is fairly restrained. "It's a pretty moral school," one student said. The social scene consists mainly of small parties in off-campus apartments where beer is reportedly easy to obtain, even though Irving County is dry.

Student government and dorm committees plan other social activities. The biggest unofficial bash of the year is Groundhog Day. On this special day, students take buses into the woods, set up kegs, and party all night, waiting for the groundhogs to come out. In the fall, the big event is Charity Week, a fundraiser for local charities, involving karaoke contests, dunking booths for professors, and student "jails." University-sponsored trips and social events are attended mostly by freshmen and sophomores; upperclassmen tend to "do their own thing."

> Some feel that coed dorms are in the highest demand, because the single-sex dorms have strict limits on visits by members of the opposite sex.

Students report that the sense of competition they feel in their academic pursuits is not quite as strong in intercollegiate athletics. UD only recently joined the NCAA Division III, and its rugby team, a club sport, has the longest reputation in the state. The women's soccer team, however, made it to the playoffs last year and is one of the more successful teams on campus. The athletic program launched its first baseball season a few years ago, and it has done very well, too. UD does not offer athletic scholarships, and as for mascots, one student said, "If we have one, you never see it at all."

Undergrads praise UD's small size and its commitment to a liberal arts educa-tion. Students have a common desire to learn, and although the school's rigorous academics and stern codes of conduct give parents peace of mind, many stu-dents like UD for the sense of spirit and adventure it instills in them.—*Melissa Chan and Staff*

FYI

The three best things about attending the University of Dallas are "small classes, close rela-tionships with professors, and the spiritual and moral awareness of the student body."

The three worst things about attending the University of Dallas are "the isolation of campus if you don't have a car, the lack of privacy in double rooms, and the attendance policy."

The three things every student should do before graduating from the University of Dallas are "go abroad, go to the Groundhog Day celebrations (wacky but worth it), and eat a meal with a professor."

One thing I'd like to have known before coming here is "start saving money early for extra travel and recreation expenses if you plan to go abroad."

University of Houston

Address: 4800 Calhoun Road, Houston, TX 77004
Phone: 713-743-1000
E-mail address: admissions@uh.edu
Web site URL: www.uh.edu
Location: urban
Founded: 1927
Private or Public: public
Religious affiliation: none
Undergraduate enrollment: 15,618
Total enrollment: 31,602
Percent Male/Female: 47%/53%
Percent Minority: 53.0%
Percent African-American: 14.0%

Percent Hispanic: 19.0%
Percent Asian: 19.0%
Percent in-state/out-of-state: 89%/11%
Percent Pub HS: NA
Fraternities: 27%
Sororities: 34%
Number of Applicants: 8,083
Percent Accepted: 74%
Percent Accepted who enroll: 57%
Entering: 5,134
Transfers: 4,045
Application Deadline: rolling
Mean SAT: 515 V, 533 M

Middle 50% SAT range: 450–570 V, 470–590 M
Middle 50% ACT range: NA
Mean ACT: NA
3 Most popular majors: psychology, education, finance
Retention: 76.0%
Graduation rate: 37.0%
Library: 1,900,000 volumes
Tuition and Fees: $1,983 in; $6,740 out
Room and Board: $4,360
On-campus housing: 40%
Financial aid, first-year: NA

Looking for a big Texas school that still provides a great liberal arts edu-cation? The University of Houston, with a new image, a new logo, and a $5 million publicity campaign designed to at-tract students, is on its way up.

Diversity in Academics

UH is a gigantic, diverse campus in every way. The school enrolls more than 30,000 undergrads, yet manages to maintain an academic program that seems to satisfy everyone. Fourteen colleges make up the UH system, each one with a specialty, such as education, business administra-tion, natural sciences and mathematics, and humanities, fine arts, and communi-cations. Students choose from classes in any of these colleges, which allows them to study a wide range of topics. One of the most respected colleges is the Conrad N. Hilton School of Hotel and Restaurant

Management, which has an on-campus hotel to give students hands-on experience.

Though a large university, UH takes its role as a liberal arts school very seriously. Core requirements make up a large portion of the underclassmen's schedules. The requirements include a total of 42 class hours, consisting of 6 hours in communication (English), 3 hours of math/logic and reasoning, 3 hours of humanities, 3 hours of visual or performing arts, 6 hours of natural sciences, 6 hours of social sciences, 6 hours of history, and 6 hours of government. While some students feel "bogged down" by these requirements, others are simply "indifferent." The requirements, though often tedious, provide students with a solid background in diverse subjects.

Of the 120 different concentrations undergrads have to choose from, students consider the most difficult to be the math-based ones, including engineering and architecture. While there are no "slacker" majors, one student believed that geology would be a safe bet "because when I took that class I skipped the second half of the semester (except the tests) and still got an A." Majors with good reputations are optometry (for which there is an entire college), engineering, and journalism. Each of the science departments wield their own reputations, as well, offering impressive resources such as the Texas Center for Superconductivity Research, now known simply as "Paul's House" in honor of Paul Chu, a UH professor who did early research in superconductivity. The theater department boasts the Pulitzer Prize–winning playwright Edward Albee, who teaches and produces shows for the entire student body.

Every year 300 hard-working students go through a thorough application process to join the Honors College. This college—the only interdisciplinary college at UH—gives selected students the opportunity to have a small liberal arts college atmosphere within a huge university setting. Members of this elite group must maintain a high GPA. In exchange for their efforts, honors students enjoy special perks, including the chance to live in the best dorms on campus, access to smaller classes, and priority registration.

For the other students at UH, there is not too much to complain about. They register for classes through a phone system, and are rarely shut out of the classes they want. While some lectures in the core system can have up to 600 students, most upper level courses enroll no more than 30 students.

A Diverse Crowd

Despite the decent dorms, good food, and quiet atmosphere, UH remains a commuter school. Less than a fifth of the students live on campus and despite strong racial and ethnic diversity, 67 percent of the student body is from the same county in Texas. Students often live in off-campus apartments, or, more commonly, choose to stay at home and drive to school. The average age of UH students is significantly higher than that of other colleges, and many students are adults taking classes part-time, or returning to school after time out in the real world.

Those who do live on campus are fairly happy with the UH culture. Because of the distance between housing complexes, solidarity develops within the four different residence halls: Cougar Place (known for housing lots of varsity athletes and containing a suite setup), Moody Towers ("the dorms that suck the most . . . with cramped rooms and communal showers"), the Quadrangle, and Cambridge Oaks (privately run on-campus apartments). Students living on campus have the opportunity to know one another better, as they are often the only ones around during weekends, without a home to "zip back to and do a load of laundry."

The UH meal plan actually allows students to eat and pay for what they want. Instead of specified meal costs, the card works like a debit card, taking money out of an account set aside for food. This allows students to eat all over campus in spots like the Horizon's Café, which features Pizza Hut, Fresh Grill, and Little Kim Son, and the new Millennium 2000 Café, which holds a Wendy's, a Taco Bell, and a coffee shop. In addition, students can use their "meal money" to shop at any of several convenience stores and make food on their own. In the past, students have protested about the food, but the administration is making efforts to improve it by adding fast-food and convenience store options.

Hanging Out Off Campus

Houston is the fourth largest city in the country and has much to offer UH students. Unfortunately, UH is not in the best area of Houston. Ten minutes from downtown (by car or the Metro, Houston's public transit) and right off the interstate, as one student put it, "UH is in the middle of the ghetto, you have to go over to Rice for things like cool coffee shops." But again, the administration is looking to change all that. With an on-campus police department and a multitude of emergency phones, crime is at a low. Nevertheless, students warn that just as you should not walk around anywhere late at night, "you don't want to walk around alone on the campus perimeter late at night." As long as students use common sense, UH is a safe campus.

Students maintain that having a car is almost essential, as there is little campus night life. Hence, many students, even those who live on campus, own cars. In Houston itself, students hang out in clubs like Numbers, which has live alternative music, and Rockefeller's. Coffee shops are ever popular with the college crowd, and in the city many frequent the new Magic Bus, a combination bar and coffee house.

During the daylight hours students can go to the museum district and learn about natural history, science, or art, or shop in the Galleria, a mall complete with an ice-skating rink. For a day trip, students may choose to go to the beaches at Galveston or to Freeport for a change of pace.

Staying On Campus

Students kick back when they're not in classes or working on assignments. A typical UH student wears jeans and T-shirts, and is "way casual." Unless you are one of the few in a Greek organization or in an academic honor society, the chances to get dressed up are few and far between. But diversity, in dress and attitude, is abundant.

The campus itself is fairly compact, yet "very beautiful." It has the country's largest sculpture garden and plenty of grassy areas and trees. One student stated, "you keep on discovering new areas of the campus every day." Statues such as the "person sitting in a box" in front of the science building add to the aesthetic appeal of the campus. The incredible new opera house/music building adds to the campus's aesthetic and makes seeing performances that much more enjoyable.

There are over 250 student organizations at UH, and they range from the Cattle Rustler, to the Young Socialists, to the Shotokan Karate Club, to the National Leadership Honor Society. The Student Program Board oversees all student social activities. In mid-April, the annual Frontier Fiesta and Cook-Off rouses school spirit with a weekend of "Broadway-like" performances, cultural dances, and food—all in a carnival-like atmosphere.

> **"I have better things to do than go watch the football team lose."**

Without any exceptional sports teams, school spirit has waned in the past few years, and is, according to one student, "not so healthy," while another comments that "I have better things to do than go watch the football team lose." The one exception is UH's baseball team, which was ranked 6th in the nation last year. According to some students, support of the sports teams is increasing. With past athletic greats like Carl Lewis and NBA MVP Hakeem Olajuwan as UH alumni, the athletic department definitely has the potential for greatness.

UH is a large, incredibly diverse school with plenty going on to suit anyone's taste. Every option is available both academically and culturally in this growing and changing institution, led by an administration set on improving in the new millennium.—*Kyla Dahlin*

FYI
The three best things about attending UH are "the honors program, Frontier Fiesta, and downtown Houston."

The three worst things about attending UH are "the parking, the lack of school spirit, and the fact that so many students commute."

The three things that every student should do before graduating from UH are "to study by the Cullen Spring fountain on a nice spring day, to hear a concert in the new opera house, and to join a club!"

One thing I'd like to have known before coming here is that "advisors don't usually know how to help you."

University of Texas/Austin

Address: Main Building, Room 7, Austin, TX 78712-1111
Phone: 512-471-3434
E-mail address: adfre@utxdp.dp.utexas.edu
Web site URL: www.utexas.edu
Location: small city
Founded: 1883
Private or Public: public
Religious affiliation: none
Undergraduate enrollment: 37,203
Total enrollment: 48,008
Percent Male/Female: 50%/50%
Percent Minority: 33.0%

Percent African-American: 4.0%
Percent Hispanic: 14.0%
Percent Asian: 14.0%
Percent in-state/out-of-state: 94%/6%
Percent Pub HS: NA
Fraternities: 5%
Sororities: 6%
Number of Applicants: 16,778
Percent Accepted: 71%
Percent Accepted who enroll: 56%
Entering: 10,858
Transfers: 1,123
Application Deadline: 1 Feb
Mean SAT: 601 V, 620 M

Middle 50% SAT range: 530–640 V, 560–670 M
Middle 50% ACT range: 22–27
Mean ACT: NA
3 Most popular majors: business management, communications, engineering
Retention: 88.0%
Graduation rate: 65.0%
Library: 1,600,000 volumes
Tuition and Fees: $3,128 in; $9,608 out
Room and Board: $4,854
On-campus housing: NA
Financial aid, first-year: 26%

In the green hills of central Texas, the University of Texas at Austin exemplifies the old saying, "Everything's bigger in Texas." The flagship state school offers a multitude of resources for its student body of nearly 50,000. "The size and the resources differentiate UT," one student said. From an exciting social scene to excellent academics, UT has a myriad of opportunities just waiting for students.

At a school as large as UT, you can find nearly every kind of person. "It's fairly diverse in terms of dress and interests. The cliques aren't there and I have met people from everywhere," said one undergrad. The student body is generally progressive, making UT a bit of an anomaly in conservative Texas. With so many students, there is a little of everything.

Academic Texan

Classes can be tough to get into, depending on your year, and students complain about the telephone registration system known as "Tex." It's not a lost hope, as one student explained. "I've found that with persistence and patience, you can get any class you want. I usually try Tex once and then I go to the department or professor."

While introductory classes like psychology and chemistry are usually large, with 200 to 500 students, upper-division classes are generally smaller. Freshmen have the option to take a freshman seminar class on topics from Ethics and Politics in Everyday Life, to Don Quixote. One freshman said, "I really enjoy my freshman seminar class. Part of class is becoming acquainted with campus and dealing with problems that come up." Freshmen also praise UT's orientation—held in three-day sessions during the summer—for easing the sometimes trying transition to college life.

UT also has an honors program called Plan 2, a multidisciplinary liberal arts major that freshmen with high SAT scores can apply to in conjunction with their application for admission. Plan 2 offers small classes and special advising. Many Plan 2 students double-major in Plan 2 and another subject. Each department also has its own honors programs. The engineering honors program is especially well known; according to one undergrad in the program, "Other than my chemistry class, all my classes are small to midsized, from about 15 to 35. At honors programs, I talk one-on-one to professors in my field and they actually listen to what I say." The engineering program evaluates GPAs for all freshman engineering majors and accepts the top 10 percent into the program. Language classes are also notoriously difficult. Government and history classes require reading and "are really hard if you don't know what you are doing," said one student.

Longhorn Living

Most freshmen live on campus, although it is not required. Because of UT's housing shortage, many prospective students put down a deposit for housing during their senior year of high school just to guarantee having a place the next year. Housing is decided by lottery, and though opinions of the dorms are mixed, students note Jester as a good place to live. Rooms in Kinsolving are nicer, but it's an all-girls dorm. And "no one wants to walk that far," one added. Jester, meanwhile, is a high-rise dorm so large that it has its own zip code. Students have the option of coed or single-sex housing. Most will agree, however, that campus accommodations are on the smallish side. "I was planning on living in the dorms next year, too, but I don't think I can deal with this small a space," said one undergrad. Other options include the women's co-op, a vegetarian co-op, and the honors dorm, Carrothers. Many upperclassmen, however, choose to live off campus in nearby apartment complexes.

Students say the food at UT isn't too bad, considering the size of the school. Undergrads do not have to buy a meal plan, but most do anyway, as there are no cooking facilities in the dorms. Dining halls serve the traditional variety of institutional food, and a salad bar is always available along with vegetarian entrees such as vegetarian jambalaya or spinach lasagna. Students can use their meal cards at any dining hall, and an express lane is available for quick lunches. Dinner is not served on Sunday nights, so students often go out with friends to nearby Austin eateries, including Kerbey Lane Cafe and Magnolia Cafe.

Nightlife, Texan-Style

Students spend weekends enjoying the city of Austin, famed for its live music. "Austin is the live music capital of the world," one senior explained. Sixth Street is a popular spot for nightclubs and restaurants, and attracts students who want to party or just enjoy the atmosphere. Student performers take advantage of Austin as well, performing in its numerous coffeehouses and clubs. Other options include exploring the city or taking a day trip to Canyon Lake, outside of Austin.

The Greek system has a noticeable presence on the UT campus, but students do not feel a tremendous amount of pressure to rush. Alcohol is prevalent on campus, but there is still plenty to do for those who don't choose to go this route. "I have a few friends who don't drink; it's not that big a deal," said one undergrad. Some fraternities are organized by interests or specialties, such as science or law.

UT is fairly compact for such a large university, and students bike, walk, or take the bus anywhere they want to go. The campus is grassy, and students spend plenty of time outdoors in the sunny Austin weather. One of the more popular spots is called the "six-pack," a lawn with three buildings on either side. The Tower is a common study spot, as is the West Mall which features a string of franchised fast food chains for those who like to munch while they study. UT's library system offers as many resources as the rest of campus, including the Undergraduate

Library and Perry Castnedal Library, shortened PCL. The campus also sports libraries for specialized subjects.

Sports and school pride are big at UT. Crowds flock to the annual football games against rivals Oklahoma and Texas A&M. The weekend of the A&M game features all kinds of traditions, including tailgating by alumni and students. The Longhorns have a strong record, and undergrads like to let the world know. The UT Tower glows orange every time UT wins a game, white when they win the championship, and "#1" for the even rarer occasions. Fans go wild no matter what shines on the Tower. In general, students consider themselves "fit," and the popularity of intramural sports reflects it. Athletic opportunities include varsity, club, and intramural teams.

"Being so big offers a lot of variety and choices for deciding where you want to be active," said one student, explaining the role of extracurriculars at the university. Some of the possibilities include the *Daily Texan*, a widely read student-run newspaper, student government, and volunteer activities. Fine arts and theater also have a big presence on campus, showcasing the talents of the Longhorns. Students mentioned being involved in everything from nursing programs to the local band scene. "If you can't find it in Austin, you can't find it anywhere."

> **"If you can't find it in Austin, you can't find it anywhere."**

Students at UT are quick to point out that your education can and will be what you make of it. Longhorns have incredible school spirit, which they attribute to the wide range of options available at the university. While students caution that it is possible to get lost in the crowd, survivors agree that UT is an unforgettable and worthwhile experience. When asked what single thought they had about UT, both a senior and a freshman had the same answer: "I love it!"—*William Chen and Staff*

FYI

The three best things about attending UT/Austin are "the women; the parties; and the size and atmosphere of campus."

The three worst things about attending UT/Austin are "it takes a month to learn how to get around; there's a lot of distractions from studying; and...is there really supposed to be three bad things about UT?"

The three things that every student should do before graduating from UT/Austin are "drink at Cain and Able's; visit the Tower; and anything else just because it's there in Austin for you to do."

One thing I'd like to have known before coming here is "rooms are *so* small."

Utah

Brigham Young University

Address: A-183 ASB, Provo, UT 84602-1110
Phone: 801-378-2507
E-mail address: admissions@byu.edu
Web site URL: www.byu.edu
Location: urban
Founded: 1875
Private or Public: private
Religious affiliation: Church of Jesus Christ of Latter-Day Saints
Undergraduate enrollment: 29,565
Total enrollment: NA
Percent Male/Female: 53%/47%
Percent Minority: 5.0%

Percent African-American: 0.0%
Percent Hispanic: 2.0%
Percent Asian: 2.0%
Percent in-state/out-of-state: 29%/71%
Percent Pub HS: NA
Fraternities: NA
Sororities: NA
Number of Applicants: 7,937
Percent Accepted: 71%
Percent Accepted who enroll: 80%
Entering: 4,508
Transfers: NA
Application Deadline: 15 Feb

Mean SAT: NA V, NA M
Middle 50% SAT range: NA V, NA M
Middle 50% ACT range: NA
Mean ACT: 27
3 Most popular majors: business management, elementary education, zoology
Retention: 87.0%
Graduation rate: 62.0%
Library: NA
Tuition and Fees: $2,830 in; $2,830 out
Room and Board: $4,350
On-campus housing: NA
Financial aid, first-year: NA

S tudents at Brigham Young Univesity have great things to say about their school. As one student noted, "it's challenging, very social, and everyone is friendly. We all have a common background. It makes you feel connected to a larger community." Perhaps this environment is indicative of the fact that an overwhelming majority of BYU students are members of the Church of Jesus Christ of Latter-day Saints, commonly known as the Mormons. For most students, shared beliefs draw them together and reaffirm their decision to attend this private religious school.

Up to the Challenge

Freshmen and sophomores spend a great deal of their time taking courses to fulfill general education requirements at BYU, "which provide a good base and are good for figuring out what you like," as one undergrad said. Students must take classes in English, natural sciences, social sciences, religion, American heritage, and the history of civilization. They must also fulfill a physical education requirement and take at least two courses in math, music, or foreign language.

With such extensive core requirements, it is not surprising that introductory and general education classes are extremely large, enrolling several hundred students per class. Most of the larger classes break into sections or labs taught by TAs, many of whom are upperclassmen majoring in the field. As students reach upper-level courses, class size dramatically decreases, ranging from 20 to 30 students per course. Some undergrads complain about the registration system, which gives priority to grad students and upperclassmen. Registration by phone has eased their pain, but some students describe waiting up until midnight the day of registration to be the first to phone in their class schedule.

Grades are reportedly "big . . . huge" on campus, particularly for students enrolled in the honors program and multiple honors societies. Anyone with a GPA of 3.7 or above qualifies for a scholarship. Students report a general feeling that professors "don't curve much." To make academic life a little easier, some students opt for electives like Introductory Ceramics or Sign Language.

Mountain Majesty

According to students, one word summarizes BYU's modern brick campus: "beautiful." Many of the buildings on campus have just recently been completed. The Ernest L. Wilkinson Center, affectionately known as "the Wilk," "looks spectacular. We all love it." The only building yet to be completed is the Harold B. Lee Library, and is not expected to be done anytime soon. Located in the heart of the Rocky Mountains, the compact Provo campus is not as sprawling as the scenery. It reportedly takes about 20 minutes to walk from end to end. Students say they feel safe on campus.

> **"Marriage is always on the mind."**

BYU does not require students to live on campus at any time. Most freshmen choose to live in campus dorms that are monitored by RAs, who reportedly are "not strict because they don't have to be," according to one student. Many upperclassmen opt to live off campus in apartments in the vicinity of campus. They are required to sign an off-campus housing code, similar to the honor code, when they move. Undergrads on campus live in small doubles and share hall bathrooms. All the dorms are single-sex, with no coed, athletic, or Greek housing available. Students are also not allowed to have members of the opposite sex in their dorm rooms. Residents say the dorms are very social places, reportedly providing unlimited opportunities for fun, but discouraging any serious in-room studying.

BYU students are fortunate in their varied selection of dining options. They can choose between the standard three meals a day in one of two cafeterias, or the more popular Dining Plus program, which gives students $10 a day in meal credit that can be spent anywhere on campus, including

vending machines. If the money is not spent, it carries over to the next semester. Popular eating spots include "the Wilk," where students can find fast-food options in Central Garden Court, or the Sky Room restaurant with its formal atmosphere. Also popular is the Creamery, which sells milk, cheese, ice cream, and eggs from the BYU Agriculture Station (one of the largest research and teaching dairy facilities in the U.S.) and bakery goods from the BYU kitchens.

Doing It All

Outside of class, BYU students do a little bit of everything. Especially popular on campus are ballroom dancing ("The team is amazing!") and community service. A large number of students hold jobs on campus, many of them as TAs for introductory classes in their major, assistants for busy professors, or custodians. And in the words of one student, "Athletics are huge!" BYU athletic facilities are outstanding and many students take advantage of them, whether through intramurals, aerobics, weight-lifting classes, or participation on varsity teams. To show their sporting spirit, many undergrads head for football games to cheer on their Cougars, particularly against rival University of Utah.

Always Something to Do

Outside the strong religious affiliation, the one thing that sets BYU apart from any other university is its social life. There is no Greek life, and alcohol, drugs, tobacco, and caffeine are forbidden by the honor code that students strictly follow. There is no traditional party scene on campus, but that doesn't prohibit students from having fun. Dances are incredibly popular (sometimes with several hosted in the same weekend), and two large formal dances are held each semester. The dating scene is nontraditional, since students usually go out on group dates, jokingly referred to as "polygamy dates." Young married couples are not unusual, and, as one student put it, "marriage is always on the mind."

A variety of activities are coordinated through the Wilkinson Center, the campus student center. Inexpensive admission $3 for most events on campus draws students to improvisational comedy routines, a cappella singing-group performances, theater, and the like. Students are also active in their ward (church congregation) and their "family," a smaller group within their ward.

Academically, socially, and spiritually, BYU students find their experience fulfilling. Although it can be difficult to find diversity in their surroundings, most see this in a positive light. As one student said, "I love it because of the teachers, the students, the spirit of the campus. Almost everyone shares the same beliefs yet we are still all so different."—*Jennifer Rogien and Staff*

FYI

The three best things about attending BYU are "the size of the school, most people having the same religious beliefs, and the cute guys down the hall."

The three worst things about attending BYU are "the general education classes, long lines everywhere, and expensive housing."

The three things that every student should do before graduating from BYU are "go to a football game, go to the Fall Fling, and hike up the Y on the mountain."

One thing I'd like to have known before coming here is "how expensive everything is."

University of Utah

Address: 200 S. University Street, Salt Lake City, UT 84112
Phone: 801-581-7200
E-mail address: admissweb_undergrad@saff.utah.edu
Web site URL: www.utah.edu
Location: suburban
Founded: 1850
Private or Public: public
Religious affiliation: none
Undergraduate enrollment: 20,344
Total enrollment: 25,803
Percent Male/Female: 55%/45%
Percent Minority: 0.0%

Percent African-American: NA
Percent Hispanic: NA
Percent Asian: NA
Percent in-state/out-of-state: NA
Percent Pub HS: NA
Fraternities: NA
Sororities: NA
Number of Applicants: 5,927
Percent Accepted: 88%
Percent Accepted who enroll: 52%
Entering: 2,729
Transfers: NA
Application Deadline: 1 Jun

Mean SAT: 487 V, 22 M
Middle 50% SAT range: 500–630 V, 500–630 M
Middle 50% ACT range: NA
Mean ACT: NA
3 Most popular majors: psychology, sociology, political science
Retention: 62.0%
Graduation rate: 43.0%
Library: NA
Tuition and Fees: $2,351 in; $7,575 out
Room and Board: $5,940
On-campus housing: NA
Financial aid, first-year: 24%

The University of Utah was once just a small university in a sleepy western state. However, Salt Lake City's growing population and its winning bid to host the 2002 Winter Olympic Games have contributed to the growth of student opportunities in recent years. Now, students at U of U can do more than just take a tour of the Mormon Tabernacle when they have time to spare. Instead, they can hit the latest downtown brew pub, take in a Jazz basketball game, or even try their hand at Olympic luge.

Do You Speak English?

Students cite the science departments, especially biology and chemistry, as the strongest departments at U of U. In fact, Pons and Fleischman, the scientists of the controversial cold fusion experiments, did their work at the University of Utah. Undergrads agree that the business, communications, and English departments have excellent professors, although some feel the philosophy department is "too research-oriented." The math department was criticized for its shortage of teachers who "speak English." For more academically gifted students, U of U offers an honors program that gives qualified students easy access to top-notch professors. One student added, however, that this program did not seem to be "too diverse."

Locals Abound

Most undergrads are from in state, and many are Salt Lake City natives (some even go home for lunch). For students in need of housing, campus facilities are described as "pretty spare" and "not too great. Most people live off campus if they can." Thus, only a very small number of undergrads live on campus. Others choose fraternity, sorority, or off-campus housing, which is abundant in the university area. However, a significant amount of dorm space is being built to house future Olympians on the U of U campus, and campus housing is "scheduled to double after the Olympics are over!" one undergrad reported. Since most students commute, parking spaces on and near campus are nearly impossible to find. As one commuter explained, "I often have to arrive on campus an hour before my first class just to find space." U of U is also predominantly "an all-white school," and one student reported that ethnic minorities are not represented in large numbers.

Campus activities provide students, especially those new to the city, with opportunities for meeting people. The "most visible social organization on campus" is the university's student association, the ASUU, which sponsors a variety of weekly speakers and monthly concerts, the most popular of which is the two-day reggaefest in May. The weekend social scene is dominated by fraternity and sorority parties, although according to one student, the Greek system "used to be stronger on campus." Students report that because the Greek scene is relatively small, there is little pressure to rush.

Finicky Support

Many undergrads socialize at the Pie, a pizza place decorated with years of graffiti and student signatures. The lobby of the Marriott Library is also considered a prime spot to hang out and meet members of the opposite sex. In spite of U of U's less-than-impressive football record, attendance at the games is strong. Students also take pride in the men's basketball and women's gymnastic teams. However, according to one student, school spirit doesn't extend to much more than "the football and basketball seasons." Less competitive students participate in various intramural sports.

Four More Years

Although Salt Lake City lacks the sophisticated urban attitude of many eastern cities, it has recently experienced a population influx, and is considered one of the best places to live in the United States. The city's cultural attractions include the locally based Ballet West, the Utah Symphony, and the Mormon Tabernacle Choir. The city attracts major rock, pop, and jazz performers as well. In the past five years, a new arena has been built for the Utah Jazz (the Delta Center) and the local ice arena and convention center were rebuilt in anticipation of the 2002 Olympics. The national ski team trains within 30 minutes of the university, and several popular ski resorts are within driving distance. Other outdoor attractions include camping, rock climbing, hiking, and mountain biking.

> However, a significant amount of dorm space is being built to house future Olympians on the U of U campus, and campus housing is "scheduled to double after the Olympics are over!"

The university recently built new facilities for the dance and communications departments (but no new parking lots, one student lamented). The communication facility is equipped with more than 300 computers in five computer labs. A new computer research facility and biology building are both currently under construction. In addition, the recently completed Huntsman Cancer Institute is the largest facility in the United States devoted to cancer research and offers students many unique opportunities to gain exposure to scientific research.

Long a school dominated by Utah Mormons, the university has recently begun to branch out, thanks to the growth of the Salt Lake City area. U of U may not be the place for those seeking great ethnic and religious diversity, but its strong sense of family, local cultural offerings, and proximity to the great outdoors will continue to draw students regardless of religion or origin.—*Brian Abaluck and Staff*

FYI

The three best things about attending the University of Utah are "the opportunity for experience and research in the field of medicine and science, the amazing view of the mountains from campus, and the available outdoor activities including skiing, snowboarding, and waterskiing."

The three worst things about attending the University of Utah are "that campus life suffers from the fact that it is largely a commuter campus, the lack of funding from the state of Utah, and the shortage of parking."

The three things that every student should do before graduating from the University of Utah are "learning how to snowboard, go to Lake Powell, and watch the sun set over the Great Salt Lake."

One thing I'd like to have known before coming here is "that there is so little in the way of on-campus housing."

Vermont

Bennington College

Address: Office of Admissions, Bennington, VT 05201
Phone: 802-440-4312
E-mail address: admission@bennington.edu
Web site URL: www.bennington.edu
Location: rural
Founded: 1932
Private or Public: private
Religious affiliation: none
Undergraduate enrollment: 511
Total enrollment: 635
Percent Male / Female: 30% / 70%
Percent Minority: 7.0%

Percent African-American: 2.0%
Percent Hispanic: 2.0%
Percent Asian: 2.0%
Percent in-state / out-of-state: 8% / 92%
Percent Pub HS: NA
Fraternities: 0%
Sororities: 0%
Number of Applicants: 782
Percent Accepted: 63%
Percent Accepted who enroll: 22%
Entering: 170
Transfers: 27
Application Deadline: 1 Jan
Mean SAT: 623 V, 543 M

Middle 50% SAT range: 570–680 V, 520–640 M
Middle 50% ACT range: NA
Mean ACT: NA
3 Most popular majors: visual & performing arts, interdisciplinary studies, literature & languages
Retention: NA
Graduation rate: NA
Library: 120,000 volumes
Tuition and Fees: $22,500 in; $22,500 out
Room and Board: $5,650
On-campus housing: 100%
Financial aid, first-year: NA

The town of Bennington may seem to be a tranquil outpost of rural Vermont, but artistic passions seethe beneath its placid surface. "What struck me about coming here is how passionate people are about what they do," one student said. "There's so much energy and raw passion." Not surprisingly, the creative energy of Bennington students often defies and overturns traditions, whether they be societal or artistic. But the college does uphold one important tradition—that of being on the cutting edge of just about everything.

Independent Thinking

No core curriculum confines students to specific courses, and majors as such do not exist; students simply must complete eight courses a year and do a senior project to graduate. This unstructured academic environment places the burden of decision making on students. "You really have to be self-motivated and self-

inspired," one student said. Another agreed, saying, "If you're not motivated enough, you're either going to leave or not do well at all." Academic flexibility allows students essentially to custom-tailor their own education; reportedly, one student concentrated on costume design and physics. This freedom also leads to a great deal of student/faculty interaction, since each student works very closely with an advisor and a "plan committee" to form his or her own individual program of concentration.

Upholding this flexible non-curriculum is a lack of a structured grading policy. Students do not receive written grades, and GPAs are nonexistent. Rather, teachers issue written evaluations of students' course work. Since students work closely with their teachers in small classes from the start of their freshman year, "the teachers remember you and your projects." Bennington's faculty is comprised of "teacher-practitioners" who work in their field while teaching. To further encourage students to bridge the gap between theory and practice, a part of the academic year is set aside as a work-study term. During this "Field Work Term" (FWT), students go out and work rather than go to school. The jobs they take vary greatly, and reflect the diversity of interest among the student body. "Not many go out and look for high-paying internships with big firms," one student said. According to her, one student took massage courses in Portugal; another worked at a bookstore; and another did research with a prominent scientist.

While this system helps students connect course work to real life experience, its implementation several years ago met with heated opposition. At the beginning of the 1994 fall term, many academic departments were eliminated, resulting in the firing of tenured faculty members. In place of the departments, the disciplines (music, art, humanities, sciences, and technology) are now taught by teacher-practitioners. The elimination of academic departments caused one student to remark, "We're in a state of total chaos." But since that time, the chaos has subsided. The class of 1997 was the last class to have witnessed the uproar caused by the changes in 1994, and students agree that the situation has improved tremendously.

Living Art

The flexibility of course work at Bennington allows students to pursue their artistic and educational aims independently. Some fulfill one student's description that "they live art, they breathe art, they are art," by essentially locking themselves in their studios. The Visual Arts and Performing Arts Center (VAPA) remains open 24 hours a day, and students work together or individually on projects at all hours of the day or night. This building houses all of the visual and performing arts spaces at Bennington (with the exception of music, for which there is a separate building called Jennings Hall), including dance studios, performing spaces, theater spaces, darkrooms, and studios for all kinds of visual art and design, from painting to architecture to ceramics. One student said, "I think that the biggest way we participate in each other's lives outside of classes would be in supporting each other in our artistic endeavors."

While the atmosphere at Bennington is eminently accepting and tolerant, it may be difficult for students who are not immersed in art to adjust. "I know that for some people who aren't interested in the arts, it can be very intimidating," one student said.

An "Alternative" Community

Echoing the freedom of the academic atmosphere, Bennington's social atmosphere is open and, according to one student, "liberal to the extreme." In previous years, some students have dressed in drag for graduation. Completely accepting of one another's lives, students report that no tension over homosexuality or bisexuality disturbs campus life. Racial tension is likewise nonexistent on the Bennington campus. Some students, however, expressed dissatisfaction over the low minority representation. "We're pretty much a bunch of whites," one said. Perhaps because of the widespread acceptance of difference at Bennington, no formalized interest groups exist. All groups are, for the most part, unstructured. "Even our literary magazine isn't really a club. People come and put something together. It's that kind of thing," one student said.

The small size of Bennington and its isolated setting have a strong impact on the social life of the college. One student described the campus as "incestuous" due to its small population. "Everybody knows who you're with, what you're doing, and who you're sleeping with," he said. The fact that everybody knows everybody else often results in a feeling of claustrophobia. Cliques develop easily, and one student warned, "I think because it's so small, it's dangerous to get yourself stuck into one group of friends." The dating scene can be dismal, although it does exist. Women comprise the majority of Bennington's population, and this lopsided statistic worsens the problem. "There isn't that much dating going on," one student claimed. "It's just a lot of people sleeping around."

Means of Escape

In order to flee Bennington's occasionally claustrophobic atmosphere, students drive to Albany or Manchester, the nearest cities to Bennington. Cars are not only a mode of transportation, but a means of escape. For those who do not own cars, trips planned by the Student Life Organization offer a good alternative. The organization plans trips to shopping malls, ski slopes, and various places in the area. "They're really good to us," one student said appreciatively.

> One student reminisced about his second or third party at Bennington, "I must have kissed about 10 people there."

On-campus options also relieve students from routine. In addition to art exhibitions, concerts, and plays, student bands perform on Friday and Saturday nights in the Cafe, which serves "amazing nachos and smoothies" in addition to providing a meeting place for students. On some weekends, major parties liven up placid Bennington. Among them, the Dress to Get Laid Party (a parody of frat parties at more "mainstream" colleges), the Redneck Party, and '70s and '80s theme parties are popular. One student reminisced about his second or third party at Bennington, "I must have kissed about 10 people there."

While campus social life can be lively, the sports scene is not alive and kicking. There are no hard-core sports at Bennington, although the college has a coed soccer team. Students report that anybody can sign up to play, "even if you've never kicked a ball in your life." Bennington might lack the "school spirit" occasioned by athletics at other schools, but students do not seem to mind. "Bennington probably has 'school spirit' in what it stands for and what it should stand for. . . . People here have always appreciated that it goes against the tide," one student said.

Food and Housing

Bennington also differs from the mainstream in its food: it actually tastes good. In addition to serving a variety of foods, the cafeteria caters to individual requests. Living is likewise surprisingly good. Nearly all students live one of the 12 houses situated on the Commons lawn. Each New England–style house (white with green shutters) accommodates about 30 people and has its own "personality." While students cannot choose their house, they are assigned according to a housing questionnaire they fill out. Some are designated smoking or nonsmoking houses, while some are unofficially recognized among students as "raise hell houses." Each house contains a little kitchenette and a large living room with a fireplace. After freshman year, all students automatically get singles in the houses. Bennington's long-standing problem of underenrollment guarantees that students have all the space they need. It also means that those who are there really want to be. "It's not for everyone, definitely," one student said. "But I've gotten so much out of this place."—*Susanna Chu and Staff*

FYI

The three best things about attending Bennington College are "getting to live in small, homey houses instead of crowded dorms, the freedom of choosing your own program, interacting with teachers who are actually versed in the ways of how their discipline functions in the real world."

The three worst things about attending Bennington College are "the claustrophobically small community, the chaos from the freedom of choosing your own program, and the difficulty of getting to a city if you don't have a car."

The three things every student should do before graduating from Bennington are "do something absolutely fabulous during FWT, try every smoothie flavor at the Cafe, check out what people are wearing at the Dress to Get Laid party."

The one I'd like to have known before coming here is "what a great community Bennington is."

M a r l b o r o   C o l l e g e

Address: P.O. Box A, South Road, Marlboro, VT 05344
Phone: 800-343-0049
E-mail address: admissions@marlboro.edu
Web site URL: www.marlboro.edu
Location: rural
Founded: 1946
Private or Public: private
Religious affiliation: 290
Undergraduate enrollment: 290
Total enrollment: 290
Percent Male/Female: 41%/59%
Percent Minority: 5.0%

Percent African-American: 1.0%
Percent Hispanic: 2.0%
Percent Asian: 1.0%
Percent in-state/out-of-state: 18%/82%
Percent Pub HS: NA
Fraternities: 0%
Sororities: 0%
Number of Applicants: 419
Percent Accepted: 73%
Percent Accepted who enroll: 42%
Entering: 128
Transfers: 29
Application Deadline: 1 Mar

Mean SAT: 610 V, 580 M
Middle 50% SAT range: 580–680 V, 500–620 M
Middle 50% ACT range: NA
Mean ACT: NA
3 Most popular majors: writing, environmental studies, theater
Retention: 78%
Graduation rate: 40%
Library: 52,000 volumes
Tuition and Fees: $18,800 in; $18,800 out
Room and Board: $6,750
On-campus housing: NA
Financial aid, first-year: 85%

The intimate quality of the college experience at Marlboro College extends beyond its rustic surroundings into the social lives of students both inside and outside the realm of academics. According to students, the tightness of the community is one of Marlboro's most attractive qualities, but also one of the "most challenging" aspects of being a student.

Rigorous Academics

Students call Marlboro academics "rigorous," often featuring one-on-one tutorials with professors. These tutorials are very popular with undergrads. Most introductory classes enroll 15 to 20 people, while the higher-level seminars are even smaller. Literature and the social science departments are reportedly strong at Marlboro, with the former ranking as one of the more popular majors. Religion, Literature, and Philosophy is considered the most difficult and rewarding course. As one student said, "It's the history of Western thought in one year: *The Iliad* in one week, *The Divine Comedy* the next."

Marlboro has few academic require-
me͟ s. Regardless of their major (or "field
͟͟ ͟centration" in Marlborian terms),
͟ s must fulfill a writing requirement
͟ eir sophomore year and submit a

20-page portfolio of their writing at the end of the semester, which is judged by the faculty. If the instructors view a submission unacceptable, the student has two more opportunities to pass the requirement. If a student fails to pass within three tries, he or she is asked to leave the college, regardless of previous academic achievements. The requirement can sound intimidating to incoming freshmen, but students describe it as a "good thing" that pressures them into writing clearly and concisely. One of Marlboro's most interesting opportunities is its World Studies Program where students focus on International Relations as an academic discipline and often study and work abroad during the first semester of their junior year. Students are required to write about their experiences upon their return.

Marlboro undergrads consider themselves "extremely lucky" to have strong relationships with the faculty. Teaching assistants are relatively non-existent, although some students often choose to co-teach a course with another student as their final "Plan of Concentration," a cumulative interdisciplinary effort of their last two years of study. Otherwise described as a "senior thesis times ten," this final work is relatively flexible—some opt for writing a 120-page paper while others produce a play. The intimacy students and their professors enjoy is a highlight of Marlboro, and it is not uncommon for students to enjoy dinner at any one of their professors' homes. Marlboro has one centrally located cafeteria, which encourages both students and faculty to enjoy one another's company at mealtimes.

Although upperclassmen receive priority during class registration, one student said that he "never heard of anyone not being able to take a class because it was full." The average class size is seven or eight students, and class sizes of three or four are not uncommon, which "makes it awfully hard to hide if you haven't done your work," remarked one student. The professors, for the benefit of the students, provide 20-minute introductory lectures during the first two days of each term. Although courses are described as "demanding," faculty advisors make sure their advisees keep up with the course load. The lack of organized athletics at Marlboro encourages students to focus on their schoolwork, "so what you do here is study," one student explained.

Beside dorm rooms, places for students to hang out on campus are limited, and those not interested in going to the Campus Center find themselves seeking a ride into Brattleboro, a small town popular for its "cultural and liberal" atmosphere, about 15 minutes from campus. The Campus Center functions as a campus coffeehouse, alternate cafeteria (with limited hours), game room, post office, and general location for all campus-wide events. For those who want a more sociable study place, the center is the place to meet.

Marlboro Living

All Marlboro undergrads are required to live on campus freshman year (although exceptions are made for married students and those with dependents), though most students live on campus all four years. Students praise the dorm rooms, some of which have balconies. The rooms are favorably sized, and usually only frosh live in triples. The priority for housing selection is based on how many credits a student has earned. All the Way is one of the more popular dorms because of its large

kitchen, while Howland is generally the least favorite due to "dumpy" conditions and higher noise levels. The thin walls in Howland "really affect your love life," one student moaned. However, dorm favorites change annually depending on who lives there. Resident advisors (RAs) live in each dorm and organize meetings to vote on "quiet hours" and other inter-dorm issues. One student remarked, "Unlike other colleges, the RAs at Marlboro are more like advisors and less like police." Dorm halls are coed, and only one dorm, Half Way, is reserved for women. Each year, one building is designated "substance-free" and one is "smoke-free." Security reportedly is not an issue at Marlboro, and some students do not worry if they forget to lock their doors.

Marlboro's isolated location limits the availability of off-campus housing. College-owned cottages are designed for students who desire a close-to-campus location and independence from typical dorm living. Each cottage, usually occupied by juniors or seniors, consists of four bedrooms. Renting houses in the woods from townspeople is another option, and Brattleboro, despite the commute, attracts many looking for alternatives to dorm housing.

The Grub

Dining hall food at Marlboro is reportedly decent. Many students complain about the lack of variety, although vegetarian and vegan options are available at every meal. There is freshly baked bread every day, which one student described as "fantastic." Student workers do the cooking, and accept suggestions by their peers. Dining hours are limited, but those who miss a meal can find snacks at the Campus Center. According to one undergrad on the meal plan, "You can eat as much as you want, and you don't have to pay per item." Every Sunday is Ben & Jerry's Night and both on- and off-campus students are welcome to partake of delicious, free ice cream.

What's Happening in Vermont?

The popular Outdoor Program allows Marlborians to take advantage of the pristine Vermont countryside. Students often suggest new activities, such as hang gliding, and as long as there are enough people (at least five) and money, the activity is organized and implemented. One student described campus athletics as "do-it-yourself sports," since no official varsity program exists. There is a soccer team, but apart from that formal competition is limited.

> Marlboro's emphasis on "self-reliance" academics makes it a particularly attractive school to those who seek a rigorous curriculum balanced with a lot of attention from faculty.

The party scene is reportedly diverse. In addition to going to parties organized by the Social Activities Council, most people spend time with friends either at private parties or in the Campus Center. The Cabaret, the main social event of the year, involves an exhibition of student entertainment. Social drinking is common on campus, and some students smoke marijuana, but as one undergrad said, "Neither drugs nor alcohol are in your face. They're not a requirement for attending parties."

The small size of the college "makes it hard to have casual sex relationships," one student said, "as you invariably see your fellow classmates quite often." Another student indicated that there are only "six couples" on campus. A lack of privacy is supposedly responsible for hindering random hookups.

Politically, Marlboro is predominantly liberal. Students say the gay community is quite vocal and is "very accepted" on campus. Participation in student groups, whatever the cause, is popular, and although the student body is not ethnically diverse, its geographical diversity lends itself to many different ideas and experiences from those willing to contribute. Environmental concerns are a hot topic among students. Recently, mass mailings and their impact on deforestation has been a subject of debate.

School spirit at Marlboro is surprisingly high for a school that lacks a formal athletics department. Most undergrads have a "fierce loyalty and love" for Marlboro, and many alumni remain active in college affairs. *The Citizen* is a bi-weekly student newspaper, and another popular group is the Live Action Role-Playing Group, a band of students who perform for the entertainment of the campus community.

Marlboro's emphasis on "self-reliance" academics makes it a particularly attractive school to those who seek a rigorous curriculum balanced with a lot of attention from faculty. The isolation of the college is great for those who want "to get away from it all," but most students warn that you really should know what you want in a school before coming to Marlboro: "Make sure you want someplace really independent," and do not forget to pack "some good sturdy shoes" for those wintertime hikes to class.—*Susannah Chu and Staff*

FYI
The three best things about attending Marlboro are "the quiet, the personal attention, and the alumni dedication to the place."
The three worst things about attending Marlboro are "the quiet, no varsity athletics, and Brattleboro."
The three things that every student should do before graduating from Marlboro are "join an environmental rally, hang at the Campus Center, and chow some yummy Ben & Jerry's."
One thing I'd like to have known before coming here is "know how to write because it makes the portfolio requirement a thousand times less stressful."

Middlebury College

Address: The Emma Willard House, Middlebury, VT 05753
Phone: 802-443-3000
E-mail address: admissions@middlebury.edu
Web site URL: www.middlebury.edu
Location: small town
Founded: 1800
Private or Public: private
Religious affiliation: none
Undergraduate enrollment: 2,265
Total enrollment: 2,265
Percent Male/Female: 50%/50%
Percent Minority: 0.0%

Percent African-American: NA
Percent Hispanic: NA
Percent Asian: NA
Percent in-state/out-of-state: 5%/95%
Percent Pub HS: 54%
Fraternities: 0%
Sororities: 0%
Number of Applicants: 4,865
Percent Accepted: 26%
Percent Accepted who enroll: 42%
Entering: 544
Transfers: 5
Application Deadline: 31 Dec
Mean SAT: NA V, NA M

Middle 50% SAT range: 680–720 V, 650–700 M
Middle 50% ACT range: 28–31
Mean ACT: NA
3 Most popular majors: English, economics, political science
Retention: 95.0%
Graduation rate: 89.0%
Library: 1,200,000 volumes
Tuition and Fees: $32,765 in; $32,765 out
Room and Board: included in tuition
On-campus housing: 100%
Financial aid, first-year: 36%

How many people get to say that they graduated from college on skis, or that while doing the stationary bike every day they looked out through a picture window onto Vermont's Green Mountains? Many Middlebury grads have done these things and more. Middlebury students are not only known for their academic prowess, but also for their active enjoyment of the natural setting that surrounds them.

Academics: A Course on Star Trek

Middlebury students must fulfill two sets of requirements: Cultural Civilization and General Academic. For the Cultural Civilization requirements, students must take one class in each of three groups: European, American, and other cultures. To fulfill the General Academic requirements, students must take classes in seven out of the following eight groups: the arts, deductive reasoning, history, sociology, philosophy, science, language, and literature. Students in general say the requirements are "easy to fulfill." One student said she had "never heard anyone complain about them."

Students report that both the foreign language and English departments are exceptional. Middlebury offers many intensive foreign-language classes, as well as a special intensive-language school in the summer. Middlebury also stresses good writing skills, and has a two-class requirement: one freshman writing seminar and a "writing-intensive" course. Popular departments include psychology, economics, history, biology, environmental studies, and political science. Students say there are no "gut" classes at Middlebury, but some of the easier options are nicknames "Physics for Poets" and "Chemistry for Citizens." Undergrads study in the main library, the Crest Room (a late-night dining hall), common rooms in the dorms, the science library, or the very comfortable and quiet music library.

All classes are taught by professors, and average class size is small, generally around 15 students, with the largest lectures, like Intro Biology, enrolling 105 students at the most. Students say they have no problems getting into all the classes they want. If a class fills up, students report that professors will often open up an extra section. Professors are known for their availability and friendliness. Undergrads go to professors' office hours, call their professors at home, see them around campus, or even baby-sit for their children.

Two distinctive aspects of a Middlebury education are the February entering class and the January Term (J-Term). Because Middlebury is so focused on foreign languages, and because the school is small, many students go abroad in the spring term. To fill their places, the administration admits an extra 100 students to Middlebury in February. Although some people have the misconception that these students are the leftovers who "didn't really get in," this is not the case. Middlebury chooses extremely active, leadership-oriented students for February admission so they will be up to the challenge of adjusting so quickly. "I know everyone in my class, and everyone at Middlebury knows not to mess with one of us, because we have 99 other people behind us," one February-class student said. January term is a chance for students to study a subject, such as a language, intensely. Many professors also offer January classes on the subjects of their independent research. Students also can opt for a more laid-back, fun January course, like a class on *Star Trek*, and spend extra time on outdoor winter activities.

Skinny-Dipping . . . in Winter?

Middlebury students are interested in outdoor activities no matter what the weather. In the spring and fall students swim and canoe on Lake Champlain, and hike and rock-climb on local trails. The Mountain Club organizes weekly outings, although students are welcome to go on their own as well. In the winter, Middlebury is an outdoor sports utopia with its own alpine ski slope, the Middlebury College Snowbowl, only 12 miles away. The college also owns a cross-country ski area called Breadloaf. The cross-country running trail turns into a cross-country skiing trail in the winter. And for those who are brave, the Polar Bear club goes skinny-dipping every Wednesday throughout the year.

What makes Middlebury students different from other college students? According to one student, it's "how well-rounded they are. They do a little of everything, academics and extracurriculars." Many participate in the student government, write for the weekly student paper, the *Campus*, attend lectures, join ISO (the International Students Organization), or start their own group. Many students also participate in community service in the town of Middlebury, where town-gown relations are not considered strained at all; "the college does a lot for the community," one student said. Many students participate in local Big Sib/Little Sib and Habitat for Humanity programs.

Middlebury students characterize their fellow classmates as generally "athletic," with everyone doing something active. Students are also required to fill a two-class PE requirement (less athletic students can choose classes like canoeing and ballroom dancing). Students call the gym facilities "spectacular," with a new hockey rink on the way, a new swimming pool that one student claimed is the "nicest in New England," a climbing wall, a private golf course, a football stadium with a view of the mountains, and a new eight-lane track. Men's ice hockey is the most popular sport, perhaps because it has won its division title for a few years in a row; fans show their school spirit by waiting all night for tickets.

While students find that the dating scene at Middlebury is "pretty nonexistent," random hookups and partying with friends are common. Many students start a weekend evening by going to a movie or concert on campus, and the Fun Club sponsors other nonalcoholic events. Upperclassmen 21 and over go to the few bars in Middlebury, such as Mr. Upps and Angelo's. Vermont alcohol policy is strict: in order to drink, you must show a Vermont State ID or a passport, so underage drinking in town is not much of an option. On the other hand, some students say they can drink in their rooms as long as the door is shut and they are not being noisy.

Social Houses: A Free Trip to Hawaii

Social houses are Middlebury's alternative to the Greek system, which was disbanded in 1990. Students rush social houses in their sophomore year, and everyone who rushes gets into at least one of them. According to one student, "A bulk of the student population, but not the majority" joins the social houses, and their parties are open to anyone. The administration gives the social houses money for events throughout the year, so IDs are checked at the door. At least one of the social houses throws a party almost every weekend, and some get wild. One social house throws an annual "tropical island" theme party and raffles off a ticket to Hawaii. Some guests bring packed suitcases.

Groups of dorms called commons organize parties and other social events, mainly for people who do not want to join a social house, although all students are welcome. Once the keg is kicked at a social house or commons party, at around 1 A.M., students, often very drunk, head over to McCollough Student Center, where a DJ dance party sponsored by the social houses, commons, or MCAB (Middlebury College Activities Board) rages until everyone gets tired and goes home.

Home for about 90 percent of the students is campus dorms. The other 10 percent live either in their social houses, in college-owned senior housing on the fringe of campus, or in one of the many cultural and specialty houses, such as the Italian House, the Chinese House, the International Student House, or the Weybridge Environmental House.

Dorms and Dining

Residents consider the dorms "fair," although some say Battelle, Coffren ("Coffin"), and the New Dorms, which are "very sterile," rank at the bottom of the pack, while Voter, Hepburn, and the top floors of most dorms (reserved for seniors) are considered the best rooms. Students report that "rooms are pretty bad, but if you like the people, it doesn't matter." After freshman year, undergrads choose their own dorms with a group of their friends. Some students choose substance-free and quiet halls. Junior counselors live in freshman dorms to answer academic questions, social questions, or anything else. Freshmen find their JCs more as friends than authority figures, and upperclassmen feel the same about RAs and Residence Life directors (recent grads in charge of the administration and maintenance of the dorms), who live in all dorms.

All full-time students are enrolled in the meal program and can choose from four different dining halls, all run by the same catering service. Students say the dining service staff seems to care about them and makes special meals once a month. For example, on Halloween, all the dining hall staff dresses in costume and prepares Halloween theme food. Proctor is the main dining hall; Lower Proctor (with pink walls) caters to the "Ultimate Frisbee and artsy crowd." Freeman serves regular dining hall food and Hamlin serves fast food, but also has a good salad bar. The Chateau dining hall has language tables at lunch. The Crest Room, located in the student center, is a snack bar where students eat, study, or hang out until it closes at two or three o'clock in the morning. Students cannot transfer their meals there, but can charge them on their ID card. The college is planning a renovation of the student center to provide it with billiards, a bar, a stage for performances, and a cybercafe. This renovation should be complete at the end of 1999. The school has also recently built the Bicentennial science center.

If students want to eat off campus, they often walk into town. Middlebury has several restaurants, many of which are family-run. Most students have cars, so if they want to go a little farther for food, go shopping, or go out at night, they take the one-hour drive to Burlington or drive two hours to Montreal.

> "You've probably seen the J. Crew jokes on e-mail."

Middlebury students tend to classify themselves as the "preppy, L. L. Bean, Eddie Bauer type. You need warm, comfortable clothes in the winter; it isn't a surprise that everyone orders from L. L. Bean," one student said. Another student remarked, "You've probably seen the J. Crew jokes on e-mail." Many students come from the New England area, although there is a large international student population. One non–East Coast student joked that nearly everyone comes from "a little town outside Boston." Students report that there is not much diversity and that this can be "frustrating" sometimes. Nor is there much political activism, although students consider themselves relatively liberal and environmentally conscious. Minority groups are well accepted, and the MOQA (Middlebury Open Queer Alliance) has a strong presence on campus.

Annual Events

Middlebury hosts many annual events, such as Winter Carnival, which centers on ski races, followed by snowman-carving contests and other winter games, and a formal ball. More recent traditions include Winter Olympics and a Charity Ball sponsored by the social houses. All social houses throw parties for Robin Hood days in the spring. Some students report that this event is an excuse for everyone on campus to get very drunk, although Middlebury also sponsors a concert that draws big-name bands. In the past, Middlebury has been host to the Dave Matthews Band and the Samples.

Middlebury's campus has recently been divided over the current president's plans to enlarge the undergraduate population of Middlebury and institute a residential college system. Within this plan falls a wide range of structural renovations to the school. Many students oppose this plan, but as one student said, "the student body is apathetic." If the president pushes this plan and the alumni with money back it up, the students might be in for a big change. But Middlebury's setting will remain the same, never described as anything less than spectacular. As one student said, "It was built in such a way that you will have a view." Middlebury's "marble buildings tucked in the background of the Champlain Valley" are breathtaking, while its academics are highly lauded, and "the openness and friendliness of the student body and professors" is unanimously praised. As one student said, "It definitely becomes home." All this plus graduating on skis—what else could the nature-loving academic want?

—Marion Ringel and Staff

FYI

The three best things about attending Middlebury are "beautiful campus, hot Ultimate players during the spring, and DJ dance parties every weekend."

The three worst things about attending Middlebury are "everyone looks like they're from J. Crew, winter is 9 months long, and Middlebury's in the middle of nowhere."

The three things that every student should do before graduating from Middlebury are "sled down the hill in front of Mead Chapel, hook up after getting drunk, and ski up the Snow Bowl."

One thing I'd like to have known before coming here is "the closest McDonald's is an hour's walk away."

University of Vermont

Address: 194 So. Prospect St.; Burlington, VT 05401-3596

Phone: 802-656-3370

E-mail address: admissions@uvm.edu

Web site URL: www.uvm.edu

Location: small city

Founded: 1791

Private or Public: public

Religious affiliation: none

Undergraduate enrollment: 7,270

Total enrollment: 10,246

Percent Male/Female: 45%/55%

Percent Minority: 5.0%

Percent African-American: 1.0%

Percent Hispanic: 1.1%

Percent Asian: 1.6%

Percent in-state/out-of-state: 59%/41%

Percent Pub HS: 66%

Fraternities: 4%

Sororities: 4%

Number of Applicants: 7,564

Percent Accepted: 80%

Percent Accepted who enroll: 30%

Entering: 1,818

Transfers: 320

Application Deadline: 15 Jan

Mean SAT: 562 V, 566 M

Middle 50% SAT range: 510–610 V, 520–620 M

Middle 50% ACT range: 21–26

Mean ACT: 23.6

3 Most popular majors: psychology, English, business administration

Retention: 81.3%

Graduation rate: 67.1%

Library: NA

Tuition and Fees: $8,044 in; $19,252 out

Room and Board: $5,620

On-campus housing: 95%

Financial aid, first-year: 50%

According to students, the University of Vermont offers a blend of free spirit and academic excellence amid some of the country's most resplendent scenery. Its abbreviation, UVM, is derived from *Universitas Virdis Montis*, Latin for "University of the Green Mountain." Described by one senior as "an adventurer's paradise," UVM is perfectly situated for outdoor activities; students can hike, bike, rock climb, or white-water raft within miles of their dorm rooms. World-renowned ski resorts Sugarbush and Stowe are also less than a 30-minute ride from campus. During Vermont's long winters, a free university shuttle transports snow-loving Catamounts to the slopes three times daily. When the weather permits, students can even participate in water sports such as snorkeling and waterskiing on nearby Lake Champlain.

Living at UVM

Whether they are on or off campus, UVM students know how to have a good time. Laid-back Catamounts take pride in UVM's reputation as one of the top party schools in the nation. With all these potential distractions, students often have trouble balancing work with play. "People have this idea when they first get here that they can ski all day and party all night. They soon discover, though, that at UVM you actually have to work hard to stay afloat," said one biomedical engineering major. Overall, students agree that the work load is challenging but manageable. Although specific course requirements vary from major to major, all students must take a hefty 15 credits: approximately five classes per semester. Before graduation, students must also complete two courses in physical education, ranging from martial arts to stress reduction. "We sit around and breathe in large foam pits. Attendance is 70 percent of our grade. There are no tests because they would be too stressful; I love it!" raved a student in the class. In addition, students in the School of Arts and Sciences (roughly half of the campus) must complete one lab science, one fine arts course, and a Race and Cultures class. Among other class offerings, Human Sexuality with Professor Barbor is "by far the best class at UVM, an absolute must," said one student, while another described the course Race Relations in the U.S. as "so incredibly stressful that one girl had to excuse herself from the midterm exam because it made her physically ill." While popular majors include business, psychology, environmental studies, and the notoriously "lenient" political science, students generally agree that UVM's true strengths lie in the sciences. Physical therapy, animal science (pre-vet), and nursing programs are praised as outstanding but extremely competitive. The Schools of Agriculture and Natural Resources (one of the few places in the country where undergrads can receive a degree in dairy production) also earn extraordinarily high marks.

The major complaint UVM students have about academics is registration. Although the university's newly adopted phone procedure is much less burdensome than the old policy of standing in line, some students still have difficulty getting into the classes they want. Enrollment is based on seniority; thus, all members of the senior class select their schedules before juniors begin. By the time sophomore and freshman registration opens, many classes are already filled. Although most students manage to complete their requirements within four years and agree that if you desperately need a class for graduation, you can usually squeeze in, a substantial portion of students at the University of Vermont opt for the "five-year plan."

The Campus

The sprawling university is composed of three mini-campuses: Main Campus, East Campus, and Redstone, each with its own character. Main Campus houses the majority of UVM freshmen in the Chittenden-Buckham-Wills complex (aka "the shoe-boxes") as well as the majority of classrooms. On the first snowfall, students pack Main Campus for a campus-wide snowball fight. Also located on Main Campus is Converse. In addition to being the unofficial study dorm (the bulk of the students who live here are in the pre-med or nursing programs), the Gothic building ("It looks like something out of *The Addams Family*") is rumored to be haunted by a former premed resident who committed suicide; superstitious students claim that their stereos have turned on by themselves, while members of the janitorial staff have reported mysterious, flying buckets.

Redstone, on the other hand, is generally considered the "party campus." Occupied primarily by upperclassmen and a bit more removed than the other areas, it is "the place you live if you want to drink 24-7." Redstone is also the site of the Primal Scream, a midnight tradition in which brave Catamounts shed their layers and run naked through the cold on the first night of final exams. Tamer than Redstone, East Campus is occupied primarily by freshmen and sophomores and is close to the gym.

Food on all three campuses is said to be average, with a plethora of vegetarian options at every meal. According to one finicky student, "It's the same food repeated constantly. And when I say the same food, I don't mean the same recipe. I mean the same actual food." For a change of pace, students can spend their dining hall points at Fred's Round Room, an on-campus eatery providing tasty alternatives to cafeteria-style entrees including a sandwich bar, in a warm, social atmosphere. The Medical Building's Atrium is also a favorite among more health-conscious students.

Although the campuses are a mere 15-minute walk from one another (a shuttle runs frequently between them during the week), the trek can be almost unbearable during Vermont's subzero winters, causing each area to be somewhat self-contained. One senior reflected, "Because the campuses are so spread out, your friends are basically determined by where you live." Living on campus is required for the first two years, after which many upperclassmen move to nearby apartments in Burlington. Other housing options include the Slade House, an environmentally oriented house in which the residents grow their own food and cook for each other, the academically driven Wright House, and the Living and Learning (L&L) program, in which groups of students with a common interest, such as tae kwon do, foreign language, or photography, share a suite within the Living and Learning complex. The L&L facilities are said to be among the best on campus, offering residents access to an art gallery, a pottery studio, and a computer lab.

Many Catamounts agree that UVM would greatly benefit from a more active student center to unite undergrads from all parts of campus. Although the current Billings center hosts several eateries and an arcade ("Basically two games of Pac-Man in a tiny room," one senior reported), it is more of a snack bar than a social hub. For socializing, students flock to the surrounding town of Burlington. The largest city in the state, Burlington is "the perfect college town; it totally caters to UVM students," one junior boasted. "It's small enough so that you can walk down the streets and see your friends and familiar faces, but large enough to be lively." In addition to providing students with a wide range of outdoor activities, shops, and cafes, the town has an active nightlife. On weekends, students flood Burlington's bars and clubs. Favorites include Rasputin's, Last Chance, RJ's, and Nectar's (the club where the band Phish got its start).

Whether it is in downtown Burlington, at frat parties, or in room gatherings, drinking is a central part of the UVM social scene. One political science major joked, "The campus mascot should be changed from a Catamount [a fierce mountain cat] to a six pack of Budweiser." Although students report little pressure to drink at parties, those who don't like the idea of being around alcohol "may tend to feel left out and have trouble meeting people." For an alternative to the party scene, the Billings center shows recent films and sponsors nonalcoholic "mocktail parties," also called Cheers Without Beers.

Athletic events are also extremely popular among all students. Hockey games "are not only a tradition but an obsession," one student reported. Women's basketball games draw similarly large crowds. Those who want to get in on the action can participate in UVM's strong intramural program that features everything from cricket to broomball. On a more artistic note, student groups also stage performances throughout the year; the Top Cats, UVM's a cappella singing group, are an on-campus favorite. Finally, non-drinking Catamounts can also opt to live in the Safe House, a completely substance-free dorm.

Because UVM is an officially dry campus, the off-campus Greeks dominate the party scene. The biggest parties of the year are said to be Oktoberfest, Halloween, and Spring Fling. Although the majority of UVM students attend Greek-sponsored parties and events, only about a third of the student body actually belongs to a fraternity or sorority. The Greek presence isn't limited to party-throwing, however. Both fraternities and sororities are openly committed to serving the community; members volunteer in local hospitals and homes for the elderly as well as host annual events to benefit AIDS awareness, cancer research, and other national campaigns. According to Catamounts, Greek participation is seen as an asset to the UVM experience, rather than a necessity.

The Vermont Student

On the whole, UVM students describe themselves as relaxed and open-minded. Due to the natural beauty of its setting and the strength of its School of Agricultural Sciences, the campus has a very environmentally conscious and "crunchy" character (all freshmen receive "Can't Use Papers, Plastics, or Styrofoam" cups to encourage recycling). "There are a lot of Birkenstocks here, even when it's below freezing," a nursing student remarked. "Phishheads" and Deadheads are also said to be in abundance. However, one senior said, "It's the one place I feel you can be yourself and totally be accepted."

> "It's the same food repeated constantly. And when I say the same food, I don't mean the same recipe. I mean the same actual food."

Dreadlock-wearing "hippies" walk alongside Polartec-clad athletes. Because UVM is one of the most expensive state schools in the country, however, the student body tends to be rather affluent. "The majority of people here are definitely from the Northeast," another student added. Consequently, cultural diversity is one of the hottest issues on campus. The number of in-state and out-of-state students is roughly equal, but because, as one student said, "Vermont is probably the whitest state in the country," less than 15 percent of the students are of color. There is great support for increased minority enrollment among both students and the administration, and although the school's high tuition and relatively isolated setting have kept the university from attracting such students in the past, minority enrollment is on the rise. The mandatory Race and Cultures class is intended to enhance cultural awareness on campus.

All in all, students find the University of Vermont a wonderful place to receive a first-class education in a relaxed and visually stunning setting—that is, if they can tear themselves away from the slopes —*Lauren Rivera and Staff*

FYI

The three best things about attending University of Vermont are "the gorgeous campus, the outdoor opportunities, and relaxed atmosphere."

The three worst things about attending University of Vermont are "the subzero winters, the lack of diversity, and the terrible food."

The three things that every student should do before graduating from University of Vermont are "go skiing; take Professor Barbor's class, Human Sexuality; and go to at least one hockey game."

One thing I'd like to have known before coming here is "that there was so much drinking."

Virginia

Address: P.O. Box 8795, Williamsburg, VA 23187-8795

Phone: 757-221-4223

E-mail address: admiss@facstaff.wm.edu

Web site URL: www.wm.edu

Location: small city

Founded: 1693

Private or Public: public

Religious affiliation: none

Undergraduate enrollment: 5,552

Total enrollment: 7,553

Percent Male / Female: 42% / 58%

Percent Minority: 21.0%

Percent African-American: 4.0%

Percent Hispanic: 3.0%

Percent Asian: 7.0%

Percent in-state / out-of-state: 64% / 36%

Percent Pub HS: 78%

Fraternities: 32%

Sororities: 29%

Number of Applicants: 6,878

Percent Accepted: 45%

Percent Accepted who enroll: 42%

Entering: 1,301

Transfers: 137

Application Deadline: 5 Jan

Mean SAT: 662 V, 651 M

Middle 50% SAT range: 620–710 V, 610–700 M

Middle 50% ACT range: NA

Mean ACT: NA

3 Most popular majors: psychology, biology, economics

Retention: 95.0%

Graduation rate: 88.0%

Library: 1,418,932 volumes

Tuition and Fees: $4,610 in; $16,434 out

Room and Board: $4,897

On-campus housing: 99%

Financial aid, first-year: 30%

It is rather ironic that at a school as historic as William and Mary, the history major should be a gut. But ironies and unintended consequences seem to run rampant in the second-oldest school in the country: an administration initiative to curb underage drinking leads to more, albeit private, drinking; a building touted as the oldest still-used academic building in the country is so overrun by tourists that it's barely used anymore; annual renovations on campus still leave freshman housing without air-conditioning. Yet despite these problems, students still give William and Mary, a relatively small college within Virginia's system of public colleges and universities, rave reviews. "I love it here to death," said one sophomore.

Changing Drinking Rules

Currently, the big issue on William and Mary's campus is the change in the drinking policy. Orientation Aides, sophomores who take frosh under their wings to teach them "how to survive" at W&M, and RAs, who live on freshman halls ostensibly, enforce the new rules, while in previous years students say most of them turned a blind eye to drinking.

A blind eye to drinking, however, is ending on campus. At the beginning of the 1998–99 school year, major changes were made in alcohol policies with the aim of making underage drinking and "dirty rushing" less prevalent. The college is trying to cut down on the traditional prerush, in which freshmen are recruited by frats before the official start of the rush. To do this, strict rules were put in place that forbid more than 30 freshmen on a fraternity's grounds at one time, and require that all Greek parties be by invitation only. Undercover enforcers circle through parties demanding to see identification and breaking up parties that don't check for

IDs. Also, the many "delis" near campus that "function as bars for the student population" card customers before allowing them to buy alcohol, depriving underclassmen of a major social activity.

It is unclear what effect these reforms will have on the social scene at W&M, since they are still relatively new. Students say people who drank previously keep doing so in the privacy of their own rooms. And though the new restrictions certainly crimp frat parties, some students assert that the Greek hold on campus social life—a typical weekend for many students in previous years has included at least one frat party—has been weakening over the past few years anyway.

Those who do not want to drink often rely on "make your own fun" nights of hanging out in dorms, wandering around campus, or sitting in the Sunken Garden, a colonial-era park in the center of campus. (According to tradition, students are supposed to run naked in the garden before graduating.) There are "not just parties jumping out at you," so those who would rather not drink can avoid it. Students involved in the artistic community point to a professional theater a block away from campus and a plethora of on-campus theater and music groups as alternatives to the party scene. W&M sports a strong a cappella community and extracurricular clubs and groups have started bringing in speakers, although most lectures are sparsely attended. A school-run cafe is open every night from seven to one and hosts events ranging from game night and bands to stand-up comedy.

Work First, Fun Later

Of course, it is not all fun and games at W&M. In fact, students are quick to point out that depending on your major, you may not have a lot of time for partying. Students profess that their work comes first: if you have work, you do it, and the fun comes later. "People do a lot of work here," says one senior. "There's a surprising amount of studying going on." Science majors—especially in biology—work particularly hard, but the history department is known for its light workload. "If you can't get work done [in history], I mean, c'mon, you just aren't concentrating," teased one junior. Psychology also is

known as an easy major, or as one student described it, "a piece of cake."

From the day frosh are assigned their Orientation Aides, W&M students start looking for knowledge from upperclassmen about good courses. People looking for easy A's find solace in an Intro Computer Science class, described as "turn on the computer, turn off the computer," and Human Sexuality, considered easy despite its heavy reading. A course called Math Powered Flight is known as a "very easy" way to get out of your science and math requirements.

At the opposite end of the spectrum are a series of classes taught by the popular Hans Tiefel, a professor in the religion department who teaches ethics courses in various fields; his classes include Religion and Ethics, Medicine and Ethics, Organizations and Ethics, and, most famously, Death. Students report that Tiefel "challenges you to think," and provides "excellent," if tough instruction. It's "a big deal when he likes your paper, and he does tell you when he likes your work." Upperclassmen warn that if you take one of his courses, you shouldn't take much else.

A typical course load is 15 credits per semester, although students tend to vary from 12 to 18. Courses like PE, labs, and music lessons tend to be one credit. Each term at least one department invites a well-known speaker to come and give a short, typically weeklong intensive class for a single credit; a recent example is Curtis Hanson, who created the movie *L.A. Confidential*. About 10 percent of each incoming class is chosen to be Monroe Scholars (another group is chosen to be Monroe Athletes) and get to live in the special Monroe dorm. Monroe Scholars get funds to pursue an independent project of their choice during the summer, and they also take advantage of the $2,000–$3,000 grants to go abroad.

The distribution requirements recently changed from basic guidelines that required a certain number of courses in each of three different groups to a more specific General Education Requirement. To fulfill the GER, students must take one course from a list of specific classes in each of seven areas. Requirements include a writing course, physical education, and foreign language. Student choose their major at the end of sophomore year but report that it is not that difficult to switch at a later time.

Freshmen must take at least one seminar each semester, and there are special seminars offered only to freshmen. People with a greater number of credits (either because they're upperclassmen or because they matriculate with AP credit) get to pick classes and rooms earlier than others, so even if you do not get into a course you wanted, chances are, students say, you will be able to get it eventually.

Waiting for the Lodges

"The freshman dorms are definitely the least appealing, but that gives you something to look forward to," says one upperclassman. Frosh must sweat through the beginning and end of school without air conditioning, although most other dorms have climate control. Each summer, a different section of campus has renovations done, and in the past four years, nearly every freshman dorm has been fixed up with new carpets and new bathrooms. Freshman year, "if you get lucky, you get lucky," and coming to W&M with lots of AP credit can result in sophomore standing for housing. However, students often say that in such a case, you miss out on bonding with a freshman hall, which several students identified as the source of their friends even in later years. After freshman year, housing is assigned by lottery. Off-campus fraternity houses are popular, as are "lodges," houses with about seven people sharing them. On campus there are apartment-style dorms with four to six people per suite, as well as two dorms with singles.

All freshmen must be on a 21-meal/week plan. However, there are a variety of other options for upperclassmen. For instance, there are plans that include lunches only and cater to the "fair amount" of students who live off campus. The food does not receive very high marks, but most students don't find the quality of food to be important. In addition, there are a variety of restaurants off campus, including the delis, which students frequent.

A Khaki World

W&M students describe themselves as preppy. "It's a very khaki world we live in here," one student said. "People just seem to dress nice." That is reflected also in the campus's conservative politics. Liberals need not fear, though: while the right is more numerous, the left is vocal, "so it doesn't seem so bad."

Students give different emphases to their extracurriculars. "There are those who don't join anything and study all the time, those who are really involved in the religious groups on campus, those who join all the intramural sports teams, super-volunteers. . . ." Students say some groups, such as a cappella singing, tend to encourage tighter friendships than other, bigger clubs that don't demand as much time. Sports are very minor at W&M. According to one student, "William and Mary doesn't inspire a lot of school pride." More alums go to football games than students, although many say there's a greater turnout for basketball. More of the student population is involved in intramurals and there is also a gym for working out at anytime with exercise bikes, a weight room, swimming pool, and tennis and basketball courts.

> **"It's a very khaki world we live in here."**

Among the most striking things about William and Mary is the diversity of experience, especially considering its small size. While frats have in the past been a popular form of entertainment, some students assert that they've never been to a frat party. Some freshman halls form groups that last through all four years of college while other students say their friends come mostly from their extracurriculars. Two things that characterize W&M students, however, are the emphasis they give to schoolwork and confusion over the new drinking policy.—*Jacob Remes and Staff*

FYI

The three best things about attending College of William and Mary are "the a capella groups, the pretty campus, and having Busch Gardens nearby."

The three worst things about attending William and Mary are "the large number of tourists in town, poor attendance at the football games, and bad freshman dorms.

The three things that every student should do before graduating from William and Mary are "go ballroom dancing, volunteer, and walk through the Muscarelle Museum of Art."

One thing I'd like to have known before coming here is "how big a school of five thousand people can be."

George Mason University

Address: 4400 University Drive, Fairfax, VA 22030

Phone: 703-993-1000

E-mail address: admissions@gmu.edu

Web site URL: www.gmu.edu

Location: suburban

Founded: 1957

Private or Public: public

Religious affiliation: none

Undergraduate enrollment: 14,234

Total enrollment: NA

Percent Male / Female: 62%/38%

Percent Minority: 36.0%

Percent African-American: 9.0%

Percent Hispanic: 7.0%

Percent Asian: 16.0%

Percent in-state / out-of-state: 91%/9%

Percent Pub HS: NA

Fraternities: NA

Sororities: NA

Number of Applicants: 6,035

Percent Accepted: 63%

Percent Accepted who enroll: 55%

Entering: 2,110

Transfers: 2,034

Application Deadline: 1 Apr

Mean SAT: NA V, NA M

Middle 50% SAT range: 460–570 V, 470–580 M

Middle 50% ACT range: 17–23

Mean ACT: NA

3 Most popular majors: psychology, administrative services, speech and rhetoric

Retention: 74.0%

Graduation rate: 51.0%

Library: NA

Tuition and Fees: $3,766 in; $12,516 out

Room and Board: $5,040

On-campus housing: NA

Financial aid, first-year: 38%

Just 30 minutes outside of Washington, D.C., George Mason University was founded in 1957 as a two-year branch of the University of Virginia. After gaining university status in 1972, it has come into its own and earned national recognition, although a large majority of its students are commuters from northern Virginia (parking lots are an integral part of the campus). The architecture is modern and new buildings are always under construction. The sprawling tree-lined campus seems barely able to contain GMU's academic and physical growth. "It used to be thought of as a backup school, but now people who come here really want to come here," one student reported.

An Academic Mall

Recent additions to the academic curriculum have propelled GMU from a regional university into national prominence. It offers over 100 undergraduate and graduate programs along with over 100 more certificate, interdisciplinary, and minor programs. One student said that the overall academic atmosphere is "not overly competitive," but she felt she was "receiving a great education at a reasonable cost."

Business, biology, and psychology are reportedly among the most popular majors. Business majors report that the recently built Enterprise Hall, with its new facilities and updated equipment, will revolutionize the department, whereas some students listed communications and theater as weaker departments. Almost all upper-level courses are taught by professors (as opposed to TAs, who do some teaching at lower levels) and are relatively small, with 20 to 30 students. GMU offers University 101 courses that allow freshmen to orient themselves to the university and the surrounding area. Registration for classes is done over the phone. Students with high GPAs can enroll in the Robinson Courses, which are taught by visiting professors. This prominent group has included journalist Roger Wilkins (Pulitzer Prize winner for coverage of Watergate scandal), anthropologist Mary Catherine Bateson, and African anthropologist John Paden, among others.

GMU has four innovative programs that are popular with students. The Plan for Alternatives to General Education (PAGE) provides an option that differs from general education courses. Faculty members from various disciplines team-teach the two-year program in small seminar-like classes. In the New Century College program, a student may design his or her own major with the help of a faculty advisor. The Linked Courses program allows freshmen to join the required composition class, English 101, with an introductory course in communication, government, philosophy, sociology, anthropology, psychology, or history. The fourth program is the Bachelor of Arts in Interdisciplinary Studies (BAIS), which allows students to major in a combination of disciplines.

Commuting to School

Undergrads report that George Mason is not the "typical college experience," because the student body includes a large number of commuters. Only about 15 percent of all students live in campus dorms. The on-campus social scene is limited to the small number of students who live there, but because they are a small group, they tend to be "very close and very active." People tend to hang out in definite cliques and "it is hard to make friends here if you don't live on campus," one student said. "You have to either be Greek or very social."

Freshmen who live on campus are required to live in President's Park, dorms that some consider "the worst on campus." Residents of Commons and student apartments consider their accommodations spacious and comfortable. The first-year dorms are officially alcohol-free, but residents reportedly interpret the rule liberally. On-campus living can provide a family-like experience. "The on-campus students bond together and have a lot of school spirit," said one undergrad. Popular hangouts include Taco Bell and Pizza Hut, as well as "the Rat," the only place on campus where students of legal age can buy alcohol. On the other hand, "most people go off campus to do stuff."

For those who live on campus, Greek life is very popular. The most active frats include Sigma Chi and AON. Alpha Xi Delta is a popular sorority. Frat parties tend to be exclusive, and while students say it is not hard for girls to get in (life is not fair), guys have a tough time. Most parties tend to be in private homes or in D.C. clubs. Alcohol figures heavily into the social scene. Despite the strict control of alcohol sales (hard liquor is sold in VA only through state-owned Alcohol Beverage Control, or ABC, centers), some students say underage drinking is easy if you "have connections."

Being in D.C.

Washington, D.C., is a great source of academic, social, and internship experiences. Many students choose to come to Mason because of its proximity to D.C. "It's close enough to D.C., but you get to enjoy the peaceful and convenient living of the suburbs." Clubbing and frequenting the bars in the Georgetown and Adams Morgan neighborhoods of D.C. are very popular for students with cars (which is just about everybody).

> **George Mason is relatively young and current undergrads have the opportunity to have a formative influence on shaping campus life.**

Other popular extracurricular activities at GMU include student government and the university's weekly newspaper, the *Broadside*. Those with rebellious blood can write for the underground independent newspaper, the *Expulsion*, which makes fun of the university's official paper. Students use these publications to get their ideas across to the administration, and many feel their ideas actually make an impact that might not be possible at an older, more tradition-bound school. Students report that there is almost always "something going on in the quad," from speakers to poets to comedians. Mason Day, an annual celebration, recently featured a concert by the Violent Femmes. Recent famous speakers have included mayor of D.C. Marion Barry, G. Gordon Liddy, Oliver North, news anchorman Ed Bradley, Candace Bergen, and Richard Dreyfus.

Diversity Abounds

Despite the high in-state population at GMU, students are impressed by their classmates' diverse ethnic and geographical origins. One student went so far as to say that "GMU is the most ethnically diverse campus in Virginia." Forty-nine states and 119 countries are represented at GMU and students of all types and ages are attracted to the city. There is a large, active gay and lesbian population on campus, and reportedly there is also much interracial dating. Many older students and part-time students take classes at

GMU although they have little contact with traditional-age undergrads.

In keeping with the "newness" of George Mason, the campus has modern architecture, and construction is under way as the college continues to expand. There are already two student centers, and the new University Center will house retail stores, a theater, a library center, lounge, eateries, and classrooms for the New Century College. The arts center has hosted such performers as Itzhak Perlman. Student tickets are free and all performances are open to the public.

Students report that contact between George Mason and the town of Fairfax is minimal. "Fairfax is not a college town like Charlottesville," complained one student, who said there is little to do in Fairfax. Students rely on D.C. for entertainment instead.

The biggest complaint students have about George Mason is the lack of traditions. But, many students see a positive side to this too because George Mason is relatively young and current undergrads have the opportunity to have a formative influence on shaping campus life. It may not have the rich, historical atmosphere of an older university, but GMU offers a college experience devoid of the stereotypes and prejudices that often accompany tradition.—*Seung Lee and Staff*

FYI

The three best things about attending GMU are "the incredible speakers who visit, the proximity to D.C., and 'the Rat.'"

The three worst things about attending GMU are "the lack of traditions that define a school, a lackluster Fairfax, and living in President's Park."

The three things that every student should do before graduating from GMU are "go clubbing in D.C., keep your eyes posted for awesome speakers, and get invited to a frat party."

One thing I'd like to have known before coming here is "that you will need a car to take advantage of D.C."

Hampden-Sydney College

Address: P.O. Box 667, Hampden-Sydney, VA 23943
Phone: 804-223-6120
E-mail address: hsapp@tiger.hsc.edu
Web site URL: www.hsc.edu
Location: rural
Founded: 1,776
Private or Public: private
Religious affiliation: Presbyterian
Undergraduate enrollment: 996
Total enrollment: 996
Percent Male / Female: 100%/0%
Percent Minority: 6.0%

Percent African-American: 4.0%
Percent Hispanic: 1.0%
Percent Asian: 1.0%
Percent in-state / out-of-state: 60%/40%
Percent Pub HS: 65%
Fraternities: 37%
Sororities: 0%
Number of Applicants: 991
Percent Accepted: 74%
Percent Accepted who enroll: 42%
Entering: 307
Transfers: 9
Application Deadline: 1 Mar

Mean SAT: 551 V, 557 M
Middle 50% SAT range: 500–600 V, 610–610 M
Middle 50% ACT range: 19–25
Mean ACT: 22
3 Most popular majors: economics, history, political science
Retention: 80.0%
Graduation rate: 64.0%
Library: 220,172 volumes
Tuition and Fees: $16,531 in; $16,531 out
Room and Board: $5,898
On-campus housing: 100%
Financial aid, first-year: 80%

Tradition, excellence, and honor: at all-male Hampden-Sydney, these are not just words. They are a way of life.

Academic Excellence

Excellence in academics comes in the form of the Rhetoric Program, a set of first- and second-year core requirements. Although many of their classes are predetermined by the Rhetoric Program, freshmen get a taste of the individual attention they will receive at Hampden-Sydney through faculty advisors who help plan their schedules.

The Rhetoric Program consists of challenging classes in English, writing, and speech, ten papers a semester, stringent grammar testing, and a final proficiency exam. A follow-up exam is given after the program to ensure that students have actually retained what they've learned. As one student put it, "The Rhetoric Program totally killed me my freshman year." However, students seem to appreciate the program and say that it helps later on with courses in their majors.

The economics, political science, and history departments are quite strong and popular. Languages and sciences are reportedly not as strong, yet students agree that most of the departments are quite challenging. As one sophomore put it, "If you get an A here, you really had to earn it."

The largest classes at Hampden-Sydney enroll about 35 people. Upper-level classes usually contain no more than 10 students. Students know all their professors well, and some professors invite students to dinner and other social events. The accessibility of professors also comes in handy when extensions on assignments are needed. As one student reported, "Since professors know all their students so well, they're usually willing to accept a late paper or reschedule an exam if need be. It's really easy to talk to the teachers." The college also runs a Writing Center, whose staff will read and critique any written assignments. Students agree that all of these personal services help them excel.

Living Quarters

Although only freshmen are required to live on campus, almost all upperclassmen remain in campus housing. Students choose their preferred dorm before attending Hampden-Sydney. One student explained that students almost always pick the dorms they stayed in during their visits as prospective students.

Cushing, the oldest and one of the most popular dorms, houses half the freshman class. "All the freshmen want to live there," one student remarked, because of its "*Animal House*, party-dorm" reputation and large rooms. Other popular dorms are Carpenter, which has carpeting in all the rooms, and the Hampden House apartments, which are complete with private bathrooms. The dorms are divided into four "passages," hallways where neighboring students form strong and lasting friendships.

Typical College Food

Pannill Commons, the main dining hall on campus, serves "typical college food not great," one student said. Most undergrads prefer the Tiger Inn restaurant, a campus hangout equivalent to a student center, with pool tables and a big-screen television. Although it's not part of the meal plan, the Tiger Inn attracts many students and even hosts bands and comedians.

> **"It does get a little old only having 900 guys around."**

Students also voyage off campus to the town of Farmville for food. Some like Charlie's and Macado's for sandwiches or steak dinners. The Hitchin' Post, right off campus, draws quite a crowd for sandwiches as well. Although Farmville has about "half a dozen good restaurants," one student said, it does not have much else for the college crowd. The nearest mall is 45 minutes away, in Lynchburg, and Richmond, the largest city nearby, is an hour's drive away. Students admit that "you really need a car here, or at least have a friend with a car." Freshmen are allowed to have cars on campus, reportedly a tremendous asset for visiting the women's schools about an hour away from Hampden-Sydney.

Where the Women Are

There are four women's colleges close to Hampden-Sydney: Mary Baldwin, Sweet Briar, Randolph-Macon, and Hollins. Long-

wood, a coed state school, is also nearby. Hampden-Sydney social functions have a "definitely noticeable" female presence. The College Activities Committee occasionally hosts frequent mixers with the women's schools, and the fraternities, which include half of the student body, throw parties with the sororities from the Universities of Richmond and Virginia. As one student remarked, "It's initially really easy to meet girls. It seems like almost everyone here has a girlfriend."

Going Out

Most parties and weekend activities occur at the Circle, Hampden-Sydney's fraternity row. Despite the administration's recent enforcement of the alcohol policy by making Cushing a dry dorm, the attitude toward alcohol among students is pretty laid-back. Fraternity parties, open to all students, provide a steady supply of alcohol.

Although Greek life is a large part of the campus scene, it is not divisive. According to one non-Greek, "People consider themselves Hampden-Sydney men first, Greeks second." The Greeks are responsible for all the big parties and social events on campus. The biggest is Greek Week, an annual spring weekend of partying and dancing. Greek Week hosts popular bands, which have included Hootie and the Blowfish, Big Head Todd and the Monsters, the Dave Matthews Band, Blues Traveler, and the Spin Doctors. Road trips to the women's colleges are also popular weekend activities.

Extracurriculars

The favorite extracurricular activity for Greeks and non-Greeks alike is intramural sports. Students organize their own teams and compete in a variety of sports, including football, basketball, and soccer. Varsity sports also receive enthusiastic student support, especially the football team, whose homecoming performance kicks off a weekend of parties with students from the competing school. The Young Republicans is one of the many popular extracurricular groups. Political sentiment on campus is conservative, and students say they are politically active. Other popular activities include the debate society, the literary organization, the

Key Club, and the Outsider's Club, which sponsors white-water rafting and adventure trips.

Honorable Men

One of the most prestigious campus organizations is the student government, which is responsible for enforcing the honor code. Hampden-Sydney has a strictly enforced honor code; students can be expelled for cheating, stealing, or dishonesty. Any infraction of the honor code is addressed by the student-run honor court, which assigns the accused undergrad a student lawyer and decides his punishment. Although very few cases come in front of the court, students take their judicial process seriously. They say the honor code allows them freedom to feel safe and govern themselves.

As a result of the honor code, students report, Hampden-Sydney has almost no crime. As one student said, "I leave my books everywhere. You can walk into your friend's room and start watching TV and no one will mind. Even the dorms are always open."

With a deeply entrenched honor code and strong sense of tradition, Hampden-Sydney students enjoy a special camaraderie on campus. Although one student remarked, "It does get a little old only having 900 guys around," most students agree that the all-male environment creates a sense of true fellowship, and that the college would lose much of its special character if women were admitted. Other students point out that relationships with the faculty, strong academics, and accessibility to the many surrounding women's colleges outweigh any disadvantages.—*Susanna Chu and Staff*

FYI

The three best things about attending Hampden-Sydney are "student pride, the honor code, and the sense of security around campus."

The three worst things about attending Hampden-Sydney are "the lack of cute girls down the hall, the core requirements, and the need for a car."

The three things that every student should do before graduating from Hampden-Sydney are "walk around the dorms in boxers, spend a night at a sorority house, have a humiliating experience during Greek Week."

One thing I'd like to have known before coming here is "you really can have fun at an all-guys college."

Hollins University

Address: PO Box 9688, Roanoke, VA 24020
Phone: 540-362-6000
E-mail address: huadm@hollins.edu
Web site URL: www.hollins.edu
Location: suburban
Founded: 1842
Private or Public: private
Religious affiliation: none
Undergraduate enrollment: 809
Total enrollment: 1,102
Percent Male/Female: 1%/99%
Percent Minority: 10.0%

Percent African-American: 6.0%
Percent Hispanic: 2.0%
Percent Asian: 2.0%
Percent in-state/out-of-state: 28%/72%
Percent Pub HS: 76%
Fraternities: NA
Sororities: NA
Number of Applicants: 650
Percent Accepted: 83%
Percent Accepted who enroll: 38%
Entering: 205
Transfers: 35
Application Deadline: 15 Feb

Mean SAT: NA
Middle 50% SAT range: 540–660 V, 500–600 M
Middle 50% ACT range: 22–27
Mean ACT: NA
3 Most popular majors: psychology, English, biology
Retention: 79.0%
Graduation rate: 68.0%
Library: NA
Tuition and Fees: $16,710 in; $16,710 out
Room and Board: $6,125
On-campus housing: NA
Financial aid, first-year: 64%

When the first frost falls on the beautiful campus of Hollins University, the entire community celebrates Tinker Day. Dorm halls are filled with the sound of seniors banging pots and pans, noise known as the Tinker Day Scares. Upon hearing the great clamor, students rise and do what classes before them have been doing for years; they go to the dining hall to eat breakfast in their pajamas. Classes are canceled for the entire day and everyone dons a crazy outfit and prepares to climb nearby Tinker Mountain, one of the many hills that surround the Hollins campus. At the top, students enjoy a huge picnic buffet and spend the rest of the day celebrating with songs and skits. Tinker Day is just one example of the many traditions observed at Hollins University. Students enjoy themselves at Hollins; they also recognize that Hollins is a place dedicated to providing a great education.

Broad-Based Academics

Hollins, a four-year women's university, divides its academic coursework into four divisions: humanities, social sciences, fine arts, and natural sciences. Each student must take eight credits from each division as part of a "broad based academic curriculum." Freshmen have to fulfill an additional writing requirement. Students praise the English department as exceptionally strong. As one undergrad said, "The department has like quadruple the number of professors of any other department." Aside from English, other popular majors include history and psychology. The political science department "is pretty good, but the professors are incomparably harder than in any other department." Although many undergraduates tend to major in the humanities, the natural sciences reportedly are "still pretty good and the facilities are up-to-date." Some students said that "easy" majors include communications and religion. Regardless of particular department credentials, most undergrads praise their professors for innovative assignments. For example, students in a sociology class were required to go into a store and write a paper on how they would steal money from that establishment. Not only do professors often "devise cool projects for

class," but many live on the Hollins campus and are "always open" to student interaction, one undergrad said.

Class registration at the beginning of each term is "straightforward and fast," according to students. Few students have trouble getting into the classes they want, although some introductory classes in psychology, computer science, and art do fill up, due to caps put on course enrollment. To help students choose classes, course and faculty evaluations from previous semesters are readily accessible. Hollins students are also positive about the small class sizes. One freshman said that most of her classes "only had 15 people and the largest class I have had here has been only 45 students."

Short Term

Hollins divides the year into two semesters plus a short, four-week term that occurs in January. "Short Term is the reason I came to Hollins," said one freshman. Many upperclassmen use this time to do internships made possible through an extensive alumni network run by the career development office. Other students stay on campus for intensive seminar courses. The school also sponsors many off-campus opportunities during Short Term, such as travel to Greece, Spain, or Germany to improve language proficiency. By graduation, each student must have accumulated four Short Term credits, although as one senior noted, "Who would want to miss Short Term anyway?"

Car—A Must Have

As for social life, Hollins students often find their options limited. Many go off-campus on the weekends to meet male undergrads at either Washington and Lee University or Hampden-Sydney College, both within an hour's drive. In fact, many students say having a car is a "major necessity" at Hollins. According to one senior, "There's just no bus system provided or sponsored by the administration. I have to say that it's really inconvenient not to have a car when a walk to the supermarket is half a mile." The student government does fund a taxi service on the weekends. "It's great," said one undergrad. "You can get $3 vouchers that take you to the mall or downtown." The area around Hollins is "a small district—a bit too provincial for my taste," one student said. Popular eating establishments in town include Macado's and the Mill Mountain Coffee House. One student complained, however, that "Roanoke just isn't really geared to students." Campus parties, particularly ones thrown by upperclassmen who are of age, reportedly are "uncool if you are under 21 because they won't let you near a keg."

Tradition, Tradition, Tradition

Many campus activities revolve around tradition at Hollins. Aside from Tinker Day, another popular event is Ring Night, which often "snowballs into a weeklong event." Juniors are put into groups and together do the seniors' bidding. After performing "idiotic gags and making morons of ourselves," the juniors are finally awarded their class rings. Another event is called Founder's Day, during which the seniors walk in their graduation gowns to the statue of the founder and place a wreath at its base. On certain occasions, members of a religious group called Freya don black robes and walk around campus in the middle of the night, advocating higher standards of morality.

Hollins students often criticize themselves for not "providing enough diversity." One student said that most people tend to think of Hollins students as "preppy, almost arrogant, and aloof," as many students come from higher socioeconomic backgrounds. One freshman said, "In my first few days, I did not see one person of color." One senior said that Hollins is particularly lacking in African-American students, and another said, "The diversity here tends to come from international students rather than from actual minority students from the U.S." Hollins is trying to change this image, however, in part by making substantive changes to the scholarship program for minority students.

Luxurious Housing, Crummy Food

At Hollins, all freshman live in one dorm comprised of singles and doubles. All of these rooms have built-in desks, dressers, closets, and mirrors, and air-conditioning and heating controls. One freshman living in a single said, "It's not huge, but I'm comfortable. The doubles, though, are huge." The most popular dorm on campus is Main Dorm (it "has two closets in each room as opposed to one"). Apartments across the street from the main campus house seniors and are considered "quite luxurious for on-campus housing." One of the less popular dorms is Randolph, which was built in the 1970s and reportedly "doesn't have the charm that all the other dorms do." As a result, some call it "the projects." After freshman year, housing is assigned through a lottery system, with preference given to upperclasswomen. Regardless of which dorm they live in, though, the women at Hollins are on the whole pleased with their accommodations.

The food, however, does not get such rave reviews. Though many students find campus food tolerable, others complain that it is "extremely distasteful." One student said, "I didn't expect the food to be so crummy or for there to be such a limited choice of food." Hollins only has one dining hall, with specific hours assigned for every meal. Some students find the hours inconvenient; dinner, for example, goes from 4:30 until 6:30. "I'm just not used to eating so early," one sophomore said. Despite these complaints, students praise the dining hall for its cleanliness and for "providing ice-cream sundaes every Friday at lunch as well as special theme nights every now and then." The Hollins meal plan is included in the cost of tuition. One freshman claimed, "Once you've paid, you can eat twice a week or 50 times a week." Also, as one student reported, "Probably any girl could come here and have a meal because they never check your ID." For other dining alternatives, students often go to the Rat, a place that serves as the Hollins student center and has food "like a McDonald's," or head over to the local, off-campus deli, Boomer's.

Campus Views

Hollins students are very enthusiastic about their surroundings. Many call the campus "absolutely gorgeous." The architecture is an elegant Southern/Georgian style with wide porches and grand white columns. As one student noted, "We're situated in a valley, and the surrounding mountains are just beautiful." Students praise the administration for constantly revamping and updating its buildings and facilities. Current renovations are being done on Moddey, the student services building, and the old library. A new library, opened in spring of 1999, is "great; it's the first literary landmark in Virginia." One student did complain that the weight room in the gym could use a little work. Another student added, "We also could use a few more male bathrooms. We do get visitors now and then." Campus security issues are also important to the administration. As one student pointed out, "Hollins is isolated and it's all girls, so security concerns are pretty high." Students are encouraged to go to officials if they feel security is lacking, and "panic boxes" are posted all over campus to connect students with campus security officers.

Active Student Body

Aside from basking in the beauty of their school, Hollins students are also extremely involved in campus life. Student Government Association is a popular activity and has multiple committees that are open to any interested students. The volunteer group SHARE is also extremely well respected by Hollins women, and coordinates the large amount of community service done by students. Many students also go into the mountains to work with various ecological programs. In addition to these groups, students participate actively in sports. The riding team consistently performs well, as do the fencing and swimming teams. Hollins recruits athletes, but any student interested in a sport can find a team to join. Even students who

are not active in organized sports make good use of the gym. As one student said "Though there's a lack of treadmills, we have a climbing wall and a really grea pool."

> **"Women who are going places start at Hollins."**

One recent area of concern on campus is that in July of 1998, Hollins changed from a college to a university. This change has reportedly come as a result of the need for more money, but has brough with it an increased selection of classes and majors, and many building upgrades However, many upperclasswomen are not pleased about the shift in status. Although Hollins already offers coed graduate programs, many fear that the undergraduate program will become coed. As one senior commented, "They've changed our bumper sticker from reading 'Women are going places' to 'People are going places.'" One freshman reported, however, "The president says that there is absolutely no way that the school is going coed, and I believe her." A sophomore explained, "Hollins is still very much a small liberal arts college dedicated to personal attention and women's education."

The students of Hollins University clearly love their campus, community, academic program, and learning from each other. Though one senior said, "I wish it weren't as hard finding guy friends and developing male relationships, but I'd definitely come here again—in a flash." —*Jeff Kaplow and Staff*

FYI
The three best things about attending Hollins are "the many traditions, the women's atmosphere (it provides a big comfort level), and the fact that all the professors know you."
The three worst things about attending Hollins are "the small course selection, the lack of diversity, and the scarce resources in the library."
The three things that every student should do before graduating from Hollins are "walk on the front quad, have a rope passed down to you, and go to the Spring Cotillion."
One thing I'd like to have known before coming here is "how limited classes at a small school are."

James Madison University

Address: Office of Admissions, Harrisonburg, VA 22807

E-mail address: gotojmu@jmu.edu

Web site URL: www.jmu.edu

Location: small city

Founded: 1908

Private or Public: public

Religious affiliation: none

Undergraduate enrollment: 13,733

Total enrollment: NA

Percent Male / Female: 47% / 53%

Percent Minority: 13.0%

Percent African-American: 5.0%

Percent Hispanic: 2.0%

Percent Asian: 4.0%

Percent in-state / out-of-state: 69% / 31%

Percent Pub HS: 95%

Fraternities: 14%

Sororities: 18%

Number of Applicants: 13,157

Percent Accepted: 59%

Percent Accepted who enroll: 38%

Entering: 2,973

Transfers: 587

Application Deadline: 15 Jan

Mean SAT: 540–630 V, 550–630 M

Middle 50% SAT range: 540–630 V, 550–630 M

Middle 50% ACT range: NA

Mean ACT: NA

3 Most popular majors: psychology, English, community health liaison

Retention: 91.0%

Graduation rate: 81.0%

Library: NA

Tuition and Fees: $3,926 in; $9,532 out

Room and Board: $5,182

On-campus housing: NA

James Madison University students cite "the warmth of the people" as a major reason for attending this charming southern college where optimism abounds. However, the benefits don't stop there. JMU's new president, Lindwood Rose, has inherited the successful legacy of his predecessor. Ronald Carrier, JMU's former president of 27 years, has recently moved on to become the school's first chancellor. He is credited with transforming what was once a teachers college for women into a regional powerhouse. Students can now proudly boast that for the fifth straight year, *U.S. News & World Report* has ranked JMU as the best regional public university in the South. The campus has recently seen the completion of new facilities such as a student recreation center, a second student center, dorms, and a premier College of Integrated Science and Technology (ISAT) academic building, with a newly completed second wing. These improvements are part of a plan to elevate JMU to a school of national prominence.

Top-Notch Academics

Students hail JMU's education as "top-notch" and "always getting better." The new general education program launched at JMU requires all undergrads to complete 40-43 credit hours of coursework in the sciences, arts, humanities, and social sciences. "Overall, JMU students have the chance to take advantage of wonderful degree programs in the traditional liberal arts, as well as the sciences, math, business, and our emerging College of Integrated Science and Technology," said one senior. Students tout that "professors are extremely approachable and are truly enthused about teaching undergrads." Teaching assistants have minimal contact with JMU students: they primarily help professors with grading. As far as class size, "some freshmen survey courses have between 100 and 150 students, but that's the exception, not the rule," noted one student. Upper level classes usually enroll 10 to 20 students. JMU's study-abroad programs in London, Paris, Florence, Salamanca are reportedly regarded as "superb." The honors program is praised for "giving you a more intimate experience." Integrated Science and Technology (ISAT) and business are considered especially innovative and challenging majors. Overall, JMU students work very hard and describe the academics as "rewarding and challenging." Students also point out that a JMU education is quite a bargain, even for out-of-state students. In fact, *Money* magazine recently listed JMU in the top 20 in its ranking of the nation's 100 best college buys.

Well-Rounded Students

Activism and community service are alive and well at JMU. Instead of relaxing during Thanksgiving, winter, or spring break several JMU students volunteer to travel to such places as Appalachia to conduct health surveys, New Orleans to work at an AIDS hospice, and Uganda to build houses. Community Service Learning (CSL) is a popular organization that provides students with opportunities to get involved in the local community. Students at JMU have more than 200 clubs and organizations to choose from. For those interested in politics, both Democrats and Republicans have active organizations on campus. The Marching Royal Dukes, "one of the best college marching bands," has performed across the country, and the Madisonians is a show choir of some repute. Students can get involved with WXJM, the campus radio, or write for *The Breeze*, the main campus newspaper. Striking a balance between their schoolwork and extensive extracurricular involvement forces JMU students to become "time-management gurus," according to one student.

Social Alternatives

Although the Greek system has a presence on campus, there is little pressure to rush. As one student noted, "the Greek scene is big but only to those in it." Greek life is just one of many social alternatives at JMU. "JMU is the type of school where anyone can have fun." Popular nightspots for upperclassmen include Dave's Taverna, BW3's, The Main Street Bar & Grill, and The Biltmore. "There are an abundance of places to go out to eat, drink, and socialize," said one junior. Aside from Greek Row (which more and more fraternities are starting to leave in favor of off campus housing) and the bar scene, partying takes place at off-campus houses and apartment complexes. Students describe the alcohol policies of the administration as strict and getting worse.

According to students "there are many alternatives to drinking," including plays, concerts, musical performances, speakers, and coffeehouses. JMU has its own on-campus movie theater offering movies almost every day of the week. Students are able to see fairly recent and popular movies for free on Sundays or only $2 on all other nights. The University Program Board (UPB) also sponsors rock concerts and other live performances as part of its plan to encourage nonalcoholic activities. Recent shows have included the Dave Matthews Band, Spike Lee, Third Eye Blind, Cracker, and Everything, the now famous musical group composed of JMU alumni.

Excellent Student Facilities

In the fall of 1996, JMU completed construction of an $18.5 million recreation center, UREC, lauded by students as "state of the art." It contains basketball courts, an indoor soccer rink, a large upscale weight room, an indoor rock-climbing wall, aerobics rooms, pool, saunas, Jacuzzi, and much more. Students describe UREC as the "mecca of wellness." The UREC Adventure program organizes outdoor trips almost every weekend. "It's a great opportunity to get off campus to hike, climb, spelunk, camp, canoe, and raft adventure!" said one senior. UREC also houses the wide variety of intramurals and club sports offered at JMU.

Sports, although not all-consuming, are an important part of life at JMU. Over 500 students represent JMU in 13 men's and 15 women's varsity teams. Football games are pretty well attended as both sporting and social events. Basketball is well supported, especially by the spirited members of the Zoo Cage. Soccer, field hockey and lacrosse are also becoming more popular due to the teams' recent successes and national rankings.

Luckily for JMU students, most of the dorms come with amenities such as computer labs, Internet access and free cable. Freshmen are required to live on campus and many are housed in an area called the Village. Rooms in the village are organized in suites that contain three doubles which students say they like because they get to know their suitemates well. The drawback is that students don't meet as many people as they would if they lived on a traditional hall. Upperclassmen have a number of housing options. Some participate in the housing lottery to remain on campus. Others are lured off campus by the relatively inexpensive and high-quality housing options. Many sophomores and juniors live in the newly constructed Chesapeake and Potomac Halls, considered the nicest dorms on campus.

One of JMU's most successful residential experiments has been Chandler Hall, a coed dorm that encourages a close relationship between faculty and students. Chandler students host guest speakers and have breakfast with professors.

Better Than Home Cooking

Students at JMU have over ten dining options to choose from. D-Hall (Gibbons) is the main dining hall and offers an all-you-can-eat buffet with a vast array of main dishes ranging from Italian to self-serve stir-fry to vegetarian. Students yearning for steak can dine at the Madison Grill, a small on-campus restaurant. Those looking for good fast food with a great social atmosphere can visit PC Dukes. Mrs. Green's is popular for lunch; it serves homemade breads, fresh hot soups, specialty salads, and other light meals. Ideal for busy students, Let's Go! is a convenient takeout place, offering great food ranging from Belgian waffles for breakfast to Mexican food for dinner. Lakeside Express is popular among students with cravings for some late-night munchies (open until 1 A.M. on weekends). One sophomore went so far as to say, "Not that my mom isn't a great cook, but when I go home, I actually find myself missing the food at JMU."

Beautiful Campus and Locale

JMU is situated in Harrisonburg, also known as the Burg, which some students describe as a "neat college town." However, other students "wish JMU were in a bigger city." It is nestled in the heart of the Shenandoah Valley near the Massanutten Mountains ski resort and the Shenandoah National Park. Students describe some of the natural surroundings of JMU such as Reddish Knob (a mountaintop overlook)

and the scenic Skyline Drive as "breathtaking." Students often venture into town to shop at the Valley Mall or visit some of the popular off campus hangouts including Luigi's, Spanky's, and the Artful Dodger.

JMU students give rave reviews to the appearance of their campus. The Quad, considered one of the prettiest places on campus, is a large open space surrounded by impressive bluestone buildings where students play Frisbee or sit and relax during the week. Folklore revolves around a big rock resting in the middle of the Quad, known as Kissing Rock. Before JMU turned coed in 1966, according to one student the story goes that, "when women came home from their dates, their boyfriends could not go any further than that rock and so that is where they received their good-night kiss before entering their dorm." It still remains a popular romantic hangout. The hill in front of D-Hall, which provides a view of the rest of campus, is another popular hangout. Newman Lake and the Edith Carrier Arboretum are favorite places for a peaceful stroll on campus.

> **Students describe the alcohol policies of the administration as strict and getting worse.**

Some students complain that JMU is too homogeneous and needs to do a better job recruiting minorities. Though on the whole, JMU students tend to be very well-rounded, and as one student says, "just about everyone came out of high school as the jock, musician, high-achiever, and Mr. or Miss Popularity." JMUers are overwhelmingly enthusiastic about their school. One undergrad emphatically proclaimed "I would totally pick JMU all over again. I love this place!"—*Jason Marino and Staff*

FYI
The three best things about attending JMU are "the girls, the breathtaking campus, and the overall friendly nature of the student body."
The three worst things about attending JMU are "the horrible parking shortage, overcrowding in some of the colleges, and the train that runs through the middle of campus."

The three things that every student should do before graduating JMU are "streak through the quad, swim in Newman Lake, and eat at least one meal in D-Hall drunk."
One thing I'd like to have known before coming here is "how the tricky general education requirements work."

Randolph-Macon Woman's College

Address: 2500 Rivermont Ave, Lynchburg, VA 24503-1526
Phone: 804-947-8000
E-mail address: admissions@rmwc.edu
Web site URL: www.rmwc.edu
Location: small city
Founded: 1891
Private or Public: private
Religious affiliation: Methodist
Undergraduate enrollment: 686
Total enrollment: NA
Percent Male/Female: 1%/99%
Percent Minority: 14.0%

Percent African-American: 7.0%
Percent Hispanic: 3.0%
Percent Asian: 3.0%
Percent in-state/out-of-state: 94%/6%
Percent Pub HS: 74%
Fraternities: 0%
Sororities: 0%
Number of Applicants: 634
Percent Accepted: 89%
Percent Accepted who enroll: 31%
Entering: 175
Transfers: NA
Application Deadline: rolling
Mean SAT: 607 V, 568 M

Middle 50% SAT range: 550–670 V, 510–630 M
Middle 50% ACT range: NA
Mean ACT: 25
3 Most popular majors: psychology, politics, biology
Retention: 78.0%
Graduation rate: 63.0%
Library: NA
Tuition and Fees: $17,080 in; $17,080 out
Room and Board: $7,010
On-campus housing: 100%
Financial aid, first-year: 61%

Lynchburg, Virginia is the home of Randolph Macon Woman's College, a small, private, single-sex institution. The campus, which has seen few changes since its construction, consists of majestic redbrick buildings surrounded by a redbrick wall. Inside this wall, lives a close-knit community of women who are as serious about their commitment to their school as they are about their studies.

Noses to the Grindstone

Academics at Randolph Macon are anything but easy. Students are required to take one course each in compositional English, literature, history, European culture, women's studies, Asian or African civilization, a physical science (including a lab), math, physical education, fine arts, and a foreign language. Students say the requirements are a strong selling point of the college, as they expose students to "courses that you wouldn't think of taking." Registration is done alphabetically by last name on a rotating basis per semester. Students claim that it is very rare to get shut out of a class, even for first-years. They also stress the benefits of their small school on student-faculty relations. Students consider the fact that there are no teaching assistants anywhere in the school to be a bonus as professors do all the grading and teaching themselves. Professors are described as "fantastic," and often become friends and mentors as well as instructors to their students. Although all departments are considered to be "academically strong," biology, math, and psychology are thought to be the most popular, primarily because these subjects encompass a wide variety of courses students find useful. Be warned, however—classes are not simple. Many science courses could be described as "death wish" classes by those who do not have a lot of time to spend on their work.

Thanks to such a demanding course load, students find themselves hitting the books more often than not. Lipscomb Library, a six-story building set in the middle of one of Macon's hills, is described as "adequate" for both studying and research. Although Lipscomb is not very large, the school offers its students a free interlibrary loan system, allowing them to obtain books from nearby schools. For those with some serious work to do, the Ethyl Center, with on-site tutors, computers, comfortable chairs, and solo study rooms, provides an ideal spot. For group work, the student center is a popular choice due to its central location.

Beautiful Rooms

Of course, students can also study in their spacious dorm rooms. While off-campus living is prohibited to those under 25, unmarried, or not living at home in Lynchburg, there are no complaints about the rooming alternatives. Room options comprise everything from singles to suites, and the rooms generally are large, carpeted, with ample windows and closet space. One student remarked, "Believe it or not, it's humongous, and bigger than my room at home!" Male visitors are allowed in the dorms until midnight Mondays through Thursdays, and allowed to stay overnight on weekends. The dorms also have TV lounges and old-fashioned "date parlors" that are used mostly for studying. The worst thing anyone reported about dorms were that they did not have elevators.

They Have Fun, Too . . .

When they are not busy studying or going to meetings for their extracurricular activities, Randolph Macon women go to coffeehouses and cafes in town, rent movies, or go to school-sponsored activities such as lectures. On the weekends, students make time for low-key partying, go to local bars, or visit nearby campuses such as Hampden-Sydney. There is no need for a car at Randolph Macon, and although the town is described as "boring" by some, there are plenty of on-campus activities to choose from. Favorite events include Tacky Party, where everyone "dresses up real tacky and plays seventies music," in November, and the Senior Dinner, a formal weekend that includes a cocktail and casino night.

Students are very active in extracurricular activities, which range from sports to writing for the school newspaper the *Sundial*, or the literary magazine *Hail! Muse*, to community service projects such as BIONIC, which stands for Believe It or Not I Care. MAC, Macon Activities Counsel, arranges the school's social activities. A recently added rugby team has proven popular among students. The Black Women's Alliance both provides support for African-American students as well as sponsors dances and other social events. The organization Bridges provides support for gay students on campus. Randolph Macon women are also fairly politically active, and the campus chapters of the Young Democrats and Republicans enjoy a large degree of student participation. The new weight-training center, an Olympic-size pool, refurbished playing fields, and tennis and basketball courts provide ample space for the Randolph Macon Wildcats to play, and those not involved in organized sports to keep in shape.

Spoiled Rotten

As the meal plan is included in the tuition, there are no real options, but students have few complaints about the food. "The food is really good," said one student. "We get spoiled rotten." The one main dining hall has both a hot food line and "stations" where the staff cooks food to students' specifications. Vegetarians can order meals without meat. The Skellar, a student-run snack bar, provides an on-campus alternative to the dining hall. On the weekends, many students go out to eat at a variety of restaurants ranging from fast-food to Meriwhethers-Godsy, a restaurant for special occasions, run by a Macon alum.

Evens v. Odds and Other Traditions

Tradition holds a very important place at Randolph Macon. The campus is filled with gardens and gazebos, and on beautiful days, students enjoy hanging out on front campus or in the Dell, an open-air amphitheater. There are no sororities, but some students join secret societies.

There is a traditional class rivalry between "evens and odds," those whose classes end in even or odd years, which involves practical jokes and spray-painting slogans around campus. Randolph Macon women are intensely proud of their school, and report feeling "overwhelmed by school spirit." One student reported that those who do not like it transfer out, leaving a cohesive group. Another student bragged about her dorm: "It's a great community—we all get along really well. It's like having 65 sisters!" The school's small size also fosters interaction between the faculty and students. As classes are rarely bigger than 20 or 30 students, and can be as small as one, professors get to know their pupils well, even too well, for the less studious: "Many professors eat at the dining hall, so you don't want to skip class and see them there," reported one undergrad.

> **Randolph Macon Woman's College is not for everyone: it is single-sex, small, and highly challenging.**

For some, however, the small size and relative isolation of the campus can be a drawback. There is not much to do in Lynchburg in terms of entertainment, especially for those used to big cities. While the school attracts students from all over the globe, Randolph Macon is still not as diverse as some might like it. One student complained the student body as a whole was "lacking certain aspects of American background. We are mostly white Christians from well-to-do families—Land's End, Eddie Bauer, and J. Crew kids."

A Warm Community

Randolph Macon Woman's College is not for everyone: it is single-sex, small, and highly challenging. Yet, for those who choose to attend, there is a lot to be gained from its selective atmosphere. Students have the opportunity to study abroad, as many do, during their junior year. The college also provides its students with a variety of popular internship programs. Undergrads even have the option to design their own major, for a more personalized program of study. They also cannot say enough about the pride and love they have for their school. Traditionally, RMWC has been like a second home for many students, and as with all Macon traditions, they want to keep it that way.—*Ann Zeidner and Staff*

FYI
The three best things about attending RMWC are "the personal attention, the camaraderie, and the even v. odd pranks."
The three worst things about attending RMWC are "the academic rigor, the absence of a male presence in the classroom, and the lack of diversity."
The three things that every student should do before graduating from RMWC are "go to Tacky Party, order from the J. Crew catalog, and make friends with a professor."
One thing I'd like to have known before coming here is "how much I like having men around."

Sweet Briar University

Address: P.O. Box B, Sweet Briar, VA 24595
Phone: 804-381-6142
E-mail address: admissions@sbc.edu
Web site URL: www.admissions.sbc.edu
Location: rural
Founded: 1901
Private or Public: private
Religious affiliation: none
Undergraduate enrollment: 710
Total enrollment: 710
Percent Male / Female: 3% / 97%
Percent Minority: 11.0%

Percent African-American: 4.0%
Percent Hispanic: 4.0%
Percent Asian: 2.0%
Percent in-state / out-of-state: 39% / 61%
Percent Pub HS: 67%
Fraternities: 0%
Sororities: 0%
Number of Applicants: 499
Percent Accepted: 89%
Percent Accepted who enroll: 38%
Entering: 188
Transfers: 18
Application Deadline: 15 Feb
Mean SAT: 580 V, 530 M

Middle 50% SAT range: 520–620 V, 470–580 M
Middle 50% ACT range: 23–27
Mean ACT: 24
3 Most popular majors: psychology, government, English
Retention: 80.0%
Graduation rate: 67.0%
Library: 474,818 volumes
Tuition and Fees: $16,585 in; $16,585 out
Room and Board: $6,715
On-campus housing: 100%
Financial aid, first-year: 93%

Sitting tranquil at the foothills of the South Ridge Mountains in Virginia, Sweet Briar College feels quaint with its old-Georgian style buildings and small town, rural setting. Rich with traditions established since its inception in 1901, Sweet Briar is also a place where "things are happening," as one student said, bringing to light the dynamic student body, the involved faculty, and the energetic environment. "You can do what you want here." Most Sweet Briar students agree that the intimate environment, the professors, and the highly motivated women make the school a tremendous learning experience and four remarkable years.

Strong Academics

As a liberal arts school, SWC emphasizes learning in a variety of disciplines with basic distribution requirements in addition to the requirements of your major. There is a core of courses in a variety of departments one must take to graduate. A student must take one course each in art and literature, non-Western study, social science, history, English, physical education, an oral- and writing-intensive course, as well as quantitative reasoning. Other requirements include foreign language and community service. "I didn't find the required classes to be a problem at all," said one student. "There are not too many requirements and they are pretty flexible." For a small college, (the entering freshman class is around 160 students) Sweet Briar offers a variety of very strong departments. A student can choose from thirty-four majors or you can construct your own major, which "is really easy to do." Being the most popular major, biology has a tremendous faculty and boasts a new wing of Guion, the science building, which houses equipment capable of chromatographic and electrophoretic analyses among other things. Another popular major is government. "After taking the prerequisites I am now doing independent work on governmental urban development with a professor," said one government major. Psychology and teaching certification are also well-liked.

Another aspect of Sweet Briar academics is the honors program. It offers a variety of honors seminars of all disciplines, which are team-taught by the top scholars in the field. In the spring of your junior year you have the opportunity to work closely with a faculty member and write an honors thesis over the course of three semesters, on a topic of your choice. Sweet Briar also offers cross-enrollment programs with the Seven-College Exchange program, a Dual-Degree Engineering Program with Columbia and Washing- ton University in St. Louis, and strong junior year abroad programs.

Amazing Professors

"Professors really care about teaching you something. And after the semester is over they still remember you and are genuinely interested in what you are doing. I'm still friends with many of my professors from freshman year," said one senior. Living near or on campus, the faculty at Sweet Briar makes the academic environment what it is, since there are no teaching assistants. With introductory classes averaging around 25, close interaction with professors begins freshman year. "They learn your name and are always accessible. They really care about what they are teaching," said one English major. The administration is also well-liked by students and is very involved in enhancing the Sweet Briar experience. "Our president even teaches a class." By interacting with professors in class, through research in the lab, or in a game of basketball, "you really learn to look to them as mentors and friends, not just people you see a few days a week for an hour. That really distinguishes Sweet Briar from other schools."

Room and Board

Virtually everyone lives on campus. There is a wide variety of housing available. Most frosh women live in dorms with some quads or triples, which have bedrooms and a common room attached. Residential advisors live among frosh women, as do professional resident coordinators. Besides having assistance with living conditions, freshmen also have key leaders, upperclassmen with expertise in a certain academic department or health issues, which can help with any academic or social problems students may have. "We are basically there if freshmen have problems adjusting to college life, have questions about academic stuff at Sweet Briar, or just want to hang out with some upperclassmen," said one RA. Upperclassmen can choose to live in corridor-style dorms

or there are also houses near or on campus that are very popular for seniors. The dorm rooms and houses are the most common hangout place for students. There are parlors and recreation rooms, complete with pool tables, Ping-Pong, TVs, and stereo systems. A new student center is also in the middle of being designed. The state-of-the art facility will include student study, meeting, and lounge areas; large multipurpose rooms for student events; student services offices; college postal, mailing, and shipping facilities; a full-service copy center; book shop; a grill restaurant; and outdoor recreational areas.

"Food here is great!" says one freshman. Prothro Commons, the cafeteria, offers a great variety of food that "tends to be nongreasy." SWC students have no complaints. "And when you don't like the hot meal, that's okay because there is a full salad and sandwich bar and side dishes to choose from."

Who Goes to Sweet Briar?

"We are really motivated here," said one student. "I think most of us are pretty serious about academics." At the same time, students are "genuinely friendly and good-natured." With a low minority presence and limited socioeconomic backgrounds, the term "Suzy Sweet Briar," the nickname given to the typical student, "who drives a nice car, dresses nicely, and wears pearls," still holds some truth. However, the administration is working to change that. The diversity of the activities makes up for the homogeneity of the student population. Activities range from SWEBOP (Sweet Briar Outdoor Program) to the "Learning on the Land" archeological-wildlife orientation program for freshwomen. Sweet Briar also has a unique collection of groups called tap-clubs, which vary in selectivity, themes, and seriousness. Some include "Aint's-N-Asses (a loud, comic group), Taps-N-Toes (for dancers and those that help with dance concerts), Ear Phones (for loud people who can't sing), Sweet Tones (an a cappella group), Chung Mungs, and Tau Phi (two community service based groups)."

There are a lot of things to do on Sweet Briar's "beautiful" campus. With "bike trails out the wazoo" and horseback riding at the on-campus Equestrian Center, "one of the best in the country," and in addition to the varsity sports SBC offers, like field hockey, lacrosse, riding, soccer, swimming, tennis, and volleyball, there is no end to the opportunities for physical fitness. Students often hang out at the Bistro, a restaurant in town that often hosts bands and DJs. Another popular joint is the Briar Patch, another restaurant near campus. A coffeehouse in the Meta Glass ("Glass") Dorm is a great place for students to get a little caffeine and socialize with friends. Parties on campus tend to be small, and underage drinking is prevented, so "when you turn twenty-one it's a big deal." The administration has been trying to work with the Campus Events Organization to increase the number of events on campus. Certain events like the four dell parties, outdoor band events, and two formals through the year draw a big crowd of men and women. SWC has been able to attract many groups to campus like Richmond Ballet, Urban Bush Women, and others for SB's Babcock season. In addition, there are a variety of traditional social events throughout the year. One is the Junior Banquet, "one of the biggest nights of the year," where juniors receive their class rings. There is also a step-singing tradition in the fall and spring. "Founders' Day and Lantern Bearing are our most beautiful traditions. For Founders' Day the seniors wear their robes and ask a sophomore to walk with them to the monument. A bagpiper leads the community on the walk to the monument where we place daisies on our founders' graves. Lantern Bearing is at the end of the year. Again, the seniors wear their robes. We ask an underclassmen to bear our lantern—a basket of flowers they get for us—as we walk around the quad at night. Then lantern bearers sing sad songs to us. This tradition definitely produces the most tears," a senior said.

> **"Suzy Sweet Briar," the nickname given to the typical student, "who drives a nice car, dresses nicely, and wears pearls," still holds some truth.**

But often Sweet Briar students must go off campus to find a social life, since the campus is "kind of dead" socially. A car is "definitely a must," as many students go to nearby colleges and universities. Some students go to Lynchburg, a twenty-minute drive away, "which has a little to be desired," or another option is the all-male Hampden-Sydney College. Nearby Washington and Lee and Virginia Military Institute are other popular destinations. "Guys are a big deal on the weekends," admits one student, "since we don't see many of them during the week."

Sweet Briar College offers tremendous academic experience in a tight-knit community of inspiring women. "This place does something to you," one student said. "When we leave here, we love Sweet Briar."

FYI
The three best things about attending Sweet Briar College are "the food, the professors, and the academics."
The three worst things about attending Sweet Briar are "being far from a city, lack of diversity, and no social life on campus."
The three things that every student should do before graduating from Sweet Briar are "get to know a professor, find a boyfriend nearby so you don't have to scramble for stuff to do on the weekends, and bear a lantern."
One thing I'd like to have known before coming here is "how homogenous this place is."

University of Richmond

Address: Office of Admission, University of Richmond; Richmond, VA 23173
Phone: 800-700-1662
E-mail address: NA
Web site URL: www.richmond.edu
Location: suburban
Founded: 1830
Private or Public: private
Religious affiliation: none
Undergraduate enrollment: 3,034
Total enrollment: 3,777
Percent Male/Female: 50%/50%
Percent Minority: 9.0%

Percent African-American: 5.0%
Percent Hispanic: 2.0%
Percent Asian: 2.0%
Percent in-state/out-of-state: 17%/83%
Percent Pub HS: 70%
Fraternities: 29%
Sororities: 50%
Number of Applicants: 6,234
Percent Accepted: 44%
Percent Accepted who enroll: 32%
Entering: 886
Transfers: 30
Application Deadline: 15 Jan
Mean SAT: NA

Middle 50% SAT range: 600–680 V, 620–690 M
Middle 50% ACT range: 27–30
Mean ACT: NA
3 Most popular majors: business, biology, political science
Retention: 92.0%
Graduation rate: 83.0%
Library: 1,068,000 volumes
Tuition and Fees: $20,140 in; $20,140 out
Room and Board: $4,530
On-campus housing: 99%
Financial aid, first-year: 34%

"Country club" is how one student described the University of Richmond. According to a freshman, Richmond is "a very trendy school where most people are generically prep." In the Richmond fashion world, J. Crew, Gap, and Abercrombie & Fitch all reign supreme. Nevertheless, the well-dressed Spiders of the University of Richmond follow rigorous academic schedules and profit from a rich social life.

Strong Academics

Academically, students are encouraged to receive a broad-based education through required classes in various disciplines. Students must take classes in science, English, symbolic reasoning (which can be satisfied by calculus), fine arts, and must demonstrate proficiency in a foreign language. In addition, CORE, a class that entails a lot of different readings from all over the world, is required, as is Wellness, a course in health. These classes can usually be completed by second semester of sophomore year, after which students devote their schedules to their majors. One sophomore said that some of the courses "are ridiculous because I already did the work in AP classes." The general opinion, though, as another student described, is

that "they're pretty beneficial. By forcing you to take a broad spectrum, you find out what you're interested in." While most students choose traditional concentrations in the arts and sciences, Richmond also boasts a strong business school, as well as the only program in the nation offering a degree in leadership studies. Although there are differing opinions regarding easy majors, all students said that science classes are the toughest. The typical response to biology majors is, as one student said, "I'm so sorry."

Whether the classes are easy or tough, though, class size is extremely small. Most classes enroll 20 to 25 people, giving students close contact with their professors. One junior said, "I think the professors are very open and ready to give you all the help you need. It differs from just being a number." Another junior said, "The professors really care about their students." Undergrads rarely have contact with TAs except in lab settings or for drill sessions in the introductory languages. Students have few negative comments about their classes, although one student did not like the attendance policies. "You can only miss three, otherwise they start taking a letter grade off." Another student simply said the worst thing about Richmond academics was "the 8:15 classes." As for the workload, one student said, "It's hard!" Academics at Richmond are strong and as one junior put it, "You get out of it what you put into it."

Social Options

When the Spiders aren't working on the weekend, they can be found engaging in the lively social atmosphere of the school. Washington, D.C., and the beach are both a little more than an hour away from campus, although most students choose to stay nearby for entertainment purposes. For those determined to leave campus, Richmond "has a lot for the arts, restaurants all around, bars, and the James River," said one student. Social life on campus, however, is by far the most popular option. Greek life is very strong at Richmond; students estimate that at least half of the student body rushes. However, non-Greeks are always welcome at parties on the weekend, so it is definitely not a necessity to join. Other than Greek parties, Richmond students have the option to go to movies shown every Thursday through Sunday, to hear guest lecturers (including a recent visit by director Spike Lee), or to concerts, all organized by the Campus Activities Board (CAB). Alcohol has a definite presence and while the administration "doesn't want anything to get out of hand, if no one is getting hurt, then they look the other way," reported one undergrad.

Country Club Kids, Country Club Campus

With regards to the student body, the general consensus is that the typical student "is really rich, has more money than common sense; the kid that Mommy and Daddy gave a credit card to before coming to Richmond." As mentioned previously, style plays an important role at Richmond, where "girls always wear black pants and no one wears sweats." Richmond students universally complain about the lack of diversity. A freshman said that Richmond "breeds naivete. Some students that come here have never seen a person of color and they think 10 percent minority is big. I would like to see more awareness of other races." With regards to diversity, one junior did say that

"it's one of the things the university is trying to change."

The University of Richmond's campus is unanimously described as "gorgeous." As one junior described it, "there are flowers everywhere, it's very well kept by the physical plant workers, and the architecture is amazing." Another student went so far as to describe the campus as the main reason why students come to Richmond. In the middle of campus is a large lake that separates the two halves of the campus. Over the lake sits Commons, a student union building that ranges in function from housing campus organizations to hosting karaoke nights in its restaurant. A gazebo also sits on the lake; legend has it that whomever you kiss in the gazebo will be your future spouse. The only way to avoid this fate is "to be thrown over the bridge into the water," said one junior. Aside from being happy with the physical appearance of the campus, Richmond students are also pleased with the security system. One junior said that "you always see plenty of policemen and there is a shuttle for students after 7 o'clock until 2 or 3 in the morning." In addition, dorms have card-only access, meaning only people affiliated with the university can come and go freely. According to one student, "The school is set off in suburban Richmond and is very secure. Everyone feels safe walking around."

The Coordinate System

The physical formation of the campus lends itself well to the living situation at Richmond, which is rather unique, with each half of the campus playing host to one of two residential colleges. The Coordinate system, as it is called, separates the campus so that men belong to Richmond College, while women make up Westhampton College. This separation provides for two separate student governments and judicial boards, allowing students of both genders to participate actively in the life of the university. Generally, students like the system and find that it is perhaps the most defining characteristic of their school. A freshman in Richmond College said, "I am a fan of it. An all-guy dorm means I can walk around in my boxers if I want. Plus, I would be too easily distracted if girls were in my dorm or on this side of campus." Another junior said, "I'm not an advocate for or against it, but it creates an atmosphere where a lot more studying gets done." For students who do not enjoy the system as much, there is little chance that there will be any changes. According to one sophomore, "Alums give us a lot money to keep the system in place, so we're stuck with it no matter what."

Almost all students decide to live on campus as part of the coordinate system. Very few students live off campus, even though it is slightly cheaper to do so. Freshmen can expect their rooms to be "the size of what's in it. You could get anything from a palace to something just adequate." For the most part, all dorms have air-conditioning, although one sophomore said that "AC is kind of a trade-off, because the bigger rooms don't have it, while the smaller ones do." After freshman year, rooms are chosen through lottery, with priority given to upperclassmen. Upperclassmen have the option of hall bathrooms or suite-style living quarters. In addition, there are two international houses, as well as substance-free dorms for both men and women. Furthermore, the university just instituted this year a smoke-free housing option. Students say that the best dorms for men are Thomas and Freeman, while for the women they are North Court and Lora Robins. At the other end of the spectrum are Marsh for men, which "smells bad and doesn't have air-conditioning," and South Court for women. Each dorm also has an RA on each floor. Though most students find them friendly and helpful, one sophomore said "they are really too strict for their own good with the girls." Despite these minor grievances, one junior said housing "is just really nice."

Students are generally pleased with the dining hall fare. One sophomore said "we're supposed to have one of the best dining halls in the country." While the food "gets repetitive, it's a lot better than some places I've been to," said another student. On campus, Richmond students can either go to the main dining hall or an alternative fast-food facility. One part of the dining hall named Harvest Place serves only vegetarian food, but students find the vegetarian options only "decent." Even though the food may be great, students are unhappy that all eating establishments on campus are closed by 8 P.M. Students can, however, use their meal card to order pizza, and the school is negotiating a deal with a local grocery store. Freshmen and sophomores must stick to the 19-meals-per-week plan, with no other options. One sophomore said, "I eat a lot in my room or off campus, so I really don't need that many meals." Students enjoy going to off-campus restaurants, the most frequented being Pasta Luna, the Strawberry Street Cafe, and Ukrops. Those more interested in a casual coffeehouse setting can go to the World Cup Cafe or the Fourth Street Cafe.

Service-Minded Students

As an outgrowth of Greek life, community service is extremely popular at Richmond. Community service is often a requirement for fraternities and sororities, although the Volunteer Action Council and Habitat for Humanity also provide such outlets for non-Greeks. Students who don't get involved with these groups might partake in a singing group, debate, or an academically related club, including computer science and physics. A number of students work on-campus jobs, which are "relatively easy to find and mostly minimum wage." Other students look for off-campus employment, although for them, a car is a necessity.

> "An all-guy dorm means I can walk around in my boxers if I want. Plus, I would be too easily distracted if girls were in my dorm or on this side of campus."

Basketball is Richmond's most followed sport. The team has consistently ranked high in its conference, which leads to a fair degree of team spirit, although one student said team spirit is "pretty low overall." Football games are also popular in the fall, but one junior said it was really "the tailgates that are a big deal." Another junior commented that "most people end up going to get drunk rather than to actually watch the game." Students interested in athletics, but not at the varsity level can participate in intramurals or club sports, popular ones including crew, soccer, Ultimate Frisbee, and equestrian. Students can also take advantage of Robins Center, the university gym, which is reportedly "really nice."

Regardless of its faults, Richmond Spiders are extremely proud and happy with their school. The small size allows for close interaction both in academics and social life. One sophomore pointed out that "it's a very close environment. I didn't expect to get to know so many people so closely." With the quaint charm of a small campus, but also the lures of nearby big cities, Richmond students prosper from a milieu that supplies all. A junior, very enthusiastic about her Richmond experience said, "I don't think I could be happier anywhere else."—*Shu-Ping Shen and Staff*

FYI

The three best things about attending the University of Richmond are "the location, the beautiful campus, and the friendly people."

The three worst things about attending the University of Richmond are "the lack of communication between students and administration, the coordinate system, and the lack of diversity."

The three things that every student should do before graduating from the University of Richmond are "go to the Pig Roast, the Ring Dance, and the Potter's Pub (but not before you're 21)."

One thing I'd like to have known before coming here is "there will be no health/sport medicine department as of next year."

University of Virginia

Address: Office of Admission, P.O. Box 400160, Charlottesville, VA 22904-4160
Phone: 804-982-3200
E-mail address: undergrad-admission@virginia.edu
Web site URL: www.virginia.edu
Location: small city
Founded: 1819
Private or Public: public
Religious affiliation: none
Undergraduate enrollment: 12,640
Total enrollment: 22,433
Percent Male/Female: 46%/54%
Percent Minority: 22.3%

Percent African-American: 10.0%
Percent Hispanic: 2.1%
Percent Asian: 9.9%
Percent in-state/out-of-state: 67%/33%
Percent Pub HS: 76%
Fraternities: 30%
Sororities: 30%
Number of Applicants: 16,461
Percent Accepted: 34%
Percent Accepted who enroll: 52%
Entering: 2,924
Transfers: 540
Application Deadline: 2 Jan
Mean SAT: 648 V, 659 M

Middle 50% SAT range: 600–700 V, 610–710 M
Middle 50% ACT range: 26–31
Mean ACT: 28
3 Most popular majors: commerce, psychology, economics
Retention: 96%
Graduation rate: 91.3%
Library: 4,588,606 volumes
Tuition and Fees: $4,130 in; $16,603 out
Room and Board: $4,589
On-campus housing: 100%
Financial aid, first-year: NA

Tradition and pride abound at the University of Virginia (UVA), founded by Thomas Jefferson in a hilly suburban area of Charlottesville. Across the board, students are vigilant about classifying themselves as "first-years," and "second-years," as opposed to freshmen or sophomores. Instead of a campus, UVA has "grounds," and you'll never hear the word "frat," always "fraternity." Other UVA traditions include Streaking the Lawn, and Burning the Rotunda.

A Greek Society

Social life at UVA primarily revolves around fraternities and sororities. With 38 Greek organizations, all lining Rugby Road, there's no denying that UVA is a major party school. First-years do report feeling pressured to go Greek, and social alternatives are pretty scarce for non-drinkers. Students who are not in a fraternity or sorority are usually non-Greek by choice, and as one student put it, "If you're looking for the Greek life, you'll find some organization here for you, since almost everyone that rushes gets into something."

Alternatives to fraternity parties include going to Newcomb Hall (Nuke 'em), which houses a dining hall, game room, movie theater, and meeting places for student organizations. Many students choose to make the 2½ hour trek up to Washington, D.C., claiming that "there's no nightlife whatsoever in Charlottesville." Each year, UVA hosts Midwinter's and Midsummer's events that attract students from many colleges. During these weekends, all the Greek organizations throw parties, and the campus turns into "an area of general mayhem," one undergrad reported.

Learning Built on Trust

UVA's academics are taken just as seriously as the social life, and students praise the quality of all the undergraduate schools, which include the College of Arts and Sciences and the schools of engineering and architecture. The education, nursing, and commerce schools, to which undergrads can apply in their third year, are also held in high regard. Students at UVA, however, report that they don't experience the sense of intense competition common at other academically challenging schools. One of the most striking features about UVA is its honor code, a code that allows professors and TAs to administer tests and quizzes under extremely casual circumstances, without fear of cheating. According to one student, "It's

so easy to cheat here, but no one does it—it's just not accepted."

When students need to hit the books, they usually go to one of two libraries specifically for them: Alderman for serious studying, and Clemons for "social study time." Graduation requirements at UVA are determined mostly by individual majors, although all students must take (or place out of, with high AP scores) a writing composition class and a historical studies or non-Western perspective course.

> **Non-Greek students must make a conscious effort to make friends early on.**

Special programs at UVA include the Echols Scholars program, which exempts qualifying students from all course or major requirements and gives scholars the option to live in special honors housing and priority on class registration, although it does not give any monetary rewards. One student remarked, however, that "Echols scholars are generally a despised bunch, since no one can get into the smaller classes because of them." The Rodman program for engineering offers special "Rodman courses," and the Jefferson Scholars Program offers full tuition, room, board, and expenses for 20 members of each entering class.

The Spirit of UVA

Extracurricular activities at UVA include volunteer programs through Madison House, student publications such as the *Cavalier Daily* and the *University Journal*, bands, choirs, theater, a cappella groups, religious organizations, and a slew of other organizations that cater to almost every type of student. Sports are a big deal at UVA, so much so that you can find guys in suits and ties and girls in dresses at the football games. Games generally attract a large percentage of the student body, and UVA pride and spirit are evident at every athletic event, many of which are accompanied by fireworks. Intramural teams sponsored by the residential colleges offer an opportunity for students to have fun and get exercise without the commitment of a varsity team.

Student Life

All freshmen live and eat together on Observatory Hill (O Hill). Upperclassmen can choose to live in language houses, residential colleges, fraternity houses, or in off-campus apartments. Hereford and Brown, the two residential colleges, house both students and faculty, have their own dining hall, and sponsor informal seminars. Both of these colleges have a selective application process, although Brown's central location makes it a more social and convenient place to live. All first-years are required to be on a meal plan, and many call the food "terrible and awful, but edible."

UVA's student body is racially diverse, but according to one student, "there is so much cliquing, especially racial cliquing,

that the diversity is pretty superficial." Other students report that groups form early, based on what you look like or how you act, and that non-Greek students must make a conscious effort to make friends early on. Many undergraduates, however, say they are happy with the friends they have made. Although UVA has a very active lesbian, gay, and bisexual coalition, attitudes toward homosexuals are mixed, and some students say there's truth to UVA's "conservative" and "traditional" reputation.

The university that Thomas Jefferson founded has evolved into a school where academic excellence, a vibrant social life, athletic distinction, and countless traditions go hand in hand. UVA offers a rich southern atmosphere, where pride and honor are stronger than ever.—*Jeff Kaplow and Staff*

FYI

The three best things about attending University of Virginia are "the rich traditions, the beautiful architecture, and the attractive student body."

The three worst things about attending University of Virginia are "the obsession with image that everyone has, not having a major city nearby, and the frat dominated social scene."

The three things that every student should do before graduating from University of Virginia are "go to Washington, D.C., at two in the morning, get dressed up and go to a football game with a date, and explore Charlottesville during the summer."

One thing I'd like to have known before coming here is "how seriously everyone takes the honor code."

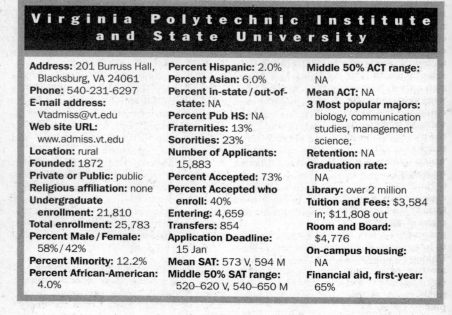

Virginia Polytechnic Institute and State University

Address: 201 Burruss Hall, Blacksburg, VA 24061
Phone: 540-231-6297
E-mail address: Vtadmiss@vt.edu
Web site URL: www.admiss.vt.edu
Location: rural
Founded: 1872
Private or Public: public
Religious affiliation: none
Undergraduate enrollment: 21,810
Total enrollment: 25,783
Percent Male/Female: 58%/42%
Percent Minority: 12.2%
Percent African-American: 4.0%

Percent Hispanic: 2.0%
Percent Asian: 6.0%
Percent in-state/out-of-state: NA
Percent Pub HS: NA
Fraternities: 13%
Sororities: 23%
Number of Applicants: 15,883
Percent Accepted: 73%
Percent Accepted who enroll: 40%
Entering: 4,659
Transfers: 854
Application Deadline: 15 Jan
Mean SAT: 573 V, 594 M
Middle 50% SAT range: 520–620 V, 540–650 M

Middle 50% ACT range: NA
Mean ACT: NA
3 Most popular majors: biology, communication studies, management science,
Retention: NA
Graduation rate: NA
Library: over 2 million
Tuition and Fees: $3,584 in; $11,808 out
Room and Board: $4,776
On-campus housing: NA
Financial aid, first-year: 65%

When the name of the school says Virginia Polytechnic, they aren't kidding about the "poly." It is not often that you find a school at which students agree that the best programs are as dissimilar as architecture and engineering. The eight colleges that make up Virginia Tech attract a wide variety of preprofessional students with diverse interests.

Eight Plus One

By the time they graduate, Hokies (as students at Virginia Tech call themselves, in reference to their giant, purple turkey mascot) must enroll in one of the eight colleges: Agriculture and Life Sciences; Architecture and Urban Studies; Arts and Sciences; Business; Engineering; Forestry and Wildlife Resources; Human Resources and Education; and Veterinary Medicine. While many students apply to the college of their choice from the beginning, many others start out in a program called University Studies, which provides students with an administrative division without forcing them to chose a college until after sophomore year. Students say that it is also not difficult to change colleges, as

long as your grades are good. Nonetheless, students caution that it's a good idea to know what you want to study because between distribution requirements (which vary within each college) and the requirements of each major, there isn't a whole lot of room for experimentation or electives. "You may have a few extra credits now and then," said one student. The business school has fewer requirements and is therefore considered easier by many undergrads.

Students report that preprofessionals make up a majority of the honors program. Based on high school grades and test scores, prefrosh are invited to apply for the program, which gives them access to small, honors-only colloquia and priority for other classes. Once they are in the program, Hokies must maintain a 3.5 GPA. Even if an applicant's high school grades aren't strong enough to get into the program at the time of matriculation to the university, anyone in the school who achieves a 3.5 is invited to apply, regardless of year.

Although most of the student body is technical-minded, students say there is room at the school for nontechnical majors. Each of the schools' requirements includes humanities classes, such as freshman English. "I've known quite a few psychology and humanities majors. The curriculum is quite diverse; it's not just technical," said one sophomore computer science major. The difficulty of classes also varies. "Some [majors] have bigger workloads than others," one student said, citing psychology and health and food services as particularly easy majors. Among the more popular gut classes is Introduction to Film. "You just go twice a week and watch movies. It's pretty slick," said one undergrad.

Students report that some elective classes can be difficult to get into, although they are quick to qualify that if a class is required for your major, you're guaranteed a spot. Advanced classes tend to have about 30 students, although some Hokies complain that many intro classes are too large, sometimes running up to 600 students. "You can usually expect them to be at least 300 people," complained one junior.

Intramurals, Graffiti Parties, and Greeks

When Hokies stop working, alcohol often comes into play, students say. "There's not much to do here if you don't drink, to be honest," said one student, who estimated that about 50 percent of campus is involved with the Greek scene. Others disputed his description of booze-soaked weekends. "Nobody forces anyone to drink," one sophomore said, explaining that even at big parties not everyone drinks. Another sophomore explained: "I expected a lot worse in terms of drinking. Once you get past your freshman year, [the dominance of frat parties] . . . turns into apartment parties for the most part."

For those who do not drink, the school is trying to increase the number of alternatives. At the beginning of the 1998–99 school year, an announcement was made by the Virginia attorney general that there would be a crackdown on campus underage drinking. In response, the administration created the Alcohol Free Programming Fund at the beginning of the 1999–2000 school year to help student groups plan dry activities. The fund has yet to see widespread use; the few student groups that know about the program have generally taken advantage of it. Students point out that "even without the new fund, every day of the week there's something going on. You can always find a concert or an organization or a movie."

For those who come from urban or suburban areas, living in tiny Blacksburg can require a bit of an adjustment. "It's definitely a change from home," said a junior from the Washington, D.C., area. Hokies occasionally travel to Roanoke to go shopping or to D.C., about three hours away, to go clubbing or see concerts. Most students at Virginia Tech have cars, although they agree that it isn't a necessity.

> **"The curriculum is quite diverse; it's not just technical."**

On the weekends, Hokies can often be found supporting their sports teams. Home football games are major occasions, particularly against rival University of Virginia. Even those not involved in "regular, full-fledged varsity sports" are often active athletes, participating in the popular intramural leagues. There are volleyball courts next to all the dorms and "there's always someone throwing a Frisbee, baseball, football, or something," said one student. In addition, students report that you can usually find a pick-up game somewhere on the Drill Field, a large courtyard around which all the residential and academic building are centered.

The First-Year Experience

All freshman Hokies must live on campus, in one of several coed-by-floor dorms; after the first year, students have the option of moving off campus. Typically, students say the number of students living on campus drops by half for sophomores, and nearly all juniors and seniors choose to live off campus. Student reviews of freshman housing are mixed, but are overwhelmingly positive about a new dorm called "The First-Year Experience," an all-freshman dorm. Other dorms include a large all-male dormitory, an athlete-only building full of suites, and a handful of upperclassman suite dorms, which have air conditioning. All the buildings are wired with an Ethernet network for Internet access.

Students have a variety of options in choosing a meal plan. Many freshmen are on a meal plan that gives them 19 meals a week at a variety of dining halls around campus. Others are on "flex," a system in which students buy points that they can use at any dining hall, including franchise restaurants in the student center, vending machines, or even the laundromat. Aside from a few horror stories about fried

chicken, Hokies are pretty happy about their food. "Virginia Tech has one of the best meal plans and dining facilities," boasted one junior.

Virginia Tech, the largest college in Virginia and a member of the state university system, is clearly a technical university. But unlike other such schools, the arts and sciences school is large enough so that there are plenty of opportunities for all types of students.—*Jacob Remes and Staff*

FYI

The three best things about attending Virginia Tech are "the laid-back atmosphere, great sports teams, and a wide range of majors."

The three worst things about attending Virginia Tech are "the boring town of Blacksburg, isolation from civilization, and having to pay to get in to a lot of parties."

The three things that every student should do before graduating from Virginia Tech are "go to the football game against UVA, go tubing on the New River, and do something outdoorsy."

One thing I'd like to have known before coming here is "how cold and windy it gets during the winters."

Washington and Lee University

Address: Lexington, VA 24450-0303
Phone: 540-463-8710
E-mail address: admissions@wlu.edu
Web site URL: www.wlu.edu
Location: rural
Founded: 1,749
Private or Public: private
Religious affiliation: none
Undergraduate enrollment: 1,729
Total enrollment: 2,096
Percent Male/Female: 56%/44%
Percent Minority: 7%
Percent African-American: 3%

Percent Hispanic: 1%
Percent Asian: 1%
Percent in-state/out-of-state: NA
Percent Pub HS: 60%
Fraternities: 82%
Sororities: 70%
Number of Applicants: 3,082
Percent Accepted: 36%
Percent Accepted who enroll: 42%
Entering: 467
Transfers: 7
Application Deadline: 1 Jan
Mean SAT: NA

Middle 50% SAT range: 630–710 V, 640–720 M
Middle 50% ACT range: 27–30
Mean ACT: NA
3 Most popular majors: economics, journalism, history
Retention: 94%
Graduation rate: 86%
Library: 503,931 volumes
Tuition and Fees: $17,105 in; NA out
Room and Board: $5,547
On-campus housing: 60%
Financial aid, first-year: NA

A re you a closet Republican? Are you an out-of-the-closet Republican? When you wake up in the morning and put on something other than a coat and tie, do you feel underdressed? If you answered yes to any of these questions,

Washington and Lee could be your dream school.

Just Say Hello

Situated in the lush foothills of the Blue Ridge Mountains, Washington and Lee

University is not your typical school. Students say the campus makes them feel transported back to a time when America was a kinder and friendlier place. Above all else, students praise W&L's honor system, under which they promise not to lie, cheat, or steal. Some students say they can leave their doors open when they are not in their rooms without worrying; all campus buildings are left unlocked; exams are unproctored. "The last time that I felt this secure must have been in my mother's womb," one undergrad said. When they are not busy in class, Washington and Lee students spend a lot of time saying hi to one another. The university's "speaking tradition" requires all students to say hello to any person that they make eye contact with while walking around campus. In the words of one student, "This isn't anyplace for a recluse."

> It is easy to surmise that General Lee would look upon this university with as much pride as current undergrads do.

There is an undeniable old-boy, bourbon-drinking, cigar-smoking Republican tradition on the Washington and Lee campus. Many students do not mind this image; in fact, many embrace it. "It is not uncommon to see students attend classes in coats and ties, or dresses," said one undergrad. The social scene reportedly is dominated by fraternities, but as one member said, "Students at other schools drink cheap beer at frat parties. Here, everyone drinks bourbon and Coke." Well over half of all W&L students go Greek, which led one student to say, "You have to be Greek to have any kind of a social life at all."

Working Damn Hard

Despite their fondness for sipping bourbon or talking about what color Jaguar they plan to buy someday, Washington and Lee students have a demanding course load. Undergrads agree that there are no "easy-A" courses to be found. "Student here work damn hard. Every A we get, we work our butts off for," said one.

Many consider the politics and history departments excellent, and students in a variety of majors have nothing but praise for their professors. "Profs here are the best. They teach all classes. They read all papers. They care, like you're one of their children," said one student. Among some of the more famous faculty members are Professors Mudd, a former anchor for CBS news, and Yoder, a Pulitzer Prize–winning journalist.

In line with the strong sense of tradition at Washington and Lee, students follow a core curriculum, which ensures that they take courses in a foreign language, English, science, and history. Students do not seem to mind studying at Washington and Lee, as they have top-notch facilities in which to learn. Leyburn Library is open 24 hours a day, and a new science center opened recently. Students also call the gym "super." The university recently spent millions of dollars refurbishing the tennis courts.

Greek Spirit

Spirit at W&L reportedly centers on the Greek system. Frats and sororities regularly compete against one another in a wide range of intramural sports. As one student said, "We have everything from shooting to water polo." In addition to intramurals, students take advantage of university-sponsored dances, especially Christmas Weekend and Mock Convention. Christmas Weekend is a week-long party with formals and a concert featuring a major performer (including such big names as Hootie and the Blowfish). The Mock Convention, in addition to being a major time for parties, is also a popular extracurricular activity. Every four years Washington and Lee holds a mock convention for the political party not in power. Students do extensive research on likely state voting trends and try to predict the candidate most likely to win each state's endorsement for the presidency. According to one student, "It's a mess of work, but all the fun we have during the convention week amply makes up for it."

Great Food

Washington and Lee undergrads love the dining hall food, which draws such comments as "great," "healthy," and "an utter joy." All freshmen eat at Evans dining hall. Upperclassmen can also eat at Evans, or at General Head Quarters (GHQ) or the co-op snack bar. Most, however, elect to eat at their fraternity or sorority house. Each house has its own team of chefs, and the food, in the words of one student, "is better than anything my mother could even hope to make." Those in search of off-campus culinary adventures often head to Palms, Spanky's, Harb's, or Lee-Hi, a 24-hour truck stop.

Not Just Resume-Padding

Washington and Lee students say they participate in as many extracurriculars as possible, not for "resume padding," but instead "to bring honor upon the university." Among the most popular activities are Mock Convention, the College Republicans (surprise, surprise), many musical groups (both vocal and instrumental), and the college's two weekly newspapers, *Ring Tum-Phi*, and the *Trident*.

The on-campus crypt of Robert E. Lee is a year-round tourist attraction. One can only imagine what this revered general would think of his namesake institution after all these years. With its tradition-laden campus, a student body tremendously respectful of these traditions, and a deep sense of honesty, it is easy to surmise that General Lee would look upon this university with as much pride as current undergrads do.—*Jeff Kaplow and Staff*

FYI

The three best things about attending Washington and Lee are "the conservative spirit, the speaking tradition, and Christmas weekend."

The three worst things about attending Washington and Lee are "you have to go Greek, drinking bourbon, and the lack of alternative, liberal viewpoints."

The three things that every student should do before graduating from Washington and Lee are "join Mock Convention, visit the crypt, and rush a frat."

One thing I'd like to have known before coming here is "how stodgy we can sometimes be."

Washington

Evergreen State College

Address: 2700 Evergreen
Parkway N.W., Olympia,
WA 98505
Phone: 360-866-6000,
x6170
E-mail address:
admissions@evergreen.
edu
Web site URL:
www.evergreen.edu
Location: small city
Founded: 1967
Private or Public: public
Religious affiliation: none
**Undergraduate
enrollment:** 3,932
Total enrollment: 4,194
Percent Male / Female:
41% / 59%

Percent Minority: 17.0%
Percent African-American:
4.0%
Percent Hispanic: 4.0%
Percent Asian: 5.0%
**Percent in-state / out-of-
state:** NA
Percent Pub HS: NA
Fraternities: NA
Sororities: NA
Number of Applicants:
1,526
Percent Accepted: 86%
**Percent Accepted who
enroll:** 86%
Entering: 462
Transfers: 835
Application Deadline:
1 Mar

Mean SAT: 588 V, 590 M
Middle 50% SAT range:
530–650 V, 480–590 M
Middle 50% ACT range:
NA
Mean ACT: NA
3 Most popular majors:
B.A. and B.S. awarded / no
majors
Retention: 65%
Graduation rate: 55%
Library: NA
Tuition and Fees: $2,757
in; $9,759 out
Room and Board: $5,136
On-campus housing:
75%
Financial aid, first-year:
44%

O pen-mindedness, liberal ideas, social consciousness, and culture of
the sixties touch every aspect of
life at Evergreen State College. Evergreen
was founded in 1971 on the unconventional idea that "Greeners" would have no
mandatory areas of study and nearly absolute academic freedom. Evergreen students choose an "area of interest" and
create their own course of study from a
wide variety of academic options. This is a
freedom these students take seriously.

Challenge Us

The academic atmosphere at Evergreen
"challenges students to challenge themselves," one undergraduate explained.
There is no grading at Evergreen; instead,
professors write evaluations of student
performance. By pinpointing areas of
strength and weakness, these evaluations
help students improve their academic
standing and learn through the process.

Some students warn that "if you're not
self-motivated, Evergreen is not the best
place for you to be." Small classes encourage student-teacher interaction, which is
evidenced by the fact that most students
call their professors by their first names.
The only requirement is a freshman core
course that teaches research, planning,
and writing by focusing on one specific
topic such as wildlife in the streams or
"modeling nature." "I really like my core
course because instead of taking a
generic chemistry course, I'm learning all
the chemistry that applies to a specific
problem. For once I feel as if I'm really applying my knowledge," said one freshman.

Evergreen divides its school year into
quarters. After the freshman core, students select programs, or areas of study
that include multiple courses running
through multiple quarters concentrating
on a particular theme. For instance, the
program "Molecule to Organism" includes

a course in organic chemistry, a course in cell biology, and a course in organismal biology; "In the Enchanted Kingdom" incorporates, among other classes, a class in Russian and Slavic folk culture and a class in the psychology of myth and legend. One junior explained, "I really feel like I come away from each program with a thorough understanding of something, not just a bunch of memorized facts that I'll forget in a few years."

The Greener Crew

Although most Greeners are Washington State residents, a considerable number come from out of state. The majority of students are Caucasian. A sizable gay and lesbian population on campus is open and supported by the rest of the student body. According to one student, "We have a whole lot of hippies here" who tend to dress in hemp and tie-dye, listen to Bob Dylan, eat organic food, and talk about Buddhism. Many discuss intellectual ideas outside of the classroom.

On weekends, "just hanging out" is popular. Students often dine out at the Corner, a student-run vegetarian cooperative that prepares food grown on Evergreen's own organic farm. Most Evergreen parties are small, private affairs, held in student rooms. There is no Greek system on campus. Super Saturday, the biggest social event of the year, showcases live music, arts and crafts, and game booths in the spring. The annual "All Freakfest Night," a 12-hour "cheesy horror film" marathon held at a local independent film theater, also attracts many students. Students say it's fairly easy to catch a ride to Olympia, Seattle, and Portland which are only an hour's drive from campus.

Students at Evergreen involve themselves heavily in extracurricular activities, even though they have a relaxed attitude about them. Free Tibet and the Washington Public Interest Research Group are two of "the many groups committed to social action." Many Greeners write for the *Cooper Point Journal* or the *Evergreen Times* newspapers. Another option is to work as a disc jockey for CHAOS, the Evergreen radio station, which plays everything from punk and industrial music to folk and contemporary jazz. Students play intramural rugby, bas-

ketball, and ultimate Frisbee, and a new varsity basketball team has drawn large crowds. However, many students argue that "sports are just here for fun."

Rainy Days

Washington's temperate rain forests engulf the Evergreen campus. "There are just so many trees here. It's gorgeous," gushed one student. Indeed, the cement buildings, which comprise most of the campus, seem to blend with the wooded surroundings. One student described the moss and algae growing on the cement buildings as "taking the landscape back to nature in a really beautiful way." The rural setting provides rock-climbing, hiking, and beach-strolling opportunities for the "very outdoor-oriented" students. This willingness to enjoy the outdoors is also attributed to the fact that most Greeners feel safe on campus.

> **Evergreen offers a nontraditional education that attracts a group of freethinking students.**

Evergreen offers students several housing alternatives: four- to six-person apartments, two-person studios, and traditional single rooms. No matter where they live, Evergreen students tend to cook for themselves and avoid the dining halls. The dorms, small apartments with living rooms and kitchens, are popular for their social atmosphere, but "it's hard to find someplace in the dorms that's quiet" to study. The "mods," or modular housing units, are set on the outskirts of campus and surrounded by thick woods. Each mod has two double bedrooms, a kitchen, a living room, a front porch, a bathroom with a bathtub, and a yard. Many living in the mods can point out the unit where Nirvana gave its first performance.

Because the buildings, including the dorms, are all located on one side of campus, students can get to all classes within five minutes. One notable feature of campus is the recreational center, open to all students, which offers activities ranging from ceramics to martial arts to yoga. The center also sports Nautilus equipment, a rock-climbing wall, a camping-gear center, saunas, racquetball courts, and an 11-lane Olympic-size pool.

Evergreen offers a nontraditional education that attracts a group of freethinking students. To get the most out of academics, students must be motivated, because "it's easy to slack off and get by. But it's ultimately up to you to learn if you want to." The independence and tolerance provided at Evergreen allow students to chart their own academic and social paths.—*Brian Abaluck and Staff*

FYI

The three best things about attending Evergreen State are "being challenged to think on your feet; emphasis on experiencial learning; and ablity to craft your own course of study through individual and group contracts."

The three worst things about attending Evergreen State are "limited number and variety of courses; Washington's pop steryotpe of a 'hippie school with no grades and lots of drugs'; and having emphases instead of majors and minors."

The three things that every student should do before graduating from Evergreen State are "experiment with all the media equipment, take only what you want to learn, and make your way into the wilderness."

One thing I'd like to have known before coming here is "that the classes offered change from year to year."

University of Puget Sound

Address: 1500 North Warner, Tacoma, WA 98416	**Percent African-American:** 2.0%	**Middle 50% SAT range:** 570–670 V, 580–660 M
Phone: 253-756-3211	**Percent Hispanic:** 2.5%	**Middle 50% ACT range:** 25–29
E-mail address: admission@ups.edu	**Percent Asian:** 11.0%	**Mean ACT:** 26.8
Web site URL: www.ups.edu	**Percent in-state/out-of-state:** 29%/71%	**3 Most popular majors:** business administration, English, psychology
Location: suburban	**Percent Pub HS:** 78%	
Founded: 1888	**Fraternities:** 35%	**Retention:** 83%
Private or Public: private	**Sororities:** 31%	**Graduation rate:** 73%
Religious affiliation: none	**Number of Applicants:** 4,138	**Library:** 463,233 volumes
Undergraduate enrollment: 2,695	**Percent Accepted:** 74%	**Tuition and Fees:** $21,425 in; $21,425 out
Total enrollment: 2,973	**Percent Accepted who enroll:** 22%	**Room and Board:** $5,510
Percent Male/Female: 39%/61%	**Entering:** 684	**On-campus housing:** 95%
Percent Minority: 17.0%	**Transfers:** 109	**Financial aid, first-year:** 72%
	Application Deadline: 1 Feb	
	Mean SAT: 621 V, 620 M	

Looking for a liberal arts college with the demanding curriculum of a major university? Amid the torrential rains (and therefore beautiful, lush greenery) lies the University of Puget Sound. As a midsize liberal arts school, UPS allows for a diverse curriculum and challenging courses in a more personalized setting. Though they often take five years to get there, graduates are well prepared for handling the challenges of the real world.

"The Work Load Is Exceptional"

UPS expects quite a lot from its students, and they tend to deliver. The school requires a basic core of classes for a bachelor of arts degree. Students must take

English, a natural science, math, communications, and physical education in order to graduate, and while this basic curriculum is regarded as necessary, "many of the core classes are lectures, and if they're not in your field of interest they can become extremely dull," as one student said.

However, as a smaller school, even the lectures seem personal. UPS only enrolls about 80 people in its largest classes, regardless of their popularity. Not that this means that you will have a hard time getting the classes you want—one student pointed out that "even the classes that are already closed aren't impossible to get into. If you speak to the professor, 9 times out of 10 you'll be admitted." TAs have actually been deemed "unconstitutional" at UPS, at least for teaching classes, so you can really build a relationship with your professors, even in the first year.

For the ambitious, UPS has a highly selective honors program available for freshmen whose SAT scores and/or high school records make them eligible. This program has the same requirements as the regular core system, but the classes are taught at a faster pace and at a more in-depth level. Honors students also must live in separate housing and write a senior thesis.

For those looking for a more diverse college experience, UPS offers an extremely liberal independent study program. Students can apply to do anything from traveling abroad for a year to working in nearby Rainier National Park as a ranger. On a more practical note, for those who find the courses at UPS too challenging or expensive (as a smaller college UPS cannot offer as much financial aid as it would like), Washington has a statewide program in which you can attend any community college in the state for a year and have your credits transfer without any hassle. As one student stated, "This way you get the same credits for the classes you don't care about, but at half the difficulty and one-fifth the cost."

As students become more entrenched in their major, the work load becomes heavier—but it's all worth it. Small classes (typically 14 students) allow for a very personal educational experience. "Stay in touch with your professors. The relationship with them becomes extremely intense due to small class sizes, and they can be of great value years after graduating," advised one senior.

Proximity to Seattle, Vancouver, Portland

"The beauty of Tacoma is its centralized geographic location to all the happenings in the northwest." Seattle is 40 minutes north, Portland is a 2 hour drive, Vancouver is 3 and a half hours, the coast is 3 hours, and Mt. Rainier National Park is a mere hour and a half away. Seattle offers everything a student could want in terms of urban life, sports, and cultural events, and if it can't be found there, any of the other cities will do.

> TAs have actually been deemed "unconstitutional" at UPS, at least for teaching classes, so you can really build a relationship with your professors, even in the first year.

This is not to say that everyone leaves Tacoma to have a good time. The small city offers several independent theaters, Narrows Alley—the local bowling center—and fantastic coffee shops like Grounds for Coffee and Shakabra. Of course, the college population has spawned many downtown bars and nightclubs, not to mention an underground party scene. According to one student, "some of the best DJs in the northwest reside here in Tacoma."

While the campus is dry, drinking "can still be fairly popular around the school." Students frequent several local bars, namely Magoo's, Engine House 9, Roselli's, and the Ram Brewery. But chemical consumption is neither expected nor pressured, and there is even a substance-free freshman dorm. Other drugs that have recently become extremely prevalent in the Northwest, such as speed and heroin, are not a problem on the UPS campus. The only substance in abundance seems to be marijuana, and "students are able to locate some of the finest bud in the world within a week of first arriving to campus." Despite this, students reiterate that UPS is a low-pressure environment, and the rumors that "mushrooms which grow on campus can be brewed into a tea for hallucinatory madness" are unfounded.

Greek Life

Fraternities and sororities play a vital role in the social life at UPS. They throw some of the coolest parties throughout the year. However, unlike those at many colleges, the UPS frats are not exclusive, nor does a majority of the student body participate. This means pretty much anyone can go to a frat party and be welcomed. Each frat throws its own formals throughout the year, but as one student stated, "the hottest party of the year is a seven-house block party called The Rail thrown every Halloween weekend." This party is open to anyone and everyone.

To counteract the frat scene, the student government throws many dances and events. One of the highlights of the year is the Xmas Mistletoast and homecoming (which includes a singing contest and a prefootball game parade). Homecoming weekend also features musical acts, which in the past have included the Stone Temple Pilots, Sky Cries Mary, and Chuck Mangione.

The Great Outdoors

If the urban scene is not your thing, the Pacific Northwest has much, much more to offer. Students often bike, hike, and walk around UPS. The Residents of the Outhouse organize backpacking trips almost every weekend. Further, the Sailing Club is extremely popular. Along with all this are ski areas, a national park, and even hunting. The weather does not hinder UPS students. As one student joked, "many students come out of March wondering what the hell that bright ball of light coming out of the sky is since we haven't seen the sun for a while."

UPS students also participate in choir, band, the radio station, and theater. While the sports teams are not necessarily as respected as they are at major universities, the women's volleyball team has a good record, and intramurals are a popular extracurricular. Popular IMs are volleyball and crew. If organized sports seem like too much effort, the Pamplin Fitness Center, built in 1994, is considered a "fantastic place to burn calories, socialize, and destress."

But Where Do I Live?

During the first year at UPS students live in campus dorms, which are considered cramped. Most of the dorms are coed; however, an all women's floor is available. After freshman year, the upperclassmen decide whether to stay in dorms or to move into a university-owned residence (these house between 5 and 6 people, whom you choose). Theme houses are popular, and range from the foreign language house to the sailing house, and even the "Outhouse" for nature enthusiasts. If you cannot find a theme house that suits your needs, it is possible to petition the school and start a new one.

While students tend to be open-minded and liberal, the student body does not necessarily reflect that. As one student put it, "A lack of diversity has been a problem for some time at this school and has been addressed, but not really solved." The student body tends to be Caucasian and middle-class, although the administration claims to be making efforts to recruit minority students from more diverse backgrounds.

Due to the lack of diversity, "interracial dating is rare," but not frowned upon. Dating does occur, or as one student put it, "Not too many are celibate here, so yeah, they date." And according to some, the campus is getting better looking with each new crop of freshmen. Homosexuality is accepted, and couples of all types are seen around campus. As one student commented, there is "lots of sex on all fronts."

UPS is a challenging liberal arts school where students work to their potential, but do not forget to unwind. Students consider UPS a strong foundation for the world beyond.—*Kyla Dahlin*

FYI
The three best things about attending UPS are "the personal relationships with your professors, the ability for any individual to make a difference on campus, and the beauty of the campus itself."
The three worst things about attending UPS are "the weather, the cost, and the small size."

The three things that every student should do before graduating from UPS are "to work, to work some more, and then relax!"

One thing I'd like to have known before coming here is "that they expect a lot from you academically, and they don't like to keep around loafers."

University of Washington

Address: 320 Schmitz Box 355840, Seattle, WA 98195-5840
Phone: 206-543-9686
E-mail address: adkuwadm@u.washington.edu
Web site URL: www.washington.edu
Location: urban
Founded: 1861
Private or Public: public
Religious affiliation: none
Undergraduate enrollment: 25,273
Total enrollment: 35,367
Percent Male/Female: 48%/52%
Percent Minority: 32.0%

Percent African-American: 3.0%
Percent Hispanic: 4.0%
Percent Asian: 23.0%
Percent in-state/out-of-state: 89%/11%
Percent Pub HS: NA
Fraternities: NA
Sororities: NA
Number of Applicants: 13,330
Percent Accepted: 60%
Percent Accepted who enroll: 48%
Entering: 3,839
Transfers: 2,900
Application Deadline: 15 Jan
Mean SAT: NA

Middle 50% SAT range: 500–630 V, 520–650 M
Middle 50% ACT range: NA
Mean ACT: NA
3 Most popular majors: business, biology, political science
Retention: 91%
Graduation rate: 69%
Library: 5,100,000 volumes
Tuition and Fees: $3,486 in; $11,508 out
Room and Board: $4,779
On-campus housing: NA
Financial aid, first-year: 36%

Founded in 1861, the University of Washington claimed only a single building on a ten-acre hill where the faculty—one professor—taught Latin, Greek, English, history, algebra, and physiology. Such humble beginnings would hardly be expected from today's dynamic university, affectionately nicknamed "U-Dub," where strong athletics and academics have given it a national reputation.

Science Bias?

As one of the largest research institutions in the country, U-Dub's specialization lies in the sciences. Students claim that the hardest but best majors are computer science, engineering sciences, biochemistry, and the natural sciences—chemistry, cellular and molecular biology, and physics. Thanks to its state-of-the-art facilities, cutting-edge faculty, and great internship opportunities, degrees in the sciences "are totally worth all the hard work." One student lamented the work that his biochemistry major required, ob-

serving that the school's average GPA for humanities was 3.1 while the average GPA for sciences was 2.8. The difference, he claimed, "speaks for itself." While students unanimously agreed that sciences are the toughest and most demanding majors, there was disagreement about the school's slacker majors. Some students contended that "psychology is a joke," and others labeled English, art, and political science courses as "wimp classes."

Despite this obvious division between the liberal arts and the sciences, U-Dub requires that students in the School of Arts and Sciences take courses in three areas: social sciences, humanities, and natural sciences. Easy classes include Psychology 101 and Music 185. These popular classes enroll nearly 800 students, while most introductory level classes enroll 300. Some students admit that they were fooled into thinking "intro equals easy." Instead, some of the classes are taught by professors who "assign homework as if you're taking only that class." But because "professors are really interested in students' learning," the workload is not overwhelmingly difficult. "After all, I've survived so far," explained one senior.

Tri-Campus System

The university operates on a three-campus system, with the main campus in Seattle and two others in Bothell and Tacoma, which have mainly evening and weekend programs. Students praise their campus as being "beautiful!" U-Dub's lakeside location provides students not only with a great view, but also with many opportunities to sail, canoe, kayak, or windsurf. The Cascade and Olympic mountains draw many students, from skiers to backpackers and other nature lovers. The campus is full of joggers and cyclists at all hours of the day, thanks to the "exceptionally safe" environment. The only complaint about the Seattle campus was the city's "nine month gray spell" and the rainy winters.

> "I had the freshman 15 . . .
> except it was negative"

The great campus has attracted an increasing number of out-of-staters, causing many undergrads to opt for campus housing. Students can opt for the "study dorm," the "party dorm," the "single-room dorm," or even the "all-nighter dorm." Most of these dorms are coed, and all are modern and comfortable: common rooms have couches and grand pianos, and computer and weight room facilities are state-of-the-art. Stylistically, the dorms are "small and concrete," claimed one student. Some students, while grateful that the rooms are furnished, wished that "there was just a little more space." The campus, however is unquestionably spacious. The size of the campus makes a bicycle a treasure, but students warn that dodging pedestrians on the sidewalk is frustrating. For those with a car, parking is expensive, and spaces in the lots are at a premium.

The most popular off-campus housing is in the nearby "U District," where rents are low and food is cheap on "the Ave" (First Avenue). Students with purple hair "flip-flopping about," make the U District, also nicknamed the "student ghetto," what one sophomore termed "the hangout for the most diverse people in the world."

Many students frequent the U District to get relatively edible food, as the school cafeterias provide only "limited choices, unpleasant service, stale ingredients, and small portions." One student conveyed the quality of the food by explaining, "I had the freshman 15 . . . except it was negative." Another student complained about his dining experience at U-Dub: "One time my pizza crust was uncooked, and the other time there was only one slice of pepperoni on my entire slice of pizza. Friends who work at the food service told me they save all the leftovers and dump it into every Friday's special 'soup of the day.'"

Students throw parties each week at the HUB (the Husky Union Building), but most generally agree that the best parties are on the Greek Row or the "big, upperclassmen apartments off campus." The Greek system at U-Dub is "less influential than WSU [Washington State University]," because frats and sororities are "only popular among themselves." For alternatives to the frats and the heavy drinking that tends to characterize such parties, the burgeoning city of Seattle offers a wealth of shops, restaurants, dance clubs, and coffee shops. The student government also offers free weekly movies, along with occasional dances and activities. One senior said, "I have never had trouble finding something to do."

Sport Shorts

That "the wave" supposedly was first introduced in the U-Dub stadium is an indication of the popularity of the school's sporting events. The Huskies football team commands great loyalty from the student body, thanks to this Pac-10 team's recent Rose Bowl appearance and perennial strength. Huge crowds come to cheer on the Huskies against their biggest rivals, the Washington State Cougars, in the annual Apple Cup showdown. To get tickets to any football or basketball game, students must endure a "minimum three-hour wait" in line, but the wait is worth it, "something every student should do."

Most students commit to some level of

sports: from club sports to intramural sports (which are "hugely popular") to a relaxing afternoon of Frisbee tossing. Undergraduates enjoy the campus's "incredibly large" recreational gym, the Intramural Activities Building, or IMA, which houses the headquarters for hundreds of competing intramural teams. Such sports as aikido, fly fishing, skiing, and snowboarding are also popular with students.

In addition to sports, U-Dub offers "every club imaginable." Students encourage the freshmen to get involved in student activities, as they often facilitate great friendships and sometimes, claimed one junior, "a date!" Among the many extracurricular options are the Swing Club, the Pagan Students Association, the Asian Dance club (which has 1,000 members), the Sci-Fi club, political groups, and Christian fellowships.

Undergrads, especially the science majors, dedicate a lot of time to their intense studying. Many find the Suzallo Graduate Study Reading Room the best place to go for "studying where it's dead quiet." On the opposite extreme is the Odegaard Undergraduate Library, which one student called the "loudest place I've ever tried to study." Despite their access to a dozen libraries, most students opt to hit the books in their own rooms.

The University of Washington, with its attractive Seattle location, its great athletic tradition, its solid academic programs, and its variety of activities, welcomes students from around the world. No longer is this school the little building on a ten-acre hill; it has evolved into a "fabulous university endowed with countless opportunities."—*Marti Page*

FYI

The three best things about attending University of Washington are "the awesome view of Mt. Rainier; the relaxed, no-dress-code atmosphere; and the strong computer science and medicine programs."

The three worst things about attending University of Washington are "rain—it's worst when weather gets colder, professors never remember you because classes are too big, and professors are hard to contact."

The three things that every student should do before graduating from University of Washington are "jump into Dumbeller Fountain at night during winter, have a caffeine overdose, get left at concerts in the Gorge."

One thing I'd like to have known before coming here is "this is a fun school, but definitely not a party school."

Washington State University

Address: Lighty 370,
Pullman, WA 99164-1067
Phone: 509-335-5586
E-mail address:
admiss@wsu.edu
Web site URL:
www.wsu.edu
Location: rural
Founded: 1890
Private or Public: public
Religious affiliation: none
**Undergraduate
enrollment:** 17,087
Total enrollment: 20,799
Percent Male/Female:
49%/51%
Percent Minority: 12.4%
Percent African-American:
2.4%

Percent Hispanic:
3.3%
Percent Asian: 5.0%
**Percent in-state/out-of-
state:** NA
Percent Pub HS: NA
Fraternities: 17%
Sororities: 16%
Number of Applicants:
12,030
Percent Accepted:
84%
**Percent Accepted who
enroll:** 44%
Entering: 4,487
Transfers: 1,923
Application Deadline:
rolling
Mean SAT: 526 V, 527 M

Middle 50% SAT range:
470–590 V,
470–580 M
Middle 50% ACT range:
NA
Mean ACT: NA
3 Most popular majors:
business administration,
communications, social
sciences
Retention: 83.0%
Graduation rate: 59.0%
Library: NA
Tuition and Fees: $3,662
in; $10,696 out
Room and Board: $4,618
On-campus housing: 97%
Financial aid, first-year:
40%

Students at Washington State University have a number of reasons for being there, but location isn't usually on top of the list. Washington State University is located in what one student called "the middle of nowhere." Despite the isolated environment, however, many students find their experiences at WSU to be better than they expected.

Farmer School? Not Really

Like many other land-grant universities throughout the United States, WSU emphasizes agriculture and engineering. The university is divided into nine colleges: the most popular include agriculture, arts and sciences, business, communications, and veterinary science. Students report that communications is the strongest department, ranking among the top programs in the region. No matter which college they choose, however, all undergraduates must fulfill a complicated system of core requirements that vary depending upon a student's major and entrance date to the school. Students with superior high school grades and standardized test scores can qualify for a selective honors program, but students in the regular program say they do not find the core requirements overwhelming.

Big Classes

Classes at WSU are relatively large. Introductory classes, especially those that meet the core requirements, can enroll as many as 500 students, and the norm in the other introductory courses is 100 to 200. Even advanced courses in popular colleges such as business or communications enroll 30 or 40 people. Students often want to sign up for the same classes and must wait to enroll in the ones they want, or even the ones they need. As a result, many undergrads need to take a fifth year to graduate.

The Town of Pullman

What on earth can a student do in Pullman for five years? "Drink, and drink, and drink" is a popular response. Despite its small size, Pullman has many bars and clubs—including Chaser's, Rico's, Doc's, and the Cavern—that attract students every weekend. The Washington-Idaho border is five miles away, and three miles beyond that is Moscow, Idaho, home of the University of Idaho. For the truly adventurous (and those with cars), Spokane is about 70 miles away, offering an even wider variety of nightlife.

Cracking the Whip

On campus, students report with some dismay that the administration's traditionally lenient attitude toward drinking has changed in recent years. The administration has banned kegs, limited fraternity and sorority parties, and prohibited alcoholic beverages at Greek functions. According to one junior, however, the rules are "broken all the time." Waterburst, a weekend party that used to take place before the beginning of school in the fall, was recently eliminated, and some students believe the traditional Greenstock Bash, WSU's version of Woodstock, will also be discontinued in future years. Many undergrads fear this could mark the demise of the active social life at Washington State, leaving little else to do on campus except drink.

Greeks? Gone

About one-fifth of WSU's undergraduate population belongs to a fraternity or a sorority, but with recent restrictions on alcohol, the Greeks no longer dominate the social scene. "If the Trojans had had this administration on their side," one student said, "they wouldn't have had any trouble with the Greeks." Nonetheless, the presence of more than 30 fraternities and sororities creates some pressure to rush.

For students who do not want to participate in Greek life, Washington State offers excellent dorms, which residents say are comfortable and foster a sense of unity. Of particular interest is the International House, which houses a culturally diverse group of undergrads. Some students complain, however, that food quality is a major drawback to dorm life—the food in the fraternity and sorority houses reportedly is much better.

The dorms are not the only facilities students praise at WSU. The CUB (Comption Union Building) is a favorite undergrad hangout, complete with a bowling alley, a game room, and a full-size movie theater. The three gyms are also popular, and the main one has a large new weight

room. The university's recent renovation of the Ernest Holland Library makes it one of the largest in the Pacific Northwest.

Extra! Extra! Read All About It!

While drinking and partying are the favorite pastimes, many WSU students get involved in extracurricular activities. The "fantastic" intramural sports program allows students to participate in anything from badminton to water polo. For those interested in writing, the school has such outlets as the *Daily Evergreen* newspaper. Cultural groups are also gaining popularity, and their activities are coordinated by a central governing body known as the Council of Minority Student Presidents.

> **Many undergrads take a fifth year to graduate.**

The popular Pac-10 football and basketball teams usually attract large crowds of undergrads to their games. While the basketball team has not performed well in recent years, many students feel it will fare better in the future, and might even make the NCAA tournament someday. The Cougars football team at WSU has had a winning record in recent years. Cougars especially enjoy annual sport battles against their state and Pac-10 rivals, the University of Washington Huskies, in the Apple Cup. Although WSU victories are rare in this showdown, the occasional victory "makes them all the more sweet," one sophomore said.

Though a geographically diverse student body is not one of WSU's strong points, since most students come from Washington, especially from the Spokane and Seattle areas, many undergraduates report that the university has a great deal to offer, both socially and academically, in a relatively relaxed and tranquil environment. The town of Pullman is not the most interesting college town, but students are confident that the years they spend at Washington State University will be the best four (or five or six) years of their lives.—*Melissa Chan and Staff*

FYI

The three best things about attending WSU are "everything's in walking distance, people are friendly, and the Greek system is large but not exclusive."

The three worst things about attending WSU are "that it's in the middle of nowhere, the campus is too hilly, and the area is too windy."

The three things that every student should do before graduating from WSU are "visit Cougar Country, go to Moscow, Idaho, and have one humiliating drunk experience."

One thing I'd like to have known before coming here is "how to pace yourself through everything."

Whitman College

Address: 345 Boyer Avenue, Walla Walla, WA 99362
Phone: 509-527-5176
E-mail address: admission@whitman.edu
Web site URL: www.whitman.edu
Location: small city
Founded: 1859
Private or Public: private
Religious affiliation: none
Undergraduate enrollment: 1,325
Total enrollment: 1,325
Percent Male/Female: 43%/57%
Percent Minority: 11.4%

Percent African-American: 1.0%
Percent Hispanic: 2.9%
Percent Asian: 6.5%
Percent in-state/out-of-state: NA
Percent Pub HS: NA
Fraternities: 37%
Sororities: 34%
Number of Applicants: 2,151
Percent Accepted: 50%
Percent Accepted who enroll: 34%
Entering: 368
Transfers: 21
Application Deadline: 1 Feb

Mean SAT: 656 V, 644 M
Middle 50% SAT range: 610–720 V, 600–700 M
Middle 50% ACT range: NA
Mean ACT: NA
3 Most popular majors: biology, English, politics
Retention: 91%
Graduation rate: 80%
Library: 282,540 volumes
Tuition and Fees: $21,742 in; NA out
Room and Board: $6,090
On-campus housing: 99%
Financial aid, first-year: 86%

With a mascot like the Fighting Missionaries, you know you are in for a strange experience when you decide to enroll at Whitman College. Whitman was founded as a mission by Marcus Whitman at Fort Walla Walla, Washington, christening its mascot. Every year, freshmen must learn the historical significance of the Whitman mission as part of the orientation program.

Studious Missionaries

Now a liberal arts college, Whitman requires its students to take a wide variety of course in six of several areas: history, literature, social science, math, fine arts, science, philosophy, religion, and linguistics. Freshmen must also take a full-year course in philosophical literature. Though all this seems overwhelming, students report that the requirements give them a broad base of knowledge that helps them

choose a major and strengthen their writing and analytical skills. Classes at Whitman are small, especially the mandatory "senior colloquiums," seminars which consist of 14 students (from various majors) and two professors who choose several novels for the group to read, discuss, and eventually write about. All classes at Whitman are taught by professors, and the small student-teacher ratio makes for excellent interaction. Some students have been invited to their professors' homes for informal study sessions.

According to undergrads, the history, English, and science departments are considered among the best. Many juniors at Whitman choose to study abroad, either through one of Whitman's own programs or through a program with another school. Whitman also offers programs in pre-law, teacher certification, and environmental studies in conjunction with other schools including Caltech, Duke, and Columbia.

Life, Missionary-Style

According to one freshman, female students had best maintain boyfriends at home because "all the good guys get taken right away." During the week, everyone is studying most of the time, though there is a good balance of academics, extracurricular activities, and just "hanging out." Compared to the neighboring Washington University, Whitman is not a huge party school, although there are parties on weekends. Different clubs often throw get-togethers. Casa Hispana has been known to host "some particularly good parties." There are also plenty of both fraternity and dorm parties where "students can get their buzz." The Marcus house, an upperclassman dorm, hosts annual parties such as the Rave. The school drinking policy encourages responsible drinking, and students describe the administration as "pretty lax." For non-drinkers, there are movies on campus and school-sponsored parties that are alcohol-free.

> Every year, freshmen must learn the historical significance of the Whitman mission as part of the orientation program.

The rooming situation is conducive to socializing mainly among people on the same floor. Students are required to live on campus for the first two years, though the majority of students decide to stay on campus for their last two years as well. Some of the dorms are very posh, which placates sorority members who have no housing of their own. Other dorms are all coed including the freshman halls, Jewitt and Anderson, which are two of the biggest dorms on campus. Most rooms on campus are doubles, with a few triples, and a couple of singles per building. About 65 people live on each floor, so there are "tons of people around all the time." The floors are split, with men occupying half of the floor and women occupying the other half of the floor. Resident advisors on each floor are "really cool" and "laid-back" and SAAs (student academics advisors) are very valuable resources for freshmen because "we can ask them what is good, bad, or indifferent."

The library is open 24 hours a day, except on weekends. There is a big computer cluster on the first floor, where students get a chance to meet friends and do their computing work. Students study either in their rooms, the libraries, or study rooms in the halls. Each hall has a study lounge and a social lounge with a kitchen. People generally prefer to study in the social lounge where "we feel much more relaxed." Students also study at coffee shops nearby, like Pangea, which is in the downtown area, and Coffee Perk.

Missionary Activism

Whitman is too small to have a football team, but takes pride in its nationally competitive ski, basketball, tennis, lacrosse, soccer, and volleyball teams. Intramurals have become more popular over the past few years; favorites include Ultimate Frisbee, football, rugby, tennis, soccer, and racquetball. The main rivals of the Fighting Missionaries are Lewis and Clark, Whitworth, and Reed. Non-athletic types contribute to campus publications, including the *Whitman College Pioneer*, also known as the *Pio*, and the *Blue Moon*, a literary magazine. Student plays and concerts are well attended, and the school tries to bring as many speakers and entertainers as possible to Walla Walla. Students also enjoy organized outdoor trips to such places as Yosemite, the Cascades, Hell's Canyon, and the San Juan Islands. Biking trips are also big among the student body, and the rural location is perfect for spring camping trips.

For a student interested in a strong liberal arts education within a small, close-knit community, Whitman College has a lot to offer. Besides, who could resist the opportunity to become known as a Fighting Missionary?—*Gautam Bahl and Staff*

FYI

The three best things about attending Whitman are "free dinners with your profs, our bike trips, and getting dirty playing rugby."

The three worst things about attending Whitman are "learning the history of the place, crazy amount of requirements, and being known as a Fighting Missionary."

The three things that every student should do before graduating from Whitman are "chill at a bunch of parties, read the *Pio*, and see Yosemite."

One thing I'd like to have known before coming here is "that this place can be very small."

West Virginia

Marshall University

Address: 400 Hal Greer Boulevard, Huntington, WV 25755
Phone: 304-696-3160
E-mail address: admissions@marshall.edu
Web site URL: www.marshall.edu
Location: suburban
Founded: 1837
Private or Public: public
Religious affiliation: none
Undergraduate enrollment: 9,304
Total enrollment: NA
Percent Male / Female: 44% / 56%
Percent Minority: 7.0%

Percent African-American: 4.0%
Percent Hispanic: 1.0%
Percent Asian: 1.0%
Percent in-state / out-of-state: 85% / 15%
Percent Pub HS: NA
Fraternities: NA
Sororities: NA
Number of Applicants: 4,452
Percent Accepted: 92%
Percent Accepted who enroll: 48%
Entering: 1,966
Transfers: NA
Application Deadline: rolling

Mean SAT: NA
Middle 50% SAT range: NA
Middle 50% ACT range: NA
Mean ACT: 21
3 Most popular majors: elementary education, biological science, secondary education
Retention: 72%
Graduation rate: NA
Library: NA
Tuition and Fees: $2,348 in; $6,294 out
Room and Board: $4,576
On-campus housing: NA
Financial aid, first-year: 42%

Green and white or blue and gold? Almost a century and a half after West Virginia split off from its eastern neighbor to fight with the north, an affiliation with either of WV's large state universities can still pit brother against brother. For over 9,000 undergraduates, the choice is clear. Marshall University, located in the heart of downtown Huntington, West Virginia, is sometimes eclipsed by the more renowned WVU, West Virginia's other large state school. Yet, Marshall's rich traditions in service, academic excellence, and student involvement easily allow it to stand proudly as a solid university with a wealth of offerings.

Seen and Herd

In recent years, Marshall has gained increased national exposure due to the overwhelming success of its football team, the *Thundering Herd*. This additional attention garnered by Marshall through the success of its athletic alums (recent NFL Rookie of the Year Randy Moss), has upped the influx of out of state applicants, an area in which the university is noticeably lacking. School spirit runs markedly high in Huntington, and students take pride in supporting their team, which boasts several consecutive undefeated seasons and multiple victories in the Mid-Atlantic Conference title game. However, as one undergrad jokingly notes, "the football games stop being fun after a while. We always win." Game day is always eventful in Huntington, and fans from around the state crowd through "Tent City" on their way to the big game. Yet, despite the success of Marshall athletic teams, the university is likely better known for the tragedy that formerly surrounded its program. The away game plane crash of 1970 in which all of the football players and coaches on board were killed is still associated with the school's name and reminders linger on campus in the form of the Memorial Student Center and an outdoor fountain commemorating the tragedy.

Academics

Coincidentally, many of those doing the reporting on Marshall are grads themselves. Marshall's journalism program is reportedly one of its most difficult and well respected. While majors give high praise to the faculty and curriculum, many of them complain of the higher grading scale that is used in many of the journalism classes. Communications and business programs typically enroll large numbers of students and health sciences are rapidly gaining popularity. In general, Marshall academics get high marks and while, as one student notes, "there are plenty of ways to slide by," most students agree that those who are looking for a challenging program should have no trouble finding their niche at Marshall.

The prestigious Yeager Scholars Program, requiring a separate application, awards full room and board for four years, a personal computer, a stipend for textbooks, and a travel abroad allowance for especially academically qualified students. Yeager Scholars also receive priority scheduling, special high level seminar courses, and a special mentor to guide them through their academic career and senior projects. Marshall has been recognized nationally for both this and other full and partial tuition scholarships, and is consistently ranked as one of America's "Best College Buys."

For such a large university, students point out Marshall's unusually small class sizes and the genuine enthusiasm of their professors. "It's great," one student gushes. "All my professors know my name!" "My math teacher is all about his office hours," another freshman remarked. "He comes to class angry if students didn't come and visit him the afternoon before." Students also report that it's not unusual for one their fellow classmates to actually be *older* than the professor. Marshall's heavy emphasis on community education often brings in adults looking to complete a degree or earn additional credit. Marshall provides students with multiple scheduling options, allowing them to register for courses in person, over the telephone, or on the Internet, although, regardless of the method, students still find registration "a giant pain in the rear."

Centralized Campus

Even if students happen to get stuck in an early morning section, however, getting to class is rarely a problem. Marshall's centralized, flat campus allows one student to "roll out of bed at 7:55 and still make it to my 8:00 class." Marshall's notorious housing shortage has made headlines in recent years when the university was forced to put up students at a local Holiday Inn while they sorted out rooming troubles. Students continue to marvel at the absurdity of a rule that requires students to live on campus for their first two years when dorms are already overcrowded. Yet, on the whole, undergrads are very satisfied with their living arrangements. Most students live in the university's massive air-conditioned Towers dorms, but its smaller rooms cause others to opt for the more spacious Buskirk and Hodges dorms. With the exception of Holderby Hall, all Marshall dorms are single-sex, and each reportedly has its tradeoffs (the Hodges males notoriously complain about their group showers). All dorms are required to observe "quiet hours" beginning at 9 P.M. on weeknights and midnight on weekends and students must sign in all guests. While students complain about rules that restrict opposite sex visitors to 11 P.M., Marshall's dorms are lauded as being very safe and are a social center for many of its students. Indeed, the campus as a whole is thought to be very secure, and many undergrads note the heavy presence of both the University Police and city officers on bike patrol.

Social Scene

When students want to get out of the dorm the surrounding area provides a lively nightlife, with Huntington's many bars pulling in the largest following, most of which line central 4th Street. Student favorites such as The Drink, The Union, and The Wild Dog attract large crowds nightly. However, students note that even with the wide variety of options, most bars take on distinct personalities and students tend to frequent their one specific venue. Fraternities and sororities also play a large role in the Marshall social scene, although students feel there is a much higher pressure for males to rush than females. For nondrinkers, the Memorial Student Center holds popular evening events and their Thursday open-mike nights typically draw several undergrads. While students don't see having a car to be a necessity, many recommend some sort of transportation to get to a "real" restaurant or to the Huntington Mall and movie theaters, which are actually in nearby Barboursville. Many of Marshall's students tend to be from nearby in-state locations, causing the campus to "almost completely clear out" on the weekends, often an annoyance for many out of state undergrads.

> **"Everyone here is so friendly. I have my home family, and then I have my Marshall family."**

Indeed, while most of Marshall's students tend to hail from West Virginia, out of state students typically don't report having trouble adjusting. However, several students do see the Marshall community as racially lopsided, with Marshall having a relatively low minority population. Students note that the undergraduate population tends to self-segregate, and the university is currently attempting to implement programs which add to campus diversity and cultural awareness. Yet, students find Marshall easy to adapt to, and praise the overall friendliness of the student body. "Everyone here is so friendly," one sophomore remarks. "I have my home family, and then I have my Marshall family."

The lively undergraduate dating scene also keeps undergrads social. While students admit that "random hookups abound," casual and serious relationships are generally easy to come by. Whether it's an evening at a concert at the Huntington Civic Arena, only blocks from campus, or a quick lunch date at the Calamity Café, Marshall students have plenty of options for their get-togethers.

Marshall's students tend to be very involved in a wide range of extracurriculars, with intramural sports, The Christian Center, and *The Parthenon*, the daily student newspaper, drawing several participants. Most undergrads also hold some type of part-time employment and several students participate in community outreach programs. Students remark on the usually high level of town-gown cooperation, and see the city of Huntington as taking an active interest in the life of the university and vice versa.

Futuristic Facilities

With a new science building and classrooms that are frequently renovated, Marshall's facilities have received lots of positive attention. One student favorite is Drinko Library, a four-floor state of the art facility which provides students with several meeting rooms and quiet study clusters which can be accessed with an ID Keycard. Drinko is also home to several classrooms with "a laptop for every student," and its first floor is open to the Marshall community 24 hours a day.

Students can eat in one of Marshall's three large dining halls, and most rate the food as at least "average." However, those who would rather dine elsewhere can head to the Student center where a Chick-Fil-A, a Pizza Hut, and a student snack shop provides additional offerings to the typical student meal plan.

As Marshall continues to pick up national momentum, its role in the collegiate world will undoubtedly increase. Students, community leaders, and the administration are cooperatively working on their "Vision 2020" plan, a course of action for the university that continues to broaden its scope and includes the construction of several new state of the art facilities. For now, however, Marshall manages to remain one of the nation's best-kept secrets as a low cost, challenging, enthusiastic university.—*Conor Knighton*

FYI
The three best things about attending Marshall are "the safe and well laid out campus, caring professors, and the 4th Street Bars."
The three worst things about attending Marshall are "overly strict dorm regulations, a self-segregating student body, and the mass exodus that occurs on the weekends."
The three things that every student should do before graduating from Marshall are "get involved, party the whole weekend of the MAC Championship, and go to at least one football and basketball game."

One thing I'd like to have known before coming here is "do all the things that sound cheesy—'Welcome Weekend' might sound dumb at first, but you'll wish you'd gone when you see how many friends your roommate made."

West Virginia University

Address: P.O. Box 6009, Morgantown, WV 26506-6009
Phone: 800-344-WVU1
E-mail address: wvadmissions@arc.wvu.edu
Web site URL: www.wvu.edu
Location: suburban
Founded: 1867
Private or Public: public
Religious affiliation: none
Undergraduate enrollment: 15,175
Total enrollment: 23,000
Percent Male/Female: 54%/46%
Percent Minority: 4.0%

Percent African-American: 3.0%
Percent Hispanic: 1.0%
Percent Asian: 0.0%
Percent in-state/out-of-state: 94%/6%
Percent Pub HS: NA
Fraternities: 16%
Sororities: 19%
Number of Applicants: 7,786
Percent Accepted: 93%
Percent Accepted who enroll: 46%
Entering: 3,331
Transfers: 1,000
Application Deadline: rolling
Mean SAT: 516 V, 515 M

Middle 50% SAT range: 470–560 V, 470–570 M
Middle 50% ACT range: NA
Mean ACT: 22
3 Most popular majors: business administration and management, journalism, psychology
Retention: 68%
Graduation rate: 56%
Library: 1,500,000 volumes
Tuition and Fees: $2,748 in; $8,100 out
Room and Board: $4,832
On-campus housing: 95%
Financial aid, first-year: 51%

"Almost heaven, West Virginia . . ." For over 22,000 proud Mountaineers, the words of John Denver's 1971 song still ring true today. Situated in the picturesque hills of Morgantown, West Virginia University boasts one of the most enthusiastic student bodies in the nation. As one student put it, "you'll never find a group of people with more school spirit than you will at WVU."

Two-Pronged Pride

Much of WVU's school spirit centers on its athletic teams. In fact, many students cite seasonal trips to Mountaineer Field as a key aspect of their college life. When not cheering on one of WVU's twenty Division I squads, students participate in a wide variety of intramural sports. As one participant explained, "you don't have to be athletic at all—everyone just comes out to have a good time. Intramurals are a great way to meet fellow Mounties."

WVU's football team draws national attention each year and often vies for one of the top slots in the Big East athletic conference. One student described the opening kick-off of the first game of the season as "the best ten seconds of the semester." The state legislature has recently mandated that the Mounties play Marshall University, WVU's state rival to the south. While football carries the largest fan base by far, sports like basketball, baseball, and gymnastics receive a smaller but equally devout following.

West Virginians take pride in their academics as well. Mountaineers are quick to point to their unusually high numbers of Rhodes scholars (sixth among public universities) and to the long-term success of graduates. The much-touted University Honors Program helps high achievers get the most out of their college experience. In addition to receiving priority housing and scheduling, honors students may take exclusive "honors only" seminars taught in small groups by the university's top faculty. To be accepted into the program, students must meet specific grade and test score requirements, although those who demonstrate success once in college can also earn their way into the program.

WVU professors are described as "very clear and precise about what they want." When confusion does arise, "professors seem to go out of their way to be helpful," noted one student. However, some undergrads complain about foreign teachers being difficult to understand. "If you're going to take a math class, be sure to bring a translator," warned one undergrad. Introductory courses have been known to enroll over 500 people, but students say that the average class size is less than 30, allowing for individual interaction between student and professor.

Unfortunately, getting into classes isn't always easy. Students gripe about the university's STAR system, a telephone course registration service and the source of endless busy signals and headaches. Often, students will sacrifice precious sleeping time in order to break through before peak calling hours and schedule the classes they want. "It's much better to wake up at 6 A.M. on the first day of scheduling than to be stuck waking up at 8:30 A.M. every day of the semester," explained one student.

In 1997, WVU entered into a partnership with the F.B.I. to create the world's first biometrics program, training students in the technical verification of one's identity. Students in this highly competitive major work with state-of-the-art technology and regularly hone their skills by sorting through mock crime scenes. Many others turn to the popular business, economics, and health sciences programs that are said to attract thousands of Mountaineers each year. With over 130 possible majors, students praise the wide course variety at WVU.

Campus Living

All freshmen are required to live on campus, with the majority living in one of two mammoth, air-conditioned dorms known as the Towers. Many freshmen apply to live in Boreman South, hoping to take advantage of the dorm's unique "suite-style" living areas. Honors students are assigned to Dadisman Hall, and females can elect to live in Boreman North, WVU's only single-sex dorm.

Unique among state universities is WVU's new Operation Jump Start program. The program matches an incoming freshman with one of WVU's nine residential "houses" ("a fancy way of saying 'dorm,'" explained one student), each functioning as a small community within the larger university. Students are placed near others with similar academic and extracurricular interests, and they frequently interact with faculty member advisors who live in on-campus houses near the dorms. Operation Jump Start also helps to coordinate Fall Fest, a giant celebration at the beginning of the first semester, featuring top musical acts as Busta Ryhmes, Puff Daddy, the Verve Pipe, and the Goo Goo Dolls.

After freshman year, some students choose to live off campus in a fraternity or sorority house, or one of Morgantown's many student apartment complexes. Of those who remain, most choose to live in Stalnaker Hall, widely regarded as the best dorm on campus.

Dining halls are generally given low marks, but Morgantown provides a wide variety of local restaurants within walking distance. Student favorites include the Boston Beanery, Pargo's, and the Mountainlair—a centrally located student union home to several fast-food chain restaurants as well as a bowling alley, a movie theater, and a game room.

> **"[You] are far less likely to gain the infamous freshman fifteen [here]."**

One student noted that Mountaineers are "far less likely to gain the infamous freshman fifteen" than their counterparts across the nation. A general source of complaints, WVU's mountainous terrain can make for a tiring hike to class. Divided into two separate campuses—the main campus is downtown and the other is in nearby Evansdale—the set-up can make getting to class a problem. Recently ranked as one of the best "people movers" in the nation, the PRT is an above-ground train that connects the two locations, running regular shuttles to several campus locations. Each fall during Mountaineer

Week, various student organizations participate in a competition to cram as many people as possible into one of the small cars (the current record is 98). While students complain of the PRT's occasional breakdowns, one student joked that "it gives us a great excuse to miss class."

WVU's extensive campus is currently under heavy renovation, and while some complain of the rampant construction, one freshman noted that "good things come to those who wait." When all is said and done, WVU will be home to a state-of-the-art 200,000-square-foot Student Recreation Center, a brand new biology building, and an addition to the central library facility.

Social Center

With a large Greek system exerting a heavy influence over social life, weekends at WVU generally revolve around fraternity and sorority parties. Pre-game football tailgates also attract thousands of students in the fall. Unable to shake its party school reputation, Morgantown is well known for its bars and dance clubs. Student favorites include Phantoms, Shooters, Dr. Longshot's, and the Brass Alley. For non-drinkers, one student quipped that "all three of us" still feel accepted and rarely have a problem finding alternate activities. WVU's new Up All Night program provides students with school-sponsored, alcohol-free activities every weekend night and generally receives high marks from the student body. Games such as Virtual Reality Soccer, Astro Bowling, and

Make Your Own Music Video—coupled with "an insane amount of free food"—make Up All Night a popular stop on a typical weekend night.

Students are quick to point out that the best part of WVU is "its people" which are described as "incredibly friendly, outgoing, and always willing to lend a helping hand." WVU students participate in a wide range of extracurriculars, with popular activities such as the Residence Hall Association, the drama club, and the student-written *Daily Athenian* enlisting several Mountaineers. However, many complain that the student body is too homogeneous; one student remembers being initially surprised by how few minority students there were at such a large university.

Getting Your Money's Worth

For the last several years, WVU has consistently remained a bargain in a field of increasingly expensive state schools. Many students remarked that while they could have gone to a more costly university, the money that they save now can be applied to the hefty price tag of graduate school down the line. Most importantly, Mountaineers seem happy about their choice. "I love it here," gushed one student. "I immediately felt like I was part of a family." A family that is proud to claim top-notch athletes, dedicated scholars, and equally dedicated socialites among its members, WVU offers a well-rounded college experience for those who are willing to bleed blue and gold.—*Conor Knighton*

FYI

The three best things about attending WVU are "the atmosphere in general (especially on football game days), the desire of the faculty to help the students succeed, and the friendly student body."

The three worst things about attending WVU are "the hills, the lack of diversity, overly large intro classes."

The three things that every student should do before graduating from WVU are "live in the dorm at least once; Attend Fall/Spring Fest; take a 'fun' course, e.g., photography, tennis, or fishing."

One thing I'd like to have known before coming here is "don't restrict yourself to a major your freshman year."

Wisconsin

Beloit College

Address: 700 College Street, Beloit, WI 53511
Phone: 608-363-2500
E-mail address: admiss@beloit.edu
Web site URL: www.beloit.edu
Location: urban
Founded: 1846
Private or Public: private
Religious affiliation: none
Undergraduate enrollment: 1,258
Total enrollment: NA
Percent Male / Female: 41% / 59%
Percent Minority: 13.0%

Percent African-American: 5.0%
Percent Hispanic: 4.0%
Percent Asian: 4.0%
Percent in-state / out-of-state: 25% / 75%
Percent Pub HS: NA
Fraternities: NA
Sororities: NA
Number of Applicants: 1,472
Percent Accepted: 70%
Percent Accepted who enroll: 30%
Entering: 309
Transfers: 60
Application Deadline: rolling

Mean SAT: 640 V, 600 M
Middle 50% SAT range: 590–690 V, 550–650 M
Middle 50% ACT range: NA
Mean ACT: 27
3 Most popular majors: anthropology, biology, English
Retention: 93%
Graduation rate: 69%
Library: NA
Tuition and Fees: $20,440 in; NA out
Room and Board: $4,628
On-campus housing: NA
Financial aid, first-year: 63%

Upon entering Beloit College, most students "realize that they have the opportunity to be treated as adults, and that their opinions really do matter," one undergrad explained. This understanding creates a "productive" atmosphere filled with a "go get 'em" attitude, as well as fostering a strong sense of responsibility. As a result, many Beloit students get involved with all sorts of school activities while keeping up with their academic work.

Challenging You to Think

Students describe the Beloit curriculum as "challenging." The strongest and most popular departments are anthropology and geology, although, as one student said, "no departments are bad here, some are just understaffed." General academic requirements include two courses in each of three divisions (natural sciences, social sciences, and humanities), which students must complete within their first two years. Upperclassmen currently take classes toward either a double major or a major and a minor, although an overhaul of the curriculum has been discussed and the requirements may change in the coming years. Class size is small: introductory classes reportedly enroll 20 to 30 students, and upper-level classes are often even smaller.

Student-faculty interaction is said to be strong and personal; one student said most professors are on a first-name basis with undergrads. Another said the faculty is "really open and willing to help with problems both during class and outside of class." Many opportunities are available for one-on-one research projects with professors, and student contact with the Beloit faculty does not end when class ends: professors often support their students by attending various school activities. One student exclaimed, "Beloit is the only place you can play poker with your professors and borrow their cars!" TAs do not teach classes, but some lead lab sessions in the natural sciences courses.

Beloit has a local chapter of the Phi Beta Kappa honor society, and students can participate in off-campus study in the U.S. and abroad. They also can choose from an urban studies program in Chicago, a political science program in Washington, D.C., or study-abroad destinations such as Indonesia, Zimbabwe, Brazil, Ecuador, Germany, France, and Japan.

Campus Architecture and Life

When they are on campus, Beloit students enjoy the architecture of their surroundings, which ranges from late-nineteenth to various twentieth-century styles. (The newest building at Beloit was constructed in 1964.) Many facilities, including the Logan Museum of Anthropology and five dorms, have undergone recent renovations. The Morse Library was modernized recently, but one student reported that it is still "not so hot." The library's resources are limited. "They are just becoming outdated and there are many periodicals which are absent and should be there," one undergrad complained. Beloit is a member of the Wisconsin Interlibrary Loan System, however, which allows students to obtain resources from any library in the state. Many undergrads do their research at the nearby University of Wisconsin at Madison.

All students must live on campus for six semesters, and most stay through their senior year. One reason for this is the scarcity of off-campus housing, and, as one student put it, "The townies don't like us." Dorms at Beloit house students from all classes together. The best dorms are reportedly the "'64 halls," which include Peet, Bushnell, Blaisdell, Whitney, and Porter. All of these dorms were recently renovated and feature carpeting and air-conditioning; they also have many singles. Most students agree that if you want a single as a frosh, these are the dorms in which to find them. Haven and Wood are among the most coveted dorms, while Aldrich is supposedly the worst place to end up, because, as one student reported, "it is noisy and there are too many frosh." Maurer is the only all-female dorm at Beloit; all others are either coed by room (such as Peet, Bushnell, and Blaisdell) or by floor (such as Haven and Wood). Other housing options include three fraternity houses and two sorority houses, language houses for French, Spanish, Russian, and German speakers, the art co-op, the Outdoor Environmental house (OEC), and the Black Students United house (BSU).

Students praise Beloit's athletic facility, the Flood Arena. One basketball player described it as the "best facility in our conference." The football and basketball teams have had good records in recent years and draw the most student support. Most athletes agree that even if the entire student body does not show up at the games, "athletes in general support their athletic friends." Intramural sports are not as popular as they once were, but two new coaches were recently hired for the women's basketball and track teams.

What's Cooking?

All first-year students must purchase a plan of 20 meals per week. After freshman year, undergrads can choose 14 or 10 meals per week. Most eat their evening meals at the Commons, a central cafeteria on the north side of campus, where almost all of the residential buildings are located. On the south side of campus, which consists mainly of academic buildings, a snack bar in the student union called D.K.'s serves fast food; students can also use their meal cards there. Popular off-campus restaurants include Domenico's (an Italian restaurant), State Street Cafe, and the local International House of Pancakes.

Town-Gown Troubles

Relations between students and residents of Beloit are reportedly poor, and most undergrads stay on campus. As one student put it, "We live in a two-block-by-two-block bubble." The Java Joint cafe is a popular spot for social study and for pure socializing. The Coughy Haus, known as C Haus to regulars, is a popular campus bar. Organizations such as BSU and the Alliance for Gay and Bisexual Students and Straight Supporters often rent the C Haus for a night to host large dance parties. Fraternities and sororities throw parties almost every weekend, and students also hang out on the quad, known as the Wall. Those looking for a mellow night out can catch a movie sponsored by the film club every Wednesday, Friday, and Sunday night. Students for a Better Education (SABE) funds other social activities. Annual Beloit parties include the Art Co-op's Deb Ball, a funky dance where women dress as men and vice versa; Folk and Blues, a two-day festival in September where bands play until midnight; and Spring Day, a Greek-sponsored festival of food and music to raise money for local charities. When students do venture off campus, they often go to Goodies, a bar (and Beloit College tradition) that recently changed locations, or Phazes, a new bar downtown. To promote responsibility, the administration encourages students to avoid dangerous situations connected to alcohol, drugs, and sex. Sex education material is readily available, especially from the resident advisors, who sell condoms and talk about sexually transmitted diseases.

Extracurricular activities play a big part in campus life. *The Roundtable*, a weekly newspaper, is the main publication on campus. Many students are djs on the campus radio station, WBCR. Syzygy is a popular Beloit poetry-reading group. Other campus groups include the Cult Movie Club; ECHO, which promotes the legalization of marijuana; the International Club; the Rock Climbing Club; and the Scuba Club.

Unfortunately, the surrounding community has its share of crime. Beloit has responded to this problem by maintaining an extensive and effective security system. Students report that the campus is always well lit, and security officers are on duty 24 hours a day. Students agree that the officers are very friendly. As one student said, "They want to get to know students better, so they try to reach out because it makes their job much easier." Just as professors and students are on a first-name basis, so are the security officers and students. "It's not just, 'There goes a security officer,' it's, 'Oh, there goes Bob.'" This close relationship makes students feel safe on campus.

> **"Beloit is the only place you can play poker with your professors and borrow their cars!"**

Most Beloit students are from Wisconsin or Illinois, but several are international students. Undergrads insist that there is no real student stereotype at Beloit; everyone is an individual. Liberalism is the main political view, though one student noted that "there are a lot of closet conservatives." Students come from a variety of backgrounds, and find many opportunities to learn from each other.

Beloit makes students work for everything, and as one senior said, "They have not taught me to think for myself—they have *pushed* me to think for myself." When students take the initiative to do something, the administration is extremely supportive. According to one student, "They say, 'You can do it!'" Another student added, "The school opens your eyes to things that you never dreamt of—different people, different ideas, and different ways of life."—*Lisa Smith and Staff*

FYI

The three best things about attending Beloit are "the push to think for yourself, the tight Beloit community, and the swingin' social scene."

The three worst things about attending Beloit are "town-gown relations, largely Wisconsin/Illinois based student body, and crappy library resources."

The three things that every student should do before graduating from Beloit are "join the Scuba club, hang out at Folk and Blues, and buy a round of drinks at Coughy Haus."

One thing I'd like to have known before coming here is "how crummy our relations are with the town."

Lawrence University

Address: P.O. Box 599; Appleton, WI 54912
Phone: 800-227-0982
E-mail address: excel@lawrence.edu
Web site URL: www.lawrence.edu
Location: small city
Founded: 1847
Private or Public: public
Religious affiliation: none
Undergraduate enrollment: 1,235
Total enrollment: NA
Percent Male/Female: 46%/54%
Percent Minority: 6.2%
Percent African-American: 1.0%

Percent Hispanic: 1.0%
Percent Asian: 4.0%
Percent in-state/out-of-state: 48%/52%
Percent Pub HS: NA
Fraternities: 35%
Sororities: 25%
Number of Applicants: 1,172
Percent Accepted: 76%
Percent Accepted who enroll: 32%
Entering: 302
Transfers: 51
Application Deadline: 1 Feb
Mean SAT: NA

Middle 50% SAT range: 570–710 V, 590–650 M
Middle 50% ACT range: 25–30
Mean ACT: NA
3 Most popular majors: biology, psychology, art and music
Retention: 81%
Graduation rate: 65%
Library: 370,000 volumes
Tuition and Fees: $20,882 in; NA out
Room and Board: $4,605
On-campus housing: 100%
Financial aid, first-year: 68%

Lawrence University, located in Appleton, Wisconsin, has been coeducational since its founding in 1847, making it the second-oldest coed university in the nation. While other schools have followed Lawrence's lead, Lawrence remains one of the leaders in coeducation. It has evolved to offer students diverse academic possibilities within the confines of a close-knit social environment.

Small Classes

The small student body strongly affects Lawrence academics. Introductory science lectures, for example, usually enroll no more than 60 students, and students cite close relationships with professors as one of the best parts of the Lawrence experience. "You spend a lot of time with your professors here," said one sophomore. "They expect a lot of you." The close student-faculty relations also provide the opportunity for students to do independent work with faculty members. Despite the small classes, few students experience any major problems enrolling in the classes that they want.

Lawrence operates on a quarter system, with students normally enrolling in three classes per term. Among the 36 courses required for graduation, students must take both introductory and upper-level classes in four distribution groups and fulfill a language requirement. All freshmen must take a two-quarter Freshman Studies, or "Great Books," course, typically containing 14 to 19 students. Undergrads consider the course "the core of [their] common experience at Lawrence." A wide range of departments receive praise from undergrads. One said the sciences are "really incredible" at Lawrence, due to the excellent instructors. "For a school of this size, the science professors are really quite good," one chemistry major said, adding, "we have really state-of-the-art science equipment." Other students praise the English, art, and philosophy departments. Lawrence undergrads refuse to describe their school as intense or stress-filled despite the rigorous academic offerings. "Students work hard, and professors expect a lot of their students, but it's definitely not cutthroat," said one senior. Another student described the academic atmosphere as "really cooperative."

In addition to a strong liberal arts and sciences program, the university has one of the top music conservatories in the country. Although the "connie" students only take about one-third of their classes in the college, they participate in Lawrence life in most other ways. Each year about 15 to 20 students take part in a five-year double degree program, which grants both a bachelor of music and a bachelor of arts degree. Lawrence also offers a B.A. in music, which allows students in the regular liberal arts college to take advantage of the conservatory programs. Students see the conservatory as a "very central and defining part of the university," and even non-musicians feel its presence.

When the atmosphere of Lawrence begins to feel too confining, students often choose to enroll in one of the "excellent" off-campus study programs. Although the university sponsors 25 programs, students can travel nearly anywhere in the world through the Associated Colleges of the Midwest program. Popular Lawrence programs include the London Study Center and the Wilderness Field Program in northern Minnesota. For those who opt to stay on campus, the library, with a small but adequate collection, is a popular place to study, and the Media Center has an excellent collection of music and movies.

Centralized Social Life

Students describe the surrounding community of Appleton, a middle-sized town in Wisconsin, as very safe. The self-contained nature of the campus led one student to remark, "I've never been afraid to walk on campus, at any time of night." However, the praise for Appleton only goes so far; one sophomore said, "The town is culturally dead, as far as I'm concerned." Another undergrad agreed that "downtown doesn't really cater to college students." On the other hand, some restaurants, bookstores, and coffeehouses have opened over the past few years on the main street, giving students an alternative to campus hangouts. Many students, for example, travel to Peggy's Coffeeshop or Zacateca's, a popular Mexican restaurant, for good food and company.

Because of the conservatory, "there're nearly always recitals and guest artists" on campus, one student said, and internationally famous classical and jazz artists often perform at the school. Many people hang out at the union, which includes the Grill, a coffeehouse, and the Viking Room bar. The Grill attracts students in search of late-night greasy food, and the new student-run coffeehouse sponsors live music nearly every weekend. Only students 21 and older can visit the Viking Room.

Although some students warn that those in search of a big party school "should not come to Lawrence," the five fraternity houses on campus often organize big parties. The Lawrence drinking policy prohibits "all kegs and keg substitutes." Even so, interested students can still reportedly find "a lot of beer" at an average weekend party. One freshman said, "If you don't want to go to frat parties, you have to create your own fun," but a senior felt that the sense of community at Lawrence makes finding a good time easy: "Sometimes it doesn't even matter what you're doing, it's just that you're doing it with friends."

All undergrads are required to live on campus, which contributes to a "centralization" of social life. One student called the housing situation merely "tolerable." Ormsby Hall, with hardwood floors and a central location, and the substance-free Kohler both rank high with students. Upperclassmen often choose Sage Hall, which has suites, quads, and singles. Despite a slight housing crunch in recent years—some study lounges have been converted into student rooms—Lawrence still guarantees housing for all. Other popular living options include the co-op house (where students prepare their own food), the five frat houses, and the five theme houses. Each year, upper-class students organize and create proposals for the theme houses, whose residents must participate in service to Lawrence or the surrounding community. Theme houses in recent years have included a feminist house, a vegetarian house, an outdoor recreation house, and a house devoted to youth outreach through the arts.

Students describe the campus food as "very predictable." "There's a lot of variety, but it can get old kind of fast," said one freshman. Regulations require that freshmen purchase a 19-meal plan, but all students (except those living in fraternity houses) must choose some form of meal plan. The main dining hall is Downer Commons, and according to Lawrence students, "the name says it all." Although the more popular facility in Colman Hall only opens for breakfast and lunch on weekdays and serves a limited menu, students appreciate the better food and table service.

Limited Diversity

About 40 percent of Lawrence students come from Wisconsin, which often creates a feeling of insularity on campus, according to several students. Although the admissions office actively recruits a large percentage of international students to campus, few describe the school as ethnically or racially diverse. "This is a very white campus," one student said. Another said that much of the student body consists of "upper-middle-class white kids." One sophomore felt, however, that the administration was making an effort to change things: "They really try to bring in a variety of people."

Because of the music conservatory, "Lawrence is very unusual in the amount of music opportunities for majors and non-majors." Music comprises a major portion of extracurricular activities on campus, with students participating in the symphony, concert band, and several student-organized recital groups. Lawrence International, the international students' organization, sponsors many activities, as does the Outdoor Recreation Club. Publications on campus include the bi-weekly *Lawrentian* and the conservative *Lawrence Review*, as well as *Tropos*, a yearly art and literary magazine. Aspiring actors often participate in one of three major productions put on at Lawrence each year. "If there isn't something here that you really want, you can start it," one sophomore said. However, some students criticize the sense of apathy on campus. "A lot of the time things don't get off the ground because students either aren't interested or don't have the time to be interested," one junior said.

> Students see the conservatory as a "very central and defining part of the university," and even non-musicians feel its presence.

Although Lawrence has a strong Division III athletic program, students agree that "the sports at this school are for the athletes and it's not a school-spirit thing." The Division III status means that "virtually anyone can participate in a sport if they're interested." Varsity teams practice at Alexander Gym, leaving the modern Buchanen-Kiewit Recreation Center open for intramural sports and general student use. "I wouldn't say the facilities are state-of-the-art, but they're better than average, especially for a school this size," said one student. Both the men's and women's swim teams ranked high in their conference last year, and the volleyball and hockey teams are also described as standout varsity sports.

In general, students describe Lawrence as a very good place to spend four years. "People say 'hi' all the time," one student said. "It's a very comfortable place." The academics offer students a challenging and stimulating undergraduate experience in a small-size setting. As one undergrad said, "A lot of the time, they expect the students to provide structure and focus for themselves." Students with enough initiative often find that at Lawrence they can do just that.—*Kathryn Eigen and Staff*

FYI

The three best things about attending Lawrence are "the music, the music, and the music."

The three worst things about attending Lawrence are "Appleton, the all white faces, and the frat system."

The three things that every student should do before graduating from Lawrence are "hang out at Peggy's, pick an extracurricular you love, and sign up for an off-campus study program."

One thing I'd like to have known before coming here is "that you better like music because you will get an ear full."

Marquette University

Address: P.O. Box 1881, Milwaukee, WI 53201-1881
Phone: 800-222-6544
E-mail address: admissions@marquette.edu
Web site URL: www.marquette.edu
Location: urban
Founded: 1881
Private or Public: private
Religious affiliation: Roman Catholic (Jesuit)
Undergraduate enrollment: 7,437
Total enrollment: 10,780
Percent Male / Female: 46%/54%

Percent Minority: 14.0%
Percent African-American: 5.0%
Percent Hispanic: 4.0%
Percent Asian: 5.0%
Percent in-state / out-of-state: 46%/54%
Percent Pub HS: 58%
Fraternities: 10%
Sororities: 8%
Number of Applicants: 6,925
Percent Accepted: 84%
Percent Accepted who enroll: 30%
Entering: 1,723
Transfers: 168
Application Deadline: rolling
Mean SAT: 576 V, 584 M

Middle 50% SAT range: 520–620 V, 520–640 M
Middle 50% ACT range: 23–28
Mean ACT: 26
3 Most popular majors: business, engineering, health sciences
Retention: 88%
Graduation rate: 72%
Library: 719,906 volumes
Tuition and Fees: $18,020 in; NA out
Room and Board: $6,086
On-campus housing: 90%
Financial aid, first-year: 84%

Whether you are interested in a traditional college atmosphere or an urban lifestyle, Marquette University offers both options. Marquette's strong religious foundation may seem incongruous with its urban setting and spirit, but students enjoy the opportunities it offers for both intellectual and social growth.

Marquette University was founded in 1881 as a Jesuit institution for a city with a large Roman Catholic population. It was named for a figure out of Wisconsin's history, Pere Jacques Marquette, a 17th-century Jesuit explorer who charted much of what is now the Midwest. The school's status as a church-related institution reportedly does not dominate its character, but students say it has a presence in campus life. The administration and faculty consider an understanding of Christian thought an integral part of a Marquette education, and this is one of the only absolute requirements in an otherwise flexible core curriculum. Few students find this an infringement of their freedom, either academic or religious. One undergrad said she regarded her theology class as "more oriented toward the philosophy of religion than specifically Catholic thought." Courses in theology are required of all students in the nine undergraduate schools and two professional schools, with the exception of Dental Hygiene. Other distribution requirements vary among the colleges.

The Curriculum

Marquette's undergraduate colleges include nursing, engineering, arts and sciences, business administration, communication, journalism, the performing arts, medical technology, and a school of education. Though business is one of the most popular majors, students say engineering is the most competitive. One junior said that the international business program is "wonderful" and that it encourages students to go abroad during their junior year to supplement their study. Other departments generally earn praise from students, although one education student complained of "a weak teaching program" that did not offer a lot of class variety. Marquette has the only dental school in Wisconsin and the only four-year curriculum available in dental hygiene. In addition, Marquette is one of the few schools in the country to offer a six-year combined bachelor's and master's program in physical therapy.

According to students, Marquette matches solid academics with accessible professors. This has recently been reflected in a sizable increase in the admissions pool, with the class of 2003 being the first to have an admissions cap imposed. Class size, however, can be an obstacle in the introductory-level courses, which often enroll 200 or more. Students must take a number of these large introductory courses to fulfill their requirements. Students report that upper-level classes have an average enrollment of about 20 to 30.

Life Outside of Class

Volunteer activity is widespread on campus, although some students think that it is "not that a lot of people are involved, just that those who are involved are very serious about their work." With a large number of religious organizations acting as a campus social-service network, there is no lack of opportunity for the service-oriented. Campus groups with church affiliation include Knights of Columbus, Campus Ministry, Marquette University Community, and Campus Crusade for Christ. Popular volunteer projects include Midnight Run, which began at Marquette to distribute food to the homeless, and construction work for Habitat for Humanity. As one junior said, "There are a lot of social problems around us, like homelessness, poverty, etc.," due to Milwaukee's urban environment, so opportunities for community service abound.

Another strong campus network is the Greek system, which is an influential part of Marquette student life. The Christian educational ethic is not daunted by the escapades of the average college student at Marquette, and many students say they "party hard." Fraternities sponsor most of the popular campus parties, which can be, as one student put it, "exclusive." Weekly house parties also are common, but according to one student, are "attended only by freshmen and people from other area colleges." Fraternities also engage in such activities as the Booze Cruise, for which members take their kegs out to the lakefront and go boating, and the Pub Crawl, in which participants go from one bar to the next along a scheduled route and do a shot at each. Although many Marquette students say they do not drink despite Milwaukee's reputation as Beer City, one senior reported that some fraternity parties "take at least two weeks to clean up."

Fraternity parties owe some of their popularity to the strict regulations against drinking in the dorms, where freshmen are required to live. Security officers stationed at entrances of dorm parties can ask dorm residents and guests to submit to a bag search for alcohol. Beer often finds its way into the dorms anyway, however, and one student said it is not uncommon "to see a keg hidden away in a garbage can." Marquette students describe their campus as "friendly." "I met my best friends here my first day at Marquette, and I continually meet new ones, " said one undergrad.

A Compact Campus

Students describe Marquette's campus as "compact." The main part of the campus measures about eight blocks long and two blocks wide. Marquette has five residence halls. Tower and East halls are popular for their spaciousness, while McCormick draws less enthusiasm from undergrads, partly because it has a reputation for wild parties. Some say it also suffers from an excess of "architectural vision"—it is a modern, circular building with small rooms in the shape of pie slices. However, one student said that McCormick is a "cool place to live because it is the only coed freshman residence hall." Priests live in the dorms to serve as advisors and friends, and also to conduct weekly masses. Most of the dorms for upperclassmen are coed, but students say that "intervisitation," or going to the rooms of those of the opposite sex, is strictly regulated. On weekends, the administration allows 24-hour visitation, but on weeknights members of the opposite sex must be out of the room by 1 A.M.

After the second year, the majority of undergrads move off campus. In past years, good off-campus housing has been expensive and difficult to find. Marquette addressed the problem by buying property near the campus and converting it into student apartment complexes, making the off-campus living experience much more pleasant. Humphrey Hall and Renee Row are popular housing options, and the new Campus Town on Wall Street has many upperclassmen excited about its coffee shops, laundry, and bowling alley.

> **With a large number of religious organizations acting as a campus social-service network, there is no lack of opportunity for the service-oriented.**

In the city of Milwaukee, as one undergrad said, "there is never a dearth of activity." Local attractions include shopping malls like Grand Avenue, which features blocks of boutiques, department stores, and restaurants; the Bradley Center, home to Marquette basketball and the NBA's Milwaukee Bucks, and Mecca Arena, which brings in big-name concerts; great restaurants, including many that represent Milwaukee's German-American population; and the nearby shore of Lake Michigan, site of many festivals and boating events. The Milwaukee Brewers also play near the campus. Those interested in the arts will not be disappointed; Milwaukee offers the Rep Theater and the Performing Arts Center, among other resources. Students with cars have easy access to Kettle Moraine, a region known for its hiking and skiing, and Chicago, which is only a two-hour drive away.

On campus, students generally hang out in the Memorial Union student center to enjoy its pub, fast food, and grand ballroom. Wells Street is home to popular restaurants and pubs like Whales on Wells, Giuliano's Pizza, and the Avalanche. Although students who live on campus must purchase a meal plan, many call the food at the cafeteria "not very good" and "unhealthy." One student mentioned a long-running campaign for low-calorie salad dressings.

The Marquette campus is constantly changing, a result of a university-led urban renewal project. One student reported that new buildings have been going up "throughout the year" in a program meant to benefit both the city and the student body. Recent additions include a theater, art museum, and a math/computer science building as well as a recreation center that one student said has "prime workout facilities" and space for Marquette's intramural games. All varsity teams enjoy strong student support. "Marquette is a basketball campus," one student said, but the men's soccer and track teams and women's tennis team also attract a following. In 1995, the basketball team made it to the NIT finals and the student body marched through the streets of the city to celebrate the team's success. Marquette does not have a football team; while some students find this to be a disadvantage, they say the situation will probably not change, as the possibility of a football team has been discussed and rejected "many times before."

A Final Look

The spiritual heart of the Marquette campus is the St. Joan of Arc Chapel, built in 1400 and brought to Wisconsin from France. Students agree that the chapel serves as an emblem of Marquette's Jesuit tradition, which characterizes the school to this day. According to students, Marquette's great basketball team, awesome gym, and city life enrich, but do not define the Marquette experience. Marquette is largely about tradition, from its predominantly religious and politically conservative faculty and student body to its close-knit, "family feel."—*Jay Munir and Staff*

FYI

The three best things about attending Marquette are "the Catholic tradition, a city rich in activities, and the energy of the campus."

The three worst things about attending Marquette are "having priests living in dorms, the visitation regulations on weekdays, and the lack of a football team."

The three things every student should do before graduating from Marquette are "take advantage of what Milwaukee has to offer, participate in the Midnight Run, get involved in a service project you believe in."

One thing I'd like to have known before coming here is "how terrific Milwaukee is."

University of Wisconsin / Madison

Address: 716 Langdon Street; Madison, WI 53706
Phone: 608-262-3961
E-mail address: on.wisconsin@mail.admin.wisc.edu
Web site URL: www.wisc.edu
Location: urban
Founded: 1836
Private or Public: public
Religious affiliation: none
Undergraduate enrollment: 27,947
Total enrollment: 40,109
Percent Male/Female: 47%/53%
Percent Minority: 12.8%

Percent African-American: 3.0%
Percent Hispanic: 3.0%
Percent Asian: 6.0%
Percent in-state/out-of-state: 60%/40%
Percent Pub HS: NA
Fraternities: 15%
Sororities: 18%
Number of Applicants: 17,260
Percent Accepted: 65%
Percent Accepted who enroll: 49%
Entering: 5,590
Transfers: 1,717
Application Deadline: 1 Feb
Mean SAT: NA

Middle 50% SAT range: 460–580 V, 460–600 M
Middle 50% ACT range: 19–24
Mean ACT: NA
3 Most popular majors: engineering
Retention: NA
Graduation rate: NA
Library: 4,800,000 volumes
Tuition and Fees: $3,650 in; $12,400 out
Room and Board: $5,250
On-campus housing: 82%
Financial aid, first-year: 28%

For many midwesterners, the choice to attend the University of Wisconsin/Madison—a midwestern powerhouse in both academics and athletics—is an easy one. But, Madison also attracts a national and international student body, as one of the country's strongest state schools, with highly ranked programs in computer science and nuclear engineering and other fields. Students love the school's resort-like environs and recognize that a school of over 26,000 undergrads is bound to have something that appeals to everyone.

The Academic Side

Undergrads praise Madison for "an incredible variety of classes to choose from," but soon find that an intricate set of requirements narrows the number of courses they can take in their first two years. Students must fulfill general education requirements in communication, quantitative reasoning, natural science, and humanities/literature/arts, which includes both social studies and ethnic studies. Specific credit requirements differ according to specific majors, and the student consensus is that the requirements are complicated and confusing. Undergrads work closely with advisors, who help them sift through the various requirements. "I understand the need for all the rules," said one undergrad, "but I think there are too many prerequisites for the interesting classes . . . you have very few selections in what you use to fulfill the requirements." Another student said the heavy requirements assure that "all the slackers are weeded out by sophomore year."

Students consider political science and math classes, especially calculus and analytic geometry, to be among the hardest offered at Madison; those looking for a lighter load supposedly take communication arts or sociology classes. Except for honor sections, lectures are almost universally "enormous," whereas discussion groups are "reasonable to small." Undergrads describe the average workload as "moderate," but say that exams are "really, really hard."

Madison professors get high ratings:

"You want to applaud when they're done lecturing," said one student. Another undergrad described impressive individual attention from Madison professors. "The dean of pre-engineering went out of his way to make me feel at home, even before I had actually decided to come here," she said. Professors are also known for being responsive to student input, especially complaints about the difficulty of exams. The only other common complaint about academics is registration. "Classes fill quickly. You'll get shut out of something even if you have a decent registering priority," said one undergrad.

Partying Hard

Madison has traditionally had the reputation of a "big-time party school." Several students are quick to oppose this notion while others take pride in the serious partying that keeps them warm throughout the frigid Wisconsin winters. Parties center on fraternities and (for the over-21 crowd) the bars on Mifflin Street. "Basically, time is determined by the bars," said one undergrad. "We have pre-bar parties, bar parties, and after-bar parties." Some of the most popular gatherings of the year include the Harvest Festival and the Mifflin Street Block Party.

Freshmen typically party at the frats or in apartments owned by upperclassmen, who "convert their basements into freshman party/money-making schemes," one undergrad reported. Some students say being underage is not usually an obstacle to drinking, except during "Operation Sting," a series of police raids at the beginning of each semester that always leave some students with hefty tickets to pay off. Undergrads report that the drug scene is mostly underground, "so if you're not interested, you rarely hear of it."

When asked about the fate of nondrinkers at Madison, one undergrad replied, "Do any exist?" Another said, "Nondrinkers don't necessarily feel left out . . . they need to decide whether they do or not." One student explained, "Most people do go to parties on the weekends, but there are plenty of people here who like to have a good time without alcohol." Alternatives include plays, shows, concerts, studying, or activities like cosmic bowling and pool, organized by the student unions. State Street is a popular hangout, offering popular restaurants and a big shopping area "good for people-watching."

Hand in hand with the popularity of drinking at Madison comes a high rate of hookups; however, students report "very little actual dating." To those looking for more than a one-night stand, one undergrad said, "The school is so big that you rarely see the same person twice just passing by, so if you want to initiate a relationship it needs to be very deliberate." Gay couples, and to a lesser extent interracial couples, are visible on campus.

Diversity

Midwesterners make up the largest group of undergrads at Madison, but diversity doesn't end there. "I couldn't believe it . . . in the first couple weeks of school I met people from Thailand, Germany, and Russia," one student said. "In some groups there's a little self-segregation," another student said, "but black-white relations are generally good." Diversity at Madison extends to personal style as well. Although students tend to stick to jeans, sweaters, sweatshirts, and baseball hats for everyday, one undergrad reported, "Pretty much anything goes . . . people are individual in the way they dress, and no one is too discriminating."

Living It Up

Dorm life at Madison is the basis for making friends and forming groups. "People usually retain their close friends from freshman year in the dorm the whole way, and they're usually the people they will choose to live with off campus," said one undergrad. Madison students can choose to live in university dorms, private apartment complexes, special learning facilities, or fraternities and sororities. Housing is guaranteed for all four years. Campus housing is divided into two areas: dorms on the lakeshore are smaller, with 60 to 80 students each, whereas dorms on the eastern half of campus are larger, less close-knit, and rowdier. Lakeshore dorms, including Elizabeth Waters, the popular all-female dorm, have beach volleyball courts, soccer fields, and baseball diamonds nearby. On the other end of campus, students find the new Kohl Center (for basketball and hockey) an exciting but distracting neighbor. All university dorms have house fellows, whose "strictness depends on the situation," said one undergrad. Most say that quiet hours are not well enforced, but HFs often report underage drinking to the police.

Good Eats

Food at Madison earns significant praise, especially the homemade ice cream and Belgian waffles. Students pay for meals on their ID cards, and can put any amount of money they choose into their account. Dining halls are open 7 A.M. to 11:30 P.M. on weekdays and 10 A.M.–11:30 P.M. on weekends, with extended hours during exams.

Madison students rave about their campus, which is "very hilly with lots of beautiful flower gardens." Because the city of Madison, and therefore the campus, is surrounded by lakes, many students compare their surroundings to a resort. "In the summer there are sailboats all over," said one undergrad, "and in the winter the lakes freeze hard and you can go ice fishing or play hockey." Students generally feel safe on campus and secure on the well-lit streets of Madison. In addition, the emergency blue-light phone system for contacting the police provides extra safety precaution. Some students complain that Madison lacks a good transportation system. Student bus passes provide free transportation on city bus lines, all of which stop running at 9:30 P.M., except the singular LN line, which acts as a SafeBus for students traveling alone late at night. As a result, students say they are forced to take taxis often.

Rowdy Wisconsin

Sports play a huge role in the extracurricular life of Madison students. The most popular spectator sport is football, with basketball and hockey following closely behind. This support was a great influence in helping Wisconsin win back-to-back Rose Bowls in 1999 and 2000. The new Kohl Center has greatly increased seating for basketball and hockey games, which are much more accessible in their new on-campus location. During games, which attract a lot of Madison residents, the student section comes alive with obscene chants, singing and dancing in the aisles, and "rowing," a spirit booster in which everyone in the section pretends to be rowing the person in front like a boat. "Madison students become fans who are wild, crazy, and loyal," said one undergrad. "We are unofficially the number one hostile football crowd in the country."

Students who do not play on varsity teams or spend all of their time cheering participate in intramurals or work out with friends. Undergrads go to the Nat to run, lift weights, and swim, or use the lake path for jogging and in-line skating. One of the most popular student groups is the Hoofers club, which organizes boating, skiing, skating, mountain climbing, and windsurfing.

> "We are unofficially the number one hostile football crowd in the country."

Many Madison undergrads have part-time jobs with tutoring services, computing centers, and food services. In fact, "there are always more jobs available than students to fill them," said one undergrad. Undergrads can also join a wide variety of clubs, or, if nothing appeals, start a new student organization. Community service opportunities, such as working with needy kids or volunteering in soup kitchens, are available "for those who are really interested," said one undergrad, "but not many people take part in them."

In general, undergrads find their experiences at the University of Wisconsin/Madison to be well-rounded. "[Madison] is extremely challenging not only in workload, but also in mere size," said one student. "There's no one to look out for you." Rigorous academic requirements, infectious school spirit, and a love of partying make life at Madison "busy and never boring."—*Liz Kukura and Staff*

FYI

The three best things about attending University of Wisconsin are "the parties, State Street, and the football team."

The three worst things about attending University of Wisconsin are "teachers who can't speak English, poor advisors, and student anonymity."

The three things that every student should do before graduating from University of Wisconsin are "fail an exam, have beer for breakfast, and go to the Nitty Gritty for a birthday."

One thing I'd like to have known before coming here is "it's more of a 5 year program than a 4 year."

Wyoming

University of Wyoming

Address: P.O. Box 3435, Laramie, WY 82071
Phone: 307-766-5160
E-mail address: mamasita@uwyo.edu
Web site URL: www.uwyo.edu
Location: rural
Founded: 1886
Private or Public: public
Religious affiliation: none
Undergraduate enrollment: 8,433
Total enrollment: 11,126
Percent Male/Female: 45%/55%
Percent Minority: 6.0%
Percent African-American: 1.0%

Percent Hispanic: 4.0%
Percent Asian: 1.0%
Percent in-state/out-of-state: 71%/29%
Percent Pub HS: NA
Fraternities: 60%
Sororities: 40%
Number of Applicants: 2,466
Percent Accepted: 97%
Percent Accepted who enroll: 51%
Entering: 1,869
Transfers: 1,107
Application Deadline: 8 Aug
Mean SAT: NA
Middle 50% SAT range: NA

Middle 50% ACT range: 21–26
Mean ACT: 23.6
3 Most popular majors: elementary education, psychology, accounting
Retention: 76%
Graduation rate: 48%
Library: 1,393,055 volumes
Tuition and Fees: $2,416 in; $7,284 out
Room and Board: $4,446
On-campus housing: 54%
Financial aid, first-year: 42%

D oes the majesty of the mountains call your name, or the serenity of the open plain whistle in your ear? If so, head west—way out west, to the University of Wyoming. Whether it's the outdoor scenery of Vedauwoo State Park, or the night life of nearby Denver, students at UW appreciate their slice of western bliss.

Studies with a Smile

"The difference between UW and my old school," remarked one transfer student, "is that even though it's a state school, the professors really care about my studies here." Although class sizes admittedly run into the hundreds, many rave over the quality of professors at UW, where long office hours and teachers interested in getting to know their pupils are the norm. Students' enthusiasm seems to lose steam when they discuss TA attention, though.

The engineering department is regarded among the university's strongest.

Students also consider UW extremely well rounded in terms of fields of study, which include UW's esteemed nursing school, tough science departments, and Latin classes. On the softer side, students consider social work to be a slack major, and any of the classes within the University Studies program to be "completely lame." University Studies is a program that is mandatory for graduation and is supposed to promote good study habits and help to make the adjustment to college life easier. Unfortunately, many students find this to be a "big joke."

For those wishing to enhance their studies, UW offers a well-regarded honors program. Available to students with a 3.7 high school GPA, or an ACT of 28 or SAT of 1240, the University Honors Program challenges its students to improve upon their thinking and writing skills. The program consists of five courses, of which two are taken freshman year, and one course during each of the remaining three years. Specific honors classes change yearly, but follow consistent themes such as "Non-Western Perspectives" and "Modes of Understanding."

Dorming and Dining

When students say UW is situated in a small town environment, they really mean it. Town-gown relations take on a new meaning when the local town of Laramie is made up primarily of students from the UW. When asked whether most students live on or off campus, one student jokingly replied "Around here, even if you live off campus, you're still pretty much on campus!" Although no one is required to live in university-provided housing, a majority of UW's freshmen and substantial percentage of upperclassmen elect to live in one of the UW's six dorms. Centrally located between most classroom buildings on West Campus and the sports buildings of East Campus, dorm living situates students in the middle of UW life. Hill and Crane house most of the UW's graduate students, while Downey, McIntyre, White, and Orr are primarily home to undergrads. Dorms are coed by wing or floor, and students can choose to live in halls with restricted visiting hours for the opposite sex and substance-free floors. Overall, students give high marks to their dorms for both size and convenience features such as sinks in rooms.

Those choosing to live on campus eat most of their meals in the Washakie Dining Hall. Located centrally to the undergraduate residence halls, Washakie contains a computer lab, game room, workout room, and a convenience store known as the Pokeskellar. More than just a store, the Pokeskellar often acts as a social center for "dormies." While Washakie is not known for its quality of food, students have many other options both on and off campus. "Laramie has your standard set of both fast-food and more sit-down oriented restaurants," reported one student, "selection really isn't a problem." Additionally, students rave over their UW Campus Expre$$ ID cards, which act as credit cards at many on campus eateries. Whether it's a mid-day burrito craving at the Taco Bell or a late night cup of joe at the local coffee spot, satisfaction is only a card swipe away.

The Rowdy Life of a Cowboy

Although most of UW's students are from Wyoming, not many return home on the weekends. More popular destinations include Denver, Ft. Collins, and the ski slopes of the Colorado Rockies. Closer to school is Vedauwoo State Park, which offers scenic trails, intense rock climbing and gorgeous views. On any given weekend though, most students stick around campus and party, especially during football season.

> **"Imagine Mayberry with many well-dressed people and no parking spots and you've got UW!"**

During the fall the UW Cowboys take center stage as they make their annual run at the Mountain West conference championship. This season is no different, with the entire school celebrating the football victory over rival Air Force Academy, snapping an eleven game losing streak that was the longest in division 1-A. Football is not the only game in this town though. Sports enthusiasm runs strongly through the veins of many Cowboys and Cowgirls, and basketball and volleyball also draw large crowds. In addition to these more common intercollegiate sports, Wyoming plays host to rock climbing, skiing, and Ultimate Frisbee teams, and its western nature shines through both the men's and women's top-ranked Rodeo Club teams.

While roping calves might not be your idea of the perfect way to spend an afternoon, UW supplies a myriad of clubs and activities to satisfy even the most discerning of students. Aspiring writers can work for the campus daily paper the *Branding Iron*, or for *Frontiers* magazine. Religious organizations, including Campus Ventures and the Intervarsity Christian Fellowship, abound on the primarily conservative campus, although liberal groups such as "Students Together in Opposition of Prohibition (of Hemp)" also make their mark. Students consider UW's relatively homogeneous population a mixed blessing. "If you fit the Abercrombie and North Face look here, you'll do fine," remarked one student, "but diversity isn't most people's first concern."

Centered on the aptly named "Fraternity Mall," the Greek system at UW is a substantial, yet non-dominating, aspect of campus social life. Greeks engage themselves in various charity events and hold parties throughout the school year, but non-Greeks do not report feeling left out. As one undergrad observed, "If you want to party, you don't need to be a Greek, but it doesn't hurt, either. Parties can be found pretty consistently around town."

Anyone Wanna Make a Snowman?

Students consider the UW campus an extremely safe place to live and work. Emergency phones are scattered throughout, and there is a nighttime campus escort service, although many female students say they feel safe even without this precaution. Many also report leaving their cars with the doors unlocked and the windows rolled down—if they are lucky enough to find a parking space. "Most people do have cars, and there is NO parking anywhere," noted one student, while another reported "imagine Mayberry with many well-dressed people and no parking spots and you've got UW!"

Students consider the UW campus attractive and scenic, with a distinct western architectural flair. Most notably among campus buildings is the Centennial Complex, which houses the University Art Museum and the American Heritage Center. Designed by internationally recognized architect Antoine Predock, the Centennial Complex reminded one student of "a big fortune cookie . . . either that or an oversized teepee." More importantly, the Centennial Complex has gathered an impressive accumulation of cultural artifacts. With collections ranging from 18th century Persian paintings to 20th century photography and sculpture, the Art Museum holds something for art lovers of all kinds, and also stages forums and lectures by invited notables. Other remarkable buildings on campus include War Memorial Stadium, home of the Cowboys, and "Old Main," the building that contained the university in its entirety in 1886 and now serves as the president's office.

There is one additional item worth mentioning about the UW campus—most of the year it will be covered in snow. The first thing every new UW student learns is that if you do not like the cold white stuff, it is going to be a long year. With subfreezing lows by the end of September, summer exits to fall pretty quickly in Cowboy country. Snowy days have even become the subject of legend around Laramie, where every good UW student knows that the first snowfall of the year can be expected on Halloween, and a blizzard will try and trap students on the last day before winter break.

With a friendly smile and easy-going nature, life out in out-of-the-way Laramie offers its students energetic professors, a safe environment, and a full social schedule, all for a bargain price. Nearby skiing, hiking, and rock climbing cater to those with an interest in the outdoors, while intellectual stimulation can likewise be found at the Art Museum and American Heritage Center. So who wants to spend four years fighting off blizzards as a Cowboy? At the University of Wyoming, everyone does.—*Robert Berschinski*

FYI

The three best things about attending the University of Wyoming are "the amazing scenery, the friendly people, and most importantly, those great apple bagels at the Union."

The three worst things about attending the University of Wyoming are "the cold, the wind, and the cold wind."

The three things that every student should do before graduating from the University of Wyoming are "learn to ski, rock climb in Vedauwoo, and go to the hot springs in Saratoga."

One thing I'd like to have known before coming here is "that everyone rides something to school. I definitely would have brought my bike if I knew I was going to able to use it all the time."

Canada

For the American student seeking the adventure of a foreign university but reluctant to travel halfway around the world, Canada may be the ideal location. A different culture, fine programs, and low tuition are just across the border. But there's more to Canada than mountain ranges, friendly people, and cold beer; before you pack your skis and buy a plane ticket, you should know what awaits you.

Don't Say We Didn't Warn You

First, let us offer these words of warning: If generalizations about all the students in a particular university are risky, then generalizations about all the universities in a particular country are even more so. As always, there will be exceptions and differences of degree with respect to everything that follows. Research everything carefully. Individual universities, as well as different programs within the universities, can vary from the exceptional to the inadequate, and it is crucial to find out as much as possible about the school that interests you before you commit.

The greatest difference between Canadian and American universities is that in Canada there are no private colleges; all Canadian schools are government-funded. This has many implications, from overt funding problems to students' attitudes about the purpose of a university and a university education. As any administrator of a state school in the United States will tell you, legislators never seem to allocate as much funding as a school thinks it needs, and Canadian schools have suffered from budget cutbacks in recent years just as American schools have. Many Canadian institutions have problems with their buildings and the quality of specialized equipment for science classes. Of course, this is not universally true, so it's important to find out which schools are strong in the subjects that interest you.

To get a general overview of all Canadian colleges, it is helpful to know if the school is situated in a French-speaking province. That can make a big difference. Ontario and British Columbia have the most colleges of the provinces, so you may want to start there in a general search.

One thing to look for in government-funded Canadian schools is a phenomenon known as "warm-body admissions." Since Canadian schools are funded based on the number of students enrolled, some schools lower their admissions standards to fill seats and raise funding. This often leads to inflated numbers of first year students and high first-year dropout rates. This generally does not occur at the better Canadian schools, such as those included in this guide. Admissions standards tend to be based more on the students' cumulative high-school grades than on other qualities, but standards vary from school to school and from program to program. It is wise to check the standards for a particular program before you apply.

Although there are now more and more exceptions, Canadian universities often lack that elusive entity known as "school spirit" or "school unity." This can be explained in part by the size of most schools and the number of students who live at home or off campus. Unlike many Americans, most Canadians don't seem to be looking for the ideal "college experience." Instead, they are looking primarily for the right education for their future careers, and convenience is an important concern. By and large, Canadian students are unabashedly preprofessional. Students view a degree as a prerequisite for a job and attend university as a means to that end.

If you decide that a unversity in Canada is right for you, there are certain procedures to follow and documents to obtain. Start early! Some schools may not be prepared to handle foreign students. For information, write or call the school and ask to be put in contact with their foreign students' office. Once accepted, you will need a visa and a student authorization. These must be obtained at a Canadian embassy or consulate in the United States, not in Canada. To get the documents, you will need proof of U.S. citizenship (usually a passport or a birth certificate), a letter of acceptance to a Canadian institution, and proof of adequate funds to support yourself while in Canada. If you decide that it's for you, strap on a sense of adventure and get ready for a unique experience, but remember that it's a four year long trek.—*Seung Lee*

Carleton University

Address: 1125 Colonel By Drive; Ottawa, Ontario K1S 5B6
Phone: 613-788-3663
E-mail address: NA
Web site URL: www.carleton.ca
Location: urban
Founded: 1942
Private or Public: public
Religious affiliation: none
Undergraduate enrollment: 14,721
Total enrollment: 17,137
Percent Male/Female: 49%/51%
Percent Minority: 0.0%

Percent African-American: NA
Percent Hispanic: NA
Percent Asian: NA
Percent in-state/out-of-state: 90%/10%
Percent Pub HS: NA
Fraternities: 0%
Sororities: 0%
Number of Applicants: NA
Percent Accepted: NA
Percent Accepted who enroll: NA
Entering: NA
Transfers: NA
Application Deadline: 10 Apr

Mean SAT: NA
Middle 50% SAT range: NA
Middle 50% ACT range: NA
Mean ACT: NA
3 Most popular majors: biology, English, political science
Retention: NA
Graduation rate: NA
Library: 2,000,000 volumes
Tuition and Fees: $2,500 in; $10,000 out
Room and Board: $4,164
On-campus housing: 20%
Financial aid, first-year: 39%

Located on the south side of Ottawa, Carleton is ideally situated for students to take advantage of the capital's offerings. The campus offers easy access to national institutions and governmental operations. Carleton offers several specialized programs such as journalism, mass communications, and aerospace engineering that greatly benefit from the university's location.

Winter Wonderland

Carleton is bounded by the Rideau River and Rideau Canal, which in winter is transformed into the world's longest outdoor skating rink. The original college was founded after World War II to educate veterans, so the university is relatively young. Although Carleton is not in the heart of the city, a 15-minute bus ride takes students downtown. Ottawa is a big city with many offerings, and undergraduates often take advantage of the opportunities for political internships in the Houses of Parliament and other government institutions. Ottawa has its own professional football team, as well as a new Triple-A baseball team, the Lynx, and an NHL team, the Senators. Ottawa also benefits from the traditional perks of capital cities, including several national museums and galleries, as well as the National Arts Centre and its orchestra. Students frequently look to the city for entertainment, and report that city-university relations are good.

Hearty snowfalls turn Carleton into a winter wonderland, especially during the ten days of Winterlude, a city-organized festival celebrating winter with the Rideau Canal as its focal point. In the spring and summer, Ottawa is a beautiful place to enjoy the many bicycle and jogging paths. As one student reported, "Walking to class can become nightmarish, as Ottawa is said to have the highest amount of bicycle traffic in North America."

Journalism and More

Journalism is among the most prestigious programs Carleton offers, attracting students from around the country and abroad; it is surely this great program that puts Carleton on the map. Students say they love it, and cite the accessibility of the faculty as one main reason. Mass communications, public administration, and political science are other strengths at Carleton. Students majoring in the aerospace and environmental studies programs can earn either a B.A. or a B.S. degree. The university also offers an aboriginal studies major as part of the Centre for Aboriginal Education and Research and Culture (CAERC), an interdisciplinary program for academic research and cultural studies of Canada's indigenous people. Carleton recently established a unique four-year Bachelor of International Business with Honours degree program that involves studies in international business as well as a foreign language. Students in this program take courses in the social sciences and spend a year at a foreign university.

Social Life

Social life often centers on the residences and on the campus pubs (the drinking age in Ontario is 19). The Unicentre, a hub of student life, includes a pub called Rooster's and Porter Hall, where various college bands perform. The residences get involved in student life by sponsoring popular intramural games and other activities. "Intramurals are fairly popular, and probably better attended than most varsity matches," said one student. A lottery system determines who will get housing (either a single or a double) in the residences, and the only on-campus housing guarantees are given to students with

at least an A-minus average. Few undergrads have trouble finding accommodation off campus, and many use the housing referral service, an innovative service provided by the university. The surrounding neighborhoods reportedly are dominated by students.

> Ottawa is a big city with many offerings, and undergraduates often take advantage of the opportunities for political internships in the Houses of Parliament and other government institutions.

Carleton students can join more than 100 campus clubs and societies. Like most Canadian schools, Carleton forbids fraternities and sororities because of their exclusive nature. But, students find other ways to fill their time, participating in organizations such as the undergraduate student paper, the *Charlatan*, the radio station, CKCU, and varsity athletics, which tend to attract spectators only when the seasons come to their respective finales. The big football game of the season is the Panda Game (named after the victory prize, originally a stuffed panda bear, but now a bronze bear trophy) against rival University of Ottawa.

As most students will admit, Carleton tries to keep its doors open to anyone who wants to learn. Most students approve of this policy—especially those who would not be in school if that were not the case—although some complain that it leads to overcrowding. Although it is relatively easy to get accepted at Carleton, students report that staying in a select program is more challenging. Spaces available in second-year classes are often limited, especially in journalism and other popular programs.

Strong fund-raising campaigns have enabled Carleton to maintain, modernize, and expand its facilities. The MacOdrum Library houses more than a million volumes as well as microfilms, archival material, maps, documents, and prints; the Carleton University Art Gallery opened in 1992 to an enthusiastic response from the community.

A telephone registration system has eliminated long lines at the beginning of each semester, although students report that "you'd better get some snacks and a blanket and prepare yourself to camp out on the phone for a good chunk of time." Another much-appreciated feature is the underground tunnel system that connects several points on campus. The tunnels provide easy access for students with disabilities and an alternative to cold cross-campus treks during those harsh Canadian winters.

Combining the advantages of the nation's capital with a variety of educational opportunities, Carleton attracts students from throughout Canada and abroad. Students can pursue their interests with diverse academic programs and extracurricular activities, all in a relaxed and friendly environment.—*Alison Pulaski and Staff*

YI

The three best things about attending Carleton are "the Unicentre, the journalism program, and spending time at the Art Gallery."

The three worst things about attending Carleton are "cold winters, the lack of a Greek scene, and having the Panda Game—come on, it's a panda!"

The three things that every student should do before graduating from Carleton are "use the tunnels when it gets unbearably cold, get an internship in Ottawa, and go to Winterlude."

One thing I'd like to have known before coming here is "how cold it gets."

McGill University

Address: 845 Sherbrooke Street West, Montreal, Quebec H3A 2T5	**Percent Minority:** NA	**Mean SAT:** NA
Phone: 514-398-3910	**Percent African-American:** NA	**Middle 50% SAT range:** NA
E-mail address: admissions@aro.lan.mcgill.ca	**Percent Hispanic:** NA	**Middle 50% ACT range:** NA
	Percent Asian: NA	**Mean ACT:** NA
Web site URL: www.aro.mcgill.ca/admissions	**Percent in-state/out-of-state:** NA	**3 Most popular majors:** psychology, political science, commerce
Location: urban	**Percent Pub HS:** NA	
Founded: 1821	**Fraternities:** 0%	**Retention:** NA
Private or Public: public	**Sororities:** 0%	**Graduation rate:** NA
Religious affiliation: none	**Number of Applicants:** 14,783	**Library:** 2,900,000 volumes
Undergraduate enrollment: 15,889	**Percent Accepted:** NA	**Tuition and Fees:** $3,168 in; $12,000 out
Total enrollment: 20,348	**Percent Accepted who enroll:** NA	**Room and Board:** $6,412
Percent Male/Female: 42%/58%	**Entering:** NA	**On-campus housing:** 28%
	Transfers: NA	**Financial aid, first-year:** NA
	Application Deadline: 15 Jan	

Located in the heart of Montreal, McGill University offers its students the best of two worlds: a college experience in a safe urban setting. Come rain or subzero weather, McGill students can always be found gracing the streets of Montreal, taking advantage of its numerous resources. About McGill's location, one student said, "Where in the States can you find an amazing university in a safe urban setting—the key word being 'safe'?" But despite its urban location, the McGill campus is no less collegiate than a suburban or rural one. Indeed, looking at McGill's luxurious lawns and plethora of trees, a student may forget that just footsteps away from campus lies one of the world's most happening cities. All things considered, it's no wonder McGill students keep coming and never want to leave!

Learning the Canadian Way

When applying to McGill, students are asked to indicate the academic field they intend to enter. At McGill, the different academic disciplines are called "faculties." The faculties cover a wide range of interests including everything from the arts to agricultural science, with each faculty having its own department and specific requirements. Most of the faculties are housed on the main campus; only agricultural studies is on MacDonald campus.

Few students complain about the requirements. Said one student, "The requirements are extremely reasonable. They truly allow one to explore what fields one is interested in without having to be loaded down." A typical four-year B.A. candidate needs about 120 credits to graduate. First-year students in the arts are required to take one class in three out of the four following disciplines—humanities, social sciences, languages, and math and science. These requirements are intended to give students a wide view of available options. After this initial year of experimentation, students declare a major and are assigned an advisor in their specific department.

But the choices given each student do not end there. Within each department, a student can choose to complete a single or double major and an honors or joint-honors degree. Honors students typically take more specialized classes and work more closely with individual professors. In addition, an honors degree might require a senior thesis, depending on the individual department.

In terms of the classes themselves, many departments require introductory lectures that, like those at other universities, tend to be quite massive. TAs help lead discussion sections, which somewhat compensates for the immense lectures. But whereas at other universities class size shrinks as courses become more advanced, at McGill classes remain large, a cause of many student complaints. At McGill, classes are taught in English, but students can elect to take tests and write papers in French.

Canadian Cutbacks

When asked about the living environment at McGill, one student replied, "All the problems with living at McGill are due to three problems, cutbacks, cutbacks, cutbacks." For instance, even though McGill's libraries house over 2.9 million volumes, the libraries themselves are described as pretty pitiful; few students actually study there.

> **"Where in the States can you find an amazing university in a safe urban setting—the key word being 'safe'?"**

What distinguishes McGill from many American universities is that few of its students actually live on campus. Most live off campus or commute from home. First priority in on-campus housing is given to international students, primarily first-years.

McGill dorms are formally called residences, but students refer to them as "rez." Four of the main residences are found on the hill, a location first-year students never stop complaining about. Said one student, "The rezes are not that near anything and you have to climb this huge hill."

Each "rez" has a unique reputation. Gardener is known as the place for quiet studious students, although current first-year students say that reputation is beginning to change; Molson, previously known as a typically rowdy dorm has become tamer in the past two years. McConnell remains the party dorm, as well as the rez with single-sex bathrooms. All three are coed. If coed living is not your thing, Royal Victoria College is an all-female dorm with a more central campus location.

Students from these three dorms eat in the same cafeteria; students in Douglas, situated slightly lower down the hill, have a separate facility. Known for its aesthetic beauty, Douglas is the favorite among many. However, due to seemingly never-ending construction, Douglas has begun to lost its charm to some.

Solin Hall, the newest "rez," is also located away from the hill. Students often complain about its location, explaining it is too far from everything. With its apartmentlike rooms, Solin offers more independent living for some; for others, it may be the cause of constant problems and hassles since Solin students have to cook their own meals.

But judging from the overall negative view of McGill food, cooking for yourself in Solin may not be such a bad thing after all; all other students are required to purchase a meal plan. McGill food was described as completely inedible and the meal plans as stingy because McGill limits what students can take at meals. In response to the sometimes ludicrous dining guidelines, one student griped, "Since when is orange juice a dessert?" For vegetarians, food options are even worse or nonexistent.

After the first year, students escape the meal plan as they move out of residences and, more often than not, into the "McGill ghetto." But don't be fooled by the name. In reality, the "ghetto" is a neighborhood of nice yet affordable apartment houses located just steps away from campus. Other popular places for upperclassmen include "The Plateau" or "The Main," which is situated near St. Laurent Street, a center of activity with its numerous bars and restaurants.

Extracurriculars Exist?

A McGill freshman asked to name organizations he belonged to could not list a single one. With the exception of sports, extracurricular activities do not enjoy high student participation, largely due to the high percentage of students living off campus. Greek life, too, has minimal campus presence. When asked to list a few clubs, most students name The Stonecutters, a popular group whose sole activity is to gather and watch *The Simpsons* together every Sunday.

Students involved in sports compete at the club, intramural, and varsity levels. An interesting fact most people don't know is that Harvard is McGill's historical rival. Indeed, the first North American football game was reportedly a McGill vs. Harvard rugby game that took a bizarre turn, leading to the "invention" of football. Nowadays, McGill's more commonly recognized

rival is Queen's University in Kingston, Ontario. And even though football is not very popular at McGill, students still get a chance to show their school spirit at the annual Homecoming game, a.k.a. the "I-didn't-know-we-had-a-football-team game." McGill students demonstrated another rare bout of school spirit when the men's soccer team won the national championship back in 1997.

For more literary minds, McGill offers several student publications. Published three times a week, the *McGill Daily* comes out twice a week in English and once in French. In addition, literary alternatives include the weekly *McGill Tribune* and the *Red Herring*, a humor magazine. But at McGill, out-of-class life typically revolves around off-campus venues.

Bars on Campus

For American natives, McGill's on-campus bar may be a strange sight. Unlike American schools where the majority of the students are underage, McGill social life truly capitalizes on the local drinking age, which is only eighteen. Whereas most freshman orientations at other schools center on talks and pizza dinners, according to one student, the goal of freshman orientation at McGill is "to get the freshmen drunk." Almost all activities revolve around drinking; even the breakfast menu features bagels and beer. Drinking is truly a central part of McGill social life.

Besides bars, other popular social spots include Peels Pub with fourteen-cent wings and shots for under a dollar. Angel's is known for great dancing. Gert's is the convenient and popular on-campus bar. Overall, clubbing and bar-hopping are the main events of a McGill student's weekend nights.

So with such a bustling social life, why would McGill students ever choose to stay in? As most McGill students would answer: the cold. Without a doubt, the freezing temperatures were one of McGill students' main complaints. But for those prospective students who are able to foresee themselves wearing woolen clothes for the next four years, McGill is the place to be.—*Alyssa Blair Greenwald*

FYI

The three best things about attending McGill are "Montreal, the people, and the legal drinking age of 18."

The three worst things about attending McGill are "the hill, the food, and the administration."

The three things every student should do before graduating are "to spend a night at Peels, to go to a McGill vs. Queens game, and to watch *The Simpsons* with The Stonecutters."

One thing I'd like to have known before coming here is "how cold it gets here."

McMaster University

Address: 1280 Main Street West; Hamilton, Ontario L8S 4L8
Phone: 905-525-4600
E-mail address: macadmit@mcmaster.edu
Web site URL: www.mcmaster.edu
Location: suburban
Founded: 1887
Private or Public: public
Religious affiliation: none
Undergraduate enrollment: 14,130
Total enrollment: 18,806
Percent Male/Female: 43%/57%
Percent Minority: NA

Percent African-American: NA
Percent Hispanic: NA
Percent Asian: NA
Percent in-state/out-of-state: NA
Percent Pub HS: NA
Fraternities: 0%
Sororities: 0%
Number of Applicants: 19,652
Percent Accepted: 66%
Percent Accepted who enroll: 29%
Entering: 3,786
Transfers: 1,004
Application Deadline: 1 May

Mean SAT: NA
Middle 50% SAT range: NA
Middle 50% ACT range: NA
Mean ACT: NA
3 Most popular majors: kinesiology, commerce, sociology
Retention: 92%
Graduation rate: 86%
Library: 1,700,000 volumes
Tuition and Fees: $3,907 in; $12,000 out
Room and Board: $5,450
On-campus housing: 70%
Financial aid, first-year: 50%

A long the highway between Toronto and Niagara Falls, there is a simple sign that leads to McMaster University. Unbeknownst to most American students, that sign also leads to one of the most academically superior institutions in Canada. Nationally recognized as a place of scholastic excellence, McMaster offers its students an extensive choice of programs in a socially and academically stimulating environment.

Exciting Academics

The first thing that attracts students to McMaster is the wide variety of possible majors. Entering freshmen can join the school of business, social science, health science, engineering, or science, each of which offers exhaustive choices. Especially popular are two interdisciplinary programs, engineering management and arts and science, the only cross-majors available in Canada. Students say that arts and science, which combines natural and

physical science with logic, the humanities, and the written word, is the absolute coolest and a guarantee to medical school admission anywhere. Engineering management grants students a degree in both engineering and business, which, according to one third-year major, is a great ticket to a job after graduation. Although this major lasts five years, most others run for the usual four years.

Some students remember being concerned about concentrating on a major at the beginning of their university career, but that worry is usually dispelled by the liberal arts requirements. In order to be awarded a degree, students have to take 30 percent of their courses outside the field of their major. One physics major lauds this requirement because it allows students to explore subjects they would never consider: It opens worlds that would otherwise be left unexplored.

Most Mac-ers feel that all of the university resources go into the science and

business faculties, while courses in the arts and humanities are neglected. The most popular introductory courses are chemistry and psychology, while undergrads say the best loved class for students of all majors is calculus. The easiest course on campus is without a doubt, Critical Thinking. While some of the first-year classes have enrollments of up to one thousand, most are under 300 and are taught almost exclusively by professors, with tutorials taught by teaching assistants. As the courses become more advanced, the classes become smaller and individual relationships with professors have room to flourish. Some of the professor teach straight out of the textbooks, but the majority are way cooler. Said one undergrad, "You can tell they are interested in what they are teaching and they really try to make every single thing interesting for us, too." Some students, especially freshmen, were surprised by the difficulty of the courses. "It is really hard to get good grades. You have to work hard even in intro classes," claimed one student.

Extracurriculars

McMaster students do not work all the time, however. There are several extracurricular options open to undergraduates, from campus newspapers to intramural sports, the Conservative Party to the Queer Club. Some students say, however, that participation is depressing. Said one junior, "There are a million and one things to get into, but nobody does." The major student-run organization is the McMaster Student Union, which basically controls all student activities, including the weekly newspaper, the *Silhouette*. The Student Union also runs two bars frequented by Mac-ites, a day-care center, a grocery store, and a radio station, all of which are staffed entirely by students.

Out and About

Indubitably, the most popular extracurricular activities at McMaster exist within the social scene. There are casual, semiformal, and formal dances throughout the year, frequent parties, two unofficial fraternity houses, and two on-campus bars. In Ontario, the drinking age is 19, which means that most students can legally enter either the Student Union or John (the bars) to hang out. Each building also has a formal and a semiformal dance, as well as being host to various other events.

The freshman orientation Welcome Week, formerly called frosh week, is one of the biggest and most fun events on campus. Students of the incoming class described it as "incredible. It was the best time I ever had." Mac freshmen tend to travel in packs, so dating is not common during the first few months. However, according to one second-year student, by January things calm down and people begin to fall into their niches.

The People Count

"The people are the most exciting things here," according to one enthusiastic freshman. Upperclassmen agree that there is no such thing as a typical student. Although there is a rather diverse population, one student was surprised by the white majority. Most Macs are from Ontario, although there is a (quite small) foreign student population. Macs are into comfort. "Don't come to Mac if you're a style queen and don't want to stand out, because you will," cautioned one undergrad.

The population of McMaster is described as big enough that you won't feel bored, but small enough that you'll recognize people walking down the street. The campus is likewise considered that perfect size, neither claustrophobic nor intimidating. Most of the buildings are on the central campus. It takes ten minutes tops to walk anywhere on campus. The university is located in West Hamilton, away from the downtown areas and industrial parks. The campus itself is surrounded by a forested conservation area, which is often used for hiking. Hamilton is only a few hours from Toronto, one of the largest cultural centers in Canada, and Mac students frequently drive into the city.

The most spectacular building at McMaster is said to be University Hall, which was one of the original McMaster structures. Mills Library is the center of a three-library system that also includes the Thode Science and Engineering libraries, both of which were recently renovated. The university has also added an art gallery to Mills.

Campus Living

There are several resident choices at Mc-Master. Most freshmen live on campus in one of the five coed dorms or in the single-sex dorms. There is also an International House for foreign students and ethnic minorities and Halycon Hall, which has mandatory quiet hours. Most upperclassmen live off campus, but those who choose to remain in rooms that are described as passable at best can live in Bates Residence, which has pre-apartments complete with kitchens and bathrooms. Any student who makes the Dean's List with an A-minus average or higher is guaranteed a single room for the next semester.

On campus, there are four cafeterias that are good for institutional grub. There are, however, some horror stories (family visits ending with mom and dad in bed ill after suspicious fish in the cafeteria). Students can also eat at one of the six fast-food kiosks around campus. Students do not have a general meal plan, but rather buy each meal, often in the main cafeteria, which has a fast-food court and is open 24/7, ideal for midnight snacks. The food is very expensive, however, so many undergraduates eat off campus.

> **The campus is neither claustrophobic nor intimidating.**

McMaster students acknowledge that they are not the most spirited school. Despite the fact that the varsity basketball team is one of the top in Canada, some students have no idea it exists. Generally Canadian league sports are good, particularly the wrestling, gymnastics, and swim teams. There is a newly renovated Wellness Center, with facilities for nonvarsity student use.

McMaster's exceptional reputation naturally leads many students to choose it. Coupled with that is a vibrant community in which members feel stimulated, not to be brainy Macs, but to expand both scholastically and socially.—*Staff*

FYI

The three best things about attending McMaster are "the people, the academic combinations, and the doors that a degree opens."

The three worst things about attending McMaster are "the academic rigor, the lack of enthusiasm for organizations, and the prices on campus."

The three things that every student should do before graduating from McMaster are "go into the city, end a date with a late night meal in the food court, and explore the outdoors."

One thing I'd like to have known before coming here is "how secluded the campus can feel if you let it."

Queen's University

Address: 110 Alfred Street, Kingston, Ontario K7L 3N6
Phone: 613-533-2218
E-mail address: admissn@post.queensu.ca
Web site URL: www.queensu.ca
Location: small city
Founded: 1841
Private or Public: public
Religious affiliation: none
Undergraduate enrollment: 10,998
Total enrollment: 15,973
Percent Male/Female: 45%/55%
Percent Minority: NA

Percent African-American: NA
Percent Hispanic: NA
Percent Asian: NA
Percent in-state/out-of-state: NA
Percent Pub HS: 89%
Fraternities: 0%
Sororities: 0%
Number of Applicants: 17,085
Percent Accepted: 47%
Percent Accepted who enroll: 32%
Entering: 2,600
Transfers: 75
Application Deadline: 15 May

Mean SAT: 558 V, 606 M
Middle 50% SAT range: NA
Middle 50% ACT range: NA
Mean ACT: NA
3 Most popular majors: commerce
Retention: NA
Graduation rate: 90%
Library: 1,900,000 volumes
Tuition and Fees: $4,540 in; $11,000 out
Room and Board: $5,600
On-campus housing: 85%
Financial aid, first-year: 55%

Do not be fooled by Queen's University's reputation as the "Harvard of the North." Although both universities boast a tradition of academic excellence, Queen's is a uniquely Canadian university, not a mere replica of its Cambridge peer. Located on the north shore of Lake Ontario in Kingston, Ontario, Queen's University is one of Canada's premier schools. Rivaling McGill University for first ranking, Queen's University demands excellence and dedication from its students, beginning at admission and persisting until graduation. Fortunately, Queen's students tend to be a driven bunch and, overall, survive and even flourish in the school's often competitive environment.

Survival of the Fittest

"Queen's academics are hard. There is no other way to describe them. But I'm not complaining," one student reported. Although requirements and course loads vary from major to major, all students should expect to be challenged academically at Queen's.

The commerce and concurrent education programs are known to be two of the best majors at Queen's. The engineering and sciences are also known to be top-notch, but are no picnic for first-year students, who often face course loads of 30-plus hours per week.

First-year courses tend to fairly large, but numbers dwindle down to about 20 people in upper-level courses. Introductory lectures usually are not overcrowded with students who simply want to meet requirements, since many departments do not require students to take courses outside of their major. In general, Queen's students report that they are pleased with the courses they are taking.

A universal comment was praise for the dedication of the professors at Queen's. Only a handful of courses are taught by TAs, and even those TAs tend to be highly qualified. Many distinguished professors, including key political thinkers, grace the halls of Queen's University, which has produced some of the most influential men and women in Canadian government.

Life Outside the Classroom

First-year students typically live on campus although a few choose to remain at home. Dorms vary from single-sex to coed. One popular coed freshman hall is Vic Hall. Some dorms have special international or "quiet" floors. Although students can request where and with how many roommates they wish to live, their requests are not always guaranteed to be met.

Residence halls were given good marks overall with few student complaints about strict regulations. Although all residential students are required to purchase a meal plan, each dorm has its own kitchen. Food is reportedly edible, but one student warned against eating the school meat. Other options for on-campus dining include Taco Bell, Pizza Hut, Subway, and Tim Horton's.

After first year, most students move off campus, though they do not tend to move far. Most students remain within one mile of campus in what is dubbed the "student ghetto apartments," named such for their cheap rents and less-than-stellar conditions. Off-campus housing in Kingston, Ontario, is not hard to come by, and most students would concur that Kingston is great a place to live. A small city with 120,000 residents, it caters to the student population thanks to an abundance of bars and restaurants. At times, however, the city's small size "can be stifling."

The campus itself has a great location right in the heart of Kingston. Bordering a lake, the campus boasts beauty in the form of wide open spaces, old limestone buildings, and a plethora of trees. Although Queen's students often get teased by their counterparts at rival McGill because of all the provincial jails located in Kingston, crime at Queen's is not a significant problem. Perhaps this is the result of the administration's tight security and strict regulations. "The regulations can be a pain, but at least you feel safe," one student said.

Unlike the majority of students at American universities, most students at Queen's are of legal drinking age, and the social life clearly reflects this fact. Frosh Week is packed with beer-drinking and partying. During the day, frosh bond at administration-organized events, but at night festivities, drinking is the focus as students kick back and meet one another. "I met some of my closest friends during Frosh Week," stated one upperclassman.

The drinking does not stop with the end of Frosh Week. Social life tends to center on three campus pubs: Clark Hall, Alphie's, and QP (the Quiet Pub). At Clark Hall, engineering students carry on the Friday noon ritual of "pounding beers til you can't get up." For those who prefer off-campus partying, the Shot receives rave reviews as did A.J.'s and Stages.

Overall, the social scene at Queen's i described as excellent. "Although Queen students may work hard during the week we sure know how to party on the week ends," one student boasted. Such partyin usually starts Thursday night and contin ues throughout the weekend.

Extracurricular Haven

Despite their busy academic schedule Queen's students still participate in a wid array of extracurricular activities. Popu lar clubs include Queen's Model Parlia ment, Alma Mater Big Brothers (AMS), student environmental coalition, and i tramurals. Students can also elect to pa ticipate in one of two weekly publication the *Queen's Journal* newspaper or th satirical *Golden Words*. Other more zar activities include the juggling club, and a though small and few in number, the Jew ish organizations on campus tend to b quite visible.

> **"Although Queen's students may work hard during the week, we sure know how to party on the weekends."**

With the Golden Gale as their schoo mascot, Queen's students are a spirite bunch when it comes to sports. Althoug the school actively recruits for athlete prospective athletes must still adhere t high academic entrance standards. Pe haps as a consequence, Queen's does n always have the strongest sports team

Some of the most popular teams Queen's are the football, rugby, an hockey teams. The annual "Kill McGil game draws huge crowds, and many stu dents come dressed in tams and overal to show their Golden Gale pride. Eng neers are known for their unusual trad tion of dying themselves purple to sho their Queen's spirit. Some students com plain about the tight security at the game but most students agree the games a "fun social events."

Even at the intramural level, spor

tend to be very popular. Students say the intramurals are very well organized and are well-divided so that anyone can pick and choose the intensity and level they wish to compete at. The only complaint is with regard to the condition of athletic facilities. Many of the stadiums are old and need to be renovated. As one student said, "We need a better sports arena in a big way."

Although many of the Queen's students are from either Toronto or Ottawa, the student body is still described as "diverse." Nevertheless, students cite the predominant Queen's student as "preppy" and from a high socio-economic background. Minorities can feel at home with the school's plethora of minority groups, but according to some students, most people tend to interact within their own ethnic group. Overall however, Queen's is not described as a cliquish school, and most students report that they are satisfied with the shape of their student body.

In fact, some students would agree that the student body is one of the best things about Queen's. "I feel I have met some of the most amazing people here, people whose friendships will last a lifetime," said one undergrad. "I love that students here are smart, but still know how to have fun. I couldn't be happier."—*Alyssa Blair Greenwald*

FYI

The three best things about attending Queen's University are "the people, the setting, and the size."

The three worst things about attending Queen's University are "the weather, the jails, and the small city living."

The three things every student should do before graduating from Queen's are "to get a Queen's jacket, to go to Stages, and to go to a 'Kill McGill' game."

One thing I'd like to have known before coming here is "how small a city Kingston really is."

University of British Columbia

Address: 2016-1874 East Hall, Vancouver, British Columbia V6T 1Z1
Phone: 604-822-3014
E-mail address: registrar.admissions@ubc.ca
Web site URL: www.ubc.ca
Location: urban
Founded: 1915
Private or Public: public
Religious affiliation: none
Undergraduate enrollment: 25,743
Total enrollment: 31,971
Percent Male/Female: 44%/56%

Percent Minority: NA
Percent African-American: NA
Percent Hispanic: NA
Percent Asian: NA
Percent in-state/out-of-state: NA
Percent Pub HS: NA
Fraternities: NA
Sororities: NA
Number of Applicants: 22,849
Percent Accepted: 48%
Percent Accepted who enroll: 29%
Entering: 3,181
Transfers: NA

Application Deadline: NA
Mean SAT: NA
Middle 50% SAT range: NA
Middle 50% ACT range: NA
Mean ACT: NA
3 Most popular majors: NA
Retention: NA
Graduation rate: NA
Library: NA
Tuition and Fees: $2550 in; $14,048 out
Room and Board: $4,516
On-campus housing: 5%
Financial aid, first-year: 16%

Located just outside of Vancouver and the sandy beaches of the Pacific Ocean and some of the greatest skiing mountains in North America, the University of British Columbia offers students the chance to experience their college years in a million different ways.

Not only does the University of British

Columbia have the reputation for being one of Canada's premiere academic institutions, but it is also one of the largest, with over 40,000 students. Accordingly, the extensive course offerings support a wide range of academic interests. The diverse social atmosphere and relaxed attitude toward underage drinking (the legal drinking age in Canada is 19, so most students can legally drink) provide numerous opportunities for students to kick back and relax at campus bars like The Pit, at popular beer garden parties, and in the fraternity houses. According to one student, the typical life of the residential dorms revolves around "party, sleep, procrastinate, party, sleep, procrastinate, intramural sport, and last-minute homework."

So Many Engineers, So Little Time

Despite the emphasis on social life within the campus dorms, course requirements at the University of British Columbia are demanding. English is required for all first year students, although freshmen claim that "it's really, really boring." Students feel the number of credits required for graduation is reasonable, even though some complained about a distribution requirement that makes students concentrating in the arts take courses in a science department (and vice versa). Sciences are particularly strong at UBC, and the majority of students major in either commerce or engineering. "There are so many engineering students here," said one undergrad. "They walk around in their stupid red jackets and play lots of pranks. And even more than engineering students, there are masses and masses of commerce students." The university also offers competitive programs in forestry and nursing. But if you are looking for an easy major, sociology, music appreciation, and French are rumored to be the slackers' favorites.

In a school as big as UBC, class size tends to be large. Lecture classes with 200 to 300 students are the norm, but classes offered in the evening can be smaller. Still, most students report being generally satisfied with the level of teaching at UBC. An undergrad noted, "All of my teachers make themselves as accessible to the students as they can in a school with 40,000 students." Large lecture classes often break up into small discussion sections run by graduate students. In one freshman English class, a TA opened a class on Margaret Atwood's *The Edible Woman* by bringing soda and cookies for the entire class.

Undergrads report that Science One (a three-course program that concurrently studies physics, chemistry, and biology), which accepts only a limited number of students, is among the most difficult classes, although some freshmen reported that Science One does not require serious work. According to one student, "The thing that thrills me the most about my classes is that there are only three, and they are easy!" Registering for classes is done by telephone and gives priority to students who make the best grades. The registration process is jokingly described as the one most difficult aspect of academic life for some UBC students.

Parties, Nude Beaches, and Drinking

Because of UBC's diversity and size, student social life varies widely. University-sponsored movies and guest lectures at the "SUB" (student union building) are reportedly well attended. Past speakers have even included a professional hypnotist. Frat parties and beer garden parties remain a favorite for most students, who generally feel that alcohol plays a significant role in most social activities at the school. The frats also host a number of theme parties throughout the year, usually featuring such events as a toga night, a "boxers" bash, and several formal affairs. Among the more unusual student hangouts is a nude beach right off campus called the Wreck. It is reported to be a "place with no laws."

Much social life at UBC is divided between students who live on campus and those who commute. Because housing is limited, many students are unable to get campus housing and a large percentage of the student body lives off campus. Vancouver's high rental rates make off-campus living fairly expensive, and many students choose to commute from home. Since a fair amount of freshman social life centers on dorm parties, many students living off campus report feeling isolated from campus life. One off-campus student observed, "It kind of takes away from the university atmosphere, that most people live far away from the school; it's also really hard to make friends here."

Thirteen Women Make a Whorehouse

Students who live on campus say the rooms are definitely livable and even nice, depending on how much you expect in a residential dorm. One major complaint, however, is that there is not enough female housing for a school some dub "the University of a Billion Chicks." Housing options include two coed complexes primarily for freshmen and a variety of apartments and family units for upperclassmen and graduate students. Single-sex and coed housing are available, and students can also choose to live in special theme housing. Fraternity houses provide additional housing for students involved in UBC's active Greek life. An old Canadian law defining houses of prostitution as those with more than 12 females under one roof prevents sororities from living together on campus.

A nighttime walking service and an on-campus bus make students feel secure on campus. Vancouver has a low crime rate for a large city, and students report they feel perfectly safe walking around campus or through the city after dark. Still, some students report that use of date-rape drugs and prowlers in the residential colleges are increasing threats to security. Unfortunately according to one student, UBC has a reputation for having "one of the highest rape rates in Canadian universities."

Dining options at the university are pretty extensive. There are cafeterias in almost every building. Students report that the food served in the dining halls is definitely edible and the veggie wraps are particularly tasty. One student even warned, "Beware of the cinnamon buns— they are highly addictive!" For those who refuse to ingest cafeteria food, the Village, an international food fair, serves everything from sushi to Subway sandwiches. All campus facilities serve only Coca-Cola products, so do not expect to find Pepsi or Snapple beverages. For those students who crave culinary diversity, Vancouver also provides a wide range of restaurants.

Pros and Cons of Diversity

Education subsidies from the Canadian government make UBC a relatively affordable institution, comparable with in-state tuition at most public colleges in the U.S. Still, many students are surprised to find a high concentration of students from upper- and upper-middle-class families. As one student noted, "The UBC student stereotype is a well-dressed commerce student. A lot of the people at this school seem to be pretty rich and quite snobby." But students from less privileged backgrounds also make up a large, if not quite as conspicuous, percentage of the student body. The UBC student body also is one of the most multicultural in Canada. Asian students form a large portion of the university's minority population, but students report that other minorities are also well represented. International students at UBC bring still more diversity to the campus, and interracial and homosexual couples are definitely accepted.

> Education subsidies from the Canadian government make UBC a relatively affordable institution, comparable with in-state tuition at most public colleges in the U.S.

However, great diversity takes its toll on school spirit. One student remarked that school spirit is only present "among engineers, forestry [students], and at sporting events." Athletic competitions are reportedly poorly advertised and rarely attended. While some students promote their Thunderbirds with pride, others do not even know that the Thunderbird is their mascot. While varsity sports are not so popular, many students do participate in the intramural sports. Undergrads describe athletic facilities for both varsity athletes and the student body at large as good, and UBC offers roughly comparable facilities to both groups. Students agree that other campus facilities are also maintained in fair condition. Although some students find the large buildings "grotesque," many others find campus aesthetically pleasing. The combination of Gothic buildings and modern glass complexes contribute to the campus's eclectic atmosphere. To nature lovers' delight, study breaks at UBC can mean taking a stroll through the botanical, rose, and Japanese gardens scattered throughout campus.

Student opinion about UBC varies as widely as its diverse population. Some students absolutely recommend the university; others complain, "it's big, it's ugly, and it's really, really lonely." While each student's perspective depends on his or her experiences, UBC has a lot to offer all its students. With a reputation for academic excellence, a unique location, and an immensely diverse student body, it's not hard to see why the University of British Columbia holds its own as one of Canada's most popular colleges.—*Letitia Stein and Staff*

FYI

The three best things about attending UBC are "how affordable it is, how safe I feel, and how strong the academics are here."

The three worst things about attending UBC are "the lack of school spirit, the commuter school mentality, and the lack of diversity."

The three things that every student should do before graduating from UBC are "tan nude at the Wreck, have a beer at the Pit, and drink lots of Coca-Cola."

One thing I'd like to have known before coming here is "how huge this place really is."

University of Toronto

Address: 315 Bloor Street West; Toronto, Ontario M5S 1A3	**Percent African-American:** NA	**Mean SAT:** NA
Phone: 416-978-2190	**Percent Hispanic:** NA	**Middle 50% SAT range:** NA
E-mail address: ask@adm.utoronto.edu	**Percent Asian:** NA	**Middle 50% ACT range:** NA
Web site URL: www.utoronto.ca	**Percent in-state/out-of-state:** NA	**Mean ACT:** NA
Location: urban	**Percent Pub HS:** NA	**3 Most popular majors:** NA
Founded: 1827	**Fraternities:** 0%	**Retention:** 96%
Private or Public: public	**Sororities:** 0%	**Graduation rate:** NA
Religious affiliation: none	**Number of Applicants:** 34,089	**Library:** 10,000,000 volumes
Undergraduate enrollment: 41,873	**Percent Accepted:** 61%	**Tuition and Fees:** $3,322 in; $9,500 out
Total enrollment: 52,796	**Percent Accepted who enroll:** 65%	**Room and Board:** $6,000
Percent Male/Female: 44%/56%	**Entering:** 13,477	**On-campus housing:** 7%
Percent Minority: NA	**Transfers:** NA	**Financial aid, first-year:** NA
	Application Deadline: 1 Mar	

Looking for great classes, a great nightlife, and 50,000 other people to share it with? At U of T, students *know* how to work and play hard, all in *da*'s largest city.

men because the enormous size of the school makes it difficult to see the same face twice. Most students, though, are able to find their own niches and are enthusiastic about their experience.

At U of T, as the university is affectionately called, everyone agrees that the education is top-notch. There are four main programs, or faculties, as they are known: engineering; arts and science; music; and

lized Attention
Size

versity of Toronto for *imidating* for fresh-physical education and health. The Arts and Science Faculty is by far the most popular program. Each has its own specific requirements, and students apply directly to the faculty of their choice. Classes at U of T are strong, and there is a wide selection available, although intro classes can be huge. "I've heard of classes with 1500 people that had to be held in Convocation Hall to accommodate everybody," commented one student. Most find class sizes become smaller and more personalized as they go up in years. One senior in engineering noted that "by fourth year you get to know the people in your program really well, since you all take the same classes year after year." The workload is demanding, but students at U of T know how to work hard. With all the choices available there is a class for everyone, and it is relatively easy for most to find a schedule that fits their needs.

> **"If you know what you want in an education, there's no better place than U of T for the number of opportunities it offers."**

The staff is also greatly admired—many professors are leaders in their field. Students agree that the faculty is highly intelligent; although some say that this doesn't necessarily make for great teaching skills. Often the number of foreign professors in the science-based departments can especially be frustrating when it comes to understanding lectures. Still, most observe that professors are generally accessible even in the biggest classes. Grading is fair, and depending on the professor, can even be somewhat stringent. One student recalled classes where only a few people passed, and a significant number failed. "There was more grade inflation in my high school," added another senior. TAs are also a helpful option, although many students grumbled about the disruption caused by a recent strike by TAs. On the whole though, most agree on the strength of teaching at U of T, and consequently on the depth of its programs.

Like at other Canadian institutions, there is a co-op program where students alternate between attending classes and working. Formally known as the "Professional Experience Year," or PY, the program is relatively young and is geared toward the engineering and computer sciences. Compared to other co-op programs where work terms last about four months, PY runs anywhere from 12–16 months at a time, which students say allows for more depth on the job. "When employers know you're going to be staying longer, they're willing to give you more responsibility, which really helps build good relationships for possible future employment," explained one student.

Life on Campus

At U of T the nine colleges make up the center of campus life. Usually it's the students in arts and science who live in the colleges, but anybody can apply. Seven of the nine are located on the university's central Toronto campus, while the other two, Erindale and Scarborough, are both about a half hour drive away. While they have their own specific religious backgrounds (St. Michael's, for example, is predominantly Roman Catholic), they are open to everyone. Also, the colleges function as somewhat autonomous units with U of T, each with its own administrative powers (registration, etc.), dining services, housing, and traditions. They serve as smaller communities within the larger one at the school, and most are enthusiastic about the sense of belonging the colleges provide that may otherwise be lacking in such a huge place. Students tend to live on campus their first and sometimes second years (housing is guaranteed for the first year), but after that many choose to live off campus. With the help of the housing office at U of T, finding a place to live outside is relatively easy and prices are affordable, if people share. Moreover, with the extensive subway system available, students don't necessarily find it inconvenient to live a distance away from campus. Since a great proportion of the student body comes from the metro Toronto area, some also choose to live at home and commute.

The food in the colleges is of typical cafeteria-style fare, and the meal plan offers flex dollars that can be transferred to local restaurants, which students praise. In any case, finding good dining in Toronto is not a problem at all—the amazing selection will satisfy anyone's palate. Furthermore, students strongly recommend checking out Chinatown, which borders the campus, for great food. There are some cooking facilities available in the colleges, too, for those who long for home-cooked meals.

After Hours

When classes are over for the day, there's a still lot to do. With such a wide variety of extracurricular activities available, "if you want it, chances are there's already a club for it," as one student commented. In a school of such mammoth size, being part of a club can be a good way to meet people. Most activities run out of Hart House, a building that boasts athletic and meeting facilities convenient for student groups to use. Still, a broad mix of students exists: while some are very involved in extracurriculars, others don't care as much about participating in campus affairs. With so many students living off campus, people find themselves separating their school lives from their outside lives. Often the sheer size of U of T, coupled with its location in a bustling city makes for a disconnected atmosphere. Students can be very businesslike at U of T, as one mentioned: "A lot of people are just here to go to class—otherwise their lives are pretty separate from the university."

There isn't a great deal of unity or support for the varsity sports teams; school spirit is mainly to be found within individual colleges or programs (such as engineering, etc.). Since each group runs its own activities and events and has its own pubs, most socializing occurs within. The divisions among colleges surprised some students. There are a number of intercollege competitions and friendly rivalries as opposed to friendships, so it can be hard to meet people from other colleges. On the upside, students of a college are often especially close and develop strong bonds with one another.

Only Toronto

If there's one thing students at U of T all agree upon, it's the umpteen number of opportunities that going to school in a city like Toronto provides. "Toronto is great," one sophomore raved; "I couldn't imagine being anywhere else." Many die-hard fans attend Maple Leafs hockey games at the new Air Canada Center, and NBA basketball at the Skydome is becoming popular. There is also a well-developed entertainment scene. From the Art Gallery of Ontario to the music of the famous Roy Thomson Hall, theater, the arts hold their own in Toronto. There is a myriad of recreational activities available—Canada's Wonderland, the country's best amusement park, is less than an hour away. Students are enthusiastic about the nightlife, too. Clubbing is the thing to do, with places like the Whiskey Saigon and The Brunswick House among some of the favorite U of T haunts. No matter what one's interests are, there is literally something for everybody in Toronto. Drinking is a popular activity but according to students, alcoholism isn't a big problem. The dating scene is, as one individual put it, "what you make of it. It's not like we lack people at U of T if you're looking for someone."

Leader for the Future

At the University of Toronto, great academics plus a great location make the school a good choice for anyone. While the size can be intimidating at first, most students are able to take initiative and carve a place for themselves somewhere. Above all students here are passionate about what they do, which helps explain U of T's high job placement rate after graduation. Many of Canada's future leaders emerge here, and with the announcement of an $80 million (CAN) grant to the university from the provincial government this year, U of T is even more firmly on the path to leading the way in Canada, if not North America, in higher education. Students on the whole give their experience two thumbs up. "If you know what you want in an education, there's no better place than U of T for the number of opportunities it offers."—*Florence Han*

University of Waterloo

Address: 200 University Avenue West. Waterloo, Ontario N2L 3G1
Phone: 519-884-4567
E-mail address: visitus@uwaterloo.ca
Web site URL: www.uwaterloo.ca
Location: urban
Founded: 1959
Private or Public: public
Religious affiliation: none
Undergraduate enrollment: 16,200
Total enrollment: 18,000
Percent Male/Female: 55%/45%
Percent Minority: NA

Percent African-American: NA
Percent Hispanic: NA
Percent Asian: NA
Percent in-state/out-of-state: 97%/3%
Percent Pub HS: NA
Fraternities: 0%
Sororities: 0%
Number of Applicants: 18,857
Percent Accepted: 46%
Percent Accepted who enroll: 40%
Entering: 3,561
Transfers: 354
Application Deadline: 1 May

Mean SAT: NA
Middle 50% SAT range: NA
Middle 50% ACT range: NA
Mean ACT: NA
3 Most popular majors: NA
Retention: NA
Graduation rate: NA
Library: 2,500,000 volumes
Tuition and Fees: $3,400 in; $14,000 out
Room and Board: $5,400
On-campus housing: 64%
Financial aid, first-year: NA

Where else can you get great academics, great work experience, and great bratwurst, all at Canadian prices? According to students at the University of Waterloo, you can get everything you want all in one place.

A Taste of the Real World

Although it is smaller than most major Canadian universities, the University of Waterloo is well-known among its peers for its rigorous and demanding academic programs. With a total of forty classes required for graduation (ten per year), there is always a lot to do, particularly for students who double-major and are struggling to fit in those extra courses. Academic programs are structured around Waterloo's six faculties: applied health sciences, arts, engineering, mathematics, environmental studies, and science; each has its own requirements. In addition, there is also an Independent Studies Program for those looking for something more specialized. While math and engineering have an especially strong reputation (Waterloo has more students enrolled in math than any other school in the world), the other departments are not slouches. There is little reported grade inflation, and professors are fairly accessible. Overall, undergrads find that the programs cater to them well. One arts student, noting the close attention students receive, commented that he could not remember taking any English classes with more than forty students per class, even freshman year.

> **Students also report that coming back to school from the "real world" after working for a term provides a better perspective on classes and university life in general.**

One of Waterloo's biggest highlights is its well-developed co-op program, where students divide the school year by alternating terms of school and employment. The co-op program is the largest of its kind in North America with over half of the student body participating. As a result, Waterloo operates on a trimester system, with classes in session all year long to allow students in the co-op program to graduate within five years. Current undergrads highly recommend the program, saying, "not only can you get some much-needed cash, but you also get work experience, which is great for future employment." Being a part of the co-op system means having the opportunity to travel—not just to nearby Toronto, but to places outside of Canada as well. Students also report that coming back to school from the "real world" after working for a term provides a better perspective on classes and university life in general. One adds that "sometimes it's nice just to get away for a change of scenery and to refocus my energies."

Building Friendships

There are two main residences for students at Waterloo, called Village One and Ron Eydt Village. There are no on-campus housing requirements, but most students spend their first and second years in the dorms. Each dorm has a resident advisor, nicknamed a "don," who is an upperclassman. Many students are very enthusiastic about living within a residential church college system. The colleges include St. Jerome's, St. Paul's, Conrad Grebel, and Renison. They are small colleges, religiously affiliated with the university. Offering both separate classes and housing spaces, the church colleges reportedly offer a "homier" atmosphere. Although each has its own religious background, students of any affiliation may apply for resi-

dence. Some say the church colleges have the most "spirit," and according to some, also have better food—try Conrad Grebel for Mennonite cooking, for one. On the whole, dorm rooms are small, but are the place where "we start to build lasting friendships so it isn't so bad—in a sense, we are all in it together."

Upperclassmen tend to live off campus—there is a lot of available housing conveniently near the school, and the cost of living is more affordable. By living off campus, students are able to avoid the meal plan which is reportedly "a total rip-off." Many find tastier food off campus as popular places to eat include East Side Mario's, Subway, Gino's, and the "plaza," which is open 24 hours a day. Gino's is particularly well known for allegedly holding the Guinness world record for creating the longest pizza.

Friendly, Outdoorsy Atmosphere

Students find the town of Waterloo, Ontario a quiet kind of university town, and are quick to differentiate it from nearby "gross, industrial, abandoned factorylike" Kitchener. For the outdoorsy types, the area around Laurel Lake provides the perfect opportunity to jog, swim, and bike. For those eager to explore the social scene, there is the Student Life Center, which organizes free movies and other recreational activities. The town of Waterloo is also famous for its great Oktoberfest celebration every year: people come from all over to sample the bratwurst, take in the dancing, and just to see what the festival is all about. Many students enthusiastically recommend the event, even if it means just taking a tour of the local breweries.

As for the night life, there is Fed Hall, Canada's largest campus dance hall, where students go to party. Thursday nights are especially popular as people line up literally hours in advance to get in. Other than that, there are the usual weekend parties with plenty of alcohol available. Waterloo may have the reputation for being a studious school, but as one student commented, "even the engineering students know how to relax once in awhile." A fair number of people leave town for the weekend and head for Toronto, which is about an hour away. However, other students were quick to point out that their peers do not go to Toronto for the weekend often, preferring to hang out with friends on campus.

Intramurals and More

Extracurricular involvement at Waterloo varies, and most students do not participate in many outside activities. Due to the co-op system, many students do not have a lot of time to pursue other activities. Extracurricular activities include an active student government and *Imprint*, the main student newspaper. Intramurals are also especially strong, given the number of fine facilities available. Any student with interest can play, and the lack of pressure on the field makes the experience enjoyable. Varsity sports are very much in the background at Waterloo.

Quest for the Pink Tie

Waterloo, like all other schools, has its own unique traditions. Among them is the quest for the pink tie, which occurs during freshman week at the start of the school year. Math students, or "mathies" as they are called, go through a mild form of initiation to get the coveted pink tie. Later, a huge pink tie is hung over the side of the math building, and this often adds to the touch of rivalry between the math and engineering departments. During frosh week, engineering students try to steal the giant pink tie, while mathies try to sneak out the "tool," the engineering faculty's prized possession. As one student said, "we love to scheme and plot, but it is really just fun and games."

A Place to Grow

At Waterloo, academics are taken very seriously. "There are lots of smart people, especially in the sciences and engineering," says one undergrad. Students head to the Dana Porter Library to study, and computer clusters are readily available on campus. While the academic atmosphere may not be cutthroat, some complain that there are people who study compulsively. One student remarked that there exists a clear separation between "half the students [who] study like crazy, and [the] half [who] have a life." Students at Waterloo can be cliquish, so school unity leaves room for improvement. However, the University of Waterloo still remains one of Canada's foremost educational institutions for the engineering, math, and arts, and those who attend rave about the good job placement rate after graduation. Above all, Waterloo students in general agree about the number of academic and social opportunities available. If there is one thing to remember about the people at Waterloo, it is that "we really know how to go after what we want." It is just that passion that keeps Waterloo growing and its students succeeding.—*Florence Han*

FYI
The three best things about attending Waterloo are "its academic reputation, extensive intramurals, and going to Fed Hall on Thursday nights."
The three worst things about attending Waterloo are "the ugly buildings, food service, and cliques among students."
The three things that every student should do before graduating from Waterloo are "go tubing in Laurel Creek, go out for a team (competitive or intramurals), and check out Oktoberfest."
One thing I'd like to have known before coming here is "that there is more to explore at Waterloo than just the academics."

University of Western Ontario

Address: Room 190, Stevenson-Lawson Building, London, Ontario N6A 5B8
Phone: 519-661-2100
E-mail address: reg-admissions@julian.uwo.ca
Web site URL: www.uwo.ca
Location: small city
Founded: 1878
Private or Public: public
Religious affiliation: none
Undergraduate enrollment: 1,916
Total enrollment: 27,722
Percent Male / Female: 46% / 54%
Percent Minority: NA

Percent African-American: NA
Percent Hispanic: NA
Percent Asian: NA
Percent in-state / out-of-state: 92% / 8%
Percent Pub HS: NA
Fraternities: NA
Sororities: NA
Number of Applicants: 23,525
Percent Accepted: 34%
Percent Accepted who enroll: 92%
Entering: 4,959
Transfers: NA
Application Deadline: 1 Mar

Mean SAT: NA
Middle 50% SAT range: NA
Middle 50% ACT range: NA
Mean ACT: NA
3 Most popular majors: sociology, psychology, biology
Retention: NA
Graduation rate: NA
Library: NA
Tuition and Fees: $3,129 in; $10,458 out
Room and Board: $5,491
On-campus housing: 50%
Financial aid, first-year: NA

Located in the west end of the province in London, Ontario, the University of Western Ontario is aptly named. Western's academic programs, which students consider "above average," encompass a broad spectrum of classes in the natural sciences, social studies, and fine arts. "It's a large school, and consequently there are a lot of departments, each with its own good facilities," one student said. In addition to strong faculties (majors), students at Western find plenty of social and extracurricular activities to round out their schedules.

Business? You're in the Right Place

Students report that business administration and kinesiology are the university's strongest faculties. The graduate school in business administration and the medical school have excellent reputations that greatly increase the academic resources available to undergrads. According to one student, the business school's "only North American equivalent is Harvard."

Introductory classes are large, reaching well into the hundreds, and can leave frosh feeling cold, but the size of third- and fourth-year courses (other than the "easy A's") are smaller; upperclassmen can expect their classes to enroll 40 to 50. Students say their professors are "very approachable people who put their teaching before their research. And, if they are unavailable, there are always plenty of TAs willing to help you with your studying or your questions." Students find their workload fairly "light" and "reasonable when you're trying to juggle athletics, academics, and extracurriculars." Potential kinesiology students are pleased that Coca-Cola funded the construction of the exercise science building, considered by those in the field to be "one of the best research centers in North America, and far and away the best in Canada." A new arts center also was recently built with a grant from the Labatt's Breweries.

The campus is a self-contained study in Gothic architecture, with a few modern buildings interspersed. In addition to the main campus, there are three affiliates: King's College, a Catholic college; Huron College, which is Anglican; and Brescia, a women's college, all located a short distance from the main campus.

London has a population of approximately 400,000. One student complained the "city itself is too homogeneous" for his liking; although the student body "reflects diverse ethnic backgrounds," this is not the case for the town of London, which is predominantly white. Others call the city "very rich and very white-collar." Many UWO students come from southwestern Ontario, Toronto, and the city of London itself; despite their "rich kid" stereotype, undergrads feel that for the most part they are "a well-balanced, well-rounded group of individuals." One did admit that, in general, "the student body is a pretty high-maintenance crowd," concerned with the clothes they wear and the way they look. In their first year at Western, most students who are not town residents live on campus. "Socially, residence life is great, but academically it's impossible to get any work done," one student reported.

Living Arrangements

Students have a choice of six residences on campus, including the infamous Saugeen-Maitland Hall, which houses 1,600-odd students. (David Letterman once named Saugeen-Maitland Hall one of the top ten "party" spots in North America.)

Students living on campus must be on a meal plan, although each residence also provides students with kitchen facilities. Cafeteria food gets a fair rating from students, who claim that "in terms of cafeteria food it's not too bad." The university food services are concerned with student feedback; the standard cafeteria fare reportedly is getting better every year because of the recent implementation of student-suggested changes. Students on the meal plan say they like being able to use their meal cards at several fast-food kiosks on campus.

Athletics are big at the University of Western Ontario, although some students say the campus has "mediocre and aging athletic facilities." If undergrads "aren't actively participating in varsity sports or intramurals, then they are at least out supporting the Mustangs," said one student. And, they support them with good reason: the football and basketball teams are consistently strong at the national level. In keeping with their image of being well-rounded, about one-third of Western students compete at different levels of intramural play from beginner to burned-out high school superstar.

Hundreds of Clubs

In addition to the strong intramural scene, Western has what one undergrad called "hundreds of clubs for students to join." From political parties to environmentalist groups, students report that these clubs are "for everyone, not just geeks." The only complaint they have is that activity clubs not funded by the university have expensive dues. Students can join political and academic groups as well as such offbeat clubs as the Water Buffalo chapter, whose members congregate in large, furry blue hats with yellow horns (just like the ones Fred and Barney wore) to "drink beer and watch reruns of *The Flintstones.*"

> "This place is amazing," one student said. "It's the only school I know of where students can party as hard as they do and still succeed in athletics and academics."

Western has something of a party-school reputation, and students agree that "it definitely could be that way if you wanted it to be." Off campus, students traditionally hang out at the Ceeps bar or dance at NAC, a hip-hop club. On campus, Centrespot student center is the hangout of choice. The Greek system is popular at Western; students report that there are "at least 21 frats and six sororities." Faculties and residences host "pubs," but otherwise, the social scene is more or less "find your own way," one student said.

Life is not always a giant party at Western, however, and undergrads agree that a "good percentage of the student body takes academics seriously." Students can hit the books in the six "excellent" libraries on campus, or in a faculty library, of which each faculty has at least one. The most popular study place is the D. B. Weldon Library; the truly hard-core academics consider its facilities and study carrels top-notch.

Ontario's Country Club?

Western has been described by more than one cynical student as a "country club," and if having a good time is what you are interested in, you can find your own little party central in London, Ontario. But at Western, you will also find self-described, well-rounded students who combine the good life with a solid academic program.

"This place is amazing," one student said. "It's the only school I know of where students can party as hard as they do and still succeed in athletics and academics." —*Amy Kappelman and Staff*

FYI

The three best things about attending Western are "the fun we have, the business program, and how involved the student body is on campus."

The three worst things about attending Western are "living in London, the prevalence of the frat scene, and having to study at the library because the dorms are too loud."

The three things that every student should do before graduating from Western are "make Centrespot a priority, join a frat, and get involved on campus."

One thing I'd like to have known before coming here is "how much I am going to miss this place when I graduate."

predominantly white. Others call the city "very rich and very white-collar." Many UWO students come from southwestern Ontario, Toronto, and the city of London itself; despite their "rich kid" stereotype, undergrads feel that for the most part they are "a well-balanced, well-rounded group of individuals." One did admit that, in general, "the student body is a pretty high-maintenance crowd," concerned with the clothes they wear and the way they look. In their first year at Western, most students who are not town residents live on campus. "Socially, residence life is great, but academically it's impossible to get any work done," one student reported.

Living Arrangements

Students have a choice of six residences on campus, including the infamous Saugeen-Maitland Hall, which houses 1,600-odd students. (David Letterman once named Saugeen-Maitland Hall one of the top ten "party" spots in North America.)

Students living on campus must be on a meal plan, although each residence also provides students with kitchen facilities. Cafeteria food gets a fair rating from students, who claim that "in terms of cafeteria food it's not too bad." The university food services are concerned with student feedback; the standard cafeteria fare reportedly is getting better every year because of the recent implementation of student-suggested changes. Students on the meal plan say they like being able to use their meal cards at several fast-food kiosks on campus.

Athletics are big at the University of Western Ontario, although some students say the campus has "mediocre and aging athletic facilities." If undergrads "aren't actively participating in varsity sports or intramurals, then they are at least out supporting the Mustangs," said one student. And, they support them with good reason: the football and basketball teams are consistently strong at the national level. In keeping with their image of being well-rounded, about one-third of Western students compete at different levels of intramural play from beginner to burned-out high school superstar.

Hundreds of Clubs

In addition to the strong intramural scene, Western has what one undergrad called "hundreds of clubs for students to join." From political parties to environmentalist groups, students report that these clubs are "for everyone, not just geeks." The only complaint they have is that activity clubs not funded by the university have expensive dues. Students can join political and academic groups as well as such offbeat clubs as the Water Buffalo chapter, whose members congregate in large, furry blue hats with yellow horns (just like the ones Fred and Barney wore) to "drink beer and watch reruns of *The Flintstones*."

> "This place is amazing," one student said. "It's the only school I know of where students can party as hard as they do and still succeed in athletics and academics."

Western has something of a party-school reputation, and students agree that "it definitely could be that way if you wanted it to be." Off campus, students traditionally hang out at the Ceeps bar or dance at NAC, a hip-hop club. On campus, Centrespot student center is the hangout of choice. The Greek system is popular at Western; students report that there are "at least 21 frats and six sororities." Faculties and residences host "pubs," but otherwise, the social scene is more or less "find your own way," one student said.

Life is not always a giant party at Western, however, and undergrads agree that a "good percentage of the student body takes academics seriously." Students can hit the books in the six "excellent" libraries on campus, or in a faculty library, of which each faculty has at least one. The most popular study place is the D. B. Weldon Library; the truly hard-core academics consider its facilities and study carrels top-notch.

Ontario's Country Club?

Western has been described by more than one cynical student as a "country club," and if having a good time is what you are interested in, you can find your own little party central in London, Ontario. But at Western, you will also find self-described, well-rounded students who combine the good life with a solid academic program.

"This place is amazing," one student said. "It's the only school I know of where students can party as hard as they do and still succeed in athletics and academics." —*Amy Kappelman and Staff*

FYI

The three best things about attending Western are "the fun we have, the business program, and how involved the student body is on campus."

The three worst things about attending Western are "living in London, the prevalence of the frat scene, and having to study at the library because the dorms are too loud."

The three things that every student should do before graduating from Western are "make Centrespot a priority, join a frat, and get involved on campus."

One thing I'd like to have known before coming here is "how much I am going to miss this place when I graduate."